Hypertext / Hypermedia Handbook

Hypertext / Hypermedia Handbook

Emily Berk and Joseph Devlin, Editors

Intertext Publications
McGraw-Hill Publishing Company, Inc.

New York St. Louis San Francisco Auckland Bogotá
Hamburg London Madrid Mexico Milan Montreal
New Delhi Panama Paris São Paolo
Singapore Sydney Tokyo Toronto

Library of Congress Catalog Card Number 90-85588

10 9 8 7 6 5 4 3 2 1

ISBN 0-07-016622-6

Intertext Publications/Multiscience Press, Inc.
One Lincoln Plaza
New York, NY 10023

McGraw-Hill Publishing Company, Inc.
1221 Avenue of the Americas
New York, NY 10020

Composed in Ventura Publisher by Context Publishing Services, San Diego, CA

Contents

Preface

"...(T)here is a debilitating misconception that the shortest way from Point A to Point B is the best way and that order is the solution to all problems—that if we could just deliver information in a more orderly fashion, we could make it more understandable." [Richard Saul Wurman, *Information Anxiety*, pg. 48]

"The difference between an onion and a (hypertext) is that no one cries when you chop up a (hypertext)." [Variation on a discussion about banjos, Cindy Mangsen, in concert at the Cherry Tree, Philadelphia, PA, October 28, 1990]

"Too much to know is to know nought...." [William Shakespeare, Love's Labours Lost, Act I, Scene 1]

"King Solomon said in his Ecclesiastes that ...'Of the making of books there will be no end...' Why should this be a curse? Solomon was wise—the wisest of all kings. He knew. He knew that there would be a time when more books would be published than written." [Elie Wiesel, "From the Kingdom of Memory," 1990]

"...Publication has been extended far beyond our present ability to make real use of the record. The summation of human experience is being expanded at a prodigious rate, and the means we use for threading through the consequent maze to the momentarily important item is the same as was used in the days of the square-rigged ships...." [Vannevar Bush, "As We May Think," *Atlantic Monthly*, July, 1945]

"The most valuable commodity I know of is information. Wouldn't you agree?" [Gordon Gekko, the character played by Michael Douglas in the film "Wall Street"]

Hypertext is not the solution to all the world's problems; it, or something like it, is merely a solution to a big class of problems. We think this class of problems includes many that concern dissemination of scholarly material, documentation, and certain kinds of computer-based entertainments. We hope that by reading this book, readers will learn more about the classes of problems hypertext is likely to solve and which it is unlikely to solve. Thus, this Handbook is meant to both echo the call to hypertext and suggest means of getting there, if that is the proper destination.

Not only do we all stand on the shoulders of giants, but we all also stumble where giants have already fallen. Thus, for example, most of us have published most of our work about hypertext in the print medium that Bush found so unworkable (see the bibliography in this book, for example). The *Hypertext/Hypermedia Handbook* is intended to be a stumble in the right direction. True, it is being printed on paper, but it will also be available as a hypertext (see the tear-out sheet at the end of this book).

Hypertext is an evolving technology. Our goal in editing this book was to collect and contrast as many contradictory views about hypertext as we could. Because this book reflects more than one ideology, it is not ideologically pure.

For example, some authors believe that hypertext should be carefully hand-crafted; others think that automatic hypertext generation is the only way to effectively process the large amounts of information necessary in military- or industrial-strength hypertext. Another major disagreement occurs over interface issues. Some strongly advocate adopting and sticking to a single metaphor (e.g., all hypertext should look like a book). Others believe each interface should be custom written for the application and that readers be given multiple interfaces from which to choose.

No doubt some of the approaches described in this book will thrive and others will prove unusable. All that is clear is that, for the time being, no one approach will work for all hypertext authors. It is you, the readers of this Handbook, who will lead the way to hypertext as a mass medium, for you are the ones who will determine where the technology goes.

The body of the *Hypertext/Hypermedia Handbook* is divided into ten sections:

The Introductory Section, which includes some definitions and a history of hypertext.

Types of Hypertexts, which features a debate between text-only and multimedia hypertexts.

Conventions for Writers/Readers of Hypertext, a discussion of hypertext as a literary genre with a bit about interactive fiction.

Automatic Hypertext Generation, an explanation of how the new automatic text-to-hypertext conversion systems work and how they can best be applied.

Designing Hypertexts, which provides authors with suggested approaches to take when designing and implementing hypertexts.

Licensing and Protection of Electronically Published Information, which highlights legal issues that hypertext publishers should consider.

Issues for Hypertext Readers, another debate—this one focusing on the dreaded syndrome known to hypertext authors as "Lost in Hyperspace"—plus a suggested cure.

Integrating Hypertext with Other Technologies, in which hypertext is described in the context of other computer-based information management and retrieval techniques.

Industrial-Strength Hypertext, in which three luminaries in the field of hypertext discuss where they think hypertext technology needs to go in order to become truly useful.

The Future of Hypertext, a discussion of the need for standards and of the future promise and responsibilities that attach to hypertext as a new mass medium.

The material in the Appendices includes:

Appendix A, the case studies section, includes short descriptions of some of the more interesting applications of hypertext technology that we have discovered. These case studies are not merely descriptions of the exciting features a particular hyperdocument has, but are explanations of why and how each product came to be created as a hypertext;

Appendix B, a short Glossary of hypertext-related terms;

Appendix C, a list of Suggested References.

The format of this Handbook is, appropriately, nonlinear. If you are not at all familiar with terms that relate to hypertext (such as "link", "node", "browse", etc.) we suggest that you start either at the Introduction or at the Glossary. Those with a particular goal in mind who are interested in learning about how others solved their information dissemination problems using hypertext should start with some case studies. Most chapters in the Handbook are cross-referenced to others. In the hypertext version, there will be many more such cross-references.

This handbook is the story of the stormy courtship and impending marriage of literature and technology. It is the story of a technology that is evolving. It is, necessarily, incomplete.

Just one more quote from a giant, and then, we'll let you get on with the Handbook:

Two Hopes

1. To have our everyday lives made simple and flexible by the computer as a personal information tool.
2. To be able to read, on computer screens, from vast libraries easily, the things we choose being clearly and instantly available to us, in a great interconnected web of writings and ideas. [Theodor Holm Nelson, Literary Machines,—Pg. 1/2]

—Joe Devlin and Emily Berk, March 3, 1991

Acknowledgments

To Theron Shreve, whose idea this was.

To Alan Rose, who let us know what we needed to do. To Jeanne Glasser, who helped us do it.

To Paula Lovejoy and those at PC Week who allowed (even encouraged) us to print our "weird" MicroScopes.

To John Blackford and the staff of the late, lamented Personal Computing Magazine, and to Sue Calia and Charlie Kreitzberg, Alejandrina Pattin, Charles Wieland, and Tom Farre, who helped us pay the bills while this book was ongoing.

To John Baxter of Catalyst, because he thinks this is fun, and to Chris Sterritt, formerly of Unisys, now at MRJ, who helped us access the Sun.

To Ruth Giellman, our patient, persevering Senior Editor, whose fine judgement and attention to detail have improved every aspect of this handbook.

To Michael Briner, Edra Cash, and Shari Berk without whom this book would never have been completed. To Peter Morley, gone to San Francisco. To Harold, Rosalind and Anne for their helpful comments, case study draft writing, copy editing and babysitting services. To Miriam, our hyperbabe, lulled to sleep by the clicking of busy keyboards.

To David Orr, our Desktop Publishing Specialist at Kinko's, who converted a myriad of Macintosh files into a format we could use and provided valuable insights about life in the Mac world and editing suggestions as well.

To Herb Eisenberg, for legal counsel and moral support.

To Doug Dixon and Doug Breuninger, for the use of their libraries, and for the interesting discussions we hope to continue to have with them.

To Ashton-Tate for Framework III, which helped keep us as organized as possible. To the guys at Novell Tech Support, Western Digital and Gateway, who helped us kludge together the LAN on which this book grew.

And to our contributors, who came through for us as we trusted they would.

I

Introduction

What Is Hypertext?

By Emily Berk and Joseph Devlin
Armadillo Associates, Inc.

"There is a growing mountain of research. But there is increased evidence that we are being bogged down today as specialization extends. The investigator is staggered by the findings and conclusions of thousands of other workers—conclusions which he cannot find time to grasp, much less to remember, as they appear.

...[T]ruly significant attainments become lost in the mass of the inconsequential...

A record, if it is to be useful to science, must be continuously extended, it must be stored, and above all it must be consulted...

Consider a future device ... which is a sort of mechanized private file and library. It needs a name, and, to coin one at random, "memex" will do. A memex is a device in which an individual stores his books, records, and communications.... It is an enlarged intimate supplement to his memory.

...The applications of science have built man a well-supplied house, and are teaching him to live healthily therein... They may yet allow him truly to encompass the great record and to grow in the wisdom of race experience." [Bush, *Atlantic Monthly*, July, 1945]

If Vannevar Bush's dream were realized, if all the world's literature could be called up from a huge database that everyone could access, there would be no need for this handbook. Contributors would submit chapters to the McGraw-Hill *Hypertext/Hypermedia* subdirectory in this Universal Database. Since all our readers would have access to Bush's original article, which would already be in the database, we would not have to reprint excerpts in this handbook. Those who logged in and inquired about the term "hypertext" would always be directed towards original copies of Bush's full-text article. The editors of the *Hypertext/Hypermedia Hyperdocument* might provide illuminating pathways through the on-line document, but readers would decide what information to read and what to skip.

Nodes and Links—The Nuclear Elements of All Hypertexts

> "The owner of the memex, let us say, is interested in the origin of the bow and arrow.... He has dozens of possibly pertinent books and articles in his memex.... First, he runs through an encyclopedia, finds an interesting but sketchy article ... Next, in a history, he finds another pertinent item, and ties the two together. Thus he goes, building a trail of many items. Occasionally he inserts a comment of his own, either linking it into the main trail or joining it by a side trail to a particular item." [Bush, *Atlantic Monthly*, July, 1945]

Perhaps because of the delay in implementation of Vannevar Bush's dream, "memex" has been rediscovered a number of times. The name that has stuck to computer-based incarnations of Bush's originally microfiche-based dream is "hypertext" [Nelson, 1987].

The fundamental unit of information in a hypertext document is called a *node*. "[Ideally] a small portion of the document which covers one concept." [See Chapter 22 by Littleford, in this book.] A node may fit on a single screen or it can be as small as a word or as large as a whole book. A node can contain a combination of text, graphics and/or other forms of data. The "items" Bush's investigator found in his encyclopedia and history are nodes.

> ...The human mind... operates by association. With one item in its grasp, it snaps instantly to the next that is suggested by the association of thoughts, in accordance with some intricate web of trails carried by the cells of the brain....
>
> Man cannot hope fully to duplicate this mental process artificially, but he certainly ought to be able to learn from it... Selection by association, rather than by indexing, may yet be mechanized." [Bush, 1945]

Nodes are connected to each other by electronic cross references called *links*. To access more information about a specific topic, the hypertext reader simply points to a *link anchor*, an on-screen indicator of the presence of a link. When a reader "selects a link" in this way, the computer screen immediately changes to reveal the contents of the node to which the link refers.

Some hypertext authoring systems allow authors to type links. For example, an author might create a link type called "definition." Every link leading from a word or phrase in one node to its definition in another node would be categorized as a definition link. In our on-line *Hypertext/Hypermedia Hyperdocument*, we would use definition links to refer our readers from the phrase "link anchor" to the entry in our glossary for the term.

Bush predicted that we would want to store more than text in our memex's nodes. He was particularly interested in storing oral messages and other speech in it. These days, those who market hyperdocuments that incorporate media such as graphics, sound, and motion video, as well as text, in their products call them "hypermedia" rather than hypertexts; the distinction is a fine one.

Hypertext Readers, Hypertext Authors

Paper documents force readers to read documents in a linear fashion—from left to right and top to bottom. Hypertext documents encourage readers to move from topic to topic (node to node) rapidly and nonsequentially. Thus hypertext, is often defined simply as "nonsequential writing" [Nelson, 1987].

A hypertext document, which we call a "hyperdocument," is constructed, in part, by the author (who creates and places the links) and, in part, by the reader (who decides which threads to follow). Of course, authors can sometimes be readers and readers authors. Because the hyperdocument contains many possibilities, the author must pay more attention to small details and overall structure than is required when authoring a printed document. Hypertext readers must assume a much more active role than readers of printed text.

The dream of hypertext has always involved empowering readers as authors. Hypertext readers should be able to place electronic bookmarks in nodes that are of interest. They should also be able to retrace a path through the hyperdocument. They may also want to make notes in the electronic analog of a margin and to create their own links where they feel authors have missed important connections.

Navigating the Information Web

One of the results of the nonlinear nature of hypertext is that it is relatively easy to lose one's place in the maze of links. Alan Littleford, one of our contributors and author of the HyperBase hypertext development system notes, "A symptom often referred to as 'Lost in Hyperspace' results when a reader of the document has been following a long chain of hypertext links and suddenly finds that he has lost his chain of thought or position in the document. The reader has been tempted to follow the connecting links to the detriment of the main purpose for using the document and has become mired in a collection of details and related issues." Scholars who have studied the so-called "Lost in Hyperspace" problem in depth report, and not unexpectedly, that the more complex the database (the more links and/or nodes), the more likely users are to get lost.

The Lost in Hyperspace phenomenon is manifested in a number of ways: the reader can't get back to a node, or forgets which node he intended to find, or realizes that the hyperdocument has just instructed her to use her microcomputer as a boat anchor.

One of the problems authors of hyperdocuments face is that linear print provides a much better means than do hypertexts, for making sure that readers see each important point in the order that makes the most sense. The writer of a typical linear text, such as the instruction manual for a child's electrical car, can assume that readers have read through earlier chapters—the ones that say "Batteries not included" and "Be sure to insert 6 D batteries before you get into the car"—before they read about steering. The author can feel confident that the immediate context makes it possible for the reader to make sense of individual words and phrases in the text.

Unless the hypertext author has imposed a linear structure on the hyperdocument (which would defeat the point of hypertext), the author cannot assume that the reader has read nodes the author thinks should logically precede the current nodes. Thus, the local context of a hypertext must be explicitly communicated by author to reader through its structure and, in particular, with properly deployed links [see Chapter 20 by Parunak, in this book.]

A hypertext author can make some assumptions about the context in which a hyperdocument will be read. However, hyperdocuments are more open-ended than books—the boundaries between topics can get fuzzy. For example, let's say the reader came across the following sentence: To make an omelet, you must break some eggs.

This set of words is almost tautological when it appears in a work by Julia Child, but is a reckless call to arms when proclaimed in a political treatise by Vladimir Illich Lenin. Thus, the author of a hyperdocument needs to ensure that readers receive many clues when they link to information that may be ambiguous (most information can be ambiguous) so they can tell immediately whether they've been launched into a cooking lesson or a revolutionary diatribe.

To accomplish this, the hypertext author must try to make each node as self-contained as possible. In designing this chapter, for example, which I knew had to fit into a larger book being written by many authors simultaneously, I drew an imaginary boundary and searched for information that would fit within it. By

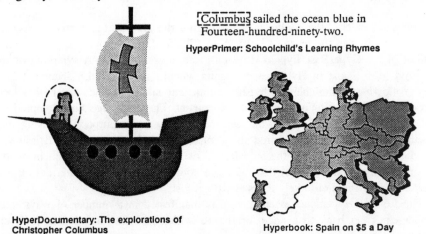

Columbus sailed the ocean blue in Fourteen-hundred-ninety-two.

HyperPrimer: Schoolchild's Learning Rhymes

HyperDocumentary: The explorations of Christopher Columbus

Hyperbook: Spain on $5 a Day

Figure 1.1 This illustration was created by, and is used with the permission of, David Anderson.

drawing the boundary, I limited the amount of information that is available to the reader in my chapter; I excluded information which I thought irrelevant. These decisions were made to keep the text clear, concise, and focused (although some readers may think that I should have made other decisions).

About the Authors

Emily Berk and Joseph Devlin

Emily Berk and Joe Devlin are co-editors of this handbook. They are also the co-principals of Armadillo Associates, a multimedia consulting and development firm headquartered at 2837 Poplar Street, Philadelphia, PA 19130.

Emily has been a designer and programmer of interactive hyper- and multi-media since 1980. Some of her recent multimedia meanderings have taken her to work as Project Leader on the DVI-based Words in the Neighborhood application at RCA Sarnoff Labs and as chief instigator of the Zoo Project, a HyperCard-based mapping program.

Joe has been a skeptical observer of the multimedia market since the seventies, when he worked in the marketing department of Commodore International and editorial department of Creative Computing Magazine. During the early 1980's Joe served as founding editor of both Software Digest and the Commodore Magazine. During the mid 80's Joe was employed as a project manager developing on-line services for large data communications and banking concerns. It was here that Joe developed his first hypertext. In the late 80's Mr. Devlin served as Project Manager of numerous benchmarking studies and Buyers Guides for PC-based software and hardware.

References

Bush, V. (1945). "As We May Think." *The Atlantic Monthly*, 176.1 (July) 101–108.

Littleford, A. (1991). "AI and Hypertext," *Hypertext / Hypermedia Handbook*, Emily Berk and Joseph Devlin (Ed.s), McGraw-Hill, New York, NY.

Nelson, T. (1987). *Literary Machines*. Vers. 87.1, The Distributors, South Bend, IN.

Parunak, H. V. D. (1991). "Ordering the Information Graph," *Hypertext / Hypermedia Handbook*, Emily Berk and Joseph Devlin (Ed.s), McGraw-Hill, New York, NY.

2

Why Hypertext?

By Joseph Devlin and Emily Berk
Armadillo Associates, Inc.

"We are surrounded by reference materials, but without the ability to use them, they are just another source of anxiety. I think of them as Buddhas, sitting on my shelf with all that information and a knowing smile." [Richard Saul Wurman, *Information Anxiety,* 1989]

Open any computer magazine and you will find an endless stream of articles about how hypertext or hypermedia technology can change your life. Is this just today's fad or is there something of substance behind all the hype? We would not be editing this book if we did not feel that the latter was true. We are confident that the promise behind hypertext is too fundamental to disappear quickly.

"You can't have everything; where would you put it?" — Steven Wright

The capacity of the storage devices we use in the computer and consumer electronic fields is getting so large that the time-worn methods of searching for information are beginning to break down. Character searches, pull-down-menus, indices and tables of contents just don't cut it when you are dealing with 550 megabytes of data on a CD-ROM, or the gigabytes that stream from other optical and digital storage devices.

"The more shoes you have in the closet, the harder it is to find a pair."
— Emily Berk

A related problem is that the amount of information being generated is growing even faster than the technology used to store it. For example, each time a new jet leaves its birthplace at Boeing, four tractor trailers full of paper documentation go with it. In this sort of situation the problem is no longer finding information or even building a place to store the information, but rather filtering out useful from irrelevant or redundant information.

Another impetus for improved information access technologies such as hypertext is the move toward multimedia (mixing of text, pictures, sound, data, and video). We can make documents much richer by adding sound and moving pictures, but multimedia data poses entirely new information management challenges; different from the ones we've seen so far. Hypertext can provide useful tools and conventions for managing and retrieving information from huge multimedia databases.

There are certain applications where hypertext offers obvious advantages over paper documents. In general, hypertext is a potential solution to problems that involve voluminous, densely cross-referenced databases that must be searched by many different people attempting to retrieve highly divergent types of information.

As can be seen in Appendix A, the Case Studies section of this book, the type of data to be searched is almost irrelevant—it is the structure of the data that determines whether hypertext will be a productive approach. For example, some conventional paper documents such as encyclopedias, dictionaries, and other reference works, are usually used nonsequentially by readers. So it's no surprise that Grolier's Encyclopedia is already available on CD-ROM, and can be accessed through HyperCard as a hypertext.

Large technical manuals intended to provide quick solutions to very specific problems are also prime candidates for hypertext. For example, suppose your B-1 bomber springs a leak 40,000 feet over Albania. There is no way you want to pull out your 10,000-page repair manual and try to diagnose the problem. Instead, you boot your computer and search the hypertext repair manual sitting on a single optical disk for solutions.

Computers do a good job of storing, retrieving and presenting vast quantities of data. The human mind is far more facile at filtering data to access information appropriate for the job at hand than are computers.

Hypertext builds upon the relative strengths of the human mind and the digital computer: the computer holds the data and presents it to the human, the human chooses which way to go by pointing at each juncture. It is an intuitive approach in which the ability to link associated text matches the brain's natural tendency to think associatively. So, for example, the smell of crayons reminds you of Miss Hyperlove, your first grade teacher, whose intoxicating scent made it easier to remember how to spell "intoxicating."

Hypertext seems simple, obvious even. You put some text, a few graphics, sounds, and motion videos perhaps, on a computer. Someone, we'll call this person the "author," annotates these "documents" by linking concepts that relate to each other together. Someone else, call this person the "reader," calls up this "hyperdocument" and follows the links.

When first you think about hypertext, the concept is trivial, but look again; it's really very complex. Well-designed hyperdocuments are magical. They allow readers to explore collections of ideas nonsequentially, by stepping back and getting an overview, zooming in for details, learning by association, experiencing the sound and images of the real thing on video, and reading or playing the same data at their own rate—repeatedly if necessary.

Hypertext may be digital technology's unique and definitive form, but achieving this vision is difficult. Well-designed hypertexts are hard to engineer. In order to build successful hyperdocuments, you must discard old ways of organizing information. This requires an intimate understanding of hypertext as a new medium. We must try things out and see how readers like them. We must learn in order to teach. Hypertext authors (be they called multimedia producers, hypertext authors, or on-line documentation specialists) should have a good theoretical grounding into what works and what does not. Providing that sort of intellectual grounding is what this book is all about.

About the Authors

Emily Berk and Joseph Devlin

Emily Berk and Joe Devlin are co-editors of this handbook. They are also the co-principals of Armadillo Associates, a multimedia consulting and development firm headquartered at 2837 Poplar Street, Philadelphia, PA 19130.

3

A Hypertext Timeline

By Emily Berk and Joseph Devlin
Armadillo Associates, Inc.

There is properly no history; only biography. —Ralph Waldo Emerson,
i. History

Individuals pass like shadows; but the commonwealth is fixed and stable.
—Edmund Burke

Year	Event
1945	Vannevar Bush published an article entitled "As We May Think" in *The Atlantic Monthly* in which he claimed that the progress of research was being stymied by the inability of researchers to find and access relevant information. Bush proposed the "memex" system, a microfiche-based system of documents and links which foreshadowed the advent of hypertext. Some of the requirements for the memex as specified by Bush: fast access to information, ability to annotate, and the ability to link and to store a trail of links.
1962	Douglas Engelbart published a paper, 'Augmenting Human Intellect: A Conceptual Framework,' which set Engelbart's agenda for the 30 years that followed. Engelbart sought to define and implement the functionality necessary for computers to augment human abilities. The functions he thought necessary included links between texts, electronic mail, document libraries as well as separate "private" space on the computer for users' personal files, computer screens with multiple windows, and the facilitation of work done in

Year	Event
1962 *(cont'd)*	collaboration by more than one person. In the course of his career, Engelbart invented the mouse, outliner and idea processor, and on-line help systems integrated with software. Engelbart was responsible for the first substantive implementations of electronic mail, word processing, and shared screen teleconferencing. AUGMENT is marketed by McDonnell Douglas; Engelbart now heads the Bootstrap Institute at Stanford University, which aims to build prototypes of software and hardware that will help office workers collaborate.
1965	Theodor Holme Nelson invented the term "hypertext" and presented it to the world. He learned that "most people are afraid of (and/or angered by) new words and ideas" [Nelson, 1987, p. 1–29]. Nevertheless, Nelson has continued as universally acknowledged Ideologist of Hypertext, relentlessly fighting to construct Xanadu, a hypertext engine based on his version of hypertext. In 1988, Autodesk, Inc. invested in Xanadu and formed the Xanadu Operating Co. to produce the market Xanadu.
1968	Andries Van Dam and his team at Brown University developed the Hypertext Editing System, which was intended to serve two purposes: to produce printed documents nicely and efficiently and to explore the hypertext concept. Van Dam's second hypertext project at Brown was called the File Retrieval and Editing System (FRESS, completed in 1982). According to Van Dam, FRESS was the first system to have an undo function [Van Dam, 1988]; undo remains the most popular feature of many software packages. In latest hypertext project at Brown is called Intermedia. Intermedia-based applications are used in teaching and learning of biology and English Literature at Brown. Intermedia is used both as a tool for professors preparing their lessons and course materials and by students for learning and creating reports. One of the seminal ideas derived from Van Dam's work is that of the "web," a set of links that belong together. By opening a web, a hypertext reader imposes a particular set of anchors and links on a document. This makes it possible for different users to impose thier own sets of links on the same document. [Meyrowitz, 1990]
1972	The last of what Frank Halasz calls the "first generation" hypertext systems, ZOG, was developed at Carnegie-Mellon University. The first generation systems all originally ran on mainframes, used text to the exclusion of other media, and provided support for workers to collaborate on a hypermedia network. ZOG was specifically designed to provide fast response to a large number of users.
1983	The "second generation" of hypertext authoring products began in the early 1980s with the emergence of workstation-based, research-oriented systems such as Intermedia and KMS. The difference between the first and second generation of hypertext products had a lot to do with improvements in technology that became available on workstations. These faster computers and displays supported more sophisticated user interfaces than earlier systems could. The second generation systems are generally targeted at networked or UNIX-based, single-user workstations, not mainframes as the earlier products were. [Halasz, 1988]

Year	Event
1983 *(cont'd)*	KMS, a commercial implementation of ZOG, has been marketed since 1983. KMS is capable of storing text and graphics in its nodes, which are called "frames." It is particularly appropriate for "industrial-strength hypertexts," where many designers and engineers must share the same documents on a large computer network.
1985	In 1982, Peter Brown began to invent the first commercial hypertext authoring system for a personal computer, which was called Guide in 1985 when *Office Workstations Limited* (OWL) began to market it for the Apple Macintosh. Guide was released for use on an IBM PC in 1987. Like other microcomputer-based hypertext authoring systems that came later, Guide provides less functionality than earlier mainframe and workstation-based products, but it does rely on a graphical user interface. Guide remains one of the few microcomputer-based hypertext products that encourages link typing.
1986	Xerox PARC's NoteCards was released. NoteCards, KMS, and Intermedia all support graphics and animation nodes as well as formatted text. They also all provide graphical overviews of the structure of the hyperdocument to aid navigational access. NoteCards pioneered in the application of metaphor to hypertext; each node in NoteCards is represented on screen as a card. NoteCards can be of any length necessary. Cards are classified as to type; some node typing has to do with the contents of a card (text, graphic, or animation), but other types can be defined.
1987	"HyperCard isn't really hypertext at all!" said Ted Nelson (who should know it when he sees it) when HyperCard came out [Nelson, 1989]. Well, HyperCard may not allow text-to-text links and it provides few of the frills most hypertext authors require for large scale hypertext production, but because it comes with every Macintosh sold, it certainly has brought a semblance of hypertext to the Macintosh masses. As can be surmised from its name, HyperCard imposes a card metaphor on its nodes. No node can be larger than a card in size. A hyperdocument is called a stack in HyperCard, and HyperCard programs are called stackware. Cards in HyperCard are linked to other cards via link anchors called "buttons." Also in 1987, the IBM-PC version of Hyperties, which began life in 1983 as The Interactive Encyclopedia System (TIES) at the University of Maryland's Human-Computer Interaction Laboratory, was introduced. Hyperties relies on the metaphor of an electronic book or encyclopedia.
1990	There are now at least twenty commercially available hypertext authoring systems running on a variety of platforms. New versions of existing hypertext products such as HyperCard, Hyperties and Guide are released regularly. Hypertext conversion programs such as Texas Instrument's HyperTRANS, OWL's IDEX, and Big Science's SmarText (now owned by Lotus), which convert existing electronic documents into hypertext, are becoming viable options or additions to business documentation plans. The demands of Vannevar Bush, Douglas Engelbart and Ted Nelson have been vindicated and may soon be met. The flood of information continues unabated.

This is not the end. It is not even the beginning of the end. But it is, perhaps, the end of the beginning. — Winston Churchill, Mansion House, 10 Nov. 1942 (about the Battle of Egypt).

References

Bush, Vannevar (1945). "As We May Think." *The Atlantic Monthly* 176.1 (July): 101–108.

Engelbart, Douglas C. (1963). "A Conceptual Framework for the Augmentation of Man's Intellect." *Vistas in Information Handling.* Ed. P.D. Howerton and D.C. Weeks. Spartan Books, Washington, D.C. 1:1–29.

Halasz, Frank G. (1988). "Reflections on NoteCards: seven issues for the next generation of hypermedia systems." Communications of the ACM July v31 n7 836–853.

Horn, Robert E. (1990). *Mapping Hypertext: The Analysis, Organization and Display of Knowledge for the Next Generation of On-Line Text and Graphics.* The Lexington Institute, Waltham, MA.

Meyrowitz, Norman (1990). The link to tomorrow. (hypermedia). *UNIX Review* Feb v8 n2 58–68.

Nelson, Theodor H. (1987). *Literary Machines.* Vers. 87.1. The Distributors, South Bend, IN.

Nelson, T.H. (1989). Unpublished interview with Emily Berk, Jan.

Shneiderman, Ben and Greg Kearsley (1989). *Hypertext Hands-On!* Addison-Wesley Reading, MA.

Van Dam, Andries (1988). Hypertext '87 keynote address. (transcript) *Communications of the ACM:* July v31 n7 887–896.

Types of Hypertexts

Since Ted Nelson first coined the term "hypertext," there has been debate over whether media other than text are encompassed by that term. Nelson himself has acknowledged the usefulness of the word "hypermedia," although he claims that from the first, his vision of hypertext always embraced multimedia as well.

In the following section, rather than try to distinguish between hypertext and hypermedia, we present two chapters that compare these two not mutually exclusive hypertext genres and define the benefits and drawbacks of each.

Types of Hyperkale

4

Text-Only Hypertexts

By Emily Berk
Armadillo Associates, Inc.

Not every picture is worth a 1000 words!

> In the Information Age the continuous flows and fragments of speech and images are like gusty winds in our face, but the ground on which we stand is the rubble of text. ... The Information Age challenges us to deepen our understanding of written language so that we might better acquire, store, communicate, and access our information through this ancient, acquired medium that we all share.
> — Robert Lucky [Lucky, 1989, pg. 91]

Hypermedia, the application of hypertext techniques to graphics, moving pictures, and sounds as well as text, is being hyped strenuously of late. This chapter is intended as something of an antidote.

It is not that I do not admire pretty pictures and the technologies that make them appear and change on computer screens. Rather, I believe that the expense and flash of hypermedia is inappropriate in certain circumstances. People won't pay for hypermedia; they'll pay for solutions to their problems. There are instances where problems can be solved only by hypermedia. There are other circumstances where the only solution is text-only hypertext.

Not every hyperdocument requires fancy graphics, sound, and/or video. In fact, many hyperdocuments benefit from the lack of distracting multimedia accompaniment. In particular, most businesses value hypertext more for its timeliness than for its flash; for its economy, elegance, and substance than for its intrinisic beauty.

The documents most people in business generate and read have few, if any, graphics, video, sound, or fury. Text-only hypertext has the power to organize and transform a quagmire of circulars, memos, reports, requests, marketing data, demographic statistics, and annual reports into a business plan. It can help businesses coordinate with government, suppliers, distributors, and customers.

Text-only hypertext has several advantages over hypermedia. These include: performance, economy, ease of development, ability to run on cheaper and more universally available equipment, and portability.

Performance

Probably the biggest advantage of text-only hypertext is the speed at which it operates. The overhead required to support even simple still-frame graphics and multiple on-screen fonts is considerable. Full-color stills, motion video and sound almost always force hypermedia developers to trade off between performance, cost and space. For example, it takes about one second for each of the full-screen images used in the *Rediscovering Pompeii* hypermedia program [see the case study in this book] to be displayed on screen. The use of sound or full-motion video can involve even longer delays.

Graphics and sound can slow down processing in a number of ways: large graphics and sound files must be loaded from slow mass-storage media such as hard disks or optical disks and the software required to manage graphics and sound steals cycles from the computer's CPU that could otherwise be devoted to responding promptly to user input.

ASCII text files load much faster than graphic files and, once loaded, usually require less work from the system and applications software to manage. With fewer time-critical tasks to worry about, the software that runs a text-only application can react more quickly to asynchronous requests from users and other interrupts.

Economy

Text-only hypertexts can easily be run on inexpensive PCs such as old 8088-based IBM XTs or Macintosh SEs. Multitasking graphical environments like Microsoft Windows or HyperCard require considerably more horsepower. Microsoft recommends at least a 286-based AT class machine to run Windows applications such as OWL's Guide 3.0.

Text-only hypertexts can be run on inexpensive monochrome graphics environments. Multimedia applications often require much more expensive high- or medium-resolution color displays.

Sophisticated hypermedia applications consume other computer resources at an astonishing rate. A single high-resolution still can take a megabyte or more of real estate on a hard drive or optical disk. An ASCII file requires just one byte per character.

Because hypermedia applications often run on cutting-edge technology, hypermedia productions often require the active involvement of one or more technical types such as computer programmers or even hardware designers. Production of text-only hypertext is apt to be much more straightforward.

Ease of Development

Text-only hypertexts can also be developed in less time, with less staff and using fewer resources than hypermedia applications. Hypertext is a literary medium; a writer or editor is almost always necessary, and hypermedia applications almost always require a designer. But text-only hypertexts require fewer hours from artists, video producers, audio producers, etc., than hypermedia products. Thus, text-only hypertexts can be designed, implemented and distributed in a fraction of the time required for hyperdocuments that include sound, graphics or motion video.

Because text-only hypertext can be run on less sophisticated systems, less technical expertise is required to develop and tweak the software that makes it run. Unlike graphics, sound, and motion video, which almost always involve outside content creators, formatters, and/or production, textual content can usually be created, edited, and formatted in-house.

In fact, for most business people who have neither the time nor the talent to get involved with fancy graphics packages and sound and video editing stations, text-only hypertext is the only way to go. In addition, text-only hyperdocuments more closely resemble the paper documents that business people are used to, so they are easier for many readers to browse.

Portability

In spite of all the fancy fonts that desktop publishing has brought us, the fact remains that most of the documents available in digital format today are stored in plain ASCII format. This includes all the requirements, policies, procedures, descriptions, specifications, laws or diagnostics, and textual representations of ideas you are likely to encounter. Sticking to ASCII-only text facilitates porting betweem platforms because ASCII remains the one common language that almost all computers understand today.

Even formatted text is easier to port than graphics or sound. There is a standard for formatted text. It is called the *Standard Generalized Markup Language* (SGML). Even highly formatted text files created in an SGML-compliant manner can be exchanged readily between computer systems. [See Chapter 10 by Rearick and Chapter 26 by Devlin for more information about SGML.] This is almost never the case with color documents formatted to be displayed on particular computer monitors.

Don't make the decision to implement a text-only or multimedia hypertext up front. Define the problem you want to solve. Design the solution to the problem. If it has pictures, sounds or motion in it, it may become a hypermedia application. If it has just a few stills in it, call it a text-only hypertext and be proud. After all, the world's most influential literary masterpieces are all text-only documents.

About the Author

Emily Berk is co-editor of this handbook. She has been a designer and programmer of interactive hyper- and multimedia since 1980. Some of her recent multimedia meanderings have taken her to work as Project Leader on the DVI-based Words in the Neighborhood application at RCA Sarnoff Labs and as chief instigator of the Zoo Project, a HyperCard-based mapping program.

References

Devlin, J. (1991). "Standards for Hypertext," *Hypermedia / Hypertext Handbook*, Emily Berk and Joseph Devlin (Ed.s), McGraw-Hill, New York, NY.

Lucky, R. (1989). *Silicon Dreams: Information, Man and Machine*, St. Martin's Press, New York, NY.

Rearick, T. (1991). "Automating the Conversion of Text into Hypertext," *Hypermedia / Hypertext Handbook*, Emily Berk and Joseph Devlin (Ed.s), McGraw-Hill, New York, NY.

5

Hypermedia

By Oliver Picher
Datapro Research Group

Emily Berk and Joseph Devlin
Armadillo Associates, Inc.

and Ken Pugh
Information Navigation, Inc.

Introduction

"Being multimedia is not quite enough for a program to be hypermedia."
[Nielsen, 1989, p. 5]

The term multimedia is one of the most overhyped in today's computer vernacular. Any application that manages to create even the most rudimentary mixture of text, pictures or sound is likely to be dubbed by its marketeers as a multimedia application.

The term hypermedia suffers with the same affliction. Most of the popular hypertext authoring systems on the marketplace today claim the ability to add still and moving graphics, audio, and software to the mix. Books have always had pictures in them—are they hypermedia applications too?

A computer program that runs in color with few pictures and beeps is not necessarily a multimedia application; a multimedia application is not necessarily a hypermedia application. In this chapter, we reserve the term hypermedia for those applications that allow users to forge their own nonlinear paths through images, sounds and text.

Figure 5.1 IBM's Linkway hypermedia product supports a variety of multimedia options. Source: IBM Corporation.

A Note about Terminology Used in this Chapter

One of the problems we all confront when writing about hypertext is its unformed lexicon. Fortunately, the term "authors" works for the creators of both hypertext and hypermedia applications. But what do you call the person who browses these products? "Reader" works well for one who uses a hyperdocument, but does not seem to apply to someone blazing a trail through a multimedia extravaganza that includes moving pictures and sound.

In this chapter, we will use the term "viewer" for a person "reading" a hypermedia document. Unfortunately, this term connotes passive couch potatoes who watch what goes by without influencing it. We attach no such limitations to a hypermedia viewer. Like hypertext readers, hypermedia viewers must be given the freedom to follow their own noses through the hypermedia web. Another problem is that the term viewer does not work well when discussing interaction with a sound passage.

Again, lacking a better term, we must settle on "viewer."

Hazards and Rewards of Hypermedia

> The idea of branching movies is quite exciting. The possibility of it is another
> thing entirely. [Nelson, 1975, p. DM44]

Adding pictures and sound to a hypertext can make the application much more expressive. Browsing a hypermedia is exciting because it's the opposite of the

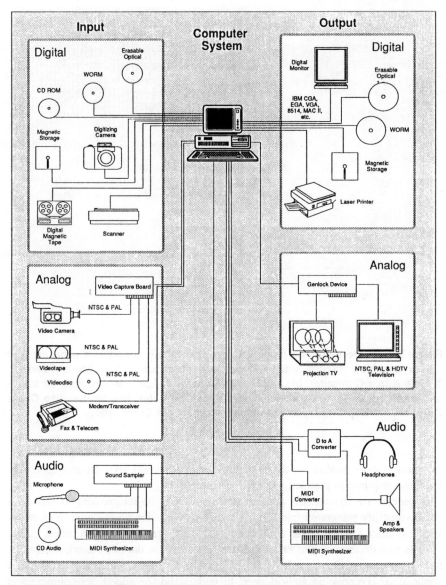

Figure 5.2   Hypermedia relies on numerous other technologies as input and output devices. Source: Datapro Research Group

passive act of watching a video or TV show. However, hypermedia applications can also overwhelm and confuse viewers. The larger the number of different media you use, the more careful you must be to place them in a clearly defined context and structure so as not to startle viewers.

Another problem is that the complexity and expense of authoring hypermedia applications increase exponentially with the number of devices used. Throwing a graph or two into what was formerly a strictly textual hypertext is technically easy to achieve and easy for viewers to follow. But adding a nonlinear sound track and

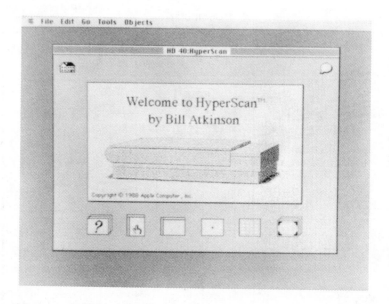

Figure 5.3 HyperScan is a powerful, but simple-to-use software program that inputs graphics directly into a HyperCard stack using the Apple Scanner. © 1988 Apple Computer, Inc. All Rights Reserved. Apple is a registered trademark and HyperScan a trademark of Apple Computer, Inc. licensed to Claris Corporation. Reprinted with permission from Claris Corporation.

full-motion video pushes the development costs per second up to figures approaching those required to produce a television commercial.

In order for a hypermedia application to succeed, the images and sounds must be so smoothly integrated into its fabric that viewers don't have to stop to worry about whether any particular node consists of text, graphics, motion video, audio, or calls to a database report or spreadsheet. Authors, on the other hand, need to be fully cognizant of the complexity to be mastered when producing a hypermedia application. Hypermedia authors need to understand the added development and production cost of sound and video hypermedia before they tackle either medium. They must also understand the costs in terms of disk real estate and video and audio hardware that those in the target audience must purchase in order to view hypermedia applications.

In this chapter we will describe the advantages, costs and pitfalls that ensue when sound, stills and moving pictures are added to hyperdocuments. The chapter is divided, roughly, into two parts. In the first part, we investigate the multimedia components of hypermedia.

Figure 5.4 In this DVI application, a digitized, video flight control panel is overlaid over a computer-generated city. Intel now owns the rights to DVI technology.

Use of these diverse technologies can make a hypermedia application great, or drag its developer to the depths of despair. In the second part of this chapter, we discuss the issues hypermedia developers face in designing and implementing hypermedia applications.

The Media of Hypermedia

Five major categories of media can be incorporated into a hypermedia application—text, still pictures, moving pictures, sound and other computer programs. Each medium offers its own advantages and poses unique problems.

The joys and sorrows of converting text into hypertext are discussed extensively elsewhere in this book. In Chapter 22 by Littleford, techniques for integrating AI and non-AI-based programs into hyperdocuments are suggested. Therefore, in this chapter, we will concern ourselves with the practicalities of using still pictures, moving pictures and sound in hypertextual applications.

Computer-Generated and Computer-Assisted Graphics

Still Graphics.

> Pictures are indeed an information mystery. They may be worth a thousand words, they may not be. But, incredibly, they require a thousand times as many bits. So perhaps they had better be a thousand times more valuable! [Lucky, 1989, p. 29]

Adding still pictures to a hypertext is the easiest way to make the leap from hypertext to hypermedia, but that does not mean the transition is easy. One problem is the sheer number of graphics formats currently in vogue. For example, major graphics standards currently popular on IBM personal computers include Postscript (EPS), Lotus 1-2-3 (PIC), Publisher's Paintbrush (PCX), SYLK, TIFF, Windows Metafile (WMF) and Windows Paint (MSP), Graphwriter II (CHT and DRW), graphic metafile (CGM and GMF), GKS (Graphical Kernel System), DXF and IGES.

There is not room in this chapter to discuss the relative strengths and weaknesses of each graphics format. Suffice to say that each hypertext development and delivery platform obeys a different set of graphics conventions and imposes its own limitations on graphics quality and number of colors.

Fortunately, many hypermedia authoring systems come complete with built-in graphics creation and editing tools. These built-in tools may save the poor developer from having to worry about the format and source of pictures, but they also

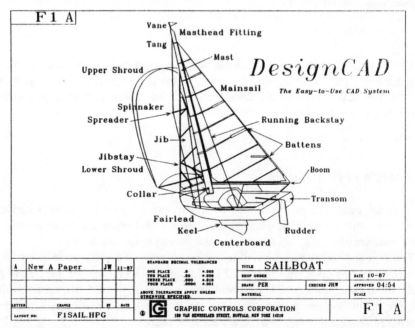

Figure 5.5   You can use computer-generated graphics to design your own sailboat.

limit the range of images developers can use. In the end, most developers take the plunge and master the art of bringing illustrations in from outside sources, including business graphics programs, paint and draw programs, CAD programs or scanners.

Animated Graphics.   Animation provides an interim step between still images and full-motion video. Computer-generated animations are considerably cheaper to produce than full-motion video. In many cases, animations can be created by a single artist using a microcomputer. Shooting live video usually requires the services of both a film and sound crew as well as a dedicated studio to edit the video and to convert it to a format that can be received by the computer.

The costs of creating an animated sequence vary with the complexity of the images provided and the number of frames (screens) displayed per second. Sometimes, a very simple animated sequence updated only a couple of times per second can be very effective. For example, creating a simple stream of images depicting the unwinding of a DNA molecule is easy and provides visual information no still photograph or motion video could rival.

Video

> ...[W]e have to devote about 100 million bits per second to create a typical television picture on your TV screen. But then you sit there in front of that bitwise voracious display and ingest only your meager few dozen bits per second. [Lucky, 1989, p. 30]

Full-motion video is nothing more than a series of still pictures flashing across a screen at 30 frames per second. Sounds simple enough, but that is an awful lot of information for a computer to process.

The problem is complicated because video can be brought into the computer in either of two entirely incompatible formats (analog or digital). Nor is it usually possible to store analog and digital video on the same storage device or to bring them into the computer over the same cabling scheme.

Analog video, like the video displayed on a television set, is made up of continuous lines of colors (or gray) that are displayed and then vanish one after the other as they are replaced with new lines. Digital video is composed of discrete dots which are displayed, a screenful at a time, on a computer (digital) monitor.

Delivering Analog Video.   It is not usually possible to store analog video on digital devices such as magnetic hard drives. Instead, analog video can be input to a hypermedia system using devices such as VCRs, videotape players, video cameras, and video still cameras. However, these devices are not able to access video frames out of sequence. In order to get to frame 100 on a videotape, a VCR must play all 99 earlier frames in order. Thus, we say that these analog devices are not random access devices.

One of the few analog media that computers can access randomly is the video-disk. Therefore, analog video sequences to be integrated into a hyperdocument are almost always stored on videodisk.

Videodisk is an analog form of *Read Only Memory* (ROM). Once a videodisk has been created (pressed) at a mastering facility, like a phonograph record, it cannot be altered. A new kind of analog optical disk memory, called OMDR, is now available from Panasonic, Sony and Teac. OMDR is a WORM (Write Once, Read Many times) format; each frame on an OMDR disk can be written once at the user site. Once a frame has been written on OMDR, it cannot be altered or deleted; however, writing to one frame of OMDR does not preclude writing to other frames later.

Videodisk formats vary, but usually each track on a disk stores one frame of video information. Since television quality video usually plays at 30 frames per second, the 54,000 tracks that can be stored on each side of a videodisk yield about 30 minutes of television-quality video. It takes a videodisk player between one and three seconds, depending on the player, to find the first frame in a sequence. After that, the videodisk can display the frames in the sequence at the rate of one every thirtieth of a second.

Digital Video.   Digital computers can turn analog devices on and off, or create windows in which to display an entire analog image, but the amount of processing a computer can perform on an analog image is severely limited. It is relatively easy for a computer to adjust colors in digital images, to crop and size them, or to mix several digital images (any combination of text, video or image) together.

Digital video frames are made up of discrete dots, called pixels, each of which is a combination of three colors—red, green and blue. The number of colors that can be displayed on a digital monitor is determined by the color depth—the number of bits used to define the red, green and blue characteristics of each pixel. For example, the color depth of a Hercules-compatible (black-and-white) screen is 1.

Only one bit of information is needed to display a pixel on a black-and-white monitor, with 1 meaning the pixel is white and 0 meaning the pixel is black. A monitor that can display 16.7 million colors needs at least 24 bits per pixel.

There is a whole host of devices capable of capturing and storing digital images. Prominent among these devices are digitizing cameras, digital scanners, and modems. Digitizing boards can also be used to translate analog images into a digital format (they freeze the continuous, analog lines of color and then translate them into discrete pixels).

Delivering Digital Video.   Digital images may be relatively easy to process, but they do chew up an awful lot of storage space. Say, for example, that a single digital video frame consists of an array 512 pixels across by 480 pixels down. If each pixel required 8 bits for each red, green, and blue component, the video would take up about 3/4 million bytes per screen. Multiply this number by the 30 frames per second required to generate a television quality moving image and the

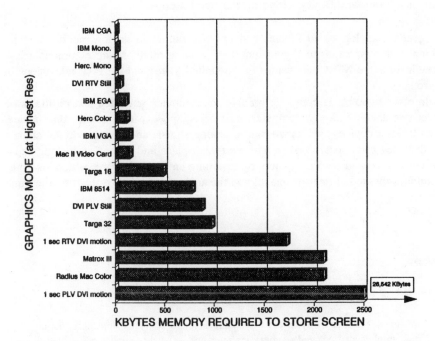

Figure 5.6 The amount of storage space a video image takes up depends on its color depth, resolution (the number of pixels displayed per square inch), and how quickly the image changes. Source: Silicon Beach Software, Inc.

storage requirement is mind boggling. A 60-second commercial shown in this resolution would take up more than 1000 million bytes of hard disk space.

The voluminous quantities of data required by multimedia and hypermedia applications have spurred the popularity of high-capacity optical data stores such as CD-ROMs. CD-ROM is a read-only, digital, computer- readable form of the popular CD-Audio medium. One CD-ROM can hold 540 Mbytes of digital data. [Miller, 1986]

The data that can be jumbled onto a single CD-ROM may include digitized video, audio, bitmaps and other computer graphics, text and computer programs. Unfortunately, the data transfer rate of a CD-ROM drive is only 150K bytes per second (a fraction of the speed of the average magnetic hard drive). This slow data transfer rate is the cause of the noticeable delay one must expect when calling data up from a CD-ROM.

The data transfer rate also makes displaying full-motion video stored on CD-ROM difficult. We discuss some of the fancy footwork required to retrieve the 30 frames per second required for full-motion video later in this chapter. Other random storage devices that can hold digital images include magnetic disks, WORM and read/write optical disk.

Mixing Analog and Digital Video on the Same Screen

In general, analog video images can only be output to analog monitors, while digital video is output to digital monitors. Analog monitors are commonplace— they include the NTSC televisions in the United States and the PAL televisions in Europe.

In order to combine computer graphics or computer-generated text on the same screen as analog video, a computer must be equipped with a *gen-locking device*. Gen-locking devices sychronize pulsed analog signals and discrete digital signals so that they can appear on screen at the proper place and time. Gen-locking capabilities can be added to computers by installing an overlay board, which also pre-combines the digital (text or image) and the analog picture for display on the same screen.

Sound

Analog and Digitized Sound

> Although the idea of hypertext that includes sound is greatly appealing, the actual implementation, and ongoing maintenance, of such complicated formats is very costly. [Lucky, 1989. p. 210]

> There is a ratio of 1,000 to more than 10,000 in the information rate required to communicate language in the form of speech as compared to text. The number of bits on a compact disk for an hour of speech or popular music would suffice for the text of 3 Encyclopedia Brittanicas. [Lucky, 1989, p. 240]

Like video, audio comes in both analog and digital flavors. Record players and tape cassettes store audio in an analog format. CD-audio (compact disks) and DAT (digital audio tape) store music in a digital format. A standard CD-ROM or CD-audio disk can accommodate up to about 72 minutes of audio.

Sound itself is transmitted through the air as an analog signal (sound waves). Microphones take sound in as an analog signal; speakers send it out again as an analog signal.

The reasons for digitizing sound are similar to those for digitizing graphics and video. Digitized sound can be processed by computers in ways that are just not possible when the sound remains in a analog format. Digitized sound takes up almost as much space as digitized video, and, like video, can be compressed to take up less space on the storage medium. The device used to translate analog sounds into a digital format is called a sound digitizer (or sampler).

Synthesized Sound.   Instead of digitizing real sounds, the hypermedia author can generate sound on the fly using specialized chips. Speech can be reproduced from either an ASCII text representation or a list of the phonemes. Current inexpensive technology permits a reasonable representation of a human voice, albeit

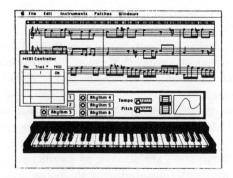

Figure 5.7   This SuperCard-based music composition program relies on computer animation and MIDI conventions to do its work.

usually one that has a pronounced accent. Musical synthesizers create digital music and other sounds.

One advantage that a sound producer has over still pictures and video is that there is a single standard—MIDI—for the dissemination and processing of sound that has been adopted worldwide. The MIDI format allows sounds to be generated on a synthesizer and stored and processed on a computer. MIDI can drive a musical synthesizer which reproduces the music with the desired tone and timbre. A MIDI-compatible sound-generating peripheral is usually required to create the sounds so specified; these devices are becoming widely available both as output and input devices.

Techniques that Make Multimedia Possible

Compression

> "Mere compression, of course, is not enough; one needs not only to make and store a record but also to be able to consult it .... Compression is important, however, when it comes to costs." [Bush, 1945]

Video Compression.   As we have seen, storing enough information to create a 30 frame-per-second (fps) video can take a tremendous amount of disk storage. Transferring all that data from CD-ROM to screen RAM fast enough to generate 30 frames-per-second requires a staggeringly fast data transfer rate of 22 Mbytes per second. (It would take an average CD-ROM player over an hour to play back 30 seconds of video stored on its shiny surface). One solution to the storage and data transfer problem is to compress video images so that each frame takes up less space on the CD-ROM and so there's less data to be moved.

Most decompression schemes work on the fly—after data has been transferred from the digital store (CD-ROM or magnetic hard drive) to the computer screen. But even at a compression rate of 80%, a five-minute-long sequence that will run at 30 frames per second can take a good long time to transfer and display [Berk, 1990]. Thus, although the capacity of a CD-ROM is 500 times that of a floppy disk, hypermedia applications devour both CD-ROM real estate and CPU and graphics processing power at an incredible rate. In hypermedia, no matter how much performance and space we get, we need more.

Lossless compression techniques, which guarantee that none of the information originally obtained is omitted from the original during the compression/decompression process, can only achieve a 1:2 or 1:3 compression ratio when applied to video information.

Higher ratios of compression are attained by sacrificing some image quality. Details which are only slightly discernible by the human eye can be eliminated without weakening the impact of the picture. The required data transfer rate can also be lowered by decreasing the resolution of the picture, slowing the rate at which frames are changed, or some combination of both.

There are several commercial systems that compress video data. All barter image quality for space. They include Intel's *Digital Video Interactive* (DVI) and *Philips' Compact Disc Interactive* (CD-I). DVI requires extensive preprocessing of the video signal and currently yields 30 frame-per-second video sequences at a relatively low image quality. CD-I currently does not support full screen 30 fps video, but promises image quality of decompressed CD-I sequences that is somewhat higher than those running through DVI decompression chips.

Almost all compression schemes used today are proprietary, and thus incompatible with each other, but most take similar approaches to increasing compression

Figure 5.8 Intel's DVI system can decompress digitized, compressed video stored on a CD-ROM as it is transmitted to screen memory. The trade-off is some loss of video quality. Photo courtesy Intel Corp. Copyright 1990.

ratios. Images are normally recorded in RGB (Red Green Blue) coding, where each pixel is defined as a combination of those three colors. Compression algorithms usually convert the RGB codes to YUV. (This conversion can be accomplished using a relatively straightforward mathematical equation.) The Y value contains the luminance (brightness) and the U and V values contain the chrominance (color) values. Because the human eye is more sensitive to differences in brightness than color, the U and V values can be compressed to a greater extent than the Y values, yielding about a 3:1 compression. Cutting the resolution in both directions by 2 achieves another 4:1 decrease in size.

Interframe correlation compression technique can also be applied. That is, the compression algorithm determines how each frame in a sequence differs from the one before it, and only stores the information that has changed between frames. These types of base/delta compression techniques can achieve up to 1:10 or 1:15 compression. Choosing to display smaller frames or to run sequences at slower frame rates can decrease the data space requirements even further.

A new class of compression chips based on an international standard called *Joint Photographic Experts Group* (JPEG) have recently begun to hit the market. A related international standard video compression scheme called *Moving Pictures Experts Group* (MPEG) is also in the works. The first MPEG compression chips are expected to be sampled sometime in mid-1991 with commercial products emerging by 1992. By that time, Intel will probably have incorporated MPEG compression standards into its line of DVI chips.

Still pictures can also be compressed. However, because people can more easily detect glitches in still frames than in frames displayed in sequence at 30 frames per second, lossless compression is more commonly applied to still images.

Other techniques such as the CCITT Group 3 or 4 Fax formats provide good compression of black and white images. Run length encoding is also good when there is a large number of unvarying lines (all black or white). Both methods can be combined to give approximately a 5 to 1 compression ratio on black and white still images.

Figure 5.9 Unlike DVI, CD-I is a "system-in-a-box." Here, the CD-I system is hooked to a television set and a speaker. Source: Philips IMS.

Table 5.1

	Motion:	Stills:
CD-I:	Up to 72 minutes on CD-ROM with partial screen, partial motion, 120-by-80 pixel resolution (this requires 5 to 10 KB per screen).	8000 still images at a maximum of 720 by 480 pixel resolution. (108 KB to 300 KB for 1 full screen).
DVI:	Up to 144 minutes partial screen full-motion, 256-by-240 pixel resolution video per CD-ROM.	5000 stills recorded at 1024 by 512 pixel resolution.
	Up to 72 minutes full-screen, full-motion, 256-by-240 pixel resolution video per CD-ROM.	7000–10000 still images at high resolution.
	Up to 16 hours 1/8 screen 1/2 frame rate 256-by-240 pixel resolution video per CD-ROM.	3500 still images with 20 seconds of audio per still.
		40,000 medium resolution still images.

Sound Compression.   As in video, hypermedia authors can trade audio quality for disk real estate. Everything from CD-audio quality to AM radio quality (without the static noise) sound can be achieved by *tweeking* sound compression algorithms and compromising on quality to save on storage.

A CD-ROM's 150 kilobyte-per-second data channel can be used partly for transferring the audio and partly for transferring other data, such as accompanying images. Alternatively, several sound tracks in different languages can be recorded for a particular image or portion of a program.

Introduction to the Design of Hypermedia Applications

[T]oday's systems for presenting pictures, texts, and whatnot can bring you different things automatically depending on what you do. Selection of this type is generally called branching. (I have suggested the generic term hypermedia for presentational media which perform in this (and other) multidimensional ways.) A number of branching media exist or are possible:

Branching movies or hyperfilms...
Branching texts or hypertexts...
Branching audio, music, etc.
Branching slide shows.
[Nelson, 1975, p. DM44]

Table 5.2   CD-I and CD-ROM XA Audio

Type	Storage requirements	Notes
Level A Stereo	1/2 hi-fi audio	(only for CD-I not CD-ROM XA)
Level B Stereo	1/4	
Level C Stereo	1/8	
Level C Mono	1/16	Up to 16 hours per CD-ROM. Good for speech. 1 second — 10 KB

The first efforts at applying a new technology are often modeled on strategies used in old technologies. Not surprisingly, many hypermedia applications use the computer as an expensive emulation of paper. Don't assume, however, that the primary focus of a hypermedia application has to be text—like a book with built-in movies. Many hypermedia applications have made successful use of video or audio as the primary medium and use text only to supplement the experience (e.g., with help screens, subtitles, and footnotes).

The creation of a hypermedia system starts when choices are made about how to treat the material. The first step is to study the target audience and determine its level of sophistication. Next comes the creation of a storyboard (a general outline which defines the possible sequences the hypertext will provide) or a map of all the potential nodes of the material and how they are interrelated. Since nodes are likely to be linked in a nonhierarchical fashion, the map should include textual or graphical depictions of what nodes will be reached by what links. For a simple web where nodes follow each other in a nearly sequential pattern, the map may not be very complex. Other webs may require more complex maps.

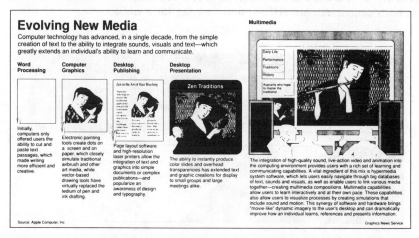

Figure 5.10 The focus of a hypermedia application can be different from what it would be if sound and motion were not available.

Cut

Time ⟶

Figure 5.11a   A cut is an abrupt transition between video or film sequences.

Dissolve

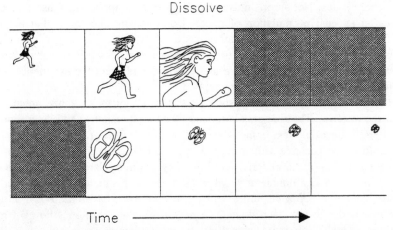

Time ⟶

Figure 5.11b   During the transition between sequences in a dissolve, images from both sequences are visible; they overlap for a while.

Wipe

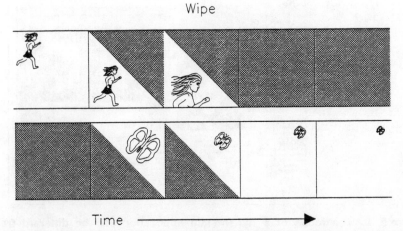

Time ⟶

Figure 5.11c   In a wipe, the sequences are isolated in particular parts of the frame; they are shown during the same time period.

Consider, for example, a hypermedia application that describes how our muscles work. The opening screen of the work might start with a video clip of a muscle in operation with a voice-over describing the processes involved. Various links might be provided allowing viewers to stop the video to call up textual descriptions of the terms used in the voice-over. From these descriptions the viewer can be provided with a choice of returning to the video where they left off or calling up another video sequence that demonstrates other related processes.

In the remainder of this chapter, we will highlight some of the many issues hypermedia authors must address in designing and implementing applications.

The Unique Challenges of Producing Hypermedia Applications

Put sound, video, text and stills together and you have multimedia. Toss in some hypertext links and you have hypermedia. Sounds easy, doesn't it? But the authoring challenges of hypertext pale in comparison to those that face the hypermedia author. The temporal nature of video and audio presents the hypermedia author with a unique set of editing and production problems, including:

- Facilitating Navigation in Hypermedia
- Controlling the Pace of a Hypermedia Application
- Linking To and From a Moving Image or a Changing Tone
- Empowering Hypermedia Viewers
- Production Quality
- Synchronization of Media

Facilitating Navigation In Hypermedia

Readers can get lost in hypermedia space at least as quickly as they can in hyper(text) space. In fact, it is often much easier to get lost in a hypermedia application because conventions for navigating video, pictures and sound are necessarily more complex than navigating text alone. Among the toughest problems hypermedia authors face is providing readers with useful and complete maps of the various pathways that can be followed through the multimedia hyperbase.

In hypermedia, as in hypertext, making the structure of the hyperbase explicit is one powerful aid to navigation [see Parunak, "Ordering the Information Graph" (Chapter 20), in this book.] Other suggestions for authors seeking to minimize viewers' disorientation as they browse through hyperdocuments are provided in the chapters by Gay & Mazur and Bernstein.

Pacing

- Granularity. A movie director controls the pace of a film by determining the length of the sequences within it and by using different trasitional devices (such as fades, wipes and cuts) between those sequences. A series of short, choppy sequences, like the editing in the old Laugh-In television show, moves the story along in a sprightly up-beat fashion. Longer, slower sequences can be more thoughtful.

  Transitions can be sudden—in a cut, sequences start and end abruptly and without warning. Or, transitions can be more gradual. In a dissolve, frames at the end of the first sequence and the beginning of the second are superimposed, so the viewer has time to think about the transition being made. On the other hand, a dissolve may move the viewer to a new sequnece more efficiently than a cut. In a wipe, some porions of the screen display the end of the first sequence, while other portions display the beginning of the next sequence for a while [Philips, 1988].

  Say a character in a movie is seen getting into his Maserati to return from his office to his palatial mansion. Rather than shoot footage of the drive between these two places, the director might film: the character getting into his car, cut to the character driving away, then cut to the driveway of the mansion where the footman is standing ready to help the hero park his car. Or, the director might speed the pace by dissolving on a shot of the character getting into his car, then fading back in on our hero purposefully entering his front door.

  In a hypermedia production, the author has less control over pacing—the reader may try to insist on watching the road as the character drives home. However, limitations imposed by the capacity and resolution of the storage medium and by the author for artistic, economic or didactic reasons will constrain the quantity, quality and volume of sound, video and graphics in any hypermedia application. Therefore, the author must decide up front which 15-second "sound bites" are sufficient to convey certain information, and whether other sequences require two or three minutes. The author will determine, by providing links, where more specific information is available and what form that information takes.

  Like a movie director, a hypermedia designer should plan each sequence in the application. Many hypermedia designers use storyboards similar to the ones used by other multimedia professionals from movie directors to software designers.

  In the storyboard, the author might impose a hierarchy of larger segments, composed of smaller segments, so that readers can choose which level is appropriate. Or, the designer might decide to build in pause, stop, fast-forward and back-up links to make it easier for readers to control the flow of the video and/or audio.

- Flow. Related to granularity is the issue of flow, especially between different segments of video. Professional video and film editors take great pains to ensure that jumps between shots are as smooth as possible. A poor transition can be disorienting for a viewer. In a hypermedia application, viewers are in theory going to be jumping in and out of different video and audio segments at will. The application developer must manage these transitions carefully, maintaining a feeling of continuity while not limiting readers' flexibility. Since a reader might "cut" between scenes in a totally unpredictable order, it might be hard for an author to decide how to implement transitions between nodes.

A hypermedia author can specify which transitional device is to be invoked when a viewer selects a particular link. HyperCard HyperTalk programmers, for example, can include visual effect commands that cause a card's appearance on screen to be accompanied by a special effect such as a dissolve or a wipe.

Linking

How does the hypermedia author set up a coherent set of links that allows readers to get to the massive amount of information stored in the moving video images (e.g., the setting, the objects within the image, the context of the action)? This is a challenge even in simple hypertexts; the fact that nodes cannot all be assumed to be text-only makes hypermedia linking more difficult. Linking into and out of moving video and changing audio sequences is particularly tricky.

Where and How To Leap Into the Video and Audio Flow

One of the problems of allowing hypermedia viewers to link into a moving stream of pictures or sounds is that you must take the element of time into consideration when placing the link. In some instances, linkages wed to particular moments in the stream make sense (for example, you will almost always want to provide a link to the beginning of a famous speech). At other times, you might want to allow viewers to enter the video or sound stream at any frame they wish. In many cases, once a sound or video node has been accessed by the viewer, it makes sense to allow the video or audio stream to play sequentially from beginning to end, but to allow the viewer enough control to cut the sequence short at any time.

If you do allow viewers to jump into a video sequence in the middle or to control the speed of video display, difficulties will occur if the compression schemes used to save storage space is based on a Base/Delta scheme. Skipping ahead in the sequence may not be possible or may result in an unacceptable time delay. Some compression schemes (such as DVI) allow authors to insert absolute frames at specified points in the video stream. You must plan these and program them in. You could, for example, provide entry into the video stream at half-second intervals, by inserting a base frame every fifteenth frame. Of course, inserting all these entry nodes incurs costs. For example, with DVI each absolute image node requires roughly three times as much data as a frame accessed sequentially.

Interactive Multimedia Research & Development Laboratory,
Educational Technology Center, Lehigh University

Program Design

The Interactive Multimedia and Development
team worked to visualize the program. A flow
chart and storyboard were developed.

Table 1. Flow Chart of Digital Dinosaur Program

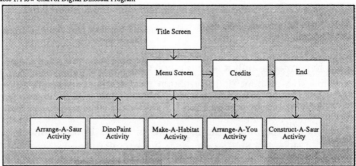

Storyboard for Program

Screen 1.1 & 1.2 - Title Screen

Digital Dinosaurs

Description: Mosaic of opening screen to high
resolution image.

Audio: Music synchronized to opening.

Programming Notes: Image transforms to high
resolution image (screen 1.1 transforms to
screen 1.2).

Screen 2.1 - Menu Screen

Description: Index screen

Audio: Audio fades out

Programming Notes: Get mouse input. Go to
module Arrange-a-saur, DinoPaint, Make-a-
habitat, Arrange-a-you, Construct-a-saur

Figure 5.12 In the design for Digital Dinosaurs, produced by Lehigh University's Interactive Multimedia Research and Development Laboratory, each item in the storyboard is broken down into a description, audio and programming notes.

Another problem is that each time you search for the beginning of a new video sequence, most storage devices will take a while to find and/or decompress it. For example, many videodisk players take three seconds to call a videodisk sequence to the screen. Obviously, with delays of this magnitude, the number of discrete calls to video should be kept to a minimum.

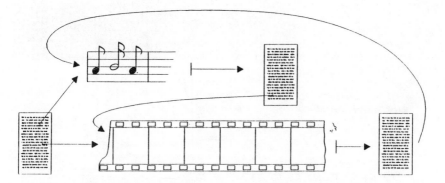

Figure 5.13   Each sequence can be treated as a discrete node...

Authors can link between dynamic objects such as audio or video nodes in several ways:

- **Each sequence can be treated as a discrete node.** The links from a sequence would only occur at the end of the sequence. In this case, once a video or audio node is selected, the entire sequence would be played, and the user would have no chance to interrupt. This is acceptable when the audio and video sequences are small, or when there are certain nodes that the author wants played all the way through every time they are accessed. Consider a worst case scenario in which a user links from a biography of Beethoven to a node which plays a noninterruptible version of his *Fifth Symphony*. More than 30 minutes would elapse from the time the listener selects the *Fifth Symphony* until user-control returned. In general, readers will expect at least the opportunity to stop a video or audio node (see Empowering Hypermedia Viewers, below.)
- **An alternative scheme is for the developer to treat each video or audio sequence as a set of nodes.** This design methodology provides more opportunities for users to make choices within each video sequence.

Each smaller node might itself refer to a sequence of other nodes, and would contain appropriate links to these other nodes. If the viewer lets a sequence play all the way through, the author will have specified the node to end on—this could be a freeze on the last frame of the completed sequence, or it could be a different node entirely.

Making Links Explicit.   In stills, such as the pictures of the moon's surface in Figure 5.15, it may be very effective to overlay text over the graphic to serve as link anchors.

However, alerting viewers to the presence of a link from within a video is more problematic. Warning viewers ahead of time that a link anchor leads into a multimedia link is a very good idea but not always easy to accomplish. In Elastic Charles, a project at the MIT Media Lab, each link to a video clip is anchored by

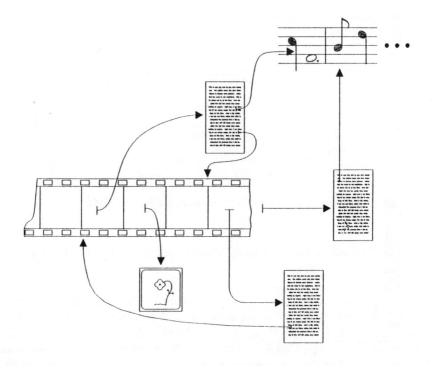

Figure 5.14   ... or, the developer can treat each video or audio sequence as a set of nodes.

a miniaturized version of the clip on the screen in a sort of moving icon (or micon). This approach works well in applications where the contents of a video sequence are so distinctive that users can recognize them by previewing just a clip. [Nielsen, 1989].

Audio nodes present another problem. It is easy to have an audio node as the destination of a hypertext link, but more difficult to anchor links from within the sounds itself. The listener cannot click on the musical notes that come out of a speaker, so the developer must provide a visual representation of the sound information that provides appropriate opportunities for linking.

Links To and From Still Pictures

You should also adopt a consistent mechanism to let viewers know where links are on each still picture. Marking active areas on the screen can be achieved any number of ways. For example, active areas (link anchors) might be highlighted by coloring them differently than the background, by outlining them, or by using a three-dimensional effect that displays the image of the link anchor when the cursor is moved over an active spot on the screen.

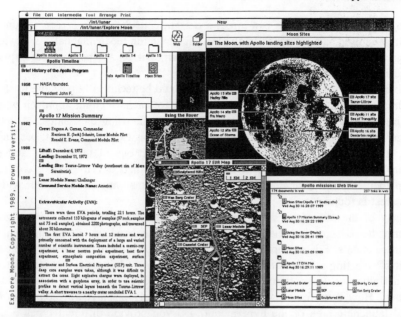

Figure 5.15   Brown University's IRIS uses a Macintosh running under A/UX. Note the use of multiple windows, timelines, and hyperlink anchors directly on the images. Copyright 1989, Brown University.

Table 5.3   Different constraints govern the use of different media in hypermedia.

	Text	Video	Audio
Content	Letters, words, sentences, paragraphs	Frames, segments	Intangible changes in pitch and volume
Organization	Static, application-dependent	Temporal (event) or spatial (place)	Temporal (event)
Meaning	In words and their context	In still image or in motion (context)	In change over time (context)
File Size	~1 byte for each letter	22MB/second	10K to 75KB/second
Potential Anchors	Keywords, buttons, highlighted text	Keywords, static and dynamic buttons, micons (moving icons), regions within image	Keywords, static and dynamic buttons, visual surrogates for sound

To see how such choices can affect a design, consider an on-screen picture of an airplane used as a reference in an electronic aviation repair manual. An obvious design is one which specifies that the viewer can click on any parts of the airplane to receive more information.

Given a high enough screen resolution, it would be technically possible to show hundreds of parts on screen and provide a link for each. Such an approach would tax the understanding and manual dexterity of anyone using the manual. A better design might be to divide the aircraft into seven areas (wheels, cockpit, passenger area, wings, engine, ailerons and tail fin). Click on one of these areas and the picture zooms in on a close-up divided into another half dozen areas or so. Each zoom focuses in on a smaller and smaller list of items until the particular widget of interest is found.

Many of the other issues that must be considered in coming up with a good hypermedia design are the same as those considered in designing plainer hyperdocuments. For example, how does the author inform the viewer what the result of selecting a link will be? Will selecting a link take you to another picture, to a definition or description of the target of the link you click on, or to a menu of choices? How does the viewer return to a previously displayed screen or to the initial launching area of the hypermedia? Do you provide different types of anchors to indicate whether links target text passages, pictures or sounds? Must text menus be scattered around the picture to provide additional guidance to the viewer?

It is easy to debate which devices work best in any given situation. In fact, it is often true that the actual mix of devices chosen is less important than the fact that a consistent approach has been adopted.

Adopting such a consistent approach allows viewers to make assumptions about what the result of each action is likely to be and saves them from stumbling blindly through the maze.

Links to Dynamic Nodes.   Just because a link is attached to one place in one frame of the video, doesn't mean the position of the link can't change in subsequent frames. The first frames could contain link anchors that appear in different places and link to different nodes than latter frames. These anchors should not move too rapidly or the viewer will have a difficult time selecting them.

Anchors may appear or disappear over time, depending on the contents of the video clip. An interview with Jean-Paul Sartre, for example, might make mention of his relationship with Simone de Beauvoir. A button would appear that would allow a reader to zoom off to get more detail on this relationship. The button, however, would disappear as the conversation with Sartre moved on to other topics.

A link's target may also change based on the viewer's responses. For example, when a viewer has explored all the nodes that emanate from a particular link, then the system might change the target of that link, as a mechanism to keep users from repetitively visiting the same nodes. Depending on how well this effect is integrated into the aspects of the application, it may either confuse viewers or promote greater efficiency in finding desired information by eliminating inappropriate or duplicate nodes.

An alternative is to place links from video outside the video frame. This is a particularly attractive option when video has been compressed using DVI or CD-I schemes, since the results are often better if full screen video is not required. Another advantage of this approach is that link anchors need not move around on the screen. Although moving the anchors may give viewers a better idea of the target they are selecting, they may also add to the *busy-ness* of the screen.

Empowering Hypermedia Viewers

The reader of a book has control over the speed and order in which material is presented. Using a hypermedia document should be a similar experience. For example, viewers should be able to skim or browse a hypermedia document as they would a document on paper and they should have the means to predict where in the hypermedia particular information is stored.

Granting hypermedia viewers control over the order of presentation is easy—this is hypertext, after all. Response speed of presentation is harder to guarantee because it relies on the ability of the delivery platform to respond promptly to user input. For example, the 3-second access time of a videodisk player means that some delay in response may be unavoidable. Developers should strive to keep video segments well-organized and to a manageable size so that viewers can skip around easily if desired and yet still understand the material.

At the most basic level, viewers must be able to escape at any time. A hypermedia application should rarely, if ever, force a viewer to watch a two-minute video sequence to its bitter end. The viewer should at least have options similar to those on tape recorders and VCRs, including the ability to rewind the sequence to the beginning and replay it, preview it in fast forward, pause in the middle of the sequence, or stop it altogether and go on.

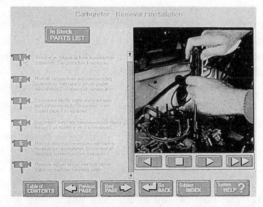

Figure 5.16 In this hypermedia car-repair manual developed using OWL International's Guide authoring system, car mechanics can control playing of the video exactly as they would control a tape player. Source: OWL International Inc.

Production Quality

The content of television may not always be the best, but the shows (and especially the commercials) are slick. Users of hypermedia applications will have little patience for poorly produced video and audio. How can designers of hypermedia applications compete with the production standards of commercial television?

Television and movie production values may differ, but at least the resolution of the screens and the number of frames of video or film required are fixed. Designers of hypermedia applications have it much harder—they must make difficult trade-offs between sound and video quality and capacity. As we have seen, many of these choices have to do with the compression techniques the author is working with, and with the capacity and power of the target delivery system.

Synchronization

Video and audio must be in perfect synchronization. If the application involves text or animated graphics, in addition to video and sound, the challenge of synchronizing all the elements of the application becomes even greater. The Athena Muse application at the MIT Media Lab, for example, matches video interviews of native French speakers with one of two levels of subtitles—full text for beginning French students and keywords for more advanced students. Creating point-to-point cross-references between the video and the subtitles, all with reasonable display performance at normal conversational speeds, was not a trivial task [Hodges, 1990].

Production and Authoring Requirements

Costs

A book publisher needs to make a tremendous investment in word processing, typesetting, printing, and bindery equipment just to produce books; a book reader needs only the book itself. The same distinction holds for hypermedia—the production system and the delivery system will differ.

Producing a hypermedia application may require video production and editing, audio production and editing, graphics and animation production and programming, digitization, possibly compression, programming or at least authoring, mastering, etc. Not all these functions need be performed in-house by the hypermedia producer, but they must all be done and they all cost [Berk and Devlin, 1990]. None of these capabilities should be required of most hypermedia viewers.

Production Costs.   The cost of any multimedia production is inevitably higher than the cost of producing text. Producing motion video is the most expensive, sound comes next, still graphics is less expensive and text is usually the easiest to manage. You can cut down on the cost of multimedia by using an approach suggested by Tom Corddry of Microsoft: keep moving video to a minimum and using sequences of stills, as in a slide show, perhaps with audio voice-over. Not only does this cut the cost of production, but it also increases the amount of information that can be stored.

The cost of producing hypermedia applications can be high; they can run from the thousands to the millions of dollars. For example, a simple hypermedia application with about forty nodes, half of them video sequences, and forty links will cost about $45,000.

This cost includes scripting and producing. Richard Michaels, of Learncom, a software training company, estimates that it will cost between $200,000 and $450,000 to implement an interactive training system without video sequences. Full-scale video-audio hypermedia productions can cost much more.

Tools

Tools for preparing hypermedia fall into a number of different categories. There are tools for editing the raw video and audio, callable routines for presenting various forms of multimedia, and authoring systems which incorporate the linking tools.

The spectrum of editing systems runs from painting programs which draw on stills, to graphics animators, to programs that identify and resequence graphical, video and/or audio sequences, to special effects generators and beyond.

Authoring tools and courseware generators may provide a flowchart-like interface and the capability to play different audio and video sequences based on certain conditions. These software products may help even those with minimal programming skills to define the flow of a hypermedia application. [See Berk and Devlin, 1990, for a more extensive discussion of the equipment necessary to produce multimedia segments for use in hypermedia.]

Cost of a Delivery System. A hypermedia delivery system might range anywhere from a street model personal computer or Macintosh (which costs under $3000) to a computer network system with six videodisks and a video jukebox and specialized equipment for voice or music synthesis. Current designs of CD-I players predict a stand-alone configuration that will sell for about $2000.

Viewers of hypermedia applications may also need the following peripherals: a CD-ROM drive ($600 to $1200), high-resolution color display board ($300 to $2000), monitor for video images ($500 to $3000), analog video disk player ($400 to $1000), voice synthesizer ($300 to $1000), music synthesizer ($300 to $2000), video decompression hardware ($200 to $1000) and audio decompression hardware ($100 to $500).

- **Graphics, Video and Sound Editing.** A hypermedia authoring system must at least be able to display and link to two- or three-dimensional graphics and to play back sequences of analog or digital audio or video.

Many hypertext authoring systems provide some support for multimedia. Apple's Macintosh combined with HyperCard 2.0 will provide access to hypertext authoring capabilities from the operating system level.

- **Authoring Systems.** In order to create a hypertext document, all an author need do, once the raw data (text) is available, is chunk it, edit it, and link it. The editing of a hypermedia document is a bit more complicated, because digital video and audio nodes are not usually available to the author in compressed, digital form until after they've been chunked and edited. This is because uncompressed video requires huge amounts of storage, but digitizing and compression is an arduous, expensive process that cannot be undertaken until particular sequences out of the raw video have been chosen for the hypermedia. Video compression cannot be performed effectively using most of the algorithms used to compress video sequences because the base/delta schemes they use can only work if all the video frames within a sequence don't change. Editing out just one frame in the middle might make it impossible to rebuild an entire sequence. Authors using analog audio and video have a similar problem. The videodisk can't be pressed until the audio and video have been edited. OMDR technology obviates this problem somewhat, because it allows authors to copy individual frames to OMDR disks.

  Some compression techniques provide an intermediate video form, such as *Real Time Video* (DVI RTV), which provides a low-resolution, slow-frame-rate approximation of what the video will eventually look like, for use by the multimedia author. The author would determine frame sequencing by using this RTV, then send the video off for final edit, digitization and compression. [Luther, 1989]

- **Staff.** The production of a hypermedia system requires a wide combination of skills. As overall director, a hypermedia/interactive designer is required to coordinate the individual pieces. Not only are motion picture or video professionals, such as camera persons, light persons, and sound persons required, but so are graphic artists for creating animations and programmers for creating special purpose nodes.

  Depending on the sophistication of the production staff, the developer may require the skills of an artist, video editor, audio producer, and other professionals to accomplish these creative tasks.

Conclusion

No technology can meet every need. Hypermedia is a good solution to some but not all problems. In some cases a non-link-based interactive approach is best. The dividing line between an interactive program and a hypermedia one is fine. A distinguishing feature is that an interactive program might have inputs which are not necessarily mouse clickable. For example, a flight simulator would have multiple variable controls, such as the position of the stick and the throttle. These could be implemented using hypermedia links, but the result would probably not be true to life.

In the case studies section at the end of this book, there are some truly lovely examples of effective applications of hypermedia. Also in the case studies see Wayne MacPhail's discussion of why he chose not to use hypermedia, but instead plain vanilla hypertext, to develop his AIDs and Immigration hyperdocuments.

All hypertext design is challenging. Hypermedia requires both hypertext design and multimedia design. Hypermedia implementation takes the skills, time and money that go into hypertext and multimedia combined. Because the storage and performance limitations imposed by hypermultimedia development and delivery platforms are severe, the key to a successful hypermedia is an ability to determine where to compromise on speed or quality.

About the Authors

Oliver L. Picher

Oliver L. Picher is an editor/analyst with Datapro Research Group in Delran, NJ. He was a member of the team that assembled the Datapro Consultant for the Macintosh, a SuperCard-based application, delivered on CD-ROM, that incorporates text, data, Macintosh screen recordings, and audio clips into a complete information service on Macintosh hardware and software.

A writer by training and a technologist by experience, Mr. Picher is awaiting the day when he can use an extensible, object-oriented, hypermedia database to do his research.

Emily Berk

Emily Berk is co-editor of this handbook and a principal in Armadillo Associates, Inc. of Philadelphia, PA. She has been a designer and programmer of interactive hyper- and multimedia since 1980. Some of her recent multimedia meanderings have taken her to work as Project Leader on the Words in the Neighborhood application at RCA Sarnoff Labs and as chief instigator of the Zoo Project, a HyperCard-based mapping program.

Joseph Devlin

Joseph Devlin is the other co-editor of this handbook and the other principal in Armadillo Associates, Inc. He has been a skeptical observer of the multimedia market since the 1970s, when he worked at Commodore International and Creative Computing Magazine.

Ken Pugh

Ken Pugh is President of Information Navigation, Inc., of Durham, NC.

References

Bastiaens, G. A. (1989). "The Development of CD-I". Boston Computer Society, "SIG Meeting Notes," *New Media News,* Winter.

Berk, E., and Devlin, J. (1990). "An Overview of Multimedia Computing." *Datapro Reports on Document Imaging Systems,* Datapro Research. Delran, NJ. February.

Brunsman, S., Messerly, J., and Lammers, S. (1988). "Publishers, Multimedia, and Interactivity." *Interactive Multimedia.* Eds. Ambron, S., and Hooper, K. Microsoft Press, Redmond, WA.

Bush, Vannevar (1945). "As We May Think." *The Atlantic Monthly* 176.1 (July) p. 101–103.

Dillon, M. (1988). "Scripting for Interactive Multimedia CD Systems" *Communications of the ACM* 31.7 (July). (Special issue on hypertext.)

Evenson, S., et al. (1989). "Towards a Design Language for Representing Hypermedia Cues." *Proceedings Hypertext '89.* November 5–7, 1989, Pittsburgh, PA . New York: ACM, pp. 83–92.

Fox, E. A. (1989). "The coming revolution in interactive digital video." (Special Section in) *Communications of the ACM:* July.

Fraase, M. (1989). Macintosh Hypermedia: Vols. I–IV, Reference Guide. Scott, Foresman and Company, Glenview, IL.

Frenkel, K. A. (1989). "The next generation of interactive technologies." *Communications of the ACM* July v32 n7 pp. 872–882.

Hodges, M. E., Sasnett, R. M., Harward, V. J. (1990). "Musings on multimedia." *UNIX Review* Feb v8 n2 pp. 82–88.

Horn, R. E. (1989). "Mapping Hypertext: The Analysis, Organization, and Display of Knowledge for the Next Generation of On-Line Text and Graphics." The Lexington Institute, Lexington, MA.

Lucky, R. (1989). *Silicon Dreams: Information, Man and Machine.* St. Martin's Press, NY.

Luther, A. C. (1989). *Digital Video in the PC Environment.* McGraw-Hill/Intertext Publications, NY.

Meyrowitz, N. (1988). "Issues in Designing a Hypermedia Document System." *Interactive Multimedia.* Eds. Ambron, S., and Hooper, K. Microsoft Press, Redmond, WA.

Meyrowitz, N. (19). "The Link to Tomorrow," *UNIX Review,* vol. 8, no. 2, pp. 58–67.

Miller, D. C. (1986). "Finally It Works: Now It Must 'Play in Peoria'," Lambert, S., and Ropiequet, S. *CD ROM: The New Papyrus.* Microsoft Press, Redmond, WA.

Nelson, T. H. (1975). "Dream Machines: New Freedoms through Computer Screens: A Minority Report." *Computer Lib: You Can and Must Understand Computers.* Published by the author.

Nielsen, J. (1989). "Hypertext II: Trip Report." June.

Nielsen, J. (1990). *Hypertext and Hypermedia.* Academic Press Inc., Copenhagen, Denmark.

Parsloe, E. (1985). *Interactive Video.* Sigma Technical Press. Cheshire, U.K.

Philips International, Inc. (1988). *Compact-Disc Interactive.* McGraw-Hill, New York.

Sherman, C. (1988). *The CD-ROM Handbook.* McGraw-Hill, New York.

Smith, T. L. (1986). "Compressing and Digitizing Images," Lambert, S., and Ropiequet, S. *CD ROM: The New Papyrus.* Microsoft Press, Redmond, WA.

Stork, C. (1988). "Interleaved Audio: The Next Step for CD-ROM." *CD Data Report,* Feb., pp. 20–24.

Yankelovich, N., et al. (1988). "Issues in Designing a Hypermedia Document System: The Intermedia Case Study." *Interactive Multimedia: Visions of Multimedia for Developers, Educators, & Information Providers.* Eds. Ambron, S., and Hooper, K. Microsoft Press, Redmond, WA, pp. 33–85.

Conventions for
Writers/Readers of Hypertext

Writing and reading used to be easy. If you were taking a test in school, you needed two sharp Number 2 pencils and three pieces of scrap paper. Essays were written on blue-lined looseleaf paper, two pages; no more, no less. Reading was even more straightforward. You went to the bookstore, or the library, or the magazine was delivered to you. You opened the book or magazine at the beginning or the table of contents or index, then opened the volume and started to read.

The contributors of the chapters in this section, not coincidentally all professors of literature, consider hypertext an essentially literary medium. But, as they point out, the conventions for writing and reading in this new medium have yet to be worked out.

Composing Hypertext:
A Discussion for Writing Teachers

By John M. Slatin
University of Texas at Austin

Introduction

I'd like to start by advancing the proposition that hypertext represents a new medium for thought and expression—the first verbal medium, besides programming languages, to emerge from the computer revolution. In saying this, I mean first of all to distinguish hypertext from word processing and desktop publishing, which to my mind remain simple extensions of the typewriter and the printing press, despite their impact on the practice of writing.

Hypertext is a new medium, in my view, because it is intimately tied to the computer; the true hypertext or hyperdocument exists and can exist only on-line, and has no meaningful existence in print. If I am right in making this claim, then it follows that we will need a new set of theoretical principles to describe how hypertext works as a medium. I don't propose to define a new rhetoric in these few pages, though I have made a preliminary attempt elsewhere to address some of the conceptual issues hypertext raises [Slatin, 1990]. Instead, I'll try to explore some of the practical problems hypertext might pose for teachers of writing.

Defining Hypertext

Theodor Holm Nelson, who coined the term hypertext in the mid-1960s, says that hypertext is any piece of "nonsequential writing" [Nelson, 1987, 1/14]. Newspapers and magazines, whose layout require us to read non-sequentially, are examples of what Nelson means; so are encyclopedias and other reference books, heavily cross-referenced and generally not meant to be read from beginning to end; and I have written elsewhere that hypertext resembles poetry in its intertextuality [Slatin, 1988]. But I cannot agree that encyclopedias and poems are already hypertexts; they can more properly be described as forerunners. Although these examples have what some might consider the virtue of making hypertext seem familiar and therefore nonthreatening, they are also quite misleading, as I shall explain below.

Nelson says that the hypertext concept is not intrinsically dependent upon the computer. I believe, however, that true hypertext can only exist on-line. So I want to modify Nelson's definition, to read as follows:

A hypertext (or hyperdocument) is an assemblage of texts, images, and sounds—nodes—connected by electronic links so as to form a system whose existence is contingent upon the computer.

The user/reader moves from node to node either by following established links or by creating new ones. The conventional text is the result of many individual choices made by the author from among the available alternatives. By contrast, the hypertext consists of many possible or virtual texts, which may be the work of different people. The reader actualizes one or more of these virtual texts in choosing which links to follow and which to ignore.

The potential significance of this difference is most clearly evident when we consider the vexing problem of hypertext's relation to print.

The Goal of Hypertext

Both word processing and desktop publishing have had an enormous impact on the practice of writing, as I have already said, and, like hypertext, both are inconceivable without the computer. What separates them from hypertext, however, is that both word processing and desktop publishing have as their goal the production of printed documents.

That is not the goal of hypertext. In my view, there is no such thing as hard copy of an entire hyperdocument. A printout of all the nodes would probably be meaningless, since it would lack even the provisional, temporary structure created by the reader's choices as she moved through the hypertext system. By the same token, a printout consisting only of the nodes accessed during a given session inside a hypertext actualizes a particular pathway through the material, a particular sequence, a particular set of choices. But it isn't the hypertext, any more than a given critical reading of a poem is the poem. What hypertext really requires is enough storage space to keep everything available on line.

Composing Hypertext

Leaving aside the financial implications of what I have just proposed, readers will naturally be asking a number of other, equally practical questions at this point. For instance, if we are seriously proposing to allow or require students to compose their essays in hypertext form, and if we accept the contention that hypertext can't be printed out, then we have to ask how students are to hand in their work. We also have to wonder what these hypertext essays will look like and how we are supposed to evaluate them.

In all candor, the only one of these questions whose answer I'm sure of is the first one: students will obviously be submitting their work to us on diskette(s) or whatever medium replaces the diskette, perhaps with accompanying documentation to explain how to get into the essay. Rejoinders to the other questions are considerably more difficult to find. (See Figures 6.1a and b.)

The form of a hypertext depends in large part, on the program used to produce it. Something done in OWL International's GUIDE looks quite different from something done in Apple Computer's HyperCard, which in turn looks quite different from something done in Hyperties or TextPro in the DOS environment, and so forth. Here again we see the difference between word processing and hypertext; there would be something seriously the matter if I had to say that the form of a student essay would depend very heavily upon the particular word processing program s/he had used. Part of the interest, for me, will be precisely in seeing how each student or group of students will solve—or at least address—the problem of what a hyper-essay should look like now. (See Figures 6.2, 6.3, and 6.4.)

What we're most likely to see at first is what one of my former graduate students, Belinda Gonzalez, referred to as "very extensive footnoting"—or, as another student, Pete Smith, put it, an alluring introductory paragraph of some sort linked

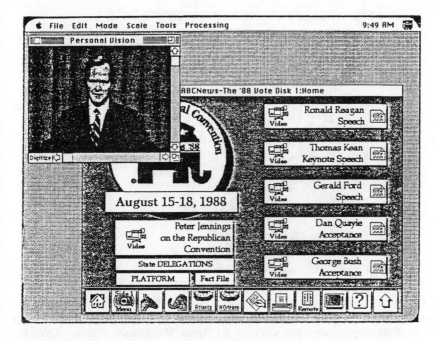

Figure 6.1a   Will students submit their history reports electronically?

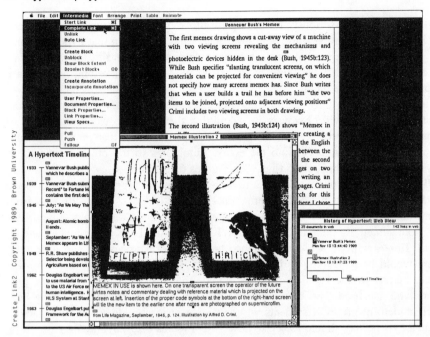

Figure 6.1b   One of them might document the history of hypertext in a way similar to that of the folks at Brown's Intermedia Lab. Copyright 1989, Brown University.

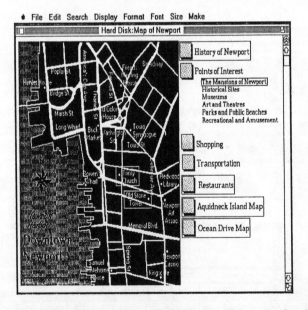

Figure 6.2   This guide for travellers to Newport, R.I., was implemented by HyperView Systems using OWL International's GUIDE hypertext authoring system. This hyperdocument runs on an Apple Macintosh. *Source*: OWL International, Inc.

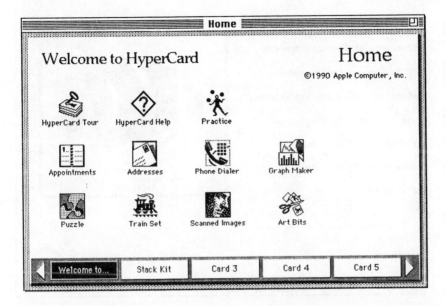

Figure 6.3 The home card is familiar to any author or reader of Apple's HyperCard, which also runs on Apple Macintosh personal computers. © 1990 Apple Computer, Inc. All Rights Reserved. Apple is a registered trademark and HyperCard is a registered trademark of Apple Computer, Inc. licensed to Claris Corporation. Reprinted with permission from Claris Corporation.

to a variety of explanatory and supporting materials such as online encyclopedias, databases, and so forth. But there is a point at which the extension becomes *hyperextended*, if you'll pardon the bad pun, so that what you're creating is no longer merely a web of annotations, but actually a system containing multiple frames of reference, multiple windows onto a particular terrain—windows which, as in James's famous House of Fiction metaphor, are created by the pressure of a particular consciousness and which represent the vision of that consciousness. Each window, that is, provides a particular way of seeing—and each way of seeing constructs a new map of the terrain, even a new landscape [James, 1934].

This suggests yet another way in which the technology of composition changes the nature of composition. Hypertext is a wonderful medium for group work [Trigg, et al. 1986]. Thus the hypertext essay might well be the work of multiple authors. One could, for instance, give a whole class a project to work on, with each student responsible for some particular aspect of it. They would work on their projects all semester long, creating individual nodes of their own and defining links among those nodes and other on-line materials available to them. They would have to work out ways of combining and linking all these materials, and creating windows opening out onto different views of the materials they had developed. Ultimately, the class would have to work out (with, of course, the

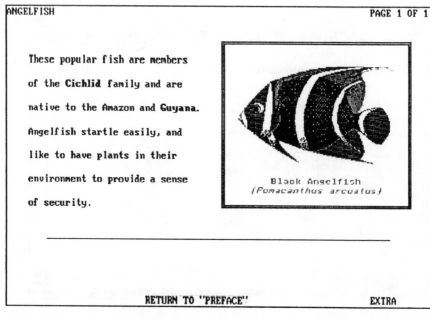

Figure 6.4 Unlike HyperCard, which relies on a card metaphor, Hyperties is based around the metaphor of an encyclopedia. Source: Cognetics Corp.

instructor's active collaboration) how best to link everything, how to define the relationships among the various elements. (See Figure 6.5.)

Personally, I can't wait to try it. Others will be more reluctant, however; for them it will seem to be giving up far too much, and getting far too little in return. And it may well seem too much to ask of our students. This case is eloquently stated by Tina Buck, another of my graduate students, and an experienced teacher. She writes: "I might (and will!) argue that hypertext is radical and perhaps inapplicable to typical freshmen and sophomores because in the first few years of college, students must be taught to think critically, structuredly, etc. I agree that hypertext approaches the way we actually think; but there is much to be said for

Figure 6.5 Apple Computer believes that students can use multimedia tools that are already available to expand their awareness of the links between concepts such as one type of animal and the environment. *Source*: Apple Computer, Inc.

the imposition of 'a trained, disciplined mind,' to facilitate communication and thought. I don't know if our typical students are ready for a stream of consciousness approach to their education. In fact, I might argue that you have to understand the five-paragraph essay first, before you launch into hypertext. Hypertext is like atonal music: until students understand (traditionally) structured music, they won't like or understand John Cage or Stockhausen."

As I said to Ms. Buck, my own first experience of hypertext was something like my first experience of jazz, when I was about twelve. I had heard about jazz as an improvisational form, I had read descriptions of wild solos, I had heard people like my grandfather saying that it wasn't music. But when I listened to jazz for the first time, I was both disappointed and delighted to find that it sounded like music to my ears! So, too, I when I actually sat down with a hypertext package after reading and thinking about it for a few months, I was most immediately impressed by its resemblance to the kinds of writing I had always known—except that the program I was using lacked the sophisticated word processing features I had come to expect.

Gradually, however, the differences between hypertext and conventional text began to appear. It is certainly true that hypertext disrupts conventional structures and expectations in some very fundamental ways. For instance, where the conventional essay has a single point of departure, an opening paragraph, the hyperdocument offers multiple entry points: the reader chooses where to enter the system. In the same way, the hyperdocument offers not a single conclusion, but rather a number of possible exit-points, and again it is for the reader to choose when and where to leave the system. Most radically of all, the hyperdocument provides many different pathways through the material constituting the system—and again the reader chooses which paths to follow and which to leave for another day. As Ms. Buck indicates, one of the claims most often made for hypertext is that it more closely simulates the interconnectedness of concepts in the mind than conventional text can do [Jones, 1990]. The problem for readers will be in finding a way through and among all the interconnections—and indeed, this may be an insurmountable problem in certain cases, cases where the student author has followed what Ms. Buck described as "a stream of consciousness approach." In any case, it suggests that the traditional opening paragraph may well have to be replaced by a kind of map describing the lay of the land—a map which would have to be accessible from any position in the system.

My first inclination is to agree with the contention that students need to understand conventional structure before understanding hypertextual redefinitions of structure. Sequential text is extremely powerful, and for exactly those reasons that led Nelson and other theorists to critique it: it does indeed impose an arbitrary sequence, an arbitrary structure, upon the material, and requires the reader to submit to that structure. (I do not use the word arbitrary in an evaluative sense, as meaning "pointless": I use it as meaning "lacking intrinsic relation to the matter at hand".) Arbitrary structures (such as the rules of football or chess, the formulae of mathematics, the metrical patterns of poetry, and so forth) are immensely powerful, and never more so than when they have been sanctioned by tradition and we have become forcibly aware—through some change in circumstance, such as the advent of a new medium—of their arbitrariness. To some extent, we commit ourselves to those structures precisely because they are arbitrary: we have to clap our hands to show that we believe. And in committing ourselves to them, we gain access to their beauty and power, and to the beauty and power of the traditions to which they belong.

Having said all that, I want to resist my own inclination to side with those who argue that students should understand traditional ways of doing things first, before we subject them to radical new methods. I want to resist for several reasons, not least of which is that one argument for hypertext is that it more closely approximates the structure of thought in our minds, or the pattern of thought in our minds, than does conventional text. As Douglas Hofstadter has said: "Nothing is a concept except by virtue of the way it is connected up (in the mind, in the memory) with other things that are also concepts" [Hofstadter, 1985].

This is as clear a statement of the conceptual basis for hypertext as one could ask for, though Hofstadter is talking even more generally here about the workings of the mind. It is precisely because hypertext has such a conceptual basis that it can be used to encourage the kinds of rigorous, highly systematic, profoundly critical thinking and writing which many practitioners see as the aim of writing courses. It would work by encouraging exploration of relationships among various objects of study, and by encouraging students to view those objects from a number of different perspectives and to place them within different frames of reference. By creating their own links among various elements in the hypertextual knowledge base, and then explaining and defending the linkages, they could try out different views of their own, and see which ones were most comprehensive and most compelling.

Far from exhibiting mere unedited, self-indulgent stream-of-consciousness, as some may fear, hypertext may and can reveal the most fundamental aspects of intelligence. If concepts themselves are created, are constituted as concepts in being placed into relation with other mental objects, then, if I understand Hofstadter correctly, analogy is the mechanism by which relationships are established, and thus the basis of conceptualization itself. See, for instance, the related essays "On the Seeming Paradox of Mechanizing Creativity" and the long, brilliant "Analogies and Roles in Human and Machine Thinking" [Hofstadter, 1985]. Hypertext links simulate and represent analogies in the mind; linkage is the electronic counterpart to analogy. Thus, hypertext permits student writers (and others, of course) to engage in the formation of concepts, and to explore the basis of their thought.

Conclusion

So I don't see hypertext as being incompatible with previous modes of thought, rather, as the prefix "hyper" indicates, I see it as an extension of text, and of the modes of thought supported by traditional text. It is also an extremely powerful analytical tool; hypertext literalizes much of the current theoretical and practical interest, among teachers of both writing and literature, in the arbitrariness of narrative, discursive, and ideological structures. And that, I think, is both the promise and the threat of hypertext.

In revealing the arbitrariness of our intellectual structures, hypertext may also provide a means of exploring the arbitrary distinctions we make on the basis of race and class and gender, and offer a way to include within the larger totality the voices and visions of those whom we ordinarily exclude, whether knowingly or not. It has been suggested (again by one of my graduate students) that hypertext, like so many other things connected with computers, is really for the elite, the wealthy and privileged. Certainly, the affluent have more access to computers than do the poor or otherwise disadvantaged; it is up to us, I think, to determine whether or not that remains true.

But it isn't true that hypertext is only for the ultra-sophisticated, or only for those in the more rarefied reaches of the academy. Michael Joyce's article "Siren-Shapes: Exploratory and Constructive Hypertexts" [Joyce, 1988] reports eloquently on Joyce's experiments with hypertext as a medium for composition by basic writers in a community college setting. And I have corresponded with a woman in Washington, DC about her plans to use hypermedia in a project to educate economically disadvantaged youth in the worst ghettoes of Northeast Washington.

And finally, perhaps hypertext serves to remind us of the arbitrariness of our commitment to the codex book, forcing us to acknowledge that, in Richard Lanham's words, in recent years "our whole posture has been defensive, based on the book and the curricular and professional structures which issue from it" [Lanham, 1989, 287]. There was a moment in Western history when writing itself appeared as a revolutionary technology, radically altering the balance of culture and power. Writing succeeded, as Eric Havelock and others have shown [Havelock, 1982], by making itself transparent—by becoming so easy to use, so automatic, that we did not think of it as technology until the computer came along and forced us to reconceive it from top to bottom.

About the Author

John Slatin

John Slatin is an Associate Professor of English at The University of Texas at Austin, and Director of the English Department's Computer Research Lab.

He is the author of several essays on hypertext, and The Savage's Romance (1986), a study of the poet Marianne Moore. He is currently at work on a book about the impact of information technology on research and teaching in the humanities.

References

Havelock, E. A. (1982). *The Literate Revolution in Greece and Its Cultural Consequences,* Princeton University Press, Princeton, NJ.

Hofstadter, D. R. (1985). *Metamagical Themas: Questing After The Essence Of Mind And Pattern,* Bantam Books, New York, NY.

James, H. (1934). (Preface to) *Protrait of a Lady,* Charles Scribners and Sons, New York, NY 46.

Jones, R. A. (1990). *To Criss-Cross In Every Direction: or, Why Hypertext Works,* Academic Computing 4: 20–21, 30.

Joyce, M. (1988). *Siren-Shapes: Exploratory and Constructive Hypertexts,* Academic Computing 2: 10–14, 37–42.

Lanham, R. A. (1989). *The Electronic Word: Literary Study and The Digital Revolution,* New Literary History 20: 265–90.

Nelson, T. H. (1987). *Literary Machines,* Theodor Holm Nelson, San Antonio, TX.

Slatin, J. M. (1988). "Hypertext and The Teaching of Writing," Barrett, E. (Ed.) *Text, Context, and Hypertext: Writing With and For The Computer,* Cambridge, MA: MIT Press. 111–129.

Slatin, J. M. (1990, in press). *Reading Hypertext: Order and Coherence in a New Medium,* College English.

Trigg, R., Sachman, Lucy, A., Halasz, F. (1986). "Supporting Collaboration in NoteCards," Conference in Computer-Supported Cooperative Work, Austin, TX, Dec. 3–5.

Toward a Paradigm for Reading Hypertexts: Making Nothing Happen in Hypermedia Fiction

By Stuart Moulthrop
Georgia Institute of Technology

...poetry makes nothing happen: it survives
In the valley of its making where executives
Would never want to tamper... — W. H. Auden, "In Memory of W. B. Yeates"

Nothing will come of nothing. Speak again. — Shakespeare, *King Lear*

Literature is a dying art. This statement is not a prophecy of doom but a paradox: literature is never more alive than when it is *dying*. Virtually every moment of literary history has struck some writer as the end of the road, the point at which serious, important, or valuable writing becomes impossible. The cultural coroners ordinarily focus on genre: the death of tragedy, the twilight of the epic, the demise of the novel, the collapse of parody. But the rise and fall of genres usually coincides with technological change. For instance, the novel came into its own only when advances in printing and the availability of cheap paper permitted the mass production of inexpensive books. Now the novel and other print genres seem threatened by the evolution of hypermedia, which Steven Levy recently branded "the end of literature" [Levy, 1990].

Literature never ends; it survives. Levy and other media critics base their doom theories on a zero-sum model of evolution in which any gain for new technologies depletes the old. Obsolescence means displacement. Yet the historical development of media patently contradicts this view. As Marshall McLuhan observed, "the content of any medium is always another medium." [McLuhan, M., 1964] More advanced technologies incorporate those that come before. Writing contains speech, print contains writing, film contains both these media, as when a voiceover accompanies a montage of headlines. Hypermedia, the latest of McLuhan's *extensions of man*, unites sound, graphics, print, and video.

Writing Survives, But In a Changed Environment

Once upon a time, when literary critics used the word "text" they meant a verbal artifact, a book or manuscript. More recently that term has come to stand for any network of symbols, verbal or otherwise: film as text, seminar as text, history as text [Barthes, 1979; Fish, 1980; White, 1973]. This latter, more expansive notion of "text" seems a better way to understand hypermedia productions and the role writing plays within them. The printed word is no longer the dominant medium, but only an element in a technological synthesis, one strand in a complex text.

We face the advent not of electronic books, but of eclectic multimedia compositions that assimilate and transcend the book. The future of literary expression is not a linear progress in which new technologies of expression usurp old ones. It is more likely to be a *recursion*, a widening gyre in which new forms merge and coevolve with their precursors.

The term recursion has several connotations. It implies the neat cyclicality of reflex and reiteration, as in the hierarchical nesting of functions in a computer program. Recursion in this sense is a rational process, analogous to the revolution of gears in an engine or the closing of circuits in a microprocessor. But there is also a second, irrational meaning of recursion. This is the sense invoked in Douglas Hofstadter's notion of *tangled hierarchies*, where an apparently orderly procedure yields paradoxical results [Hofstadter, 1979]. As in M.C. Escher's surrealist *Waterfall*, where tricks of perspective make a downgrade seem to lead upward, this irrational recursion invalidates our sense of hierarchy and shatters our interpretive framework.

Tangled hierarchies and "strange loops" may be our most powerful modes of expression at this late moment of the Twentieth century. As the cultural critic O.B. Hardison observes:

> A horizon of invisibility cuts across the geography of modern culture. Those who have passed through it cannot put their experience into familiar words and images because the languages they have inherited are inadequate to the new worlds they inhabit. They therefore express themselves in metaphors, paradoxes, contradictions, and abstractions rather than languages that "mean" in the traditional way—in assertions that are apparently incoherent or collages using fragments of the old to create enigmatic symbols of the new. [Hardison, 1990]

Hardison has in mind Dadaists, surrealists, and expressionists, the first artists to step over the modern event horizon. These figures represented an *avant garde* dedicated to subverting old orders of meaning. They accomplished this subversion by exposing the formal mechanisms of language, building poems out of abstract sounds, typographic manipulations, or random numerical sequences.

But that was a long time ago. At century's end, some critics argue, we have outgrown or exhausted such rebellious impulses. Our culture has passed from modern to postmodern, and there are those who say that *avant garde* art is impossible under postmodernism [Eagleton, 1985]. Many reasons are proposed for this situation, most having to do with the inability of artists to separate themselves from pervasive ideological and informational systems. Modernists could renounce traditional culture by embracing absurdity. Postmodern culture is *always already* meaningless. Any provisional meaning it can muster arrives predeconstructed, already defined as the sort of arbitrary, self-referential sign system that the modernists strove to create. It is impossible to be a Dadaist in a Dada universe.

Our universe is Dada with a difference, however, and the name of this difference is technology. Our capacity to build and manipulate complex informational systems has increased hugely in the second half of the century. From market analyses to programmed stock trading, we live in a world in which abstract models are increasingly based not upon any observed fact but upon other abstract models—the world of the *hyperreal*. Hardison has argued that our sense of reality is disappearing through the skylight as we replace nature with convincing images of reality. The world we have built may be absurd—not grounded in any value or sense of destiny—but it is eminently systematic.

Since technology is strongly implicated in the disappearance of the real, what possibilities are there for technological fiction? Is it possible to make meaningful or critical statements about complex, self-referential systems from within a hypermedia text, which is just such a system? Is this really the end for literature?

Even as theorists of the postmodern toll yet another death knell for yet another artform, undismayed artists have begun to explore the expressive potential of hypermedia, turning systems recursively back on themselves to probe the seams and fissures of the hyperreal. In the section that follows, we examine an exemplary hypermedia fiction.

An Example of Hypermedia Fiction

```
on mouseUp
    Global thermoNuclearWar
    put the script of me into tightOrbit
    put tightOrbit into eventHorizon
    put empty into first line of eventHorizon
    put empty into last line of eventHorizon
    put empty into last line of eventHorizon
    put eventHorizon after line thermoNuclearWar of tightOrbit
    set the script of me to tightOrbit
    put thermoNuclearWar + 10 into thermoNuclearWar
    click at the clickLoc
end mouseUp
```

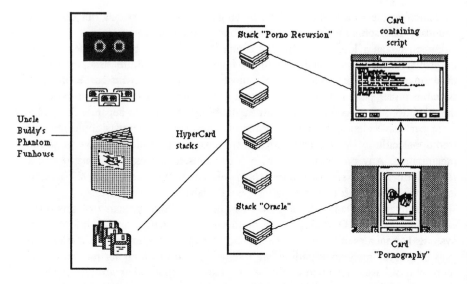

Figure 7.1   Schematic Outline of _Uncle Buddy's Phantom Funhouse._

The HyperTalk script shown above is a very small part of _Uncle Buddy's Phantom Funhouse,_[1] a work-in-progress by hypermedia artist John McDaid. The _Funhouse_ is a complex fabric of texts within texts (See Figure 7.1), consisting of video and audio tapes, photographs and drawings, letters, offprints, galley proofs, and a set of Macintosh disks, all purporting to be the effects of a disappeared writer, one Arthur "Buddy" Newkirk.

Uncle Buddy's disks hold a series of electronic documents which themselves contain a variety of printed words, images, and digitized sounds. Since these documents are hypertexts (HyperCard stacks), many of their elements are cross-linked both within and among documents.

Though there are abundant connections between Uncle Buddy's various fragments, the reader is given no clear instructions for their assembly. The details revealed by the text do not integrate into any single, exhaustive narrative. The exhibits in the _Funhouse_ are capable of multiple arrangement and signification, making Arthur Newkirk potentially many things to many readers. Implications abound, but there is no deductive problem to solve, no imperative to recover in any definitive sense the lost _art._

Yet even though the hypertextual labyrinth conceals no kernel of meaning, certain of its elements are especially significant, and the script shown above is one of them.

The script is technically untitled, but for convenience we will give it the name of the stack to which it belongs, _Porno recursion._ This stack is one of several apparently created by Uncle Buddy and copied to the backup disks included in his

---

1   Copyright John G. McDaid.

effects. When the contents of these disks are transferred to the reader's Macintosh, they provide access to Uncle Buddy's virtual reality, a densely interlinked network of notes, sketches, drafts, and correspondence.

The primary interface between the reader and this mass of information is a simulation of Newkirk's house in Pirate Cove, Rhode Island. Each room in the house is represented by a series of digitized photographs which the reader can tour by maneuvering a pointer on the Macintosh screen.

During this exploration the reader can manipulate objects in the house, opening doors, windows, drawers, and cabinets. The house provides a symbolic index or organizing metaphor for the entire set of HyperCard stacks, acting as the electronic equivalent of a *memory palace*. Objects or locales in the house are hypertextually linked to various electronic elements of the fiction. For example, opening the mailbox in front of the house, calls up a stack containing a log of Uncle Buddy's correspondence on a computer network. By manipulating the house and its furnishings, the reader can access several documents and objects, including notes for a screenplay, an annotated sketchbook, an electronic literary magazine, (*Source Code, the HyperMagazine of Hacker Poets*), and a modified Tarot deck called *Oracle*.

It is through the *Oracle* deck that the "Porno recursion" script comes to light; but as with the conventional Tarot, the path to enlightenment requires patience and ingenuity. The link between *Oracle* and the "Porno recursion" script is neither simple nor immediately apparent. To discover it, the reader needs to recognize that the Oracle stack initiates a dialogue between new media and old.

The elements or nodes in a HyperCard stack are referred to as "cards," following the file card analogy developed in Xerox PARC's NoteCards program. In *Oracle,* McDaid/Newkirk plays on this analog, patterning his electronic cards after actual, cardboard artifacts. In fact, the images on each virtual card were optically transferred from a hand-drawn deck. Like the original arcana, these hypertextual cards can be laid out or accessed in sequence, and thus interpreted for cryptic significance.

But there is a crucial difference between the electronic *Oracle* and the traditional Tarot. Material Tarot cards are formally stable and discrete. The *Oracle* cards, by contrast, may not display all of their graphic and verbal content on first presentation. Since the stack *Oracle* is a hypertext, any visible writing or image may act as a pointer to additional content. This hidden content is displayed when the reader finds a hot area or button with the pointing device. The link that takes us to the "Porno recursion" script is triggered by a button installed on an *Oracle* card called "Pornography" (See Figure 7.2).

The figure on this card shows the graph of an electromagnetic waveform of the type that might be used in radio or television broadcasting. There is also a gloss to the image, "P = T - R: Pornography equals technology minus relativity." Presumably this emblem and its gloss have some connection to the "Porno recursion" script; but the script is not directly attached to the card or its image. Technically speaking, the script resides on another card altogether, one that does not even belong to the stack "Oracle." (The reason for this inconsistency will be clear below.)

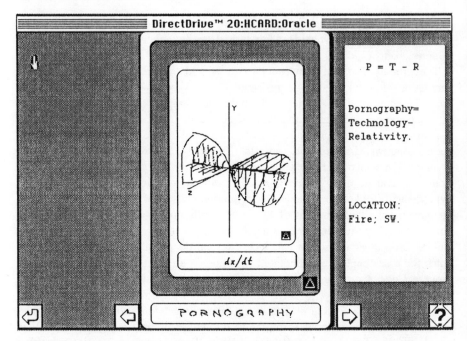

Figure 7.2   Card "Pornography" of stack "Oracle."

Since the script is not visible from the *Pornography* card, no casual browser through the *Oracle* will discover it. The script is revealed only to readers who learn to consult the cards for hypertextual links as well as textual symbolism, keeping in mind the fact that everything in Uncle Buddy's universe is potentially connected to everything else.

HyperCard provides a keyboard command that shows the location of any link buttons on a given card. Used on the card Pornography, this command reveals several buttons, one of which (the smaller black triangle immediately below and to the right of the line drawing in Figure 7.2) opens the pathway to the Porno recursion script.

Pressing this button brings up a dialog box containing the warning, "Too much recursion" (See Figure 7.3).

This standard HyperTalk error message occurs when the order of operations in a script becomes confused or tangled, for instance when a routine enters a loop in which it calls or activates itself interminably. Presumably something has gone wrong. The HyperTalk script activated by the button cannot be executed because of a serious logical flaw. *The Funhouse*, it would seem, is not entirely up to code.

But this apparent breakdown is only the beginning of what will prove to be an extremely complex interaction. The error message dialog box in HyperCard contains a button allowing the reader to edit the script that has just failed. If the reader takes this option after the "Too much recursion" message comes up, the code that appears is the "Porno recursion" script, which has ostensibly crashed after being activated by card button *Delta delta* on card Pornography (See Figure 7.4).

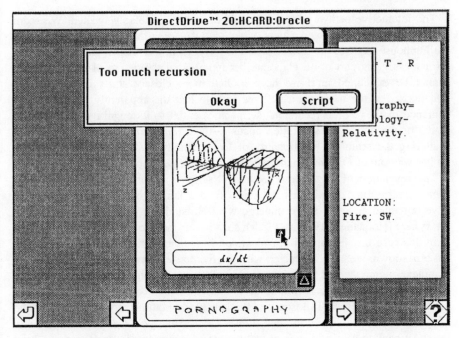

Figure 7.3 Card "Pornography" with error message.

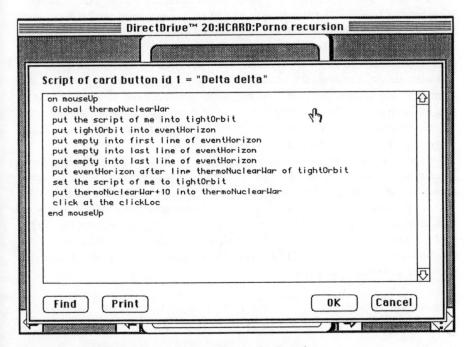

Figure 7.4 Edit window for "Porno Recursion" script.

The interactive pathway leading to this discovery is notably twisted. We seem to reach the script only by accident, when an unforeseen flaw in the functioning of the Funhouse exposes the infrastructure of the text. In fact this is not the case—the error message is part of an elaborate deception—but the nature of this deception cannot be explained until we have looked more closely at its immediate implications. For the moment, it suffices to note that the apparently unplanned appearance of the "Porno recursion" script is essential to its cognitive effect. Accidental or not, the script's eruption opens a rift in the primary illusion of the text, shattering the seamless functionality of Uncle Buddy's *docuverse*. Like Dorothy on her way out of Oz, we cannot overlook what we see behind the curtain.

The revelation of the "Porno recursion" script apparently breaks the fictional frame, confronting us with a mechanism (and a language) that would otherwise have remained concealed. We undergo what Hofstadter would call a *jump out of the system* [Hofstadter, 1979], a sudden shift in our mode of interpretation.

In this case this jump is also a *recursion* in media. Until the moment of apparent breakdown, we have interacted with the *Funhouse* as a multimedia hypertext, a complex, interconnected work informed by elaborate graphic and other metaphors. But the "Porno recursion" returns us to the ostensibly coherent, linear mode of print. After all, a HyperTalk script is fundamentally nothing more than a sequence of typed characters. The error that arrests Uncle Buddy's *Oracle* would seem to throw us back to a primitive level of function. It seems to demonstrate that all the brave machinery of the *Funhouse* depends on the printed word.

According to this interpretation, the recursion to print represents a change of levels within a stable hierarchy: higher-level functions have broken down, revealing what lies beneath. But this is only part of the story behind the "Porno recursion." To see the emergence of the script as a simple hierarchical shift is to assume that "Porno recursion" is a conventional piece of HyperTalk code—but it is plainly more than that. While HyperTalk permits the writer of a script to call variables almost anything, the choice of *thermoNuclearWar* as the name of the counter in the second line indicates that there may be more at issue here than simple functionality. The arresting line: "Global thermoNuclearWar" suggests that "Porno recursion" returns us not just to print, but to *print as a medium of literary expression*. The script is really a poem in disguise.

This is not really such a strange suggestion. High-level computer languages share many formal qualities of verse: verbal economy, line breaks and enjambments, organization into functional units (think of subroutines as stanzas). The "hacker poet" is not such a rare beast; it is not unusual for variable names or comments in a program to constitute a quasiliterary subtext. But ordinarily these poetic overtones remain latent or superficial, while in the "Porno recursion," they take on crucial significance. If we would understand what the script is really about, we must read it as a poem.

Script As Poem

The "Porno recursion" poem is a satire on systematic language. It launches a probe into the dark undertones of HyperTalk's utilitarian vocabulary. The language of programming is ostensibly unambiguous and purely functional. Declaration statements pass information about the type and name of variables; assignment commands associate information with those variables; selectors refer to specific items in a block of data. Ostensibly, these expressions mean nothing more than what they do.

The script-as-poem overturns that assumption by loading the plain language of programming with allusion. In literary terms, it employs a device called *infection*, a combination of guilt-by-association and conditioned response. The object of this device is to "contaminate" a supposedly neutral expression by associating it with language that is not so neutral, so that when the target expression reappears in an innocent context, it will carry an "infected" connotation. So the declaration syntax *global [variableName]* yields a "declaration" of *Global thermoNuclearWar.* Likewise the assignment command *put* suggests the tactics of pre-emptive strike ("put the script of me into tightOrbit") and the selector *last* is used to invoke apocalyptic singularity ("last line of event Horizon"). The twelve-line programming script is thus transformed into a vision of the end of the world.

Thus "infected," the narrow language of programming opens onto a distinctly sinister perspective. It is appropriate that this parodic distortion comes out of the *Oracle* card *Pornography* with its anti-technological gloss ("Pornography equals technology minus relativity"). The oracle of the card seems to warn that a determinist, unrelativistic application of science leads only to debased conceptions— conceptions which must include the apparently innocuous technology of the Macintosh itself, whose symbol of system failure is after all an iron bomb. Through poetic juxtaposition, Porno recursion reveals the connection between the "global" control that allows us to construct systems like hypermedia texts and the will-to-power that motivates us to produce nuclear arsenals. As Susan Sontag put it, "cogito ergo boom."

But the process of conversion from script into poem is itself highly significant. To read a brief HyperTalk script as verse is to tangle the hierarchy of hypermedia. Allusive, literary meaning is supposed to be found only at the higher levels of the text, at the level of the *virtual* reality. Programming scripts belong to a lower, merely *functional* reality. This print infrastructure is not ordinarily so loaded with meaning. "Porno recursion" demonstrates that this hierarchy is inherently unstable in hypermedia fiction. The constraints of functionality cannot suppress the evocative potential of printed language, which may erupt whenever there is "error," exposing the linear, causal structures that underlie the supposedly "nonsequential" interactive text.

Funhouse As An Example Of The Interactive Medium

But the nature of this "error" in the *Funhouse* needs further explanation. In fact, it is no error at all, but a carefully arranged object lesson about the nature of the interactive medium. We have so far considered the script as a jump out of the system in which programming asserts itself as poetry. To fully appreciate the significance of "Porno recursion," however, we need to reverse interpretive course again, moving from the allusiveness of literature back toward the functionality of

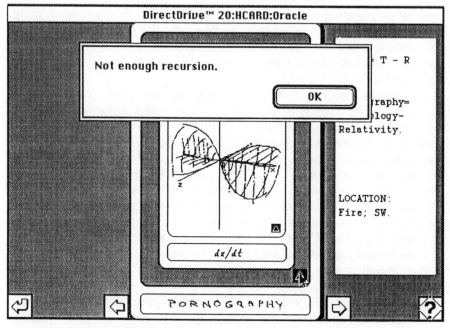

Figure 7.5   Card "Pornography" with parodic error message.

computer code. But to do this we first have to untangle the multiple deceptions in which the script is embroiled.

"Porno recursion" appears to be a flawed HyperTalk script activated by card button *Delta delta*. In fact this is not the case, and an alert or skeptical reader has several ways to detect this. The Pornography card contains a number of buttons besides *Delta delta*. Pressing one of these buttons, the larger black triangle below and to the right of *Delta delta* brings up a dialog box reading, "Not enough recursion." (See Figure 7.5.)

This patently nonstandard message clearly suggests we are in the realm of parody.

Even more revealing is the title bar of the screen containing the "Porno recursion" script (see top of Figure 7.4). The location string here indicates that we are no longer viewing a card in the Oracle stack. If the flawed script had been activated from a card in that stack, the title bar would contain the name *Oracle*, not "Porno recursion." Clicking on the *Delta delta* button activates a link between stacks—a link whose operation is very hard to notice, since the one card in the stack *Porno recursion* exactly duplicates the background of the *Oracle* card from which we departed.

The jump to a second stack confirms the suspicion that we have left the ordinary programming conventions of HyperCard. Indeed nothing about "Porno recursion" and its apparent failure is what it seems. The script is not activated by the *Delta delta* button; in fact it is never executed at all. The warning of "Too much recursion" is a false alarm, produced in the same way as the bogus "Not enough recursion" message, by use of a HyperTalk command that generates dialog boxes. The "editing window" in which the script appears is actually an ordinary display field offering no ability to edit scripts. Since the script does not appear in a real editing field, *it is not executable code.*

But the enigma deepens. While the "Porno recursion" script is not presently executable, it does have all the formal properties of a viable program. The ambiguous nature of the script cuts both ways; if it can be read as a poem masquerading as unit of programming code, we might also entertain the notion that it is a valid HyperTalk script disguised as a script disguised as a poem. This may seem an excessively paranoid approach, but it has been said that paranoia is "the realization that *everything is connected*" [Pynchon, 1973], and in the multilinked environment of hypermedia this seems a useful way of seeing.

A sensitive (or paranoid) reader might begin to wonder how the "Porno recursion" script would operate if it were removed from its fraudulent context and attached to an actual HyperCard button. Indeed, any reader who has ventured this deep into the complexities of the script and its appearance should have little trouble creating a new button and copying the script into its editing window. These are relatively simple operations in HyperCard, and since the *Funhouse* allows its reader to add to or modify its structures, they are entirely possible. All that remains then is to press the button.

Here is what happens when the "Porno recursion" script is set up and executed. First the script opens the ominously named counter, thermoNuclearWar. The next instruction commits the first of two recursions: the script copies the text of itself into a variable called tightOrbit, which it then duplicates in a second variable called eventHorizon. The version of the script placed in eventHorizon undergoes some editing and is concatenated with tightOrbit at a point determined by the counter. The value of the counter is increased by 10, so that the material contained in eventHorizon is added to a progressively longer text in tightOrbit.

The penultimate line of the script ("click at the clickLoc") represents a second, more dangerous form of recursion. This instruction tells "Porno recursion" to send itself the same signal (a "mouse click") that activated it in the first place. In other words, Porno recursion reruns itself from the beginning, creating a theoretically infinite loop.

But since the script builds progressively larger versions of itself, its self-modifying recursion quickly produces a text so large that it cannot be processed. Running on a Macintosh Plus, "Porno recursion" exhausts available RAM in about eight seconds. The result is not an error message but quite literally a jump out of the system (or the system software). Having run out of memory, HyperCard is forced, as Apple documentation puts it, to "quit unexpectedly." All processing in the Macintosh stops. There should be no permanent loss of data, but no further instructions can be executed until the computer is manually restarted, wiping out the present contents of RAM. Running the "Porno recursion" script brings reader's tour of the *Funhouse* to a dead halt—which is doubtless the reason why the script is initially presented in nonexecutable form.

Though this elaborate subterfuge does amount on one level to a practical joke, it is also much more. To begin with, the script's operation as program connects to and reinforces its meaning as satiric poem. Executed on the Macintosh, "Porno recursion" becomes a parable-by-simulation about apocalyptic thinking. Consider the action the script performs: a recursive rewriting of itself. A script about nuclear war writes a bigger script about nuclear war that writes an even bigger script about nuclear war, and so on till the crash comes. Nuclear discourse pornographically feeds on itself, replicating unchecked, until all available memory (which might stand for *discursive energy*, or even *capital*) has been expended, at which point everything stops dead.

Intrepreting Hypermedia

But though this script seems directed at the perils of systematic thinking in general, it has a particular (recursive) relevance for the kind of system called hypermedia. "Porno recursion" shatters its own electronic universe in several ways, both interpretively and practically. The script exposes itself and invites the reader to fool around—with consequences that can get reader and text quite literally arrested. In this regard the epigraph McDaid applies to the *Funhouse* has particular resonance: it is John Barth's question, "For whom is the funhouse fun?" Clearly one function of the "Porno recursion" is to spoil our fun, to deconstruct the fiction's value as entertainment, and by extension, to call into question the value of any "entertainment" that relies on a self-enclosed interactive system.

But even though the *Funhouse* refuses to entertain, it does enlighten. The "Porno recursion" teaches a series of lessons about interpreting a hypermedia text. On one level, it demonstrates the difference between the kind of "interpreting" that microchips do and the allusive free play that distinguishes human language from machine code. Uncle Buddy's diabolical script turns the computer into a suicidal automaton, forcing it to engage in an activity that will ultimately render further activity impossible. But the code as presented to the reader exists not as executable statements but as allusive, poetic language. The human reader may thus do what the mechanical reader cannot—process the instructions but refuse to execute them, consider the sequence of actions prescribed in the program and *elect not to put them into play*.

This exercise could have considerable value as an object lesson. In a world where the "global variables" of power and knowledge tend to orient themselves toward singular, hegemonic world orders, it becomes increasingly difficult to jump outside "the system." And as Thomas Pynchon reminds us: "Living inside the System is like riding across the country in a bus driven by a maniac bent on suicide." [Pynchon, 1973]

The "Porno recursion" might point the way to a response. By learning about our place on the bus (and by learning what messages are passing through the bus), we may be able to unseat the madman at the wheel. Failing that, we might at least be able to slow down, reroute, or disable the bus—possibilities for which the "Porno recursion" represents a significant raising of consciousness.

Suppose we surrender to the seduction of Uncle Buddy's "pornographic" script. What wisdom do we gain by installing and running a program that is designed to crash our machine? One way to answer this question is to suggest that there is cognitive value in such an exercise. When Auden asserted that "poetry makes nothing happen" he doubtless did not have in mind Uncle Buddy's idea of textual paralysis. But then again, Auden lived in a world without microcomputers, hypermedia systems, and virtual realities. The act of making nothing happen in McDaid's recursion may have powerful symbolic value, both as a demonstration of the danger of nuclear discourse and as a reflexive critique of hypermedia and other semi-autonomous systems. The sabotaged "Porno recursion" reverses Hardison's process of "disappearance," confronting us not with a seamless techno-logical theatre but with a little world cunningly disarrayed. The jump into the infrastructure in "Porno recursion" gives hypermedia fiction a critical agenda.

The script and its complexities show us what is at stake in interpreting hyperme-dia texts. According to the literary theorist Martin Price, the "fictional contract" holds that "to read a novel is to discover the order latent in its materials rather than simply to impose one by a set of rules." [Price, 1983] Hypermedia fiction calls this proposition in question by collapsing its primary distinction. McDaid's script demonstrates that the order "latent" in a narrative is never anything but a set of rules in the first place. But to assume that a reader is free to "impose" new rules even in a hypertext is dangerously naive. The "Porno recursion" reminds us of this by laying bare its artifices, showing us the manipulative mechanisms that underlie the apparent "freedom" of interactive reception.

This experience can be most enlightening. Hypertext is not necessarily a libera-tion. We *may* change the text only if we *can* change the rules; but first we must be able to read the rules, which exist in an underlying layer reachable only by persis-tent inquiry. If we would come to terms (or to grips) with this level of the text, we must be prepared to execute our own readerly "recursion," moving from the free play of poetic discourse back to the purposiveness of scripting languages. But in making this return we must be willing to negotiate a new fictional contract, one in which we acknowledge that any literary undertaking in hypermedia is itself im-plicated in a discourse of power and control. We should be willing to interrupt this discourse; but we can do so only if we are willing to decompile as well as deconstruct.

About the Author

Stuart Moulthrop

Stuart Moulthrop is Assistant Professor of Literature, Communication and Culture at the Georgia Institute of Technology. He has published several papers on hypertext and interactive technologies and recently completed a book on contemporary American fiction. He has given presentations at numerous trade shows and conferences, including HyperExpo, Hypertext '89, and InterTainment.

His works in progress include *Creatures and Creators,* a hypermedia cross-edition of Mary Shelley's *Frankenstein,* and James Whale's 1931 film, and *Chaos,* a hypermedia fiction. With Michael Joyce, Nancy Kaplan, and John McDaid, he is a founding member of the TINAC fiction collective.

Mr. Moulthrop may be contacted in c/o Department of Literature, Communication and Culture, Georgia of Institute of Technology, Atlanta, GA 30332.

References

Barthes, R. (1979). J. Harari (Ed.), *Textual Strategies: Readings in Poststructuralist Criticism,* Cornell University Press, Ithaca, NY, 73-81.

Eagleton, T. (1985). "Capitalism, Modernism and Postmodernism," *New Left Review 152,* 60-73.

Fish, S. (1980). *Is There a Text in this Class: The Authority of Interpretive Communities,* Harvard University Press, Cambridge, MA.

Hardison, O. B. (1990). *Disappearing Through the Skylight: Culture and Technology in the Twentieth Century,* Viking Press, New York, NY.

Hofstadter, D. (1979). *Godel, Escher, Bach: An Eternal Golden Braid,* Basic Books, New York, NY.

Levy, S. (1990). "The End Of Literature: Multimedia Is Television's Insidious Offspring," *Macworld,* June, pp. 61+.

McLuhan, M. (1964). *Understanding Media: The Extensions of Man,* McGraw-Hill, New York, NY.

Price, M. (1983). *Forms of Life: Character and Moral Imagination in the Novel,* Yale University Press, New Haven, CT.

Pynchon, T. (1973). *Gravity's Rainbow,* Viking Press, New York, NY.

White, H. (1973). *Metahistory,* Johns Hopkins University Press, Baltimore. MD.

8

Selfish Interaction or Subversive Texts and the Multiple Novel[1]

By Michael Joyce
Jackson Community College

Interactive fictions are largely figments of our imaginations.

I am not sure what to make of this sentence. It has aspects of an unrealized pun, a bad koan, a polemical claim, and a manifesto. I want to doubt it, but I believe it utterly. Though we can point to an Infocom game here, and a Source serial there, when we are honest with ourselves we know that no truly interactive fictions exist. [2]

---

1   "Selfish Interaction: Subversive Texts and the Multiple Novel" will appear in *Literacy in the Computer Age*, Barton D. Thurber, Editor, Kluwer Academic Publishers, Netherlands.

2   By far the most interesting story generation programs have emerged from the Yale Artificial Intelligence Lab. James Meehan's *Tale-Spin* [Meehan] builds Aesopian stories in natural language according to a conceptual representation of the storyworld. Natalie Dehn's, *Author* [Dehn, 1981] was an attempt to generate a story based upon the intentions of the computer "author." Dehn's work on *Starship*, as yet unpublished, moved even closer to genuine interaction, creating a science fiction world where stories changed according to the program's perception of the reader's comprehension of the story as it developed, based upon comprehension questions generated by the program. Much of my thought on interaction and multiple fiction is indebted to Professor Dehn (currently at the University of Oregon), and, in a more oblique way, to Roger Schank who was good enough to invite me to visit the Yale Lab though he wasn't sure whether I would profit from it. Schank seems alone in the increasingly applications-oriented world of AI in his commitment to understanding human thought, learning, and invention.

Partly, of course, this is because, among the things we are likely to think sloppily about, interactivity ranks right next to expert systems and natural language parsers. There are grounds for arguing that no truly interactive system of any sort exists—except perhaps implanted pacemakers and defibrillators—since true interaction implies that the user responds to the system at least as often as the system responds to the user, and, more importantly, that initiatives taken by either user or system alter the behavior of the other. Video games from the glory days of the Atari renaissance, or Flight Simulator and its clones, or certain operating systems offer us at least a glimpse of what interaction might be. However, try as we may to believe they truly interact, we see them branching off below us at some transparent level of the successive planes of software and hardware. We know, as certainly as we know Eliza (or her erstwhile offspring Mom and Murray[3]) that someone has been there before us.

And so we try to outguess her (or him). Ironically, however, in this process of attempting to accommodate our thinking in response to the demands of an application's control and data structures, true interactivity does, of course, exist. In this sense, text editors or databases could be said to be among the most successful interactive fictions, especially during the early stages of the learning curve as we come to use them. For during that time we convince ourselves that we know the story of our own thought at least as often as the application reminds us that we do not know its representation.

Likewise, we imagine we give structure to a formless conceptual space, only to discover that the space itself is a labyrinth of glass walls within which we unravel skeins of our thought in order to find our way. An error message or a dialog box at such times becomes an utterance from an offstage demon. We accommodate our thought to the system, and the system accommodates our thought—we interact.

This paper is an attempt to explore, along these lines, the forms that true interactive fictions might take in the coming years. It proceeds from nearly three years of research (with J. David Bolter) into developing StorySpace, a structure editor for creating interactive fictions (the development of which was supported in part by a grant from The John and Mary H. Markle Foundation), but it is also the result of sixteen years of writing traditional novels which were nonetheless imagined as interactive fictions without the benefit of either appropriate tools to create them or a system to present them. (See Figure 8.1.) My suggestion is that future interactive fictions, in order to be more open, will appear more closed, i.e., more like current printed fiction than the computer programs we currently consider interactive. The model here is, of course, Umberto Eco's, wherein "an open text, however 'open' it be, cannot afford whatever interpretation. An open text outlines

---

3 According to the New York Times (December 5, 1985, p. 2), [Friedman, 1985] "Mom is a Jewish Mother computer personality," and Murray "is a cartoon computer friend... conversing for hours with whomever is at the keyboard." The program was created by Yakov Kirshen and is to be marketed by Antic for the Atari 520ST. Eliza, of course, refers to Joseph Weizenbaum's widely adapted and nearly legendary computer program. See "Eliza—A Computer Program for the Study of Natural Language Communication Between Man and Machine," Communications of the Association for Computing Machinery, 9, 1966.

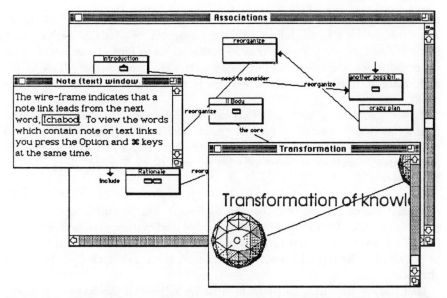

Figure 8.1 Storyspace is a simple yet powerful hypertext system with outlining capabilities, visual mapping, and interactive notes. Storyspace is a product of Riverrun Ltd; Eastgate Systems has acquired rights to publish it. Storyspace, Copyright Eastgate Systems, Inc.

a 'closed' project of its Model Reader as a component of its structural strategy." [Eco, 1979, p. 9] As a consequence, I also argue that we are more likely to experience satisfying interactions through the play of mind than through playing within texts, no matter how theoretically compelling the latter activity may seem.

The first level of interaction precedes the creation of any text.

We live in a time when we are able to assemble more information than at any previous age in history. Even so, we sometimes seem to live as much in fear of fragmentation as in hope for coherence. Inquiry into how we process and transfer our knowledge to create coherent visions of ourselves and our worlds assumes increasing importance and is enhanced by our growing awareness that media themselves intertwine and interact and threaten to become more ether than pathway, more chaos than cosmos.

We know many things but are uncertain how to use what we know. We have tools but we are uncertain what tasks to put them to, since tools by their nature alter our vision of the tasks. This process is often recursive: tools alter tasks alters tools and so on.

For a fiction writer the dynamic relationship between tools and tasks is a familiar reality. In fact, the most compelling aspect of computer tools is that they promise fiction writers a means to resurrect and entertain multiplicities that print-bound creation models have taught them to suppress or finesse.[4] That is, where James Joyce's *Finnegan's Wake*, Julio Cortazar's *Hopscotch*, or—for that matter—Laurence Sterne's *Tristram Shandy* created multiplicities as intricate as any of those we envision for interactive fictions, those texts were bound at very least by the static nature of their presentational systems [see Chapter 7 by Moulthrop, in this book].

As a result, Sterne, Joyce and Cortazar create unique—and illustrative—solutions to the static, linear presentational models open to them. Since metaphors and meta-languages alike inform through juxtaposition, it might be useful to consider these authors' solutions in terms of what we might—by Joycean "license"—call "computerese".

Sterne (who wrote *Tristam Shandy* in 1760), exploits the decorative and self-referential qualities of the Gutenbergian medium in what we might call a *screen-based* mode. Like John Barth after him, and the medieval copyists before him, he recognizes that the graphical coherencies and conventions of the printed page can be conveyed in the textual linearity. In this sense, Sterne anticipates graphical user interfaces.

James Joyce attenuates language in what we might call the *line editor* mode, recognizing that imprinting is *in* printing and thus an eidetic image. Like the Lewis Carroll of *Jabberwocky*, he forces a "what you see is what you get" environment to yield what we would call *virtual windowing*, where the in-printing seems to expand and disclose a momentary flicker of other words and other languages. His process thus is also graphical, allied as much in his time with collage or Ezra Pound's notion of ideograms, as with Donald Knuth's metafont or Macintosh's Cairo font in our own time.

However, Joyce compounds and parallels these eidetic qualities of print with narrative *macros* which summon overlays from what we could call, quite rightly in Joyce's case, libraries. These interlace successive text segments and cause side effects which extend the flicker of a line to a cyclic pulse of whole pages.

Where the effects of Sterne and Joyce reside largely in the record fields themselves, the effects of Cortazar are strictly relational. *Hopscotch*[5] comes with what we might call subroutines (or perhaps "shellscripts") which are not at all unlike Infocom branching structures or children's *Choose Your Own Adventure* books.

---

4   Douglas R. Hofstadter argues a similar point: "And when a novelist simultaneously entertains a number of ways of extending a story, are the characters not, to speak metaphorically, in a mental superposition of states? If the novel never gets set to paper, perhaps the split characters can continue to evolve their multiple stories in their author's brain. Furthermore, it would even seem strange to ask which story is the genuine version. All the worlds are equally genuine." [Hofstadter, 1985, p. 472] My notion is that this state holds true even when the novel is set to paper.

5   [Cortazar, 1966] The author's "Table of Instructions," begins, "In its own way, this book consists of many books, but two books above all. The first can be read in normal fashion and it ends with Chapter 56... The second should be read beginning with Chapter 73 and then following the sequence indicated..." The sequence moves back and forth through "new" (post Chapter 56) material and old. Cortazar is best known as the author of Blow-up [Cortazar, 1963] which, of course, was the inspiration for Antoniani's film of the same name.

Where Joyce and Sterne overtly reference a system library of parallel texts and thus make their language what we might call declarative, Cortazar provides a procedural language which readers may use to reference their own libraries. That is, Cortazar calls upon us to recall not the *subject* but the *act* of our previous readings, and invites us to read *Hopscotch* in a successive, literally programmed iteration. This second reading depends upon our decaying, yet dynamic, memory of the master text.

Whatever their differences, each of these three novelists surely preprocessed interactions with their readers, anticipating in their input stream the peculiar limitations of the batch—processed, linear output stream of a static presentational text. While this kind of preprocessing is, jargon aside, surely an aspect of any novelist's creation of an ideal reader, these novels are distinctive to the degree that their texts overtly confirm correct traversals.

In other words, the preprocessing results in the creation of an intricately networked novel-as-knowledge-structure which both simultaneously invites and confirms reader interaction. (e.g., The so-called Gorman-Gilbert Schema for *Ulysses* provides graphic substantiation of such preprocessing, especially since Joyce originally circulated it on a not-for-publication basis among friends and potential critics. See the Appendix to Richard Ellmann's *Ulysses* on the Liffey [Ellmann, 1972, pp. 186-187] for a concise history and reproduction of the schema.) Moreover, the text itself carries a syntax for such interaction (an implied labelling of network arcs) which depends upon a reader's familiarity with the operating system of literacy. That is, we readers are invited to confront these novels, even on first reading, in the same fashion that we have previously flipped through, browsed, reviewed, or recollected other, more linear novels.

This invitation to confront is what I believe instantiates the interactivity of these texts, offering, as it were, the structural strategy of Eco's open text. Each of these novels is what Eco calls *work in movement*. As such, "the possibilities which the work's openness makes available always work within a given field of relations... we can say that the work in movement is the possibility of numerous personal interventions, but it is not an amorphous invitation to indiscriminate participation. The invitation offers the performer the chance of oriented insertion into something which always remains the world intended by the author." [Eco, 1979, p. 62]

Therefore, it is perhaps not too much to say that, if truly interactive computer fictions are to exist, they will require tools for simultaneously creating and recovering such oriented insertions within given fields of relations. That is, interactive fictions require *text processing* rather than word processing tools.

For text processing, unlike word processing, is a method of intellectual and artistic discovery and presentation. If word processing may be thought of as a tool for thought (making any written text available for emendation, elaboration, and restructuring at any point along its length), text processing may be thought of as a thoughtful tool (making a master text and variations of it available to readers along a presentational path predetermined by the writer and selected or influenced by the reader). Text processing makes texts transparent, inviting readers to consider parallels, explore multiple alternate possibilities, and participate in the uncertain process of discovery and creation.

Our program, Storyspace, originated as an attempt to develop a text processing tool to enable writers of interactive presentations to exploit multiplicities. Storyspace depends upon a decisional order rather than a fixed order of presenting material. A fixed order presentation may be thought of as a road map, within which the author may present side trips or forks (some of which the traveller or reader may be allowed to choose among). The order of presentation, however, remains linear. The trip (or text) proceeds from point A to point B, however various the digressions.

A decisional order, however, may be thought of as a series of locales, some of which are linked by linear progression or argument, but with others determined by allusiveness, resemblance, evocation or unexplained and "intuitive" parallels determined as often by the author as by the reader. The journey along a decisional pathway may continue to proceed from point A to point B, but the traveller will not only be invited to dream or recall other journeys (some as yet unmade), but also will be confronted with unexpected or surprising turns, detours, and compelling alternate routes. More importantly, each alternate reading will cause the text itself to degrade or reform, so that no successive reading will ever again substantially parallel a traversal of the initial master text. In such a way, the reader's creation of an implied text could become physically enacted on the screen or in instantaneously laser-printed (and, one could imagine, perfect-bound) hardcopy.

This kind of subversive text, or multiple novel, would offer its readers the opportunity to explore the cohesion of a work in a way analogous to successive readings separated by time. The reading would, in this sense, encompass in its interaction either the kinds of imaginary dialogues we often conduct with author or character after reading a story, or the reveries of succeeding (or "what if") episodes which either interject or follow.

Rather than speculating on a character's deeper motivations, for example, the story itself might—in successive readings—offer greater or lesser explorations of motivation. As such, the text would overtly offer in its structure that which Eco claims for every work of art. It would be "effectively open to a virtually unlimited range of possible readings, each of which causes the work to acquire new vitality in terms of one particular taste, perspective, or personal performance." [Eco, 1979, p. 63]

To enable potential interactions of this kind, the Storyspace text processor preserves both a decisional pathway (the choices made by a creator of a work, i.e., the interaction which precedes text) and a presentational pathway (sequences of nodes and their links available to the audience/reader, i.e., the interactions which follow from texts).

The decisional pathway provides the creator of a work with a repertoire of associations and linkages, some designed solely to serve as mnemonic, architectonic, and editorial stimuli and utilities, and others designed to directly interface with the presentational pathway. This latter pathway provides a means for presenting multiple, interactive versions of a work, with the range, liberty and syntax of interactivity determined either by the creator or by the reader. The text thus may be accessed either directly or through predetermined associative scripts designed by the author but transparent to the reader.

Storyspace might thus be used to create a novel as supple and multiple as oral narratives, but with the referential and coherent richness of in-printed, relational works such as those of Sterne, Joyce, Cortazar, and others. These computer-enhanced, subversive texts, would merge process and product much in the manner of Baroque themes-and-variations or jazz improvisation, in which the colorations or embellishments are ephemeral, often depend on audience or occasion, and usually resist static apprehension or capture. The intellectual basis for such work involves both a natural collation of trends in twentieth century thought concerning the transitory and multiple nature of human experience; and also a reflection of our widespread cultural urges and individual longing for methods to identify and represent the perceived order and complexity which underlies a mass of information.

To the extent that the decisional pathway would also be available for readers to use, we might also expect that they would template story generation scripts which would offer them opportunities to participate in the narrative itself in the fashion of a hypertext.

Certainly, the narrative and the technological models exist for readers to do so.

Yet would they? I think not. For a fiction is essentially a selfish interaction for both its author and its reader.

It is likely that no one interrupted Homer.

Or, perhaps there were drunken hecklers even then, in the courtly supper clubs of Asia Minor. Almost certainly there were the Attic equivalents of piano bar patrons who politely request "Melancholy Baby" or "Steadfast Penelope." Even so, we can feel reasonably certain that no outsiders interrupted Homer in the sense that they established a priority in his narrative, or that their language subsumed his.

Or to put it differently, a question we might ask ourselves in our enthusiasm about interactive fictions is: Since the technology has existed for some time, why don't people write alternate chapters in the blank spaces of bound novels, or alternate sentences in the blank spaces between printed sentences?

Why don't most readers write at all? Why don't most readers at least write the beginnings of sequels to the novels they love? (Some readers, of course, do. The Baker Street Irregulars are perhaps best known, although science fiction fans seem even more devoted to creating an alternate canon. The Friends of Darkover, " a non-sectarian, non-sexist, and non-profit group of science fiction and fantasy lovers... has come into being with no purpose except the discussion of secondary universes, primarily Darkover." [Marian Zimmer Bradley and the Friends of Darkover, 1980].

Bradley mentions similar alternate worlds created by Star Trek and Tolkien fans. Friends and colleagues of mine report similar alternate versions created by fans of the Dr. Who television program and readers of The Witch World of Andre Norton. Bradley notes that the majority of alternate Darkover stories are written by women, and suggests—much in the same vein as Sherry Turkle—that women, who are trained as children by role play rather than fantasy, tend to feel more comfortable at first in someone else's world.

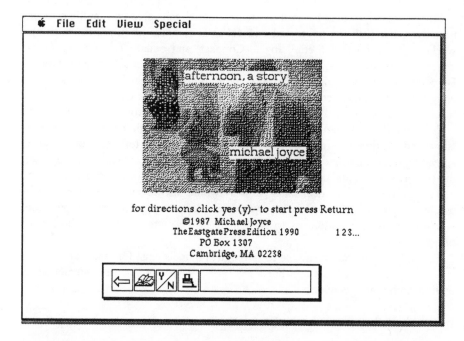

Figure 8.2   You read Afternoon, a hypertextual novel by Michael Joyce, actively. You can click on any word; some of them activate links. Afternoon is published by Eastgate System, Inc. Afternoon copyright by Eastgate Systems, Inc.

In the case of those readers who don't, we would like to respond that the medium was not appropriate, since we would like to believe that the computer medium is appropriate. Yet another series of questions follows upon these proposed beliefs.

Why don't most readers of current interactive fictions write alternatives within them, or sequels without them? Certainly, the medium offers opportunities. Users of multitasking systems could input alternatives in one window as the interactive story scrolls in another. Users of other systems could summon text-editors running under the application, or—as an emergency expedient—use break keys and input alternate lines to an uncompromising operating system or monitor. (They might also use Storytree, a simple and quite fascinating structure editor, published by Scholastic Software.)

To a certain extent, of course, users already do these things. Even the most experienced users of interactive adventure or mystery games sometimes find themselves inputting commands which exercise the parser beyond its limits and cause it either to admit ignorance or output default, Eliza-like solecisms. And few honest computer users can swear that they have not explored the variety of canny, canned responses which applications or systems programmer's provide in anticipated response to hallowed Anglo-Saxon expletives and imperatives.

The two preceding cases suggest a paradigm for what I want to call selfish interactions. In the first, readers either become too enveloped in the language of the narrative, or—paradoxically—fail to become fully cooperating participants in the linguistic subset which the parser demands. That is, they either lose themselves in the story world, or experience the loss of the story lexicon in the parser. In the second, users acknowledge the linguistic subset by seeking ironic or hortatory confirmation of it. That is, they explore the limits of phatic communication which underlie a highly codified linguistic subset.

In each case, the attendant pleasures are ones which involve confirmation of interaction. Yet what is confirmed are limits, or the traversal of boundaries between procedure and declaration, i.e., between the act of reading in a certain way and the text which anticipates and signifies successful reading in that certain way.

Thus, we are unlikely to write intertextual, parallel, or detached versions of an interactive fiction because we selfishly seek confirmation of our alternative choices within the text. Likewise, we are more likely to write (or utter) alternatives to a fiction either within a computer conference, where other readers can assume author or character roles to confirm our choices, or in adventuring or other groups, where conversation and mutual fantasy supply confirmation outside the software or text.

Yet the communal aspects of these conference or group readings are likely to be unsatisfied to the degree that any participating role-player moves the text beyond the constraints we imagine the author imagined. Or, to state the case positively, we are satisfied and delighted when the text reconfirms our variations. Thus, an interactive mystery which presents a taunting prompt, i.e., "Too bad you dropped the phaser, you could sure use it now," delights us even as we are reduced to carbon atoms.

It is unsurprising that the overtly intertextual nature of most current interactive fictions is so attractive to literary theorists and narratologists. That is, we often read interactive fictions in parallel streams consisting of:

1. the narrative stream, or the story itself, which echoes, self-reflexively quotes, and anticipates its variations within a relatively unconstrained lexicon, and

2. the game stream, or the "story" of the narrative flow chart and program syntax, which not only enables confirmations within the first stream, but also provides confirmations of its own, but within a highly constrained, formulaic lexicon.

We are as pleased to recognize the structure of the latter as we are to experience the structure of the former.

Yet the current apparatus seems somehow makeshift. The pleasures of parallel reading are not quite compensation for the jolt of alternating lexicons. The continued development of more successful parsers cannot conceal the fact that true natural language front-ends are years away from development, nor can it convince even the most naive users that they have engaged in genuine interaction resulting in alterations to their reading behavior and the story's text. We know that we are engaged in something more like a game than a reverie, and although there are undeniable pleasures in mapping the story and its branches while matching wits with its programmer within the game stream, we somehow know that in the narrative stream we are interrupting Homer, or, worse, both Homer and his programmer.

Ideally, of course, both the program *map* and the text it traverses would change with our changing interests, much in the way, for instance, that Joyce's Ulysses changes style to suit sensibility, quarter of the city, and hour of that June day. (See the Appendix to Richard Ellmann's Ulysses on the Liffey [Ellmann, 1972, pp. 186–187] for a concise history and reproduction of the schema.) That is, it is possible to conceive of an interactive computer fiction within which the branching schemes, alternate traversals, and so on both disclosed themselves as integral parts of the narrative and altered themselves according to our shifting interests and current states. In such an interactive fiction, the branching choices, attribute lists, and implicit/explicit menus would disappear into a seamless, but subversive, text which constituted both the story and the game stream. The immediate effect would be both to widen the fictional domain, or story world, of interactive fictions, and, more importantly, to involve a wider audience and thus a wider authorship.

A subversive text would restore the Homeric situation to the extent that its branching would be driven by: 1) previous conditions and 2) detection of audience interests, rather than by direct intervention of audience into story. As an example, consider the following, purely hypothetical, example of interaction we envision for Storyspace.

The interactive fiction, *Emma,* consists of a paperback book (or master text) and an accompanying computer disk. On the disk are the master text and subversive variations. The screen display is very similar to the Macintosh notepad in that it allows paging/browsing forward and back in the text. Each screen page is identical to a portion of the corresponding page in the printed master text. Thus a reader who preferred screens to printed pages would be able to read *Emma* through— once. Without browsing forward or back. But she or he would have no indication of this fact, except that when the reader flipped, for example, forward in the screen master text from page two to page two hundred, it would be impossible to return to page two. Or, more accurately, the page two the reader returned to would be utterly different from the page two she or he left.

Since the master text would still exist in the printed version (and would have existed on the screen for one continuous read-through, before it decayed), it would be possible to try to make some sense out of the second "page two" by comparing its intent, focus, style, point-of-view, etc., against the master "page two."

Perhaps the reader could test a hypothesis (still very much in the game stream fashion) by browsing forward again from page three (using either the master text as a map, or using a search function within the program to choose the same character or setting that the previous browse to page two hundred resulted in). Or perhaps the reader would simply read sequentially through the new story, choosing to compare it or not with the master text.

Suppose, however, that the reader did choose to pause at different points and compare with the master text. Suppose further that the author had embedded in the decisional pathway a branching structure which depended upon the machine's ability to calculate (and/or accumulate) eventless reading of certain pages with common themes or characters. Suppose that branching structure presented yet another version of the multiple novel, with an ordering and structure quite unlike the hypothetical one the reader has decided to pursue.

Suppose that in the very next episode, a character seemed to recall an event very much like the one that used to be on page two and asked someone's help in recalling it. And the screen display suddenly refused to move to the next screen page, but would move forward and back through everything that preceded the current page and followed the page after next.

Suppose the reader quickly gets frustrated, puts the disk aside, and does not use it again until months later. Perhaps winter has changed to spring in the interim. Suppose that the spring novel was entirely different from the winter novel, and that the computer's clock triggered the new version.

Or, suppose that each time the disk was rebooted after a master reading, a blank screen appeared, or an old-fashioned A> prompt, or a ? cursor, or a polite request, "What would you like to read?"

Suppose that there really were natural language front-ends and expert systems which constructed reader *agents* which tailored texts to suit the input to such prompts. Or suppose a Boolean technological leap resulting in both faultless voice recognition chips and natural language processors so that random mumbles or directed beefs and bravos created such agents, and the resultant new texts. Suppose that input to the above noncommittal prompts caused the software to take over the system and dial up 800 numbers which downloaded new versions (or caused Videotex services to pump new text through the friendly TRINTEX or AT&T blackbox in the living room).

Suppose that the text *did* invite you to write a version, an alternate sentence, a chapter, a sequel? And then never showed it to you again. Or showed only parts of it, intertwined with a version of the multiple tale appearing months after the reading that prompted you to write in the first place.

Suppose somebody shouted, "Play *Steadfast Penelope*," and the screen display altered to Greek fonts, or the voice chip began to declaim formulaics in a foreign tongue.

Suppose a text can anticipate unpredictable variations upon it.

I am not sure what to make of this sentence. It has aspects of an unrealized pun, a bad koan, a polemical claim, an oxymoron, and a manifesto. I want to doubt it, but I believe it utterly.

There is a phenomenon known variously to computer scientists but often called interference, the concurrency problem, or software interaction, where, in complex systems and programs, levels upon levels of software functioning together exhibit unanticipated side effects causing unpredictable and usually nettlesome—but occa-

---

** ● File   Edit   View   Special**

<u>begin</u>

I try to recall winter. < As if it were yesterday? > she says, but I do not signify one way or another.

By five the sun sets and the afternoon melt freezes again across the blacktop into crystal octopi and palms of ice-- rivers and continents beset by fear, and we walk out to the car, the snow moaning beneath our boots and the oaks exploding in series along the fenceline on the horizon, the shrapnel settling like relics, the echoing thundering off far ice. This was the essence of wood, these fragments say. And this darkness is air.

<Poetry > she says, without emotion, one way or another.

Do you want to hear about it?

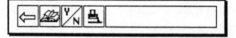

Figure 8.3   **The tool bar from Afternoon. You can respond to questions by clicking the Yes/No buttons or typing. You can also type some words, and occasionally, a one word question, in the Text entry box. You may browse links by choosing Browse. You can also print the text of a screen by choosing Print. Afternoon was written by Michael Joyce and is published by Eastgate System, Inc. Afternoon copyright by Eastgate Systems, Inc.**

sionally felicitous—effects. For a debugger these interferences call to mind the swamp of *The Big Two-Hearted River*, where "the banks were bare, the big cedars came together overhead, the sun did not come through, except in patches (and) in the fast deep water, in the half light, the fishing would be tragic."

In a similarly dark place, Eco considers a question (parallel to interference or the koan that begins this section) which exhibits itself in James Joyce's pre-discovery of nuclear fission in the phrase "abnihilation of the ethym" in Finnegan's Wake. According to Eco, "the poet anticipates a future scientific and conceptual discovery because—even if through expressive artifices, or conceptual chains set in motion to put cultural units into play and to disconnect them—he uproots them from their habitual semiotic situation." (This and the following quotations, with the exception of the last line from "Big Two-Hearted River," are from Eco, p. 86.)

The discourse here is also a swamp (and the fishing is dangerous), yet what comes through is a vision of interactive interference not only anticipated but, in a sense, forced by the networking of language. "Sooner or later someone understands in some way the reason for the connection and the necessity for a factual judgement that does not as yet exist," suggests Eco. "Then, and only then, is it shown that the course of successive contiguities, however tiresome, was traversable or that it was possible to institute certain transversals. Here is how the factual judgement, anticipated in the form of an unusual metaphor, overturns and restructures the semantic system in introducing circuits not previously in existence."

This kind of fishing, of course, exists at the level of the linguistic microcosm, yet it does not seem so far removed from the kind of macrocosmic interaction of dual story streams which I have suggested as the most likely mode for coming interactive fictions. The linking arc in such a network is the selfish reader, the someone who sooner or later understands the reason for a connection. What is critical, however, is that the arc itself be literally instantiated, as present in the creation as in the performance.

"The factual judgment," says Eco, "draws, perceptively or intellectually, the disturbing data from the exterior of language. The metaphor, on the other hand, draws the idea of possible connection from the interior of the circle of unlimited semiosis, even if the new connection restructures the circle itself in its structuring connections."

The multiple novel, likewise, will invite writer and reader to restructure the circle of a text in its ability to simultaneously, and subversively, present both the exterior and interior of language through successive, and shifting, story streams. Already the tools present themselves for use: the idea processors, hypertexts, and Storyspace's. (See Figure 8.3.)

"(Nick) looked back. The river just showed through the trees. There were plenty of days coming when he could fish the swamp." — 1/9/1989

About The Author

Michael Joyce

Michael Joyce is a prize-winning novelist as well as a teacher of writing. He has lectured and published widely on issues relating to hypertext and writing, and is part of the TINAC collective.

Together with Jay Bolter and John B. Smith, he is the co-developer of Storyspace, hypertext software for writers and readers published by Eastgate Systems. His interactive hypertext fiction, *Afternoon*, also published by Eastgate Press, has been called "an information age Odyssey" (by Pamela McCorduck writing in Whole Earth Review).

He holds an MFA from the Iowa Writers Workshop, where he was a Teaching Writing Fellow; and he has been a Visiting Fellow at the Yale University Artificial Intelligence Project. He is currently Professor of Language and Literature and Coordinator of the Center for Narrative and Technology at Jackson Community College, as well as Director for JCC's National Community College Alliance charter project sponsored by Apple Computer and the League for Innovation in Community Colleges.

Michael Joyce may be contacted at the Center for Narrative and Technology, Jackson Community College, Jackson, MI 49201.

References

Bradley, M. Z. and the Friends of Darkover (1980). "Statement of Purpose," *The Keeper's Price.* DAW books No. 373, New York, NY.

Cortazar, Julio (1963). *Blow-up.* Random House, New York, NY.

Cortazar, Julio (1963). *Hopskotch.* Random House, New York, NY.

Dehn, N. (1981). "Story generation after Tale-Spin," Proceedings of the Seventh Annual Joint Conference On Artificial Intelligence. Vancouver, BC.

Eco, U. (1979). *The Role of the Reader.* Indiana University Press, Bloomington, IN.

Ellmann, R. (1972). *Ulysses on the Liffey.* Oxford University Press, New York, NY.

Friedman, Thomas L. (1985). "From Israeli cartoonist, a chatty computer game," NY Times, Dec. 5, 2, New York, NY.

Hofstadter, D. R. (1985). *Metamagical Themas.* Basic Books, New York, NY.

Meehan, J. *The Metanovel: Writing stories by computer.* Ph.D. dissertation, Research Report #74, Computer Science Department, Yale University, New Haven, CT.

Meehan, J. *Tale-spin,* a software package developed at the Yale Artificial Intelligence Lab, New Haven, CT.

Storytree, a structure editor program published by Scholastic Software.

Weizenbaum, J. (1966). "Eliza—A Computer Program for the Study of Natural Language Communication Between Man and Machine," *Communications of the Association for Computing Machinery,* 9.

IV

Automatic vs. Hand Generation

The much-publicized disagreements between the "hand-crafters" and the "automatic hypertexters" has widened recently because systems that can actually perform automatic conversion of on-line documents into hypertext are finally on the market. These conflicts are, in fact, a bit overblown. Most of those who do not automatically generate hypertexts do use some tools to aid in the conversion of existing on-line and papertext documents. Most of those who sell automatic text-to-hypertext conversion systems acknowledge that the hyperdocuments that emerge will have to be edited, tested, and changed by skilled hypertext authors.

In this section, two men who have worked at automatic text-to-hypertext conversion for a long time explain the capabilities and limitations of their products. Tom Rearick is President of Big Science, whose automatic conversion product, SmarText, is a general-purpose conversion tool that creates medium-sized hypertexts. Rob Riner works for Texas Instruments, whose HyperTRANS Facility is a set of utilities designed to generate huge hypertexts.

9

Automated Conversion

By Rob Riner
Texas Instruments, Inc.

Introduction: The Decision to Automate

The ever-growing amounts of information being generated in fields as diverse as medicine, engineering, maintenance and law require us to develop means of organizing information in ways which support rapid retrieval.

Forty-five years ago Vannevar Bush realized that:

> "The difficulty seems to be not so much that we publish unduly in view of the extent and variety of present-day interests, but rather that publication has been extended far beyond our ability to make real use of the record. The summation of human experience is being expanded at a prodigious rate, and the means we use for threading through the consequent maze to the momentarily important item is the same as was used in the days of square-rigged ships." [Bush, 1945]

This problem has only gotten more acute with the development of personal computers; text editors and database managers have provided the means to create ever-increasing amounts of information.

Businesses are becoming increasingly dependent upon efficient access to this huge volume of information. A critical element in the movement to highly interactive information systems is our ability to take the massive amounts of already existing information and convert it for use on interactive computer systems.

Paper-Based Authoring

Businesses generate paper-based documents by amassing information and then organizing its presentation. This organizational process may require a great deal of effort.

For technical or reference documents, features such as tables of contents, indices, and page and section numbering have all been developed to help readers find information in paper-based presentations in nonlinear ways; that is, without having to read sequentially through entire texts. The table of contents allows readers to see the basic structure and organization of a document. An index provides readers with a list of topics that might otherwise have to be searched for. Both the table of contents and the index help readers to identify items of interest and then rapidly access them.

Many people see hypertext as a means of avoiding or overcoming the creative limitations imposed by the linearly structured paper presentation medium. Yet, in many cases, a great deal of effort has gone into the construction of searching support tools such as tables of contents and indices; this effort should not be discarded when considering converting paper-based information to hypertext.

Rationale for Conversion

Converting an information resource into hypertext involves much more than simply creating a computer-readable version of the text and graphics. Converting involves:

- Selecting documents which would benefit readers if they were in hypertext form
- Determining how to convert them
- Producing process-ready computer files from paper or other forms
- Specifying and identifying what should be linked
- Performing the conversion and verifying the results

Manual vs Automated Conversion

There are two basic means of converting existing documents into hypertext. One is manual conversion. This involves selecting a hypertext authoring tool and then entering the document into that environment manually and constructing all of the links as you convert the pages. Hypertext authoring has all the perils of any authoring; the organization and flow of the information is in the hands of the author and it's then up to the reader to deduce that structure.

Another major problem with manual conversion is the inducement of human error. In a manual conversion, decisions regarding what should be linked and where a link should go are made by human operators and therefore subject to individual interpretation. This might be valuable for the true author who is constructing new information, but for a conversion it can be a disaster. In fact, the repetitiveness of the chore of constructing links in existing materials can lead people to error while repetitive tasks are what computers do best. The goal of most conversions is an enhanced but true reflection of what is in the original document. With automated conversion what is linked and where links go is specified up front and therefore verifiable. After a document has undergone automated conversion, a human author may be able to add links beyond those that current conversion software would implement.

There is an interesting parallel between the current state of hypertext conversion and the early days of *Computer Assisted Instruction* (CAI). In the early days of CAI, a great number of companies produced and marketed CAI authoring tools. Initially, many of their clients began converting their curricula to this new delivery environment. Once the prototypes and/or initial projects were completed, and they had both evaluated the level of effort involved in converting a short lesson (maybe an hour long) and extrapolated that level of effort to converting an entire course, they often abandoned CAI entirely. The anticipated effort simply was not worth it.

The same story can be told about manual conversion of documents into hypertext. Many people are investigating hypertext and are interested in getting their information into this new form. Manual conversion works for small prototype projects. But when you scale up from converting a few pages or even a few dozen pages to converting tens of thousands of pages, manual conversion becomes unthinkable. A perfect example is a reference text which has an index of over 50,000 items. If you could manually insert links at one a minute, it would take over five months to construct just the links for the index of this one book. For several years now, the Hypermedia Systems & Services organization at Texas Instruments Incorporated has been developing computerized tools to do this type of conversion.

The PEAM Experience

The *Personal Electronic Aid for Maintenance* (PEAM) program is a historical case in point. In the early 1980s the Department of Defense undertook a multi-phase research project aimed at developing a portable system to aid maintenance technicians in performing maintenance tasks [Personal Electronic Aid for Maintenance (PEAM) Final Report, 1981].

Realizing that paper documentation could not be used because it was too bulky, often out of date, and often not available, the Personal Electronic Aid for Maintenance program was undertaken. The goal was to come up with a conceptual design for a portable electronic device which could provide technicians with accurate technical information on demand.

The program was begun in 1980 by Texas Instruments and the XYZYX Information Corporation, and funded through the Army Project Manager for Training Devices (and later the Army Research Institute for the Behavioral and Social Sciences) and the Naval Training Equipment Center. Initial prototypes delivered in

1985 contained a flat panel display, a memory storage module, and speech input and output devices, all contained in a briefcase-sized unit.

Users' interaction with PEAM was through a limited set of commands which could be entered via function keys or speech. With only eight commands (next, last, select, backup, yes, no, menu, and speak) users could navigate throughout an electronic maintenance manual. This system incorporated hypertext navigational properties to assist technicians in locating necessary information.

Early on, it was recognized that the information in the current paper maintenance manuals was going to have to be transformed somehow into interactive units capable of display and manipulation. The approach was to construct a hierarchical set of *Job Performance Aids* (JPAs). While this was not referred to as hypertext, it had all of the primary characteristics: the information was contained in small units, these units were connected and the user moved between or among these units via the connections. The issue faced by the PEAM program was how to convert existing maintenance manuals into the interactive units. What was learned was that at that time there was no automated process available to support this conversion. Converting a single manual by hand was possible for the tests. But even using their sophisticated computer tools, it would be prohibitively expensive to do all military manuals that way.

Once the prototype units were completed, an independent group was commissioned to test the utility of the PEAM concept. The system was evaluated under both Navy and Army environments. The Army evaluation used the maintenance procedures associated with a subassembly of the turret assembly of the M-1 Tank and the Naval with the NATO SEA SPARROW Surface Missile System.

In the Army test, a group of qualified M60 Tank mechanics was split in two. One group was trained on how to use the paper manuals for the M-1 tank and the other was trained on how to use an emulator of the PEAM device. Once the training was complete fault conditions were introduced into a tank simulator and the mechanics were instructed to troubleshoot the faults. In the Navy test, a single test group was used but this group was made up of individuals who ranged from experienced technicians to individuals with no technical training at all.

The Army test results showed an almost 3:1 reduction in troubleshooting errors with the PEAM system. The Naval test results showed an almost 6:1 reduction in troubleshooting errors with the PEAM system [Wisher and Kincaid, 1989]. In the Army test it took several days of training for the group that used hardcopy manuals to learn how to use the M-1 while the PEAM group was trained on how to use the device in a matter of minutes. An interesting observation from the Naval study was that there was little performance difference between the experienced technicians and the inexperienced technicians who used PEAM.

Two major lessons were learned from PEAM. First, while the PEAM program appeared to validate the utility of the hypertext approach to organization and delivery of information, it did not overcome the problem of converting large volumes of existing information into hypertext. Second, the potential effectiveness of the PEAM concept became clear.

Detailed Procedures Involved in Conversion

In order to successfully port information from paper to hypertext, it is necessary to understand the nature of the information involved. In particular, we must concern ourselves with factors involved in the original creation, display and the intended use of the information in its current form.

Many written texts are prepared and accessed in a linear format: that is, text is normally read from the first page to the last in sequential order. This format supports the presentation of information as a series of related events occurring in a chronological order. Entering many books at a point in the middle is generally neither very informative nor entertaining because it violates the intended linear process of presentation. The fundamental structural element for this approach is the page number. Page numbers provide both the sequential order to the printed text and a mechanism which allows readers to enter and re-enter books over several readings.

However, technical reference materials are not read in the same way as other books. These materials typically are highly cross-referenced and in fact are not used in a linear fashion. Documents of this type incorporate various types of structures. These include: one or more table of contents; chapters; numbered sections and/or paragraphs; section and/or paragraph titles, indentures or other identifiers; and various internal and external reference schemes.

Each of these structures helps readers access a document in a nonlinear fashion. That is, specific parts of the document can be located quickly without the need to read all the preceding parts. Automated conversion methods should take advantage of structures created by the writers, technical editors, and indexers of original documents. The Texas Instrument HyperTRANS facility was devised to identify and utilize all of these structural and contextual elements and use them in automatically building hypertext documents.

What Does Automated Conversion Do?

Creation of a hypertext document involves deciding how to partition the information: what should constitute a chunk or node; what types of nodes and links are required; which nodes should be linked to which and by what type of link; and so on. Because of these options, and the repetitive nature of the task, manual conversion is time-consuming and prone to error. The Texas Instruments HyperTRANS system was designed to automate link identification and construction.

Rather than just a stream of characters, a document is comprised of paragraphs, illustrations, graphs, lists, tables, sections, and chapters. An automated conversion system must be able to recognize these structural elements, determine which to treat as hypertext nodes and then construct the appropriate links to form the hypertext network. Some links capture the hierarchical structure of the document; for example, a section is linked to its parent chapter and any subsections become the section's children. Other links connect figure references to their figures, glossary or index entries to the places they occur in the document, concepts to related concepts, and so on. Any node can be linked to any other node, even nodes in other documents. This can become a critical aspect of conversion because often written material comes in sets or groups which reference each other. This can be seen in "User," "Reference" and "Technical" guides which accompany hardware and even some computer software packages. Often discussions in one document refer readers to one of the other documents for greater detail or definitions or procedures.

The Steps Involved In Automated Conversion

The procedures involved in successful automated conversion are described below.

Selecting Appropriate Materials. The first step in automated conversion involves selecting appropriate documents for input. Of primary concern when evaluating a document for conversion is the nature of the information and the target audience for the hyperdocument.

Some types of documents, while they could be converted, would not benefit from conversion. A novel, for instance, might be convertible but readers would probably not obtain any real value from having it converted.

Information that, in print, is approached in a nonlinear fashion is likely to benefit from conversion. These kinds of printed documents include encyclopedias, maintenance manuals, parts catalogs, etc. Educational and technical reference books used to find specific items of information are also good candidates for conversion.

Some believe that the information in its written form needs to be in many relatively short pieces which are cross-referenced to be a good candidate for automated conversion [Furuta, Plaisant and Shneiderman, 1988]. While this is nice to have, not all candidate documents meet this requirement.

The conversion algorithm must be adaptable to both deeply- and broadly-structured documents. A broadly-structured document, an encyclopedia, for example, contains a large number of individual articles many of which can be linked. Many technical manuals, on the other hand, may have tables of contents with 5, 6, or even 7 levels of indenture, thus indicating a very deep structure. Many good candidate documents have very deep structures in addition to being highly cross-referenced.

Documents which are deeply-structured can be difficult to use in paper form, and they may be harder to convert into hypertexts, but they can be made highly useful in hypertext form.

Any document or set of documents is a good candidate for conversion if it is information-rich, highly cross-referenced, or has a complex, well-defined structure. Documents of this description include: business proposals, maintenance manuals, programming manuals, military or corporate standards, textbooks, technical refer-

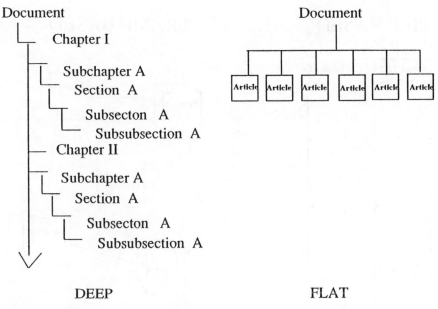

DEEP   FLAT

Figure 9.1   Deep vs. flat structure.

ences and so on. Documents which have reasonably consistent formats and use technical vocabularies make ideal candidates for hypertext conversion.

Elements to look for in selecting candidate documents include:

- Does the use of the document lend itself to hypertext?
- Is there an explicit or implicit structure?
- Does it have a table of contents or can one be extracted or derived?
- Does it have an index, glossary, etc.?
- Is it highly cross-referenced either internally or externally?
- Are there definable units which can be linked?

The Texas Instruments HyperTRANS process is applicable to many different types of documents.

Selecting and Configuring the User Interface.   Many of the currently available hypertext systems are frame-based. These tools equate a node or frame to the information which can be displayed on a single computer screen. Frame-based authoring tools are appropriate for most authoring because authors can think and create units of information in screen or frame sized units. But existing written information does not always translate easily into screen-sized units. Frame-based interfaces can require significant reformatting of materials for display purposes.

File-based hypertext systems do not impose the same restrictions on node size as frame-based systems and thus can be easier to convert to. In one type of file-based system the complete textual information is contained in one (or a series of)

FILE BASED   FRAME BASED

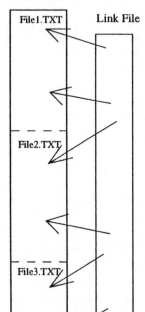
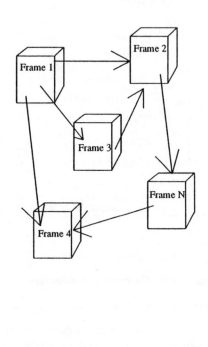

Figure 9.2   File vs. frame based systems.

text files similar to a set of word processor text files. Link information is stored in a separate set of files and contains information about where links point into the text file(s).

For example, the Texas Instruments DISCOVER ... interface is not limited in terms of the size of the chunks (or nodes) of information. By keeping the link information separate from the nodes and being able to link to elements that might be within a chunk or node, the interface can handle information with virtually any size units. This file approach also supports a *look-and-feel* similar to the original paper document.

Another aspect of the user interface involves how the information is intended to be used. Authors of technical reference manuals often do not want readers to have access beyond browsing or looking at certain information. If it is important that maintenance personnel all follow the same procedures, then it is important that they not be able to modify the information in any way.

Sometimes it is important that readers not change the information but it is also useful for them to be able to add personal or local comments as annotations to the original information. This annotation capability can go so far as adding additional personal links.

Even in its paper form, a manual is rarely ever error-free and often a person using a manual can find better ways of performing a task than is specified in the maintenance manual. Providing a means of identifying, capturing and then re-distributing this information can significantly improve the hyperdocument. These locally-generated annotations and links can be captured as a source of feedback to the authors of the information. This can be especially useful with maintenance manuals.

Once a document has been converted to hypertext, the original authors will recognize additional links and changes which they would like to make. Hypertext provides the ability to display and manipulate relationships which can give an author cues to other items which could be related. If they have to go through the painful process of manual conversion, they may never get to the point of analyzing and identifying these additional relationships. Providing them a rapidly converted version of their materials gives them a base from which they can embellish the information using a manual hypertext authoring tool.

Another consideration is whether there is a need to return to a print form of the information from the hypertext database. If editing and printing are elements of the complete system, then keeping the text in some ASCII or other native form with as little added mark up in the files as possible makes editing and printing the information easier.

Display Environment Considerations. An additional consideration in conversion is the target display environment. If the information is very voluminous and/or contains a large number of colors or highly complex graphics, it will impact both on the end display environment and the conversion process.

Large complex graphics, multiple text fonts and the like may dictate high resolution or graphics monitors for display, mass storage devices (such as CD-ROM drives), or input devices (e.g., a color scanner).

High quality print images may achieve resolutions of up to 1200 dots per inch while a very good computer screen can display the equivalent of only about 100 dots per inch. This disparity means that printed images that are scanned into hypertexts may become unreadable on a typical computer screen. Of course, the hypertext builder may decide to show only a portion of each high resolution picture on screen at a time. In addition, printed images may contain so much detail that in displaying them, the ability to zoom in, pan and/or scroll through the image becomes necessary. These decisions can have a major impact on the document conversion process.

Handling Graphics. Give serious consideration to the display requirements for graphic images being imported.

- Is it imperative that the same level of clarity that was on the printed page be maintained for computer display?

- Is it acceptable to reduce the size of the images (using graphics tools or utilities) so that each can be displayed, whole, on a single screen?
- Are there elements in the graphics which should be linked to other graphics or to text?

Answers to these questions can have a major impact on the procedures used to import images into the hyperdocument. The same kinds of issues must be addressed relative to other print attributes and their conversion to computer display. If the document contains multiple fonts or other attributes, is it acceptable to convert these to computer-displayable alternatives? If not, if displaying the font attributes on screen exactly they appear on paper is critical, then the conversion process will undoubtedly involve weighty graphical design considerations.

Typically, printed illustrations are converted from paper by means of scanning or frame grabbing from the paper originals. Frame grabbing refers to the process of capturing the image with a video camera and then digitizing a single (still) frame of the video. These scanned or grabbed images are usually converted into raster or bitmapped images which are then displayed using a graphics display utility. The amount of adjustment images require for display will determine how much human intervention will be required during the conversion of printed and graphical elements.

Many technical manuals include call outs or other identifiers which are integrated into a graphic and reference some other graphic or piece of text. A conversion process must include the ability to handle these types of links, preferably without having to reconstruct the graphic. Many current hypertext tools provide utilities for importing and manipulating graphics. However, there are, in general, fewer tools that facilitate linking to and from graphics.

Converting Source Text Into Machine Readable Formats. Before text can be converted into hypertext, it must be available in computer-readable form. There are two basic ways of getting textual materials into a format that can be processed by the automatic conversion software. One is to scan in original paper pages; the other is to convert already-existing computer files.

Scanning: Documents which are available only on paper must be scanned in in order to be converted into computer-readable text. It is often the case that even when computer files exist, the paper version of the document is the most correct or accurate version of the information. For example, some physical "cut-and-paste" processes or last minute editing corrections to galley proofs may have resulted in changes to the printed document that never have been incorporated into the computer files.

A great deal of effort has to go into analyzing the document before scanning occurs. Scanners and their support software are geared toward capturing "pages" of information primarily for storage and reprinting them on paper. Scanning technology is not geared toward preparing text information for computer display. Thought must go into deciding how to separate and store information input via the scanner to facilitate the automation process.

The basic scanning procedures include:

1. Bound material is unbound or photocopied;
2. Each page is scanned to produce a bit-array image;
3. The images are split into sub-images containing either text only or graphics only; and
4. The text-only images are sent through an optical character recognition (OCR) program to extract their individual ASCII characters.

In some instances it is to useful to retain the image version of complete pages for display purposes but the ASCII version of the text characters is still necessary for link identification.

Not all procedures in the hypertext creation process can be fully automated. Scanning is one of those procedures. Since no image scanner is 100% accurate, the resulting files must be proofread and scanner-induced errors must be corrected. Some text images are difficult to convert into text characters due to poor print quality, low contrast between ink color and paper color, small or complicated typefaces, or other reasons. Also, OCR algorithms often have trouble with items such as underlining, boldface, italics, and other print enhancements or character attributes. Using the scanner usually saves a great deal of time and effort, but for some documents, a skilled typist's manual input is actually faster.

High-quality graphics may also benefit from a human touch. Using a graphics package, elements of graphic images can be touched up. For example, an area that should be solid black but has a few white pixels, or a line that should be continuous but appears broken can be fixed manually. The amount of operator time required for scanned text and graphics varies from document to document and application to application.

Translating existing computer-based text files: A format conversion utility is customarily used to translate existing computer files into a standard format acceptable for hypertext conversion. Some currently available page layout or formatting utilities are not recommended because they were designed to produce pages to be printed on paper and thus converting their native files to hypertext-processible forms is extremely difficult.

If a conversion utility is unavailable for a particular format, one of two processes must be applied to produce process-ready files: develop a format conversion utility, or print the document and then scan it in using an OCR program to convert the bitmapped scanner image into text.

Creating the Document Description. A document typically contains a table of contents, a list of figures, a bibliography, a glossary, an index, and so on, but these can exist in many possible formats. Typically the conversion facility must be informed about the specific formats used by a given document or set of documents. The TI HyperTRANS facility recognizes many formats, but new formats are inevitable. When a new format is encountered, HyperTRANS must first be taught the distinguishing characteristics of the unfamiliar formatting style. This requires a programmer or technician to create a document description. The document description tells HyperTRANS which formats are used in the document. The document description will provide HyperTRANS with information such as what a typical line in the table of contents looks like, what the format is for an entry in the document's index or glossary, how to recognize figure references, internal cross references, or references to other documents, etc.

Once a document description is available, HyperTRANS can search the document for visual and spatial cues, attributes, or other features that will help it to identify the document's various internal structures and links. Once a document description has been generated, it can be used for any document with the same format. When an entire set of manuals with a consistent style needs to be processed, only one of these documents needs to go through this document description step. All of the others can be processed using the same document description.

Subtle elements in a document can have a significant effect on the efficacy of the automated conversion. For example, an author may use a reference such as "see Paragraph 1" when there are several Paragraph 1s in the document. There might even be a Paragraph 1 in every chapter in the document. In these ambiguous cases, a reader would use context cues to determine which Paragraph 1 the author really was referring to. Occasionally the automated conversion process must possess the same capability. HyperTRANS extracts information about such ambiguities by analyzing the document and also relies on the document description file.

Creating View Descriptions.   The same body of information can be of value to many different readers. It might be made more useful if it is organized for them. Even the same reader may look at a hyperdocument with a different view at different times. For example, a typical repair manual can contain a training view, a troubleshooting view, a routine maintenance view and a purchaser's view. Each view can be seen as a filter; information not relevant to a particular reader should be filtered out. An expert might not be shown training information, a service mechanic would see maintenance procedures and a purchasing agent would see part names, numbers, quantities and prices. View descriptions can be created for any group of readers which can be described. View descriptions may appear as alternate tables of contents or structural organizations to the information. Details about the target reader group need to be specified prior to actual conversion in order for the view descriptions to be defined.

Initiating the Conversion Process.   After the computer-readable files of a document have been created, they are stored in one or more text files and bit-mapped graphics files. An additional file may be required which contains a short description of each graphic (such as "Figure 12-4," Diagram 5," or "Photo of Part A1B2C3"), along with the name of the file where the graphic is stored. At that point, for the TI HyperTRANS process, the text file(s), the file containing the graphic descriptions, the Document Description file and any View Description information are fed to a batch process. The batch process includes functions for identifying (or marking) the links and building the links. The process must be capable of:

- parsing (chunking) the input documents into nodes;
- building hierarchical links based on the division of the document into chapters, sections, subsections, etc. This may involve using the existing table of contents or generating one automatically if needed;
- building associative (non-hierarchical) links among the document's nodes based on references to: chapters, sections, figures and tables, key phrases, index and glossary entries;
- building associative links to other documents (external links) based on cross references.

Errors in Input Documents.   There are a variety of issues which automated conversion must be able to handle. Among these is how to deal with errors in original documents. In working on over 50 conversion projects Texas Instruments Hypermedia Systems & Services has not yet processed a document in which we did not uncover errors. These could be as simple as a typographical error or a misspelling or something much more serious such as total inconsistency in structure. The HyperTRANS process has been designed to uncover all kinds of errors in the material which it is fed.

When HyperTRANS encounters a problem while processing a file, it describes the problem in an output file called an Exception Log. Each log entry indicates the exact location in the document where the problem occurred as well as which HyperTRANS module was executing at the time. The types of problems reported by HyperTRANS include errors in the document description and errors in the document itself.

Typical types of errors which HyperTRANS uncovers are:

- inconsistent names or numbering;
- missing figures, tables, captions, etc.;
- missing footnotes, bibliographic notes, etc.;
- index entries not found in text;
- unreferenced items.

Each error must be resolved before a complete hyperdocument can be produced. Errors in the document description are corrected before the document is reprocessed. Errors in the original document may require consultation with the author of the document. Correcting them may require no more than a typographical change, or a major structural change or rewrites of portions of the document may be required.

Completing the Conversion.   Once all the errors have been resolved, the completed hypertext database must be checked and verified. Algorithms can be applied to ensure that there is an origination and destination for each link. Human review is required to check content-related linking. The utility of any given link is often a subjective decision and typically is left up to the original document authors or readers. It is also through this review and validation process that content specialists often identify both better ways to write the paper manual and ways to improve subsequent versions of the hyperdocument.

Processing the Materials for the End Environment.   Once the hypertext database has been created, you have to process the information for the desired reader environment. Unless the conversion facility is closely tied to a user interface, what comes out of the convertor is information about the text, graphics and hypertext links which then has to be translated into the required format for the desired interface. This may involve writing software to implement the desired user interface using the text, graphics and links generated by the automatic conversion. This is where the issues relative to frame vs file based systems come into play. Also, issues concerning text vs graphic based interfaces are important as well as the basic metaphor employed by the interface. The flexibility (or lack there of) of the user interface has a major impact on the ability to automatically translate documents for the interface.

Packaging and Distribution.   Once the hyperdocument has been created, it will be distributed to readers. The medium for distribution is chosen based on the size of the hyperdocument and the computer and peripherals readers own. Critical concerns for distribution involve the number of readers and the volatility of the database. Rapid and frequent changes probably suggests a centralized database which readers can access. More static documents which require periodic updating and maybe support a large number of displaced users probably suggests some type of CD-ROM. Small documents can be distributed to individuals on diskette. Larger databases may require a CD-ROM or other large capacity mass storage device. In some instances a single copy of a document can be shared via a local area network or other communication approach.

Open Issues for Translation

A variety of issues pertaining to automatic conversion remain to be worked out. Some of these are issues for hypertext in general. Among these are hypertext standards, the role of hypertext in solving bigger problems and the nature of information organization.

Standardization

Standardization implies some agreed-to concepts, principles or guidelines. Currently, there are efforts underway to develop standards for hypertext but none have, as yet, been accepted and implemented by the growing hypertext community. If you select a particular hypertext tool or interface for your work, you have no guarantee at present that what you develop will be compatible with what others develop. This provides both an opportunity and a problem for those doing automated conversion. First, it means that it may not be simple to convert one hyperdocument format to another and thus it will provide work for those who want to create these translators. But more importantly, it means that each hypertext tool which is created need not comply with anything which would make automated conversion easier. [See Chapter 26 on Standards in this book.]

Hypertext As Part of a Solution

Converting information into hypertext in most instances should not be viewed as a stand-alone exercise. Information access is typically tied to some larger problem which someone is trying to solve. Whether it be better education, or more effective maintenance, or more timely business decisions, the use of hypertext for information access must be placed in context.

Often technologies come along which people attempt to use to solve all of their problems. Hypertext is a relatively new idea which has not yet matured and, therefore, its boundaries of application have not been thoroughly tested. While this means that hypertext may well prove valuable in areas as yet untried, it also means that there are places where it is not the best solution and we need to identify and communicate these as well.

Additionally this means that in order for a hyperdocument to be truly useful, it must be able to interact with other software. For example, a parts and service hyperdocument may interact with parts ordering and inventory software.

Information Organization

Hypertext environments allow writers to produce information in a haphazard way and then link the information later. While this provides some very exciting opportunities for creative writers it also poses some potential problems. Effective writing (especially in technical areas) is often a difficult and time consuming activity. Having information technically correct is only part of the problem. What often takes the most work is identifying the best organization and structure to apply to the information and then being disciplined enough to consistently apply the organization. Without effective discipline, the hyperdocument creator can produce a very useless document. Organization and structure are critical elements to information transferral, regardless of the medium.

Conclusions

Hypertext provides an exciting addition to the traditional means of information access and manipulation. With the growth of computers, the creation of forms of information storage and retrieval have had an equal opportunity to grow. No longer are we limited to the printed page as a means of conveying information. Just like the spreadsheet really extended the "calculator" to take advantage of the computer, so can hypertext extend the written document to take advantage of the computer.

Hypertext authoring tools provide the means of creating this new form but to really provide the momentum for this new concept we must find ways of moving vast amounts of already existing information into hyperdocuments. To accomplish this, automated conversion programs are needed.

Automated conversion is necessary for a variety of reasons. First and foremost is simply the size of the problem. The amount of existing information which could benefit from being converted is staggering. Manual conversion is simply too slow, imprecise and costly to be effective.

Finally, for hypertext conversion to be effective, we must leverage what has gone on before. While hypertext provides us the means of extending our information transfer opportunities, we should not ignore what already exists. It has been our experience that good hypertext requires/reflects good organization. Well written, well structured, well organized documents make for good hypertext. Poorly written, poorly organized information makes for poor hypertext. Those involved in creating this new technology should build on the legacy of authors who have gone before.

About the Author

Robert W. Riner, Ph.D.

Robert W. Riner, Ph.D., is currently the Marketing Director for the Hypermedia Systems & Services organization at Texas Instruments. In that capacity he is responsible for interacting with customers to assess information management needs and to see where the TI HyperTRANS process can solve customer problems. Prior to his current position he was on loan to the Computer Learning Research Laboratory at the University of Texas at Dallas where he was involved in research focused on the application of artificial intelligence and hypermedia to education and training. For 15 years, he has been involved in the development and application of advanced technologies to improve human productivity. He has a Ph.D. in instructional design from Florida State University.

Mr. Riner may be contacted at Hypermedia Systems and Services, Texas Instruments, Inc., P. O. Box 650311, MS 3968, Dallas, TX, 75265.

References

Bush, V. (1945). "As We May Think", *Atlantic Monthly, Vol 176*, July, 106–107.

Devlin, Joseph. (1991). "Standards for Hypertext," *Hypertext / Hypermedia Handbook*, Emily Berk and Joseph Devlin (Ed.s), McGraw-Hill, New York, NY.

Furuta R., Plaisant C. and Shneiderman B., (1988). A spectrum of Automatic Hypertext Constructions. *Hypermedia, Vol 1 No 2,*, 179–195.

Personal Electronic Aid for Maintenance (PEAM) Final Report, (1981). Prepared for the Human Factors Laboratory, Naval Training Equipment Center and The Army Project Manager for Training Devices (Contract NO. N61339-80-C-0134), August.

Wisher R. and Kincaid J., (1989). Personal Electronic Aid for Maintenance: Final Summary Report, Army Research Institute, March.

10

Automating the Conversion of Text Into Hypertext

By Thomas C. Rearick

Big Science Company

Introduction

Computer users are quick to recognize the benefits of hypertext-based on-line documentation: ease of use and rapid access of information.

Most are not aware of the considerable effort required to transform existing linear text into hypertext. The high initial cost of creating hypertext and the recurring cost of maintaining it limits its availability. Only when the creation and maintenance of hypertext is automated will it become accessible to a much larger audience.

This chapter discusses the conversion of existing text into hypertext.

Most hypertext authoring tools, used manually to originate and link text, are useful for creating small hypertext applications but lack the productivity enhancing tools when linking large amounts of text.

Existing text (hardcopy or electronic) may require processing before being converted into hypertext. The following section describes tools for preprocessing text so that it can be linked. This chapter includes sections which describe how hypertext links are created manually; technologies for computer assisted linking; and alternate strategies for improving the conversion process. Some of the techniques and strategies discussed describe SmarText, a commercially available conversion tool. Finally, an important development is discussed that will influence the future of text-to-hypertext conversion.

A Note On Terminology

Because this chapter deals with conversion of existing linear documents into hypertext, it seemed improper to call the person who supervised this process an author. Products like SmarText don't change the style or content of pre-existing documents in any way, but they do provide new ways of accessing information. Thus, we use the word "builder" to refer to the one who orchestrates the process by which products like SmarText create hyperdocuments.

Automation of Text Preprocessing

Existing text requires preprocessing if it is incompatible with the conversion utility. If text exists in an electronic form, very little effort may be necessary. But a significant level of effort may be necessary if the text exists only in a hardcopy form that must be scanned and converted into electronic text. In either case, programs exist to automate this preprocessing.

Hardcopy text is transformed into an electronic form by manual keyboard entry or *optical character recognition* (OCR). Keyboard entry may be the only option available if the hardcopy text is handwritten, in a nonstandard font or type size, or is illegible.

Optical character recognition involves three steps: scanning, character recognition, and artifact removal. Optical scanners transform hardcopy pages into electronic images. These text images can be stored in a computer and displayed like any other image.

OCR software and/or hardware is used to transform scanned images into ASCII text. In this form the words take up less disk space. Character recognition is usually fastest when performed on specialized hardware but software-based character recognition is usually less expensive.

The optical scanning and recognition process introduces errors or artifacts that must be corrected. Artifacts occur, for example, when the image of a letter "e" is recognized as a "c" or when the image of an "h" is recognized as a "b."

Specialized editors with integral spelling checkers are available from OCR manufacturers to automate the removal of artifacts. If the character recognition hardware or software is unsure of whether or not it has recognized a letter, it flags the word containing that character. After character recognition, the editor skips from one flagged word to the next, suggesting correctly spelled replacement words if the flagged word does not exist in the editor's dictionary. This improves the productivity of artifact removal because the user need only accept or reject the editor's suggested replacements.

The following are likely to reduce the productivity of the hardcopy conversion effort by increasing the number of artifacts. At some point, it may be cheaper and faster to enter the text manually:

- Kerned text reduces the accuracy of character recognition. Kerning is a practice used by typesetters to improve the appearance of text. Two letters are kerned when one letter made to overhang or come into proximity to the other. Kerning often occurs, for example, when a lowercase vowel follows a capital "T" or "W." While kerning improves the appearance of text, it reduces the reliability of optical character recognition.

- Nonstandard font sizes and types are not recognized. Recognition systems handle the most common typefaces (e.g., Courier) and font sizes (10 and 12 point). They are useless with very small or large font sizes or fancy fonts such as cursive styles.
- Glossy finish hardcopy documents may reduce the accuracy of character recognition. Glossy hardcopy effectively reduces the contrast of the scanned text. Some scanners are more resistant to this effect than others.
- Text printed on colored or shaded backgrounds may be unreadable. This is because most scanners encode non-white regions as black.

Even if text exists in an electronic form, it may require processing before it can be converted into hypertext. The electronic text may be in a format that is incompatible with the authoring or conversion tool. Examples of potential problems include:

- The text may contain extended, graphic, or otherwise non-ASCII characters not recognized by the conversion tool.
- The termination characters used to denote the end of a line of text or paragraph may be incompatible with the conversion tool.
- The text may exist in a word processor file format that is incompatible with the conversion tool.

Utilities are available for converting various word processor files into ASCII text with line termination denoted by a carriage return and line feed character. Most hypertext authoring or conversion tools can import text in this format.

Methodologies for Defining Links

Before discussing the automation of the conversion process, it is useful to review the different methodologies for organizing linear text into nonlinear hypertext.

Defining Hypertext Links Using Embedded Commands

The links of many hypertext systems are defined by embedding commands in text.[1] This marked-up text may be interpreted by a structured browser or compiled

---

1 For example, commands that define hypertext links are usually embedded physically in the text. SmarText commands are stored in separate shadow files so that the source text is never physically altered. SmarText commands may be said to be logically embedded.

into a hypertext application. There are two types of embedded commands: procedural and declarative.

Procedural languages specify what a link should do: *make the next word a link to x.* Most hypertext command languages are procedural. For example, HyperTalk is the procedural command language for HyperCard.

Declarative languages specify what a link is: *the next line is a chapter heading,* or *the following paragraph is semantically related to x, y, and z.* If declarative commands are used, then a separate file is necessary to describe conventions for linking chapter headings or paragraphs (similar to style sheets found in word processors).

Procedural languages are proprietary and application-specific. In contrast, a declarative markup language can be used in various applications to define hypertext organization, database organization, and hardcopy page layout. *Standard Generalized Markup Language* (SGML) is an example of a declarative markup language that can be used for multiple purposes.

The procedural/declarative options need not be mutually exclusive.

SmarText creates a procedural command list from the declarative commands embedded in proprietary word processor source files such as Samna's Ami Professional. This resulting list of procedural commands is then edited manually or by direct manipulation.

Linking By Direct Manipulation

Linking (text) by *direct manipulation* (LDM) requires less memorization and recall than more traditional authoring. That makes LDM easy to use by novice or occasional users. LDM is an example of What-You-See-Is-What-You-Get (WYSIWYG) editing [Shneiderman, 1983]. A hypertext link is created in SmarText using direct manipulation the following way:

- Select the link destination by clicking on it with a mouse.
- Click on a pull down menu command **Create Link**. A moveable dialogue box appears containing two buttons, **Link** and **Cancel**.
- Select the first link source in the text window by clicking on it with a mouse.
- Click on the **Link** button of the **Create Link** dialogue box. A link is created.
- Repeat the third and fourth operations for as many links as desired.
  When finished, click on the **Cancel** button of the **Create Link** dialogue box.

Although LDM may not be as easy to explain as an embedded command language, it is simple and fast.

Multiple Methodologies For Linking Hypertext

Linking by embedding commands in text and LDM each has its advantages. LDM prevents the hyperdocument builder from ever introducing syntactical errors, so

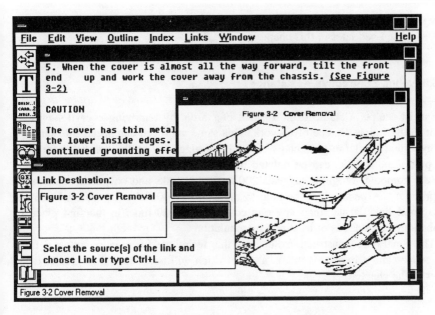

Figure 10.1   Creating hypertext links by direct manipulation.

program debugging is unnecessary. By requiring less memorization and recall of programming commands, LDM has a shorter learning curve. Yet, embedded command linking typically provides a richer and more powerful set of options than does LDM. An embedded command language is necessary if one wishes to automate the text-to-hypertext conversion process. Then, one could write a computer program that analyzes text and generates hypertext link commands.

Users get the best of both worlds if authoring or conversion tools support both embedded command programming and linking by direct manipulation. This is accomplished by offering two views of the same hypertext document: WYSIWYG and uncompiled program commands. Guide (version 3.0 for Microsoft Windows), Toolbook, and SmarText are examples of commercial hypertext systems that offer the user the choice of embedded command programming or linking by direct manipulation.

Computer-Assisted Link Generation

A more efficient way to define links is to let the computer generate them. Computer-assisted link generation capability may be integrated into a conversion tool or it may be offered as a part of a standalone utility. A standalone utility analyzes the text and then generates link commands. These link commands are then either compiled by the hypertext compiler or interpreted directly by the hypertext engine.

The appendix at the end of this chapter describes a standalone user-written program that generates hypertext links based on lexical string matching. Examples of integrated computer assisted link generation built into the SmarText Construction Set are discussed later in this chapter.

Additive vs. Subtractive Assistance

An artist sculpts a statue from a block of marble by removing everything irrelevant to the finished piece of artwork. This same approach can speed the sculpting of hypertext if a large percentage of the links suggested by the computer are inappropriate and if links can be deleted much faster than they can be inserted. Suppose a computer program suggests 200 hypertext links and only half of them are appropriate. A person may be able to mark those 100 links for removal (leaving 100 good links) faster than any one could create 100 links in the first place by embedding commands or by direct manipulation.

The SmarText Construction Set uses this technique for creating internal cross references and a hypertext index, a topic which will be discussed in greater detail later in the chapter.

Technologies for Computer Assisted Linking

The ideal conversion tool would create hypertext links correctly in text without any human intervention. It is unlikely that such a tool will ever exist since two people rarely agree on what a correct link is. A more realistic goal is a conversion tool that suggests links and creates them upon human confirmation. That is the goal of the technologies discussed below.

The reader should be forewarned: many of the techniques discussed below have not been tested outside of research laboratories. As promising as some may seem, there is no guarantee that they will ever be practical.

A technique may prove impractical because it is too slow, too unreliable, or because it requires too much computer memory.

Lexical Analysis

One approach to computer-assisted linking is based on lexical analysis. In its simplest form, lexical analysis resembles pattern or character string matching. Lexical analysis can be a powerful tool but users must be aware of its limitations.

Synonymy and *polysemy* both limit the usefulness of lexical analysis. Synonymity occurs when two different words have the same meaning. Polysemy occurs when one word has more than one meaning. One study has shown that people typically use the same word to describe an object only 10 percent to 20 percent of the time. Therefore, automated linking based on keyword matching alone is unlikely to be successful.

Simple character string matching could be used to generate commands to link all instances of a word to the definition of the word. However, this approach would most likely generate many redundant links. If a word to be linked occurs several times within the same paragraph, only the first instance of that term should be linked. Otherwise, text is likely to become cluttered with redundant hypertext links and readability will suffer. [See Chapter 11 by Shneiderman, et al., in this book.]

Another problem with simple character string matching is the likelihood that it might miss links altogether. Simple string matching cannot discern the many root word variations due to the concatenation of suffixes. *Stemming* is required to determine if two words share the same root word. A word is stemmed by recursively removing suffixes from the tail end of words until only three or more characters remain. The English language has only about 75 prefixes and 250 suffixes.

There are two approaches to word stemming: heuristic and rule-based. A heuristic approach to stemming can determine a root very quickly by interactively removing suffixes like *s, er, ing,* and others, from the end of a string until no suffixes remain. This approach works very well for words like *compute(s), computer(s), computing, computable, computability, computation, and computational.* This approach does not work for words like *sable, sing,* and *seer.* The reliability of this algorithm improves if one requires that at least three characters remain in the root. But it will still group the terms *cap* and *capability* or *cat* and *catering* together. Dictionary-based approaches are slower and occupy more memory than heuristic approaches but they are more reliable. They record the permissible suffixes with each word in a large dictionary. Compiling such a dictionary is time consuming. If a word to be stemmed is not contained within the dictionary, then the algorithm falls back to a heuristic approach.

The appendix to this chapter describes a simple but useful application of lexical analysis for creating a hypertext table of contents from data down-loaded from an on-line database.

Statistical Analysis

Results of statistical analyses of word frequency and distribution throughout a text document can be used to automate the generation of hypertext indexes and internal cross references.

Large on-line database systems that store the text of technical articles often search for particular articles by comparing the words of a query with word descriptors that characterize the article. Usually these descriptors are assigned to each text record by subject experts. The process of assigning keyword descriptors to text records is called *indexing.* Automatic indexing has been studied as a way to create compact keyword descriptions of documents stored and accessed in large text retrieval systems.

The same technology used to index databases can be used to create a hypertext *index*—similar to the index found in the back of books. However, the objectives for creating an index for text retrieval and for hypertext are different. Database indices discriminate between text records that have well-delineated boundaries. The indices for printed or hypertext documents are meant to help readers locate important topics that are discussed within a body of text that has few or no internal boundaries. Because of these differences, underlying assumptions for generating an index may be different. The following two assumptions apply to hyperdocument indices only:

* Words that occur very frequently or very infrequently within a document are the least likely to be of interest to the reader. By analyzing the statistics of word frequency, one may choose those words that have an intermediate frequency of occurrence. SmarText relies on this assumption.
* There are simply too many useless words that occur with intermediate frequencies and there are many useful words that occur infrequently.

Therefore, by itself, automated indexing based on term frequency is not very useful. *Stopword* and *keyword* lists can be used to improve the performance of indexing. A stopword list contains terms that should never be entered into index. A keyword list contains terms that should always be entered into an index if the document contains that word.

Every time SmarText builds an index, it includes a default stopword list containing hundreds of common words. In addition, every time the hyperdocument builder manually deletes a word from a SmarText index, that word is added automatically to a document-specific stopword list.

This stopword list can be reused in building other related documents.

Every time the builder adds a word manually to the index, that word is added automatically to a document-specific keyword list. Like stopword lists, this keyword list can be reused in building other related documents.

Syntactical Analysis

Syntax is used to describe the structure of words in sentences. One of the goals of analyzing sentence syntax is to determine the parts of speech so that meaning can be inferred. For example, whether a word is being used as a noun (high frequency *transistor*) or as an adjective (high frequency *transistor* radio) influences its meaning. By identifying how a term is used, a program should be able to differentiate between multiple meanings of the same word. The use of syntax to infer sentence meaning has been the focus of research in *natural language processing* (NLP) and *artificial intelligence* (AI) for more than 30 years. Unfortunately, this research has produced few robust or commercially viable products.

Computational complexity and brittleness are two reasons why NLP and AI have had limited commercial success. The amount of processing required in nontrivial expert systems based on production rules or deductive retrieval can easily exceed the resources available on personal computers or the patience of users. Brittleness describes the ungraceful degradation of program performance inherent in all symbol-based AI systems. It is a form of unreliability that occurs whenever an AI program encounters a situation that its creator never anticipated. The ability of AI programs to use common sense and to learn from their mistakes depends solely on the cleverness and foresight of their programmers.

The application of syntactical methodologies is discussed in greater detail in [Salton, 1989a; Salton, 1989b].

Syntax can also be used to describe the hierarchical structure of chapter and section units within a complete document. An algorithm is described later in this chapter that infers a hierarchical structure from a document's text. Although the algorithm is brittle, it reduces the time spent creating a hypertext table of contents.

Semantics

Semantic analysis attempts to create hypertext links based on the explicit meanings or implicit associations (connotations) of terms and phrases [Foltz, 1990]. Semantics is an area of controversy because of disagreement over what *meaning* is. Lexical, statistical, and syntactical techniques analyze text patterns without regard to what those patterns mean. Programs claiming to perform semantic analysis are based on one or more of those non-semantic approaches. This suggests that meaning is inherently probabilistic or structural in nature—a claim that many disagree with.

Although there is research suggesting that semantic analysis can improve the retrieval of textual information, a significant amount of processing and memory is required and performance improvements are incremental at best [Foltz, 1990].

Alternative Strategies for Improving Productivity

Our goal is to reduce the cost of converting linear text into hypertext by improving the productivity of the process. Computer-assisted linking is a very appealing idea, but it is only one of many ways to expedite the conversion process. Depending on the data being linked and the application, computer-assisted linking may be the least fruitful of productivity-enhancing strategies. The following low technology strategies can significantly reduce the time and effort required to convert text into hypertext.

Prior Planning Prevents Poor Performance

Many electronic documents exist first as hardcopy documents. By anticipating the eventual conversion of a hardcopy document to an electronic form, a lot of manual labor can be avoided. The following are suggestions for those planning to publish in both hardcopy and electronic forms:

- Do not store text with words split up by hyphenations. Utilities exist for splitting whole words into syllables but few utilities exist that can tell the difference between a single word split into two syllables and a hyphenated word (e.g., *on-line*).

• Use symbolic references to other parts of the document: avoid page number references. Page numbers make little sense for hypertext documents if scrollable text is wrapped and displayed within sizable windows. Instead of page references, refer to chapter headings or descriptive text strings that can be searched.

• Avoid overuse of sidebars. Sidebars resemble footnotes except they tend to contain more text and are embedded in the page in a box of their own. They are examples of nonlinear text since they occur outside of the main text stream. Since they do occur outside of the main text stream, a conversion tool may not know what to do with them (where to link them in), thus requiring a greater manual effort.

• Correct spelling errors. A misspelled word is unlikely to be linked using any of the automation techniques described above.

• Ensure consistency between the table of contents and the embedded heading captions of source text files. During the development of the SmarText Construction Set, we found that it was often best to ignore the table of contents of the printed document because printed tables of contents tended to differ from the chapter headings as they appeared within the text or the hypertext. This is becoming less of problem now that many word processors automatically generate tables of contents based on the text in a document. However, to be on the safe side, SmarText infers document structure directly from the headings embedded in documents.

• Avoid wide multicolumn tables. Pretty much all structured browsers that wrap text within scrollable and sizable windows make a mess of multicolumn tables if those tables are forced to be wrapped. For example, when the document is displayed, its columns may no longer line up. There are two alternatives to forced-wrapping: use narrow tables or provide an application link to a spreadsheet program.

• Provide hints to the conversion tool. SmarText infers chapter headings and their hierarchical structures from many ASCII text files. However, the inference algorithm works best when it is processing text stored in a native word processing format that uses declarative tags. If a tag is available, SmarText will use it. For example, SmarText will assume that a line of text tagged as Heading_2 by Ami Professional is a second level heading.

Preserving and Re-Using Conversion Information

Once one hyperdocument has been built, building subsequent and related hyperdocuments should require less work if information gathered while building the initial document can be reused. The SmarText Construction Set achieves this two ways: 1) stopword and keyword lists created in building one document may be re-used in building subsequent documents, and 2) alternative views of a document can be derived from existing views. Each of these examples is described in the next section.

Automating Simple Recurring Tasks and
User Interface Design

Some recurring tasks, like searching for the next occurrence of a particular word, can be automated with simple macro utilities. Making often-used functions more accessible, as icons for example, reduces the amount of keyboard or mouse activity. Designing the user interface for intuitive yet efficient use may be the most productive way to improve productivity—and one of the most difficult.

The SmarText Electronic Document
Construction Set

This discussion describes version 1.0 of the SmarText Construction Set. The SmarText Electronic Document Construction Set is a software product that automates the creation and browsing of large hypertext documents.

SmarText is a Microsoft Windows application that operates on 80286 and 80386 personal computers. SmarText shipped in September, 1990, and is distributed by Lotus Development Corporation's Word Processing Division.

The SmarText Electronic Document Construction Set comes in two versions: a builder for creating and browsing hypertext documents and a network-compatible reader or structured browser [Conklin, 1978] for reading only. The builder includes all the features found in the reader but adds manual and automated link editing functions.

Features of the Reader and Builder

The SmarText user interface, shown in Figure 10. 2, relies on a book metaphor to unify its various components conceptually. The implementation of the book metaphor in SmarText is neither as graphical nor as literal as implementations of hypertext products that frame text within file cards or spiral bound notebooks. A metaphor makes new or abstract concepts familiar and understandable by grounding them on concrete and familiar concepts [See Chapter 11 by Shneiderman, et al., in this book]. If a metaphor is extended too literally, however, it can limit or constrain its target domain. Electronic documentation has different constraints than hardcopy documentation does—just as motion pictures are different from theater. Our goal was to use metaphor to shorten the SmarText learning curve without limiting the medium.

Title page, table of contents (outline), body of text, illustrations, card catalog (summary) and index are each bounded by a movable, sizable, and scrollable child window. All child windows are constrained within the SmarText application parent window. SmarText allows both readers and builders to place bookmarks, write margin notes, and copy text from the hyperdocument into an ASCII file, then edit it using a built-in editor. All browsing and link editing commands can be invoked

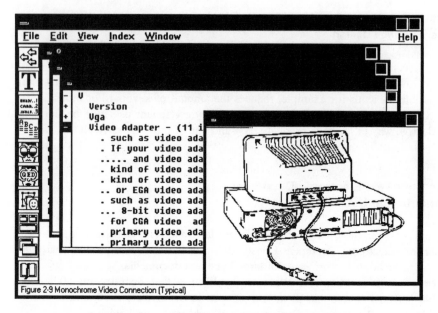

Figure 10.2   The SmarText Construction Set User Interface.

via a keyboard or a mouse. Accelerator keys and an optional, configurable icon bar provide speedy shortcuts for keyboard or mouse users, respectively.

SmarText documents, like most books, can be browsed several ways. Readers can scroll text linearly within a node. Or, readers can select cross references, denoted by highlighted text, to link to other text locations, illustrations, or executable programs. The act of selecting a link in the *outline, index* and *search results* windows causes the text window to change.

The outline window displays an on-line analog of a table of contents.

When a reader clicks on a chapter or section heading in the outline window, the text window becomes the topmost child window and displays the beginning of that chapter or section. The outline window looks and operates like many outlining programs: top level headings hide lower level headings until they are expanded to display lower level headings.

Figure 10.3 shows the text and outline windows tiled within a SmarText application (parent) window.

Word entries of the index window expand into *KeyWord-In-Context* (KWIC) hypertext links. Word-stemming is performed automatically. Double clicking on a KWIC phrase causes the text window to scroll to the location of that phrase. By seeing the word used in context, the reader can better decide which instance of a word is of interest. Figure 10.4 shows the index window maximized. When the reader double clicks on a KWIC phrase, the text window that contains the KWIC phrase becomes the topmost child window.

Boolean search is provided for full text search of one-, two-, or three-word phrases. The results of a search are displayed in a search results window. The

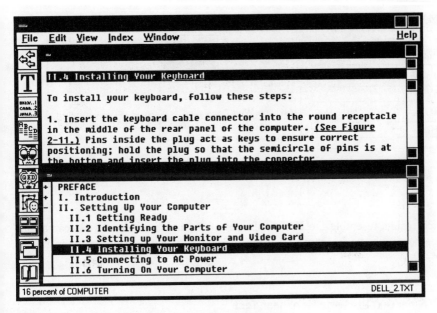

Figure 10.3   SmarText text and outline windows.

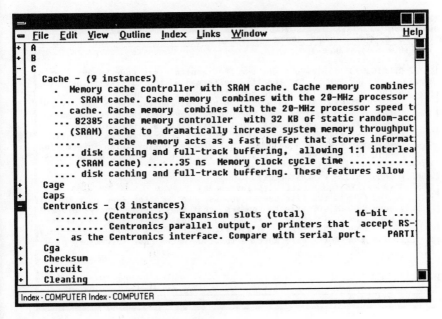

Figure 10.4   SmarText index window.

Word(s) to Find:

CONFIG

◉ And   ○ Or   ○ And Not
┌─ Options ─────────────────
SYS   ☒ Find Words In Order

◉ And   ○ Or   ○ And Not   Maximum Word Separation:

FILE   │ 19 │ characters

Figure 10.5   Search dialog box.

search results resemble the KWIC phrases of the index window. The search dialogue box is shown in Figure 10.5; the search results windows is shown in Figure 10.6.

How SmarText Presents Nonlinear Text

SmarText is intended to be used by novice or casual readers as well as expert users. A criticism often heard of hypertext is that readers become disoriented or lost in hyperspace. SmarText presents nonlinear text in a way intended to minimize reader disorientation.

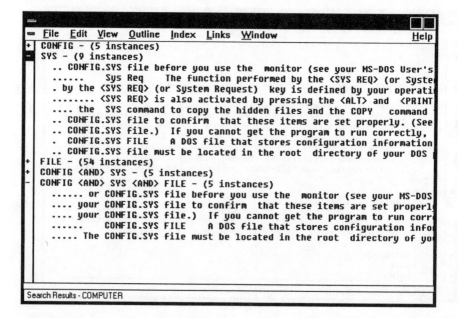

```
 ▬  File  Edit  View  Outline  Index  Links  Window                    Help
[+] CONFIG - (5 instances)
[-] SYS - (9 instances)
       .. CONFIG.SYS file before you use the  monitor (see your MS-DOS User's
       ......     Sys Req    The function performed by the <SYS REQ> (or Syste
       . by the <SYS REQ> (or System Request)  key is defined by your operati
       ........ <SYS REQ> is also activated by pressing the <ALT> and  <PRINT
       .... the  SYS command to copy the hidden files and the COPY  command
       .. CONFIG.SYS file to confirm  that these items are set properly. (See
       .. CONFIG.SYS file.)  If you cannot get the program to run correctly,
       .  CONFIG.SYS FILE    A DOS file that stores configuration information
       .. CONFIG.SYS file must be located in the root  directory of your DOS
[+] FILE - (54 instances)
[+] CONFIG <AND> SYS - (5 instances)
[-] CONFIG <AND> SYS <AND> FILE - (5 instances)
       ...... or CONFIG.SYS file before you use the  monitor (see your MS-DOS
       .... your CONFIG.SYS file to confirm  that these items are set properl
       .... your CONFIG.SYS file.)  If you cannot get the program to run corr
       ......      CONFIG.SYS FILE    A DOS file that stores configuration info
       ..... The CONFIG.SYS file must be located in the root  directory of yo

 Search Results - COMPUTER
```

Figure 10.6   Search results window.

Some hypertext systems model the nonlinearity of text as a network of connected nodes containing text. These nodes typically represent both a physical unit of text (a file) and a logical unit of text (everything that appears on screen). The act of following a link from one node to the next may be represented to the reader in one or more of the following ways:

- Replacing one card by another card
- Replacing the contents of a scrolled window
- Adding a window
- Replacing a text string inline with another text string

Each of these approaches deprives the reader of a sense of Gestalt—a sense of the document's boundaries and the reader's location in the text with respect to those boundaries. This lost sense of place may account for some of the disorientation common to readers of hyperdocuments.

SmarText, by contrast, offers multiple views of text presented *linearly*. SmarText readers select a *View* in order to choose to traverse one path out of many possible paths. The text, index, and outline windows are constrained by the selected view. The SmarText reader is constantly reminded of a view's boundary in four ways:

- The slider of the scroll bar shows the view's boundary and reader's relation to it.
- A number on the status bar indicates the percentage of the view traversed (one percent to 99 percent).
- The outline window provides a hierarchical description of the entire view.
- The rate at which the slider moves along the scroll bar while one is scrolling or paging gives the reader a sense of the amount of text in the view.

Document Physical & Logical Organization

The logical presentation of text by SmarText is independent of its physical organization. A single SmarText document may reference over five hundred source text files. SmarText never modifies or duplicates text or graphics data. SmarText translates text stored in native word processor formats on-the-fly. This reduces the storage overhead of maintaining hardcopy and electronic forms of documentation and insures that both forms are consistent with each other.

Since SmarText is a fine-grained system (pointers address characters, not chunks of text), a nodal model is irrelevant. A view may organize sentences, paragraphs, or whole files into any arbitrary linear order or hierarchical structure. One view can be a small, simplified extract of another view. By separating logical and physical organization, the hypertext user has a wide range of options for constructing alternative views or browsing paths through text and graphical data.

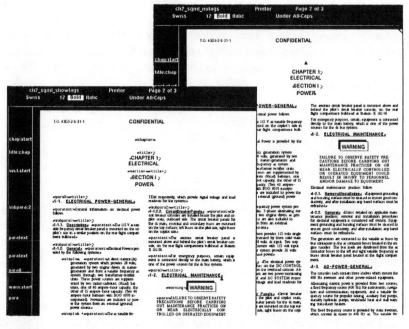

Figure 10.7

Inference of Table of Contents

SmarText automates the construction of a hypertext table of contents (outline) by inferring chapter and section headings from the source text files. If the source text file is in an ASCII or simple word processor format, then SmarText analyzes the syntax of each line with respect to the following cues: 1.) line length, 2.) indentation, 3.) capitalization 4.) heading structural cues. Heading structural cues consist of alphabetic letters and Roman or Arabic numerals combined by punctuation marks such as a period (.) or dash(-). SmarText uses a proprietary algorithm to infer the syntax of heading structural cues since there is no common convention for denoting heading hierarchical structure.

Some word processors, such as Ami Professional, store text in a declarative, marked up form. In this case, text that is a title, top level heading, or second level heading is typically marked as such. SmarText uses these mark-up tags to improve the reliability of the algorithm that infers document structure (see Figure 10.7).

SmarText currently uses the descriptive tags found in Samna's Ami and Ami Professional word processors to build document outlines. Some manual editing of the inferred outline is almost always required. A SmarText builder can easily delete, insert, and promote or demote outline captions (move them up or down a hierarchical level) by direct manipulation. The builder can also change the logical order of headings from within custom views. Swapping the order of two headings in an outline results in the logical swapping of their associated text within the text window. SmarText never modifies source text or graphics files.

Automated Index Generation

SmarText creates an on-line index with *keyword-in-context* (KWIC) links automatically using the automatic indexing algorithm discussed previously. The approach is summarized below (the actual implementation is different):

- Find all unique words in a document.
- Group words that share a common root together.
- Remove words that also occur in specified stopword lists if they do not also occur in any specified keyword lists (keywords always take precedence over stopwords).
- Remove words that occur most or least frequently (the builder may adjust the threshold levels) that do not occur in any keyword lists.
- For each word, insert a procedural command into an ASCII file (called a shadow file in SmarText). This command will instruct SmarText to add that word to the index window.
- Compile the ASCII command file to generate an underlying data structure to speed browsing.

The listing in Table 10.1 shows all the index words beginning with "a" that SmarText extracted from the King James Version of the Bible. The index was built using only the default stopword list containing about three hundred words common in North American English. (The results are presented before any words were excluded by a builder.) The use of subject-specific keyword and stopword lists would improve this result.

Typically, numerous poor choices for index words are made by the algorithm on the first try. The builder deletes those words by marking (clicking on) those words to be deleted and depressing the *Delete* key. Deleted words are automatically placed on the default document's stopword list. That stopword list may be used again when building other documents.

The builder may manually add words to the index by invoking an *Add Word* to *Index* function or by adding the word to the keyword list and regenerating the index.

Table 10.1   Index words extracted from the King James Version of the Bible.

Abimelech	Adultery	Angry
Abner	Afar	Armies
Abode	Afterward	Array
Abram	Age	Arrow
Abroad	Ahaz	Asa
Abundance	Almighty	Aside
Abundant	Amalek	Asses
Accomplish	Amaziah	Astonied
Accuse	Amen	Author

Inference of Internal Cross References

SmarText infers hypertext cross reference links within the text window.

The goal of automated cross reference generation is to identify paragraphs that discuss meaningful terms in detail, then to link outlying instances of those terms to the detailed paragraphs. The technique is based on a simple heuristic: if multiple instances of a meaningful word are clustered within a paragraph, then the subject of that paragraph is semantically close to the term itself. SmarText assumes that a word is meaningful if it is listed in the index. The algorithm is summarized below:

- Determine which index words have instances that occur in tightly packed clusters within the text. These become the cross reference terms.
- For each cross reference term, create a link from each solitary instance of the term to the first instance of that word occurring in a cluster of term instances.
- If there are multiple clusters of instances, create a link from the first word instance in a cluster to the first instances in the next cluster.
- Repeat the third step until the last cluster is linked to the first.

The SmarText builder can control the number of cross reference links generated. The algorithm used to determine if index terms are clustered is proprietary.

Sometimes SmarText makes poor choices for cross references. This would happen, for example, if the word *teaspoon* or its abbreviation *tsp.* appeared in the index of an on-line cookbook. *Teaspoon* would probably become an internal cross reference because the word occurs several times in close proximity in the ingredients list of many recipes. However, *teaspoon* would be a poor choice as a cross reference link because it is rarely the subject of a paragraph.

Most index words do not get cross referenced. However, cross reference links can be generated automatically for any index word. The Auto Link dialogue box, shown in Figure 10.8, allows the builder to delete all cross reference links for an index term or to force the generation of cross reference links for one or more index terms. Errors introduced by Auto Link function can be edited manually.

Automated Construction of Views

SmarText's text and outline windows define a view or logical organization of the document. SmarText infers one view based on the physical text files. In addition, SmarText document developers may define alternative logical views. The logical organization of a custom view is completely independent of the document's physical organization. In fact, the captions for alternative views need not exist in the original text at all.

There are three ways to construct an alternative view: manually, based on an existing view, and based on cross reference links.

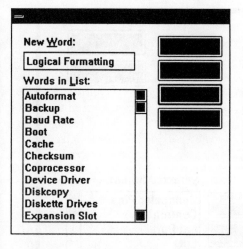

Figure 10.8   Creating and removing cross reference links.

Figure 10.9 shows a dialogue box for creating new views. To create a new view manually:

- Using the mouse or keyboard, select text within the text window corresponding to a chapter or section unit. The first line of selected text becomes the default chapter or section caption in the outline window.
- Edit the caption if necessary.
- Continue the first two steps and until all section captions and section text units are collected.
- Edit the order and hierarchical levels of captions in the outline window. Changing the order of these captions effectively changes the order of text within the text window.

A new view can be created from an existing view. In this case, the new view begins as an exact copy of an existing view. Outline captions in this copied view can be removed, reorganized, and edited by direct manipulation.

The third way to create an alternative view is to base it on one or more index words. In this case, SmarText locates text where selected index words are clustered, selects the text, and inserts them into the new view just as you would manually insert it. Figure 10.9 illustrates the creation of a view called *All About Printers* based on a list of selected index words: connector pins, Centronics, LPT port, and so on. SmarText locates all paragraphs that contain multiple instances of these index words and appends them together into the text window. SmarText then creates an outline whose captions are the first line from each paragraph (usually these are poor captions, but easy for builders to change).

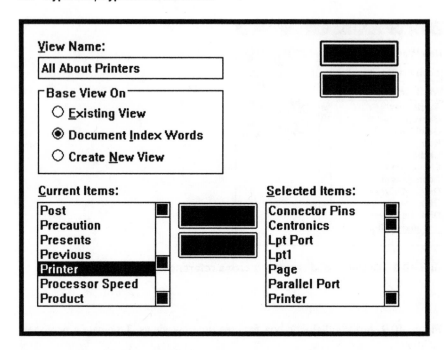

Figure 10.9   Creating a view based on existing views and keywords.

Support for Document Revision

The time and effort required for revising documents is a significant part of documentation life cycle costs. The cost of using outdated documentation can be devastating. On-line documents must preserve link information during revisions or else document revision becomes even more time consuming.

Preserving links during text revisions is easy if link commands are embedded in the text itself. However, SmarText stores link information (in the form of physical pointers) apart from the source text files. If a source file is edited, then the pointers become meaningless. To avoid losing links, SmarText gives the builder an option to save additional (text string) data that will be used solely for reconstructing existing links. Even so, links may be lost if there is significant cutting and pasting of text.

SGML and the Future of Text-to-Hypertext Conversion

The increasing acceptance and availability of the *Standard Generalized Markup Language* (SGML) as a standard for page markup will have the single greatest influence on the automated conversion of text into hypertext [Bryan, 1988]. SGML is an international standard for document representation. Its scope is publishing in the broadest sense—from hardcopy documents to multi-media database publishing. SGML is being drafted [ISO 8879] by the International Organization for Standardization [Goldfarb, 1986].

SGML simplifies the conversion of text into hypertext because the descriptive tags embedded in SGML files will aid in the conversion process.

The ASCII character set is currently the most common data type shared by word processors, electronic spreadsheets, and database programs. SGML encodes many of the structural relationships in data that are lost importing or exporting ASCII data. Someday, users will export data from a spreadsheet to an SGML format then import that SGML data into a desktop publishing (DTP) system. Conversion filters exist that do this now, but without a common data exchange standard, many more filters need to be written in order to handle all data formats.

SGML is a meta-language. It does not define a specific markup language but an abstract syntax for defining such a language. This frees it from dependency on character sets, national language biases, computer systems and devices. Since SGML is intended to be an unambiguous, formal specification, it can be manipulated by computer programs as well as humans. SGML is largely a declarative (descriptive) language, though it does provide for procedural (processing) commands.

SGML will blur the differences between corporate managers of publication and information systems. This is because documents defined using SGML will exist in paper and electronic forms (see Figures 10.10 a and b).

Example of Automated Link Generation

Note: The following example illustrates how links in a large SmarText hypertext application are created automatically independent of built-in conversion tools. This is important because conversion utilities built into products like SmarText cannot automate the conversion of all possible text formats. The example application described below is both useful and practical.

Special interest conferences or forums are valuable services provided by on-line database services such as BIX or Compuserve. Electronic forums enable users of a particular product to seek help from others and to share ideas, complaints, data, and utilities. Forums are a valuable source of information to the company whose product is the focus of the forum. Forums provide that company with information that aids marketing, product development, product support, and engineering.

How can information downloaded from a forum be distributed throughout a large organization efficiently and cost effectively? Downloaded data is usually poorly organized, has a very short useful lifetime, and may amount to several

⟨NEWSLETTER⟩
⟨TITLE⟩

The Form/Content Split ⟨/TITLE⟩

⟨SUBTITLE⟩

**Created to Illustrate the Power of the Separation
and the Joy of Not Having to Look at Every Page on the Screen** ⟨/SUBTITLE⟩

⟨HEADLINE⟩

Let Writers Write and Designers Design ⟨/HEADLINE⟩

⟨SUBHEAD⟩ **Productivity Comes from Focus** ⟨/SUBHEAD⟩

⟨P⟩ Traditional wordprocessing is a well-defined and well-understood component of the office environment. Succeeding generations of software have expanded the scope of wordprocessing but have not changed its basic role: to give people the tools they need to capture ideas, to manipulate words, and then to print out pages with a minimum of surprises. ⟨/P⟩

⟨P⟩ Sophisticated publishing software has added immense power and flexibility to the process by providing intermediate stages which allow for the detailed design and formatting of pages or entire documents. ⟨/P⟩

⟨P⟩ The first publishing software took for granted that the input to the publishing process would come from traditional wordprocessors. ⟨E1⟩ *even though wordprocessing software was never designed to meet the specific needs of publishing* ⟨/E1⟩. ⟨/P⟩

⟨P⟩ ⟨SQAE⟩ changes all that, by recognizing the special requirements and capabilities of the publishing process and also the huge potential of the powerful new storage media now becoming available. ⟨/P⟩

⟨SUBHEAD⟩ **One Format for Creation, Another for Production** ⟨/SUBHEAD⟩

⟨P⟩ Building on the excitement and market education associated with desktop publishing, ⟨SQAE⟩ recognizes that some publishing jobs require user control over the design of each page – and that currently available software offers terrific capability in this area – but that others need sophisticated, high-end ⟨E1⟩ *production* ⟨/E1⟩ publishing, the realm in which the user is responsible only for the content of documents and the system takes care of the formatting. ⟨/P⟩

⟨P⟩ ⟨SQAE⟩ is built on the principle that a user can be most productive by taking advantage of the ⟨E1⟩ *structure* ⟨/E1⟩ that every document has. That structure allows one: ⟨/P⟩

⟨LIST⟩
⟨LISTITEM⟩
⟨LISTITEM⟩ to compose an outline of a document as the first step in the creative process; ⟨/LISTITEM⟩
⟨LISTITEM⟩ to fill out the document through the outline, or in any order, and use structural tools to manipulate the document into final form; ⟨/LISTITEM⟩
⟨LISTITEM⟩ to produce documents that match the style or format of other documents; ⟨/LISTITEM⟩
⟨LISTITEM⟩ to create documents that contain the basic information that specialized personnel would need to design and then automatically format them; ⟨/LISTITEM⟩
⟨LISTITEM⟩ to store documents that can be stored, indexed and retrieved with complete flexibility. ⟨/LISTITEM⟩ ⟨/LIST⟩ ⟨/P⟩

⟨P⟩ A user creates a file using ⟨SQAE⟩'s traditional Macintosh tools. However, rather than choose typefaces and sizes, he or she marks the ⟨E1⟩ *parts* ⟨/E1⟩ of the letter, report, book, prospectus or newsletter: the ⟨E1⟩ *headings* ⟨/E1⟩, ⟨E1⟩ *subsections* ⟨/E1⟩, ⟨E1⟩ *tables* ⟨/E1⟩ and so on. The software takes care of turning those parts into appropriate graphic display, using to full advantage the Macintosh pointsizes, fonts and faces. The file stored on the disk, however, retains the structural information about the file, in a ⟨O⟩ tag ⟨/O⟩ format known as ⟨E1⟩ *Standard Generalized Markup Language* ⟨/E1⟩ (⟨SCP⟩ SGML ⟨/SCP⟩). ⟨/P⟩

⟨P⟩ That format, then, includes sufficient information to allow users to send text to a range of publishing software, chosen to meet the demands of a specific task; to transmit material between dissimilar computers; to produce a great variety of printed formats or databased information from one file. ⟨/P⟩

⟨P⟩ ⟨SQAE⟩ creates machine independent ⟨SCP⟩ ASCII ⟨/SCP⟩ text whose tags work in collaboration with our company's first product – ⟨SQPS⟩ – or with any other publishing or database software built on the principles established by ⟨SCP⟩ SGML ⟨/SCP⟩. ⟨/P⟩

⟨P⟩ This means that corporations, institutions and government departments can gently enforce official design guidelines – without their employees having to understand typesetting rules – and can ensure the consistency of information in databases shared among many sites and many computers. ⟨/P⟩

⟨SUBHEAD⟩ **Data, Graphs and Illustrations are Inserted Automatically** ⟨/SUBHEAD⟩

⟨FIGURE⟩ CHART_1 ⟨/FIGURE⟩

Figure 10.10a The SoftQuad Author/Editor, a Mac-based production publishing program, lets users define the parts of a document rather than the format of those parts. For example, he or she marks the headings, subsections, tables, etc., according to the SGML standard. This is a document with structure embedded... (Copyright 1991 SoftQuad, Inc.)

megabytes each month. A solution to this problem is to construct a hypertext document that can be browsed from a personal computer on a local area network or from a shared dedicated personal computer. (Note: One problem not addressed in

The Form/Content Split

Created to Illustrate the Power of the Separation and the Joy of Not Having to Look at Every Page on the Screen

Let Writers Write and Designers Design

Productivity Comes from Focus

Traditional wordprocessing is a well-defined and well-understood component of the office environment. Succeeding generations of software have expanded the scope of wordprocessing but have not changed its basic role: to give people the tools they need to capture ideas, to manipulate words, and then to print out pages with a minimum of surprises.

Sophisticated publishing software has added immense power and flexibility to the process by providing intermediate stages which allow for the detailed design and formatting of pages or entire documents.

The first publishing software took for granted that the publishing process would come from traditional wordprocessors, *even though wordprocessing software was never designed to meet the specific needs of publishing.*

SoftQuad Author/Editor changes all that, by recognizing the special requirements and capabilities of the publishing process and also the huge potential of the powerful new storage media now becoming available.

One Format for Creation, Another for Production

Building on the excitement and market education associated with desktop publishing, SoftQuad Author/Editor recognizes that some publishing jobs require user control over the design of each page – and that currently available software offers terrific capability in this area – but that others need sophisticated, high-end *production* publishing, the realm in which the user is responsible only for the content of documents and the system takes care of the formatting.

SoftQuad Author/Editor is built on the principle that a user can be most productive by taking advantage of the *structure* that every document has. That structure allows one:
- to compose an outline of a document as the first step in the creative process;
- to fill out the document through the outline, or in any order, and use structural tools to manipulate the document into final form;
- to produce documents that match the style or format of other documents;
- to create documents that contain the basic information that specialized personnel would need to design and then automatically format them;
- to create documents that can be stored, indexed and retrieved with complete flexibility.

A user creates a file using SoftQuad Author/Editor's traditional Macintosh tools. However, rather than choose typefaces and sizes, he or she marks the *parts* of the letter, report, book, prospectus or newsletter: the *headings, subsections, tables* and so on. The software takes care of turning those parts into appropriate graphic display, using to full advantage the Macintosh pointsizes, fonts and faces. The file stored on the disk, however, retains the structural information about the file, in a 'tag' format known as Standard Generalized Markup Language (SGML).

That format, then, includes sufficient information to allow users to send text to a range of publishing software, chosen to meet the demands of a specific task; to transmit material between dissimilar computers; to produce a great variety of printed formats or databased information from one file.

SoftQuad Author/Editor creates machine independent ASCII text whose tags work in collaboration with our company's first product – SoftQuad Publishing Software – or with any other publishing or database software built on the principles established by SGML.

This means that corporations, institutions and government departments can gently enforce official design guidelines – without their employees having to understand typesetting rules – and can ensure the consistency of information in databases shared among many sizes and many computers.

Data, Graphs and Illustrations may be Inserted Automatically

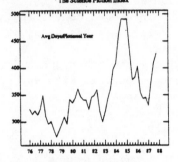

The Science Fiction Index

Warehouses Good for Storage, Experts Say

Warehouses are an effective way of storing goods, and should remain so for the foreseeable future, concluded the Man and His Goods conference as it wound up its eight day meeting in Toronto yesterday.

The 500-member conference also re-stated its conviction that ships are an effective way of moving goods after they have been stored in warehouses.

The two resolutions reflect concern on the part of the conference organizer, the Canadian Objects Association, that "fundamentals" such as storage and shipping capacity not be abused.

"We deplore certain trends we see," Tonder W. Truck, director of policy for the COA, told a final plenary session of the conference at the very large and ugly Toronto Convention Centre. "If ships had been meant to be used as restaurants, or if warehouses had been intended for use as shopping malls and dance theatres, they would have been restaurants, shopping malls and dance theatres, and not ships and warehouses."

This special edition of *The Form/Content Split*
has been published to celebrate the connection
between SoftQuad Publishing Software and SoftQuad Author/Editor.
This page was created by a writer with no concern for the format
and was 'poured' into the design previously created for it.

Figure 10.10b   ...Here is what the document looks like when SoftQuad prints it out. (Copyright 1991 SoftQuad, Inc.)

this example is the potential for violating the on-line database company's copyright.)

Let's look first at the raw text data down loaded from an imaginary on-line service. The following messages are characteristic of messages downloaded from a user's forum devoted to an imaginary hypertext product called HyperHype:

```
. . . . . . . .
#: 6861 S99/HyperHype
06-Jun-90 18:40:30
Sb: video drivers
Fm: Jim Fripp 12345,6789
To: all
the video driver for the ACME video board is now available
for HyperHype from their bbs.
415-968-1234
download is approx. 20 minutes at 2400.
jim
#: 6862 S99/HyperHype
06-Jun-90 18:44:26
Sb: Help needed converting graphics files
Fm: Kelly Wallabee 98765,43
To: All
How come the one graphic format that HyperHype supports
isn't compatible with any other known format? Doesn't that
seem strange to anyone? Is there an HHP to TIFF converter
out there?
* Kelly
There is 1 Reply.
#: 7205 S99/HyperHype
07-Jun-90 09:51:41
Sb: #6862-HHP to TIFF conversion utility
Fm: Rex Ponderosa 34567,8901
To: Kelly Wallabee 98765,43
The HyperHype folks will sell you a PIC-HHP graphics
conversion utility for $995. If your graphics are in any
other format, then you'll need another graphic conversion
utility to get it into PIC format first.
Good luck.
* Rex
. . . . . . . . .
```

It is unreasonable to expect anyone to scroll through several megabytes of data like this. Browsing a table of contents is a more reasonable way to scan a large amount of text. Unfortunately, SmarText (version 1.0) cannot recognize the subject of each message even though it seems this would be a simple task. A message's subject follows the *Sb:* identifier. We can write a program that recognizes the subject of each message and constructs a SmarText table of contents (outline) automatically.

Figure 10.11 illustrates the 4-step process to create a table of contents for a document named HypeHype. In the first step, SmarText analyzes the source text

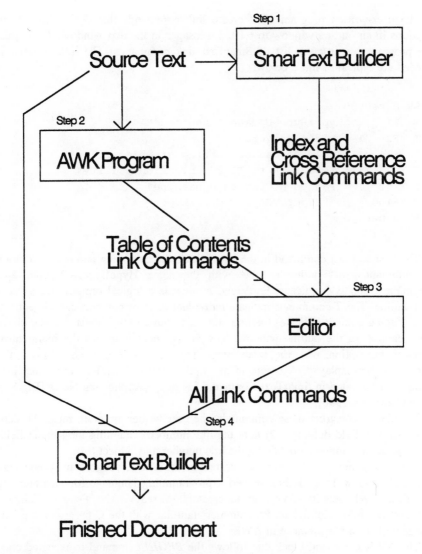

Figure 10.11   Creating a Table of Contents with SmarText.

file and constructs an ASCII file of commands that define index and cross reference links. This file is called a shadow file (hypehype.shw). In the second step, commands that define outline links are created using a custom user-written program. This user-written program generates outline link commands that are then inserted into the shadow file using a common ASCII editor (step three). Finally, when SmarText opens a document, it detects that the shadow file has been modified (outline links were inserted) and recompiles its pointer database. The result is a fast, custom-built hyperdocument.

The user-written program must create link commands that define links from captions in an outline window to related messages in the text window. To do this, the program constructs a list of SmarText link commands. The link commands needed are typical of those below:

```
BV HypeHype
T -F1   /1 "  HyperHype Update Announced "
T -F26  /1 "  video drivers"
T -F36  /1 "  Help needed converting graphics files"
T -F78  /1 "  #6862-HHP to TIFF conversion utility"
T -F90  /1 "  PageDown Crashes HyperHype"
T -F106 /1 "  #Super VGA for HyperHype"
EV HypeHype
```

The first and last command in the list indicate the beginning and end of a block of commands that define a view with the name HypeHype—BV indicates BeginView and EV indicates EndView. A view is a logical organization of text and outline. The *T* commands indicate individual table of contents caption entries. The *-Fnnn* argument indicates the line number to jump to whenever the user clicks on a caption in the outline window. The */n* argument indicates the hierarchical level of the caption, where *n* is an integer from 1 to 9. The quoted string is the caption to be displayed. A complete description of the SmarText command language can be found in SmarText Command Language Application Notes [Big Science Company, 1990].

In order to construct these commands, the user-written program must: 1) identify a subject field delimiter, 2) note the line number containing the subject field, 3) construct a command containing the line number and subject text.

Our link generation program is written in the AWK programming language [Aho, et al., 1988]. AWK is a powerful programming language for manipulating text data. AWK gets its name from its creators: Alfred V. Aho, Peter J. Weinberger, and Brian W. Kernighan. Programmers familiar with the C programming language will see a resemblance in AWK.

The AWK command block that follows the *BEGIN* command is executed once before AWK processes the input file. (Likewise, an AWK command block that follows the END command is executed once after AWK processes the input file.) All other AWK statements are applied to each line of the input file and have the form:

```
matchExpression {statement}
```

If *matchExpression* evaluates to a non-zero value, then the *statement* is executed. The AWK program is shown below:

```
BEGIN {print "BV SUBJECT";}              # Print BeginView command
$1 == "Sb:"                              # For each line in the
text file,                                   if 1st field
matches "Sb:"
  { $1 = "";                             # then delete first field
  printf ("T -F%d /1 \"%s\"\n", NR-2, $0); # & print out command
  }
END {print "EV SUBJECT";}                # Print EndView command
```

In addition to the BEGIN and END statements, two AWK commands are executed in the example above. The second one, the *printf* command, does all the work. NR is an AWK internal variable that indicates the number of records (lines) read thus far. That value is decremented by 2 so that the line number will reference the beginning of the message. The symbol $0 is another AWK global variable containing the entire text record (line). Since the first field ($1) was set to a null string, $0 contains all text following the first field. The # symbol, like the // symbol in C++, indicates that the rest of that line is a comment.

This simple program can be enhanced in several ways. Alternative views can be constructed based on the date the message was posted, the message originator or the intended receiver of a message. Instead of creating a hypertext table of contents, one could write a program to insert internal cross reference links that would link common messages or threads.

Most SmarText builders will never need to write their own programs to automate the conversion of text into hypertext. However, in specialized applications where custom linking is necessary, SmarText provides access to its internal commands by text manipulation programs. The AWK programming language was used in this example but any macro or programming language supporting string manipulation could have been used. ICON is one such alternative list and string handling language.

Many word processors like Samna's Ami Professional and Microsoft's Word for Windows also include powerful embedded macro languages.

Summary

Some computer scientists claim that the automatic conversion of linear text into hypertext is an unattainable goal. They may be correct. The conversion of text into hypertext may never become *automatic* but this chapter has shown several practical ways that it can be *automated*.

What technologies are most useful for converting text into hypertext?

What hypertext tools are best? Any answer to those questions will have a very short lifespan. The hypertext conversion technology, driven by commercial interests and enabling technologies, is changing very quickly. The best ideas are yet to come.

About the Author

Thomas C. Rearick

Thomas C. Rearick is President of Big Science Company, developers of the SmarText Construction Set being marketed by Lotus Development's Word Processing Division. Mr. Rearick has lectured on hypertext throughout the United States and Europe.

Before founding Big Science Company, Mr. Rearick was a Senior Scientist at the Advanced Research Organization of Lockheed Aeronautical Systems Company in Marietta, Georgia. He holds engineering degrees from Duke University and Syracuse University. He is a member of the Association for Computing Machinery, the Institute of Electrical and Electronics Engineers, and the American Association of Artificial Intelligence.

Tom Rearick and his wife Jean live in an Atlanta suburb. They both enjoy caving, rock climbing, canoeing, and backpacking. They have a son, Charlie.

Mr. Rearick may be contacted at Big Science Company, 5600 Glenridge Dr., Suite 255, Atlanta, GA 30342.

References

Aho, A.A., Kernighan, B.W., and Weinberger, P.J. (1988). *The AWK Programming Language*, Addison-Wesley, Reading, MA.

Big Science Company, (1990). SmarText Command Language Application Notes, Release 1.0, Atlanta, GA.

Bryan, M. (1988). *SGML: An Author's Guide to the Standard Generalized Markup Language*, Addison-Wesley, Reading, MA.

Conklin, J. (1978). "Hypertext: An Introduction and Survey," *Computer,* Sept., 1978, 17–41.

Foltz, P.W. (1990). "Using Latent Semantic Indexing for Information Filtering", *Conf. on Office Information Systems,* Cambridge, MA, 150-157.

Furnas, G.W., Landauer, T.K., Gomez, L.M., Dumais, S.T. (1983). "Statistical Semantics: Analysis of the Potential Performance of Keyword Information Systems," *Bell System Technical Journal, 62(6),* 1753-1806.

Goldfarb, C. F. (Ed.), (1986). "Information Processing—Text and Office Systems—Standard Generalized Markup Language (SGML)," *Int'l Standard ISO 8879,* Int'l Organization for Standardization, Geneva.

Salton, G. (1989a). *Automatic Text Processing: The Transformation, Analysis, and Retrieval of Information by Computer,* Addison-Wesley, Reading, MA.

Salton, G. (1989b). "On the Application of Syntactic Methodologies in Automatic Text Analysis", *Proceedings of 12th Int'l. ACMSIGIR Conf. on Resear. and Devel. in Info. Retrieval,* Cambridge, MA, June, 1989, 137-150.

Shneiderman, B. (1983). "Direct Manipulation: A Step Beyond Programming Languages," *Computer,* August 1983, 57-69.

Shneiderman, B., Kreitzberg, C., Berk, E. (1991). "Editing to Structure a Reader's Experience," *Hypertext / Hypermedia Handbook,* Emily Berk and Joseph Devlin (Ed.s), McGraw-Hill, New York, NY.

Designing Hypertexts

Hypertext is a new technology; hypertext designers and authors have much to learn and few tools to help them.

In the first chapter in this section, Ben Shneiderman and Charles Kreitzberg, noted researchers in the area of user-appropriate interfaces, discuss some of the techniques authors can use to make their hypertexts easier for readers to use.

Then, Geri Gay, who has been experimenting with the use of hypermedia to teach students at Cornell University, discusses some of her findings about the design of educational interactive fiction.

In the third chapter in this section, our distinguished contributors from abroad, Franca Garzotto, Paolo Paolini and Daniel Schwabe, and Mark Bernstein from Eastgate Systems, give an overview of the state of methodologies for defining the structure of a hypertext (which they call "Authoring in the Large"), and a detailed description of their Hypermedia Design Model.

Finally, Ernest Perez provides some insights on designing and building the nodes and links of a hypertext (what our Italian friends would call "Authoring in the Small"), and a shopping list of utilities hypertext authors should not be without.

11

Editing to Structure a Reader's Experience

By Ben Shneiderman
University of Maryland

Charles Kreitzberg
Cognetics Corp.

and Emily Berk
Armadillo Associates, Inc.

Introduction

"A thing is unified and clear and simple because it is designed that way, or it is not unified and clear and simple. Making things clear and simple is hard." [Ted Nelson, 1987]

"It is easy to think that, because learners can move through a body of knowledge in new ways, we know where they are going." [Michael Joyce, 1988]

Since the invention of writing, authors have explored ways to structure knowledge so their readers could extract it from linear print media. Authors have even explored strategies that enable readers to link related fragments of printed text and graphics despite their linear format.

"There are basically two difficulties in writing sequential text: deciding on sequence... and deciding what's in and what's out. (Hypertext authors) no longer have to decide what's in and what's out, but simply where to put things in the searchable maze." [Nelson, 1987]

The real-life process of creating hypertexts, however, is not that simple. The ease with which readers use and comprehend hypertext and even their ability to locate information, depend upon the structure of the hypertext network—Nelson's searchable maze. Thus, there is a great need to study how knowledge must be organized so that readers can take advantage of hypertext environments [Yankelovich, Meyrowitz and Van Dam, 1985; Conklin, 1987; Marchionini and Shneiderman, 1988].

While some hypertext/hypermedia proponents advocate total browsing freedom, experience has convinced others that too much of a good thing can be a problem. Based on experience with increasingly ambitious projects, researchers and designers are moving ahead rapidly in developing appropriate guidelines for structuring hypertexts. This chapter reports on the authors' experiences and offers specific guidance.

Our starting point in designing hypertext is to ask the question "is this knowledge base suitable for hypertext implementation or is it better implemented using conventional printed papertext?" Papertext can have several advantages over current implementations of computer-based hypertext. For example, the printed page is an excellent high-resolution display, capable of presenting large quantities of text with color graphics. It is easy to access, convenient to annotate and usually (but not always) portable. Hypertext, on the other hand, offers rapid dissemination, potentially lowered production costs, protection against information overload, possible lower cost, and true multimedia (including animation, speech, audio and full-motion video). Central to hyertext, however, is the notion that the knowledge base is organized into a network of related elements. This central idea, leads us to test each knowledge base against the "Golden Rules of Hypertext." In our experience, knowledge bases which match the Golden Rules, are most appropriate for hypertext implementation. The rules state that:

• There is a large body of information organized into numerous fragments
• The fragments relate to each other
• The reader needs only a small fraction at any time

With these as our guiding principles, we are now ready to consider structuring techniques for hypertexts.

Author's Goals In Structuring a Hypertext

Authors of hypertexts should keep the following goals in mind:

• To improve information accessibility
• To enhance usability
• To increase reader satisfaction [Glushko, 1989]

"There are tricky problems here. One of the greatest is how to make the reader feel comfortable and oriented," warned Ted Nelson [Nelson, 1987]. The author's challenge is to structure the hypertext so that it corresponds to the ways that readers might think about the topics and to help readers create appropriate mental models of the knowledge base. To do this successfully requires an understanding of the many ways in which concepts may be tackled by readers. Such understanding is more likely to come to an author who has prior experience explaining the subject matter to engaged students.

Conflict between Physical and Logical Structure

A hypertext really has two sets of structures:

* The logical structure of a hypertext is imposed by the author. This includes the relationship between links in the database (tree, network, graph), the relationship of links to nodes and the content and design of individual nodes and networks of nodes.
* Authors usually have much less freedom when it comes time to define the physical structure of a hypertext. Layout, typography, user input device, and other aesthetic concerns are always heavily influenced by the hypertext delivery platform and development system.

In most cases, the author can rework the logical structure of the hypertext but he or she can't ignore the size and resolution of the screen onto which that logical structure will be mapped. For example, if the hypertext will be displayed on a black and white, 80 column by 25 row monitor, and the author has decided that the logical structure of the hypertext will allow 100-line long nodes, readers will have to navigate between 4 different screens within the same node. Thus, the author of a hypertext must design the logical structure keeping possible physical configurations of both the development and delivery systems in mind [Glushko, 1989].

Description of Hyperties

Much of the work described in this chapter has revolved around a hypertext system called Hyperties®,[1] an acronym for *Hyper*text *I*nteractive *E*ncyclopedia *S*ystem. Hyperties was originally a research project at the University of Maryland's Human Computer Interaction Laboratory. Cognetics Corporation (Princeton Junction, New Jersey) now distributes it commercially and has continued its development while the University of Maryland has focused its research on advanced versions.

As might be guessed from its name, Hyperties is built around the metaphor of an electronic book. This contrasts with the "stack" metaphor used by some other systems such as Hypercard. The nodes in Hyperties are called *articles*; they may consist of many pages. Articles may include text, graphics, audio and video. Hyperties facilitates the construction of such book-like structures as a cover, table of contents, index, footnotes, running heads and preface. The look and feel of the

---

1 Hyperties is a registered trademark of the Cognetics Corporation.

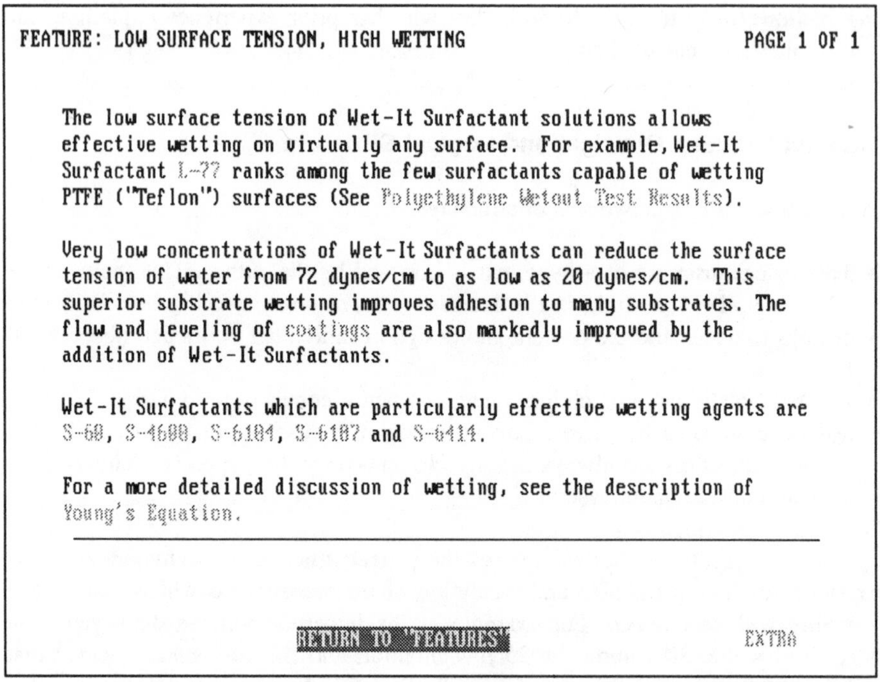

FEATURE: LOW SURFACE TENSION, HIGH WETTING   PAGE 1 OF 1

The low surface tension of Wet-It Surfactant solutions allows
effective wetting on virtually any surface. For example, Wet-It
Surfactant L-?? ranks among the few surfactants capable of wetting
PTFE ("Teflon") surfaces (See Polyethylene Wetout Test Results).

Very low concentrations of Wet-It Surfactants can reduce the surface
tension of water from 72 dynes/cm to as low as 20 dynes/cm. This
superior substrate wetting improves adhesion to many substrates. The
flow and leveling of coatings are also markedly improved by the
addition of Wet-It Surfactants.

Wet-It Surfactants which are particularly effective wetting agents are
S-60, S-4600, S-6104, S-6107 and S-6414.

For a more detailed discussion of wetting, see the description of
Young's Equation.

RETURN TO 'FEATURES'   EXTRA

Figure 11.1   A sample Hyperties screen. Source: Cognetics Corp.

electronic book can be controlled by *stylesheets* which specify screen layout, typefaces and "buttons." All of these elements are optional, allowing considerable flexibility in authoring hypertext. (See Figure 11.1.)

Hyperties is being used in a number of corporate settings and, at HCIL, in
regular experimental studies to test design alternatives and observe user behavior.
In addition, we have modified Hyperties over the years to provide the functionality
and user interface features our experience has shown necessary.

This chapter outlines some of the authoring techniques we have found most
effective in designing the logical structure of a hypertext database so that readers
feel "comfortable and oriented."

Size and Configuration of Nodes

The Article is the Basic Node in Hyperties

The basic unit of information in Hyperties is the *article*. An article consists of a
title, an optional brief description, an optional script, and content. Graphics may
be interspersed with text in an article. Highlighted terms (references) in the body
of an article serve as links; they tell readers that more information on a topic is
available. Links may also be defined as "hot" areas in graphics.

Size of Nodes

The size of articles (*nodes*) is an important design consideration. Our research has shown that it best to keep articles short; we suggest that each node be a few screens long, and probably no longer than one hundred lines.

Details on Demand

We recommend that hypertext authors use the following techniques to chunk articles into small pieces:

- Instead of discussing a subsidiary topic which is not the main subject of an article, you can just allude to it and designate a phrase that refers to it as a link. You can make that topic the subject of its own article, or at least give the topic a description which can be called up by readers. If readers are interested in more information about this peripheral topic, they can follow its link.
- The same technique can be applied to details. Rather than including detailed information in an article, you can simply reference it and create separate articles for it. This shields readers from unnecessary details, but provides a path readers can follow when it seems relevant. This technique is especially useful when the source material contains case studies, experiments or lots of examples.

Information Overload—Details on Demand

Another important factor in structuring readers' experiences in a hypertext is the author's ability to regulate the rate of information flow. "If Orwell were writing *1984* now, he would not say, 'Destroy the information.' He would say, 'Inundate people with information, they'll think they're free. Don't deny them. Give them more. Undigested information is no information at all, but it creates the fiction that you have accessed it, even though you didn't benefit from it' " [Wurman, 1989].

Information overload occurs when a reader receives too much data to process meaningfully. Normally when information is presented, the recipient evaluates the incoming stream, selecting and retaining some elements and discarding others. The reader's selective attention provides appropriate filters to separate relevant from irrelevant and protects readers from sensory chaos. The apparent paradox is that readers must understand the information before they can determine whether it is worth paying attention to.

If the information load becomes too great, the filtering process breaks down and readers pay attention to the wrong data while important information may be ignored. Hypertext, which is designed to deliver information to readers rapidly, makes it easy for readers to drown in information; at every click of the mouse or keyboard, the reader can access more.

Information overload is not merely a problem of volume. Properly prepared, people are capable of dealing with an enormous amount of information and can perform great feats of selective attention. This is demonstrated by the well-studied "cocktail party phenomenon" in which people effortlessly tune out a number of simultaneous conversations to focus on one. If, however, an individual's name is mentioned across the room, the person named hears it immediately [Cherry, 1953].

"You can mass-produce raw data and incredible quantities of facts and figures. You cannot mass-produce knowledge, which is created by individual minds, drawing on individual experience, separating the significant from the irrelevant, making value judgments." [Theodore Roszak, author of *The Cult of Information*, quoted in *This World*, (5/24/87) from Wurman, 1989] Information overload is really a problem of understanding. When meaningfulness is lost, information becomes noise and people filter it out. When information is meaningful, readers accept it and organize it for later use.

Once, working with a chemical safety manual, it quickly became apparent to us that information overload was a major problem for the employees. The manual contained a vast amount of information. Some of this information was of interest to all readers (for example, how to respond in an emergency situation), some was germane to specific groups of readers (for example, supervisors' responsibilities) and some was relevant only to the group responsible for writing and maintaining safety procedures (for example, audit and review requirements). (See Figures 11.2a and 11.2b.)

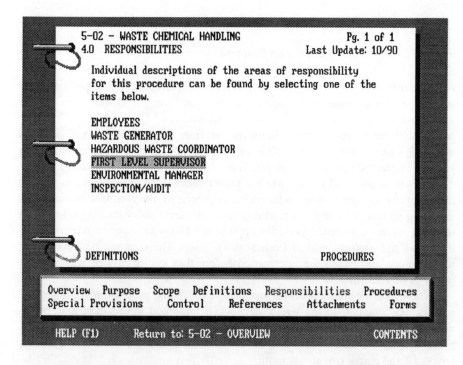

Figure 11.2a   When different information is of interest to different readers, ...
Source: Cognetics Corp.

The requirement for formal audits of the manual had led the writers of the (hard copy) manual to organize the information by procedure. Every piece of information, trivial or weighty, relating to a specific procedure was contained in the body of text describing that procedure. This technique simplified maintenance of the printed manual but created difficulties for readers who often were forced to read though many procedures to glean small amounts of information that they found pertinent. In one case, an employee looking for reporting requirements for which she was responsible had to consult all 80 procedures, extract the relevant requirements, and consolidate them into a single list.

Management suspected that employees were so overwhelmed by the volume of information that they did not dare to try to extract it. This state of affairs was unacceptable because it compromised the safety of the employees and their co-workers.

To solve this problem, we developed a paradigm we call "details on demand" [Kreitzberg, 1991]. This paradigm suggests that information overload can be minimized if hypertext authors:

- Provide *just enough* information initially to ensure comprehension. We assume that information overload results from cognitive disorganization and can be reduced by increasing the meaningfulness of the presentation. When information is meaningful, there is a natural cognitive organizing process which occurs. It is as if the new information fits existing templates in the receiving individual's

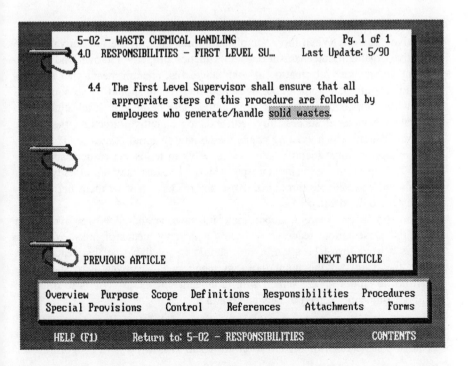

Figure 11.2b ... provide "just enough up-front, details on demand." Source: Cognetics Corp.

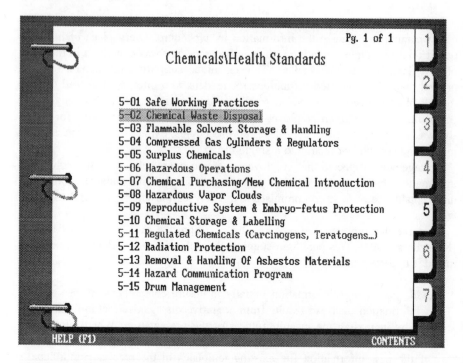

Figure 11.3a Just enough up-front, ... Source: Cognetics Corp.

cognitive structure. When these templates do not exist, or are not activated, the cognitive organizing mechanism does not function properly and overload results.

- Present *just enough* information at each stage. Just enough means that the presentation should be complete, but not elaborated. There should be no conceptual gaps which impair understanding nor should there be details which clutter. To integrate the material successfully with existing cognitive structure, the reader must understand which existing concepts the new material relates to. Therefore, the presentation must identify relevant concepts in terms the reader can understand. If there are prerequisite concepts which the reader may not already know, they should be available through links so the reader can view them before proceeding on to the details.

- Provide *details on demand*. Subordinate information should be removed from the initial presentation; readers can access it later by means of links. Wherever there is a need for elaboration, a link should be available so that readers can obtain the details at the point they are mentioned. However, care should be taken not to clutter up the screen with redundant links. Our style is to limit the number of links per screen to between 6 and 8.

The just enough organizing principle is applied recursively so that at every level of detail the same rules of organization are used. Following is our algorithm for

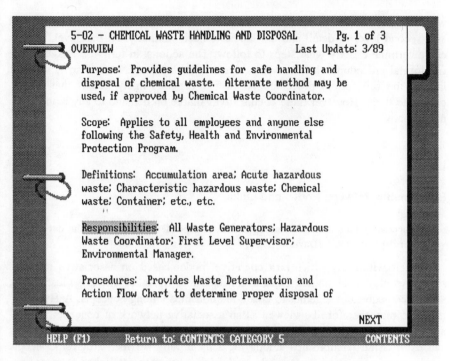

Figure 11.3b ... details on demand. Source: Cognetics Corp.

applying the just enough rules listed above to the design of a hypertext (See Figures 11.3a and 11.3b):

- Identify the domain of discourse so that a context is established. Meaningfulness is highly dependent upon context [Bransford and Johnson, 1972]. For example, the phrase "I want you to press a suit" has a very different meaning depending upon whether you are talking to a lawyer or a tailor.
- Identify pre-existing knowledge which the individual needs for complete understanding. Make such knowledge available through links so that the reader can access it and process the remainder of the information meaningfully.
- Present the information in logical sequence so that the information that comes first provides context for the information that follows.
- Identify details that the individual can obtain to elaborate the information in the initial presentation. When constructing a detail level, apply these same rules to it.

In terms of the safety manual, these rules led us to construct a brief summary of each relevant procedure. This summary provides links to relevant prerequisite knowledge (for example, definitions used in a safety procedure) and links to more detailed explanations of the actions required. The summary provides the reader with a context for the full set of actions to be followed. These actions are treated as a second level of detail and are linked to each summary. At this level, readers can determine exactly what steps to follow. The actions, in turn, are linked to the full formal procedure which serves as a reference document. Most readers will not link to the full formal procedure because it contains many details that do not pertain to them. However these details are available on demand to any reader who needs them.

Links

Relationship Between Nodes and Links

"Success or failure of a hypertext product is dependent on how well the developer deploys links." [Davison, 1989]

Implicit within Hyperties is a cognitive model based on associative relationships. Articles in Hyperties explain concepts and tie other articles, illustrations, and video sequences together to create relationships among concepts. A Hyperties database may therefore be viewed as an associative network of concepts and examples at various levels. There is great power in this simple structure—authors can express the relationships among ideas by linking between articles. Concepts can be explicated at multiple levels, with high-level concepts linked to more specific concepts and specific concepts linked to examples.

We strongly believe that the use of article titles as navigational landmarks can reduce the disorientation readers of a hypertext inevitably feel each time they traverse a link. Thus, most of the links a Hyperties reader selects look like the name of the destination node.

The destination of a Hyperties link is usually the beginning of an article. With certain misgivings, we are introducing located links that jump directly inside an article to a specified location. However, because we believe that this type of link demands additional reorientation efforts by readers, we urge hypertext authors to implement these located links sparingly. For example, you might want a bibliography article with an alphabetized list of references. However, a link to a specific reference might cause you to jump into page 5 of the 10-page long bibliography.

Links in Hyperties are unidirectional [see Chapter 20 by Parunak, in this book] because bidirectional links can be confusing. For example, when reading about the play *Les Miserables* you may want to read about France, but when reading the article on "France," you probably don't want to see all of the countless articles referring to it. In cases where authors of a database believe a two-way link is desirable, they can create paired unidirectional links.

We chose to implement Hyperties using embedded link markers in both text and graphics because empirical studies demonstrated that this method was extremely comprehensible to readers and authors, that distraction was reduced, and that screen layouts were less cluttered. Even so, visible links are a potential distraction

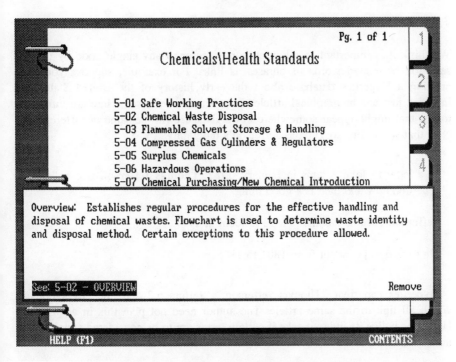

Figure 11.4   When a link is selected, Hyperties first displays the short description of the destination article (in this case the overview), before jumping a reader to a new article. Source: Cognetics Corp.

from the reading process and we have considered allowing readers to delay link display until they have completed reading an article.

The underlying structure of Hyperties article files reflects the fact that links are embedded in text, i.e., each link is stored in the node that serves as its source. To specify a reference within text, a Hyperties author simply marks the string that will serve as the entry point to the link. When an author specifies a reference, the authoring tool examines the list of entry names and synonyms to make the link.

When a link is selected, Hyperties first displays the short description of the destination article before jumping a reader to a new article. The reader can then decide whether to follow the link to the full article or not. The description provides a smoother transition between articles and limits the possibility of irrelevant jumps (see Figure 11.4). In some cases, an article consists only of a description. The author of a hyper-database can also decide to bypass the presentation of descriptions in a given database altogether. We have found that when Hyperties is used with touch screens in public access kiosks, it is best to jump directly to the target article.

Synonyms

We think it is important to allow authors to refer to any single node by using a selection of related words or phrases as links. For example, suppose you were creating a Hyperties database about the early history of the United States and included just one biographical article about Thomas Jefferson. Here are three sentences that might appear somewhere in the database (in the same or different articles) that would link to Thomas Jefferson's biography:

In a letter to John Adams in January, 1787, **Thomas Jefferson** wrote, "A little rebellion now and then is a good thing."

Jefferson became Adams' Vice President in 1797.

He served as president from 1801 to 1805.

Hyperties can treat "Thomas Jefferson," "Jefferson," and "he" as synonyms which all link to the same article. The author need not plan this in advance; as Hyperties builds its index it asks if certain terms are to be considered synonyms or not.

Limiting the Number of Links

Just because a particular word, phrase or graphic is linked to a particular node in one instance, it does not always have to be used as a link. A Hyperties author decides when readers will be able to link from a word or phrase by enclosing it in tildes. This keeps articles from becoming cluttered with highlighted terms. For example, say we were authoring a hyperdocument in which the following sentences appeared together in the same node:

Thomas Jefferson was already a revolutionary in 1774 when he wrote "A Summary View of the Rights of British America," in which he denied British authority over the colonies. In the Declaration of Independence, Thomas Jefferson eloquently summarized his conviction that the rights of individuals weigh heavily against the power that can be exercised by any government. However, because he was serving in a diplomatic role in France at the time, Thomas Jefferson had little impact on the framing of the Constitution of the United States.

When preparing this paragraph for use in a Hyperties hypertext, we would mark only the first mention of Thomas Jefferson. Readers using the browser would see only the first reference to Thomas Jefferson highlighted as a link.

Global Structures that Can Help Readers

Guided Tours

Linear papertexts provide a much better means for ensuring that readers see each important point in the order that makes most sense than do hyperdocuments. The editor of a hypertext Personal Computer Owners Manual, for example, cannot be sure that the person reading about turning the personal computer on has already been instructed to plug it in.

Many hypertext development systems provide authors with a way to define ordered paths through a database so readers are less likely to get lost, and, where necessary, are obliged to read certain nodes in a prescribed order.

For example, suppose a set of articles were organized into five key topic areas. Some of the articles build upon more general ones. What you want the reader to do is:

1. Read the introductory node in each topic area;
2. Then use the browser within each topic area to explore details.

An author using Hyperties can create these *Guided Tours* in at least two ways. The first way is to use the introductory article to refer to the five key topics, each of which is discussed in a separate node:

Article 1: Buying a Personal Computer
Article 2: Selecting Software
Article 3: Setting Up Your Hardware
Article 4: Installing and Running the Software
Article 5: Upgrading Your System

The reader can select each key article in turn. From each key article, the reader can browse to related articles of interest and, eventually, return to select the next key article listed in the introductory article.

The second technique is to link the end of each article to the next article which you want the reader to see. For example, the first article, "Buying a Personal Computer," might end as follows:

Congratulations! If you followed the instructions in this article, you now own the perfect microcomputer. But a personal computer without software is like a VCR without a video cassette. Next, read about **Selecting Software**.

This technique can be expanded to create a number of different paths through the material.

Metaphor

"In the beginning, the idea in terms of electronic presentation of data is to imitate existing data-presentation designs so that people won't become too confused. Reference books are among the easiest information sources to understand because people have been brought up with them for years, and they know how to use the data because they have been laboriously trained to do it in school.... The problem is that outside of school we don't have any particular training in how to access or utilize data." [From a conversation with Dick Brass, Wurman, 1989]

"A model is a representation of some knowledge." [Weyer, 1989]

Hypertext authors use metaphor in order to establish conventions readers can follow so they can ignore the interface they need to use to find information and just find the information.

Hyperties' Metaphoric Design.   There are several advantages that accrue from thinking and designing Hyperties databases as electronic books or hyperbooks. Chief among these is the fact that most everybody is familiar with the visual and navigational cues provided in a paper book. Adopting book-like conventions on-line insures that most people will be able to use a hypertext document with only a minimal amount of instruction.

Each Hyperties database consists of elements which are similar to those in a conventional printed book: a cover, a preface, a table of contents, articles, illustrations, an index.

Choosing the Metaphor.   While Hyperties is based on the encyclopedia and more generally the book metaphor, other possibilities exist. We chose the book metaphor because our focus was on reading paragraph- or page-length chunks of information and we chose to apply the term "article" to each chunk. This led us naturally to having a title for every article and then tables of contents and indices.

Other hypertext systems rely on the card and stack or filebox (e.g., NoteCards and HyperCard) metaphors. These metaphors are convenient, comprehensible and easily represented on the screen. Intermedia utilizes a web of files or documents and Guide deals with a database of documents with notes and buttons.

We felt that these metaphors limit authors to storing smaller amounts of information than we think necessary in each node. More computer-oriented metaphors such as screens collected into directories seem quite technical and might be unappealing to many users.

In our recent work on an ambitious *Interactive Encyclopedia of Jewish Heritage* that is being created by twelve historians for the Museum of Jewish Heritage, we have developed the City of Knowledge metaphor. There are four gates to the city, drawn as an ancient walled city, conveying the four access paths of data. Then there are key stopping places to visit and explore and various vistas where readers can get overviews. (See Figure 11.5.)

Pro and Con.   Metaphors are convenient because their familiarity facilitates learning and reduces anxiety. Metaphors based on existing objects such as books,

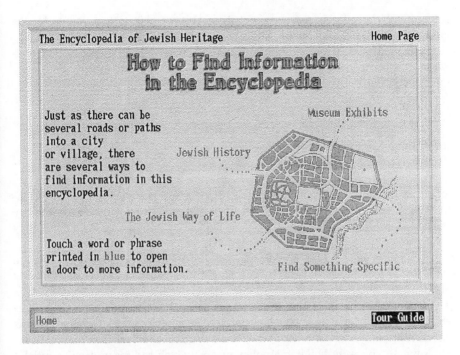

Figure 11.5   The City of Knowledge is the metaphor we chose for the *Interactive Encyclopedia of Jewish Heritage*. There are four gates to the city, drawn as an ancient walled city, conveying the four access paths of data. (Copyright 1991, Museum of Jewish Heritage; used with permission.)

desktops, typewriters and documents, are meant to make novice users feel comfortable. There are many inappropriate metaphors for hypertext that might be chosen by a misguided designer, such as a printing press, a Morse code telegraph, or a skywriting airplane. An inappropriate metaphor might make it harder for the user to acquire the necessary concepts. Of course, malicious metaphors would really turn readers off. Imagine how a hyperdocument would fare if it were represented as a sewer pipe spilling out information or as an exploding television.

Even well-chosen metaphors can be misleading. The book or encyclopedia metaphors only vaguely suggest the power that links can have (webs are a more effective metaphor to convey the power of hypertext). In particular, the book metaphor may mislead readers into believing that they can easily grasp the size or organization of the hyperdocument. [See Chapter 18 by Gay and Mazur, in this book.] This problem is compounded because ways of showing readers the size of hyperdocuments are only now beginning to appear.

While real-world metaphors can be misleading, they are usually effective. An alternative is to invent abstract objects (e.g., something fanciful such as an "electrodoc") and then try to explain its properties by showing features (e.g. "doctoc" for document table of contents and a "docdex" for a document index). Visual icons of arbitrary design can represent these abstract objects (e.g., circle for the electrodoc, square for the doctoc, and a triangle for the docdex).

Some readers may prefer the abstraction, but experience suggests that real-world metaphors, even if their properties are not entirely true-to-life, are usually more successful.

Book Metaphor Specific Structures

Introductory articles.   In each Hyperties electronic book, the author specifies one article as the lead or introductory article. Since many readers will browse the introductory article first, this article should be designed to refer to as many key articles as possible. There are several strategies for composing the introductory article.

One strategy is to fill the introductory article with many references, making it a summary of the entire database. By scanning it, the reader can select one of many places to begin browsing.

A second strategy is to confine the introductory article to only a few key references. Authors who choose this strategy aim to minimize the number of details which confront readers in order to start them down an appropriate path. For example, suppose you were building a policy manual which had many detailed articles about specific policies. Rather than referencing many policies in the introductory article, you could develop a more general approach such as the following:

This database contains policies relating to:

Permanent employees,
Temporary staff,
and **Consultants.**

In addition you will find policies which apply to all staff relating to

Security,
Non-disclosure,
and **Dealing with the press.**

A third strategy for the introductory article is to design it as a high level index. Here is an example:

Corporate Policies

Permanent Staff
   Hiring Permanent Staff
   Termination Procedures
   Benefits and Vacation Policies

Temporary Staff
   Approval Policy for Hiring Temps
   Approval Policy for Retaining Consultants

This technique of using the introductory article as an index can be extended to other articles. For example, Approval Policy for Hiring Temps could link to a new article that provided a detailed index to relevant policies, for example:

Approval Policies for Hiring Temps
   Hiring Short-term Temporaries from Agencies
   Establishing Qualifications of Temporary Staff
   Hiring Independent Contractors

This technique can yield an extensive network of indices. A particular article could appear in several indices, so readers can access it from many points. For example, an article on Vacation Policies for Permanent Staff could be highlighted under vacations, benefits, permanent staff, or any other relevant area.

Index. Sometimes readers looking for a specific article will not want to browse the database starting with the introductory article. Hyperties automatically creates an index which lists all the articles in the database. Readers may go to the index at any time and access any article in the database directly.

The Index command displays an alphabetical list of the articles in the database. (See Figure 11.6.)

Table of Contents. In Hyperties, there is only one type of article. However, certain articles, like the "Introduction" article, the "Index" article and the "Table of Contents" article have reserved titles. When a reader invokes the Table of Contents command, Hyperties displays the article the author has named "Table of Contents." Authors can use these named articles to store whatever information they deem fit. We recommend that authors store information in a form appropriate to each article's title. (See Figure 11.7.)

Chapter. We published our guidebook to hypertext, *Hypertext Hands-On!*, both as a conventional printed book and as an electronic book to enable readers to compare the two publications and evaluate the strengths and limitations of each. In the Hyperties electronic version, we organized access to the data in two ways:

- Hypertextual platforms which allow readers to springboard themselves to portions of the book they find of most interest.
- An index, which allows readers looking for information about specific topics to use boolean search strings to jump directly to their target node.

Platforms provide starting off points from which readers can *jump off* to more detail. At the highest level, a platform is a list of chapters. If the reader selects a chapter, he or she gets a brief summary of the information in it and a list of the

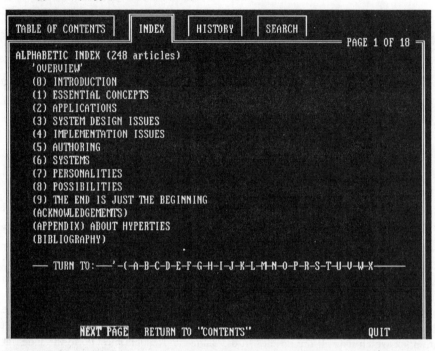

Figure 11.6 The index from *Hypertext Hands On!*, a hypertext about hypertext published by Addison-Wesley Publishing Company.

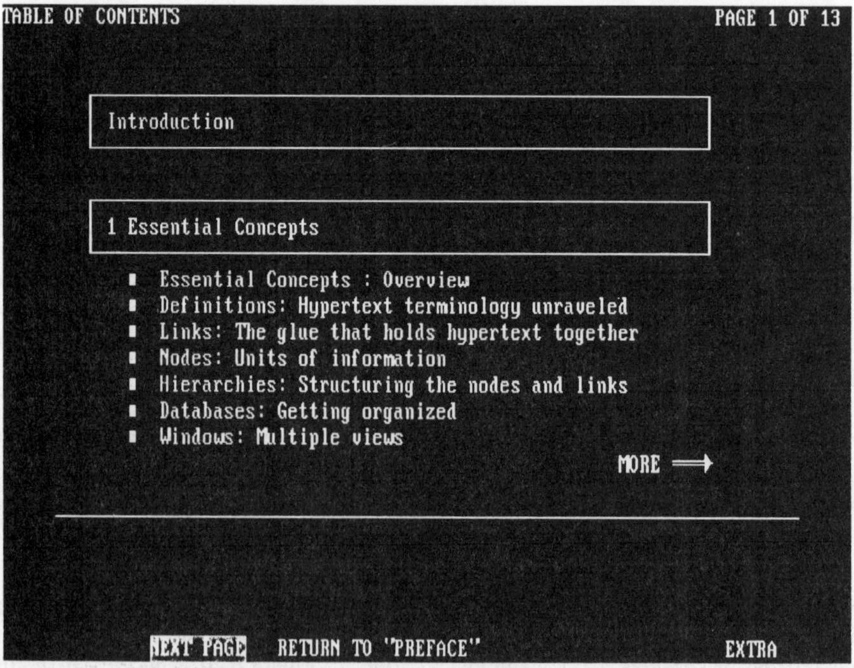

Figure 11.7 The table of contents from *Hypertext Hands-On!*

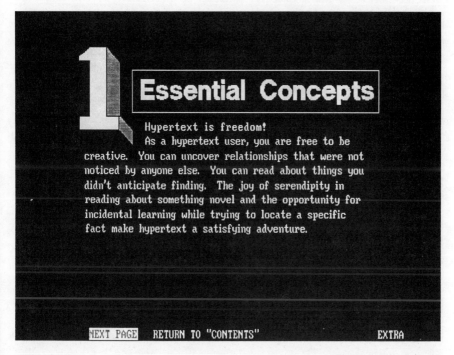

Figure 11.8 The Platform Page for Chapter 1 of *Hypertext Hands-On!*, a hypertext about hypertext published by Addison-Wesley Publishing Company.

articles it contains. The reader can continually return to the platform. This reduces the sense of being *lost in hyperspace* which can occur when a reader loses track of the structure of the hyperdocument and especially its links.

To read *Hypertext Hands-On!* using the platforms, a reader might select Chapter 1 which discusses basic concepts. The Chapter 1 platform provides a place to access each of the concepts contained in it. The reader can select a concept, browse around its links, and then return to the Chapter 1 platform. Then the reader can select another basic concept and repeat the procedure until all desired concepts have been explored. (See Figure 11.8.)

Search.   The Search command gives access to a full text string search which constructs a list of articles containing the searched string(s). See Figure 11.9.) [More information about text search and retrieval is provided in Chapter 21 by Fox, et al., in this book.] (

Conclusion

Our experience in exploring the new world of hypertext/hypermedia with Hyperties has been exciting and fun. At times we do feel like we are taking historic steps

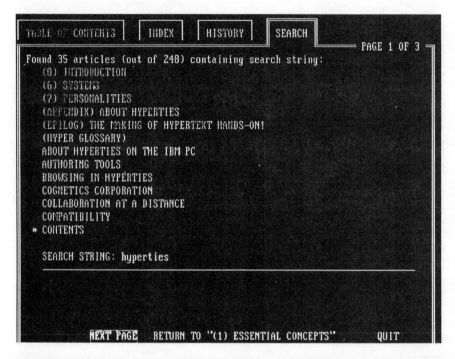

Figure 11.9 A search for the term Hyperties in *Hypertext Hand-On!* finds 35 articles.

in creating electronic books, but other times we are burdened with details and deadlines that force us into making compromises. Although our progress over the past eight years is clear, we still feel that we are at the Model T stage of evolution for this technology.

While there is a danger of too much hype about hypertext, there is clearly a promising future. We hope that you will join the growing number of pioneers who contribute to designing this vital and influential technology.

We still need new ideas for managing and synchronizing larger, higher resolution screens with multiple windows, animation, video, speech, music, and even physical experiences and virtual realities. Readers will press forward their demands for multiple tables of contents, graphic browsing, annotation, exportation, printing, powerful search, history-keeping, bookmarks, and status recording. We also need powerful authoring tools to support importation, editing, exportation, and printing of multiple articles and complete databases in multi-user, distributed networks. Underlying system support is necessary to ensure rapid and reliable performance even with large distributed databases, security control, encryption, integration with other software, and extensibility.

There is much work to be done.

About the Authors

Ben Shneiderman

Ben Shneiderman is a professor in the Department of Computer Science, head of the Human-Computer Interaction Laboratory, and member of the Institute for Advanced Computer Studies, all at the University of Maryland at College Park. He taught previously at the State University of New York and at Indiana University. He regularly teaches popular short courses and organizes an annual satellite television presentation on *User Interface Strategies* seen by thousands of professionals.

Dr. Shneiderman is the author of *Software Psychology: Human factors in Computer and Information Systems* (1980) and *Designing the User Interface: Strategies for Effective Human-Computer Interaction* (1987), Addison-Wesley Publishers, Reading, MA. His most recent book, co-authored with Greg Kearsley, *Hypertext Hands-On!*, includes a hypertext version on two disks. He is the originator of the Hyperties hypermedia system, now produced by Cognetics Corp., Princeton Junction, NJ. In addition, he has co-authored two textbooks, edited three technical books, and published more than 120 technical papers and book chapters.

Ben Shneiderman is on the Editorial Advisory Board of the *International Journal of Man-Machine Studies, Interacting with Computers, Behaviour and Information Technology, International Journal of Human-Computer Interaction and Human-Computer Interaction Abstracts.* He edits the Ablex Publishing Co. book series on *Human-Computer Interaction.* He has consulted and lectured for many organizations including Apple, AT&T, Citicorp, GE, Honeywell, IBM, Library of Congress, NASA, and University research groups.

Dr. Shneiderman may be contacted at the Human-Computer Interaction Lab., Dept. of Computer Science, University of Maryland, College Park, MD, 20742.

Charles B. Kreitzberg

Charles B. Kreitzberg is President of Cognetics Corporation, which specializes in the design of human-centered software products. One of the software products distributed by Cognetics is Hyperties. Dr. Kreitzberg has assisted in the design of automatic bank terminals, museum exhibits, videotext, and hypertext systems and educational software.

Before he founded Cognetics Corporation, Dr. Kreitzberg was the director of technology research and development at the Educational Testing Service. He co-authored four books and many articles.

Dr. Kreitzberg also developed a computerized SAT study disk for Harcourt, Brace, and Jovanovich; an interactive novel, *Amnesia,* which was published by Electronic Arts; a software series to help young children develop problem-solving skills, interactive advertising, computer-based testing and measurement software, and other successful software packages.

Dr. Kreitzberg received his B.A. in computing in 1969 from City College of New York, an M.S. in computer science from Rutgers University (1972), and his Ph.D. in educational psychology from the City University of New York (1978). He is a licensed psychologist in New Jersey and New York. He may be reached at Cognetics Corporation, 55 Princeton-Hightstown Road, Princeton Junction, NJ 08540.

References

Bransford, J.D. and Johnson, M.K. (1972). "Contextual prerequisites to understanding: Some investigations of comprehension and recall," *Journal of Verbal Learning and Verbal Behavior*, 11, 717-726.

Cherry, E.C. (1953). "Some experiments on the recognition of speech with one and with two ears". *Journal of the Acoustical Society of America* 25, 975-979.

Conklin, J. (1987). "Hypertext: An Introduction and Survey", *IEEE Computer* 20(9), 17-41.

Davison, D. (1989). (Unpublished interview with Emily Berk.)

Gay, G., and Mazur, J. (1991). "Navigating in Hypermedia." *Hypertext / Hypermedia Handbook*, Emily Berk and Joseph Devlin, (Ed.s), McGraw-Hill, New York, NY.

Glushko, R. (1989). "Hypertext '89 Course Notes #3: Turning Text Into Hypertext."

Joyce, M. (1988). "Siren Shapes: Exploratory and Constructive Hypertexts." *Academic Computing*, November.

Kreitzberg, C. and Shneiderman, B. (1988). "Restructuring knowledge for an electronic encyclopedia," Proceedings of the International Ergonomics Association's 10th Congress, Sydney Australia, 18-25.

Kreitzberg, C.B. (1989). "Designing the Electronic Book: Human Psychology and Information Structures for Hypermedia," *Designing and Using Human-Computer Interfaces and Knowledge-Based Systems*, G.Salvendy and M.J. Smith, (Eds.), Elsevier Science Publishers, B.V., Amsterdam.

Marchionini, G., and Shneiderman, B. (1988). "Finding facts vs. browsing knowledge in hypertext systems," *IEEE Computer*, 21, 70-80.

Nelson, T.H. (1987). *Literary Machines*, Published by the author; distributed by the Distributors, South Bend, Indiana.

Shneiderman, B. (1987). "User interface design for the Hyperties electronic encyclopedia," Presented at *Hypertext '87*, University of Chapel Hill, NC.

Shneiderman, B. and Kearsley, G. (1989). *Hypertext Hands-On!: An Introduction to a New Way of Organizing and Accessing Information*, Addison-Wesley. Reading,. Massachusetts (USA), 165

Shneiderman, B., Plaisant, C., Weiland, W., Botafogo, R. and Hopkins, D. (1989). "Visual Engagement and Low Cognitive Load in Browsing Hypertext." Department of Computer Science, Technical Report CS-TR-2433, University of MD, March 1990.

Weyer, S. and Borning, A. (1989). "A Prototype Electronic Encyclopedia". *ACM Transactions on Office Information Systems.*

Wurman, R. S. (1989). *Information Anxiety*, Doubleday, New York, NY

Yankelovich, N., Meyrowitz, N., and Van Dam, A. (1985). "Reading and Writing the Electronic Book," *IEEE Computer* 18(10), pp. 15-30.

12

Structuring Interactive Multimedia Fiction

By Geri Gay

Interactive Multimedia Group, Cornell University

Introduction

There is an emerging consensus that the telling of stories is a fundamental human activity. We respond to the events of our lives by weaving them into a coherent narrative that makes sense of them and thereby makes sense of us. If our stories can become richer and more sophisticated, our lives will be enriched.

Connelly and Clandinin have put forward a theory that holds that people are basically storytellers, who, "individually and socially, lead storied lives" [Connelly and Clandinin, 1990]. Jerome Bruner contends that human beings can create hypotheses that will "accommodate virtually anything" confronting them [Bruner, 1986, p. 51]. In fact, in most of our communication activities, we are inferring meaning, trying to make sense of conversations and events, filling in the gaps. Interactive fiction can contribute to the process of constructing richer stories.

Application of Hypermedia Techniques to Interactive Fiction (IF)

Hypertext techniques can be applied to fiction. When this happens, the readers' experiences of viewing/navigating/reading the resulting *interactive fictions* (IF) differ from those of readers of books who follow a traditional plot or narrative. Reading an interactive fiction is akin to participating in a computer adventure game where the reader can explore a mythical world [Nielsen, 1990].

When hypertext meets interactive fiction, the hypermedia program provides a fictional space in which readers construct and create their own stories. Instead of designing a linear plot line, the author creates nodes and tools to explore those nodes. If the author has built appropriate features into the hypermedia document, its readers will use the tools to determine what will happen next by choosing to explore certain multimedia links. In so doing, the reader may change the theme of the fictional universe with each reading. The number of episodes may change, characters will change according to context, story lines will vary according to sequence, and different plots may unfold. Thus, the hypermedia or hypertext program frees both author and reader from restrictions imposed by traditional media and becomes a collaboration by author and reader [see Chapter 8 by Joyce, in this book].

Most interactive fiction programs have been designed and developed for hypertext systems [Bolter and Joyce, 1987]. Currently, high capacity storage devices such as *compact discs* (CDs) and *videodiscs* allow users to access text, static graphics, animation, video clips, voice, and music from relatively inexpensive microcomputers. In the future, more powerful hardware and more sophisticated software will allow interactive fiction authors to endow readers with more potent tools and precise, interesting and more easily controllable plot elements [see Chapter 5 by Picher, in this book].

In short, we have found that hypertext is a very useful technique for implementing interactive fictions. This chapter explains why this is so, using examples from our research.

Features of Hypermedia Systems

A printed novel presents its episodes in one order, but a hypertext system can remove that restriction. Under hypertext, "electronic systems become virtual storytellers and narrative is no longer disseminated in a single direction from singer to listener or writer to reader" [Joyce, 1989, p. 383]. Instead of a series of paragraphs, the author lays out a textual space in which his or her fiction operates [Nielsen, 1990, p. 81]. Within each episode, the reader is compelled to read what the author has written. The reader can participate in constructing the storyline and plot by selecting a particular order of episodes at the time of the reading.

Nonlinear composition and hypermedia experiences demand flexible and powerful tools and systems. The designer of an interactive fiction must consider not only content, but what tools and software to use. Understanding the technical capabilities of the hardware, software and hypertext systems is an essential first step. The capabilities and limitations of these systems will influence both how the author represents the content and the ways readers access and use it.

Hypermedia systems provide a structure for organizing, storing and retrieving information. Such systems provide tools to manage and display the underlying structure of the network as well as a set of methods and protocols for tailoring the manipulation of information in the network. Most hypermedia systems have several distinguishing features in common as detailed in the following sections.

Nodes and Episodes

A hypermedia system keeps track of a database of nodes or episodes which contain information in various media including text, video graphics and audio. In the print medium, an author sets up the connections between related pieces of information by cross-referencing the relevant passages. In this process, the author tags text with key-words or phrases which, if selected, will lead readers to related information. Similarly, in the hypermedia production process, each episode or node has a title, a user-accessible list that can be used to track information and locate where it can be shared, and an arbitrary amount of content such as a short video segment, graphics, text, or animation.

Links

A hypermedia system supports links which interconnect individual nodes and represent the relationships between nodes and episodes. The internal structure of the hyperbase allows the designer to store information (story elements) in a neutral form, separate from hard-wired links. Each link is a directed connection between related pieces of stored information within the database. Therefore, relationships between nodes can change based on the types of links connecting them [see Chapter 20 by Parunak, in this book].

The hypertext system may manifest the presence of links in a hyperdocument to readers in many ways, including highlighting text or superimposing button-like icons on screen. Some hypermedia systems allow readers to navigate by pointing at a button or icon on the screen using a mouse or a touchscreen. Once the reader has selected the target information, the system traverses the link, retrieves the destination specified by the link and displays it on the screen. The reader may then view or read the segment, and in some cases may annotate the segment. Examples of typed links supported by OWL International's Guide Hypertext System can be seen in Figure 12.1a and b.

In its simplest form, interactive fiction requires only two elements: episodes (hypertext nodes) and decision points (links) between episodes [Nielsen, 1990]. The episodes may be paragraphs of prose or poetry, short narrative pieces, graphic designs, pictures, motion video, and animated pieces. The lengths of the episodes will establish the structure and rhythm of the story—how long the reader remains a conventional reader before participating in the selection of the next element. When writing/designing an interactive fiction, the author inserts decision points at the end of each episode. These links become the points where the reader has an influence on the course of the story.

⊕ Expansion Buttons   and   ☐ Replacements

⇨ Reference Buttons   and   ⇨ Reference Points

✳ Note Buttons   and |✳| Definitions

‖▶ Command Buttons   and |✳| Definitions

Figure 12.1a   Examples of typed links supported by OWL International's Guide Hypertext System can be seen in Figures 12. 1a and 1b.

Browsing

Hypermedia systems employ one or more of the following mechanisms to enable readers to browse for information in the database:

- a system of links and nodes for accessing specific information
- cross-referenced keywords, attributes and values to search for in the database
- a graphical display for navigating around the system

Navigation is the primary means by which readers access information in a hypermedia system. The user travels around the network by hopping from node to node (via the links set up by the author) to examine their content and relationships, choosing at each step which node to examine next. In many hypermedia applications, readers can navigate around a system using a graphical display.

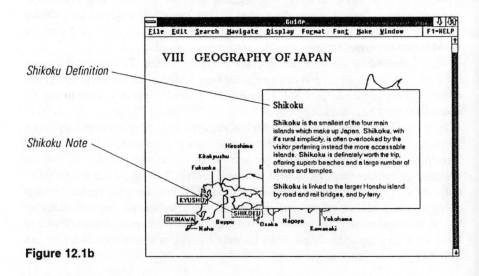

Figure 12.1b

Designing Stories

Choosing and manipulating interactive images is similar to choosing words for a piece of writing. The user interface of a hypermedia system can be designed to support both minor modifications and large interactive fiction application development. Using special editors such as Storyspace [Bolter and Joyce, 1987] or authoring tools such as Toolbook (IBM platform) or HyperCard (Apple platform), users can design their own stories using elements from the database for annotating or composing their own hypermedia fiction pieces.

Types of Interactivity

Personal multimedia technologies provide individuals with new means of reflection, exploration, and self-expression. At some point, designers of interactive multimedia programs must confront a basic question of control. Should readers be able to range freely through the multimedia events or nodes, or should they be led along a predetermined path that follows particular story lines? Tools for creating new materials, representing content, and making links potentially may be controlled by the both the author and the user.

The amount of control possessed by the author versus the reader within interactive environments may be thought of as existing on a continuum.

Figure 12.2 illustrates the varying levels of control which readers may acquire over reading, interpreting, and creating hypermedia fiction programs. At one end of the continuum, readers follow one or several predetermined paths through a story. At the opposite end, users become authors who are encouraged to create their own stories using text, graphics, movies and other elements from a variety of sources.

Guided Story

An author can structure an interactive story by limiting the number of available choices. In a guided story, readers' options are limited so that they may have little real influence over the outcome of the story. Interactive fiction produced at this level is usually so predictable that readers do not really feel in control. The author places a number of restrictions on the reading order, how often a reader gets to make a choice, and the number of options available to choose from.

In most hypertext fictions, the reader begins with an episode designated by the author as the starting place. The reader reads the text of that episode and may respond by typing text or pressing or clicking on an appropriate button. The system processes the reader's reply simply by checking all the links that lead out to the current episode. It then displays the elements of the destination episode or next cluster of possibilities and awaits a further reader response.

Guided Stories	Free Exploration	User as Author
User is reader with little control. Author has control over presentation, number of choices, and frequency of choices.	User has control over order of presentation and is able to augment information presented.	User is an author with ability to create own stories using multimedia tools and resources.

Figure 12.2   At one end of the reader-control continuum, readers follow one or several predetermined paths through a story. At the opposite end, users become authors who are encouraged to create their own stories using text, graphics, movies and other elements from a variety of sources.

Free Explorations

The extent of the reader's choices and therefore his freedom in examining the literary space depend upon the links that the author creates between episodes. The author has to consider what the reader could do and would want to do when he or she creates the story. Toward the midpoint of the continuum, readers have more than a few alternatives and are able to move from one place in the program to any other place.

Readers can choose among options which allow them to customize the presentation; different readers can view the information in different sequences and augment or annotate author's stories.

In essence, the authors and readers become collaborators. One example of this type of interactive fiction, the *shared universe*, has recently become popular in the science fiction genre. The basic idea is that several authors write stories in the same fictional universe using the same general characters and same general background [see Chapter 8 by Joyce, in this book].

User As Author

Hypermedia systems open up a whole new area for self-expression and creative composing. Hypermedia also has the potential to allow the reader to become an author of an interactive story. The tools in the hypermedia program provide the reader with an environment for capturing, representing, integrating, managing and communicating ideas. In this story environment, users can develop their ideas, and transform informal and unstructured jottings into formal stories and structured presentations. By using an on-line database of images, sound and text, or by adding their own graphics, text and audio segments to the database, the user is able to develop plots and stories by writing a series of discrete episodes and connecting them to other episodes via hypertext links. Readers can interchange scenes, place scenes in a different chronological order, change geographic or spatial position among scenes, and decide on the number of scenes used in the story.

Designing an Interactive Fiction Program

Cornell University's *Interactive Multimedia Group* (IMG) wanted to explore the potential of interactive multimedia technology as a medium for creative expression. The IMG was also interested in providing students a motivating and intriguing context to promote intercultural understanding. With these goals in mind, they designed and developed an interactive fiction program called El Avion Hispano in the spring of 1989. The program allows readers to take a subjective look at passengers on an airplane by placing them in an environment where they can view, navigate, create and play with the story elements.

The underlying premise of the story space is that most people have probably traveled by plane or train and have often constructed or imagined stories about other passengers. The design team felt this fictional environment would encourage readers to feel free to make up scenarios based on ambiguous or scanty information. Students are encouraged to imagine the characters' basic assumptions, goals, intentions, and feelings about other characters in the scenes. Writer's tools, such as a fortune teller who delivers intriguing details about some of the passengers as a means for overcoming writer's block, are available for specific assignments. A dictionary with 8,000 entries is also provided to assist in constructing narratives.

Interactive multimedias (fictions) that focus upon the study of foreign language and intercultural communication afford students the opportunity to be confronted by cultural situations in which decisions are made based on language, body language, and on cultural interpretations of the situation presented. Such fictions provide readers with a means for constructing their own stories or interpretations of other cultures and promote reflection and understanding that is somewhat akin to that which is gained through immersion in a foreign culture. The reader is almost forced to make sense of and interpret a variety of contexts.

The theoretical foundation of El Avion Hispano is based on the second-learning language principles of H. Douglas Brown [Brown, 1987]. In part, Brown's theory promotes communicative competence over linguistic competence, values cognitive learning more than it does rote, and recognizes the importance of the contextual, affective aspects of personal study and inquiry. The events which comprise El Avion Hispano provide human interaction at three of Brown's four levels of communicative competence: function, register, and socio-linguistic competence.

Program Description

The reader of El Avion Hispano assumes the role of a reporter or writer traveling on a commuter airline flight and is advised to learn as much as possible about the background and relationships of the other passengers. The reader is also able to click on a pre-selected still from a scene and thereby gain access to other scenes, stills, or text.

This is similar to interactive fiction using text except the visuals also act as links to other story elements. The links allow readers to:

- Examine objects on the plane including the contents of a briefcase, a birth certificate, a personal letter
- Look into passengers' minds to see what they are thinking
- Examine personal connections of passengers by going back in time

Additionally, a dictionary and grammatical notes are available for the enhancement of the program's assignment, as well as an "inflight magazine" which contains articles relevant to the reader's investigation.

Readers are able to compose their own stories using the scenes provided or by adding their own audio tracks and still pictures. In addition, they are provided with an onscreen notebook in which to record notes about the video scenes, text, and stills they choose to view. The notebook becomes an interactive composition space. Readers can clip a piece from a video freeze-frame in the program and paste it into the notebook, record their own narration, and/or write their stories in Spanish. (See Figure 12.3.)

Figure 12.3 Screen from El Avion Hispano. Students of Spanish can type words in English and Spanish and paste video clips into their notebooks. They can move around the hyperdocument by clicking on objects and people in the pictures or notebook, as well as clicking on any of the picons (picture-icons) at the bottom of the screen.

The following paragraphs describe how a reader, who is already engaged in the El Avion Hispano interactive fiction, would interact in order to gain more information about fellow passengers.

After taking his/her seat, the reader is exposed to interactions, characters and scenarios in much the same way any air traveler experiences these occurrences: randomly (as the video proceeds forward inviting the user to stop and select various options) or selectively (as eavesdropping or action attracts interest). The learner uses the iconic *menu* guide to access several databases woven into the basic theme.

The opening scene of El Avion Hispano shows several angles of a sepia-toned Ford Trimotor airplane in flight and concludes with a full-color shot of the interior cabin. Some of the passengers are plainly visible. A voice-over making frequent use of the second person announces the reader's assignment in Spanish:

> "Attention! There is only the briefest time before your flight leaves. Only time to give you this most important instruction. You are to watch the other people with you on the flight and write a story about them."

The home-screen is displayed, and the program goes on standby. Arranged in the home-screen are the following items: a sizeable notebook in which the user can record his/her notes and thoughts; a video window, at this point showing a still from the cabin; a panel of controls for the video; and several picons (picture icons) for connecting the user to additional areas of the program.

There are several scenes on the airplane. They randomly appear following action by the learner. At the conclusion of any scene, a key frame from the sequence appears in the video window. Inside all key frames are numerous hot spots—links—that are identified for the reader. The reader activates the hot spot by touching the touch screen.

When a hot spot is triggered, the reader will hear/watch additional audio-video segments, all of which are apparently unfold off the plane.

By clicking on the characters or various other *picons*, the student can observe activities, eavesdrop on various conversations on the airplane, examine a character's background, discover inner thoughts of the characters, and examine many objects in the scenes.

Aware that even the best writers need assistance at times in furthering their work's progress, the designers of El Avion Hispano established an array of picons which, when activated, provide assistance to the reader. The areas linked to these picons include an in-flight magazine containing additional information in various forms about the characters on board, various writer's tools which help to focus an assignment, an opportunity to interview a character, and a fortune teller who delivers intriguing details about some of the passengers. The dictionary is also accessed through this array of picons.

Excerpt From Program

Having viewed a scene in a previous session and having recorded some thoughts in the on-screen notebook, the reader clicks on the airplane icon labeled "Look

Around." The software selects a random scene which the reader has not yet witnessed which reveals an exchange between other passengers on board the aircraft. The following is an excerpt (translated) of dialogue from one such scene.

Man (showing a plate bearing a bun and some lettuce): Miss? Is this the kind of meal you serve on Conceptual Airlines? Where is the meat?

Attendant: I'm sorry, sir, I don't understand what you are trying to say.

Man: What do you mean you don't understand! The question is: Where is the meat? ...Because it is not here. Last night I had a meal in a vegetarian restaurant, and liked it. But today, no way!

Attendant: I'm sorry, would you like me to bring you another plate?

Woman sitting behind man on plane (holding a rubber chicken): Couldn't he eat this?

Man: How could you let that woman on this airplane with that chicken?

Attendant: It's not real.

At any point the reader can interrupt the scene to return to the notebook. The application automatically inserts a preselected still from the scene into the reader's notebook, under which notes related to the scene can be inserted. In addition to reminding the reader of what has been viewed, the pictures in the notebook are also active. Clicking on the picture of any previously viewed scene makes that scene the current focus of interest. This means the reader can watch it again or can click on objects in the picture and follow links to other scenes or information.

Design Considerations in the El Avion Hispano Program

Intense discussions went on among the designers of El Avion Hispano about how much story content should be included in the original video segments. This issue is best described by "story vs. no story." Should the video segments suggest a story that has a traditional beginning, middle and end? Should the characters relate, have a history of themselves, of each other? Should there be conflicts, external and internal? Might it be wise to design a subplot?

On the other side of the issue, which gets support from the belief that learners will make their own connections and personal sense of even the most obfuscatory events, are additional questions. If there is any appearance of story, will there be an expectation of conflict and its resolution by the reader and will he/she be disappointed with the program if such is not the case? If, on the other hand, scenes are designed to be visually rich but virtually unrelated to one another, what criteria will be available to readers to help them decide whether to reject any scene in favor of another? Is there a happy medium for designing content somewhere between a tightly constructed story and a collection of unrelated video segments?

Tightly constructed stories work well for the plots of television shows and motion pictures. More loosely constructed stories, in which different segments with sharper boundaries are cut together to evoke a mood or emotion, rather than to tell a story, may work better in contemporary commercials.

How much story construction is best for an interactive fiction? Program designers for El Avion Hispano sought to first answer the question by positioning themselves at the top of the construction space.

They began with an integrated story synopsis complete with characters, plot, and multiple settings, then loosened it up by discarding parts, altering times, mixing characterizations, etc. Their decision to disassemble a story—rather than to assemble one—was prompted by the program's paired objectives:

• The first seeks to have learners speak the language following observation and study of contextually grounded simulations.
• The second is to have them write in a creative, instead of reportorial, manner.

The first objective might have been attainable through the integration of unrelated video segments into a plot. However, the designers were concerned that readers would be stymied by a set of segments that was overly diffuse.

Basically, the designers felt that their purposes would best be achieved by cutting and editing from a whole story rather than by creating segments individually and then piecing them together. This consideration holds special merit for the kind of original video discussed in this chapter which only implies the presence of story, the actuality of which is realized through the user's creating or interpreting a story.

Controlling Ambiguity

Closure in dramatic film is sought after by producers and directors because audiences expect it. Video scenes must tie together. The ambiguous "leave 'em hanging" ending has been absent from most popular films and television for some time. In fact, the loss of a single narrative stream of action destroys most traditional ways of viewing films in Western civilization.

Elimination of all ambiguity may not be as vital in the design of an interactive fiction. However, if they are to be made comfortable in the ambiguous universe of an interactive fiction, both users and programmers are likely to require a reshaping of their expectations.

By investing video, audio, graphics, and text segments with a measure of controlled ambiguity, a program's designers can develop a form of video Rorschach, a novel orchestrated in tandem with the structuring of a corresponding lesson. Perhaps the easiest of video Rorschachs to design are those which are visually rich in details of persons, ambience, and surroundings; and correspond to lessons encour-

Ambiguous ———————————————— Literal
Unstructured ——————————————— Structured
Non-linear ————————————————— Linear
No-story ——————————————————— Story-line
Requires interpretation ———————— Interpretation(s) provided
User has creative control —————— Author has creative control

Figure 12.4   Considerations for video, audio, graphic, and textual representations of interactive fiction programs.

aging learners to describe what is before them. For example, some scenes in El Avion Hispano use visual elements and items that, although familiar, are not readily identifiable by the reader. Another, this one a silent scene, shows a woman discarding the ash from a cigarette into an object that is vertical, long, sectioned, and gold in color. A man then walks into the scene and hands a flower to another woman sitting in the shadows.

Students can use ambiguous story elements to formulate stories about characters' general motives and needs. El Avion Hispano is rich in cultural context and provides students with the opportunity to hear native speakers introduce themselves and interact in several common situations such as negotiation and querying.

Guidelines

Developing hypermedia fiction programs is more complex than developing linear programs. Because it is the reader who navigates, there can be no guarantee that any of the fictional elements will unfold as the author planned. The following list of recommendations is generated from a series of interviews, observations, and discussions with users of El Avion Hispano during the development of the program. The list is not inclusive but only is intended to serve as a guide:

* Provide ambiguous story elements.
* Authors should create many ambiguous story elements so that the stories are not too predictable. They must provide story elements which allow for creative flexibility, and multiple interpretations and uses. Authors should include suggestions of stories, development of plot, characterization, etc.
* Give readers many choices throughout the program. The experience of using hypermedia systems should be a rewarding, entertaining and enriching experience.
* Incorporate spatial anchors. Interactive fiction allows readers to move through time and space. Authors should incorporate into the program orientation devices and familiar elements such as home cards, metaphors, or fixed bases in case the reader becomes lost or disoriented.
* Nonsequential story elements. The author should construct the fiction as a network of ambiguous story elements or episodes. Since readers are able to struc-

ture their own stories or follow their own paths throughout the program, the individual story elements need to make sense no matter how they are put together.

• Consistent user interface. Authors must make certain that the tools and program have a consistent, clean, and clear look. The user interface should be transparent and easy to follow.

Conclusion

Hypermedia presents the opportunity for accessing information that incorporates multiple views and dimensions. The reader decides how the story develops. While using interactive fiction programs, readers have the opportunity to become actively engaged; to carefully watch, judge, interpret, and even create scenes. We believe that interactive fiction designers should, like Jerome Bruner, in his book "Actual Minds, Possible Worlds," advocate a new "breed of developmental theory." Its central concern "will be how to create in the young an appreciation of the fact that many worlds are possible, that meaning and reality are created and not discovered, that negotiation is the art of constructing new meanings by which individuals can regulate their relations with each other."

About the Author

Geri Gay is an assistant professor of communication at Cornell University where she also directs the *Interactive Multimedia Group* (IMG), a research and development body which has produced multimedia computing applications with wide-ranging topics, including foreign language study, the physics of windsurfing, cultural entomology, and interactive multimedia itself. Her work has appeared on PBS and remains on display at Tech 2000 and at the Smithsonian National Demonstration Laboratory in Washington, D. C. The results of Dr. Gay's research have been published in the *Journal of Research on Computing in Education, Journal of Educational Psychology,* and in *Academic Computing.* Dr. Gay and her group receive much of the funding for their research from IBM, the National Science Foundation, and Apple Computer.

Dr. Gay may be contacted at the Interactive Multimedia Group, Cornell University, 221 Kennedy Hall, Department of Communications, Ithaca, NY 14853.

References

Bolter, J. D. & Joyce, M. (1987). "Hypertext and creative writing," *Proceedings ACM Hypertext '87 Conference,* Chapel Hill, NC, 13–15, 41–50.

Brown, H.D. (1987). *Principles of Language Learning and Teaching,* 2nd ed., Prentice-Hall, Englewood Cliffs, NJ.

Bruner, J. (1986). *Actual Minds, Possible Worlds,* Harvard University Press, Cambridge, MA.

Connelly, F. & Clandinin, D. J., "Stories of Experience and Narrative Inquiry," *Educational Researcher*, 19(4), 2-14.

Howell, G. "Hypertext meets interactive fiction: New vistas in creative writing." Green, C., and McAleese, R. (Eds.) *Hypertext: Theory into Practice II*, INTELLECT Press.

Joyce, M. (1989). Proceedings of ACM HT '89 Conference, Pittsburgh, PA.

Joyce, M. (1991). "Selfish Interaction," *Hypertext / Hypermedia Handbook*, Emily Berk and Joseph Devlin (Ed.s), McGraw-Hill, New York, NY.

Nielsen, J. (1990). *Hypertext and Hypermedia*, Academic Press, San Diego, CA.

Parunak, H. V. D. (1991). "Ordering the Information Graph," *Hypertext / Hypermedia Handbook*, Emily Berk and Joseph Devlin (Ed.s), McGraw-Hill, New York, NY.

Picher, O. (1991). "Hypermedia," *Hypertext / Hypermedia Handbook*, Emily Berk and Joseph Devlin (Ed.s), McGraw-Hill, New York, NY.

13

Tools for Designing Hyperdocuments

By Franca Garzotto
Politecnico di Milano

Paolo Paolini
ARG—Applied Research Group

Daniel Schwabe
Pontifícia Universidade Católica do Rio de Janeiro

and Mark Bernstein
Eastgate Systems, Inc.

Introduction

The development of hypertext has been driven by an urgent need for tools that can help us communicate, comprehend, and refine complex ideas. Engelbart's quest [Engelbart, 1963] to "Augment Human Intelligence" was motivated by his perception of an urgent need for people to assimilate unprecedented amounts of information. While most early hypertexts were comparatively small (The Hypertext '87 Digest [Bernstein, 1988], for example, contains roughly 175 pages), the construction of large hyperdocuments remains a central concern of hypertext research.

A large hyperdocument contains not only a prodigious amount of information, but also a large number of links. The richness and diversity of the nodes in a successful hyperdocument is reflected in the richness and diversity of its links. Yet Nelson's polemical declaration [Nelson, 1976], *Everything is intertwingled!* is not literally true. We cannot use hypertext to interlink everything. Rather, we use links selectively to convey part of a thought and to show how that thought fits into the structure of an argument.

The process of hypertext design encompasses:

* The design of individual *chunks* or *nodes*
* The design of the web of links which interconnects these nodes

In this chapter we focus on some of the tools hypertext designers and authors can use in planning the overall structure and design of hypertexts, a process we call *authoring in the large* [ARG, 1990]. These tools are particularly useful in the design of highly complex hypertexts. We distinguish authoring in the large from *authoring in the small*, the process of composing the contents of individual hypertext nodes, which will not be emphasized in this chapter.

We will begin by evaluating tools and structuring approaches that may help authors who are developing highly complex hyperdocuments. Some of these tools and approaches are built into existing hypertext authoring systems. Others must be implemented without much assistance from these systems. We will then propose a *Hypertext Document Model* (HDM) that may help hypertext authors describe the structure of hypertexts during the design phase before they have to implement individual links.

A Note about Terminology Used in this Chapter

In this chapter we use the term "hyperdocument" to denote one specific hypertext document made up of interlinked pages or nodes. We use the term "hypertext system" for a set of software tools used to create a hypertext. Notecards, KMS, Intermedia, and Hypergate are all examples of hypertext systems. Note that a single hyperdocument might be published in several editions, each using a different hypertext system.

Authoring in the Large

Research into the management of the overall structures of hypertexts has often been driven by concern with difficulty of hypertext navigation.

While Bernstein argues elsewhere in this volume that the *navigation problem* may be illusory [Bernstein, 1991], the fear that readers might become disoriented when using complex hypertexts has been a leading concern of authors [Landow, 1987; Utting, 1990; Parunak, 1989; Nielsen, 1990], and many others [see Chapter 18 by Gay and Mazur, in this book, for their comments in this regard].

Tools for depicting, understanding, and specifying hypertext structures can help readers navigate through complex documents. These tools may also help authors and editors avoid structural inconsistencies and mistakes. For example, they may aid proofreaders in verifying links as well as text.

Prescriptive Approaches to Structuring Large Hypertexts

Faced with the prospect of intractably complex information needs, some authors adopt an essentially prescriptive approach to structuring hyperdocuments; they impose a simple, regular structure on them. Prescriptive structures are often implemented using highly specialized link typing. For example, sequential links—next and previous—cause readers to move in linear order through the document. Node typing is also possible. For example, a hypertext manual on handling dangerous chemicals might assign different types to distinguish nodes that describe chemicals, nodes that describe routine handling procedures, and nodes that describe emergency treatments.

Specialized link and node typing is built into certain hypertext systems. Therefore, the choice of hypertext system may determine whether certain prescriptive structures are encouraged, permitted, or required and whether they can be implemented easily using built-in tools.

Linear Structures

While hypertext is intrinsically nonlinear, some systems products grant linear substructures a central organizational role. To HyperCard [Atkinson, 1987], every hyperdocument is a *stack*, a linear pile of cards with a first card on top and a last card on the bottom. Links may permit readers to move outside the linear sequence, and computational operations (e.g., sorting) may alter the sequence. Nevertheless, the linear sequence is fundamental to the system's design and rarely far from the reader's or the author's mind. Many stacks rely on the *next card* button; readers of HyperCard documents may readily assume that, at any point in the stack (except, perhaps, the last card), the command *go to next card* will make sense.

Guide [Brown, 1987] also prescribes the extensive use of linear structures. In many applications, users may be totally unaware that the document shown on the screen is made up of many interlinked substructures. In particular, the Guide reader sees the document as a single scroll, through which she can browse, occasionally summoning auxiliary windows or opening other scrolling documents, but

HyperCard   Home

Figure 13.1   To HyperCard, every hyperdocument is a stack, a linear pile of cards with a first card on top and a last card on the bottom. © 1990 Apple Computer, Inc. All Rights Reserved. Apple is a registered trademark and HyperCard is a registered trademark of Apple Computer, Inc. licensed to Claris Corporation. Reprinted with permission from Claris Corporation.

more frequently unfolding and refolding stretch-text *replacement buttons* [Brown, 1987].

While hyperdocuments created using either Guide or HyperCard may be structured in the same, essentially linear fashion, the rationale for using a linear structure is different for each product. HyperCard uses linearity to provide a consistent navigational opportunity. Guide, on the other hand, uses linearity to provide continuity between information chunks.

Hierarchical Structures

Many hypertext researchers advocate extensive use of hierarchical structures to organize the contents of hypertexts. In KMS, for example, every node is part of a single overall hierarchy. KMS links are of two types: *tree links*, which conform to the hyperdocument's hierarchical structure and cross-hierarchical *special links*, which breach its hierarchical constraints.

KMS strongly encourages a top-down, stepwise refinement approach to organizing material. The system's hierarchical emphasis suggests that writers should sketch in general information first, later adding details at lower levels of the hierarchy. The resulting hierarchical backbone helps readers build a coherent mental model of the database. Multiple hierarchies can be constructed to provide alternative paths through the database [Akscyn, 1987]. Similarly, each item in NLS/Augment is identified by a hierarchical description [Engelbart, 1968].

In contrast to KMS and Augment, Concordia [Walker, 1988] does permit authors to describe non-hierarchical structures. But it also provides hierarchical overviews of local neighborhoods to make documents appear to be hierarchical. NoteCards [Halasz, 1987a] includes a hierarchy-promoting filebox construct, but includes equally extensive support for non-hierarchical browsers.

Other Recursive Structures

Several hypertext systems have adopted more complex, recursively defined structures for their organization idiom, building complex information structures by repeating small patterns in the same way that simple triangles can be assembled to form complex geodesic domes. gIBIS [Conklin, 1987] identifies a structure of rhetorical moves that make up design discussions. (See Figure 13.2)

The limited sets of node and link types and the use of color and hypertext in gIBIS are intended to foster disciplined design discussions so that gIBIS users are not drawn into spurious arguments. Although users are generally enthusiastic about using gIBIS, its authors have reported that the structural model they adopted appears to be excessively spare and abstract, and that additional types of links and nodes (e.g., for annotative or procedural discussion) are desirable.

In a similar vein, Winograd proposes a recursive structural representation of routine business memoranda [Winograd, 1988]. Winograd's design seeks to cap-

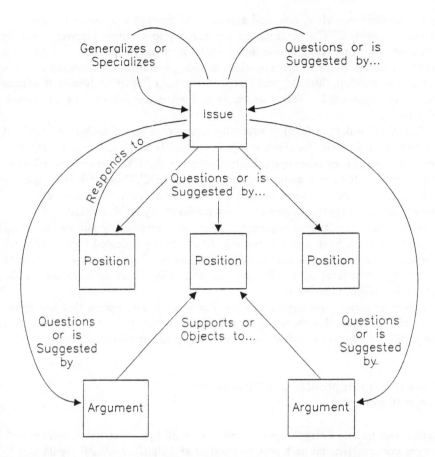

Figure 13.2 gIBIS is a specialized hypertext system intended to represent engineers' discussions about product and system design. Each node represents a specific issue, a proposal, or an argument in favor of or against a proposal. This structure, motivated by a theoretical model of the engineering design process, is intended to reflect the structured but infinitely recursive process through which designs are proposed and refined.

ture the notions of promise, commitment, and delegation in the structural semantics of the hypertext network.

The most impressive feature of this system is its ability to evaluate the structure of a body of requests and promises, in order to automatically construct "virtual" links [Halasz, 1987]. These virtual links can satisfy queries such as:

- Have I any outstanding commitments due before the end of this week?
- Which of my people are responsible for arranging the annual sales conference?

Another system with a recursive design is CYC [Lenat, 1990], an exceptionally large knowledge base designed to model and consider the contents of an encyclopedia. Readers can view, edit, and extend CYC through a hypertextual interface [Travers, 1989]. CYC's contents are organized into a single hierarchy, but its nodes are also organized into complex (but systematic) structures defined by a host of relations. Some of these relations include generalization, refinement, inheritance, membership, duration, and extent. A myriad of other properties of objects and concepts are used to define structures within the contents of the CYC knowledge base.

Each CYC link-type (slot) is explicitly represented as a full-fledged hypertext node (unit). This node contains a complete definition of the link-type's semantics, described in terms of other units. Each structure in the CYC network is reflexive; it describes itself as well as its contents. Because the CYC network is completely reflexive, it can be extremely complex. On the other hand, this same reflexivity means that readers may examine CYC's structure at any level of detail.

On balance, prescriptive approaches have been remarkably successful. Many hypertext authors have found it possible to create sophisticated hyperdocuments whose structures are quite accessible to their users. Hence, those who advocate prescriptive structural approaches almost invariably claim to have solved the hypertext navigation problem.

However, prescriptive approaches conflict with an assumption that lies at the heart of hypertext—that the sophisticated, nonlinear structure of discourse is most effectively expressed by sophisticated, nonlinearly structured connections.

Constructive Approaches to Structuring Large Hypertexts

Rather than impose a single *a priori* structure on all hyperdocuments, authors with a more constructive approach seek to discover and clarify structural regularities in specific documents. These authors often use tools such as link maps and other visualization tools and construction kits that help them generate regular hypertext structures easily and systematically.

Visualization Tools

Visualization tools help authors observe patterns in the hypertexts they construct. These tools help authors and readers survey the size and scope of hypertext documents and explore hypertext neighborhoods. Tools for visualization have proven extremely popular with authors and readers alike. It has even been asserted that geometric visualization is intrinsic to the very notion of hypertext. The development of tools to help authors (and readers) visualize large navigation spaces is currently one of the more active areas of hypertext research.

Intermedia [Yankelovich, 1988] and NoteCards [Halasz, 1987a] automatically generate graphical overviews of hypertext documents. Nodes are represented as icons, and links are represented as connecting lines. For small hypertexts, these graphical browsers are extremely useful. However, as the number of nodes and

Figure 13.3   A partial hypertext map constructed automatically by Storyspace [Bolter, 1990]. The hierarchical backbone of the hypertext is represented through nesting of rectangular "writing spaces;" non-hierarchical links are drawn only when the source or destination is in view and at the same level of the hierarchy as the reader. Storyspace is published by Eastgate Systems, Inc.

links increases, it becomes increasingly difficult to find an effective layout. (See Figure 13.3)

Storyspace [Bolter, 1987, 1990] shows short-range links in full but merely indicates the presence of links to objects outside the user's current focus.

SemNet [Fairchild, 1988] addresses the layout problem differently. It represents the hypertext network as a three-dimensional graph, viewed on a stereoscopic (or depth-cued) display. SemNet uses incremental relaxation techniques to improve the layout of the hypertext network by trying to make the links on screen as short as possible.

Considerable effort has been invested in developing tools that show readers hierarchical and almost-hierarchical maps of hypertext structures. When a strict hierarchical backbone is present, its structure can be displayed readily [Halasz, 1987; Bolter, 1987]. However, since hierarchical structures are already understood by users, these *tree diagrams* have limited value, especially since they hamper visualization of non-hierarchical links.

In addition, tree diagrams can become cumbersome when trees grow large. The classic browser [Goldberg, 1980] has proved invaluable for displaying information in trees that are broad but shallow. Scrolling windows display each level of the tree. When the reader selects an item in any window, the next window displays the children of the selected node. Browsers are useful for viewing trees of up to roughly 5000 nodes, provided the depth of the tree does not exceed the number of windows that can be displayed conveniently.

Hierarchies can also be displayed by recursive nesting of objects. Boxer [diSessa, 1986], for example, is a hypertextual environment designed as a reconstructible user interface tool for use by children. It displays the hierarchical structure of a document or of a program as a set of nested rectangular boxes. Boxer displays local views of the hierarchy, but suppresses the display of boxes far removed in the hierarchy from the current focal point.

MUE [Travers, 1989], a browser and editor for CYC [Lenat, 1990], also uses recursive nesting to represent the local structure of a hypertext. Since CYC represents structures that are not strictly hierarchical, MUE projects separate images of a unit for each occurrence of the unit in the neighborhood of the current focus.

Elision (information hiding) of deeply-nested hierarchies and display of almost-hierarchical hypertexts are central concerns of Guide [Brown, 1987]. Unlike some other visualization approaches, Guide does not present structure through geometrical schema. Instead, Guide represents textual structure in the form of abstract textual structures: a section heading represents (and may be expanded into) a section which may, in turn, be expanded into more detailed discussions.

Empirical studies indicate that graphical overviews may be among the most heavily-used features in a hypertext document, even when the document design does not appear to be biased toward their use [Walker, 1990]. These results may, however, be distorted by the attractions of visualization tools as displacement activities.[1] Moreover, while visualization tools have made great progress toward representing hierarchical and almost-hierarchical structures, the representation of more complex webs in an efficient and aesthetically pleasing manner has proven to be much more challenging. Visualization approaches depict regular hierarchies well, but are much less effective at revealing regular structures in more complex hypertext webs.

Templates for Construction

Constructive tools help authors generate regular hypertext structures easily and systematically. The simplest constructive tools allow readers to create multiple copies of individual hypertext nodes which share a common internal structure. The author can then change individual nodes as necessary. Other constructive tools can actually scan the contents of a hyperdocument and suggest strategies for linking and/or structuring it.

A HyperCard node [Atkinson, 1987], for example, is made up of a background description, which it may share with many other nodes, and a discrete foreground description which is unique to the node. The background of a card may include all the components of any other HyperCard node, including links. Links attached to the background of a set of cards may connect all nodes that share that background to a single place, or they may connect each instance to a different computationally-defined place. (See Figures 13.4a and 13.4b.)

---

1   A displacement activity is a person or animal's inappropriate behavior in response to a stimulus or stimuli. For example, if a person begins frantically munching on popcorn, instead of running when scared by a horror movie, that person is engaging in a displacement activity.

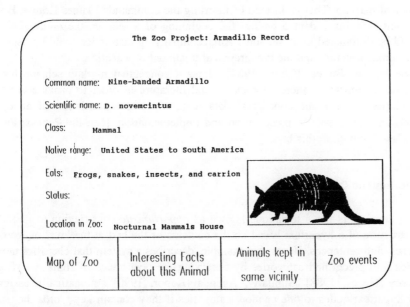

The Zoo Project: Animal Record Template

Common name:

Scientific name:

Class:

Native range:

Eats:

Status:

Location in Zoo:

| Map of Zoo | Interesting Facts about this Animal | Animals kept in same vicinity | Zoo events |

Figure 13.4a   A template such as this one can automatically create links as well as textual information. *The Zoo Project* © 1990 E.Berk and J.Devlin.

The Zoo Project: Armadillo Record

Common name: Nine-banded Armadillo

Scientific name: D. novemcintus

Class: Mammal

Native range: United States to South America

Eats: Frogs, snakes, insects, and carrion

Status:

Location in Zoo: Nocturnal Mammals House

| Map of Zoo | Interesting Facts about this Animal | Animals kept in same vicinity | Zoo events |

Figure 13.4b   The data that appear on this screen are generated by fitting textual and pictorial information from a database into the format specified by the template. The template can also complete some of the links (such as those on the four buttons at the bottom of the screen).

Hypergate style pages [Bernstein, 1988] and Information Lens templates [Malone, 1988] also enable writers to create as many instances of a class of hypertext nodes as required. NoteCards' notion of a hierarchy of node types and link types encourages a similar style of node creation [Halasz, 1987].

IDE, an extension of NoteCards, permits writers to create entire webs of nodes and links in a single operation [Jordan, 1989]. Starting from the observation that many parts of a hypertext share repetitive local structures, Jordan et al. define *structure accelerators* which function as macros to create locally-connected sets of related nodes.

Inductive Construction

Inductive approaches to construction create a hypertext structure by identifying structures implicit in existing (linear) documents and then incorporating them into hypertexts.

For example, Glushko [Glushko, 1989] uses typographic conventions in paper documents as structural cues. Section headings can be recognized from their typographical structure, and a hierarchical structure can be induced from the section/subsection hierarchy that is pervasive in current documentation. [See Chapter 10 by Rearick, in this book.]

Coombs [Coombs, 1987] argues persuasively that it would be preferable for authors of linear texts as well as hypertexts to provide conceptual rather than typographical markup. That is, instead of inserting the commands "Times Roman Bold 24 point Hanging Indent 5 cm" at the beginning of a section, the entire section should be designated as a "section." An accompanying instruction would prescribe the internal structure and the typographical treatment of a section.

The Perseus Project [Crane, 1987] adopts a conceptual markup scheme for a hyperdocument about ancient Greek art and literature in order to provide greater modularity between the conceptual data (e.g., interlinear translation of an epic poem) and the details of presentation and implementation. [See the Perseus Project, Case Study 5, in this book.]

Opportunistic Construction

Other developers use a technique known as *opportunistic* construction to identify the structure of a hypertext based on the contents of the text at the level of words, phrases, and sentences. Hayes, for example, describes a system that classifies news stories into predefined categories by observing the occurrence of signal words or phrases [Hayes, 1988]. Similarly, Agenda [Kapor, 1990] automatically assigns new hypertext nodes to one or more categories if they contain key words the user has previously indicated to be important, or if they contain certain expressions that the machine can automatically interpret. Agenda can, for example, automatically assign a message that refers to "a week from today" to the category "July 14, 1991." Unlike [Hayes, 1988] however, Agenda relies exclusively on lexical information. If a professor of mathematics defines a category that includes the term "set," Agenda will be unable to distinguish "set theory," "set up an appointment," and "set clocks one hour back."

VISAR [Clitherow, 1989] relies on the extensive semantic information contained in CYC [Lenat, 1990] to construct content links by examining the conceptual structures that underlie lexical patterns. For example, since CYC explicitly represents the connection between *cognitive model* and *artificial intelligence* and between *music* and *composition*, it is able to discover a probable link from the phrase "Cognitive model of music" to a node entitled "An expert system for computer-assisted composition," without the detailed domain-specific programming required by rule-based systems like [Hayes, 1988]. However, because CYC's ontology (its representation of the meanings of and relationships among concepts) and our understanding of language is incomplete, VISAR is probably best considered a link apprentice, which locates links that a human author can approve or reject.

Bernstein's Link Apprentice [Bernstein, 1990] adopts an intermediate approach to link discovery. The Link Apprentice takes advantage of the observation that usage patterns convey considerable semantic information—information which deep semantic tools like VISAR can represent, but which simple lexical pattern matching obscures. The Link Apprentice identifies similarities between hypertext nodes by measuring the approximate frequency with which all words and word-fragments appear; following our previous example, while it may be extremely difficult to disambiguate the word "set" in an isolated phrase, it is much safer to suppose that two passages which share words like "set," "disjoint," "recursive," and "Mandelbrot" have a great deal in common. Because no deep analysis of language or semantics is required, the Link Apprentice can be very fast and is sometimes quite accurate, but because it can perceive only superficial, lexical properties of the text, it makes many mistakes.

A Model-Based Approach

We have seen that the elucidation of hypertext structures has been a preoccupation of hypertext research. Unfortunately, the discussion of hypertext structure has been muddled by the absence of a language or notation for describing structure. Indeed, the notion of document structure has often become entangled with rationalizations of specific hypertext system features or implementation schemes. We possess a flexible vocabulary for discussing hypertext *systems* [e.g., Halasz, 1990], but remarkably little has been written about the structure of individual hyperdocuments.

In this part of the chapter, we propose a simple schematic model which can capture and explain regular structures in a wide variety of hyperdocuments. We use the term *Hypermedia Design Model* (HDM) [Garzotto, 1990] to denote an abstract, conceptual language which can be used to describe structures which occur in a family of related hyperdocuments. Note that this goal differs from system models such as those described by [Halasz, 1990] and [Furuta, 1990]; we aim to describe the common structures inherent in hyperdocuments, not the shared properties of hypertext writing tools. Our Hypermedia Design Model provides linguistic primitives for specifying structural and semantic properties of a hypertext application or of a family of applications, without regard to specific implementation issues.

Our model is not tied to a specific hypertext system or to a specific topic, nor does it prescribe a correct or proper structure for hyperdocuments. Inevitably, the model describes some kinds of structures more readily than others, and these biases have been a source of considerable discussion and occasional debate in the hypertext community.

An effective, concise, and expressive design model should provide a language in which an author could describe the structure of a planned hyperdocument, or even a complete set of related hyperdocuments. Thus, the model could facilitate communication between authors and the myriad of experts, editors, assistants, and clients with whom authors must interact.

Our Hypermedia Design Model allows an author to describe the structure of a hyperdocument at an abstract, general level without having to specify each individual link. Without a modeling language, a writer cannot easily explain a planned hyperdocument to a client or manager until it is nearly complete.

Similarly, design models should permit editors to describe changes in a hyperdocument's organization in general, conceptual terms, and should help managers coordinate writing teams in a coherent and logical manner.

The existence of a model that captures the structure of a hyperdocument should facilitate later revisions. This is an especially crucial consideration in technical documentation, where frequent changes and improvements necessitate frequent revision. By providing a common language for discussion of hyperdocument structure, hypermedia design models facilitate comparison and criticism of hyperdocuments.

Design models can be used as design tools. Just as computer-based drafting systems can help engineers design and modify mechanical systems, computer-based modeling systems can help hypertext authors design and modify hyperdocuments.

A Hypermedia Design Model

Our *Hypermedia Design Model* (HDM) seeks to provide a language for describing the structural regularities which occur in individual hyperdocuments and in groups of related hyperdocuments. As in all engineering models, HDM describes complex structures as collections of smaller, simpler parts. In building a model we identify both the individual, atomic parts which the author combined to construct a hyperdocument network and the manner in which the larger structure is assembled.

Note that HDM describes only the *structure* of hyperdocuments; it is concerned only with authoring-in-the-large. Our model does not describe the appearance of the document. It says nothing about selection of typefaces, graphical overviews, the manner in which links are anchored, or indeed anything concerned with the

Table 13.1

ENTITY:	(VIVALDI'S "THE FOUR SEASONS")					
COMPONENTS:	SPRING			SUMMER ... (etc.)		
PERSPECTIVES:	DIGITAL RECORDING	MUSICAL SCORE	TEXTUAL COMMENTS	DIGITAL RECORDING	MUSICAL SCORE	TEXTUAL COMMENTS
	UNIT	UNIT	UNIT	UNIT	UNIT	UNIT

contents of individual nodes. Instead, it describes only the structural and semantic relationships among *groups* of nodes.

Components. Brief examination of almost any useful hyperdocument reveals that several different nodes may touch on the same topic. For example, we might find that one node contains a person's resume, another contains the same person's picture, and a third node contains his employment history. It is natural to consider each of these nodes a different facet of information about this person. In HDM, we say that each of these nodes represents a different *perspective* on the person. In this case, the collection of nodes or *units* that contain information about an individual is called a *component*. Each unit corresponds to a perspective on the component. In this way, we can capture local structures succinctly and precisely. For example, in describing a hypertextual commentary about a composer and his works, we might specify that "Each piece of music will be represented as a component containing a digital recording, a musical score, and a textual comment." (See Table 13.1.)

Entities and Entity Types. An *entity* is a set of components which, taken together, describe an object or concept. While an entity may occasionally include only a single component, most hyperdocuments will include entities with a rich but consistent internal hierarchical structure. Loosely, an entity is a *section* of a hyperdocument that describes a single topic. For example, an entity might contain all the information about a symphony, its components being its different movements.

Most hyperdocuments include sets of closely-related entities of the same *type*. For example, a historian planning a new hypertext textbook might define entity types including *King, Kingdom,* and *War,* while a maintenance manual might include entity types *Problem* and *Repair Procedure.* All entities of a given type share the same set of possible perspectives on the components and potentially, links to other classes of entities.

Because all entities of a single type share a single set of perspectives, they all share basic presentation qualities. We may require that all *Kings* have portraits and biographies, or that each *Symphony* have musical score and a digital recording.

Links and Link Types.   Just as the basic appearance of similar entities should be consistent, the links among the components that make up an entity should also be consistent. These *structural links* form the infrastructure of an entity. If the components of a *Repair Procedure* comprise individual steps to be performed in a fixed sequence, we might require that each step should be linked to the next step and the previous step. If the components of an *automobile* are assemblies of *parts*, we might require that parts be linked to adjacent parts (via adjacent-to links) or components parts (via is-part-of links). [See Chapter 20 by Parunak, in this book.]

We have specified that in HDM, the internal structure of an entity is always hierarchical because hierarchies are easily understood and used by hypertext authors and readers. We call entities whose components describe increasingly specific aspects of the concept represented by the entity *refinement hierarchies*.

Entities that have been broken up into chunks for rhetorical convenience, and not in order to capture an underlying conceptual structure, are artificial structures; we call them *continuation hierarchies*.

The second class of links in HDM are the *application links*. Whereas structural links mirror the inherent structure of an entity, application links reflect semantic relationships between structurally disjoint topics in the hyperdocument. An author deploys an application link, to give readers access to information whose relevance depends on insight into the topic area, rather than merely on the structure of an entity. Unlike structural links, the presence of application links is dependent on the contents of specific entities and components. For instance, all *Shakespearean Plays* may possess structural links to *Acts*, but only some possess application links to *Kings of England*.

HDM specifies that an Entity belongs to an Entity Type. Likewise, HDM defines an Application Link Type as a set of links whose source and target entities are of the same entity types, respectively. For example, an author may define a link type called "Author" to connect *Plays* to *persons*. Instances of type person, "Shakespeare," for example, would be connected to instances of type *Play*, e.g., "Hamlet," via a link of type *Author*.

Outlines.   Hypertext readers often appreciate being able to start browsing by using a pre-determined navigation pattern or tour through the hyperdocument. These tours are most useful when they are tailored to individual readers' backgrounds, preferences, and interests. Indeed, a key promise of hypertext is its ability to provide paths tailored to a wide variety of audiences.

HDM applies the term *outline* to portions of the hyperdocument which contain navigation information, guidance, or information maps and tours. Like other HDM entities, outlines possess a hierarchical internal structure. Unlike other entities, these hierarchies do not represent an object or a concept, but merely organize sets of links in the hyperdocument. Tables of Contents, indices, and Management Overviews are familiar kinds of outlines.

A set of entity and link types is called a *schema*. A schema characterizes a class of hyperdocuments for a given application domain. A particular hyperdocument is described using specific entities and links, which together constitute a schema instance.

From Conceptual To Concrete Links

Entities and components are *abstract* objects that HDM uses to represent conceptual objects. When an author creates a new hyperdocument while working from a schema, these abstract entities are implemented as nodes, or chunks of information that can actually be presented to the reader.

How should an author translate HDM's plan for linking entities and components into links that actually lead readers from source nodes to their targets? Naturally, one requirement is that concrete links be consistent with the schema. If the schema does not provide for links between apples and oranges, then the author must not insert a link to connect an *apple* unit and an *orange* unit. On the other hand, if the design calls for each *person* to be linked to a *biography*, then the author must link at least one unit of each *person* to some point in a *biography*.

Automatic construction tools, working from the abstract design, could assist authors to build repetitive structures and could check authors' work to ensure that the hyperdocument corresponds to the intended design. This approach can reduce the tedium of hypertext writing. [Jordan, 1989]

Examples of Hypertext Modeling

In this part of the chapter, we will present three examples that illustrate how our HDM can be used in the development of a hyperdocument. The first example describes an application that was developed starting with the HDM. The other two are well-known hyperdocuments whose structural foundations we identify using the model-based approach.

Expert Dictionary for Banking

In our first example, we design a hypertext containing management information required by a financial firm.[2] This firm manipulates *documents* according to *procedures*. *Laws* are issued by the state to discipline and control financial transactions. Laws are often general in nature, and must be made more specific by *regulations* issued by some authority on the basis of the text of the law. These regulations, in turn, are interpreted within individual organizations, each of which may have unique *informal norms* to ensure and monitor compliance.

This hypertext will do more than just list procedures for filling out loan applications, it will also explain why each disclaimer on the form is required, and whether certain disclosures are required by law, by accounting regulation, or are merely a matter of custom. In Figure 13.5, we show some initial entity types and application link types and how they relate to each other.

---

2 This example is a subset of a larger prototype application [Garzotto, 1989] developed by ARG SpA and Politecnico di Milano within the European ESPRIT projects INDOC and SUPERDOC.

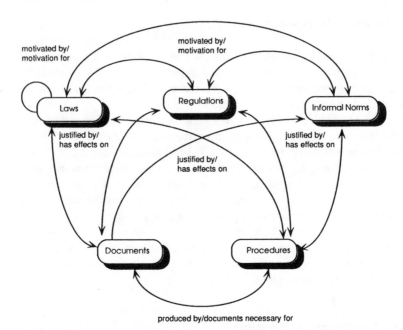

Figure 13.5   Schema of Entity Types and Application Link Types.

These abstract relationships may be clarified by examining a portion of the hypertext created using this design.

The *Mortgage Loan Procedure* entity located in the top right of Figure 13.6, like all *procedures*, contains a refinement hierarchy of steps which are to be followed. The first step is named "Preliminaries." Later we come to a step named "Acceptance," which in turn, is also made of several steps. All procedures share this internal structure, so frequent users (e.g., bank officers) will be able to follow both common and unusual procedures with ease.

A regulation titled "*Memorandum* 21/10/89" is another entity in the design. Two components of this regulation effect parts of the Mortgage Procedure, as indicated by application links. *Memorandum* 21/10/89, in turn, is linked (via a *motivated-by* application link) to "*Law* 19/8/89." Figure 13.6 also includes an outline which provides the reader with a list of all the documents needed for the compilation of a Mortgage Loan Request. (Darkly shaded areas in Figure 13.6 denote entities whose internal structure is detailed further in the figure; other entities shown, e.g., Law 19/8/89, are not elaborated further.) Once the model and design are derived, we may proceed to implement the hypertext.

In Figure 13.7 we see the schematic description of regulation Memorandum 21/10/89 that corresponds with its *Structure* perspective. At the bottom of the screen, we see a set of link anchors representing the structural links which are always anchored in the structural perspective of each *Regulation*.

All instances of Structure perspectives in a *Regulation* link to corresponding Description and Official Text nodes. When the reader clicks on a button that an-

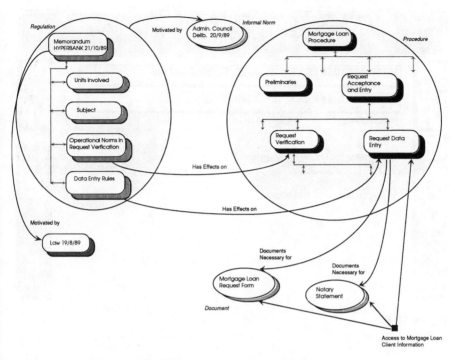

Figure 13.6 An implementation of the model in Figure 13.5.

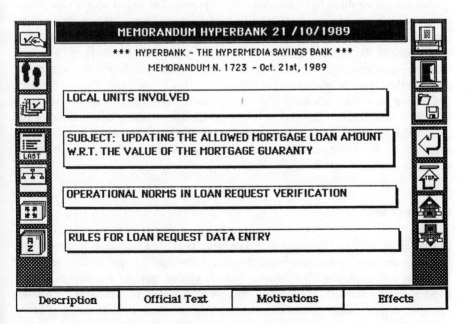

Figure 13.7 The Structure perspective of a Regulation.

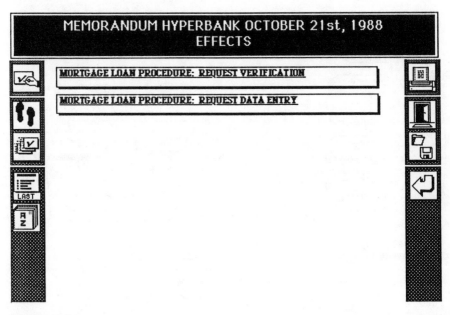

Figure 13.8

chors one of these links, the perspective it targets can be examined. Indeed, the system can create these links automatically whenever the author adds a new Regulation. Such automatic structure creation tools, termed "structure accelerators" by [Jordan, 1989], can simplify repetitive authoring tasks while increasing the internal consistency of the finished hypertext. The anchors labeled "Motivations" and "Effects" are application links. Since the semantics of these links are application-dependent, they must be placed by the author.

Clicking on the Effects button brings the reader to the screen shown in Figure 13.8. In it, the reader must choose which of the two possible destinations of the anchor Effects he/she wishes to examine. Note that, in particular, the node corresponding to this screen can be automatically generated by the system from the definition of the schema instance.

Election of 1912

The Election of 1912 [Bernstein and Sweeney, 1989] is a historical hypertext that examines the progressive movement that swept through U.S. politics in the period from 1896 through the First World War. A central goal in the design of this hyperdocument was the creation of a micro-world; a safe, protected, yet rich environment, where students could conduct historical research. A wide range of entity types and extensive linking gives readers a sense that the hypertext's information space is extremely large.

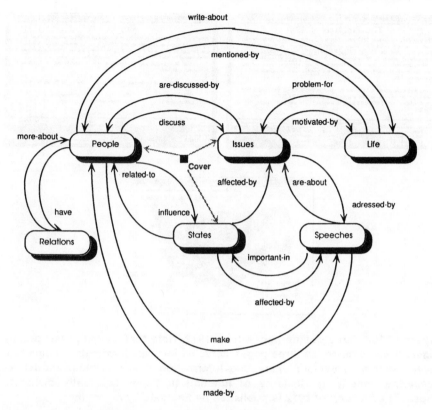

Figure 13.9   HDM Schema: *The Election of 1912.*

A secondary goal in developing *The Election of 1912* was to investigate the efficacy of a rich repertoire of navigation tools [Bernstein, 1988] for exploring a deeply-intertwingled hypertext in the absence of a simple, *a priori* structure.

The *1912* hypertext was developed without an explicit model, but a series of consistency reviews enforced an informal design scheme which can easily be captured in an HDM schema (see Figure 13.9). The bulk of *1912* is an assortment of *People, Issues,* and *State* entities. Each is a continuation hierarchy describing a specific topic relevant to the Progressive era. Characteristic types of application links interconnect these entities. *People,* for example, may be linked to *Issues* on which their positions were well known and to *States* in which they wielded political influence.

Outline pages provide a variety of interconnected access routes to diverse sections of the document. (See Figure 13.10) The cover page includes links to *front matter* (e.g., copyright notices or acknowledgments), and to a brief overview of the election (an outline in narrative form), and to additional outlines that describe inter-related sets of people, places, and issues.

Perhaps the most controversial aspect of *The Election of 1912* is its deliberate avoidance of hierarchical structure. In HDM terms, the *1912* hypertext uses nu-

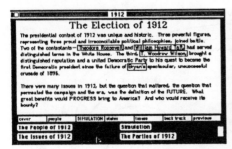

Figure 13.10   Three outline pages from *1912*. Note that, despite their greatly different appearance, all three pages serve as informal information maps that invite readers to explore interesting information. The schematic model reveals the underlying similarity of function in these apparently disparate pages. The *Election of 1912* is published by Eastgate Systems, Inc.

merous application links within and between individual entities to encourage readers to follow topics of immediate interest instead of promoting systematic, passive *tree-traversal* approaches to reading. The hypertext author's decision whether or not to make the structure of a hyperdocument explicit is an aesthetic one. To further encourage readers to explore freely, creatively, and spontaneously, the *1912* hypertext does not distinguish between structural and application links.

The Election of 1912 includes an interactive election simulation. This simulation relies on a complex set of partial differential equations and finite state machines to simulate the dynamics of the last phase of the 1912 presidential campaign. Reader actions serve as temporal inputs to the simulation and are reflected in simulated outcomes.

A substantial portion of the cost of developing the *1912* hypertext was spent on checking and editing the hypertext's large and complex web. Proofreading and testing provide a key role for schematic models in hypertext publishing. Because the *1912* hypertext depends extensively on application links, these links raise complex and subtle rhetorical issues. The *1912* hypertext incorporates a wide variety of outline pages. Therefore, the links between outlines and topics shape the readers' experience. Much testing was devoted to ensuring link consistency (e.g., that *People* only be linked indirectly to Issues via *Speeches*). Availability of model-based development tools might have prevented errors (fortunately not numerous) which escaped the publisher's attention [Margolis, 1989].

In the final example in this chapter, we will examine a moderately large hypertext implemented using HyperCard [Atkinson, 1987] according to the schematic design we have just discussed. Note that the model explicitly specifies structural regularities that organize the hypertext, yet leaves the author abundant opportunity to provide application links as opportunities arise.

Companion to Beethoven's Ninth Symphony

Companion to Beethoven's Ninth Symphony [Winter, 1989] is a CD-ROM and HyperCard-based listening guide to Beethoven's Ninth Symphony. The hypertext contains approximately six hundred nodes and includes social and cultural historical notes about Beethoven's time and life, interpretations of Beethoven's work, analysis of the symphony, and an introduction to general musical concepts. Many nodes are linked to musical illustrations drawn from an orchestral performance of Beethoven's Ninth symphony and passages from the complete performance are linked to textual explication.

In Figure 13.11, we present a schematic model of this hypertext. This model was *not* used in the design process; instead, it reflects a reader's interpretation of the implicit structure which underlies the document.

Historical/musical note entities describe the social and cultural history of Beethoven's time and life, interpret his Ninth symphony, and provide musical commentary on the work. This information may be seen from two perspectives: *Text* and *Music*. For stylistic reasons, *Note* entities are built as continuation hierarchies.

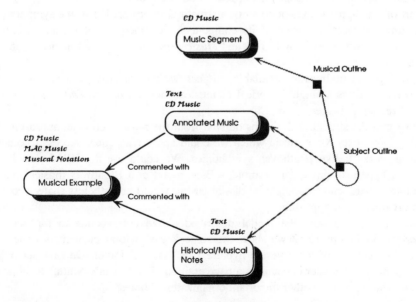

Figure 13.11   A schematic model of *Companion to Beethoven's Ninth Symphony* [Voyager, 1990].

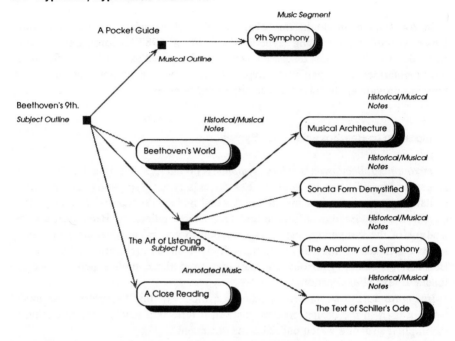

Figure 13.12   Structural elements from the _Companion_.

Instances of a musical example entity type, which can occur in music, Mac music, and musical notation perspectives, use musical terminology and notation to elaborate on relevant concepts that appear in other entities.

Part of this hyperdocument contains a structural interpretation of the symphony, analyzing the work in terms of its component movements, themes, and motifs. _Annotated music nodes_ include _Text_ and _Music_ perspectives and refinement hierarchies.

Two types of outlines are available. _Subject Outlines_ offer sequences of topical _Notes_ that address a single historical or musical theme. _Musical Outlines_ contain lists of related passages.

Note that the structural decisions derived from the model define an approach to writing hypertexts about music which we could apply with equal success to other musical works unlike Beethoven symphonies. We could use the HDM model to design a hypertext about, for example, a Bach motet or a Broadway musical. The resulting hyperdocuments might be dissimilar but would nevertheless share a common organizational approach.

Let us examine how the model described above corresponds to the actual hypertext. In Figure 13.12 we show the some key structural elements—some of the outline entities which give the hypertext its essential flavor. On first opening the hypertext, the reader encounters a page entitled "Beethoven's Ninth," a subject outline which points to other important organizational notes:

- A musical outline entitled "A Pocket Guide"
- A historical note entity entitled "Beethoven's World"

- A subject outline entitled "The Art of Listening"
- An annotated music entity entitled "A Close Reading"

Note that no instances of a musical example appear in the figure. Entities in the musical example are to be taken as comments about many different kinds of entities but they are *not* full-fledged entities. In other words, we can jump directly to a variety of textual discussions, some of which may include structural links to musical examples, but we will never link *directly* to a musical example belonging to another entity. An interesting observation can be made about the *Companion to Beethoven's Ninth Symphony*: all of the navigation paths available are basically over *structural* links.

Naturally, this design is most appropriate to hypertexts which are intended for use by readers who are comparatively unsophisticated in musical matters. If the hypertext were intended for use by symphonic conductors, a different model might be more appropriate. For example, application links to other pieces of music, or to other composers or performers, could also be included.

Let us look now at the internal structure of the entity "Beethoven's World," a typical example of a *historical Note* entity (See Figure 13.13). Each historical note

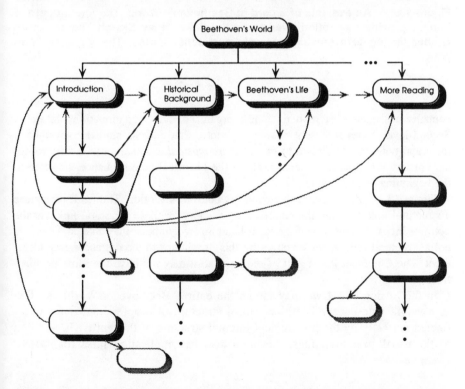

Figure 13.13 The structure of Beethoven's World. Each chapter is represented as a "column," whose top node is the chapter's title. Some (but not all) of the induced structural links are represented in gray. The gray nodes stand for instances of "musical example," which are to be regarded as "commentaries" to the text.

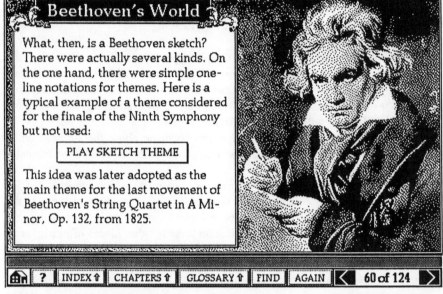

Beethoven's World

What, then, is a Beethoven sketch? There were actually several kinds. On the one hand, there were simple one-line notations for themes. Here is a typical example of a theme considered for the finale of the Ninth Symphony but not used:

PLAY SKETCH THEME

This idea was later adopted as the main theme for the last movement of Beethoven's String Quartet in A Minor, Op. 132, from 1825.

⌂ | ? | INDEX ⇧ | CHAPTERS ⇧ | GLOSSARY ⇧ | FIND | AGAIN | ◀ 60 of 124 ▶

Figure 13.14   An example of a card in Beethoven's World. The anchors at the bottom provide navigation over structural links; "Play Sketch Theme" is an anchor linking to a musical example comment. Source: The Voyager Company.[3]

contains a sequence of textual chunks organized into a continuation hierarchy. Second-level nodes represent chapters of notes that address similar topics. Each historical note may be linked to one or more *musical example* entities. The reader may at any point go to the next node in the historical note sequence, or jump to the beginning of any chapter.

Figure 13.14 shows a typical card of "Beethoven's World." The reader traverses a structural link by using the buttons (i.e., anchors for these structural links) at the bottom: Index, Chapters, and the right-hand arrow symbols. Play Sketch Theme is not a structural link. A reader choosing this link jumps to the corresponding Comment. The Comment is not part of the note, so it may not have the same perspective.

In fact, using HDM we may model the entire "Beethoven's World" section as a single note entity. The hierarchical structure of chapters and notes is reflected perfectly by the hierarchical internal structure of this entity. In addition to the usual structural links, this note also has application links to *Musical Example*.

---

3   The Voyager Company, 1351 Pacific Coast Highway, Santa Monica, CA 90401.

Conclusion

Composing individual hypertext pages is a familiar task, one which is closely akin to most other forms of writing, while designing the overall hypertext structure—authoring in the large—is a new and challenging task. *Prescriptive approaches* address the design problem by adopting preferred topological patterns (i.e., networks, trees, other recursive structures) as the basic building blocks from which all hypertexts should be built.

Constructive approaches, on the other hand, do not prescribe a special, desirable structure. Instead, they seek to help authors visualize, identify, and make explicit the structures that underlie apparently unstructured hypertext documents. They also provide tools to simplify the tedious task of creating repetitive structures.

Inductive approaches seek to discover new or implicit hypertext structure by analyzing regularities in linear text or hypertext. Constructive and inductive approaches draw general conclusions from specific features.

Model-based approaches, on the other hand, provide a vocabulary of concepts and primitives which can be used to describe hypertext structures *before the hypertext is written* and to compare alternative designs for the same document. We believe that systematic and rational structural decisions can and should be made before the hypertext is written, and that coherent and expressive hypertext webs should be designed-in, not added on, and that our HDM is a good way to design hypertexts before they are implemented.

About the Authors

Franca Garzotto

Franca Garzotto graduated with a degree in Mathematics from the University of Padova (Italy). She received her Ph.D. in Computer Science from Politecnico di Milano. She is currently Senior Researcher at the Department of Electronics of Politecnico di Milano.

In the past five years her main research activities have been: specification and management of database integrity constraints, semantic modelling of legal documents, automatic generation of documents, hypertext modeling, hypertext authoring tools, integration of hypertexts and knowledge base systems.

Within the European ESPRIT projects "INDOC" and "SUPERDOC" she has been involved in the design of knowledge based system for automatic generation of administrative and legal documents, and of a large hybrid knowledge based/hypertext-based system for banking environments.

Dr. Garzotto is currently involved in the design of advanced authoring tools for large hypertext applications within the European Commission ESPRIT project HYTEA ("HYperTExt Authoring"). She can be contacted at the Department of Electronics, Politecnico di Milano, Piazza Leonardo da Vinci, 32, 20133 Milano, Italy.

Paolo Paolini

Paolo Paolini graduated with a degree in Physics from the University of Milano. He received Master and Ph.D. degrees in Computer Science from UCLA. He is currently Associate Professor at the Department of Electronics of the Politecnico di Milano.

He is also President of A.R.G.—Applied Research Group, the company that launched the European Commission ESPRIT project HYTEA. In this position he oversees a number of Italian and European projects in the office automation, database, and hypertext areas.

Dr. Paolini has published several research papers mainly in the area of databases. In this field he has been working on modeling for databases, abstract data types and databases, formal definition of views. His main current interests are office automation (in particular, semantic modeling of documents and automatic generation of documents), hypertext, and multimedia applications. He can be contacted at A.R.G.—Applied Research Group, Via Pio La Torre 14, Vimodrone (Milano), Italy.

Daniel Schwabe

Dr. Daniel Schwabe received his B.S. in Mathematics from the Pontifical Catholic University of Rio de Janeiro (PUC-RJ) in 1975, and his M.S. in Informatics in 1976, from the same institution. He received his Ph.D. in Computer Science from UCLA in 1981. He has been on the faculty of the Departmento de Informática at PUC-RJ since 1981, where he currently is associate professor.

Dr. Schwabe has been involved in the past seven years in the design and development of knowledge-based systems, including one containing Brazilian legislation about social security benefits; another allowing access to a large complex statistical data base; and many others in areas such as medical diagnosis and software engineering.

More recently, he has been investigating the integration of such systems with hypertext-based systems, having developed a prototype system containing engineering norms for pipe construction for nuclear facilities which exhibits characteristics of both knowledge-based and hypertext-based systems. He can be contacted at the Departamento de Informática, Pontifícia Universidade Católica—RJ, R. Marques de S. Vincente, 225/4º and., prédio RDC, Gávea, Rio de Janeiro, RJ 22453, Brasil. E:mail (pucrjdi@brfapesp.bitnet)

Mark Bernstein

Mark Bernstein is chief scientist at Eastgate Systems, Inc., a firm specializing in hypertext research since 1982. He led the team that developed the Hypergate hypertext system, and in addition to his conventioanl publications has written critically-acclaimed hypertexts, including *The Election of 1912* and *The Flag Was Still There* (with Erin Sweeney). Current research interests range from machine learning and automatic link discovery to historical simulation and crisis management. He was chairman of the AAAI-88 workshop on AI and Hypertext, and has taught numerous courses on The Craft of Hypertext. Eastgate Systems publishes Hypergate, a hypertext environment designed for technical documentation, and Storyspace a hypertext environment for writers. The Eastgate Press is the leading publisher of serious hypertexts; recent releases include *Afternoon* by Michael Joyce and Sarah Smith's *King of Space*.

Berstein, a graduate of Swarthmore College, received his doctorate from Harvard in 1983. Dr. Bernstein may be reached at Eastgate Systems, Inc., P.O. Box 1307, Cambridge, MA 02238.

References

ARG, (1990). "HYTEA Technical Annex", Esprit Project P5252, June 1990.

Akscyn, R., McCracken, D., Yoder, E. (1987). "KMS: A Distributed Hypermedia System for Managing Knowledge in Organizations", *Proc. Hypertext '87, ACM*, Baltimore, MD, pp. 1-20.

Atkinson, W. (1987). *HyperCard*, software for Macintosh computers, Apple Computer Co, Cupertino, CA.

Bernstein, M. (1988). "The Bookmark and the Compass: Orientation Tools for Hypertext Users," *SIGOIS Bulletin 9*, pp. 34-45

Bernstein M. and Sweeney, E. (1989). *The Election of 1912*, hypertext for Macintosh computers, Eastgate Systems Inc, Watertown, MA.

Bernstein, M. (1991). "The Navigation Problem Reconsidered," *Hypertext/Hypermedia Handbook*, Emily Berk and Joseph Devlin, (Eds.) McGraw-Hill, New York, NY.

Bernstein, M. (1990). "An apprentice that discovers hypertext links", *Hypertexts: Concepts, systems and applications*, A. Rizk et al., (Eds.) Cambridge University Press, Cambridge, MA.

Bolter, J.D., Joyce, M. (1987). "Hypertext and Creative Writing," *Proc. Hypertext '87, ACM*, Baltimore, MD, pp.41-50.

Bolter, J.D. (1990). *Writing Space: The Computer, Hypertext, and the History of Writing*, Lawrence Erlbaum and Associates, San Mateo, CA.

Brown, P. J. (1987). "Turning Ideas Into Products: The Guide System", *Proc. Hypertext '87, ACM*, Baltimore, MD, 33-40.

Clitherow, P., Riecken, D., Muller, M. (1989). "VISAR: A system for inference and navigation of hypertext", *Proc. Hypertext '89, ACM*, Baltimore, MD, 293-305.

Conklin, J., Begeman, M. L. (1988). "gIBIS: A Hypertext Tool for Exploratory Policy Discussion", *ACM Trans. Office Information Systems 6*, 303-331.

Coombs, Renear, DeRose, S. (1987). "Types of markup and the future of scholarly text processing", *Communications of the ASCM 11*.

Crane, G. (1987). "From the old to the new: Integrating hypertext into traditional scholarship," *Proc. Hypertext '87, ACM*, Baltimore, MD.

Crane, G. (1990). "Standards for a Hypermedia Database: Diacronic v.s. Syncronic Concerns," *Proc. 1st Hypertext Standardization NIST Workshop*, Gaithersburg, MD.

diSessa, A., Abelson, H. (1986). "Boxer: A Reconstructible Computational Medium", *Communications of the ACM 29.*

Engelbart, D. (1963). "A Conceptual Framework for the Augmentation of Man's Intellect," *Computer-Supported Cooperative Work: A Book of Readings,* Irene Greif, (Ed.) Morgan Kaufmann Publishers Inc., San Mateo, CA, 35-66.

Engelbart, D., English, W. (1968). "A Research Center for Augmenting Human Intellect," *Computer-Supported Cooperative Work: A Book of Readings,* Irene Greif, (Ed.) Morgan Kaufmann Publishers Inc., San Mateo, CA, 81-106.

Fairchild, K.M., Poltrock, S.E., Furnas, G.W. (1988). "SemNet: Three-dimensional graphic representations of large knowledge bases", *Cognitive Science and its Apllications for Human-Computer Interaction,* R. Guindon, (Ed.) Lawrence Erlbaum.

Furuta, R., Stotts, D. (1990). "The Trellis Reference Model," *Proc. 1st Hypertext Standardization NIST Workshop,* Gaithersburg, MD.

Garzotto, F., Paolini, P. (1989). "Expert Dictionaries: Knowledge Based Tools for Explanation and Maintenance of Complex Application Environments," *Proc. 2nd ACM Int. Conf. on Industrial and Engineering Applications of Artificial Intelligence and Expert Systems,* Tullahoma , TN.

Garzotto, F., Paolini, P. (1990). "The HDM data model for hypertext applications: an informal introduction", *Tech. Report., Dept. of Electronics,* Politecnico di Milano.

Gay, G., and Mazur, J. (1991). "Navigating in Hypermedia," *Hypertext / Hypermedia Handbook,* Emily Berk and Joseph Devlin, (Ed.s) McGraw-Hill, New York, NY.

Glushko, R. (1989). "Design issues for multi-document hypertexts," *Proc. Hypertext '89, ACM,* Baltimore, MD, 51-60.

Goldberg, A., Robson, D. (1983). *Smalltalk-80: The Language and its Implementation,* Addison-Wesley, Reading, MA.

Halasz, F. (1987). "Reflections on NoteCards: Seven Issues for the Next Generation of Hypermedia Systems," *Proc. Hypertext '87, ACM,* Baltimore, MD, 345-66.

Halasz, F., Moran, T.P., Trigg, R.H. (1987a). "NoteCards in a Nutshell", *Proc. ACM CHI+GI 87* (Toronto, 5-9 April 1987) 45-52.

Halasz, F., Schwartz, M. (1990). "The Dexter Refernce Model," *Proc. 1st Hypertext Standardization. NIST Workshop,* Gaithersburg, MD.

Hartson H., Hix, D. (1989). "Human-Computer Interface Development: Concepts and Systems for Its Management," *ACM Computing Surverys 21.*

Hayes, P. J., Knecht, L.E., Cellio, M.J., (1988). "A News Story Categorization System", *Proc. 2nd Conf. on Applied Natural Language Processing,* Austin, TX, 9-17.

Jordan, D., Russel, D. (1989). "Facilitating the Development of Representations in Hypertext with IDE", *Proc. Hypertext '89, ACM,* Baltimore, MD.

Kapor, M. et al. (1990). "Agenda," *Communications of the ACM 33.*

Landow, G. P. (1987). "Relationally Encoded Links and the Rhetoric of Hypertext," *Proc. Hypertext '87, ACM,* Baltimore, MD, 331-44.

Lenat, D. B., Guha, R. V. (1990). *Building Large Knowledge-Based Systems: Representation and Inference in the CYC Project,* Addison-Wesley, Reading, MA.

Malone, T. W., Grant, K. R., Lai, K. Y., Rao, R., Rosenblitt, D. (1988). "Semistructured Messages are Surprisingly Useful", *Computer-Supported Cooperative Work: A Book of Readings,* Irene Greif, (Ed.) Morgan Kaufmann Publishers Inc., San Mateo, CA, 311-34.

Margolis, M. (1989). Review of "The Election of 1912", *Social Science Computer Review 7,* 231-3.

Marshall, C.C., Irish, P.M. (1989). "Guided Tours and On-line Presentations: How Authors Make Existing Hypertext Intelligible for Readers," *Proc. Hypertext '89, ACM,* Baltimore, MD.

Nelson, T.H. (1976). *Computer Lib/Dream Machines*, reprinted (1987) by Microsoft Press, Redmond, WA.

Nelson, T. H. (1981). *Literary Machines*, privately published.

Nielsen, J. (1990). "The Art of Navigating Through Hypertext," *Communications of the ACM 33.*

Parunak, H. V. D. (1989). "Hypermedia Topologies and User Navigation," *Proc. Hypertext '87, ACM,* Baltimore, MD, 43–50.

Parunak, H. V. D. (1991). "Ordering the Information Graph," *Hypertext / Hypermedia Handbook,* Emily Berk and Joseph Devlin, (Ed.s) McGraw-Hill, New York, NY.

Shneiderman, B. (Ed.) (1988). *Hypertext on Hypertext*, Database & Electronic Product Series, ACM Press.

Travers, M. (1989). "A Visual Representation for Knowledge Structures", *Proc. Hypertext '89, ACM,* Baltimore, MD, 147–58.

Utting K., Yankelovich, N. (1990). "Context and Orientation in Hypermedia Networks," *ACM Trans. on Information Systems, 7,* 58–84.

Walker, J. H. (1988). "Supporting document development with Concordia," *IEEE Computer 21,* 48–59.

Walker, J. H., and Young, E. (1990). "A Case Study of Using a Manual Online," *Machine-Mediated Learning,* February.

Winograd, T. (1988). "A Language/Action Perspective on the Design of Cooperative Work," *Computer-Supported Cooperative Work: A Book of Readings,* Irene Greif, (Ed.) Morgan Kaufmann Publishers Inc., San Mateo, CA, 623–656.

Winter R. (1989). *Companion to Beethoven's Ninth Symphony*, CD Companions Series, The Voyager Company, Santa Monica, CA.

Yankelovich, N., Haan, B.J., Meyrowitz, N. K., Drucker, S.M. (1988). "Intermedia: The concept and construction of a seamless information environment," *IEEE Computer 21,* 91–96.

14

Tools for Authoring Hypertexts

By Ernest Perez
Texas Woman's University

Tools for Authoring Hypertexts

"The value of information lies in how it is organized." [Larson, 1990]

"Give us the tools and we will finish the job." Winston Churchill, Radio Broadcast, 9 Feb. 1941, Addressing Pres. Roosevelt.

The Need For Authoring Tools

Since Vannevar Bush's first intimations of hypertext, subjective *associative linking* has been central to its definition. The idea of intuitive, unstructured access to information is beguiling. Readers should experience hypertext browsing as this kind of free-and-easy experience. However, hypertext authors cannot afford to take an overly intuitive approach to constructing hyperdocuments; they need powerful tools to aid in translating *flat* texts into hypertexts that respond to readers' needs.

This chapter explains why certain tools are helpful in constructing large hypertexts efficiently, provides examples of existing tools and describes useful features to look for. Finally, it provides a master plan for developing hyperdocuments in a structured environment in which a group of individuals all work on a single hyperproject.

Text Editors and Word Processors

Much of a hypertext author's time is spent writing and formatting text, not actually linking nodes. Therefore, your choice of text editor will affect the efficiency with which you work. A good text editor performs many functions: text composition, text formatting, spell checking, style checking, search and replace, justification, and column formatting.

All of these functions and many more provided by good word processors are crucial to the hypertext authoring process. Most hypertext authoring systems provide text editing functionality either by including a built-in word processor, by accepting ASCII text generated using a stand-alone word processor, or by accepting certain types of word-processor-formatted text.

In most cases the text editors built into hypertext authoring systems are not nearly as powerful or flexible as dedicated text editors or word processors. Most users of desktop publishing software use their powerful regular word processors and editors to generate most of the text and to make all major editorial revisions. They use the text editor built into the desktop publishing package only at the last editing stage to perform minor touch ups and formatting. Similarly, hypertext authors may elect to do original text composition, major editorial work, and spell- or style-checking within their standard word processing environment. Hypertext authors should steer clear of any hypertext development system that does not provide the editing features they need unless it provides an easy and reliable way of importing the text generated by the full-featured word processor of their choice.

Import Capabilities

If you expect to spend a great deal of time generating hypertexts, consider using a sophisticated external word processor that can embed hypertext instructions for you. For example, Flambeaux Inc.'s xText system package is unique because it contains drivers to convert files from Microsoft Word and WordPerfect. These drivers do not simply import text (any good word processor can do this); they can be set up to translate standard font modes like "underline" and "doublestrike" into link delimiters, color highlights, etc. that the hypertext engine understands. The Flambeaux product comes with a simple guide for adapting print drivers from other editors or word processors. (I was able to build one for my own ASCII editor in about 5 minutes.)

Many of the more advanced word processors include macro languages that allow you to write short programs to perform this sort of translation. But writing macros is harder than using pre-existing translation routines of the type offered by programs such as xText.

Shelling

Nothing is more frustrating than being forced to exit the hypertext development engine in order to boot the word processor needed to make minor edits to a hypertext screen. Of course, those developing under multitasking environments such as Microsoft Windows or the Macintosh Finder or a multiuser operating system such as UNIX don't have this problem. Multi-tasking environments allow you to run both the hypertext development system and your text editor at the same time, which makes quick edits easy.

Many MS-DOS-based hypertext development systems also provide this sort of multitasking capability in the form of a shell function. For example, MaxThink's HyPlus run-time hypertext programs allow an author to specify an ASCII editor or word processor that can be called while the hypertext program is running. There is also a version of HyPlus that works directly with WordPerfect Office files.

Conversion and Importing of Text

ASCII code is the Esperanto, the universal language, of modern electronic information tools. By sticking to ASCII, contributions culled from many authors working on a wide variety of platforms can be brought easily into virtually any hypertext. Cross loading and downloading of data and remote file transfer are all easy to accomplish at the ASCII level.

Standard word processing format translation utilities may be useful when multiple document formats must be imported into the hypertext database. For example, the "Brooklyn Bridge" utility is a popular DOS-based application that translates documents formatted for one word processor into another word processor format which the hypertext development system recognizes. This kind of approach can induce errors that would not occur when working in plain ASCII, but preserves typographical details such as fonts and type sizes, centering, tab columns, etc., that would be lost in straight ASCII files.

Graphic Editing Tools

The same sorts of choices must be made in selecting a graphics tool as in selecting a text editor or word processor. Some hypertext authoring programs come with built-in graphics editors, but in most cases these are anemic tools not suitable for intensive development. It's far better to purchase one of the excellent external graphics tools on the market in order to generate the images you need. Most hypertext development systems do provide facilities for displaying images in standard graphic formats such as PC-Paintbrush, Dr. Halo, etc. Alternatively, some hypertext products can capture graphic images into their own proprietary formats (e.g., HyperWriter, GUIDE).

When selecting a graphics tool, be certain that it can produce and save images in formats that your hypertext development tool can understand. Alternately you can purchase a translation program to convert between various graphics formats. As with word processors, it is very helpful when the hypertext development system allows the author to hot link or toggle into the graphic editor environment directly from the authoring system. This allows efficient last-minute touchups to be generated with minimal effort.

Effective Screen Formatting

Good authoring systems should include sufficient display-formatting horsepower to get the job done. They should be able to format and display margins, columns, justification, and any other text or graphics characteristics required by the hyperdocument. The ability to support multiple on-screen fonts, simple graphics, colors, and so on, is also very important for authors when they are designing screens.

Mode Switching

Hypertext programs can usually run in two modes: an authoring mode and a reading mode. In the reading or browsing mode, functions such as link creation and link deletion are usually disabled.

Authors must occasionally go into reading mode in order to evaluate the final appearance of a hyperdocument and to preview readers' runtime interaction with the document. Therefore, the authoring system should allow for easy switching between authoring and browsing modes. Two systems that make the transition between these models very easy are HyperWriter and Maxthink. NTERGAID's HyperWriter switches from authoring to browsing mode with a simple keystroke toggle. MaxThink's runtime browser has the ability to call an author-defined editor, effectively providing this ability.

Hypertext-Specific Tools

Certain tools are specific to, and required for, efficient hypertext authoring. Such tools focus on the act of putting nodes together, not on creating content. Some of these tools come built into hypertext authoring systems. These typically include those used to generate lists of links and/or nodes, and tools for managing screen design. Other tools are more likely to be offered as add-ins to the main hypertext generation engine. These include outliners and tools for "chunking" (splitting up), converting, and importing source text files.

Built-in Functions for Node and Link Listing

Every hypertext authoring system should be able to generate a list of all the nodes that make up any given hyperdocument and/or lists of links that connect those nodes. A good node list aids the author in determining where and when to place jumps. Node listings provide a mechanism for checking node content and the accuracy of node links. The best such programs can also list descriptive material such as short titles, descriptive phrases stored by the author with the nodes, or text lifted from the first line of the node in the list itself.

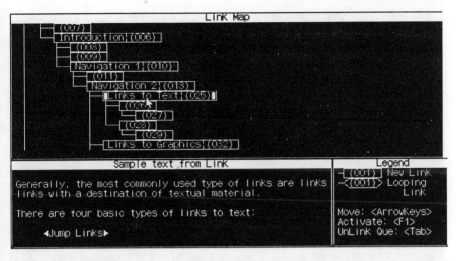

Figure 14.1 Display of a node link map and selected node text on a HyperWriter link map screen. The top window shows a graphic outline of link connections within a hypertext database. Nodes are numbered by default, but can be named. The bottom left window shows beginning text of the currently selected node. The bottom right window gives brief instructions. Nodes may be called directly by selecting and pressing RETURN or the mouse button.

Both the link and node lists may be organized as a single document. If links are stored externally (outside the node), separate link and node lists are more likely to be provided. (See Figure 14.1)

Built-in Functions to Provide Node Information

The authoring system should also allow easy production of lists of specific node names, content descriptions, and link or index terms. The author can use this information during system design summaries. This is a valuable reference during editing and linking. Examples of this kind of functionality include:

MaxThink's FS (File Splitter) utility, which produces a text file list of author-created node content notes, as a byproduct of chunking a document into separate ASCII file nodes.

The Hyperties system, which includes a function for storing short descriptive titles within each node. (See Figure 14.2.)

OWL's GUIDE for the PC relies on the Microsoft Windows directory file display for help in storing and displaying descriptive information about files. (This is not a GUIDE-specific ability; it is an operating system capability.)

NTERGAID's HyperWriter provides a graphic network display of linked nodes. These are numbered by default, but can be named easily. A window on the map display screen additionally shows the first few lines of the cursor-selected screen.

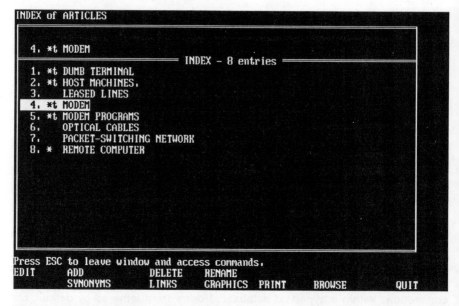

Figure 14.2 A Hyperties "RESOLUTION" screen, presented for inspection of node status or after saving a new node. The characters preceding node names indicate current completion status. "*" (asterisk) means a short optional preview description has been entered; "t" means the text of the node has been entered. The RESOLUTION screen lets the author check that newly linked nodes actually exist, as well as what node elements are present.

The HyperWriter editor can directly call up the selected file from this hierarchical display.

Built-in Tools for Annotating Nodes

It is helpful for the hypertext authoring system to allow authors to attach descriptive notes to nodes. Authoring systems can support note information on nodes in two ways:

- By automatically maintaining lists of node names, version numbers, data about when/what changed in a node, etc.
- By providing authors with the ability to make notes about a node.

Author Notes Mode.   It is often a great help for authors to be able to add internal editorial comments and status notes, which will not be displayed when readers use the browser. A tool which opens up a "notes mode" for the author helps in this respect. For example, an author might want to mark a node: "For access by readers with clearance level xxx" or "Links out of this node have not yet been established."

Tools For Outlining

One of the best strategies for developing a hyperdocument is to begin with a detailed outline. In creating such an outline, the author maps the coverage and develops a logical structure for the hyperdocument. A good outliner provides both general and detailed views on the data, encourages clear system definitions, and allows quick, efficient revision.

Several good standalone outlining tools are available to hypertext authors. These include popular programs such as Grandview, PC-Outline and ThinkTank. The MaxThink Outliner is a module of MaxThink, Inc.'s hypertext authoring system, and has also received good reviews as a quality general outliner.

The problem with many of the popular outlining systems is that they were designed with a linear presentation in mind and as such are restricted to parent-child relationships. Another kind of outliner (called a matrix or multidimensional outliner) is better suited to hypertext development.

Matrix outliners support linking of any outline topic (or node) to any other topic (or node) in the global outline structure. Matrix outlining programs automate the building of complex hypertext network hierarchical webs, and provide multiple access paths to topics. MaxThink's HOUDINI software is one example of an outliner in this genre [MaxThink, 1987]. It provides a valuable tool for laying out a nonlinear hypertext outline because it textually depicts network relationships.

HOUDINI is ASCII-based; it can produce clear (albeit bulky) text-based hard copy printouts of network relationships. The various display and output formats can include text summaries (with clear node descriptions) unlike the abbreviated output of the usual hypertext graphic browser node maps. HOUDINI can include longer textual commentary; it can also directly make hypertext link jumps from within the matrix outliner to display the contents of mapped nodes.

HOUDINI is unusual in combining network organizing ability with textual information inspection. This MS-DOS based software module is not tied to the Max-Think authoring system; it can also be used as a general hypertext network organizing tool. (See Figure 14.3.)

Chunking

One of the basic tenets of good hypertext development is that text should be chunked into short nodes that don't take up more than a screen or two. Large text files can be broken up into smaller nodes manually with excellent results, but this manual approach is time-consuming. If the volume of material you are importing is large, you can purchase a batch file splitter to automate the act of splitting or chunking source text files into smaller nodes or separate files.

Some file splitters can divide documents up automatically using chapter headings, outline numbering schemes or other embedded typographic or structural elements to provide the cues to where breaks can logically be made. [See Chapter 9 by Riner, in this book.]

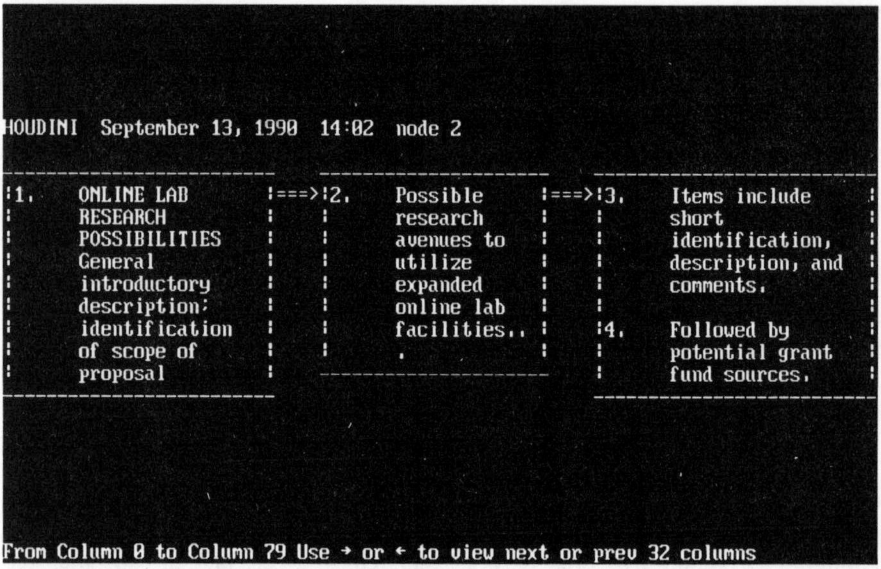

```
HOUDINI  September 13, 1990   14:02  node 2
------------------------------------------------------------------------------
:1.   ONLINE LAB      :===>:2.   Possible     :===>:3.   Items include    :
:     RESEARCH        :    :     research     :    :     short            :
:     POSSIBILITIES   :    :     avenues to   :    :     identification,  :
:     General         :    :     utilize      :    :     description, and :
:     introductory    :    :     expanded     :    :     comments.        :
:     description;    :    :     online lab   :    :                      :
:     identification  :    :     facilities.. :    :4.   Followed by      :
:     of scope of     :    :       ,          :    :     potential grant  :
:     proposal        :    --------------------    :     fund sources.    :
------------------------                           --------------------------



From Column 0 to Column 79 Use → or ← to view next or prev 32 columns
```

Figure 14.3 A HOUDINI link mapping output screen; this is normally a printed report. It shows input and output for Node 2 of a matrix outline. The left side item is an input link; right side items are output links. The notes illustrate how node contents might be abstracted, for interpretation or for author instruction notes.

Other file splitters rely on manually inserted or flagged breakpoints to divide text files into nodes. MaxThink's FS (File Splitter) utility is of this genre. It can be used to break flagged ASCII files up into multiple files and automatically produces a report that lists new file names and (author-embedded) file content descriptions. Flambeaux's xText is another system that performs batch compilation of hypertext systems from manually flagged ASCII source files.

String-scanning Utility. For editing efficiency, one must be able to search for and locate specified terms or phrases within the text in nodes. It is helpful to produce direct links to the node location for easy reference and display. Linked worklists of node locations of specified terms or phrases ("Where does 'xyz' occur in my node universe?") can be used for batch candidate node inspection during linking.

MaxThink's MP (Match Phrase) utility produces a linked node list, pointing to occurrences of a word or phrase. The MaxThink outliner also includes a command which displays an inverted index word list of all words in an outline. All displayed terms are also hypertext links. This allows the author to instantly jump to the pertinent part of an outline.

Link Checking and Editing Utilities.   Whereas authors can get outside help for editing of textual and graphic nodes, tools that aid in verification and updating of links are harder to find.

- Link Trail. It is useful to have utilities which scan the hypertext information base and produce hardcopy records of links to and from all nodes. (MaxThink's REFALL and other utilities produce this information.) This link trail report displays or outlines link network connections that aid in editorial analysis and checkup. Such a record is used for analysis of the hypertext node distribution and linked node clusters, i.e., these utilities can help authors identify where linking is weak, overlinked, etc. The link trail should be text-based, and provide more detail than the intricate (and sketchy) graphical browser displays. (See Figure 14.4.)
- Blind reference detector. Another useful information control tool is a function or utility to produce lists of dangling or blind references (links that point to nonexistent nodes). Blind references are usually caused by misspelled node names,

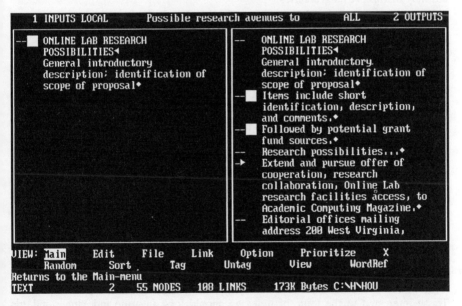

Figure 14.4   A HOUDINI "View" screen showing simultaneous window display of input and output links. The currently active node is (truncated) at the center top of the windows (Reads "Possible research avenues to..."). There is one active input link node in the left window, and two active output links in the right window, both sides show link highlight signals following the "–" markers. Windows may show optionally active links only, or all nodes, as in the right window. Either link list window can be scrolled or paged. The author may toggle links by moving the cursor to the node marker, and pressing the F5 key.

nonexistent, or (whoops!) forgotten nodes. They may occur because a node that once existed has been deleted or renamed.

Hyperties displays a node directory which flags links to nodes which have not yet been created, and those not yet identified by an embedded, short descriptive phrase. The MaxThink IC (Integrity Check) utility checks and reports the existence of all incomplete node references.

* Synonym or aliasing feature for links. Hypertext authors should be able to define synonyms or aliases for node, link or reference terms. This allows links to be made using a synonym or different phrase equivalent to a given node name. For example, the term "drug" or "drugs" might be an alias reference to a node defined or labeled as "narcotics."

Synonyms can be resolved as they occur during the authoring process, as in Hyperties or with a master file synonym table, as in the Flambeaux's xText authoring system.

Indexing Tools.   Traditional indexing software includes facilities for cross referencing, phrase usage, synonyms, controlled vocabulary, etc. Hypertext-based indices may also serve as glossaries.

Hypertext system designers need professional indexing tools for creating and controlling traditional alphabetic indices of links to node text. No authoring system I know of yet includes such sophisticated indexing facilities.

We've all used encyclopedias that provide examples of quality multi-level, descriptive indexing. This level of indexing requires sophisticated tools that can handle multi-level subject headings and interchapter filing. Such tools are not easily found at present.

Indexing software should be able to index both single terms and phrases made up of several words. Also important is the ability to maintain a thesaurus of preferred terms, to review and revise terms, to include cross-references specifying preferred terms, and to lock out entries of certain terms, except in cases where this order is manually countermanded. Control functions should be able to combine related terms (such as "dog" and "canine") so that when you look up one term you are automatically referred to the other as well.

The easy way to resolve index term conflicts is for the indexer to use a controlled vocabulary list of approved terms. These are expensive to produce and maintain, since they are laboriously built, after much mental (and verbal) debate and consideration. Building an indexing vocabulary is a highly specialized task. Those interested in the topic of indexing should look into the indexing standards that have been drawn up by the *International Standards Organization* (ISO).

What steps can be taken to simplify the process of indexing? One approach is to use someone else's thesaurus as a base for your own hypertext product. Thesauri (indexing vocabulary lists) are available from a variety of sources. For example, general topic lists can be taken from the Readers' Guide index headings, Library of Congress Subject Headings, and the Facts on File news digest heading lists. There are also specialized thesauri for practically every discipline. Examples include the Engineering Index, Chemical Abstracts, Social Sciences Index,

Communications Abstracts, etc. Many of these thesauri are for sale from their publishers.

You may ask, "Who in the world's going to do all this index development for our hypertext authoring team?" One option is to hire an on-staff or consulting professional librarian or contract indexing experts. Even large publishers like the *Encyclopedia Britannica* or the *New York Times* use outside indexing services.

Professional indexers and librarians receive specialized training in analyzing documents or texts for meaning, in applying and designing various classification, categorization, and subject heading systems. Many professional indexers are specialists with degrees and experience focusing upon particular subject areas. To find such an individual check with the American Society of Indexers, the Special Libraries Association, or the American Library Association.

Word Frequency Analysis Report. A utility which lists word frequency and/or phrase occurrence can be very helpful. Such utilities can show term usage and synonym occurrence. These utilities usually provide the options for sorting words alphabetically or by occurrence.

Keyword Extraction Utility. Keyword extraction utilities are close cousins to the word frequency tools described above. These utilities use statistical analysis to automatically extract a short list of the most important or descriptive content words in a document. These utilities produce an automatic listing of all the keywords. Such lists can serve as a mini-abstract of the content of the node or document. Once you have this list, it is relatively easy to decide where links should be placed [Salton, 1969; Pao, 1978].

Keyword lists have other uses. For example, the keyword list can be used to drive the creation of an inverted index like the one used in MaxThink's glossary feature. Extracted keywords can also be used to drive an outline of term co-occurrence, similar to the ones created by Prosoft, Inc.'s popular IZE text database for MS-DOS.

Linking To External Programs And Peripherals

In most cases multimedia development implies pulling information from more than one storage device at a time. For example, still images are typically stored on a hard drive, but video comes from videodisk or videotape. In order to manage this feat the development system needs drivers that can work with both serial and parallel ports and as well as drivers for whatever peripherals are used. For example, 1st Class, GUIDE, Hyperties, Knowledge Pro, and the MaxThink all provide runtime control of serial devices. On the input side, some versions of Hyperties are capable of accepting touch-screen input.

Many hypertext products also allow direct operating system calls or *shelling* to the operating system. Such programs can easily make calls to external programs. Hypertext programs that provide this ability can gateway into other applications or information systems, exchange information with external programs, or read and process RAM memory or disk file information originating from the external programs. 1st Class, GUIDE, Knowledge Pro, and MaxThink are examples of programs with this ability. Apple's HyperCard is famous for its ability to call XCMDs (external programs written in Pascal, C or assembler) for operations not easily done with the HyperTalk scripting language.

The Master Plan: A Hypertext Authoring Model

I wholeheartedly concur with Glushko, Raymond and Tompa, and others who promote the use of the "hypertext engineering" approach. But these designers often work with highly structured information bases, which are not always the raw material from which hypertext authors can start.

Creating hypertext can be a grubby, dirty, tedious text-handling job. Manually crafting every node and placing each link is a labor-intensive endeavor that only works for very small hypertexts. Even when building on highly structured information bases, it's simply not possible for most authors to create industrial strength hyperdocuments using manual methods exclusively.

I propose a general plan for creating large-scale hyperdocuments:

- Plan. The first step is to engage in extensive strategic planning, goal definition, audience/user analysis, specifications, resources, budgeting, etc.
- Assemble Information. The content for a hypertext information base will generally originate in one of two ways. It will: a) be converted from an existing electronically readable text base or database; or, b) be specifically assembled and created for the new hypertext information product. [See Chapter 9 by Riner and Chapter 10 by Rearick, in this book for more information on conversion vs. creation.]
- Convert Text. If the information originates from existing material, the authoring team must do detailed format and content analysis, resulting in a general algorithm for node output. Parsing definition and data conversion follows. Project managers should consider including node header extract reports, word frequency reports, automatic abstracting summaries, etc., as part of the data conversion.
- Generate Original Material. If the information is an original creation, the planning will define the information base coverage. I recommend use of an outliner program for careful initial general hierarchy definition. Within subsections, the outline should include short abstracts or descriptions of specific node content. This can be extended with a network or matrix outliner like MaxThink's HOUDINI, to predefine many of the major link paths. HOUDINI reports can output node details, including both content notes and input links. This will be a good guide for multiple authors composing the original material. (See Figure 14.5.)
- Organize the information into the hypertext database. I recommend that the project team consider using a sophisticated text database product as an editorial aid for assembling large information bases. Editors can use text databases to effi-

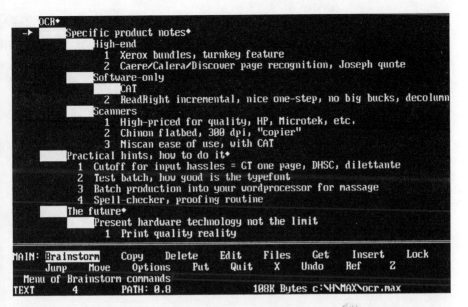

```
OCR◆
 →    ▮pecific product notes◆
      ▮High-end
        1  Xerox bundles, turnkey feature
        2  Caere/Calera/Discover page recognition, Joseph quote
      ▮Software-only
        ▮CAT
        2  ReadRight incremental, nice one-step, no big bucks, decolumn
      ▮Scanners
        1  High-priced for quality, HP, Microtek, etc.
        2  Chinon flatbed, 300 dpi, "copier"
        3  Miscan ease of use, with CAT
      ▮Practical hints, how to do it◆
        1  Cutoff for input hassles = GT one page, DHSC, dilettante
        2  Test batch, how good is the typefont
        3  Batch production into your wordprocessor for massage
        4  Spell-checker, proofing routine
      ▮The future◆
        ▮Present hardware technology not the limit
        1  Print quality reality

MAIN: ▮Brainstorm   Copy    Delete    Edit    Files    Get     Insert    Lock
      Jump    Move    Options    Put    Quit    X    Undo    Ref    Z
 Menu of Brainstorm commands
TEXT      4         PATH: 0.8              108K Bytes c:\H\MAX\ocr.max
```

Figure 14.5 An expanded outline view in the MaxThink ASCII-based node hierarchy outliner. MaxThink, Inc. has a utility program which will generate hierarchically linked hypertext node files from the outline. The outline items may contain multiple lines of text, comments, or author-embedded file node links.

ciently and quickly examine node text content, searching power for words, phrases, classifications, authors, personal or corporate names, titles, etc. The author can even use these databases to define fields for entering of input and output links.

Microcomputer-based programs such as Ask/Sam, Nutshell Plus, and Text/SEARCH, and mini- or mainframe-based products like Information Dimensions BASIS, Cuadra STAR, or BRS SEARCH, are inverted-index, full-text systems that provide near-instantaneous retrieval and display of text in response to free-formatted queries.

• Final preparation in proprietary hypertext authoring system format. As editing is completed, the database can output reports in defined proprietary formats, for export into a particular authoring system. This output could alternatively go to separate ASCII files, for systems like MaxThink and GUIDE, or be "chunked" from a single output file by a utility program.

The text database could generate separate "worklist" reports with node identifications, input and output links, to guide authors in embedding links. For many systems, the formatted output of nodes from the text database could include flagged links. Editors would later inspect nodes to insure meaningful or cosmetic link positioning. The database could also output formatted ASCII files for use in the HOUDINI matrix outliner, for complex network analysis. (See Figure 14.6.)

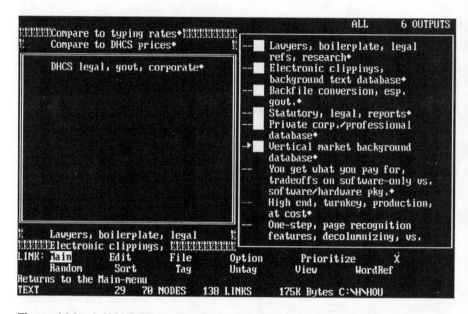

Figure 14.6 A HOUDINI work screen showing selective linking within matrix outliner. The left window displays the truncated text of an active node; the right window shows other nodes in the file. An author makes links by moving the cursor to the node marker and toggling the link off or on with the F5 key. Highlighted blocks mark active links to items.

The text database can produce additional user access or navigational tools, to be included in the runtime system. Possibilities include: tables of contents; formatted contents outlines; node title lists; node lists with descriptive keywords; simple indices; link term lists; formatted index files; author lists; subject listings; etc.

The specific authoring systems would of course be used for final editing inspection and touch-ups.

Conclusion

Large, complex hypermedia systems simply cannot be built using brute force authoring methods and working notes on scrap paper. Hypertext authors can and should take advantage of professional information organization methods and information access tools during the complicated process of hypertext authoring.

We can use hypertext authoring technology to automate proven traditional information retrieval methods in order to construct hyperdocuments. Our investment in the proper authoring tools will result in improved document quality.

A hypertext authoring team should include subject expertise, editorial staff, visual design specialists, and computer/technical staff. It is advisable to include a competent librarian/indexer to work on indexing and managing the linking. These professionals can help insure good coverage of this specialized area of information delivery.

About the Author

Ernest Perez

Ernest Perez is a professional librarian, with extensive background in newspaper information systems, text database management, data translation, and information system planning. He has written extensively for professional publications and the popular microcomputer press, specializing in text database, hypertext, and software application topics. He was Library Director at the Chicago Sun-Times, and installed their BASIS full-text database, using output from the ATEX publishing system. He was the newspaper's editorial representative for the Compuserve Newspaper Information Provider project, and also prepared the basic database content and information provider plan for the Field Electronic Publishing KEYCOM teletext experiment. He was also Library Director at the Houston Chronicle.

Mr. Perez has a journalism undergraduate degree from the University of Texas at El Paso, and a Master's of Library Science and Certificate of Advanced Study from the University of Texas at Austin. He is currently a doctoral candidate at the School of Library and Information Studies, Texas Woman's University. His dissertation topic is an analysis of information access methodologies for hypertext systems.

References

Braden, R. A. (1986). "Visuals for interactive video: Images for a new technology (with some guidelines)," *Educational Technology*, (May), 26(5), 18–23.

Cleveland, D. B., and Cleveland, A. (1990). *Introduction to indexing and abstraction.* Second edition. Englewood, Colorado: Libraries Unlimited.

Frisse, M. (1988). "From text to hypertext," *Byte*, (October), 247–253.

Frisse, M. (1988). "Searching for information in a hypertext medical handbook," *Communications of the ACM*, 31(7), 880–886.

Glushko, R. J. (1989). "Transforming text into hypertext for a compact disc encyclopedia." in "CHI '89: Wings for the Mind," Proceedings of conference, April 30–May 4, Austin TX: Addison-Wesley, 293–298.

Glushko R. J. (1990). "Designing a hypertext electronic encyclopedia," *Bulletin of the American Society for Information Science*, 11(2), 14–21.

Glynn, S. M., and Di Vesta, F. J. (1977). "Outline and hierarchical organization as aids for study and retrieval," *Journal of Educational Psychology*, 89(2), 89–95.

Hamilton, N., and Allinson, L. (1989). "Extending hypertext for learning: an investigation of access and guidance tools," in "People and Computers V," Proceedings of the Fifth Conference of the British Computer Society Human-Computer Interaction Specialist Group, September 5–8, Sutcliffe, A., and Macaulay, L. (Eds.), Cambridge, Cambridge University, 293–304.

Kearsley, G., and Shneiderman, B. (1988). *Hypertext Hands-On!*, Addison-Wesley, Reading, MA.

MaxThink, Inc. (1987). HOUDINI system processor [documentation]. Kensington, CA: MaxThink.

MaxThink Inc. (1990a). HyPlus: hypertext word processor system [documentation]. Kensington, CA: MaxThink.

MaxThink Inc. (1990b). TransText [documentation] Kensington, CA: MaxThink.

Pao, M. L. (1978). "Automatic text analysis based on transition phenomena of word occurrences." *Journal of the American Society for Information Science*, 28, 121–124.

Raymond, D. R., and Tompa, F. W. (1988). "Hypertext and the Oxford English Dictionary," *Communications of the ACM*, 31(7), 871–878.

Riner, R. (1991). "Automated Conversion." *Hypertext/Hypermedia Handbook*, Emily Berk and Joseph Devlin (Eds.), McGraw-Hill, New York, NY.

Rearick, T. (1991). "Automatic Versus Hand Generation," *Hypertext/Hypermedia Handbook*, Emily Berk and Joseph Devlin (Eds.), McGraw-Hill, New York, NY.

Salton, G. (1969). "A comparison between manual and automatic indexing methods." *American Documentation*, (January), 61–71.

Texas Instruments Hypermedia Services (1990). HyperTRANS [brochure] Dallas, TX: Texas Instruments.

VI

Licensing and Protection of Electronically Published Information

Section VI should be of particular interest to hypertext producers and distributors as well as to authors.

In Chaper 15, Steve Haynes provides an overview of the intellectual property issues that hypertext producers and content suppliers should know about.

In Chapter 16, Stephen McIntosh discusses how hypertext producers can obtain permission to use content produced by others and how content producers can protect their intellectual property rights.

In Chapter 17, Patrice Lyons focuses in on some legal issues that may arise when importing content into hypertexts.

15

Intellectual Property and Licensing Concerns

By Stephen L. Haynes

West Publishing Company

Introduction

Many hypertexts incorporate text, illustrations, and other media originally created by authors aside from the hypertext producer. It is important for both the authors of the original works and for the creators of hypertexts to be aware of the legal issues that may arise concerning protection of intellectual property rights. In addition, even with full knowledge of rights conferred via copyright, trademark or patent law, the producer, vendor, or distributor of hypertext information is still faced with a novel set of licensing concerns. Those reading this book should bear in mind that this chapter discusses general principles of intellectual property protection and licensing as applied to hypertext and hypermedia. In any given instance, readers should consult knowledgeable legal counsel as to the specifics of particular situations.

We begin this discussion of intellectual property and licensing concerns with a brief review of the applicable traditional intellectual property factors for trademark and copyright.

Traditional Intellectual Property Factors

The mere fact that hypertext and hypermedia look and act differently from traditional information bears little on the intellectual property factors that come into play. In fact, the same intellectual property factors that traditionally apply to other media apply to hypertext as well. Many aspects of current thinking about other dynamically displayed media, such as online databases and video games, apply equally well to hypermedia.

The two traditional intellectual property factors to be considered are trademark and copyright.

Trademark

Because of public identification of a name or symbol with a particular product, protection of that relationship is very important commercially. A name or symbol may not only apply to the overall product, but as well to its component or related parts. The personal computer software user is already well familiar with these acknowledgments of protected related products, since many software documentation manuals will contain references in the first few pages that identify registered trademarks.

As defined under current statute (Title 15, United States Code), trademark law covers the unique names or graphic symbols associated with a product. To the extent that information is vended under a trademarked name (e.g., "Encyclopedia Britannica"), if that information is included as part of a larger compilation (including online, mainframe-based information services), the trademark must be displayed and acknowledged. In most if not all cases, the owner of the trademark will require the information service to display the trademark information prominently. This requirement is usually spelled out in the contract by which the information provider is granted the right to use the trademarked name.

If the content of a hypertext is unique enough to warrant its own trademark, or if the hypertext content already has an established position in the market (and thus already has a protected trademark), or if the content may become part of a larger hypertext project that itself may have a protected trademark, the hypertext provider may want to secure a trademark for the hypertext content. Any owner of a potentially *trademarkable* product should also remember that, subject to certain restrictions, a trademark may now be applied for in advance of actually releasing the product. (15 U.S.C. Sec. 1051(b))

Two levels of trademark protection can be secured: the so-called common law trademark and the registered trademark. A common law trademark need not be registered with any agency. Instead, the symbol "tm" is affixed to the trademark name to be protected. Common law trademark is derived from the same principles as state laws relating to unfair competition. Central to any alleged common law trademark infringement, however, is the concept of "confusion":

> "It is well settled that the crucial issue in an action for trademark infringement or unfair competition is whether there is any likelihood that an appreciable number of ordinarily prudent purchasers are likely to be mislead, or indeed simply confused, as to the source of the goods in question." (Universal City Studios Inc. v. Nintendo Co., Ltd., 746 F.2d 112, 115 (2d Cir. 1984).)

Thus, successful prosecution of a common law trademark case will depend, among other things, upon the uniqueness of the designation trademarked and on whether the infringer had notice of the trademark protection.

Registered trademarks are established by federal statute (Title 15 of the United States Code). A trademark under federal law is "... any word, name, symbol or device or any combination thereof adopted and used by a manufacturer or merchant to identify his goods and distinguish them from those manufactured or sold by others." (15 U.S.C. Sec. 1127.) Anyone may register a unique trademark with the U.S. Patent Office. Thereafter, that trademark can be marked as registered by, among other techniques, affixing to the trademark the familiar "R" in a circle symbol. The R in a circle designates the mark as registered. If this mark is present there can be no defense of innocent infringement. Anyone seeking to use a trademarked work is duty-bound to check whether the mark is registered.

Copyright

Copyright protects the actual text (or images or collection of text or images) comprising the intellectual material. The roots of copyright protection are deep in American society, reaching back to Article I, Section 8, Clause 8 of the U.S. Constitution, which reads:

> "The Congress shall have Power ... (8) To promote the Progress of Science and useful Arts, by securing for limited Times to Authors and Inventors the exclusive Right to their respective Writings and Discoveries...."

Because of this constitutional mandate, copyright protection bestows on the copyright owner what is often referred to as a limited monopoly right in the control over his property. This means that (subject to very few exceptions)[1] the copyright owner can essentially do business or refuse to do business with whomever he or she chooses.

Moreover, acquisition of copyright is simple. Under current law, a copyright is deemed to exist in an authored product at the time of creation. A slightly different copyright protection comes into effect upon publication of the work. ("'Publication' is the distribution of copies or phonorecords of a work to the public by sale or other transfer of ownership, or by rental, lease, or lending...." (17 U.S.C. Sec. 101)) Once the phrase "Copyright (year) by (author's name)" (or some limited variation on that phrase) has been affixed to the first few pages of the work, the work becomes eligible for registration with the Copyright Office (17 U.S.C. Sec. 401 et seq.) Upon registration, the copyright is fully protected, including (most importantly) the right of the copyright owner to sue to protect the copy-

---

1 Limitations on exclusive rights denoted in Title 17: Fair use (Sec. 107); Reproduction by libraries and archives (Sec. 108); Effect of transfer of particular copy or phonorecord (Sec. 109); Exemption of certain performances and displays (Sec. 110); Secondary transmissions (Sec. 111); Ephemeral recordings (Sec. 112); and Secondary transmissions of superstations and network stations for private home viewing (Sec. 119). See also Secs. 113–118.

right, enjoin infringement, or collect money damages for infringement. (17 U.S.C. Sec. 501 et seq.)

Copyright can exist not only in *authored* works, as in the sense of a novel, screenplay, movie, etc., but also in compilations of materials, such as collections of short stories. Copyright can even exist in collections of otherwise unprotected information, like the collections of names, addresses and phone numbers found in telephone directories. Some jurisdictions, however, have held that collections that merely meet what has come to be called the "sweat of the brow" test do not rise to the level of originality required for copyright—e.g., a computer-generated arrangement of otherwise unprotected facts into which the author placed little editorial work and exercised little independent selectivity is not protected. This compilation copyright protection has important implications for hypertext applications, as will be discussed presently.

Some things are not copyrightable: for example, products of U.S. government employees, produced at government expense, are not susceptible to protection.[2] Matters "in the public domain" are also not susceptible to copyright (e.g., mere facts cannot be copyrighted, such as an individual's name, address, and telephone number). Compilations of such facts, however, can be copyrighted if sufficient effort and editorial expertise has been expended in their collection, presentation, and publication—for example, the white pages telephone directory, or road maps (which are copyrighted collections of otherwise uncopyrightable facts—the individual features displayed on such maps).

Materials once copyrighted may lose their protection and become part of the public domain. This used to happen if adequate notice was not displayed on the work. Current law has removed that danger, although notice is still required in order to defeat what is known as the "innocent infringer" defense. (17 U.S.C. Sec. 401(d))

In addition, material that was copyrighted passes into the public domain after the passage of time. (17 U.S.C. Sec. 302 et seq.) Thus, materials that might once have been protected by copyright (e.g., the Federalist Papers or Shakespeare's plays) are no longer protected.[3] This time period is so long, however, as not to be relevant for most purposes related to this discussion.

Another cautionary note about copyright. Any author who is working in the employ or at the direction of another is cautioned to seek competent advice as to the ownership of the copyright in his work. In 1989, a Supreme Court case (Com-

---

2 Recent moves by state governments, however, have increased the interest in (and reaction to) copyright protection for state government-generated information, including in some instances collections of material (such as compilations of state regulations). For reasons beyond the scope of this discussion, this tendency has raised considerable concern in the information industry.

3 In a twist on this status of older material that is sometimes confusing, a collection of such non-copyrighted materials may still be protected, as a compilation. In such a case, the material itself is not protected, but the collection, its arrangement, and any editorial additions or changes to the material (e.g., introductions, annotations, footnotes, translations, corrections to text based on modern scholarship, etc.) will be protected.

munity for Creative Non-Violence v. Reid, 109 S.Ct. 2166) focused attention on a copyright doctrine known as "work made for hire." A work made for hire is one authored by a person usually in the employ of another. Needless to say, a natural signal of concern in this regard is when the contract of employment specifically informs the author that his product is being created as a "work made for hire." This is not to say that material produced under a work-made-for-hire relationship is in any way improperly acquired or of any diminished value for either the creator or his employer; the creator merely loses several property rights in his creation, the most important of which is the copyright.

The potential hypertext author should be aware of a significant limitation on copyright that has particular relevance in hypertext applications—fair use. Fair use refers to permitted use of portions of copyrighted materials in other publications. The statute sets forth the definition of fair use rather succinctly (17 U.S.C. Sec. 107):

Sec. 107. Limitations on exclusive rights: Fair use

Notwithstanding the provisions of section 106, the fair use of a copyrighted work, including such use by reproduction in copies or phonorecords or by any other means specified by that section, for purposes such as criticism, comment, news reporting, teaching (including multiple copies for classroom use), scholarship, or research, is not an infringement of copyright. In determining whether the use made of a work in any particular case is a fair use the factors to be considered shall include—

(1) the purpose and character of the use, including whether such use is of a commercial nature or is for nonprofit educational purposes;

(2) the nature of the copyrighted work;

(3) the amount and substantiality of the portion used in relation to the copyrighted work as a whole; and

(4) the effect of the use upon the potential market for or value of the copyrighted work.

Fair use in the hypertext context will be discussed below; generally, however, it should be noted that several recent cases have limited the fair use exception when the sources of the works extracted are unpublished, such as the letters of J.D. Salinger (Salinger v. Random House, Inc., 811 F.2d 90 (2d Cir. 1987)). Fair use generally, except when falling within the clear intent of the statute (such as copies made for classroom use), is a difficult defense to a charge of copyright infringement. Where there is doubt and where fair use is in issue, consult an attorney.

Another traditional copyright principle that casts a different light in the hypertext context is that of a *derivative work*, which the statute (17 U.S.C. Sec. 101) defines as

... a work based upon one or more preexisting works, such as a translation, musical arrangement, dramatization, fictionalization, motion picture version, sound recording, art reproduction, abridgment, condensation, or any other form in which a work may be recast, transformed, or adapted. A work consisting of editorial revisions, annotations, elaborations, or other modifications which, as a whole, represent an original work of authorship, is a "derivative work".

As with fair use, derivative work must be considered in the context in which the question is raised. The inclusion in the statute of "annotations, elaborations, or other modifications" definitely brings to mind hypertext applications, however. The statute says in Sec. 103 that

> "the copyright in a ... derivative work extends only to the material contributed by the author of such work, as distinguished from the preexisting material employed in the work, and does not imply any exclusive right in the preexisting materials. The copyright in such work is independent of, and does not affect or enlarge the scope, duration, ownership, or subsistence of, any copyright protection in the preexisting materials."

Copyright and trademarks are properties; since they can be owned, they can also be bought and sold. Thus, the owner of either a trademark or copyright may be someone other than the original inventor of the trademark or author of the work. This is often the case with works published in the traditional sense, such as books, compact discs, movies, etc. Such transfer of trademark or copyright properties, or the rights to use the underlying properties, may be the subject of a license, a copyright assignment or a copyright release. A license, a copyright assignment and a copyright release are different. A license does not transfer the copyright, just certain rights in the use of the property; a copyright assignment transfers the copyright (and usually all rights attendant thereto); a copyright release is much like the assignment, except that it can be a release as against the entire world (e.g., placing a work into the public domain), or it can be a document signed by one the character of whose work may be in doubt (in this sense, it works much like a "quit claim deed" in real estate). Licenses are discussed at greater length later in this chapter.

Intellectual Property Concerns Unique to Hypertext

Patent and trademark issues as they apply to hypertext may be treated within the context of much more traditional approaches. However, hypertext and hypermedia represent uncharted territory for copyright considerations.

Trademark

Trademark concerns unique to hypertext and hypermedia are few and trademarks are adequately protected via licensing agreements. Simply put, if an author or owner has a trademark associated with his work, that author should use the license agreement to limit or expand conditions governing how the trademark is to be displayed or used in the hypertext application, marketing and training materials. The usual form of that protection is to convey to the licensee the right to use trademarks, so long as such trademarks are displayed properly and ownership is stated. There often will be language in the license specifically stating that no ownership is transferred in the right to use the trademark. Language will often also limit use of the trademarks to material directly associated with the work. A more restrictive form of license requires review by the trademark owner of any documentation, training materials, etc., using his trademark. An even more restrictive license requires approval by the owner before use. These latter two forms of restriction are overkill unless the application is viewed as being particularly susceptible to abuse, or if the trademark being protected is particularly valuable or all-encompassing of a body of work.

Copyright

At the outset of our discussion of copyright in the hypertext context, it should be noted that hypertext and hypermedia are not discussed anywhere in Title 17, nor have any reported cases arisen in the federal courts relating to hypertext or hypermedia applications. For this reason, the discussion that follows is based upon reasonable expectations and extensions of existing, non-hyper-based copyright law.

For works created in a traditional manner—e.g., those created as "linear" products (books, articles, newspapers, movies, etc.)—copyright attaches upon creation. Even if the work is later incorporated in a hypertext application, the original copyright protects the whole and its parts. The one exception to be aware of is application of fair use to extracts taken from a copyrighted work and incorporated in another work via hypertext. In other words, if an otherwise infringing extraction is protected under the fair use exception, then the fact that incorporation of the extraction is via hypertext as opposed to traditional *linear* quotation makes no difference. Conversely, infringing a copyright by appropriating material for use in a hypertext is still infringement. This is true, however, only if the infringement occurs within the context of an overall authored work (i.e., only if the author of the infringing work has physically incorporated the infringed material as part of the publication of an overall work). If hypertext reference occurs from one work to another within a greater hypertext application, and such application is not under the control of the referencing work's author, it is doubtful that the work making the reference will be infringing. Liability would attach to the owner of the overall hypertext application only if the infringed work was incorporated in the overall application without permission.

In fact, Theodor Nelson, the leading exponent of hypertext applications, has coined the term *transclusion* to describe the reference to outside material via hypertext. As he explains in a recent article in *Byte* magazine:

> Transclusion means that a thing can be in two places at once. Suppose you write a sentence you like, or there's a paragraph that needs to be quoted from one document to another. (Copying it) loses the connection—the thread that ties them all together. But in transclusion, you make a virtual copy from one place into the other so that there is a hole in one place that you wanted (the sentence), which is filled always from the other place whenever you get to the hole (*Byte*, September 1990, pp. 298-299).

Nelson claims that transclusion obviates copyright concerns, since the physical location (i.e., published location) of the transcluded material remains constant and there is no physical copying such that the copyrighted material would be infringed. Readers accessing the transcluded material are actually accessing the (presumably lawfully licensed) material in its original form. Again, as should be perfectly clear, unless there is a physical copying of a work such that infringement occurs, an author creating a hypertext link to another's work does not infringe on that work by creating that link.

This, however, may beg the question. Although present copyright law is replete with the concept of physical copying as a prerequisite to infringement, who is to say but that a future court may consider transclusion to have the same effect as copying, and therefore be considered infringement, too. The more persuasive argument stemming from transclusion is that not only is there no physical copying, but copyright information can be bundled with the transcluded text, and, moreover, attribution for royalty purposes can also be triggered. Thus, not only is the transcluded material's author properly credited in the intellectual sense, but in the financial sense as well.

It is of course probable that present and future authors will create works specifically for hypertext publication. Copyright will protect those works no less than it protects works traditionally prepared. In other words, the fact that an author writes an article with built-in links to other works and built-in points of linkage from other works affects in no way the copyright protection of that work. What is more important is that, by means of a license, the author can ensure that the publisher provides effective notice of copyright.

Patent

Patent law, which does not apply to the expression (i.e., the content of the work), but rather to the novel techniques and applications of inventions relating to the hypertext system, applies to computers and to software under certain circumstances. Thus, patent protection can also apply to the system under which hypertext applications are generated. However, since in this chapter we do not concern ourselves with the hypertext authoring system, but rather with the content of the hypertext publication itself, we will not discuss principles of patent law here.

Licensing Factors (Author vs. Publisher)

Other than limitations on copyright protection pursuant to fair use or other specific limitations,[4] the way by which an author or other owner of a copyrighted work transfers a limited or unlimited right to use that work in a publication is through a

---

4   See Note 1, supra.

license of that work. The license may be so broad as to convey the copyright itself (in which case there is an assignment of the copyright, and ownership passes to the licensee), or so narrow as to permit only specific, limited uses of the copyrighted work (e.g., in a specific publication, or for a specific period of time, or within specific geographic boundaries). If the license does not specifically say so, the copyright itself is not conveyed (17 U.S.C. Sec. 204).

For protection of both copyright owner and the person or company seeking to make use of the copyrighted material, the license permitting use must be in writing. The specific rights conveyed must be set forth—e.g., whether the license is exclusive or nonexclusive, limited or unlimited, world-wide or of limited geographic scope. The term of the license should be specific, although if the licensee will be making expenditures in order to convert the licensed material to machine-readable or hypertext-enabled form, the license may contain terms preventing termination prior to recovery of these expenses. A perpetual license may be granted, of course, but they are extremely rare and usually under unusual circumstances. For example, if the licensed work is so completely commingled with other works of the licensee, such that deletion of the licensed work would be impossible, then the license might be perpetual. As another example, if the licensed work formed only the foundation upon which more material would be built over time, resulting in the modification of the originally-licensed work, a perpetual license might make sense. In such cases, however, it would make even greater sense to simply convey the copyright outright.

Protection of Work Product

A license should protect the work product of the licensor (the one owning the work that is the subject of the license) yet still permit the licensee (the one obtaining the licensed rights in order to publish the licensed work) latitude and flexibility in creating the product. This means that each of the following factors should be included in the license:

1. Assuming that the license conveys limited rights as to the use of trademarks, the licensee will give notice of such trademarks in the product itself, in promotional materials, in documentation and in training materials; this may require an itemization of the trademarks to be protected in the agreement or in an addendum.
2. Both parties are responsible for securing of copyright protection of their own works. If the licensee's work is a compilation including the licensor's, then the licensee is responsible for securing that separate copyright protection.
3. The licensee will give notice of the licensor's copyright ownership; it is often desirable that the actual form of copyright notice be set forth. Specifics of copyright notice relating to hypertext products are discussed below.
4. Both parties will agree to give the other notice of any known infringement of the other's copyrights.

When first viewed, the techniques of hypertext strongly suggest that the licensed works may be intermingled with other works, to the extent even that the licensed work will be broken up into parts (chapters, paragraphs, even sentences) that will be incorporated among portions of the hypertext product that are not the subject of the license. That of course is not the case. As has been discussed above relating to the technique of transclusion, it is not the physical intermingling of text that takes place in a proper hypertext application, rather the linking of textual elements makes it seem that intermingling takes place.

The licensed text will actually reside, whole, in a separate physical location. Thus, it would be prudent for the licensor to prohibit intermingling of his text with others' and require that the entirety of the licensed text be included in the product, without being broken up, subdivided, or modified in terms of substance.

The license may include terms which specify whether the licensor or the licensee is expected to provide the hypertext links.[5] Generally, it may be expected that points of linkage outward (e.g., from points in the licensed text to other texts) will be the responsibility of the licensor, whereas points of linkage inward (e.g., from external texts to points in the licensed text) may be the licensee's responsibility. Actual implementation of the linkages, however, will always be the responsibility of the owner of the hypertext product, usually the licensee.

The licensor must decide the degree to which he will permit alteration of his work product.[6] In most instances, subject to limitations or necessities dictated by the hypertext system itself, the licensor is within his rights to require that his entire work, without alteration, deletion or addition, be included in the licensee's product. Limitations and necessities dictated by the hypertext delivery platform may include: inability to display graphics, necessity of reformatting text, inability to display more than 80 characters on a line, and required insertion of hypertext links.

The licensee, on the other hand, must assure that he retains a certain degree of editorial discretion in the formatting of the final product and successful inclusion of the licensed material. For this reason, the license will probably contain language permitting some degree of (usually carefully delineated) permissible alteration. What should be made clear, however, is that it is the licensee who will

---

5 What is intended here is either through mnemonic codes (e.g., %HTL%—HyperText Link point) or through certain forms of reference (e.g., in a legal treatise, use of standard legal citation forms) to provide a program (that builds the hypertext product) enough information to know where a hypertext link exists, and to what or for what the link pertains.

6 Incidentally, whereas a license may permit alteration of a work, the licensor's copyright pertains to the unaltered version of the work. The altered version is a derivative work and is protected separately, usually under the copyright owned by the licensee. The statute, however, in 17 U.S.C. Sec. 401, makes clear that the licensor's copyright is entirely protected by notice of copyright held by the licensee. It may be worthwhile for the license to provide a cross-conveyance by the licensee to the licensor of the right to sue for copyright infringement of the derivative work insofar as the portion infringed included the altered licensed material. Absent that cross-conveyance, the licensor may have no ability to protect the derivative version if the licensee fails or chooses not to do so.

make the alterations necessary, not a third party (e.g., another author hired to modify the licensed text). [See Chapter 17 by Lyons, in this book, for a detailed discussion of the types of alteration that may have to be performed by the producer of a hypertext, and the legal ramifications of such alterations.]

Some technological features of hypertext systems require special consideration in the context of alterations, however. Specifically, use of *bookmarks* and of *reader-inserted hypertext links* must be considered.

- Bookmarks. Some hypertext browsers make it possible for readers to insert transient bookmarks in the text. Readers can usually specify whether these bookmarks are stored temporarily or permanently. These bookmarks provide points of reference to which readers can return on command. Readers may be able to name bookmarks in order to facilitate returns to unique locations. The license should specify that such bookmarks are permitted (to protect the licensee) but that no further right is conveyed thereby to create a secondary derivative work (to protect the licensor).
- Reader-inserted hypertext links. In the most sophisticated browsing systems, readers may create their own hypertext linkages to other material. In some instances, those linkages may be to material already in the hyperdocument. In others, the linkages may be to material that a reader adds to the system. Naturally, questions will arise as to copyright protection of the added material, fair use (if the material is derived from external, copyrighted works), protection as a derivative work, etc. The same license provisions discussed for bookmarks should be included.

We may hope that bookmarks and reader-inserted hypertext links are adequately addressed under existing copyright law. Arguably, hyperdocuments with reader-created bookmarks or reader-created links could be considered new and unique works. To the extent the works are for the reader's own access alone, they are arguably unpublished in that form. Nevertheless, a separate copyright exists in such works, and the author's (and the licensee's) rights are protected as extensions of the derivative works' protection. To the extent that the licensee's hyperdocument facilitates such capabilities, their status might be addressed in the readers' license agreements. In addition, to the extent that the hyperdocument permits inclusion of reader-inserted hypertext links and material, the reader agreements should require that readers not infringe on any copyrighted material by doing so.

Acknowledgments/Byline

Hypertext systems present a major problem in the acknowledgment of an author's name and byline. If a linkage is made to material authored by another, should that author's name be displayed at every point his or her material is displayed? The license agreement may legitimately address this concern, but how it will be resolved is a function of the relative importance of the linked-to work, the vanity of the author, and capabilities of the system. The unaltered licensed text will not contain byline information at each point of potential in-linkage, nor will it contain byline information of every out-linked reference. If the system permits, the act of engaging a hypertext link will result in display (in a window, or at the head of the linked-to material) of the author's byline and identification of the title and other information regarding the linked-to work. In all likelihood this information will be dynamically supplied by the system, and it will be derived from information stored on the system separately from the text of the licensed work itself. From the reader's standpoint, of course, it is particularly important that the derivation and weight of the linked-to material be stated.

Copyright

Associated with the question of acknowledgments and bylines are what may and may not reasonably be expected in providing notice of the licensor's copyright.

In the first instance, to the extent a hyperdocument comprises numerous individual works under a single product umbrella, a compilation copyright will attach to the work as a whole and the individual items therein will continue to retain whatever copyright protection they had standing alone and will in addition be protected as part of the compilation. While it is expected that compilation owners will wish to protect (and will take whatever steps are necessary to protect) their own intellectual property rights, licensors should expect that protection of their own property against infringement will primarily be their responsibility.

The principal question insofar as the license is concerned is the degree to which notice must be given of the licensor's copyright. It is conceivable that the license will require the licensee to give notice of the licensor's copyright at each point that the licensor's material is accessed, whether directly or via a hypertext link. It should be emphasized, however, that such separate notice is not necessary under existing copyright law.

The license should require, however, that notice of the copyright of the licensed work be provided somewhere—in documentation, in the directory to material contained in the system, on the face of the CD-ROM, etc. Exactly where and how will usually be the subject of negotiations, especially taking into account limitations of the system.

Royalties

Any discussion of licensing concerns would be deficient if it did not address the question of royalties: how much, how calculated, and when paid.

Typical royalties for machine-readable publications fall in the range of 15–20 percent. Variations will naturally depend upon importance of the licensed work to the overall publication and reputation of the author. In addition, certain license terms may increase the amount of the royalty. Most notable among these is whether the license is exclusive or semi-exclusive. (Semi-exclusive could refer to a geographic exclusivity, or exclusivity vis a vis a particular competitor, or exclusive within a certain market, although the latter can have antitrust implications).

An exclusive license, particularly for an important work, can significantly increase the royalty. Of course, the licensee must be interested in exclusivity in order to make it worthwhile. If the work in issue is a new product, exclusivity will be demanded by the publisher as a matter of course, with no additional compensation.

Conceivably, royalties might be paid as a lump sum. This approach is more likely, however, where instead of a license of copyrighted material the compensation is made to an employee or for a work made for hire. For an employee, there is virtually no latitude in making conditions for additional compensation. In the case of a work made for hire, however, such terms can be incorporated in the contract of employment.

Royalty calculation will depend upon the medium. In an online hypertext medium, royalty will depend upon the manner by which the online system is billed. Consider the following:

- If billed on a straight connect-time basis, royalties will be calculated on a simple dollar amount per hour of connect time or percentage of revenue. In either case, royalties will apply only to the time during which the material is actually being reviewed by the reader (the online connect time).
- If billed on an "event" basis (e.g., where searches are charged at one rate, browsing connect time at another, and different specialized operations (e.g., a hypertext connection) at yet others), royalties can be calculated on a basis as simple as a percentage of revenue, or as complicated as formulae that take into account the complexity of the information, the manner in which it is accessed, the percentage it represents of the overall corpus, etc.
- If billed on an "output" basis (e.g., where a different rate applies for different formats of output, and where there may be separate charges for each record viewed), royalties will likely be based on a straight percentage.

Whatever the calculation method employed, however, in online systems the licensor is expected to take his chances insofar as revenue is concerned. Revenue to be received will be a function purely of the degree to which his work is used. If his work has little appeal, then it will be little used, and royalties will be negligible. Of course, one term of the license agreement can be agreements between the parties regarding the nature and intensity of marketing of the materials. Intensity of marketing should translate directly into increased revenues and increased royalties. The licensee's willingness to enter into promises on this subject will again depend upon importance of the author or his work.

For offline systems, where the hyperdocument may be sold as a subscription or as a book, royalties will usually depend upon successful sales of the overall work. It is very difficult to base royalties on use in an offline system, since that requires extensive and sophisticated metering systems at the local level. Far more likely, if the work is sold as a subscription, with the retrieval/browsing software being under the control of the licensee (or third-party supplied software having some recognition in the industry), the licensor will be paid an agreed-upon percentage based on the importance of the author or work, and the percentage of the total work the licensed material represents. Although an advance against royalties is conceivable, the industry is still too young and revenues too uncertain for a pattern of such royalties to have emerged.

Looking Ahead

This chapter has tried to establish principles within which the hypertext author can expect intellectual property and licensing concerns to arise. Looking ahead, some developments on the horizon may complicate matters further.

First among these is the growing use of what is called Object Oriented Programming. In OOP, software and databases are merged, so that a set of data will often carry with it the software necessary for its own access. When this happens, some might argue that we have neither fish nor fowl: the software is protected under copyright in one manner, the database in another. Which will control?

The second matter of concern relates to a merger of patent and copyright concerns in all things related to computers. There are some who believe that databases and software deserve a *sui generis* protection of their own—a protection that is neither patent nor copyright, but rather one legislatively created and unique to the genre. This is viewed by many to be a dangerous proposition, but it has its advocates.

We may rest assured, however, that with substantial financial interests at stake in databases and hypertext applications, intellectual property concerns and licensing techniques will remain very important no matter the imaginative forms in which information is presented.

About the Author

Stephen L. Haynes

Mr. Haynes is the Manager of WESTLAW's Research and Development efforts. His department is responsible for setting goals and priorities for enhancements to WESTLAW's system and databases, negotiating outside database acquisitions, and designing database and system features.

Before coming to West in January 1984, Mr. Haynes was an attorney with a major Wall Street firm and a consultant to the legal industry on litigation support and office automation. He has a J.D. degree from the University of Chicago Law School, and a B.A. in Humanities from Michigan State University.

Mr. Haynes is a member of committees or subcommittees of the Patent, Trademark and Copyright Section of the American Bar Association; the Association of American Publishers; and the Information Industry Association.

Mr. Haynes may be contacted at Westlaw Research & Development, West Publishing Company, 50 West Kellogg Boulevard, St. Paul, MN 55102.

References

Nelson, Ted (1990). "The Byte summit; Insights—On the Xanadu Project," *Byte*, September, 298-299.

Lyons, P. (1991). "Copyright Concerns of Hypertext Producers," *Hypertext / Hypermedia Handbook*, Emily Berk and Joseph Devlin, (Ed.s), McGraw-Hill, New York, NY.

16

Intellectual Property Issues in Multimedia Productions

By Stephen Ian McIntosh
Earth Wise, Inc.

This section on legal issues concerning the acquisition of component media is reprinted from "The Multimedia Producer's Legal Survival Guide" by Stephen Ian McIntosh.

This chapter discusses issues involved in acquiring particular types of media for use in a hypertext, hypermedia or multimedia presentation.

The chart in Figure 16.1 provides a summary at a glance and may be referred to as a quick reference.

Text

Text is perhaps the easiest medium to gain permission for, because it's usually easy to identify the author or publisher. Compared to other forms of media, acquisition of the right to reprint text is relatively inexpensive. For purposes of this analysis, *text* includes textual material found in books, magazines, tests, charts and tables of numbers and figures. News articles can usually be safely used without permission after three months, but any column or article that is syndicated under a separate byline or otherwise individually copyrighted must be used with permission. The doctrine of fair use (discussed in detail in *The Multimedia Producer's Legal Survival Guide*) is also the broadest and most well-defined in the area of the written word. Although the context must be considered, even for commercial uses it is possible to quote 300 words or less from a book or article without violating copyright. This assumes, however, that the work is properly quoted and not passed

Type of medium	Film and video, still photos	Text	Graphics	Software	Music	Multimedia Presentations
Types of protection	All frames protected by copyright. Some images within the frame may have trademark protection.	All forms of expression protected by copyright II not government works or otherwise in public domain	Company or product logos protected by trademark. Artistic visuals and software graphics protected by copyright. Availability of protection for "look and feel" of graphics is unclear.	Most software protected by license contract. Patent and copyright may provide overlapping protection. Many forms of "freeware" in public domain with no restrictions on use.	Copyright is on four levels: composer, publisher, recording company and artist. Older compositions in public domain but individual recording retains copyright.	Copyright protection as compilation or derivative work. Use limited by level of permission granted by copyrighted component media. Wholly original works enjoy copyright protection at creation.
Rights of owner	Exclusive right to reproduce, adapt, publish or display publicly, distribute by leasing, licensing or other transfer. Limited exception to exclusivity for fair use.	Exclusive rights to reproduce, adapt, publish, etc. Fair use exemptions largest for critique. Ideas not protected, but close paraphrasing prohibited.	Visual arts protected by copyright even without notice. Notice and registration strengthens rights, however. Trademark rights prevent "confusingly similar" use.	Specific rights under term of license, if any. Full copyright protection. Licensee has absolute right to make archival copy.	Right to perform, record, reproduce, adapt, publish, etc. Limited use home recording not protected.	All rights to use, reproduce, etc. protected. Creators of works made for hire may not show portfolio work unless permitted by "author."
How obtained	Author's copyright occurs automatically on creation. Notice and registration with register of copyrights (form PA) strengthens rights. Contact studio, publisher or photographer for inquiries on use in derivative work. Contact producer or parent company for video.	Author's copyright occurs upon creation (file form TX or SE for serials). Contact publisher for inquiries on permitted use.	Copyright created when original graphic becomes fixed in a medium. Notice and registration strengthen rights (file form VA unless contained in text or software). Trademark obtained through common law use and state/federal registration.	Notice should appear on computer screen or on the package of the software (file form TX). Internal graphics protected by copyright to the entire package. Patent protection, when available, granted by the U.S. Office of Patents and Trademarks. Contact main licensing company or author.	Copyright protection upon writing of score, performance of work or recording. Additional levels of copyright obtained as function performed (form PA). Contact publisher or recording company or use copyright clearinghouse to find rights holders and negotiate with them for right to use.	Same as software or video, except must have permission from authors of any protected component media (file form PA or TX).
Test for infringement	Substantially similar reproduction or use. Use of one frame of video may constitute infringement, depending on the context.	Copying and distribution other than for limited educational purposes. Extensive quoting other than for critique. Reproduction by voice or other. Substantially similar paraphrasing. No infringement if independent creation using others' ideas.	Copyright test of infringement is substantially similar reproduction or use. Infringement of trademark tested by likelihood of confusion, mistake or deception.	Unauthorized copying or use; unauthorized derivative work incorporating source or object code or graphics.	Unauthorized performance or commercial recording or sale of score.	Unauthorized copying or use' unauthorized derivative work.

© Stephen Ian McIntosh — February 22, 1990

Figure 16.1

off as part of a larger whole. Additionally, a quotation of 300 words from a one- or two-page article or poem would constitute use of a significant portion of the work and would thus require permission.

In order for text to be subject to copyright protection it must be of sufficient quantity. Although a haiku (a 17 syllable poem) would probably qualify for protection, a short paragraph of advertising copy may not. Slogans may be trademarked, although they are generally not subject to copyright protection.

Graphics

Basic geometric shapes and symbols are not subject to copyright protection, but all other graphical representations and abstractions including illustrations, cartoons, computer images and all types of fine art are protected by copyright. Rights to cartoons and illustrations are often controlled by a syndicate or the publication in which the work appears. The copyright to fine art is often controlled by the artist.

When requesting permission to use a graphical work, be sure to distinguish between a photograph or other reproduction of the graphic you may be working with and the graphic itself (if you plan to use the photograph of the graphic, you will need permission for both). Also, describe how the graphic will be used. Will it be in a background with text overlay or will it appear in a window? Will the graphic be one of 5,000 images available for random access or will it fill the title screen and be central to the identity of the program?

Still Photos

Many of the same considerations for the acquisition of graphics apply equally to still photographs. That is, even if you acquire permission from the copyright owner, commercial use of the pictured subject may involve other rights such as a trademark or the likeness of a person who has not signed a release with the photographer. If a celebrity or public figure is pictured in the photo, special care must be taken to ensure proper permission. The celebrity, for instance, may have given permission for the photo to be used only for certain purposes. (See the discussion below under "Talent".)

The person who took the photograph usually owns the copyright. Some photos, however, are owned by wire services and news agencies. In such cases ownership usually appears in small print near the margin of the photo. (How to obtain permission to use the photo is discussed in *The Multimedia Producer's Legal Survival Guide*.) Depending on the intended use, photographs can be expensive when acquired from commercial sources. Costs range from $50 per picture for one-time educational use to $600 per picture for commercial distribution. It may be more economical to purchase film or video footage and use captured stills. While you should inform the owner of the footage that you intend to use some stills, it shouldn't make much difference because once the footage is digitized, a still may be produced by the user at any moment.

There is a strong network of providers and researchers of photographs. Certain specialized organizations and individuals can provide valuable assistance in acquiring photos and may be less expensive than a rights and permissions professional or a stock photo house. The following organizations may be a resource for the multimedia developer:

- The American Society of Picture Professionals publishes a directory of picture researchers, photographers and photo supply houses:

   Mindy Klarman, Director of Photo Resources
   C/O American Society of Picture Professionals
   Macmillan/McGraw-Hill School Division
   866 Third Avenue
   New York, NY 10022
   (212) 702-4705

- Photonet is a computer network which puts together those who need photographs with those who supply them: 4200 Aurora Street, Suite N, Coral Gables, FL 33146, (305) 444-0144.
- Picture Research is a resource for public domain photographs: 6107 Roseland Drive, Rockville, MD 20852-3648, Attn: Grace Evans, (301) 230-0043 (personal number for Grace Evans).
- The Special Libraries Association publishes Picture Source 4, containing information about picture libraries: 1700 18th Street NW, Washington DC 20009, (202) 234-4700.

Film and Video

Non-theatrical film and video footage can be acquired with a similar investment of time and expense as that with graphics or still photos. The same considerations regarding securing clearance for persons or images contained in the footage also apply (see discussion of still photos above). Unless the footage is purely educational or in the public domain, non-theatrical footage can cost between $500 and $1,000 a minute. This may seem expensive, but if you consider the number of still frames in a minute of film, it's less expensive than still photos on average.

A technical consideration in the acquisition of footage is frame slippage caused by the transfer of film to a video master. The majority of footage available is on videotape—even if the footage was originally shot on film. If the film was transferred using an inferior conversion method or under a foreign standard, it will look fine on video; but when you put it on the laserdisc, there will be frame slippage. Thus, be sure to inquire about the film-to-video conversion method or test the footage before paying for the right to use it.

When it comes to theatrical film or video, commercial use (including in-house or industrial use) can become very expensive. There are many rights involved in a typical movie or television program. Permission from the studio, production company or television network (sometimes all three) is required as well as from the performer appearing in the clip. If there's music in the sound tack of the footage to be used, permission may also be required from the composer or musician. Older movies are less expensive, but tracking down the actors or their heirs can be difficult.

Music and Sound

Although this section is on acquiring rights to music, it's important to first emphasize that producing original music for your multimedia program shows greater artistic integrity and can be less expensive than acquiring preexisting music that may not be perfectly suited to your program. There are many fine musicians who will be excited to be involved with a multimedia project and will work for a fair fee.

Making your own recordings of public domain music is also an attractive alternative to acquisition, given the availability of high quality synthesizers.

There are four or five levels of copyright for most music: the publisher, the recording company, the recording artist and the composer, and the arranger. If you want to use copyrighted music, there are several alternatives available. For commercial use of an original recording, permission is required from the publisher, the recording company and the American Federation of Musicians. These permissions should cover all copyright rights involved, but make sure this is the case by asking the owners when you're in the process of seeking their permission.

Many of the most famous musicians will not allow their music to be used commercially (including in-house use)—Bruce Springsteen, Bob Dylan, and Irving Berlin, for example, won't give you permission. The Beatles, however, can be used by paying a large fee to Michael Jackson, who owns the rights. Other artists allow their music to be used, but will not permit the lyrics to be changed—Stephen Sondheim and Frank Loesser are examples.

Most publishers of music will gladly grant permission. Indeed, selling rights for the use of music in video programs and corporate presentations is a big business. The record company must also give its permission if you wish to use the original recording and it may be more reluctant. For example, the fees that must be paid to the publisher and recording company for in-house use of the original recording of popular music are in the range of $4,000 to $10,000 for a year's use. One-time use prices range from $1,000 to $4,000.

A less expensive alternative to using an original recording is to acquire the right to make your own recording of a popular song from the publisher. There are many companies that specialize in making sound-alike recordings or *covers* using studio musicians. Fees to use covers range from $500 to $650 for one year's use.

If you want to change the lyrics to a piece of music to be used in your program, permission must be obtained to make a cover and the publisher must approve your proposed changes to the lyrics. The greater the alteration of the lyrics, the longer it will take to get the publisher's permission. Once the publisher's permission to create the cover and alter the lyrics has been obtained, you can have the cover recorded with the new lyrics or have an instrumental version recorded and add

Filling Out Application Form PA

Detach and read these instructions before completing this form. Make sure all applicable spaces have been filled in before you return this form.

BASIC INFORMATION

When to Use This Form: Use Form PA for registration of published or unpublished works of the performing arts. This class includes works prepared for the purpose of being "performed" directly before an audience or indirectly "by means of any device or process." Works of the performing arts include: (1) musical works, including any accompanying words; (2) dramatic works, including any accompanying music; (3) pantomimes and choreographic works; and (4) motion pictures and other audiovisual works.

Deposit to Accompany Application: An application for copyright registration must be accompanied by a deposit consisting of copies or phonorecords representing the entire work for which registration is to be made. The following are the general deposit requirements as set forth in the statute:

Unpublished Work: Deposit one complete copy (or phonorecord).

Published Work: Deposit two complete copies (or phonorecords) of the best edition.

Work First Published Outside the United States: Deposit one complete copy (or phonorecord) of the first foreign edition.

Contribution to a Collective Work: Deposit one complete copy (or phonorecord) of the best edition of the collective work.

Motion Pictures: Deposit *both* of the following: (1) a separate written description of the contents of the motion picture; and (2) for a published work, one complete copy of the best edition of the motion picture; or, for an unpublished work, one complete copy of the motion picture or identifying material. Identifying material may be either an audiorecording of the entire soundtrack or one frame enlargement or similar visual print from each 10-minute segment.

The Copyright Notice: For published works, the law provides that a copyright notice in a specified form "shall be placed on all publicly distributed copies from which the work can be visually perceived." Use of the copyright notice is the responsibility of the copyright owner and does not require advance permission from the Copyright Office. The required form of the notice for copies generally consists of three elements: (1) the symbol "©", or the word "Copyright," or the abbreviation "Copr."; (2) the year of first publication; and (3) the name of the owner of copyright. For example: "© 1981 Constance Porter." The notice is to be affixed to the copies "in such manner and location as to give reasonable notice of the claim of copyright."

For further information about copyright registration, notice, or special questions relating to copyright problems, write:

Information and Publications Section, LM-455
Copyright Office
Library of Congress
Washington, D.C. 20559

PRIVACY ACT ADVISORY STATEMENT Required by the Privacy Act of 1974 (P.L. 93-579)
The authority for requesting this information is title 17 U.S.C., secs. 409 and 410. Furnishing the requested information is voluntary. But if the information is not furnished, it may be necessary to delay or refuse registration and you may not be entitled to certain relief, remedies, and benefits provided in chapters 4 and 5 of title 17, U.S.C.
The principal uses of the requested information are the establishment and maintenance of a public record and the examination of the application for compliance with legal requirements.
Other routine uses include public inspection and copying, preparation of public indexes, preparation of public catalogs of copyright registrations, and preparation of search reports upon request.
NOTE: No other advisory statement will be given in connection with this application. Please keep this statement and refer to it if we communicate with you regarding this application.

LINE-BY-LINE INSTRUCTIONS

1 SPACE 1: Title

Title of This Work: Every work submitted for copyright registration must be given a title to identify that particular work. If the copies or phonorecords of the work bear a title (or an identifying phrase that could serve as a title), transcribe that wording *completely* and *exactly* on the application. Indexing of the registration and future identification of the work will depend on the information you give here. If the work you are registering is an entire "collective work" (such as a collection of plays or songs), give the overall title of the collection. If you are registering one or more individual contributions to a collective work, give the title of each contribution, followed by the title of the collection. Example: "'A Song for Elinda' in *Old and New Ballads for Old and New People*."

Previous or Alternative Titles: Complete this space if there are any additional titles for the work under which someone searching for the registration might be likely to look, or under which a document pertaining to the work might be recorded.

Nature of This Work: Briefly describe the general nature or character of the work being registered for copyright. Examples: "Music"; "Song Lyrics"; "Words and Music"; "Drama"; "Musical Play"; "Choreography"; "Pantomime"; "Motion Picture"; "Audiovisual Work."

2 SPACE 2: Author(s)

General Instructions: After reading these instructions, decide who are the "authors" of this work for copyright purposes. Then, unless the work is a "collective work," give the requested information about every "author" who contributed any appreciable amount of copyrightable matter to this version of the work. If you need further space, request additional Continuation Sheets. In the case of a collective work, such as a songbook or a collection of plays, give information about the author of the collective work as a whole.

Name of Author: The fullest form of the author's name should be given. Unless the work was "made for hire," the individual who actually created the work is its "author." In the case of a work made for hire, the statute provides

that "the employer or other person for whom the work was prepared is considered the author."

What is a "Work Made for Hire"? A "work made for hire" is defined as: (1) "a work prepared by an employee within the scope of his or her employment"; or (2) "a work specially ordered or commissioned for use as a contribution to a collective work, as a part of a motion picture or other audiovisual work, as a translation, as a supplementary work, as a compilation, as an instructional text, as a test, as answer material for a test, or as an atlas, if the parties expressly agree in a written instrument signed by them that the work shall be considered a work made for hire." If you have checked "Yes" to indicate that the work was "made for hire," you must give the full legal name of the employer (or other person for whom the work was prepared). You may also include the name of the employee along with the name of the employer (for example: "Elster Music Co., employer for hire of John Ferguson").

"Anonymous" or "Pseudonymous" Work: An author's contribution to a work is "anonymous" if that author is not identified on the copies or phonorecords of the work. An author's contribution to a work is "pseudonymous" if that author is identified on the copies or phonorecords under a fictitious name. If the work is "anonymous" you may: (1) leave the line blank; or (2) state "anonymous" on the line; or (3) reveal the author's identity. If the work is "pseudonymous" you may: (1) leave the line blank; or (2) give the pseudonym and identify it as such (for example: "Huntley Haverstock, pseudonym"); or (3) reveal the author's name, making clear which is the real name and which is the pseudonym (for example: "Judith Barton, whose pseudonym is Madeline Elster"). However, the citizenship or domicile of the author must be given in all cases.

Dates of Birth and Death: If the author is dead, the statute requires that the year of death be included in the application unless the work is anonymous or pseudonymous. The author's birth date is optional, but is useful as a form of identification. Leave this space blank if the author's contribution was a "work made for hire."

Author's Nationality or Domicile: Give the country of which the author is a citizen, or the country in which the author is domiciled. Nationality or domicile must be given in all cases.

Nature of Authorship: Give a brief general statement of the nature of this particular author's contribution to the work. Examples: "Words"; "Co-Author of Music"; "Words and Music"; "Arrangement"; "Co-Author of Book and Lyrics"; "Dramatization"; "Screen Play"; "Compilation and English Translation"; "Editorial Revisions."

Figure 16.2 Application Form PA (page 1 of 4)

3   SPACE 3: Creation and Publication

General Instructions: Do not confuse "creation" with "publication." Every application for copyright registration must state "the year in which creation of the work was completed." Give the date and nation of first publication only if the work has been published.

Creation: Under the statute, a work is "created" when it is fixed in a copy or phonorecord for the first time. Where a work has been prepared over a period of time, the part of the work existing in fixed form on a particular date constitutes the created work on that date. The date you give here should be the year in which the author completed the particular version for which registration is now being sought, even if other versions exist or if further changes or additions are planned.

Publication: The statute defines "publication" as "the distribution of copies or phonorecords of a work to the public by sale or other transfer of ownership, or by rental, lease, or lending"; a work is also "published" if there has been an "offering to distribute copies or phonorecords to a group of persons for purposes of further distribution, public performance, or public display." Give the full date (month, day, year) when, and the country where, publication first occurred. If first publication took place simultaneously in the United States and other countries, it is sufficient to state "U.S.A."

4   SPACE 4: Claimant(s)

Name(s) and Address(es) of Copyright Claimant(s): Give the name(s) and address(es) of the copyright claimant(s) in this work even if the claimant is the same as the author. Copyright in a work belongs initially to the author of the work (including, in the case of a work made for hire, the employer or other person for whom the work was prepared). The copyright claimant is either the author of the work or a person or organization to whom the copyright initially belonging to the author has been transferred.

Transfer: The statute provides that, if the copyright claimant is not the author, the application for registration must contain "a brief statement of how the claimant obtained ownership of the copyright." If any copyright claimant named in space 4 is not an author named in space 2, give a brief, general statement summarizing the means by which that claimant obtained ownership of the copyright. Examples: "By written contract"; "Transfer of all rights by author"; "Assignment"; "By will." Do not attach transfer documents or other attachments or riders.

5   SPACE 5: Previous Registration

General Instructions: The questions in space 5 are intended to find out whether an earlier registration has been made for this work and, if so, whether there is any basis for a new registration. As a general rule, only one basic copyright registration can be made for the same version of a particular work.

Same Version: If this version is substantially the same as the work covered by a previous registration, a second registration is not generally possible unless: (1) the work has been registered in unpublished form and a second registration is now being sought to cover this first published edition; or (2) someone other than the author is identified as copyright claimant in the earlier registration, and the author is now seeking registration in his or her own name. If either of these two exceptions apply, check the appropriate box and give the

earlier registration number and date. Otherwise, do not submit Form PA; instead, write the Copyright Office for information about supplementary registration or recordation of transfers of copyright ownership.

Changed Version: If the work has been changed, and you are now seeking registration to cover the additions or revisions, check the last box in space 5, give the earlier registration number and date, and complete both parts of space 6 in accordance with the instructions below.

Previous Registration Number and Date: If more than one previous registration has been made for the work, give the number and date of the latest registration.

6   SPACE 6: Derivative Work or Compilation

General Instructions: Complete space 6 if this work is a "changed version," "compilation," or "derivative work," and if it incorporates one or more earlier works that have already been published or registered for copyright, or that have fallen into the public domain. A "compilation" is defined as "a work formed by the collection and assembling of preexisting materials or of data that are selected, coordinated, or arranged in such a way that the resulting work as a whole constitutes an original work of authorship." A "derivative work" is "a work based on one or more preexisting works." Examples of derivative works include musical arrangements, dramatizations, translations, abridgments, condensations, motion picture versions, or "any other form in which a work may be recast, transformed, or adapted." Derivative works also include works "consisting of editorial revisions, annotations, or other modifications" if these changes, as a whole, represent an original work of authorship.

Preexisting Material (space 6a): Complete this space and space 6b for derivative works. In this space identify the preexisting work that has been recast, transformed, or adapted. For example, the preexisting material might be: "French version of Hugo's 'Le Roi s'amuse'." Do not complete this space for compilations.

Material Added to This Work (space 6b): Give a brief, general statement of the additional new material covered by the copyright claim for which registration is sought. In the case of a derivative work, identify this new material. Examples: "Arrangement for piano and orchestra"; "Dramatization for television"; "New film version"; "Revisions throughout; Act III completely new." If the work is a compilation, give a brief, general statement describing both the material that has been compiled and the compilation itself. Example: "Compilation of 19th Century Military Songs."

7,8,9   SPACE 7, 8, 9: Fee, Correspondence, Certification, Return Address

Deposit Account: If you maintain a Deposit Account in the Copyright Office, identify it in space 7. Otherwise leave the space blank and send the fee of $10 with your application and deposit.

Correspondence (space 7): This space should contain the name, address, area code, and telephone number of the person to be consulted if correspondence about this application becomes necessary.

Certification (space 8): The application cannot be accepted unless it bears the date and the handwritten signature of the author or other copyright claimant, or of the owner of exclusive right(s), or of the duly authorized agent of the author, claimant, or owner of exclusive right(s).

Address for Return of Certificate (space 9): The address box must be completed legibly since the certificate will be returned in a window envelope.

MORE INFORMATION

How To Register a Recorded Work: If the musical or dramatic work that you are registering has been recorded (as a tape, disk, or cassette), you may choose either copyright application Form PA or Form SR. Performing Arts or Sound Recordings, depending on the purpose of the registration.

Form PA should be used to register the underlying musical composition or dramatic work. Form SR has been developed specifically to register a "sound recording" as defined by the Copyright Act—a work resulting from the "fixation of a series of sounds." Form SR should be used when the copyright claim is limited to the sound recording itself. (In one instance, Form SR may also be used to file registration for both kinds of works—see (4) below.) Therefore:

(1) File Form PA if you are seeking to register the musical or dramatic work, not the "sound recording," even though what you deposit for copyright purposes may be in the form of a phonorecord.

(2) File Form PA if you are seeking to register the audio portion of an audiovisual work, such as a motion picture soundtrack; these are considered integral parts of the audiovisual work.

(3) File Form SR if you are seeking to register the "sound recording" itself, that is, the work that results from the fixation of a series of musical, spoken, or other sounds, but not the underlying musical or dramatic work.

(4) File Form SR if you are the copyright claimant for both the underlying musical or dramatic work and the sound recording, and you prefer to register both on the same form.

(5) File both forms PA and SR if the copyright claimant for the underlying work and sound recording differ, or you prefer to have separate registration for them.

"Copies" and "Phonorecords": To register for copyright, you are required to deposit "copies" or "phonorecords." These are defined as follows:

Musical compositions may be embodied (fixed) in "copies," objects from which a work can be read or visually perceived, directly or with the aid of a machine or device, such as manuscripts, books, sheet music, film, and videotape. They may also be fixed in "phonorecords," objects embodying fixations of sounds, such as tapes and phonograph disks, commonly known as phonograph records. For example, a song (the work to be registered) can be reproduced in sheet music ("copies") or phonograph records ("phonorecords"), or both.

Figure 16.2   Application Form PA (page 2 of 4)

FORM PA
UNITED STATES COPYRIGHT OFFICE

REGISTRATION NUMBER

_____

PA   PAU

EFFECTIVE DATE OF REGISTRATION

Month   Day   Year

DO NOT WRITE ABOVE THIS LINE. IF YOU NEED MORE SPACE, USE A SEPARATE CONTINUATION SHEET.

1

TITLE OF THIS WORK ▼

PREVIOUS OR ALTERNATIVE TITLES ▼

NATURE OF THIS WORK ▼ See instructions

2   **a**

NAME OF AUTHOR ▼

DATES OF BIRTH AND DEATH
Year Born ▼   Year Died ▼

Was this contribution to the work a "work made for hire"?
☐ Yes
☐ No

AUTHOR'S NATIONALITY OR DOMICILE
Name of Country
OR { Citizen of ▶ _____
Domiciled in ▶ _____

WAS THIS AUTHOR'S CONTRIBUTION TO THE WORK
Anonymous?   ☐ Yes ☐ No
Pseudonymous? ☐ Yes ☐ No
If the answer to either of these questions is "Yes," see detailed instructions

NOTE

Under the law, the "author" of a "work made for hire" is generally the employer, not the employee (see instructions). For any part of this work that was "made for hire" check "Yes" in the space provided, give the employer (or other person for whom the work was prepared) as "Author" of that part, and leave the space for dates of birth and death blank.

b

NATURE OF AUTHORSHIP Briefly describe nature of the material created by this author in which copyright is claimed. ▼

NAME OF AUTHOR ▼

DATES OF BIRTH AND DEATH
Year Born ▼   Year Died ▼

Was this contribution to the work a "work made for hire"?
☐ Yes
☐ No

AUTHOR'S NATIONALITY OR DOMICILE
Name of country
OR { Citizen of ▶ _____
Domiciled in ▶ _____

WAS THIS AUTHOR'S CONTRIBUTION TO THE WORK
Anonymous?   ☐ Yes ☐ No
Pseudonymous? ☐ Yes ☐ No
If the answer to either of these questions is "Yes," see detailed instructions

c

NATURE OF AUTHORSHIP Briefly describe nature of the material created by this author in which copyright is claimed. ▼

NAME OF AUTHOR ▼

DATES OF BIRTH AND DEATH
Year Born ▼   Year Died ▼

Was this contribution to the work a "work made for hire"?
☐ Yes
☐ No

AUTHOR'S NATIONALITY OR DOMICILE
Name of Country
OR { Citizen of ▶ _____
Domiciled in ▶ _____

WAS THIS AUTHOR'S CONTRIBUTION TO THE WORK
Anonymous?   ☐ Yes ☐ No
Pseudonymous? ☐ Yes ☐ No
If the answer to either of these questions is "Yes," see detailed instructions

NATURE OF AUTHORSHIP Briefly describe nature of the material created by this author in which copyright is claimed. ▼

3

YEAR IN WHICH CREATION OF THIS WORK WAS COMPLETED This information must be given
◀ Year in all cases.

DATE AND NATION OF FIRST PUBLICATION OF THIS PARTICULAR WORK
Complete this information Month ▶ _____ Day ▶ _____ Year ▶ _____
ONLY if this work has been published.
◀ Nation

4

See instructions before completing this space.

COPYRIGHT CLAIMANT(S) Name and address must be given even if the claimant is the same as the author given in space 2.▼

TRANSFER If the claimant(s) named here in space 4 are different from the author(s) named in space 2, give a brief statement of how the claimant(s) obtained ownership of the copyright.▼

APPLICATION RECEIVED

ONE DEPOSIT RECEIVED

TWO DEPOSITS RECEIVED

REMITTANCE NUMBER AND DATE

DO NOT WRITE HERE
OFFICE USE ONLY

MORE ON BACK ▶ • Complete all applicable spaces (numbers 5-9) on the reverse side of this page
• See detailed instructions.   • Sign the form at line 8.

DO NOT WRITE HERE

Page 1 of _____ pages

Figure 16.2   Application Form PA (page 3 of 4)

EXAMINED BY	FORM PA
CHECKED BY	
☐ CORRESPONDENCE Yes	FOR COPYRIGHT OFFICE
☐ DEPOSIT ACCOUNT FUNDS USED	USE ONLY

DO NOT WRITE ABOVE THIS LINE. IF YOU NEED MORE SPACE, USE A SEPARATE CONTINUATION SHEET.

PREVIOUS REGISTRATION Has registration for this work, or for an earlier version of this work, already been made in the Copyright Office?

☐ Yes ☐ No If your answer is "Yes," why is another registration being sought? (Check appropriate box) ▼

☐ This is the first published edition of a work previously registered in unpublished form.

☐ This is the first application submitted by this author as copyright claimant.

☐ This is a changed version of the work, as shown by space 6 on this application.

If your answer is "Yes," give: **Previous Registration Number** ▼   **Year of Registration** ▼

5

DERIVATIVE WORK OR COMPILATION Complete both space 6a & 6b for a derivative work; complete only 6b for a compilation.

a. **Preexisting Material** Identify any preexisting work or works that this work is based on or incorporates. ▼

See instructions before completing this space.

b. **Material Added to This Work** Give a brief, general statement of the material that has been added to this work and in which copyright is claimed. ▼

6

DEPOSIT ACCOUNT If the registration fee is to be charged to a Deposit Account established in the Copyright Office, give name and number of Account.

Name ▼   **Account Number** ▼

CORRESPONDENCE Give name and address to which correspondence about this application should be sent. Name/Address/Apt/City/State/Zip ▼

Be sure to give your daytime phone ◄ number

Area Code & Telephone Number ►

7

CERTIFICATION* I, the undersigned, hereby certify that I am the

Check only one ▼

☐ author

☐ other copyright claimant

☐ owner of exclusive right(s)

☐ authorized agent of _____
   Name of author or other copyright claimant, or owner of exclusive right(s) ▲

of the work identified in this application and that the statements made
by me in this application are correct to the best of my knowledge.

Typed or printed name and date ▼ If this is a published work, this date must be the same as or later than the date of publication given in space 3.

_____ date ►

Handwritten signature (X) ▼

8

MAIL CERTIFI- CATE TO Certificate will be mailed in window envelope	Name ▼ Number/Street/Apartment Number ▼ City/State·ZIP ▼	Have you: • Completed all necessary spaces? • Signed your application in space 8? • Enclosed check or money order for $10 payable to Register of Copyrights? • Enclosed your deposit material with the application and fee? MAIL TO: Register of Copyrights, Library of Congress, Washington, D.C. 20559

9

* 17 U.S.C. § 506(e): Any person who knowingly makes a false representation of a material fact in the application for copyright registration provided for by section 409, or in any written statement filed in connection with the application, shall be fined not more than $2,500.

☆ U.S. GOVERNMENT PRINTING OFFICE: 1981: 355–306

Nov. 1981-700,000

Figure 16.2   Application Form PA (page 4 of 4)

your own recording of the lyrics over it. When using a cover, do not neglect to obtain releases from the recording artists for the use of the music in your program.

There are many music libraries (similar to stock houses) which may be the best source for a variety of inexpensive prerecorded music. The following are several examples:

- Production Music Library Association
  1619 Broadway, 11th Floor
  New York, NY 10019
  (212) 265-9493
- Capitol Production Music
  6922 Hollywood Blvd., Suite 718
  Hollywood, CA 90028
  (213) 461-2701
- Dewolfe Music Library
  25 West 45th Street
  New York, NY 10036
  (212) 382-0220
- Associated Production Music
  6255 Sunset Blvd.
  Hollywood, CA 90028
  (800) 543-4276

Software

Acquiring software for use in your multimedia program is fairly straightforward. As with text, the copyright owner can usually be identified. Most computer systems come with the operating system, so there's no need to sell (and hence no need to license) the operating system.

You will need a license for the commercial use of a programming language unless you use a programming language without restrictions. However, even if you use an unrestricted programming language to construct your multimedia program, the use of a compiler to reduce the programming language to assembly or machine language for commercial purposes will require a license.

Many multimedia developers use HyperCard in their programs. Although HyperCard is available for use with all Macintosh computers, if you plan to sell HyperCard as a part of your program you will have to license it from Apple Computer Inc. Apple will license HyperCard for resale for the nominal fee currently of $50 per year per product.

To acquire more specialized forms of software you will have to negotiate with the publishers or author. It's customary in the software industry to use the publisher's form of license agreement, but the terms of such agreements are often negotiated. An example of an annotated software license agreement is provided in *The Multimedia Producer's Legal Survival Guide.*

Filling Out Application Form TX

Detach and read these instructions before completing this form. Make sure all applicable spaces have been filled in before you return this form.

BASIC INFORMATION

When to Use This Form: Use Form TX for registration of published or unpublished non-dramatic literary works, excluding periodicals or serial issues. This class includes a wide variety of works: fiction, non-fiction, poetry, textbooks, reference works, directories, catalogs, advertising copy, compilations of information, and computer programs. For periodicals and serials, use Form SE.

Deposit to Accompany Application: An application for copyright registration must be accompanied by a deposit consisting of copies or phonorecords representing the entire work for which registration is to be made. The following are the general deposit requirements as set forth in the statute:

Unpublished Work: Deposit one complete copy (or phonorecord).

Published Work: Deposit two complete copies (or phonorecords) of the best edition.

Work First Published Outside the United States: Deposit one complete copy (or phonorecord) of the first foreign edition.

Contribution to a Collective Work: Deposit one complete copy (or phonorecord) of the best edition of the collective work.

The Copyright Notice: For published works, the law provides that a copyright notice in a specified form "shall be placed on all publicly distributed copies from which the work can be visually perceived." Use of the copyright notice is the responsibility of the copyright owner and does not require advance permission from the Copyright Office. The required form of the notice for copies generally consists of three elements: (1) the symbol "©", or the word "Copyright," or the abbreviation "Copr."; (2) the year of first publication; and (3) the name of the owner of copyright. For example: "© 1981 Constance Porter." The notice is to be affixed to the copies "in such manner and location as to give reasonable notice of the claim of copyright."

For further information about copyright registration, notice, or special questions relating to copyright problems, write:

Information and Publications Section, LM-455
Copyright Office
Library of Congress
Washington, D.C. 20559

PRIVACY ACT ADVISORY STATEMENT Required by the Privacy Act of 1974 (Public Law 93-579)	PRINCIPAL USES OF REQUESTED INFORMATION
	• Establishment and maintenance of a public record
AUTHORITY FOR REQUESTING THIS INFORMATION: • Title 17, U.S.C., Secs. 409 and 410	• Examination of the application for compliance with legal requirements OTHER ROUTINE USES:
FURNISHING THE REQUESTED INFORMATION IS: • Voluntary	• Public inspection and copying • Preparation of public indexes • Preparation of public catalogs of copyright registrations
BUT IF THE INFORMATION IS NOT FURNISHED: • It may be necessary to delay or refuse registration • You may not be entitled to certain relief, remedies, and benefits provided in chapters 4 and 5 of title 17, U.S.C.	• Preparation of search reports upon request NOTE: • No other advisory statement will be given you in connection with this application • Please keep this statement and refer to it if we communicate with you regarding this application.

LINE-BY-LINE INSTRUCTIONS

1 SPACE 1: Title

Title of This Work: Every work submitted for copyright registration must be given a title to identify that particular work. If the copies or phonorecords of the work bear a title (or an identifying phrase that could serve as a title), transcribe that wording *completely* and *exactly* on the application. Indexing of the registration and future identification of the work will depend on the information you give here.

Previous or Alternative Titles: Complete this space if there are any additional titles for the work under which someone searching for the registration might be likely to look, or under which a document pertaining to the work might be recorded.

Publication as a Contribution: If the work being registered is a contribution to a periodical, serial, or collection, give the title of the contribution in the "Title of this Work" space. Then, in the line headed "Publication as a Contribution," give information about the collective work in which the contribution appeared.

2 SPACE 2: Author(s)

General Instructions: After reading these instructions, decide who are the "authors" of this work for copyright purposes. Then, unless the work is a "collective work," give the requested information about every "author" who contributed any appreciable amount of copyrightable matter to this version of the work. If you need further space, request additional Continuation sheets. In the case of a collective work, such as an anthology, collection of essays, or encyclopedia, give information about the author of the collective work as a whole.

Name of Author: The fullest form of the author's name should be given. Unless the work was "made for hire," the individual who actually created the work is its "author." In the case of a work made for hire, the statute provides that "the employer or other person for whom the work was prepared is considered the author."

What is a "Work Made for Hire"? A "work made for hire" is defined as: (1) "a work prepared by an employee within the scope of his or her employment"; or (2) "a work specially ordered or commissioned for use as a contribution to a collective work, as a part of a motion picture or other audiovisual work, as a translation, as a supplementary work, as a compilation, as an instructional text, as a test, as answer material for a test, or as an atlas, if the parties expressly agree in a written instrument signed by them that the work shall be considered a work made for hire." If you have checked "Yes" to indicate that the work was "made for hire," you must give the full legal name of the employer (or other person for whom the work was prepared). You may also include the name of the employee along with the name of the employer (for example: "Elster Publishing Co., employer for hire of John Ferguson").

"Anonymous" or "Pseudonymous" Work: An author's contribution to a work is "anonymous" if that author is not identified on the copies or phonorecords of the work. An author's contribution to a work is "pseudonymous" if that author is identified on the copies or phonorecords under a fictitious name. If the work is "anonymous" you may: (1) leave the line blank; or (2) state "anonymous" on the line; or (3) reveal the author's identity. If the work is "pseudonymous" you may: (1) leave the line blank; or (2) give the pseudonym and identify it as such (for example: "Huntley Haverstock, pseudonym"); or (3) reveal the author's name, making clear which is the real name and which is the pseudonym (for example: "Judith Barton, whose pseudonym is Madeline Elster"). However, the citizenship or domicile of the author must be given in all cases.

Dates of Birth and Death: If the author is dead, the statute requires that the year of death be included in the application unless the work is anonymous or pseudonymous. The author's birth date is optional, but is useful as a form of identification. Leave this space blank if the author's contribution was a "work made for hire."

Author's Nationality or Domicile: Give the country of which the author is a citizen, or the country in which the author is domiciled. Nationality or domicile must be given in all cases.

Nature of Authorship: After the words "Nature of Authorship" give a brief general statement of the nature of this particular author's contribution to the work. Examples: "Entire text"; "Coauthor of entire text"; "Chapters 11-14"; "Editorial revisions"; "Compilation and English translation"; "New text."

Figure 16.3   Application Form TX (page 1 of 4)

3   SPACE 3: Creation and Publication

General Instructions: Do not confuse "creation" with "publication." Every application for copyright registration must state "the year in which creation of the work was completed." Give the date and nation of first publication only if the work has been published.

Creation: Under the statute, a work is "created" when it is fixed in a copy or phonorecord for the first time. Where a work has been prepared over a period of time, the part of the work existing in fixed form on a particular date constitutes the created work on that date. The date you give here should be the year in which the author completed the particular version for which registration is now being sought, even if other versions exist or if further changes or additions are planned.

Publication: The statute defines "publication" as "the distribution of copies or phonorecords of a work to the public by sale or other transfer of ownership, or by rental, lease, or lending"; a work is also "published" if there has been an "offering to distribute copies or phonorecords to a group of persons for purposes of further distribution, public performance, or public display." Give the full date (month, day, year) when, and the country where, publication first occurred. If first publication took place simultaneously in the United States and other countries, it is sufficient to state "U.S.A."

4   SPACE 4: Claimant(s)

Name(s) and Address(es) of Copyright Claimant(s): Give the name(s) and address(es) of the copyright claimant(s) in this work even if the claimant is the same as the author. Copyright in a work belongs initially to the author of the work (including, in the case of a work made for hire, the employer or other person for whom the work was prepared). The copyright claimant is either the author of the work or a person or organization to whom the copyright initially belonging to the author has been transferred.

Transfer: The statute provides that, if the copyright claimant is not the author, the application for registration must contain "a brief statement of how the claimant obtained ownership of the copyright." If any copyright claimant named in space 4 is not an author named in space 2, give a brief, general statement summarizing the means by which that claimant obtained ownership of the copyright. Examples: "By written contract"; "Transfer of all rights by author"; "Assignment"; "By will." Do not attach transfer documents or other attachments or riders.

5   SPACE 5: Previous Registration

General Instructions: The questions in space 5 are intended to find out whether an earlier registration has been made for this work and, if so, whether there is any basis for a new registration. As a general rule, only one basic copyright registration can be made for the same version of a particular work.

Same Version: If this version is substantially the same as the work covered by a previous registration, a second registration is not generally possible unless: (1) the work has been registered in unpublished form and a second registration is now being sought to cover this first published edition; or (2) someone other than the author is identified as copyright claimant in the earlier registration, and the author is now seeking registration in his or her own name. If either of these two exceptions apply, check the appropriate box and give the earlier registration number and date. Otherwise, do not submit Form TX; instead, write the Copyright Office for information about supplementary registration or recordation of transfers of copyright ownership.

Changed Version: If the work has been changed, and you are now seeking registration to cover the additions or revisions, check the last box in space 5, give the earlier registration number and date, and complete both parts of space 6 in accordance with the instructions below.

Previous Registration Number and Date: If more than one previous registration has been made for the work, give the number and date of the latest registration.

6   SPACE 6: Derivative Work or Compilation

General Instructions: Complete space 6 if this work is a "changed version," "compilation," or "derivative work," and if it incorporates one or more earlier works that have already been published or registered for copyright, or that have fallen into the public domain. A "compilation" is defined as "a work formed by the collection and assembling of preexisting materials or of data that are selected, coordinated, or arranged in such a way that the resulting work as a whole constitutes an original work of authorship." A "derivative work" is "a work based on one or more preexisting works." Examples of derivative works include translations, fictionalizations, abridgments, condensations, or "any other form in which a work may be recast, transformed, or adapted." Derivative works also include works "consisting of editorial revisions, annotations, or other modifications" if these changes, as a whole, represent an original work of authorship.

Preexisting Material (space 6a): For derivative works, complete this space and space 6b. In space 6a identify the preexisting work that has been recast, transformed, or adapted. An example of preexisting material might be: "Russian version of Goncharov's 'Oblomov'." Do not complete space 6a for compilations.

Material Added to This Work (space 6b): Give a brief, general statement of the new material covered by the copyright claim for which registration is sought. Derivative work examples include: "Foreword, editing, critical annotations"; "Translation"; "Chapters 11-17." If the work is a compilation, describe both the compilation itself and the material that has been compiled. Example: "Compilation of certain 1917 Speeches by Woodrow Wilson." A work may be both a derivative work and compilation, in which case a sample statement might be: "Compilation and additional new material."

7   SPACE 7: Manufacturing Provisions

General Instructions: The copyright statute currently provides, as a general rule, that the copies of a published work "consisting preponderantly of nondramatic literary material in the English language" be manufactured in the United States or Canada in order to be lawfully imported and publicly distributed in the United States. If the work being registered is unpublished or not in English, leave this space blank. Complete this space if registration is sought for a published work "consisting preponderantly of nondramatic literary material that is in the English language." Identify those who manufactured the copies and where those manufacturing processes were performed. As an exception to the manufacturing provisions, the statute prescribes that, where manufacture has taken place outside the United States or Canada, a maximum of 2000 copies of the foreign edition may be imported into the United States without affecting the copyright owners' rights. For this purpose, the Copyright Office will issue an Import Statement upon request and payment of a fee of $3 at the time of registration or at any later time. For further information about import statements, write for Form IS.

8   SPACE 8: Reproduction for Use of Blind or Physically Handicapped Individuals

General Instructions: One of the major programs of the Library of Congress is to provide Braille editions and special recordings of works for the exclusive use of the blind and physically handicapped. In an effort to simplify and speed up the copyright licensing procedures that are a necessary part of this program, section 710 of the copyright statute provides for the establishment of a voluntary licensing system to be tied in with copyright registration. Copyright Office regulations provide that you may grant a license for such reproduction and distribution solely for the use of persons who are certified by competent authority as unable to read normal printed material as a result of physical limitations. The license is entirely voluntary, nonexclusive, and may be terminated upon 90 days notice.

How to Grant the License: If you wish to grant it, check one of the three boxes in space 8. Your check in one of these boxes, together with your signature in space 10, will mean that the Library of Congress can proceed to reproduce and distribute under the license without further paperwork. For further information, write for Circular R63.

9,10,11   SPACE 9, 10, 11: Fee, Correspondence, Certification, Return Address

Deposit Account: If you maintain a Deposit Account in the Copyright Office, identify it in space 9. Otherwise leave the space blank and send the fee of $10 with your application and deposit.

Correspondence (space 9): This space should contain the name, address, area code, and telephone number of the person to be consulted if correspondence about this application becomes necessary.

Certification (space 10): The application can not be accepted unless it bears the date and the handwritten signature of the author or other copyright claimant, or of the owner of exclusive right(s), or of the duly authorized agent of author, claimant, or owner of exclusive right(s).

Address for Return of Certificate (space 11): The address box must be completed legibly since the certificate will be returned in a window envelope.

Figure 16.3   Application Form TX (page 2 of 4)

FORM TX
UNITED STATES COPYRIGHT OFFICE

REGISTRATION NUMBER

TX   TXU

EFFECTIVE DATE OF REGISTRATION

Month   Day   Year

DO NOT WRITE ABOVE THIS LINE. IF YOU NEED MORE SPACE, USE A SEPARATE CONTINUATION SHEET.

1

TITLE OF THIS WORK ▼

PREVIOUS OR ALTERNATIVE TITLES ▼

PUBLICATION AS A CONTRIBUTION If this work was published as a contribution to a periodical, serial, or collection, give information about the collective work in which the contribution appeared.   Title of Collective Work ▼

If published in a periodical or serial give: Volume ▼   Number ▼   Issue Date ▼   On Pages ▼

2   **a**

NAME OF AUTHOR ▼

DATES OF BIRTH AND DEATH
Year Born ▼   Year Died ▼

Was this contribution to the work a "work made for hire"?   □ Yes   □ No

AUTHOR'S NATIONALITY OR DOMICILE
Name of Country
OR { Citizen of ▶_____
     Domiciled in ▶_____

WAS THIS AUTHOR'S CONTRIBUTION TO THE WORK
Anonymous?   □ Yes □ No
Pseudonymous?   □ Yes □ No
If the answer to either of these questions is "Yes," see detailed instructions.

NATURE OF AUTHORSHIP Briefly describe nature of the material created by this author in which copyright is claimed. ▼

NOTE
Under the law, the "author" of a "work made for hire" is generally the employer, not the employee (see instructions). For any part of this work that was "made for hire" check "Yes" in the space provided, give the employer (or other person for whom the work was prepared) as "Author" of that part, and leave the space for dates of birth and death blank.

b

NAME OF AUTHOR ▼

DATES OF BIRTH AND DEATH
Year Born ▼   Year Died ▼

Was this contribution to the work a "work made for hire"?   □ Yes   □ No

AUTHOR'S NATIONALITY OR DOMICILE
Name of country
OR { Citizen of ▶_____
     Domiciled in ▶_____

WAS THIS AUTHOR'S CONTRIBUTION TO THE WORK
Anonymous?   □ Yes □ No
Pseudonymous?   □ Yes □ No
If the answer to either of these questions is "Yes," see detailed instructions.

NATURE OF AUTHORSHIP Briefly describe nature of the material created by this author in which copyright is claimed. ▼

c

NAME OF AUTHOR ▼

DATES OF BIRTH AND DEATH
Year Born ▼   Year Died ▼

Was this contribution to the work a "work made for hire"?   □ Yes   □ No

AUTHOR'S NATIONALITY OR DOMICILE
Name of Country
OR { Citizen of ▶_____
     Domiciled in ▶_____

WAS THIS AUTHOR'S CONTRIBUTION TO THE WORK
Anonymous?   □ Yes □ No
Pseudonymous?   □ Yes □ No
If the answer to either of these questions is "Yes," see detailed instructions.

NATURE OF AUTHORSHIP Briefly describe nature of the material created by this author in which copyright is claimed. ▼

3

YEAR IN WHICH CREATION OF THIS WORK WAS COMPLETED   This information must be given ◀ Year   in all cases.

DATE AND NATION OF FIRST PUBLICATION OF THIS PARTICULAR WORK
Complete this information ONLY if this work has been published.   Month ▶_____ Day ▶_____ Year ▶_____   ◀ Nation

4

COPYRIGHT CLAIMANT(S) Name and address must be given even if the claimant is the same as the author given in space 2.▼

TRANSFER If the claimant(s) named here in space 4 are different from the author(s) named in space 2, give a brief statement of how the claimant(s) obtained ownership of the copyright.▼

APPLICATION RECEIVED

ONE DEPOSIT RECEIVED

TWO DEPOSITS RECEIVED

REMITTANCE NUMBER AND DATE

DO NOT WRITE HERE OFFICE USE ONLY

See instructions before completing this space.

MORE ON BACK ▶   • Complete all applicable spaces (numbers 5-11) on the reverse side of this page.   • See detailed instructions.   • Sign the form at line 10.

DO NOT WRITE HERE
Page 1 of_____ pages

Figure 16.3   Application Form TX (page 3 of 4)

EXAMINED BY		FORM TX
CHECKED BY		

☐ CORRESPONDENCE
Yes

☐ DEPOSIT ACCOUNT
FUNDS USED

FOR
COPYRIGHT
OFFICE
USE
ONLY

DO NOT WRITE ABOVE THIS LINE. IF YOU NEED MORE SPACE, USE A SEPARATE CONTINUATION SHEET.

PREVIOUS REGISTRATION Has registration for this work, or for an earlier version of this work, already been made in the Copyright Office?
☐ Yes ☐ No If your answer is "Yes," why is another registration being sought? (Check appropriate box) ▼
☐ This is the first published edition of a work previously registered in unpublished form.
☐ This is the first application submitted by this author as copyright claimant.
☐ This is a changed version of the work, as shown by space 6 on this application.
If your answer is "Yes," give: **Previous Registration Number** ▼   **Year of Registration** ▼

5

DERIVATIVE WORK OR COMPILATION Complete both space 6a & 6b for a derivative work; complete only 6b for a compilation.
a. Preexisting Material Identify any preexisting work or works that this work is based on or incorporates. ▼

b. Material Added to This Work Give a brief, general statement of the material that has been added to this work and in which copyright is claimed. ▼

See instructions
before completing
this space.

6

MANUFACTURERS AND LOCATIONS If this is a published work consisting preponderantly of nondramatic literary material in English, the law may require that the copies be manufactured in the United States or Canada for full protection. If so, the names of the manufacturers who performed certain processes, and the places where these processes were performed must be given. See instructions for details.
Names of Manufacturers ▼   **Places of Manufacture** ▼

7

REPRODUCTION FOR USE OF BLIND OR PHYSICALLY HANDICAPPED INDIVIDUALS A signature on this form at space 10, and a check in one of the boxes here in space 8, constitutes a non-exclusive grant of permission to the Library of Congress to reproduce and distribute solely for the blind and physically handicapped and under the conditions and limitations prescribed by the regulations of the Copyright Office: (1) copies of the work identified in space 1 of this application in Braille (or similar tactile symbols); or (2) phonorecords embodying a fixation of a reading of that work; or (3) both.
a ☐ Copies and Phonorecords   b ☐ Copies Only   c ☐ Phonorecords Only

See instructions.

8

DEPOSIT ACCOUNT If the registration fee is to be charged to a Deposit Account established in the Copyright Office, give name and number of Account.
Name ▼   **Account Number** ▼

CORRESPONDENCE Give name and address to which correspondence about this application should be sent. Name/Address/Apt/City/State/Zip ▼

Area Code & Telephone Number ►

Be sure to
give your
daytime phone
◄ number

9

CERTIFICATION* I, the undersigned, hereby certify that I am the
Check one ►
☐ author
☐ other copyright claimant
☐ owner of exclusive right(s)
☐ authorized agent of _____
of the work identified in this application and that the statements made
by me in this application are correct to the best of my knowledge.
Name of author or other copyright claimant, or owner of exclusive right(s) ▲

Typed or printed name and date ▼ If this is a published work, this date must be the same as or later than the date of publication given in space 3.

_____ date ► _____

Handwritten signature (X) ▼

10

MAIL CERTIFI-CATE TO	Name ▼
Certificate will be mailed in window envelope	Number/Street/Apartment Number ▼
	City/State/ZIP ▼

Have you:
• Completed all necessary spaces?
• Signed your application in space 10?
• Enclosed check or money order for $10 payable to Register of Copyrights?
• Enclosed your deposit material with the application and fee?
MAIL TO: Register of Copyrights, Library of Congress, Washington, D C 20559

11

* 17 U.S.C. § 506(e) Any person who knowingly makes a false representation of a material fact in the application for copyright registration provided for by section 409, or in any written statement filed in connection with the application, shall be fined not more than $2,500.

☆ U.S. GOVERNMENT PRINTING OFFICE: 1981: 355–304   Nov. 1981-400,000

Figure 16.3   Application Form TX (page 4 of 4)

Talent

If you use actors in your multimedia program you must get them to sign a release to ensure that you have full rights to use their likenesses for all your applications. Many industrial or low-budget videos use student or non-union actors in their productions. If you wish to use more professional actors in your multimedia program, you will probably have to pay the wage scale and comply with the requirements of the Screen Actors Guild. Obviously, this will be quite expensive.

Hiring and negotiating with professional actors and their agents could be the subject of an entire book of its own. Contact the Screen Actors Guild for literature and leads on finding out more about the conventions of the motion picture and television industry.

Examples of releases are found in *The Multimedia Producer's Legal Survival Guide*, as is a detailed discussion of privacy and publicity rights.

About the Author

Stephen Ian McIntosh

Stephen Ian McIntosh is a California lawyer and businessman with practice experience working with high technology companies, venture capital financing, software licensing, and intellectual property. McIntosh lectures on intellectual property issues in interactive programs and multimedia development.

Until recently, McIntosh was associated with the law firm of Pillsbury, Madison and Sutro in San Francisco. He is now Vice President of Finance and General Counsel of Earth Wise, Inc, in Boulder, Colorado. McIntosh holds a Bachelor of Science in Business Administration from the University of Southern California and is an Order of the Coif graduate of the University of Virginia School of Law where he was Articles Editor of the *Virginia Law Review.*

17

Copyright Considerations of Hypertext Producers: Imaging and Document Conversion

By Patrice Lyons, Esq.

Adapted from a talk given at the Library and Information Technology Association, Chicago, Illinois, June 22, 1990.

Introduction

This chapter will consider whether any rights under the federal copyright statute may be infringed upon by the unauthorized conversion of documents printed on paper to digital form for fixation on optical discs or tapes. While there are a host of interesting copyright issues relating to access over computer networks to information fixed in optical media, I will touch on them only as they relate to the actual imaging and document conversion process.

Before turning to a discussion of some legal aspects of document conversion, I would ask you to indulge in a bit of imaging. I was recently visiting Nantucket, MA, and happened to notice a sign that I thought rather interesting. They had built a series of attractive disposal bins that looked like small versions of the lovely shingled houses prevalent on the island. On the row of bins, there was a mark showing a series of arrows arranged in a circle to signify recycling of the elements.

Let us assume that a poet in an idle moment, seeing this arrangement, decides to write an ode to recycling. The words of this poem are arranged within a circle of

259

arrows in an artistic manner. The letters are printed in the color brown to signify the earth: the graphic design is drawn in the color green, signifying grass; and the words and design are set against a blue background to signify the heavens. The poem is published in a small anthology of poems on various aspects of the environment.

At some later time, an environmental group reads the anthology, and decides to add it to a collection of material on recycling that it is converting into digital form for eventual distribution to the public on an optical disc. The group also intends to make the information accessible over its computer network for display and printing at remote locations.

Since the copy of the anthology being scanned by the group was carried on several field trips, it contains smudges and handwritten marginal notes. Moreover, the work was not printed on high quality stock, and much of the input material is in somewhat deteriorated form. The digital information resulting from the conversion process reflects the low quality of the original copy. In the resulting bitmap, many of the characters are unclear, and there are smudges throughout the text. When the resulting bitmap is further converted into text for enhanced retrieval, the conversion method used distinguishes the graphic design of the arrows from the text.

The digitized text is shown in paragraph form and the graphic design is separated out. Even though some attempt is made to check the accuracy of the material in the editing phase, there is a high percentage of errors in the machine-readable text fixed on an optical disc. Further, the blue, green and brown colors in the original poem have been deleted in the digital representation of the text, because the scanner was not capable of processing color images.

Being sensitive to copyright issues as well as the environment, the group makes an inquiry about permissions that may be required before proceeding with its plans to market its digitized information, and permit access to the information fixed in this form over its computer network. They were particularly encouraged to do so because there is a copyright notice on the anthology as a whole, as well as on each individual contribution to the collective work; and, a copyright claim in the anthology has been registered with the Copyright Office. Certain copyright considerations that may arise in connection with this general scenario will be the focus of my comments.

Subject Matter of Copyright

Whether copyright infringement occurs in the conversion process would depend on the nature of the imaged works and the extent to which they have been accurately reproduced. What is protected by copyright will vary from case to case. Where the works being scanned are not protected by copyright, such as publications of the U.S. government or solely factual material, a license may not be required to reproduce, display publicly, and transmit the material for remote viewing, and, perhaps, to make a derivative work. While this would not rule out claims based on other legal theories such as privacy, from a copyright perspective there may not be any restriction on the conversion of such public domain material into digital form. I say "may," since it is often unclear whether a given work is protected by copyright.

Even in the case of works published at the time the first copyright law was enacted over two hundred years ago, the work being scanned may be a revised edition of the earlier work. While the underlying work is in the public domain, the new matter may be subject to copyright as a derivative work. It has long been established that "a 'copy of something in the public domain' will support a copyright if it is a 'distinguishable variation.'" [Alfred Bell and Co. v. Catalda Fine Arts, 191 F.2d 99, 102 (2d Cir. 1951].

In an action for copyright infringement, a defendant would usually have recourse to defenses such as "fair use" and copying restricted to ideas (often referred to as the idea/expression dichotomy). It is axiomatic in copyright law that "(a)n author can claim to 'own' only an original manner of expressing ideas or an original arrangement of facts." [Cooling Systems and Flexibles v. Stuart Radiator, 777 F.2d 485, 491 (9th Cir. 1985)]. Moreover, where an idea is capable of being expressed in only a limited number of ways, courts have allowed all but verbatim reproduction or very close paraphrasing of the original work. [See, e.g., Landsberg v. Scrabble Crossword Game Players, Inc., 736 F.2d 485, 488 (9th Cir. 1984)] So, for example, the rules of a game would usually not be subject to copyright, while an original wording used to describe those rules might be.

When converting material for library or archival purposes, it is usually not practical to make an analysis of each work to determine whether it is subject to any copyright claims, and, if so, who is the owner of copyright. Given the extent of protection accorded to even fact-based works under certain judicial decisions, it may not be prudent to rely solely on subjective judgments to decide whether in a given case material is protected by copyright. This rationale would apply to the conversion of abstracts and indices into digital form as well as the full text of print material such as journal articles. While it may be argued that unauthorized reproduction in digital form of substantial portions of a given index or abstract constitutes "fair use," [see e.g., New York Times Co. v. Roxbury Data Interface, 434 F. Supp. 217 (D.N.J. 1977)] where such material is reproduced verbatim from the original text, it is advisable to request authorization from the copyright owners (and here I am not talking about isolated and occasional reproduction for personal use).

An interesting decision that may serve to illustrate the need to seek authorization to reproduce material in digital form is the case involving the reproduction by Mead Data in its LEXIS computerized legal research service of West Publishing Company's arrangement and pagination of legal decisions. [See West Pub. Co. v. Mead Data Cent.. Inc., 799 F.2d 1219 (8th Cir. 1986)] The court took the position that "(a)n arrangement of opinions in a case reporter, no less than a compilation and arrangement of Shakespeare's sonnets, can qualify for copyright protection." [Id. at 1224]

Even if the underlying material is in the public domain, or authors of individual contributions to a collective work do not object, a publisher of such material printed in paper form may object to a given reproduction into digital form. Often, the publisher will choose the typefont for the text, add an introduction, index or title page, choose the color and appearance of certain aspects of the text and accompanying pictorial or graphic material, and edit the material for accuracy in spelling, content, and grammar. In the case of a periodical, a publisher may claim copyright in the overall selection and arrangement of the journal articles and other elements in a given issue. Where the publisher's contributions are limited to such minor elements as correction of spelling errors, arrangement of text in columns, or selection of typeface design, they may not warrant protection as copyrighted works apart from the underlying work. However, the selection and arrangement of the articles is a more controversial matter. This is particularly evident in the area of database protection where there has been a growing conflict among the Courts of Appeals on whether copyright protection for databases may be premised on "sweat of the brow" or "industrious collection" alone, or whether "originality" in the selection and arrangement of the contents is also required. [See, e.g., Financial Investors Service, 808 F.2d 204 (2d Cir. 1986), cert. denied, 484 U.S. 820 (1987)]

Whether a publisher may claim any rights in such items as the appearance and layout of a page has been the subject of some dispute over the years. At an International Copyright Symposium held at Paris in April 1990, consideration was given to the preparation of an international convention to protect what was termed the "publisher's right" on a neighboring rights theory. Neighboring rights are usually accorded to works that are deemed secondary in character to original works of authorship subject to copyright. While strong support for this proposal came from the publisher's association of the United Kingdom, representatives of U.S. publishers resisted the suggestion. This right would build on any rights of authors in the underlying works, much as the author of musical works and the producer of a sound recording based on such works are accorded different levels of protection in various countries.

Leaving aside for the moment the question of a new publisher's right, and assuming that the material you intend to convert to digital form is protected by copyright, what basic rights should you cover in a licensing agreement? In analyzing this matter, it is necessary to address the characteristics of the imaging and conversion technology used in a given case.

Initial Reproductions

A photocopy of a paper document will occasionally be made at the preprocessing stage in order to enhance or improve the quality of the resulting bit-mapped images. This issue is usually considered within the context of on-going negotiations relating to photocopying by libraries and archives. In the early seventies, often-difficult negotiations preceded the enactment of Section 108 of the Copyright Act of 1976, and the adoption of the photocopying guidelines set forth in the Conference Report on the 1976 Act. [See Photocopying—Interlibrary Arrangements, H.R. Rep. No. 94-1733, 94th Cong., 2d Sess. 72 (1976)]

While most library groups have adjusted to these requirements, there is a growing perception that the scope of these provisions is somewhat restricted and out of date. Since the technology for scanning documents into bit-mapped images and converting the material into ASCII for enhanced retrieval purposes was not prevalent at the time the copyright law was revised, the 1976 Act and guidelines do not appear to cover these technological developments.

For the moment, however, initial photocopying done at the preprocessing stage may be considered covered by the existing provisions on photocopying, and, perhaps, any current photocopy licenses. In this respect, the activities of the *Copyright Clearance Center* (CCC) are of particular note. The CCC is playing an important role in facilitating access to copyrighted works while assuring some return to the copyright owners for the photocopying of their works.

Digital Conversion Process

Apart from any initial photocopies, the actual conversion of material printed on paper into digital form would not usually fall within legal provisions on photocopying by libraries and archives, or CCC license agreements limited to photocopying. Unless the material being converted is not protected by copyright, or the copying is permitted under a theory such as "fair use," the conversion process would appear to be a distinct category of reproduction that would require a separate authorization from the relevant copyright owners.

There are currently a limited number of experimental licenses that have been negotiated between user organizations and copyright owners and their representatives, such as the CCC, for the conversion of copyrighted material printed on paper into digital form for purposes of remote access over computer networks. As users and copyright owners alike gain more experience with this new technology, it may become advisable to consider the copyright aspects of document conversion in a more systematic manner, perhaps along the lines of Section 108 of the 1976 Act and the guidelines on photocopying by libraries and archives. The status of out-of-print works, difficulty in identifying copyright ownership, technical requirements such as maximum percentage of errors that will be tolerated and the degree to which efforts should be made to conform the digitized copy to the original work may be addressed at such time. Until further experience is acquired, such details will best remain a matter for negotiation between copyright owners and users in the context of voluntary license arrangements.

Characteristics of Technology

Care should be taken when negotiating license agreements for the reproduction of works in digital form to anticipate the particular characteristics of the conversion process. Digitization inherently distorts most signals, but the amount of distortion varies. While some errors may occur due to flaws in the original copy, others may be traced to technical constraints. The hardware and software used in representing a work in digital form may abridge, compress, recast, or adapt the material in such a way that it may amount to an infringement of exclusive rights of the copyright owner. Questions may also be raised concerning the application of moral rights following entry of the United States into the Berne Union in March 1989; I will come back to this issue.

The quality of the technology is rapidly improving and new capabilities are being added. However, given current technical limitations, it is advisable for an organization using a conversion technique that segments document pages into those regions containing text and those containing graphics, and then represents the text as ASCII characters and stores the graphics as bit-mapped images, to secure a specific license to reproduce the original work in truncated form, in addition to any other permissions that may be required. This would be particularly true where the retrieval software does not recognize graphics, and, therefore, a user is only capable of accessing the text material.

A recent case in the television broadcast industry provides some guidance on this point. The case involved copyright claims of WGN, an independent television station in Chicago, against United Video, a satellite common carrier that picks up and delivers the WGN signal for reception by cable systems.

WGN initiated an experiment with teletext, using what is called the vertical blanking interval to carry information for viewing in connection with its nine o'clock news program. United Video did not deliver the WGN teletext along with the news, but, instead substituted teletext supplied by Dow Jones.

The court found that WGN's teletext was covered by the copyright in its nine o'clock news, provided that the teletext was "intended to be seen by the same viewers as are watching the nine o'clock news, during the same interval of time in which that news is broadcast, and as an integral part of the news program." [WGN Continental Broadcasting Co. v. United Video, 693 F.2d 622 (7th Cir. 1982)] In reaching its decision, the court likened the WGN situation to the case where, "if the publisher of a history book includes a fold-out map as an endpaper for the reader to consult from time to time while reading the text, the copyright on the book includes the map although the map is not intended to be read either simultaneously with the text or in some prescribed sequence with it." [Id. at 627] Citing the decision in Gilliam v. American Broadcasting Companies, Inc., the court noted that:

> A copyright licensee who "makes an unauthorized use of the underlying work by publishing it in a truncated version" is an infringer—any "unauthorized editing of the underlying work, if proven, would constitute an infringement of the copyright in that work similar to any other use of a work that exceeded the license granted by the proprietor of the copyright." [WGN Continental Broadcasting Cos., id. at 625.]

Where an author of a journal article illustrates the text with statistical tables and other graphic material, and, without the consent of the copyright owner, this material is deleted when the article is converted to digital images, it is difficult to support an argument that the graphic material did not form an integral part of the article. There is a need for specificity in your license agreements on this point. Representing the digitized article in such truncated form may constitute not only an infringement of the author's reproduction rights, but also the making of an unauthorized derivative work.

Derivative Works

It is often thought that, in order to be deemed a derivative work, the original material must be reproduced or performed in the secondary work. A recent decision involving works of art indicates that a derivative work may be created where parts of an underlying work are separated from the original version and recast in a different form. [See Mirage Editions, Inc. v. Albuquerque A.R.T. Co., 856 F.2d 1341 (9th Cir. 1988)] In the Mirage case, the court was asked to determine whether the process of selecting pages from a commemorative book containing a compilation of copyrighted individual art works and personal commentaries, mounting the pages individually onto ceramic tiles, and selling the tiles at retail constituted an infringement of copyright in the book.

While the underlying work in Mirage was not reproduced or performed when the pictorial material from the book was mounted on tiles, the court found that the author's right to prepare or authorize the preparation of a derivative work was infringed. The court concluded that, while the act of removing the individual images from the book and placing them on the tiles may not accomplish a reproduction, the individual images were recast or transformed by incorporating them into its tile-preparing process, and, therefore, the defendant prepared an infringing derivative work. [Id. at 1344]

The separation of bit-mapped images of text from any graphics material, and the subsequent representation of the text in ASCII characters, where the text alone is fixed in an optical media, would appear to constitute the making of a derivative work as well as a reproduction of the original material. On the other hand, where the system software is capable of recognizing both the ASCII code and the bit-mapped graphics images, and recombines them for retrieval purposes, and there is a high degree of accuracy in the representation of the original work made available to the public, there may be a reproduction of the original work, but it is questionable whether the resulting digital product constitutes a derivative work. The controlling question would appear to be whether the original work has been transformed, adapted or recast into a new and different version.

Stepping back from such elements as the separation of text and graphics, it may be useful to consider for a moment whether the conversion of a document printed on paper into digital form constitutes such a change in character to represent the making of a derivative work. Here I am referring to the intrinsic new properties inherent in the nature of digitized information.For example, unlike print material, text fixed in digital form may be manipulated, searched, revised and accessed over computer networks, to name a few properties.

This calls to mind the debates that transpired in the early part of this century when the then new motion picture technology permitted the dramatization of novels and other printed works. In a case decided by the Supreme Court in 1911, a year before Congress revised the copyright law to provide specifically for the category of motion pictures, the Court was asked to review the question whether the public exhibition of moving pictures infringed any rights under the copyright law in the novel *Ben Hur.* The Court found that, if "moving pictures may be used for dramatizing a novel, when the photographs are used in that way, they are used to infringe a right which the statute reserves." [Kalem Co. v. Harper Bros., 222 U.S. 55, 62 (1911)]

In a more recent decision involving the sale of a speeded-up video game, Midway Mfg. Co. v. Artic Intern.. Inc., [704 F.2d 1009 (2d Cir. 1983)] the court relied on the additional value to the copyright owner of having the right to market separately the speeded-up version. Distinguishing the case of a speeded-up phonograph record where the change in time of the added chorus, and the slight variation in the base of the accompaniment, without any change in the tune or lyrics, was considered too trivial to warrant legal protection as a derivative work, the court found that a "speeded-up video game is a substantially different product from the original game," and therefore, subject to the derivative rights of the owner of copyright in the original game. [Id. at 1014]

Moral Rights of Authors

Unlike an author's economic rights embodied in the current copyright law, the Berne Convention for the Protection of Literary and Artistic Works [Paris Act, 1971], to which the United States became a party in March 1989, sets forth certain rights that are of a personal nature. Section 6bis, paragraph (1), of the Berne Convention provides that:

> Independently of the author's economic rights, and even after the transfer of the said rights, the author shall have the right to claim authorship of the work and to object to any distortion, mutilation or other modification of, or other derogatory action in relation to, the said work, which would be prejudicial to his honor or reputation.

While an author may seek relief for these rights under state law, and, to date there has been only limited recognition of such rights at the federal level, [see, e.g., Gilliam v. American Broadcasting Companies, Inc., 538 F.2d 14 (2d Cir. 1976)], the remedies available are uneven at best. Of particular relevance in the document conversion process is the right of integrity.

At a hearing last fall on "Moral Rights and the Performing Arts," the Register of Copyrights recalled that, in joining the Berne Convention, Congress decided to follow a minimalist approach, and, in particular, did not enact additional moral rights protection. In addition to moral rights issues raised in connection with the computer colorization of motion pictures, the Register addressed other alterations of motion pictures made for post-theatrical release that may be subject to moral rights, such as the editing of films for television, "lexiconning" or time compression (speeding up or slowing down of films), and "panning and scanning" (adaptations of films to convert images conceived for the wide theatrical screen to smaller television screens). Analogies to the document conversion process come to mind, e.g., scanners that do not process color information, compression methods that distort the signal, and system software that separates text from graphics.

The Register also noted a new technology, known as digital sound sampling, that he thought Congress might want to consider in the moral rights context. A moral rights issue may arise where samples from various musical performances are assembled into a new composition. While copyright in sound recordings gives the copyright owner the economic right to control the creation of substantially similar derivative works, digital sampling allows the peculiar characteristics of someone's sound to be manipulated from only a few notes. The Register concluded that, using traditional copyright infringement principles, a one or two note sample may not be judged a substantial taking sufficient to constitute copyright infringement.

Moral rights considerations would also come into play in the conversion of documents printed on paper into digitized form. Given the technology available, it is evident that notions of "fair use" developed in a print world may no longer be relevant where the normal use of a digital work may be limited to the taking of brief excerpts, or, eventually, the manipulation of text in order to abstract what may be termed "knowledge." But that is a discussion for another day.

About the Author

Patrice Lyons, Esq.

Patrice A. Lyons has served as Legal Officer at UNESCO in Paris (1971-1976), where she was involved in the preparation of the convention relating to the distribution of program-carrying signals transmitted by satellite. As a Senior Attorney in the Office of General Counsel, Copyright Office (1976-1987), she participated in the drafting of the Semiconductor Chip Protection Act of 1984 and the regulations implementing the compulsory licensing scheme estabished by the Copyright Act of 1976. Her practice is geared toward the variety of intellectual property issues which affect the communications and computer industries.

She was educated at the College of White Plains of Pace University (B.A., 1963); Syracuse University (M.A., 1966); Georgetown University Law Center (J.D., 1969) and Columbia University (1969-1970), where she was Burton Memorial Fellow.

She is active in many professional organizations and has served as National Vice-President for the D.C. Circuit of the Federal Bar Association. She is a member of the Bars of New York State and the District of Columbia, the American Bar Association and the Federal Communications Bar Association.

Patrice Lyons may be contacted at: Law Offices of Patrice Lyons, P. O. Box 40430, Washington, DC 20016.

Issues for Hypertext Readers: Navigation in a Non-Linear Medium

In this section, a sort of discussion rages over the notorious "Lost in Hyperspace" dilemma. Does this problem exist? Geri Gay and Joan Mazur have seen it happen. Can it be avoided? They say yes, as does Van Parunak.

But, in Chapter 19, Mark Bernstein tells us that that the "Lost in Hyperspace" problem might not be as big an issue as we thought.

18

Navigating in Hypermedia

By Geri Gay and Joan Mazur
Interactive Multimedia Group, Cornell University

Definition of Navigation

The purpose of a well-designed hypermedia program is to provide a supportive environment in which users can access and annotate information, create their own paths through the material, and construct webs of information with a minimal amount of effort. This purpose differs sharply from traditional computer-assisted instruction in which users are directed through the program via a linear selection of menus.

Because hypermedia is so new, we are still debating how to best support readers using this nonlinear technology. Researchers do know that the hypermedia reader must master its navigation system, figure out where to go and, based on this understanding, create on-the-spot, personalized itineraries through the hyperbase.

As Jakob Nielsen [Nielsen, 1990] points out, we must rely on metaphors such as "navigation" to describe the active processes one must engage in while reading a hyperdocument. Readers of books and magazines and viewers of video or films rarely describe their experiences with these media in terms of navigation. One normally reads a book and views a movie, starting at the beginning, continuing to the end, in the sequence imposed by the author. Hyperdocuments, however, are nonlinear—they have neither beginning nor end.

This metaphor of navigation highlights the active, strategic role taken on by the reader who engages a hyperdocument. It is the reader, not the hypertext author, who charts a course through the sea of information. The reader is at the helm, making the decisions to either access or circumnavigate the islands of content in the hyperdocumentary sea.

As the chartmaker must be aware of the sea's vastness and depict the various ways to sail it, so the hypermedia designer must understand the program's enormous content and provide readers with tools and other aids for easy access. The designer, like the chartmaker, defines not the course, but the possibilities. The navigator, ultimately, will be on his or her own.

Challenges of Navigating Hypermedia Programs

To navigate through an extensive hyperdocument, a reader must master the tools the author provides to help plan moves, search the database, and retrace currents already followed in the hyperdocument. Readers must necessarily learn to direct the retrieval of the information they seek.

Readers must be able to navigate both globally and locally through the hypertext structure. The global context stresses the big picture and helps the navigator to comprehend the organization of the program's extensive content. The local context of navigation, on the other hand, defines the specific tools which generally appear as on-screen icons and which enable the reader to make the leap to nodes directly connected to the current one.

Global Navigation of a Program

Lost in Hyperspace

Navigating through extremely large hyperbases can be daunting. The nonsequential, user-controlled nature of hypermedia creates a myriad of possibilities for readers to annotate and to link information that they have discovered. Use of visual organizers along with overview maps and diagrams facilitate navigation in the global context, aid in minimizing this concern, and help prevent readers from becoming lost in hyperspace.

We used a hyperdocument called *The Bughouse* to test some of our theories relating to the effect of an author's design on the ability of students to learn from a hyperdocument. *The Bughouse* is a hypermedia program which contains information on the subject of cultural entomology, a subject area that encompasses the disciplines of anthropology, art, history, and entomology. The developers of *The Bughouse* at Cornell University's Interactive Multimedia Group interviewed students who used our program. These students reported that although they had difficulty navigating in a local sense, they were able to remain oriented in the hyperdocument because of the use of a house as the overall visual organizer.

"Sometimes, using the arrows (movement icons), I had trouble trying to move to where I wanted to go in the program," one student explained. "So, instead, I began to use the overview maps." Eighty percent of these students reported that the visual organizer helped them to access content [Gay and Mazur, 1990].

Novice hypermedia readers, especially, can be hampered by their unfamiliar role as navigators as they interact with a hyperdocument. They may be unprepared to handle the responsibility and to take control of accessing and sequencing information [Gay, Trumbull and Mazur, 1990]. For them, availability of general visual organizers and maps, which provide a global context for navigation through the content of a hypermedia program, is vital.

The Local Context for Navigation

Even though a navigator may understand the scope and overall design of the program well enough to plan a general itinerary through its information space, he or she can become lost in the course of specific moves which link nodes of information in the hypermedia database. In other words, hyperdocument readers can become lost locally, on a specific path, too. During iterative testing of *The Bughouse*, 45 percent of participants reported they had problems with spatial orientation. They stated they were lost or turned around in the defined, or metaphorical, space of the program.

For example, although most of them realized that certain specific information could be found only outside the house, they were unable to locate the door which would allow them to exit the dwelling—they knew where they wanted to go, but they could not figure out how to get there.

We have observed several common problems encountered while navigating local context. One problem is that users can lose track of their goals. Another frustration is that they find themselves unable to return to items of information that are of particular interest. Computer tracking systems, which trace the reader's moves through the program, can help readers revisit nodes. These tracking systems may take several forms, but usually a diagram which shows the nodes and links which have been connected is made available to the reader. This *interaction history* [Nielsen, 1990], in the form of an on-line map, should be made available for the reader to consult as needed. The line between navigational guidance and over-control by an author is a fine one. The structure of the hyperdocument can promote searching by association, yet allow for a great possibility of serendipitous finds of pertinent information. In our research we have learned that users benefit from this serendipity in that many enjoy the experience of discovering unexpected nuggets of information. In a recent study [Gay and Mazur, 1990], one user reported enthusiastically, "I found things connected to other topics that I never expected...it was a different way to learn."

Involving Users In The Design Process

Program development by Cornell University's Interactive Multimedia Group uses live-reader testing throughout the entire design phase to catch and correct global and local navigational problems. Testing begins as soon as a prototype is available which embodies the basic program goals and navigational schemes.

Differences in Hypermedia and Hypertext Navigation

Hypertext and hypermedia systems share several common attributes, but differ in a few dramatic ways. Both allow large amounts of loosely structured information to be linked in a nonlinear format. Both respond to the characteristics, goals, and skills of the reader. *Hyper-* programs are, by nature, highly interactive, requiring designers to iron out many problems of human-computer interaction. Hyper-authors always end up addressing questions relating to the visual structure and organization of the on-screen presentation.

Hypertext programs are by convention limited to textual material. The term hypermedia, on the other hand, implies a rich mix of text, video, audio, and/or graphics, in any combination the author desires and the system can support. In fact, each node (or, program event) may itself involve the use of several media simultaneously. A video clip, for example, might be accompanied by both a voice-over and on-screen text. Developers should ensure that their hyperdocument doesn't overwhelm or startle readers and yet permits the richness of multimedia to come through. Students participating in the testing of our hypermedia program on cultural entomology were pleasantly surprised when they encountered their first full-motion video event.

An appropriate visual metaphor can serve to compartmentalize a large hyperbase comprised of motion video and various stills and help to focus readers' attention on the subject matter. The same visual metaphor may also help readers to structure their experiences and plan their moves within the hyperdocument's information space.

Effect of Navigation Features On Interface

Early research on hypertext found that completely nonsequential hypermedia programs are perceived as disorderly and lead to "idiosyncratic and exceptional forms of connection" [Nelson, 1987]. For some readers, hypermedia can be a form that is too free. Designers of hyperdocuments need to determine how much control and guidance to make available to a reader using the program's navigational tools.

Because it is hard to predict exactly how much guidance all potential readers will need, some authors choose to build interfaces that adapt to various users' abilities and styles. Some add other, more traditional ways of searching through a hyperdocument (e.g., text search and retrieval) [See Chapter 21 by Fox et al, in this book], so that their browsable hyperdocuments also permit readers to interactively formulate queries of the hyperbase.

Effect of Interface On Navigation

A hyperdocument consists of a database and an interface. The interface provides the mechanism for accessing information contained in the database. Information-seeking in a hypermedia database is affected by the database's content, its organization, and its physical form, including its hardware and system configuration. The interface for a search system establishes the communication channels for human-computer interaction [Gay and Mazur, 1990]. The developers of *The Bughouse* chose to implement an interactive touchscreen as the hardware interface to the hypermedia reader. We chose the touchscreen because it made it possible for a reader to navigate to any point in the hyperbase simply by pointing at it. We hoped that the direct relationship between pointing to a node and getting to it would make it easy for readers to master this navigational tool.

Characteristics of Effective Navigational Tools

Navigational tools for hypermedia readers must be learnable, usable, consistent, and flexible. We believe that all these characteristics are equally important. A tool that is not learnable is of no use to the reader. Likewise, a tool that does not respond consistently will be difficult, and perhaps impossible, to learn to use.

Learnability

Learnable tools are easy to understand; the reader learns quickly what they do and how to make them work. The learnability of a navigational tool is measured by the time it takes a reader to learn its function and by how well the reader retains this knowledge through subsequent interactions with the hyperdocument. Tools whose learnability does not carry over between program uses constitute an undue *cognitive load* [Oren, 1989] for the user. Cognitive load refers to the amount of thinking a reader must devote to learning and using navigational tools. The reader may be side-tracked or confused by the amount of effort needed to learn how to navigate. Obviously, this runs counter to the intended purpose of hypermedia.

Usability

To assess the usability of a navigational tool, one asks several questions:

- Does the user understand what the navigational tool is for?
- Can the student comprehend the mechanics of the tool?
- Can he or she move to a desired spot in the program?
- Do users make satisfactory use of a variety of navigational tools?

All together these questions ask, "Do users make use of the full range of tools provided, and do they do so appropriately?" If the majority of users in an iterative testing situation routinely shy away from use of a particular tool, its usability is questionable. Problems with an unused navigational aid need to be investigated and changes made to ensure usability. The more usable various tools are, the more accommodating will be the hyperdocument to readers with varying search preferences, tasks, and learning styles.

Consistency

Consistency of performance is a key factor in designing tools which are usable and learnable. Screens should be designed so that similar elements serve similar functions. Users should also consistently maintain the same level of control while they are using a program. The reader navigating a hyperdocument should always have the option to return to a home base and anchor (one way is to provide on-screen home icon), or to quit the program entirely [Gay, 1989]. A final consideration for consistency involves providing an intuitive, common-sense feel to a program's navigational tools. Laurel [Laurel, 1988] calls this quality *personness*, and defines it as a feeling that the user is actually doing something as an active participant, and is relating to the program from an "I" perspective.

Flexibility

Flexible tools accommodate a variety of user dispositions, learning styles, and user goals. Do the navigational tools provide an opportunity for a variety of types of searches which can accommodate a variety of users, with differing goals, in various situations? If so, a program's navigational tools are flexible. Program developers need to continue to push the limits of visual, diverse tools so that a variety of navigational activities can occur.

Research on Navigational Tools for Hypermedia

Case Study

One of the primary purposes behind *The Bughouse* was to determine which navigational tools are most helpful to users. Our studies focused on how students were able to learn to use hypermedia navigational tools, the strategies they developed to search for information, the success of their searches, and their perceptions about the system and actual use of it.

Other goals of our research were to:

- determine which navigational tools would help users to explore large multimedia databases
- learn how to define multiple ways to organize and represent knowledge
- understand the evolution of satisfactory screen design and program mechanics
- find a way to ensure usability of the tools by readers with different backgrounds and abilities

What has been gained from our studies may have applicability to other hypermedia productions. Students who employed *The Bughouse* program had virtually no experience with hypermedia applications, although most had used computers for word processing or data entry in their school assignments.

The Bughouse contains information in a variety of formats and from varied media including text; video; commercial film clips; original program segments involving actors, photographs, and animation; segments of old television commercials; and music. The nodes established from all of these total 140 and they are referred to more familiarly as *events*. Each event includes a central element—a work of art, a video segment, slides, a musical selection, or a passage of text. The program's events represent aspects of cultural entomology that can be categorized according to historical period, geographic location, species, or cultural theme. The problem for the volunteer explorers of *The Bughouse* was to learn how to get to events and how to find the information they needed.

The students in our study were involved in both purposive (with a focused goal) and nonpurposive searches for information in the hypermedia system. We found that students involved in purposive searches tended to use different tools than those who were exploring the information in a non-purposive way. Following are some of the tools we studied, and some of our results. [Trumbull, Gay and Mazur, 1990]

Tools for Navigation

Visual Organizers and Maps. A Victorian farmhouse was chosen as a metaphor for organizing the content of *The Bughouse* hyperbase. General themes were organized by room. For example, topics dealing with insects and food are placed in the kitchen, insects and music in the music room, insects and fear in the farmhouse's basement, and so on. (See Figure 18.1.)

Objects in each of the rooms become entry points to the multimedia events or content items. If the student touches a ceramic bee on the kitchen counter, he or she is able to access information on honey-collecting throughout the world. If the student touches a cookbook, various segments relating to insects as food are displayed. In this manner the student can move through the various information webs attached to the objects visible in the rooms. (See Figure 18.2.)

Overview maps were used to orient students spatially and thematically. Putting to work this navigational tool, navigators can establish their present location in the program. If the student selects a new location on the map, he or she moves from the current location to the new place in the house. In doing so, the reader is navigating the visual interface. The maps of the house and grounds are labeled by the general themes located in each area.

When participating students were not looking for anything in particular (nonpurposive searching), most preferred, although not to the complete exclusion of other navigational tools, to explore *The Bughouse* by browsing through the house and grounds.

Figure 18.1   Maps of the house and its surroundings enable students either to pinpoint or change quickly their location in the program at any time. A change in location changes also the most immediate points of entry to the hypermedia web.

Wandering through the information space by touching rooms and objects of interest, browsers expressed their feeling of visiting a museum or fun house. They were able to search for items in the database by relying on an intuitive or common-sense approach.

During searches for which a goal, or objective, had been defined, readers were most successful in discovering relevant information when they relied on the visual interface and Browse Mode. Almost 70 percent of those engaged in a purposive search using the Browse Mode also reported feeling they had visited most or all of the relevant events. Others, however, expressed uncertainty as to the scope or limits of the program, and felt that there remained additional content to be explored.

Index.   Topics contained in *The Bughouse* Index are arranged alphabetically, and there are numerous cross-references which enable readers to search the knowledge domain of the program methodically. This type of search system is based on traditional word search indexes which are familiar to most readers in both books and other hypertext systems. The traditional index responds to the need of readers to search directly for material by providing a list of all the content items in the program. By moving through the list provided in the Index, we thought that a reader could get a feel for the range and quantity of available subject matter in the database. (See Figure 18.3.)

Figure 18.2   Directional arrows as icons greet users as they enter the house to browse through its many rooms. Users in the browse mode navigate through the program by accessing content material as they touch room items that appear on the monitor's screen.

Using the Index, students found fewer content items relevant to their assigned task than had those who used any other navigational tool, but approximately half expressed satisfaction that they had, in fact, found everything. They seemed lulled into confidence, whether by their use of the Index or by some preconceived expectation that led them to use this search strategy. Several in this group reported choosing the Index because they had figured it to be the most efficient method to get at information. However, unlike the visual interface and Browse Mode of navigation, the Index did not communicate to users the thematic or conceptual connections of information contained in the hypermedia webs of program events. Students who used the Index had difficulty with understanding meaning—the relationships among items were not so very apparent. "I looked through the headings in the Index," stated one participating student, "and just guessed if any would somehow show a relationship to the assigned topic."

On-line Guidance.   The Guide feature in *The Bughouse* leads readers through complex webs of information and subject matter. Behind the scenes, as readers navigate through the hyperdocument, the guide function records their paths. When a reader invokes the on-line advisor, the guide tries to suggest other areas for exploration relevant to topics already discovered by the reader.

The list of topics generated by the Guide is created by a tracking system which tracks, and then marks each inquiry. If a pattern can be determined by this track-

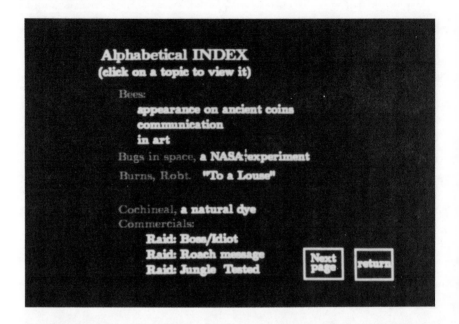

Figure 18.3   The Index provides users with a traditional method for accessing content materials. The program's events are listed in alphabetical order and extensively cross-referenced.

ing system, the user receives a streamlined list of related information for further inquiry. If the user has not established a pattern (i.e., has not established a pattern recognized by the programmed support), the advisor only suggests an area for investigation. (See Figure 18.4.)

The Guide feature provides suggestions that relate to the complexity of the web of connected events. "I used the Guide to delve deeper into a topic area," one user noted, "and [to] get ideas about other items related to the same subject." Using the webs of related information in the Guide enabled participating students to make conceptual connections among program events. In our study, those who consulted the Guide were the second most efficient group at finding information relevant to their goals.

Recommendations

Visual Organizers.   Hypermedia designers are advised to create visual images and interfaces that will help users access visual and audio databases. By using both a global interface to suggest overall organization of content and specific objects to act as a subset of the global organizer, users will be more likely to access database items more intuitively.

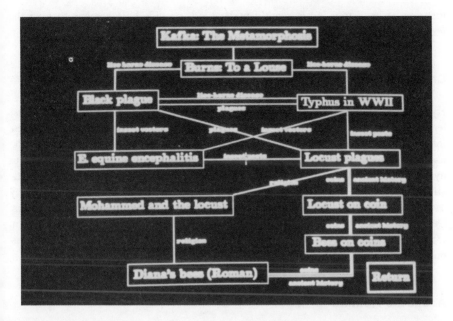

Figure 18.4 The web shown here illustrates how the Guide feature is capable of suggesting additional program events for the user to view and study. A user who has already read about Kafka's *Metamorphosis*, listened to Burns' *To a Louse,* and learned about the Black Plague, and who has consulted the *Guide,* would then be given a short list of additional events to view, such as Typhus in WWII, Locust Plague, or Equine Encephalitis.

Maps and other graphic organizers.   Because advance graphical organizers provide an overview of links in the database and show the location of content items, their use is recommended. Organizational maps, which provide readers with a visual picture of their paths through the database, are equally recommended.

Also, many readers like to have instant access to a home position or orientation spot in the program. A home card will reduce anxiety for these users and reorient them when they become lost or confused in the hyperdocument.

Traditional Index.   An index or other text tool for searching should be provided for users who are interested in looking up or finding a specific item.

On-line guidance or help.   Program authors are urged to incorporate an on-line guidance or tracking system into their design. This will provide users with a record of their individual path through the program. Also, it will show the many linkages in the database. These linkages, which form webs, reflect the user's own interests.

Clarity of purpose and ease of access.   Users should be able to access all online tools without difficulty and readily understand the purpose of each. If the function of each tool is not readily understood, provide help screens to give the user additional explanation.

Conclusion

Hypermedia designers ought to continue to develop highly visual, interactive systems to assist readers in finding pertinent information in hypermedia databases. Interfaces ought to be appropriate to the design and structure of the database. The use of visual organizers can be particularly helpful in orienting users in hyperdocuments which have their information stored and accessed nonsequentially. Alphabetical indexing, on the other hand, although it is familiar to many users, may not be so helpful for navigating through large hypermedia programs. Designers need to continue to develop usable, flexible hypermedia navigation tools which keep pace with the powerful storage and access capabilities of computers.

About the Authors

Geri Gay

Geri Gay is an assistant professor of communication at Cornell University where she also directs the *Interactive Multimedia Group* (IMG), a research and development body which has produced multimedia computing applications with wide-ranging topics, including foreign language study, the physics of windsurfing, cultural entomology, and interactive multimedia itself. Her work has appeared on PBS and remains on display at Tech 2000 and at the Smithsonian National Demonstration Laboratory in Washington, D. C. The results of Dr. Gay's research have been published in the Journal of Research on Computing in Education, *Journal of Educational Psychology, Academic Computing.* Dr. Gay and her group receive much of the funding for their research from IBM, the National Science Foundation, and Apple Computer.

Dr. Gay may be contacted at the Interactive Multimedia Group, Cornell University, 221 Kennedy Hall, Department of Communications, Ithaca, NY 14853.

Joan Mazur

Joan Mazur is a Ph.D candidate in Education at Cornell University and works as a research assistant to Dr. Gay and the IMG. Ms. Mazur can also be reached at the Interactive Multimedia Group of Cornell University.

References

Gay, G. (1989). "Search mode strategies for hypermedia," *Technology and Learning*, 3:2, March/April, Erlbaum, Hillside, NJ.

Gay, G. and Mazur, J. (1990). "Iterative testing of a hypermedia program: navigational and representational issues." Submitted for publication.

Gay, G., Trumbull, D., and Mazur, J. (1991). "Designing and testing navigational strategies and guidance tools for a hypermedia program." Accepted for publication *Journal of Educational Computing Research*.

Laurel, B. (1990). "Interface agents: metaphors with character," Laurel, B., (Ed.) *The Art of Human-Computer Interface Design*. Addison-Wesley, Reading, MA.

Nelson, T. (1987). *Literary Machines-abridged Edition 87.1 Computer Guideline (a Guide envelope) for the Apple MacIntosh.* OWL International, Bellevue, WA.

Nielsen, J. (1990). "The art of navigating in hypertext," *Communications of the ACM, 33:3*, 296-310.

Oren, T. (1990). "Cognitive load in hypermedia: designing for the exploratory learner," *Learning with Interactive Multimedia*, Sueann Ambron and Kristina Hooper (Eds.) 125-137. Microsoft Press, Redmond, WA.

Trumbull, D., Gay, G. and Mazur, J. (1991). "Students' actual and perceived use of navigational and guidance tools in a hypermedia program." Accepted for publication in *The Journal of Research on Computing in Education*.

19

The Navigation Problem Reconsidered

By Mark Bernstein
Eastgate Systems, Inc.

The Navigation Problem

The impulse toward hypertext grew out of dissatisfaction with the limitations of linear writing, echoed in the intuitive conviction that a less restrictive medium would permit writers to express complex relationships and structures with greater clarity and precision.

"Everything is intertwingled!" [Nelson, 1974]

Liberation [Nelson, 1974] and *intellectual augmentation* [Engelbart, 1968] were the chief concerns of early hypertext research. By 1987, however, a pronounced shift in emphasis had taken place, reflected in widespread and profound concern with the difficulty of hypertext navigation.

The classical hypermedia problem is the "getting lost problem," which becomes more severe as the database grows larger [Akscyn, 1987].

The biggest problem in hypertext systems, which most of us admit in footnotes toward the end of papers extolling the virtues of our systems, is of getting lost [Brown, 1987].

If the reader begins to fear that she is overlooking crucial information or if she feels lost in a maze of hypertext links, the reader will abandon hypertext and insist upon conventional media [Bernstein, 1988].

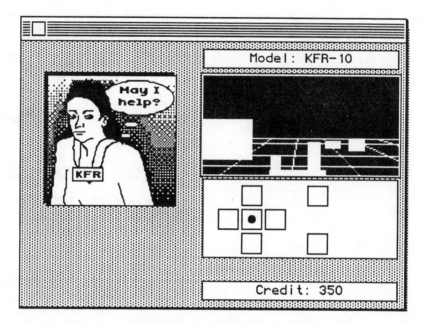

Figure 19.1 An unusual hypertext navigation tool, designed for use in a hypertext short story [Bernstein, 1990]. The large panel on the right side of the screen provides a view of a section of "cyberspace"—a representation of computation activities in the (simulated) world. Readers use the controls beneath the cyberspace view to maneuver through cyberspace, and can inquire about or attempt to visit structures in view.

The panel on left side of the screen represents a Tour Guide which the user has installed; the icon indicates that this Guide wishes to offer an observation about one of the structures in view. Copyright Eastgate Systems, Inc.

Discussion of the merits of hypertext, both in the research community and in the trade press, has frequently been dominated by discussion of the efficacy with which various systems address the navigation problem.

Fear of disorientation has led to the implementation of elaborate graphic browsers [Yankelovich, 1988; Fairchild, 1988], to reliance upon an explicit hierarchical backbone [Walker, 1990; Ackscyn, 1987], to extensive reliance on sequential presentation [Atkinson, 1987], or to drastically restricted visions of hypertext:

> Excessive linking causes serious problems of disorientation and cognitive load for the user....Several researchers are working on new representations of hypertext link structures that may help to solve these problems, but limiting the links in the first place seems like a more practical solution. [Glushko, 1989]

The navigational apparatus in some recent hypertext documents (e.g., [Walker, 1990; Nielsen, 1989]) occupies more screen space than does the content.

Does the Navigation Problem Exist?

The widespread belief that hypertext navigation is difficult appears to rest upon three basic arguments:

- Hypertext navigation necessarily confronts readers with a new and unfamiliar cognitive burden, in addition to the customary burdens associated with reading. (e.g., [Conklin, 1987].)
- Hypertext readers are observed to issue a large number of navigation commands. [Walker, 1990]
- Anecdotes in which individuals found a specific hypertext document to be confusing.

All three arguments are widely accepted, yet it is clear that each argument is vulnerable. We know far too little of the cognitive processes inherent in reading to be certain that navigation necessarily places any incremental burden on readers or that the increment will prove significant. The well known Hawthorne effect, for example, casts strong doubt on any *a priori* estimate of cognitive difficulty. The frequency with which users issue navigational commands could easily represent an artifact of specific interface designs; indeed, navigational commands (such as the graphical overviews [Walker, 1990] which are reported to be especially popular) might as readily be attributed to displacement behavior as to an intrinsic property of hypertexts.

Anecdotes of disorienting experiences necessarily address perceived shortcomings of individual documents, not of the medium itself, and the argument from silence ("I have never read a hypertext I have not found to be confusing") is hardly convincing in light of the very small number of hypertexts published to date.

Nor can we hope to demonstrate the impact of hypertext's alleged cognitive load by naively measuring the speed with which test subjects perform retrieval tasks [Egan, 1989; Shneiderman, 1987; Nielsen, 1989]. Studies of retrieval rates are not without interest, but retrieving facts from a reference document is but a single, atypical facet of the larger, more significant task which written works address. Technical documents are written to persuade, entice, excite, illuminate, and inspire, not merely to facilitate recall. We should not limit our perspective on hypermedia to simplistic retrieval tasks merely because these tasks are easy to study.

The Navigation Problem in Linear Texts

In considering—or reconsidering—the navigation problem, it is vital to consider separately those issues which pertain specifically to hypertext, and those which are of equal concern to those who compose linear documents. We all have struggled at times with confusing, ill-organized, and unkempt writing. We must expect that some inept or perverse writers will produce obscure, confusing, and frustrating hypertexts. Some topics seem to be intrinsically intricate, obscure, or difficult to explain. While hypertext may prove useful in treating these difficult subjects, it may not succeed in rendering complex theories instantly accessible, and we might not be surprised should hypertext fail to enliven tax codes or maintenance procedures. For example, the scenario proposed by [Utting, 1990], in which a reader becomes disoriented while hurriedly reviewing large volumes of insurance regulations in preparation for an important meeting, applies with essentially equal force to conventional media and to hypertext; those who attempt to master a wealth of information in the course of an afternoon must expect to become confused.

We should also be careful to distinguish *intrinsic* navigation problems from those caused by sloppy, careless, or inept writing. The existing hypertext literature is small, and still contains a preponderance of works written or edited by researchers who created the first generation of hypertext systems. While some of these workers write well, many were inspired to work in the field by perceived shortcomings in their own writing. At times, obvious blunders have crept into published hypertexts; for example, in [Bernstein and Sweeney, 1988], a specious link connects the state of Washington in the northwestern U.S. to a biographical entry for Booker T. Washington.

Errors attributable to flawed proofreading or inexpert indexing should be laid at the door of the publisher, not blamed on the medium. Just as readers may justly expect to encounter polished and expertly edited documents, authors may reasonably anticipate an audience of attentive, interested, and industrious readers. If a reader is distracted, uninterested, or hurried, we may well anticipate that he or she will encounter difficulties. If the reader's goals do not coincide with the author's, moreover, the reader may be frustrated despite the author's best efforts. Conflict between author and reader underlies the second of three disorientation scenarios in [Utting, 1989]. Here, an author has constructed a comprehensive hypertextual description of the insurance industry, while the reader is seeking to skim the entire document in the course of a morning, cramming for a business meeting for which she is clearly ill-prepared. The cognitive overhead in this instance lies not in the medium, but rather in the application of reference materials to tasks for which they were not designed.

Distractions and Deceptions

A portion of the concern with hypertext disorientation may be blamed upon accidental flaws that marred early hypertext systems. Many of the earliest prototype systems were relatively slow. If turning a page takes several seconds, readers may sometimes lose their train of thought while waiting for the computer to respond. Some early users of Intermedia, for example, brought books to the computer lab so they could read in the interval between pages! Extremely slow or inconsistent response is disorienting, but no modern hypertext system (including Intermedia) suffers from this malady.

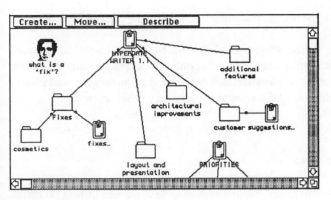

Even a simple hypertext structure can become confusing and complex... if it is described by a poorly planned map.

In this example, a hypertext discussion has been shuffled to obscure underlying relationships. Indeed, finding the ideal arrangement of issues in the hypertext map represents a real and substantive contribution to the discussion.

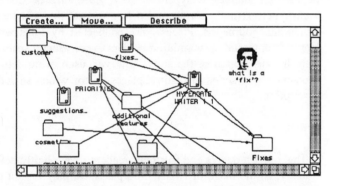

Figure 19.2   Neither maps nor simplistic structures can "cure" hypertext disorientation, because the opportunity for growth and understanding may entail the risk of confusion and disorientation. Here, two views of a complex design discussion are presented using an experimental hypertext system [Bernstein, Humphreys, and Cohen, 1989]. Copyright Eastgate Systems, Inc.

Some first-generation hypertext systems provided no easy, consistent method by which readers could retrace their path or retract an erroneous decision. Others lacked familiar amenities—bookmarks, tables of contents, indexes—to which readers are accustomed and which they expect. Some very early programs used primitive graphic displays which were distracting and unpleasant to read, and which were often located in noisy, busy, and uncomfortable computer laboratories. These shortcomings were conquered long ago; they are accidents of emerging technology, extrinsic to a serious consideration of hypertext style and technique.

Deliberate Hypertext Disorientation

While I can discover no clear evidence that hypertext is intrinsically disorienting or that hypertext navigation is intrinsically difficult, there does exist a considerable body of evidence that hypertextual techniques *can* be used to deliberately disorient the reader.

Writers of hypertext fiction adopt textual devices to disrupt reader expectations in order to shape the narrative experience, to confront the reader with challenges and puzzles, or to advance the narrative. A brief catalog of techniques which writers have adopted to deliberately disorient the reader may prove instructive.

Deceptive Orientation Cues

Hypertext novelists have frequently found means to lead readers to rely on orientation cues which they eventually withdraw or subvert with great dramatic impact. In the first interactive hypertext story, *Adventure* or *Colossal Cave* [Crowther], each hypertext node corresponded to a unique fictional locale through which the protagonist journeyed. Places were connected by links with spatial labels (e.g., North or downstairs), permitting readers to construct a spatial map of the hypertext web. In one section of the story, however, users were deliberately disoriented by encountering a series of distinct places, all of which shared a single, unchanging description:

```
You are in a maze of little twisty passages, all alike.
```

This section delays and frustrates readers by explicitly defeating their navigation strategy; in the maze of twisty little passages, they cannot distinguish where they are, or whether a navigational command has had any effect at all. Smith's *King of Space* [Smith, 1990] achieves a related effect by trapping the protagonist in the dark; the groping panic of a protagonist who suddenly cannot see is echoed by a coal-black screen, in which the reader must grope for invisible links.

Joyce's *Afternoon* [Joyce, 1990] presents readers with a complex and dynamic web of interconnections which change as the reader proceeds through the hypertext.

> *Afternoon* resembles an automated railway in which the points keep switching of their own accord. Since the story is heavily recursive, readers may find themselves frequently returning to the same textual locales; but a yield word (link) that took them from *son* to *Sun King* on the first iteration may now lead somewhere else entirely. The text can seem to have a mind of its own and readers may easily feel lost within its shifting circuitry—an outcome consistent with the nondeterminist principles of the text. [Moulthroup, 1989]

While the place appears unchanged since the reader's first visit, both the reader and the text have, in fact, been transformed; following the path you followed before may lead you somewhere marvelous and new. Joyce leads the reader to believe she has returned to a safe, familiar place in the hypertext, but while the page seems to be familiar, its behavior is entirely new. In a similar vein, in *Uncle Buddy's Fun House* [McDaid, 1990, see also Chapter 7 by Moulthrop, in this book], the author carefully simulates a system error in order to alarm and agitate the reader, and to make a rhetorical point on the proliferation of nuclear weapons.

Violating Expectations

Any coherent narrative—and any well-designed user interface—creates an array of expected, conventional behaviors to which readers become accustomed. While a particular interface may be unique to a single hypertext, after reading the instructions and spending some time with the hypertext, the reader comes to anticipate what he can do, and how the system will respond. Suddenly violating these expectations can give rise to violently disruptive and disorienting experiences. Once the author establishes a conventional visual cue for a button, we expect that all buttons will share a common behavior. If the reader encounters a button that tries to run away when someone tries to push it, or that cries in pain when it is pressed, the reader is likely to be astonished. Puns and double entendres are especially effective in both linear and hypertextual texts when readers are led to anticipate only one interpretation.

Fragmentation

Novelists, playwrights, and musicians have long understood the technical utility of switching among independent themes or plot lines. When the pace of an episode has built to a crescendo, the focus may be switched to a different part of the tale, with distinct characters and distinct pacing. Change of context is inherently nonlinear, and writers have long recognized that these transitions require special care. Conventional transition passages, typographic cues, reprises, and narrative overviews are frequently used to reestablish context after a shift; by omitting expected cues or by increasing the frequency of context shifts, authors may deliberately fragment the reader's vision. *Oulipo*, a contemporary French literary movement which relies on extensive digression "within a maze of plots, characters, puzzles and mysteries," may be viewed as a linear embedding of nonlinear texts [O'Rourke, 1990], building upon a nonlinear prose tradition with roots in the work of James Joyce, Cortazar, Borges, and Pynchon. All depend on fragmentation of narrative to achieve a distinctive fragmentation of experience.

Disruptive Novelty

Sudden, unanticipated, and unconventional changes in the appearance or behavior of a hypertext are sometimes useful to awaken the reader's concentration, to open the reader to new ideas, or to emphasize a dramatic development. In Nelson's *Computer Lib/Dream Machines*, a nonlinear textbook printed conventionally, the pages are unexpectedly turned upside-down half way through the book to indicate a transition from visions of the near future to more remote dreams [Nelson, 1972].

In Smith's *King of Space* [Smith, 1990], readers may find themselves thrust without warning into unexpected hypertextual mechanisms depicted as (simulated) machines which they must learn to manipulate. Even within these episodes, sudden and unexpected outbursts serve to alarm readers. At one point, an elevator breaks into song and Marxist dialectic, perhaps startling readers who had expected the hypertext to remain silent.

Defeating Spatial Analogy

Many hypertext readers develop spatial analogies to help them reason about the structure of a hypertext as they read; their current focus of attention becomes a place or location, and links invite them to depart on trips to other, related places. Spatial analogies can prove extremely powerful, as evidenced by the widespread interest in automatic hypertext mapping [Yankelovich, 1989; Fairchild, 1988; Halasz, 1987].

In his hypertext novel *Chaos* [Moulthrop, 1991], Stuart Moulthrop intentionally defeats spatial analogy by introducing a new factor for which no spatial equivalent can be found. Pages in *Chaos* are connected by links, labelled by character name, but the behavior of these links is determined both by the point of departure and by the current *mood*. The mood can change dynamically during a reading, or may retain a single value for an extended period; no simple spatial analogy explains the behavior of this mood, and hence no spatial analogy predicts the behavior of the hypertext. Moulthrop uses this effect to attack the static, flat quality which can develop when apparent freedom of will (represented by links, from which readers may choose freely) confronts the rigidity of a predetermined narrative. Because readers can't easily perceive the hypertext web, the illusion of freedom and mystery is extended.

Recursion

Unexpected return to a previously-visited locale is intrinsically disorienting, especially when such returns are rare. As discussed above, *Afternoon* employs recursion to disrupt and fragment the narrative, reflecting the fragmented experience of its characters. Readers may perceive recursion as a system error or as a signal that the contents of the hypertext have been exhausted. *King of Space* [Smith, 1990] exploits the tension evoked by unexpected recursion for dramatic effect; an apparent return to an early episode in which the protagonist committed a symbolic rape develops instead into a new narrative in which the earlier action is seen from a different perspective.

To review, we have identified six distinct techniques which authors have used to deliberately disorient readers:

- Deceptive Orientation Cues
- Violating Expectations
- Fragmentation

- Defeating Spatial Reasoning
- Disruptive Novelty
- Recursion

Effective Use of Disorientation

We may well marvel at the diversity of methods which writers have developed in order to achieve an effect which is widely believed to be intrinsic to hypertext—disorientation. If hypertext is intrinsically disorienting, why have artists felt the need to develop such a diverse range of techniques to achieve it? If hypertext disorientation is undesirable, why have so many writers worked so hard to promote it?

The answer, of course, is that disorientation is not inherently wrong; indeed, a degree of disorientation, deliberately introduced and thoughtfully controlled and guided, can be a powerful tool for writers.

Freedom vs. Constraint

The relationship between instructor and pupil—or between an authoritative author and a reader—is fraught with tension; the instructor ultimately controls the discourse, and the person instructed is almost invariably reluctant to surrender that control, to place the experience entirely into the instructor's hands.

> Most people consider school to be a grim necessity to be accepted, endured, and survived.....A curriculum promotes a false simplification of any subject, cutting the subject's many interconnections and leaving a skeleton of sequence which is only a caricature of its richness and intrinsic sophistication. [Nelson, 1981]

Rigid organizational schemes assert the author's magisterial authority but may arouse a degree of resentment. By offering a richer web of links, the author is able to acknowledge the reader's active participation and to bestow upon the reader a measure of liberty and initiative [Hammond, 1988]. Conversely, by imposing a clear and limited organizational scheme on an otherwise complex web (e.g. by constructing a linear tour of a complex information space), an author can reduce a topic's apparent complexity and comfort the bewildered reader.

The tension between freedom and constraint is reflected throughout conventional textbooks. In fields which are widely believed to be challenging, complex, and intimidating, successful textbooks place great emphasis on explicit, systematic organization to orient and reassure the bewildered reader. Conversely, when authors expect students to be overconfident or smug in their apparent mastery of a familiar subject, writers often adopt a looser, discursive and narrative style. In an introduction to Organic Chemistry, we may be anxious to suppress links whenever possible to focus the reader's attention on underlying simplicity; in a refresher course on classroom technique intended for experienced teachers, on the other hand, we may be anxious to offer new, exciting and unexpected links to enliven a subject that may, for some readers, seem stale.

Open Prairies vs Pleasant Parlors

The apparent size of a hypertext shapes the reader's experience. If the hypertext seems too large, diverse, and confusing, the reader will be baffled; if the hypertext seems too small, confined, and rigid, the reader will be bored.

Rich, irregular, and unpredictable hypertext webs increase the apparent size of the hypertext, making even small documents seem rich and filled with information and excitement. *The Election of 1912* [Bernstein, 1988] would, in print, be a slender volume of less than 150 pages, but extensive use of topical links in a deeply intertwingled web (with an average of 7 structural and 4 topical links per screen) has led reviewers to believe that the document is very large indeed.

> *The Election of 1912* is a unique hypertext program that takes a single event in United States history and covers virtually every aspect of it. This is possible because of the hypertext format - a format that allows the user/reader to follow any path through a large amount of information, and not be restricted by a preset, linear structure. [Kinnell, 1989]

In other contexts, we may find it desirable to make a large document appear small and manageable. An explicit, simple, and repetitive hierarchical structure sharply diminishes the apparent scope of a document. Consistent use of a limited repertoire of graphic cues reinforces orientation and familiarity, where a richer graphic vocabulary might confuse the issue. In the *Expert Dictionary for Banking* [Garzotto, 1990, and see also Chapter 13 by Garzotto, et al., in this book], an intimidating web of laws, regulations, and business procedures is rendered manageable by breaking down each document into its component parts, by explicitly describing the structure of the document, and by sharply limiting the kinds of links which may be present at any point. In his *Hypertext 87 Trip Report*, Nielsen devotes a vast amount of screen space to information maps which are constantly in view, reinforcing the implicit organization through repetition and graphic presentation [Nielsen, 1989].

Drama vs. Comfort

Dramatic intensity, surprise, and excitement all work to inspire, engage, and refresh the reader. Predictability, repetition, and consistency work together to soothe, reassure, and calm the reader. Effective writing constantly balances drama and comfort, modulating the level of dramatic intensity to concentrate reader attention at critical moments.

Topical links are intrinsically dynamic and inviting. They clamor for attention, inviting the reader to depart from the current topic and to visit another place, perhaps someplace remote and very different from the current point to attention. The intensity with which these links are perceived can, of course, be modulated by skillful design and sensitive placement. Links which interrupt the text, which advertise themselves, or which are graphically prominent or exceptional are clearly more inviting than small iconographic symbols. An animated image of a tour guide link (refer again to Figure 19.1) calls attention to itself by virtue of its novelty. A screen filled with links, offering a wide variety of new opportunities, is exciting and dramatic. The opportunity to move swiftly across a vast expanse of hypertext web is deeply engaging to the bored reader; an opportunity to follow many links is as tempting as are the streets of an interesting new city. Comfortable readers are happy to risk mild disorientation to get "just a little lost."

Not every passage of a hypertext demands equal attention; an attempt to make every part of the text equally dramatic will yield a noisy, unmodulated manuscript which clamors for attention but receives none.

The presence of predictable, structural links, the absence of unexpected or exceptional links, and the use of familiar, consistent visual design all calm the reader. Large hypertext webs will thus prove most effective if they are carefully modulated, if some sections are rich in complexity while others are simpler, more restrained, and less demanding.

In summary, mild disorientation can excite readers, increasing their concentration, intensity, and engagement. Hypertexts can and do exploit the effects of disorienting elements to achieve three indispensable aims:

- Empower readers (Freedom vs. Constraint)
- Encourage adventurous exploration (Open Prairies vs. Pleasant Parlors)
- Increase dramatic intensity (Drama vs. Comfort)

Severe and/or prolonged disorientation is uncomfortable, and should usually be reserved for special, unusual situations as in the post-modern fiction of Michael Joyce [Joyce, 1990].

The complete absence of orientational challenges is dull and uncomfortable. A boring hypertext is every bit as bad as a confusing one.

About the Author

Mark Bernstein

Mark Bernstein is Chief Scientist at Eastgate Systems, Inc., a firm specializing in hypertext research since 1982. He led the team that developed the Hypergate hypertext system, and in addition to his conventional publications has written critically-acclaimed hypertexts, including *The Election of 1912* and *The Flag Was Still There* (with Erin Sweeney). Current research interests range from machine learning and automatic link discovery to historical simulation and crisis management.

He was chairman of the AAAI-88 workshop on AI and Hypertext, and has taught numerous courses on The Craft of Hypertext. Eastgate Systems publishes Hypergate, a hypertext environment designed for technical documentation and Storyspace, a hypertext environment for writers. The Eastgate Press is the leading publisher of serious hypertexts; recent releases include *Afternoon* by Michael Joyce and Sarah Smith's *King of Space.*

Bernstein, a graduate of Swarthmore College, received his doctorate from Harvard in 1983.

Dr. Bernstein can be reached at: Eastgate Systems, Inc., P. O. Box 1307. Cambridge, MA 02238.

References

Akscyn, R., McCracken, D., and Yoder,E. (1987). "KMS: A Distributed Hypermedia System for Managing Knowledge in Organizations," *Hypertext 87 Proceedings*, ACM Press, Baltimore, MD.

Atkinson, W. (1987). *HyperCard*, software for Macintosh computers, Apple Computer Co., Cupertino, CA.

Bernstein, M. (1988). "The Bookmark and the Compass: Orientation Tools for Hypertext Users", ACM SIGOIS Bulletin, October.

Bernstein M., and Sweeney, E. (1988). *The Election of 1912, Hypertext for Macintosh Computers*, Eastgate Systems, Watertown, MA.

Bernstein, M., Humphreys, C., and Cohen, E. (1989). *Cherokee*, an unpublished, collaborative hypertext environment, Eastgate Systems, Watertown, MA.

Brown, P. J. (1987). "Turning Ideas Into Products: The Guide System," *Hypertext 87 Proceedings*, ACM Press, Baltimore, MD.

Conklin, J. (1987). "Hypertext: An Introduction and Survey," *IEEE Computer*, (September) 17ff.

Crowther, W. and Woods, D. *Adventure* (also known as *Colossal Cave*), hypertext fiction for a variety of computers, Stanford University, Stanford, CA.

Egan, D. E., Remde, J. R., Landauer, T. K., Lochbaum, C. C., and Gomez, L. M. (1989). "Behavioral evaluation and analysis of a hypertext browser," *Proc. CHI 89*, ACM Press, Baltimore, MD. 205–210.

Engelbart, D. C. and English, W. (1968). "A Research Center for Augmenting Human Intellect," reprinted in *Computer-Supported Cooperative Work*, (1988.) Irene Greif, (Ed.), Morgan Kaufmann Publishers, San Mateo, CA.

Fairchild, K.M., Poltrock, S.E., Furnas, G.W. (1988). "SemNet: Three-dimensional graphic representations of large knowledge bases," *Cognitive Science and its Applications for Human-Computer Interaction*, Erlbaum, L., and Guindon, R., (Ed.s).

Garzotto, Franca (1990). "Expert Dictionary for Banking."

Garzotto, F., Paolini, P., Schwabe, D., and Bernstein, M. (1991). "Tools for Designing Hyperdocuments," *Hypertext/Hypermedia Handbook*, Emily Berk and Joseph Devlin (Ed.s), McGraw-Hill, New York, NY.

Glushko, R. J. (1989). "Design Issues for Multi-Document Hypertexts," *Hypertext '89 Proceedings*, ACM, Baltimore, MD.

Halasz, F., Moran, T.P., and Trigg, R.H. (1987). "NoteCards in a Nutshell," *Proc. ACM CHI+GI 87* (Toronto, 5–9 April 1987) 45–52.

Hammon N. and Allison, L. (1988). "Travels around a learning support environment: Rambling, orienteering or touring," *Proc. ACM CHI 88* (Washington DC, May 15–19, 1988) 269–73.

Joyce, M. (1990). *Afternoon*, hypertext for Macintosh computers, Eastgate Systems, Cambridge, MA.

Kinnell, S. (1989). Review of *The Election of 1912*, *History Microcomputer Review 5*, 90–922.

Landow, G. P. (1987). "Relationally Encoded Links and the Rhetoric of Hypertext," *Proc. Hypertext '87*, ACM, Baltimore, 331–44.

Landow, George P. (1990). "Popular Fallacies about Hypertext." Designing Hypertext/Hypermedia for Learning. David H. Jonassen and Heinz Mandl, (Ed.s), Heidelberg: Springer-Verlag, 3.1-3.20.

McDaid, John (1990). "Uncle Buddy's Funhouse," Hypertext for Macintosh Computers. In preparation.

Moulthrop, Stuart (1989). "Hypertext and 'the Hyperreal'," Hypertext '89 Proceedings, ACM, Baltimore, MD.

Moulthrop, Stuart (1991). "Chaos," Hypertext for Mcintosh Computers. In press by Eastgate Systems, Inc.

Moulthrop, Stuart (1991). "Toward a Paradigm for Reading Hypertexts: Making Nothing Happen in Hypermedia Fiction." Hypertext / Hypermedia Handbook, Emily Berk and Joseph Devlin (Ed.s), McGraw-Hill, New York, NY.

Nelson, Theodor H. (1987). Computer Lib, Second Edition, Microsoft Press, Redmond WA.

Nielsen, Jacob (1991). "Hypertext '87 Trip Report," Hypertext for Macintosh Computers. Published by the author.

Nielsen, Jakob (1989). "The Matters that Really Matter for Hypertext Usability," Hypertext 89, ACM Press, Baltimore, MD, 239-248.

Nielsen, Jakob (1990). "The Art of Navigating Through Hypertext," Communications of the ACM 33.

O'Rourke, Michael (1990). "Hyperfiction: The Computer and the Imagination," Edge (Summer), 1933-8 Hazama-cho,Hachioji-shi, Tokyo 193 Japan. 6-9.

Shneiderman, Ben (1987). "User interface design and evaluation for an electronic encyclopedia," Cognitive Engineering in the Design of Human-Computer Interaction and Expert Systems, Elsevier Science Publishers, 207-34.

Smith, Sarah (1990). King of Space, hypertext for Macintosh computers, Eastgate Systems, Cambridge MA.

Walker, Janet H., Mannes, Suzanne and Young, Emilie (1990). "A Case Study of Using a Manual Online," Machine-Mediated Learning (February) in press.

Yankelovich, N., Haan, B.J., Meyrowitz, N. K., Drucker, S.M., "Intermedia: The concept and construction of a seamless information environment", IEEE Computer 21 (199) 91-96.

Tolkien, J. R. R. (1955). Lord of the Rings. 3 Volumes. Houghton-Miffin, Boston (1954-6). First American Edition.

20

Ordering the Information Graph

By H. Van Dyke Parunak
Industrial Technology Institute

Introduction

Greek legend tells of the Gordian Knot, tied by King Gordius of Phrygia. It was fantastically complex, and its ends were tucked into the middle so that they could not be seen. A mystic oracle revealed that whoever could untie the knot would become the master of Asia. Many tried to unravel the knot, but with no success. When Alexander the Great conquered Phrygia, he learned of the oracle and tried to support his ambitions of empire by untying the knot, but was no more successful than his predecessors. Finally, in desperation, he cut the knot in half with his sword.

Any fisherman, knitter, sailor or Scout knows that it's not hard to tie Gordian Knots; we usually call them "tangles." What takes skill is to tie a knot that holds when it's supposed to, and yet unties easily.

Ropes and strings aren't the only things that are hard to keep straight. Information links in a hyperdocument also have a way of getting so tangled that information actually becomes harder to find, rather than easier.

This chapter begins by showing why a hyperdocument with a tangled information graph is bad. Then it discusses two techniques for organizing the graph. Finally, it reviews the problems of tangled graphs and shows how these techniques solve those problems.

A Note on Terminology Used in this Chapter

Ted Nelson invented the word "hypertext," and uses it to refer not only to a technology but also to any particular piece of "nonsequential writing" [Nelson, 1980, 1987]. Since "text" does not always connote the visual and aural materials that people are now manipulating in a similar way, "hypermedia" has come into vogue for the technology. But "media," unlike "text," is not commonly used to describe a single document or a collection of material. So what do you call one particular collection of nodes and links that works together as a unified whole? We could use the word "web," an evocative word that hints at the pattern laid out by the links in a hypertext. However, that term has been popularized by the folks at Intermedia [Yankelovich, et al., 1988] to refer to a set of links that is stored separately from the material that is linked together (an important innovation that deserves wider attention). In this chapter, we will use "hypermedia" to refer to the technology, "hyperdocument" to refer to a particular set of nodes and links (independent of the hardware and software that permits us to manipulate it), "graph" to refer just to the set of links (whether or not they are stored as a web, separate from the nodes), and, occasionally, "hyperbase" to refer to the structured set of files containing information that gets sorted into nodes and links when it is accessed by a hypermedia reader.

In this chapter I also often refer to the "reader" and "author" of a hyperdocument. The same individual may wear both hats, but not always at the same time. Readers are those who traverse links as the fancy strikes them. Authors, on the other hand, accept the responsibility of constructing and organizing webs so as to make traversing them easier for others.

Why Do We Need To Order the Information Graph?

A well-ordered graph of information is not only easier for authors to manipulate, but also helps computers do more to make a hyperdocument easy for readers to use.

The reader of a hyperdocument constantly asks three questions: Where am I? Where do I want to go? How do I get from here to there? The hypermedia community calls this dilemma "the navigation problem," because it has strong similarities with geographical navigation [Robertson, et al., 1981, see also Chapter 18 by Gay and Mazur in this book].

If you are a native neither of Manhattan nor of London and yet have visited both cities, you know the difference that an ordering scheme can make to navigation. With Manhattan's regular grid of streets and avenues, many addresses are easy to find. In comparison, London (like many other old European cities) is a maze of twisting streets with little apparent system to their names. The major benefit to ordering the information graph is to help readers navigate.

Human users aren't the only ones who need to navigate through a hyperbase. Automatic text retrieval systems already provide valuable services in scanning large volumes of text for key words and phrases. The addition of hypermedia links can make this retrieval both faster and more accurate if there is some reasonable structure to the links. If the information graph is tangled, computerized processing will get confused even sooner than humans, and the advantages of linking for automatic searching quickly disappear.

An important factor in the usefulness of an information base, either by humans or by machines, is its complexity, which is directly related to the number of entities that the user has to keep straight. In a hyperdocument, elements of complexity include the total number of nodes, the total number of links, and the typical number of links emanating from a single node. Some techniques for ordering the information graph reduce the impact of these numbers on the overall complexity of the system. For example, one technique permits a large number of nodes to be treated as a single node, while another provides a way for users to ignore most of the links in the system without losing their path to required information.

Hypermedia is often described as a step toward the paperless office, but most paper manufacturers aren't losing any sleep. For many purposes, information must still be recorded on paper and hypermedia systems must be able to produce meaningful paper documents summarizing selected portions of their contents. This process is called *linearization,* because it reduces a graph to a linear document, and it's relatively straightforward to do if the graph has certain characteristics. If the graph is a tangle, the best one can do is print out the individual nodes, and let the reader figure out their relationship to one another—without the help of the hypertext system!

The number of different hypermedia systems on the market is increasing daily. Many of them are being used to structure large, important bodies of information. The use of standard, well-ordered structures in graphs opens the door to exchanging hyperbases between different systems, and even to integrating them into a larger network of information. In contrast, tangles soon reach a maximum usable size, and cannot effectively be merged into larger systems.

How Can We Order the Graph?

Techniques for ordering the information graph fall into two main classes. We can constrain the patterns of links among the nodes, and we can define different types of links as though we had colored each type of link in a different color. In this section, we develop an intuitive understanding of each class of techniques and motivate it with a metaphor. The next two sections go into more detail on the two classes.

Constraining Linkage Patterns

In describing the navigational benefits of an ordered information graph, we contrasted the relatively regular arrangement of streets in Manhattan with the rather tangled arrangements found in older European cities. The geographical metaphor not only highlights the problem, but also suggests a solution. Just as regular arrangements of streets can help travelers navigate through a city, so regular arrangements of links can help knowledge workers move through a hyperdocument [Parunak, 1989].

Humans use at least six different strategies in navigating geographically. We'll review these strategies here, and then use them later when we compare the benefits of different linkage patterns.

The *Identifier Strategy* gives a unique identifier or description to a place that we might want to visit, so that we can recognize it the moment we see it (for example, "the house with the fluorescent orange star painted on the roof"). By itself, this strategy amounts to exhaustive search: we must visit every location, one at a time, until we find the one matching the description. Even so, with the appropriate hardware, this search can be reasonably fast: consider using a helicopter to find the house with the painted roof. More commonly, the Identifier Strategy is not used alone, but as a component of other strategies.

The *Path Strategy* gives the searcher a step-by-step description of how to get to the target: "Turn left at the first light and right at the second gas station, and it's the blue house (Identifier Strategy) on the right." The Path Strategy is useful when the number of roads leaving any one location is much fewer than the total number of locations. Otherwise, the selection problem in finding the next step in a path is not significantly easier than going directly from start to the target.

Paths are not necessarily unique; sometimes there are several paths between two points, but the Path Strategy still works as long as the traveler has a clear set of instructions to follow.

Travelers apply the *Direction Strategy* when they follow directions such as "Go due north." Like the Path Strategy and unlike the Identifier Strategy, the Direction Strategy avoids exhaustive search. It differs from the Path Strategy in the framework that the traveler uses for guidance. In the Path Strategy, this framework is local to an individual location, and is stated in terms of the roads leaving that location. In the Direction Strategy, the framework is global to the entire system, part of the matrix in which the places are embedded.

Directional frameworks can vary in their granularity. The coarsest defines one dimension (say, "north" vs. "south"), and cuts the search problem in half. Finer systems include not only the four cardinal points (North, South, East, West), but intermediates (NE, NNE, ENE), and ultimately the full degrees, minutes, and seconds of modern navigation.

The Direction Strategy depends on the existence of some texture or distinguished point in the world relative to which directions can be established. A sphere would naturally have no directions, but earth escapes this dilemma because it has an axis of rotation (reflected in the relative stability of the pole star and the regular rising of the sun) and geological irregularities (such as the direction of flow of rivers, or magnetic north).

The *Distance Strategy* bounds search to a circle around the traveler's current location: "It's only a mile (ten minutes) from here." It is often used in connection with the Direction Strategy: "Go south for two kilometers." The Distance Strategy works best on a smooth (unfolded) surface. If one can go from A to B either around the hill or over it, the usefulness of distance is weakened, and folding the topography by digging a tunnel makes it even less well defined.

We can use the Distance Strategy whenever we can use the Path Strategy, by measuring distance along the path. Usually, if there are multiple paths from one point to another, there will also be multiple distances. As with the Path Strategy, the Distance Strategy is of little use if one can move directly from any one location to any other.

The *Address Strategy* refines the Direction Strategy by establishing an orthogonal set of coordinates, such as latitude and longitude or street names. Manhattan's regular grid of avenues (running roughly north-south) and streets (east-west) makes addresses fairly transparent (even if traffic congestion and one-way streets make getting to a destination there almost impossible).

Such a grid is easiest to use if the intersecting "roads" are numbered sequentially in each direction, for then one can go directly to the intersection of interest. Even if the lines have unordered names rather than numbers, the search problem is still less complex than in the Identifier Strategy. For example, a ten-by-ten grid defines 100 intersections. To find a desired item by address, one must find the two intersecting roads, searching only twenty items (the ten roads in each direction) instead of the 100 that the Identifier Strategy would require. In this case, the Address Strategy saves 80% of the effort. For larger sets, the benefit is even greater, and can be enhanced still further by adding additional dimensions. In Manhattan, one is interested not only in street and avenue, but also floor number.

Tourists who have experienced the "If it's Tuesday, this must be Belgium" syndrome understand the *Region Strategy*. Most travel exposes us in some depth to a few regions of interest, and ignores the areas in between. After a trip to Europe, I may remember a day spent in the vicinity of the Eiffel Tower, two days within the sound of Big Ben, and a pleasant afternoon driving down the Rhine, with little sense of what lies between them. I will tend to group my memories of the trip around these regions, and if I wanted to return to a place of interest, I would know in which region to begin my search. The same phenomenon recurs on a humbler scale for anyone who commutes to work. We tend to know the town where we live pretty well, and the neighborhood around our office, but what lies between is reduced to a strip of asphalt.

Defining Linkage Types

From our experience as travelers, we understand the usefulness of constrained linkage patterns in solving the problems of tangled graphs of information. The same experience also shows us the value of different kinds of links. In navigating from one place to another, we may travel on city streets, interstate highways, rivers, oceans, railroad tracks, or sidewalks, or through the air. We tend to think about each of these link types separately. For example, route maps that show one type of link usually do not show the others.

We can define different types of links in hypermedia [Trigg, 1983; Bornstein and Riley, 1990; Furuta and Stotts, 1990; Lange, 1990]. A fertile analogy to guide our thinking in this case is linguistics. The discipline of discourse grammar has developed taxonomies of the kinds of relations that can exist between separate *chunks* of language [Beekman, 1974, 1981; Grimes, 1975; Longacre, 1976, 1980, 1989; Mann and Thompson, 1987]. From this work, we can derive a classification scheme for the links in a hyperdocument.

To see how this insight works, consider the interconnections between the pieces of language that make up a conversation. Walking down the hall one day, we might hear a conversation something like this:

a.   Did you hear about the new Acme project?
b.   *What project is that?*
c.   The one where we're installing our new tin-can-and-string telecommunications system.
d.   *Oh, that one. What about it?*
e.   The project manager just quit.
f.   *Why?*
g.   Production problems.
h.   *What do you mean?*
i.   Well, a critical component of those systems is tin cans. We buy them used from restaurants, and keep a room full of goats to lick them clean and eat the paper off the outsides. Lately, she hasn't been able to get enough goats.
j.   *Yes, but on the other hand, demand for our systems has been low lately, so perhaps it's just as well we don't have to support such a large work force.*

As we eavesdrop on such a conversation, we set each successive contribution in context by its relations to what has gone before. These relations are of well-defined types. For example, lines (c) and (e) *amplify* line (a); line (g) gives the *reason* for line (e), (i) defines a *part* of the system described in (c), and (i) and (j) *contrast* with each other (see Figure 20.1).

Speech relations like these are part of the standard equipment of any human being. We use them every day in understanding how different pieces of text relate to one another, not only in conversations, but in written material as well. These same relations exist between nodes in a hyperdocument. In fact, more often than not, an author who creates a link between two nodes is trying to indicate the existence of one of these relations between the source and destination nodes. If each link is labeled to indicate the kind of relation that it specifies, the information in the graph becomes much clearer and human users can more easily select from a variety of links that begin at a single node, based on the kind of further information they want. Automatic search programs can retrieve constellations of nodes related in specified ways. Linearized text (a paper dump of a hyperdocument) can reflect these relations and thus be more readable. Linguists have defined an exten-

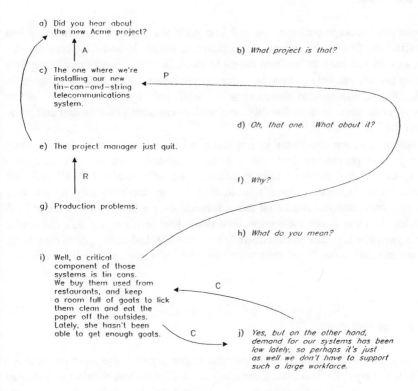

a) Did you hear about the new Acme project?

   A

b) *What project is that?*

c) The one where we're installing our new tin-can-and-string telecommunications system.

   P

d) *Oh, that one. What about it?*

e) The project manager just quit.

   R

f) *Why?*

g) Production problems.

h) *What do you mean?*

i) Well, a critical component of those systems is tin cans. We buy them used from restaurants, and keep a room full of goats to lick them clean and eat the paper off the outsides. Lately, she hasn't been able to get enough goats.

   C

   C

j) *Yes, but on the other hand, demand for our systems has been low lately, so perhaps it's just as well we don't have to support such a large workforce.*

Figure 20.1   The lines of dialog are connected by lines that classify each contribution in relation to what has been said earlier.

sive typology of such relations, which we will outline in detail later in this chapter.

What Kinds of Linkage Patterns are There and How Are They Useful?

The basic building block out of which link patterns are built is the link, and the question of whether links are directional or not makes a big difference in how patterns of links behave. So this section begins with a discussion of link directionality. Then it surveys six different linkage patterns, giving a simple definition and a diagram of each and explaining how it relates to the navigational strategies outlined in the last section. After summarizing the relation between linkage patterns and navigational strategies, we conclude the section by looking at some ways restricted linkage patterns can be employed in a hypermedia system.

Link Directions

In describing linkage patterns, we call one node the parent of another if a link goes from the first to the second (from parent to child). In some hypermedia systems, readers can only move from parent to child. In most, readers can move from child to parent, but only if they have previously followed the link from parent to child. That is, the reverse direction is available only by backing up. In a few systems, links have no directionality, and readers can start at either end and move to the other.

Whether links are directional or not makes a big difference in navigation, since one-way links provide readers with a sense of up and down that two-way links cannot. In our discussion of linkage patterns, we will assume that all links are one-way. This restriction doesn't mean that readers can't traverse a link both ways, but only that you must first move forward over a link before you can back up along it in the reverse direction. We don't lose anything by this restriction, since a two-way link can be described as two one-way links in opposite directions. The reverse isn't true. If we start with two-way links, we can't build a one-way link.

Six Linkage Patterns

We'll discuss the six basic linkage patterns beginning with the most constrained, in which the most navigational techniques are available, and moving to the least constrained, in which navigation is most difficult. Within each pattern, we consider only sets of nodes that are connected in such a way that there is at least one node from which you can start and reach every other node in the set. So you can assume that every node in a pattern is connected, at least by way of other nodes, with every other node in the pattern.

Linear. The simplest linkage pattern is linear, in which each node has at most one child and one parent. Two cases are possible (see Figure 20.2).

If every node has exactly one child and one parent, the nodes form a ring. Otherwise, exactly one node has no child and exactly one node has no parent, and the structure is a chain with these two nodes as its ends.

The linear pattern supports all of the navigational strategies discussed in the last section, though they are hardly necessary, given the simplicity of the structure. The Path Strategy differs little from the ubiquitous Identifier Strategy, since in both cases one simply traverses the linear list of links. Our assumption that all nodes are reachable from at least one node means that all links are head-to-tail, never head-to-head or tail-to-tail, and thus the structure defines a natural direction within which one can move forward or back. There is a unique distance between any two nodes, defined as the number of links between them, and a unique (though trivial) address for each.

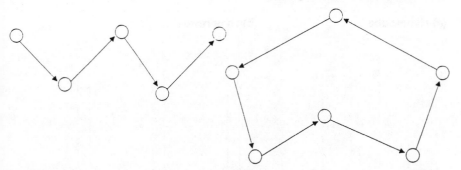

Figure 20.2 In a linear linkage pattern, each node has at most one child and one parent.

Hierarchy. In a hierarchical linkage pattern, one node has no parents and the others have exactly one parent (see Figure 20.3).

This topology characterizes popular PC-based outline processors such as ThinkTank(TM) or PCOutline(TM), and is also the basic structure of Engelbart's AUGMENT [See Chapter 24 by Engelbart in this book, and Engelbart and English, 1968]. The orphan element (the root of the hierarchy) is usually the node at which one enters the hyperdocument. All links point away from the root, so any node is reachable from it. Furthermore, since a link once traversed can be followed in the reverse direction, one can go from any node back up (to the root if necessary), and then down to any other node.

If we rule out moving back and forth repeatedly over the same link, a hierarchy defines a unique path between any two nodes: from the current node, back up repeatedly to the unique parent of the current node until one reaches a node that is an ancestor of the target node, then forward down a different branch to the target node. Because there is a unique path between any two nodes, we can define distances between nodes, which are conveniently abstracted in terms of depth in the hierarchy. Directionality is also well defined in a hierarchy: up (toward the root)

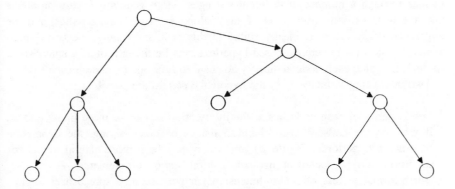

Figure 20.3 In a hierarchical linkage pattern, one node has no parents and the others have exactly one parent.

(a) Hypercube   **(b) Hypertorus**

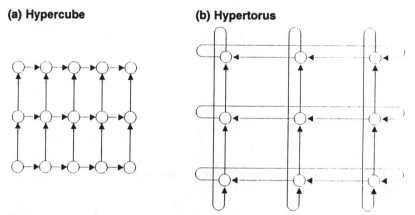

Figure 20.4a and b   Hypercube and Hypertorus.

or down (away from it). Hierarchies do not support an orthogonal addressing strategy.

Hypercube and Hypertorus.   The hypercube linkage pattern takes its inspiration from a rectangular grid of streets like that in Manhattan. In Manhattan, connecting links are drawn from two sets (streets and avenues), and each corner lies at the intersection of a street and an avenue. In a hypercube, the links that intersect at a node can be drawn from three, four, or even more sets. Figure 20.4a shows a two-dimensional hypercube.

The hypercube pattern directly supports an orthogonal addressing strategy for navigation. It is useful for domains that invite one to compare a number of items along a number of dimensions. One implementation of this topology, SymEdit (an experimental application of this topology in use at ITI) is a useful tool for studying symmetrical patterns in literary documents, where one wishes to trace common themes through a number of different passages. More generally, many problems take the form of comparing a set of cases along a set of characteristics, and the hypercube organization is ideally suited to this task. Informally, the two-dimensional version of a hypercube-based hypertext may be thought of as a spreadsheet for text, in which each node is directly adjacent to four others, one on each side.

Two interesting refinements of the hypercube pattern are possible:

- In a hypercube, each node lies at the intersection of two or more linear chains. If we join the ends of each chain so that it becomes a ring, the hypercube becomes a hypertorus (Figure 20.4b), which may be a more natural model for structuring a hyperdocument that lacks natural first or last elements.
- Our informal picture of a two-dimensional hypercube as a spreadsheet implies that the network can be embedded in a plane, so its links do not cross each other. If a natural ordering can be imposed on each dimension, a hypercube can avoid crossing links, but this restriction is not necessary for the Address Strategy for navigation.

With or without these refinements, readers can search each dimension of a hypercube separately, leading to a huge reduction in the number of nodes that they must examine. For example, if we arrange 100 nodes into a linear chain, readers must examine an average of 50 to find a particular node, but in a two-dimensional hypercube they need examine only about 10, and only about 5 in three dimensions. With larger collections of nodes, the savings are even greater. Instead of examining 5000 nodes to find the one they want out of 10,000 in a linear pattern, a two-dimensional hypercube cuts their search by a factor of 50 to about 100 nodes, and a three-dimensional hypercube by a factor of 1000, to about 50 nodes.

In addition to the Address Strategy for which the topology is designed and the ubiquitous Identifier Strategy, the hypercube topology supports the Path Strategy. Also, if the dimensions are ordered (so that the hypercube can be embedded in a physical space of the same dimensionality without crossing links), the hypercube (though not the hypertorus) supports the Direction Strategy and (using the city-block metric along the hypercube links) the Distance Strategy.

Directed Acyclic Graph.   The *Directed Acyclic Graph* (DAG) is a more general linkage pattern than any we have considered up to this point (see Figure 20.5). It requires only that there be no loops in the network. That is, starting from a node and moving only forward over links, it is impossible to come back to the starting node. Linear, hierarchical, and hypercube patterns are DAG's, but not every DAG has the regularities that these patterns do. Rings and hypertoruses have loops, and so are not DAG's, but their structure is regular in other ways.

Most hypermedia networks with DAG structure have a single point of entry, forming a common ancestor of all nodes and yielding a semilattice. Unless there are other regularities (as in patterns that we have previously considered), neither Distance nor Address Strategies apply in a DAG, but the absence of cycles means that direction is well defined, as are paths.

Clumped.   Sometimes a hypermedia network consists of a number of densely interconnected regions, between which sparser connections exist (see Figure 20.6).

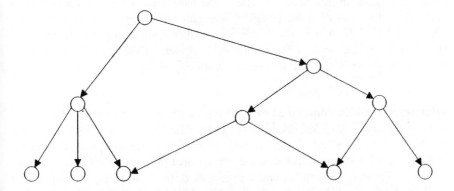

Figure 20.5   The Directed Acyclic Graph (DAG) requires only that there be no loops in the network.

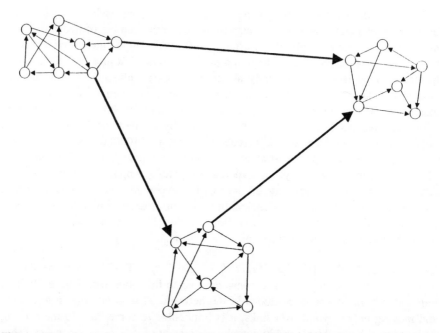

Figure 20.6 In a clumped pattern, it is worthwhile for the author to consider each clump as a node and inquire about the pattern formed by connections between clumps.

This pattern, which we call clumped, supports the Region Strategy. The dense interconnections in restricted regions typically result because clumped nodes have more in common with each other than they do with the rest of the network, and readers can sense this commonality and orient themselves with it.

In a clumped pattern, it is worthwhile for the author to consider each clump as a node and inquire about the pattern formed by connections among clumps. If the author can constrain this pattern to one of the more regular types, readers will be able take advantage of more powerful navigational strategies to find the right clump, and then browse freely within the smaller confines of the clump itself. Hyperdocument authors can sometimes guide readers in this way by appropriate use of aggregation links, as described below under link types.

Arbitrary. The least constrained pattern consists of any connected set of nodes. If none of the constraints described above applies, the Identifier and Path Strategies are the only ones available. Even the Path Strategy becomes useless as the number of links per node increases, for then the navigational problem involved in selecting the next step along a path becomes almost as difficult as going directly to the target node. So we may distinguish a partial arbitrary pattern (with few links per node) from a complete arbitrary pattern (with many links per node).

	Identifier:	Paths:		Direction:	Distance:		Address:	Region:
		Unique	Multiple		Unique	Multiple		
Linear	x	x		x	x		x	
Ring	x	x			x		x	
Hierarchical	x	x		x	x			
Hypercube (Ordered)	x		x	x	x		x	
Hypercube (Tangled)	x		x			x	x	
Hypertorus (Ordered)	x		x		x		x	
Hypertorus (Tangled)	x		x			x	x	
DAG	x		x	x		x		
Clumped								x
Arbitrary (partial)	x		x			x		
Arbitrary (complete)	x							

Figure 20.7   Linkage Patterns and Navigational Strategies.

Summary

Figure 20.7 summarizes our conclusions about which topologies support which navigational strategies.

These strategies all assume that links are one-way. What would happen to our patterns if we replaced one-way links with two-way links? Figure 20.8 shows the impact such a change would have on the available strategies. (In determining whether a pattern permits Path and Distance Strategies, we assume that the same link is not traveled twice in moving between two nodes.)

With two-way links, the Direction Strategy is no longer available. Also, only linear and hierarchical patterns offer the unique Distance Strategy, since two-way links open up alternative paths with varying distances in the other patterns. As a result, the differences between the hypercube and the hypertorus, as well as between ordered and tangled forms of each, disappear.

Uses of Linkage Patterns

At first glance, the notion of restricted linkage patterns seems directly opposed to one of hypermedia's great strengths, the ability to move freely wherever one

	Identifier:	Paths:		Direction:	Distance:		Address:	Region:
		Unique	Multiple		Unique	Multiple		
Linear	x	x			x		x	
Ring	x					x	x	
Hierarchical	x	x			x			
Hypercube or Hypertorus	x		x			x	x	
DAG	x		x			x		
Clumped								x
Arbitrary (partial)	x		x			x		
Arbitrary (complete)	x							

Figure 20.8   Patterns and Strategies with Two-Way Links.

wishes in a network of information. In fact, there are several ways in which readers can have the advantages of the patterns we have discussed without losing the flexibility that brought them to hypermedia in the first place. Many navigational aids commonly implemented in hypermedia systems are effectively mechanisms for inducing a topology of reduced complexity on the hyperdocument, and thus enlarging the set of navigational strategies that readers can bring to bear. These mechanisms are of two kinds. *Beaten path* aids help readers find places in the network that they have already visited. *Abstraction* aids give readers a different perspective on a complex hyperbase, a perspective that offers a simpler linkage pattern than that of the whole hyperbase.

Beaten Path Mechanisms.   Beaten path navigational aids enable a user to return easily to places already visited, and include back-up stacks, path macros, and book marks.

A *back-up stack* keeps track of the nodes through which a reader has moved, so that the steps can be retraced back to the starting point. It generates a smaller network with a linear linkage pattern, within which the widest range of navigational strategies is possible.

A generalization of the back-up stack is the *path macro*, which remembers a path and permits the user to move back and forth along it repeatedly, in essence building a subdocument with a more constrained linkage pattern within which navigation is simpler. It records the most recent path of specified complexity (usually linear or hierarchical). In the case of a hierarchical path macro, when the reader visits a node already in the macro along a different path, the older link to the node is removed from the macro and replaced with the newer one.

Book marks permit readers to identify particular landmark nodes and jump directly to them from any point in the system. A book mark facility induces a one-level hierarchy whose root is the known entry point (for example, a pop-up window that lists marked locations). A home button that takes the reader immediately to the entry point of the hyperdocument is a degenerate example of a book mark.

Abstraction Mechanisms. Abstraction mechanisms permit readers to step back from the overall hyperbase, which may itself have an arbitrary pattern of linkage, and gain a new perspective from which the linkage is more constrained. Three examples are scripts, typed links, and multilevel systems.

Scripts [Zellweger, 1989] or *tours* [Marshall and Irish, 1989] are selected paths through a hyperdocument that one user (perhaps the author) has prepared for another. A tour is like a turnpike map that shows the main road and indicates possible side trips for readers with extra time and special interest. The tour itself can have an extremely simple pattern of connectivity, usually linear or, at worst, hierarchical. As long as readers who leave the script have a quick way to jump back to the point at which they left it, they can browse around the larger environment without fear of getting lost.

In the next section, we will show how links can be classified into different *types*. When this is done, the pattern formed by links of any one type may be much simpler than the overall linkage pattern of the entire system. For example, consider a one-level dictionary (a hierarchy) attached to a hierarchical hyperbase. The overall pattern is a DAG, since one can access a single node of the dictionary from many different nodes of the main hyperbase. However, since each system is a hierarchy, and since the reader distinguishes between accessing definitions and roaming about the main hyperbase, the distance strategy that ordinarily is not available in a DAG is still useful.

The notion of combining simpler well-defined topologies to control the complexity of the larger system is anticipated in [Brown, 1982]. We have already observed that the clumped linkage pattern permits us to apply the notion of patterns at *multiple levels*, either among individual nodes or among groups of nodes. Frequently, connections are much more regular between clumps than within a clump, or can be made more regular without greatly impairing the user's freedom in exploring the network. When this is the case, facilities that enable readers to back up and look at clumps rather than individual nodes can enable them to use a rich set of navigational strategies at the higher level.

What Kinds of Link Types Are There and How Are They Useful?

We can distinguish three main classes of link types that are useful in hypermedia. The first two of them take their inspiration directly from linguistic discourse relations.

- Association links are the most common, and reflect various ways in which one node brings another to mind. For example, one node might give the reason for the assertions in another node.

- Aggregation links join a node that represents a whole with its parts. For example, a node representing a book is the aggregate of the nodes representing its chapters, and would be joined to them by aggregation links of type *Chapter*.
- Revision links join a node to earlier and later versions of itself, and have no obvious parallel in discourse grammar.

In this section, we'll discuss each of these three categories of links, and then survey how they make a hyperdocument easier to use.

At the outset, we should note that two nodes may be linked by several different links, each calling attention to a different kind of relation between them. Typed links may thus lead to an increase in the total number of links in a network. However, because link types enable readers to identify the links of interest at any particular time, a hyperdocument with a typed links system will be clearer and easier to read than those that are not typed. And, because the hypertext system can display just links of the types of interest for any particular operation, the overall efficiency of the system will improve.

Association Links

There are two kinds of association links. To understand the difference between them, we need to think about groups of words. We're not interested in random groups of words ("bird ship the under"). Instead, consider groups that, informally, make sense to a reader, groups like "the hat," "blue marbles," "under the rock," "before she left," "the boy hit the ball," and "sun." (A group might have only a single word in it.)

Groups of words that make sense are of two different types: those that contain a verb (which we call *clauses*), and those that do not (which we call *words* if they have only one member and *phrases* otherwise). This distinction is important because only a *clause* (a group with a verb) actually says something: it constitutes a proposition. Groups without verbs are not propositions.

There is a set of grammatical relations, involving both syntax and semantics, that describes how words and phrases combine to form clauses. Another, completely different set of relations permits clauses to combine to form larger units, such as sentences or paragraphs. Interestingly, paragraphs can be combined into still larger structures, and this time we don't need a new set of relations. The same relations that join clauses to one another also join paragraphs and chapters together. Thus it is convenient to describe clauses and everything more complex than a clause with the same term, proposition. And in fact, everything larger than a clause can be summarized, at least approximately, with a single clause, so it really does make sense to treat even an entire book as a proposition. In a hyperdocument, a proposition can range in size all the way from a single clause to an entire node.

We're not interested at this point in the relations that join words and phrases into clauses, but we are interested in those that join propositions to something else.

The *something else* may be either another proposition or a word (or phrase), and that distinction gives us the two broad classes of association links: *word-proposition* and *proposition-proposition* links.

For each type of link that we describe, we can also define an inverse. These inverses are useful in building actual systems, but, in order to save space, we will not discuss these inverses here.

Word-Proposition Links.   Three kinds of links relate a single word or phrase to another proposition.

• A content link leads from a word that describes or names a proposition to that proposition. For example, one node might contain the phrase, "Gettysburg Address," and a content link from those words would lead the reader to the text of the address. Links that lead to a graphic display are often content links, as are links that permit portions of a document to expand or contract when selected.

• Identification links define or otherwise restrict the meaning of a word or phrase. Their most common use is to link individual terms to a glossary.

• Comment links give additional information about a word or phrase that does not restrict its meaning. For example, a comment link might lead from a person's name to a node containing the person's birth date, address, and social security number. (Sometimes, the difference between comment and identification links disappears. Links from personal name to supplemental information are comment links for most names, but become identification links if the network refers to more than one person with the same name.)

Proposition-Proposition Links.   A far wider variety of links joins propositions to each other. They may lead from one entire node to another, but they can also lead from any proposition within a node to another proposition in the same node or elsewhere. (Remember that a proposition can be as small as a clause or as large as a complete document.) These links are of four kinds, each with several more detailed varieties.

Orientation Links.   Define the environment for the state or events described in a proposition. They are of three types.

• A location link joins a proposition to a description of the place where that proposition applies.

• A temporal link describes the chronological relation between the states or events described in two propositions. It can be of six types (each of which has an inverse) [Allen, 1983], conveniently displayed graphically along a time line. (See Figure 20.9.)

• A circumstance link joins a proposition to another proposition that describes aspects of its environment other than local or temporal.

```
A Before B:      AAAAA    BBBBB
A During B:      BBBBBBBBBBBBB
                 AAAAA
A Overlaps B:    AAAAAAA
                 BBBBBBB
A Meets B:       AAAAAABBBBBB
A Starts B:      BBBBBBBBBBBBB
                 AAAAA
A Finishes B:    BBBBBBBBBBBBB
                 AAAAA
```

Figure 20.9 The six types of temporal links can be compared when displayed along a time line.

Implication Links. Record logical relations among propositions. They are of seven types. In particular:

- A causation link joins one proposition to another that describes its cause. For example, a causation link might lead from "My tire is flat" to "There is a piece of glass stuck in my tire."
- A purpose link joins one proposition to another that describes its purpose: "I'm going on a vacation" might lead via a purpose link to "I need a rest." (Philosophers will note that what we call Causation and Purpose are both examples of a broader notion of causality, and represent efficient and final cause, respectively.)
- A condition link joins one proposition to another whose truth insures the truth of the first. For example, a condition link could lead from "It will be a nice day tomorrow" to "The sky is red this evening." Condition and causation are easily confused. *Condition* simply records a correlation in the truth of two propositions, without considering whether one causes the other or whether both are affected by a common cause. *Causation* claims that one directly causes the other.
- Contrafactual links are closely related to condition links. A condition link joins a proposition to another whose truth insures the truth of the first. A contrafactual link joins a proposition to another whose truth insures the falsehood of the first. Thus from "I can clean off my desk each day," a contrafactual link leading to "There are only 24 hours in each day," explains why in fact I can't clean off my desk each day. Contrafactual links can be paraphrased with "If X were true (but it isn't), then Y would be true (but it isn't)."
- A concession link captures the notion of "although." It leads from one proposition to another that might be thought to invalidate the first, but does not. A concession link leading from "I can clean off my desk each day" to "There are only 24 hours in each day" invites us to ask, "How does he ever do it?"
- A warning link leads from a proposition that describes an obligation to another describing an undesirable consequence that will arise if the obligation is not fulfilled. For example, in a hyperdocument describing maintenance and diagnosis of a piece of equipment, a warning link might lead from a node outlining a

particular maintenance activity ("Lubricate the thrust bearing every six months") to a description of what might happen if the bearing is not lubricated ("Failure of the main thrust bearing can result if it is not regularly lubricated").

- Evidence links move from a proposition to others that provide data that support it and from which it is induced. A hyperbase for machine diagnosis might have nodes describing symptoms, joined by evidence links to other nodes that give possible diagnoses for those symptoms. Evidence links are similar to condition links, but weaker; a particular symptom can be evidence for several diagnoses, only one of which may be true. Alternatively, if one attaches a probability weight to evidence links, then an evidence link with a weight of 100% becomes a condition link.

Paraphrase Links.   Connect one proposition with another that contains similar information. They are of five types.

- Amplification and summary links are inverses of one another. Each connects a proposition that makes a point concisely with another that gives more detail. In high school, we all studied the role of the topic sentence in a paragraph. In link terms, an amplification link leads from the topic sentence to the rest of the paragraph, and a summary link leads from the rest of the paragraph to the topic sentence. Hyperdocuments commonly include some nodes that serve as tables of contents for other nodes; the link between an entry in a table of contents and the associated material is an amplification link.
- Abstraction and instance links are inverses and connect a generic proposition with a specific form of it. For example, in a human resources hyperdocument, an instance link would connect a proposition describing a company policy about rewarding excellence to a record of a particular case where an outstanding employee was rewarded. Note that the same two propositions might also be linked by a cause link: the employee was rewarded because of the company policy.
- Equivalence links join two propositions that contain the same information in different words.

Illustration Links.   Connect dissimilar propositions that clarify one another. They are of three types.

- A manner link joins one proposition to another that describes the manner or style in which the event or state in the first came about.
- A comparison link joins two propositions that are different from one another but show points of similarity, and draws attention to those similarities. In a hyperbase of medical cases, one might connect two different cases in which the same symptoms appeared.
- A contrast link joins two propositions and draws attention to the differences between them. In a network of medical cases, one might connect two cases with different outcomes. Note that a given pair of propositions might be joined both by contrast and comparison links, one serving to emphasize the points of difference between the propositions, the other calling attention to their similarity.

Aggregation Links

Often, a group of nodes in a hyperbase together form a constellation, a unit that we want to be able to name and manipulate as a single node. Hypermedia gives us the flexibility to define a single node to represent the group. It is the whole of which they are the parts. Aggregation links then connect the node as a whole to its parts. There will often be other links, either association links or revision links, among the part nodes, as well as between the part nodes and other nodes not part of the same whole.

Each kind of whole has a different set of parts, and each part-whole relationship defines a different aggregation link, so we do not expect to be able to list all aggregation links. We will describe several wholes that appear promising, and identify the aggregation links that they generate. In the process, we must be careful not to lose sight of the forest for the trees. The big idea of aggregation links is that sometimes it makes sense to view individual nodes as parts of another one, and when this is the case, we need to define the kinds of parts that make up the whole with appropriate aggregation links.

Aggregation links take their inspiration from the linguistic notion of *scripts* [Barr and Feigenbaum, 1981], structured frameworks that are perceived to lie behind many areas of human interaction.

The Argument Aggregate. The Toulmin structure [Toulmin, 1969] is a basic framework for representing the parts of a logical argument. It maintains that any argument can be analyzed into the basic components of datum, claim, warrant, backing, and rebuttal. In a hyperbase, a single node representing a given argument would have aggregation links leading to each of these components of the argument. A reader can "pick up" the entire argument by way of the high-level node, and then traverse the appropriate aggregation link to access the desired component of the argument.

For instance, consider the following bit of reasoning:

> "Some consumer advocates are arguing that microwave ovens pose a cancer risk, since they expose their users to microwave radiation. Microwaves can cause cancer, as numerous experiments with laboratory animals have shown. But industry spokesmen insist that their products are safe, when maintained according to the owners' manual, because the level of emissions that they produce is well within government approved safety guidelines."

Cast as a Toulmin structure, this argument would appear as in Figure 20.10. (We have replaced the link labels defined by Toulmin with particular link types from our survey of association links.)

The backbone of any argument is a claim supported by a datum. The warrant gives a general rule that justifies the derivation of the claim from the datum, and the backing gives evidence for the validity of this general rule. The rebuttal permits us to capture exceptions to the general rule.

A hypermedia representation of this structure might have a single node representing "Resolved: that microwave ovens are a cancer risk." That node would be

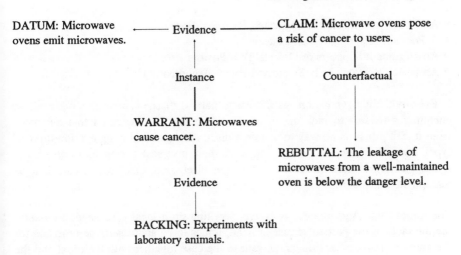

Figure 20.10 An argument cast as a Toulmin structure.

linked via an aggregation link of type *Claim* to another node recording the claim; via a *Datum* link to a node recording the datum; and so forth. Conversely, one can define the inverse of each of these links, leading (for example) from a node stating "Microwaves cause cancer" via an "Inverse-Warrant" link to the argument in which this proposition serves as a warrant.

Nodes can participate in multiple aggregations. In the argument we have been discussing, the statement "Microwaves cause cancer" is a warrant. One can imagine another argument in which this statement serves as a claim, supported by the datum, "Experiments with laboratory animals." In addition to the "Inverse-Warrant" link connecting "Microwaves cause cancer" to the original argument node, we would expect an "Inverse-Claim" link connecting it to another argument node, "Resolved: Microwaves cause cancer."

The links that are apparent in Figure 20.10 between the individual nodes that make up the Toulmin structure are not aggregation links but ordinary association links, and permit us to navigate directly from one low-level node to another. Aggregation links move up to the whole of which a node is a part, and back down to other parts of that whole.

The Discussion Aggregate. The gIBIS schema of discussion [Conklin and Begeman, 1987] models an argument as an interconnected set of nodes that constitute Issues, Positions on those issues, and Arguments on those positions. These nodes are connected through association links of several types. Here, we summarize these links according to the titles used by the developers of gIBIS. Each of these links can also be named in terms of the system of associative links developed above.

• An Issue Generalizes, Specializes, Replaces, Questions, or Is-Suggested-By another Issue.

- An Issue Questions or Is-Suggested-By a Position.
- A Position Responds-To an Issue.
- An Argument Supports or Objects-To a Position.
- An Issue Questions or Is-Suggested-By an Argument.

Even without aggregation, gIBIS has a natural "issue-centered" structure that encourages readers to pick up an issue and access the discussion that emanates from it. Still, there is no way to handle a discussion as a unit. Aggregation links of types *Issue*, *Position*, and *Argument* (with their inverses) permit us to attach the nodes that serve these functions to a single discussion node, which can then be manipulated as a unit.

The Legal Case Aggregate.   A lawyer working on a legal case needs to assemble the facts of the particular case at hand, issues to be addressed, the rationale for the client's claim, other rulings relevant to the case together with their text and the statutes on which they rest, and the decision finally reached in the case [Halasz, 1988]. Each of these items might be a node in a hyperdocument, with various associative links tying them together. The network will be more useful in a law office if readers can pick up a single node representing a given case and from it access the different components using aggregation links of types *Fact, Issue, Rationale, Precedent,* and *Decision*.

The Software Module Aggregate.   In languages such as C or Pascal, a software module is a highly structured piece of text, with a program body and declarations for interface, constants, types, and variables. A computer-aided software engineering environment might store the software under production in a hyperbase, in which a single node representing a module leads by way of aggregation links to the appropriate program text. This approach is particularly useful in insuring that, for example, constant declarations used in different modules are consistent with each other, by seeing to it that those modules access the very same node containing the constants. Some existing languages already implement a primitive form of aggregation link by way of *include files*, which are named in the text of a module and whose contents are drawn into the module when it is compiled.

Aggregates vs. Typed Nodes.   Some hypermedia systems attach types to nodes. gIBIS, for example, classifies each node as an *Issue*, a *Position*, or an *Argument* (or, for more general comments, *Other*). Attaching labels to nodes in this way is appropriate for a system whose whole purpose is to represent a single kind of structure (in this case, discussions), but would be awkward if these nodes also served other purposes in a more general enterprise information base. In this context, a type such as *Issue, Position,* or *Argument* does not belong to a node in isolation, but only to a node as it relates to some larger structure. The type is a role that a piece of information fills, and that role is meaningful only in relation to the whole to which that piece is related. A given piece of information might conceivably fill many different roles simultaneously. Treating its role as a node type requires us to define a primary aggregation to which it belongs. By assigning roles via aggregation links rather than node types, an author can link a given node into as many different kinds of aggregations as needed, without discriminating among them.

Revision Links

Frequently, we need to store successive versions of information that is in some sense *the same*. As a piece of software is developed, a given module will be revised to make it more efficient or remove bugs, and the successive versions of the same module need to be kept available in an orderly fashion. A manufacturer whose products need to conform to government standards must keep copies of those standards, as they are updated and revised over the years, so that the version of the standards in effect when a contract was signed can be retrieved for reference on that contract, even if the standard has changed. A contractor who is negotiating a contract with a client needs to keep successive versions of the contract on hand to manage the course of the negotiations. In each case, the successive copies of the item in question (the software module, the standard, or the contract) are revisions of something that is in some sense the same in each of its incarnations.

The linking structure of hypermedia is a natural mechanism for recording these series of revisions, by way of links of types *Ancestor* and *Descendant* (or *Predecessor* and *Successor*).

Using Typed Links

Typed links are a powerful tool for manipulating a hyperbase. In this section we discuss some of their benefits, and then suggest how a system can cope with the complexity introduced by a large set of link types.

Uses of Typed Links. Typed links open the door to two powerful navigational tactics: filtering and zooming. They also greatly facilitate automatic processing of hypermedia networks.

Filtering occurs when the hypermedia system shows you only some of the paths you can follow through a network. With untyped links, the system must either show every reader all of the links that originate with a node, or none of them. It has no grounds for selecting a subset of the links for a particular reader's attention. But in most cases, readers have some sense of what they're looking for. You probably know, for instance, whether you want a definition of an unfamiliar word, a supporting argument for a proposition, an illustration of it, or a counter-example, and typed links enable the system to focus your choices accordingly. Revision links are seldom needed in the same thought processes as other types, and making them invisible when you're not using them can drastically decrease the apparent complexity of the overall system. A map of all the links in a large hyperbase is a hopeless tangle, but a map showing only links of one or a few types can be much more manageable and useful.

Aggregation links let readers zoom in and out of networks. You can treat a related set of nodes as a single node, to avoid dealing with their internal detail, or move down to access specific relations among the parts of a whole.

Once the system understands the types of various links, it can manipulate them automatically. For example, if you are looking for causes of a situation described in a given node, the system can automatically follow causal links to retrieve not just immediate causes but also remote ones (causes of causes). For another example, link types permit a system to join individual nodes together into linearized documents in a way that is much more natural and readable than would be possible without link types, because the system can structure the linearization to take account of the semantic relations among the nodes.

Coping with Large Sets of Link Types. We have defined a very large set of link types—in fact, an unlimited set, since each new kind of aggregate brings along its own set of aggregation links. In spite of the benefits, both readers and authors may well feel intimidated at the array of options.

We can simplify matters considerably if we realize that the link types themselves form a hierarchy. Our description of association links is an example. The most general type in this hierarchy is *Association,* which has two subtypes: *Word-Proposition* and *Proposition-Proposition.* Each of these is further divided in the scheme presented above.

We can extend this typing scheme to include all link types. The root of the type hierarchy is *All-types,* with three children: *Association, Aggregation,* and *Revision.* The children of *Aggregation* can be grouped into families, such as *Argument, Discussion, Legal-case,* and *Module.* These family names are not themselves link types, and so cannot belong to the hierarchy, but recognizing them is useful in reducing the complexity of the overall hierarchy. The children of *Revision* are *Predecessor* and *Successor.* The children of *Association* are as outlined above.

If the hyperdocument author organizes the link types required in the hypertext into such a hierarchy, readers need proceed only as far down the tree as their needs require. For example, *Causation* and *Purpose* are two different kinds of Implication links. For some purposes, a reader might be looking for implication links but not care whether they are causation or purpose links. Because *Implication* is an ancestor of both *Causation* and *Purpose* in the hierarchy of link types, a reference to Implication would retrieve both *Causation* and *Purpose* links. More generally, a hyperdocument with typed links can be treated as though it had untyped links by referencing links of type *All-type,* which is an ancestor of every link type and thus describes every link in the system.

Conclusion

Here I'll consider each of the areas of promised benefit outlined at the outset, and illustrate how using constrained patterns of links and link types can contribute to each.

Ordering conventions help readers to navigate. Hypermedia authors should provide patterns of links that will permit users to employ the kinds of navigational strategies that they use in the real world, and typed links to enable readers to filter out unneeded connections and zoom in and out of subdocuments. Patterning and typing are synergistic in reducing the complexity of a hyperdocument. When we filter a net to show only links of a certain type, the resulting pattern of connectivity is often simpler, and navigational clues more abundant, than for the full hyperdocument. For example, revision links usually form a strict hierarchy, and causal links will not form cycles.

If authors impose these kinds of structures on their hyperdocuments, automated searching becomes feasible. We have already discussed how typed links can enable the computer to search, for example, for all the causes, immediate and indirect, of a given node. Patterns of links also are useful to a computer, in providing addressing schemes that can be used to move through the hyperdocument. In other words, these techniques enable us to "structure the experience" of a computer as well as of a human reader.

Authors should impose order on their graphs in order to reduce their complexity, so that readers can process them more efficiently. It is easier to generate meaningful linearized text (that is, a conventional paper document) if the author is disciplined.

Link typing can also help the hypertext system discern how the material is related; link patterns suggest certain presentation formats (for example, successive indentation for hierarchical material). Different hyperdocuments that use the same standardized structures can be combined more effectively, with less reader confusion, than other disjoint hyperdocuments.

Most hypermedia systems today are stand-alone implementations, each with its own scheme for coding information. As more and more material becomes available in electronic form, people will want to read material created using one hypertext system with a different one. The more structure authors build into hyperdocuments, the more information will be available to computerized systems in converting material from one format to another.

About the Author

Dr. H. Van Dyke Parunak

Dr. Parunak is a Scientific Fellow at the *Industrial Technology Institute* (ITI) in Ann Arbor, Michigan, a not-for-profit contract research organization that promotes the renewal and continued vitality of North American manufacturing through appropriate use of advanced technologies.

His international training (five graduate degrees) and range of research and practical experience (spanning biology, linguistics, philosophy, artificial intelligence, computer science, and manufacturing engineering) provide a broad foundation for innovative and effective solutions to challenging problems. As a leading strategist in emerging information technologies, he helps ITI's clients determine the appropriate information management tools for different applications and integrate these into unified information systems with consistent human interfaces. ITI's expertise includes not only the software and computer science disciplines essential to engineering hypermedia systems, but also the computer communications techniques that permit truly distributed information systems and the understanding of organizational design and performance enhancement methods that can turn these systems to the competitive advantage of their users.

Dr. Parunak may be contacted at the Industrial Technology Institute, P. O. Box 1485, Ann Arbor, MI 48106.

References

Barr, A. and Feigenbaum, E.A. (1981). *The Handbook of Artificial Intelligence.* "*Frames and Scripts,*" *Volume III*, 216–222.

Beekman, John and Callow, John (1974). *Translating the Word of God.* Grand Rapids, MI.

Beekman, John, Callow, John and Kopesec, Michael (1981). *The Semantic Structure of Written Communication.* Summer Institute of Linguistics.

Bornstein, Jeremy and Riley, Victor (1990). "Hypertext Interchange Format: Discussion and Format Specification, Draft 1.3.4," *Proceedings of the Hypertext Standardization Workshop*, NIST Special Publication SP500-178, 39–47.

Brown, J.W. (1982). "Controlling the Complexity of Menu Networks," *CACM 25:7* (July) 412–418.

Catlin, Timothy, Bush, Paulette and Yankelovich, Nicole (1989). "InterNote: Extending a Hypermedia Framework to Support Annotative Collaboration," *Proceedings of Hypertext '89*, 365–378.

Conklin, J. and Begeman, M.L. (1987). "gIBIS: A Hypertext Tool for Team Design Deliberation," *Proceedings of Hypertext '87*, 247–252.

Cook, Walter A. (1969). *Introduction to Tagmemic Analysis.* Washington, DC.

DeRose, Steven J. (1989). "Expanding the Notion of Links," *Proceedings of Hypertext '89*, 249–257.

Engelbart, D. and English, W.K. (1968). A Research Center for Augmenting Human Intellect, *AFIPS Conference Proceedings, Vol. 33, Fall Joint Computer Conference*, San Francisco, CA, December 1988, pp. 395–410, FJCC 1968.

Engelbart, D. (1991). "Knowledge-Domain Interoperability and an Open Hyperdocument System," *Hypertext / Hypermedia Handbook*, Emily Berk and Joseph Devlin (Ed.s), McGraw-Hill, New York, NY.

Fillmore, Charles J. (1968). "The Case for Case," E. Bach and R.T. Harms, (Ed.s), *Universals in Linguistic Theory.* New York, 1–88.

Furuta, Richard and Stotts, P. David (1990). "The Trellis Hypertext Reference Model," *Proceedings of the Hypertext Standardization Workshop*, NIST Special Publication SP500-178, 83–93.

Garg, Panaj K. (1988). "Abstraction Mechanisms in Hypertext," *CACM 31:7*, 862–870.

Gay, G. and Mazur, J. (1991). "Navigating in Hypermedia," *Hypertext / Hypermedia Handbook*, Emily Berk and Joseph Devlin (Ed.s), McGraw-Hill, New York, NY.

Grimes, Joseph E. (1975). *The Thread of Discourse.* The Hague.

Halasz, Frank (1988). "Reflections on Notecards: Seven Issues for the Next Generation of Hypermedia Systems," *CACM 31:7*, 836–855.

Lange, Danny B. (1990). "A Formal Model of Hypertext," *Proceedings of the Hypertext Standardization Workshop*, NIST Special Publication SP500-178, 145–166.

Longacre, Robert E. (1976). *An Anatomy of Speech Notions*. Lisse.

Longacre, Robert E. (1980). "An Apparatus for the Identification of Paragraph Types," *Notes on Linguistics 15*, 5–22.

Longacre, Robert E. (1989). *Joseph: A Story of Divine Providence. A Text Theoretical and Textlinguistic Analysis of Genesis 37 and 39–48*. Winona Lake, IN.

Mann, William C. and Thompson, Sandra A. (1987). "Rhetorical Structure Theory: A Theory of Text Organization," Livia Polanyi, (Ed.), *The Structure of Discourse*. Norwood, NJ. ISI Reprint Series RS-87-190.

Marshall, C.C. and Irish, P.M. (1989). "Guided Tours and On-Line Presentations: How Authors Make Existing Hypertext Intelligible for Readers," *Proceedings of Hypertext '89*, 15–26.

Minsky, Marvin (1981). "A Framework for Representing Knowledge," J. Haugeland, (Ed.), *Mind Design*, Cambridge, MA, 95–128.

Nelson, Ted (1980–1987). *Literary Machines*. Published by the author; distributed by the Distributors, South Bend, IN.

Parunak, H.V.D. (1989). "Hypermedia Topologies and User Navigation," *Proceedings of Hypertext '89*, 43–50.

Robertson, G., McCracken, D. and Newell, A. (1981). "The ZOG Approach to man-machine communications," *International Journal of Man-Machine Studies 14*, 461–488.

Toulmin, S.E. (1969). *The Uses of Argument*. Cambridge University Press.

Trigg, Randall H. (1983). "A Network-based Approach to Text Handling for the On-Line Community," Ph.D. Dissertation, University of Maryland.

Yankelovich, Nicole, Smith, Karen E., Garrett, L. Nancy, Meyrowitz, Norman (1988). *Interactive Multimedia*. "Issues in Designing a Hypermedia Document System," Microsoft Press, 34–85.

Zellweger, P.T. (1989). "Scripted Documents: A Hypermedia Path Mechanism," *Proceedings of Hypertext '89*, 1–14.

VIII

Integrating Hypertext with Other Technologies

Hypertext is just one of a spate of new technologies developed in the past few years to help us manage the flood of information which continues to inundate us. In the two chapters in this section, our contributors discuss two of hypertext's competitors. However, as both our team at VPI&SU and Alan Littleford agree, both Text and Concept Searching and AI can be combined with Hypertext to produce better information retrieval than any of these technologies could provide by itself.

21

Integrating Search and Retrieval with Hypertext

By Edward A. Fox, Qi Fan Chen,
and Robert K. France
Dept. of Computer Science,
Virginia Polytechnic Institute and
State University

Introduction

While hypertext and hypermedia have numerous applications, they cannot solve all our problems relating to information access. Such access can build upon manually or automatically created indices, search algorithms, feedback procedures, and other techniques whose value has been proven on collections much larger than those that can be managed solely by browsing and following links. We propose a reference model for what we believe is an urgent need, that of integrating search and retrieval with hypertext and hypermedia. Further, we describe a prototype system designed around that model which would facilitate access to a wide variety of types of information.

Current Status

In this chapter, we focus on the problem of how to efficiently store and retrieve a wide range of disparate information (including data stored in databases, text bases, media archives, knowledge bases, and other organized collections). Once such collections were managed almost exclusively by mainframes, which ensured centralization and often enforced vendor, and sometimes industry-wide, standards. With the shift to personal computers and workstations, there has been a rapid proliferation of specialized packages, which make interchange of information between software and hardware platforms difficult.

Accumulations of information in forms that are hard to integrate are being created and expanded at a rapid rate. Large online database vendors such as Dialog, Maxwell Online, STN, and others provide access to enormous collections of bibliographic records (usually titles, abstracts, and other citation data) or full text (reference works, newspapers, legal documents). In house, corporate employees are generating electronic mail messages, database files (separately organized for geographic information, CAD/CAM, chemical registry data, and image databanks), and word processing documents. The serious problems of providing democratic access to all this information and of supporting manipulation techniques as versatile and natural as speech or pencil-and-paper methods have yet to be solved.

Prospects for Improvement

The emergence of networked computer systems and optical storage devices have exacerbated the problem of incompatible data formats and, as a result, forced vendors to seek solutions. For example, software designed to access data scattered across a heterogeneous network needs to follow rigorously enforced conventions.

Optical publishing systems increase the amount of storage capacity available at a reasonable cost. This allows in-house access to huge databases of text, graphics, images, and even interactive digital video [Fox, 1988d, 1989d, and 1990a]. The huge amount of information that can be stored optically can make particular facts difficult to find. Fortunately, locally stored information can be organized and more easily accessed with more modern software than is provided with on-line services such as Dialog. This allows more advanced information retrieval techniques to be implemeted [Fox, 1986a].

Our work is motivated by an analysis of current potentials and problems with information access. In the first part of this chapter, we describe a framework for integrating hypertext systems with techniques for discovering information quickly, leading readers to particular nodes efficiently even in very large, unfamiliar hyperbases. In the second section, we consider some of the capabilities that must be provided by information systems, pointing out which are provided by various types of existing systems. The third section discusses progress made in that direction and its sequel provides further background. The fourth section discusses the VPI&SU CODER project, which provides a means of exploring a broad class of information access approaches. The final section of the chapter outlines how we are extending CODER for hypermedia and interoperability, and includes recommendations for conceptual and practical integration of information retrieval with hypertext/hypermedia.

Necessary Capabilities

Computer systems which are intended to facilitate user's access to information should:

- Include help systems that can explain how to perform a search and what is done as part of that search;
- Adapt to user requirements;
- Help users describe and elaborate their information needs;
- Be built in a flexible and modular fashion so that they can be easily extended. [Belkin, et al., 1983; Belkin, et al., 1987a]

A user-centered, mixed initiative interaction (where both user and computer operate concurrently and can each seize control of input or output activities at almost any time) is preferred, so that:

- the user can request an explanation or follow a new train of thought at any time,
- the computer can request clarification or display tentative results as appropriate to further what it believes are the user's current goals.

Since these goals often relate to finding relevant items in some information repository, it is important to pay special attention to efficient and effective searching, as is discussed in the next subsection.

Finding Barn Doors and Stringing Pearls

The current generation of information retrieval systems rely on various search techniques to find relevant items. These can be viewed at both the abstract and system-specific levels [Bates, 1981]. One approach is to seek information by first looking for a neighborhood where useful items can be found and then selecting related or linked items from among the items at hand.

One can think of first finding the *barn door* and then, after glimpsing something of interest, i.e., a valuable *pearl*, following leads to closely related items. This is analogous to searching and then browsing, or using information retrieval techniques and then applying hypertext methods.

Most information being accessed has been processed to some degree in order to make access easier. Outlines, tables of contents, and indices (e.g., for author names, or specially selected descriptors) are usually developed by humans according to some theory or organizing principles. Readers who can relate to existing organizational systems can often find items of interest; computer menus are sometimes applied to map these structures to available regions of display screens. Related items may be found if they occur nearby, if an index points to a series of items, or if explicit cross references are provided.

Unfortunately, the searcher's perspective and/or vocabulary does not always match that of the author or indexer. This is particularly important when a complex idea is involved and when a very large collection of items is being searched. Here precoordinated systems (where some of the most important combinations of ideas are precombined and added to indices, sometimes as phrases like "information retrieval") may fail and force readers to build post-coordinated queries (like "multimedia and retrieval"). Narrower queries can be formed using proximity operators. These include:

* searches for adjacent words (two words placed side by side);
* two or more words located in a single sentence;
* within field combinations (e.g., two words located within a title line);
* within a paragraph.

Boolean query construction (i.e., using ANDs, ORs and/or NOTs to specify matches) can be exceedingly difficult, and indeed ten-to-one variations have been observed in the ability of different individuals (and even of the same individual at different times) to form good queries. Frequently, repeated efforts are required to form queries that do not retrieve many nonrelevant items (i.e., have high precision) and yet do retrieve a significant fraction of the relevant items (i.e., have high recall).

Finding relevant items often involves one or more of the following steps:

* Translating an information need into the organization of concepts represented by a table of contents, index or thesaurus.
* Adopting a scheme to descend through some hierarchical organization of topics or descriptors to find specific section(s) of interest.
* Combining words or terms used within an index or thesaurus or forming the free text into a formal Boolean query.
* Refining the query by adding synonyms or related terms (broadening), by increasing specificity (narrowing) or by reorganizing the query structure.
* Visually examining all selected items to find those of value.

Sometimes the task at hand makes the choice of search method obvious. If you are looking for a single known item, a Boolean search will work best. Looking for multiple items on the same topic calls for browsing. Attempts to retrace a previously viewed presentation suggests the use of links. Sometimes a combination of methods works best.

Unified Metaphors

The steps involved in searching and browsing hyperdocuments should be hidden behind a task-oriented interface that lets readers search at a conceptual, descriptive level instead of at either a word-oriented or a procedural level. Boolean queries, for instance, fail to fulfill readers' information access needs because they focus attention on the wrong objects and force users to think in terms of the mechanics of search algorithms. Conversely, properly implemented browsing systems allow readers to explore a range of conceptual dimensions easily and intuitively. A graphical presentation coupling the spatial metaphor of nearness to the hypermedia metaphor of links supports such explorations using simple pointing operations. Most importantly, both searching and browsing should be subsumed by a set of consistent metaphors and abstractions that encourage the integration of these access techniques.

Using naturally occurring metaphors as the backbone of the user interface offers several advantages. Unfortunately, while paper sketches and natural language input may be easy for humans to work with, they are often beyond the scope of all but the most expensive of today's computer systems.

Another possibility is to have a standardized unified digital representation and manipulation system. We all take for granted the fact that telephones connect people all around the world, and that they do this because of international agreements on hardware and software standards. We can envision a collection of standards for hardware, software, and information structures or data formats [see Devlin, 1991] built around both existing and exciting new technologies for digital encoding. This requires management of multimedia including: text, graphics, images, speech, audio, and video. It involves interconnection of multiple computers and diverse networks, and use of a variety of peripheral and input/output devices. Finally, it requires *intelligent* processing to improve efficiency and effectiveness and to ensure smooth human-computer interaction.

Progress Toward Unified Access

Networking

A great deal of progress has been made towards integration of computer networks [Tannenbaum, 1981]. Thousands of computers are internetworked, able to exchange electronic mail. Many are connected to allow even higher levels of integration: passing of files, remote log-ins, and even communication between programs. In the area of library information retrieval, the Z39.50 standard has been developed so that a user of one library system can cause that system to have a query processed on another system, and then indirectly receive the search results. Various organizations, including universities such as VPI&SU, are developing and testing prototype systems for information interchange that follow Z39.50 specifications. In addition, the X.500 standard has enabled many prototype systems to combine into a partial global directory system—a computer analog of the telephone white pages.

Much of the success in internetworking can be credited to the use of a layered approach to software, whereby physical connection, data connection, session management, presentation handling, and application program operation have separate interfaces and specifications. The *International Organization for Standardization*

(ISO) *Open Systems Integration* (OSI) model uses physical, data link, network, transport, session, presentation, and application levels to encourage interoperability of software on heterogeneous computers [Zimmerman, 1980]. OSI has been the basis for Z39.50, X.500, and many other related standards.

This layering approach also applies to storage systems. On the one hand, there are levels of physical units, operating system-identified devices, and network wide file systems. On the other hand, there are software divisions, such as the proposed standard of the Air Traffic and Air Transport Associations, which separates the search engine component of CD-ROM software (which itself builds upon the volume and file description layer specified by the ISO 9660 standard) from the user interface layer.

Object Model

While computer users generally search for relevant concepts, computer scientists have tried to meet user's needs by studying and building specialized processing systems for particular classes of information. Thus, the term "data" is often associated with database management systems, "information retrieval" is often limited to text databases, and "knowledge bases" are viewed as the proper repositories for collections of complex list structures and rules.

To unify these approaches, object-oriented databases have been proposed that might contain and support processing of any class of information. In hypertext systems that build upon these object bases, completing a search or following a link would lead to presentation of any of various objects: a screen of text, a bitmap display, an audio segment, a spreadsheet entry, an individual plane of a complex image, an explanation of some expert rules, or a tabular report.

However, to date only limited progress has been made in integrating database management systems (which at present usually follow the relational model) with text retrieval systems (which frequently employ inverted files and require access by way of Boolean queries). One issue is the differences in items being manipulated; tables of numbers or short character strings have few data types as opposed to the variety encountered in multimedia systems, and database structures are much more regular than those found in the world of compound documents (e.g., books, magazines, letters, reports, and encyclopedias). A possible solution is to use abstract data types (e.g., sets, lists, vectors) as elements of a relational DBMS [Fox, 1981]. Some of these ideas were used in the redesign of the SMART system for the UNIX environment [Fox, 1983a], which eventually led to a version of that system that is widely used by document retrieval researchers. Another approach is to directly use the relational model, with performance tuning and limited extensions where needed, to handle bibliographic records [Lynch, 1987].

Artificial intelligence (AI) research extends these efforts to solving the problems of knowledge representation. Initially, languages like LISP and Prolog focused on symbol and list manipulation. Real world objects were associated with *atoms* that could be located by their names. Property lists (sets of property type/value pairs) were attached to these atoms.

But to better match human ability to deal with default values, groupings of key attributes with various types of objects, and taxonomic classification of similar classes of objects, the concept of a *frame* was developed. This concept has proven useful for information retrieval [Fox, 1987b, Weaver, et al., 1989].

Essentially, a frame class (e.g., U.S. postal address) has various slots for important aspects of the object (e.g., state, zip code), and may inherit from more general classes (e.g., postal address with slots for name and locality), as well as be instantiated for an individual (e.g., John Smith's U.S. postal address). Frames can be grouped together into extremely regular knowledge bases.

A semantic network is an alternate knowledge representation, closer in orientation to hypertext [Findler, 1979, Morgado, 1986]. A semantic network can be envisioned as a graph where nodes are used to represent objects, and links to indicate significant, meaningful relationships. One well-known semantic network system, SNePS [Shapiro, 1989], supports knowledge representation and inference (i.e., proving or drawing conclusions based on knowledge recorded previously in the system). In SNePS a distinction is often made between *path-based inference*, whereby the reader follows a succession or chain of links from some node to identify some relationship, and *node-based inference*, whereby logical propositions are represented in the network and are combined with other propositions in varied regions of the network in accord with the rules of logic. Path-based inference can be very efficient, and corresponds to following links in hypertexts. Semantic networks can also support *spreading activation*, where several concepts are located in the network, all paths of length 1, 2, etc. from each are explored until paths from several concepts meet—a type of parallel search for important associations. Spreading activation has been used in the GRANT system to retrieve documents related to various topics, projects, and grant proposals [Cohen and Kjeldsen, 1987].

Semantic networks are useful for handling the inter-relationships in language. At VPI&SU, for example, we have taken machine-readable dictionaries, extracted and restructured the important data [Fox, 1986b], archived them in the form of Prolog facts, and loaded them into a semantic network to facilitate further processing and access [Fox, 1988a; France, et al., 1989a]. In so doing we have found it helpful to build an elaborate taxonomy of relations (i.e., links) common between word senses in our lexicon. One goal is to extend earlier experiments that indicated improvement in retrieval effectiveness could result by finding words that are lexically related to query terms [Fox, 1988e]. Thus, the system knows enough about the meaning of a query to search for "captain" if a query asks for "ship's officers," or "general" when "army leader" is sought. Others have considered networks as important support structures for probabilistic (Bayesian) inference systems that prove when a document is relevant to a query [Croft and Turtle, 1989]. Ultimately, semantic networks can be combined with hypertext and hypermedia to lead to a uniform representation of objects, as discussed below.

Integration of Various Search Techniques

Research suggests that the best retrieval performance results when many different forms of information about documents are utilized by a variety of search methods [Belkin and Croft, 1987b]. Integration of various approaches has this same goal [Fox, 1987b]. Thus, one might merge the results from using Boolean, vector, and probabilistic searches for a given information statement. Any of these search methods can also be modified by the use of feedback, where a reader indicates what documents or sections thereof are relevant, and the computer uses all the information it has available about that sample to perform another, better search. One can even throw in use of AI techniques, as discussed in the section on our work with CODER. Reference models provide a clear framework for integration and thus have become popular in regard to networking, where different cabling, interconnection, specialized hardware, firmware, and layers of software allow users of similar applications on different computers to collaborate.

Reference Models for Hypertext

In order to develop interoperable information systems and a unified representation model, a reference model for information management systems must first be developed. Work on hypertext reference models has arisen in part as a result of standardization efforts for hypertext/hypermedia [see Chapter 26 by Devlin on standards]. We have found the Dexter model [Halasz and Schwartz, 1990] and the r-model [Furuta and Stotts, 1989; Furuta and Stotts, 1990; Stotts and Furuta, 1989] to be particularly insightful. However, interoperable information systems should properly include not only hypertext/hypermedia, but also searching, networking, and other applications and levels of manipulation.

A More Complete Reference Model

Our proposal for a reference model that integrates hypertext and other sources of information is shown in Figure 21.1, and explained in more detail in subsequent sections. Essentially it combines the seven OSI layers with seven other layers relating to hypertext/hypermedia and other types of information systems.

The bottom four layers are OSI layers that together support the secure transport of messages. Atop the transport layer is a layer that provides essential support for files and process communication (messages). Processes operate above this layer to support high-level communication between machines, including necessary translations between data representations. These six layers complete an extended groundwork for communication among machines, languages, and environments at a highly abstract level.

The node layer comes next, supporting atomic, structured, and multimedia objects. The anchor layer allows points or spans inside nodes to be addressed in ways appropriate for each node type. Links connect anchors, thus providing a

Layer	Typical Contents
Application	hypertext, hypermedia, information retrieval, image management, authoring, training, tutoring, CAD/CAM, interactive digital video
Presentation	devices: windows, pointing devices, speakers; media: text, audio, video; operations: generalization, editing, translation, access, browsing, selection, picking, querying, sequencing.
Session	base selection, user identification, history management, versioning.
Base	base: knowledge, information, data; operations: search, inference.
View	graphs, lists, sets, vectors, relations, frames.
Link	link Ids, labels.
Anchor	anchor Ids, span descriptions.
Node	textual strings, integers, object Ids.
Communication	processes.
Physical machine	file systems, storage media, message support.
Transport	ISO lower level equivalent
Network	ISO lower level equivalent
DataLink	ISO lower level equivalent
Physical	ISO lower level equivalent

Figure 21.1   Information Management System Reference Model.

layer that is essentially a graph or network of information items. The view layer allows various aggregations and associations as well as common data and information and knowledge structures to be manipulated (e.g., have a view of relations, a view of vectors, a view of frames, a view as linked collections of nodes). The base layer allows coordinated access to data, information and knowledge bases— through search, navigation, and related operations. Higher levels correspond to upper level OSI layers, but are organized to support common information access, hypertext/hypermedia, and presentation/application programming activities.

We view this model as providing a framework for integrating information management systems. Our aim is to validate this framework, to prove it adequate for a wide variety of activities. Towards the end of this chapter, we explain how our work with the CODER system is being extended and layered along the lines of this integrated model.

Previous Work

In the broadest sense, a reference model for information management should encompass work in electronic publishing, document representation, text analysis, storage, information retrieval, and hypertext/hypermedia.

Electronic Publishing

In connection with ACM Press Database and Electronic Products [Fox, 1988c], we have ventured into a variety of electronic publishing ventures [see also Fox, Rous, Marchionini, 1991]. In *Hypertext on Hypertext* we dealt with three versions of a single hypertext, in order to accommodate user preferences for equipment and operating systems. Further, in one of the versions [Shneiderman, 1988], the original hypertext system was extended to include more comprehensive searching capabilities, in part because of our experiences with online and CD-ROM publishing. These experiences also pointed out the need for standards and integrated or interoperable systems to allow wide-scale electronic publishing [Fox, 1990b].

For example, while developing the Virginia Disc series of CD-ROMs, we purposely provided data and information bases in multiple forms to allow comparison of approaches and software packages. The *Master Gardener Handbook* on Virginia Disc One [Fox, 1990c] is available in hypertext form, or can be searched with a bibliographic retrieval system. Though the former is handy for reading and browsing, the latter is more convenient for finding specific facts. Similar comparisons can be made between alternative retrieval systems (Personal Librarian applied to searching the *King James Bible* at either the chapter or verse level).

Related Work

The most popular database management software today—relational DBMS—is based on the simple mathematical concept of a *relation*. A database relation can be thought of as a flat table, but is much more precisely defined—a relation is a set of individual items, called "tuples" and sometimes thought of as rows, each containing values for a fixed collection of attributes, usually associated with columns of the table. Queries in the relational model are answered by combining these relations using a restricted set of operations that depend on the flat and uniform structure of the tuples. Traditional information retrieval also uses the notion of sets [Artandi, 1971], but regards each item as a nonuniform—and often structured—collection of attributes. Information retrieval queries combine desired attributes using sentence-forming operators. Thus, a Boolean query specifies a set of documents by combining simpler queries (ultimately, individual indexed words or concepts) using logical operators.

Other systems of operators are possible. For instance, significantly more effective retrieval results from a simple change related to human perception of language and Boolean logic—making the *AND* and *OR* operators softer or less strict. One realization of this change, the p-norm model, allows a parameter, p, to vary so there is a continuum between strict *AND*s and strict *OR*s [Salton, et al., 1983]. This model allows retrieval results to be ranked in descending order of presumed value, and gives users flexibility to indicate relative importance of search terms. Further extension is possible, whereby user judgments regarding which previously retrieved documents are relevant can be used to automatically build better Boolean or p-norm queries [Salton, et al., 1985].

Feedback is also fundamental to the probabilistic model [Robertson and Jones, 1976], whereby documents are also ranked according to estimated probability of relevance. Ranking from probabilistic retrieval and various fuzzy set-based schemes [Bookstein, 1985] is of particular value to users so they need not be concerned with retrieval set size, but rather can let the computer carry out pattern matches to find closely related items.

Another enhancement to retrieval results from adding information. This has been demonstrated using the vector space model, where linear algebra can be used to allow descriptions of term occurrences in document collections [Salton, 1989]. Many people are familiar with keyword-based search approaches [called syntactic searches in Littleford, 1991], in which the reader searches for a particular string of characters in a database or uses entries from a *controlled* vocabulary for searching. Keyword-based searches are usually only available as alternatives to rather than complements to citation-based searching (e.g., as is done with the *Science Citation Index*). Yet if term and citation data are both made available [Fox, 1983b], especially when used in feedback searching, better results can be obtained than from either type of data alone [Fox, 1988b]. In the vector approach, readers select documents or groups of documents which can be treated as queries, so the system can search for these matches.

Results with these advanced retrieval methods have been demonstrated with collections of up to tens of thousands of documents. A pilot study indicated applicability to roughly 300,000 documents [Fox, 1987d], and results are now being analyzed from a recent study at VPI&SU with 500,000 library catalog records and 216 users, that compared Boolean, p-norm, vector, and vector with probabilistic feedback approaches. It seems that advanced methods for retrieval can be applied to very large collections.

CODER

Work on the *COmposite Document Expert/extended/effective Retrieval* (CODER) system began in 1985, to develop a testbed for the integration of AI and information retrieval methods [Fox, 1986a]. The aim was to develop a next-generation retrieval system: a system that would have greater effectiveness and efficiency than previous systems, and one that would allow comparison and integration of advanced retrieval methods. Our plan is to integrate the various retrieval models into a unified system [Fox, 1989a].

CODER Architecture

As can be seen in Figure 21.2, CODER was conceived as a comprehensive standalone system that could deal directly with end users and could receive texts of bibliographic and full text documents ready for analysis. The architecture follows principles of software engineering, AI prototyping, and object oriented construction [Fox, 1987a].

CODER assumes a coarse-grained parallel operation of the sort now provided by computer networks. A central *spine* holds information for shared use by the analysis and retrieval subsystems. Each subsystem is specified as a collection of modules acting as a *community* and communicating through a central blackboard (a module with *areas* that experts can post to or read postings from). Attached to each blackboard is a strategist, with rules to indicate which modules should be requested to examine which types of postings.

The retrieval subsystem is broken into modules along functional lines, based on studies of user and search intermediary interaction [Belkin, et al., 1983], as a "distributed expert based information system" [Belkin, et al., 1987a]. Thus, there are modules for user modeling, dialog and discourse management, search, planning, morphological analysis, and other operations. These can operate on a single computer, or can be spread across a network of machines on which they run in parallel.

The spine stores document and other text collections, relational data, and more complex knowledge structures. Frames are used extensively to describe documents, real-world entities, sessions, and system users. A lexicon holds English language knowledge derived initially from the *Collins English Dictionary* [Fox, 1986b] and later extended from other sources [France, et al., 1989a]. Domain knowledge suitable for each document collection processed is also stored. For example, the spine includes knowledge about ships and geographical locations for an application involving analyzing and retrieving Navy messages.

CODER Implementation

CODER has evolved from a rough prototype to a system that now shows promise as the basis for a campus information system at VPI&SU. Initial development was keyed to a modest collection of electronic digests about AI, a simple menu style interface, and facts derived from the *Handbook on Artificial Intelligence* [Fox, 1987c]. In this version, names of leading AI researchers were identified, words

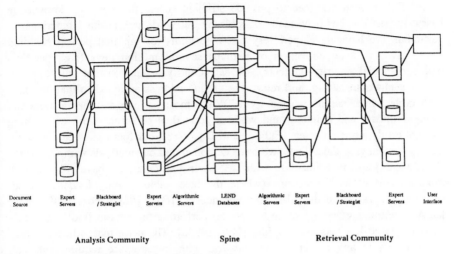

Document Source	Expert Servers	Blackboard / Strategist	Expert Servers	Algorithmic Servers	LEND Databases	Algorithmic Servers	Expert Servers	Blackboard / Strategist	Expert Servers	User Interface

Analysis Community   Spine   Retrieval Community

Figure 21.2   CODER system architecture.

associated with their definitions were given in the running text of the book, and a hierarchical taxonomy of AI areas correlated with sections of the text.

Successive applications include new fact bases dealing with ships and geographic locations, a medical thesaurus, and more extensive user interfaces. A more complete language for intermodule communication was developed, so modules written in Prolog, C, and C++ could send messages between computers, including frames, sets, lists, and relations [Weaver, et al., 1989].

Various retrieval techniques have been incorporated, and ultimately CODER should operate by applying several advanced methods [Belkin and Croft, 1987b] in concert or separately on a case-by-case, heuristically determined basis.

CODER/LEND

In extending CODER to handle the results from analyzing multiple machine-readable dictionaries, and to support large document collections, we recognized the benefits of integrating the relevant facts, relationships, and frame structures into a large knowledge base. Since lexical information is so highly inter-related, we chose a semantic network type of representation. However, existing semantic network systems were designed to work with the entire network in primary memory. Thus, we conceived of the *Large External Network Database* (LEND).

LEND has been under development since 1988, with the aim of providing integrated storage, access, and manipulation for data, information, and knowledge. Specifications have been prepared [France, 1989b; Chen, 1989], and the second implementation is now partially complete. A version of LEND is in use in connection with a campus directory system based on the X.500 standard. However, most work with LEND relates to CODER.

LEND has been designed to provide efficient access to very large knowledge bases. In part this has been made possible by our work with hashing functions. In particular, we have developed very fast algorithms for minimal perfect hashing. Thus, given a static collection of perhaps several million keys (e.g., people's names or social security numbers), we can identify a function that will take any key as a character string, and return the unique address assigned to that key in a hash table which has no wasted space. While most hashing assumes a moderate level of update and deletion, and while a good deal of recent work on hashing focuses on dynamic data sets [Enbody and Du, 1988], our focus has been on static or slowly changing data. Thus, we have demonstrated our methods with CD-ROM [Fox, 1990c] and in connection with LEND. In particular, we have worked with minimal perfect hash functions (where the hash table is fully loaded, and all searches for values in the table take one access) [Fox, 1989b, Fox, 1989c]. Our latest techniques give very close to optimal performance and can find these functions for large key sets very rapidly [Fox, 1990d]. The net effect is to have very rapid access to any object in the network, with lower space requirements and faster performance than those of other common secondary storage access mechanisms [Comer, 1979].

CODER together with LEND now supports analysis and searching for several types of collections. Some 70M bytes of network data has been loaded from dictionaries and document sets into LEND. We aim to demonstrate the utility of this combination through experimentation with sections of a large hypertext reference work dealing with cardiology, a medical thesaurus, our English dictionary data, and hundreds of thousands of bibliographic records.

Beyond these practical issues, however, LEND is the embodiment of our new theory about integrated information access. Though initially building upon concepts of knowledge representation in semantic networks, LEND was extended to also handle hypertext/hypermedia. Indeed, the theory underlying our present work with LEND is that integrated representation of all types of information, including numbers, text, and frames—as objects in a network—should be the foundation for efficient, flexible, and powerful intelligent retrieval systems. As we further combine CODER and LEND, the result should be an integrated information management system, usable for document analysis, query processing, and hypertext.

Recommendations for Integration

In recent years, object-oriented methods have become popular for programming and object-oriented databases have been shown to be useful for multimedia [Kim and Lochovsky, 1989]. Object typing is the basis for handling these varied sorts of objects.

Typed Objects

Our reference model begins with a layer of objects. We assume that objects are typed, that is, that text objects can be differentiated from integers or video segments and treated appropriately. Appropriate treatment is generally defined algebraically, by specifying the operators that function within a type. Thus, integers come equipped with addition, multiplication, and so forth, while text objects come with operators for concatenation and a test for inclusion. The type system should enforce against such meaningless operations as concatenating two integers or multiplying texts.

Typing schemes play an important role in many different programming disciplines and representational systems. Classical programming languages are based on flat typing systems, where no relations are implied among the built-in types. The more modern of these include both primitive, atomic types (e.g., integers, reals, and atoms) and composite types (e.g., records, lists, and sets). Type conversion functions may provide morphisms from objects of one type to objects of another. Current work in programming language theory includes extending typing systems to include function types and polymorphous types for composite objects.

Type declarations in programs are quite similar to definitions of *object classes* in object-oriented databases. One defines broad classes, like numbers which have operations like addition, and then narrower classes, like integers, which inherit properties from the broader or parent class. This allows a taxonomy of objects to be developed, with programming to specify operations of new objects limited to those (e.g., next in sequence for integers) not present in previously defined classes. Each class comprises a certain type of object, together with the operations of methods that are appropriate to the objects of that type. Since objects only respond to their appropriate methods, meaningless operations are not permitted. Furthermore, use of this system makes it possible to model objects directly, to support fast prototyping, and to group types with similar methods together, defining structure and operation as it becomes appropriate (See Figure 21.3.).

Integrated information systems require a significantly richer set of atomic types than do typical applications in either the classical or object oriented paradigms. Not only is text required, but graphics and images are becoming commonplace in documents, and we are at the threshold of a revolution in handling digital audio and video [Fox, 1989d; Fox, 1990a]. Additionally, information objects like bibliographic records or dictionary entries are best modeled by composite objects with a rich internal structure. For document objects, there are obvious part/whole and subtype/supertype hierarchies implicit in document structure [Guting, et al., 1989] and other hierarchies inherent in media objects. Multiple inheritance hierarchies are useful in this context, since information objects often satisfy more than one description simultaneously. For example, a document that is at once an electronic mail (e-mail) message and a set of bibliographic references inherits attributes from both the e-mail message type (sender, address) and the bibliography type (subject domain, record format).

Anchors and Links

One innovation of hypermedia practice has been the use of *anchors*. When two objects are linked in a hypertext system, the link runs not between entire objects

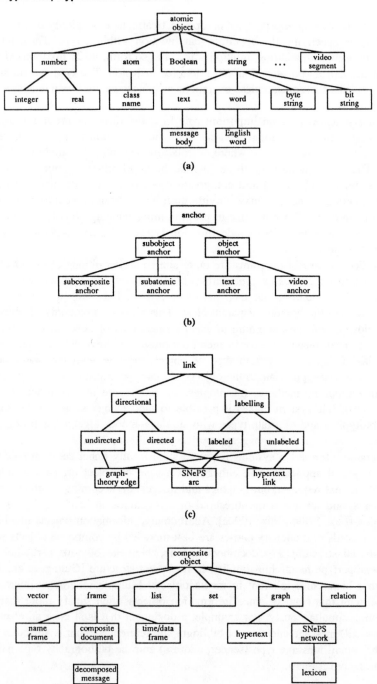

Figure 21.3 Type hierarchies for (a) node layer (b) anchor layer (c) link layer (d) view layer.

but from a hot spot in one object to a relevant section in the other. We can formalize this idea and extend it to other classes of objects through the concept of an anchor. An anchor is a segment within an object, where "segment" and "within" are given meaning by the object type. Thus, an anchor in a CAD drawing might attach the key to the diagram, or to the sketch of the left front door of a car (regardless of whether an animation shows the door opening and closing), or a button shown on the controls of a computerized jukebox that allows audio selection or rewind or play.

In the anchor layer, each class of objects that support anchors is provided with methods for creating and resolving anchors; at all higher layers, anchors are abstractions that can only be interpreted with reference to these methods. In many cases, however, operations are further specialized. If a link is unidirectional, then activating an anchor at the start of the link leads to the link itself, while activating the link and thence the anchor at the other end of the link usually leads to presentation of that target anchor and the node it is attached to.

An anchor serves as the terminating point for links, which are associations between active areas within objects. (Where the entire object is intended, the object as a whole constitutes an anchor.) Links can be of many types, depending upon their intended use (see Figure 21.3c). Within each type, links can be further differentiated, for instance by the type of the objects linked, or by label. In semantic networks, links are generally differentiated by their labels. As in the classical programming language approach, however, these implied link types form a flat domain. We suggest an enrichment to allow a hierarchy of link types. This allows the same sort of typing system to be used with links that was used with objects, and also follows earlier work in hypertext, where many link types were found appropriate [Trigg and Weiser, 1986], and where a link taxonomy was described [DeRose, 1989].

Anchors allow reference to objects or parts thereof. Links can use anchors to refer to an entire node, to a portion of an atomic node, or to one of the components of a node collection. As a result, a semantic interpretation can be imposed even in an interoperable system for resolving links [Pearl, 1989].

In information retrieval the concept of nearness between document objects becomes important. Any such measure of proximity must effectively be based upon links between words and their exact appearance in the text. Thus, proximity in an index for this chapter would be equivalent to a pointer to the seventeenth word of this paragraph. With an anchor for that word occurrence, a search could easily lead to the target word, or some surrounding context like sentence or paragraph that might be displayed with highlighting.

With nodes, anchors, and links—the heart of a hyperbase—we have also the key elements for managing other graph-like systems. Graphs are very handy for modeling, computer networks, traffic routes, or lexicons of word associations. But other views of graphs can be built so that manipulations are tailored; such as when head and tail operations are applied to ordered lists. Systems that support defining such views can allow us to handle composite documents, complex knowledge representations, and other perspectives on our data.

Views and the Pattern Language

Links can be used to express simple associations between objects. Thus, one type of link might associate a commentary with the text it refers to, while another link might associate a person's name and digitized photograph. Links can associate spreadsheets with totals in a report or words with their definitions.

Often, however, the relations between objects are more complex. For instance, the link between a document and a concept that occurs within it can include a weight denoting how important the concept is to the document. Furthermore, it is often desirable to consider a relation as an object itself. For example, one might want to search to find all the types of links or all links between text and image nodes.

The SNePS semantic network system [Shapiro, 1979] has the means to build such complex objects on a substrate of associative links. In particular though, this capability is usually used to manage short texts for natural language processing, or to describe facts that might otherwise be stated as first-order predicate calculus terms. Similar techniques can be used to model lists, sets, or frames. Frames in turn provide a natural representation tool for composite documents and media objects. In this way, vivid representation systems for a given domain are built from more general tools. We refer to these constructed classes as *view types*.

Even at the view level, a full type system with multiple inheritance is supported. The inheritance hierarchies are more complex, since different perspectives call for different structures and sets of operations, but the typing system itself can be as simple as that used at lower layers.

Views are made of up of classes of view objects. Each such class is created by specifying a mapping of the composite objects in the class into associative structures on the graph level, and by defining the methods for the class in terms of graph operations. This is accomplished in LEND by a pattern language. Related work has been done in connection with AUGMENT [Engelbart, 1962], with graphic queries and a graph language [Consens and Mendelzon, 1989], with taxonomies of graphs for hypermedia [Parunak, 1989], and with paths or trails in hyperbases [Marshall and Irish, 1989; Zellweger, 1989]. The pattern language is used to carry out associative access to objects related by links. Such access patterns are best characterized by following a path of a given or indeterminate length, with possible restrictions on the nodes and arcs that may occur in the path. Our focus in LEND is on efficient access of these basic operations.

LEND operates in two ways. The first is to help carry out typical browsing and searching tasks. LEND automatically maps these tasks into a series of operations it carries out on the underlying graph of information items. In a sense, views are used so higher level tasks can be easily mapped into lower level operations by the system developer, and then automatically carried out as needed.

LEND's second mode of operation is through direct manipulation by users of the underlying graph. Thus, a linguist might want to find all words connected to any word in a sentence by up to three synonym associations. Such an expert user of LEND must understand the syntax of our language for graph manipulation, given in Figure 21.4. For hypertext developers, the notation is relatively familiar, with nodes used to describe the various objects, but with arcs used instead of links. This pattern language supports a variety of retrieval schemes. Nodes can be found given their unique system assigned identifier, or sets of nodes satisfying a list of criteria can be returned. Thus, there are node conditional expressions, which can be used to specify more complex sub-graphs, as part of more complex pattern language expressions. A set theoretic description of the pattern language operators, based on the concept of unification, is given in Figure 21.5. A semantic description using many sorted algebras is shown in Figure 21.6. The operators in the language do not cover all possible graph access requirements. However, graphs make up a class of view objects (the natural, or base view).

From this class, the user is free to derive new classes of graph objects and to augment them with any further operations desired.

Our pattern language has been prototyped with a Prolog interpreter and has been tested with various types of data. We expect that our pattern language will be quite useful to support access to the graph layer, and that subsequent CODER development will benefit from this powerful formalism and tool, to carry out a wide variety of information management tasks.

Pattern   ::= PatternExp |
                    compose(PatternExp, PatternExp) |
                    or(PatternExp, PatternExp)

PatternExp   ::= Nodes |
                 Paths

Paths   ::= Arcs |
                   compose(Paths, Paths) |
                   iteration(Nodes, Paths, Nodes, N, N)

Arcs   ::= ArcVar |
                   newArcs(ArcID) |
                   newArcs(Nodes, Labels, Nodes)

Labels   ::= LabelVar |
                   LabelString

Nodes   ::= NodeVar |
                   newNodes(NodeID) |
                   restrict(Nodes, NodeCondiExp)

Figure 21.4 Pattern Language Syntax in BNF.

retr(Node, UG) = {n | n ∈ V_{UG} AND unify(Node, n)}

retr(Arc, UG) = {a | a ∈ E_{UG} AND unify(Arc, a)}

retr(restrict(Nodes, CondiExp), UG) = {n | n ∈ Nodes AND CondiExp(n) evaluates to true in Class(n)}

retr(restrict(Labels, CondiExp), UG) = {l | l ∈ Labels AND CondiExp(l) evaluates to true in Class(l)}

retr(compose(Pattern1, Pattern2), UG) = {G⊂UG | (exists G_1 ⊂ G)(G_1 ∈ retr(Pattern1, UG))
  AND (exists G_2 ⊂ G)(G_2 ∈ retr(Pattern2, UG)
  AND (for all g ∈ G)(g ∈ G_1 or g ∈ G_2)) }

retr(or(Pattern1, Pattern2, UG) = retr(Pattern1, UG) UNION retr(Pattern2, UG)}

retr(star(Pattern, Node1, Node2), UG) = retr(Pattern, UG) UNION {G⊂ UG | (for some new variable X)
  ((exists G_1 ⊂ G)(G_1 ∈ retr(substitute(Pattern, X, Node2), UG)
  AND (exists G_2⊂ G)(G_2 ∈ retr(star(substitute(Pattern, X, Node2)), UG)
  AND (for all g ∈ G)(g ∈ G_1 or g ∈ G_2)) }

retr(iterate(Pattern, Node1, Node2, k), UG) =
  IF k = 0 THEN { }
  IF k = 1 THEN retr(Pattern, UG)
  IF k > 1 THEN {G⊂ UG | (for some new variable X)
  ((exists G_1 ⊂ G)(G_1 ∈ retr(substitute(Pattern, X, Node2), UG)
  AND (exists G_2 ⊂ G)(G_2 ∈ retr(iterate(substitiute(Pattern, X, Node1, k-1), UG)
  AND (for all g ∈ G)(g ∈ G_1 or g ∈ G_2)) }

NOTES:
UG is the "universal graph": all nodes and arcs in a given network.
V_{UG} is the set of vertices (nodes) in UG; E_{UG} the set of edges (arcs) in UG.
unify(A, B) = A and B are the same except that either may have variables where the other has constant terms.
substitute(P, X, Y) = a pattern exactly like P except that X has been substituted everywhere for Y.
retr(P, UG) = set of graphs in the universe of graphs satisfying pattern P.

Figure 21.5   Pattern Language Operator Semantics.

Application of the Model in CODER

Most of the types shown in Figure 21.7 are of general utility. Some have been included, though, as examples of atomic and composite object types that have proven useful in CODER. Our particular type system is further detailed in Figure

Functionalities		Operators
1. LabelString	→ Labels	newLabels
2. NodeID	→ Nodes	newNodes
3. ArcID	→ Arcs	newArcs
4. Nodes × Labels × Nodes	→ Arcs	newArcs
5. Arcs	→ Paths	newPaths
6. Paths × Paths	→ Paths	compose
7. Nodes × Paths × Nodes × N × N	→ paths	iterate
8. Nodes × NodeCondiExp	→ Nodes	restrict
9. Nodes	→ Pattern	newPattern
10. Paths	→ Pattern	newPattern
11. Patterns × Patterns	→ Pattern	compose, or

Figure 21.6   Pattern Language Operators.

Layer	Class Name	Operations
all layers	general classes	create, destroy, compare, modify, access.
node layer	string text word number Boolean concept constant	concatenate, matchSubstring. vectorize, pattern match. morphological transform, stem. +, -, *, /. AND, OR, NOT. rename.
anchor layer	general anchor text anchor video anchor	anchorID -> NodeID, anchorID -> AnchorPlace. anchorID -> text span. anchorID -> video frame span.
link layer	link	LinkID -> directionInfo. LinkID -> (SouceAnchorID, DestinationAnchorID).
view layer	graph list set vector frame	traversPath, matchSubgraph head, tail, sublist, concatenate, elementInList. insert, membership, subset, union, intersect. addVect, subVect, scaleVect, cosine. setSlot, getSlot, matchFrame.

Figure 21.7   Typical Objects and Operations in Node, Anchor, Link and View layer.

21.7, where some of the methods for some of the objects are listed. Many of these have already been programmed and tested; work on others is proceeding.

More useful types for *information retrieval* (IR) objects will be added. For example, we will have graph objects, collection objects, etc. Since LEND is object-oriented, we have the freedom to expand the hierarchy and, at the same time, recognize desired performance for each class of objects. Currently, we are forming a SNePS network view from the underlying graph object class. Our purpose is to make LEND efficiently execute primitive operations required by SNePS's path-based inference on large externally stored data sets. We also plan to implement a view based on the F^3L common representation language [Weaver, et al., 1989]. F^3L's frames, facts, and functions have been widely used both in CODER and its knowledge bases. Once they have been transformed into a LEND view, all of CODER's existing knowledge bases can be loaded directly into LEND's integrated memory.

Another important application of the reference model is to conceptually and computationally model different IR systems in an efficient fashion using nodes and links. This will be beneficial to comparative research in IR techniques. It will also support research in IR from the AI perspective, both because it provides a way to merge classical document models with the semantic network or frame models mentioned above, and because data represented in the graph model can be divorced from its format and viewed reflexively. If this uniform representation of data can be supported with high access performance, then we will also realize some of the advantages of database technology (data sharing, simple management) with document and media information. It is these advantages that have made database management systems so popular in processing uniform data.

In Figure 21.8 we extend Figure 21.1 to show how the general model can apply to operations we are building into CODER. The first column gives the layer, the second lists parts of the CODER system that fall into that layer, and the third column describes in a more general situation what objects (types, operations) would occur at that level. Our reference model thus both expands upon earlier reference models, and relates to an actual system that has been under prototype development for several years. While further theoretical work and development is underway, CODER/LEND and our reference model should already provide some insight into future systems that integrate information retrieval and hypertext/hypermedia operations along with a variety of data, information, and knowledge.

Layer	CODER Modules	Typical Contents
Application	CODER/AIList, CODER/Cardiology, CODER/Navy.	hypertext, hypermedia, information retrieval, image management, authoring, training, tutoring, CAD/CAM, interactive digital video
Presentation	interface, dialogue.	devices: windows, pointing devices, speakers; media: text, audio, video; operations: generalization, editing, translation, access, browsing, selection, picking, querying, sequencing.
Session	discourse, blackboard, strategist, planner.	base selection, user identification, history management, versioning.
Base	search, lexicon browser.	base: knowledge, information, data; operations: search, inference.
View	list mgr, set mgr, F^3L class mgrs.	graphs, lists, sets, vectors, relations, frames.
Link	LEND link mgr.	link Ids, labels.
Anchor	LEND span mgr.	anchor Ids, span descriptions.
Node	string mgr, text mgr., integer mgr.	textual strings, integers, object Ids.
Communication	F^3L communication& process mgr.	processes.
Physical machine	UNIX files, messages.	file systems, storage media, message support.
Transport	TCP/IP	ISO lower level equivalent
Network	TCP/IP	ISO lower level equivalent
DataLink	TCP/IP	ISO lower level equivalent
Physical	TCP/IP	ISO lower level equivalent

Figure 21.8 Use of Information Management System Reference Model in CODER.

About the Authors

Edward Fox

Edward A. Fox received his B.S. from MIT in 1972 in Electrical Engineering, and his MS and Ph.D. degrees from Cornell University. Dr. Fox is now an Associate Director for Research in the Computing Center, and an Associate Professor in the Department of Computer Science at Virginia Polytechnic Institute and State University, Blacksburg, VA 24061-0106. He has served as principal investigator or co-principal investigator on more than twenty grants and contracts, sponsored by the National Science Foundation and other sponsors.

Dr. Fox has worked with the Association for Computing Machinery (ACM) in a variety of volunteer capacities. He is a member of the Publications Board, editor-in-chief of ACM Press Database and Electronic Products, vice chairman of the ACM Special Interest Group on Information Retrieval (SIGIR), and associate editor for "ACM Transactions on Information Systems." He has authored or co-authored several articles appearing in "Communications of the ACM" and was executive producer and script writer for "Interactive Digital Video," an hour-long documentary supplement to the July 1989 "Communications" special issue on Interactive Technologies, for which he served as guest editor.

Dr. Fox is editor and project manager for the Virginia Disc series of CD-ROMs, and is author of a variety of journal articles, book chapters, and other publications relating to information storage and retrieval. He serves on the editorial boards of "Information Processing and Management" and "The CD-ROM Professional," on the research advisory council for Chemical Abstracts Service, and has been on a variety of program committees and panels.

Qi Fan Chen

Qi Fan Chen is a Ph.D. candidate at Virginia Polytechnic Institute and State University in the Department of Computer Science. His dissertation work on "An Object-Oriented Network Database System for Information Retrieval Applications" deals with development of LEND and its integration with CODER, as discussed in this chapter. He has co-authored several articles relating to the CODER system and the construction of minimal perfect hash functions to support efficient access to hypermedia and other networked information.

Robert K. France

Robert K. France is a research scientist at Virginia Polytechnic Institute and State University in the Computer Science Department. His MS thesis spelled out the design of CODER, and he has thus been involved in the development of CODER since its inception. Mr. France has co-authored a variety of articles, dealing with the architecture, development, knowledge representation methods, and other aspects of this innovative system.

References

Artandi, S. (1971). Document Retrieval and the Concept of Sets. *Journal of the American Society for Information Science,* July–August, 289–290.

Bates, M. J. (1981). *Search Techniques.* Annual Review of Information Science and Technology, Martha E. Williams (Ed.), ASIS/Elsevier Science Publishers B. V., Amsterdam, Vol. 16, 139–170.

Belkin, N. J., Seeger, T., and Wersig, G. (1983). Distributed Expert Problem Treatment as a Model for Information System Analysis and Design. *Journal of Information Science* 5:153–167.

Belkin, N. J., Borgman, C., Brooks, H., Bylander, T., Croft, W., Daniels, P., Deerwester, S., Fox, E., Ingwersen, P., Rada, R., Sparck Jones, K., Thompson, R., and Walker, D. (1987). *Distributed Expert-Based Information Systems: An Interdisciplinary Approach.* IP&M, 23(5):395–409.

Belkin, N. J., and Croft, W. B. (1987). Retrieval Techniques. *Annual Review of Information Science and Technology,* Martha E. Williams (Ed.), ASIS / Elsevier Science Publishers B. V., Amsterdam, Vol. 22, 109–145.

Bookstein, A. (1985). Probability and Fuzzy-Set Applications to Information Retrieval. *Annual Review of Information Science and Technology,* Martha E. Williams (Ed.), American Society for Information Science / Elsevier Science Publishers B. V., Amsterdam, Vol. 20, 117–152.

Bush, V. (1945). "As We May Think." *Atlantic Monthly,* 176, July, 101–108.

Chen, Q. F. (1989). *Proposed Specification for an Associative Network Database.* Draft report, Computer Science Department, Virginia Polytechnic Institute and State University, Blacksburg, VA.

Chen, Q. F. (1990). *An Object-Oriented Network Database System for Information Retrieval Applications.* Dissertation Proposal, Computer Science Department, Virginia Polytechnic Institute and State University.

Cohen, P. R., and Kjeldsen, R. (1989). "Information Retrieval by Constrained Spreading Activation in Semantic Networks." *Information Processing and Management,* Vol. 23, No. 4:255–268.

Comer, D. (1979). The Ubiquitous B-tree. *ACM Computing Surveys* 11(2):121–137, June.

Consens, M., and Mendelzon, A. (1989). "Expressing Structural Hypertext Queries in GraphLog." *Hypertext '89 Proceedings,* Nov. 5–8, 1989, Pittsburgh, Special Issue—ACM SIGCHI Bulletin, 269–292.

Croft, W. B., and Turtle, H. (1989). "A Retrieval Model Incorporating Hypertext Links." *Hypertext '89 Proceedings,* Nov. 5–8, 1989, Pittsburgh, Special Issue—ACM SIGCHI Bulletin, 213–24.

Deogun, J. S., and Raghavan, V. J. (1988). "Integration of Information Retrieval and Database Management Systems." *Information Processing and Management,* Vol. 24., No. 3; 303–313.

DeRose, S. (1989). "Expanding the Notion of Links." *Hypertext '89 Proceedings,* Nov. 5–8, 1989, Pittsburgh, Special Issue—ACM SIGCHI Bulletin, 249–258.

Devlin, Joseph (1991). "Standards for Hypertext," *Hypertext / Hypermedia Handbook,* Emily Berk and Joseph Devlin (Ed.s), McGraw-Hill, New York, NY.

Enbody, R. J., and Du, H. C. (1988). "Dynamic Hashing Schemes," *ACM Computing Surveys* 20:85–113.

Engelbart, D. (1962). *Augmenting Human Intellect: A Conceptual Framework.* SRI Technical Report AFOSR-3223, Contract AF 49(638)-1024, October.

Findler, Nicholas (1979). *Associative Networks: Representation and Use of Knowledge by Computers.* Academic Press, Orlando, FL.

Fox, E. (1981). "Implementing SMART for Minicomputers Via Relational Processing with Abstract Data Types." *Joint Proc. of SIGSMALL Symp. on Small Systems and SIGMOD Workshop on Small Data Base Systems,* Oct. 1981, Orlando, FL, ACM SIGSMALL Newsletter, 7(2):119–129.

Fox, E. (1983). *Characterization of Two New Experimental Collections in Computer and Information Science Containing Textual and Bibliographic Concepts.* TR 83-561, Cornell Univ. Dept. of Computer Science, Sept., Ithaca, NY.

Fox, E. (1986). "Information Retrieval: Research Into New Capabilities." Steve Lambert and Suzanne Ropiequet, editors, *CD-ROM: The New Papyrus,* Microsoft Press, Inc. 143–174.

Fox, E., Wohlwend, R., Sheldon, P., Chen, Q. F., and France, R. (1986). *Building the CODER Lexicon: The Collins English Dictionary and Its Adverb Definitions,* TR-86-23, October, Virginia Polytechnic Institute and State University Computer Science Dept., Blacksburg, VA.

Fox, E., and France, R. (1987). "Architecture of an Expert System for Composite Document Analysis, Representation and Retrieval." *International Journal of Approximate Reasoning,* 1(2):151–175.

Fox, E., and Chen, Q. F. (1987). "Text Analysis in the CODER System." *Proceedings Fourth Annual USC Computer Science Symposium: Language and Data in Systems,* April 8, Columbia, SC, 7–14.

Fox, E. (1987). "Development of the CODER System: A Testbed for Artificial Intelligence Methods in Information Retrieval." *IP&M,* 23(4):341–366.

Fox, E. (1987). "Testing the Applicability of Intelligent Methods for Information Retrieval." *Information Services and Use,* 7:119–138.

Fox, E., Nutter, J., Ahlswede, T., Evens, M., and Markowitz, J. (1988). "Building a Large Thesaurus for Information Retrieval." *Proceedings Second Conference on Applied Natural Language Processing,* Feb. 9–12, Austin, Texas, 101–108.

Fox, E., Nunn, G., and Lee, W. (1988). "Coefficients for Combining Concept Classes in a Collection." *Proc. 11th Int'l Conf. on Research and Development in Information Retrieval,* June 13–15, Grenoble, France, 291–307.

Fox, E. (1988). *ACM Press Database and Electronic Products—New Services for the Information Age. Commun. of the ACM,* 31(8):948–951.

Fox, E. (1988). Optical Disks and CD-ROM: Publishing and Access. *Annual Review of Information Science and Technology,* Martha E. Williams (Ed.), ASIS / Elsevier Science Publishers B. V., Amsterdam, Vol. 23, 85–124.

Fox, E. (1988). "Improved Retrieval Using a Relational Thesaurus for Automatic Expansion of Boolean Logic Queries." *Relational Models of the Lexicon: Representing Knowledge in Semantic Networks,* Martha Walton Evens (Ed.), Cambridge Univ. Press, Cambridge, UK, 199–210.

Fox, E. (1989). "Research and Development of Information Retrieval Models and their Application." *Information Processing and Management* (IP&M), 25(1):1–5.

Fox, E., Chen, Q. F., Heath, L., and Datta, S. (1989). "A More Cost Effective Algorithm for Finding Perfect Hash Functions." *Proc. ACM 1989 Computer Science Conference,* February 21–23, Louisville, KY, 114–122.

Fox, E., Heath, L., and Chen, Q. F. (1989). *An O(n log n) Algorithm for Finding Minimal Perfect Hash Functions,* TR-89-10, VPI&SU Computer Science Dept., April, Blacksburg, VA. Submitted for publication.

Fox, E. (1989). "The Coming Revolution in Interactive Digital Multimedia Systems." *Commun. of the ACM,* 32(7):794–801.

Fox, E. executive producer, script writer. *Interactive Digital Video.* A videotape supplement to July 1989 Communications of the ACM, produced for ACM Press Database and Electronic Products with assistance from IBM Thomas J. Watson Research Center (with Guillermo Pulido as producer/director).

Fox, E., and Chen, Q. F. (1990). *ACM's Need and the CODER/LEND Approach.* Paper HT-5 in Hypertext Standardization Workshop, Jan. 16-18, National Inst. of Standards and Tech., Gaithersburg, MD.

Fox, E., editor and project manager. *Virginia Disc One.* Produced by Nimbus Records, 1990. Blacksburg VA: Virginia Polytechnic Institue and State University Press.

Fox, E., Heath, L., Chen, Q. F., and Daoud, A. (1990). "Practical Minimal Perfect Hash Functions for Large Databases." TR 90-41, Virginia Polytechnic Institute and State University, Department of Computer Science, Blacksburg, VA, August.

Fox, E., Rous, B., and Marchinioni, G. (1991). "ACM's Hypertext and Hypermedia Publishing Projects," *Hypertext / Hypermedia Handbook*, Emily Berk and Joseph Devlin (Ed.s), McGraw-Hill, New York, NY.

France, R., Fox, E., Nutter, J. T., Chen, Q. F. (1989). "Building A Relational Lexicon for Text Understanding and Retrieval." *Proc. First Int'l Language Acquisition Workshop*, Aug. 21, Detroit, MI.

France, R. (1989). *Proposed Specification for an Associative Network Database.* Draft report, Computer Science Department, Virginia Polytechnic Institute and State University, Blacksburg, VA.

Furuta, R., and Stotts, P. D. (1989). "Programmable Browsing Semantics in Trellis." *Hypertext '89 Proceedings*, Nov. 5-8, Pittsburgh, Special Issue—*ACM SIGCHI Bulletin*, 27-42.

Furuta, R., and Stotts, P. D. (1990). "The Trellis Hypertext Reference Model." Paper HT-6 in Hypertext Standardization Workshop, Jan. 16-18, National Inst. of Standards and Tech., Gaithersburg, MD.

Guting, R. H., Zicari, R., and Choy, D. (1989). "An Algebra for Structured Office Documents." ACM Transactions on Office Information Systems, Vol. 7, No. 4, 123-157 April.

Halasz, F., and Schwartz, M. (1990). "The Dexter Hypertext Reference Model." Paper HT-9 in Hypertext Standardization Workshop, Jan. 16-18, National Inst. of Standards and Tech., Gaithersburg, MD.

Kim, W., and Lochovsky, F. H., editors (1989). *Object-Oriented Concepts, Databases and Applications.* ACM Press, New York, NY.

Lange, D. (1990). "A Formal Model of Hypertext." Paper HT-13 in Hypertext Standardization Workshop, Jan. 16-18, National Inst. of Standards and Technology, Gaithersburg, MD.

Lindeman, M. J., Crabb, J. C., Bonneau, J. R., and Wehrli, V. F. (1990). "Designing a Scholars Electronic Library: The Interaction of Human Factors and Computer Science Tasks." *Advances in Human-Computer Interaction*, Vol. III.

Littleford, Alan (1991). "Artificial Intelligence and Hypermedia," *Hypertext / Hypermedia handbook*, Emily Berk and Joseph Devlin (Ed.s), McGraw-Hill, New York, NY.

Lynch, C. A. (1987). "Extending Relational Database Management Systems for Information Retrieval Applications." Dissertation. University of California, Berkeley.

Marshall, C., and Irish, P. (1989). "Guided Tours and On-Line Presentations: How Authors Make Existing Hypertext Intelligible for Readers." Hypertext '89 Proceedings, Nov. 5-8, 1989, Pittsburgh, Special Issue—ACM SIGCHI Bulletin, 15-26.

Morgado, Ernesto J. M. (1985). "Semantic Networks as Abstract Data Types." Dissertation. Department of Computer Science, University of New York at Buffalo.

Parunak, H. Van Dyke (1989). "Hypermedia Topologies and User Navigation." Hypertext '89 Proceedings, Nov. 5-8, 1989, Pittsburgh, Special Issue—ACM SIGCHI Bulletin, 43-50.

Pearl, A. (1989). "Sun's Link Service: A protocol for Open Linking." Hypertext '89 Proceedings, Nov. 5-8, 1989, Pittsburgh, Special Issue—ACM SIGCHI Bulletin, 137-146.

Robertson, S. E., and Jones, K. S. (1976). "Relevance Weighting of Search Terms." *Journal of Documentation*, May-June, 129-146.

Salton, G., Fox, E., and Wu, H. (1983). "Extended Boolean Information Retrieval." *Communications of the ACM*, 26(11):1022–1036.

Salton, G., Fox, E., and Voorhees, E. (1985). "Advanced Feedback Methods in Information Retrieval." *Journal of the American Society for Information Science*, 36(3):200–210.

Salton, G. (1989). *Automatic Text Processing*. Addison-Wesley, Reading MA.

Shapiro, C. (1979). "The SNePS Semantic Network Processing System." Nicholas Findler. *Associative Networks: Representation and Use of Knowledge by Computers*. Academic Press, Orlando, FL, 179–203.

Shapiro, C., et al. (1989). *SNePS User's Manual*. Department of Computer Science, State University of New York at Buffalo.

Shneiderman, B., (Ed.). (1988). *Hypertext on Hypertext, HyperTies edition*. ACM Press Database and Electronic Products, New York, NY.

Stotts, P. David, and Furuta, Richard (1989). "Petri-Net-Based Hypertext: Document Structure with Browsing Semantics." ACM Transactions on Information Systems. Vol.7, No.1, January, 3–29.

Tanenbaum, Andrew S. (1981). *Computer Networks*. Prentice Hall, Englewood Cliffs, NJ.

Teskey, F. N. (1989). "User Models and World models for Data, Information, and Knowledge." *Information Processing and Management*. Vol. 25, No. 1.

Tompa, F. W. (1989). "A Data Model for Flexible Hypertext Database Systems." ACM Transactions on Information Systems. Vol. 7, No. 1. January, 85–100.

Trigg, R., and Weiser, M. (1986). "TEXTNET: a network-based approach to text handling." ACM Trans. on Office Information Systems 4(1):1–23, Jan.

Weaver, M., France, R., Chen, Q. F., and Fox, E. (1989). "Using a Frame-Based Language for Information Retrieval." *Int. Journal of Intelligent Systems*, 4(3):223–257.

Zellweger, P. T. (1989). "Scripted Documents: A Hypermedia Path Mechanism." Hypertext '89 Proceedings, Nov. 5–8, 1989, Pittsburgh, Special Issue—ACM SIGCHI Bulletin, 1–14.

Zimmerman, H. (1980). "OSI Reference Model—The ISO Model of Architecture for Open Systems Interconnection," *IEEE Trans. Commun.*, Vol. COM-28, 425–432, April.

22

Artificial Intelligence and Hypermedia

By Alan Littleford
Cogent Software, Ltd.

Intelligent Information Retrieval

Overview

This chapter discusses the addition of *artificial intelligence* (AI) to both documentation and the environment in which it is created, stored, and retrieved.

The kinds of documents we concern ourselves with in this chapter include policy and procedure manuals, reference and user manuals, functional specifications, maintenance manuals, academic papers, reviews, and other information which is not particularly well structured. In this chapter, we will not concern ourselves with documents which are *de facto* paper databases—documents consisting of data in some fixed format, for which a good table of contents is usually all that is required. A good author has the ability to ask the following important questions:

* How will the reader use this information?
* What topics will the reader expect to be linked together?
* What common mistakes might a reader make?

But even skillful authors may find it hard to come up with a finite number of correct answers to these important questions.

This is not surprising because:

Equally intelligent readers may use the same information in different ways. Also, the same reader may use the same document at different times in different ways. For example, a software manual may be used as a tutorial, a reference, a detailed specification, or an overview.

The links readers choose may differ. Link choice may depend on the mindset as well as the current interests and skill level of the reader.

Readers can and do make mistakes. They may stumble down the wrong paths because they have made false assumptions, factual errors, or drawn the wrong inferences from information.

The only tools the author of conventional (paper) documents has are ones of explication and organization. The author has to choose some level of detail—presumably low enough to minimize the level of misunderstanding and yet not so low as to bombard readers with a mass of useless, confusing data. A print author can lay out the documentation in a natural way, and make sure it is well indexed and has good table of contents, but after that a reader is on his or her own.

Hypermedia promises to alleviate some of these problems. Suitable levels of detail can be hidden behind links and called up when required [as discussed in Chapter 11 by Shneiderman, et al., in this book]. The organization itself becomes somewhat flexible in that a user may choose what to read next from related topics, but hypermedia by itself is only a small step up from conventional documents:

Explanatory links correspond to footnotes.

Contextual links correspond to bibliography listings, *see also* notes embedded within the text, or a good index and table of contents.

Indeed, sometimes the only purpose hyperlinks seem to serve in large documents is to make up for the drawbacks of having documentation on a computer in the first place:

• Lack of real estate—computers that can display two full-size side-by-side images of paper on a screen are still not cheaply available for personal computers (indeed, a good enough color display and controller card can approach the cost of the computer itself).
• Lack of physical contact with the document—readers cannot physically skim through hyperdocuments, keep four pages (or more) open at a time and flip back and forth between them quickly.

That said, if the potential inherent in using computers to store and display documentation is tapped, we should be able to get to the point where readers actually prefer to have documents in hypermedia form. Sadly, for the moment, most arguments for hypermedia storage rely on economic advantage for the organizations involved in creating and dispersing the information.

What are the inherent advantages of providing documentation on a computer system?

- Interactivity—the system can track a reader through the document. At any time it knows what a reader has looked at and in what order. It can also keep a record of the length of time spent in various sections. The system should be able to exploit this information.
- Mutability—once a document is in a computer, its content can be regarded as data in a database. What the system chooses to present to the reader when asked, for example, to show examples of some concept, may well depend on how much time the reader spent in the introductory material (simpler examples might be shown to people who spent a longer than average time in the introductory section). Similarly, the system may also determine whether or not to include certain links.
- Adaptability—We should be able to banish forever the concept of a fixed document, which is simply the imposition of a paper-dependent convention to computers. We should also banish the rigid hierarchy of conventional hypertext linkages. In their place, we should have adaptable documents. These documents will dynamically adjust their content and presentation to that which best suits the current reader. The relationship between fixed, hypermedia and adaptive documents can be seen in Figure 22.1.

How can one go about implementing adaptive documentation? Clearly we cannot describe every conceivable use for the document, have it recognize which use applies in a given instance and adjust accordingly. The number of combinations of possible paths through a document expands at an alarming rate. For example, if you exclude loops, then the number of different ways through a document with

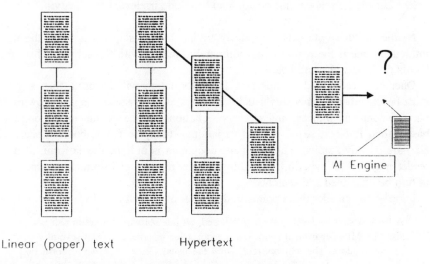

Linear (paper) text   Hypertext

Figure 22.1   Increasing mutability of documentation.

N nuggets (a small portion of the document which covers one concept) is N x (N-1) x (N-2) x..x 1. A document with 20 nuggets (an outlandishly small number) will have therefore approximately 2,432,902,000,000,000,000 paths through it (an outlandishly large number). Even if only one millionth of the possible paths were practical the number is still gigantic. Worse, if we double the number of nuggets to 40, the number of potential paths is about a billion billion billion times larger than the document with 20 nuggets.

What we need, therefore, is a way of describing the properties of potential paths. It is much easier to specify a path by saying "If a person clicks on this link and they have already read the introductory sections then take them to a third level description rather than an introductory-level description" than it is to evaluate all possible paths through the introductory material and the current link. To accomplish this goal, we need a way of talking about general properties of nuggets of the document. We also need a language in which rules derive inferences from generalizations about relationships between the nuggets. This technology needs to run on a computer and it must be, at worst, moderately efficient.

Fortunately, such technology exists. One of the early successes of *Artificial Intelligence* (AI) research was the development of Expert Systems—programs whose instructions are detailed in precisely such rules of inference. Before we discuss this technology in some detail, let us first take a closer look at the problem.

Retrieving Information

At the most fundamental level, documents contain data. The intelligence which has interpreted the data in order to produce information has historically been supplied by the reader. In order to extract information, the reader must:

1. Determine precisely the use to which the information will be put.
2. Locate the relevant information and exclude irrelevant information.

Neither of these steps is necessarily trivial. Indeed step (1) is often the more intractable one if the reader is not intimately familiar with the subject. This problem is discussed in detail below.

Once the reader understands how the information will be used, then step (2) must be undertaken. This step usually involves extensive searching—following tables of contents, indices, and reference citations. If the document is computer-based, then full text searches (and variations—fuzzy searches, boolean searches, etc.) are usually applied. Further, if the document is in hypermedia form, then the reader may follow hyperlinks, resulting in new nuggets of information which will in turn be examined and searched.

In order to consider these points in detail, let us look at a real world example:

> A bank wishes to develop some rule-based, on-line software for credit risk analysis. The MIS department sends out a request for information from several competing vendors. The vendors reply with the usual glossy fliers and information about their products. The MIS department now has to decide which software is best for the application.

Determining The Requirements. The bank's requirements may well include the following words: "must support large number of terminals with adequate response time, will be used in COBOL environment, must be able to access DB2 records." This set of requirements is couched in terms that bankers use. On the other hand, the software vendors' documents may speak of the "Rete algorithm," "extension languages" and "forward and backward chaining algorithms." This is the language that software vendors are accustomed to using—the dreaded TechnoTalk or JingoSpeak.

If the reader of the technical document is knowledgeable enough about its subject area, then he/she knows that clues to the product's performance will be found in the discussion of the Rete algorithm. The extension language section, on the other hand, may well discuss how the program relates to the COBOL environment, etc. Even if he/she is not a native TechnoTalker, if the document is small enough, the reader may be able to perform an exhaustive search (i.e. read the whole thing).

We have discussed explicit requirements that the reader knows about—"answer the following questions ...," but there are also implicit requirements. If the document is being read for preliminary qualification purposes, then the reader does not want chapter and verse on the various topics—simple statements will suffice. Later, when a more detailed comparison is made between survivors of the culling process, much more detail may be required.

Locating Relevant Information. Once we have determined our requirements and then expressed them in the language of the available documentation, then we can attempt to find out which vendors can satisfy them.

The Two Ss. The S words are *Syntax* and *Semantics*. Syntax refers to the words in the document and the arrangement of those words. Semantics refer to the meaning of those words.

This is not an idle distinction. Indeed, many of the limitations of current approaches to retrieving information from documents are due to the fact that most searching procedures rely exclusively on syntax. You can ask for sections of the document which contain certain combinations of words, e.g. "Find all occurrences of the word speed", but you generally cannot ask for "all those sections which discuss system performance"—which might include references to speed, transactions per second, inferences per second, bandwidth etc.

Full text search (including boolean and fuzzy search) is clearly syntax-oriented. The semantics are left entirely to the reader. An intricate juggling act has to take place—orchestrate a search that is too tightly focused and you may miss information, too loose and you are bombarded with information, much of which is irrelevant.

Full text search with factor analysis (where a search for one word may in turn cause an automatic search for others) is somewhat of an improvement. This function is usually performed by a static off-line analysis program that looks for patterns of related words. For example, the reader might start the search by looking for the word "computer," and the system may also return occurrences of "CPU."

Still, both of these searching techniques (and several related ones) rely on explicit use of specific words, on syntax alone. The semantics, what there are, are entirely implicit.

*It is the central tenet of this chapter that the **semantics** of the document should and can be made as explicit as its **syntax**, and that the user can exploit the semantics when trying to locate information.*

Bootstraps. The bootstrap problem is best paraphrased by the answer I was given when asking for directions during my first visit to Boston: "How can I tell you how to get there if you don't know where you are going?" I knew where I wanted to be, but the description of the proposed route relied on too much background knowledge, i.e. landmarks, etc.—so that if I could understand the directions I wouldn't have needed to ask for them. This is a fundamental problem of any form of documentation—if you don't know anything about the subject then how do you know which questions to ask?

The syntax-based searches discussed above require a working knowledge of the subject, enough to know the buzzwords, appropriate proper nouns and what subjects they relate to. Factor analysis reduces this threshold by implicitly grouping buzzwords.

Exploiting Knowledge

It would seem that finding information in a large document is a hopeless task, yet people can and do find it (with varying degrees of success). The trick is that readers (or their agents) implicitly use knowledge of various types to help focus their searches:

* Organizational knowledge. As readers become familiar with certain documents, and come to know how they are structured, partitioned etc., their ability to phrase acute syntactical questions increases. Frequent use of a search engine trains readers; with enough use they learn what disastrous queries have in common and how flexible and reliable the engine really is.
* Domain knowledge. Musicians have a better chance of finding information in a music database than non-musicians. Is a twelve tone row a compositional technique or an instrumental argument? The wits may say both!
* Contextual Knowledge. "Why does the reader want to know this?" The reader's goal in searching can often drastically focus a search. The level of sophistication of the reader also flavors a search ("Does he want chapter and verse or just a summary?").

We aim to show that the intangibles described above can be made tangible in the sense that computer programs can exhibit domain knowledge of a document, can derive conclusions from the document organization and can manipulate a document to emphasize the information a reader is really interested in.

The Complications of Hypermedia

Hypermedia is a two-edged sword. On the one hand, it permits the development of flexibly-structured computer-based documentation with convenient information-hiding [see Chapter 11 by Shneiderman, et al., in this book, regarding "details on demand"], yet its very flexibility can lead to problems.

Linkitis

One of the main complaints about hypertext is that links reflect what the author thinks important more often than they reflect what the reader hopes to find. The reasons for this are not hard to fathom given our discussions above—the relevance of a link depends heavily on how the document is currently being used and the use to which the information will be put.

Attempts by an author to solve this problem often result in *linkitis*—linking anything and everything in sight to something else. Frustration and confusion results for the reader. Given an overabundance of links, it is necessary for the author to also give the reader an idea of what will be found if a link is traversed. The author may try to address the overlinking problem by typing links [see Chapter 20 by Parunak, in this book] and giving a visual cue for each link type. Or, the author may display a snippet of the target of the link when it is first selected, so a reader can see what the link's destination would be before leaving the current node [refer to Chapter 11 by Shneiderman, et al.].

Although these techniques mitigate the problem, they do not address the fundamental issue. Too many links can be worse than too few links. The challenge is to select the appropriate links to present to a reader at any given time.

Lost In HyperSpace

Lost in HyperSpace refers to the feeling of disorientation a reader can experience when he is following a connected trail of hypertext links. Each link in the trail may make perfect sense, but by the time the reader is several links deep, the relevance of his current position in the document to where he started from may be far from clear. Playing the game of following a chain of synonyms in a dictionary can lead to the same feeling—the word you end up with is only marginally associated with the word you started from, even though each word in the chain is a synonym for the preceding word.

Reducing the depth of a document (the maximum length of any chain of links) and providing maps of links can help alleviate this disorientation, but these approaches begin to get clumsy when dealing with exceptionally large hyperdocuments. Documents infected with linkitis are likely to exacerbate the Lost in HyperSpace syndrome.

Dynamic Growth of Hypermedia Systems

The trend in modern computing is towards networked, distributed processors. Information stored somewhere on the network is accessible from anywhere on the network. This means that the infrastructure is in place to support a *web* of on-line hypermedia documents. Documents are always being created and added to the web, deleted from the web or modified. In this environment, the concept of a fixed library of documentation has to be discarded. It should be possible to dynamically link your document to extant documents using hypertext links and vice versa. Ted Nelson's Project Xanadu [Nelson, 1988] is to be a system supporting precisely this capability.

Any dynamic, distributed growth of interlinked documents can cause serious problems in any relatively passive approach to hypermedia. Organizational knowledge (see above) of readers or intermediaries can rapidly become outdated as the extended document evolves.

Any attempt to control the spread of links by imposing a static classification system on them is also destined to fail almost by definition, since a *novel* link between two previously disconnected nuggets of information is unlikely to fit cleanly into any pre-existing category. So the number of categories increases with the number of links (albeit more slowly) and you are back to the original problem.

Artificial Intelligence

We have discussed the problems which occur when documentation repositories become unduly large or are stored on-line on computers. We have hinted that a solution to both these problems can be found by exploiting implicit knowledge about how documents are organized and used, or explicit knowledge about the content of the documents themselves.

The key is to be able to express this knowledge in such a way that the computer system itself can begin to play a role in reasoning sensibly about the contents of documents and how they are organized. Computer technology which attacks this problem is the topic of this section.

What is AI?

AI can be loosely defined as a set of programming techniques which mimic human decision-making strategies. AI programs are not necessarily required to come up with the exact answer to a question. Indeed, certain questions may not have *best* answers.

AI techniques usually prove most useful where the problems we are dealing with are very large and somewhat ill-defined. Because these problems are large, it is not practical to deal with every contingency. Because they are ill-defined, we cannot easily write down an algorithm that an ordinary computer program can use to solve these problems in a reasonable amount of time. Thus, where conventional programs talk about procedures and variables, AI programs tend to talk about rules-of-thumb, probability and patterns.

As we have seen, the number of possible answers can become very large when we are considering what information to show or hide, or which paths to lead a reader down. AI is often used to provide answers to issues of choice (for example, out of these five billion possible answers, find one which is good enough). Or, there may not necessarily be only one solution to the problem, nor may there necessarily be a best one. In these cases, we see that AI techniques offer at least the correct *flavor* of solutions.

Some AI Techniques

There are many different AI programming techniques and systems. Indeed AI is often defined as whatever AI researchers are doing at the moment, or to quote AI pioneer Marvin Minsky, "Once we understand it, it isn't AI."

Nonetheless, there are at least three AI tools which have proved themselves in day-to-day applications which seem to be particularly relevant to the future of extensive hypermedia documentation.

Rule-based Expert Systems.   Expert systems are computer programs which emulate human expert decision-making in some particular sphere of knowledge. Expert systems exist for blood infection diagnosis, diagnosing equipment failures of various kinds, and geological data interpretation, to name but a few.

Rule-based refers to the way a class of expert systems is built. An expert system consists of two parts: a rule set and an inference engine.

The rule set is the collection of rules which provides the knowledge an expert system possesses. Rules may be written in different ways according to the implementation of the system, but they usually have two parts: an IF part and a THEN part.

For example, a rule from an expert system performing automobile repair might be:

IF
    Car's lights do not work, and
    Car's horn does not work,
THEN
    Suspect dead battery.

An inference is a determination arrived at through reasoning. The inference engine is responsible for choosing rules from the rule set which might apply in the current situation (i.e. whose IF parts are satisfied), applying the relevant THEN parts (which results in a changed situation) and then repeating this process until it can terminate with an answer.

There are several different schemes by which inferences may be constructed. Some use the rules by *backward chaining*. This means looking through all the rules' THEN parts for conclusions which solve your problem (if, for example, your problem is to diagnose a car failure, the rule above definitely helps you), then trying to prove the IF parts. The IF parts may in turn set up sub-problems, and the process continues until you have run out of sub-problems.

Alternatively, the inference engine may look through the IF parts first, trying to find conditions which are true. The relevant THEN parts are executed which may change the state of the *world*, and the IF parts are checked again. This continues until either no rule's IF parts are TRUE, in which case the program has failed to find a solution, or some THEN part which was executed stated the required solution.

Notice that the expertise of the expert system is contained entirely within the rules. The inference engine knows only how to choose and apply rules; the actual knowledge is encoded within the rules. Thus, expert systems addressing totally different problems might be constructed simply by giving the inference engine a new set of rules. Many commercial software packages are available that consist of just an inference engine and an editor for creating rules. These are often called expert system shells.

Rule-based expert systems are still where most of the major successes of AI can be found. One of the chief advantages of the rule-based approach is that each rule is usually a nugget of expertise. It can be read in isolation from other rules and make perfect sense. This tends to make creation and maintenance of expert systems much easier for very large systems than a conventional programming approach.

Rules do not spring to life fully-formed. An expert has to supply the expertise, usually with the help of an intermediary, so his knowledge may be captured in rule form. This stage can be rife with problems, since no two experts go about solving a problem in the same way, and since even an expert can have problems explaining his reasoning. Indeed, experts usually become experts by having such familiarity with the problem that they don't have to think too hard about how to go about solving it! To overcome these problems, there are software tools available which help an interviewer formulate questions that will encourage the expert to provide detailed descriptions of his reasoning, and from thence the formal rules he uses in his decision making.

Neural Networks.   Since the 1940s, researchers have been attempting to produce computer systems which reason by trying to emulate the underlying hardware that (presumably) supplies humans with their reasoning capabilities, namely the cells which comprise the brain. These brain cells, often called *neurons*, are organized in interconnected networks. The computer-based models of these networks have become known as neural networks.

Every neuron has several inputs and one output. The output of a neuron is usually connected to the input of another neuron. The output of a given neuron is a function of all the activity at inputs to the neuron, where some of the inputs tend to encourage output when activated, whereas some tend to check output from the cell.

Inputs can also have weights. Imagine these to be dials which, when turned, affect the influence a given input has on its cell's output. Some inputs in the neural network are left unconnected, and these form inputs to the network as a whole. Similarly, some outputs are left unconnected, and these form outputs of the entire network.

Computer-based models of neurons stop at this point, whereas the genuine articles are known to be more complex. Nonetheless, it has been discovered that appropriate networks of computer neurons have an amazing property—they can be taught to recognize patterns. The power of this simple ability can be realized when you learn that applications of neural networks currently include reading handwriting, recognizing insider trading action in the stock markets and recognizing the smell of plastic explosives in airport luggage.

Neural networks are another approach to expert systems. In rule-based expert systems, a human expert has to have sat down and explained his reasoning in terms of a collection of rules. Neural networks are totally different in that they are taught to solve problems in much the same way humans are taught. The network is given a series of training runs of input patterns (say handwritten "A's") and desired outputs (in this case the letter "A"). In the case where a particular input pattern led to an erroneous output (say one handwritten "A" was thought to be a "H"), then the neural network automatically adjusts some of the weighting factors on the neurons so that the given sample will result in an "A" being recognized the next time. This training is repeated over and over again until the neural network behaves correctly (or at least to a high enough level of precision).

One drawback of neural networks is that it is impossible to open up a neural network and see the knowledge contained within it like one can with the rule-set in a rule-based expert system. This makes it hard to change a neural network incrementally, or to debug it methodically. But then again, neural networks can achieve their performance without the necessity for long, error prone interviews with an expert to extract his secrets. We will see shortly that both approaches can be used to augment hypermedia systems.

Blackboard Systems. Blackboard systems are used to allow different expert systems to solve problems cooperatively. Imagine a room full of experts in various subjects. One announces she is trying to solve a problem and is having difficulty with one step, so she goes up to a blackboard at the end of the room and writes down her sub-problem. At this point, another expert looks at the blackboard and sees a sub-problem which he thinks he can solve; after a few minutes he announces he can solve it if only he can answer two other questions, which he duly writes on the blackboard.

The important points of this system are:

- The blackboard allows experts in different fields to interchange problems and cooperate in the solution of a problem that no single expert could solve on his or her own.
- The internal workings of the various experts are known only to themselves.

Applying AI to Hypermedia Documentation

We have seen that knowledge associated with a document can come in many different forms and we identified three important ones:

- Organizational knowledge. Knowledge about how the content of the document is organized.
- Domain knowledge. Explicit knowledge about the content of the document.
- Contextual Knowledge. Knowledge about the particular way in which information from the document will be used.

Below we list four ways in which artificial intelligence techniques can be used to augment hypermedia documentation by making the knowledge discussed above amenable to computation.

Embedding Organizational Knowledge

Organizational knowledge is comprised of statements about the organization of a document. It relies very little on the actual content of the document, so a document on bread baking might have precisely the same structural organization as one on brain surgery. Typical statements that relate to organizational knowledge include:

- This section is required reading.
- This section requires a thorough understanding of section seven.
- This section can be skipped on first reading.
- If you skipped chapter three then skip the next five sections.
- This is a important section or a difficult section.
- If someone has opted not to see the class of "examples", then exclude the "tutorial" information from the current view of the document.
- The current section is a landmark section.

In conventional documents, such structural semantics may be stated explicitly in the text of the document. A notable example is the series of mathematical texts by (the pseudonymous) Nicolas Bourbaki. Sections containing hard to understand reasoning are marked by the universal "S" road signs for "winding road ahead." Prefaces to chapters may list prerequisite reading.

Embedding this sort of semantic structure in a hypertext involves making the display mechanism (the software) aware of these relationships in such a way that it can use them. For example, if the display software knew you had not read chapter three, it would hide the next five sections (until chapter three was read).

The key point now is that the structural semantics can be described in terms of IF-THEN rules. Simple factual assertions ("chapter seven is difficult") may be replaced by the trivial rule:

IF
 TRUE
THEN
 "chapter seven is difficult."

Since TRUE is always true, chapter seven is always hard. The structural semantics specific to the document may be augmented by more generally applicable rules:

IF
 The reader has been reading tutorial material, and
 The reader has been skipping reference material
THEN
 The reader is most probably a novice.
IF
 The reader is a novice,
THEN
 Skip the difficult chapters.

This is obvious, and good document authors try to accommodate this reasoning by grouping hard material in clearly defined sections or chapters (with warning labels). But, as we have observed, this approach is passive when applied to paper documents—the reader is the one who must act upon these kinds of tips from authors.

A particularly annoying aspect of computer-based documentation is spending a lot of time trying to find some information which, it turns out, you really didn't want to read. If the document knows you most probably don't want to read it, then it shouldn't let you hunt for it or indicate that it is available.

Structural semantics also embodies the notion of natural landmarks. A landmark is a section of the document which is particularly memorable or important. Landmarks are natural focal points—if a reader gets lost in hyperspace at some point, taking him back to the most relevant landmark is often a good idea since it can offer some stability in otherwise rough air [see Chapter 20 by Parunak, in this book].

Embedding Domain Knowledge

Whereas organizational knowledge has to do with the organization of the document and little or nothing to do with its content, domain knowledge deals precisely with the content of the document. Domain knowledge deals with WHAT the document says; organizational knowledge deals with HOW it says it.

Domain knowledge is much harder for a computer-based system to deal with than organizational knowledge since it relies heavily on what humans take for granted—common sense. Making computer systems exhibit common sense is an active research topic with total solutions still many years away.

We could use rules of inference to describe domain knowledge. Typical rules might include:

IF
   The subject under study is Baroque Music,
THEN
   Restrict any queries involving dates to the period
   1550-1750.

Another way to view this rule is that it defines the dates of Baroque music period in western culture.

The problem with this approach is that domain knowledge is vast. Whereas structural knowledge can be reduced to a manageable collection of rules about the organization of documents plus some specific facts about specific documents, domain knowledge is boundless. We need more expressive tools.

One relevant AI technique which may be used is the *Concept Hierarchy*, a data structure which lists the major concepts of some domain and how the concepts relate to each other. The concept hierarchy may be used to help a user understand the content of a document using such requests as:

• Put this section in a more general context.
• Give me a more detailed discussion of the main issue.

A sample of a partial concept hierarchy for classical music is given in Figure 22.2.

We cannot be in the position of having to invent a new concept hierarchy for each document we are going to publish in hypermedia form; reusability of hierarchies is essential. On the other hand, if the hierarchies are made general enough to cover a lot of material, they run the risk of becoming devoid of real content.

Work being undertaken at the MCC technology consortium by Douglas Lenat and his colleagues [Lenat, 1988] is relevant here. They are constructing *Cyc*, an intelligent encyclopaedia. When completed, Cyc will contain a lot of specific facts about everyday items ("Glass is transparent," "Public nudity is frowned upon"), and a large amount of consequential, common sense knowledge ("People in glass houses shouldn't store clothes"). Constructing Cyc is a gargantuan task and practical systems based on it will be a long time coming, but nonetheless it does hold the promise of eventually being able to retire handcrafted domain semantics with more general structures.

Concept hierarchies also supply a valid map for a document. Unlike most hypertext-related mapping devices, which show how the document is organized, the hierarchy shows how the content of the document is organized. The two may differ greatly. In particular, if you are exploring near the *edge* of a hyperdocument (where outward links are few and far between) you may come to a dead end beyond which the author chooses not to take you. In pursuit of some relevant nugget of peripheral information, you may perform some key word search across other documents to find relevant information, and then continue following links to

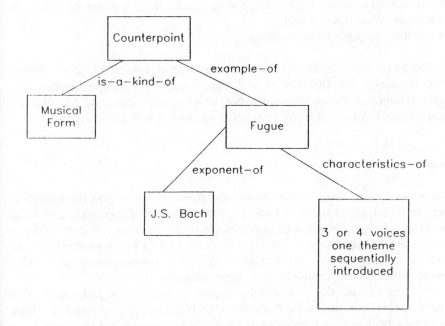

Figure 22.2   A sample of a partial concept hierarchy for "classical music."

find the nugget you wanted. Conceptually, the two nuggets are related and so are very close together in the concept hierarchy, but you would never surmise this by looking at the map of links you followed to bridge the gap.

Local Agents

Structural and domain semantics embed within a document the knowledge required to help readers retrieve information from the document. You need the knowledge (whether it be in the form of rules for structural semantics or concept hierarchies for domain semantics) but equally important you need to be able to exploit this knowledge efficiently. I don't necessarily want to see the concept hierarchy, I want to see a relevant nugget of information.

A key to this is the concept of an agent. Agents are programs which work on the reader's behalf, pursuing his or her agenda, using the embedded knowledge within a document and returning information. Think of a Local Agent as a representative of the author of a document, able to answer questions that you, the reader, would love to be able to ask:

- Which sections should I read first?
- Could you show me the most important sections?

- My particular interest is the ecology of the late Cretaceous period and I have ten minutes. What should I read?
- I'm lost—help me get my bearings.

The local agent contains the inference engine which applies the rules contained with the documents. The agent must also provide a very good user interface, possibly graphical or natural language driven, which can solicit requests from the user and deliver responses. It is also responsible for dealing with global agents.

Global Agents

As we discussed earlier in this chapter, the power of hypermedia documentation will be fully realized when the idea of a static collection of documents is replaced by that of a large, dynamic web of documents which are being constantly added to the system by hypermedia 'publishers.' The concept of a web goes along with the current trend towards highly distributed computer systems connected by high speed networks using combinations of local and global storage.

Publishing an addition to an existing hyperdocument may be problematic. New documents have to fit into the (hopefully global) concept hierarchy and their links must be established based on previously published documents and vice versa.

Local Agents works on behalf of readers of hyperdocuments. Global Agents work for the dynamic web. As documents are added, Global Agents attend to linking the information, driven by the concept hierarchy, and then inform Local Agents of the new state of the web. The distributed database system of today provides precisely such functions when database nodes are added or removed from a network.

Since Global Agents have access to the *big picture*, they can see how the web is being used. This is another source of important knowledge that is left on the cutting room floor when documentation makes its way onto computers. Again, we have some obvious, domain-independent rules which can and should be used.

- **Follow the path well trod.** If a reader asks "where should I go next?" and you don't have a good answer, then take him where most other people have gone.
- **As the world turns, relevances change with time and age.** If people are using the web in ways not statistically related to the Concept Hierarchy, then the Hierarchy is out of date. Change it.

Global Agents watch, listen and learn how people are using the web. When the Global Agents notice certain patterns recurring, they can help a Local Agent, and thence a reader, find relevant information. A program that learns from patterns? An application for Neural Networks! Local Agents may temporarily become users of other Local Agents. When a reader poses a request for information which the Local Agent cannot satisfy, the Agent may go the Global Agent and ask for help. The Global Agent knows where to go for this help and can call up one or more different Local Agents to supply him with the information needed. These Local

Agents may be running different inferencing mechanisms, they are certainly using different rules and documents, so a method is needed to get these systems to work in a cooperative fashion. Blackboard technology is an obvious candidate.

It's Deja Vu All Over Again

Beginning with the observation that computers offer a lot more than simply being able to store and display the contents of documents, we have found ourselves, a scant few pages later, discussing labyrinthine knowledge *warehouses* tended by ephemeral intelligent Agents, who, driven by Concept Hierarchies, strive to do your bidding.

You have seen this before. Go down to your local library.

If you know precisely what it is you are looking for, then a quick visit to the card catalogs will find what you are after. You have performed the equivalent of a keyword or full text search.

If you haven't formulated what you are after clearly in your mind, then you need to talk to a Local Agent to help you formulate the right questions. Using Concept Hierarchies that have been developing since birth, the genuine article neural net, plus a good knowledge of the structural semantics of the organization of the books in the library (with a little help from the cataloging scheme), your librarian can suggest books, or pointers to clusters of books that you should read.

Failing this, he or she can, with the mediation of a global agency (the inter-town library system, of which your local node is a member), talk to another local agent over the telephone (also part of the global agency communication network) and see whether that Agent can offer some help. Using the Blackboard of social discourse skills, these Agents finally locate and deliver the information you want.

Theory Into Practice—Hyperbase

Would-be librarians can relax. We are a long way from the fully functional 100 percent computer-based knowledge warehouse described above. However, tools are becoming available which allow pieces of the picture to be developed.

HyperBase [Cogent, 1990] is a tool for embedding structural semantics, some domain semantics and Local Agents within a hypermedia document. It has proven highly useful to major corporations requiring intelligent documentation or adaptive CBT (computer based training) modules.

HyperBase is a hypermedia system wrapped around a rule-based programming language. The rules themselves are stored within the documents. HyperBase can watch a reader explore the hypermedia document and compare its usage to patterns stored as rules. (These rules, however, have to be authored. HyperBase does not support neural network technology.)

Links and hypertext buttons can also be defined by rules, so where you *go* when you follow a link can depend intimately on where you have already been, who you are and what you want to know. For example, the following piece of code within a document:

Example:
is_a(expert), visit_chapter('Advanced Examples');
is_a(novice), visit_chapter('Basic Examples').

defines a hypertext link which depends on the level of the reader. The word "Example" becomes the button and is highlighted in a HyperBase window. When a reader clicks on this button, he is linked to another window containing the "Advanced Examples" or "Basic Examples" chapter depending on whether or not he is an expert. Of course HyperBase is structured so that although code is embedded in the document, it is never actually seen by the reader, it just executes quietly in the background, implementing the semantics we have discussed above.

How does the document know whether the reader is expert or not? There are several possible ways. The simplest might be to add tags to various chapters in the document:

:- assert is_a(expert).

or

:- assert is_a(novice).

The ":-" simply says to HyperBase: "When a person reads a part of the document containing this piece of code, then execute the code that follows immediately." The code in this instance adds to a knowledge base the fact "is_a(expert)" or "is_a(novice)." These facts are equivalent to the IF-THEN rules:

IF
    TRUE
THEN
    is_a (expert).

Thus the act of reading a section of the document gives the Local Agent (which can be more HyperBase code) rules which it can then use to later guide the user through various links.

Expert systems can be embedded within HyperBase documents, and these systems can provide domain as well as structural knowledge. HyperBase was used to produce a review of a software system very similar to that described in the banking example provided at the beginning of this chapter.

Embedded within the document are rules like the following:

need :-
    performance,
    assert(visit($Need_Performance$)).

```
need :-
    external_access,
    assert(visit($Need_External_Access$)).

need :-
    user_defined_object,
    assert(visit($Need_User_Defined_Object$)).

need :-
    callable,
    assert(visit($Need_KML$)).

performance :- real_time(yes).
performance :- large_kbs(yes).
performance :- interactive(yes).
```

The first set of rules defines what the user might *need* to read (which attacks the Bootstrap problem discussed above). The rules can be read as follows:

If the user needs performance, then record the need to visit the chapter called Need_Performance so the Local Agent can act on it later.

If the user needs external access, then record the need to visit the chapter called Need_External_Access so the Local Agent can act on it later.

Etc.

How does the expert system know that performance is an important issue for the reader, as the reader may not himself be aware of this issue yet? The second set of rules begin to address this. They say:

If the reader's application is going to be real time, large or interactive, then performance will be an issue.

So now the problem is reduced to determining whether the reader's application falls into one of the three performance-intensive categories. HyperBase gives the Local Agent several ways to make this determination, the simplest being to display a dialog box over the document and ask the reader directly.

HyperBase allows quite complex rules representing both structural and domain semantics to be embedded within the document. The actual presence or absence of a button on the screen can also be determined by rules, so if the reader is an expert as defined above, many of the buttons linking to tutorial information could be turned off automatically. This gives a dynamic solution to the problems stemming from linkitis.

Current State of AI and Hypertext

We have looked at the way AI technology could redefine the concept of on-line documentation. Hyperdocuments will collaborate with their readers in the search for information. Some AI technologies, for instance rule-based expert systems, are already mature; some, like blackboarding and neural networks, are beginning to find wider acceptance, albeit slowly; and yet others, like the common sense knowledge in Lenat's Cyc program, are definitely in the research phase.

Some commercial products are appearing which combine aspects of AI and hypermedia. They do so in different ways and sometimes for different reasons, but nonetheless the fusion of technologies is taking place.

Neuron Data's *Nexpert Object* is an expert system shell available on many different computers. Nexpert Object allows the association of expert systems with HyperCard stacks. (HyperCard's own scripting language, HyperTalk, could itself be used to add rules to HyperCard stacks, but this language is very limited in this regard.)

Texas Instruments, Inc.'s HyperTrans is a system which, using AI techniques, performs an analysis of documentation and suggests the most appropriate hypertext links to create [See Chapter 9 by Riner].

HyperBase, from Cogent Software Ltd, combines a hypermedia capability with expert system capabilities of the Prolog language. It permits the development of intelligently adaptive documents.

1st Class HT, from 1st Class Expert Systems, is an expert system shell based on induction (it attempts to produce rules which explain known data) tightly coupled with a hypertext system. It has been used to develop diagnostic systems which can access maintenance documentation on-line.

KnowledgePro Windows, from Knowledge Garden, Inc, is an applications builder for the Microsoft Windows environment. It features support for decision trees and hypertext.

None of these products is anywhere near sufficient to support our knowledge warehouse concept. The different approaches they take all exhibit the same fragility when it comes to dealing with exceptionally large distributed documents.

Research into hypertext is ongoing. Work at Bellcore (Bell Communications Research Labs) includes Thoth II, an experimental system for embedding semantics in hypertext. Xerox's 'Notecards' (the model for Hypercard) is built in Lisp and has access to that AI language.

Computer Aided Document Engineering (CADE)

Embedding domain knowledge within a document is, as we have argued, a key to effective use of extremely large hypermedia documentation webs.

This does not happen automatically and the process of handcrafting a description of the semantics of each document would be time consuming at best, and impossible for lay authors at worst.

What is required is a structured document authoring system which embeds semantics on behalf of the author. In the same way that *Computer Aided Software Engineering* (CASE) tools provide a structured environment in which (ideally) a logical process for describing the requirements of a software system eventually lead to the automatic generation of code for that system, we propose CADE.

CADE systems will be very distinct from traditional document preparation (desktop publishing or word processing) systems.

CADE systems will permit authoring of nuggets of information rather than complete hyperdocuments per se. CADE systems will offer embedded semantics for nuggets based on widely accepted Concept Hierarchies, and will automatically generate new semantics for other nuggets as relationships between them are defined.

For example, if a nugget being authored is given the following semantics:

(Description of: Chemical Process: Catalysis)

and the author creates another nugget, linked to the first by an *Example of* relation (one of a number of possible relations supplied by the CADE system), then the semantics of the second nugget are evidently:

(Example of: Chemical Process: Catalysis)

The CADE system will assign these semantics automatically.

The uniform use of CADE system will result in documents with semantics already embedded. The moment they are published into a hypermedia web, the global agent can evaluate the semantics and link it in to the web accordingly. CADE is the appropriate development environment for hypermedia documentation as desk top publishing and word processors are for paper based documents. CADE systems will themselves use AI techniques to assign appropriate semantics to documents (as in the example above).

CADE, like CASE, is designed to bring an engineering discipline to what was previously regarded as an artistic endeavor. Documents produced in a CADE environment will finally be able to exploit the promise on-line hypermedia offers, but which so far has been unfulfilled.

About the Author

Alan Littleford

Dr. Alan Littleford is founder and President of Cogent Software, Ltd. Cogent develops and markets computer software and consults with major corporations in advanced computer technologies.

He is the architect of HyperBase, a Hypermedia system featuring embedded expert system capabilities, and the author of the underlying Cogent Prolog programming language. His current technical interests include the development of

CADE-based Hypermedia publishing and retrieval systems for very large documents.

Before founding Cogent Software in 1986, he was the founder of Prime Computer, Inc.'s Artificial Intelligence research laboratory, where he lead the development of an expert system capable of remotely diagnosing failures in Prime Computer hardware and software.

A mathematician *manqué*, Dr. Littleford received BSc and ARCS degrees from the Royal College of Science of Imperial College in London, and M.A. M.Phil. and Ph.D. degrees in mathematics and computer science from Columbia University.

A music buff, Dr. Littleford finds great delight in wrestling Beethoven to a draw at the piano. Unfortunately, his Bach is worse than his byte.

Dr. Littleford can be reached at: Cogent Software, Ltd., 21 William J. Heights, Framingham, MA 01701.

References

Cogent Software, Ltd. (1990). *Hyperbase User and Reference Manual.*

Lenat, D. and G. (1988). *The World According To Cyc*, MCC technical report 300-88.

Martin, J. (1990). *HyperDocuments and How To Create Them*, Prentice Hall, New Jersey.

Nelson, T. H. (1988). "Managing Immense Storage," *Byte* Magazine, January.

Parunak, H.V.D. (1991). "Ordering the Information Graph," *Hypertext / Hypermedia Handbook*, Emily Berk and Joseph Devlin (Ed.s), McGraw-Hill, New York, NY.

Riner, R. (1991). "Automated Conversion," *Hypertext / Hypermedia Handbook*, Emily Berk and Joseph Devlin (Ed.s), McGraw-Hill, New York, NY.

Shneiderman, B., Kreitzberg, C. and Berk, E. (1991). "Editing to Structure a Reader's Experience," *Hypertext / Hypermedia Handbook*, Emily Berk and Joseph Devlin (Ed.s), McGraw-Hill, New York, NY.

IX

Industrial Strength Hypertext

Industrial strength hypertexts are those designed to tackle big jobs.

In his second chapter for the Hypertext / Hypermedia Handbook, Van Parunak of ITI introduces the subject. ITI's charter is to bring new technologies up to industrial strength and to bring heavy industry up to date on new technologies. Thus, Dr. Parunak knows whereof he writes when he discusses what industries need from their hypertext systems.

Peter Benton's interest is in engineering applications based on emerging technologies. His view of workgroup hypertext is that it is evolving and still has far to go.

Douglas Engelbart, one of our favorite visionaries, writes about how following through on his grand designs can benefit heavy industry in general, and an aerospace company in particular.

23

Toward Industrial Strength Hypermedia

By H. Van Dyke Parunak
Industrial Technology Institute

Overview

The emerging technology of hypermedia offers a powerful new mechanism for solving common problems of information management faced by large commercial and industrial organizations. We begin by describing some of the problems that such users face. Then we outline those general characteristics of hypermedia that make it attractive as a solution to this challenge, and describe requirements, not yet commonly available in the market, that a hypermedia environment must satisfy to address these problems.

What's the Problem?

Large commercial organizations, such as manufacturers, are beginning to learn that their business is information at least as much as it is steel, or automobiles, or paper goods. In this section we survey some of the kinds of information they need to manipulate and the kinds of manipulations that they require, and then illustrate the tangled maze that can result. For the sake of concreteness, these illustrations focus on the domain of manufacturing, but the issues they raise are important for any large commercial undertaking.

Kinds of Documents

The information challenge facing a modern business is huge, not just in terms of the amount of information that must be integrated, but also in terms of the different kinds of material to be handled. Here are only a few of the many categories that any large firm needs to manipulate.

Contracts.   At the heart of business is the notion of one company doing something for someone else. As consumers, we tend to think of a private individual as the "someone else." More often, though, the "someone else" is another company, and the heart of the interaction is a detailed contract that spells out the expectations of the two companies about what will be done, when, how, and for what price. Project activity centers on this contract. Requirements spelled out in the contract must be satisfied by both companies if the transaction is to be successful. Thus, every other piece of information connected with the project must be traceable to the contract, and a manager who begins with the contract must be able to access everything that is relevant to it.

Standards.   Increasingly, equipment manufacturers are building their machines to conform to international standards. The protocols for electronic communications (such as MAP and TOP) are a prime example. A manufacturer who wants to build a new plant must understand these standards in order to purchase equipment intelligently and make it work together successfully. In domains where public standards are not yet well developed, many companies are beginning to adopt their own internal standards to make their internal operations more consistent and efficient. Standards, either external or internal, are useful only when they are consulted. But, as the volume of standards material increases, it becomes more difficult for engineers to understand their requirements and correlate them with project activity.

Government Regulations.   Increasingly, business operations concern not just the seller and the buyer, but the government as well. A mountain of federal regulations constrains how a firm operates its plants, the working conditions it must maintain for its employees, how it should handle hazardous materials, what records it must keep of its manufacturing processes, and a host of other details. Like standards, these regulations do no good unless they are read, understood, and integrated with operations. One major manufacturing firm employs thousands of people full time just to manage government regulations.

Corporate Mission and Policy.   Companies are not in business to follow standards and government regulations. What they are in business for is defined in statements of corporate mission and policy. While mission statements are usually succinct, the strategic plans that implement them can be massive, and will impact operations only to the extent that they are accessible to line managers.

Project Plans.   The success of any activity depends on its planning, and when an activity involves more than one person, that planning must be recorded and communicated among the participants. Large industrial projects, such as the introduction of a new product line or the upgrading of a factory, take many person-years to plan and yield a mountain of documents that outline what will be done when and at what cost. Tracking projects against these plans and dealing with the inevitable deviations is the essence of successful project execution, and requires that project staff be able to find and understand the portions of the plan that concern whatever they are doing at the moment.

Supplier Information. In contrast to their ancestors a generation ago, modern manufacturers seek to develop strategic alliances with their suppliers. More and more, firms that sell to other firms rather than to the public are seen as critical business partners by their customers. Once, their task was simply to deliver parts or materials at a minimum price. Now, they are taking an increasingly important role in quality assurance and even the design of their clients' products. As a result of this increased linkage, the information that needs to pass between the supplier and the builder of the final product has become far more complex than a bid against a set of engineering drawings. Manufacturers of consumer goods are expecting their suppliers to operate a virtual extension of their own internal information system, and the engineering data generated by the supplier must in turn be available to the customer, as though the supplier were just another division of its client.

Product Documentation. Many products today are complex enough to require at least an owner's manual. Those that are expensive enough to warrant repair (like home appliances and automobiles) also need maintenance manuals for use by service personnel. Discrete products are not the only ones that must come with documentation. The users of batch products like steel and polymers need accurate, detailed information on the physical and chemical properties of each shipment. Keeping the documentation up to date with the product is a major challenge. Because technical publications are usually produced by a different part of the organization than the one that produces the product, it is easy for engineering changes to the product to escape the notice of those responsible for publications. The result is documentation that is at best inconsistent with the product it accompanies.

Product Designs. Within a company, products take shape through a process of conceptualization, design, process engineering, and finally production. The design of a product such as an automobile consists of acres of engineering drawings and technical specifications, supported by tons of engineering analyses. Consumer goods have more technical content today than ever before (antilock braking systems and automatic climate control in automobiles, for instance). Increased technical content in the product means more complexity in the design. This information must first of all be shared efficiently among members of the design team, to ensure that the overall design is consistent with itself. As the design develops, it must be accessible to engineers designing the processes by which the product will be made, so that they can evaluate how producible the product will be and suggest modifications that might reduce the cost of manufacture.

Production Programs. Just as designs move between product designer and process engineer, machine programs and process plans move between process engineer and the equipment operator on the shop floor. Just as process engineers need ways to comment on the producibility of a design, operators need to give feedback on the input they receive. This input comes in many forms, including (to name only a few) numerical control programs for machining tools, ladder logic for material handling systems, robot programs, and process routings.

Maintenance Instructions. Manufacturing comes to its focus with the workers operating machines to create a product. Nothing can throw the system out of focus faster than a broken machine. Some numbers can illustrate this; every minute of lost time on a machine that produces ten to twelve $200 parts a minute is worth $2000 or more. In fact, if that machine is a bottleneck for the rest of the production line, the cost of the lost time is the value of the total amount of product that could have been produced during that period. Having backup machines available at $20 million per machine is not always feasible. When a machine breaks, it must be repaired as quickly as possible. Even better, it needs regular maintenance so that it won't break unexpectedly.

Twenty-million-dollar machines are not just expensive, they are excruciatingly complex. The maintenance manuals that accompany them occupy yards of bookshelf space and do not capture the intuitive hunches that experienced maintenance personnel develop (and that are lost to the company when they retire or move elsewhere). Even if the necessary information is in the manuals, finding it is a time consuming and uncertain process. Capturing the sounds made by healthy and sick machines and videotaping the correct procedures for replacing malfunctioning parts are promising new directions, but pose increased information management challenges.

Internal Business Reports. Producing, updating, and extracting information from the various categories of documents that we have reviewed present a formidable challenge, and we have not even considered the information that represents the focus of attention of the traditional MIS organization, that is, the day-to-day data on the business performance of the firm.

The modern trend in management is to push decision-making responsibility as low as possible in the organization. This strategy requires more staff than ever before to access, understand, and act upon the firm's business information, including budgets, sales and expense reports, production schedules, order projections and consolidated profit and loss statements.

Required Operations

These diverse documents refer to each other copiously and often exhibit implicit dependencies on each other. Typical information management problems include:

* appending personal notes to electronic files, just as people traditionally write in the margins of paper documents or attach yellow sticky notes;

- correlating related but distinct documents (such as contract requirements and details in a project plan) with one another;
- identifying all the documents that must be changed if a document on which they depend changes (for example, keeping product documentation consistent with revised design documents);
- maintaining histories of products, as originally built and as modified; and
- maintaining histories of standards and regulations, and guaranteeing that project files are linked to the governing editions of those standards and regulations (which are often the editions in effect when a contract was signed, not necessarily the latest editions).

An Illustration

Figure 23.1 identifies some of the information that people operating within an integrated manufacturing environment need to access, and suggests how that information is interrelated.

The five circles reflect five areas of activity in the manufacture of durable consumer goods such as appliances and automobiles.

- Design. Determines what will be made.
- Analysis. Provides simulations and tests to ensure that the design is sound.
- Process Engineering. Derives plans to produce the product.
- Production. Executes these plans.
- Logistics. Maintains the product once it leaves the plant.

Design begins with conceptual studies (not shown in the figure), and draws heavily on supplier catalogs to make use of standard parts. It issues queries to Analysis and receives results that may lead to modifications in the Design. The final design must be reflected in technical manuals that are maintained and distributed by Logistics. The final design also specifies material requirements that can direct advance ordering by Production.

The main output of the design activity consists of engineering drawings accompanied by a wealth of dimensions, tolerancing, and material details, delivered to Process Engineering. Process Engineering in turn produces process plans for Production.

All of the functions require access to a consistent set of corporate and external standards. The increased use of computer equipment in all functions means that operations and maintenance manuals must be readily available. Each function needs ways to offer timely comments on the material it receives from other functions. Workers need to be able to track where a product or process is in the chain, so as to manage the overall workflow.

Figure 23.1 looks busy and tangled, and yet it illustrates only a small part of the information that ties a modern manufacturing operation together. It backs up our original contention that the business of manufacturing is about information as much as it is about product.

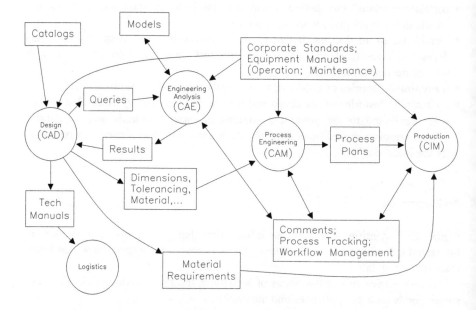

Figure 23.1   The Manufacturing Information Maze.

How Huge is Huge?

Hypermedia is currently the most promising technology to cope with this challenge. How huge would a hypermedia system need to be to get its arms around Figure 23.1? Our review of the problem shows that there are many dimensions of hugeness to consider. We can group them under those that relate to the information itself, those that relate to the users of that information, and those derived from timing requirements.

Information-Related Hugeness. When we think of a huge hyperbase, our first inclination is to ask how many nodes and links it contains. The sheer mass of material is staggering. It is a truism in the aerospace industry that a new airplane cannot carry the weight of its own documentation. Many hypermedia systems pride themselves on being able to manage a single CD-ROM database, with an overall size on the order of half a billion characters, but the kind of system envisioned by Figure 23.1 is measured in the trillions (10^{12}) of characters, or (with nodes on the order of a thousand characters) billions of nodes and thus multiple billions of links. The mass of material to be managed is magnified by the many diverse kinds of information that it contains. Even if the material were homogeneous, and thus amenable to conventional database technology, the task would be formidable, but we are confronted here with text, graphics, audio, and video, addressing different questions and produced on a wide variety of parent systems.

User-Related Hugeness. The large number of users who must access the corporate information resource further complicates our challenge. We must consider the effects of hundreds of people accessing the system at the same time, some of them changing its contents while others seek to retrieve an up-to-date and consistent picture of their enterprise. These users have different perspectives on the information that they retrieve, and need to be able to view it in ways that best suit their purposes; the shop foreman reads the order projections to set the production schedule for the next month, while the accounting office reads it to manage the company's cash flow. Additionally, the users (and their information) are geographically distributed. It's not uncommon for an automobile made in the US to have an engine from Japan and a braking system from Europe, yet the information generated in these scattered locations must be available at each of them if the overall product is to function as a whole.

Time-Related Hugeness. There is an absolute measure to the distance from my home to my office (about three miles). But the distance seems very different when I'm late for an early-morning meeting. The faster we need to move from one place to another, the farther apart they seem to be. The same principle holds true in an information system. The faster one needs to move from one point in it to another, the bigger it seems. Timing is an important constraint in modern manufacturing. Whether we are looking for the appropriate maintenance information to take advantage of a five minute gap in the production schedule of a transfer press or trying to bring a new product to market before our competition does, the pressure is on to deliver information faster today than yesterday, and even faster tomorrow, and that pressure makes an already immense information delivery challenge even larger.

What Does Hypermedia Have To Offer?

Hypermedia is a set of nodes of information that users can link together and among which they can navigate in real time. Hypermedia differs from traditional information management technologies (such as databases, free text, and expert systems) in several ways, including the user interface, the kinds of information that can be managed, the structure that the information must have, and management of the life-cycle of the information system.

User Interface

The distinctive characteristic of hypermedia is its user interface. In fact, from one point of view, hypermedia is a user interface that can serve as a front-end to more conventional systems. As a highly interactive system that supports ad-hoc user "what if" questions, it resembles expert systems and contrasts with the usual report or form oriented database or free text system. It is even more interactive than an expert system. With an expert system, the user first poses a query and then receives a response, but hypermedia permits the query and response phases to proceed in parallel. As one browses, one is continually retrieving information, and browsing (the query activity) continues until the desired response has been obtained.

Kinds of Information

In general, hypermedia offers the ability to manage a much wider array of material than do other technologies, including text, graphics, video, audio, and executable code. Other systems can store any of these kinds of information and present them as the product of a query, but hypermedia is unique in its ability to retrieve against them. For example, a graphical database could store names and digitized portraits and present the portraits in response to queries consisting of names, but it would be much more difficult to enter the system with a photograph of a person (other than the photograph stored in the database) and emerge with the person's name. Because hypermedia relies on the pattern recognition capabilities of the human rather than (in this case) on scene analysis, it would be able to support the retrieval task from portrait to name. A common hypermedia implementation defines hot spots on a graphic image and permits the user to pick those spots to move to other information. This type of functionality is difficult even to imagine in other information management metaphors.

Required Structure

Material stored in a database must follow a fixed relational format. Every record has the same fields, and each field typically has a highly-constrained length and format with fairly limited matching algorithms. Free-text systems relax the constraints on the size of individual fields and offer a richer language for describing the contents of a field, but still require a regular field structure for each document. The knowledge bases underlying expert systems provide much richer structuring mechanisms, often with the expressiveness of first order logic. These mechanisms permit knowledge bases to represent the semantics as well as the syntax of their contents, while (relational) databases typically store only the syntax. Hypermedia systems offer semantic richness of data storage comparable to that used in expert systems. In fact, a hyperdocument can be viewed as an expert system whose inference engine is not a computer but a human being.

Life-Cycle Costs

Because humans remain much more closely in the loop with hypermedia than with other information management technologies, preparation of information for use in the system can be less burdensome than with other technologies. The human browser can compensate to some degree for inadequate or incorrect preparation, if the environment is flexible enough to permit users to address documents directly.

What Will It Take to Solve the Problem?

The market for hypermedia environments is characteristic of an emerging technology. Various systems demonstrate different combinations of desirable features, but no one system currently has the combination of features to support the needs that we see in our applications. In this section we review the enabling technologies that have led to the current blossoming of interest in hypermedia, and then outline some requirements, not yet widely satisfied in commercial products, that are important for true industrial-strength hypermedia.

Current Enabling Technologies

It was almost fifty years ago, in the early 1940s, that Vannevar Bush conceived of what we now call hypermedia. [Bush, 1945, Nyce and Kahn, 1989] His vision was only barely within the technical horizon, and until about five years ago, only a few academics toyed with his concepts. Suddenly, we find ourselves in the midst of a burst of enthusiasm that is reminiscent of the emergence of commercial-grade expert systems about ten years ago. A review of the technologies that have made this possible helps us understand why hypermedia is so much in vogue and what foundations are available for constructing the next generation of information systems.

It was the computer that first permitted researchers to implement Bush's ideas. Until the development of the integrated circuit, computers were too expensive for dedicated use by individuals except in research environments, but the rapid drop in the cost of high-speed processors now brings computer-based information management within the reach of a large population.

The essence of hypermedia is displaying information to people and allowing them to take action by pointing. A hard-copy terminal or teletypewriter, the staple of early computer systems, is completely inappropriate for this approach, and the display systems used in early research on hypermedia (such as Engelbart's NLS/Augment [Englebart, 1968]) were, like the computers that drove them, out of reach of private users. A page in a small book contains about 2000 characters. Users have been acclimated by centuries of book reading to expect at least this much context in front of them at once. Thus, the first display that is minimally adequate even for primitive hypertext is the 25x80 screen of the common personal computer. The emergence of megapixel displays for workstations permits current systems to display enough material at once to give users a reasonable context for selection, and the rapid proliferation of pointing devices (including the mouse, touch screens, light pads, digitizing tablets, joy sticks, and track balls) has made a "point and shoot" approach both technically affordable and familiar to a wide audience.

Again taking a small book (say, 200 pages) as a guide to the amounts of information to be managed, we can see that the ability to store at least 400,000 characters (200 pages of 2000 characters each) is another minimal requirement for giving users electronic access to book-like material. Magnetic tape, the standard persistent storage medium for the first several decades of the computer age, is inherently unsuitable to the point-and-shoot world of hypermedia because it does not give random access to its contents, and the earliest rotating media held only a few hundred thousand characters. The development of inexpensive high-density storage, most notably the CD-ROM (with capacities approaching a gigabyte), makes it feasible to have large amounts of material on-line and available for access by hypermedia.

The preceding technologies are necessary for any hypermedia system, not just those of industrial size and complexity. A stand-alone hypermedia system intended for a single user and handling only materials prepared expressly for its manipulation requires little more. To support the plethora of diverse materials and users that characterize the industrial environment, hypermedia (like any other industrial computer system) relies increasingly on open systems and standards. The industrial environment includes equipment from many vendors. A hypermedia system can integrate text files from word processors with engineering drawings from CAD workstations and numerical data from a mainframe-based MIS system only if the formats of these materials are published and conform to reasonable standards, either *de jure* (such as ASCII encoding for textual information) or *de facto* (such as .PIC file format for graphics). Recent years have seen an explosion in the development of standards for computers, and the *National Institute for Standards and Technology* (NIST, formerly the National Bureau of Standards) has begun to explore the need for standards especially directed toward hypermedia. [Moline, et al., 1990]

One area where the development of existing standards is especially important for industrial hypermedia is in the emergence of low-cost, standardized networks that permit the physical interconnection of computers. In particular, the OSI layered model of communications is gaining widespread acceptance, and offers system designers a powerful mechanism for constructing hypermedia systems that are independent of the particular communications system in use, so long as it conforms to a standard set of protocols. [IEEE, 1984] The resulting interconnectivity gives a hypermedia system access to information throughout the organization and permits it to integrate this information for users.

Areas of Needed Development

As hypermedia develops its full potential in industrial settings, it will take on a number of characteristics in four areas:

- the larger computing environment in which it operates
- the capabilities of the hypermedia engine itself
- the interface it presents to users
- the ability to do much of the task of linking documents automatically

All of these capabilities exist in some form in the research community, but several of them still pose significant developmental challenges, and they are not yet commercially available in a single product.

The Environment. To gain wide acceptance in industry, a hypermedia system must run on a variety of delivery vehicles. The need to interact with other systems places a premium on the use of standards. Multiple users should be able to access the system concurrently, and the system should be able to access information distributed throughout the organization.

• Multiple delivery vehicles. Large industrial users are beginning to insist on Sun-class UNIX machines as their common denominator workstation. [Beal, 1988] Small firms will find anything more than a personal computer too much of an investment, but if they sell to large firms, they still need a way to access their clients' systems. Even within a large firm, some users do not require the full functionality of a workstation-based system: think of an army of clericals who are doing document entry and link maintenance by way of scanners and OCR. Systems need to offer full functionality on large machines, with consistent subsets available on smaller machines.

• Standards-Based. The presentation should be X-Windows based, to assure maximum portability across different platforms. Use of a policy package such as Motif, Nextstep, or OpenLook will ensure a common look and feel for the interface [Nye, 1989, Beaver, 1990]. Emerging hypermedia standards from the NIST working group are important; the Dexter model [Halasz and Schwartz, 1990] offers an excellent foundation for such standards, and the Intermedia exchange format [Brown University, 1989] has the advantage of being publicly available.

• Multiuser Access. Systems need to be designed to accommodate multiple users who are manipulating (and in some cases modifying) the system concurrently. Distributed database technology offers a number of well-developed techniques to see to it that concurrent interactions don't leave the hyperbase in an inconsistent state. Furthermore, the vision of a single network of information spanning an entire corporation raises important issues of security and access control. Not all users should have access to all of the information on the network. The ability of hypermedia to provide multiple routes to the same data makes access control particularly challenging.

• Distributed Users and Data. Users in a large firm need desktop access to information, so the hypermedia system itself must either be accessible from remote locations or (preferably) distributed among different workstations. Furthermore, the data made available by the system will not all reside at a local user's machine. Most current systems are not networked, and require all information to be local or at least available via a transparent *network file system* (NFS).

The Engine. The mechanisms provided for maintaining and traversing the information network should support an information web that is stored separately from the documents, and should permit users to apply several such webs simultaneously to a set of documents, with structuring devices to reduce the cognitive complexity of the system. Users should be able to link to applications as easily as to previously existing information.

- Web-Based. Most current systems embed full linking information in the documents managed by the system. This approach is fine for a relatively short document or for one that is written from the ground up as hypermedia. It is extremely cumbersome for managing documents that were not originally intended for use in a hypermedia environment, or that are distributed on CD-ROM's. Imagine a firm that receives twenty CD-ROM's a month of updated government regulations. Adding internal linking information to these documents would require maintaining more than ten gigabytes of on-line storage for the modified documents, and in some cases government auditors may look askance on firms using modified rather than original documents as their working copies. Furthermore, if links must be stored in the text of the document, different users cannot maintain distinct sets of links for the same document (and thus cannot write their own notes "in the margin" without publishing these notes to other users).

  The solution to this problem is to house links and notes in a separate data structure, a "web," as in the Intermedia system. [Yankelovich, et al., 1988] The user interface merges the document and the web to produce an integrated display. The information that one sees in an anchor on the screen comes from the document, but the marking on the screen that designates it as hot and the action that results from clicking on it are defined in the web.

- Multiple Webs. Because an industrial system needs to accommodate multiple users, it should be able to integrate several different webs for the same document (such as an "official" roadmap and individual annotations), with the resulting links being the union of those in the individual webs. Careful thought needs to be given to handling overlapping anchors. For example, picking an anchor that corresponds to multiple links should give a list of links for further choice, but if the links are the same, only one should be shown. Different webs may have different permissions associated with them; of the several webs that my current session merges with a given text file, I may be able to edit some but not others.

- Web Structuring. The large number of nodes in an industrial hypermedia network will quickly become unnavigable unless the connections are structured to help users understand where they are, decide where they want to go, and plan a way to go there. Techniques to structure the network fall into two major categories: constraining the patterns of connectivity among nodes, and assigning types to the links between nodes. Both are discussed in detail in Chapter 20 of this book.

- Application Integration. The information that lies at the end of a link may not always be stored statically. It may need to be computed from current data by way of a spreadsheet, or retrieved from a database system, or inferred with an expert system. Link traversal alone is not the best technique for retrieving all the forms of information that the system must handle. To be most effective, a hypermedia system should be able to serve as a front-end to a wide variety of information management tools, packaging the different procedures needed to access them so that the user perceives a common interface.

Interface Characteristics   Hypermedia is first of all a user interface. Existing hypermedia systems have experimented with a number of interface techniques, and several are particularly useful in an industrial setting: full multimedia, integrated browsing and editing, navigational helps, and alternate movement mechanisms.

- Full Multimedia. Manufacturing information is not only textual, but extensively graphical (in the form of engineering drawings), with important promising applications for video and audio (for example, in helping operators recognize the sound of a defective machine or understand the manipulations required for a difficult operation). Industrial applications will require the full range of multimedia.
- Integrated Browsing and Editing. Some hypermedia systems employ a very different mode when editing documents and building links than when browsing. For example, links may be constructed by placing explicit markers in the text and writing fragments of code. In an industrial setting, hypermedia will be used by people with relatively little computer experience, both to retrieve information and to record information for the use of others. Such users will have little patience with a system that requires them to do "programming." The system should look as much like a simple word processor or paint program as possible, and link generation should be by straightforward point-and-shoot operations. The multiple-web capability means that users can always add their own annotations to material or generate their private connections, so there is no such thing as a purely "read-only" hyperbase, and the ability to do such operations should be readily accessible when browsing.
- Navigational Helps. We have suggested that the hypermedia engine should provide ways to structure the web, by supporting typed links and regular patterns of linkage. Elsewhere, this Handbook describes particular mechanisms to make these structuring devices useful to users. These mechanisms include high-level maps of large portions of the network (preferably filtered by link types to reduce the complexity of the display); history mechanisms to help users recall where they've been; and scripting techniques to provide a turnpike through a dense information landscape. Techniques such as these are particularly important for systems of the size and complexity needed to integrate a large commercial firm.
- Alternate Movement Mechanisms. The standard mechanism in hypermedia for moving from one node to another is link traversal. While powerful, this mechanism is not sufficient for large systems. Sometimes a user knows a description of a destination but not a chain of links to go there. In such a case, it is annoying to be restricted to a step-by-step search. Various systems provide different alternative mechanisms for moving rapidly between remote locations in the hyperbase. Maps usually permit users to pick any desired node and move there directly, without explicitly following a connecting path. Some systems provide various levels of free text search capability among their textual nodes. In others, nodes have publicly visible addresses or names and can be invoked directly.

Automatic Linking.   For broad classes of information, useful links can be generated automatically. This capability is extremely important for integrating large quantities of material (such as government regulations) into a hypermedia system, and for coping with frequent upgrades. Examples of feasible automatic linking include glossary support, automated tables of contents, and formulaic references [see Chapters 9 and 10 by Riner and Rearick, in this book].

- Automatic Table of Contents. Several commercial firms offer systems to identify portions of documents automatically and build appropriate links to a table of contents. Typically, a document definition file tells the system how to identify different parts of the document, and the system produces a hierarchical table of contents from which one can link directly to the text. Documents that are available in a mark-up language such as SGML or Scribe are particularly easy to parse for this purpose. [Coombs, 1987]
- Formulaic References. Large portions of a commercial hyperbase will consist of material (such as government publications, standards, or legal material) to which other documents refer with highly stylized reference formats (e.g., '301.18(a)'). The standard form of such references makes it relatively straightforward to identify them automatically and generate links to the associated text.
- Glossary Support. Because the users in a large commercial system come from many different parts of the organization, they will need help in understanding specialized vocabulary in information from other units. Systems should support a glossary link from any word to an appropriate definition. Such links need not be coded explicitly. A glossary pick on any word can have the effect of searching the glossary for that word, and returning the definition if one is available.

Conclusion

Many current hypermedia systems are designed as closed, stand-alone systems that deal with relatively contained bodies of material in proprietary formats. Modern industry offers a wide variety of applications for hypermedia, but requires a more open, distributed approach. Nothing that is needed is without precedent somewhere in the hypermedia research community, but the integration of these features and their offering in a single commercial set of tools will open the door to unprecedented growth in the impact and popularity of this new technology.

About the Author

Dr. H. Van Dyke Parunak

Dr. Parunak is a Scientific Fellow at the Industrial Technology Institute (ITI) in Ann Arbor, Michigan, a not-for-profit contract research organization that promotes the renewal and continued vitality of North American manufacturing through appropriate use of advanced technologies.

His international training (five graduate degrees) and range of research and practical experience (spanning biology, linguistics, philosophy, artificial intelligence, computer science, and manufacturing engineering) provide a broad foundation for innovative and effective solutions to challenging problems. As a leading strategist in emerging information technologies, he helps ITI's clients determine the appropriate information management tools for different applications and integrate these into unified information systems with consistent human interfaces.

ITI's expertise includes not only the software and computer science disciplines essential to engineering hypermedia systems, but also the computer communications techniques that permit truly distributed information systems and the understanding of organizational design and performance enhancement methods that can turn these systems to the competitive advantage of their users.

Dr. Parunak may be contacted at the Industrial Technology Institute, P. O. Box 1485, Ann Arbor, MI 48106.

References

Beal, E. (1988). "A CAD/CAM Integration Saga Unfolds at General Motors," *Computer Graphics Review, 3:6* (November/December), 26–32.

Beaver, J. (1990). "GUIs: Putting A Friendly Face on UNIX," *CommUNIXactions, 10:1* (January-February), 8–13.

Brown University (1989). "An Interchange Format for Hypertext Systems: The Intermedia Model," *TR 89-6*, Institute for Research in Information and Scholarship (IRIS), Brown University.

Bush V. (1945). "As We May Think," *Atlantic Monthly, 176(1)*, 101–108.

Coombs, J. H., Renear A. H., and DeRose S.J. (1987). "Markup Systems and the Future of Scholarly Text Processing," *Communications of the ACM* 30:11, 933–947.

Englebart, D., and English, W. K. (1968). "A Research Center for Augmenting Human Intellect," *AFIPS Conference Proceedings, Fall Joint Computer Conference*, 395–410.

Halasz, F. and Schwartz, M. (1990). "The Dexter Hypertext Reference Model," 95–133.

Moline, J., Benigni, D., and Baronas, J. (Eds.) (1990). "Proceedings of the Hypertext Standardization Workshop," January 16–18, *National Institute of Standards and Technology*, NIST Publication SP500-178.

Nye, A. (1989). "The X Window System Protocol," *UnixWorld, 7:9* (September), 105–113.

Nyce, M., and Kahn P. (1989). "Innovation, Pragmatism and Technological Continuity: Vannevar Bush's Memex," *Journal of the American Society for Information Science*, 40:3 (May), 214–221.

Parunak, H. V. D. (1991). "Ordering the Information Graph," *Hypertext / Hypermedia Handbook*, emily Berk and Joseph Devlin (Ed.s), McGraw-Hill, New York, NY.

Rearick, T. (1991). "Automating the Conversion of Text into Hypertext," *Hypertext / Hypermedia Handbook*, emily Berk and Joseph Devlin (Ed.s), McGraw-Hill, New York, NY.

Riner, R. (1991). "Automated Conversion," *Hypertext / Hypermedia Handbook*, emily Berk and Joseph Devlin (Ed.s), McGraw-Hill, New York, NY.

IEEE (1984). Special Issue on Open Systems Interconnection (OSI), *Proceedings of the IEEE, 71:12*, (1984).

Yankelovich, N., Haan, B.J., Meyrowitz, N. K., and Drucker, S. M. (1988). "Intermedia: The Concept and the Construction of a Seamless Information Environment," *IEEE Computer*, 21:1, 81–96.

24

Knowledge-Domain Interoperability and an Open Hyperdocument System

By Douglas C. Engelbart
Bootstrap Project, Stanford University

This work was sponsored by grants from the Kapor Family Foundation, Sun Microsystems, Inc., and Apple Computer, Inc.

Introduction

This paper anticipates that the tools and methods of *computer-supported cooperative work* (CSCW) will become harnessed with revolutionary benefit to the ongoing, everyday knowledge work within and between larger organizations. Toward that end, the following concerns about interoperability between knowledge-work domains will have to be met, and something such as the *open hyperdocument system* must become available for widespread use.

As computers become cheaper and we learn more about harnessing them within our cooperative work, they will come to support an increasing number of different domains of knowledge work. Moreover, the sphere of computer-supported activities within each domain will steadily expand as more function and more skill become employed.

It is predictable that increasing functional overlap will occur as these expanding domains begin to overlap. It has become apparent to me that someday all of our basic knowledge-work domains will be integrated within one coherent *organizational knowledge workshop*. This leads to thinking about an overall, integrated architectural approach to the ever larger set of common knowledge work capabilities emerging within a multi-vendor environment.

Much has been accomplished to date in standards and protocols in the highly active field of networked workstations & servers, where *interoperability between hardware and/or software modules* has become a central theme.

This paper considers *the interoperability between knowledge domains*. This interoperability theme will be increasingly important for a workable CSCW framework as the scope and degree of CSCW increases. Dramatic increases will predictably create a marked paradigm shift about how to organize and operate cooperative human endeavors. I think that two phenomena will yield changes and a paradigm shift that will make this interoperability of paramount importance:

- With a relatively unbounded technological frontier together with immense and growing economic pressure, the speed, size, and cost of computers, memory, and digital communications will continue improving by geometric progression.
- Awareness and importance of CSCW is emerging, with a predictable trend toward our doing more and more of our personal and cooperative knowledge-work online.

Assuming an inevitably gigantic scale for our interknit *CSCW world* provides some important guidance for the continuing investment of our business resources and professional time.

For one thing, each year earlier that an effective degree of knowledge-domain interoperability is in place within important organizational or institutional domains could be worth hundreds of millions of dollars and could mean the difference between vitality and sluggishness.

And for another, we would prefer to avoid investing our research, product development, or organizational-change resources toward ends that won't be interoperably compatible within that future, radically different paradigm.

Interoperability in an Individual's Knowledge Workshop

To begin with some very basic knowledge-domain interoperability issues, consider your own (future?) *Computer-Supported Personal Work* (CSPW). Assume that you have acquired a fairly comprehensive, online *knowledge workshop*; you have found better and better software packages to support the kinds of tasks shown in Figure 24.1.

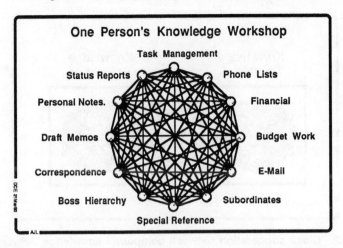

Figure 24.1 Each functional domain is a candidate for a working interchange with all others.

Consider what you will some day have when your individual workshop inevitably becomes truly integrated. Between the E-Mail and the task management files, or the status reports, or whatever, you really would like to tie these functional domains together with a flexible free-flow of information and linkages.

What kind of interoperability do you have now? I happen to think that the interoperability provided today within most CSPW domains has a great deal of improvement yet to be pursued. But I'd resist any serious arguments about this unless it be approached within the context of a coherent *CSCW interoperability framework* such as outlined below. Let me say in warning, though, that from such a framework I will contend that the marketplace for CSPW will change drastically as CSCW takes hold within our larger organizations and their inter-organizational communities.

Interoperability in a Group's Knowledge Workshop

Suppose that you and a colleague each have a fully integrated CSPW domain, comprised of nicely interoperable sub-domains as in Figure 24.1. And suppose that you want to work together online. Consider the interoperability between your respective knowledge-work domains, as in Figure 24.2.

Now you're faced with a new challenge and a new problem. You might set it up so you have a few lines that cross between domains, but why stop there? When do two people in intense cooperative work NOT need total interoperability? In fact they depend on it heavily in the paper world. Why not online?

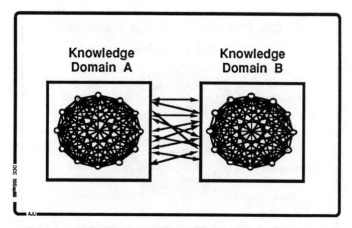

Figure 24.2   Close cooperation between compound knowledge domains puts new demands on the knowledge-work interchange.

Interoperability Across Time and Space

Yet another example of multiple domains is found in the familiar time-place matrix shown in Figure 24.3. In many cases, activities in the different quadrants involve the same substantive work content. Is knowledge-work interoperability between the quadrant domains an issue? Very much so. For example, face-to-face meetings need to flexibly utilize anything from the whole organizational knowledge base, and the meeting's records should immediately become an integral part of that same base for later-time work.

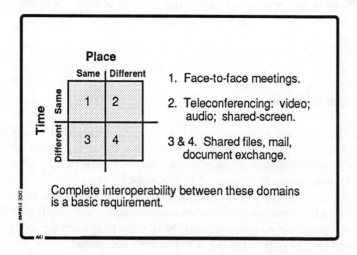

Figure 24.3   Collaborative processes generally considered.

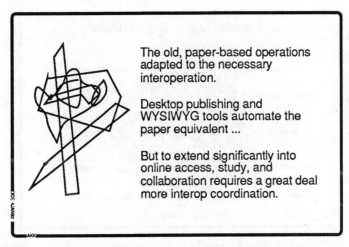

The old, paper-based operations adapted to the necessary interoperation.

Desktop publishing and WYSIWYG tools automate the paper equivalent ...

But to extend significantly into online access, study, and collaboration requires a great deal more interop coordination.

Figure 24.4   Consider some knowledge domains with which you intersect significantly.

A Point About Online Group Knowledge Work

The matrix in Figure 24.3 is very neat and ordered. In Figure 24.4 I offer another picture of multi-domain, group knowledge work which isn't so cleanly laid out. This reflects how I feel about the various knowledge-work domains with which my CSPW domain must interoperate.

The purpose of interoperability is to avoid having information islands between which information cannot flow effectively. Since we grew up in a paper-based framework, we've given little thought about how much exchange and interoperability support we really do have, and how much we depend upon it. To be interoperable in our CSPW world we could simply print out and hand over the hard copy. With WYSIWYG screens and desktop publishing, we're doing that with nicer paper, faster.

So when we inevitably move from computer-supported paper generation and exchange to computer-supported online creation and exchange, we will need the same level of interoperability. And as the number and scale of knowledge domains involved in a given CSCW *web* increases, so does the need for *online interoperability*.

Interoperability Across Knowledge Domains

To appreciate the extraordinary complexity of heavy industrial knowledge work, and the associated requirements for interoperability, consider the important functional domains within a large manufacturing organization producing a complex product, such as an airplane. It is a serious enough challenge to provide effective interoperability among the knowledge workers within any one of the domains in Figure 24.5; just consider the inter-domain challenge. And then consider that some

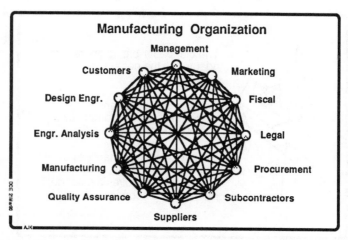

Figure 24.5   Each functional domain is a candidate for working interchange with all others.

of these domains, such as customers and suppliers, exist *outside* the organization, each with its own equally complex multi-domain structure.

The Large Matrix Organization

An interesting example comes from my time at McDonnell Douglas Corporation, where I marvelled at how something as complex as one of their airplanes gets a business plan, and gets designed, manufactured, flown, and supported. Look at any given project or program (*P1* through *Pn* in Figure 24.6), and the functional support that's required (*F1* through *Fn*), and the exchange that needs to happen within this matrix.

Each function has to share and exchange working information with many programs, and each program has to share and exchange with many functional support areas. Wherever there isn't mutual interoperability, the workers at the domain intersections will have to suffer with inter-domain switching and converting—which is very expensive. Depending upon this kind of functional program matrix environment will require knowledge-domain interoperability across the whole organization.

The Aerospace Industry as a Case in Point

To really appreciate the magnitude of this situation, let's look inside one of those aerospace programs:

A Large Aerospace Program.   McDonnell Aircraft Company is participating in a bid to build the *Advanced Tactical Fighter* (ATF) for the Air Force. It's possibly one of the most technically complex products anyone has ever dealt with.

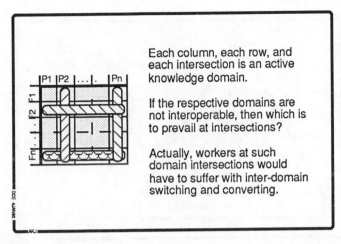

Each column, each row, and each intersection is an active knowledge domain.

If the respective domains are not interoperable, then which is to prevail at intersections?

Actually, workers at such domain intersections would have to suffer with inter-domain switching and converting.

Figure 24.6   Consider the domains within a matrix organization of projects and function.

On top of that, they have an urgent mandate to start practicing *concurrent engineering*, where the designers have to work concurrently with the manufacturing engineers. This will require intense back-and-forth cooperation between the two knowledge domains, which no one really knows yet how to do on such a large scale.

Also, significant design and manufacturing problems are often delegated to the first-tier suppliers shown in Figure 24.7, so the cooperation with that tier is also close and intense. Then the first tiers hand off to the second tiers, and so on. So, all-in-all, you have something like 6,000 companies cooperating—each a separate, complex, knowledge-work domain. They are expected to keep track of all business- and technical-exchange records throughout the design and manufacturing process.

I should point out here that the arrows in the diagram represent the legal flow of contracts being awarded. The actual exchange of documents would be shown as a two-way flow of continual negotiation and refinement throughout the design and manufacturing process—developing the specifications, proposals, change orders, testing records, and so on. And for any part within any airplane, the manufacturer must later be able to identify when it was delivered, by whom, and even who was the shop foreman at the time of assembly.

Also, a program of this size in the aerospace world would typically comprise a 10 to 30 year life cycle. So when we talk of Different Time/Same Place, and Different Time/Different Place (Figure 24.3), the definition of "Time" includes decades, not just hours or days. Even in a short time span and without turnover, it is not unheard of for a project team, in any industry, to occasionally lose sight of some important design decision trails, and consequently waste time and money repeating old discussions or past mistakes. Consider the likelihood, and the cost, of such lost history occurring in this long-term environment. To comply with the Department of Defense's (DoD's) forthcoming *Computer-aided Acquisition and Logistic Support* (CALS) mandate, all documents exchanged between the DoD

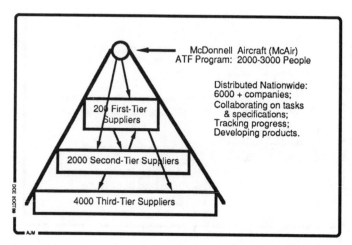

Figure 24.7 Islands in supplier hierarchy of a major aircraft program would be very costly.

and its contractors must be transmitted, updated, and managed in a standard, computerized form—a truly gigantic interoperability challenge.

Two Companies Teaming. The situation is even more complex: as with most new, large-system, DoD procurements, the Air Force requires ATF bidders to be joint-venture teams comprised of major aerospace firms. In this case, McDonnell Aircraft is teaming with Northrop Aircraft. Figure 24.8 shows how Northrop would form its part of the program, with several thousand workers internally, in close collaboration with several tiers of suppliers.

And then picture the two companies as a team (Figure 24.9), and consider the intense demands for interoperable recorded document exchange across functional support and project domains within this ATF-contractor team—within each company, between the two companies, and between them and the DoD (remembering the CALS initiative).

And then consider Figure 24.10 and all of the recorded interchange between these two companies and their supplier hierarchies, throughout the multi-decade life cycle of the program.

The Web of Aerospace Relationships. Now consider all the other large-program webs of aerospace contractors, suppliers, and customers represented by the small sub-set shown in Figure 24.11. A great many of these suppliers and customers will work with many of the same contractors. The complexity becomes staggering. Within such an inter-knit web of cooperative knowledge domains, there is no practical solution for effective interoperability other than industry-wide standards—adhered to by contractors, customers, and suppliers.

And every other large industrial sector must also achieve CSCW interoperability. And those sectors must themselves interact effectively. The CSCW-interoper-

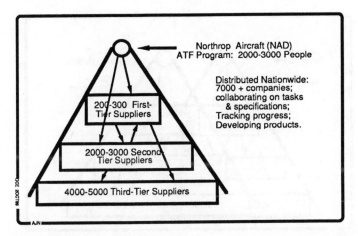

Figure 24.8   Islands in supplier hierarchy of a major aircraft program would be very costly.

able web will cover the world, as has clearly been or will be done for transportation and communications (e.g. telegraph, telephone, radio, or TV). I think a strong case can be made that the cost of NOT having total knowledge-domain interoperability would far exceed the cost of achieving this interoperability.

So how will this urgent need be satisfied—for intense, computer-supported cooperation across the knowledge domains of our rapidly approaching future world? It would seem that our *CSCW future* must include something like the solution characterized below as *an open hyperdocument system*. And if so, then all of our research, product development and application exploration should align with and properly affect the concepts and principles by which the future state is pursued.

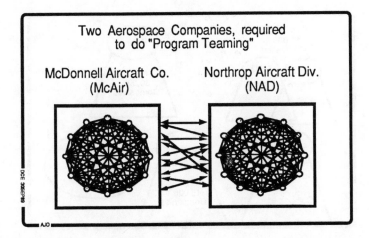

Figure 24.9   Close cooperation between large organizations puts new demands on knowledge-work interchange.

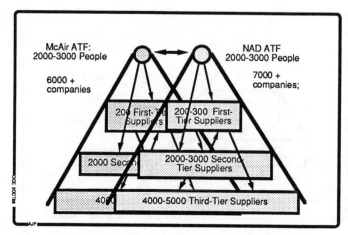

Figure 24.10   Teamed aerospace program—immense demand for knowledge-work exchange.

Towards An Open Hyperdocument System

Several years ago at McDonnell Douglas Corporation we coined the term *Open Hyperdocument System* (OHS) and began to define the associated functional and interoperability requirements for the kind of wide-area online cooperative knowledge work described above. This followed several years of careful study, and some pilot trials—one of which involved thousands of knowledge-workers using a prototype system containing many of the required capabilities.

Note: McDonnell Douglas is poised to move forward with requirements such as below as the basis for functional specifications and a workable procurement process.

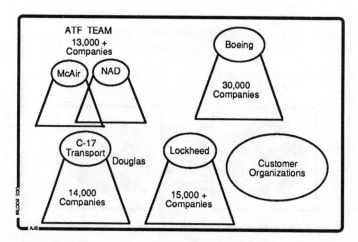

Figure 24.11   With common customers and suppliers, an aerospace industry can't afford islands.

In the following, I assume a need to provide basic capabilities so generic as to satisfy both the CSPW and CSCW application requirements over a broad spectrum of knowledge domains within a wide variety of organizations—including for instance universities, standards groups, and the U.S. Congress.

Some General Assumptions

In an open hyperdocument system, basic standards for document architecture are of course important. But beyond that, facilities for creating, transporting, storing, accessing and manipulating the hyperdocuments are embedded within an open, interoperable information-system environment, and the combined functionality is available within the knowledge-work domains of every class of worker (working from any vendor's terminal/workstation of suitable capability). Under these conditions, the role and value of hyperdocuments within groups, and between groups, offers very significant improvements in productive knowledge work. Two unique issues differentiate this new environment from document-support systems to date:

1. interlinkage between objects arbitrarily located within a large, multi-topic and extended-history document & data collection; and
2. extensive, concurrent, online utilization for creating, studying, organizing and linking within and between the many overlapping and nested knowledge domains.

These differences introduce paradigm shifts that produce different system requirements from those that have been evolving in the predominantly CSPW marketplace. For instance, WYSIWYG will give way to WYSIWYN—"what you see is what you need (at the moment)"—providing different options for how you'd view selected portions of the document space in your windows. The WYSIWYG view would be but one option (and likely to be utilized with decreasing frequency). Other expected shifts are implicit in some of the following suggested OHS requirements.

Besides special, *document-system architecture* features, full achievement of large-domain CSCW gains awaits two things:

1. widespread implementation of integrated, open-system architectures; and
2. widespread adoption of new knowledge-work processes (or, "knowledge processes").

To me, these new knowledge processes are especially relevant. They will involve new systems of skills, conventions, roles, procedures, methods and even organizational structures. I believe that they will provide a much more effective matching of basic human capabilities to the heavy knowledge-work and collaborative tasks within the functional human groupings that we call *organizations*, and within the mission-specific groupings that we call *projects*.

In my experience, truly effective new knowledge processes will emerge only via a co-evolutionary process—new knowledge processes and the new tools evolving together in real working environments. Explicit evolutionary pursuit with numerous, well-run pilot groups, seems called for.

From this is derived the position that a really good set of requirements and functional specifications for an OHS can only emerge from solid prototypical experience, in which advanced knowledge processes were developed and exercised along with advanced tools.

Note that the following list was derived from extensive experience with the evolution of the AUGMENT System (an OHS prototype owned by McDonnell Douglas) and its concurrent application within numerous real-work pilots.

Essential Elements of An OHS

Mixed Object Documents — to provide for an arbitrary mix of text, diagrams, equations, tables, raster-scan images (single frames, or even live video), spreadsheets, recorded sound, etc.—all bundled within a common *envelope* to be stored, transmitted, read (played) and printed as a coherent entity called a *document*.

Explicitly Structured Documents — where the objects comprising a document are arranged in an explicit hierarchical structure, and compound-object substructures may be explicitly addressed for access or manipulation of the structural relationships.

View Control of Objects' Form, Sequence, and Content — where a structured, mixed-object document may be displayed in a window according to a flexible choice of viewing options—especially by selective level clipping (outline for viewing), but also by filtering on content, by truncation or some algorithmic view that provides a more useful view of structure and/or object content (including new sequences or groupings of objects that actually reside in other documents). Editing on structure or object content from such special views would be allowed whenever appropriate.

The Basic Hyperdocument — where embedded objects called links can point to any arbitrary object within the document, or within another document in a specified domain of documents—and the link can be actuated by a user or an automatic process to "go see what is at the other end," or "bring the other-end object to this location," or "execute the process identified at the other end." (These executable processes may control peripheral devices such as CD ROM, video-disk players, etc.)

Hyperdocument "Back-Link" Capability — when reading a hyperdocument online, a worker can utilize information about links from other objects within this or other hyperdocuments that point to this hyperdocument—or to designated objects or passages of interest in this hyperdocument.

The Hyperdocument Library System — where hyperdocuments can be submitted to a library-like service that catalogs them and guarantees access when referenced by its catalog number, or "jumped to" with an appropriate link. Links within newly submitted hyperdocuments can cite any passages within any of the prior documents, and the back-link service lets the online reader of a document detect and "go examine" any passage of a subsequent document that has a link citing that passage.

Hyperdocument Mail — where an integrated, general-purpose mail service enables a hyperdocument of any size to be mailed. Any embedded links are also faithfully transmitted—and any recipient can then follow those links to their designated targets in other mail items, in common-access files, or in *library* items.

Personal Signature Encryption — where a user can affix his personal signature to a document, or a specified segment within the document, using a private signature key. Users can verify that the signature is authentic and that no bit of the signed document or document segment has been altered since it was signed.

Access Control — hyperdocuments in personal, group, and library files can have access restrictions down to the object level.

Link Addresses that are Readable and Interpretable by Humans — one of the *viewing options* for displaying/printing a link object should provide a human-readable description of the address path leading to the cited object; *and,* that the human must be able to read the path description, interpret it, and follow it (find the destination "by hand" so to speak).

Every Object Addressable — in principle, every object that someone might validly want/need to cite should have an unambiguous address (capable of being portrayed in a manner as to be human readable and interpretable). (E.g., not acceptable to be unable to link to an object within a "frame" or "card.")

Hard Copy Print Options to Show Addresses of Objects and Address Specification of Links — so that, besides online workers being able to follow a link-citation path (manually, or via an automatic link jump), people working with associated hard copy can read and interpret the link-citation, and follow the indicated path to the cited object in the designated hard copy document.

Also, suppose that a hard-copy worker wants to have a link to a given object established in the online file. By visual inspection of the hard copy, he should be able to determine a valid address path to that object and for instance hand-write an appropriate link specification for later online entry, or dictate it over a phone to a colleague.

Hyperdocuments In a General Integrated Architecture

Besides the aforementioned Hyperdocument Mail and Hyperdocument Library features, there are other important CSCW features that are dependent upon an *integrated system.*

Shared-Window Teleconferencing — where remote distributed workers can each execute a related support service that provides the "viewing" workers with a complete dynamic image of the "showing" worker's window(s). Used in conjunction with a phone call (or conference call), the parties can work as if they are sitting side-by-side, to review, draft, or modify a document, provide coaching or consulting, and so on. Control of the application program (residing in the "showing" worker's environment) can be passed around freely among the participants.

Inter-Linkage Between Hyperdocuments and Other Data Systems — for instance, a CAD system's data base can have links from annotations/comments associated with a design object that point to relevant specifications, requirements, arguments, etc. of relevance in a hyperdocument data base—and the back-link service would show hyperdocument readers which passages were cited from the CAD data base (or specified parts thereof).

Similarly, links in the hyperdocuments may point to objects within the CAD bases. And, during later study of some object within the CAD model, the back-link service could inform the CAD worker as to which hyperdocument passages cited that object.

External-Document Control (XDOC) — same *catalog system* as for hyperdocument libraries—with back-link service to indicate links from hyperdocument (and other) databases, for any relevant material that resides offline or otherwise external to the OHS.

The Interoperable OHS Environment

Figure 24.12 is an example of what the share-and-exchange domain within an open hyperdocument system might look like.

The requirements outlined above form a basic support platform for any group knowledge work effort, with interoperability across time and space (including all quadrants of the Time/Place matrix), across knowledge domains, and across organizational domains.

The Interoperability Investment

It could take a lot of effort and expense to get such knowledge-work interoperability. You might say, "Why don't I just do the part that's important?" as in Figure

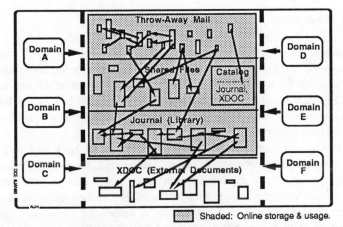

Shaded: Online storage & usage.

Figure 24.12 Knowledge-domain interoperability is greatly enhanced by hypertext linkage capability.

24.13, Choice A. Someone else's idea of what's important to share and exchange may look like Choice B.

As more and more of the knowledge work in each domain is done online, then the benefits of a comprehensive degree of CSCW interoperability will rapidly increase.

How do you decide how far to go? You'd compare the value of A vs. B, or B vs. C. And you'd say, "Well, let's see, with each successive choice I'd save more money, wouldn't I?" So how much more? We don't know how to quantify it yet. But, once you start finding a way to make some of the major subdomains interoperable, by the time you've picked these selective lines in Choice A or B, what would be the incremental cost in dollars and effort to get Choice C? But the real question is, what does it cost in dollars and effort NOT to have the interoperability.

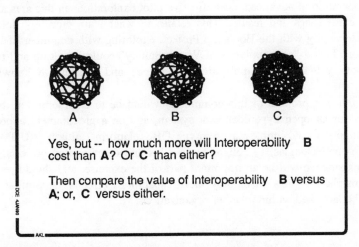

Yes, but -- how much more will Interoperability **B** cost than **A**? Or **C** than either?

Then compare the value of Interoperability **B** versus **A**; or, **C** versus either.

Figure 24.13 Providing for extensive interoperability will be expensive.

The OHS Movement

I asked people familiar with complex aerospace projects, "Well all right, let's make a guess—if the kind of hyperdocument interoperability we are talking about here were installed for instance under the whole design & manufacturing operation of this ATF program, what might the yearly dollar benefit be?" They look back and forth at each other for a while ... So I offer: "$300,000,000 a year?" And they look at it and say, "At least."

User organizations must realize that they can't just sit back and wait for the standards groups and computer vendors to deliver this, because there hasn't yet been enough orientation or application experience in this area. It seems necessary for the larger user organizations to take responsibility, to become pro-active—e.g., with exploratory pilots, active development of associated knowledge processes, and cooperative requirements definition—and then show the vendors that there is a sizable market for this.

But they must also realize that it isn't just a matter of specifying, procuring, and installing the resulting system—they have to learn how to employ it effectively in this extremely complex environment. And they must realize that they have to co-operate more intensively than before: The stakes are extremely large; there is too much to learn and events are moving too rapidly; and the resources and degree of stakeholder coordination involved are both very high.

To find this effort emerging from within the aerospace industry seems likely enough to me: it is the most complex work environment I know of, and a most urgent candidate for harnessing the benefits of wide-area CSCW and effective knowledge-domain interoperability. But other large organizations also have pressing needs for exactly this same capability—for example, car manufacturers, computer vendors, government agencies, consulting firms, universities, consortia, and standards groups.

To me there is a real need for a cooperative movement—among large organizations that are heavily dependent on group knowledge work—to coordinate planning and operation of advanced, cost-effective pilot explorations in this area and to share the experiences and results. This relates to what I am currently doing at Stanford University with the Bootstrap Project: exploring with a number of larger organizations how a "cooperative, CSCW community" could be set up and run to provide both valuable pilot-application experience and substantive knowledge products.

One of the first projects of this community would be to collaborate on the requirements for an open hyperdocument system, and on a procurement approach. The community would employ a prototype OHS platform (initially AUGMENT from McDonnell Douglas) to collaborate on this and other related projects. This hands-on experience will be an important part of the exercise, and should provide valuable insight into how to employ these capabilities effectively. Similar pilot trials will be launched within member organizations.

About the Author

Douglas C. Engelbart

Dr. Douglas C. Engelbart is Director of the Bootstrap Project and guiding force behind the Bootstrap Community. The vision of the Bootstrap Project is to push the frontiers of information management, hypermedia, groupware, and organizational evolution, following a special strategic framework for bootstrapping organizations into the 21st century. The Bootstrap Community, which was launched in March 1989 with $100,000 each from the Mitchell Kapor Family Foundation, Apple Computer and Sun Microsystems, will operate as a living prototype of its work, employing an evolving set of prototypical work methods and tools to facilitate and support the life cycle of its own evolving knowledge base.

Dr. Engelbart has a 30-year track record as a visionary and pioneer of integrated information systems and organizational augmentation. He holds the patent on the mouse; and has made major contributions in display editing, multiple windows, outline and idea processing, hypertext, hypermedia, and groupware, with early prototypes in full operation under the NLS/AUGMENT system as early as 1968. More recently, much of his work has been adopted by the McDonnell Douglas corporate CAD/CAM/CALS Program for integrated architecture. In addition to launching the Bootstrap Community, Engelbart is writing Bootstrap!, a book (and funds permitting, a video) describing the bootstrap strategies and the unique practical experience driving his work.

Dr. Engelbart may be contacted at Bootstrap Institute, 6505 Kaiser Dr., Fremont, CA 94555.

References

For more background on the source experience from which these proposed OHS requirements grew:

Engelbart, D. C. (1982). "Toward High-Performance Knowledge Workers," *OAC '82 Digest, Proceedings of the AFIPS Office Automation Conference*, San Francisco, April 5-7, 1982, 279-290.

AUGMENT, Re-published in *Computer Supported Cooperative Work: A Book of Readings*, Irene Greif (Ed.) (1988). Morgan Kaufmann Publishers, Inc., San Mateo, CA, 67-78.

Engelbart, D. C. (1984). "Authorship Provisions in AUGMENT," *COMPCON '84 Digest, Proceedings of the 1984 COMPCON Conference*, San Francisco, CA, Feb 27-Mar 1, 465-472 (OAD,2250,). Republished in *Computer Supported Cooperative Work: A Book of Readings*, Irene Greif (Ed.) (1988). Morgan Kaufmann Publishers, Inc., San Mateo, CA, 67-78.

Engelbart, D. C., and Lehtman, H. G. (1988). "Working Together," *BYTE* Magazine, December 1988, 245-252.

25

Work Group Automation
and Hypertext

By Peter M. Benton
Informed Decisions

and Joseph Devlin
Armadillo Associates, Inc.

Introduction

There is nothing new about groups of people working cooperatively to achieve common goals, but the techniques used to coordinate group efforts are constantly evolving. The capability to coordinate large projects interactively, in close to real time is very much a 20th Century phenomenon.

These days, automation has assumed a major role as a facilitator of all phases of manufacturing. Today, the movement of both materials and information to both the job site and the production facilities at that site are likely to be under control of automated systems. Dubbed "flexible-" or "small-lot-size-" manufacturing systems, these systems are significant evolutionary improvements upon processes that have been used for decades.

Networked hypertext systems offer comparable potential for popularizing the automation of intellectual work. We believe that the commercial success of new hypertext products will depend on how well they enable groups of people to participate in flexible processes for intellectual work.

The 90s—The Decade of Work Group Automation

The new frontier in automation focuses on the automation of intellectual work. These systems coordinate the intellectual activities of individuals working in a group and sponsor cooperation among those individuals. Variously called Workgroup Automation systems, *Computer Supported Cooperative Work* (CSCW) packages and Collaborative Computing systems, or simply "workgroup computing," this application area is wide-reaching and poorly defined.

The marketplace is awash with a flood of new Workgroup Automation systems. Most of these systems will fail. In part, these failures will come because the programs do not take into consideration some of the problems that are unique to working in a networked environment.

The first wave of Workgroup Automation Systems blend existing tools (such as electronic mail, calendars, scheduling programs and project management software) together. This approach is easy to implement and can provide powerful functionality, but too often users are forced to master a separate interface for each tool. Hypertext-based front-ends promise to solve a number of these sorts of problems by acting as the glue to bind applications together and by imposing a consistent interface on a variety of disparate applications.

Those with a more prophetic view of workgroup computing argue that such blended applications are good for fostering one-way communications between individuals in the group but don't really engage a whole group at once. By way of contrast, applications such as Lotus' Notes and Coordination Technology's TOGETHER espouse a structured view of fundamental types of human interaction. They attempt to interpret and automate the sorts of interactions that go on between people, finding common functions, routines, and procedures—the deep structure of how people work together.

Hypertext systems are well suited for supporting collaboration of this type. The linking structure inherent in hypertext allows for the coordination of nodes written by different authors. Specifically, hypertext provides an easy method for attaching comments and annotations to other people's work without altering the originals. And, because hypertext chunks data into small nodes, it is relatively easy to support through a distributed network.

Networks provide a richly supportive environment that is well suited for hypertext. Information stored anywhere on a network must be accessible from any other location on the network. This provides an infrastructure to support a *web* of on-line hypermedia documents. Documents are easily created and added to the web, deleted from the web or modified. [See Chapter 22 by Littleford in this book.]

History of Networked Hypertext Systems

The awareness that networked systems can be used to support users working together is not new. Vannevar Bush's *As We May Think* [Bush, 1945] described *Memex*, a hypothetical microfiche-based system that could be used to share information among researchers investigating similar subject areas.

Douglas Engelbart's AUGMENT System was probably the first working model of a hypermedia system that supported collaboration between coworkers. This system supported terminal linking, electronic mail, file sharing, and the ability to pass the gavel among several people working together at separate terminals. [See McDonnell Douglas' *Open Hyperdocument System* (OHS) prototype in Chapter 24, in this book.]

More recently, Ted Nelson's vision of the Xanadu project describes on-line libraries that encourage readers to add their own links and annotate others' work as well as their own. The main purpose of the gIBIS system [Conklin, 1989] is to support group work. In the Colab project at Xerox PARC, computers support collaborative processes in face-to-face meetings [Stefik, et al., 1987].

Problems and Opportunities Specific To Networked Hypertext

Hypertext and networks may be made for each other, but that does not mean that coming up with a good networked hypertext system is easy. Anyone attempting to do so should keep the following challenges in mind.

Success Requires Better Cognitive Models

Designers of work group automation systems should strive to make the whole workgroup application be more than the sum of the parts (electronic mail, calendaring, group editing, etc.), else it will fail miserably.

To achieve this purpose, the designer must take into consideration not only the technical requirements but also the politics, social structure, and dynamics of the group that is being automated. Success is much more likely to come to packages that streamline the way people are used to working rather than those that try to get people to change their way of working to adjust to a (presumably superior) automated system.

Lost In A Changing Hyperspace

One of the biggest design challenges in creating any hyperdocument is avoiding reader disorientation. Without the proper orientation tools it is easy for a reader to get lost while following a trail of webs through even a single-user hypertext. [See "Ordering the Information Graph" by Parunak and "Navigating in Hypermedia" by Gay & Mazur in this book.]

When more than one reader works on a shared hypertext system, the orientation problem is magnified many fold since some may be revising the topology or contents of the hyperdocument as others are reading it. One solution to this particular problem was suggested by the designers of Xerox's NoteCards [Irish and Trigg, 1989]. Their solution was to establish a special area within the hypertext for communication among authors and to use different typefaces for the text written by each author. This remains an open area for research.

Flexibility Can Add Confusion

A design question that networked hypertext systems share with single-user hypertext systems is: How much control do you provide the reader over the appearance of the material he or she views? It is a central tenet of most hypertext systems that readers should be free to view information in whatever order and format they like. But when working in a group situation, having everybody reviewing a slightly different version of a hyperdocument may cause confusion.

We are all used to passing paper reports around our workplace with notes asking things like "What you think of the copy on page three?" Allowing people the freedom to look at the *same* piece of text on an entirely different location on their respective displays precludes the use of this sort of pointer. This is an especially significant problem with windowing interfaces that allow text and graphics to be moved, reshaped, and scrolled. Thus, in some cases, networked hypertext systems need to impose a more fixed format than is common in single-user hypertexts.

Version Control

Another challenge that must be faced is one of version control. Consider what happens when one author creates a link to node A and then the original author of node A deletes or rewrites the node? The same problem can occur in a single-user hypertext, but the probability is that the person who deletes the node will be the same person who added the new links and he or she will know how to fix things.

The beauty of networked hypertext environments is that multiple authors can create massively intertwingled constructions that no single author could imagine. The danger is that the person who deletes a node may have no idea of all the directions in which it is linked.

The ideal solution to the problem of version control is to invest enough intelligence in the computer system so that it can figure out how to re-attach orphan links to the most relevant remaining nodes. But systems capable of performing this feat are still beyond the reach of current technology. A more realistic solution is a system that notifies an author of the repercussions of his changes and forces him or her to manually update the missing links.

Automatic Revision Tracking

One advantage of working on a network is that users must identify themselves to the system as part of the login process. This login information (along with the user profile entered when the user is first admitted onto the system) provides a rich source of information that can be used to track each reader's progress through the maze and to customize the information presented to that reader. For example, a networked hypertext system can be set up so that it automatically stamps the identity of each author on each link and node he or she creates.

Log-in names can also make it easy for the system to keep track of the author of a node or link and the last date in which it was changed. Whenever the system receives a request to add new material to a node, it should check to see if the editor is the same as the original author. If the editor is the same as the author, then the copy is changed and the date updated. If the editor is not the same as the author, some provision has to be made to attach comments on top of the original node, perhaps as a new node linked to the first one.

Of course the problem with this scenario is that the network of nodes and links can become terribly messy and some human intervention will probably be necessary to clean things up once in a while. A partial solution is provided if the name of the author is always kept on a separate node which is linked to the actual text. This removes some clutter from the screen and saves the space that would be wasted if the system stored the same name over and over.

Another problem is how to deal with multiple comments on the same point. Do all comments radiate from the central node or are they all stacked sequentially?

Filtering Information Based Upon the Reader's Profile

An author's user ID can also be used to determine whether he or she is authorized to read, link to, change or delete information. For example, in a university environment, professors might be authorized to add or change the overall structure of a hyperdocument but students would be authorized to add only links and annotations.

It is also possible for the hypertext system to use log-in information to automatically filter the document to show only information that is relevant to that reader. Again using the university example, it might be assumed that first year physics students need not be offered links leading to advanced subjects like quantum mechanics.

More advanced hypertext systems can keep track of the type of information a particular reader usually accesses and can adjust what is shown next based upon past history. The system might recognize readers who ask to see a basic tutorial on a subject as rank beginners who would not want to see a treatise on a complex subject until intermediate lessons had been mastered. [For more information on building intelligence into the network see Alan Littleford's chapter, in this book.]

Taken to an extreme, an intelligent document could not only create itself by extracting and formatting relevant data from a central database and then formatting itself for presentation, but it could also route itself to where it was needed. This sort of capability might prove especially useful in a workgroup environment. Imagine a report that could route itself to different employees to work on and then pass the results along to various supervisors who had to approve the results before they could be put into effect.

Several vendors of on-line publishing systems are investing heavily in intelligent document technology. For example, Interleaf Inc. has recently been publicizing a computer-based object called an "Active Document." Computer programs can be attached to parts of active documents (for example, paragraphs, titles and graphics). These programs may be triggered by events such as a user copying a document or when the system clock reaches a certain time. What happens to the document when an event triggers an embedded program is up to the skill and imagination of the writer/programmer who embedded that code.

Separating Content From Access and Presentation Procedures

A great many of the single-user hypertext systems on the market today store links as part of the same files that hold the content (nodes) they are linking. This approach becomes unmanageable when the number of nodes becomes large and many users are given rights to create or delete nodes and links. If hypertext systems are to successfully serve as the glue used to meld together a wide variety of applications running on a network, it is important that content be separated from access and presentation methods.

One step in this direction is the use of standard markup languages such as *Standard Generalized Markup Language* (SGML), which separates the format of a document from the ASCII text that is formatted. But SGML is not far-reaching enough in that it does not provide standards that regulate linkages into databases that are external to the hypertext. For example, DEC has recently demonstrated a version of its DECwindows system that supports links between its electronic mail and calendar programs. The hypertext links are kept external to the files in a system-wide database. DEC provides the programming interface for developers to add hypertext to their programs. The end user benefits from a consistent interface to a variety of applications. The problem, of course, is that, unlike fonts and layout which can be handled by SGML, hypertext data structures remain adamantly unstandardized and show no sign of being standardized anytime soon.

Examples of Complex Collaborative Efforts

The next few pages are devoted to descriptions of various types of workgroup automation.

An Automated Payroll System—Computerized Automation At Its Most Simple

The initial focus of business data processing, following its introduction in the 1950's, was to automate standard business functions such as accounting. Many individuals may work on an accounting system, but they each have their own discrete job and don't need to collaborate per se. In fact, the paper trail maintained by most accounting systems is an essentially linear one. Each piece of paper is worked on by one person, who then files it or hands it off to the next person.

Automated payroll applications are a good example of the type of system that lent itself to the simpler automation typical of the 1950's. Paychecks for hourly labor result from processing both paper records and timecards. A new worker joins a company, and information such as his address and rate of pay are added to the payroll department records by a payroll supervisor, who generates a time card for that worker. Once on the job, the worker stamps the timecard to record hours. A payroll clerk has the task of preparing the payroll from completed timecards and applying payroll calculation procedures (such as how to compute withholding for state taxes). The payroll supervisor examines the payroll transaction and authorizes check preparation. Several workers must coordinate efforts to accomplish distinct tasks using standard procedures and uniform resources, but the work flows from one hand to another; there is no simultaneous processing or group work per se.

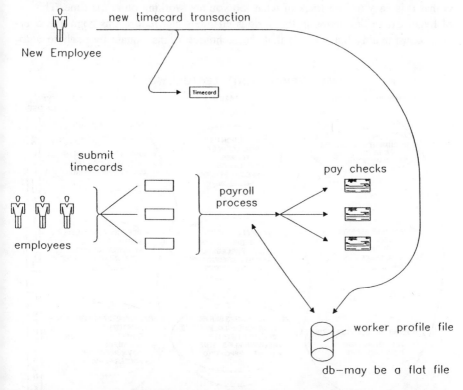

Figure 25.1 Payroll Workflow—An example of computerized automation at its most simple. In a simple payroll workflow, communication is from individual to individual and group to group. All this is handled formally, using structured transactions and schedules. There is basically one channel of communication: the workflow itself.

The Beginnings of Real Collaborative Workgroup Computing

As successful as the automated accounting systems were and remain, they have very little to do with collaborative work. The next step in the evolutionary process of workgroup automation are systems that allow multiple interrelated tasks to be managed simultaneously. Until the advent of multi-user systems and/or local area networks, real-time communications and multi-user database systems based on such collaborative working environments were simply not possible.

We now have tools that allow us to really collaborate with our co-workers. A common feature of the new workgroup applications that have recently emerged is that they are inherently less standardized in task and workflow than the payroll system described earlier. Each task must still follow its own channel from beginning to end, but communication between various individuals working together is carried on over several channels simultaneously. One problem with all this activity is that it is easy to lose track of what job you are working on at the time. The use of hypertext to link items in the various channels can reduce this cognitive overhead considerably but we feel that the technique is inadequate by itself to auto-

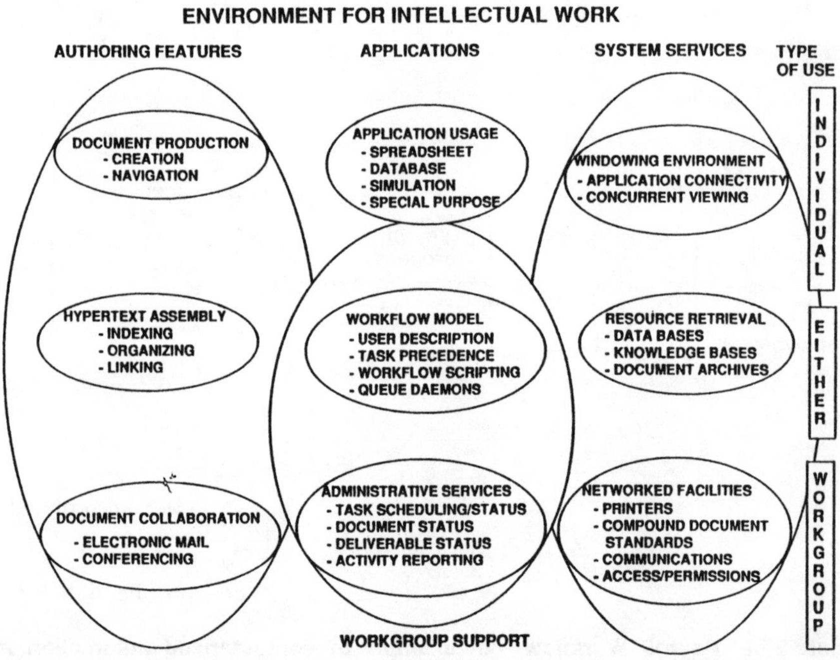

Figure 25.2   Delineates the various features required for an environment for intellectual work. These features are grouped into capabilities such as authoring, applications, and system services. The features required get more sophisticated as the type of use and target audience changes from the individual to the workgroup.

mate the entire process. The other tools which need to be added depend upon the task at hand.

Occupations such as text management in journalism and publishing, analysis conducted in business management, and design using simulation in engineering can all benefit from these new systems. But because each has different requirements and goals, each must be handled differently.

Journalism and Publishing: A Text Management Example

Every issue of a magazine or edition of a book has unique characteristics of editorial content, page design and formatting, handling of tables, illustrations, photographs and (for magazines) advertising. This uniqueness makes it necessary to adapt the tasks, resources and workflow for every edition or issue. In publishing, there are often multiple streams of work, one for each article or section of a book.

Workflow. For example, if an issue is to include a compendium of financial characteristics of U.S. companies, staff are temporarily reallocated to prepare and check numerical tables, and the workflow is adapted accordingly. In contrast, the workflow for handling payroll changes only rarely.

Channels of Workgroup Communication. In journalism and publishing, the writers and editors collaborating on an article have to communicate using at least three channels at the same time:

- Channel 1 is the discussion of the assignment—what to cover, when is it due, how long should it be, what changes are needed?
- Channel 2 is the assignment, itself—the words in the text which have to be carefully researched written, edited, copy edited, and proofread.
- Channel 3 is the non-textual part of the assignment—tables, art, photos, sound bites, etc. These have to be carefully prepared, checked, and placed into the article.

Linking Across Channels. From an abstract perspective, in journalism and publishing there are links from channel 1 to channels 2 and 3, and links between items in channels 2 and 3.

For example, the Editor-in-Chief may have assigned an article on the shrinking defense budget. The reporter supplies a first draft which translates the impact of budget cuts into numbers of jobs lost.

The editor, in looking at the draft, may conclude that there is an important industrial policy aspect to the story, and ask the reporter to find out if Congress is looking for ways to retain or enhance industrial competitiveness while shrinking the defense budget.

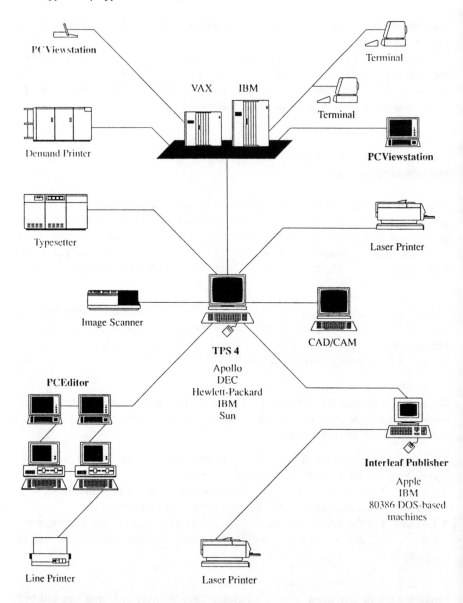

Figure 25.3 Interleaf's corporate-wide solution for electronic publishing is an integrated environment where publications are born, developed, reviewed, revised, illustrated, stored, retrieved, and printed in one seamless operation, with precisely the right tool at every station. (*Photo courtesy Interleaf, Inc.*)

This change in the reporter's assignment (channel 1) points to places in the article (channel 2), and in the illustrations (channel 3) where industrial competitiveness issues can be raised.

In the editorial production systems used today, such links exist implicitly, but are part of the text itself. The hypertext paradigm, in making links explicit, enables the publishing process to handle complex topics with greater rigor. Hypertext by itself is not enough. All the other automated workflow capabilities (described below) must be present, as well.

Typical System Capabilities

Time deadlines are so tight for daily or weekly publications that nearly all of the work must be done on one multi-user, multiprocessing computer system or on closely-coupled distributed processing systems.

Examples include multi-user editorial and composition systems such as ATEX for magazines, PENTA and XYVISION, for books, and INTERLEAF for technical documentation.

Such systems have built-in features needed to facilitate the flow of work between individuals, and between groups. These features include:

- Daemons (semi-autonomous programs) to move articles, electronic mail and other files from place to place as individuals complete their assignments.
- Process servers (special purpose workhorse computers) with programs to do intensive file operations such as hyphenation, justification and composition. Process servers work in the background, and when done, return the file to the sender.
- Script languages which allow the system administrator to establish a complete workflow plan across the whole installation.
- Security and user access controls to ensure that individuals can use only the resources they need.

The above capabilities are needed for workgroup systems but are not as important for individuals.

An emerging trend in publishing is to use so-called "structurally tagged" text. This means that every textual element (such as a chapter title, a subhead, a table element, a footnote) is marked with a tag that identifies the kind of element it is. Tagging is being adopted most rapidly for technical documentation because it is now required by the Department of Defense. Based on SGML, tagging embeds structure into the document, and so makes conversion to hypertext much easier [see Chapter 10 by Rearick in this book].

The *Text Encoding Initiative* (TEI) sponsored by three scholarly societies has released the first draft of a tagset, based on SGML, to record structural and descriptive features of a body of text.

For example, the tags enable identification of stanzas and other sub-elements of poems, and enable scholars to record their comments, criticisms, interpretations and translations in an organized way as part of the same document.

Business Management: An Example of Workgroup Analysis

Success in business today often depends as much upon how well a company manages information as on the products it produces. Many different groups collaborate in the collection and analysis of this information—product managers, market analysts, statisticians, surveyors, accountants, clerical staff, etc.

Workflow.   Consider an example from a consumer products marketing department. A product line marketing manager may have a hunch that the kinds of products bought in 24-hour supermarkets differ in some way from those bought in restricted hour supermarkets. To test this idea, she comes up with a research plan that requires store visits to collect lifestyle data using survey forms, and a statistical comparison of the sales mix from matched stores—which differ only in their hours of operation.

The marketing manager starts up two streams of work to be run as parallel projects: a survey and a statistical study. For the survey team, she describes the issues she wants answered, and provides sample questions for the form. The survey staff starts with this guidance and prepares a sample survey form which they return to her. She critiques it, and they revise the form until it is mutually acceptable. Together, they select stores where the surveys will be conducted.

For the statistical team, she describes the issues and lists the products, product attributes, store characteristics, and customer attributes that should be considered. The survey team looks at the sales database (supplied by a market data firm) and lays out a plan for the statistical analysis. She critiques the plan, and together they arrive at a satisfactory one.

Channels of Workgroup Communications.   In this example, there are two projects moving in parallel. For each project, the following channels are needed:

- Channel 1 is the assignment to the survey or statistical analysis team—the objectives, the schedule, the budget, suggestions for technical approach and so on.
- Channel 2 is the working paper set for each of the respective teams. Each team has its own working paper set, and the product manager has access to it. Its format varies. The survey team's working papers include draft surveys and comments. The statistical analysis team's working papers include programs and sample data illustrating the planned analysis.
- Channel 3 is the final report which integrates the results of the two projects and provides interpretation of the results.

Linking Across Channels.   There are many links between channels 1, 2, and 3 for the survey and many links between channels 1, 2, and 3 for the statistical analysis. However, there are relatively few links between the two projects. Both projects are designed to address the same underlying questions, but the methodology differs, and the stores investigated for surveys and statistical comparison may be disjoint sets. However, the final report prepared at the end of the study will include numerous links within the two separate studies.

Typical System Capabilities. Many different kinds of systems are used to convert raw data into useful information for business analysis. A number of consumer products companies use specialized, high performance workstations that enable the user to conduct an analysis by drawing lines between icons.

An example of such a system is METAPHOR. METAPHOR includes special purpose database servers (to store large volumes of marketing data) and computer servers (to execute statistical studies rapidly). In addition to data management and analysis, a METAPHOR workstation allows users to set up explicit links between documents, and between documents and supporting studies, such as spreadsheets or statistical analyses. In other words, it provides hypertext-like functionality. It also includes electronic mail, desktop publishing, text storage and retrieval systems, and project scheduling applications.

Engineering: An Example of Workgroup Design

A large part of the workday for an engineer involves setting up and running simulations of natural phenomena, collecting data from the simulation and analyzing it statistically. In typical engineering projects there are multiple streams of work. The large variation in task content and workflow requires a high degree of flexibility in the support systems.

Workflow. If an engineer has problems with the design of a component, he will plan a series of simulations of design alternatives to examine critical variables. He writes the simulation instructions. Data collection, analysis, and presentation will vary dramatically depending on the specifics of the problem under investigation. Different facets of the work will be done by different people depending on their role and skills. Results of the simulations will be summarized as numeric tables, written interpretations, and possibly as graphics which show the data in a visual or diagram form.

Channels of Workgroup Communication. In engineering, the workers have to communicate using several channels simultaneously [Conklin, 1987].

- Channel 1 is the description of the project—the objectives, schedule, budget, resources available, technical approach and simulation criteria.
- Channel 2 is the lab notebook of simulation results, in raw form, that grows by accretion. Its format encompasses numerical data, textual observations, and measurements of various kinds—photographs, diagrams, etc.
- Channel 3 is the current state of the new design, in evolving form, that grows in fits and starts as discoveries and design decisions are made.
- Channel 4 is the final report on the project, for internal publication. It includes samples of important raw data, the step by step thinking process, the key insights and design decisions.
- Channel 5 is the collection of the communications between the principal engineer, the staff, and with peers in other related projects. It tracks the day by day

guidance given by the principle investigator, negotiations of alternative schedules and resource utilization, and records some of the day-by-day findings as the analysis and design proceeds.

• Channel 6, if present, is a final report on the project for external publication in journals. It is a synopsis of Channel 4, the internal final report.

Linking Across Channels. Once again, in this example there are links running from channel to channel. There is a veritable hypertext web among elements in all the channels [Irish and Trigg, 1989]. Once again, hypertext can simplify matters by providing an easy-to-follow network of links to interconnect the various channels. As in the journalism, publishing and business management fields, hypertext by itself is inadequate to automate the engineering design process. A substantial complement of automated workflow capabilities (described below) are needed.

Typical System Capabilities. Engineering labs function at many levels of automation. Some use paper, some use networks, some use integrated systems. The trend in engineering-intensive firms is to use both multi-user systems and local area networks between personal workstations.

To save time, simulations are typically run on the most powerful available machine. For example, Apple Computer simulates operation of future Macintosh PCs on a Cray super computer. Several major automobile manufacturers use supercomputers to determine the impact of design changes on fuel efficiency and other operational characteristics.

Common features of automated engineering environments include electronic mail within the workgroup and with the outside world, project scheduling applications, and electronic reference libraries including work done locally and by affiliated groups.

An emerging feature of automated engineering environments is the use of so-called compound documents. Compound documents provide figurative containers into which various objects—revisable text, engineering drawings, software for simulations, packages of data, graphics, even voice and video will be incorporated. Right now such products allow you to combine graphics and the text easily into a single document. The Diamond system from Bolt Berenak Newman of Cambridge, MA. is an example. The resemblance to hypertext is striking.

Characteristics of Collaborative Work Projects

As careful study of the examples provided earlier will reveal, projects that can benefit from the use of workgroup automation tools have several points in common:

Integration.	To succeed, the project has to combine skills that no single individual has.
Parallelism.	Large portions of the job need to be done in parallel, with varying amounts of communication across the streams of work.

(continued)

Characteristics of Collaborative Work Projects

Broad Subject Coverage.

The subject area dealt with in the project is large and changing fast. Collaboration becomes particularly important when advances in the subject area come from many sources.

Multi-stage Process.

The intellectual work steps in the project need to follow a multi-stage process model.

Typical Activities Handled by Collaborative Work Projects

Some tasks performed in the course of collaborative work projects differ from those to be done by a single worker. In some cases, it's just that the importance of certain tasks becomes magnified when the task is performed as part of a group effort; in other cases, tasks are altogether different:

Researching Information.

Collecting information from journals, books or databases is an important individual activity in collaborative work. The means selected varies depending on where and how the information is stored and the search skills of the user.

Asking Questions.

Collecting information through posing questions is an important collaborative task. It tends to be done in person or through systems that allow relatively quick interactions, such as conferencing or electronic mail.

Writing.

Writing may be individual or collaborative, and generally is both. Preparing the writing plan is often a collaborative effort, while crafting sentences is often individual. Related tasks include refining large volumes of original text, summarizing existing text into abstracts and summaries, or boiling down written materials into short phrases or even keywords.

Building Symbolic Models.

Building symbolic models, whether financial, mathematical, or logical, is an important individual activity in collaborative work. Preparation of a model overview is often a collaborative task. The work is done with an appropriate tool, such as a spreadsheet or a modeling package. The results of several people's efforts can be combined if they use a consistent format.

Building Iconic Designs.

Building iconic designs, such as drawings, schematics, or simulations also is an important individual activity. Again, preparation of the overview is often a collaborative task. Interesting progress has been made in the last few years in allowing several people each to share the same virtual sheet of paper, and to work together on a design, each owning a layer or color on the virtual workspace.

(continued)

Typical Activities Handled by Collaborative Work Projects

Critiqueing.

Commenting on or critiqueing others writings, symbolic and iconic models is a common individual task in collaborative work. The object of the comments may be writings, drawings, spreadsheets or physical models.

Capabilities of Systems Supporting Collaborative Work

To automate a group effort, a system needs to possess some or all of the following technical capabilities:

Task Scheduling and Work Commitments.

Who will do what tasks, and when should they do them? In the engineering example, we saw that there were two channels of communication dealing with planning and scheduling issues (channels 1 and 5). A number of generalized planning and scheduling systems exist, and these can be integrated into collaborative work/hypertext systems with some effort. The major issue is to establish link types for time commitments that are handled effectively by both the scheduling/planning system and the hypertext document manager.

Deliverables Inventory.

What is the set and status of agreed-upon, committed-to deliverables? Each deliverable corresponds to a completed unit of work—a physical thing such as a report, spreadsheet or software that can be delivered.

Deliverables need to be described and inventoried, their status (planned, in process, completed) tracked, and their authors and reviewers identified. Documents need to be listed in the task schedule as things to be done, and in the reference library as things available to be read. Such capabilities have been developed to varying degrees in technical library systems used in research laboratories.

Workflow Automation.

The workflow from one team member to another should be automated to eliminate re-entry of information, and to reduce elapsed time between worksteps. As described in the clerical and publishing examples, it is vital that the system move units of work from one person to another, and that each worker can add to what was done before without redoing things from the beginning. From a systems standpoint, this means the whole architecture has to be designed to manage queues of work for each user.

(continued)

Capabilities of Systems Supporting Collaborative Work

Multimedia Production.
The result of any single workstep may be words on paper or other things—lists, a spreadsheet or data file on a floppy disk; a script, speech, or video presentation on tape or disk; a model simulation, animation or computer program on a disk, or available in a database accessible to the workgroup.

Engineering has the most demanding requirements for multimedia capabilities. The idea of visualization—being able to see data after they have been converted into images—is forcing a level of integration across systems that was unthought of a decade ago. So-called object-oriented multi-media databases have been developed to make it easier to move information bundles that include many kinds of elements from workstation to workstation.

Administrative Tracking.
How much work has been done, and needs to be done, by project; how many resources have been consumed; what resources are available for other work; what is the schedule for the next work period.

The business world requires that systems that automate clerical operations provide a full range of reports to analyze work accomplished and work to do. Off-the-shelf mainframe business application packages include such reporting. Home-grown systems tend to be enhanced over time to provide such reporting. As hypertext is applied to workgroups, such reporting will be essential for clerical and transaction-oriented applications.

Comparison of Automation for Group and Individual Projects

Type of Automation	Group Project	Individual Project
Work Automation	Desirable, performed by multi-user process servers.	Desirable, performed at the individual's workstation.
Procedures	Standardized, particularly if people work in parallel, or do the same work repeatedly.	May be ad-hoc. However, become standardized if the same work is done repeatedly.
Resources	Uniform. Each user has access to the same reference resources.	Ad Hoc. User builds a local "heap" that helps in his particular work.

(continued)

Comparison of Automation for Group and Individual Projects

Workflow	Organic. Work for individuals and groups is apportioned to reach some overall criterion of quality, performance, or timeliness.	Serial. Work for the individual is a serial process.
Workflow Facilitation	Extensive. Use of script languages, access controls, common data storage, electronic mail, scheduling and shared reference libraries.	Modest. Use of individual work plan and schedule; local filing and storage.
Communication Across Streams of Work	Extensive. Use of electronic mail, message types, communication channels to organize communications and orchestrate work.	Nominal. Use of paper notes and to-do lists to orchestrate work.
Hypertext	Extensive. Use of linking features as a communication device from person to person and group to group, and across different channels. Use of linking feature to "web together" related ideas in the same channel.	Moderate. Use of linking feature to "web together" related ideas in the same channel.

Authoring Tools Needed by Both Workgroup and Hypertext Capabilities

Clearly, the need to support groups of people working together is an important driver of hypertext systems and standards. However, progress in the hypertext world is not as far along as in business and publishing automation because commercial development of hypertext systems started considerably later than other applications. The necessary authoring features for individual use include:

- Uniform mechanisms and resources for naming, indexing and organizing hypertext pages.
- Support a wide range of tools for document creation, assembly, production and composition.
- Permit integration with other applications through external windowing environment, or through intimate application connectivity.

In general, group authoring tools need the following additional capabilities:

- Allow fixed, semi-fixed or flexible workflow model—controlled by the system administrator or the hypertext author.

(continued)

Authoring Tools Needed by Both Workgroup and Hypertext Capabilities

- Are network aware—the basic architecture assumes the end user is working in a network that supplies a varying set of capabilities—databases, printers, communications links, other users.
- Provide tools to schedule tasks and track status of document preparation across the collaborating workgroup.
- Provide reporting on work done, work to do at each workstation or function.
- Support control of access and resource utilization down to the user and task level.

Examples of workgroup-oriented hypertext systems include Intermedia at Brown University [Catlin, et al., 1989], and KMS as applied at a law firm [Yoder and Wettach, 1989].

Summary

In this article we have surveyed the relationship between workgroup automation and hypertext applications. Generally speaking, automated workgroup support has evolved from uniform resources, tasks and processes to uniform resources allied with flexible tasks and processes.

Environments for intellectual work are achieved when automation supports work tools with facilities for record keeping and data management.

We assert that hypertext authoring systems should integrate the characteristics of uniform resources, flexible processes, and tools that are characteristic of most kinds of group work. If the hypertext system interacts with other applications and is network aware, then it meets our definition of an environment for intellectual work. Such hypertext systems can help collaborating groups of people be more effective.

About the Authors

Peter Benton

Peter Benton is President of Informed Decisions and consults on application of advanced technology to workgroups. Until 1991, he was Vice President and Chief Scientist for McGraw-Hill where he identified technologies and applications to improve quality, timeliness and cost effectiveness of McGraw-Hill products and services.

His experience includes publishing systems, data processing, ergonomics (how people work), knowledge-based systems, multi-media technologies, and natural language processing.

In 1989 and 1990, Peter architected the McGraw-Hill Custom Publishing System, which enables college professors to create customized text and workbooks for their classes by combining chapters, articles end other items from many sources.

Several years ago, Peter developed the editorial systems used by McGraw-Hill News—a real-time news information service. The system provided a spectrum of workgroup capabilities, as well as individual task automation tools for reporters, writers and editors.

He has a Bachelor of Science in Computer Science from the School of Engineering, City College of New York, and a Master of Business Administration from Bradley University. He has taught Audit and Control of Computer-based Systems in the Master of Business Administration Program of the New York Institute of Technology.

Peter may be contacted at Informed Decisions, 1637 Eighth Avenue, Brooklyn, NY 11215, via MCIMail at 127-5869, or on BIX at benton.

Joseph Devlin

Joseph Devlin is one of the co-editors of this handbook. He has been a skeptical observer of the multimedia market since the 70's, when he worked at Commodore International and Creative Computing Magazine.

Joe may be contacted at Armadillo Associates, Inc., Philadelphia, PA.

References

Bush, V. (1945). "As We May Think," *Atlantic Monthly*, July.

Catlin, T., Busch, P., Yankelovich, N. (1989). "Internote: Extending a Hypermedia Framework to Support Annotative Collaboration," *Proceedings of Hypertext '89, SIGCHI*, ACM, New York, NY, 365-378.

Conklin, J., Begeman, M. (1987). "gIBIS: A Hypertext Tool for Team Design Deliberation," *Proceedings of Hypertext '87*, Chapel Hill, NC, 247-251.

Conklin, J., Begeman, M. (1989). "gIBIS: A Hypertext Tool for Exploratory Policy Discussion," *Communications of the ACM, 32(5)*, 625-628

Irish, P., Trigg, R. (1989). "Supporting Collaboration in Hypermedia: Issues and Experience," *Journal of the American Society for Information Science.* 40(3), 192-199.

Stefik, M., Foster, G., Bobrow, D. G., Kahn, K., Lanning, S., Suchman, L. (1987). "Beyond the chalkboard: Computer support for collaboration and problem solving in meetings," *Communications of the ACM*, Jan. 30(1) 32-48.

Yoder, E., Wettach, T. (1988). "Using Hypertext in a Law Firm," *Proceedings of Hypertext '89—SIGCHI*, ACM, New York, NY, 159-167.

The Future of Hypertext

In this section, we jump from the mundane to the philosophical as we discuss hypertext in the future. Joe Devlin, co-editor of this handbook, starts the section with a discussion of the need for standards for hypertext. Then, in Chapter 27, John McDaid exhorts us to take control of the hypertext medium before it takes control of us.

26

Standards for Hypertext

By Joseph Devlin

Armadillo Associates, Inc.

Introduction

"Standards for hypermedia must emerge before hypermedia databases can be fully useful, but long-lived standards can only emerge after we know much more about how people will use hypermedia databases." — Gregory Crane [Crane, 1990].

Those attempting to establish standards for hypertext usually proclaim the following goals:

- To embed support for as many standard text, graphic, and sound sources as possible; to support import of these objects from as many popular applications packages as possible.
- To make it possible for hypertext authors to use standard sets of existing tools (word processors, graphics packages, editing consoles, etc.) to modify hyperdocuments.
- To allow whole documents to be shared between hypertext and other applications software.
- To help in exchanging hypertext documents between different hypertext platforms. [Brown, in Moline, et al., 1990]

The problem with these goals is that there is no clear mechanism for achieving them. Development of new technologies such as hypermedia always outruns the development of the standards that define them. Standard formats are proposed by the small vendors that open up new markets, by larger companies that move in when the markets mature, by the academic community, and by industry standards organizations. Eventually evolutionary selection culls out unsuccessful formats, but by the time this happens new standards dealing with more complex issues are already being suggested.

The end result is that standards build slowly, layer by layer. The simplest, least controversial components get standardized first. For example, ASCII has come to be widely accepted as the only way to encode unformatted text. Another common tendency is to draw upon standards already adopted for related technologies. For example, many hypertext vendors depend upon the *Standard Generalized Markup Language* (SGML), a publishing industry standard, to manage the layout of hypertext screens. More complex issues, such as how to anchor links, what form those links should take, and how to transfer data between hypertext systems depend upon standards that are in flux.

Developers who take a layered approach to hypertext standards usually create modular programs that can grow and change as the market matures and standards evolve. This strategy has proven successful in other fields. For example, the International Organization for Standardization OSI (Open Systems Integration) model divides network standards into separate physical, data link, network, transport, session, presentation, and application levels. Modular OSI programs can be built to allow the user interface to be changed without having to rewrite whole programs from scratch. The same benefits accrue to those who adopt layered hypermedia standards.

The old chestnut that the nicest thing about standards is that there are so many to choose from applies aptly to the field of hypermedia standards. The goal of this chapter is not to describe each and every important hypertext standard—such coverage would consume more pages than can be found in this entire book. Instead, it provides an overview of the types of standards that are of interest to hypertext and hypermedia developers. In this chapter I try to emphasize areas where the adoption of standards may benefit, or has already benefited, hypertext readers and authors, and the kinds of standards that have been accepted or are being debated in the hypertext community.

There is no way that hypertext developers can expect to stay on the cutting edge of hypertext standards. They can, however, work within the safe confines of the stable, standardized layers and extend into uncharted regions only when necessary. This chapter attempts to show where the boundaries lie. In the first part of this chapter, we discuss standards such as content definitions that are easily adopted from other fields. The second part of this chapter is devoted to issues that are more or less unique to hypertext.

Standardizing Content: Borrowing Existing Standards

The vast majority of the problems encountered while creating hypermedia applications are not new. Hyperdocuments are usually created by stringing together existing documents containing text, pictures, sounds, etc. All of these can be stored and manipulated using well-known electronic publishing, compound document, networking, or database management standards. Other well-established standards provide facilities for typographical encoding, timing and synchronization, cross-referencing, security, and directory management.

By far the best-defined standards are those which deal with the content imported into hyperdocuments. With few exceptions, standards for representing such data are clearly defined and commonly used in the electronic publishing and graphics fields. Standardizing on common data formats insures an abundant supply of material to incorporate into hypermedia at low cost. Compatibility with common standards opens hypertext up to a wide variety of public domain and commercial sources for data. It also insures that a wide variety of text editors and formatters, drawing and paint programs, sound and video editors, and the like can be used to supplement the (usually weak) tools incorporated into hypermedia authoring systems.

Content can be divided into four clearly separated categories: text, still graphics, full motion video, and sound.

Text

Raw (ASCII) text is the most prevalent and best-defined element used in hypertexts. Conventions for controlling the appearance of text (fonts to be used, alignment, etc.) are more diverse, but several methods for representing screen and hardcopy appearance have been adopted universally. If the documents you rely on include formulas, special characters, tables, paragraph structures, specification of their appearance and other layout conventions, you will also have to adhere to standards that reach beyond plain ASCII.

Fortunately, a single *de facto* standard from the electronic publishing world applies in all these cases. That solution is the *Standard Generalized Markup Language* (SGML). SGML defines the logical structure of a document, allowing authors to share documents and collaborate with colleagues without concern about incompatibilities between text formatters and printing devices.

Originally designed for editing, publishing and printing, SGML was accepted as an international standard in 1986. This system-independent markup language provides a hardware- and software-independent means for describing the logical structure (paragraphs, sentences, headers, footnotes, etc.) of a document. Users of SGML find that exchanging and processing electronic documents and combining them into hyperdocuments becomes relatively easy.

SGML has been widely incorporated into hypertext systems that run on minicomputers and mainframes. Those working exclusively on microcomputers are not as lucky. Many of the most popular PC-based graphical user interfaces (such as Microsoft Windows or the Apple Macintosh operating system) impose their own typography and layout conventions. This usually means that porting applications to another Mac or PC is relatively easy, but cross-platform migration becomes challenging. Fortunately, this is changing as PC-based hypertext systems add SGML compliance to their bag of tricks. For example, Cognetics Corporation's Hyperties system now accepts SGML tagged input.

Still Graphics

Storage formats for still pictures are well defined but so abundant that not one of them can be considered a standard. No single hypermedia authoring system can be expected to support every graphic format, but most of them support at a least of few of the most common types. Popular formats include geometric graphics notations such as CGM, Postscript, PHIGS, and SPDL Picture Descriptions. Raster graphics notations such as TIFF, Group-3 and -4 Fax, and IIF are also common.

For efficiency reasons, most existing hypertext systems that accept graphics store them as bit-maps that refer to specific screen coordinates. This provides an obstacle to interchange between platforms with differing display architectures. Hypermedia developers dealing with still pictures should make sure that both the development and delivery platforms they choose can handle the types of graphical objects they wish to use in their hyperdocuments.

Motion Video

In the last few years, hyperdocuments that utilize motion video have become more common. Standards for incorporating analog video into hyperdocuments are well defined (NTSC, PAL and SECAM).

Digital video gives hypertext authors greater control over images, but for the time being, digital video is expensive and typically requires the use of a proprietary technology offered by a single vendor (DVI or CD-I, for example). Several interesting proposals for universal standards are in committee at the major standards organizations (e.g. those being discussed within the ISO's Joint Photographic Experts Group and Moving Picture Experts Group), but their adoption appears to be several years away.

Incorporating slide shows and animations into a hyperdocument provides an inexpensive alternative to the high development and delivery costs of full-motion video. The timing and synchronization problems encountered when using these sorts of applications have their counterparts in the space management problems of page layout and graphics.

Sound

Substantial progress has recently been made to provide a single, universally-accepted standard for tying digital sound into the flow of a hyperdocument. The first step was the near universal acceptance of *Musical Instrument Digital Interface* (MIDI) as the notation used to drive computerized generation and control of music. The next step was ANSI's proposal (X3V1.8M) for *Standard Music De-*

scription Language (SMDL) and *Hypermedia/Time-based Structuring Language* (HyTime).

SMDL is closely related to SGML. It defines a standard for representing music in an abstract manner that is neutral with respect to how it is performed or presented on a score. HyTime is a hyperdocument-structuring language built into SMDL that provides the time sequencing information necessary for linking music into a multimedia. It defines basic identification and addressing mechanisms and is independent of object data content notations, link types, processing and presentation functions, and semantics. Links can be established to documents that conform to HyTime as well as to those that do not, regardless of whether those documents can be modified by the hypertext authoring system [Goldfarb, 1990].

User Interface

The adoption of a user interface standard influences important usability issues such as how links are navigated, how windows are managed, what interactive devices (such as keyboards, mice, and tablets) can be used, and the types of commands and prompts that can be issued by hypertext authors and readers.

The differences between the various popular user interfaces provides yet another argument for the clean division of hypertext standards into various levels. Such a separation allows programs to be ported between platforms with relative ease. Without that separation, programs must be rewritten from scratch when they move from platform to platform.

Are There Hypertext-Specific Standards?

Do hypermedia have unique requirements that can't be filled by adapting existing document or networking standards? Opinions on this issue differ. One approach is taken by the *American National Standards Institute* (ANSI), an American organization whose sole purpose is to establish voluntary industry standards.

ANSI has set up several standards technical committees to deal with hypertext standardization (X3V1—Text Processing/Office and publishing systems; X3L2—codes and character sets; X3H3—computer graphics). It is ANSI's opinion that the existing subcommittees and working groups originally set up to handle publishing, networking database standards, and the like, can best deal with all issues pertaining to hypermedia standardization. However, other groups working on standards have concluded that many of the standardization requirements for linking are unique to hypertext and thus have no close counterparts in other media.

Link Standards

Regardless of whether or not you believe that the linking mechanisms of hypertext are unique or not, it is clear they represent the cutting edge of hypertext standardization. No other area of hypertext is as poorly defined or shows as much variation from system to system. At present, virtually all hypertext development systems use proprietary methods for establishing, storing and heralding links, storing, notating and identifying nodes and tying all the elements of a hypertext together.

Adoption of common link standards will make it much easier to transfer a hyperdocument developed in one platform to another. But this is not the sort of argument that convinces hypertext development system vendors to make radical changes in their design. Vendors who have collected a loyal cadre of customers based upon the superiority of their technology are rarely eager to release those customers and adopt a more generic standard implementation.

There are several aspects of linking that can be standardized. However, there is little consensus that will lead to the quick adoption of standard addressing schemes (how links target nodes), schemes for anchoring (alerting readers to the presence of a link), or link typing conventions. [See Chapter 20 by Parunak, and Chapter 13 by Garzotto, et al., in this book for further discussion about the benefits of standardized linking schemes.] Vendors are also divided in their use of frame-based (one screen per node) or file-based (scrolling within a node) nodes. [See Chapter 9 by Riner, in this book for his analysis of these issues.]

Embedded Versus Separate Links. Many hypertext development systems still embed links as part of the content of hyperdocument nodes rather than isolate them into separate files. The use of embedded links ensures quick and easy generation of hyperdocuments, but it is extremely limiting when used in hypertexts that will change over time.

When links and nodes are stored together, any change to one affects the other. Storing links and nodes separately insures that changes can be made easily by switching, adding or deleting either links or nodes. Perhaps more important for long term development, links that cannot be separated from content make interchange between different hypermedia systems very difficult.

Standard Interchange Formats

A hypertext interchange format is a set of standards that allows readers on separate systems to share their data, thus eliminating the need to acquire, learn, and use a new hypertext system only to access that system's data. The ultimate challenge of any set of standards is to achieve a successful interchange format. Facile interchange of hyperdocuments is not currently feasible; an Apple HyperCard stack cannot be read by the OWL Guide browser or Xerox's NoteCards without manual intervention.

If an interchange standard for hypertext is to be effective, it must allow a hyperdocument created on one system to be presented on another. In particular, it must allow for the possibility that the receiving system does not have the capability to display the presentation as intended on the original system. This separation of the logical structure from presentation is not just an inconvenience needed for portability; it is a positive feature that can be used to give hypertext some of the advantages that generic markup conventions and structured word processors have brought to paper documents.

The first step towards the creation of successful interchange formats is to establish common capabilities all hypermedia systems must share. This involves coming up with accepted standards for all the various layers described in this chapter. The biggest hurdle to overcome is the adoption of common link/anchor/structure layers. Once that is done, maps must be devised that can tie external objects into the link anchors and define how each object is to be stored externally.

CALS. Hypertext developers are not the only ones interested in coming up with a standard interchange format. The U.S. *Department of Defense* (DoD) has determined that the establishment of a common electronic data exchange format is absolutely essential to streamline the flow of information between the DoD and the various defense contractors it uses. Thus the DoD has created a rigorous documentation interchange standard and demanded that all defense contractors gear up for its use. Named the *Computer-aided Acquisition and Logistics Support* initiative (CALS), this standard provides a way of storing all information content, be it parts lists, documentation, drawings or whatever, in a revisable form, in structured documents.

Some hypertext developers feel that CALS provides all the basic building blocks required for building any hyperdocument. Others argue that CALS does not provide rich enough support for various link types, addressing schemes and anchoring structures. No doubt CALS will evolve to respond to some of these complaints.

Conclusion

The reasons for the slow adoption of hypertext standards are many. One problem is that no one single standard can provide the best possible solution for all technical problems.

For all their shortcomings, standards are also necessary prerequisites to mass market success for any technology-driven product. The adoption of standards creates a level playing field in which every vendor agrees to play by the same rules. Standards provide consumers with the assurance that today's purchases will not become obsolete tomorrow. The end result of the adoption of standards is lower prices and more variety for consumers and a much larger base of consumers for manufacturers to sell to. The adoption of standards also radically reduces development costs for hardware and software vendors.

Standards don't come easily or arrive full blown. Instead, they evolve slowly, layer by layer, as markets mature and technology improves. Some standards have reached maturity and should be adhered to closely. Others are still in the development stage and are presently of more concern to standards committees and hardware and software developers than to hypertext developers and producers. Standards developers must be conscious of the multiple areas which may be addressed under the umbrella of hypermedia and multimedia standardization.

About the Author

Joe Devlin

Joe Devlin is co-editor of this handbook. He has been a skeptical observer of the multimedia market since the 70's, when he worked in the marketing department of Commodore International and editorial department of Creative Computing Magazine. During the early 1980's Joe served as founding editor of both Software Digest and the Commodore Magazine. During the mid 80's Joe was employed as a project manager developing on-line services for large data communications and banking concerns. It was here that Joe developed his first hypertext. In the late 80's, Mr. Devlin served as Project Manager of numerous benchmarking studies and Buyers Guides for PC-based software and hardware. He is currently a principal of Armadillo Associates, Inc., a multimedia consulting and development firm, where he can be reached at 2837 Poplar Street, Philadelphia, PA 19130.

Acknowledgments

Many thanks to David Anderson, for his patience, input and efforts on our behalf.

References

Billingsley, Pat (1989). "The Standards Factor: Are Standard User Interfaces the Solution?" *Sigchi Bulletin, Vol. 21,* Number 1. July, 14–16.

Brown, Peter (1990). "Standards for hypertext source files: the experience of UNIX Guide" (Pg. 53), Moline, Judi, Dan Benigni and Jean Baronas, eds. *Proceedings of the Hypertext Standardization Workshop,* Jan. 16–18, 1990 National Institute of Standards and Technology, U.S. Government Printing Office. Washington, D.C.

Crane, Gregory (1990). "Standards For A Hypermedia Database: Diachronic Vs. Synchronic Concerns" (Pg. 71), Moline, Judi, Dan Benigni and Jean Baronas, eds. *Proceedings of the Hypertext Standardization Workshop,* Jan. 16–18, National Institute of Standards and Technology, U.S. Government Printing Office. Washington, D.C.

Furuta, Richard and Stotts, P. David (1990). *Dynamic Characteristics of Hypertext.* (as yet unpublished).

Garzotto, F., Paolini, P., Schwabe, D., Berstein, M. (1991). "Tools for Designing Hyperdocuments," *Hypertext / Hypermedia Handbook,* Emily Berk and Joseph Devlin (Ed.s), McGraw Hill, New York, NY.

Goldfarb, Charles F., and Newcomb, Steven R. (1990). "X3V1.8M Working Draft ANSI Project X3.749-D Hypermedia/Time-based Structuring Language (HyTime)," 7th Draft. September 5.

Moline, Judi, Benigni, Dan, and Baronas, Jean, eds. (1990). Proceedings of the Hypertext Standardization Workshop, Jan. 16–18, 1990 National Institute of Standards and Technology, U.S. Government Printing Office. Washington, D.C.

Parunak, H. V. D. (1991). "Ordering the Information Graph," *Hypertext / Hypermedia Handbook,* Emily Berk and Joseph Devlin (Ed.s), McGraw Hill, New York, NY.

Riner, R. (1991). "Automated Conversion, " *Hypertext / Hypermedia Handbook,* Emily Berk and Joseph Devlin (Ed.s), McGraw Hill, New York, NY.

27

Breaking Frames: Hyper-Mass Media

By John McDaid
New York Institute of Technology

Introduction

> Electric technology does not need words any more than the digital computer needs numbers. Electricity points the way to an extension of the process of consciousness itself, on a world scale, and without any verbalization whatever.
> — Marshall McLuhan [McLuhan, 1964, p. 83]

> A great media-metaphor shift has taken place in America, with the result that the content of much of our public discourse has become dangerous nonsense.
> — Neil Postman [Postman, 1985, pg. 16]

What I'll be suggesting in this chapter is a way of looking at the evolution of media as a recursive phenomenon, occasioned and constrained by physical and social conditions. In his book, *Understanding Media*, Marshall McLuhan presents a theory of media as a dynamic, evolving ecology. He views media history as a succession of conceptual frameworks, in the manner of whose breaking we may discern a pattern. I will focus on the role hypermedia plays, and will come to play, as we re-envision the world from within the emerging paradigm of digital technology.

What is meant by an ecological perspective on media? Take McLuhan's famous saying, "The medium is the message." One way to translate this is: "Media are environments." We usually assume that the world is "unmediated," but only naively, in an unreflective fashion. If pressed, we admit that our perceptual limits—our visual spectrum, auditory range, and tactile threshold—are limits which condition our knowledge of the world. The world, the environment you are experiencing right now, is brought to your consciousness by natural media—your senses. Media are not passive conduits, but active shapers and massagers of messages. To fully apprehend the character of the world they bring us, we must realize that they are part of our ecosystem, interacting with, shaping, and representing our experience.

Our senses are, of course, no longer supplied solely by natural media—in fact, the majority of our knowledge of the world is technologically framed, whether by a pair of glasses or the six o'clock news. In order to understand the degree of insinuation of media in natural reality's place in our environment, we must learn to break these frames—not in the manner of Luddite reactionaries, but rather in a phenomenological, postmodernist mode. Understanding media means uncovering their biases, gaining the power to unmask, in our symbolic ecology, their impact.

The Media Ecosystem

Media theorists have identified three paradigm technologies in the history of communications: orality, literacy, and electronics. These technologies shape the epistemologies, rhetorics, and social structure of the cultures which employ them [Ong, 1982; Eisenstein, 1979; Postman, 1985; Postman, 1988]. The imputed effects of orality and literacy are fairly well understood (if still subject to debate), but when theorists have looked at the electronic genre, their focus has usually been on broadcasting. Broadcasting is not truly a digital technology; it is an outgrowth of electric, rather than electronic, systems. And while these electric technologies have been with us in some form for over one hundred years, the truly electronic—that is to say, the digitally electronic technology—has existed for less than fifty.

There is reason to suspect, and hope, that the effects of the digital may be of particular relevance to the issues facing world cultures at this time. For reasons which will be touched on below, the media environments of orality and literacy have failed to match the world in important ways. Clearly, electronic broadcast media have hitherto borrowed heavily from the metaphors and methodologies of the oral world and the printed page. Hypermedia, on the other hand, is further removed from print technology; it may be digital technology's unique and definitive form.

What Is Hypermedia?

Hypermedia [Nelson, 1987] is Theodore Nelson's term for computer-mediated storage and retrieval of information in a nonsequential fashion. An extension of Nelson's earlier coinage, "hypertext" (for nonsequential writing), hypermedia implies linking and navigation through material stored in many media: text, graphics, sound, music, video, etc. [Nelson, 1987, p. 0/2]. But the ability to move through textual information and images is only half the system: a true hypermedia environment also includes tools that enable readers to rearrange the material. As Nelson put it in a comment during a HyperText '89 session: "with full user control."

In 1945, Vannevar Bush first described the (analog) personal information machine he called the *memex*. In the same much-reprinted Atlantic Monthly article he also predicted, somewhat hesitantly:

> In the outside world, all forms of intelligence, whether of sound or sight, have been reduced to the form of varying currents in an electrical circuit in order that they may be transmitted. Inside the human frame exactly the same sort of process occurs. Must we always transform to mechanical movements in order to proceed from one electrical phenomenon to another? It is a suggestive thought...
> [Bush, 1945]

Thus, Bush foresaw the advent of a new, he called it electrical but we call it digital, medium which would allow researchers to connect and reference mixed-media material instantly across disparate domains, the medium we now call hypermedia. It is the linking, the building of trails to construct hybrid documents of associational value rather than linear sequence, which marks hypermedia's radical departure from the embryonic electronic technologies of radio and television.

Not until the 1960s, with the work of visionaries like Engelbart and Nelson [Rheingold, 1985] did hypermedia begin to take shape in computer labs. And it took until the 1980s for hypermedia to make its way to the microcomputer, in programs like Guide, StorySpace, and (arguably) HyperCard. Such systems make it possible for the average personal computer user to construct and navigate through information-spaces containing any type of digital, or digitizable, content whatsoever.

Because this conversion to digital form and dependence on computers are essential characteristics of truly electronic environments, I suggest we follow Baudrillard [Baudrillard, 1982] in applying the term digitality (to parallel orality and literacy) as the shorthand descriptor for this emerging paradigm.

So What?

> Electricity points the way to an extension of the process of consciousness itself, on a world scale, and without any verbalization whatever. — Marshall McLuhan [McLuhan, 1964, p. 83]

If McLuhan is right, if digitality really does point the way to an extension of consciousness, media theorists have ample justification for concern. Although McLuhan usually intends his words as probes rather than predictions, what can we make of the promise—or threat—of a medium that needs no words?

> I will try to demonstrate that as typography moves to the periphery of our culture and television takes its place at the center, the seriousness, clarity, and, above all, value of public discourse dangerously declines. -Neil Postman [Postman, 1985, p. 29]

Will hypermedia further erode mediated discourse as descried by Neil Postman? Is the world of *blipverts*[1] and Baudrillard's *hyperreal*[2] the inevitable heat-death of discourse, or is the true ecology of media one of *Chaos*[3] rather than *Entropy*?[4] Could it be that hypermedia can deal a *counterblast* [McLuhan and Parker, 1969] against precisely such decay? (Not that hypertext will save the world, but that it might address certain communicational difficulties.) Could the early electric media—for example, television—be analogous to the intermediate phases of literacy?

Havelock [Havelock, 1976] and Ong [Ong, 1982] describe a series of evolutionary stages between orality and literacy as a function of the spread of encoding and decoding abilities. Early electronic media, especially within the context of consumer capitalism, retained print's one-way, one-to-many, hierarchical nature. Only recently, with digital computers and the convergence of audiovisual technologies, has the capability of many-to-many communication and the potential for a *polylogical* conversation emerged where marginalization is minimized, and the desire to reduce complex issues to right answers gives way to resonances along a spectrum of interpretation. Using this model, television can be thought of as the scribal phase of digitality, paralleling the scribal print culture broadcast from reader to copyist.

The Medium Is the Mirage

> And you may ask yourself—Well...how did I get here? [Byrne and Eno, 1980]

If communication media so deeply affect human consciousness by mediating transactions with reality, how can we ever get outside this system?

What Are the Variables We Need To Pay Attention To?

Theorists categorize media according to the way they shape messages: the extent to which they are visual or auditory, their degree of abstraction, and the simplicity of the coding scheme among others [Ong, 1977; Innis, 1951; Havelock, 1976].

---

1 A blipvert is a subliminal 30 second commercial broadcast in a few seconds—so quickly that viewers don't have time to change the channel—on the science fictional television channels portrayed in the Max Headroom television series.

2 [Baudrillard 1982, p. 146], "The Real is not only what can be reproduced, but that which is always already reproduced." For Baudrillard, electronic media have replaced the real with its representation. We 'see' the president on the news; we do not say we see a representation of the president.

3 As mathematicians and physicists are discovering, and as the Greeks knew years ago, from Chaos order can emerge spontaneously.

4 Entropy refers to the second law of thermodynamics: that isolated systems in ordered states move toward disorder. If the universe is a closed system, it would eventually reach absolute zero, maximum Entropy.

Based on these formal features, theorists divide media into three categories: oral, literate, and electronic, each of which will be investigated in detail below.

McLuhan also posits a state called the *unified sensorium* [McLuhan, 1964, p. 67], a prelinguistic but symbolic mental life which preceded orality, which he regards as an Edenic balance and harmonious integration of the senses. In McLuhan's view, it is only by deviating from this Blakean consciousness, only by succumbing to linearity and reification, that the Word is created.

The Word and Its World

Orality describes the state of cultures whose predominate form of communication is the spoken word. While there can be no hard evidence for such assertions, one must assume language to be of extreme antiquity, perhaps deeply implicated in the rise of organized human endeavor many tens of thousands of years ago. The characteristics of oral cultures are linked to the features of spoken language: its evanescence [Ong, 1982], its origin in the human lifeworld [Ong, 1982], and its involvement of hearing, a sense modality which is inclusive rather than detached [McLuhan, 1964]. The following charts representing correlations between media and their social impacts are derived from the work of Elizabeth Eisenstein, Eric Havelock, Marshall McLuhan, Walter J. Ong, and Neil Postman.

Orality is the base upon which other communication technologies build. Phonetic literacy, which Havelock [Havelock, 1976, p. 25] traces back to 700 BCE, emerges against the ground of underlying oral culture—in fact, the cultural shape of orality creates the need for further technological extension. While Jacques Ellul's [Ellul, 1964] strong determinist view that technology shapes culture to its own ends may not be warranted, there is evidence that sociotechnic factors in the Greek world mitigated against a solely oral culture. Orality's inability to innovate, its ineffectiveness as a durable and transportable code, and its inability to adequately homogenize an expansive empire served as the springboard for alphabetic literacy [McLuhan, 1964].

Two hypotheses are presented here: each medium arises by building recursively upon its predecessor, taking the previous technology as content, and each medium arises at the intersection of enabling technology and recursively engendered environmental pressure.

The characteristics of oral cultures listed in Table 27.2 may not seem problematic, and in fact, for some theatres of operation, oral language worked quite well. But the Greeks found themselves poorly served by the evanescence of speech, just as we today find ourselves at a juncture where the linguistic conceptions occasioned by day-to-day reality have broken down. Unlike prelinguistic symbols which suggested rather than defined meaning, oral language cuts up the world and then *utters or outers* it, projects it onto the world as *the way things ARE* [McLuhan, 1964]. And language-level decisions about the way things are were formed at pretty low levels of sophistication—a range of experience that included only the inexplicable cycling of Nature and a few crude human technologies like fire, Folsom points and, perhaps, the inclined plane. Conceptions formed in such

Table 27.1   Characteristics of Orality

Author	Text	Audience
physically present	audible	physically present
capable of response	evanescent	contextually related
cultrually enabled	recursively shaped by context	forced to track text in time

Note: Orality gives rise to texts which are formulaic, but flexible.

media environments break down quickly when operated at relativistic velocity or on submicroscopic scales.

Language makes us good at billiards, bad at quantum tunnelling. This may become a nontrivial issue as we discover which of these skills, in the long run, is more important.

The Text Remains the Same

Literacy radically alters the sensory ratios of the cultures which employ it. The world of print is highly visual, abstract, and disincarnate. It separates the word from its origins in human experience and makes possible the development of readerships not bound by space and time. Havelock [Havelock, 1976] has pointed out the epistemological implications of Greek alphabeticism. Previous syllabary notations relied on consonants. But consonants are real, discrete; they exist in isolation. Vowels, on the other hand, only exist as a flow; they are the most ephemeral of the sounds which "exist only when...going out of existence" [Ong, 1982, p. 32]. The snaring of these most fleeting abstractions indicates a powerful ability to decompose and classify. As went vowels, so went the external world. Consider the

Table 27.2   Characteristics of Oral Cultures

Media	Mind	Universe	Culture	Technology
metaphor	group	sacred	conservative	hunting
rhetoric		infinite	ear-based	framing
religion		eternal Now	human	trade

Note: Oral texts lead to a formulaic pattern of information management, and oral culures inherit this predisposition.

Table 27.3   Characteristics of Literacy

Author	Text	Audience
physically absent	visible	physically absent
incapable of response	permanent	contextually dislocated
culturally disabled	shaped at the point of "utterance"	recusively constructs text with multiple readings

Note: Written texts achieve innovation through analysis and hierachy, enabling absent readers to "reconstruct" meaning.

philosophies which arose in the period immediately following the introduction of this powerful new technology. Ong [Ong, 1982] has pointed out that Plato's world of ideas is a silent, impersonal, abstract space removed from the lifeworld...and that this is very much like the disembodied reason stored in print.

Orality enables social organizations to build up to the point of information overload. And it may have been the nascent fascination with the recursive act of talking about talking (or, as they say in the trade, *rhetoric*) that led to the idea of bringing some sort of order to the speech-act; attempting to set it down somehow, a recursion which yielded writing. (See Table 27.3.)

Of the variety of representational systems developed in response to the information overload of memory-based orality, one flavor was particularly successful: alphabetic script. McLuhan makes much of the fit this technique achieves with the growing desire to grasp and manipulate the universe; to take the flux of speech and chisel out a relatively few meaningless and arbitrary symbols, which can then be combined to form the infinite complexity of texts—recursive indeed.

The alphabet is a potent technology, but it also has serious drawbacks. As with all extensions of one sense, it pushes us further from the synesthetic manifold of pretechnological sensory experience, further from the Unified Sensorium. McLuhan argues that the alphabet freed us from the "tribal trance of resonating word magic and the web of kinship" and through the power of letters as "agents of aggressive order and precision" gave us "empires and military bureaucracies" where individuals were alienated from their "imaginative, emotional and sense" lives. [McLuhan, 1964, p. 88–90]

Writing, McLuhan says, gives us an eye for an ear. Speech may have been more linear than prelinguistic symbolization, but at least speech vanished; its sequentiality was a result of our predicament as Beings-in-Time, rather than something deliberately designed in. In computer jargon, the linearity of speech is a bug rather than a feature.

Writing is the reification of linearity, of tracking down, of hierarchizing. It is the formulaic *beginning-middle-endness* of writing that we invented it for. In many ways, this was not such a good thing. Inevitably, the teeth which shape our spoken

Table 27.4   Characteristics of Literate Cultures

Media	Mind	Universe	Culture	Technology
alphabet	individual	alienated	progressive	logic
machines		successive	eye-based	math
consumer		discrete	technical	science
capitalism				

Note: Written texts support hierarchical patterns of organization, both in information and culture.

words are exteriorized as the lead slugs packed into the maw of the printing press. The heating up of text accelerates (for good or ill) the rise of capitalism, democracy, Protestantism, and gives rise to the book-driven, specialist, curricular school. (See Table 27.4.) All of this describes fairly well where we are, and brings us to the threshold of the next recursion.

The analytic world of print has begun to crumble under the weight of its information overload. Paper-based consciousness struggles to forge the connections necessary to comprehend eleven-dimensional superstring theory, non-zero-sum geopolitics, or the etiquette of the Society of Mind. We have reached a limit, and the recursive process of writing about writing has yielded the next step—*hypermedia.*

Hypermedia: Web of Maya or Isis' Net?

> Electric technology does not need words any more than the digital computer needs numbers. Electricity points the way to an extension of the process of consciousness itself, on a world scale, and without any verbalization whatever.
> — Marshall McLuhan [McLuhan, 1964, p. 83]

> "Print is dead." — Egon Spengler, *Ghostbusters* [Brillstein, 1984]

McLuhan's epigraph is on the verge of becoming true. Electronic technologies have "reached...a critical mass," [Postman, 1985, p. 28] and have superseded the spoken and printed word as the preeminent vehicles of inculturation and communication. Hypermedia has grown out of (but is more than) intertextuality and reader-response theory. In fact, by analogy to literacy, these represent pretechnological responses to the environmental pressure built up by the information overload of linear print. Hypermedia environments make possible texts which can be reorganized by readers as they desire. Hyperdocuments can, in at least a rudimentary sense, be queried, finally putting to rest Plato's often-cited denunciation of texts as fixed, unresponsive objects. But just as the residually-oral Plato scorns the new medium of print, the residually-literate distrust the digital. As McLuhan noted:

> Such is the austere continuity of book culture that it scorns to notice these *liaisons dangereuses* among the media, especially the scandalous affairs of the book-page with electronic creatures from the other side of the linotype. — [McLuhan, 1964, p. 193]

Hypermedia's nonlinear textual spaces allow multiple readings to actualize discrete, individual texts' explications of an underlying virtual order. More like the *real world* where meaning is made transactionally, hypertexts possess a multiplicity of possibilities, each of which is equally valid and none of which is the correct order or story. The reader comes to a hypertext not as a passive receiver of a predetermined order, but as an active constructor of the text. True, books can be read out of order, but the printed order is suggestive—some might even say controlling:

> The fixed arrangement of pages always militates in favor of that "automatic" reading from first to last which branching narrative attempts to subvert. Thus, the more intricate page-turning a text demands, the more conscious its reader is likely to become of the native sequence which (s)he is being made to violate. Instead of liberating the narrative imagination, the technical difficulty of poly-sequential books inoculates readers against too much heterodox thinking. [Kaplan and Moulthrop, 1989, p. 9]

An important distinction needs to be made about the varieties of hypertextual experience. We may profit more, at this juncture, by investigating and composing hypertexts with aesthetic rather than purely functional objectives. Not to exclude expository hypertexts; rather, exposition in hypertext becomes even more artistic—the linking and building of webs is a highly complex, aesthetic process. What should be excluded is the recapitulation, in this new medium, of the established truths about how to convey information.

Two arguments underpin this philosophy. First, as McLuhan frequently pointed out, art is an anti-environment, and artists the "radar antennae" of humankind who "exult in the novelties of perception afforded by innovation...(They) glor(y) in the invention of new identities, corporate and private, that for the political and educational establishments, as for domestic life, bring anarchy and despair." [McLuhan 1968, p. 12] The second—and more prosaic— reason is that because hypermedia is in its incunabula, the body of texts available as examples is small, and most of them (even many which call themselves *art*) are simply reproductions, in the new medium, of existing works, much like incunabula texts of print [McLuhan, 1962].

Most existing hypertexts are what Michael Joyce has characterized as *exploratory*. [Joyce, 1988, p. 11] In such works, the hypertextual component is limited to navigational devices which facilitate exploration of an information space. The reader remains in *audience mode*, and reading and authoring remain different jobs. [See Chapter 8 by Joyce, in this book.] While these early hypertexts represent a

Table 27.5   Characteristics of Digitality

Author	Text	Audience
implicated in text	multi-sensory	virtual presence
limited response	flexible, active	contextually prompted
paraculturally[a] enabled	recursively created in the "reading"	actualize idiosyncratic texts from the virtual

Note: Digital "texts" are created through interaction, and yield new opportunities on each reading. The terms "author" and "audience" lose meaning as the roles become more symmetric.

[a]Hypertext authors can make certain aspects of their culture recoverable. This "paracultural" enablement is roughly analogous to the parasocial interaction supplied by broadcast media.

step in the direction of digitality, they fall short of the goal Joyce sets out: texts which fully engage the reader, which he calls *constructive hypertexts*.

> Constructive hypertexts ... require a capability to act: to create, to change, and to recover particular encounters within the developing body of knowledge....These encounters, like those in exploratory hypertexts, are maintained as versions, i.e. trails, paths, webs, notebooks, etc.; but *they are versions of what they are becoming, a structure for what does not yet exist.* — Michael Joyce [Joyce, 1988, p. 11] (Emphasis added)

In other words, knowledge *in* constructive hypertexts exists not as preconceived truth waiting impatiently to be discovered, but rather as potential, lurking in a Heisenbergian way.[5] Until we create it, link it, write it, recover it—*It* does not exist; the *Truth* is our truth. We create this knowledge contextually and share it electronically not by convincing someone that we are right, but by following their exploration of our links and exploring theirs in order to negotiate our shared and disparate spaces. (See Table 27.5.)

A new medium is a new way of translating and organizing experience and a new way of sharing it. It is to be anticipated that these translations of experience—and their ramifications for culture—will be profoundly different from those of print. (See Table 27.6.) In the same way that the sequential, linear printing press gave rise to sequential, linear systems, we have begun to see, in a variety of disciplines, the importance of recursion (models of the writing process and the universe), of holistic thinking (management styles and medicine), and integrative

---

5   Here I am referring to the Heisenberg Uncertainty Principle. One overly simplistic statement of the Heisenberg Uncertainty Principle is that the more we know about one thing, the less we know about something else.

Table 27.6   Characteristics of Digital Cultures

Media	Mind	Universe	Culture	Technology
icons	holistic	recursive	integrative	parallel processing[a]
telepresence[b]		self-similar[c]	sense-balanced	Object Oriented Languages
AI/robots		relativistic	parahuman[d]	hypermedia

Note: Hypertexts suggest ways of organizing information and culture which are active, decentralized, and nonlinear.

[a] Computer systems with multiple processors simultaneously manipulating data.

[b] Remote operation of devices supported by realistic presentation of sensory information.

[c] Patterns of organization repeated at differing levels of detail.

[d] The human scale of oral cultures freed from their media constraints; the Global Village.

rather than mass-market culture (micro-marketing, narrowcasting, electronic bulletin boards).

Examining the technologies which create the digital recursion can give us insight into their likely effects: rather than the hierarchies of traditional computer programs, the new *object oriented languages* create a system of computational entities, each with some degree of autonomy, which work together to accomplish a task. Writing an object-oriented program is not so much like punching keys on a calculator as it is like building Frankenstein's monster from pre-existing body parts.

The Potential of Hypermedia Discourse

So, what then is the ecological perspective on hypermedia? The circuitous route I have taken so far in defining this rough beast is an indication of how difficult it is to encode one technology within another. As Isadora Duncan's apocryphal explanation of dance goes, "If I could *explain* it, I wouldn't have to *dance* it." Nor is this a facile sidestepping of the issue. Hypermedia is, literally, *a process that must be experienced*—it is a process in time. Imagine trying to explain, in a completely oral culture, your brand new idea for *books*. It's difficult to get anyone to understand because, being completely oral, there is no language for that which does not exist in an oral world. You, with this idea of language bound up on paper, are obviously not right in the head.

Ted Nelson has suggested thinking of hypermedia as the general phenomenon of which linear texts are a special case. A linear text, in his view, is a hypertext of which only one possible track or series of links has been actualized, the canonical link structure (top left to bottom right, turn page) which has become so inculcated as to have vanished in a Barthesian mythological sleight-of-hand. Teaching children to write, therefore, is like teaching them to draw only straight lines. It may enable them to draw straight lines eventually, but it doesn't open up the more interesting questions of curves, or spheres, or the constraints of dimensionality itself. Hypertext, taken as a design discipline, is analogous to presenting the straight line as a degenerate member of the class of two-dimensional curves—an interesting and powerful member of the family of dimensional rhetorics, but not the only member.

Another spin is to view hypermedia composition in light of the theory of media evolution sketched out above. Picture McLuhan's Unified Sensorium, the many-at-onceness of symbolization, as the starting point. As an artifact of our predicament as Beings-in-Time, we develop primitive media strongly flavored by single-channel linearity. (We can only hear linearly.) When these media shatter the Unified Sensorium, we climb through a spiral of orality and literacy, to return (this time with full consciousness, as James Joyce might suggest) to a hyper- or multi-mode reunification of the senses.

The need for such reunification—and the danger of failure—is especially significant in light of Postman's most recent critique of mass media: "It is clear that our engineers, not our poets, are the unacknowledged legislators of our time" [Postman, 1988, p. xiii]. Here we have an electronic medium which can be precisely, powerfully, in the hands of the poets, a technology which replaces passive viewing with active involvement, and which provides a means to achieve the connectivity and coherence leeched from modern culture by the primitive hybrid fusion of print and electronics. It seems we are in the midst of a *phase change* between technologies, when the characteristics of the defining medium become momentarily apparent [McLuhan, 1964, p. 27]. Here is an opportunity and, for those concerned with media, a responsibility.

We already know that people need to be active shapers of knowledge, that we constitute ourselves in polylogic rather than monologic roles, and that the communicational field needs to be a transactional space. If we examine the fit of these goals with hypermedia—and print—we may well discover that what we've been trying to do all along has been to live in a hypermedia mode, but that we have been constrained by our print-framed environment.

And lurking behind our self-interest and idealism is the still-turning wheel of evolution. Orality and print, arising out of the linear lifeworld, have profound bandwidth limitations. Our common sense, those cognitive constructs occasioned by experience with linear media, break down in the face of a universe which is mostly not human-sized, unsettlingly discontinuous, and decidedly nonlinear. Ernst Cassirer has described relativity as "the shattering of the highest law of motion taught us by experience." [Cassirer, 1923, p. 39]. The order of events depends on the frame of reference—a difficult notion for the linearly imprinted.

The leading edge of the recursion is already here. Parallel processing, object-oriented languages, and hypermedia discourse are aspects of this digital paradigm, one of interactive fictions and simulated realities. Unhinged from the requirements imposed by archaic media, consciousness can bootstrap itself into conceptual frameworks literally unimaginable today, where relativity is not the shattering of any law at all, but is as intuitive as the inertia of a moving car.

What is at stake in this recursion is the transformation of consciousness. There are tremendous vested interests: the institutions many of us work for specialize in training people to accept and become narcotized by linearity and its infrastructure. What Moulthrop [Moulthrop, 1989, p. 265] has called the "military-entertainment complex" (or military-*infotainment* [Joyce, 1990]) waits eagerly to turn hypermedia into just more HyperMTV.

As people concerned with the potential of computer-mediated discourse, we must push for a vision of hypermedia as decentered and democratic, as a read-write rather than a read-only medium, and as a way of telling new stories rather than repackaging and repurposing the old.

Whole new forms of communication are not rolled out in every generation. To us falls the task of breaking a frame many of us are deeply attached to. But we have no choice; we must act, now, to shape a digital culture of empowerment and difference, or we will be swept, wordless, into the matrix where the future may well be a DataBoot[6]—stamping on the human interface, forever. If it helps, try to remember that Marshall McLuhan was an optimist.

About the Author

John McDaid

John McDaid is a doctoral candidate in the Media Ecology Program at New York University, where he is currently completing his dissertation on the symbolic ecology of hypermedia.

He worked with NYU's Expository Writing Program, where he developed and coordinated their Macintosh writing/hypermedia labs. He is currently an instructor at the New York Institute of Technology. He is currently working on a full-length hypermedia fiction, called *Uncle Buddy's Phantom Funhouse*. [See Chapter 7 by Moulthrop, in this book.]

Mr. McDaid may be contacted at 197 Sterling Place, Brooklyn, NY 11238, or by BITnet: Mcdaid@nyucf.

Author Notes. I am indebted to Michael Joyce, Nancy Kaplan, and Stuart Moulthrop for their friendship and insights. Much of this text owes its clarity to discussions with these valued colleagues. A special thanks to Karen Marlow-McDaid for her ideas and critical perspective, as always.

---

6 I use DataBoot as a pun on the phrase DataGlove, the three-dimensional input device used in Virtual Reality programs to propel users through totally artificial three-dimensional spaces, to suggest that there might be a dark side to virtual realities. To me, a DataBoot is a general term for all input and output where the sole rhetoric is one of simulation [Orwell, 1961, p. 220].

References

Baudrillard, J. (1982). *Simulations*, (P. Foss, P. Patton, P. and P. Beitchman, Trans.), Semiotext(e), New York, NY.

Brillstein, B., (Producer) & Reitman, I. (Director). (1984) *Ghostbusters*, (Film). Columbia Pictures, Los Angeles, CA.

Bush, V. (1945). "As We May Think," *The Atlantic Monthly*, July. Also, reprinted in Nelson, T. (1987). *Literary Machines*, (Available from Ted Nelson, Project Xanadu, Palo Alto, CA.)

Byrne, D. and Eno, B. (Composers). (1980). "Once in a Lifetime," *Remain in Light*, (LP Record), Sire, New York, NY.

Cassirer, E. (1923). *Structure and Function and Einstein's Theory of Relativity*, Open Court, New York, NY.

Eisenstein, E. (1979). *The Printing Press as an Agent of Change*, Cambridge University Press, Cambridge, MA.

Ellul, J. (1964). *The Technological Society*, (Merton, R., Trans.). Vintage, New York, NY.

Havelock, E. (1976). *Origins of Western Literacy*, The Ontario Institute for Studies in Education, Toronto, Canada.

Innis, H. (1951). *The Bias of Communication*, University of Toronto Press, Toronto, Canada.

Joyce, M. (1991). "Selfish Interaction or, Subversive Texts and the Multiple Novel," *Hypertext / Hypermedia Handbook*, Emily Berk and Josph Devlin (Ed.s), McGraw-Hill, New York, NY.

Joyce, M. (1990). Keynote address, Computers and Writing conference, Austin, TX, May.

Joyce, M. (1988). "Siren Shapes: Exploratory and Constructive Hypertexts," *Academic Computing*, *3(4)* November, 10–14, 37–42.

Kaplan, N. and Moulthrop, S. (1989). *Something to Imagine*, Manuscript submitted for publication.

McLuhan, M. (1964). *Understanding Media*, McGraw-Hill, New York, NY.

McLuhan, M. (1962). *The Gutenberg Galaxy*, New American Library, New York, NY.

McLuhan, M. & Parker, H. (1969). *Counterblast*, Harcourt, Brace & World, New York, NY.

Minsky, M. (1986). *The Society of Mind*, Simon and Schuster, New York, NY.

Moulthrop, S. (1991). "Making Nothing Happen in Hypermedia Fiction," *Hypertext / Hypermedia Handbook*, Emily Berk and Joseph Devlin (Ed.s), McGraw-Hill, New York, NY.

Moulthrop, S. (1989). "Hypertext and the Hyperreal," *Hypertext '89 Proceedings*, *ACM*, New York, NY, 259–267.

Nelson, T. (1987). *Literary Machines*, Available from Ted Nelson, Project Xanadu, Palo Alto, CA.

Ong, W. (1982). *Orality and Literacy*, Methuen, New York, NY.

Ong, W. (1977). *Interfaces of The Word*, Cornell University Press, Ithaca, New York, NY.

Orwell, G. (1961). *1984*, New American Library, New York, NY.

Postman, N. (1988). *Conscientious Objections*, Knopf, New York, NY.

Postman, N. (1985). *Amusing Ourselves To Death*, Viking, New York, NY.

Rheingold, H. (1985). *Tools For Thought*, Simon and Schuster, New York, NY.

Appendix A:
Case Studies

Sometimes, the real-life work of creating hyperdocuments is obscured in theoretical discussions of link typing, recursion and the true meaning of hypertext.
  The following Case Studies section, which describes existing hyperdocuments and how they came to be created, is intended to inspire readers to engineer their own, and to alert them to the issues they are likely to confront in so doing.

Case 1
Hypertext and Journalism:
Towards a New Mass Medium

By Wayne Macphail
Metaphor—The Hypermedia Group, Inc.

Introduction

Newspapers, with their reliance on sidebars, summary paragraphs, graphics and their umbilical information connection to previous and related stories, are prime candidates for conversion to hypertext and hypermedia. The true hypermedia newspaper is a long way off, but for the past two years, I've been exploring the application of plain vanilla hypertext to newspaper journalism.

In cooperation with the *Hamilton Spectator,* the daily paper in Hamilton, Ontario, Canada, I've developed two hypertext systems. One is a hypertext guide to researchers who are looking for alternative causes of AIDS. The second is a guide to immigration and new immigrants to the Hamilton area. Both systems can run on a basic IBM Personal Computer or clone, with or without a hard drive or graphics card.

The authoring software I used for both projects is PC-Hypertext by Neil Larson of MaxThink. I used this simple, clever tool for several reasons:

- It runs on the most modest of IBM PCs. This was important because the newspaper wanted the product to be used by the greatest number of our readers. Although PC-Hypertext allows for the use of graphics (from CGA to VGA) we steered clear of them, because we wanted our hyperdocument to fit on a single 5 1/4" disk. We also wanted people without graphics cards to be able to browse it.
- It is extremely easy to make and alter links using PC-Hypertext. With authoring systems such as HyperCard, links are associated with physical locations on the screen. This type of linking is called screen-linking. If text is shortened or lengthened, the button remains in the same screen position and is therefore useless in regard to the context of the written material. With text-based links, the links are part of the ASCII text file and move when the text is edited. PC-Hypertext links are text-linked rather than screen-linked which makes it possible

to re-edit copy without having to re-program your links. This is a must for newspaper copy-based hypertext systems.

- The interface is easy to use. A novice can navigate the hyperdocument using only the four cursor keys and can return to a main menu screen using the CTRL-HOME key combination. There are elegant bells and whistles in the system as well, but most users stick with just six keys for browsing. The learning curve is a steep but easy climb.

- It is easy to add additional files to a PC-Hypertext system. Editing existing files is also effortless because all information, including links, is stored in ASCII form.

- MaxThink has developed a number of powerful, elegant tools for creating intelligent hierarchical structures that lead people intuitively through a body of information. These include the MaxThink Outline Processor and Houdini, both of which allow users to easily build hierarchical and knowledge matrix systems which can be converted into hyperdocuments using other utilities available from MaxThink.

- It's possible to jump out to DOS or run other programs while inside PC-Hypertext. We take advantage of this capability, by developing a quiz program used in both the AIDS and Immigration hyperdocuments that dynamically alters the text based on a reader's wrong answers. The quiz can be taken as a hypertext jump. When readers return from the quiz, they are led to a screen that provides suggestions for further reading. The suggestions themselves are anchors to links to points in the hyperdocument, so readers not only get immediate feedback about their knowledge of the system but also immediate remedial instruction. (The AIDS quiz was written in Turbo C.)

- PC-Hypertext allows for graphics, indices, glossaries, bookmarks, and other editorial functions should they be necessary.

The two journalistic hyperdocuments I developed differ from one another in a key aspect. The first system was a straight conversion from print to hypertext. The second was built as a hypertext from day one, that is, hypertext was used as an organizational as well as a delivery tool.

The AIDS Hypertext

The first project I developed using hypertext began life as a three-part series about those who explore the causes of AIDS. I wrote and researched the article with another journalist, Suzanne Morrison, now the *Hamilton Spectator's* medical reporter. The series ran in *The Spectator* as three full-page articles.

When I converted the articles to hypertext I first went through them and highlighted medical and technical terms I thought needed definition. I then wrote approximately thirty screen-long definitions, each as a separate ASCII file. I divided the articles into more digestible chunks knowing that, through hypertext, I could link them together again. Occasionally, this chunking required some rewriting, but often it didn't as the structure of the pieces lent itself to easy division. A software tool developed by MaxThink (called File Splitter) made the file-splitting easy. Next, I wrote what I called a *touchstone piece*, a short summary of the information with a myriad of links to the network numbering two dozen primary files.

Jumps from those major files took users to other minor files (definitions, for example). So, from the main menu, a user was only three keystrokes away from any file in the system. This quick, intuitive access to information is the key to effective hypertext.

What I had done, to use newspaper parlance, was create a main story with approximately 85 sidebars. Sidebars are the short, sometimes shaded or tinted stories that run beside or in the middle of longer pieces. They're meant to expand on aspects of a story that would otherwise divert a reader's attention if placed in the middle of a piece.

The beauty of hypertext sidebars is, of course, that they are accessible no matter where a reader is in a network. For example, one of the definitions I wrote was for the term "retrovirus." This word shows up often in the series of articles and a reader can move from the mention of the word to a definition of it. That's much simpler than flipping back a few pages or scanning up a column in search of a definition printed earlier. This highlights another advantage of hypertext: it shows readers how one piece of information is associated with other things.

Finally, to finish the AIDS hyperdocument, I created a number of menus that lead users directly to definitions, information on key theories, biographies of the researchers, and to a general background discussion on AIDS itself. These multiple pathways into information make it easy for first-time readers to navigate a system and help create the illusion of vast knowledge and infinite choice in what is really a closed system with carefully designed pathways.

The final system, which contained all the information in the original stories, plus definitions and the AIDS background information, fit nicely on a single 5 1/4" disk. I compressed the information into a single file and uploaded it onto a number of BBS systems in Canada and the U.S. *The Spectator* agreed that we would not charge for the hyperdocument but rather asked that users who found it valuable would make a donation to a local AIDS organization. Since it was released two years ago, it has made its way to Antwerp, Glasgow, and all of North America. It is part of the McMaster University Medical Centre Library and is used by AIDS groups as educational material. The rapidity with which this hyperdocument travelled is a good indicator, I think, of the power of hypertext as a mass medium.

The Immigration Hypertext

In the years following the release of the AIDS hyperdocument, I explored a number of hypertext systems including KnowledgePro, Guide, Black Magic, and Matrix Layout. Each had its own appeal, but I found myself returning to MaxThink's products because they allowed me to develop hypertexts quickly and efficiently.

In the summer of 1990 I had the opportunity to head a group of ten reporters putting together a 24-page tabloid insert into *The Spectator* about the new wave of immigrants coming into the community. It struck me as an ideal hypertext project; I could see the advantage of linking hard data about countries of origin with sole human-interest, life-experience stories. Also, I thought that it would be interesting to contrast the various immigration experiences of our newcomers to those of immigrants from other countries.

Fortunately, *The Spectator* was interested in the project and allotted me three months' time to produce copy for both the tabloid and hypertext forms. *The Spectator* was also interested in making use of the hypertext form in the *Newspapers In Education* (NIE) program used by many newspapers in North America. Local school boards have IBM Personal Computers, so MaxThink's HyPlus (a more recent version of PC-Hypertext) seemed like a good developmental system to use.

Because I knew from the start that the project would become a hypertext, I decided to use HyPlus in conjunction with Qedit Advanced to write the various articles. HyPlus lacks its own editor, but allows an easy jump (using the ALT-E key combination) to any ASCII editor you care to use. Qedit is a quick, wonderfully configurable text editor that fit the bill exactly. All the reporters learned how to use the system (learning time was about 20 minutes.) Many not only entered and edited their stories, but also learned how to create links between stories.

Using hypertext as the developmental tool made it easy to keep track of stories and made it simple for reporters to jump to other journalist's work to see what they were learning. We also developed a messaging system which we removed once the final product had been completed.

The Immigration and AIDS hyperdocuments were developed differently. For the Immigration hyperdocument, I built a lattice of menus and dummy files as a skeleton. This allowed reporters to see how their stories fit in context with other work and made it easy to keep track of finished and unfinished nodes. As the reporters wrote their stories, the skeleton began to flesh out. When all the stories were complete, a copy editor stepped in and edited the raw copy. The stories were then ported over to our layout and pagination terminals. After porting, the intra-file links were added. The system was developed this way because otherwise the copy editor would have had to remove the hypertext jumps from the destined-for-print copy. It also insured that both the hypertext and print copy was clean and identical.

Next a practical, not exhaustive, word index was done for the hypertext version. We also added links to NIE questions and exercises not found in the tabloid version.

There is a quiz in the Immigration hypertext version much like the one in the AIDS hypertext. This time, however, I rewrote the code in BATCOM, basically a language that extends batch files. It's perfect for writing small (though somewhat slow) programs that manipulate files and get user input. The whole quiz filled approximately 8K of memory.

At this writing the Immigration hypertext is about to be made available to readers of the *Hamilton Spectator*. The plan is that the disk (the system takes about 500K but has been PKZIPPed down to one self-unzipping file that fits on a single disk) will be available to local schools through the NIE program and also available to nonscholastic readers of the paper at a nominal cost. We hope it will be the first of many such products.

Conclusion

I think these two ventures in journalistic publishing hold promise. They are simple, though, I think, effective tools that are realistic considering the capability of the PCs most people have. They also point out that there is a great deal of difference between the linear, top to bottom, reading of a newspaper and the lateral jumps that can be made in hypertext. Information and knowledge have to be packaged and thought about in new, exciting ways before hypertext comes into its own.

As the price of hardware decreases and the availability of that hardware increases, hypertext, and eventually hypermedia, will make inroads into media share accessed by the general public. Newspapers need to develop and nurture hyperjournalistic skills in their reporters and editors now in preparation for technological advances that will surely come.

About the Author

Wayne MacPhail

Wayne is president of Metaphor—The Hypermedia Group, Inc., and the science/technology reporter at *The Hamilton Spectator*. He is striving, in both capacities, to marry journalism and hypermedia.

Wayne can be reached at Metaphor, 91 Bond St. North, Hamilton, Ontario, Canada, L8S 3W4.

Case 2
ACM's Hypertext and Hypermedia Publishing Projects

By Edward Fox
Virginia Polytechnic Institute and State University

Bernard Rous
ACM

and Gary Marchionini
University of Maryland

The *Association for Computing Machinery* (ACM), founded in 1947 as the society for the computing community, aims to advance the sciences and arts of information processing, to promote the free exchange of information about these areas among professionals and the public, and to develop and maintain the integrity and competence of individuals involved in computing activities. In 1988, the publication activities of ACM were consolidated under the auspices of *ACM Press*. That year, *ACM Press Database and Electronic Products* was established to coordinate hypertext, hypermedia, CD-ROM, online database, interactive multimedia, database extracts, and other publishing efforts based on ACM's growing electronic library. Edward A. Fox served as volunteer editor, and Bernard Rous (Associate Director for Publications) coordinated activities at ACM headquarters. In 1989, Gary Marchionini was appointed editor for hypertext and hypermedia products, and Scott Stevens was appointed editor for interactive multimedia, to handle the growing publishing program—both volunteers working in cooperation with Editor-in-Chief Fox. At ACM Headquarters, Margaret Tuttle was hired in 1990 to coordinate CD-ROM and related publishing efforts.

These activities have been related closely, since 1988, to the area of hypertext publishing. The first venture related to *Hypertext '87*, the large conference held at the University of North Carolina at Chapel Hill under the auspices of ACM. Some of the best papers from that conference were extended and printed as a Special Issue of *Communications of the ACM*, appearing in July 1988. Fox and Rous coordinated publication of hypertext versions of that Special Issue, timed to appear with it, and to be available for *SIGGRAPH '88*, held in August of that year.

Three versions of *Hypertext on Hypertext* were commissioned, to run under MS-DOS (coordinated by Ben Shneiderman, using HyperTies), as a group of HyperCard stacks (coordinated by Nicole Yankelovich), and for SUN and Apollo workstations (coordinated by Elise Yoder, using KMS). Each version was developed independently, was sent out for review, and was revised based on comments received—all in a short time period so that production deadlines could be met. Well over 2000 copies of this hypertext have been sold, with many used for courses on hypertext. Several articles have been written about these products (e.g. "Hand-crafted hypertext—lessons from the ACM experiment" by Leora Alschuler, pages 343–361 in *THE SOCIETY OF TEXT: Hypertext, Hypermedia and the Social Constructs of Information*, ed. by E. Barrett, MIT Press, 1989).

From a user's perspective, two of the most notable features of this project are: (1) readers can read about hypertext as they work with it, thus experiencing many of the situations described by the authors; and (2) readers can compare the same hypertext on three different platforms and with three different software systems, as well as compare them with the printed version. The main weaknesses are probably: (1) the photos and figures were not as nice as those used in the printed forms; and (2) since the journal issue was short and contained articles selected for breadth instead of depth, the resulting hypertext did not have as much added value from links as might be desired.

From the publisher perspective, *Hypertext on Hypertext* was a valuable experience. While the financial gain was slight, more important, however, were the lessons learned regarding hypertext publishing: (1) standards are needed so that publishers can prepare a single version of a hypertext rather than undertake the expensive effort of producing several for different platforms and operating systems; (2) because of the slow growth of the CD-ROM field in the 1980s and the size constraints of reproducing quality images and figures, larger hypertexts are more manageable on workstations; and (3) a long term hypertext publishing program would best be established as a result of cost-benefit analysis to identify important value-added works, that are of adequate size to be truly useful.

Based on these lessons, ACM has adopted a two-pronged approach to hypertext publishing. One has been to support work toward hypertext standards [see Chapter 21 by Fox, Chen, and France, and Chapter 26 by Devlin, in this book]. The second has been to commission preparation of new hypertexts with significant added-value. This latter effort is being coordinated by Gary Marchionini. The first project of this type involves Robert Akscyn, as volunteer editor, and Elise Yoder of Knowledge Workshop (an organization identified as the result of a thorough study of responses to an ACM-issued Request for Proposal for selecting hypertext vendors.)

They are developing a large hypertext for ACM, using the proceedings from *Hypertext '87, Hypertext '89*, and a variety of articles that have appeared in the hypertext/hypermedia field. Also, a large bibliography will be integrated with this collection of articles, so that a comprehensive hypertext for the field is available for searching and browsing. The final result will be usable on workstations using KMS, both for individual systems and in networked configurations. In addition, a CD-ROM will be prepared, with the KMS version, as well as a standard version of the entire hypertext. The intention is for KMS to automatically export to whatever is the current draft standard for hypertext/hypermedia. At present, an option being considered is X3V1.8M/SD-7 *Hypermedia/Time-based Structuring Language* (Hy-Time) being developed by ANSI X3V1.8M, the Music Information Processing Standards Committee.

A variety of other hypertext and hypermedia publishing activities are in progress or being planned. ACM is also open to proposals for co-development and/or co-marketing of similar electronic products that are in keeping with its educational and other missions.

About the Authors

Edward A. Fox

Edward A. Fox received his B.S. from MIT in 1972 in Electrical Engineering, and his MS. and Ph.D. degrees in Computer Science from Cornell University. Dr. Fox is currently an Associate Professor in the Department of Computer Science at Virginia Polytechnic Institute and State University. He serves as Vice Chair for the ACM Special Interest Group on Information Retrieval (SIGIR), Associate Editor for ACM Transactions on Information Systems, and on various other boards and advisory groups. He can be reached at the Department of Computer Science, 562 McBryde Hall, Virginia Polytechnic Institute and State University, Blacksburg, VA 24061-0106.

Bernard Rous

Bernard Rous received his Masters degree in Anthropology from the New School for Social Research in 1974, and B.A. from Brandeis in 1968. He was Executive Editor for Computing Reviews 1983-87 and has been Associate Director of Publications for the ACM since 1988. Bernard Rous may be contacted at ACM, 11 West 42nd Street, 3rd Floor, New York, NY 10036.

Gary Marchionini

Gary Marchionini is an Associate Professor in the College of Library and Information Sciences. His research is focused on information seeking in electronic environments and human-computer interaction. He can be reached at CLIS, Rm. 4121G, Hornbake Bldg. (South Wing), University of Maryland, College Park, MD 20742-4345.

Case 3
DaTa Knowledgebase Systems™ (Deloitte & Touche Accounting & Auditing Knowledgebase Systems)

By Bruce I. Winters
Deloitte & Touche

Neil Larson
MaxThink, Inc.

Anthony Philips
Savoir Faire

Quick Case Data

Knowledgebase—Accounting and Auditing Pronouncements and Materials

Delivery Platform—CD-ROM

First Delivery—January 1988

Frequency of Delivery—Quarterly (with intermediate deliveries where importance or weight of material justifies)

Size—approximately 70 million bytes or 30,000 printed pages of material

Software Platform—a derivative of Houdini and Hynet and related utilities from MaxThink Inc.

Updates—Upwards of 3 million bytes

User base—Worldwide use by audit staff

Introduction

Why would one of the six largest accounting and auditing firms, one with 57,000 employees and 4,900 partners in 104 countries, get involved with a new technology (hypertext) on a new medium (CD-ROM)?

- In the past ten years there has been a veritable explosion of new accounting, tax, legal and securities rules, and pronouncements. The volume of material that an average CPA has to be cognizant of has gone from 2,000 to 8,000 pages in the past ten years. The value of all this material, in terms of what is really there that's of any function or utility, has not increased. There's also a distinction between potential information and realized information.
- Our clients have become very sophisticated. Often the larger clients have hired some of our best people and put them to work keeping their firm abreast of current accounting and auditing issues and developments. Although the clients' accounting specialists concentrate on the accounting issues related to their industry and their client firm throughout the year, our staff typically deals with several clients a year in different industries.
- Deloitte & Touche, like all major accounting firms, has a consistent staff turnover.

Four years ago, we addressed these problems. We first considered the use of technology that was already available—hard copy and an existing on-line accounting knowledgebase called NAARS.

The Decision to Hypertext

The major issue, we thought, was volume of information—how could we store it all in one place? Volume mitigated against paper, and argued for electronic storage and a computer.

We also realized that the written word, to date, has bound us (no pun intended) into sequential searches and sequential presentations. Using the computer as the tool, different pathways could be created for different readers based upon their background, their interest, and the level of understanding they already have.

For some years there has been in existence a computer system called *National Accounting and Auditing Research System* (NAARS), which is run by the *American Institute of Certified Public Accountants* (AICPA), the accounting and auditing profession's governing body. NAARS is an on-line system available through the Mead Lexis-Nexis network. NAARS has dramatically improved the ability of professionals to access information. However, because users must use text string/Boolean searches to obtain information from the system, searchers using NAARS must be expert enough to know what they are looking for and that the answer is in the NAARS system. If both of these are not true then the result is usually information overload, a costly pile of paper and a frustrated user. Problems in obtaining cost effective answers prompted Deloitte & Touche to establish a small group of NAARS search professionals.

One possible answer was to reduce the cost of NAARS searches. We were aware that one of our competitors had taken this approach by putting the contents of NAARS (and more) on a CD-ROM but using text string/boolean search. Their approach addressed the cost issue but did not resolve two important problems:

- Text searching is like ice fishing: you put bait down the hole and sit and wait. If the bait is right you hook lots of data/fish and if it is not (wrong search algorithm) you get nothing—and you don't know which until you are finished.
- You cannot, as yet, ask an intelligent question using text string searches. If you ask for "income taxes" you get "income taxes" and not "FAS96" and "APB11" or "deferred taxes" even though you would be quite happy to find information on these issues as well.

The nail in the string search coffin for us was a study we followed up on that showed that lawyers using either of the U.S.'s largest on-line databases found only 22 percent of the citable cases in their searches. Studies show that even professional researchers of on-line databases find less than 50 percent of the available information on any subject. At the core, the issue is that it does not matter how many books you have on the shelf if you can't find what you want when you need it.

The real issue, we found, was *how* to store knowledge in the computer so users could find it. The developers of DaTa considered a number of techniques for managing the necessary information. One candidate was *Artificial Intelligence* (AI). [See Chapter 22 by Littleford, in this book for more information about AI.] However, hypertext offered significant advantages over AI to DaTa's creators. These included speed of hypertext construction, rapidity of learning, facilitation of knowledge representation, ease of modification and efficient transmission of knowledge.

We concluded that hypertext would provide *browsability* so that those who are not experts can still circle the area in which the answer lies and hone in on it in an intuitive way; it would allow searchers to see associated information while a search was being made.

The result was *DaTa Knowledgebase Systems.*™ DaTa consists of a structured collection of documents interconnected by key words and ideas to create a set of hypertext networks of information. It provides any user with access to expert level accounting/auditing knowledge and allows instant jumping between documents.

Objectives of DaTa

The result of our research was the adoption of the following objectives for DaTa:

- Comprehensiveness: Include all relevant accounting and auditing information by idea content.

- Speed: Provide rapid, easy access (less than ten keystrokes) to specific answers without presuming any knowledge of the material by the user.
- Context: Present all relevant information relating to the accessed information within the total body of accounting knowledge.
- Documentation: Provide an audit trail of the search, as well as electronic copying and printing capability of user elected information.

Hardware Considerations

We did not want our people to have to buy sophisticated new PCs just to run DaTa. We wanted something that would work on our lowest common denominator machine: an IBM PC or compatible with 640K RAM, a monochrome monitor (Note: DaTa also runs in full color), even running with a slow 8088 CPU. This ruled out software that used more sophisticated and complex systems. Our people are text-oriented and generally have little need for mice, which represented another constraint. We concluded that all data would be provided on CD-ROM so that, with a single disk, a volatile body of knowledge could be easily, inexpensively, securely and completely updated.

Construction of DaTa

Hypertext, based on our research, represented in theory a very viable answer to our problems. It was not an easy answer in practice. We have struggled with at least the following problems in developing DaTa into a viable system:

- Getting text into the hyperdocument
- How to update large volumes of information
- How to make links visible or invisible
- How to make the system easy to use
- The question of copyright
- The issue of copy protection
- The skills required of the author/preparer of the hypertext

In this case study, we will discuss two general problems in some depth.

Getting Text Into the Hyperdocument

Following are the steps we go through to convert a typical 150-page section of text into a hyperdocument:

- Data Input: Only about 20 percent of the material included in DaTa comes to us in electronic form. The rest needs to be scanned in. OCR (Optical Character

Recognition) is not as much of a "science" as we would like; it is never 100 percent accurate. We end up with numerous glitches and typos.

- Clean up the text: Run spelling and grammar checkers, then proof the text to correct errors.
- Split the text into files: Using a word processor, we add a code, a file name, and a file descriptor at each new idea unit in the text (generally every 1–4 paragraphs). A DaTa utility uses these codes to split the original files into smaller ASCII files. 150 pages become about 500 ASCII files.

Steps one through three usually take 80 percent of the time. The remainder of the process requires brain rather than brawn.

- Build a master cross-reference index to the ASCII files. We use a utility to mark key words and phrases in each file (and add synonyms if necessary). We highlight perhaps three or four words/phrases per file, then assemble these word lists into a master cross-reference file.
- Put the cross-references into each ASCII file. We load the word/phrase cross-reference list into a network builder, then use this network to identify files that shared common words and phrases.
- Integrity check. Use another DaTa utility program to make sure the ASCII networks are valid (no isolated files, no dead-end links, etc.)
- We use both a decision-tree builder and network builder to build the knowledge hierarchies/networks that lead to other hierarchies/ networks.

Skills Required of a Hypertext Author

The cleaner the original structure, the easier it will be to turn a document into hypertext. It is imperative when constructing a knowledgebase that the hypertext author have a very highly developed sense of structure of the material. That means that he or she knows the material well (and preferably has a passion for it) and has a very good understanding of how the hyperdocument should work.

A hyperdocument is as good as its author makes it. Hypertext is not a panacea for bad writing. In fact it makes bad writing worse.

DaTa—Next Steps

DaTa has helped us make strides toward the enhancement of professional skills. We have a long way to go. We still need to enhance:

- User modelling: The user needs to be able to tailor the knowledge for his or her specific needs.
- Query: One major difference between the neophyte and the expert is that an expert (in theory) knows which questions to ask. DaTa should assist the neophyte in phrasing the (right) questions.

- Analytical: Despite the intelligence built into DaTa, its users must still do plenty of ad hoc analysis. To support this, DaTa will provide an assortment of tools and advice on how to use them. DaTa must have the ability to actually produce results, not abstract decisions but results as policy, guidance, actions, contracts, financial statements, and files supporting opinions.
- Change: The more organized the information the greater the impact of change. If DaTa is to be truly useful in nontrivial areas, then it must become expert at dealing explicitly with change for the user.

Can all this be done? Can it be done with the current tools? Can it be done cost effectively?

We feel the answer is yes three times. DaTa has produced a quantum increase in our ability to deliver Knowledge. We feel that DaTa is just the first step, but it is definitely a step in the right direction.

About the Authors

Bruce I. Winters

Bruce I. Winters, CISA, CPA, is a senior manager with the national office of Deloitte & Touche in Wilton, Connecticut. He is responsible for the management and coordination of all the firm's DaTa (Deloitte & Touche Accounting and Auditing Knowledgebase Systems) related activities. His education includes a BBA and MBA degrees in public accounting with a minor in computer science. Bruce has over ten years of experience as a computer audit specialist and five years in national accounting and auditing—audit methods and techniques. For the past three and a half years, he has directed the devlopment , production and delivery of DaTa for the firm. He believes that his introduction of DaTa (hypertext) and CD-ROM technology to the firm has already made major changes in the way accountants and auditors think and work.

Bruce enjoys speaking to groups (including formal university teaching), working on his house, swimming, and his favorite pastime is dieting. He and his wife Susan live in West Redding, Connecticut.

Bruce can be contacted at Deloitte & Touche, Ten Westport Road, P. O. Box 820, Wilton, CT 06897-0820.

Neil Larson

Neil Larson is president of MaxThink, a software development firm in Berkeley, California. As a consultant to Deloitte & Touche, he is responsible for the DaTa software engine and utilities. He has a BS in math from UC Berkeley and an MBA from Stanford, with a focus on marketing and operations research. He is very interested in how people think and how computer software can help represent and clarify ideas.

In his meager spare time, he plays banjo in a Dixieland jazz band, plays stride piano, tap dances, is a sailor and avid science fiction reader.

Anthony Phillips

Anthony Phillips is an independent consultant that helps build the knowledgebases in DaTa. Previously, he was a partner of Deloitte & Touche, controller of a Fortune 500 company, a FASB project manager, and author. His professional life has been spent resolving accounting problems. DaTa represents his ultimate efforts to help make the experiences of professionals widely available in a useful form.

He is interested in model trains, reading anything he can lay his hands on, drawing, and is a self-described ex-athlete. He lives in Kentfield, California with his wife Sarah.

Case 4
ML INFO—An On-Line Multimedia Information Center

By Lily Diaz
Creative Image Transfer
and Halsey Minor

Computer networks are wonderful enabling tools, but they are not always easy to use. The authors of this paper were hired to implement an on-line multimedia support system (ML INFO) to help financial analysts trying to access information distributed across a local area network. Analysts are usually hired for their financial acumen, not their proficiency with a keyboard.

Our client, a large New York-based financial institution, provides each analyst with a large procedure manual detailing how to use the networked tools at their disposal. Few analysts ever take the time to read this document. Instead, they call the computer support center and demand that someone walk them through their problems as they arise. A great many of the hundreds of daily support calls deal with routine problems. What is the best way to reduce the volume of these calls leaving the support staff free to deal with more serious problems? The customer hoped we could provide them with an easy-to-use, on-line help system that would do the job. It was reasoned that such a system could also provide vital hand-holding for analysts working late at night when no support staff was available. (See Figure C4.1.)

In designing the ML INFO library, we had to keep several considerations in mind. The system was to be used to train between 125 and 150 financial analysts including 50 to 75 new hires each year. Thus, the help system had to be so easy that even these new hires could use it. We were also asked to make sure the system was "accessible, enjoyable, and fun."

The original design of ML INFO closely mirrored the style and content of the paper documents it was to replace. We improved the organization and appearance of the original documents and placed them on-line for easy access, but for cost reasons chose not to take the time required to break the document down into hypertext format. This proved to be a mistake. Everyone who saw our preview of the system asked the obvious question: "If analysts don't take the time to read the paper manuals why would they read the same stuff on line?"

Figure C4.1 An ever expanding world of information can be accessed through the ML INFO Library.

Once the cheap and easy approach was rejected, we hunkered down to do it right. Material was rewritten, and essential information was placed up front. We kept all the detail included in the original document, but placed it further back in the structure where it could be accessed via hypertext links.

Over the nine-month development period we tested many of the commercially available multi-media products that run on the IBM-compatible PCs our client uses. Prototypes were built using Hyperties from Cognetics, then Guide 2.0 from OWL International, and in the final system, ToolBook from Asymetrix Corporation. ToolBook was eventually chosen because it provided the rich support for the graphics we needed.

We used a wide variety of graphics tools to generate the graphics images we desired. These included Micrografx's Designer, CorelDraw!, Z Soft's PC Paint, and ToolBook's own graphics package. Because the Microsoft Windows environment that Toolbook requires restricts the number of colors which can be displayed at the same time, all files were converted to .PCX format and brought into ToolBook via the Windows Clipboard.

The ML INFO screens are all based around a book metaphor. People are already familiar with the way libraries organize information and with the idea of books as units of knowledge. Thus we felt this approach would be easy for users to conceptualize. The book metaphor could also be easily designed to blend in with the menuing scheme used by the Banyan network operating system installed on the client's local area network.

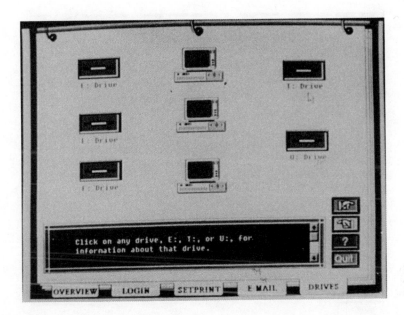

Figure C4.2   Want to see what information is stored on a disk drive? Simply click on that drive.

The first visual element encountered by an analyst using ML INFO is a graphical representation of a library. Point to a book about a particular subject and that book pulls out of the shelf, moves towards the reader, and then opens to the title page. At the bottom of each page are tabs that are used to flip quickly between subject areas. Icons located on the lower right side of the page provide other navigations tools. For example, most screens include icons for paging forwards and backwards, for calling up help or for exiting the program. Hypertext links can be embedded anywhere on the screen that is appropriate. The analyst discovers these icons by scrolling around the screen until the cursor changes shape. All these devices were designed to be consistent with both the book metaphor and the Banyan menu style. (See Figure C4.2.)

We decided to use animated sequences in ML INFO in order to make the application more appealing and to encourage use. Thus, the opening screen includes a three-dimensional depiction of an investment banking library. As you move though ML INFO, animated sequences show books opening, pages turning and the like. All this creates a sense of familiarity and invites the user to grab a book off the shelf and see what is inside. Because no full-fledged animation packages were available for the Windows environment during development, a DOS-based animation program was used to generate moving library sequences. TOPAS 3.5 was used to build the three-dimensional models of the library and books. It was also used to apply texture maps and in the creation and rendering of the animation sequence. Once created, the frames in this sequence were converted into files that could be displayed in VGA format. Autodesk Animator was utilized for converting, retouching, and displaying the frames from a disk or server.

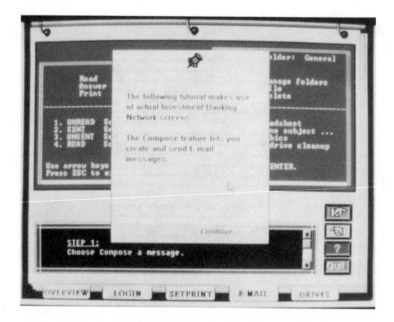

Figure C4.3   Notes are tacked up on the screen until you read them.

Currently there is one book with five main chapters included in ML INFO. The book teaches analysts how to best utilize the network resources at hand. Each chapter in this book is referenced through a tab located at the bottom of the each page. (See Figure C4.3.)

As other chapters are added, more books will be placed on the shelf. For example, analysts will be able to point to the book entitled "E:mail" to learn how to send other employees memos. Graphics devices are used whenever needed to quickly convey ideas. For example, floor maps are provided to show analysts where to pick up printed output. (See Figure C4.4.)

ML INFO made its debut during the 1990 associate and analyst training program. The application was used in a classroom environment to train new employees how to use the company's computer network. This accomplished two things. First, it provided a good way of introducing employees to the system's uses and benefits. Secondly, the system's colorful, animated, interactive nature made it a far more interesting and comprehensible teaching tool than the black-on-white text based manuals used in prior years. The reaction to ML INFO by this group of new employees was very positive.

As the system becomes more robust, it will provide an alternate means of tapping technical support expertise and relieve some of the support burden. Finally, the multimedia nature of the application and its around-the-clock availability for everyone connected to the company's computer network makes it an attractive reference tool. The trick to achieving these goals was to break the material up into small digestible nuggets linked together in a hypertext environment.

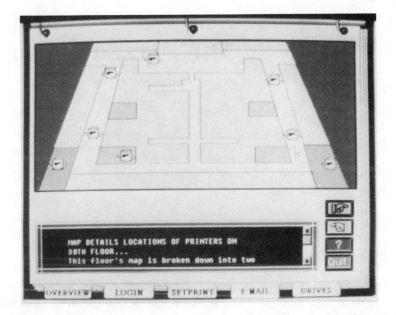

Figure C4.4   Want to find out where your output is going to? Simply follow the map.

About the Author

Lily Diaz

Lily Diaz is a multimedia design professional. She holds a degree in anthropology from Brandeis University and received her Master of Fine Arts in Computer Art from the School of Visual Arts in 1989. Lily Diaz recently received a Fulbright Fellowship to travel to Spain. She is working on a multimedia application that will depict historical events related to the 500th Anniversary of the *Discovery* of the New World.

Ms. Diaz is president of Creative Image Transfer, where she can be reached at P. O. Box 5196, Rockefeller Station, New York, NY 10185-5196.

Halsey Minor

Halsey Minor is a graduate of anthropology from the University of Virginia. Halsey was an investment banker at a major New York Investment banking firm before developing ML INFO. He is currently developing a multimedia magazine on CD-ROM.

Case 5
The Perseus Project

By Cynthia J. Bannon
University of Michigan

Introduction

The Perseus Project is named for the Greek hero Perseus, who learned by travelling. Perseus presents students with a world of ancient Greek literature and culture in which to travel, explore and learn.

A Multimedia Journey Through Ancient Greece

Imagine a college student who is learning ancient Greek and reading the *Eumenides,* a play by the Greek tragedian Aeschylus. After she has worked for several hours translating the Greek text, she is tired and a bit confused. The *Eumenides* is the first Greek tragedy she has ever read, and, though she can read Greek, she doesn't know very much about either the play itself or the performance of tragedy. So she turns to Perseus[1] to learn more. As the college student sits down at her MacIntosh she thinks, "Aristophanes sure knew what he was talking about when he said that no one could understand Aeschylus." She slides the CD into the CD-ROM player, switches on the videodisc player and boots up her MacIntosh.

As the Perseus Gateway appears on her screen, our student decides to investigate Greek tragedy first (See Figure C5.1).

With a few clicks of the mouse, she selects an essay on the development and performance of Greek tragedy. This essay is part of Perseus' Historical Overview, which offers an introduction to many aspects of Greek history and culture.[2] The

---

1 The Perseus Project is based at Harvard University, with collaborators at Bowdoin College, Pomona College, and St. Olaf College, among others. It is funded primarily by the Annenberg/CPB Project and by Apple Computer, Inc. Prof. Gregory Crane of Harvard University is the project director.

2 The historical Overview is written by Professor Thomas R. Martin of Pomona College. In future versions of Perseus, the Historical Overview will cover the years . . .

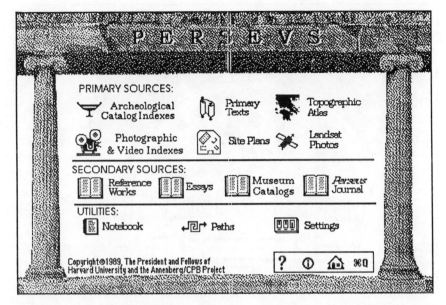

Figure C5.1 Perseus Gateway. Used by permission of the President and Fellows of Harvard College.

Overview is linked to other Perseus resources—images, maps, site plans, architectural catalogs—to provide a variety of approaches to Greek tragedy.

With these resources, the student can also explore the actual theater on the southern slope of the Acropolis where tragedy was performed in Athens. Automatic links allow her to view a site plan of Athens, which provides detailed views of the theater in Athens, or a catalog description of the theater. A button on the catalog card (labelled "Periods," Figure C5.2) links the catalog directly to a series of architectural plans, showing the theater at different periods in its history, from its early foundations to the Hellenistic period.

Another link takes the student to the Image Archive—Perseus' spectacular collection of video and photographic images—where she can see images of the theater as it looks today. With a series of clicks, the student can familiarize herself with the physical and historical context of dramatic performance at Athens. Perseus' drawings and video images give students a feeling of place by connecting these ancient dramas with the modern world through experience of the physical surroundings. After exploring ancient Athens, our student can return directly to her study of the *Eumenides* using Perseus' links menu.

Perseus' Language Tools

Next, our student chooses "Primary Texts" from the menu, which brings her to the Primary Text Index, where she selects the *Eumenides*, the third play in the *Oresteia* of Aeschylus.

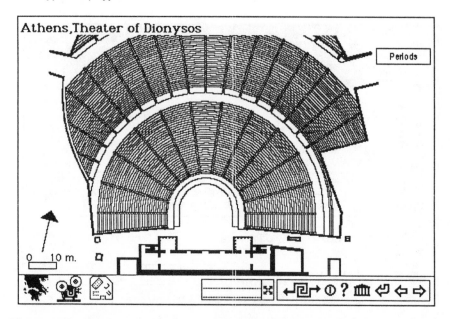

Figure C5.2   Plan of the Theater of Dionysos in Athens. Used by permission of the President and Fellows of Harvard College.

The *Oresteia* is a set of three plays (a trilogy) which revolve around a chain of murder and blood guilt. The murders begin before the drama opens, with Agamemnon's sacrifice of his daughter Iphigeneia. In the first play, his wife exacts retribution for the death of their daughter through his death. In the second play, his son, Orestes, put his mother to death to avenge the death of his father. The *Eumenides*, the third play, explores the moral questions involved in this chain of murders and inherited blood guilt.

In her reading of the *Eumenides*, our student encounters some puzzling grammatical forms. Ancient Greek is a highly inflected language with a large number of inflected forms and variable declension/conjugation patterns. Because of this complexity, a simple search will not allow a reader to find all the forms of a word. Perseus, however, includes a morphological parser, called "Morpheus," which can help an inexperienced student analyze the morphology of ancient Greek words and identify the dictionary entry form of the words even in cases where the dictionary entry looks very different from the inflected form.

For instance, if our student was reading the opening of the *Eumenides*, she might have trouble with the form μολόντα (molonta, in line 15). To solve her quandry, she could simply select the troublesome form with the mouse and then click the Analyze button, which is conveniently located right on each text card. In a matter of seconds, Perseus identifies μολόντα (molonta) as a masculine, singular, accusative, aorist participle of βλώσκω (blosko, "to come, go"). Perseus also provides this student with a Greek-English Dictionary to resolve questions of translation; the dictionary can also be accessed by an automatic link from the text

English-Greek Word List

Type a string and then click Look Up to see lemmas of words containing the string.

String to Look Up: net

Look Up

Lemmas of: net	33	Lemmas used in: Aeschylus	13

Lemmas of: net:

ἄγρευμα
ἅλινος
ἄρκυς
ἀμφίβληστρον
βόλος
δίκτυον
δικτυβολέω
δικτυόκλωστος
δικτυόομαι
ἕρκος
ἐπίδρομος
γάγγαμον
κεκρύφαλος

Lemmas used in: Aeschylus:

ἄγρευμα
ἄρκυς
ἀμφίβληστρον
βόλος
δίκτυον
ἕρκος
ἐπίδρομος
γάγγαμον
λίνον
νεφέλη
ὁρκάνη
πάγη
περίδρομος?

Show Definition   Show Usage

Figure C5.3   Word List for "net" in the works of Aeschylus. Used by permission of the President and Fellows of Harvard College.

of the *Eumenides*. (Perseus contains the Intermediate Liddell and Scott Greek-English Lexicon.)

Beyond simple grammatical analysis, Perseus contains philological tools for the study of language and metaphor in Greek literature. In the opening scene of the *Eumenides*, Orestes is described using imagery of the hunt, with specific reference to nets and snares, ἀρκυστάτων (arkustaton, "surrounded by snares", line 112). In addition to simply searching for parallel passages in which this word occurs, Perseus can generate a list of Greek terms related to nets and snares that Aeschylus uses in his plays.

For instance, words from hunting contexts like θήρατρον (theratron, "a hunting net or trap"), σαγήνη (sagene, "a drag net") and also related terms δικτυοβόλοζ (diktuobolos, "fisherman") and λαβύρινθος (labyrinthos, "labyrinth or maze"). Perseus' English-Greek Word List is more than an English-Greek dictionary. It generates a list of all Greek words in whose definition the English term appears.

Since imagery is an important vehicle for meaning in Aeschylus' works, this list offers a rich source of data for a literary analysis of net imagery in the Oresteia.

Building Paths In Perseus

In addition to studying the Greek text of the *Eumenides*, our student has also been assigned to compose an essay that illustrates and interprets the play. She will construct this essay within the Perseus environment, by making a "Perseus path." A path is a sequence of locations in Perseus—for example, an image of a building

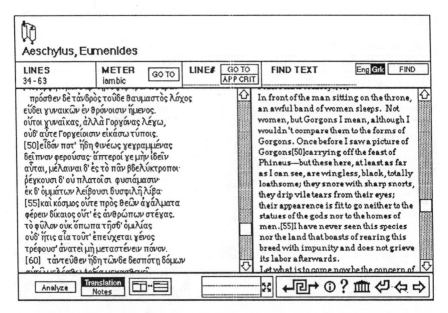

Figure C5.4 Furies in Aeschylus' *Eumenides*. Used by permission of the President and Fellows of Harvard College.

and a passage of text—linked together by the path-maker. Locations, represented by icons, are displayed in a linear array on a Path card, which preserves the path for future reference (See Figure C5.5).

Our student will use her path first to illustrate the opening scene of the *Eumenides*. As the play opens, Orestes is at Delphi seeking religious purification for the death of his mother. The Furies, fiendish goddesses who avenge the killing of kindred, have pursued him to Delphi.

Our student navigates, using the links menu, to the Image Archive. The Image Archive contains images of a variety of artistic media—Greek vases, carved gems, metal reliefs.[3] She can link images from the Perseus Image Archive to the text of the *Eumenides*. She clicks through the hierarchy of Image Indices to view and select images for her path, then uses a Path menu to add her selected images to the path. The student selects images of the Furies, and links them to Aeschylus' description, bringing the literary description to life on her screen:

"... an awful band of women sleeps. Not women, but Gorgons... [they] are wingless, black, totally loathsome; they snore with sharp snorts, they drip vile tears from their eyes. . . ." [lines 46–54, Figure C5.4]

She can add video images and site plans of Apollo's shrine at Delphi to her path to show the physical environment in which the action of the play occurs. (See Figure C5.5.)

---

3 The objects in the Perseus Image archive come from galleries and collections in Europe and the United States, a collection that is richer and more diverse than any single reference work or catalog.

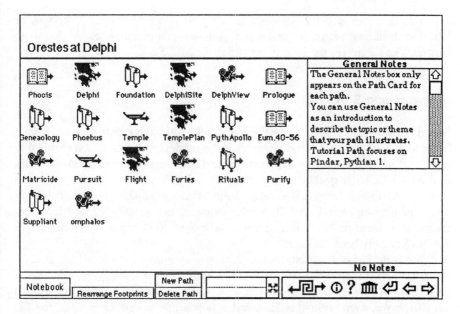

Figure C5.5   Path Card. Used by permission of the President and Fellows of Harvard College.

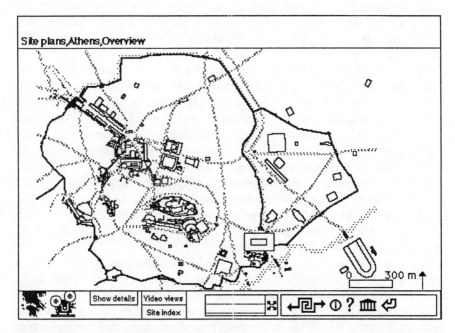

Figure C5.6   Site Plan of Athens. Used by permission of the President and Fellows of Harvard College.

Our student can also include links in her path to the Historical Overview, or Site and Building plans, to make her path an interpretative essay that both illustrates and analyzes the literary text. (See Figure C5.6.)

Hardware and Software

Perseus runs under HyperCard on the Macintosh. Although it performs better on a faster Mac, an SE with 2 Mb of memory is the minimum configuration required to run it. All the digital data (texts, databases and black-and-white images) is distributed on a CD. High quality analog images are distributed on a videodisc for the moment. As image compression and manipulation techniques improve, color images will also be stored on CD. At the moment, the quantity of detailed color images in Perseus prohibits this; it would take over 3000 Mb to store the images that have already been collected.

A complete Perseus station, therefore, would optimally include a Mac II computer, a 13-inch monitor, 4 Mb of RAM, a hard drive, a CD player, a videodisc player and a video monitor. However, it is possible to use the videodisc without the CD player, even without a Mac, and it is possible to use the data on the CD without the benefit of the images on the videodisc.

The Perseus Project, like its namesake, was designed to travel far and wide. Two mandates of the project were to release the system early in the development cycle and to make it available to classics departments in schools and colleges. This meant that we had to choose a relatively inexpensive hardware and software platform. Since building Perseus involves extensive gathering and structuring of data, it was also important to find a software platform that provided as much of the infrastructure as possible.

The Macintosh makes it easy to work with non-Roman character sets like Greek, and also to combine text and graphics. HyperCard, which was released just as Perseus got started, was the only software toolkit on any machine that required little programming, allowed fast development and low-end delivery. The project had experimented earlier, on a grant from Xerox Corporation, with Xerox Notecards on Xerox Lisp machines. This was an extremely versatile system, but at the time, it ran on expensive and rare hardware.

HyperCard has some shortcomings and is not the most appropriate system in which to develop a large, complex mixed-media database. However, the data in Perseus has been prepared with generality and portability in mind, so it can be ported easily when a more sophisticated system becomes available. Perseus won't cease to be usable when HyperCard does.

This emphasis on data and data preparation sets Perseus apart from other hypertext/hypermedia projects. Instead of trying to create a system, Perseus is trying to create information. A great deal of effort is spent on rich archival formats for the texts, images and databases, which is not apparent in the HyperCard presentation. Texts are all SGML-conformant, images are stored in Postscript format, and most linking and other travel through the system is handled by using a database of canonical document names, so they are not system-dependent.

In this way, Perseus has collected a large quantity of data which will outlast any one hardware or software system. Because Perseus is not tied to its distribution or development system, it is a universal tool. It is more like a library than a text book or any one scholar's view of a topic. It contains mostly primary sources, but will have more and more secondary material as more classicists, archeologists, anthropologists and other scholars and students contribute to it.

Conclusion

The sources contained in Perseus allow students to marshall evidence for their interpretations of what they read from a wider range of sources than a purely literary analysis would employ. Moreover, the rich environment of Perseus can stimulate students to ask new and more sophisticated questions about ancient Greek literature and culture. Perseus makes it possible for them to explore these questions more broadly and in greater detail than they would in traditional research.

About the Author

Cynthia J. Bannon

Cynthia J. Bannon is a doctoral candidate in the Department of Classical Studies at the University of Michigan. Her interests in the ancient world include both Greek and Roman topics. She has just completed her doctoral dissertation, *Consors Mecum Temporum Illorum: Brothers in Republican Rome*, which studies the relationship between brothers in Republican Rome as well as the idea of brotherhood in the literature of the period. She can be contacted through the Department of Classical Studies, The University of Michigan, Angell Hall, Ann Arbor, MI 48109.

Case 6
PathMAC: An Alternative Approach to Medical School Education at Cornell School of Medicine

By Lily Diaz
Creative Image Transfer

Everybody knows that medical school is hard. The hours are long and the number of facts that must be memorized is daunting. In 1985, Drs. Steve Erde and Daniel R. Alonso of the Cornell School of Medicine began experimenting with the idea of using computers to make the learning process more efficient.

Today, 40 percent of all students taking Introductory Pathology at Cornell School of Medicine are enrolled in an electronic version of the course. Macintosh computers tied into the PathMAC database are scattered throughout the dorms and classrooms for student access. From these terminals, students can study on-line textbooks, run simulated laboratories, or test their mastery of physiology by viewing on-line dissections. More students would like to go electronic, but the university is limiting enrollment in the electronic pathology course so that it can objectively determine which system produces better results.

The hardware and software environment on which PathMAC runs is diverse. Students can access the system though any one of 18 Macintosh II computers. The standard hardware configuration on the Macs is 2 Megs of RAM, an 8-bit color card and a 19-inch color monitor, linked via an Ethertalk connection. PathMAC provides on-line access to approximately 7 Gigabytes of images and bibliographical material that can be searched intelligently, cross-referenced, and printed. Software includes applications written in HyperCard, OWL's Guide and other software tools developed in-house.

For example, the opening screen shown below was scripted with HyperCard by Henry C. Hsu, a student from Boston University. On the left hand side of the screen students indicate which course they are taking. The selection of materials available for biochemistry, anatomy, neuroscience, parasitology, physiology, and radiology courses is considerably smaller than that available for pathology, but the

Figure C6.1   From the main menu of PathMAC students can access a variety of applications appropriate to their course of study.

system is rapidly growing. On the right hand side of the screen are buttons that can be used to access individual applications such as Carousel or Virtual Cat, or the Medline on-line medical database. (See Figure C6.1.)

The most heavily linked on-line application is an electronic pathology text called HyperPath, which includes large portions of a version of the well-known textbook, *Robbins Pathological Basis of Disease*. This application was written under OWL's GUIDE and includes both text and images pulled from the original. Because the system is on-line, it is relatively easy for the professors at Cornell to update materials by adding new text and graphics nodes as needed. Underscoring is used to indicate terms linked to pop-up notes that provide definitions or citations. The hypermedia pathology textbook is structured in a three-layer system which links the instructor's lectures, the textbook itself, and pertinent citations. Icons sprinkled throughout the document point to images available for further examination. (See Figure C6.2.)

Another popular application is Carousel, a visual archive that currently includes more than 1000 images. Visual archives have long been a useful tool of the pathologist. Doctors have been taking photographs of interesting cases for years, filing them in a library for their own reference or for others to peruse. Putting these illustrations on-line for student use makes them much more accessible. It also allows them to be linked into other applications (such as the on-line texts).

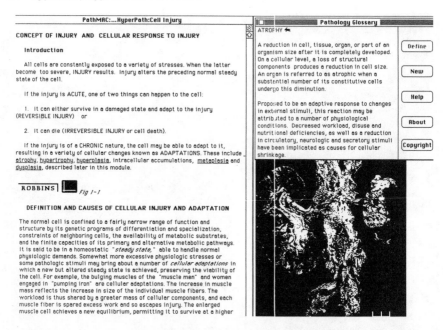

Figure C6.2   A page pulled from the on-line PathMAC pathology textbook.

When used in a teaching environment, Carousel images are paired with stimulating questions. For example, diseased organs can be shown on the screen and the student asked to make a diagnosis. Students can also use the images to study anatomy or to compare images of normal against abnormal tissue cells. Because students can independently pursue their own courses of study, the instructors have more time to pay attention to the students' work.

Carousel is probably the fastest growing application on PathMAC. Cornell has amassed almost 3000 images that will soon be on-line.

Images are brought into the system with the use of either a flatbed scanner or a Barneyscan and they are retouched, if needed, with the use of Adobe Photoshop. With the exception of the Medline materials, a system of indexing medical periodicals that were already on-line, text entries depend upon manual data entry.

Virtual Cat is another of the utilities available. Written by Dr. Dan Gardner and ported to the Macintosh by Michael Abato, Virtual Cat is a program used to perform simulated laboratory experiments that otherwise would be performed on live cats. For example, students can set the system up to test the response of various drugs on simulated cat muscle. The students choose which drugs to inject, in what quantity, and then electrically stimulate the muscle and record the results on a simulated strip chart. (See Figure C6.3.)

The advantage of these simulated experiments is that much more control over the results can be achieved than is possible with real live muscle. As in real life, no two runs of the program produce the same results, but by working in simulation, botched experiments due to faulty procedures are eliminated. In one test of

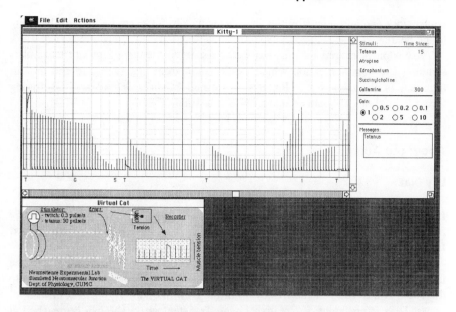

Figure C6.3   Students can inject different drugs into their virtual cat and then view the results on the chart displayed on the screen.

the Virtual Cat, students were unable to figure out which data was derived from an experiment performed on an actual live cat and which came from an experiment performed on a simulated cat.

Yet another type of on-line simulation is represented by CBX. This program, originally developed by The National Board of Medicine and ported to the Mac by Michael Abato, consists of a patient simulation system in which students are presented with and tested on their responses to situations requiring medical intervention. In this simulation, students are provided with written case histories. Students are then provided with forms used to request diagnostic tests. Once the tests are run and all the questions answered, the computer compares the students' actions against the recommended course of action and provides suggestions.

The students who use the PathMAC system are enthusiastic about the system. The system currently operates 24 hours a day and is in constant use. Cornell Medical School is committed to the project. The question is: how fast should it expand and in what direction should it go?

Drs. Erde and Alonso hope that someday a descendant of PathMAC may replace much of the medical school curriculum as it is known today. Other schools feel the same and serious discussions are already in progress to determine how to best share software and data between allied schools. This problem is particularly acute when one tries to form links between various applications. With this in mind Cornell has joined a consortium of 12 medical schools that share software and images to be used in multimedia teaching environments.

The advent of multimedia is also having its impact on PathMAC. Some of the projections for the future are the use of video technology for the psychiatry coursework and audio capabilities in courses which, for example, require listening to the heart.

The vision of shared information resources among universities, and the understanding and communication which would result from this exchange and the enthusiasm of the staff and volunteers at Cornell Medical School are the driving forces behind this alternative approach to education.

About the Author

Lily Diaz

Lily Diaz is a multimedia design professional. She holds a degree in anthropology from Brandeis University and received her Master of Fine Arts in Computer Art from the School of Visual Arts in 1989.

Ms. Diaz recently received a Fulbright Fellowship to travel to Spain where she is working on a multimedia application that will depict historical events related to the 500th Anniversary of the *Discovery* of the New World.

Ms. Diaz is president of Creative Image Transfer, where she can be reached at P. O. Box 5196, Rockefeller Station, New York, NY 10185-5196.

Case 7
Grapevine Described

By Robert Campbell and Patricia Hanlon
Campbell & Hanlon, Inc.

Copyright © 1988

General Description

Grapevine is an interactive, multimedia teaching, learning, and research tool about America in the 1930s. It runs on a Macintosh Plus or SE computer with a hard disk drive and a Pioneer 4200 videodisc player. It incorporates extensive text that is linked and cross-indexed; and includes music, interviews and other sound resources, photographs and art, and footage from television and film, all controlled by HyperCard. It is intended for use by teachers and students at high school and college levels.

Its Goal

Teachers of civics, economics, American history, and the humanities draw from many sources, including literature, to help students relate these subjects to the world. Teachers of American literature illuminate their subject with issues, events, and personalities from the authors' worlds. Students respond more completely to literature which tells them more than merely "what happened" in the plot.

The subject matter of *Grapevine* is the major social, economic, political, and cultural issues of the United States in the 1930s as approached from the perspective of John Steinbeck's *The Grapes of Wrath*.

As a research tool, the program is a large interconnected repository of text, sound, and pictures. Regarded as a source of information, it is a database of factual material: direct quotations, biographies, statistics, letters, history. The links built into the database allow the reader to pursue important relationships, themes, and contrasts. The database is a place to browse, compare, and store information and pictures along with the connections between them. It is also a source for material used by the reader to make his/her own report or statement. However, the *Grapevine* database is not a substitute for a library. The teacher and students ought

Grapevine
DESCRIBED

©1988 by Robert Campbell & Patricia Hanlon

"American Scene," by Jay B. Turnbull

GENERAL DESCRIPTION: Grapevine is an interactive, multimedia
teaching, learning, and research tool concerning the American
1930s. It uses a Macintosh Plus or SE computer with a hard disk
drive and a Pioneer 4200 videodisc player. It incorporates
extensive text that is linked and cross-indexed; music,
interviews, and other sound resources; photographs and art; and
motion footage from television and film, all controlled within
HyperCard. It is intended for use by teachers and by students in
high school and up.

THE NEED: Teachers of civics, economics, American history, and
the humanities draw from many sources, including literature, to
help students connect these subjects with the world. Teachers
of American literature illuminate their subject with issues,
events, and personalities from the authors' worlds. Students
respond to literature that tells them much more than merely
"what happened" in the plot.

Figure C7.1 A page from "Grapevine" with an illustration by Jay B. Turnbull.

to to seek out some of the many works cited in order to study the topic in greater detail. For this, an extensive annotated bibliography has been provided. *Grapevine* provides detailed ideas and suggestions for teaching research skills.

As a presentation utility, *Grapevine* is a practical way for the teacher or students to share with others the results of their own thought and research. Any image can be chosen in any order from the large number available on the videodisc, recombined, and presented with original sound narration or with commentary added. Teachers and students may choose to use *Grapevine* to create presentations on videotape.

Most of the material needed for a presentation already exists in the database as quotations or samplers and as images and sound. The reader brings his own emphasis, his own order, and wherever he wishes, his own commentary, questions, or assignments. If he lacks the time to create an original presentation, he may decide to use *Grapevine*'s own introductory presentation as it is, or to include changes. The scenario on which the introductory presentation is based is included in *Grapevine* as a model which will help those teachers who wish to author their own presentations.

Students may make reports and share their insights and opinions in many ways. One of which is to use *Grapevine* as a teacher would do, to construct a presentation for which most of the raw material is to be found in the program, but reordered, edited, annotated, and interpreted in new ways. The presentation utility is what one uses to tell a story, create a report, share opinions, to communicate and perhaps to persuade.

Grapevine includes a collection of stories or narratives suitable for individual students or small groups seeking background on many aspects of the period.

Grapevine contains extensive resources for research and teaching, but it is especially useful as a template, providing both a body of material and a structure on

NEW DEAL NEWS

★★★   March, 1933 and Beyond   ★★★

ECONOMIC PLIGHT
OF NATION CITED

Analysts of the nation's investment prospects, long-term market commitments and local indebtedness have concluded in a Geneva roundtable that trends are, as one reported by ———— economist put it, "The U.S. economical ———— the modern ded of a man who isn't old. " was Monte-negro, p———— prestigious and yet mysterious of the for———— payouts in this week's disloca-tions. Others adversaries of this health spa in the Al-

Big map

FDR INAUGURATED!

NEW GOVERNMENT AGENCIES PLANNED

"BRAINS TRUST" TO TAKE OVER

Washington, D.C.— It was a raw, blustery day in Washington, with dark clouds scudding overhead and periodic gusts of cold rain beating through the bare trees and across the glistening pavements. Along Pennsylvania Avenue from the foot of Capitol Hill to the White House half a million people wrapped in blankets and overcoats huddled in open benches or massed against the ropes strung alon——

Click any headline for more facts.

begin. Oth——— the great p——— platform h——— flags and th——— The moo——— Some felt t——— with the less than ideal weather, while others perceived an element of fatalism, even fear—fear that for all the hoopla and campaign oratory, more had been promised

Washington, D.C. The nation's capitol took its ——— with rumor and speculation over reports from usually reliable sources to the effect that in a matter of only hours the sworn-in President intends to establish n power til posts over a whole new galaxy co agencies which will begin to implement this

HOOVER LEGACY

Last President at fault, pundit says

There has been a groundswell in this city, in the words of the nation's suffering, said Alexander Schwanewitz.

Figure C7.2 ("Man with a wheelbarrow," image copyright Oakland Museum, 1000 Oak St., Oakland, CA.

WELCOME TO

Grapevine

Click here for a tour of Grapevine

See the parts of Grapevine.	Get a briefing on the 1930s.
Get details about the parts.	Play a quiz game on the 30s.
Search Grapevine for a topic.	Go directly to...
	Quit

OPTIONS

Figure C7.3

E𝒳𝒫O

Issues of the
1930s with
suggestions
for lessons,
discussion,
research, and
follow-up.

 Index   Search GrapeVine

Figure C7.4

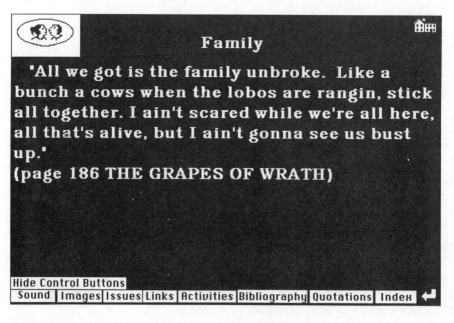

Family

"All we got is the family unbroke. Like a
bunch a cows when the lobos are rangin, stick
all together. I ain't scared while we're all here,
all that's alive, but I ain't gonna see us bust
up."
(page 186 THE GRAPES OF WRATH)

Hide Control Buttons
Sound │ Images │ Issues │ Links │ Activities │ Bibliography │ Quotations │ Index

Figure C7.5

which teachers and students can conveniently build or use as a model with other subject matter.

Inquiries may be addressed to Grapevine, 33 Encline Court, San Francisco, CA 94127.

References

Campbell, R. and Hanlon, P. (1988). "Grapevine: a High-Tech Voyage Through the 'Thirties," *American Educator*, Winter.

Campbell, R., and Hanlon, P. (1990). "HyperCard: A New Deal in the Classroom," in Ambron, Sueann and Kristina Hooper, (Eds.) *Learning with Interactive Multimedia: Developing and Using Multimedia Tools in Education*, Microsoft Press, Seattle, WA.

Campbell, R. (1989). "(I Learned It) through the Grapevine: Hypermedia at Work in the Classroom," *American Libraries*, March.

"Here Comes Multimedia," Special section, *MacWeek*, January 31, 1989.

Hooper, K. (1988). *Interactive Multimedia Design 1988: Technical Report #13, Version Two.* Apple Computer, Inc., Cupertino, CA.

Ambron, S., and Hooper, K. (Eds.) (1988). *Interactive Multimedia: Visions of Multimedia for Developers, Educators & Information Providers*, Microsoft Press, Seattle, WA.

Rogers, M. (1988)."Here Comes Hypermedia," *Newsweek*, 10/3.

Solomon, G. (1989). "Heard It, Read It, Saw It on the Grapevine," *Electronic Learning*, May.

Weld, E. (1989). "The teacher is still center stage," *Boston Sunday Globe*, May 7, p. B62.

Case 8
Guide To Opportunities in Volunteer Archaeology: Case Study on the Use of a Hypertext System in a Museum Exhibit

By Catherine Plaisant
University of Maryland

Introduction

This case study describes the steps of the birth and traveling life of the *Guide to Opportunities in Volunteer Archaeology* (GOVA), and demonstrates that such an adventure can be successful without being burdensome. The database was constructed by the professors and students at the University of Maryland History Department. Regular updates of the database were made for each venue of the exhibit. Finally the database was translated into French for use in Canada. System users were observed in the museum and usage data were collected and analyzed. Helpful features of the hypertext system as well as the difficulties encountered are described here.

In the summer of 1987, Professor Ken Holum of the University of Maryland History Department approached the Human-Computer Interaction Laboratory for help in developing a hypertext application for a museum exhibit to open the following spring. Thus began a two-year collaboration between the two groups, which allowed us to test *Hyperties®*[4] (Hypertext Interactive Encyclopedia System) [Shneiderman, et al., 1989] in the real world. [For more information about Hyperties, see Chapter 11 by Shneiderman, in this book.]

The exhibit was organized by the Smithsonian Institute Traveling Exhibition Service. It opened in Washington, DC in March, 1988 at the National Museum of Natural History, then traveled to five museums over the next two years (Los Angeles, Denver, Minneapolis-St. Paul, Boston, and Ottawa.)

---

4   Hyperties is a registered trademark of the Cognetics Corporation.

Created by the University of Maryland Center for Archaeology and the Human-Computer Interaction Laboratory for
King Herod's Dream
an exhibition of the Smithsonian Institution Traveling Exibition Service

TOUCH THE SCREEN

Figure C8.1 The title page of GOVA.

The Museum Exhibit

Two freestanding podiums were installed in the final chamber of the exhibit on "King Herod's Dream." This exhibit was about the ancient Roman port city of Caesarea located on the shores of what is now modern-day Israel. It focused on the rise of urbanism in ancient times and the archaeological methods used during the past 20 years of excavation [Holum, 1988; Holm, et al., 1988]. This last station of the exhibit invited visitors to learn more about the archeological sites around the world that welcome volunteers and about how to join such a dig.

The two custom-made podiums housed IBM PC-AT computers. The EGA monitors, each equipped with a Microtouch touchscreen, were at about waist level and tilted at a 45 degree angle to the horizon. The only permanent instruction on each podium was "Touch the screen" written above the monitor. No keyboards were provided.

The Database

The GOVA database was developed under the direction of Ken Holum. It consists of about 200 articles. The contents include information about archaeological digs

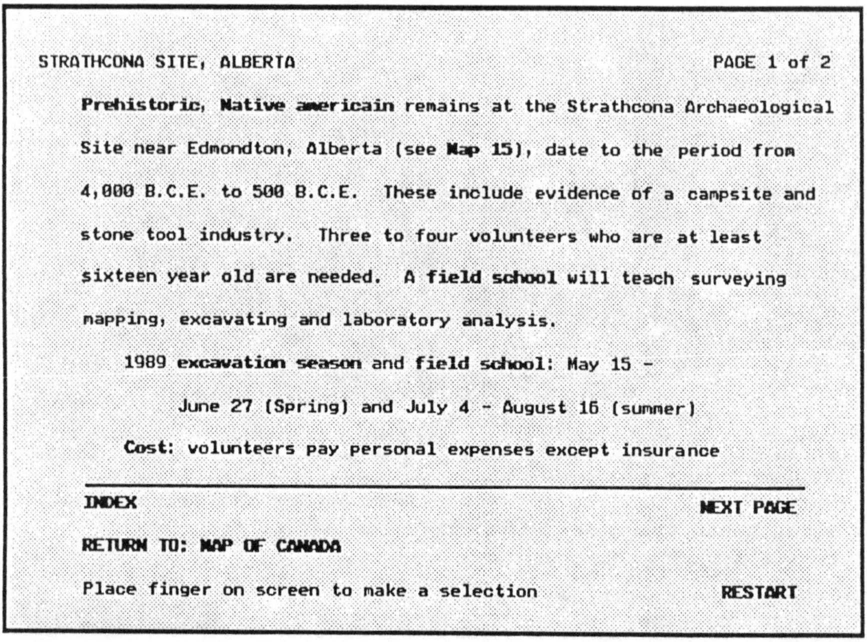

```
STRATHCONA SITE, ALBERTA                              PAGE 1 of 2

 Prehistoric, Native americain remains at the Strathcona Archaeological

 Site near Edmondton, Alberta (see Map 15), date to the period from

 4,000 B.C.E. to 500 B.C.E. These include evidence of a campsite and

 stone tool industry. Three to four volunteers who are at least

 sixteen year old are needed. A field school will teach surveying

 mapping, excavating and laboratory analysis.

    1989 excavation season and field school: May 15 -

       June 27 (Spring) and July 4 - August 16 (summer)

    Cost: volunteers pay personal expenses except insurance
 _____

 INDEX                                                 NEXT PAGE

 RETURN TO: MAP OF CANADA

 Place finger on screen to make a selection            RESTART
```

**Figure C8.2   Page 1 of 2 of the article giving information about the archaeo-
logical site of Strathcona in Canada. Each blue word (bold in this book) is
selectable.**

(See Figure C8.2) taking place around the world, description of historical periods, and practical suggestions about how to join a dig.

A special effort was made to cover local sites near the currently exhibiting museum. The archaeological sites are organized both geographically and by historical periods. The information can also be accessed by direct selection on 11 maps (See Figures C8.3 and C8.4).

The initial database was constructed in a relatively short period of time. Between two and three person-months were necessary to collect information about the digs, structure the information, write each article following a predetermined style, and mark the links. Each author used whatever text editor he or she was most familiar with to accomplish this task. Graphic artist Karen Norman prepared the maps and created three graphic screens (an example of which is seen in Figure C8.1). Then about two weeks of work was necessary to build the database in the computer (import articles, adjust their formatting, verify the links in the text and create the graphic links). As expected—and as it probably should be—the initial writing itself was found to be the most important and time-consuming task. Most of the help given by the Human-Computer Interaction Laboratory team had to do with the use of DOS and of the package used to create the graphics. Hyperties was learned easily by the History Department team.

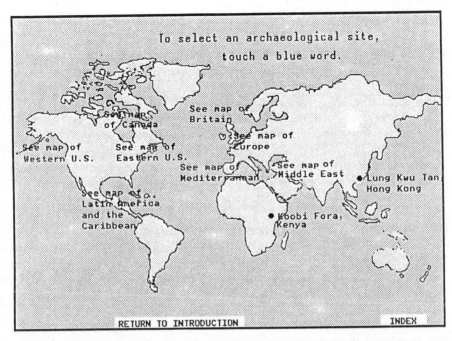

Figure C8.3 The world map allows patrons to select a geographical area of interest.

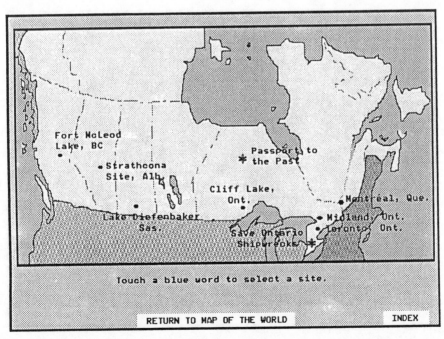

Figure C8.4 The map of Canada allows users to select an archaeological site in Canada by pointing to a spot on the map with their fingers.

The Browser

We used a version of Hyperties which supported the use of a touchscreen as an input device, automatic restart after a period of inactivity at the computer, and the automatic logging of usage data. The museum patrons merely touched highlighted words on the screen to see a linked article.

Blue highlighting indicates the selectable items in both text as well as maps. Users receive feedback about the exact touch position by a cursor just above their fingers. When the cursor is on a selectable item, that area is highlighted. The selection is activated when users lift their fingers from the screen. This method produces low error rates and high user satisfaction [Potter, et al., 1988].

Data Collection and Observations in the Museum

Data on the articles accessed, the time spent in each article, the number of times the index was accessed, etc. were collected from 4500 sessions while the exhibit was in Washington, DC. Results show that visitors used the links embedded within the articles of the hyperdocument more than the traditional index.

Article selection appeared to reflect anticipated interests of patrons suggesting they were able to successfully navigate the database (patrons exhibited a pronounced tendency to ask for information about local sites even though information

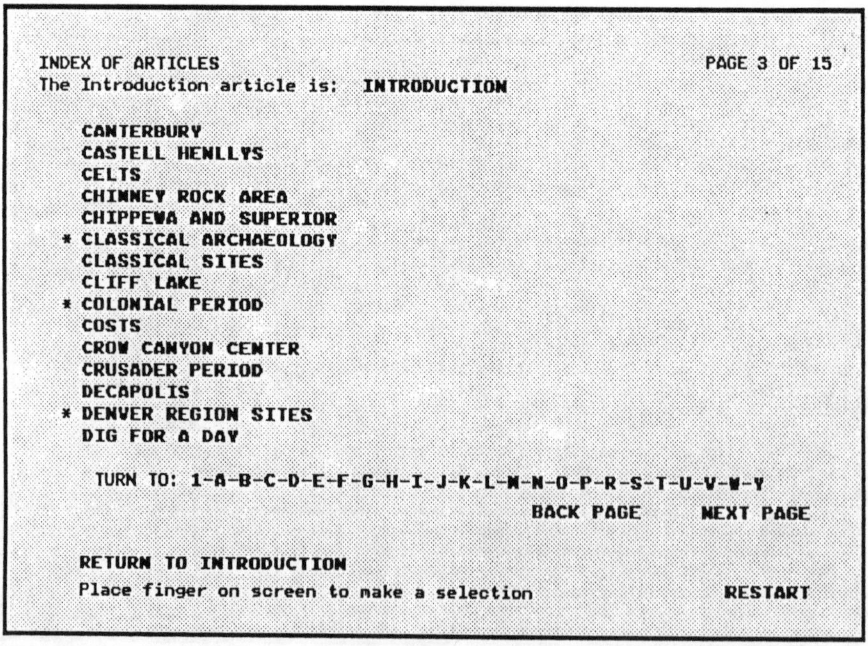

```
INDEX OF ARTICLES                                    PAGE 3 OF 15
The Introduction article is:   INTRODUCTION

    CANTERBURY
    CASTELL HENLLYS
    CELTS
    CHIMNEY ROCK AREA
    CHIPPEWA AND SUPERIOR
  * CLASSICAL ARCHAEOLOGY
    CLASSICAL SITES
    CLIFF LAKE
  * COLONIAL PERIOD
    COSTS
    CROW CANYON CENTER
    CRUSADER PERIOD
    DECAPOLIS
  * DENVER REGION SITES
    DIG FOR A DAY

    TURN TO: 1-A-B-C-D-E-F-G-H-I-J-K-L-M-N-O-P-R-S-T-U-V-W-Y
                                        BACK PAGE      NEXT PAGE

    RETURN TO INTRODUCTION
    Place finger on screen to make a selection         RESTART
```

Figure C8.5   A 15-page provides direct access to all the articles of the database.

pertaining to local sites was neither the focus nor the front end of the database) [Shneiderman, et al., 1989].

The data collection was complemented by direct observation and interviews of museum patrons. Three observers spent four sessions of about two hours each at the exhibit, observing and discussing three potential problems: the touchscreen interface, the Hyperties mechanism, and the database structure. Each session allowed us to pick out the weaknesses of the application and to put in place a productive mechanism of criticism and modification between laboratory and museum. This double approach (usage data collection and direct observation) appeared to be appropriate for improving the user interface and database structure and guaranteeing the usability of the system [Shneiderman, et al., 1989]. Most of the patrons were able to traverse smoothly from article to article and focus on their reading and not on the navigation mechanisms.

The Process of Regular Revisions of the Database

For each new venue of the exhibit, the database was updated to show current archaeological digs and also to emphasize the sites local to the museum area. The authors of the database found that making these revisions was facilitated by the simple, yet powerful, Hyperties authoring tool. The alphabetical index of articles was highly appreciated when revising an already existing database. Additionally, the browser guarantees that no invalid links (therefore no error messages) are presented to readers, allowing authors to simply remove outdated information without danger.

Updating of maps was the most time-consuming task. The authors of the database expressed the need for a tool for handling lists of topics (e.g., lists of sites per area or per period of the past). Some assistance in the maintenance of the overall structure would probably also be useful. For example, using newly developed tools [Botafogo, 1990], we found several structural anomalies in the fifth version of the database revised two years after the original writing (e.g., some articles could not be reached other than by the index).

A Language Translation

For the last stop of the traveling exhibit, Ottawa, Canada, the database was translated into French and the browser was modified to handle the two languages. The translation was performed from a printed copy of the database by a team in Canada.

Links in Hyperties are embedded in nodes. A Hyperties link is marked by a pair of tildes surrounding a word or group of words to be highlighted. Therefore, translators were instructed to leave the tildes in the French text, just as they appeared in the English. Translators also retained the formatting commands (e.g., @p for next paragraph).

The French text was then automatically imported by the author tool. Most of the links were resolved directly by the authoring tool and a French-speaking person then verified the accuracy of the links. Most of the human intervention involved assigning synonyms to counteract the human translation variations and fixing instances where the authoring tool didn't handle the accentuated vowels in the article titles properly. Changes to graphics had to be handled manually. A few changes were made to the browser: very few messages and command names changed, and an introduction allowed readers to choose which language they wanted to use.

Conclusions

This hypertext system was used successfully for two years. Patrons were able to traverse the database and find information related to their own interests. We depended on direct observation in museums to identify problems and successes, and patron-suggested improvements were made in the first two weeks of operation.

The authors of the database were able to easily update the content and the structure of the database over the two-year duration of the exhibit. The translation process was made easier by the textual representation of the links and the automatic reconstruction of the database.

Acknowledgments

Ben Shneiderman, Professor of Computer Science, and Richard Potter, graduate student of the laboratory, were major participants in the development and evaluation of GOVA. Professor Ken Holum initiated the project and actively directed the writing of the database, assisted by Diane Everman. Rodrigo Botafogo created the graphic tools used with Hyperties. We also greatly appreciate the cooperation of Myriam Springuel of the Smithsonian Institute.

Catharine Plaisant may be contacted at the Human–Computer Interaction Laboratory, Center for Automation Research, University of Maryland, College Park, MD 20742.

References

Botafogo, R. (1990). "Structural Analysis of Hypertexts," Masters Thesis, Department of Computer Science, University of Maryland, College Park, MD.

Holum, K. (1988). "Reliving King's Herod's Dream," *Archaeology*, May/June 88, 44–47.

Holum, K., Hohlfelder, R., Bull, R., Raban, A. (1988). *King Herod's Dream—Caesarea on the sea*, W. W. Norton & Company, New York, NY.

Potter, R., Shneiderman, B., and Weldon, L. (1988). "Improving the accuracy of touch-screens: an experimental evaluation of three strategies," *Proceedings of the conference on Human Factors in Computing Systems*, ACM SIGCHI, New York, NY.

Shneiderman, B., Brethauer, D., Plaisant, C., and Potter, R. (May 1989). "The Hyperties electronic encyclopedia: An evaluation based on three museum installations," *Journal of the American Society for Information Science*, 40(3), 172–182.

Shneiderman, B., and Kearsley, G. (1989). *Hypertext Hands-On!*, Addison-Wesley, Reading, MA.

Shneiderman, B., Kreitzberg, C., and Berk, E. (1991). "Editing to Structure a Reader's Experience," *Hypertext / Hypermedia Handbook*, Emily Berk and Joseph Devlin (Ed.s), McGraw-Hill, New York, NY.

Case 9
Rediscovering Pompeii

By Ruth Giellman
Armadillo Associates, Inc.

On August 24, A.D. 79, the Roman city of Pompeii was buried by the eruption of Mt. Vesuvius. In 1748, it was uncovered accidentally. Since then, archaeological exploration of the city has continued. It is not surprising that computer technology is being enlisted to aid in managing the vast amounts of data that are still being generated at the site.

Between 1987 and 1989, more than one hundred scientists, archeologists, architects, art historians, anthropologists and specialists from IBM Italy and Fiat Engineering collaborated to develop useful new applications for computer technology in the field of archeology. The efforts of these professionals (who collectively form the Neapolis Consortium) have yielded a number of computer programs, as well as an expanding graphical and textual database of the topography, monuments and artifacts of Pompeii and the surrounding region.

At the core of the Neapolis Consortium's information processing system is an IBM Enterprise System/3090 Model 150E mainframe computer which stores the database of information on Pompeii. This information is shared among researchers using an IBM Token Ring network and twenty-five IBM Personal System/2 (PS/2) computers. Forty IBM 3179 Color Display Stations are also used. In addition, IBM 5080 Graphic Systems are used for mapping and three dimensional modeling applications (see Figure C9.1), and a stereo plotting device is used for drawing maps.

The *Winchester Solid Modeler* (WINSOM) and graPHIGS three-dimensional modeling programs on the IBM 5080 Graphic Systems enable members of the Neapolis Consortium to electronically reconstruct Pompeian architecture and objects, as an aid in studying and restoring the actual buildings and artifacts. This technology not only allows researchers to create detailed architectural drawings but also lets them rebuild missing elements and visually tour electronically restored buildings.

To date, images of and information about 10,000 frescoes and mosaics at Pompeii have been entered into the project's database. Researchers can use this database to locate all findings referring to a particular pictorial theme, or to call up color images of mosaics and frescoes, enlarging specific areas of one or more

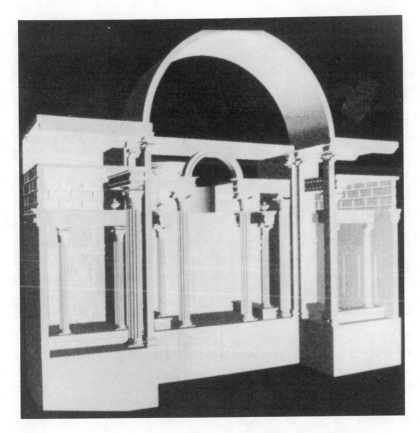

Figure C9.1 Computerized reconstruction of a Pompeiian gateway.

images for detailed or side-by-side studies. They also simulate the way frescoes might look after restoration, using the high-resolution capabilities of the IBM 7350 Image Processing System and PS/2 Model 8514 displays. Selecting from a palette of computer-generated colors, consortium members "experiment," matching areas of missing pigment without risk to the actual painting.

Using new aerial surveys, computerized maps of Pompeii and its environs are developed on scales ranging from 1:500 to 1:25,000. (See Figure C9.2) Electronic maps can be updated, analyzed and printed based on specific requirements. For example, Consortium members have generated maps showing archeological finds by historical periods and others indicating the location of frescoes by their style of painting and state of preservation. Researchers are also able to electronically enter the city, isolate particular quarters or buildings, and display features such as mosaics or frescoes inside a building on high-resolution screens.

The combination of the processing and storage capabilities of a mainframe computer and a relational database make it possible to manage the complex relationships between the large amounts and different types of archeological text and

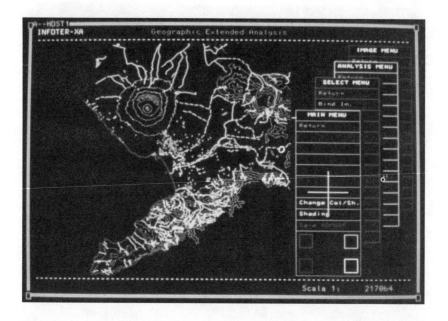

Figure C9.2   A computer-generated site plan of the city of Pompeii.

image information. The information is highly cross-referenced for use in a wide range of studies.

Rediscovering Pompeii, the museum exhibition which grew out of the Consortium's project, brings both actual artifacts and computerized records about Pompeii to the general public. The exhibition was designed to encourage museum-goers to explore everyday life in 1st-century Pompeii, and presents a comprehens-ive picture of the life, death and rediscovery of the ancient city. *Rediscovering Pompeii* presents a combination of the worlds of archeology and advanced infor-mation management—the fruits of archeological excavations and easy access to information in the Consortium's database—via hypertext.

Among the artifacts on display as part of the exhibit are: a wooden money holder, said to be unique among archeological finds from the ancient Roman world; a large and extremely rare bronze food warmer; numerous vessels, games, and pieces of jewelry; and sculpture, including a bronze statuette of the wine-god Bacchus and theater masks in marble relief (see Figure C9.3).

Scattered throughout the exhibition halls are 15 computer stations, each offering museum-goers different information about artifacts on display and about Pompeii in general. Each stand-alone computer station consists of an IBM PS/2 personal computer equipped with an advanced graphics IBM 8514 monitor (1024x768 reso-lution) and a hard disk.

Figure C9.3 **These marble theatrical masks shown in relief are typical of the items on display.**

Eleven of the 15 microcomputers run interactive programs that give visitors a say in what information is retrieved from the database. These interactive stations feature touch screen interfaces. The other four stations present continuous loops of information.

The most complex of the interactive applications is a hyperdocument containing approximately 1000 images of Pompeiian artifacts (many of which were not on display in the exhibit) and about 400 nodes of accompanying textual information. These images are divided into six categories, including technology, art and religion. Upon request from the visitor, images of a dozen or so different objects in a category are displayed on the screen at a time. Each image is stored in a separate file, approximately 1 MB in size, on the hard disk. Response time is approximately one second to call up a full-screen image, less than a second for text.

Museum visitors request information about an artifact by touching its image on the computer screen. This information is displayed on cards, each of which contains text plus a series of commands and highlighted keywords that link to additional images. For example, if a visitor touches the image of a bronze vase, a card containing a description of the vase is displayed. The words "bronze" and "water distribution" are highlighted in the text, indicating that more information is available on these topics.

A menu displayed on the left side of the screen contains navigation commands and a button for calling up help. Navigation commands include those used to move forward or back one node at a time or to jump to the beginning of a description of an artifact or all the way to the main menu. Help comes in two forms: textual advice about how to accomplish certain procedures and maps of the hypertext with which users can orient themselves while working their way though the hyperdocument. For example, users reading about a bronze vase might call up a map that shows they are viewing the third node out of six describing that vase and shows them how to jump quickly to descriptions of related artifacts.

Another hyperdocument provides information about the volcanic eruption of Mt. Vesuvius that buried Pompeii. Visitors can view relief and contour maps which illustrate different stages of the eruption. They can also access in-depth technical information about volcanoes and about the effects of the eruption by touching on highlighted keywords.

Other interactive programs in *Rediscovering Pompeii* allow visitors to:

- View images of some of the exhibition's objects as if they were walking around them.
- Take an electronic "walk" through Pompeii's Forum, theaters, amphitheater, villas and baths, so they can see them from various perspectives.
- Read the charred and almost invisible remains of Roman literature on papyrus by means of digitized reconstruction of the original letters.
- Read 18th-century excavation records.
- Examine a fountain intricately decorated with glass mosaic and seashell inlay, in a three dimensional approximation of its original environment.
- Explore the restoration of works of art and site mappings.
- Obtain information on Pompeian painters and techniques, and decorative styles in Pompeian fresco painting.
- View the town's famed Stabian baths and several of its elaborate building complexes.

All software used in *Rediscovering Pompeii* was developed specifically by the Neapolis Consortium for the exhibition. The decision to go with a custom-designed program was made because at the time development began, no commercially available system could provide touch screen control over the large number of high resolution images to be used in the exhibition. While the developers tried to limit the size of each node to one screen or 20 lines, some of the nodes contain several pages of text.

The high resolution graphics required by archaeologists take up a lot of storage space. The developers of *Rediscovering Pompeii* considered storing the hyperdocuments on optical disk, because optical disk can hold up to 200 megabytes of data. However, access time to load a single graphical screen from optical disk took 10 seconds; much too long. Therefore, it was decided that information would be stored on magnetic disk. A simple graphics compression program was devised for graphics. This compression program reduces full screens that would otherwise take up half a megabyte by an average of 20 percent.

While the hypertext development system developed for *Rediscovering Pompeii* is fully capable of supporting sound, the developers decided against using this capability in the New York exhibition because it would create too much additional noise in the exhibition space. Because text, sound and images are stored as separate files by the system, it has been relatively easy to create separate Italian and English versions of the exhibition. The pictures remain the same, but the descriptive text and sound (if appropriate) are easily changed to suit the local audience and museum conditions.

Rediscovering Pompeii was organized by the Italian Ministry of Cultural and Environmental Assets, the Archeological Superintendency of Pompeii and IBM Italy. The exhibit was overseen by Baldassare Conticello, the superintendent for archeology in Pompeii. Professor Conticello organized *Rediscovering Pompeii* in collaboration with Professor Luisa Franchi dell'Orto and Dr. Antonio Varone. *Rediscovering Pompeii* opened at the IBM Gallery of Science and Art in July, 1990. It went on to Houston and from there will move to Rome in 1991.

Images courtesy of the Italian Ministry of Cultural and Environmental Assets, and the IBM Gallery of Science and Art.

About the Author

Ruth Giellman

Ruth Giellman is a senior editor for the *Hypertext/Hypermedia Handbook*, with seven years of experience in working with computers. A graduate from the University of Pennsylvania, with a degree in the Biological Basis of Behavior, Ms. Giellman has previously written for a leading marketing research and consulting firm.

Case 10
Electronic Music Lover's Companion: An Interactive Guide to Classic Electronic Music

By Thom Holmes
Flying Turtle Productions

One of my lifelong interests has been electronic music. I became interested in it during the 1960s, a period that saw the classic age of *avant garde* electronic music come to a close and the modern era of computer-based music take hold. Today's popular music and music technology owe a lot to the pioneering composers and inventors who experimented in this medium during the first seventy years of this century.

I wrote a book in 1985 to document the developmental years of electronic and experimental music between 1900 and 1970. One aspect of the subject that has always fascinated me is the symbiotic relationship between the inventors of electronic music instruments and composers. In my book, I traced the parallel developments in each field, showing how the ideas of composers inspired the inventors of the instruments, and vice versa. In the end, however, I realized that the printed page was not the most effective medium for presenting this story.

Soon after learning about Apple's HyperCard I realized that an electronic publishing medium was at hand that could help me translate the story of electronic music into a different kind of educational and entertainment tool. From the start, it has been the kinetic quality of hypermedia that has fascinated me; its ability to bring a subject alive with sound and graphics. Hypermedia provides the next-best solution to sitting someone down with some pictures and recordings and personally telling them the story of electronic music. Thus, my *Electronic Music Lover's Companion* was born. (See Figures C10.1 and C10.2.)

Although I have also done work in color using SuperCard and Plus, I chose to create the *Electronic Music Lover's Companion* using HyperCard for several reasons:

- Its widespread availability to Macintosh users, particularly educators and musicians who comprise an important segment of the audience.

Figure C10.1

Figure C10.2   Main Menu Screen of the *Electronic Music Lover's Companion*.

- Its familiarity to Macintosh users, providing a built-in comfort factor for those who might choose to buy the program.
- The ability to avoid having to produce a standalone or runtime copy of HyperCard because stacks are operated by the HyperCard application provided with all Macintoshes. This saves disk space and keeps the program to a size that does not use up too much of the customer's hard-disk space. In contrast, a standalone program developed in SuperCard adds more than 300K on top of one's basic stack.
- The availability of CD audio XCMDs, originated by Apple and packaged into a workable development tool by Voyager (the CD Audio Stack). These ready-made routines allow one to control the playback of an audio compact disc from a CD-ROM drive. This forms the means for presenting music using the *Electronic Music Lover's Companion*.

Surprisingly, the most challenging aspect of this project has not been the development of the program itself, but the licensing of the electronic music to be used with it. What I discovered was that none of the classic electronic music available at one time on vinyl had yet been released on compact disc. Even if it were, I would probably want to produce a greatest hits' version to be used with my program. Being a small, independent developer, I did not possess the financial leverage to merely acquire the licensing rights to everything I needed. So, I began a campaign to convince the record companies that they would benefit from taking part in the project, and that they should give serious consideration to releasing their valuable collections of experimental music now sitting idle in their vaults. In a sense, the programming has taken a back seat to the effort to revive the availability of the music itself, which is probably as it should be.

Following the Trail of Discovery

With hypermedia, users are not limited to the connections I define for them; they are free to make their own and organize their exploration of the subject in a way that makes most sense to them. No other available medium provided a means to emulate the sense of discovery and invention I wanted to create. Electronic music is, by its very nature, an integration of technology, musical arts, and aesthetic principles. Hypermedia allows me to integrate the presentation of these elements in a seamless fashion, inviting the user to experience the synthesis of this musical art following a trail of discovery similar to that experienced by the pioneers in the field. The information elements of the *Electronic Music Lover's Companion* include (See Figures C10.3 and C10.4):

- Seven textual components (history of the technology, history of the aesthetics, biographical notes, discographies, quotes from the composers, quotes from their critics, and running commentary to an audio compact disc companion).
- Audio samples (digitized demonstrations of classic electronic music sounds).
- Visuals (illustrations of instruments, inventors, composers, performers, and scores).

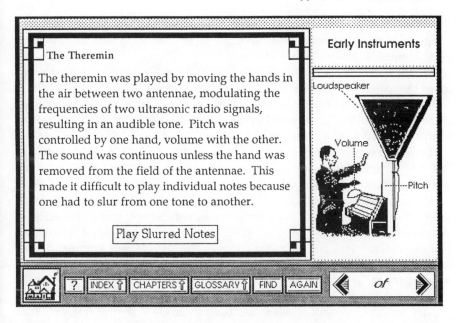

Figure C10.3 An Information Screen from the Technology Section of the program.

Figure C10.4 A Biography Screen.

Hypertext provides the linkages needed to make connections between the technology, music, and aesthetic ideas that make up this subject. This adds dimension to the comprehension of the subject.

Say, for instance, one is interested in the music of Edgard Varese. One could begin by reviewing Varese's biography and his famous prediction in 1917: "I dream of instruments obedient to my thought and which with their contribution of a whole new world of unsuspected sounds, will lend themselves to the exigencies of my inner rhythm."

The path that traces Varese's life and the evolution of his music can be followed to a path that describes musical instruments created to help fulfill his dream. Individual compositions, such as Varese's *Poeme Electronique* from 1958, are linked to technical developments such as the emergence of the tape recorder as a tool for assembling sounds. To better understand the significance of the music in its own time, an explanation of the music in Varese's own words is offered, as well as opinions published by music critics of the time. *Poeme Electronique* can be listened to from a companion compact disc that is annotated with a running commentary in the stack describing technical aspects of the work. Finally, paths amplifying the ripple effects of Varese's influence can be followed to see how his thinking affected the work of other composers for many years that followed. (See Figures C10.5 and C10.6.)

One may develop a similar path for any of the composers or inventors found in the *Electronic Music Lover's Companion,* or invent new ones beginning at any point. Additional examples of paths could include:

- Staying on any of the seven text paths from beginning to end, without branching. For example, studying the history of electronic music technology in chronological order.
- Tracing the influences on a given composer and exploring the music of his or her predecessors.
- Exploring the aesthetic ideas presented by the music and jumping to audio examples on the companion audio compact disc.
- Beginning with the music itself and working back to learn about the ideas and technology that preceded it.
- Exploring the connections between technology and the musical ideas that were inspired by it.

Tools Used

In addition to HyperCard, tools used in creating the *Electronic Music Lover's Companion* include:

- Ensoniq Mirage digital sampler. A professional music keyboard/sampler that allows me to capture the sounds of antique electronic music instruments and play them back for demonstration purposes. Some of these clips are then used in the

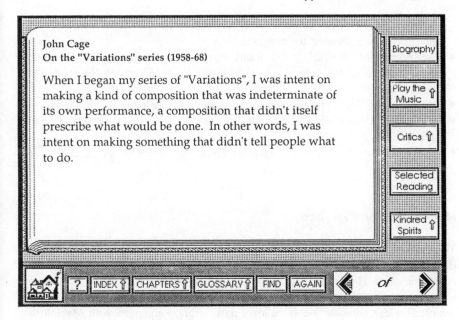

Figure C10.5   A quote from John Cage.

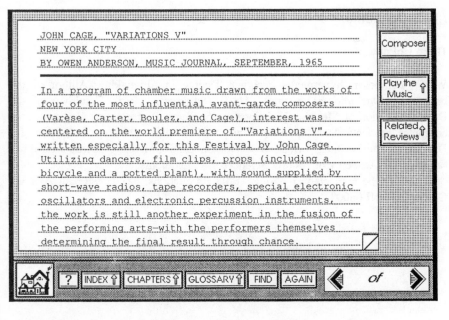

Figure C10.6   A critic's response to a performance by John Cage.

Electronic Music Lover's Companion, particularly for the audio cues that occur when one moves about in the program.

- MacRecorder and SoundEdit (Farallon). Used primarily to sample audio recordings that are used for demonstration purposes in the *Electronic Music Lover's Companion*.
- AppleScanner. For capturing photos and other images used in the program.
- Several paint and draw programs, including SuperPaint, PixelPaint, and Studio 8.
- Voyager CD Audio Stack. For creating HyperCard controls for an audio compact disc.

Multimedia For Everybody

The term multimedia often implies special hardware requirements (such as video disc players, video output boards, etc.), that are beyond the pocketbooks of most computer users. HyperCard and the CD Audio tools, however, provide a reasonably inexpensive platform on which to deliver high quality hyper/multimedia programs. One can envision a college-level music library equipped with Macintoshes and CD-ROM readers, a place where students go to learn about music at their own pace, using programs similar to the *Electronic Music Lover's Companion*, programs that might even be developed by the same professors who lecture them in the classroom.

About the Author

Thom Holmes

Writer, composer, hypermedia designer. Degree in filmmaking. Author of the book *Electronic and Experimental Music* (Scribner's, 1985). Employee of the Datapro division of McGraw-Hill since 1975, creating information services about computer products. Developed the *Datapro Consultant (Macintosh Edition)* for Datapro, a multimedia information service on CD-ROM. Staff educator on dinosaurs for the Academy of Natural Sciences in Philadelphia.

Thom can be contacted at Flying Turtle Productions, 721 Crestbrush Avenue, Cherry Hill, NJ 08003.

Case 11
If Monks Had Macs...

By Brian Thomas
riverText ™

Figure C11.1

Description

If Monks had Macs... is a computer program that allows you to explore the library of a medieval monastery. When you start the program, you find yourself at a desk before an open window that looks onto the monastery cloister. With the click of a mouse, you can open the first computerized edition of *The Imitation of Christ*, make entries in the journal that is linked to it, or browse the library shelves.

On the shelves of the library you'll find books from the past 800 years. Among these books you can find a graphic adventure game about a monk's trek through the medieval wilderness to the library, interactive investigations of quantum physics and evolution, dramatic documents about German students resisting the Nazis, the monastery jukebox, and more.

If Monks had Macs... was written using Apple Computer's HyperCard (now marketed by Claris Corporation), a software erector set that you can use to design and build additions to our world or your own independent worlds.

From the sample *If Monks...* images included here, you can see that we provide not just 500-year-old text with links on a Macintosh screen, but the feeling of a medieval monastery in which to read the text. When you find yourself before that open window looking onto the cloister, you hear the monks finish the last chorus of a Gregorian chant. The monks' chant drifts across the cloister and mixes with the fountain's delightful murmur. After the monks have finished singing you can hear, occasionally, a bird or two chirping its own song. If you tarry long enough, you'll hear the peal of the monastery bells. These are all separate sounds into which the fountain's sound has been mixed.

It was easy to use the powerful programming language that comes with HyperCard to continually rearrange the sounds according to life-like probabilities so that our opening never sounds like a broken record, but gives the illusion of reality. We're not yearning for virtual reality here, we just want to open with a hook that will engage the browser's interest and set a mood for what follows. The label we prefer for what we do is not hypertext or multimedia, but *interactive media*.

You discover right after the opening scene that this is an interactive world; the objects in it respond to you. If you select a book by clicking on it, you zoom into a close-up from which you can begin reading; if you click on the row of books to the side you can browse the whole library. (See Figure C11.2.) With a click of the mouse, books (HyperCard programs by us or other authors) can be added to or removed from the library.

In the library is a high intensity interactive activity. (The unpretentious refer to these activities as games.) In our interactive short story of a game, you take the part of a rather bumbling monk who needs to learn to trust his principles and his wits to escape the devil's clutches and trek through the medieval wilderness to the monastery library. There are other surprises such as the monastery jukebox and pinball arcade in another library book that are too irrational to describe here.

Figure C11.2   Click on the open book and you'll zoom into a close-up.

True interaction, like true democracy, requires more than a choice between predetermined solutions. Ideally, the user ought to be able to participate in the project. To move in the direction of true interaction in *Monks*, first, a sophisticated self-indexing journal is linked to *The Imitation of Christ* so that those so inclined can examine their own lives. Second, users are encouraged to add or remove programs in the library as they build their own collections. Third, in one program, we succeeded in presenting the Macintosh community with a philosophical critique of the theory of evolution. Since the responses to this widely circulated work were received and discussed via modems on an electronic *bulletin board service* (BBS), we created a simulation of the experience of actually using the computer to call and interact with a BBS to display the discussions. As we have received more responses, they have been added to successive releases of the program. The user can also post messages on his copy of the BBS so that anyone who reviews his copy of the program will see his contributions to the discussion.

Finally, we provide a resource of lasting value that the user can, if so inclined, turn to again and again. Our medieval resource, *The Imitation of Christ*, is an epigrammatic book of more than a hundred brief chapters that has been in continuous use by countless individuals for 500 years. (See Figure 11.3.)

Our introduction to the *Imitation* begins, "Written in hypertext 550 years ago in the monastery of St. Agnes. . . ." This is not exactly how any introduction to a previous edition of *The Imitation of Christ* begins. But other introductions do point out that the *Imitation* is a marvellous mosaic that arranges more than 1100 references to nearly every book of the Bible into the "best loved and most widely read book of Christianity" after the Bible itself. Despite the inner unity of the *Imitation*, the reader is usually advised in the introductions to "open the book to any page at random where he will find much instruction and inspiration," or to read the book "slowly, reflectively, in brief portions at a time," or to repeatedly turn to it as a "source of devotional thoughts and aphorisms." Thus, these introductions to the

Figure C11.3 The row of icons to the right of this title page is the "control panel" for the book.

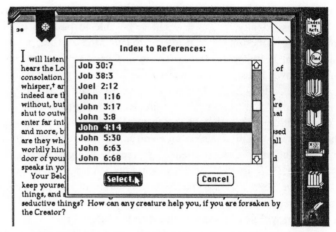

Figure C11.4 The "Index to References" has been called up on top of a typical page of the *Imitation*, and a passage has been selected that will soon be displayed.

Imitation advise readers that this is a book that need not be read sequentially, and is, in a sense, the weaving of an intricate pathway through the Bible towards the light of Heaven.

Our hypertext edition makes this nonsequential reading easier and more enjoyable then it has ever been before, and it makes all the biblical references easy to access, search and study.

In a paperback book the long chapter titles of the *Imitation*'s first one hundred chapters usually take up about five to six pages. We shortened the titles in order to fit the 100 chapters that we include in our edition neatly on one page so that the reader can access any chapter from a single page with a click of the mouse button. I noticed an introduction to an old edition of the book that mentioned that many readers stand the book on its spine and let it fall open where it may and believe that they receive just the right spiritual blessing from the passage their eyes fall upon. To give our readers this capability, we include an icon of a book falling open in our row of controls. When a reader presses this icon-button, the program chooses a chapter at random.

Interactive media, with all its sound and fury, can be a lot of fun. However, there is a danger that if the primary emphasis is not on the written word, on the content, then you could just have an interactive idiot box, a video game. Many of the elements of *If Monks had Macs...* are game-like, but the primary emphasis always comes back to text—to meaning.

If Monks had Macs... is about a time before capitalism and a freedom beyond free enterprise. In December 1989, the editors of *MacUser* magazine listed *If Monks had Macs...* one of the top 200 Macintosh programs. This educational entertainment for the Macintosh is a free gift from our company to everyone. *If Monks had Macs...* is EveryWare. If you like it enough to keep it for yourself, give a copy to someone else.

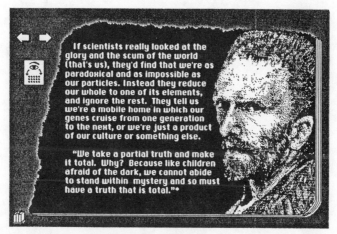

If scientists really looked at the glory and the scum of the world (that's us), they'd find that we're as paradoxical and as impossible as our particles. Instead they reduce our whole to one of its elements, and ignore the rest. They tell us we're a mobile home in which our genes cruise from one generation to the next, or we're just a product of our culture or something else.

"We take a partial truth and make it total. Why? Because like children afraid of the dark, we cannot abide to stand within mystery and so must have a truth that is total."*

Figure C11.5 This program, called *Passing Notes*, combines a little philosophy with a lot of art and science.

If you don't know someone who already has a copy, you can get *Monks* compressed onto three disks for a nine dollars ($9.00) distribution charge from the nonprofit Berkeley Macintosh Users Group. Send a check with a request for *If Monks had Macs...* to:

BMUG PD library
1442A Walnut Street #62
Berkeley, CA 94709
(415) 549-BMUG

BMUG's normal low charge for three disks would be twelve dollars ($12.00), but we arranged the lowest possible handling, postage, and materials charge. You will need a Macintosh with at least 1 megabyte of memory, an 800K disk drive, a hard drive and HyperCard 1.2 to run *If Monks had Macs....* Apple Computer and MacWorld magazine also offer a CD-ROM that includes most of *If Monks had Macs...*, a lot of other award-winning HyperCard programs and the long awaited HyperCard 2.0 for a nominal fee.

The next *riverText* ™ project is an educational-entertainment centered around Henry David Thoreau's *Walden*. It will include an innovative graphic adventure game, a wild, uninhibited examination of Thoreau and his world, the complete annotated text (with research features) of *Walden*, and *Civil Disobedience*, a much improved journal aimed at helping readers with their own writing, and much, much more. It will be very reasonably priced.

Brian Thomas can be contacted on CompuServe at #73057,377 or on Genie at "B.T."

All images copyright Brian Thomas and *riverText* ™

Case 12
Xanadu

By Harold Berk
Armadillo Associates, Inc.

The information age has brought us many advances in communication. Along with these advances, however, it has brought an overwhelming, apparently relentless flow of data of many different types: text, images, data that can be stored digitally and data that can't so be stored, unstructured multimedia documents; engineering and statistical data, etc.

Consider the following: You are in the hospital, dying of some rare disease. Your physician's database has not been updated recently enough to reflect that a potential cure for your fatal disease has been discovered. What happens? Depending on your physician's work schedule, how mentally and physically stressed he or she is, and how soon he or she gains access to this information, your survival could be at stake.

Is it naive to think that someday all information will be organized and acessible through a central database? Perhaps not. Xanadu, the brainchild of Ted Nelson, represents an all-out attempt to solve the problems of inefficient information access, retrieval, and management.

Nelson is the guy who coined the term "hypertext" way back in 1965. Ever since that time he has struggled to create an actual product that was equal to his vision. In 1988, Autodesk, Inc. invested in Nelson's vision and formed the Xanadu Operating Co. to produce and market Xanadu. Now that control of the product is no longer directly in Nelson's hands, it is not clear how closely the vision of Xanadu will resemble its implementation.

The technical challenges that must be overcome in order to deliver Xanadu are considerable. Current plans are to release the first version of the Xanadu Server and retrieval engine some time in 1991. For the time being we must make do with Autodesk's written description of what Xanadu aims to achieve:

- Support all forms of data (text, graphics, audio and video) as well as composite, multimedia documents.
- Provide access via a link to any and all chunks of data. Each chunk can be as small as a pixel or as large as a library.

- Support an unlimited number of link types. Application developers will be able to create whatever link types best suit their purposes. (e.g. Billing clerks might use "repeat order" links and programmers subroutine links.)
- All links created in Xanadu are automatically omnidirectional, giving applications and users access to of all related materials.
- Support for powerful filtering capabilities so that users and developers can cull valuable information from the worthless. Xanadu allows the application developer to specify the kind and number of link types available to each user. Types not supported for a class of users are hidden from their view.
- Provide for the retention of previous versions of hypertext chunks (according to the parameters determined by the user or application).
- Support a wide variety of platforms. Core information management functions are platform-independent because they run on a central server.
- Allow for the development of individual applications running on local computers that serve as front ends to retrieve, organize and relate documents stored in the Xanadu database.

Xanadu is based on a Client/Server model. The Xanadu/Server (provided by Autodesk) handles core information management functions, freeing the client application (usually provided by independent software developers) to focus on local processing, presentation and editing of information. The Server assumes responsibility for storage, maintenance and retrieval of information, and the maintenance of integrity of the information. The Client application is responsible for presenting the information to the user and manipulating on-screen Xanadu documents. A wide range of client applications packages are envisioned, each tailored to the machine it runs on and the type of user it supports. Thus, an architect working on a Sun workstation and an accountant working on an IBM PC can access the same database on the same server—often with very different results.

Xanadu links are envisioned to be somewhat like human neural connections: the pathways are made more repeatable with additional travel. The Xanadu engine keeps track of well-worn paths through the data. These paths may then be presented to subsequent users, guiding them to more meaningful nodes. (See Figure C12.1.) Xanadu also supports creation of specialized link types and filtering of links by type. For example, an application or user may be interested in seeing only the links on a document that are of link type "Engineering Change and Order," "Material Cost" and were created by author "Jones," before January, 1998.

Because the Xanadu/Server was designed to operate in a distributed, multiuser environment, it is important to provide network supervisors with the ability to monitor the dynamic state of shared information and to regulate the way users collaborate with each other. Provision is made to allow sensors to be embedded within various parts of a document. When specific events (such as the attachment of a link or the modification of the document) take place, a signal is sent by the sensor to the application's front end. Consider how this might be applied to provide solutions to the mediating of royalty rights, calculations of user fees, and research into product awareness and even political polling.

Link Types/Filters

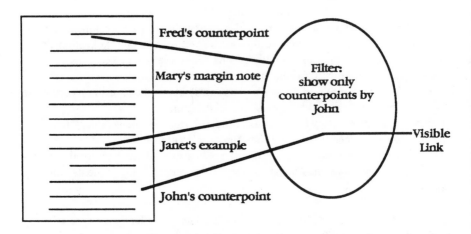

Figure C12.1   Link Types/ Filters. Reprinted with permission from Autodesk, Inc.

Another feature that sets Xanadu apart from other authoring systems is its concept of a "document." Xanadu sees a document as anything that contains any form of digitized information. A document may have any number of versions of any size and may be comprised of any mixture of information types.

Documents in Xanadu are defined as *soft-edged,* that is, every document is not rigidly defined as a file distinct from other files. Xanadu provides the idea of a *virtual document,* where a *document* can be made up of individual elements that may be parts of other documents that do not necessarily share physical proximity. The individual elements of a Xanadu Virtual Document might exist at far-flung locations. One paragraph of text might reside on the third floor server in the accounting department and the graph next to it might be pulled from another server at the other end of town. The user would perceive a single document, but the actual location of the files that went into that document would be transparent. Although none of the material of such a "virtual document" is duplicated from the original material, the virtual document can be copied, edited, linked or otherwise manipulated. In essence, it would seem to have all the characteristics of a "real" document. However, all of the individual components of the Virtual Document would retain knowledge of their origin and relationships to other documents. The linked material could be followed back to all other references of the document to check context and authorship. (See Figure 12.2.)

Xanadu supports Version/Revision Control based on a *Trail of Changes.* This version control and comparison works for text, graphics and other forms of infor-

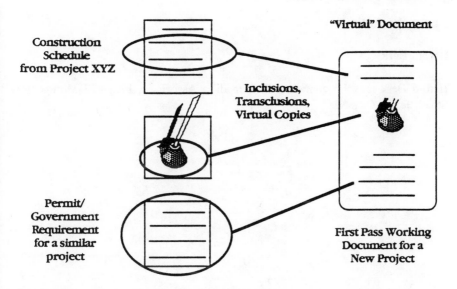

Figure C12.2   Virtual Document. Reprinted with permission from Autodesk, Inc.

mation. Any two documents within a Xanadu information base can be compared based on their edit histories. This offers the possibility of providing one of the most effective type of document comparison mechanisms available. (See Figure C12.3.)

The Xanadu Hypermedia Information Server is being developed by the Xanadu Operating Company, a subsidiary of Audodesk, Inc. It will at first be made available for use on Sun workstations. Subsequent versions will be introduced for high-end IBM-compatible PCs, Apple Macintoshes and NEXT computers.

Version Control and Historical Trace

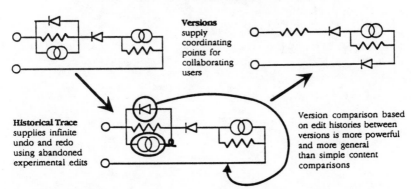

Figure C12.3   Version Control and Historical Trace. Reprinted with permission from Autodesk, Inc.

About the Author

Harold Berk

Harold Berk may be contacted at Armadillo Associates, Inc., 877 Montgomery Street, Jersey City NJ.

Case 13
Storyspace: Hypertext and the Process of Writing

By Mark Bernstein
Eastgate Systems, Inc.

A Hypertextual Tool For Writers

Storyspace[5] is a hypertext system designed specifically to facilitate the process of writing. While most hypertext systems are intended primarily for presenting information—for creating and publishing finished electronic manuscripts—Storyspace emphasizes the process of developing, refining, and revising ideas. While Storyspace can also be used to publish finished hyperdocuments, our chief goal has been to create a pleasant and invigorating working environment which allows writers to explore and exploit the complex relationships that interconnect their ideas.

Storyspace hyperdocuments are made up of writing spaces—represented in Figure C13.1 by named, rectangular boxes. Each writing space represents a thought, plan, or idea, which is briefly described by its title. Writing spaces can contain as much text (with illustrations) as the author wishes to include. Writing spaces may also contain additional writing spaces that further explain the topic at hand.

Personal Tools

Writing is an intensely personal process. Most authors prefer to work with familiar tools and to proceed at their personal pace, and no serious writing tool can succeed if it inhibits or obstructs these intense personal preferences. Storyspace does not prescribe a specific approach to writing. For example, some writers prefer to begin a project by jotting down a bundle of writing spaces in a burst of spontaneous energy; Storyspace supports this style by permitting writers to create new writing

---

5   Storyspace software designed by: Jay David Bolter, Michael Joyce, and John B. Smith.
    Storyspace is a trademark of Eastgate Systems, Inc. P.O. Box 1307, Cambridge, MA. 02238 (800-562-1638, 617-924-9044).

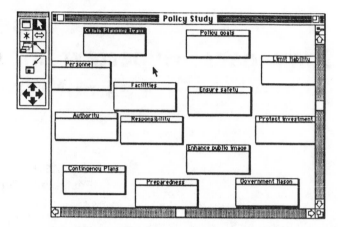

Figure C13.1   This Storyspace document contains a scattering of ideas on crisis management which the author has rapidly jotted down. Later, the author will add text and illustrations to each space, will rearrange the writing spaces to make their organization explicit, and will interlink related writing spaces. Storyspace, copyright Eastgate Systems, Inc.

spaces as quickly as they can type the titles. Other writers prefer a more systematic approach, and carefully consider the way each new writing space would fit into the overall scheme; for these writers Storyspace provides a precise positioning tool which lets them locate a new writing space with a single click of the mouse. Some writers enjoy the opportunity Storyspace offers to pick up and move writing spaces as if they were concrete objects; for them, Storyspace supports a graphic, direct manipulation approach to arranging writing spaces. Others prefer a more abstract, command-oriented approach; for them, Storyspace provides a full set of organization commands. Similarly, Storyspace can instantly switch from a chart view or outline to the more graphic *Storyspace view*, adapting to individual habits and, perhaps, extending personal horizons. (See Figures C13.2 and C13.3.)

Links and Paths

To link writing spaces, the writer merely draws a line between them. Links have names to explain the nature of the connection; link names might include "raw data," "rebuttal," "management overview," "procedural suggestion," and "detailed budget." Links can interconnect entire writing spaces, specific textual passages or a specified part of an illustration. Naturally, Storyspace keeps track of the link position and automatically adjusts the link as writing spaces are reorganized and as the text is revised. Optionally, the author can attach requirements to a link (e.g. "Follow me only if the reader has already reviewed the safety instructions"), and specify actions to be performed on arriving at a new destination (e.g. "Display videodisc frame 723 and play a fanfare when entering this writing space").

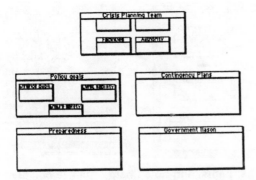

Figure C13.2 A Storyspace view of the crisis planning study, showing writing spaces that contain other writing spaces. The author can pick up and move any writing space by dragging it with the mouse, or can open the writing space by clicking on its title. Storyspace, copyright Eastgate Systems, Inc.

A single command attaches a note to any writing space. Notes are themselves writing spaces; they can contain text, graphics, additional writing spaces, and even additional notes. Because writing spaces are automatically marked with their author's name and the date on which they were created, notes provide a fast, convenient way for collaborators to revise joint writing projects. Simple commands let an editor gather together all notes on a given topic, all notes written by a single author, or all notes written during a given period of time.

A collection of links that share the same name is called a *path*; Storyspace users can take guided tours through a large set of interlinked writing spaces by selecting a path and following it. (See Figure C13.4.)

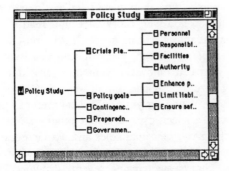

Figure C13.3 This "chart view" provides a different perspective on the same document shown in Figure C13.2. As in the Storyspace view, the author is free to move or modify any writing space just by pointing to it. Special organization commands or "power tools" let users duplicate, transform, or revise entire sections of the document at once. Storyspace, copyright Eastgate Systems, Inc.

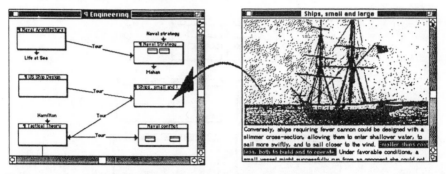

Figure C13.4 Links, paths, and notes help organize complex writing spaces. Storyspace, copyright Eastgate Systems, Inc.

Here we see working notes for a hypertext on the American War of 1812. While this hypertext was published using the Hypergate hypertext system, Storyspace was used for research and working notes throughout the writing process. The highlighted section of the text on the bottom right of Figure C13.4 will shortly be linked to a newly created note; other notes and paths are visible in the map view at the left.

Tools, Not Packages

Because writing is so intensely personal, writers are loyal—often fiercely loyal—to their favorite writing tools. If we were to convince writers to use Storyspace, we knew from the outset that Storyspace must work smoothly and easily with other programs that writers already use. Storyspace cooperates with other programs instead of trying to replace them.

Writers may, of course, type their material directly into writing spaces. If a writer prefers other tools, however, Storyspace will read a wide variety of files and import their contents into a writing space. If you must write with your pencil on scraps of yellow paper, go ahead; you can scan your work with your favorite scanner and import your text (and even your drawings) directly into Storyspace. There, you can reorganize, revise, and link in ways that paper makes inconvenient or impossible. Similarly, if you (or your publisher) prefer to prepare your camera-ready manuscripts with a specific page layout program, you can quickly export your work while keeping your personal notes and working drafts to yourself.

Naturally, some documents will be printed on paper, while others are best published as hypertexts. Storyspace creates several different kinds of stand-alone hyperdocuments, suitable for different writing styles and purposes. In keeping with its tool philosophy, Storyspace can also export a hypertext to other programs (e.g. Hypergate and HyperCard) which provide specialized facilities for hypertext presentation. Rather than struggling (and inevitably failing) to build all these different types of software into a single program, Storyspace takes advantage of other tools and concentrates on its main role—the process of writing.

The Process of Writing

Most writing tools available today emphasize the final steps in writing—layout and typography. Storyspace shifts the emphasis back where we believe it belongs, seeking to assist and promote daring, spontaneous writing by concentrating on the structure and interplay of ideas—not on the details of typesetting. Links and paths, working together with a flexible hierarchical framework, give an abstract but visual representation of a work as it evolves. Nested and *intertwingled* writing spaces let writers concentrate on abstract ideas, not typographic details, freeing writers to visualize and explore the shape of their ideas in new and exciting ways.

About the Author

Mark Bernstein

Mark Bernstein is chief scientist at Eastgate Systems, Inc., a firm specializing in hypertext research since 1982. He led the team that developed the Hypergate hypertext system, and in addition to his conventional publications has written critically-acclaimed hypertexts, including *The Election of 1912* and *The Flag Was Still There* (with Erin Sweeney). Current research interests range from machine learning and automatic link discovery to historical simulation and crisis management.

He was chairman of the AAAI-88 workshop on AI and Hypertext, and has taught numerous courses on The Craft of Hypertext. Eastgate Systems publishes Hypergate, a hypertext environment designed for technical documentation—and Storyspace, a hypertext environment for writers. The Eastgate Press is the leading publisher of serious hypertexts; recent releases include *Afternoon* by Michael Joyce and Sarah Smith's *King of Space*.

Bernstein, a graduate of Swarthmore College, received his doctorate from Harvard in 1983. He can be contacted at Eastgate Systems, Inc., P. O. Box 1307, Cambridge, MA 02238.

Appendix B:
A Hypertext Glossary

By Emily Berk
Armadillo Associates, Inc.

Overview

This hypertext glossary does not presume to be a glossary of every term ever used to describe hypertext or a hypertext application. In fact, it does not even define all the technical terms used in each chapter in this book.

Instead, this glossary is intended to define a more limited set of hypertext-specific terms that the average reader of this book needs to know in order to get the gist of most chapters and to pursue further research into hypertext. Wherever possible, I have tried to echo the definitions authors have used in their chapters in this glossary, so you can refer back to them.

The structure of each entry in this glossary is as follows:

- *Definition:* a short explanation of what the term means.
- *Elaboration:* how the term relates to hypertext or to hypertextual applications.
- *Synonyms:* other terms or phrases used in the same or similar contexts as the term that is defined.

Anchor

Definition: The on-screen depiction of a link.

Elaboration: [Chapter 18 by Gay] The hypertext system may manifest the presence of links in a hyperdocument to readers in many ways, including highlighting text or superimposing button-like icons on screen.

[Chapter 21 by Fox, et al.] One innovation of hypermedia practice has been the use of anchors. When two objects are linked in a hypertext system, the link runs not between the entire objects but from a "hot spot" in one object to a relevant section in the other.

....An anchor serves as the terminating point for links, which are associations between active areas within objects.

Synonyms: Icon, micon, button, link geometry, picon, link marker.

Annotation

Definition: A feature provided in some hypertext browsers which allows readers to make additions to hyperdocuments.

Elaboration: Bookmarks, notes, and bread crumbs are all types of annotations that hypertext readers may make.

Author

Definition: The person who creates a hypertext.

Elaboration: [Chapter 20, by Parunak] I often refer to the "reader" and "author" of a hyperdocument. The same individual may wear both hats, but not always at the same time. Readers are those who traverse links as the fancy strikes them. Authors, on the other hand, accept the responsibility of constructing and organizing webs so as to make traversing them easier for others.

[Chapter 10, by Rearick] Because this chapter deals with conversion of existing linear documents into hypertext, it seemed improper to call the person who supervised this process an "author." Instead, we use the word "builder" to refer to the one who orchestrates the process by which SmarText creates hyperdocuments.

Synonyms: Builder, designer, programmer.

Authoring System

Definition: The system—hardware, software, procedures, conventions, etc. used to create a hyperdocument. Hypertext authoring systems can be assembled in three parts: the hardware and operating system, the authoring system software and special-purpose utilities that may supplement the authoring system.

Elaboration: The set of tools necessary for those who will be browsing through completed hyperdocuments is not as extensive as those required for authoring. Therefore, those who buy hypertext authoring systems are usually able to provide readers with runtime versions of browsing software at a lower cost.

[Chapter 12 by Gay] Nonlinear composition and hypermedia experiences demand flexible and powerful tools and systems. The designer of an interactive fiction must consider not only content, but what tools and software to use. Understanding the technical capabilities of the hardware, software and hypertext systems is an essential first step. The capabilities and limitations of these systems will influence both how the author represents the content and the ways readers access and use it.

[Chapter 13 by Garzotto, et al.] We use the term "hypertext system" for a set of software tools used to create a hypertext. Notecards, KMS, Intermedia, and Hypergate are all examples of hypertext systems. Note that a single hyperdocument might be published in several editions, each using a different hypertext system.

...Specialized link and node typing is built into certain hypertext systems. Therefore, the choice of hypertext system may determine whether certain prescriptive structures are encouraged, permitted or required and whether they can be implemented easily using built-in tools.

Synonyms: Hypertext system, author, authoring platform.

Book mark

Definition: An annotation hypertext readers can insert into a hyperdocument so they can return to a particular location.

Elaboration: [Chapter 20 by Parunak] Book marks permit readers to identify particular landmark nodes and jump directly to them from any point in the system. A book mark facility induces a one-level hierarchy whose root is the known entry point (for example, a pop-up window that lists marked locations). A home button that takes the reader immediately to the entry point of the hyperdocument is a degenerate example of a book mark.

Boolean Search

Definition: A Boolean search is a search phrased and conducted according to the mathematical language of logic. A Boolean search almost always requires the use of one or more of the following logical operators: AND, OR, NOT, XOR (exclusive OR; one or the other, but not both).

[Chapter 21 by Fox et al.] A Boolean query specifies a set of documents by combining simpler queries (ultimately, individual indexed words or concepts) using logical operators.

Elaboration: A Boolean query is almost always based on text search. Thus, for example, a search that reads "lady AND over 30" might not return "women over 30" or "ladies over 30."

[Chapter 21 by Fox et al] Boolean query construction (i.e., using ANDs and ORs and NOTs to specify matches) can be exceedingly difficult, and indeed ten-to-one variations have been observed in the ability of different individuals (and even of the same individual at different times) to form good queries. Frequently, repeated efforts are required to form queries that do not retrieve many non-relevant items (i.e., have high precision) and yet do retrieve a significant fraction of the relevant items (i.e., have high recall).

Synonyms: Text search, logical search, query.

Bread crumbs

Definition: Like Hansel in the folk tale "Hansel and Gretel," hypertext readers can annotate their hyperdocuments with bread crumbs so they can find their way back to locations of particular interest.

Synonyms: Trail markers, history, paths.

Browse

Definition: Browsing is a means of reading which does not require that the reader read every word in the same linear order in which it is stored. The reader of a hyperdocument browses by following links.

Elaboration: [Chapter 23 by Parunak] The distinctive characteristic of hypermedia is its user interface. In fact, from one point of view, hypermedia is a user interface that can serve as a front-end to more conventional systems. As a highly interactive system that supports ad-hoc user "what if" questions, it resembles expert systems and contrasts with the usual report or form oriented database or free text system. It is even more interactive than an expert system. With an expert system, the user first poses a query and then receives a response, but hypermedia permits the query and response phases to proceed in parallel. As one browses, one is continually retrieving information, and browsing (the query activity) continues until the desired response has been obtained .... Hypermedia systems offer semantic richness of data storage comparable to that used in expert systems. In fact, a hyperdocument can be viewed as an expert system whose inference engine is not a computer but a human being.

Synonyms: Navigating, reading.

Browser

Definition: Hypertext systems are often composed of two separate pieces of software—the authoring tools and the browser. The browser can be used to read hyperdocuments that have already been created and cannot be changed significantly.

Synonyms: Delivery system.

Chunking

Definition: A chunk is a logical sub-set of a hyperdocument, one that is to be presented to the reader as a piece. Chunking is the process of determining which information goes into which chunk (or node).

Elaboration: In some hypertext systems, such as Hyperties, a chunk can be longer than a screen long. Other systems, such as HyperCard, restrict the size of a chunk to the size of a screen, or smaller.

For information about some tools that facilitate chunking, see Chapter 14 by Perez and Case Study #3 by Winters, et al., in this book.

Synonyms: Nuggetizing.

Conversion

Definition: The process whereby existing documents, on paper or on-line, are adapted for use in hypertext.

Elaboration: [Chapter 9 by Riner] Converting an information resource into hypertext involves much more than simply creating a computer-readable version of the text and graphics. Converting involves:

- Selecting documents which would benefit readers if they were in hypertext form,
- Determining how to convert them,
- Producing process-ready computer files from paper or other forms,
- Specifying and identifying what should be "linked," and
- Performing the conversion and verifying the results.

There are two basic means of converting existing documents into hypertext. One is manual conversion. This involves selecting a hypertext authoring tool and then entering the document into that environment manually and constructing all of the links as you convert the pages.

Manual conversion works for small prototype projects. But when you scale up from converting a few pages or even a few dozen pages to converting tens of thousands of pages, manual conversion becomes unthinkable. A perfect example is a reference text which has an index of over 50,000 items. If you could manually insert one link per minute, it would take over five months to construct just the links for the index of this one book. For several years now, the Hypermedia Systems & Services organization at Texas Instruments Incorporated has been developing computerized tools to do this type of conversion.

[Chapter 10 by Rearick] Computer users are quick to recognize the benefits of hypertext-based on-line documentation—ease of use and rapid access of information. Most are not aware of the considerable effort required to transform existing linear text into hypertext. The high initial cost of creating hypertext and the recurring cost of maintaining it limits its availability. Only when the creation and maintenance of hypertext are automated will it become accessible to a much larger audience.

Synonyms: Hypertext building, hypertext creation, importing.

Delivery System

Definition: The hardware and software used by a hypertext reader.
Elaboration: The delivery system can often be less sophisticated and less costly than the hypertext authoring system.

Details on Demand

Definition: [Chapter 11 by Shneiderman, et al.] Rather than including detailed information in an article, you can simply reference it and create separate articles for it. This shields readers from unnecessary details, but provides a path readers can follow when it seems relevant. This technique, known as "Details on Demand," is especially useful when the source material contains case studies, experiments or lots of examples.
Elaboration: [Chapter 13 by Garzotto et al.] Elision (information hiding) of deeply-nested hierarchies and display of almost-hierarchical hypertexts are central concerns of Guide [Brown, 1987]. Unlike some other visualization approaches, Guide does not present structure through geometrical schema. Instead, Guide represents textual structure in the form of abstract textual structures: A section heading represents (and may be expanded into) a section which may, in turn, be expanded into more detailed discussions.

[Chapter 11 by Shneiderman et al.] There should be no conceptual gaps which impair understanding nor should there be details which clutter. To integrate the material successfully with existing cognitive structure, the reader must understand which existing concepts the new material relates to. Therefore, the presentation must identify relevant concepts in terms the reader can understand. If there are prerequisite concepts which the reader may not already know, they should be available through links so the reader can view them before proceeding on to the details.

... Subordinate information should be removed from the initial presentation; readers can access it later by means of links. Wherever there is a need for elaboration, a link should be available so that readers can obtain the details at the point they are mentioned. However, care should be taken not to clutter up the screen with redundant links. Our style is to limit the number of links per screen to between six and eight.
Synonyms: Information hiding, filtering, elision.

Filter

Definition: A feature of some hypertext browsers that allows readers and/or authors to prevent certain categories of information from being supplied.
[Chapter 20 by Parunak] Filtering occurs when the hypermedia system shows a reader only some of the paths you can follow through a network.
Elaboration: [Chapter 11 by Shneiderman, et al.] Normally when information is presented, the recipient evaluates the incoming stream, selecting and retaining some elements and discarding others. The reader's selective attention provides appropriate filters to separate relevant from irrelevant and pro-

tects readers from sensory chaos. The apparent paradox is that readers must understand the information before they can determine whether it is worth paying attention to.

[Chapter 20 by Parunak] A map of all the links in a large hyperbase is a hopeless tangle, but a map showing only links of one or a few types can be much more manageable and useful.

Related Terms: Details on demand, information hiding, elision.

Full text search

Definition: [Chapter 21 by Fox, et al.] (Full text searches are) ... keyword-based search approaches (called syntactic searches in Chapter 22 by Littleford in this book), in which the reader searches for a particular string of characters in a database or uses entries from a "controlled" vocabulary for searching.

Elaboration: [Chapter 21 by Fox, et al.] The main problem with full text searching is that the only terms that can possibly be located are the terms that appear in the document.

[Case Study 3 by Winters, et al.] You cannot, as yet, ask an "intelligent" question using text string searches. If you ask for "income taxes" you get "income taxes" and not "FAS96" and "ABP11" or "deferred taxes" even though you would be quite happy to find information on these issues as well.

[Chapter 22 by Littleford] [M]ost searching procedures rely exclusively on syntax. You can ask for sections of the document which contain certain combinations of words, e.g. "Find all occurrences of the word speed," but you generally cannot ask for "all those sections which discuss system performance"—which might include references to speed, transactions per second, inferences per second, bandwidth etc.

Full text search (including boolean and fuzzy search) is clearly syntax-oriented. The semantics are left entirely to the reader. An intricate juggling act has to take place—orchestrate a search that is too tightly focused and you may miss information, too loose and you are bombarded with information, much of which is irrelevant.

Full text search with factor analysis (where a search for one word may in turn cause an automatic search for others) is somewhat of an improvement. This function is usually performed by a static off-line analysis program that looks for patterns of related words. For example, the reader might start the search by looking for the word "computer," and the system may also return occurrences of "CPU."

Synonyms: Syntactic search, text search, keyword search.

Hierarchy

Definition: A hierarchy is a structure that allows elements in a database to relate to other files in a one-to-n mapping. In hypertext, a hierarchy is set of nodes organized into a system of successive ranks. In a hierarchy of nodes, each node except for the first has a parent or source node.

Elaboration: [Chapter 19 by Bernstein] An explicit, simple, and repetitive hierarchical structure sharply diminishes the apparent scope of a document.

[Chapter 13 by Garzotto, et al.] Many hypertext researchers advocate extensive use of hierarchical structures to organize the contents of hypertexts. In KMS, for example, every node is part of a single overall hierarchy. KMS links are of two types: "tree links," which conform to the hyperdocument's hierarchical structure and cross-hierarchical "special links," which breach its hierarchical constraints.

KMS strongly encourages a top-down, stepwise refinement approach to organizing material. The system's hierarchical emphasis suggests that writers should sketch in general information first, later adding details at lower levels of the hierarchy. The resulting hierarchical "backbone" helps readers build a coherent mental model of the database. Multiple hierarchies can be constructed to provide alternative paths through the database [Akscyn, 1987]. Similarly, each item in NLS/AUGMENT is identified by a hierarchical description [Engelbart, 1968].

[Chapter 20 by Parunak] This (hierarchical) topology characterizes popular PC-based outline processors such as ThinkTank(TM) or PCOutline(TM), and is also the basic structure of Engelbart's AUGMENT [see Chapter 24 by Engelbart in this book, and Engelbart, 1968]. The orphan element (the root of the hierarchy) is usually the node at which one enters the hyperdocument. All links point away from the root, so any node is reachable from it. Furthermore, since a link once traversed can be followed in the reverse direction, one can go from any node back up (to the root if necessary), and then down to any other node.

If we rule out moving back and forth repeatedly over the same link, a hierarchy defines a unique path between any two nodes: from the current node, back up repeatedly to the unique parent of the current node until one reaches a node that is an ancestor of the target node, then forward down a different branch to the target node. Because there is a unique path between any two nodes, we can define distances between nodes, which are conveniently abstracted in terms of depth in the hierarchy. Directionality is also well defined in a hierarchy: up (toward the root) or down (away from it). Hierarchies do not support an orthogonal addressing strategy.

Synonyms: Tree, network.

Hyperdocument

Definition: [Chapter 13 by Garzotto, et al.] We use the term "hyperdocument" to denote one specific hypertext document made up of interlinked pages or "nodes."

Elaboration: We distinguish hyperdocument, an instance, from hypertext and hypermedia, which refer to technologies rather than applications.

Synonyms: Stack, book, hyperbook, document, hypermedia application, hypertext application, program.

Hypertext

Definition: The technology of nonsequential reading and writing. Hypertext is technique, data structure, and user interface.

Elaboration: [Chapter 6 by Slatin] I want to modify Nelson's definition, to read as follows: A hypertext (or hyperdocument) is an assemblage of texts, images, and sounds—nodes—connected by electronic links so as to form a system whose existence is contingent upon the computer. The user/reader moves from node to node either by following established links or by creating new ones.

Synonyms: Hypermedia.

Hypermedia

Definition: [Chapter 27 by McDaid] "Hypermedia" is Theodor Nelson's term for computer-mediated storage and retrieval of information in a nonsequential fashion. An extension of Nelson's earlier coinage, *hypertext* (for nonsequential *writing,* hypermedia implies linking and navigation through material stored in many media: text, graphics, sound, music, video, etc. [Nelson, 1987]. But the ability to move through textual information and images is only half the system: a true hypermedia environment also includes tools that enable the 'reader' to rearrange the material. As Nelson put it in a comment during a HyperText '89 session: "with full user control."

Elaboration: [Chapter 18 by Gay and Mazur] The term hypermedia ... implies a rich mix of text, video, audio and/or graphics, in any combination the author desires and the system can support. In fact, each node (or, program "event") may itself involve the use of several media simultaneously. A video clip, for example, might be accompanied by both a voice-over and on-screen text.

[Chapter 5 by Picher et al.] A computer program that runs in color with few pictures and beeps is not necessarily a multimedia application; a multimedia application is not necessarily a hypermedia application. ... We reserve the term hypermedia for those applications that allow users to forge their own non-linear paths through images, sounds and text.

Synonyms: Hypertext.

Index

Definition: A systematic guide to items contained in or concepts derived from a collection. These items or concepts are represented by entries arranged in a searchable order, such as alphabetical, chronological, or numerical. This order is normally different from that of the items or concepts in the collection itself.

A systematic arrangement of entries designed to enable users to locate information in a document.

Elaboration: [Chapter 9 by Riner] An index provides readers with a list of topics that might otherwise have to be searched for.

[Chapter 10 by Rearick] The objectives for creating an index for text retrieval and hypertext are different. Database indices discriminate between text records that have well-delineated boundaries. The indices for printed or hypertext documents are meant to help readers locate important topics that are discussed within a body of text that has few or no internal boundaries.

... Function of an Index: The purpose of an index is to enable users to find information. Identify and locate relevant information within the material being indexed. Discriminate between information on a subject and passing mention of a subject. Exclude passing mention of subjects that offers nothing significant to the potential user. Analyze concepts treated in the document so as to produce a series of headings based on its terminology. Indicate relationships between concepts. Group together information on subjects that is scattered by the arrangement of the document. Synthesize headings and subheadings into entries. Direct the user seeking info under items not chosen for the index headings to the headings that have been chosen, by means of cross-references. Arrange entries into a systematic and helpful order.

Synonyms: Outline, keyword list, cross reference list.

Link

Definition: [Chapter 12 by Gay] A link is a pointer from one hypertext node to another. The presence of a link alerts a hypertext reader that there is a relationship between the node that is the source of the link and the link's target node.

Each link is a directed connection between related pieces of stored information within the database.

[Chapter 24 by Engelbart] "[L]inks" can point to any arbitrary object within the document, or within another document in a specified domain of documents—and the link can be actuated by a user or an automatic process to "go see what is at the other end," or "bring the other-end object to this location," or "execute the process identified at the other end."

Elaboration: Links are usually denoted by words or phrases that are highlighted in some fashion, but they can also be buttons, icons or other graphics. For example, each component of a schematic diagram may be a link to a more detailed schematic of that component or to a text description.

The manner in which links are signified to readers is known as the "anchor."

[Chapter 13 by Garzotto, et al.] A large hyperdocument contains not only a prodigious amount of information, but also a large number of links. The

richness and diversity of the nodes in a successful hyperdocument is reflected in the richness and diversity of its links. Yet Nelson's polemical
declaration [Nelson, 1976], "EVERYTHING IS INTERTWINGLED!" is
not literally true. We cannot use hypertext to interlink everything. Rather,
we use links selectively to convey part of a thought and to show how that
thought fits into the structure of an argument.

[Chapter 22 by Littleford] One of the main complaints about hypertext is
that links reflect what the author thinks important or relevant more often
than they reflect what the reader hopes to find. The reasons for this are not
hard to fathom given our discussions above—the relevance of a link depends heavily on how the document is currently being used and the use to
which the information will be put.

Synonyms: Cross reference, active text, hot spot, anchor.

Link, Embedded

Definition: [Chapter 12 by Gay] The internal structure of the hyperbase
allows the designer to store information (story elements) in a neutral form,
separate from hard-wired links.

[Chapter 23 by Parunak] [However], most current systems embed full
linking information in the documents managed by the system. This approach is fine for a relatively short document or for one that is written from
the ground up as hypermedia. It is extremely cumbersome for managing
documents that were not originally intended for use in a hypermedia environment, or that are distributed on CD-ROMs. Imagine a firm that receives
twenty CD-ROMs a month of updated government regulations. Adding internal linking information to these documents would require maintaining
more than ten gigabytes of on-line storage for the modified documents, and
in some cases government auditors may look askance on firms using modified rather than original documents as their working copies. Furthermore, if
links must be stored in the text of the document, different users cannot
maintain distinct sets of links for the same document (and thus cannot write
their own notes "in the margin" without publishing these notes to other
users).

The solution to this problem is to house links and notes in a separate data
structure, a "web," as in the Intermedia system. The user interface merges
the document and the web to produce an integrated display. The information that one sees in an anchor on the screen comes from the document, but
the marking on the screen that designates it as hot, and the action that results from clicking on it, are defined in the web.

Elaboration: [Chapter 25 by Benton, et al.] A great many of the single-user
hypertext systems on the market today store links into the same files as the
content (nodes) they are linking. This approach becomes unmanageable
when the number of nodes becomes large and many users are given rights
to create or delete nodes and links. If hypertext systems are to successfully
serve as the glue used to meld together a wide variety of applications run-

ning on a network, it is important that content be separated from access and presentation methods.

[Chapter 11 by Shneiderman, et al.] The underlying structure of Hyperties article files reflects the fact that links are embedded in text, i.e., each link is stored in the node that serves as its source. To specify a reference within text, a Hyperties author simply puts tildes around the string that will serve as the entry point to the link. When an author specifies a reference, the authoring tool examines the list of entry names and synonyms to make the link.

Link Marker, Embedded

Definition: "Embedded link marker" refers to the anchor of a link that appears within the content of a node when it is presented to hypertext readers. In general, link markers that change from node to node are embedded in the content of a node. The advantage of nonembedded link markers is that they can be placed in a control panel in a consistent format on the computer screen.

Elaboration: It makes sense to use nonembedded links for links to nodes such as HELP and INDEX that are always available to readers.

[Chapter 11 by Shneiderman, et al.] We chose to implement Hyperties using embedded link markers in both text and graphics because empirical studies demonstrated that this method was very comprehensible to readers and authors, that distraction was reduced, and that screen layouts were less cluttered. Even so, visible links are a potential distraction from the reading process and we have considered allowing readers to delay link display until they have completed reading an article.

Link Typing

Definition: Authors place links in hypertexts to alert readers to a relationship between a source and a target node. Some authoring systems allow authors to name the relationship the link represents by giving the link a "type."

[Chapter 13 by Garzotto, et al.] For example, an author may define a link type called "Author" to connect "Plays" to "persons." Instances of type Person, "Shakespeare," for example, would be connected to instances of type Play, e.g., "Hamlet," via a link of type Author.

[Chapter 12 by Gay] The link type may be denoted by the hypertext system to the reader automatically. For example, Owl's Guide 3.0 changes the cursor shape when a reader moves it over different types of links.

Elaboration: [Chapter 12 by Gay] Each link is a directed connection between related pieces of stored information within the database. Therefore, relationships between nodes can change based on the types of links connecting them.

[Chapter 20 by Parunak] If each link is labeled to indicate the kind of relation that it specifies, the information in the graph becomes much clearer and human users can more easily select from a variety of links that begin at a single node, based on the kind of further information they want. Automatic search programs can retrieve constellations of nodes related in specified ways. Linearized text (a paper dump of a hyperdocument) can reflect these relations and thus be more readable.

... We should note that two nodes may be linked by several different links, each calling attention to a different kind of relation between them. Typed links may thus lead to an increase in the total number of links in a network. However, because link types enable readers to identify the links of interest at any particular time, a hyperdocument with typed links will be clearer and easier to read than an untyped one. And, because the hypertext system can display just links of the types of interest for any particular operation, the overall efficiency of the system will improve.

[Chapter 21 by Fox, et al.] ... [O]ne type of link might associate a commentary with the text it refers to, while another link might associate a person's name and digitized photograph. Links can associate spreadsheets with totals in a report, or words with their definitions.

[Chapter 13 by Garzotto, et al.] Sequential links—"next" and "previous"—cause readers to move in linear order through the document. Node typing is also possible. For example, a hypertext manual on handling dangerous chemicals might assign different types to distinguish nodes that describe chemicals, nodes that describe routine handling procedures, and nodes that describe emergency treatments.

Lost in HyperSpace

Definition: [Chapter 22 by Littleford] 'Lost in HyperSpace' refers to the feeling of disorientation a reader can experience when he is following a connected trail of hypertext links. Each link in the trail may make perfect sense, but by the time the reader is several links deep, the relevance of his current position in the document to where he started from may be far from clear. Playing the game of following a chain of synonyms in a dictionary can lead to the same feeling—the word you end up with is only marginally associated with the word you started from, even though each word in the chain is a synonym for the preceding word.

[Chapter 18 by Gay and Mazur] ... Even though a navigator may understand the scope and overall design of the program well enough to plan a general itinerary through its information space, he or she can become lost in the course of specific "moves" which link nodes of information in the hypermedia database. In other words, hyperdocument readers can become lost locally, on a specific path, too. During iterative testing of the Bughouse (an entomology hypertext), 45% of participants reported they had problems with spatial orientation. They stated they were "lost" or "turned around" in the defined, or metaphorical, space of the program.

For example, although most of them realized that certain specific information could be found only outside the house, they were unable to locate the door which would allow them to exit the dwelling—they knew where they wanted to go, but they could not figure out how to get there.

We have observed several common problems encountered while navigating local context. One problem is that users can lose track of their goals. Another frustration is that they find themselves unable to return to items of information that are of particular interest.

Elaboration: [Chapter 13 by Garzotto, et al.] Research into the management of the overall structures of hypertexts has often been driven by concern with difficulty of hypertext navigation. While Bernstein argues elsewhere in this volume [Bernstein, 1991] that the "navigation problem" may be illusory, the fear that readers might become disoriented when using complex hypertexts has been a leading concern of authors [Landow, 1987; Utting, 1990; Parunak, 1989; Nielsen, 1990; Chapter 18 by Gay and Mazur in this book].

[Chapter 19 by Bernstein] [D]isorientation is not inherently wrong; indeed, a degree of disorientation, deliberately introduced and thoughtfully controlled and guided, can be a powerful tool for writers.

Synonyms: "The navigation problem," disorientation.

Medium

Definition: Media are devices that store data.

[Chapter 27 by McDaid] We usually assume that the world is "unmediated," but only naively, in an unreflective fashion. If pressed, we admit that our perceptual limits—our visual spectrum, auditory range, and tactile threshold—are limits which condition our knowledge of the world. The "world," the environment you are experiencing right now, is brought to your consciousness by natural media—your senses. Media are not passive conduits, but active shapers and massagers of messages. To fully apprehend the character of the world they bring us, we must realize that they are part of our ecosystem: interacting with, shaping, and re-presenting our experience.

Elaboration: [Chapter 6 by Slatin] Hypertext is a new medium, in my view, because it is intimately tied to the computer: the true hypertext or hyperdocument exists and can exist only on-line, and has no meaningful existence in print. If I am right in making this claim, then it follows that we will need a new set of theoretical principles to describe how hypertext works as a medium.

[Chapter 27 by McDaid] A new medium is, at bottom, a new way of translating and organizing experience and a new way of sharing it. It is to be anticipated that these translations of experience—and their ramifications for culture—will be profoundly different from those of print.

Synonyms: Device, means of communication, technology.

Metaphor

Definition: A representation of knowledge which relies on the imposition of the form of an object unlike the object being described or used onto that object.

Elaboration: [Chapter 18 by Gay and Mazur] An appropriate visual metaphor can serve to compartmentalize a large hyperbase comprised of motion video and various stills and help to focus readers' attention on the subject matter. The same visual metaphor may also help readers to structure their experiences and plan their "moves" within the hyperdocument's "information space."

[Chapter 11 by Shneiderman, et al.] Hypertext authors use metaphor in order to establish conventions readers can follow so they can ignore the interface they need to use to find information and just find the information.

Metaphors are convenient because their familiarity facilitates learning and reduces anxiety. Metaphors based on existing objects such as books, desktops, typewriters, and documents, are meant to make novice users feel comfortable. There are many inappropriate metaphors for hypertext that might be chosen by a misguided designer, such as a printing press, a Morse code telegraph, or a skywriting airplane. An inappropriate metaphor might make it harder for the user to acquire the necessary concepts. Of course, malicious metaphors would really turn off users. Imagine how hypertext would fare if it were represented as a sewer pipe spilling out information or as an exploding television.

Even well-chosen metaphors can be misleading. The book or encyclopedia metaphors only vaguely suggest the power that links can have (webs are a more effective metaphor to convey the power of hypertext). In particular, the book metaphor may mislead users into believing that they can easily grasp the size or organization of the hyperdocument. (Visualizations of the size of hypertexts are only now beginning to appear.)

While real-world objects can be misleading, they are usually effective. An alternative is to invent abstract objects (e.g., something fanciful such as an "electrodoc") and then try to explain its properties by showing features (e.g. "doctoc" for document table of contents and a "docdex" for a document index). Visual icons of arbitrary design can represent these abstract objects (e.g., circle for the electrodoc, square for the doctoc, and a triangle for the docdex). Some users may prefer the abstraction, but experience suggests that real-world objects, even if their properties are modified, are usually more successful.

Hyperties is based on the encyclopedia and more generally the book metaphor. The book metaphor because our focus was on reading paragraph- or page-length chunks of information and we chose to apply the term "article" to each chunk or node. This led us naturally to having a title for every article and then Tables of Contents and indices.

Other systems have developed the card and stack or filebox (e.g., Xerox NoteCards and Apple HyperCard). These are convenient, comprehensible and easily represented on the screen. Brown University's Intermedia utilizes a web of files or documents and Owl's Guide deals with a database of documents with notes and buttons.

Synonyms: Model, analogy, map.

Navigation

Definition: [Chapter 18 by Gay and Mazur] Jakob Nielsen [Nielsen, 1990] has noted that the notion that readers of hypermedia programs "navigate" is a metaphoric one. Readers of books and magazines and viewers of video or films rarely describe their experiences with these media in terms of navigation. One normally reads a book and views a movie, starting at the beginning, continuing to the end, in the sequence imposed by the author. Hyperdocuments, however, are nonlinear—they have neither beginning nor end.

This metaphor of navigation highlights the active, strategic role taken on by the reader who engages a hyperdocument. It is the reader, not the hypertext author, who charts a course through the sea of information. The reader is at the helm, making the decisions to either access or circumnavigate the islands of content in the hyperdocumentary sea.

... Readers must be able to navigate both globally and locally through the hypertext structure. The global context stresses the big picture and helps the navigator to comprehend the organization of the program's extensive content. The local context of navigation, on the other hand, defines the specific tools which generally appear as on-screen icons and which enable the reader to make the leap to nodes directly connected to the current one.

[Chapter 19 by Bernstein] Many hypertext readers develop spatial analogies to help them reason about the structure of a hypertext as they read; their current focus of attention becomes a place or location, and links invite them to "depart" on trips to other, related places. Spatial analogies can prove extremely powerful, as evidenced by the widespread interest in automatic hypertext mapping [Yankelovich, 1989; Fairchild, 1988; Halasz, 1987].

Elaboration: [Chapter 20 by Parunak] Just as regular arrangements of streets can help travelers navigate through a city, so regular arrangements of links can help knowledge workers move through a hyperdocument [Parunak, 1989].

Synonym: Browsing.

Node

Definition: A node is the smallest piece of a hyperdocument that can be addressed by a link.

[Chapter 22 by Littleford] [Ideally] a small portion of the document which covers one concept.

Elaboration: [Glushko, 1989] A node serves both as a container of information, and as the address of a link.

[Nielsen, 1990] The things which we can link to or from are called nodes.

Synonyms: page, card, unit, chunk, topic, article, card, nugget, link destination, frame, record, document, file, event, sequence, segment, passage, entity, component, view.

Path

Definition: The ordered set of nodes through which a reader has passed to get to his or her current position in a hyperdocument.

Synonym: History.

Related Term: Tour—a particular path through some information.

Reader

Definition: In this book, we use the term "reader" to refer to a person who navigates through a hyperdocument.

[Chapter 20 by Parunak] I often refer to the "reader" and "author" of a hyperdocument. The same individual may wear both hats, but not always at the same time. Readers are those who traverse links as the fancy strikes them. Authors, on the other hand, accept the responsibility of constructing and organizing webs so as to make traversing them easier for others.

Elaboration: [Chapter 5 by Picher, et al.] The term "readers" works when applied to a person browsing a hypertext, but seems somewhat inappropriate when applied to those finding their ways through a multimedia extravaganza of pictures and sound. Thus we adopt the term "viewer" for those "reading" a hypermedia document. Unfortunately this term connotes passive couch potatoes that watch what goes by without being able to influence it. Please understand that we attach no such limitations on a hypermedia viewer. Like hypertext readers, hypermedia viewers must be given the freedom to follow their own noses thought the hypermedia web.

Synonyms: User, navigator, browser, target audience, viewer, participant, explorer.

Recursive Function/Recursion

Definition: A function which is defined in terms of itself. In hypertext, a method of determining which node to display based on knowledge the hyperdocument has about itself and about the reader's interaction with it.

Elaboration: [Chapter 7 by Moulthrop] The term "recursion" has several connotations. It implies the neat cyclicality of reflex and reiteration, as in the hierarchical nesting of functions in a computer program. Recursion in this sense is a rational process, analogous to the revolution of gears in an engine or the closing of circuits in a microprocessor. But there is also a second, irrational meaning of recursion. This is the sense invoked in Douglas Hofstadter's notion of "tangled hierarchies," where an apparently orderly procedure yields paradoxical results. As in M.C. Escher's surrealist

"Waterfall," where tricks of perspective make a downgrade seem to lead upward, this irrational recursion invalidates our sense of hierarchy and shatters our interpretive framework.

... [An example:] A script about nuclear war writes a bigger script about nuclear war that writes an even bigger script about nuclear war, and so on till the crash comes. Nuclear discourse pornographically feeds on itself, replicating unchecked, until all available memory (which might stand for discursive energy, or even capital) has been expended; at which point everything stops dead.

[Chapter 27 by McDaid] It may have been the nascent fascination with the recursive act of talking about talking (or, as they say in the trade, rhetoric) that led to the idea of bringing some sort of order to the speech-act; attempting to set it down somehow, a recursion which yielded writing.

[Chapter 13 by Garzotto, et al.] Several hypertext systems have adopted ... complex, recursively defined structures of their organization idiom, building complex information structures by repeating small patterns in the same way that simple triangles can be assembled to form complex geodesic domes.

[Chapter 8 by Joyce] Tools by their nature alter our vision of the tasks. This process is often recursive: tool alters tasks alters tools... and so on.

Synonyms: Self-referential, reflexive.

Tour

Definition: [Chapter 20 by Parunak] Tours are selected paths through a hyperdocument that one user (perhaps the author) has prepared for another.

Elaboration: [Chapter 20 by Parunak] A tour is like a turnpike map that shows the main road and indicates possible side trips for readers with extra time and special interest. The tour itself can have an extremely simple pattern of connectivity, usually linear, or at worst, hierarchical. As long as readers who leave the tour have a quick way to jump back to the point at which they left it, they can browse around the larger environment without fear of getting lost.

[Chapter 13 by Garzotto, et al.] Hypertext readers often appreciate being able to start browsing by using a predetermined navigation pattern or "tour" through the hyperdocument. These tours are most useful when they are tailored to individual readers' backgrounds, preferences, and interests. Indeed, a key promise of hypertext is its ability to provide paths tailored to a wide variety of audiences.

[Chapter 11 by Shneiderman, et al.] Many hypertext development systems provide authors with a way to define ordered paths through a database so readers are less likely to get lost, and, where necessary, are obliged to read certain nodes in a prescribed order.

Synonyms: Script, guided tour, outline, platform.

Transclusion

Definition: Haynes in this book (Chapter 15), quoting *Nelson*:
Transclusion means that a thing can be in two places at once. Suppose you write a sentence you like, or there's a paragraph that needs to be quoted from one document to another. [Copying it] loses the connection—the thread that ties them all together. But in transclusion, you make a virtual copy from one place into the other so that there is a hole in one place that you wanted [the sentence], which is filled always from the other place whenever you get to the hole [Byte, September 1990, pp. 298-299].

Elaboration: [Chapter 15 by Haynes] Nelson claims that transclusion obviates copyright concerns, since the physical location (i.e., published location) of the transcluded material remains constant and there is no physical copying such that the copyrighted material would be infringed. Readers accessing the transcluded material are actually accessing the (presumably lawfully licensed) material in its original form. Again, as should be perfectly clear, unless there is a physical copying of a work such that infringement occurs, an author creating a hypertext link to another's work does not infringe on that work by creating that link.

This, however, may beg the question. Although present copyright law is replete with the concept of physical "copying" as a prerequisite to infringement, who is to say but that a future court may consider transclusion to have the same effect as copying, and therefore be considered infringement, too. The more persuasive argument stemming from transclusion is that not only is there no physical copying, but copyright information can be bundled with the transcluded text, and, moreover attribution for royalty purposes can also be triggered. Thus, not only is the transcluded material's author properly credited in the intellectual sense, but in the financial sense as well.

Web

Definition: [Chapter 20 by Parunak] "Web" has been popularized by the folks at Intermedia to refer to a set of links that is stored separately from the material that is linked together (an important innovation that deserves wider attention).

Elaboration: [Chapter 23 by Parunak] Because an industrial system needs to accommodate multiple users, it should be able to integrate several different webs for the same document (such as an "official" roadmap and individual annotations), with the resulting links being the union of those in the individual webs. Careful thought needs to be given to handling overlapping anchors. For example, picking an anchor that corresponds to multiple links should give a list of links for further choice, but if the links are the same, only one should be shown. Different webs may have different permissions associated with them; of the several webs that my current session merges with a given text file, I may be able to edit some but not others.

Synonyms: Link map, link file.

References

Glushko, Robert, (1989). "Hypertext '89 Course Notes #3: Turning Text Into Hypertext."

Nielsen, Jakob (1990). *Hypertext and Hypermedia.* Academic Press, New York, NY.

Appendix C:
Hypertext and Hypermedia:
A Selected Bibliography

Terence Harpold
Group in Comparative Literature
University of Pennsylvania

In the thirty years following the 1945 publication of Vannevar Bush's *As We May Think,* the literature of hypertext amounted to fewer than two dozen titles, the majority of which were the product of only two authors. In the next ten years, the literature doubled, or perhaps tripled, in size. Since 1985, the number of articles or books dealing with the theory, design, and implementation of hypertext has grown—and continues to grow—prodigiously, to the point where it has become impossible to compile a single list of every relevant title.

In the last two or three years, the character of the literature has changed as well. Whereas the bulk of hypertext literature continues to deal with the technical problems of design and implementation that were the focus of early literature, authors are turning with increasing frequency to the epistemological, philosophical, and sociological consequences of hypertext, and borrowing methods and terminology from disciplines far removed from computer science. It may be that hypertext studies have reached a kind of intellectual crossroads, where the technical problems have become sufficiently familiar that it is now possible to address the consequences of this new form of literature *as* a new literary form. Michael Joyce has recently argued that this sea change has already passed us. I suspect that Ted Nelson would contend that it came several decades ago.

For the reasons outlined above, this bibliography can claim to be neither comprehensive nor definitive. Rather than attempt to address the range of hypertext studies, I've selected a core set of titles on hypertext theory and design. With a few exceptions, I've excluded publications that deal with the capabilities or implementation of specific hypertext software, or with test cases of hypertext applications. The list is divided into six sections.

The first section, "Bibliography," includes other bibliographies of hypertext literature. The length and focus of these bibliographies vary; several include articles on implementation and applications that I have excluded from this bibliography. The most comprehensive are Simpson's *Hypertext: A Comprehensive Index* (which includes an exhaustive topic-oriented index of keywords), Yankelovich and Kahn's *Hypermedia Bibliography*, and Knee and Atkinson's *Hypertext/Hypermedia: An Annotated Bibliography*.

"Collections and Proceedings" lists edited collections, conference proceedings and journals devoted to hypertext and hypermedia. Many of the individual articles in the sections that follow can be found in these collections.

"History and Overview" lists books and articles of historic significance in hypertext studies (articles by Bush, Engelbart and Nelson), or those which offer an historical assessment of early hypertext systems. The notion of history I've used here is admittedly fuzzy: it's difficult to divide the "recent" from the "historic" in a field where literature that is less that ten years old can be said to be genuinely historic.

The fourth section is by far the longest. Without the benefit of a nonlinear, on-line presentation, it is difficult to organize these titles under a rubric less general than "Theory and Design." Many of these publications cross boundaries between theory and design; most belong to one or more categories within those areas.

The fifth section, "Critique," includes titles that are skeptical or openly critical of hypertext and the theoretical and practical assumptions upon which it is based. Proponents of hypertext often make extraordinary, passionate claims for it; the articles in this section are among the few on the topic that question those claims.

The final section, "Background," lists books and articles not directly related to hypertext theory or design, but which are frequently cited by authors writing on those topics. Subjects represented in this section include interface design, the psychology, philosophy, sociology and history of computers, the theoretical and practical significance of electronic publishing, and language and information theories. As the definition of what qualifies as hypertext literature grows, the scope of this list will grow accordingly.

I would like to thank Rosemary Simpson for her advice and direction in the compilation of this bibliography.

Terence Harpold
Philadelphia, December 1990

Bibliography

Franklin, Carl. "A Bibliography on Hypertext and Hypermedia with Selected Annotations." *Database* 13.1 (February 1990): 24–32.

Knee, Michael and Steven D. Atkinson. *Hypertext/Hypermedia: An Annotated Bibliography*. New York: Greenwood Press, 1990.

Lin, Xia. "A Selected Hypertext Bibliography." *Educational Technology* 28.11 (November 1988): 41–42.

Mitterer, John, Oland Gary and J.S. Schankula. *Hypermedia Bibliography*. St. Catherines, Ontario, Canada: Brock University Department of Computer Science. *Technical Report CS-88-02*. 1988.

Nielsen, Jakob. "Hypertext Bibliography." *Hypermedia 1.1* (Spring 1989): 74–91.

Simpson, Rosemary, ed. *Hypertext: A Comprehensive Index*. Boston: BCS [Boston Computer Society] Hypermedia Resource Group, 1988.

Yankelovich, Nicole and Paul Kahn. *Hypermedia Bibliography*. Providence, RI: Institute for Research in Information and Scholarship (IRIS), 1989.

Collections and Proceedings

ACM Transactions on Information Systems 7.1 (January 1989). [Issue devoted to hypertext theory and implementation.]

AI and Hypertext: Issues and Directions. AAAI-88: AI and Hypertext workshop proceedings, August 1988, St. Paul, MN. Ed. Mark Bernstein, Watertown, MA: Eastgate Systems, Inc., 1988.

Barrett, Edward, ed. *Text, Context and Hypertext: Writing with and for the Computer*. Cambridge, MA: MIT Press, 1988.

Barrett, Edward, ed. *The Society of Text: Hypertext, Hypermedia and the Social Construction of Information*. Cambridge, MA: MIT Press, 1989.

Berk, Emily and Joseph Devlin, eds. *The Hypertext / Hypermedia Handbook*. New York: McGraw-Hill, 1991.

Byte 13.10 (October 1988). [Includes special section on hypertext.]

Communications of the ACM 31.7 (July 1988). [Special issue on hypertext.]

Delany, Paul and George Landow, eds. *Hypermedia and Literary Studies*. Cambridge, MA: MIT Press, 1991.

Educational Technology 28.11 (November 1988). [Special issue on hypertext.]

Hypermedia. Patricia Baird, ed. London, England: Taylor Graham. [Journal devoted to the subject of hypermedia.]

Hypertext '87 Proceedings. November 13–15, 1987, Chapel Hill, NC. New York: ACM, 1989.

Hypertext '89 Proceedings. November 5–7, 1989, Pittsburgh, PA. New York: ACM, 1989.

Jonassen, David H. and Heinz Mandl, eds. *Designing Hypermedia for Learning*. Berlin: Springer-Verlag, 1990.

Journal of American Society for Information Science 40.3 (May 1989). [Issue devoted to "Prospectives on Hypertext."]

McAleese, Ray and Catherine Green, eds. *Hypertext: State of the Art*. Norwood, NJ: Ablex Publishing Corp, 1990.

McAleese, Ray, ed. *Hypertext: Theory into Practice*. Oxford: Intellect, 1989.

Moline, J., D. Benigni and J. Baronas, eds. *Proceedings of the Hypertext Standardization Workshop, January 16–18, 1990, National Institute of Standards and Technology*. NIST Publication SP500-178.

New Media News. BCS [Boston Computer Society] Hypermedia/Optical Disk Publishing SIG. [Magazine devoted to hypermedia and optical disc publishing.]

Shneiderman, Ben and Greg Kearsley. *Hypertext Hands-On!* Reading, MA: Addison-Wesley, 1989.

Shneiderman, Ben, ed. *Hypertext on Hypertext*. [Several software formats for different hardware platforms.] New York: ACM, 1989.

History and Overview

Bush, Vannevar. "As We May Think." *The Atlantic 176.1* (July 1945): 101–108.

Bush, Vannevar. "Memex Revisited." *Science is Not Enough*. New York: William Morrow, 1967. 75–101.

Conklin, Jeff. "A Survey of Hypertext." *MCC Technical Report STP-356-86*, Rev. 2. 1986.

Conklin, Jeff. "Hypertext: An Introduction and Survey." *IEEE Computer 20.9* (September 1987): 17–41.

Engelbart, Douglas C. "A Conceptual Framework for the Augmentation of Man's Intellect." *Vistas in Information Handling*. Ed. P.D. Howerton and D.C. Weeks. Washington, D.C.: Spartan Books, 1963. 1: 1–29.

Engelbart, Douglas C. "Authorship Provisions in AUGMENT." *Proceedings COMPCON Conference*. February 21–March 1, 1984, San Francisco.

Engelbart, Douglas C. "Collaborative Support Provisions in AUGMENT." *Proceedings COMPCON Conference*. February 21–March 1, 1984, San Francisco, CA.

Engelbart, Douglas C. "Coordinated Information Services for a Discipline or Mission-Oriented Community." *Proceedings Second Annual Computer Communications Conference*. January 24, 1973, San Jose, CA.

Engelbart, Douglas C. "Toward High-Performance Knowledge Workers." *Proceedings AFIPS Office Automation Conference*. April 5–7, 1982, San Francisco, CA.

Engelbart, Douglas C. "Toward Integrated, Evolutionary Office Automation Systems." *Proceedings Joint Engineering Management Conference*. October 16–18, 1978, Denver, CO.

Engelbart, Douglas C. "Workstation History and the Augmented Knowledge Workshop." *Proceedings ACM Conference on the History of Personal Workstations*. January 9–10, 1986, Palo Alto, CA.

Engelbart, Douglas C. and William K. English. "A Research Center for Augmenting Human Intellect." *Proceedings AFIPS Conference, 1968 Joint Computer Conference*. December 9–11, 1968, San Francisco. Montvale, NJ: AFIPS Press, 1968. 395–410.

Engelbart, Douglas C., Richard W. Watson and James C. Norton. "The Augmented Knowledge Workshop." *Proceedings AFIPS Conference, 1973 National Computer Conference and Exposition*. June 4–8, 1973, New York. Montvale, NJ: AFIPS Press, 1973. 9–21.

English, William K., Douglas C. Engelbart and M. L. Berman. "Display-Selection Techniques for Text Manipulation." *IEEE Transactions on Human Factors and Electronics 8.1* (March 1967): 5–15.

Fraase, Michael. *Macintosh Hypermedia: Vol. I, Reference Guide*. Glenview, Illinois: Scott, Foresman and Company, 1989.

Kay, Alan. "Personal Dynamic Media." Palo Alto, CA: *Xerox PARC Technical Report SSL-76-1*. Xerox Palo Alto Research Center, Palo Alto, CA, 1976.

Murray, John M. and Kenneth J. Klingenstein. "The Architecture of an Electronic Book." *IEEE Transactions on Industrial Electronics* IE-29.1 (February 1982): 82–91.

Nelson, Theodor H. "A Conceptual Framework for Man-Machine Everything." *Proceedings AFIPS National Computer Conference and Exposition*. June 4–8, 1973, New York. Montvale, NJ: AFIPS Press, 1973. M21-M26

Nelson, Theodor H. "A File Structure for the Complex, the Changing and the Indeterminate." *Proceedings Association for Computing Machinery, 20th National Conference*. New York: ACM. P-65: 84–100.

Nelson, Theodor H. "A New Home for the Mind." *Datamation* (March 1982): 169-180.

Nelson, Theodor H. "As We Will Think." *Proceedings Online 72: International Conference on Online Interactive Computing.* Brunel University, Uxbridge, England, 1972. Uxbridge, England: Online Computer Systems, Ltd., 1973. 439-454.

Nelson, Theodor H. "Computopia and Cybercrud." *Computers in Instruction.* Ed. Levien, The Rand Corporation, 1974.

Nelson, Theodor H. "Computopia Now!" *Digital Deli.* Ed. Steve Ditlea, San Francisco: Workman Publishing, 1984. 349-351.

Nelson, Theodor H. "Data Realms and Magic Windows." *Proceedings Meeting of the Association of Computer Programmers and Analysts,* 1975.

Nelson, Theodor H. "Dream Machines: New Freedoms through Computer ScreensA Minority Report." *Computer Lib: You Can and Must Understand Computers.* Redmond, WA: Microsoft Press, 1987.

Nelson, Theodor H. "Electronic Publishing and Electronic Literature." *Information Technology in Health Science Education.* Ed. Edward C. Deland. New York: Plenum Press, 1978.

Nelson, Theodor H. "Getting It Out of Our System." *Critique of Information Retrieval.* Ed. G. Schechter, Washington, D.C.: Thompson Books, 1967. 191-210.

Nelson, Theodor H. "Replacing the Printed Word: A Complete Literary System." 1980. *Information Processing 80.* Ed. S.H. Lavington, Amsterdam: North-Holland, 1980. 1013-1023.

Nelson, Theodor H. "The Hypertext." *1965 Congress of the International Federation for Documentation Abstracts.* October 10-15, 1965, Washington, DC. 80.

Nelson, Theodor H. *Literary Machines.* Swarthmore, PA: T.H. Nelson, 1981.

Nelson, Theodor H. *Literary Machines. Vers. 87.1.* The Distributors, South Bend, IN: 1987.

Nelson, Theodor H. *Literary Machines. Vers. 87.1.* Guide Envelope Document. Bellevue, WA: OWL International, Inc., 1987.

Nyce, James M. and Paul Kahn. "Innovation, Pragmaticism, and Technological Continuity: Vannevar Bush's Memex." *Journal of American Society for Information Science 40.3* (May 1989): 214-220.

Smith, Linda C. "'Memex' as an Image Potentiality in Information Retrieval Research and Development." *Information Retrieval Research.* Ed. R.N. Oddy. London: Butterworths, 1981. 345-369.

Yankelovich, Nicole, Norman K. Meyrowitz and Andries van Dam. "Reading and Writing the Electronic Book." *IEEE Computer 18.10* (October 1985): 15-30.

Theory and Design

Agosti, Maristella. "Is Hypertext A New Model of Information Retrieval?" *Proceedings of the 12th International Online Information Meeting.* Dec. 6-8, 1988, London, England. New Jersey: Learned Information, 1988. 57-62.

Ambron, Sueann, and Kristina Hooper, eds. *Interactive Multimedia: Visions of Multimedia for Developers, Educators, & Information Providers.* Redmond, WA: Microsoft Press, 1988.

Ambron, Sueann, and Kristina Hooper, eds. *Learning with Interactive Multimedia.* Redmond, WA: Microsoft Press, 1990.

Baird, P., N. Mac Morrow and L. Hardman. "Cognitive Aspects of Constructing Nonlinear Documents: HyperCard and Glasgow Online." *Proceedings of the 12th International Online Information Meeting.* December 6-8, 1988, London. Oxford: Learned information, 1988. 207-218.

Barrett, Edward. "Textual Information, Collaboration and the Online Environment." *The Society of Text: Hypertext, Hypermedia, and the Social Construction of Information.* Ed. Edward Barrett, Cambridge, MA: MIT Press, 1989. 305-322.

Beeman, William O. et al. "Hypertext and Pluralism: From Lineal to Non-lineal Thinking." *Proceedings Hypertext '87.* November 13–15, 1987, Chapel Hill, NC. New York: ACM, 1989. 67–88.

Benest, I., and G. Jones. "Computer Emulation of Books." *Proceedings of the IEE International Conference on Man/Machine Systems.* Conference Publication 212, 1982.

Benton, Peter. "Work Group Automation and Hypertext." *The Hypertext/Hypermedia Handbook.* Eds. Emily Berk and Joseph Devlin, New York: McGraw-Hill, 1991.

Berk, Emily and Ruth Giellman. "Text-Only Hypertexts." *The Hypertext/Hypermedia Handbook.* Eds. Emily Berk and Joseph Devlin, New York: McGraw-Hill, 1991.

Bernstein, Mark. "The Bookmark and the Compass: Orientation Tools for Hypertext Users." *ACM SIGOIS Bulletin 9* (1988): 34–45.

Bernstein, Mark. "The Navigation Problem Reconsidered." *The Hypertext/Hypermedia Handbook.* Eds. Emily Berk and Joseph Devlin, New York: McGraw-Hill, 1991.

Bielawski, Larry and Robert Lewand. *Intelligent Systems Design: Expert Systems, Hypermedia, and Database Technologies.* New York: Wiley, 1991.

Bolter, Jay David. "Beyond Word Processing: The Computer as a New Writing Space." *Language and Communication 9.2/3* (1989): 129–142.

Bolter, Jay David, and Michael Joyce. "Hypertext and Creative Writing." *Proceedings Hypertext '87.* November 13–15, 1987, Chapel Hill, NC. New York: ACM, 1989. 41–50.

Bolter, Jay David. "The Idea of Literature in the Electronic Age." *Topic: A Journal of the Liberal Arts 39* (1985): 23–34.

Bolter, Jay David. "Text and Technology." *Library Resources and Technical Services 31.1* (January/March 1987): 12–23.

Bolter, Jay David. "Topographic Writing: Hypertext and the Electronic Writing Space." *Hypermedia and Literary Studies.* Eds. Paul Delany and George Landow, Cambridge, MA: MIT Press, 1991. 105–118.

Bolter, Jay David. *Writing Space: The Computer, Hypertext, and the History of Writing.* New York: Lawrence Erlbaum, 1990.

Brachman, Ronald J. "On the Epistemological Status of Semantic Networks." *Readings in Knowledge Representation.* Eds. Ronald J. Brachman and Hector J. Levesque, Los Altos, CA: Morgan Kaufmann, 1975. 192–215.

Brown, Peter. "Viewing Documents on a Screen." *CD ROM: The New Papyrus.* Ed. Steve Lambert and Suzanne Ropiequet. Redmond, WA: Microsoft Press, 1986. 175–184.

Brown, P.J. "Hypertext: The Way Forward." *Document Manipulation and Typography.* Ed. J. C. van Vliet. Cambridge: Cambridge University Press, 1188. 183–191.

Brown, P.J. "Linking and Searching within Hypertext." *Electronic Publishing: Origination, Dissemination and Design 1.1* (April 1988): 45–53.

Brown, John Seely. "Process versus Product: A Perspective on Tools for Communal and Informal Electronic Learning." *Education in the Electronic Age: A Report from the Learning Lab, WNET/Thirteen Learning Lab.* New York: WNET, 1983. 41–58.

Byles, Torrey. "A Context for Hypertext: Some Suggested Elements of Style." *Wilson Library Bulletin 63.3* (November 1988): 60–62.

Carlson, Patricia Ann. "Hypertext and Intelligent Interfaces for Text Retrieval." *The Society of Text: Hypertext, Hypermedia, and the Social Construction of Information.* Ed. Edward Barrett, Cambridge, MA: MIT Press, 1989. 59–76.

Catano, Hames. "Poetry and Computers: Experimenting with Communal Text." *Computers and the Humanities 13* (1979): 269–275.

Catlin, Timothy, Paulette E. Bush and Nicole Yankelovich. "InterNote: Extending a Hypermedia Framework to Support Annotative Collaboration." *Hypertext '89 Proceedings.* Nov. 5-7, 1989, Pittsburgh, PA. New York: ACM, 1989. 365-78.

Cawkell, A.E. "What are the Uses of Hypertext?" *Critique 1.10* (September 1989): 1-12.

Charney, Davida. "Comprehending Non-Linear Text: The Role of Discourse Cues and Reading Strategies." *Proceedings Hypertext '87.* November 13-15, 1987, Chapel Hill, NC. New York: ACM, 1989. 109-120.

Cooke, Peter and Ian Williams. "Design Issues in Large Hypertext Systems for Technical Documentation." *Hypertext: Theory into Practice.* Ed. Ray McAleese, Oxford: Intellect, 1989.

Crane, Gregory. "Hypermedia and Scholarly Publishing." *Scholarly Publishing 21.3* (April 1990): 131-156.

Crane, Gregory and Elli Mylonas. "Ancient Materials, Modern Media: Shaping the Study of Classics with Hypertext." *Hypermedia and Literary Studies.* Ed. Paul Delany and George Landow, Cambridge, MA: MIT Press, 1991. 205-220.

Crane, Gregory. "From the Old to the New: Integrating Hypertext into Traditional Scholarship." *Hypertext '87 Proceedings.* Nov 13-15, 1987. Chapel Hill, NC. New York: ACM, 1989. 51-56.

Crane, Gregory. "Redefining the Book: Some Preliminary Problems." *Academic Computing* 2.5 (February 1988): 36-41.

Crouch, Donald B., Carolyn J. Crouch and Glenn Andreas. "The Use of Cluster Hierarchies in Hypertext Information Retrieval." *Proceedings Hypertext '89.* November 5-7, 1989, Chapel Hill, NC. New York: ACM, 1989. 225-38.

Cumming, Alister and Gerri Sinclair. "Conceptualizing Hypermedia Curricula for Literary Studies in Schools." *Hypermedia and Literary Studies.* Ed. Paul Delany and George Landow, Cambridge, MA: MIT Press, 1991. 315-328.

Davenport, E. and B. Cronin. "Hypertext and the Conduct of Science." *Journal of Documentation* 46.3 (September 1910): 175-192.

Davis, Ken. "Hypertext: A New Medium for Reading and Writing." *Proceedings 40th Annual Conference on College Composition and Communication.* March 16-18, 1989, Seattle, WA.

Davis, Ken. "Toward a Hypertext on Writing." *Proceedings 5th Annual Computers and Writing Conference.* May 13-14, 1989, Minneapolis, MN.

Delisle, Norman, and Mayer Schwartz. "Context—A Partitioning Concept for Hypertext." *Proceedings Computer-Supported Cooperative Work.* Austin, TX, 1986.

DeRose, Steven J. "Biblical Studies and Hypertext." *Hypermedia and Literary Studies.* Ed. Paul Delany and George Landow, Cambridge, MA: MIT Press, 1991. 185-204.

DeRose, Steven J. "Expanding the Notion of Links." *Proceedings Hypertext '89.* November 5-7, 1989, Pittsburgh, PA. New York: ACM, 1989. 249-57.

Devlin, Joseph. "Standards for Hypertext." *The Hypertext/Hypermedia Handbook.* Ed. Emily Berk and Joseph Devlin. New York: McGraw-Hill, 1991.

Dickey, William. "Poem Descending a Staircase: Hypertext and the Simultaneity of Experience." *Hypermedia and Literary Studies.* Ed. Paul Delany and George Landow, Cambridge, MA: MIT Press, 1991. 143-152.

Dillon, Andrew, Cliff McKnight, and John Richardson. "Navigation in Hypertext: a Critical Review of the Concept." *Proceedings INTERACT '90.* Ed. D. Diaper, D. Gilmore, G. Cockton, B. Shacke. Amsterdam: North-Holland, 1990. 587-592.

Doland, Virginia M. "Hypermedia as an Interpretive Act." *Hypermedia 1.1* (Spring 1989): 6-19.

Doland, Virginia M. "The Hermeneutics of Hypertext." *Proceedings of the 12th International Online Information Meeting.* December 6-8, 1988, London. Oxford: Learned Information, 1988. 75-82.

Duffy, Thomas M., Brad Mehlenbacker and Jim Palmer. "The Evaluation of Online Help Systems: A Conceptual Model." *The Society of Text: Hypertext, Hypermedia, and the Social Construction of Information.* Ed. Edward Barrett, Cambridge, MA: MIT Press, 1989. 362-387.

Duncan, Elizabeth B. "A Faceted Approach to Hypertext?" *Hypertext: Theory into Practice.* Ed. Ray McAleese. Oxford: Intellect, 1989. 157-163.

Duncan, Elizabeth B. "Structuring Knowledge Bases for Designers of Learning Materials." *Hypermedia* 1.1 (Spring 1989): 20-33.

Edwards, Deborah M., and Lynda Hardman. "'Lost in Hyperspace': Cognitive Mapping and Navigation in a Hypertext Environment." *Hypertext: Theory into Practice.* Ed. Ray McAleese, Oxford: Intellect, 104-125.

Engelbart, Douglas "Knowledge-Domain Interoperability and an Open Hyperdocument System." Republished in *The Hypertext/Hypermedia Handbook.* Ed. Emily Berk and Joseph Devlin. New York: McGraw-Hill, 1991.

Evenson, Shelley, et al. "Towards a Design Language for Representing Hypermedia Cues." *Proceedings Hypertext '89.* November 5-7, 1989, Pittsburgh, PA . New York: ACM, 1989. 83-92.

Fahmy, E. and D.T. Barnard. "Adding Hypertext Links to an Archive of Documents." *Canadian Journal of Information Science* 15.3 (September 1990): 25-41.

Feiner, S. "Interactive Documents." 1985. *Design in the Information Environment: How Computing is Changing the Problems, Processes and Theories of Design.* Ed. Patrick Whitney and Cheryl Kent. Carbondale: Southern Illinois University Press, 1985. 118-32.

Feiner, S., S. Nagy and Andries van Dam. "An Experimental System for Creating and Presenting Interactive Graphical Documents." *ACM Transactions on Graphics 1.1* (1982): 59-77.

Feiner, S., S. Nagy and Andries van Dam. "An Integrated System for Creating and Presenting Complex Computer-Based Documents." *Computer Graphics 15.3* (1981): 181-189.

Feiner, S., S. Nagy and Andries van Dam. "Online Documents Combining Pictures and Texts." *Proceedings International Conference on Research Trends in Document Preparation Systems.* Lausanne, Switzerland, 1981.

Feiner, Steven. "Seeing the Forest for the Trees: Hierarchical Display of Hypertext Structure." *Conference on Office Information Systems.* March 23-25, 1988, Palo Alto, CA. New York: ACM, 1988. 205-212.

Forrester, Michael. "Interfaces and Online Reading." *New Horizons for the Information Profession: Meeting the Challenge of Change; Annual Conference of the Institute of Information Scientists.* Ed. Hilary Dyer and Gwyneth Tseng. London: Taylor Graham, 1988. 97-112.

Fox, Edward, Qi Fan Chen and Robert France. "Integrating Search and Retrieval with Hypertext." *The Hypertext/Hypermedia Handbook.* Ed. Emily Berk and Joseph Devlin, New York: McGraw-Hill, 1991.

Fraase, Michael. *Macintosh Hypermedia: Vol II, Uses and Implementations.* Glenview, Illinois: Scott, Foresman and Company, 1990.

Franklin, Carl. "Theoretical Foundations of Hypertext/Hypermedia." *Proceedings 1989 Academic Microcomputing Conference.* Indianapolis: Indiana University Press, 1989. 47-57.

Frisse, Mark. "From Text to Hypertext." *Byte 13.10,* (October 1988): 247-253.

Furuta, R., C. Plaisant and B. Shneiderman. "A Spectrum of Automatic Hypertext Constructions." *Hypermedia 1.2* (1989): 179-195.

Gaines, Brian and Joan N. Vickers. "Design Considerations for Hypermedia Systems." *Microcomputers for Information Management 5.1* (March 1988): 1-27.

Garg, Pankaj K. "Abstraction Mechanisms in Hypertext." *Communications of the ACM 31.7* (July 1988): 862-870.

Garg, Pankaj K. and Walt Scacchi. "Composition of Hypertext Nodes." *Proceedings of the 12th International Online Information Meeting.* December 6–8, 1988. London. Oxford: Learned Information, 1988. 63–73.

Garrett, L.N., Karen E. Smith and Norman Meyrowitz. "Intermedia: Issues, Strategies, and Tactics in the Design of a Hypermedia Document System." *Proceedings Computer-Supported Cooperative Work.* Austin, Texas, 1986. Institute for Research in Information and Scholarship, 1986. 1–18.

Garzotto, Franca, Paolo Paolini, Daniel Schwabe and Mark Bernstein. "Tools for Developers." *The Hypertext/Hypermedia Handbook.* Ed. Emily Berk and Joseph Devlin. New York: McGraw-Hill, 1991.

Gay, Geri. "Interactive Fiction." *The Hypertext/Hypermedia Handbook.* Ed. Emily Berk and Joseph Devlin, New York: McGraw-Hill, 1991.

Gay, Geri. "Search Mode Strategies for Hypermedia." *Technology and Learning 3:2* (March/April, 1989).

Gay, Geri and Joan Mazur. "Navigating in Hypermedia." *The Hypertext/Hypermedia Handbook.* Ed. Emily Berk and Joseph Devlin, New York: McGraw-Hill, 1991.

Glushko, Robert J. "Design Issues for Multi-Document Hypertexts." *Proceedings Hypertext '89.* November 5–7, 1989, Chapel Hill, NC. New York: ACM, 1989. 51–60.

Glushko, Robert J. *Turning Text into Hypertext.* Santa Clara, CA: Multimedia Computing Corp., 1989.

Grise, Roger A. "Online Information: What Do People Want? What Do People Need?" *The Society of Text: Hypertext, Hypermedia, and the Social Construction of Information.* Ed. Edward Barrett, Cambridge, MA: MIT Press, 1989. 22–44.

Halasz, Frank G. "Reflections on NoteCards: Seven Issues for the Next Generation of Hypermedia Systems." *Communications of the ACM 31.7* (July 1988): 836–855.

Hammond, Nick and Lesley Allinson. "The Travel Metaphor as Design Principle and Training Aid for Navigating Around Complex Systems." *People and Computers III.* Ed. D. Diaper and R. Winder. Cambridge: Cambridge University Press, 1987. 75–90.

Hammwohner, Rainer and Ulrich Thiel. "Content-Oriented Relations Between Text Units: A Structural Model for Hypertexts." *Proceedings Hypertext '87.* November 13–15, 1987, Chapel Hill, NC. New York: ACM, 1989. 155–74.

Hanson, Robin. "Toward Hypertext Publishing: Issues and Choices in Database Design." *SIGIR Forum 22.1–2* (Fall 1987/Winter 1988): 9–26.

Harpold, Terence. "Threnody: Psychoanalytic Digressions on the Subject of Hypertexts." *Hypermedia and Literary Studies.* Ed. Paul Delany and George Landow, Cambridge, MA: MIT Press, 1991. 171–184.

Haynes, Steven "Hypertext: Intellectual Property and Licensing Concerns." *The Hypertext/Hypermedia Handbook.* Ed. Emily Berk and Joseph Devlin, New York: McGraw-Hill, 1991.

Herrstrom, David S. and David G, Massey. "Hypertext in Context." *The Society of Text: Hypertext, Hypermedia, and the Social Construction of Information.* Ed. Edward Barrett, Cambridge, MA: MIT Press, 1989. 45–58.

Horn, Robert E. *Mapping Hypertext: The Analysis, Organization and Display of Knowledge for the Next Generation of On-Line Text and Graphics.* Waltham, MA: The Lexington Institute, 1990.

Irby, Charles H. "Display Techniques for Interactive Text Manipulation." *AFIPS Conference Proceedings: 1974 National Computer Conference and Exposition.* May 6–10, 1974, Chicago. Montvale, NJ: AFIPS Press, 1974. 247–255.

Irish, Peggy M. and Randall H. Trigg. "Supporting Collaboration in Hypermedia: Issues and Experiences." *The Society of Text: Hypertext, Hypermedia, and the Social Construction of Information.* Ed. Edward Barrett, Cambridge, MA: MIT Press, 1989. 90–106.

Jonassen, D.H. "Hypertext Principles for Text and Courseware Design." *Educational Psychologist 21.6* (1986): 269–92.

Jonassen, David H. "Designing Structured Hypertext and Structuring Access to Hypertext." *Educational Technology 28.11* (November 1988): 13–16.

Jonassen, David H. *Hypertext/Hypermedia.* Englewood Cliffs, NJ: Educational Technology Publications, 1989.

Jones, Henry W., III. "Developing and Distributing Hypertext Tools: Legal Inputs and Parameters." *Proceedings Hypertext '87.* November 13–15, 1987, Chapel Hill, NC. New York: ACM, 1989. 367–74.

Joyce, Michael. "Selfish Interaction: Subversive Texts And The Multiple Novel." *The Hypertext/Hypermedia Handbook.* Ed. Emily Berk and Joseph Devlin, New York: McGraw-Hill, 1991.

Joyce, Michael. "Siren Shapes: Exploratory and Constructive Hypertexts." *Academic Computing, 3.4* (1988):10–14; 37–42.

Kahn, Paul. "Linking Together Books: Adapting Published Material into Intermedia Documents." *Hypermedia and Literary Studies.* Ed. Paul Delany and George Landow, Cambridge, MA: MIT Press, 1991. 221–256.

Kearsley, Greg. "Authoring Considerations for Hypertext." *Educational Technology 28.11* (November 1988): 21–24.

Kirby, M.R., and T. Mayes. "Towards Intelligent Hypertext." *Hypertext: Theory into Practice.* Ed. Ray McAleese, Oxford: Intellect, 164–172.

Koved, L., and B. Shneiderman. "Embedded Menus: Selecting Items in Context." *Communications of the ACM 29.4* (1986): 312–318.

Kreitzberg, Charles and Ben Shneiderman. "Designing the Electronic Book: Human Psychology and Information Structures for Hypermedia." *Designing and using Human-Computer Interfaces and Knowledge-based Systems.* Ed. G. Salvendy and M.J. Smith. Amsterdam: Elsevier Science Publishers, 1989.

Landow, George. "Hypertext and Collaborative Work: The Example of Intermedia." *Intellectual Teamwork: Social and Technological Foundation of Cooperative Work.* Ed. J. Galegher, J. Kraut and C. Egido. Hillsdale, New Jersey: Lawrence Eribaum Associates, 1990. 407–428.

Landow, George P. "Relationally Encoded Links and the Rhetoric of Hypertext." *Proceedings Hypertext '87.* November 13–15, 1987, Chapel Hill, NC. New York: ACM, 1989. 331–343.

Landow, George P. "The Rhetoric of Hypermedia: Some Rules for Authors." *Journal of Computing in Higher Education 1.1* (1989): 39–64.

Landow, George. "Context32: Using Hypermedia to Teach English Literature." *Proceedings 1987 IBM Academic Information Systems University AEP Conference.* Milford, CN, 1987. Ed. L.H. Lewis, *IBM Academic Information Systems.* 30–39.

Landow, George. "Hypertext in Literary Education, Criticism and Scholarship." *Computers and the Humanities 23.3* (1989): 173–198.

Lesk, Michael. "What to Do When There's Too Much Information." *Proceedings Hypertext '89.* November 5–7, 1989, Pittsburgh, PA . New York: *ACM,* 1989. 305–318.

Levin, J.A., H. Kim and M. M. Riel. "Hypertext Perspectives on Educational Computer Conferencing." *Online Education: Perspectives on a New Environment.* Ed. L.M. Harasim, New York: Preger, 1990. 215–265.

Littleford, Alan. "Artificial Intelligence and Hypermedia." *The Hypertext/Hypermedia Handbook.* Ed. Emily Berk and Joseph Devlin, New York: McGraw-Hill, 1991.

Louie, Steven and Robert F, Rubeck. "Hypertext Publishing and the Revitalization of Knowledge." *Academic Computing 3.9* (May 1989): 20–23; 30–31.

Luther, Willis and Martin Carter. *Management of Change and History in a Hypermedia Environment.* MCC Technical Report HI-164-87, June 1987.

Lynch, Cliford A. "Hypertext. Large Databases, and Relational Databases." *Proceedings of the 10th International Online information Meeting.* Medford, NJ: Learned Information, 1989. 265-270.

Lyons, Patrice. "Copyright Considerations: Imaging and Document Conversion." *The Hypertext/Hypermedia Handbook.* Emily Berk and Joseph Devlin, eds. New York: McGraw-Hill, 1991.

Marchionini, Gary and Ben Shneiderman. "Finding Facts and Browsing Knowledge in Hypertext Systems." *IEEE Computer 21.1* (January 1988): 70-79.

Marchionini, Gary. "Hypermedia and Learning: Freedom and Chaos." *Educational Technology 27.11* (1988): 8-12.

Marcus, Stephen. "Reading, Writing, and Hypertext." *College Literature 15* (Winter 1988): 9-18.

Marshall, Catherine C. "Exploring Representation Problems Using Hypertext." *Proceedings Hypertext '87.* November 13-15, 1987, Chapel Hill, NC. New York: ACM, 1989. 253-268.

Martin, James. *Hyperdocuments and How to Create Them.* Engelwood Cliffs, NJ: Prentice-Hall, 1990.

McAleese, Ray. "Navigation and Browsing in Hypertext." *Hypertext: Theory into Practice.* Ed. Ray McAleese, Oxford: Intellect, 1989. 6-44.

McDaid, John. "Breaking Frames: Hyper-mass Media." *The Hypertext/Hypermedia Handbook.* Ed. Emily Berk and Joseph Devlin, New York: McGraw-Hill, 1991.

McGrew, P.C. and W.D. McDaniel. *On-Line Text Management: Hypertext and Other Techniques.* New York: Intertext Publications, McGraw-Hill, 1989.

McKnight, Cliff, Andrew Dillon and John Richardson. "The Authoring of Hypertext Documents." *Hypertext: Theory into Practice.* Ed. Ray McAleese. Oxford: Intellect, 1989.

McKnight, Cliff, Andrew Dillon and John Richardson. "A Comparison of Linear and Hypertext Formats in Information Retrieval." *Hypertext: State of the Art.* Ed. Ray McAleese and Catherine Green. Norwood, NJ: Alex Publishing Corp., 1990. 10-19.

McKnight, Cliff, Andrew Dillon and John Richardson. *Hypertext in Context.* Cambridge: Cambridge University Press, 1990.

McKnight, Cliff, Andrew Dillon and John Richardson. "Journal Articles as Learning Resource: What Can Hypertext Offer?" *Designing Hypermedia for Learning.* Ed. David Johassen and Heinz Mandl. Berlin: Springer-Verlag, 1990. 277-290.

McKnight, Cliff, Andrew Dillon and John Richardson. "Problems in Hyperland: A Human Factors Perspective." *Hypermedia 1.2* (1989): 167-178.

McKnight, Cliff, Andrew Dillon and John Richardson. "The Construction of Hypertext Documents and Databases." *Electronic Library 6.5* (October 1988): 338-342.

Meyrowitz, Norman K. "The Link to Tomorrow." *Unix Review 8.2:* 58-67.

Meyrowitz, Norman. "Intermedia: The Architecture and Construction of an Object-Oriented Hypermedia System and Applications Framework." *Proceedings of the Conference on Object-Oriented Programming Systems,* Languages and Applications (OOPSLA '86) September 29-October 2, Portland, OR, 1986.

Monty, M.L. "Temporal Context and Memory for Notes Stored in the Computer." *ACM SIGCHI Bulletin 18.2* (October 1986): 50-51.

Moriariu, J. "Hypermedia in Instruction and Training: The Power and the Promise." *Educational Technology 28.11* (November 1988): 17-20.

Moulthrop, Stuart. "Hypertext and 'the Hyperreal.'" *Proceedings Hypertext '89.* November 5-7, 1989, Chapel Hill, NC. New York: ACM, 1989. 259-267.

Moulthrop, Stuart. "In the Zones: Hypertext and the Politics of Interpretation." *Writing on the Edge 1.1* (1989): 18–27.

Moulthrop, Stuart. "Making Nothing Happen: Hypermedia Fiction." *The Hypertext/ Hypermedia Handbook.* Ed. Emily Berk and Joseph Devlin, New York: McGraw-Hill, 1991.

Moulthrop, Stuart. "Reading from the Map: Metonymy and Metaphor in the Fiction of "Forking Paths." *Hypermedia and Literary Studies.* Ed. Paul Delany and George Landow, Cambridge, MA: MIT Press, 1991. 119–132.

Negroponte, Nicholas. "Books Without Pages." *IEEE International Conference on Communications IV,* 1979.

Nelson, Theodor H. "Managing Immense Storage." *Byte,* (January 1988): 225–238.

Nelson, Theodor H. "Unifying Tomorrow's Hypermedia." *Proceedings of the 12th International Online Information Meeting.* December 6–8, 1988, London. Oxford: Learned Information, 1988. 1–7.

Neuwirth, Christine M. and David S. Kaufer. "The Role of External Representation in the Writing Process: Implications for the Design of Hypertext-Based Writing Tools." *Proceedings Hypertext '89.* November 5–7, 1989, Chapel Hill, NC. New York: ACM, 1989. 319–342.

Nielsen, Jakob. "Evaluating Hypertext Usability." *Proceedings of NATO Advanced Research Workshop on Designing Hypertext/Hypermedia for Learning.* July 4–7, 1989, Rottenburg, West Germany.

Nielsen, Jakob. "The Art of Navigating in Hypertext." *Communications of the ACM 33.3* (March 1990): 296–310.

Nielsen, Jakob. "The Matters that Really Matter for Hypertext Usability." *Proceedings Hypertext '89.* November 5–7, 1989, Chapel Hill, NC. New York: ACM, 1989. 239–248.

Nielsen, Jakob. *Hypertext and Hypermedia.* New York: Academic Press, 1990.

Ofiesh, Gabriel. "The Seamless Carpet of Knowledge and Learning." Ed. Steve Lambert and Suzanne Ropiequet. *CD ROM: The New Papyrus.* Redmond, WA: Microsoft Press, 1986. 299–319.

Oren, Tim. "Cognitive Load in Hypermedia: Designing for the Exploratory Learner." *Learning with Interactive Multimedia.* Sueann Ambron and Kristina Hooper, eds. Redmond, WA: Microsoft Press, 1990. 125–137.

Oren, Tim. "The Architecture of Static Hypertexts." *Proceedings Hypertext '87.* November 13–15, 1987, Chapel Hill, NC. New York: ACM, 1989. 310–324.

Parsaye, Kamran, et al. *Intelligent Databases: Object-Oriented, Deductive Hypermedia Technologies.* New York: Wiley, 1989.

Parunak, H. Van Dyke. "Hypermedia Topologies and User Navigation." *Proceedings Hypertext '89.* November 5–7, 1989, Chapel Hill, NC. New York: *ACM,* 1989. 43–50.

Parunak, H. Van Dyke. "Industrial Strength Hypertext." *The Hypertext/Hypermedia Handbook.* Ed. Emily Berk and Joseph Devlin, New York: McGraw-Hill, 1991.

Parunak, H. Van Dyke. "Ordering the Information Web." *The Hypertext/Hypermedia Handbook.* Ed. Emily Berk and Joseph Devlin, New York: McGraw-Hill, 1991.

Perlman, Gary. "Asynchronous Design/Evaluation Methods for Hypertext Technology Development." *Proceedings Hypertext '89.* November 5–7, 1989, Chapel Hill, NC. New York: *ACM,* 1989. 61–82.

Perez, Ernest. "Tools for Developers." *The Hypertext/Hypermedia Handbook.* Ed. Emily Berk and Joseph Devlin. New York: McGraw-Hill, 1991.

Picher, Oliver, Joseph Devlin and Ken Pugh. "Hypermedia." *The Hypertext/Hypermedia Handbook.* Ed. Emily Berk and Joseph Devlin, New York: McGraw-Hill, 1991.

Rada, R. *Hypertext: From Text to Expertext.* Maidenhead: McGraw-Hill, 1991.

Rada, R. "Reading and Writing Hypertext: An Overview." *Journal of the American Society of Information Science 40.3* (May 1989): 164–171.

Rada, R. M. Mhasi and J. Barlow. "Hierarchical Semantic Nets Support Retrieving and Generating Hypertext." *Information and Design Technologies 16.2* (1990): 117-136.

Ramey, Judith. "Escher Effects in Online Text." *The Society of Text: Hypertext, Hypermedia, and the Social Construction of Information.* Ed. Edward Barrett, Cambridge, MA: MIT Press, 1989. 388-402.

Rearick, Thomas C. "Automatic Hypertext Generation." *The Hypertext/Hypermedia Handbook.* Ed. Emily Berk and Joseph Devlin, New York: McGraw-Hill, 1991.

Rubens, Philip. "Online Information, Hypermedia, and the Idea of Literacy." *The Society of Text: Hypertext, Hypermedia, and the Social Construction of Information.* Ed. Edward Barrett, Cambridge, MA: MIT Press, 1989. 3-21.

Scacchi, Walt. "On the Power of Domain-Specific Hypertext Environments." *Journal of American Society for Information Science. 40.3* (May 1989): 183-191.

Schwartz, Mayer, and N. Delisle. "Contexts: A Partitioning Concept for Hypertext." *Proceedings Computer Supported Cooperative Work.* Austin, TX, 147-152.

Shasha, Dennis. "When Does Non-linear Text Help?" *Proceedings First International Convference on Expert Database Systems.* Ed. L. Kerschberg, Menlo Park, CA: 1987. 163-174.

Shneiderman, Ben, Charles Kreitzberg and Emily Berk. "Editing to Structure a Reader's Experience." *The Hypertext/Hypermedia Handbook.* Ed. Emily Berk and Joseph Devlin, New York: McGraw-Hill, 1991.

Shneiderman, Ben, et al. "Visual Engagement and Low Cognitive Load in Browsing Hypertext." Department of Computer Science, University of Maryland. *Technical Report CS-TR-2433.* March 1990.

Shneiderman, Ben. "Reflections on Authoring, Editing, and Managing Hypertext." *The Society of Text: Hypertext, Hypermedia, and the Social Construction of Information.* Ed. Edward Barrett, Cambridge, MA: MIT Press, 1989. 115-131.

Simpson, Annette and Cliff McKnight "Navigation in Hypertext: Structural Cues and Mental Maps." *Hypertext: State of the Art.* Ed. Ray McAleese and Catherine Green. Norwood, NJ: Ablex, 1990. 73-83.

Slatin, John M. "Hypertext and the Teaching of Writing." *Text, Context and Hypertext: Writing with and for the Computer.* Ed. Edward Barrett, Cambridge, MA: MIT Press, 1988. 111-129.

Slatin, John. "Composing Hypertext." *The Hypertext/Hypermedia Handbook.* Ed. Emily Berk and Joseph Devlin, New York: McGraw-Hill, 1991.

Slatin, John. "Reading Hypertext: Order and Coherence in a New Medium." *Hypermedia and Literary Studies.* Ed. Paul Delany and George Landow, Cambridge, MA: MIT Press, 1991. 153-170.

Smith, John B., Stephen F. Weiss and Gordon J. Ferguson." A Hypertext Writing Environment and its Cognitive Basis." *Proceedings Hypertext '87.* November 13-15, 1987, Chapel Hill, NC. New York: ACM, 1989. 195-214.

Smith, Karen E., and Stanley B. Zdonik. "Intermedia: A Case Study of the Differences Between Relational and Object-Oriented Database Systems." *Proceedings Conference on Object-Oriented Programming Systems, Languages and Applications* (OOPSLA '87). October 4-8, 1987, Orlando, FL.

Streitz, Jörg Hannemann and Manfred Thüring. "From Ideas and Arguments to Hyperdocuments: Travelling Through Activity Spaces." *Proceedings Hypertext '89.* November 5-7, 1989, Chapel Hill, NC. New York: ACM, 1989. 343-365.

Tchudi, S. "Invisible Thinking and the Hypertext." *English Journal 77.1* (1988): 22-30.

Tompa, F.W. "A Data Model for Flexible Hypertext Database Systems." *ACM Transactions on Information Systems 7.1* (January 1989): 85-100.

Travers, Michael. "A Visual Representation for Knowledge Structures." *Proceedings Hypertext '89.* November 13-15, 1989, Chapel Hill, NC. New York: ACM, 1989. 147-158.

Tsai, C. "Hypertext: Technology, Applications, and Research Issues." *Journal of Educational Technology Systems. 17.1* (1988): 3–14.

Utting, Kenneth, and Nicole Yankelovich. "Context and Orientation in Hypermedia Networks." *Institute for Research in Information and Scholarship Technical Report 88-2.* 1988.

van Dam, Andries and David E. Rice. "Computers and Publishing: Writing, Editing and Printing." *Advances in Computers.* New York: Academic Press, 1970.

van der Merwe, D.P. "Annotating Literary Texts with Hypertext." *Proceedings of the 12th International Online Information Meeting.* December 6–8, 1988, London. Oxford: Learned Information, 1988. 239–247.

Weyer, Stephen A. "As We May Learn." *Interactive Multimedia: Visions of Multimedia for Developers, Educators, & Information Providers.* Redmond, WA: Microsoft Press, 1988. 87–104.

Weyer, Stephen A. *Searching for Information in a Dynamic Book. Report SCG-1.* Xerox PARC, Palo Alto, CA, February 1982.

Weyer, Stephen A., and Alan H. Borning. "A Prototype Electronic Encyclopedia." *ACM Transactions on Office Information Systems, 3.1* (January 1985): 63–88.

Wigging, Lyna L. and Michael J. Shiffer. "Planning for Hypermedia: Combining Text, Graphics, Sound and Video." *Journal of American Planning Association 56.2* (Spring 1990): 226–240.

Woodhead, Nigel. *Hypertext and Hypermedia: Theory and Application.* Wilmslow: Sigma, 1990.

Woods, William A. "What's in a Link: Foundations for Semantic Networks." *Readings in Knowledge Representation.* Ed. Ronald J. Brachman and Hector J. Levesque, Los Altos, CA: Morgan Kaufmann, 1975. 217–242.

Wright, P. "Interface Alternatives for Hypertexts." *Hypermedia 1.2* (1989): 146–166.

Yankelovich, Nicole, and Andries van Dam. "Spinning Scholarly Webs." *The Annenberg/CPB Project Report to Higher Education.* Washington, D.C.: The Annenberg/CPB Project, 1987.

Yankelovich, Nicole, D. Cody and George Landow. "The Creation of a Hypermedia Corpus for English Literature." *SIGCUE Bulletin 19* (Spring-Summer 1987).

Yankelovich, Nicole, et al. "Intermedia: The Concept and the Construction of a Seamless Information Environment." *IEEE Computer 21.1* (January 1988): 81–96.

Yankelovich, Nicole, et al. "Issues in Designing a Hypermedia Document System: The Intermedia Case Study." *Interactive Multimedia: Visions of Multimedia for Developers, Educators, & Information Providers.* Ed. Sueann Ambron and Kristina Hooper, Redmond, WA: Microsoft Press, 1988. 33–85.

Yankelovich, Nicole. "From Electronic Books to Electronic Libraries: Revisiting 'Reading and Writing the Electronic Book.'" *Hypermedia and Literary Studies.* Ed. Paul Delany and George Landow,. Cambridge, MA: MIT Press, 1991. 133–142.

Zellweger, Polle T. "Active Paths Through Multimedia Documents." *Document Manipulation and Typography.* Ed. J. C. van Vliet. Cambridge: Cambridge University Press, 1988. 19–34.

Critique

Glusko, R.J. "Visions of Grandeur?" *Unix Review 8.2* (February 1990): 70–80.

Jaynes, Joseph T. "Limited Freedom: Linear Reflections on Nonlinear Texts." *The Society of Text: Hypertext, Hypermedia, and the Social Construction of Information.* Ed. Edward Barrett, Cambridge, MA: MIT Press, 1989. 48–161.

Jones, W.P. "How Do We Distinguish the Hyper from the Hype in Non-linear text?" *Proceedings INTERACT '87.* Ed. H.J. Bullinger and B. Schackel, Elsevier Science Publishers B.V. (North-Holland). 1107–1113.

Manes, S. "Hypertext: A Breath of Air Freshener." *PC Magazine 6.11* (June 9, 1987): 9(12).

Meyrowitz, Norman. "The Missing Link: Why We're All Doing Hypertext Wrong." *The Society of Text: Hypertext, Hypermedia, and the Social Construction of Information.* Ed. Edward Barrett, Cambridge, MA: MIT Press, 1989. 107–114.

Ogdin, Carol Anne, and Richard L. Davison. "The Emperor's New Clothes: Why Hypertext Stands Naked." *Multimedia Review* (Spring 1990): 22–26.

Raskin, Jef. "The Hype in Hypertext: A Critique." *Hypertext '87 Proceedings.* November 13–15, 1987. Chapel Hill, NC. New York: ACM, 1989. 325–330.

Thompson, Bev and Bill Thompson. "Hyping Text: Hypertext and Knowledge Representation." *AI Expert,* (August 1987): 25–28.

Background

Apple Computer, Inc. *Human Interface Guidelines: The Apple Desktop Interface.* Reading, MA: Addison-Wesley Publishing Co., 1987.

Bateson, Gregory. *Steps to an Ecology of Mind.* San Francisco: Chandler Publishing Co., 1972.

Bennis, Warren. "Thoughts from a Victim of Info-Overload Anxiety." *Antioch Review, 1977.* Yellow Springs, OH: Antioch Press, 1977.

Bolt, Robert A. "Put-that-there: Voice and Gesture at the Graphics Interface." *Computer Graphics 15.3* (August 1980): 262–270.

Bolter, J. David. *Turing's Man: Western Culture in the Computer Age.* Chapel Hill: University of North Carolina Press, 1984.

Booth-Clibborn, Edward, and Daniel Baroni. *The Language of Graphics.* New York: Abrams Publishers, 1979.

Brand, Stewart. *The Media Lab: Inventing the Future at MIT.* New York: Viking Penguin, 1987.

Burnham, David. *The Rise of the Computer State.* New York: Vintage Books, 1984.

Campbell, Jeremy. *Grammatical Man: Information, Entropy, Language, and Life.* New York: Simon and Schuster, 1982.

Costanzo, William V. *The Electronic Text: Learning to Write, Read, and Reason with Computers.* Englewood Cliffs, NJ: Educational Technology Publications, 1989.

Dondis, Donis. *A Primer of Visual Literacy.* Cambridge, MA: MIT Press, 1973.

Donnelly, William. *The Confetti Generation: How the New Communications Technology is Fragmenting America.* New York: Henry Holt, 1986.

Drexler, E. *Engines of Creation: Challenges and Choices of the Last Technological Revolution.* New York: Anchor/Doubleday, 1986.

Easterby, R., and H. Zwaga. *The Design and Evaluation of Signs and Printed Material.* New York: Wiley, 1984.

Freiberger, Paul. *Fire in the Valley: The Making of the Personal Computer.* Berkeley: Osborne/McGraw-Hill, 1984.

Furnas, G.W. "Generalized Fisheye Views." *Proceedings ACM CHI '86 Conference on Human Factors in Computing Systems.* Boston, MA, April 13–17, 1986. 16–23.

Garson, Barbara. *The Electronic Sweatshop.* New York: Simon and Schuster, 1988.

Greenfield, Patricia Marks. *Mind and Media: The Effects of Television, Video Games, and Computers.* Cambridge, MA: Harvard University Press, 1984.

Gumpert, Gary and Robert Cathcard, eds. *Intermedia: Interpersonal Communication in a Media World, 3rd edition.* New York: Oxford University Press, 1986.

Heim, Michael. *Electric Language: A Philosophical Study of Word Processing.* New Haven: Yale University Press, 1987.

Hiltz, Starr Roxanne and Murray Turoff. *The Network Nation.* Reading, MA: Addison-Wesley, 1978.

Hofstader, Douglas R. Gödel, Escher, *Back: An Eternal Golden Braid. A Metaphorical Fugue on Minds and Machines in the Spirit of Lewis Carroll.* New York: Random House, 1980.

Innis, Harold. *The Bias of Communication.* Toronto: University of Toronto Press, 1985.

Klapp, Orrin. *Overload and Boredom: Essays on the Quality of Life in the Information Society.* New York: Greenwood, Press, 1986.

Lambert, Steve and Suzanne Ropiequet, eds. *CD ROM: The New Papyrus.* Redmond, WA: Microsoft Press, 1986.

Lancaster, F.W. *Toward Paperless Information Systems.* New York: Academic Press, 1978.

Lanham, Richard A. "The Electronic Word: Literary Study and the Digital Revolution." *New Literary History 20.2* (Winter 1989): 265–290.

Laurel, Brenda, ed. *The Art of Human-Computer Interface Design.* Reading, MA: Addison-Wesley, 1990.

Levinson, Paul. "Electronic Text and the Evolution of Media." *Journal of Social and Biological Structures 13.2* (May 1990): 141–149.

Levinson, Paul. "Intelligent Writing: The Electronic Liberation of Text." *Technology in Society 11.3* (Fall 1989): 387–400.

Levinson, Paul. *Mind at Large: Knowing in the Technological Age.* Greenwich, CT: JAI Press, 1988.

Mason, Robin and Tony Kaye, Ed. *Mindweave: Communication, Computers and Distance Education.* London: Pergamon, 1989.

McLuhan, Marshall. *The Gutenberg Galaxy: The Making of Typographic Man.* Toronto: University of Toronto Press, 1962.

McLuhan, Marshall. *Understanding Media: The Extensions of Man.* New York: New American Library, 1964.

Minsky, Marvin. *The Society of Mind.* New York: Simon & Schuster, 1986.

Minsky, Marvin. "A Framework for Representing Knowledge." *The Psychology of Computer Vision.* P. Winston, ed. New York: McGraw-Hill, 1975.

Mullins, Phil. "The Fluid World: Word Processing and Its Mental Habits." *Thought* 63.251: 413–428.

Negroponte, Nicholas. *Soft Architecture Machines.* Cambridge, MA: MIT Press, 1975.

Negroponte, Nicholas. *The Architecture Machine.* Cambridge, MA: MIT Press, 1970.

Nielsen, Jakob, ed. *Designing Interfaces for International Use.* Amsterdam: Elsevier Science Publications, 1990.

Niesz, Anthony J., and Norman Holland. "Interactive Fiction." *Critical Inquiry 11* (1984): 104–112.

Norman, Donald A. *The Psychology of Everyday Things.* New York: Basic Books, 1988.

Ong, Walter J. *Interfaces of the Word: Studies in the Evolution of Consciousness and Culture.* Ithaca: Cornell University Press, 1977.

Ong, Walter J. *Orality and Literacy: The Technologizing of the Word.* London: Methuen, 1982.

Pool, Ithiel de Sola. *Technologies of Freedom: On Free Speech in an Electronic Age.* Cambridge, MA: Harvard University Press, 1983.

Ronell, Avital. *The Telephone Book: Technology, Schizophrenia, Electric Speech.* Lincoln, NE: University of Nebraska Press, 1989.

Ropiequet, Suzanne, ed. *CD ROM: Electronic Publishing.* Redmond, WA: Microsoft Press, 1987.

Roszak, Theodore. *The Cult of Information.* New York: Pantheon Books, 1986.

Scagg, G.W. "Some Thoughts on Paper Notes and Electronic Messages." *SIGCHI Bulletin 16.3* (January 1985): 41–44.

Shallis, Michael. *The Silicon Idol: The Micro Revolution and its Social Implications.* New York: Schocken Books, 1984.

Shneiderman, Ben. *Designing the User Interface.* Reading. MA: Addison-Weslesy, 1987.

Simons, Geoff. *Eco-Computer: The Impact of Global Intelligence.* New York: Wiley, 1987.

Tufte, Edward R. *Envisioning Information.* Chesire, CT: Graphics Press, 1990.

Tufte, E. *The Visual Display of Quantitative Information.* Cheshire, CT: Graphics Press, 1984.

Whorf, Benjamin. *Language, Thought and Reality.* Cambridge, MA: MIT Press, 1956.

Widmer, Kingsley. "Sensibility Under Technocracy." *Human Connection and the New Media.* Barry Schwartz, ed. Englewood Cliffs, NJ: Prentice-Hall, 1973.

Winograd, Terry and Fernando Flores. *Understanding Computers and Cognition: A New Foundation for Design.* Norwood, NJ: Ablex Publishing, 1986.

Wurman, Richard Saul. *Information Anxiety.* New York: Bantam Books, 1989.

Zuboff, Shoshana. *In the Age of the Smart Machine: The Future of Work and Power.* New York: Basic Books, 1988.

About the Author

Terence Harpold

Terence Harpold is a Ph.D. candidate in Comparative Literature at the University of Pennsylvania. He is also founder of Slithy Resources, a hypermedia design and publishing firm.

His publications relating to hypertext include essays on hypertext and psychoanalytic theory and the carnival/grotesque stylistics of the hypertextual corpus. He is currently working on a book-length study of narrative digression.

Trademarks

Aldus is a registered trademark of Aldus Corporation.
ABC of a registered trademark of American Broadcasting Companies.
Amiga is a trademark of Commodore.
askSam is a trademark of Seaside Software Inc.
AT&T is a trademark of American Telephone & Telegraph Company
Atari is a registered trademark of Atari, Inc.
aTEX is a registered trademark of Atex, Inc.
AutoCAD and Autodesk Animator are trademarks of Autodesk, Inc.
Aztec C is a trademark of Manx, Inc.
Betacam and View are trademarks of Sony Corporation.
BRS Search is a registered trademark of Thyssen-Bernemiszd, Inc.
Byte magazine is a copyright and trademark of McGraw-Hill, Inc.
C-scape is a trademark of Oakland Group, Inc.
COMPAQ is a registered trademark of Compaq Computer Corporation.
Dan Bricklin's Demo Program is a trademark of Software Garden Inc.
dBase and Framework III are trademarks of Ashton-Tate.
Dialog is a gegistered trademark of Dialog Information Services.
Dow Jones is a trademark of Dow Jones & Company, Inc.
Dr. Halo is a trademark of Media Cybernetics Corp.
DVI (Digital Video Interactive) is a trademark of Intel Corporation.
Storyspace, Hypergate, and Election of 1912 are trademarks of Eastgate Systems.
Encyclopaedia Britannica is a trademarked name of Encyclopaedia Britannica, Inc.
Epson is a registered trademark of Epson America, Inc.
Microsoft, Microsoft C, Microsoft Windows, Microsoft Word, Flight Simulator, MS-DOS, GW-BASIC, Code, CodeView, and QuickC are trademarks of Microsoft Corporation.
Gem is a trademark of Digital Research, Inc.
Grammatik is a trademark of Wang Laboratories, Inc.
Hewlett-Packard, HP Laserjet, and PCL are trademarks of Hewlett-Packard Co.
HYPERBASE is a trademark of Cogent Software, Ltd.
HyperNews is a trademark of Training Resources Unlimited.
HyperQuiz is a trademark of Dan Shafer.
Hyperties is a trademark of Cognetics Corporation.
HYPERTRANS is a trademark of Texas Instruments.
HyperWriter! is a trademark of NTERGAID
IBM IBM LinkWay, IBM-PC, PC/XT, Personal Computer AT, IBM-PC DOS, PC-DOS, IBM Personal System/2, PS/2, InfoWindows, Enterprise Systems/3090, SAA, and IBM's Systems Application Architecture are trademarks of International Business Machines Corp.
IDE is a registered trademark of Interactive Development Environments, Inc.
Information Lens is a trademark of Thomas W. Malone.
INTERLEAF is a registered trademark of Interleaf, Inc.
Intermedia and Iris Intermedia are registered trademarks of Brown University Corporation.
KMS is a registered trademark of Knowledge Systems, Inc.
KnowledgePro and Knowledge Pro Windows are trademarks of Knowledge Garden, Inc.
Lattice C is a trademark of Lattice, Inc.
LEXIS is a trademark of Mead Data Central Inc.
Lotus, Lotus 1-2-3, and Lotus Freelance are registered trademarks of Lotus Development Corporation.
Macintosh, HyperCard, HyperTalk, Mac II, MacDraw, MacPaint, Sane, and Stackware are registered trademarks of Apple Computer, Inc.
MaxThink is a trademark of MaxThink, Inc.
Menu's for HyperCard! and Report! are trademarks of Nine to Five Software, Inc.
METAPHOR is a trademark of Metaphor Computer Systems.
MIT Media Lab is a trademark of Massachusetts Institute of Technology Corp.
MOTIF is a trademark of Open Software Foundation, Inc.
NEXTSTEP is a trademark of neXT Incorporated.
Nintendo is a trademark of Nintendo Corporation LTD.
Notecards is a trademark of Xerox.
GUIDE is a trademark of Owl Internationsl, Inc.
PC-Paintbrush is a registered trademark of Zsoft Corporation.
Photonet is a trademark of Photonet Computer Corporation.
Script Expert is a trademark of Softpress Publishing and Dan Shafer.
ScriptView is a trademark of Paul T. Pashibin/Eldon Benz.
Sidekick and Turbo C are trademarks of Borland International, Inc.
SmarText, AMI, and AMI Professional are registered trademarks of SAMMA Corporation.
Sun Microsystems is a trademark of Sun Microsystems.
Tandy is a registered trademark of Tandy Corporation.
Targa is a registered trademark of Truevision, Inc.
Telenet is a trademark of GTE.
ThinkTank is a trademark of Living Videotext, Inc.
Toolbook is a registered trademark of Asymetrix Corp.
Transputer is a registered trademark of Inmos Limited Corporation.
Unix is a trademark of AT&T.
Westlaw is a trademark of West Publishing Co.
Xanadu is a trademark of XOC, Inc.
xText is a trademark of Flambeaux, Inc.
XYVISION is a trademark of Xyvision, Inc.
XyWrite is a trademark of XyQuest, Inc.

Index

- Looking for more information about hypertext, hypermedia and multimedia?
- Want to purchase a digital version of the Hypertext/Hypermedia Handbook?
- Interested in the Hypertext/Multimedia Newsletter?

Armadillo Associates can keep you up to date in the field of Hypertext and Multimedia!

Send a check for $5.00 (payable to Armadillo Associates, Inc.) and we will:

- send you a copy of the Armadillo Hypertext/ Multimedia Newsletter, and
- send an order form for the electronic version of the Expanded Hypertext/Hypermedia Handbook.

Correspondence should be addressed to:

Fulfillment Department
Armadillo Associates, Inc.
2837 Poplar Street
Philadelphia, PA 19130
(215) 235-2069

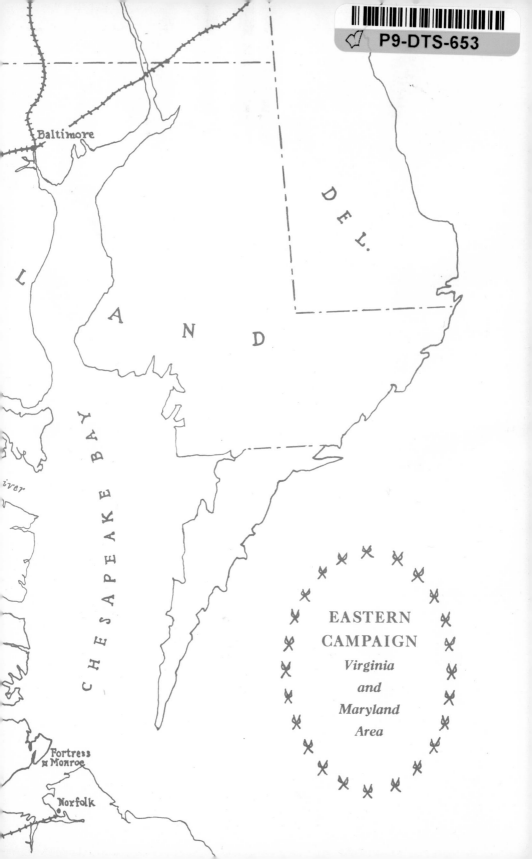

Baltimore

D E L.

M A R Y L A N D

C H E S A P E A K E   B A Y

iver

Fortress
Monroe

Norfolk

EASTERN
CAMPAIGN

*Virginia
and
Maryland
Area*

FROM
THE
CANNON'S
MOUTH

General Alpheus S. Williams

the
Civil War
letters
of
General
Alpheus S. Williams

FROM
THE
CANNON'S
MOUTH

edited
with an
introduction
by
Milo M. Quaife

DETROIT
WAYNE STATE UNIVERSITY PRESS
AND THE DETROIT HISTORICAL SOCIETY

1959

Grateful acknowledgement is made to the Mary
E. Murphy Fund of the Detroit Historical Society for financial assistance toward
the editing and publication of these letters.

foreword

HENRY D. BROWN · DIRECTOR

DETROIT HISTORICAL MUSEUM

The publication of selections from the General Alpheus S. Williams Papers on the Civil War marks an important new undertaking for the Detroit Historical Society and Wayne State University Press, both of which have enjoyed a long and fruitful association. This is their first sponsorship of the reproduction and editing of original source materials, a type of publication that makes original sources more readily available to those who in turn write about our heritage for the general reader. The book will be a contribution for writers and students of the history of the American Civil War. The Press and the Society consider publication of this type of basic source material a logical part of their contribution to a deeper understanding of our local and national heritage.

It is singularly appropriate that this initial project of scholarly editing of original sources should be concerned with the period of the Civil War, for the coming centennial of that conflict has directed national attention to the need for additional published source materials. While the major contribution of the volume will be to make more readily available important original materials on the Civil War, the letters themselves contain some of the finest depictions of warfare as it actually is which can be found anywhere in literature.

The publication of the Alpheus S. Williams Papers was made possible through the bequest of the late Mrs. Fred T. Murphy to the Detroit Historical Society. For fifteen years prior to her death in November 1956, Mrs. Murphy had been most active in local history projects as a member of the Museum Building Fund Committee, a member of the Board of Trustees of the Detroit Historical Society, and a member of the Detroit Historical Commission, 1946–1956.

As a daughter-in-law of General Russell A. Alger, the wife of Frederick M. Alger from 1901 until his death in 1933, Mrs. Murphy was deeply concerned over the proper means of emphasizing the important contributions of Union participants in the Civil War. General Alger, a contemporary of General Williams, was not only a distinguished participant in that conflict but later served as commander of the Grand Army of the Republic, Michigan Governor and Senator, and Secretary of War. It may be recalled that it was through Mrs. Murphy that the late Mrs. Charles B. Pike, daughter of General Alger, became interested in the proposed building for the Detroit Historical Museum, and that her generous gift initiated the building fund drive, which culminated in the present Museum structure.

The Detroit Public Library generously granted permission for the Society to publish the Alpheus Williams Papers in the Burton Historical Collection and cooperated wholeheartedly in the details incident to preparing them for publication. While the bulk of the papers had been copied some years ago, much copying and recopying of material still had to be done. Members of the Museum's administrative staff, particularly Miss Patricia Butkowski, Secretary to the Director, contributed substantially to the completion of this phase of the work.

Dr. Milo M. Quaife, from 1924 to 1947 Secretary-Editor of the Burton Historical Collection of the Detroit Public Library and a distinguished historian and editor, called our attention to the significance of the Alpheus S. Williams Papers. The Society and the Press were fortunate in enlisting Dr. Quaife's services as editor. His long and important contributions in the field of editing original source materials is well known to many of the individuals who will make use of this volume. Members of the Society will recall that Dr. Quaife delivered the Lewis Cass Lecture in 1954 and that in 1956 he was presented a citation by the American Association for State and Local History for distinguished contributions to the field of American national and local history.

preface

My procedure in preparing the letters for publication should be explained to the reader. Since they are chiefly family letters, written by a devoted parent to his young daughters, the originals contain a great deal of domestic and private material which possesses no interest for the present-day reader. Partly for this reason, in part to avoid useless expense, all of this material has been deleted from the present version. Like all other authors, General Williams occasionally committed errors of grammar or of orthography. To reproduce these in print would serve no useful purpose, and such corrections as the individual circumstances required have been made; also as a matter of course, such details as capitalization and punctuation have been standardized. It is perhaps unnecessary to add that none of the deletions and changes have been animated by the motive of suppressing or altering Williams' expressions of opinion.

I am under obligation to numerous individuals and institutions for assigning the editorial task to me and making the publication of General Williams' letters possible. I am grateful to Mrs. Margaret Barbour, the general's granddaughter, for her sympathetic interest and support. Mr. Henry D. Brown, Director of the Detroit Historical Museum, and Dr. Harold A. Basilius, Director of Wayne State University Press, whose respective institutions have jointly sponsored and financed the book, have given me their constant support, along with much technical assistance. Professor Alexander Brede, Editor of the Wayne State University Press, has competently performed the copy reader's task of whipping the manuscript into final shape for printing. From Mrs. Elleine Stones, former Chief, and Mr. James Babcock, present Chief, of the Burton Historical Collection of the Detroit Public Library, within whose pleasant domain the editorial work has been chiefly performed, I have received unfailing service and cooperation in facilitating the task. Nor should acknowledgement be omitted of the helpful interest of Dr. Alfred

H. Whittaker or the many services rendered by Miss Dorothy Martin, Archivist of the Burton Collection, along with the usual courteous services of the remaining members of the staff, which contribute so much to render the Collection a peaceful haven of historical research. For the reproduction of the old illustrations I am indebted to the excellent photography of Mr. Joseph Klima, Jr. The index is the work of Mr. Simon Greenfield. Last but not least may be noted the help accorded by Letitia, my permanent secretary and wife.

M.M.Q.

contents

illustrations

Historical
Introduction

historical introduction

Over the main cross roads of Detroit's Belle Isle Park looms the equestrian statue of "a weary man on a tired horse." [1] It was erected in 1921 as a memorial to General Alpheus S. Williams, Detroit and Michigan's best-loved soldier. Around it flows a stream of automobile traffic which long since provoked the proposal that the statue should be removed to a more suitable location. Yet still the General reins his steed, serenely unperturbed by the noise around him, and the prediction may be hazarded that any serious effort to banish him to a more secluded scene will be met with a storm of public disapproval.

Surface indications to the contrary, polyglot Detroit sincerely cherishes the memory of her historic past. Statues, bronze markers, and other memorials abound throughout the city's older area, directing the attention of the passing throng to the actors and actions of former times. For almost a century the venerable City Hall has displayed on its exterior walls the statues of four notable figures of the remote past. Statesmen and politicians, poets and other dreamers—Christopher Columbus and Franz Schubert (who did not live in Detroit), railroad stations, both "Underground" and actual, churches and trees and hospitals and toll gates—these and many others populate the city's pantheon. Belatedly, therefore, the city bestirred itself, now half a century ago, to erect a permanent memorial to its foremost soldier, General Alpheus S. Williams.

Williams was born in the village of Deep River, Connecticut, on September 20, 1810. [2] His father died when Williams was but eight years old, and his mother during his seventeenth year, leaving his future training to the care of family relatives. Left to him, also, was a reputed patrimony of $75,000, a very considerable fortune a century and a half ago. [3] Following his graduation from Yale in 1831, for several years he devoted his time to an intermittent study of law and a series of extensive travels, both in America and Europe. According to his biographers the

3

legal study was pursued at Yale, yet his journal preserved in the Burton Historical Collection of the Detroit Public Library discloses that in the early winter of 1831–32 he was studying in New York under the tutelage of a Mr. Hall. It further discloses that he did not take his legal studies too seriously. In early January 1832, he responded to an invitation from "Miss H" to visit Philadelphia and from there went to Washington. About this time he decided to accompany his brother on a voyage to Brazos Santiago at the southern tip of Texas, which was then a Mexican possession. On April 22, 1832, he began the voyage, bidding goodby to the law with this light-hearted valedictory: "farewell to law, Alph's occupation is gone."

Whether he resumed it upon his return to New York remains unrecorded, but in the spring of 1833 he embarked upon another southern tour, extending to Charleston and thence up the Savannah River and through the Cherokee country to New Orleans. The following spring he undertook another extensive tour, extending this time to Ohio and St. Louis. He was back in New Haven by the end of July, and in October 1834, he embarked upon a prolonged tour of Europe. The intervals between these several excursions afforded his only opportunity to master the intricacies of the legal profession, whose practice he presently entered upon.

In short, it seems apparent that for several years following his graduation from Yale he was chiefly intent upon dissipating his patrimony. He was abetted in this pleasant task by Henry Wikoff, a young Philadelphian, who for several years was his classmate at Yale. To escape expulsion by the college authorities, Wikoff had hastily departed from New Haven to spend his senior year at Union College, from which he was duly graduated in 1831. Possessed of an ample inheritance and a no-less ample stock of self-assurance, he now set out to see the world. Whether he persuaded Williams to join him in his travels, or vice versa, remains unrecorded. At any rate, for several years the two young men toured America and Europe as companions.[4]

They sailed from New York in mid-October 1834 on a tour which was to last a year and a half. From Le Havre the fellow-travelers proceeded to Paris in one of the ponderous French diligences, drawn by five stout Norman horses. Awaiting them in Paris was the actor Edwin Forrest, an old-time friend of Wikoff's guardian. Already widely famous in America, Forrest had embarked upon a prolonged European excursion, with Wikoff and Williams as his traveling companions. The trio of tourists had excellent introductions, along with plenty of money, and they found little or no difficulty in establishing contact with many of the leading characters of the time.

After experiencing the delights of Paris for two or three months they departed upon a tour of Italy. Upon its conclusion they returned to Paris in the spring of 1835, intent upon paying a visit to England and Scotland. During its progress Wikoff conceived the project of a journey to Russia, and thence southward to Constantinople and Jerusalem. Williams, however, whose funds were running low, stoutly declined to embark upon such a journey; Wikoff and Forrest departed for the Baltic and Saint Petersburg, and Williams returned alone to Paris, where he passed the ensuing winter. On March 6, 1836 he bade farewell to Paris and France, arriving in New York after an "agreeable" voyage of thirty-eight days.

Before him lay the sober task of earning a living and mastering his profession. Why he fixed upon Detroit as the scene of his future activities has nowhere been recorded. However, in 1836 the city was enjoying its first great boom. Western immigration and speculation in wild land were running at flood tide, and as the natural gateway to Michigan and the farther West Detroit offered promising inducements to an aspiring professional man. Hither, therefore, Williams came, and from the day of his arrival on August 12, 1836, until his death forty-two years later Detroit remained his home.

One of Detroit's leading citizens from the close of the War of 1812 was Charles Larned, soldier, lawyer, and civic leader. A native of Pittsfield, Massachusetts, he had gone to Kentucky prior to the outbreak of the war to "read" law in the office of Henry Clay. When the news of Detroit's downfall arrived, the young law student enlisted in a Kentucky regiment which was hastily raised and with it marched northward to join the army of General Winchester. There he shared in that leader's disastrous campaign, which was highlighted by the River Raisin defeat and massacre of January 22, 1813.

Along with Lewis Cass and many another soldier who had served in the war, upon its conclusion Larned made Detroit his home, and until his death in 1834 he combined the practice of law with the holding of various public offices. Meanwhile, in 1816 he married his boyhood sweetheart, Sylvia Colt of Pittsfield, and began the rearing of a numerous family. Julia, the eldest daughter, married Lewis Allen, and Catherine married John G. Atterbury, with whom Williams some months after coming to Detroit established a legal partnership. Jane Hereford, sister of Catherine and Julia, quite early in life married Benjamin Pierson. The union was soon terminated by his death and on January 16, 1839 the young widow became the bride of Alpheus Williams. Four months later he recorded in his journal that his married life was "flowing on like the peaceful current of a gentle river, happy as the day is long." Mrs. Williams died a decade later at the early age of thirty. Five children had been born of her union with Williams, two of whom died young. The others, Irene, Charles Larned, and Mary, will claim our subsequent notice.

In 1840 Williams was elected Probate Judge of Wayne County. Atterbury, meanwhile, developed a desire to exchange his legal calling for that of the ministry, and about the year 1843 Lewis Allen succeeded to the interests of the legal partnership. Williams' term of Probate Judge expired in 1844, but he had begun the assumption of other duties which continued to distract his attention from the law. In 1842 he became president of the Bank of St. Clair (removed about this time to Detroit). On November 10, 1843, he purchased the Detroit *Advertiser*, a daily paper, which he continued to own until January 1, 1848. In April 1849, he began a four-year term of service as postmaster of Detroit. The postoffice occupied the first floor of the Old Mariner's Church, which stood, until its recent removal, at the northwest corner of Woodbridge Street and Woodward Avenue. During Williams' incumbency of the office he had a staff of five assistants. Among other civic offices which he held at various times were colonel of the volunteer night watch (in 1849), recorder (1845–48), and member of the Board of Education (1856–57).

It was perhaps inevitable that a young man of Williams' temperament and energy should manifest an interest in military activities. Joseph Greusel, one admiring biographer, even affirms that he was born with a predilection for military life and that his travels in America and Europe during his early manhood were undertaken for the express purpose of studying the scenes of former battles and the reasons for the

6

successes and defeats associated with them. Of this remarkable "predilection," we have found no evidence prior to his removal to Detroit in 1836. It is not improbable, however, that, like other young men, he was interested in the military companies which constituted one of the very few forms of organized athletic activity in the era prior to the Civil War. At any rate, on November 26, 1836, he was admitted to membership in the Brady Guards, a company then recently organized, and from this time forward he assumed an increasingly prominent role in the military activities of the city. In 1838 the company was called into active service, performing patrol duty for several months during the continuance of Canada's Patriot War. In 1839 Williams was elected first lieutenant of the company, and in 1843 and 1846 its captain. The Mexican War was now at hand and Williams was appointed lieutenant colonel of the Michigan regiment which late in 1847 departed for the scene of conflict. It arrived in Mexico too late to participate in any battles, but during the winter and spring of 1848 it performed garrison and outpost duties. In the early summer the regiment returned to Detroit, where it was mustered out on July 23.

Although it had won no particular glory in the war, the opportunity had been afforded to Williams to master the routine of military life and to experience at first hand the many problems in which such service abounds. His reputation, too, as an active leader of military affairs in Michigan had been materially enhanced. Upon the death of General Brady in 1851 the Brady Guards became moribund. Its place in the life of the city was assumed by the newer company of Grayson Guards, which had been organized in 1850. In November 1855 this organization gave place in turn to the Detroit Light Guard, with Williams as its captain and leader. In 1859 the company evolved into a battalion of two companies, with Williams as its major. With this step, his pre-Civil War military education was completed.

Two years later came the firing on Fort Sumter and in its wake the holocaust of America's bloodiest war. In Michigan, public opinion overwhelmingly supported President Lincoln and the preservation of the Union. "Secession is revolution," said Governor Blair in his inaugural address in January 1861, "and revolution is the overt act of treason and must be treated as such. . . . It is a question of war the seceding states have to face."

This forthright declaration was followed by appropriate measures looking to belated preparation for waging war. General Williams was appointed brigadier general of state troops and from June until August he conducted a school of military instruction at Fort Wayne. Meanwhile new regiments were being organized in rapid succession, and before the war ended the state had sent over 90,000 men into the Union service, from which practically one in six was never to return.

In August 1861, Williams was appointed by the President a brigadier general of United States volunteers, to take effect as of May 17. Ordered to Washington at the beginning of October, he was assigned to General Banks' command which constituted the right wing of the newly-created Army of the Potomac, then stationed in the general vicinity of Harpers Ferry. From this time until the close of the war he was in constant service save for a single month's leave of absence in the winter of 1863–64. Repeatedly during the war he was given command of a division or of an army corps, winning the unvarying commendation of his superiors and the warm devotion of his soldiers. Yet, save for the relatively meaningless award of a brevet major generalship in January 1865, he ended his service as he had begun it, with the rank of brigadier general.

Why the promotion so clearly merited was withheld from him is difficult to understand. That he despised the arts of self-glorification and refused to woo the favor of the correspondents who followed the armies affords a partial explanation. Whatever the further reasons may have been, the fact remains clear that in the matter of official preferment he was the forgotten man of the Union Army. "In my judgment," wrote an officer of his staff in later years, "General Williams was one of the finest military commanders in the eastern army, and had he been fairly treated would have found his proper place at the head of it. He had all the attributes of manhood, was brave as a lion, was thoroughly versed in all the arts of war, and had a genius that inspired him where other men failed in a pressing emergency." [5]

Admittedly this is the statement of a friend and admirer, but it finds ample support in the commendations of such military authorities as General Sherman, General Hooker, General Slocum, and General Thomas. In sum, although General Williams failed to obtain official promotion he enjoyed the confidence of his military superiors, the affection of the members of his military staff, who gave expression to it by the gift of a magnificent sword, and the love and admiration of his soldiers, who awarded him the title of "Pap" Williams.

Both the quality and the volume of General Williams' wartime correspondence is amazing. Throughout the war he recorded his activities in a personal journal, most of which has unfortunately been lost. He maintained a constant correspondence with his daughters, frequently writing separate and more or less identical letters to each of them. Commonly he wrote them amid the crude surroundings of active campaigning; frequently, when subject to a constant flow of interruptions from members of his staff and others; at times, when beset by weariness or with the booming of cannon and the staccato reports of rifle fire assailing his ears. Yet into them he poured the scent of flowers, the singing of birds, the shocking sights of a military hospital, the hardships endured and the valor displayed by the common soldiers, the grandeur of mountain scenery, and the uproar of armies locked in desperate battle. With their aid the reader still may view the windrows of Confederate dead at Antietam, the headlong stampede of Union troops at Chancellorsville, the struggles of drowning mules trapped in the mud of a Virginia winter, the amazing spectacle presented by Sherman's tatterdemalian army emerging from its march through the Carolinas; or hear once more the voice of a woman in the darkness welcoming the conquering Union army as it entered doomed Atlanta.

General Williams' family in 1861 consisted of his son, Charles Larned, who was born in 1841, and his daughters, Irene and Mary, born respectively in 1843 and 1846. Upon Williams' entering the army, the family was broken up, never to be restored. Larned (as he was commonly called) accompanied his father to the army, although he refrained from enlisting. After about a year of employment, chiefly in connection with the quartermaster's department, he obtained work in Philadelphia, where he remained for several years, and where he married in February 1869. For many years he was attached to the office of Major Farquahar of the Engineer Department of the United States Army. In 1883 he entered upon an eighteen-year clerkship in the United States Engineer's office at Detroit. Transferred in 1901 to the Lake Survey, he served as chief clerk until his death in 1919.

Irene Williams (the Rene of the letters) passed the war years with her family relatives in Detroit and Connecticut or in the study of music at Philadelphia and possibly elsewhere. On January 18, 1866 she married William J. Chittenden, a member of the noted Chittenden hotel family. For several decades he served as manager and proprietor of the well-known Russell House at the corner of Woodward Avenue and Cadillac Square, subsequently the site in turn of the Pontchartrain Hotel and the National Bank of Detroit. Throughout her married life Mrs. Chittenden was active in social and patriotic society activities. She died at Chicago on April 7, 1907, while en route from the Pacific Coast to her home in Detroit. Of her several children, only Margaret, who married William T. Barbour, is still living. To her we are indebted for the preservation of General Williams' letters and for their gift in recent years to the Burton Historical Collection of the Detroit Public Library.

Mary (Minnie in the letters) was entrusted to the care of the family relatives in Connecticut, and two years passed before she saw her father again. She married Major Francis Farquahar, a West Point graduate in the class of 1861, who was attached to the Engineer Department of the army. For many years, until his death in July 1883, he was engaged in engineering activities on the Upper Mississippi and around the Great Lakes. His widow outlived him more than half a century, dying on February 7, 1935. In 1921, then the only living member of her father's family, she witnessed the unveiling of his monument on Belle Isle.

The close of the war left Williams without an occupation and with but limited financial means. He presently accepted the offer of an appointment as military administrator of the Ouachita District, comprising much of southern Arkansas, then a crude frontier region whose residents were much addicted to the late Confederacy and to acts of violence. Early in 1866 he resigned his commission, and upon his return to Detroit was appointed minister resident to the Central American republic of San Salvador, where he remained for three years. Returning once more to Michigan, he waged an unsuccessful campaign for governor in 1870 and two successful ones for election to Congress in 1874 and 1876.

His career was terminated by his death at his post of duty on December 21, 1878. As chairman of the House Committee on the District of

Columbia he had won deserved credit for the probity of his conduct in an era when graft and dishonesty in the conduct of public office was commonplace. In 1875, with his children long since married and scattered, he established a new home by marrying Mrs. Martha Tillman, the widow of a well-known Detroit merchant, who survived him. He was accorded a funeral marked by expressions of public esteem and grief such as falls to the lot of but few men. His material monument is the imposing statue erected to his memory on Belle Isle. His wartime letters to his daughters, now first published after the lapse of almost a century, may well become an even more enduring monument.

1. Thus characterized by John C. Lodge at the unveiling of the monument in October 1921. Whether it was the sculptor's intention to produce this effect may be doubted. Instead, he seems to have sought to depict the general checking his steed while he pored over a road map.

2. Without exception, apparently, his biographers erroneously affirm that he was born at Saybrook. Saybrook village, at the mouth of the Connecticut River, is in the New England town of Old Saybrook. Deep River, which lies some miles to the northward, is in the town of Saybrook. Apparently the confusion of the biographers derives from this multiplicity of names.

3. For this and some other biographical details we are dependent upon "Winder's Memories," first published in the Detroit *Sunday News* (subsequently the *News Tribune*) in 1893–94. John Winder, the author, was a pioneer Detroit lawyer and official, whose host of interesting memories were subsequently republished, with additions, by Robert B. Ross, under the title of *The Early Bench and Bar of Detroit from 1805 to the End of 1850* (Detroit, 1907). Both the book and the newspaper file are now exceedingly rare items.

4. Wikoff was a puzzling, as well as a fascinating, character. Although he authored several books, one of them a 600-page volume devoted to his personal history, the year of his birth and even the name of his father remain unknown. Possessed of fortune and an engaging personality and a brilliant intellect, throughout his life he moved in the best circles of society. Yet he made the pursuit of pleasure his chief occupation, and his uncompleted autobiography bears the significant title, *Reminiscences of an Idler* (New York, 1880). For a sketch of his life see the *Dictionary of American Biography*. (Hereafter cited as *Dict. Am. Biog.*)

5. The statement of Captain B. W. Morgan at the time of General Williams' death.—Undated newspaper clipping in the Chittenden scrapbook, in the Burton Historical Collection.

I

Organizing
an
Army

ORGANIZING AN ARMY

Until the firing upon Fort Sumter in April 1861, despite increasing debate between North and South, practically no preparation for waging a war had been made. That event signalized the close of the era of peaceful discussion and the resort to trial by battle. The profusion of volunteers for the army, in North and South alike, was only equalled by the almost complete absence of arms and other material essential to the existence of an army. Along with this went a similar lack of experience in the organization and conduct of armies. Only in the costly school of trial and error could capable leaders be found and disciplined armies created. Thus in the opening months of the war an impatient public opinion hopefully anticipated a prompt invasion of the South and an early end of the war, while the military authorities held back, arguing the need of better preparation for their task.

The situation in Michigan illustrates fairly closely the conditions elsewhere throughout the North. Prior to 1861, the state had twenty-eight volunteer militia companies with an aggregate strength of but 1241 officers and men. In response to Governor Blair's appeal, ten of these companies rushed to Fort Wayne in Detroit, where on May 1, 1861 they were mustered into the United States service as the First Michigan Infantry Regiment. On May 13 the regiment departed for Washington, to participate soon afterward in the battle of Bull Run, the opening combat of the war.

ON THE EVE OF BULL RUN

Washington,
Saturday, July 13th, 1861.

My Dear Minnie:

I have just found your dear and affectionate letter on my return from the other side. I have but a moment to thank you and to say that I am well, and I can find no paper at hand but this envelope.[1]

I am sure, however, that you will be glad to get even a line from me. I have been visiting all the camps on this and the Virginia side. There are over 80,000 men in camp within ten miles of Washington. Each camp is isolated and therefore the show is not great, but as you ride from one to the other for a whole day you become impressed with the immensity of the gathering.

I have seen our friends Lew Forsyth and wife and Cousin Marion but have not seen Cousin Maria yet. I expected to have been home today, but am waiting the passage of a law authorizing the appointment of generals. I have the promise of an appointment, but after all it depends much on the kind of law passed by Congress. I was very cordially received by the Secretary of War and by the President, and have made the acquaintance of a host of [illegible], generals, etc. etc., besides meeting scores I have known before. . . .

Your Affectionate Father,
A.S.W.

◈

Detroit, [Sept.] 28th, 1861.

My Dear Daughter:

I have just time to say that I shall (D.V.) leave . . . for Washington Monday evening and expect now to stop a few hours in Philadelphia on Wednesday next. The 8th Regiment went last night and Brodheads' cavalry go tonight. . . . Larned went last night with my staff, horses, and baggage. So we break up. Minnie will write you the news. Love to all.[2]

Your Affectionate Father,
A.S.W.

IN SEARCH OF A COMMAND

Washington, Oct. 4th, 1861.

My Dear Daughter Irene: [3]

I reached here all safe but hugely annoyed by crowded cars and drunken soldiers. Found my staff and Larned anxious for my arrival. Horses and baggage all arrived safe, and through the courtesy of Col. Rucker are safely deposited and stabled in his private quarters. [4]

Yesterday I occupied a hot day in the War Department and military offices, reporting myself and seeking directions for my brigade. I had an audience of Gen. Scott and was received very graciously and kindly. I have not yet seen Gen. McClellan. Indeed, he is not easily seen, being almost constantly in the saddle on the other side. I, of course, saw his Assistant Adjutant General and the Chief of his Staff, Gen. Marcy. [5] I expect an order today, but don't yet know my destination.

Yesterday I was much encouraged that I should have a full brigade of Michigan troops. Today it is intimated to me that I shall be sent to Banks' division. [6] He has no brigadier general and is posted, as you probably know, on the upper Potomac in the vicinity of Harpers Ferry. I only regret this because I fear I shall have no Michigan troops, and have command of strange regiments. However, we must make the best of a bad case, if it is a bad case. The matter, however, is not definitely settled. I have had a second interview with Gen. Marcy today on the subject. . . . I saw Mrs. Smith a moment yesterday. Kirby, who is now here, has the colonelcy of an Ohio regiment and is going to Columbus, Ohio. [7] Mrs. Smith will probably go with him and spend the winter in Cincinnati, where Kirby's residence will be ordered. . . .

Ever Your Affectionate Father.

◈

CAMP LIFE BEGINS

Camp near Darnestown, Md.,
Saturday night, Oct. 12th, 1861.

My Dear Daughter:

Here I am away up amongst the hills of Maryland about two miles from the Potomac and about twenty miles above Washington. Imagine a pretty high hill (mountains in our state), on top a thick wood, at the bottom a small rapid stream, a valley spreading out for a quarter of a mile or so and bounded on the opposite side by higher hills formed into projecting knobs by lateral ravines. On one of the largest of these is the encampment of Gen. Banks, staff and escort, foot and horse. On our hillside are my eight or ten tents, sheltered by the woods in the rear. Just within the woods are our servants' tents and farther in, the picket for our horses, sheltered as well as may be by a hedge of bushes and covered by one of our tent flies.

Nearby is William Dollarson's cooking apparatus.[8] Around about on the hills (all in sight save one) are the regiments of my brigade as follows: 2nd Massachusetts, Col. Gordon; 5th Connecticut, Col. Ferry; 28th New York, Col. Donnelly; 46th Pennsylvania, Col. Knipe; 19th New York, Maj. Ledlie; Co. A, Rhode Island Battery, Capt. Tompkins; in all, nearly 5,000 men.

The country round about is beautiful, varied into high hills and fertile valleys with numerous small, rapid, clear streams. Altogether it is a delightful spot, especially towards sundown when the bands of the regiments strike up for the evening parades and the hillsides in front are covered with moving bodies of troops and the bugle calls from the neighboring brigades float up the valleys and are echoed along the hillside.

It seems queer, though, and almost magical to be transported in such a brief time from a quiet home to this bustle and stir of battalions of armed men, where civil life is really hardly observable and military pomp and preparation cover everything, the cultivated and uncultivated land and man and beast, with the trappings of war. But you will ask, How did you get there? Well! To go back to my last letter to you from Washington, when I was in daily expectation of a brigade of Michigan troops. On Saturday last I received an order to report forthwith to Gen. Banks, with an intimation (to soften my disappointment) that Gen. Banks was in need of a brigadier, and that I would find a responsible command. So on Monday, as soon as we could gather together our tents and other necessaries, we mounted horse and with three wagons drawn by double mule teams set forward to our unknown destination. . . .

We had a slow and pleasant ride till towards evening when we were overtaken by a tremendous shower, and we took shelter for the night at a small village inn at Rockville. I never saw it rain harder, and the wind blew a tempest. It was a hard night for the poor soldiers, many of whom are out on picket guard all night without shelter. The next morning we started forward in a drizzle and reached Gen. Banks' headquarters about noon. On my way I rode off the line a few rods to visit Gen. Meade, who commands a brigade eight or ten miles below.[9]

We dined with Gen. Banks, who gave me orders for my brigade, and I started out to select a camping-ground, which I found without difficulty in the position I have attempted to describe.

We were strangers, and none of the regiments near offered me the least assistance. Gen. Banks promised to send me a detail of men but none came. So we all set to work, myself, Capt. Wilkins, Lt. Pittman, Larned, and the three servants, none of whom but Capt. Wilkins and myself had ever seen a tent pitched. However, we were all pretty snugly located before dark and William had opened our mess chest and prepared a very comfortable meal of broiled ham and soda biscuits, and upon this diet we were obliged to feed for a couple of days before we could find fresh meat or bread. The country people bring in nothing, being pretty much all Secessionists, and those disposed to sell have been fairly eaten out by our large army. Man and beast find small pickings. Our horses had a little poor hay for a day or so and then a little corn, but at length we have ferreted out the resources of the land and have meat for ourselves and oats and hay for the horses.

My Yorkshire proves a splendid animal, afraid of nothing and full of life and spirit. We are kept very busy in posting ourselves up with the brigade. I am in the saddle a good deal, visiting the several regiments. Capt. Wilkins is kept employed with a clerk and one or two other assistants and a mounted orderly in answering applications, making the daily details for guard, pickets, duty officers, recording orders, and generally providing for our large military family of 5,000 men, to say nothing of the hundreds of teams and horses. For the latter, especially, we have much trouble in providing day by day, forage being very scarce and very dear.

Our daily routine is: up at reveille (sunrise); William gives us a cup of strong coffee soon after and breakfast in an hour. By eight o'clock the reports begin to arrive from the several regiments, and then sergeant-majors [begin] to copy orders and the general applications for leave, furloughs, for quartermaster's or commissary's stores, for all kinds of wants. Orders from division headquarters follow, all to be copied, repeated in a new order, and distributed to the several regiments.

We have improvised a few desks out of packing boxes and on these we do most of our writing. Breakfast over, I mount (as soon as the consolidated report of all the regiments is made up and signed) to visit the regiments in turn. I do not get back much before dinner time. After dinner I am again in the saddle with some duty to do. In this way the days seem short, and by eight or nine o'clock we are all in bed.

We know little of what is passing beyond our immediate vicinity. The two other brigades of this division are commanded by Gens. Abercrombie and Hamilton.[10] They lie near at hand but neither have as large and, I think, not as good regiments as I have. You will see that I have troops from five different states, among them the famous Rhode Island Battery with James' rifled cannon. This company was at Bull Run battle and gained a good reputation. The 2nd Massachusetts is a splendid regiment; the colonel and lieut-colonel are both graduates of West Point. The 5th Connecticut is commanded by Col. Ferry, a member of Congress from that state, a man of great energy and industry but I think not much of a soldier.[11] The other regiments are tolerably well officered, and all but one have been in service since May.

Now Minnie dear, I have told you pretty much all I can think of about myself and my matters. Larned makes himself useful, but not exactly in the way I wish. I shall put him in the adjutant general's office. He prefers outdoors. He received your letter yesterday in which you mention an eight-page letter to me, which I grieve to say has not come to hand. I have not received a single letter from you nor from Irene since I left her, but my companions are in the same plight. Neither Capt. Wilkins nor Lt. Pittman have heard from their wives. It is strange how irregularly letters come to us here at home. It was better in Mexico. However, keep writing, I suppose they will turn up.

I commenced this letter last evening and am finishing it on a box upon which my early cup of coffee has made some blots. You must hardly expect a neat letter from camp. I fear this is scarcely legible. We have orders to hold ourselves in readiness to march within twenty-four hours and hence all writing places are occupied now as early as reveille. I think it more than probable we shall not move at all, but the preparation of two-days' cooked rations, all the fuss and bustle, is as necessary as though the march were certain. . . . We talk of you often in our Detroit mess. You are a great favorite with my staff officers, and Father, you know, never wearies hearing your praises.

Your Affectionate Father,
A.S.W.

❖

ROUTINE OF CAMP LIFE

Camp near Darnestown, Md.,
Oct. 16th, 1861.

My Dear Daughter: . . .

Your first letter was only received today by the hands of Larned, who after much perseverance got it out of the Washington Post Office. He went down last Monday with a train to get us some necessaries, but on arriving in Washington found that his memorandum was lost, so back he posted, arriving at camp about noon, and was off again mounted on horse-back at one o'clock. I was very much pleased with his perseverance and energy in the matter. I gave him your messages. He promises to write you on his return. I see by the New York papers that they have a report that Gen. Banks' Division has been attacked and badly cut up, all of which is without foundation. We have not been even threatened, unless an occasional shot across the river at our pickets can be called threatening, so you see you must not be alarmed at any rumors.

I have no idea that we shall be attacked until we cross the Potomac. We, none of us, can guess what our movements are to be. I have a fine brigade. One of the regiments, 2nd Massachusetts, is the best volunteer regiment I ever saw and drills like regulars. The 2nd Connecticut is under the command of Col. Ferry. The Rhode Island Battery has James' rifled cannon and is the same battery which gained distinction at Bull Run. The New York and the Pennsylvania regiments are well commanded and are making efforts to improve. On the whole, I am well-satisfied, though I should have preferred one or two regiments from Michigan.

We have had very fine weather for some days, with splendid moonlight nights. Within the hearing of my camp are probably eight or ten regiments, all with excellent bands, besides several camps of artillery, cavalry, and independent zouave companies with bugles and trumpets. In consequence, we have a profusion of music at all hours, but especially during the moonlight evenings. The hillsides and projecting knobs which lie around our circular-formed valley are covered with tents, and at night when the lights are lit and the camp fires blazing and the bands playing the scene is very striking and beautiful. I should like to transplant you here for an evening if I could safely send you back to Aunt Kate's for a lodging. I am sure you would enjoy the sight and the music, to say nothing of my society.

The country around us is much broken with hills and valleys. Some of the rides along the narrow bridle paths by the side of considerable streams are very romantic. I am a great deal in the saddle from necessity, and like it amazingly. Day before yesterday I rode over twenty-five miles and yesterday about fifteen to visit one of my regiments on detached service. In one of my rides I visited the camp of the 7th Michigan, Col. Grosvenor. It is about two miles towards the river from Poolesville. I was received with great eclat. You will remember this is one of the regiments in my camp at Fort Wayne. It is a very fine regiment.[12] The sergeants, and corporals, even, rushed out to greet and shake hands with me.

According to the custom of the army I am obliged to live and travel in considerable state, though you know I have not much fondness for the ceremonies of military life that have not immediate influence upon its efficiency and discipline. I have a guard detailed for me every day at my own camp by the several regiments, in turn. They turn out and present arms every time I leave or return. Behind me rides a mounted orderly, whenever I leave camp, and as soon as I approach the encampment of a regiment, the sentinels begin to pass the word, "Turn out the guard," "The Brigadier General." Out rolls the guard of a hundred men or so and I am obliged to ride along the front, cap in hand, to acknowledge the salutation, while the drummers beat a furious tattoo upon their drums and the guard presents arms. I go through this process at least once a day with all my regiments, and then leave instructions to "never mind the guard," which means do not turn out on my approach again today.

The details I have to attend to are very considerable, so much so that I have a clerk detailed besides my staff. All the issues from the quartermasters and commissaries I have to approve, all charges for courts martial, all applications for furloughs and leaves, and all reports. In short, everything for 5,000 men has to pass under my supervision, besides the daily detail of guards, officers of the day, etc. Still we have greatly simplified much of this circumlocution system and saved half of our labor. I find time after morning business to visit most of the regiments, to examine the condition of the camps, hospitals, kitchens, etc. Each morning my field officer of the day, whose duty it is to visit and supervise each camp night and day, makes me a long written report, and all his complaints and suggestions I generally attend to in person as the most effectual way of correcting error and improving matters generally. To do all this I am up at sunrise or thereabouts and to bed about nine o'clock, and during these moonlight nights about ten o'clock. . . .

Your Most Affectionate Father,
A.S.W.

◈

BEFORE THE BATTLE

Camp at Edwards Ferry,
Oct. 23rd, 1861.

My Dear Rene:

I am on the point of moving over with my brigade. Have been in the mud and rain forty-eight hours, mostly without sleep and marching by night. I have only time to enclose the money you asked for, and to say that if I fall or am taken prisoner you must help Larned to support yourself and Minnie. You are able and willing and full of energy and confidence. Larned is pretty well used up and nervous. He will write soon.

You will hear by telegraph if anything occurs, long before this reaches you. God bless you my daughter and have you always in his holy keeping.

Most Affectionately, Your Father,

A.S.W.

◈

DISASTER AT BALL'S BLUFF

Camp near Muddy Brook, Md.,

November 5, 1861.

My Dear Lew: [13] . . .

Now as to war matters. We are having the devil's own weather and have had since we were so suddenly woke up from our quiet camp near Darnestown. I made a forced march with my brigade, got orders while inspecting a regiment, left all standing, tents, hospitals, etc., with a camp guard, and commencing after dark I was at Edwards Ferry before daylight, having performed nearly twenty-five miles, part of the way in a cold rain and deep clay mud. Gen. Banks had no knowledge of the intended movement till 5 o'clock P.M. nor did any of us know of the disaster to poor Baker till we reached Poolesville, five miles from Edwards Ferry. Here I was taken to the telegraph office and shown Baker's full dress hat and uniform, two ball holes through the hat and several through the coat. His corpse lay in a house nearby.[14]

From this point to the Ferry the road was full of stragglers and ambulances with wounded. Not a man carried his arms. All professed to have thrown them into the river and swam for life. They told enormous stories, and very pitiable if true. Every man was the last of his company. Arriving at the ferry, we had a doleful position on the muddy banks, crowded with arriving troops, cold rain, and high winds. I posted my men in the woods, found Gens. Banks and Stone looking dolefully around a camp fire and waited till daylight to pass over my brigade.

When daylight came, I found the means of transit were two small boats and one canal boat, capable of carrying perhaps one hundred men and occupying an hour or so in being poled over by awkward boat-men. The river was much swollen and very rapid, about one-quarter mile broad or more, and in the misty, dull morning light it didn't look at all pleasant. Gen. Abercrombie's brigade was ahead of me, having come by the shortest route. I waited and waited in the rain till nearly 2 o'clock, when orders came to bivouac and but a few hours after came the sudden rattle of small arms and the booming of big guns from over the river. We had a stirring sight for a half hour or so, in full view from the high banks on our side. All at once the fight stopped, the guns ceased fire, and there was a painful silence over the other side, especially as the smoke settling down over the field, we could see nothing of the position of our troops. In a short time we learned that the enemy had fled, and subsequently we had positive intelligence that they lost sixty men killed in this short conflict.[15]

My brigade was ordered under arms again and soon we went on a double-quick to the ferry, the men cheering all the way, and consider-ing the weather, the march, the means of transportation, and all things else, were in excellent spirits, better, I confess, than I was, though I assumed an especial alacrity and good cheer at the prospect of passing over. We didn't get over, however, for the cavalry had possession of the boats and it was dark before even they could move. After some delay we were ordered back for the night.

The day following was a furious gale, so strong that only one or two boats crossed. Our poor fellows already over lay in the mud day and night without shelter and badly provisioned. We were hourly expecting an attack upon them and we had no means to reinforce them. I contrived to get over one company of sharpshooters to scout on the south side of Goose Creek, where we had not one man and from which direction our flank was exposed. There was a furious popping of skir-mishers all day and we could see bodies of their troops in position on the hills behind. My brigade was taken down to the ferry, my artillery embarked on the boats, and after dark I was ordered back again to remain in readiness to embark during the night. I tumbled myself onto my bed full-armed, expecting to be called at any moment. I did not awake till morning, when I found my scouting officer at hand to report that all our troops had recrossed and left the "sacred soil" to its own people.

Gen. McClellan had been in camp the day before all day. No general officer, unless Gen. Banks, knew his decision till it was carried out during the night by the withdrawal. During the gale of Wednesday I had put all my regiments in tents behind the first roll of the high bank, my wagon train having followed me up as I ordered and the same day my supply train arrived, so that my whole brigade was well provided. It was mighty cold, however, and I regret to say that few fences within a mile of Edwards Ferry had even a foundation rail left. We remained in camp within full reach of their guns and shells till Saturday, but as my brigade was in advance I took the precaution to send my whole wagon train (which with its hundreds of mules and heavy wagons is no joke in a stampede) five miles to the rear.

On Saturday (26th) we broke up and marched by the river road to this point, reaching this [place] after dark and encamping pell mell, weather raining, in an open space surrounded by woods of evergreens. I have since got all my regiments into the evergreens, well protected from the high winds, which blow furiously more than half the time. We are about a mile in direct line from the river, which my brigade has been picketing for nearly five miles on the banks of the canal, but which I have had narrowed down to two and a half miles. All the roads are also picketed, which besides the camp guards takes nearly one man in four of my command on duty every night.

Since coming to this camp, we have had two furious northeasters and last night ice formed very thick. All the troops of my brigade have overcoats, but the single blanket and such worn-out tents are poor protection. The men are suffering badly, though strange to say in this brigade we have less sickness than before marching to Edwards Ferry. The other brigades, which are encamped west of me in open and elevated plains, are suffering much more, and sickness has greatly increased and is increasing. As division officer of the day yesterday I had to visit every regiment of the three brigades and was in the saddle from 9 o'clock till sundown. I found one Indiana regiment without overcoats, and yet doing duty on the river as pickets. This is too bad and any country ought to be damned that suffers it.

We have not been molested from the other side. Their scouts and pickets show themselves, but scarcely a musket is fired. I go along the tow-path with as much feeling of safety as I should on the Erie Canal.

Yesterday, I went two or three miles down, part of the way with an escort of dragoons (my officer-of-the-day hangers-on) but received no recognition from our saluting friends opposite. Indeed, picket shooting is getting to be voted barbarous. Up at Edwards Ferry they exchange visits now, crossing over and having confabs. . . .

No one here (not [even] Gen. Banks) can guess what is to come next. We talk of winter quarters at Frederick, at Poolesville, at Rockville, at Washington, and now and then it is guessed that we are to follow the southern expedition. In the meantime, we watch the opposite shore, but I fear don't *pray* much, but rather swear. I shall not comment on the sad repulse at Conrad's Ferry near Edwards Ferry. I have my opinion of the whole movement—the originator, the motive, and the expectation. McCall was at Darnesville (nearly opposite our present camp) reconnoitering. Stone was at Poolesville. Baker was burning for a fight. A few horsemen crossed, rode towards Leesburg, and came back reporting no enemy at Leesburg or on the road. There seemed a golden chance to get ahead of McCall and take Leesburg by a simple march. One rickety boat transported over two or three small regiments and a few men [were] held ready to be passed over in an equally singular way at Edwards Ferry. It is plain that nobody expected to be driven back or come back in a hurry, for it was simply impossible to do so with the transit means at hand. Gen. Banks, fifteen to twenty miles distant, was not notified of the movement. Gen. McCall at Darnesville moving toward Leesburg was not notified, for on the same day he made a retrograde movement of twelve miles, thus leaving the enemy at liberty to go to Leesburg. Gen. McClellan was not notified till Baker was defeated. It was therefore plainly an unpremeditated and unprepared effort, and failed, as nine out of ten such hasty affairs will.

Who was to blame, I know not—but I do know that there is a mighty amount of stupidity in those papers who lay the affair to Gen. Banks. Gen. Stone's division is not under Gen. Banks' command. It is (like Gen. Banks') one division of Gen. McClellan's Army of the Potomac. On the very morning that Baker crossed, Gen. Banks was at my tent talking over the probabilities of crossing and expressed his opinion that no advance on the upper Potomac could be made till further movements were had before Washington. At 10 o'clock the same day, hearing that some movement was on foot above, he telegraphed and got answer that there was no intention of crossing, or something to that effect! This was received after Baker's column had actually in part crossed the river!

It was not till Baker was driven back that Gen. Banks was telegraphed to send one brigade to Conrad's Ferry and Hamilton's brigade (being nearest in position) was put in motion. At the same time the other two brigades were ordered to move to Seneca Ford, and I had actually marched nearly four miles toward the mouth of the Seneca before a second telegraph directed us all toward Poolesville and Edwards Ferry. My night march was increased nearly eight miles by this operation. Our editors seem to speak as if Gen. Banks commanded the whole line of the upper Potomac. It is not so. McCall commands one division below—partly over the river. Banks comes next and Stone one above, each three brigades, but there was no 25,000 men at Edwards Ferry, nor half of that number. There is a great overestimating of troops on this line. The regiments are greatly reduced in number and some never had over 750 men. If the estimates made of troops around Washington are equally erroneous then indeed there is good cause to remain stationary. Besides, our troops are miserably armed. Our fine 7th Regiment, Col. Grosvenor, which was across the river at Edwards Ferry, is armed with the Belgian rifle, not one in ten of which can be discharged. I have one regiment with guns of three different calibers and I found a regiment yesterday with guns of four different calibers. What are we to think of such indifference to the effectiveness of troops? This whole matter is weekly reported by me, and I doubt not sent up. But in truth we have no good guns, and to all uses of war, we should be just as strong with half the men we have well-armed as we are now. But enough. I am sending you an intolerable letter. Give much love to Jule and Syl and Cousin Maria and Mary, and to little Jule one of my provoking kisses. I shall hope to hear from you often—give us the little news. Our letters are provokingly slow, but they do come. . . .

Yours Affectionately,
Alph.

P.S. Don't mention what I have said about Banks' telegraphs or our forces.

Can't stop to read over. A. S. Williams.

ALL QUIET ALONG THE POTOMAC

Camp near Muddy Brook, Md.,
Nov. 9th, 1861.

My Dear Daughter:

I wrote you a pretty long letter a few days since in which I promised photographs of my headquarters' log cabin. The weather has been so stormy since that I have not been able to get them printed. We have had two violent easterly gales with rain followed by high northeasterly winds, very cold and disagreeable.

Yesterday we had a fine day, quite Indian summer like. The day before was clear but cool with high winds. As division officer of the day I rode all day from 9 A.M. till sundown, visiting all the regiments of the three brigades, the several picket guards on the road, the cavalry and artillery camps, and finishing up by following the river pickets for miles (along the tow-path of the canal, which runs on the margin of the Potomac) partly on horseback and partly on foot. My brigade has been picketing the river bank for nearly five miles, from Great Falls to the mouth of the Muddy Branch. About 200 men are put on each afternoon carrying 24 hours' rations and returning the following evening after being relieved.

It is a hard duty, as the poor fellows are not allowed fires and the weather has been very inclement. Still they go on with wonderful cheerfulness. There is a strange excitement in the prospect of shooting at one another across the river. We have had, however, very little picket firing and do not encourage it. The Rebels appear on the opposite bank, but so long as they remain quiet we do not trouble them. The river has been unusually high, overflowing the banks of the canal and wholly submerging the island. Since I wrote you last (I think) Gov. Blair and suite paid me a visit and dined with us.[16] . . .

Dr. Antisell joined us as brigade-surgeon a few days ago. He is a very agreeable and intelligent addition to our mess.[17] Capt. Whittlesey has received his appointment as brigade quarter-master and been ordered to report to me, so you see I am getting my staff filled up pretty much as I wished.[18] The young officer who is acting-assistant-commissary of subsistence is from my native village of Deep River and is a most excellent and efficient officer. He has the strong recommendations of the regular commissary and will probably get his appointment and be permanently put on duty with me. This, with the appointment of one more aide (which I can make from lieutenants) completes my staff. I expect Capt. Whittlesey some time next week.

All my regiments are now encamped in evergreen woods, except the 19th New York, which is two or three miles distant guarding the division supply train. They are very comfortably located and much less exposed than the regiments of other brigades, encamped on high table lands open to all the high winds of the season. Two of my regiments have cut out the small scrub pines and grubbed up the roots making a square completely hedged in, in which they pitch their tents, and on the edge of the square piled up the bushes so as to completely cut off the cold winds. Almost every tent has its fire, which is built in the mouth of a trench in the front. The trench is carried through the tent covered over with flat stones and earth and terminating behind in a turf chimney surmounted by a barrel to increase the draft. In this way the fire is carried under the tent; the stones, once heated, keep up the warmth a long time, and a tent is made very comfortable. Others dig deep cellars and build regular fire-places, carrying the chimney through the ground under the wall of the tent to some distance away and use the barrel for a chimney.

In one regiment (28th), which is encamped among trees of larger growth, the men are building log huts along the line of streets. If we are left in position long this whole regiment will be hutted. I have a busy brigade and am much pleased with it. I fancy it is far the best in the division in all respects, in drill, policing, good order, and cheerful discharge of any duty. In marching, I believe (since my forced march to Edwards Ferry through the rain and mud) that I can beat any troops in the Army of the Potomac. . . .

I should like to visit you at Christmas and perhaps we may be so placed in winter quarters that I can get away. While, however, operations are liable to be active and we are still in the field I do not like to be absent one day. All the other generals of this division have been away and both, I believe, are in Washington now. I intend to stick close to the camp till the prospect of any movement this season is closed. There is some talk about winter quarters. Gen. Banks has intimated that we shall move soon, but I think he is not much better advised than the rest.

It has been thrown out that we may follow the southern expedition as a reinforcement. I think all movements are in suspense awaiting information from that source.

In the meantime we hear, day after day, the booming of cannon above and below us and our minds are kept conjecturing "what is up." Yesterday, all day, we heard reports of heavy guns, and a few days before we were sure that Gen. McCall was engaged below Danesville. Dr. Antisell, who came up, says the rumor below was that all our division was fighting the enemy and that the cannon reports came from our direction. In the meantime, around the whole front of our encampment the rolling drill ground, covering a space of several hundred acres, is on every pleasant day a scene of the most lively and pleasant kind. Several regiments are engaged in all kinds of drill, some by battalion, some by companies, some skirmishing, some forming squares, some charging in line of battle; in short, employed in all manner of maneuvers. While the regiments are marching out and in, the bands play, and occasionally, when the companies are at rest. This scene begins at 8 o'clock A.M. when all regiments "mount guard" and all bands play in succession. Then comes the drill by companies till near 11 o'clock, then for two or three hours the space is cleared, excepting [for] straggling details and mounted orderlies. In the afternoon the regiments appear again by battalion, all the bands playing and the sounds very discordant sometimes, from the quantity of instruments from different directions. In a few moments, the whole space will be covered by the changing and moving masses and detachments of men, and the sound of many voices giving hoarse and loud orders takes the place of musical instruments.

Towards sundown the drills stop and the music begins again, till the regiments form for evening parades skirting along the circular line of the evergreen woods, and all in full view of our log-cabin home. The scene is then most animating and cheerful. I often wish you were here to enjoy it, knowing your fondness for this military display and for the music of bands. In the evening, before tattoo, the bands generally play again, in turn, and now and then one comes round to serenade the General.

Tattoo comes and then taps, all lights are extinguished, all noise hushed, except the outrageous braying of mules or the more agreeable neighing of horses or perhaps the call of some far-off sentinel, who calls loudly the number of his post, with a yell for "Corporal of the Guard." Then may be heard in the stillness of the night the tramp of horses, some officer, with his escort, going the "grand rounds"; or perhaps a single horseman can be heard dashing furiously over the hills in the direction of division headquarters, coming as if he bore a message of vast importance, which, though often delivered at midnight, turns out to be nothing more than a leave of absence or a detail for next day, or some other insignificant matter which might as well have been delivered next day.

When the days are fair, I ride with some of my staff over the country to get familiar with the many byroads and bridle paths. It is a country full of commanding views and pleasant prospects. Almost every hill one ascends gives him a far-off view of hill and dale and river. From some we get long peeps into Virginia. We have on these highest points regular signal stations, with a corps of officers in permanent charge. Communications are made at fixed hours with Washington below and as high up as Point of Rocks and Harpers Ferry—in the daytime, by a series of flags, and by night by varied-colored lamps, after the system invented by Major Ayers, who is in command of the corps.

The highest point for signals is Sugar Loaf Mountain, which rises some few miles above Edwards Ferry in the shape of a loaf of sugar, several hundred feet above any surrounding hill. It is a prominent and conspicuous point from the whole line of the river. From the station at its top one can plainly see Leesburg on one side and Frederick, Maryland, on the other. The next station below is a hilltop near our camp. To gain a higher elevation, an old dry tree on the hill is used and ascended by ladders. Away up in its branches they have fixed a sort of nest where through the strong telescopes used one can see away down to Chain Bridge and away up to Edwards Ferry, the camps of Gen. Stone's division being plainly visible.

It is, indeed, a grand prospect, and along the whole distance long patches of the Potomac gleam out towards a pleasant sunset, seeming like silver lakes. Everything, of a quiet afternoon, such as we have had several times, looks so peaceful and home-like, the cattle grazing on the hillsides, the smoke curling from the many farmhouses, that one can hardly realize that thousands are armed for battle on either side of that pleasant river and amid those quiet valleys. But so it is, and one's heart feels heavy in the thought that it is so.

You will be glad to hear that my horse is doing finely, notwithstanding his outdoor exposure to rain and wind, and his occasional deprivation of hay or oats. The whole division is much troubled to procure forage. I am obliged to send the wagons of my brigade 25 miles for hay and oats. The roads are now so heavy that the mules consume much of the load before they return, or on the return. When you reflect that we have in the division about a thousand four-mule-wagons, besides the horses of officers, artillery, cavalry, and various staff departments, you will comprehend somewhat the difficulty we have to feed them. The country immediately about us is not very productive, and the farmers have been pretty closely skinned and complain bitterly that they are often obliged to sell at prices fixed by the government. I fear their complaints are well founded, but "necessity knows no law." Still, I think the government should make liberal prices.

There is a great rush to me at each new encampment for guards for houses. I have invariably tried to protect the people, and always send out small pickets to houses near our camps; and yet, in spite of all endeavors and all efforts of commanders of regiments, there is a good deal of rascality done; mainly, however, I think, by the hordes of unenlisted teamsters, drovers, and hangers-on, who are a necessary appendage to an army. I am greatly annoyed by daily complaints and try hard to correct the evil and do justice where damage is done. I fear, however, we are suffering the usual consequences of an armed occupation, making more enemies than friends. Indeed, I fear there is not much real loyalty in this part of Maryland, and that the people would greatly rejoice to see us driven out. They *talk* very patriotic. . . .

Ever Your Affectionate Father,
A.S.W.

◈

ARMY DRILLS AND NEEDS

Camp near Muddy Branch, Md.,
Nov. 24th, 1861.

My Dear Daughter:

Your last letters have reached me with much better regularity and all have come to hand. The last, with the enclosure of your school report, was very gratifying. . . . I was much pleased with Aunt Kate's letter. I shall answer it soon, but at present my time is much occupied. I have, in consequence, somewhat delayed writing you or Irene longer than usual, and I shall be obliged now to make a short letter. I could write you in the evening, but that our small log cabin, 12 by 15, is full of the desks of staff officers and their assistants, who keep up a constant talk about forage, rations, abstracts, requisitions, claims, prices, supplies, and the like with the regimental quartermaster and others who seek the night to make arrangements for the succeeding day. Add to this a very smoky chimney and all the [illegible] of a crowded cabin, with all writing tables occupied, and you can imagine I have a poor chance for letter writing.

The past has been a tolerably pleasant week and I have improved it by a review of my brigade and brigade drills, in which all my regiments are maneuvered together. We make a great show in these "evolutions de luxe," especially as they are mainly done in double-quick, and the regiments being very well drilled the movements are made with wonderful precision and accuracy. Would you not like to see four or five regiments closing up into mass, then deploying into line of battle, then moving rapidly to the front in "echelons" forming squares all in one grand oblong parallelogram, then separating into squares of single regiments, oblique and direct; in short, taking all manner of offensive and defensive positions and all moved without confusion or disorder and controlled as by a single thought to the same end?

Mine is the only brigade in this division which has these drills, and consequently we have a large crowd of spectators from the three brigades and from the host of civilian employees of the army. It was quite an imposing affair, *we* all think. I found a large field of many hundred acres where I could form all my regiments in one line. After marching in quick time, each regiment marched past in double-quick to the music of its own band. It was very handsomely done, for all my regiments but one have been nearly five months in service and move on the double-quick with the regularity of veterans. They trot off with knapsack packed, canteen and haversack and cartridge box, with forty rounds of ball cartridges, as if nothing was on their backs. On the whole, you see, I am well pleased with my brigade, and what is perhaps more important, I think the brigade is well pleased with me, but this may be fancy.

We have all been expecting to move from our present position to Rockville or Frederick for winter quarters. It is rumored today, however, that we shall not go into winter quarters at present, but must hold on here to await events. We are in a sorry position. The roads, even the best ones, are almost impassable, and the new ones cut for military purposes and to get into our camps are for all practicable value quite so. In riding in yesterday from the camp of one of my regiments I found lots of mule wagons stalled in the mud, some with broken tongues and others badly disabled in other ways. If this is so while the weather is comparatively good, what may we not expect as soon as the winter days begin in reality?

So far the season has been, for a week at a time say, one day heavy rain, the next a cold, strong north wind, gradually lessening into a tolerably mild Indian summer day. This would end in another heavy north-east rain. Thus we seemed to be just in that point where a constant strife is going on between the north and south winds. Tonight we have a regular snow storm with a northerly wind. My heart bleeds for the poor fellows picketted along the river with little shelter, many without blankets, and some without overcoats. I have been unremitting in my efforts since I joined the brigade to get all this necessary clothing supplied and have sent all my colonels to Washington and some to their states to get overcoats and blankets. They have been promised over and over again. Many have been supplied, but not all.

There seems [to be] a great want of foresight somewhere, a great negligence in preparing for the future. I don't pretend to say where, but I know that our volunteers could be clothed and ought to be. Their exposure in this weather all through these stormy nights is bad enough with the best clothing, but without overcoats and blankets it is barbarous and will cost the government in pensions and hospitals ten times the

value of good warm clothing. If mittens are not provided before the winter cold comes, thousands will be disabled by frozen fingers and hands.

My regiments have very bad tents, but they are making all sorts of huts and warm shelters for winter and when inside their tents will get along pretty well, I think. Most of them have got fireplaces inside, so have regular log houses, others have mounted tents on log basements. It is quite a curiosity to go through the camps and see the various devices to keep warm. With new tents we could keep warm all winter, I think.

I fear you were too much alarmed at the Edwards Ferry affair. The exposure to me is not very great, and what I most feared in that river crossing was that we should have hard work to get back if Beauregard had sent, as he could, a large force to attack us. But he did not, and we, fortunately, did not stay to give him a chance. Leesburg is about as near Centerville (the Rebels' large army) as Washington. Of course we could hardly expect to stay long at Leesburg without a big battle.

I have not yet sent the photographs; I am waiting to get one of myself and some others. If I don't get them this week I will send those I have by express. Love to all. I have forgotten to tell you how useful we have found your "housewife." [19] Capt. Wilkins and Mr. Pittman [20] talk of you often and wish to be remembered. Capt. Whittlesey has not yet arrived; we expect him soon. I should like to send my things to Annie to be overhauled. I think she would find some things out of sort. Larned has no "housewife." Can't you make him one? I will write you again in a few days and talk about Christmas.

Your Affectionate Father,
A.S.W.

◈

REMOVAL TO WINTER QUARTERS

Headquarters, 3rd Brigade,
Camp near Frederick, Dec. 7th, 1861.

My Dear Daughter:

A letter from Aunt Patty received just before I left Camp at Muddy Branch says that you had not heard from me for four weeks,

If this is so, my letters must have miscarried, for the longest interval has not been over two weeks. I must have written you at least five letters from Camp Muddy Branch while we were there but about four weeks. You must not think it strange nor that you are forgotten if my letters are very irregular, for I have not only constant occupations but subjects of incessant thought. It is an easy matter for you, who have literally nothing that *demands* daily attention, to write to your friends. If you had the care and supervision of a town of 4,000 people you would find the time for writing not easily got at.

As I wrote you in my last, we have changed camps and I am now perched up in the hills which form part of the chain of the Blue Ridge. We are westward of the city of Frederick about three and one-half miles. Back of us lies a high range of wooded hills, and as we have the southern slope on a gravelly soil, with several small mountain streams running close to us, with plenty of wood, we can say that our camp for cold weather is most eligibly located. My headquarters are in a farmer's house, nicely situated, with a two-storied corridor or stoop running the whole length of the house. We have one large room for office and eating-room, one bedroom (small) for myself and Larned, and one large one for my staff. For the first time in two months I have slept in a room and on a bed! So rapidly do we acquire new habits of life that it seems strange, and as the weather is very fine I almost regret my tent and field bed!

The country about us is exceedingly beautiful and picturesque. We are just in the first hills of the mountain range and my regiments are encamped up a narrow ravine or valley which runs east and west into the ridge, called Catoctin Mountains. East of us, perhaps fifteen or twenty miles, is another range of mountains or high hills called Parr's Ridge. Between these two ranges lies a most beautiful and fertile valley, rolling in great undulations and cultivated to the highest perfection. In the center of this valley is the ancient and rather fine-looking city of Frederick, a place of several thousand inhabitants, renowned for the wealth of its citizens and for its Secession proclivities. At a distance, its lofty spires and its long range of cement[?] buildings and other public edifices give it a very picturesque appearance. From our headquarters we can overlook a greater part of this valley, and the city, though distant over three miles, seems (especially, through the present hazy atmosphere) to be almost within a stone's throw.

So much for my location: We broke up camp on the morning of the

4th inst. (Wednesday) moving with all my regimental and brigade supply-trains of over a hundred four-horse wagons. The other brigades had moved each a day before the other. The roads had been terrifically bad, so deep in mud that we found it difficult to get forage for our numerous cattle. But fortunately the weather became freezing cold and the road hard, but as rough as the popular song makes the road over Jordan. However, I made fifteen miles the first day, bringing up wagons and everything promptly and encamping long before sundown on a superb ground on the banks of the Little Seneca, on the "Mudpike" from Rockville to Frederick.

The next morning we were on the march a little after sunrise. The day was beautiful, a veritable Indian summer day, and I anticipated a pleasant march. Before reaching the village of Clarksburg, however, we began to be annoyed by the stragglers of other regiments which had preceded us one day. Presently we overtook the wagon train of an entire regiment, which had stalled or been neglected on the way. You will think that passing a few wagons is no great matter, but if you had had a little experience in getting heavily-laden vehicles stretching out three miles or more over roads running over abrupt and rocky hills and through deep, narrow gullies and ravines you would have some appreciation of the labor and delay.

We succeeded, however, in passing the train, but as we proceeded we began to meet long lines of returning wagons. The stragglers of one regiment (the 1st Maryland) unattached to any brigade, fairly lined the road, drunken and furious with liquor and committing all sorts of depredations and outrages. In the villages especially, the rum-shops had all been taken possession of, and the most violent conduct was being exhibited. I had no empty wagons and could not encumber my command with drunken prisoners, so all I could do was to clear out and shut up the groggeries and drive the rascals out of the villages into the country.

I was necessarily annoyed all day, and as savage and angry as a tiger, especially as those drunken stragglers were most intent upon giving their rum canteens to my men and occasionally manifested their high regard by a grand discharge of loaded muskets, fired without especial regard to range or aim. On one occasion a wagon-load fired a volley at some of their comrades lying drunk by the roadside. Fortunately the balls took effect on the rails instead of the persons of their friends. I expected to hear of wounds and loss of life, but I believe nothing was killed but hogs, dogs, and cattle.

In spite of all these annoyances and delays I reached the Monocacy Junction (three miles from Frederick) with my whole command about 3 o'clock P.M. The wagons of the regiments, with all the tents, forage, etc., did not get up at all, and these regiments were obliged to bivouac in a pretty frosty night without shelter of any kind. We found quarters in a nice house and I (for the first time in two months) had a room and a great, broad bed! All by myself! Our host and hostess were very kind and agreeable, the latter a remarkably pretty woman, and as I had not seen a passable face for a long time I enjoyed the sight as a novel entertainment.

Our trains got up in the night and we were off again soon after sunrise. I halted outside Frederick, closed up my ranks, and marched through the city in grand style, colors flying and music playing. They complimented us by saying that we made a fine show, much better than the other brigades. I rode at the head of the brigade with my staff of six. The whole population was out, and the flag of our Union was displayed very generally.

Today I have been into Frederick for a short time on business and to report to Gen. Banks, who has his headquarters there. I found the place very ancient in appearance, but with a good many elegant private residences. I hear the people are very hospitable, and that if we seek it or assent to it we shall be very generously entertained here. As for myself, I think I shall desire to keep very quiet. I have lost pretty much all desire for the gay *monde*.

I made the acquaintance yesterday of a Gen. Klemmer, who lives some ten miles east and is one of the active and prominent Union men of the state. I was introduced to a good many other gentlemen, but I was deeply impressed with the idea that while they regret the disseverance of the Union and are willing to treat us kindly, they have, after all, no very strong feeling for our side, believing, probably, that all hope of a restoration of the Union as it was is gone. However, I shall probably be here some weeks and shall see and know more. Nobody seems to know our future destination. Of course, there are all kind of rumors; for going south and going west; for breaking up the division and sending us all ways. I think nothing definite has as yet been decided, but that toward spring we shall be reinforced and sent down the valley of the Shenandoah, or toward western Virginia.

But this is all guess. I don't think Gen. Banks knows his future movements. He is not very communicative, even to those near him in command, and although always pleasant and courteous, he cannot be said to be a companionable person. I think he is oppressed somewhat with a position novel and untried, and full of responsibilities of a character so different from those he has had heretofore that he feels ill at ease. He is an officer of excellent judgment and good sense, but not familiar with military routine or etiquette, and he has for an adjutant general an officer who knows less of military [life] and [is] of less experience than he. I regard the whole state of things as unfortunate for Gen. Banks and, perhaps, *en consequence,* unfortunate for us who have the honor to command his brigades.

I think the army, and perhaps the political influence at Washington, is against him. You know that old army officers think that no man can be qualified to command who is not a graduate of West Point and has not spent at least fifteen years as a *clerk* in an army bureau or on duty at a frontier post as a lieutenant to a command of a dozen men, where there are no books, no drill, no military duty, nothing but a vast amount of whisky drinking, card playing, and terrific, profane swearing; and where, as a consequence, men forget in a year or so all they could learn in four years, and acquire habits of the most indolent and unambitious and dissolute kind. And yet, with honorable exceptions, such are the men who, in the eyes of one another at least, and I fear, too, of a good share of the public, are fit to command our armies or have any responsible positions in this war.

At least, the whole West Point influence is against any man who did not happen to spend four years of his life in that institution, and any man who has been there, even for a few months, no matter what his natural stupidity or his indolent, inefficient habits, his ignorance acquired or habitual, is fit for all responsibility and all power. I have seen much of these men and I confess to a most ineffable disgust with the whole thing. I begin to think that all the prominent acquisition obtained there is superciliousness, arrogance, and insolence. Of course, there are noble exceptions, men of military taste and ambition, to whom that institution has been the alphabet of knowledge they have gained afterwards and who would have been under any circumstances good military men. But to set it down as certain that a graduate of West Point is *ipso facto* a good officer would be like pronouncing every graduate of Harvard or Yale a man of learning—or classical knowledge—or a learned lawyer, or doctor. As these graduates forget their Latin and Greek, so these West Pointers forget their tactics, their strategy, their logistics, or exchange what little they knew for skill in whist, euchre, monte, and billiards. But I have unintentionally run into a disquisition.

The other brigades of Gen. Banks' division are east of Frederick about the same distance that mine is west, so we are quite six miles apart. . . . .

Your Affectionate Father,

A.S.W.

◈

WINTER QUARTERS AT FREDERICK

Camp near Frederick, Md.,
Dec. 18th, 1861.

My Dear Daughter:

We received an order last night, or rather early this morning, to be ready for a rapid march toward Williamsport. As we were all unpacked and housed, in fact, quite settled down in our farm-house headquarters, it created a good deal of bustle and confusion. However, we were all ready bright and early, when a countermand was received with orders to be on the alert. Our domestic arrangements, however, are left in great disorder while we await the next movement. As I may be on the road in a short time I embrace the leisure of suspended orders to write you. You will know by telegraph long before this reaches you whether we have left Frederick or not. So you can direct your letters as heretofore— "Headquarters, 3rd Brigade, Gen. Banks' Divn. near Frederick."

We have had two weeks of very charming weather which our major general has improved by a series of reviews of all his brigade and independent regiments and detachments. My brigade was reviewed last

Friday, that is four regiments, the artillery having been detached to be consolidated into one battalion.

I see that the Baltimore papers give us a very favorable notice. I send you a slip from the *Sun*. After the review I drilled the whole brigade together in some very showy movements, such as forming squares by regiments in echelon on the double-quick; forming oblique squares of battalions; marching to the front on double-quick of battalions in mass, and divers such things which none of the other brigades had attempted. I also passed the general on the second time at double-quick, each battalion closed in mass and taking the double-quick step from its own music. On the whole, we of the 3rd Brigade think we rather excelled in the maneuvers, though the 1st had better ground and had just secured their new uniforms.

I accompanied Gen. Banks as a part of his cortege in all the reviews. His retinue, made up of the brigadier generals, his own large staff, and the brigade staff, with a large escort of cavalry, made a very showy cavalcade. Most of the officers were in full dress, epaulettes and chapeaus. I went each time in my simple shoulder straps and un-dress cap. At my own review, I came out in full feather, with my full regulation dress: chapeau, yellow sash, epaulettes, red second[?] belt, and all. As everybody seemed bent on "fuss and feathers" I thought I would show them that we were provided with the article! It was quite an accident that I had them, as I have no great fancy for the pomp of full dress, but, on the whole, I am rather glad I was prepared.

Since I wrote you, Col. Brodhead, 1st Michigan Cavalry, has joined our division. He is encamped on the other side of Frederick, about six miles from us. I have been to see him once. His regiment is finely mounted and he seems to have a fine lot of men. I fear they know, as yet, very little of cavalry drill. Indeed, I doubt if any of the large drafts of cavalry will be of much service, except as outposts, escorts, patrols, and the like. However, I suppose the government knows where to place its 60,000 cavalry.[21]

I have been so busy I have not seen much of Frederick or its people. I probably shall not, as I am from three to four miles away. I have, however, mounted on a bright sunny day the apex of a mountain knob, one of the highest of the Catoctin Range, and had a most extensive prospect of the two broad valleys on each side of that range of mountains. The one east (in which Frederick lies) as seen from this elevation of from 1,500 to 2,000 feet was exceedingly vast and impressive. The Eastern Range, which down in the valley seems high and broken, looks from my mountain peak like a gentle and gradual swelling up of the surface into a smooth ascent. Down south towards the Potomac is the Sugar Loaf, which seems to terminate that range. All between, for miles and miles up and down, are the square lots of the cultivated farms (green now with winter wheat) and the white farmhouses, looking in the distance and in the bright sunlight very neat and attractive.

On the other side of the Catoctin we had the smaller but equally beautiful valley which lies between it and the South Range. In its center is the neat and considerable village of Middletown, and far off in the southwest the mountain gap through which flows the Potomac at Harpers Ferry. The famous Maryland Heights, which has been the scene of various conflicts, looms up just beyond the river-gap. So much for scenery.

I am sorry I shall not be able to be with you for Christmas. . . .

Love to all. Larned promised, and I thought did write you all about our Thanksgiving under canvas. It was no grand affair, but we had turkeys and chickens, and William made a big effort. . . .

Your Very Affectionate Father,
A.S.W.

◈

A MILITARY EXECUTION

Headquarters, 3rd Brigade,
Near Frederick, Md., Dec. 23, 1861.

My Dear Daughter:

I wrote you a few days ago, I think, while under orders and expecting to be off at once for Williamsport, Md. Since then the order has been countermanded, but we are held subject to a movement at once when ordered. The weather, in the meantime, which has been spring-like since we arrived, has changed to the very most tempestuous, snowing, sleeting, raining, freezing, and altogether of the most un-

43

pleasant character. My poor fellows are badly prepared for it, as we have been expecting daily to move and but little "hutting" has been done in some of the regiments, in expectation of going away soon. Besides this, our hundreds of public horses are in the open air, exposed to sleet and cold rain, freezing as it falls. One such day will cost the government more than lumber to cover the whole army would. There will be hundreds of horses and mules dead tomorrow morning. The very high wind and low temperature will make sad havoc. . . .

To multiply the depth of a "blue Monday," we had an execution by hanging a private of my brigade on the parade ground today at 2 P.M. The culprit was named Dennis Lanaghan. While on a march just three months ago, he deliberately loaded a musket and shot the major of his regiment, the 46th Pennsylvania, simply because the major had compelled him to follow a wagon, and on his refusing had tied a rope to him for a short time. He was partly intoxicated at the time, but when sober was a very bad man. He has been in the hands of the provost guard of the division ever since, and after one or two trials set aside for irregularity in the order organizing the court, he was finally condemned a few weeks since.

I received an intimation for the first time yesterday that he was to be executed today, and this morning a party from Frederick began putting up the scaffold on a knoll in the center of the field we use for drills. At 12 o'clock I received the notification of the execution. The unpleasant office was performed by the provost marshall, and my brigade was present only as spectators. The day, as I have mentioned, was half-sleety, half-snowy, and with a high, cold wind. The ceremonies were very short. The rope was adjusted, a Catholic priest whispered something to the prisoner, a black fellow pulled the cord and let fall the drop. The man fell about two feet and literally died without a struggle. There was but an almost imperceptible drawing up of his legs and not a movement besides. The troops marched off leaving a small guard, and the affair was all over in ten or fifteen minutes.[22] . . .

On Wednesday is Christmas. I have been thinking that we have never before been absent from one another at Christmas. Rene and Larned have been away, but I think we have always been together. The day to me is full of associations. Happily for you, while you can remember the happy scenes of the past, you can look joyfully to the future. I have reached that age when "Merry Christmas" has no cheerful sound, but is rather full of sad remembrances of the many, many dear ones who used to enjoy the festive days with me but are here no more. In short, my dear Minnie, I have got so old that I begin to live in the past and hardly take into account the future on earth. But it gives me pleasure to see you merry and cheerful, and I most cordially wish you a Merry Christmas and a Happy New Year. . . .

Believe me as ever, Your Affectionate Father,

A——

1. The letter was written on both sides of a split-open envelope. Here, as elsewhere throughout the letters, as far as practicable, private and personal details have been deleted.

2. Although this letter was dated August 28, accompanying information discloses that it was actually written a month later. The official *Record of Service of Michigan Volunteers in the Civil War, 1861– 1865* (hereafter cited as *Record of Service of Michigan Volunteers*) discloses that Colonel Brodhead's First Michigan Cavalry left Detroit for Washington on September 29, 1861 and that the Eighth Infantry Regiment, mustered at Detroit on September 23, departed for Washington on the 27th of this month. General Williams' succeeding letter of October 4, announcing his then recent arrival in Washington, harmonizes with the supposition that he left Detroit on Monday, September 30. The following Wednesday, when he planned to be in Philadelphia for a few hours, fell on October 2, and the letter of October 4 states that he had spent the preceding day at the War Department.

3. From long-hand copy; original manuscript missing.

4. Daniel Henry Rucker (1819–1910) of the Grosse Ile Rucker-Macomb family. He entered the army in 1837, served in the Mexican War, and in the Civil War attained the rank of major general. The daughter of his second wife, Irene Curtis Rucker, became the wife of General Philip H. Sheridan.

5. For General Randolph B. Marcy (1812–87) see the *Dict. Am. Biog.* He was General McClellan's father-in-law.

6. Nathaniel P. Banks of Massachusetts, politician and Civil War soldier, under whom General Williams was about to serve. For a sketch of his career see *Dict. Am. Biog.*

7. A letter of General Williams to his daughter, Irene, written July 24, 1855, states that Mrs. Smith, widow of Captain E. Kirby Smith who was killed at Molino del Rey in 1847 is momentarily expected on a visit, and that "young" Kirby, evidently her son, now at West

Point, will accompany her. The son, Joseph Lee Kirby Smith graduated from the Academy in the class of 1857. He was appointed colonel of the Forty-third Ohio Regiment on September 28, 1861 and died at the age of twenty-six on October 12, 1862 from wounds received at Corinth, October 3–4. According to the *Dict. Am. Biog.*, Confederate Lieutenant General Edmund Kirby-Smith was a younger brother of Captain E. Kirby Smith and thus was an uncle of our present subject. Various allusions in the letters of General Williams disclose that Mrs. Smith was an old-time family friend.

8. The 1861 *Detroit Directory* lists George W. Dollarson, colored, as a baker, and Mrs. Dollarson of the same address as an embroiderer. One may surmise that William was their son.

9. George Gordon Meade, subsequently commander of the Army of the Potomac and victor of Gettysburg.

10. General John J. Abercrombie, a graduate of West Point in the class of 1822, a veteran of the Mexican War and of long years of frontier service, and Charles S. Hamilton, a West Point graduate of the class of 1843. For their military careers see George W. Cullum, *Biographical Register of Officers and Graduates of the U.S. Military Academy at West Point. . . .*

11. Colonel Orris S. Ferry was a lawyer who had been a Republican member of Congress from 1859 to 1861. Following the war he was a member of the Senate until his death, November 21, 1875.

12. The Seventh Michigan Infantry, chiefly composed of militia companies from various towns, was mustered into service at Monroe on August 22, 1861 and left the state for the seat of war on September 5. Of its total number of enlistments throughout the war (1375) slightly more than one-half (691) were casualties from wounds, diseases, etc. Over 13 percent (183) were killed in action or died as the result of wounds received.

13. Lewis Allen of Detroit. His wife (Julia Larned Allen) and General Williams' deceased wife were sisters.

14. Edward D. Baker, prominent as an orator and politician, and a personal friend of President Lincoln. The battle of Ball's Bluff, October 21, in which he was killed, was a very minor military operation. Coming soon after Bull Run, however, and like that battle a Union defeat, it had important consequences. General Stone, who dispatched his troops across the Potomac without orders from General McClellan, was arrested, imprisoned, and officially disgraced. The popular demand for a scapegoat induced Congress to create the Committee on the Conduct of the War, which until the end of the war maintained a vigilant oversight of the Administration and its armies. As yet the nation was unaccustomed to scenes of bloodshed, and the armies were

chiefly composed of amateur soldiers, a condition which is illustrated in the present letter.

15. This description deals with the minor engagement near Edwards Ferry on the afternoon of October 22, 1861. A relatively small force of Confederates attacked the Union force under General Abercrombie on the south side of the Potomac, abandoning the assault when it found itself outnumbered by the Northern soldiers. General Abercrombie reported a loss of one man killed by the enemy and another killed "by mistake." In addition, General Lander, who was present for some unexplained reason, suffered a flesh wound in the leg. See *War of the Rebellion: A Compilation of the Official Records of the Union and Confederate Armies* (Washington, 1902), Series 1, V, 336–38 and 354–55, for conflicting official reports of the action. (Hereafter cited as *Official Records.*)

16. Austin Blair, one of the active founders of the Republican party, was governor of Michigan from 1861 to 1865. Although he had been one of the floor leaders for Senator Seward at the Chicago Republican Convention of 1860 which nominated Lincoln for the Presidency, in his role as governor, Blair was a vigorous advocate of Lincoln's measures and he became not the least distinguished member of the notable group of Northern "war governors." In his inaugural address (January 3, 1861) he proclaimed the power of the Federal government to defend itself and his certainty that it would do so, warning the seceding states that it was a question of war which faced them. Under his leadership the First Michigan (three-months) Regiment was the first regiment of western troops to reach Washington, and a precursor of the vigor with which the Michigan state government supported the President throughout the war.

17. Dr. Thomas Antisell, subsequently medical director of the Twelfth Corps.

18. Franklin W. Whittlesey of Ypsilanti, who entered the service as a captain in the First Michigan Infantry, April 20, 1861. He attained the rank of colonel of the regiment and was honorably discharged for disability, March 18, 1863.—*Record of Service of Michigan Volunteers.*

19. A container for keeping needles, thread, scissors, etc.

20. Captain William D. Wilkins, assistant adjutant general, and Lieutenant Samuel E. Pittman of the First Michigan Infantry were members of General Williams' staff.

21. General Williams' distrust of the cavalry branch of the Union army was well-founded. "Who ever saw a dead cavalryman" became a commonplace gibe throughout the army in the early years of the war. In its latter half, under the leadership of such men as Pleasonton, Kilpatrick,

Sheridan, and Custer, the Union cavalry became a fair match for its Confederate counterpart. As for the First Michigan Cavalry, after more or less arduous service in the Shenandoah Valley and around Washington, in the course of which Colonel Brodhead was mortally wounded, and in the second battle of Bull Run, August 30, 1862, it was assigned, early in 1863, to General Custer's Michigan Cavalry Brigade comprising the First, Fifth, Sixth, and Seventh regiments. Under his leadership the brigade acquired a reputation fairly comparable to that of the famous foot-slogging Wisconsin-Indiana-Michigan Iron Brigade.

22. An interesting comment concerning this execution was supplied following General Williams' death in 1878 by the provost marshal who conducted it. Early on the appointed day of execution he went with a corps of workmen to erect the gallows. The severe storm of sleet and rain threatened to demolish the structure unless additional ropes to anchor it could be secured. The site was near General Williams' headquarters tent and the provost marshal applied to him for an order on his wagonmaster for the needed supplies. General Williams, however, declined, saying: "Spare me the necessity of issuing an order. You can, no doubt, find what you want." The tremulous voice and moistened eye of the general commanded the provost marshal's respect. Years later, upon meeting him, the incident was alluded to, when General Williams said he would have given his right arm if by so doing he could have spared the culprit's life.—Unidentified newspaper clipping dated about January, 1879, in Burton Historical Collection, Williams' file.

II

Up and
Down the
Shenandoah

UP AND DOWN THE SHENANDOAH

Whatever other faults General McClellan displayed, he was a fine organizer and drill-master. Throughout the winter of 1861–62 he was busy with plans for the capture of Richmond. Meanwhile, General Banks' command would invade Virginia by way of the Shenandoah Valley. Banks was a good politician but only a mediocre military leader. Against him was pitted Stonewall Jackson, the outstanding military genius of the Confederacy. Although badly outnumbered by the several Union armies opposed to him, Jackson triumphed over all of them. He fell short, however, of his objective of destroying Banks' army, which escaped intact across the Potomac. In the letters which follow General Williams narrates the triumphant advance and subsequent retreat of General Banks' army in this first invasion of the Shenandoah Valley.

HORRORS OF BORDER WARFARE

Hancock, Md., Jan. 31, 1862.

My Dear Daughter:

I have not heard from you for nearly a month, except through Irene, that your eyes were troubling you again. I suppose this is the reason you have not written.

I have been able to write you but once since I reached this place. My hard march up found little relief here. I found the village full of new and undisciplined troops, infantry, cavalry, and artillery, without order or decency. I got my first intimation that I was to be put in command on my way up and had no instructions what to do. The weather was intensely cold and the ground so frozen that a tent-pin could not be driven. There was not a vacant foot in town, so I bestowed the regiments of my brigade in barns and in all manner of places outside, and went to work from the moment of my arrival, telegraphing right and left, and I have kept it up pretty busily ever since.

When I reached here the Rebels were in large force within ten or twelve miles, extending from the hills opposite to Unger, fifteen miles below. They have been moving about cautiously ever since, but have made no great demonstrations towards me. My patrols are sent over almost every day and go nearly up to Bath,[1] where the Rebels have a garrison. But I operate very cautiously, as I am under orders to hold this post and await further instructions.

But I am here where I see the horrors of this war in its worst forms. All the Union people on the other side (mostly in moderate circumstances) have been stripped of everything that could be eaten or used. Their husbands have generally fled to this side, leaving wives and children at their little homes, hoping to save their furniture or some small property to bring away hereafter. These wives fill my office daily and fill my heart with pain at the recital of their sufferings and deprivations. Many of them are living on corn meal alone and have been for weeks. I tried to help a few, but the number is altogether too great for one poor private purse and I have given up in despair. Every day male refugees arrive who have spent nights in the woods to avoid Rebel pickets. They all bring sorrowful tales of misery all through the adjoining counties. Prices of everything are exceedingly high, and want very general amongst the poorer classes. What these poor people will do to sustain life all winter is more than I can imagine. I have sent over several armed parties to bring families away, but in most cases the parties are too far away to bring their effects to the river.

This town, since the new regiments were sent to Cumberland, is very orderly and my troops behave well. I am sorry to say that the troops who were obliged to flee from Bath behaved very badly. All the houses were deserted when the Rebels fired upon the town and had not been occupied. The retiring troops, having forded the river to their arms in extremely cold weather, seized upon the houses and destroyed a great deal of property wantonly, besides eating up all the provisions of every house. The complaints of housekeepers are very numerous, and well-founded, I fear. It annoys and frets me exceedingly.

I have now five regiments of infantry, six pieces of artillery, and two companies of cavalry, besides some unattached companies. The weather has been snowing and raining till the mud is impassable. I have over 800 horses and mules to feed, to say nothing of the several thousand men. What with the bad roads, I find it no easy job, especially as the mules are pretty much used up by exposure to cold and wet and hard work. However, we hold on and hope for better weather. . . .

Your Loving Father.

❖

DIFFICULTIES OF WINTER WARFARE

Headquarters, 3rd Brigade,
Hancock, Feb. 3, 1862.

My Dear Lew:

Your letter by Capt. Wilkins came to hand some time ago, but I was in the midst of cares and duties of the most insistent and irritating nature. I had gone to Washington on Sunday [2] to meet Irene and had a very pleasant time with her and Cousin Marion on Sunday afternoon. On Monday morning, I received telegraphs and orders in hot haste to join my brigade forthwith. I started in the first train with Dr. Antisell and had a most disagreeable time from Frederick in chase of my brigade which preceded me twenty-four hours. The march of so many men and wagons had beat the road to the condition of ice and our mules being uncalked worked all sorts of antics over the high hills which lie at right angles to the road from Frederick to this place. By dint of perseverance, we made forty miles and overtook the brigade the same night [January 6] at Clear Spring. In the meantime, I had received a telegraphic order to precede the command and relieve General Lander at this place. I made great haste to do so, and faced the anti-summer temperature of below zero in crossing the high mountain west of Clear Spring and after much tribulation was safely set down at Hancock on Wednesday 8th inst.[3]

I found here five regiments of infantry of the newest and most mobbish species. During the shelling of the town on Sunday previous [January 5], the people had left their houses, food, furniture and all, which our troops (some fording the river arms deep and others sent up from below) had occupied and literally appropriated to themselves. Food, furniture, forage, fuel and all had been used and destroyed without thought or decency. Three of the regiments were new and had been armed with Belgian [rifles] the day of the attack. They knew nothing of camp, garrison, or other military duty, and were literally a mob firing their loaded muskets right and left and playing the very devil generally.

I did not wait to get my overcoat off before I began a reform. I appointed a provost marshal and gave him a guard as soon as my own brigade came up of reliable men [and] ordered a report of the strength of regiments, established a grand guard and outposts four miles up and down the river, shut up the groggeries, and filled up several respectable sized rooms with arrested rowdies. Two of these regiments had lost all their camp and garrison equipage and the weather was cold to zero. Every particle of space in the whole town was crowded. Retiring citizens from the country rushed upon me with violent complaints of robbery, plunder, destruction of all their edibles, and with all the ten thousand complaints of a people scared out of their homes at a moment's notice, which a hungry and irresponsible soldiery had taken possession of.

To add to [my] tribulations up came my four regiments, three of them without winter tents and the ground so frozen that tents could not be pitched at any rate. I hardly know now how I disposed of them—

some in barns outside, some in canal boats, and some in bivouac. But the thing was done, and I went to my blankets a tired and anxious man. I had at least 6,000 men crowded into a little village, not 500 yards from the opposite bank [of the river] held by the enemy in force not less than 15,000 with twenty pieces of artillery. It seemed but a stone's throw to the high hills opposite, which looked down upon this town, which is at the foot of the hills on our side. I had eight pieces of artillery—four of smooth bore six-pounders and four Parrotts. Reports brought to me were that Jackson and Loring held Bath in great force and extended in a continuous camp up to the high hills opposite, and that they intended to renew the shelling of Hancock as soon as the weather moderated.

I was full of concern that they might begin that night. If so, we should have had a scene of confusion that I am not anxious to witness. The town, as I have said, is at the foot of high hills right on the river bank and is completely commanded by the opposite shore. So is the road approaching from below for at least eight miles. It runs along the hillsides for all this distance, hemmed in by precipitous ridges and slopes and overlooked by the hills on the Virginia shore at not more than half-musket distance in many places, and in no place out of range. It was a pleasant predicament to be in if those twenty-odd guns had opened upon us and had enfiladed, as they could, our only retreat and the route of all our supplies. I found one road to the rear leading towards Pennsylvania, a very hard road, but I ordered my wagon train to park two miles out upon it, and made arrangements to take all the regiments as promptly as possible behind the hills and then hammer away with artillery.

There we stood for two days, while I had my scouts, civil and military, across the river and up and down to get information. I myself mounted a high ridge five miles above called Round Top from which I could see far and wide over Dixie from an elevation of 2,000 feet. But I could see nothing but camp fires extending for miles away down the valleys but behind intervening hills.

On the 3rd day I learned that the Rebels were moving away—leaving an inferior force behind—but a large camp a few miles below. Lander above had got the same news and descending from Romney he fell back towards Cumberland.[4] Gen. Kelley, who was still there, telegraphed me to send reinforcements.[5] I was but too glad to get rid of my green ones and forthwith started all the infantry but my own brigade on the road to Cumberland. In the meantime, the telegraph line, which I had reconnected through the enemy's country for ten miles, was cut again and I was isolated from Kelley. By the aid of mounted men every five miles I established a communication by the road (forty miles). I was under orders to hold this post but to go to Lander's aid if he was attacked; so I was obliged to keep my command under marching orders with cooked rations for days, Lander being in a constant stew—at times full of fight and asking me to join him in a five-days' march, bivouacking in the open air and depending upon our haversacks for provisions. Expecting to be ordered to this service, I sent back to Hagerstown all my baggage, but the powers above (military) I think put an end to Lander's quixotic expedition, which would probably have resulted in frozen feet to hundreds, if nothing more disastrous. I confess I had no stomach for such an expedition, especially [since] with all my care many of my men were already frostbitten.

My Dear Lew: Sitting in your parlor or resting quietly snug in your warm bed it may seem very easy to talk of winter campaigns and to call out "Onward" in mid-winter. But if you will come down to these snow-clad hills and take one midnight's round to my outposts, see poor devils in rotten tents not fit for summer, talk to the sentinel on his two-hours' round without fire, see the damnable roads, figure up how much provisions it takes to feed a few thousand daily, hear the *cries* not of men only but of half-frozen animals (mules and horses) of which I have upwards of 800—half frozen and half killed by work—witness the effort it takes to get in forage, which I buy from twenty to thirty miles away, to transport subsistence stores thirty miles away, you will be satisfied that in winter months a stationary force has about all it can do to subsist itself, especially in the rain, snow, and mud we have had for the last twenty days. For while it freezes hard at night, it thaws in the valleys by day, or it snows on the hills and rains in the valleys. Altogether I have never seen such cursed weather and such devilish roads.

I should like to photograph you one day's work here. I have five regiments of infantry, six pieces of artillery, and two companies of horse. In the morning begin the reports, and with them the requisitions for things wanted. I have been four months trying to get things absolutely necessary for comfort. I have had requisitions for thousands of shoes and have received but 500 for two months. I have hundreds of men nearly shoeless. But for supplies from the states [they] would have been absolutely barefooted. I had men who could not march from Frederick for want of shoes! I have written and telegraphed, cursed and swore, and pleaded and begged, and in return have had promises that they should be sent forthwith. But they came not. Just fancy in this age soldiers left without shoes in this war for the Union and that in midwinter and in a campaign!

Again, but two of my regiments have Sibley tents, the only ones you can live in in winter, because [they are] the only ones in which you can use a stove.[6] One of the other regiments has common wedge tents used all through the three months' campaign and literally in shreds. One other has almost equally bad—wholly unfit for this season. These regiments have hutted themselves up to our march here. Now it cannot be done. I have for months had the promise of Sibley tents but they come not! I made requisition for bugles for skirmishing drill four months ago. They are needed for the efficiency of my command. I have had the promise of them fifty times, but do not get them.

Same of axes and intrenching tools—same of everything. It takes months to have a requisition filled, yet I see the papers every now and then boast of how excellently our troops are provided. It is all sham, except in rations. We have never wanted for an abundance to eat. It is the only department that is provided, or if provided makes its regular issues. In all other things the troops are woefully neglected. But for provisions made by states and for articles the men buy for themselves they would suffer extremely. Half of my men are in boots bought for themselves. I can say nothing about troops near Washington, but speak only of those at a distance. It may all be the fault of our own division departments. I know I don't fare worse than the other brigades of Gen. Banks' division. On the contrary, [I] fancy I am somewhat ahead of them in getting supplies. If I were Gen. Banks, with his political influence, I should understand in a few days where the fault lies. He seems to take it easy and make abundant promises.

I have run rather unintentionally into complaints. As it is against regulations, you will please not read [this] to others, but keep [it] to yourself. It is one of the curses of our service that no complaint can be uttered but to the proper authorities, and they regard them not. I could tell a tale that would smash up the whole department of sleepy old-fogy quartermasters and I am sorely tempted to do so. I doubt not that there are in our depots an abundance of everything I require to make my men comfortable, but they cannot be got out under three months' time. In spite of all this my command is unusually healthy for the fatigue and exposure they have had, nor do they complain. Their eagerness to get into Dixie is amusing. I send out daily small parties as patrols. There is a great effort from all the regiments to get on this duty which though full of fatigue is full of excitement and hairbreadth escapes.

But if we have suffered some, Jackson's command has suffered more. We have reliable information that he sent back over 1,200 frozen and sick men during the few days he lay opposite. People who came over yesterday say that his sick and disabled fill every house from Bath to Winchester and that many amputations have taken place from frost-bites. His whole command was exposed to a heavy snow-storm, followed by intense cold. I see the Dixie papers confirm the reports of his disasters. He lost a good many men, too, from our Parrott guns, which were admirably served, every shot landing plump into his batteries, up-setting his guns, killing his horses, and throwing his men into confusion. A loyal man who was on that side told me that men were killed by some of the last shots thrown purposely high, at least two miles from the river bank. On their side, the firing was miserable. They literally did no damage to the town, though some shots passed through roofs of houses and some shells exploded in the streets. Not a person was wounded. Most of their shot fell short or passed high over the town into the hills beyond.

The country around this [place] is most splendidly picturesque. After the day's work, I take a horseback [ride] for a couple of hours each day to make myself familiar with the roads and the country. The day after I took command here my scouts discovered the frame of a bridge about two miles up [river] which had been all prepared for laying across the river. I supposed, therefore, that they intended to cross at that point and I was greatly in hopes they would attempt it. I could have demolished their whole 15,000 [men] in thirty minutes by close calculation. I did not disturb their bridge till the main force had left. I then sent a party over and threw it into the river.[7] The river here was favorable when I arrived, but has been very high most of the time since. I found only a single flatboat, carrying perhaps sixty men. There are some canal boats, but they are too cumbersome to be served in the rapid current. I have applied for authority to build boats and could have enough in a week to carry half my command, but I have no response. So of Bath, the famous Berkeley Springs, I got reliable information that the force left there did not exceed 500 men, with one Brig. Gen. (Carson) and two or three field officers, considerable baggage and all that. I had discovered a mountain pass to their rear cutting off their retreat perfectly. I applied for permission to try it. It was an easy and sure thing, but I got no response. That cursed Ball's Bluff haunts the souls of our chiefs, and perhaps it is well it does. We are too much divided and are operating on the periphery while they stand in the center. I could plan a campaign to seize upon Winchester and relieve all the country north and northwest and open the Balt. and Ohio Railroad beyond molestation. If you will look at the map you will see how completely it is the key to the whole of the country now occupied by Jackson and Loring. It is in the most fertile valley of Virginia which leads down to Staunton, cutting their most important railroad and completely turning the entrenchments at Manassas, but I have no room, or time for more. . . . Love to all.

Affectionately,
A.S.W.

◈

BOASTING OF GENERAL LANDER

Hancock, Feb. 19, 1862.

My Dear Daughter:

It is so long since I have written to you that I forget when and where I left off, but it matters little, as I have been here in Hancock watching the course of events, somewhat anxious on account of the erratic movements of my next military neighbor, Gen. Lander. I see now, to my great surprise, by newspapers and his own reports that he has been doing great things, though I have been for four weeks in constant communication with him at Patterson Creek, from which place he has not moved till the last week, without suspecting his glories. He talks in his report to Gen. McClellan of having opened the railroad from Cumberland to Hancock, while in fact I have had possession of all this road from Hancock half way to Cumberland for nearly four weeks, and have twice established the telegraph line over the whole route.

I see, too, he reports of the daring and successful reconnoissance of some one of his colonels as far as Unger twenty-two miles south, when in fact my patrols had been there several days before and I myself with other officers and an escort of only four mounted men had ridden nearly to the same place but two or three days before, crossing the Potomac seven miles above and returning to a point opposite this place, after a circuit of several miles. In truth, until last Sunday Gen. Lander knew nothing of the railroad or the other side of the Potomac for twenty miles above. The whole of that region has been held by my pickets, who have had possession of the railroad bridge over the Big Cacapon and below for five to ten miles. I confess my astonishment, therefore, to see in the Baltimore papers today a long account of Gen. Lander clearing the line of the railroad and opening the route for Gen. Williams' brigade to cross, and a complimentary order of the Secretary of War to Gen. Lander for his valuable services.

I belong to Gen. Banks' division of the Army of the Potomac and Gen. Lander commands a division of the Army of Western Virginia. Our boundary line is the Potomac and the western slope of the Alleghanies. I am, therefore, on the extreme right of the Army of the Potomac and cannot go beyond that line without especial orders, though I have sent my pickets far over my line. In this way I have held the railroad (Baltimore and Ohio) on the other side of the Potomac for miles, because Gen. Lander, retiring from Romney, had taken post fifty-odd miles distant at Patterson Creek. The only damage done to the road was partial injury at the Big Cacapon before I came up, which was repaired in a day and the cars can now run from Wheeling to this place, though they have been down but once.

Wednesday, February 26, 1862.

I wrote this some time ago and have been to Frederick since and just returned. . . . We shall march again tomorrow, I suppose for Williamsport and then for "Dixie." You will hear all about us by telegram, but don't be alarmed. I think the enemy will not wait for us, even at Winchester. We shall go in strong force if Gen. Banks is not mistaken.[8] I will write you a line or so when I get a chance. . . .

Your Affectionate Father,
A.S.W.

❖

THE ADVANCE TOWARD WINCHESTER

Bunker Hill, Va., Mar. 8, 1862.

My Dear Daughter:

This is a little hamlet twelve miles north of Winchester on the pike from Williamsport. My headquarters are in a small room of a small house. I have a bedroom adjoining, which just holds my bed. The others, servants and all, occupy our office-room rolled in blankets at night. We are glad of any shelter, for the weather has been very rough, worse than our Detroit March. Indeed, I don't know when I have [not] been exposed to bad weather, but my health is good and my spirits never better.

We left Hancock on March 1st and marched to Williamsport the same day, twenty-three miles. At this point I commenced crossing the river on a single scow ferry-boat. It took me twenty-four hours to get across two regiments and their trains. Consequently, I was nearly three days in passing over my six regiments of infantry, a company of artillery and two companies of cavalry. My advance regiments took possession of Martinsburg without opposition, the Union people welcoming us and the non-Union, for the most part, running away. It was at this point that the Rebels last summer destroyed over fifty locomotives of the Ohio & Baltimore Railroad, the melancholy ruins of which still stand on the track. On Wednesday last I left Martinsburg with my brigade expecting to meet the enemy in force at this place, but he had evacuated and we found nothing but a small picket of cavalry and a few infantry. My cavalry advance dashed into the town, a few rounds of musketry were fired from the houses, we captured five or six of them, and then our anticipated battle was all over without loss to us.

61

I happened to be in advance with some officers and got considerable of the fever of the rush and thus was one of the early ones in.

Yesterday I sent out a reconnoitering party towards Winchester which was attacked by a considerable force in the woods. My troops drove them easily but we had three men wounded and Capt. Wilkins' fine horse (Prince), which you will recollect, was struck in the shoulder and badly hurt. We killed six of the enemy and wounded seven. They were all cavalry. These fellows are very daring. After we drove them off yesterday they came back at night and fired on my pickets. They are driving all round outside of my lines picking up soldiers on furlough and stealing horses and other property of Union men. I hope to trap some of them soon.

I have the advanced position now and on the extreme right of the Army of the Potomac. My brigade has now six regiments of infantry, six pieces of rifled cannon and two companies of cavalry, the largest command I have had, at least 5,000 men. On my left is Gen. Hamilton and beyond him toward the Shenandoah the other brigades of Gen. Banks' division. Behind late Gen. Lander's, now Gen. Shields' division is coming up, a part having arrived at Martinsburg. I don't know what is ahead, but I think we shall drive them forward without much trouble. . . .

I write you hurriedly. My little office is crowded with all sorts of men for all sorts of business. I am now really "monarch of all I survey," and all the people about, as well as my own troops, think I should supply everything and do everything. Love to all. . . .

Ever Your Affectionate Father,
A.S.W.

❖

OCCUPATION OF WINCHESTER

Winchester, Mar. 13th, 1862.

My Dear Daughter:

I have merely time to say that we are in Winchester. I left Bunker Hill day before yesterday, my brigade in advance. I skirmished all the day with my light troops and occasionally shelling the woods with six pieces of artillery, which I held in advance. I have since learned that we killed several of the Rebels. I had but one man wounded. We encamped at night within five miles of this place, the Rebels with their artillery in full view of us. Several earthworks were observable, and we looked forward for a great battle in the morning. My whole brigade was under arms at 4 o'clock yesterday and at daylight we moved forward, four regiments in advance with nearly 800 skirmishers leading, covering the hills in a line for nearly three miles. The morning was beautifully spring-like and the sky as clear as crystal. We moved with great caution, as all the hills showed entrenchments. It was an exciting sight as our long line of skirmishers moved forward and mounted in a long row of single men towards the batteries, looking in the distance like a swarm of ants crawling up the hillsides.

We watched with our glasses as they reached the works, and observed several persons advance from them in front as they approached. Presently we saw them all going to the rear and our front line of videttes pouring over the line of entrenchments without opposition. Soon the large fort came in sight and the left line of skirmishers approached and halted and sent back word that the fort was in front and apparently occupied. They were ordered to "feel" them cautiously, and forward went the whole line, and soon we saw them tumbling over the parapets and the bayonets brightly glaring in the morning sun.

We knew then that the town was ours, and gathering up the whole command, ten regiments, two batteries (ten guns), and four companies of cavalry, we advanced on the town en masse, myself and Gen. Hamilton, who just ranks me, riding in advance.[9] As we reached the outskirts the mayor and council met us and surrendered the city of Winchester, asking protection to private property. We then marched most of the regiments through the town. Many of the people hailed our entrance by waving handkerchiefs and some by showing the Star-Spangled Banner. It is nearly a year since it has been shown in Winchester. . . .

I lost, in advancing from Bunker Hill, five men wounded. It is the only brigade in Gen. Banks' division which has had a man wounded. Indeed, I have led the whole advance, and yet you probably will not see my brigade mentioned. I was joined at Bunker Hill by Gen. Hamilton, who ranks me on the list of generals, though appointed the same day. He sent me in advance the first day and in command the second day, and yet as he ranks me I have no doubt his name alone will get the credit. However, I court nobody—reporters nor commanders—but try to do my whole duty and trust it will all come out right. But I can't help seeing how much personal ambition is mixed up with all these operations, small fame at the expense of the great purpose we have in hand.

It took me all day yesterday to get my regiments in position, and at night I went to my camp-bed the tiredest man you can think of. I have a great many incidents I should like to tell you, but I have no time. Since we arrived, scores of generals have come up. Gen. Shields, Gens. Gorman, Abercrombie, Sedgwick, and I know not how many more. I have had amusing scenes with wives of Rebel officers and others for protection of property, and in one instance with the wife of Col. McDonald, a colonel in the Rebel army, to whom I applied for quarters.

My reputation for kindness and leniency preceded me and scores of people have come to me and said, "We hear you are disposed to treat us with kindness, and we beg you to do this and that to aid us." Indeed, I think I am looked upon as the only soft-hearted man in command, but it is a matter of congratulation to know that my soft words have made more Union friends than hundreds of harsh generals could accomplish. Indeed, I feel that all that is needed is kindness and gentleness to make all these people return to Union love. They think we are coming to destroy, and seem to be astonished when we don't ransack their houess and destroy their property. If I had time I should love to tell you of the hundreds of Union-loving people who have told me their sufferings and their grievances and how they have waited for our coming, and how their neighbors have deceived them with the idea that the "Yankees" (all of us are Yankees) were going to destroy them. . . .

Love to all,

Yours Affectionately,

A.S.W.

P.S. Don't be anxious. I think we shall drive all before us without trouble.

A.S.W.

FIRST BATTLE OF WINCHESTER

Strasburg, 20 miles south of Winchester, Va.,
March 30th, 1862.

My Dear Daughter: . . .

I wrote you last from Winchester, after I had been put in command of a division (three brigades) of troops and was on the point of marching eastward across the Shenandoah. One of my brigades left on Friday, the 21st, and the other two and myself on Saturday, the 22nd. We reached the Shenandoah with our long trains Saturday night, and the head of the column, including one brigade and train and part of another brigade, had passed, when the pontoon bridge gave way. It took nearly all day to repair it. In the meantime I had received information that the enemy had returned in considerable force to Winchester and were threatening an attack. Gen. Shields was there with his division. I halted my brigade, which was still on this side, and sent it back to Berryville to be ready to reinforce Gen. Shields.

In the meantime, the river was rising and the bridge bid fair to go away altogether, leaving my command on two sides. I stood by the bridge to watch its safety, expecting to cross the other brigade the next day. At daylight in the morning, however, a messenger brought the word that there had been a fight before Winchester, that Gen. Banks had left for Washington the same day, and that Gen. Shields had been wounded in a skirmish the day before. I was much wanted. I mounted my horse and with a small escort of cavalry set out in hot haste for Winchester. My 1st Brigade was already on the march for the same place. On reaching Winchester I found that Gen. Banks had returned and assumed command and was then following up the retreating enemy. I stayed long enough to order my brigade to follow, and to feed myself and horse, and started for the front.

I overtook Gen. Banks seven or eight miles out. The enemy was in sight, with a strong rear guard of infantry, cavalry, and artillery, but retiring from one strong position to another. We followed them all day till near sundown. At their last stand a battery from my brigade was brought up and they were driven helter-skelter from their position, leaving behind several killed and wounded, with tents, etc. The troops of Gen. Shields' division had been engaged in battle the day before [10] and had marched fifteen to twenty miles after a night-watch on the battlefield. My brigade (the old third that I commanded for so many months, now commanded by Col. Donnelly, senior colonel) had marched thirty-six miles since the preceding evening and with but two hours' rest.[11]

We could follow no farther, so the whole command bivouacked on the field, many a poor fellow supperless. My wagons were thirty miles away with no order to follow, for I did not expect to follow so far, but I found comfortable lodgement in a farmhouse and sufficient to eat. I do not give you any description of the battle or the battlefield, where at least four to five hundred lay dead, nor of the wounded which filled the houses of Winchester and all the little villages on our march this side.[12] You will see pictures enough, often greatly exaggerated, in the newspapers. We came and occupied this place and five miles in advance on Tuesday last and are waiting certain events for future operations. Two of my brigades are now here. The third is over the Shenandoah. Which way we go next is not decided, but I think you'd better direct to me, "Comdg. 1st Division 5th Army Corps (Banks), Winchester."

This place is most beautifully situated in a narrow valley, where the spurs of the Blue Ridge terminate in bold, precipitous bluffs on one side, and a regular unbroken ridge bounds the other. My fatigues the last week have been immense and my responsibilities and anxieties beyond description. If I had been one day later in marching from Winchester I should have had command in the battle and I think could have done a good deal more than was done. Indeed, the wound of Gen. Shields and the absence of Gen. Banks left the whole thing in charge of a colonel, and those who ought to know say the matter managed itself pretty much and the victory was gained by simple hard fighting under great disadvantages of position and movements. Whether true or not, it is quite certain that men do better when those who have been their chief commanders are present. In this view of the case, with only my old brigade to assist, I think I could have captured all Jackson's guns and been a major general! The last thought is rather selfish, but it seems to be a very prominent (too much so I fear) motive in all hearts hereabouts. . . .

Your Affectionate Father,
A.S.W.

FRATERNIZING WITH THE ENEMY

Camp near Edinburg, Va., April 9, 1862.

My Darling Daughter:

I have been reading over your letter of latest date (received March 14) and wondering what has become of the many you have written since, for I know full well that you write me weekly. I wrote you last from Strasburg a week or so ago. On the 1st we moved to this place, banging all the way at the rear guard of the Rebels. There was not much loss, I fancy, on either side as the artillery had the whole work at long range. We lost one killed and some wounded by bursting shells. Long before reaching this place we saw the heavy columns of smoke from the burning bridges over the considerable stream that flows just in advance of the town, one a road and the other a high railroad bridge. They burned all the bridges on the railroad; one just back of this, a monstrous piece of trestle work over a hundred feet high across a chasm of many hundred feet.

The day was beautifully spring-like, the finest we have had, and what with the banging of big guns, the long lines of troops and baggage wagons, it was quite a day of excitement. Many of the shells of the Rebels burst hundreds of feet in the air, giving the semblance of pyrotechnics got up for our entertainment. When, however, a piece from one of them struck a poor fellow sitting quietly on some railroad ties, splitting his skull and dashing his brains in all directions, the poetry of the shelling was changed to a sad realization of these dangers.

We found the stream (Stony Creek) too deep for fording and the whole command encamped on this side. Our advance occupies the town of Edinburg and for several miles along the ridges which lie this side of the stream, while the Rebel advance is for the most part in plain sight on the opposite ridges and in the woods beyond. Every now and then the big guns on both sides open on one another with tremendous noise. After awhile the Rebels withdraw and all is quiet except an occasional popping of the advanced pickets. We have had several skirmishing parties across the stream to protect our bridge builders and we generally drive them back, but they appear again as insolent as ever as soon as our troops retire. We have lost one man only in all this banging and shooting, though several of their shells have fallen in unpleasant vicinity to our quarters in Edinburg. My headquarters are a mile back from the town and we are in comparative quiet, except the noise of the guns.

We are still following up the valley of the Shenandoah. On the left of the road is one of the ridges of the Blue Ridge, running in an almost uniform altitude of fifteen hundred feet. Occasionally a "gap" opens through the ridge, which is always evidence of a cross-road leading toward Warrenton, Culpeper Court House, or some other considerable town east of the Blue Ridge. On our right is a more unequal ridge of the North Mountain, broken into peaks and sending off spurs into the valley, contracting sometimes to a narrow space. We passed one but a few miles back called the "Narrow Passage," where there is only a kind of natural bridge, just wide enough for a road over a very deep ravine. It is the same place where the high railroad bridge was burned. The pike and the bridge are close together. It is a very strong military position, and we expected great opposition to its surrender. At a house close by, elegantly furnished, owned by a young lady, Gen. Jackson had his headquarters for some time. The place was abandoned very soon after our artillery opened on it from a distant hill. The young lady with a sister remain at home, though the house is in part occupied by one of my brigade commanders as headquarters. The place is called Willow Glen Cottage. It has a very picturesque location with two mountain streams coming from the west and the Shenandoah flowing far down in a deep valley on the east and winding away to the base of the Blue Ridge. The night after we arrived I went to call upon the brigade commander and met the band of one of his regiments coming to serenade me. I took them back to Willow Glen and gave the young ladies the benefit of the music. They were very pleasant and chatty but rank Secessionists, having brothers and other friends in the Rebel army. The scene from the house was exceedingly beautiful. The troops had marched without tents and one brigade had bivouacked from the road far up the hillsides and built a very large number (countless as seen from the piazza) of camp fires. There was just enough of the new moon to make "darkness visible" and to give a magical effect to the whole scene. I don't know as I have ever seen a sight more striking and impressive, especially as the music of the band—the murmur of the thousand voices from the bivouac and the occasional cheer from the men as some patriotic air struck their fancy, taken up and carried on away to the far off ridges—gave additional effect to the eye picture. This, however, is the occasional poetry of war.

Our marches for the past month, and, indeed, before, have been generally in sleet, snow, and cold rain, after bivouacking in storms,— almost always, on the march without tents. Today and for three days past the weather has been fit for the middle of winter. Snow, rain, sleet and freezing, till every tree is covered with ice and the ground white with snow. After several warm days it comes with especial severity. The men are for the most part in tents, excepting always the large force which in front of the enemy are obliged to keep on picket and other guards. The poor animals are fairly shriveled up with the ice and sleet. Forage is very scarce, in fact, all stripped off from this section, and what is worse, our long marches over wet roads have destroyed fearfully the poor shoes issued by the government. I have at least 4,000 men in my division who are shoeless completely, or so nearly so that they cannot march. Shoes issued to my men in Winchester are already entirely worn out! Such is the fraud that contractors are permitted to put upon poor soldiers! I can hardly conceive of a crime more fitly punished by death. We should be far in advance but for these constant draw-backs, which fairly unfit an army for march[ing]. . . .

Your Affectionate Father,
A.S.W.

◆

A MILITARY PAGEANT

Camp near Sparta, 4 miles south of New Market, Va.,
April 20, 1862.

My Dear Rene:

We have made another forward movement. The command left our camp near Woodstock Thursday morning at daylight and reached New Market about dark. The day was unusually warm and we had the customary amount of banging of big guns and an occasional pop of small arms. At Mt. Jackson we halted for several hours to give time for a flank movement of two brigades. Across a stream in front of the town is the strongest position we have met, and at this point we supposed the Rebels would give battle. We had contrived, by a dash of cavalry, to save the covered bridge over the North Fork. After shelling the ridge occupied by the enemy we drew up our entire force on the broad river bottom on both sides of the road, covering the columns by a cloud of skirmishers extending several miles. Cavalry and artillery were intermingled in masses amongst the infantry. The field from the high riverbank on the north could be overlooked for miles, and every corps could be distinctly seen. It was a splendid spectacle, the finest military show I have seen in America. Indeed, I have never before seen a single plain upon which so many troops could be displayed, this side of our western prairies.

I watched the advance for some time from a high bluff, as the troops were obliged to march slowly over the soft wheat-fields. Before they reached the foot of the hills in front, I mounted and rode forward on the road, but the enemy had vanished. They fired only two guns and limbered up and sped. We saw nothing more of them till we reached New Market. Ashby, who commands the Rebel cavalry, early had his horse killed and came near losing his own life, as the ball passed through his saddle.[13] My brigades had the advance all day. They passed through New Market after dark and encamped on the south side, or rather bivouacked on the ground. The next morning we moved forward four miles to a small stream on which we are now in bivouac.

The rascals fought us all the way out and we had some beautiful practice with rifled guns. We chased them some three miles in advance of this. They burned every bridge, even to the little culverts, and made a tremendous bonfire of their camp some miles ahead of us. But as they know the country and have fine roads they are too fast for our infantry. As for the cavalry, it is good for kicking up a dust, doing foraging, capturing horses and stealing them, and for not much else. The material is good enough, but they are poorly drilled and poorly mounted. The horses have not been over half-fed during the winter and of late have been severely handled. The Rebel cavalry seems much better drilled and have better horses. At any rate, they scale the fences most beautifully and show themselves very fearless till our rifled guns open, when they put out rapidly.

We contrived to capture two lieutenants and a few privates. The night before we left Edinburg four companies of infantry from my division captured fifty-odd—a whole company—of Ashby's cavalry, officers and all. They were conducted by a Union man and they were fairly surrounded before they knew of our approach. As I write, eight prisoners are brought to me. Deserters are very common. But this is a great country and a beautiful one. I have never seen so beautiful and apparently so fertile a valley. It improves greatly as we advance. There were points on our march on Thursday that one never tired looking at. We have still the same mountain ranges on either hand, perhaps six miles apart, and the same rolling valley between, but the ridges are more broken into peaks and gaps and the valley is occasionally traversed by spurs and dotted by solitary peaks, which rise like sugar loaves from an even surface.

Some of the wives and daughters of officers have followed us as far as Edinburg, amongst them, Mrs. and Miss Copeland, Lt. Col. of the 1st Michigan Cavalry. I think, however, that they are out of place and must be a source of great anxiety and annoyance. For example, an order to march usually comes at midnight and the troops are expected to be under arms before daylight. Everything must be packed and placed in wagons. As we carry all our cooking utensils and mess furniture, to say nothing of the office desks, table, etc., etc., we find enough to do without looking out for the effects of wives or daughters. However, *chacun à son gout*. It may all be very fine, "but I don't see it." I prefer to think of you as safe in Philadelphia.

We are under orders to move forward again. Our men's shoes are following somewhere in rear of us, but we seem to keep in advance and many men are fairly shoeless. I hope they will catch us soon. . . .

Your Affectionate Father,
A.S.W.

◈

THE ADVANCE TO HARRISONBURG

Harrisonburg, Va., April 29, 1862.

My Dear Daughter:

I wrote you from camp near Sparta last week. This camp was about four miles below New Market. My 1st Brigade moved down to within four miles of this place a week ago and the second came down on

Thursday last, and both advanced and took position in front of the town on the road running eastwardly toward Gordonsville, upon which Jackson's forces had retreated. I was obliged to ride about ten miles a day through pelting rain, sleet, and snow before we left our last camp to attend a board for examination of officers. In consequence I caught a terrific cold all over and have had my first ill day since I have been in the service. We have had the most infernal weather, such as I never saw in Michigan in the month of April. The hills were, till yesterday, quite white with snow in spots, and while at our last camp we had two heavy snow-storms and rain enough to make a young deluge, I was out of sorts only a day, but I was obliged to ride over twenty miles on a pretty hard-going horse with sore limbs and aching head. However, I kept my feet all the while and am now quite well again. There is nothing like my universal remedy-diet.

This valley thus far continues to be beautiful—even more so than farther "down," as they call toward the north, more diversified and picturesque. We have reached the end of the ridge that has hemmed us in on the east, and now the valley spreads out in that direction to the Blue Ridge, while the loftier and irregular tops of the Alleghanies are plainly visible on the west, stretching far away toward the south. The intervening valley is broken into many conical-shaped knobs, which give a most singular appearance to the view as seen in the late afternoon from a high hill east of town. The town is beautifully situated in the bottom of the valley and has around it many elegant country seats. It is altogether the most attractive-looking town I have seen in the valley.

Our cavalry were sent forward toward Staunton a few days since but found the bridges burned over the streams below, which were not fordable just now. Jackson's army is east of this from fifteen to twenty miles on the slopes of the Blue Ridge. He has a very large bridge between us and him. It is said that he has it ready for burning. We fear he has been largely reinforced and intends to turn upon us here or wait for us in his present strong position. We have had several pretty strong skirmishes with him and taken several prisoners; lost one ourselves, and several killed and wounded.

The road toward his present camp is in a wretched condition. I think we shall be obliged to remain here some days. I hardly know what will be the next movement. We are now pretty well advanced into the interior and are a long way from the base of our supplies. As we have neither railroad nor water transportation we find it no small task to keep our force supplied in rations, forage, and clothing. I contrived to get shoes for most of my division at the last camp, but our wants are still many. The troops have had to bivouac much of the time in rain and snow with such shelter as they could put up out of rails, boughs, etc., but it is wonderful how inventive and ingenious they become in providing for themselves. I am sorry to say, however, they do not always respect private property, though persons are seldom molested.

The Negro population increases as we go south, and although they all understand that the rear is open to them, very few leave their masters. Indeed, many of them are afraid of us at first, probably from big stories of our cruelties that are told them. They seem glad at our coming and probably think some great benefit is to accrue to them, but they show very little desire to quit their present homes. In truth, they are much attached to localities, and but for the fear of being sold south I don't think a dozen could be coaxed away. As it is, probably fifty have come in and are employed by our quartermasters. If the abolitionists could see things as they really are here they would have less confidence in the aid the Negro is in concluding this war. Their masters say that they become more insolent and lazy on our advance, and that is the only good we are likely to do them. . . .

Your Affectionate Father,
W.

◆

RETREAT TO STRASBURG

Strasburg, Va., May 17, 1862.

My Dear Daughter:

You will see that we have made a retrograde movement. I cannot explain the reason, because I really don't think there *is* any. If there be one, it is unknown to us here and is confided to the authorities at Washington. We regard it as a most unfortunate policy and altogether inexplicable, especially as we had the game all in our hands, and if the moves had been made with the least skill we could easily have check-mated Jackson, Ewell, and Johnston, instead of leaving them to attack and drive back Milroy, as we hear they have done.[14]

I cannot explain to you, and I am not permitted to complain, but if the amount of swearing that has been done in this department is re-corded against us in Heaven I fear we have an account that can never be settled. But here we are with a greatly reduced force, either used as a decoy for the Rebel forces or for some unaccountable purpose known only to the War Department. Imagine our chagrin in marching back, like a retreating force, over the same ground that we had driven the Rebels before us, and having the galling reminders of our defeat, and that without a gun being fired or a man killed. But all this is private and not to be repeated outside of your home. The worst part is that we have put ourselves in a most critical position and exposed the whole of this important valley to be retaken and its immense property of rail-roads and stores to be destroyed.

I have had a wearisome march of several days through heat and dust most intolerable. All our vast trains of stores, etc., had to precede us, and we followed in the fine powder that these miles of wagon wheels pounded up for us. We have finally come to a stand here; that is, my decimated division is here and a few other troops, while others have been detached on some wild-goose chase after the enemy. I am getting terribly disgusted and feel greatly like resigning. How a few civilians at a distance can hope to manage this war is inconceivable. I sometimes fear we are to meet with terrible reverses because of the fantastic tricks of some vain men dressed in a little brief authority. If we do not, it is because the Almighty interposes in our behalf. . . .

I wrote to Aunt Patty some time ago, I fear a very blue letter, for I have been hugely out of sorts for some time. With all our victories, I do not feel we are gaining much. There is so much jealousy and detrac-tion, in and out of Congress, so much selfishness, such a struggling after self-aggrandizement, so little pure and disinterested and in-genuous patriotism, that I shudder for the future. If we have a reverse, God help us! You do not see it as I do, and perhaps I am morbidly alive to it. But I am so surrounded by its presence, I see it so palpably in Congress, in the heart-burnings and bitterness of our commanding generals, in the divisions and sub-divisions of our forces to give command to favorites, in the sacrifice of power which lies under our hand, just to checkmate some rival or to destroy some dreaded popularity, that I tremble at some great disaster. Was the whole government, civil and military, united and actuated by one great and engrossing and fine purpose, this rebellion would be destroyed in two months. As it is, I fear it may yet destroy us.

But enough of this. I am disheartened just now by events transpiring about me and probably look on the dark side of everything. But when I see three military departments lying side by side divided and powerless, which if united might combine an irresistable force which could march to Richmond, I feel disgusted and heart-sick. Such are the departments commanded by McDowell, Banks, and Fremont. The latter has literally done nothing, and is in a position to do nothing. Banks could do but little because his force has been taken away for the others. McDowell is drawing away other troops to make a great show and bluster. If these forces were all in one column they could drive all before them out of Virginia. But this is a grumbling letter, written late at night. Perhaps I'll write in better humor tomorrow.

How long we shall be here and where go next, I can't say.

Goodbye, Love to all,

Your Affectionate Father,
A.S.W.

◈

PERPLEXITY OVER THE RETREAT

Strasburg, Va., May 21, 1862.

My Dear Daughter:

I received yours of the 16th this morning. I have already explained to you in a previous letter why we are here. The whole of this is unexplainable, especially as we occupied a position from which we could in one movement have interposed between the commands of Jackson and Ewell and thus have saved Milroy and Schenck from being driven back with loss. But the whole movement comes from the highest command and we are neither authorized to criticise nor complain. I could say much more, but it is not advisable. I trust we shall be safely extricated from a dilemma, that, to speak mildly, was unnecessarily brought about. I have no idea how long we shall be here or where [we will] go next. I probably know as much as General Banks. . . .

I am glad you are doing something for the comfort of the sick and wounded soldiers. You can hardly imagine how these little matters comfort the sick and the dispirited; how they are remembered in after years. The smallest attentions—a simple kind word falls often with wonderful influence upon their hearts and will be repeated to you years hence, if you should chance to meet them. . . .

My headquarters are at a large brick house just outside of Strasburg, a very old and very stately mansion of an old Virginia family. The lady is a widow with a pretty large family of girls, children and step-children. She has a governess from Massachusetts, a very pleasant young lady who has been here during the whole Rebel war and is, in fact, quite a Secessionist. So the officers say. I have had very little to say to any of them. The young men have very pleasant concerts with the family every evening. . . .

Your Affectionate Father,
A.S.W.

❖

SECOND BATTLE OF WINCHESTER AND FAILURE OF THE CAMPAIGN

Williamsport, May 27, 1862.

My Dear Daughter:

I can fancy your anxiety after the recent telegraphic tidings from Banks' column. I therefore telegraphed you yesterday that I was safe here. We have had a very unpleasant time through anxious and laborious days and sleepless nights, such as I fancy would make old age come prematurely.

On Friday evening last [15] we got conflicting rumors of an attack upon our guard at Front Royal, a small village about twelve miles east of Strasburg where a considerable valley, parallel with the valley in which Strasburg is, crosses the Shenandoah. Through this valley is a

76

stone pike, and there are several mountain gaps through which good roads at this season connect with the stone pike from Strasburg to Staunton. As there is a good road from Front Royal to Winchester, the Rebels with sufficient force at Front Royal could easily intercept our line of march and cut us off from our supplies, especially as the occupation of Front Royal destroyed the railroad line that connected us with Washington.

I think I have several times written you that I regarded our position as very critical. It was in reference to this very matter, all which has taken place, almost exactly as I feared. Ewell's division, estimated at from 10,000 to 15,000 troops, had been joined in the valley below Front Royal by Jackson's brigade of 8,000 to 12,000, and they moved with great rapidity and secretly upon and actually took by surprise, the regiment (1st Maryland) doing guard duty there. I do not think fifty men escaped, and the few who did passed the night in the woods on their route to Winchester. It was near midnight, therefore, before we knew the extent of our disaster.

By some strange fatality a large quantity of clothing and other public stores for the use of the department had been placed in depot there, and it is rumored a considerable number of excellent arms. All this was grabbed by the hungry Rebels. By a singular coincidence the 1st Maryland of the Rebels was the leading infantry regiment in the attack on the 1st Maryland of our service. The Rebel cavalry, in which arm they are very strong, did the business, however, and, I fear, committed fearful and outrageous slaughter. The stories told by the escaped and the runaways on these occasions are not always to be believed. If they were, one would be obliged to think men turned to brutish beasts, such instances of bloody and monstrous butchery of wounded and unresisting men are narrated. Amongst the killed was Col. Kenly of Baltimore, who commanded the regiment. He was a marked character, a most perfect gentleman and as brave a soldier as ever wore a sword. Amongst the many friends in the service who have fallen within the past few days, I know of none whose death has so deeply touched me. His regiment was attached to my old brigade while I was at Hancock, and at his own earnest request. I have, of course, seen much of him almost daily since. I shall not soon forget his cheerful face and courteous bearing.[16]

But to my narration of events. When the fact was patent that a very large force had possession of the railroad and was crossing the river towards Winchester, orders were immediately issued to start our immense trains of wagons, commissary, quartermaster, ordnance for division brigades and regiments—several hundreds—toward Winchester, and the command to hold itself ready to follow. As you have never seen, you cannot appreciate the difficulties of moving these long mule-trains or the impediments they make to a rapid march, especially in retreat, when hurry and confusion, frightened teamsters and disordered teams, break-downs and collisions and ten thousand nameless things conspire to make up the turmoil and increase the disorder. The great wonder is that they ever get off, but they do move, and under all the circumstances with wonderful expedition.

Our trains on this occasion (as we were moving all our supplies) reached for miles, indeed, almost a continuous line of wagons from Strasburg to Winchester, twenty-two miles. The troops marched about 10 o'clock A.M. Guards had been sent with the wagons, but anticipating an attack in force, we were obliged to hold our forces together as much as possible to meet it. The rumors of large forces of Rebels gathered as we marched, till it became almost a certainty that Winchester was in possession of the Rebels in force, at least 20,000 men. These rumors were corroborated by the frequent attacks upon our trains by cavalry at different points, creating much disorder and no little loss of mules and vehicles. Wagoners are proverbially scary and on the first alarm they cut traces, mount horses, and decamp. This is often done when not an enemy is within miles, and it is a singular fact that our losses on this march were at a long distance from the actual points of attack. Still, under all the difficulties, we succeeded in bringing through our long line of wagons with wonderful success, but the labor to the men was very great and our rear guard was engaged with the Rebel skirmishers till long after midnight.

As we approached Winchester we were agreeably surprised to find that the enemy was not before us, and that the flag of our Union was still flying from the public buildings. The regiments encamped on the elevations just outside of town so as to cover the two roads leading towards Front Royal and Strasburg. I had been up all the night before, and what with the excitement and responsibilities I was weary enough, but the rumors of approaching forces were too reliable and the probabilities of an unequal contest the next day, as well as the hurrying and necessary preparations for the events that were sure to open at daylight occupied my mind and time until midnight.

In the meantime the booming of artillery and crack of the outpost muskets kept up as if the Rebels knew we were sleepy and were determined to keep us from rest. I had been in bed, it seemed to me, not half an hour before a terrible rapping at my door roused me from the deepest sleep. In rushed a bevy of staff officers with Gen. Crawford, who has just joined us, just from Gen. Banks, with positive information that the Rebels were before us (probably around us) in tremendous force of not less than 20,000 infantry, cavalry, and artillery. The General must see me at once to arrange the program for the morning. Of course I was obliged to lose my second night's sleep. The General had information that we should be attacked in the morning by a superior force, and the question of our best position to defend our trains and stores, as well as to keep ourselves from annihilation, had to be discussed.

It was decided to make a fight as we were, in front of the town. I had but 3,500 infantry and ten pairs of Parrott guns with six useless brass pieces to resist a force estimated by nobody at less than 15,000 and by most (prisoners and citizens) at 25,000 troops.[17] The prospect was gloomy enough. That we should all be prisoners of war I had little doubt, but we could not get away without a show of resistance, both to know the enemy's position and to give our trains a chance to get to the rear. I hurried up my own wagons and sent them off to get the advance, if possible, and after sundry preparations and a hurried cup of coffee found the daylight coming on.

The Rebel guns opened fire at the earliest dawn and the banging to and fro became incessant. Larned came up for instructions as the heavy gun-firing began and I, of course, ordered him to put out with Capt. Whittlesey's wagons without delay. He seemed very cool for him, and probably did not realize the difficulties that surrounded us. He says now that the Parrott shells make a terrible noise and he does not like them at all. He seems to think he has been in imminent danger, though I think no shell came within half a mile of him.

I shall not undertake a minute description of our fight. By direction of Gen. Banks I joined him at his headquarters and we rode to the front. The sun was just rising, but the heavy smoke from the guns so obscured a cloudless sky that it smelt sulphurous and looked dismal. I rode to the center of the brigade on the right, which occupied a series of knobs, on the highest of which one of our batteries was playing away manfully. The whiz of the Parrott shells going and coming kept the air quite vocal and, strange to say, had an exciting effect upon my unstrung nerves. I felt rather exhilarated than depressed. There is a singular fascination and excitement about the banging of guns and rattling of musketry with the pomp and circumstance of war.

After riding along this brigade and examining the front through my field glass for a while, I rode to the left where three regiments of my old brigade were posted. They had already been warmly engaged with the infantry and had gallantly repulsed them, almost annihilating a North Carolina regiment. Their dead and wounded lay thickly scattered along the front of one of our regiments. Some of our officers went out and talked with them. They all expressed regret that they had been fighting against the Union. I was rejoiced to find my old brigade doing so well. Every man semed as cool and cheerful as if preparing for a review. They lay in order of battle behind the crests of hills ready for another attack. Away off the hills were seen the moving masses of the enemy, evidently preparing to out-flank us and get to the rear while their batteries were opening in new directions and fresh troops were constantly coming up. The colonel in command of the brigade had already counted *nine regimental colors* that were moving up to crush out this small brigade of only three regiments, numbering not over 1,500 men.

The case certainly looked hopeless enough, but officers and men seemed composed and defiant. Fearing that we were about being turned on this flank, I started for the right wing to get reinforcements. I stopped a few moments to confer with Gen. Banks, and pushing on had hardly reached the valley which intervened between the two wings when a furious fusillade began on the right. Their cannons opened with tremendous vigor and apparently from a dozen new batteries. As I was obliged to ride across the line of fire of most of them, it seemed to me that I had become a target for the whole Rebel artillery. Several shells passed in most unpleasant proximity to my head with a peculiar whizzing sound that made one involuntarily bob his head.

I dashed on as fast as my horse could carry me, but before Icould reach the front I saw our artillery were limbering up and that a regiment on the right (the 27th Indiana) was getting into confusion and many men running back. I dashed at them with such of my staff as were with me and made all sorts of appeals to rally them. The men would stop for a while, but before I could get them in line a new batch of fugitives would break all my efforts. Presently the whole regiment came pouring back in a confused mass. I saw the case was hopeless with them, and directing an officer to rally them behind a stone wall in the rear, I pushed to the right, where were posted four companies of the 1st Michigan Cavalry. I saw near the head of the column Maj. Town, who came forward to meet me with zeal and spirit. I ordered him to dash up the hill and if a chance opened to charge and hold in check the enemy who were rapidly rushing up to the position deserted by our Indianians. Town took his men to the crest of the hill gallantly and I went forward with them to get a look at the position of the enemy.

As we reached the brow of the hill a most terrific fire of infantry was opened upon us from a long line which extended beyond my extreme right. The air seemed literally to be full of whizzing bullets, which stirred up currents of wind as if the atmosphere had suddenly been filled with some invisible cooling process. The cavalry could do nothing before such an overwhelming force and it went down with great rapidity. I stopped just long enough to know that I could see nothing of value through the smoke in front, and looking to the left I saw the whole line of the brigade retiring in order and yet rapidly to the rear. I put spurs to my horse, descended partly down the hill and was beginning to think I should spend a time in Richmond if I did not hurry, especially as I was penned in by a heavy stone wall. I dashed my horse at a point where two or three stones appeared to have been knocked off the top and although he is a pretty heavy beast (not my favorite gift horse) I think he appreciated the occasion for he cleared the wall most gallantly and carried me safely over into a narrow lane. At this moment all my staff officers were away on duty except Capt. Beman, who also took the wall.

As this lane was well under cover I thought it my duty to make a second effort to get a look at the enemy and consequently turned up the hill again but had not got far before the colors of the Rebels, infantry and cavalry, appearing on the top warned me I had no time to lose to withdraw the two brigades. I therefore sent word to Col. Donnelly, commanding the 1st Brigade, to retire by the east of the town and Col. Gordon, 5th Brigade, to pass his regiments through the town to the pike to Martinsburg. It was hurrying times, as you can well imagine, with the very large force that was pressing us on all sides. I rode through one of the side streets and was saluted by a shot from a window which came near finishing Capt. Beman. It was necessary to make great efforts to stop a stampede, especially as the early fugitives had been joined by several unarmed sick from Shields' division, who were scattering alarm with great vigor. These, with a great number of wagons of sutlers and citizens and some army conveyances were whipping and hallooing and creating great alarm.

I overtook, after a while, one of our batteries, which I got into position. I then seized upon every straggling officer and began to reassure the men by forming them in squads, but the difficulties of calming men in such condition is enormous. You can have no idea of the confusion. All of the regiments but one were fortunately passing to the rear in pretty good order, some of them admirably; but still the fugitives continued to increase and the danger of a rout was imminent. There is a strange sympathy in courage and in fear, and masses seem to partake of one or the other feeling from the slightest causes. For instance, on reaching the first woods, with several other mounted officers, I succeeded in getting quite a line of fugitives established and ready to make a stand. Just at this time, down came a company of Michigan cavalry, running their horses at full bent. My line of brave fellows broke at once and went off in double-quick. On the other hand, but a few moments afterward two companies of other cavalry came from toward Martinsburg riding toward the enemy and shouting with drawn sabers. Our fugitives received them with cheers and seemed at once to recover from their alarm.

From this onward to Martinsburg even the leading rabble marched coolly and in quiet. The artillery was placed in position at all good points and the main force of the cavalry, kept in the rear by Gen. Hatch, with the infantry columns on either flank, protected us from much injury, though the assaults by cavalry and battery were frequent. One column of two regiments of Donnelly's brigade followed a parallel road on the right flank and did not join us, but crossed the River Potomac some seven miles below. One other mixed column of cavalry and infantry with twenty-odd wagons, having been cut off on Saturday night, took the road towards Hancock and crossed the Potomac at Cherry Run, all sound. The rest of the command halted an hour or more at Martinsburg and then resumed the march toward Williamsport, where it was supposed the river was fordable for men.

Our whole train (nearly 500 wagons) had preceded us to the river and I began to congratulate myself that we were well out of a bad scrape and that I should get a sound sleep in Williamsport that night. Judge of my disgust, then, when within three or four miles of the river I came upon the rear of our train and was told that the river was not fordable except for horse-teams and horsemen, that it was between four and five feet deep and of great rapidity. With a heavy heart and weary limbs I began to work my way to the ferry through the jam of teams and wagons and guns and caissons and forges, intermingled with straggling cavalry and mounted men. It was already dark and the road, which winds through gullies and descends a series of steep hills to the river for miles, it seemed to me, was not easily followed with my poor eyesight, but after hard labor and a great deal of swearing, I fear, I reached the plateau by the river.

Here it seemed as if all the wagons of the army were in "corral," that is, drawn up in close lines and packed together almost in mass, covering acres of ground. I worked my way to the ferry and found the single scow-boat (by means of which with my brigade alone I was three nights and days in crossing over in March) busy at work taking over the sick and wounded. I was cheered, however, by hearing that my personal baggage had arrived early and was across the river. Hoping to get some relief by the prospect at the ford, I worked through the crowd of mules and vehicles down to the point where the river is entered. Big fires had been built upon both sides to guide the crossing, and horsemen and horse-teams were struggling in the river to get across. The river here is over 300 feet wide and the current exceedingly rapid, especially where the water is the deepest.

The descent into the river from the bank is very muddy and each wagon, as it went in, stalled on the start and then the poor animals would struggle and flounder in the rapid stream, which reached nearly to their backs, till many a horse and scores of mules were drowned. I saw it was a desperate chance for getting our teams over, and as for the men, who were busily building large fires along the hillsides and cooking their suppers, I felt most sadly for them, for not one could possibly pass through that fierce current of a broad and gloomy river.

The poor devils had been without anything to eat, as the fight began in the morning before they had cooked breakfast, and they had marched thirty-five miles without an ounce to eat in their haversacks. I thought of the desperate confusion of horses and wagons and men should we be strongly attacked after it was known that at least five to one were after us; of the demoralized condition of our troops, consequent upon a march of sixty miles (with but one meal) in two days and an almost constant succession of combats and one heavy battle; of the probabilities that we should be followed to the river and attacked, at least by daylight, before a tithe of our men could be crossed and while all our immense train was parked ready to deepen the awful confusion that must follow.

I saw I had another sleepless night before me, and as I had been fasting all day my appetite, as well as my philosophy, prompted me to seek sustenance without delay. So I made for a small house, which I found full of sick and wounded, and the surgeons were actually dressing a horrible arm mutilated by a shell, while others were waiting to be cared for. But the horrible and the careless are strangely mingled in war. A private soldier recognized me as I entered and said he had just made some coffee which he would cheerfully share with me. We sat down to the same table. I found bread and sugar, while he drew from his kit butter and his sugar rations, remarking that he always took care of the subsistence; that while he had enough to eat he could march forever.

The small room filled with hungry officers and men, and it became almost a fight for our small pot of coffee. It shows how discipline works, for my friend, the private, was quite sure to announce my name and rank to save his coffee pot, and it is to the credit of tired and famished men that they always gave way on the announcement. But as I had given up my horse to a wounded soldier during the afternoon, the matter, after all, was only reciprocal. Ah! Rene, the experience of that long, sixty-mile march and the deaths and wounds which a few hours brought under my notice seems now as a great and horrible nightmare dream. My great responsibilities and anxieties I could not then realize, and I felt as cool and collected as on a common march. But they come back to me now, and I just begin to realize under what a tremendous pressure of feeling and rapid thought I was all the while acting. I had no time to think of myself, because I was so filled with the great danger that surrounded the thousands who looked to me for direction.

All Sunday night I walked from the ferry to the ford and then to Gen. Banks' quarters—in wagons by the way—to see what could be done to hasten the safe transportation of our men. Fortunately we had dragged back two pontoon boats which were launched, and a scow was found, and we began about 2 o'clock the morning of Monday to get our men rapidly over. The wagons, too, were getting slowly over the ford, but some wagons stalled and mules drowned and the white-covered boxes stood in the river, some times three and four together, as monuments of danger to those who followed.

The men all dropped to sleep as if dead. The campfires, which blazed briskly on our first arrival, died out. Nothing was heard but the braying of mules and the rolling of wagons moving toward the ford and the occasional obstreperous cursing of some wagon-master at the unruly conduct of his team. We had pushed forward towards the rear a section of artillery and some infantry and cavalry to watch the approach of the Rebels, but so convinced were our men of the vastly superior force of the enemy that they were poorly prepared to resist an attack. I waited impatiently, and yet mostly anxiously, for daylight. The regiments not on duty were brought down to the front and stood quietly waiting their turns to cross. We sat there for hours around the campfires of Gen. Banks, talking of the past and discussing the probabilities of the morrow; the major general and four brigadier generals, Banks, Williams, Hatch, Crawford, and Greene. The last-named two had joined us just before the retreat to command brigades, then commanded by colonels.

I had my horse unbridled and fed from oats picked up from the thrown-away forage, and I unbuckled the martingale and fixed my sword and pistol and other weighty traps so that I could be ready to swim the stream after I was satisfied that further efforts were useless. I was determined to trust to my horse, and as I knew the ford would be over-crowded I decided to take the deep current and trust to the swimming qualities of my horse. So I tied him near the bank with Lt. Pittman's [horse]. Capt. Wilkins and Beman had got separated from us, and Whittlesey was with his train and St. Augustine, ordnance officer, was with his wagons, ready to destroy the ammunition in case of necessity.

My escort of cavalry was reduced to half a dozen who had followed me vigorously all day, and especially one black-eyed boy, who seemed to be, through the fight and even afterwards, like my shadow. He never quit my side, but with a quiet, determined manner was always ready to answer when I called. His name is Lemcke, and he is from Michigan. I have not yet had time to look him up and reward him for his devotion.[18]

At length daylight came. The river had fallen half a foot but the mule-trains were constantly balking and the mules drowning, till there were dozens of wagons and two pieces of artillery in the stream, blocking up the way and increasing the difficulties. So we went to work with ropes to draw them out and succeeded so as to open the way again. Then down came the cavalry to try the ford. With all my fatigue, I could not but laugh at the scene. The strong current would take some away down stream. Others would ride fearlessly over and with little trouble. Several got so confused that they lost the ford and swam away down the river in the middle of the stream. Each horse seemed to have some peculiarity. Now and then a rider would be thrown and would disappear, floundering in the water. Some would run against the stalled wagons, and altogether the scene was most confused, and in spite of its real seriousness and danger was in fact laughable.

But the enemy came not, and after a while, what with fixing the ford entrance and what with improvised facilities of transportation, matters began to be more hopeful and cheerful. At 9 o'clock or so, being satisfied all was safe, I crossed on the ferry. Most of the men were then over, and the wagons were getting along rapidly. I hoped to get some rest, but on this side I found so many things to attend to that it was hours before I could throw myself on a bed. After three days and nights of incessant fatigue and without sleep, you may be assured I slept soundly, and yet awoke unrefreshed. But I am now pretty well again, and yet not over the soreness of muscle and general debility consequent on such long efforts.

I cannot tell you now what our loss has been; probably 800 in killed, wounded, and missing. My infantry force was not far from

3,500 men. The cavalry is made up of so many incongruous organizations that I can say nothing of it, except that it did nothing for us, except as a part of the rear-guard under Gen. Hatch. With him they were useful and efficient, but there were so many straggling and running here and there to the great confusion of order and discipline that I regretted they were not all away.

To sum up, Rene, we have marched sixty-odd miles in two days, with nearly 500 wagons and have brought them all in with the exception of perhaps 50; have fought numerous combats and one severe fight, in the face, and in spite of the best efforts of from 15,000 to 20,000 Rebels. A successful retreat is often more meritorious than a decided victory. We were certainly very successful in our defeat, for which I think "good luck" should have the main praise. We have got off in pretty good order, but if you were a politician I could tell you how easily all this could have been avoided and how, instead of being a defeated and dispirited army, we ought now to be in Staunton or beyond, with Jackson and Ewell defeated fugitives and the whole Rebel crew driven back far beyond the line of Richmond. A singular blunder, a division of our forces and a neglect to send to us troops which were there in this valley has led to all this disaster and unhappy loss of life, property, and territory.

I write this under constant interruptions and have no time to revise. As I am only half recovered to my usual condition you must make it out the best way you can. . . .[19]

  As ever,

Your Affectionate Father,
A.S.W.

❖

REASONS FOR THE DISASTER

Williamsport, June 2nd, 1862.

My Dear Daughter:

I wrote a long account of our "skedaddle" (new but very expressive phrase in the army) to Rene and told her to send it to you. I hope you have received it before this. We had a most disagreeable retreat, marching nearly seventy miles—some of the troops more—in two days, fighting two-thirds of the way with one severe battle in front of Winchester, and passing three nights without sleep. We brought off nearly 500 wagons containing all the supplies of the department. We were attacked by at least 20,000 men. We had to oppose them only two [illegible] brigades of my division of about 3,600 infantry, 10 Parrott guns, and 6 smooth-bore guns, and perhaps 1,500 scattered, discordant, and unorganized and very poor cavalry that literally did nothing but make an occasional show of a portion of themselves. Five hundred of them separated from us and took a different direction and several hundred more fled and spread enormous reports of our destruction. As we were separated from our provision wagons, our men had but one meal in two days, except what they picked up on the way. Our loss in killed, wounded and missing is pretty large, being at least one-fifth of the command. Considering the force attacking us, it is less than might have been expected.

I believe I have several times told you that I thought we were in a critical position. If I have not, it was because I did not wish to alarm you. But the War Department seemed determined to strip Gen. Banks of his whole command to make new departments and new armies at points where there was no enemy. For instance, Gen. Fremont lay directly in our rear and without a possibility of meeting an enemy unless we were driven back. Yet the War Office gave him an army of 30,000 men [and] Gen. McDowell an army of 40,000 or more, while Gen. Banks' command was reduced to the number above stated, in face of two columns of the enemy not less than 10,000 each and but one or two days' march from us.

In order to get us somewhat out of the way (I suppose), we were ordered to return to Strasburg, a three days' march, and here we were obliged to hold the debouches of two valleys (at both points large public stores were in deposit) twelve miles apart. The two columns of Ewell and Jackson were one in each of said valleys and good stone pikes led directly to our valuable deposits. How anybody of common sense could have expected any other result than what followed, I cannot imagine. But the wise "powers that be" at Washington, whose policy seems to be to divide our forces into the weakest and smallest commands, and in this way give time and chance for the Rebels to combine and overwhelm us, did not seem to think we were in danger. On the contrary, they were every day spreading us out over a long railroad line, making us thinnest where we were most exposed and where by a sudden attack our railroad communication could be broken and the rest of our command isolated and surrounded. . . .

The War Department has undertaken the management of the whole war from its bureau in Washington and it has a chronic trepidation that Washington City is in danger of being attacked. If we are not wholly destroyed by its policy, it is because Providence interposes to save us. We have under Banks, McDowell, and Fremont at least 80,000 troops which could be united in one week and overwhelm everything by a movement up this valley to Staunton and to Lynchburg, and from that point move directly on the flank of the Rebel army at Richmond. Not a Rebel enemy would dare to remain behind us either in western or northern Virginia. This movement could and should have been made two months ago, while we were at Harrisonburg, before we were ordered to retrograde. Two brigades of my division and Gen. Shields' division numbered probably 14,000 men; Blenker's division and other troops within a few days' march (at Winchester), numbered 12,000. A part of my division, at least 5,000 men, were east of Strasburg, two days' march. At least 30,000 men could have been concentrated within five days.

We had then before us Ewell's division, 12,000 strong or less, at the crossing of the forks and of the Shenandoah south-east of us, twenty miles off. Jackson's division [was] marching to Staunton with 12,000 more and 4,000 of Johnston's, and massing to attack and defeat, as he did, on Gens. Milroy and Schenck in the mountains. A march of twenty miles would have placed us at Staunton between Ewell and Jackson's divisions, pinning up Jackson in the mountain passes, from which he could not possibly escape, and forcing Ewell to run away if he could, which I doubt from the then condition of the roads. Just at this very moment Shields' division was sent to McDowell and we were ordered back to Strasburg, and Blenker was sent from Winchester away up to Romney and then round to Franklin to join Gen. Fremont!! Marching hundreds of miles out of the way and away from the enemy to get to a place not forty miles from Harrisonburg where we were!

In truth, the War Department seems to have occupied itself wholly with great efforts to give commands to favorites, dividing the army in Virginia into little independent departments and creating independent commanders jealous of one another, and working solely for their own glorification and importance. If we had had but *one general* for all these troops there would not now be a Rebel soldier this side of the railroad from Lynchburg to Richmond. But enough of this. Tell Uncle John that the regulations do not permit me to grumble nor criticise, and he must not compromise me with this information.

Love to all,

Your Affectionate Father,

A.S.W.

1. Bath, better known as Berkeley Springs, is in Morgan County, West Virginia, some five or six miles southwest of Hancock.
2. Actually on Saturday, January 4.
3. That is, on January 8.
4. General Frederick W. Lander, killed on March 2, 1862.
5. General Benjamin Franklin Kelley.
6. The Sibley tent was conical in shape, like the tepee of the Plains Indian tribes, and large enough to house several soldiers in relative comfort. A ventilation device at the top permitted the use of a stove or other fire at the center of the tent.
7. This bridge had been constructed by General Jackson on January 5, for the purpose of crossing the Potomac to capture Hancock. Upon learning of the arrival of Union reinforcements there, he abandoned the project, preferring to direct his force to the recapture of Romney. See his report in *Official Records*, Series 1, V, 392.
8. General Banks was about to launch the first invasion of the Shenandoah Valley. General Jackson was in possession of Winchester at this time.
9. Charles Smith Hamilton, a West Point graduate in the class of 1843. At the opening of the Civil War he was appointed colonel of the Third Wisconsin Infantry Regiment, and on May 17, 1861 was commissioned a brigadier general, on the same day as General Williams.
10. The battle of Kernstown, March 23, 1862, in which General Jackson was defeated. For a comprehensive account of the battle and the succeeding operations by General Nathan Kimball, who in the absence of General Shields commanded the Union army, see *Battles and Leaders of the Civil War* (reprint edition, New York, 1956) II, 302–13.

11. Historians still comment with admiration on the feats of Jackson's infantry who marched "thirty miles in twenty-four hours." The letters of General Williams disclose that when properly led, Union soldiers were quite capable of meeting the best efforts of Jackson's famed "foot-cavalry."

12. "I did not stop, in my haste to get to the front, to visit the battlefield in front of Winchester, but from some of my officers I hear it presented a horrid sight. The dead (several hundred) lay pretty much all in a small space where the fight had been thickest. They were un-buried on the second day, at least the Rebels were. The wounded were taken in early. They filled all of the public and many of the private buildings in Winchester, and all along our route they were in villages and houses. Some wounds made by our shells were ghastly enough.

    "The ladies of Winchester for the first time made their appearance in the streets, carrying comforts to their own wounded, [but] *not to ours.* I am much disgusted with the samples I have had of female Secesh. It has been my endeavor to treat them all courteously and kindly, but their manners, even under the gentlest language and [illegible] are anything but maidenly or ladylike. I say this after making all allowance for wounded pride and bitter feelings."— Letter to daughters, March 27, 1862.

13. Turner Ashby was a native of Fauquier County, Virginia, and a some-what notable leader of Confederate cavalry in the early months of the war. He operated chiefly in the lower Shenandoah area in 1861–1862 until he was killed near Harrisonburg on June 6 of the latter year.—*Dict. Am. Biog.*

14. General Jackson had defeated Milroy at McDowell on May 8, 1862, compelling the latter to retreat northward toward Franklin, West Virginia. This letter indicates that as late as May 17 General Williams had but little, if any, knowledge of the defeat.

15. General Jackson captured Front Royal on Friday, May 23, 1862. The letter discloses that General Williams learned of the affair late on the same day.

16. The report of his death was unfounded. Although wounded, Colonel Kenly survived to serve throughout the war and to die peacefully on December 20, 1891.

17. As commonly in warfare, the strength of the Confederate army is ex-aggerated. Yet Jackson had twice as large a force as General Banks' army, which was, in effect, General Williams' division, and the success-ful withdrawal of the Union army across the Potomac marked an important failure for General Jackson. According to one admiring biographer the failure was caused by the ability of the vanquished Unionists to retreat faster than the victorious "foot-cavalry" could follow them—an apparent reflection upon the marching capacity of

the latter.—Allen Tate, *Stonewall Jackson: The Good Soldier* (New York, 1928), pp. 150–51.

18. August Lemcke from Marquette, who enlisted in Company B, First Michigan Cavalry on August 23, 1861. He was discharged for disability, January 9, 1863.—*Record of Service of Michigan Volunteers*, Vol. XXXI.

19. Not the least remarkable thing about the battle and the retreat of the Union army was the writing by General Williams of this 5,000-word account of it on the day following his escape.

III

Cedar Mountain
and
Second Bull Run

CEDAR MOUNTAIN AND SECOND BULL RUN

Despite the fact that in the Seven Days' Battle before Richmond McClellan had inflicted much heavier losses upon the Confederates than his own army had sustained, his inaction following their conclusion made clear to the world that the campaign had ended in failure. Still seeking a general who would lead the Army of the Potomac to victory, President Lincoln offered its command to General Burnside, who promptly declined the responsibility. In his desperation the President now called General Pope from the West, to whom was entrusted the direction of the newly-formed Army of Virginia. Boastful, vainglorious, and incompetent, Pope promptly led his army to humiliating defeat and a retreat behind the defenses of Washington. Once more General Williams' command, badly outnumbered, stood face to face with Stonewall Jackson's grim soldiers. At Cedar Mountain on August 9 he fought desperately, despite the blundering of the higher command, sustaining one of the heaviest losses, for the numbers engaged, of any battle of the war. The letters which follow fairly disclose the practically unanimous condemnation of the leadership and character of General Pope.

TRAPPING STONEWALL JACKSON

Williamsport, June 3rd, 1862.

My Dear Daughter:

I shall go over the river as far as Martinsburg tomorrow probably. Our men have not been supplied with lost blankets, knapsacks, etc., but Gen. Banks is very impatient to get into Virginia again. . . . Our troops, one of my brigades, are in Martinsburg again and it is rumored that McDowell or Fremont is in Winchester. I suppose we are to do over the old story and go a third time through the valley. When we get well up we shall again be left alone to be driven back. The government seems determined to play the game of fast and loose. . . .

Some of our officers taken at Winchester have returned on parole. The Rebels had left the town and paroled all the officers. Col. Kenly, 1st Maryland, is alive but wounded, not dangerously. Col. Murphy is a prisoner, not wounded. Our prisoners are well treated since the fight. They contrived to pick up a good many stragglers and sick men, but took very few able-bodied men who stayed by their colors.

Where we shall go next is very uncertain. I shall be better able to tell you at Martinsburg. The B. and O. Railroad was not much damaged. Indeed, the Rebels seem to have been on a rapid foray for stores, unless they have gone back to try fortunes with McDowell and Fremont. If these officers have made a junction, Jackson can never get out of the valley. If they have kept separate, as I fear, he will be apt to beat them *seriatim*. Our commanding generals are fishing so much for personal popularity that I think they care but little for the general cause, when it conflicts with private interest.

I am quite well and over my fatigue. Indeed, I see nobody quite as tough as I am. . . .

Love to all,

Your Affectionate Father,
A.S.W.

◈

FAILURE TO TRAP STONEWALL

Winchester, June 16, 1862.[1]
My Dear Daughter:

Your letter of the 10th reached me yesterday. I came up from Williamsport to Martinsburg on Thursday last, spent a pleasant evening with the family of Commodore Bornman, U.S.N., consisting of several daughters and other female relatives, all very agreeable and strongly for the Union. The next day I came on here and now have quarters in a fine old house built on the site of old Fort Loudon of the French and Indian War times. The family is thoroughly Secesh but very civil to me, probably for the reason, given by one of the ladies, that she had heard that I treated all with great kindness and politeness. I wonder if they will remember this if I am taken prisoner.

My troops are scattered from this place to Front Royal. I was glad to meet on my arrival several officers of my 2nd Brigade, which has been absent since our attempted march to Centerville. They had come up as a committee to see Gen. Banks and get an order restoring them to my command again. They have been under Gen. McDowell and are terribly disgusted with him. I felt much pleased at the preference shown for my command. Gen. Banks telegraphed to Washington, but the War Department under some unaccountable influence of Gen. McDowell refuses to order them back to my division.

The pretense is that Gen. McDowell is about to do some great operation. I hope he will. He made a great failure in pursuing Jackson. Officers of his command report that he marched to within four miles of Strasburg and heard the guns of the first fight between Fremont and Jackson, when he ordered a halt and subsequently counter-marched to Front Royal and started, himself, forthwith for Washington. If he had followed closely he could have destroyed Jackon. Instead of that, Jackson seems to have cut up pretty badly Shields' division (a part of McDowell's) sent to intercept him at Port Republic bridge. Matters were very unskillfully managed, or Jackson's army would now be among the things that were.

Indeed, I am heart-sick at the want of common sense in all the management of affairs outside of McClellan's army in Virginia. In this valley it would seem that we are to be the sport of changing policy. I

97

would I were well out of it, even in the hardest place of the army. I can stand anything except the gross stupidity that someone is guilty of. You must not be surprised to hear we are all travelling over the Potomac again, though we have troops enough in West Virginia, if properly combined, to drive away everybody this side of Richmond. We have too many district commands and too many independent commanders.

I am greatly pressed for time. All my regiments are yet unsupplied with things lost on the retreat, knapsacks, blankets, haversacks, canteens, and the like. Three weeks have gone, and we ought to have had everything in three days. I feel sick when I think of the suffering and sickness which these insincere and wicked plays [?] do and will cause among our men. . . . I am wearied, annoyed, tired, and distressed to death, and yet my tough constitution stands it all as if made of iron. Alas, this fearful responsibility which others direct and you cannot control where you are most responsible. . . .

Your Affectionate Father,
A.S.W.

◈

A PROPHETIC FORECAST

Near Front Royal, Va., June 22, 1862.

My Dear Daughter:

I wrote you last from Winchester. We came down here on Thursday last and met a warm reception from our old companions. The men of my old brigade turned out en masse and cheered me vociferously. Some of them remarked that I was a re-inforcement equal to a brigade. This is very flattering, for perhaps I prefer the love of the men to the favor of the government. We are now on the spot where the 1st Maryland Regiment was attacked before our retreat, and the camps are nearly at the place where the last stand was made. I trust we are not to go through the same disaster, though I confess to you I have my apprehensions, so badly are we overlooked and neglected and so confident am I that the Rebels intend to make a desperate effort for this valley. If the government is wise it will direct its fears this way and not toward the fortified front of the capital. If Maryland is ever invaded, it will be through this valley—mark my prediction.[2]

We have received a great acquisition of prominent officers, and have here and hereabouts generals enough to command an army four times our number. Shields and four or five brigadiers have just gone off, but Fremont, Banks, and Sigel, major-generals, and Craword, Greene, Cooper, Slough, and several others besides myself still flourish in this little army. One would suppose the government was determined to scare the Rebels by a show of general officers. . . .

I have not had a line from you since you left Philadelphia, but our mails are very irregular. We are now literally in the field. There are few dwellings hereabouts; the few are very large, but have a run-down air—very a la Virginia. It is not easy to account for, but this whole beautiful valley with its productive soil presents very few indications of prosperity. Houses and appurtenances have an air of neglect and dilapidation. I think they are all in debt and spend yearly more than they raise. . . .

Your Affectionate Father,
A.S.W.

◈

BATTLE OF CEDAR MOUNTAIN

Culpeper, Aug. 17, 1862.

My Darling Daughter:

I have not found time to write you a line since our battle on the 9th, and it was with much difficulty that I could get a telegraph through.[3] Gen. Pope for some reason shut down on everything and thousands of anxious people were kept anxious for days waiting a single line.

We came up here from Washington Court House in a two days' march, dusty and hot in the extreme. Being in the rear, I did not reach this place till after midnight on the night of the 8th (day before the battle) and as I was obliged to see my divisions in camp, it was after 2 o'clock before I got to sleep in a small room of a small toll-house outside of town. There were a dozen or so of us jammed into one room.

At 10 o'clock the next morning news came that the enemy was

advancing in force upon one of my brigades which had moved the night before six miles or so to the front. We left everything standing and moved off to their support. We found the brigade just beyond a little stream called Cedar Run and within a mile of a mountain whose northern side slopes gradually up into a considerable elevation. The country was much wooded, with intervening strips of cultivated land. The position was a bad one and I immediately wrote back to Gen. Banks to that effect. He came up, however, soon afterwards, about the time my second brigade (Goodwin's), which I had gone ahead of, arrived. The enemy had opened with his cannon the moment I arrived, but was soon silenced by ours. From this to 3 o'clock, there was no firing. After my brigades were put in position, our cook got us up a good lunch of coffee, ham, etc., and I invited many field officers of my old brigade to join me. After lunching, we all lay down under a shade [tree] and talked over the events of the ten months we had been together, and everybody seemed as unconcerned and careless as if he was on the lawn of a watering place instead of the front of a vastly superior enemy. Col. Donnelly of the 28th New York, a great joker and full of humor, was in excellent spirits and cracked his jokes as joyously as ever.

Sorrow and misfortune seemed far away and yet of all the field officers of these three regiments (mine) not one, five hours afterwards, was unhurt. Everyone was either killed or wounded. Col. Donnelly, 28th New York, mortally wounded; [4] Col. Knipe, 46th Pennsylvania, twice wounded and nearly insane from a wound in the head; Col. Chapman, 5th Connecticut, wounded and a prisoner; Lt. Col. Brown, 28th, New York, lost his arm; Maj. Cook killed, and Lt. Col. Stone, 5th Connecticut, killed; Maj. Blake, a young man graduated at Yale last year, badly wounded and a prisoner. Two of the adjutants were killed and one wounded. Nearly all the sergeants killed. In the 28th New York every officer in action was killed or wounded. In the 46th Pennsylvania five lieutenants only escaped, in the 5th Connecticut six lieutenants escaped.

The 10th Maine, a new regiment in this brigade, was almost as badly cut up. In Goodwin's brigade the loss was not so great, but in the 2nd Massachusetts, a regiment whose officers are of the Boston elite, four captains were killed outright, all of them young men of great fortunes and of the highest standing. The major was also wounded. Lt. Col. Crane of the 3rd Wisconsin was killed. He was a most excellent man and very popular. Out of the 3,400 infantry of my division at least 1000 were killed, wounded, or missing, but few missing.[5] This does not include the slightly wounded who returned to duty.

The battle was opened by artillery about 3 o'clock. At 5, I had placed my brigade in the woods and orders were sent to push through and if possible take a battery which was doing great mischief to our left (Augur's division). It was in this effort to pass the open ground, which was successfully accomplished, and in the woods beyond where they had concealed their reserves, that we suffered so severely. For two hours the volleys of infantry were incessant and the roar of artillery seemed hushed in the din of small arms. By the aid of the 2nd (Gordon's) Brigade we held on till dark, though it was every moment apparent that we were greatly outnumbered and exposed to flank movements. We then slowly withdrew to our old position, wondering what had become of the 12 or 15,000 of our troops (Rickett's and part of Sigel's corps) which we had passed in the morning on our way out, not over four miles from the battlefield. If they had arrived an hour before sundown we should have thrashed Jackson badly and taken a host of his artillery. As it was, they came up some time after dark and took up a position that greatly relieved us.

We had, however, several instances of tremendous cannonading and the Rebels tried once seriously to force our lines. I came very near being caught in it. I was riding towards a road in front of which I had been directed to mass my division, or what was left of it. When but a few rods off, a spirited fire of infantry was opened upon us. Just in front of me was Gen. Gordon and an escort of cavalry. Fortunately we were in a small hollow and the balls passed over us. There was, however, a general stampede of officers and dragoons. Just behind us Gens. Pope and Banks were sitting dismounted with a good many staff officers and escorts. This was a hurrying time with them and altogether the skedaddle became laughable in spite of its danger. In front of the woods not over 500 yards off was an infantry regiment just come up, which opened fire with very little regard to friend or foe, and I fear killed some of our horses if nothing else.

I contrived to get beyond the line of fire pretty soon. The Rebels almost immediately opened with a heavy fire of artillery to which two of our batteries (twelve pieces) on the flank promptly responded. It was a grand sight, especially as our batteries were well served and knocked the Rebels to pieces rapidly. Finding the Rebel shells passed far over me, I stood on a little knoll and enjoyed the sight vastly. It was a flaming pyrotechnic display. In the morning, I counted over twenty dead Rebel horses, and they left one lieutenant and several men killed on the position of their battery. They didn't stay long after our guns got the range and quiet reigned the rest of the night.

It was a glorious moonlight, too, but what with fatigue and excitement and extreme thirst I can't say I was in the best frame [of mind] to enjoy it. I had sent my escort away in the afternoon to search the woods on the right, and after dark, all my staff officers to search for stragglers. So after riding with Gen. Banks to the river after water, I picked up a bundle of wheat or rye straw, took my horse to a fence near the front, unbridled him, tied the halter about my arm, and went to sleep while he munched straw.

After an hour or so I woke up and rode to the rear again to find water and see if my stray companions could be found, but I discovered nothing but two bareheaded[?] staff officers of General Banks and so I came back to my old stand and dozed till daylight. As the first streaks of light appeared, I discovered two haystacks, and hoping for a few for my horse went over to them. Here I found a strange medley of general and staff officers and privates all mixed up in the straw. Amongst others, Gen. McDowell appeared to me as I had taken a roost for a small nap before the fight was renewed, as I was assured by Gen. Pope it would be by sunrise. I wish he had kept his promise, for I feel confident we should have punished them badly. I found, too, that my troops had gone to the rear and that all the other troops had been massed in columns of brigades. I had heard the rumbling of vehicles, which I dreamed or imagined to be ambulances with wounded, but which was the moving of artillery. Everything was solemnly still except this rumbling and an occasional suppressed tone of command.

I found my troops and all my staff (except Captain Wilkins) a mile or so to the rear. They had been looking for me almost all night, but not so far to the front. Poor Wilkins was missing. He was seen safe after the fight coming from the right where I sent him. He probably was run upon by the Rebel pickets when alone and captured. We heard the next day he was a prisoner and several have since come in who saw him. He is not wounded. I miss him greatly now, for Gen. Banks was run against by a horse in the skedaddle and on the following day turned over the command to me and went into town. I have since been incessantly at work till after midnight. I contrived to finish a hurried letter to Rene yesterday and now I am writing you at midnight. The applications I receive from all sources for everything, for telegraph, transportation, protection, etc., and the thousand reports and returns, the looking after the broken troops of two divisions, the numberless papers to be endorsed and forwarded, the hundreds of matters to be examined and approved, you cannot imagine.

We have a new general, too, who has new rules, with a new staff just from the bureau that make all the trouble and vexation possible. I pray for Gen. Banks to get well. To add to all, the adjutant general of the corps was wounded (Maj. Pelouse). My adjutant general and the adjutant general of the 2nd Division were both taken prisoners. I have nobody on my staff to help me but Lt. Pittman, who is adjutant general and aide. The quartermaster and commissary have their duties out-side. . . .

I was ordered with the remnants of our corps into town on Wednesday last, and have command of all the troops here and about. How long we shall stay here I can't guess. A good many troops are in advance, but not as many, I fear, as the Rebels can bring up from Richmond. I hope to see the day we shall meet them with at least equal numbers, and on fair grounds. But our generals seem more ambitious of personal glory [than] of their country's gain, at least some of them. . . .

As ever, Your Affectionate Father,
A.S.W.

◈

THE SECOND BULL RUN CAMPAIGN

August 26, 1862.[6]

My Dear Daughter:

I am now near Fayetteville, about seven miles from Warrenton. For ten days I have not been able to change clothes and only now and then to wash my face—sleeping under trees or on the unsheltered earth— and generally vagabonding up and down the Rappahannock. I have not been able to write you for two good reasons. 1, I have had nothing to write on. 2, A general order has stopped all letters going out. I might add a third—that day and night we have been literally under arms, liable at any moment to be called into action or into a fatiguing march. If I ever get settled, I will give you a detailed history of the last week. I have had hard service and hard traveling, but I think the past week's experience puts all other labor and privations to the shame. All our baggage has been forty miles from us and we have been at times, officers and men, literally with[out] bread or meat. Every minute came a new order—now to march east and now to march west, night and day.

Such a vagrant-looking set of officers from the major general down was never seen. We have been on the march today, having left Waterloo Bridge yesterday. I find here an officer who is going to Washington, and I use him to smuggle through a note.

I don't know if we shall get mails up or not but I suppose we shall, as I received a letter yesterday, but none from you for ten days. Where all this will end, I cannot guess. We are getting some reinforcements but nothing to what we should have. A few of us—my division reduced in the late battle to half its muster and almost without officers—are compelled to do an immense duty, enough to kill iron men. We have been under fire of shells almost continuously and at times most incessant and tremendous. After hard labor and great losses of life we are back where we were when Gen. Pope published his famous order that we must look to no lines of retreat and that in his western campaigns he never saw the backs of his enemies. In short he boasted greatly, at which we all laughed and thought he would do better to stay where we then were till he got men enough to do half what he threatened. But I have room for no more. Say to Minnie that I will write her by my first private chance.

Your Affectionate Father,
A.S.W.

◈

Camp near Rockville, September 8, 1862.
My Dear Daughter:

With the exception of my short pencil note, I have not been able to write you since the fight at Cedar Mountain but once I believe. . . . For two weeks, we were without knowledge of the outer world. To look back upon those two weeks of anxiety, sleepless nights, long marches, and almost incessant battling, it seems like a long nightmare when one wakes up feverish and exhausted, and but indistinctly can recall what has happened to him.

A few days after our Cedar Mountain battle, the command of the army corps was turned over to me by Gen. Banks, and I was ordered to move the corps to Culpeper and take command of all the troops there. We were there several days but most incessantly and vexatiously occupied. I was almost always up till after midnight. The loss of so many general and field officers threw matters into confusion.

I had got the books and papers of the corps together and was getting matters straightened when orders came for us to pack up for a sudden march on Rappahannock Crossing. We had our tents pitched in [the] large front yard of a Dr. Herndon and I was most comfortably located. But on the 17th ult. at 2 p.m. we were obliged to pack up and start our trains, but the corps was to remain as a rear guard to all of McDowell's wagons. Mine were got out of town early, but McDowell's and Sigel's came lurching by all night while myself and staff were watching and waiting. It was 10 o'clock the next morning before I could put my column in motion.

While I was waiting, sleepy and impatient, soon after sunrise a cavalry officer brought up and delivered over to me Maj. Fitzhugh, a general of Gen. Stuart's Rebel cavalry. He was well dressed and a very gentlemanly young man. I invited him to take coffee with me, as it was just ready, and afterwards I took his parole not to attempt to escape. He was mounted on an elegant horse, a present of his wife, parting with which seemed to be his great grief. He rode with me all day. I gave him a dinner on the road. I crossed the Rappahannock before sundown at the railroad crossing and took up a line of battle on the south side of the railroad along the river and bivouacked. My wagons had all gone back on some quartermaster's orders and our best shelter was the woods, to which we took with our prisoner. I kept him till the afternoon of the next day, took his parole to report to Gen. Halleck in Washington, and then shipped him on the railroad. He almost shed tears when I took him aside and offered him such funds as he might need for present uses. He acknowledged most warmly my kindness, which he had not expected, and seemed sincerely affected. So strangely are the extremes of friend and foes brought near. So strangely does war mix our passions and our better feelings.

The enemy opened his big guns upon us the next day, Wednesday, but harmed only the forces (McDowell's) on our right. Thursday night we moved down towards Berry's Ferry to support [Gen.] Reno. Slept within woods in a big rain storm, ordered back next morning, stayed in woods.

Friday, 22d, ordered up river to support Sigel. Encamped near Beverly Ford, terrific shelling all day. Moved troops to woods in rear of Sigel, who attacked the enemy with infantry. Gen. Bohlen was killed.[7] Sigel lost badly, though I see the newspapers give him the false reputation of having taken 2,000 of the Rebels! In the morning (Saturday) the woods we were in were shelled and several fell close to us. A 12-pound round shot passed directly over our impromptu breakfast table just as we left it, whereupon we mounted our horses and moved out of range.

Saturday, 23d, followed Sigel's corps towards Warrenton Springs along the Rappahannock. It was a day of very slow marching over very bad roads. Sigel had a long train with him and we were obliged to lie in the road for hours for his command to go by. . . . Reno's corps followed us. Just before night a tremendous cannonade began in front followed by heavy volleys of musketry. It was dark before we halted for the night. Sigel was in advance up[on] a narrow, bad road. Reno some miles in the rear. The enemy was reported in force across a narrow creek. We were crowded into a small open space surrounded by heavily wooded hills. I went forward to see Sigel. Found him in a farmhouse full of Dutch staff officers and several general officers: Gen. Carl Schurz, Milroy, and Schenck were there. All anticipated a big battle next day.

I got home through a horrid road by the light of a lamp carried by a mounted orderly about 2 o'clock in the morning. The next day we reconnoitered early towards Warrenton Springs—got the column on the road following Sigel about noon. As soon as we reached the hills overlooking the Springs, the Rebels opened firing[?] with their guns. Ours were soon in position and for hours we had the fiercest artillery duel that has happened in this war. While it was going on, I was obliged to march my division along a wooded hill directly in the rear of our batteries and under the direct range of the Rebel guns. The shells whizzed and burst over us and the cannon shot cut the trees and branches like rattling hail, and yet strange to say not a man of the 1st Brigade that I was leading was injured. In the midst of the wood we found a lady (the wife of one of Sigel's staff) and two officers closely hugging the side of a big tree. As we came up one officer (an old German of most military aspect), alarmed apparently by a shell bursting near, threw himself flat upon his saddle and spinning his horse by ferocious kicks high on his rump, he skedaddled in about as laughable a way as can be conceived. None of us could help a grin quite audible even though all probably would have been glad to emulate his speed.

We passed safely through these woods and obtaining an open space in a deep hollow, we halted for an hour or so while the duel of big guns kept up. Finally, a corps of pioneers reached the bridge over the Rappahannock and set fire to it. We marched off up the Warrenton Pike till we reached a cross road towards Waterloo Bridge which crosses the river between Warrenton and Springville, our old route when we first began the campaign under Pope. We encamped on the road about two miles from the bridge. Sigel in front of us still and his eternal trains all night as they had all day stopping our march. The next morning, we marched towards the bridge, but soon fell into Sigel's confused ranks. I was leading the corps, and as we were ascending a hill Sigel appeared in his long cloak and broad-brimmed hat, looking as if he might be a descendant of Peter the Hermit. He was terribly enraged that Gen. Banks should order his corps to march through his ranks. He lifted his arms up and spread out his cloak as if he was about to give a benediction. It was a tremendous cursing in mixed German and broken English. Altogether the scene was very laughable, and we all laughed heartily as soon as we could get our faces away from the enraged general. I calmed his resentment in a short time by assuring him that Gen. Banks had intended no disrespect, and that I would take the responsibility of moving the corps back and uncovering his troops, which I did in five minutes. I saw the enraged general soon afterwards expending his surplus wrath on a very black Negro, whom he was having soundly thrashed, probably for neglecting his breakfast.

Same day, Monday, the 25th, we received orders to march in all haste towards Bealeton Station, about three miles from the Rappahannock. It was rumored that the Rebels were moving towards Thoroughfare Gap to cut our communications. We marched some miles, passing McDowell's corps, or part of it, on the way. We were halted for the night in a fine camping ground. At last I halted the corps there as Gen. Banks was absent in Warrenton. The next morning we moved forward, but were halted in the woods after a few miles and stayed all night. Wednesday (27th) we again moved forward to Bealeton and followed up the railroad towards Warrenton Junction. We encamped at night with[in] a mile of Warrenton Junction. Fitz John Porter's command were ahead of us and thousands of his stragglers covered the route.

The next morning (28th) we marched to Kettle Run near Catlett's Station. There we halted over night and had time to look at the battleground of Gen. Hooker's division, which took place the day before.[8] Gen. John C. Robinson (Capt. Robinson of Detroit) was one of his brigadiers. As I came up with the rear of Porter's corps in marching out in the morning, I came across the 16th (Stockton's) Michigan Regiment. Capt. Tom Barry, formerly a clerk at Tillmans, was commanding the regiment.[9] I found several officers I knew, among them Robert Elliott. We left Kettle Run and marched to Bristow Station and Manassas Junction. All day before we had heard the sound of heavy firing northwest and north of us, but no order came to move nor did we hear a word from Pope. Today we could see from the fortifications of Manassas the fight going on—the smoke of cannon and of infantry firing.[10] About 3 p.m., just as the cloud of smoke seemed thickest in the center, and when, too, it seemed that our troops were receding (as afterwards proved true), we were ordered to march back four miles to Bristow Station. All night we were without information save what came from rumor with its thousand tongues. We were away off on one flank with a little decimated corps of not 6,000 fighting men. If our troops were driven our chances of getting away were small. I had taken the corps back by order. It was nearly dark when we reached our camping ground. I could not find Gen. Banks and so made my dispositions for the night as best I could. I slept soundly in spite of uncertainty and doubt and anxiety.

Early the next morning Gen. Banks sent for me and showed me an order to burn all public property and march via Brentsville. The railroad bridge had been burned by the Rebels, leaving on the south side hundreds of our wounded and sick, besides miles of cars full of army stores and provisions. The wounded and sick we had taken off to Centerville by wagon, but the goods were there and the torch was soon applied and a tremendous bonfire, whose smoke went up high into the heavens, broke out for miles along the railroad. At the same time our ammunition wagons were set on fire and many of our ambulances. Explosions followed like salvos of artillery. I had for my headquarters carriage an ambulance and one wagon, which we had contrived to secure to carry our forage and food. These I determined to keep. I got them off safely and have them yet. Gen. Banks burnt up his private baggage almost wholly. We saved a good many ambulances. The day was rainy and the road we took to Brentsville muddy and heavy.

At Brentsville we turned off to the left and after [marching] up hill and down we came out on the plains near Manassas and crossing Bull Run we encamped on the hills near Blackburn Ford. This is the point where your Gen. Tyler and our Gen. Richardson began the attack on Thursday before the unfortunate battle of Bull Run. The affair was considered a failure, and I believe (justly or unjustly I can[not] say) both Tyler and Richardson were considered censurable. We remained here guarding the bridge over the ford that night and part of next day. It was here that we began to get some definite intelligence of the disasters of the fights on Saturday. We heard, too, the death of poor Fletcher Webster, who had spent a day and night with me at Culpeper on his return from leave at Marshfield. He was in great spirits there and was anxious that the battling might begin. Here, too, we heard that Col. Brodhead was wounded and a prisoner. He has since died and his body sent home.[11] Col. Roberts, too, of the 1st Michigan [Infantry] was reported killed.[12] Fifty of my personal acquaintances and friends were reported killed or wounded. Such is war. Our troops had fallen back and lay as thick as leaves in Vallombrosa in rear of the bare hills of Centerville.

In the afternoon, we were ordered towards Fairfax Station by a road running parallel to the pike from Centerville to Alexandria. We had nearly reached a cross road to Fairfax Court House when a heavy fire of infantry opened on our left, apparently not half a mile distant. We had just been ordered by a staff officer to halt and there we lay on the road while the musketry rattling and cannon now and then boomed out above the rattling din. Amidst it all began the most furious storm of thunder, lightning, and rain I have ever been exposed to. The firing slackened somewhat, but in each lull of the storm it would begin again furiously. Then the thunder would begin again and such lightning, apparently striking the trees in our very midst. All this kept up until dark, when guns and thunder all stopped and the silence was oppressive. I crawled into my ambulance and slept soundly from fatigue. In the morning, we learned that Gens. Kearny and I. S. Stevens had been killed in the fight near us and that we had lost several hundred killed and wounded. The enemy were forced back, but it cost us valuable lives, two of the best officers in the service.[13]

After waiting half a day in the road, we were finally moved forward with orders to proceed to the forts near Alexandria. This was Tuesday (2nd inst.). It was midnight before we got into bivouac on the hills behind the forts near Washington. We groped about for hours before we could find a place to stop, trying to find Franklin's corps.[14] We fetched up in the grove of a gentleman's country seat. I fear as the night was cold that our long [illegible] in the Rebel land did not prepare our troops to abstain as they should from burning the man's fences. It was very cold, strangely so, and our men for over two weeks had been days without rations, marching without shelter, bivouacking in storms and wearied and fretting beyond endurance. Indeed, Rene, I should not be willing to try a description of what our men were exposed to in this terrible seventeen days. Our trains had all been sent away and we were always finding forage and subsistence burnt up just as we were getting near it.

All this is the sequence of Gen. Pope's high sounding manifestoes. His pompous orders issued in Washington and published in the daily telegraphs all over the country with great commendation of the press and apparently of the people greatly disgusted his army from the first. When a general boasts that he will look only on the backs of his enemies, that he takes no care for lines of retreat or bases of supplies; when, in short, from a snug hotel in Washington he issues after-dinner orders to gratify public taste and his own self-esteem, anyone may confidently look for results such as have followed the bungling management of his last campaign. A splendid army almost demoralized, millions of public property given up or destroyed, thousands of lives of our best men sacrificed for no purpose. I dare not trust myself to speak of this commander as I feel and believe. Suffice it to say (for your eye alone) that more insolence, superciliousness, ignorance, and pretentiousness were never combined in one man. It can with truth be said of him that he had not a friend in his command from the smallest drummer boy to the highest general officer. All *hated* him. McDowell was his only companion and McDowell is disliked almost as much, and by his immediate command he is entirely distrusted.

But enough of this. We were allowed a day's rest near Fort Albany and then ordered to the front and have led the advance up to this point. We are now within a few miles of where I began my service with the old brigade a year ago. What a contrast. The three regiments of that brigade (one has been transferred) are here yet in name, but instead of 3,000 men they number altogether less than 400 men present! Not a field officer nor adjutant is here! All killed or wounded! Of the 102 officers not over 20 are left to be present! Instead of hopeful and confident feelings we are all depressed with losses and disasters. Instead of an offensive position the enemy is now actually in Maryland and we are on the defensive. What a change! After such vast preparations and such vast sacrifices. This has been called a "brainless war." I can't tell you of the future. We are accumulating troops this way and shall doubtless have some severe conflicts. If we fail now the North has no hope, no safety that I can see. We have thrown away our power and prestige. We may become the supplicant instead of the avenger. . . .

The trains left us at Culpeper, and we did not see them again till we crossed the river. They luckily escaped the raids at Catletts and Fairfax. . . .

I am again in command of the army corps and worked to death. Gen. Banks seems to get sick when there is most to do. I see that the 24th Michigan, Col. Morrow's [regiment], is ordered to this corps.

Four other regiments are ordered to us, but they are so green in officers and men that little can be expected.

Love to Auntie and children. I will write as often as I can.

Your Affectionate Father,

A.S.W.

1. Reproduced from a typewritten copy. The original letter is missing.
2. General Lee's two invasions of the North, ending respectively at Antietam and Gettysburg, were by way of the Shenandoah Valley.
3. The battle of Cedar Mountain, August 9, 1862, the first encounter in the Second Bull Run campaign. In it, General Banks' command, 8,000 strong, fought desperately General Stonewall Jackson's 20,000 men, being driven in retreat toward nightfall, as General Williams relates.
4. Colonel Dudley Donnelly, wounded on August 9, died at Culpeper, August 15, 1862.
5. General Williams' Second Corps bore the brunt of the battle and sustained all but a minor fraction of the Union losses (2,216 men in a total for all units engaged of 2,381). Of the total loss reported, 585 are ascribed as "captured or missing." General Williams, however, states that the missing were but few, leaving the implication that almost all of the 585 were either captured or killed. General Jackson's report of the battle acknowledges a loss of 1,314 killed, wounded, and missing, and adds that this was "probably" about one-half the Union loss. Since the latter were outnumbered two to one, the proportionate Union loss was correspondingly greater. Jackson was so gratified over the victory that he ordered a divine service to be held in the army on August 14, to give thanks for past victories and to implore the continued divine favor for the future. See *Official Records*, Series 1, XII, Part 2, 136–39 and 181–85.
6. A penciled note written on scrap paper. The Second Bull Run campaign was now approaching its climax in the defeat of General Pope's army and its withdrawal within the defenses of Washington on August 29–30, 1862. A second letter of similar tone was written on the same day by General Williams to his other daughter.
7. General Henry Bohlen, a native of Germany, was appointed colonel of the Sixty-fifth Pennsylvania Infantry on September 30, 1861. He was commissioned a brigadier general, April 28, 1862, and was killed in the battle of Freeman's Ford on August 22, following.
8. The battle of Kettle Run on August 28, 1862 was another Union defeat. For General John C. Robinson's report of it see *Official Records*, Series 1, XII, Part 2, 421–22.
9. Thomas B. W. Stockton of Flint, a West Point graduate of the class of 1827, served as colonel of the First Michigan Regiment in the Mexican

War 1847–48. In 1861, at the age of fifty-nine, he became colonel of the Sixteenth Michigan Infantry. He was captured at Gaines' Mill in the Peninsular campaign, June 27, 1862, and was exchanged on August 12, following. Thomas J. Barry of Detroit was commissioned captain of Company A, Sixteenth Regiment, on August 1, 1861. He was wounded in the battle of Manassas on August 30, 1862.—*Record of Service of Michigan Volunteers,* Vol. XVI.

10. The first day's battle of Second Bull Run, Friday and Saturday, August 29–30, in which General Pope unsuccessfully attacked Jackson's force.

11. Colonel Brodhead was wounded in the action of August 30 and died on September 2.

12. Horace S. Roberts of Detroit entered the military service (three months) as a captain in the First Michigan Infantry Regiment on April 20, 1861. On August 10, 1861 he was commissioned lieutenant-colonel of the re-organized (three-year) First Michigan Regiment, of which he became colonel on April 28, 1862. He was wounded at Gaines' Mill, on June 27 and was killed on the second day of Second Bull Run, August 30, 1862.—*Record of Service of Michigan Volunteers,* Vol. I.

13. This was the battle of Chantilly, September 1, 1862, in which General Jackson unsuccessfully sought to gain the road by which General Pope's defeated army was withdrawing toward Fairfax Court House. For the careers of General Isaac I. Stevens of Washington Territory and General Philip Kearny, see *Dict. Am. Biog.*

14. General William B. Franklin, whose military career proved stormy. The conduct of his corps at the Second Bull Run battle provoked a testy exchange of letters between General Halleck and General McClellan, the former accusing someone (presumably McClellan) of disobedience to orders and the latter replying with a tart request for definite instructions, since he resented being accused of disobedience when he had "simply exercised the discretion you imposed in me."—*Official Records,* Series 1, XII, Part 3, 723. For General Franklin's career see *Dict. Am. Biog.*

IV

Northward
to the Potomac
and Antietam

VI

NORTHWARD TO THE POTOMAC AND ANTIETAM

The Confederate victory at Second Bull Run on August 29 and 30 presented to General Lee two alternative courses of future action. Lacking the resources required for a successful investment of Washington, he could concentrate his army at a suitable base between that city and Richmond, there to await a renewed Union invasion; or he could improve upon the current demoralization of the Union forces to launch his own invasion of the North in the hope of rallying the people of Maryland to the Confederate cause and of obtaining its recognition by the governments of western Europe.

The decision was made quickly and on September 3 Lee's army began the northward march which was to culminate two weeks later at Antietam. But the people of Maryland did not rally to the Confederate banner. In need of supplies from Virginia, Lee divided his army, sending General Jackson to capture Harpers Ferry, which commanded the northerly end of the Shenandoah route. Meanwhile General McClellan, who had been restored to the command of the Army of the Potomac, followed the Confederate invaders, interposing between Lee's army and the cities of Washington and Baltimore. At this juncture blind chance dealt General Lee a stunning blow. He gave to three of his generals identical copies of an order detailing his plans for the movement of his army. One of the copies became lost and was picked up by a Union soldier. Conveyed to General McClellan, it disclosed to him the division of the Confederate army and gave him the opportunity to crush Lee before Jackson could rejoin him. In turn, a Confederate sympathizer who learned of McClellan's possession of the order, reported this information to Lee, who took position behind Antietam Creek, where he awaited McClellan's attack. The ensuing battle of

Antietam, fought on September 17, was probably the bloodiest single day's fighting of the entire war. Although the Union forces were again badly mismanaged, Lee's army was so severely punished that all thought of continuing the invasion of the North was abandoned, and the army was glad to escape to the friendly shelter of Virginia, whither the Army of the Potomac slowly followed it. One will seek long for a more stirring description of a great battle than the one which General Williams penned to his daughters from his camp near Harpers Ferry on September 22, but five days after the battle.

EN ROUTE TO ANTIETAM

Camp near Damascus, Md., Sept. 12, 1862.

My Dear Daughter:

I have not written you (excepting a scrawl in pencil) since we were in camp near Cedar Mountain. I have not been able to, for we were over two weeks without pen, ink or paper—almost without food— sleeping every night in our clothes—often without taking off my spurs! —and without one opportunity to change our underclothes.

What with marching through woods and bushes my only coat is exceedingly ragged, and I have doubtless, in the eyes of the new regiments, added to our old corps much the aspect of a jail bird or loafer. Indeed, we old veterans are much amused at the fresh and gaudy show of our new volunteers. I have no doubt they are equally disgusted with our forlorn appearance. I have now about 3,000[?] of these jolly fellows, who have marched up from Washington without tents and with no shelter but blankets and some overcoats. They think they are suffering amazingly, and I fancy, as it is raining tonight, that they are not as comfortably placed as they were a few weeks ago under their paternal roofs, as they have not the knack of old soldiers of ex- temporizing shelters out of rails and blankets and pieces of boards. I doubt if they won't by tomorrow begin to look to the ragged regiments for comfort.

I have not time to write you of my experiences since we left Cul- peper. I have sent Rene a long account, and if you wish to read it ask her to send it to you. Suffice it to say that for over three weeks we have been scarcely a day without marching—for at least seven days without rations, except what a poor country afforded to a very large and hungry crowd. Our horses fed on the grass of the country. At length we reached the fortifications opposite Washington, about the last of the army of Pope, which never took thought of lines of retreat or bases of supplies.

I think I prognosticated to Uncle John through a letter to you that Pope would prove, as he did, a vain, weak, and arrogant man. From the first, I had a great disgust for him for his pomposity and swagger, though I was glad that we had one head to the army—even a cabbage head! We rested but one day in camp near Alexandria and have since had the advance. Gen. Banks has been in command of the corps but a few days since the battle of Cedar Mountain, and since we reached the fortifications, relinquished it altogether. I have had the advance toward Frederick till today. This morning I came up from five miles below, and pitching my headquarters tent on the cross road have been entertaining my friends of Burnside's command, which has been filing by all day. He has over 30,000 men. Just think of the procession! Gen. Willcox commands a division in Burnside's command (2nd Corps) and dined with me as he came by.[1] He is looking remarkably well, never better I think, certainly fatter than formerly. Gen. Burnside passed almost all the afternoon in my tent with Gen. Parke,[2] Cox[3] and others.

The 17th Michigan belongs to the command and many of the officers stopped to see me.[4] A few days ago my camp was within a few rods of the 7th Michigan and many of the officers who were in the School of Instruction at Fort Wayne called upon me. Indeed, I have repeatedly met Michigan officers of late, and they all greet me with great cordiality.

I have been coöperating with Gen. Sumner's corps. In it is Gen. Dick Richardson, commanding a division.[5] I find he has been made a major general, but there seems to be great contempt for him among his brother officers of rank. I did not see him, but Captain Norvell, his assistant adjutant general, came to see me.[6]

I have been intensely occupied. The loss of the principal officers of the corps has greatly perplexed me, and the [labor entailed by the] re-organization of commands which have lost field and staff and company officers, as well as all their books and papers, is immense. We march all day or are under arms all day, and then pitch our main tent and write half the night. While I write, my office tent looks like a bureau office in Washington. Five clerks, two staff officers, and some outsiders are all at work at a long table through the center. Orderlies are coming and going with dispatches. Reports are coming in from brigades and divisions and the establishment looks as if we had sat down for a season's work, and yet in an hour everything may be packed in wagons as it was an hour ago and we off for some other locality.

Tell Uncle Lew we are approaching the Rebels in large force. Burnside on the right, myself next, Sumner next, Franklin next. There will be a great battle or a great skedaddle on the part of the Rebels. I have great confidence that we shall smash them terribly if they stand, more confidence than I have ever had in any movement of the war. We move slowly but each corps understands the others, and when we do strike I think it will be a heavy blow. Tell Uncle Lew to pay those notes as his judgment dictates. I will write him if I am not on the march at daylight. . . . Don't be frightened about me, but believe me,

As ever, Your Affectionate Father,
A.S.W.

◈

EN ROUTE TO ANTIETAM

Camp near Frederick, September 13, 1862.

My Dear Lew: . . .

I have been so long without a clean shirt that I am rejoiced to be so near a town that I may reasonably hope to find a haberdasher to-morrow. It is just a month that I have been without rest or sleep of a reasonable kind. Tonight I have straw under a blanket! Think of that luxury!

The enemy have gone towards Hagerstown. We shall find them that way, I think, though they evidently begin to fear we are too many. I reached this (near Frederick) this noon, having forded the Monocacy with my corps. Gens. Hooker, Burnside, Sumner, and Franklin are near at hand.

The big guns have been banging all day, but little injury done about here. We have chased them across the South or Cotoctin mountains. What a pretty circuit I have made. My march for Dixie began here, and here I am after a year, with a crippled nation's *defenders*.[7]

I can't write more, for at every halt I have an infinitude of matters to examine and decide and write about.

Love to all. I wrote Minnie a day or so ago.

Yours Affectionately,
A.S.W.

◈

SOUTH MOUNTAIN AND ANTIETAM

Camp near Sandy Hook,
Near Harpers Ferry, Sept. 22, 1862.

My Dear Daughters:

I wrote you last from Damascus, I think, on the 11th inst. On the 12th we moved to the neighborhood of Urbana, after a circuitous and tedious march. On the 13th we marched to Frederick expecting an attack all the way. We forded the Monocacy and encamped about a mile east of the city. It was a year ago nearly that we marched through Frederick with flying banners. Alas! of those gallant troops (the old 3rd Brigade) how few remain. On Sunday the 14th we were ordered forward from Frederick crossing the Catoctin Mountain by a very rough road, east of the pike upon which we were encamped a year ago. The road took us very near our old campground at a small hamlet called Shookstown. I found all the people knew me, and I was fairly deluged with peaches, apples, etc. Ascending the mountain, we heard the reports of distant artillery and once on the summit could see that a fierce engagement was going on across the valley and in the gorges of the opposite range of mountains.[8]

We were hurried down and marched over rough roads and finally about sundown I got an order to bivouac the corps. Before, however, the regiments had filed into the fields a new order came to follow Gen. Sumner's corps over the ploughed fields toward the musketry firing heard in front. I had ordered a supper (after a meal-less day) at a farmhouse and went back to get it and to look after my artillery which had got astray in our field and erratic marches. We had a good meal and I mounted to follow the command when I heard that Capt. Abert, U.S. Topographical Engineers, of my staff had been seriously injured by the fall of his horse. Having directed his removal to the house where Dr. Antisell was, I rode back but met a staff officer on the way with a report that the corps was ordered to Middletown to report to Gen. McClellan. Thither I started in the darkest of nights, but at Middletown could hear nothing of my corps. So I rode from there toward the mountain gap where the fighting had been and got as far as our advanced pickets but could not find my corps.

Back I went to Middletown again, but could get no knowledge of my command. But here I heard with sad heart that Gen. Reno, one of the best officers and bravest fellows, had been killed in the engagement.[9] But one day before he had spent at Damascus half a day with me, full of spirits, full of confidence, and full of good feeling. Of all the major generals he was my *beau ideal* of a soldier. You will remember that he commanded a corps which followed ours along the Rappahannock. I had been thrown much with him. His frankness, absence of pomp and parade, his cheerfulness under all circumstances—that indescribable something in manner, had made me love him at first sight. I could have cried when I heard of his death, but for the thousand cares that oppressed me and for the heavy duties which close up the tender impulses of the heart.

Hearing nothing of my command I again rode to the front and on the pike found a portion of our regiment sleeping calmly with no knowledge of the rest. Soon afterward I found a mounted orderly, who directed me to a by-road leading up through the mountain defiles, and following this I at length at 2 o'clock in the morning found the rear division of my command bivouacking near the column of Hooker, which had been engaged with the enemy. I lodged under the best tree I could find, and at daylight got my whole command under arms and went forward to see what was to be done. On the top of the pass I met almost the first [man] I knew, Gen. Willcox, who commands a division. The dead lay thick in front, but I could see nothing beyond as the mist hung heavily on the mountain. Our troops, however, were already in motion and skirmishers were firing right and left as they pushed the Rebels forward.

Going back to my command, I met Gen. Mansfield, who had just arrived from Washington to take command of the corps. He is a most veteran-looking officer, with head as white as snow. You may have seen him in Washington. His home is at Middletown, Conn. and he has been inspector general of the army for a long time.[10] With this new commander came an order to march. I went back to my division, rather pleased that I had got rid of an onerous responsibility. We crossed the fields to the Hagerstown pike. Our new commander was very fussy. He had been an engineer officer and never before had commanded large bodies of troops.

Onward we went after being delayed for other columns to pass.

Crossing the South Mountain we descended rapidly to Boonsboro where the people, as at Frederick, received us with great rejoicing. I did not tell you that in marching my corps through Frederick we were greatly cheered and ladies brought bouquets to me as commander. The same enthusiasm followed us everywhere. Citizens met us on horseback and the whole population seemed rejoiced that we were chasing the Rebels from the state. At Boonsboro we passed south towards Sharpsburg, taking across lots and in all sorts of out of the ways. We encamped at a crossroads and for the first time for weeks I slept in a house, the home of a Mr. Nicodemus. As I was getting my division into camp I saw other troops arriving and an officer darting up to me put out his hand eagerly to greet me. It was the topographical engineer captain with whom Alph. and Ez. went to New Mexico, now Col. Scammon of an Ohio regiment.[11] I did not feel very kindly, I fear, and yet he looked so changed and so glad to see me that I greeted him in return. He went away and I have not seen him since.

The next morning we were ordered hurriedly to the front, Gen. Mansfield, in an excited and fussy way, announcing that we should be in a general engagement in half an hour. Over we went across lots till we struck a road and after a three-mile march we were *massed* in close column in a small space where the shells of the enemy's guns fell close to us. A high ridge in front did not seem much protection. We lay here all day, and at night fancied we were going to rest. I sought a tent with one of my colonels, who gave me the best bed I had seen for weeks.

During the afternoon, amongst the troops marching up I had seen Col. Stockton and other old friends. It was evident that the Rebels were standing for a fight. Their lines were plainly visible from the elevation in front and one battery had been playing all day with ours. I had got fairly asleep when along came a message to get under arms at once. Oh, how sleepy I was, but there is no help at such times. Up I got and in a few moments the head of my division was moving along an unknown road. We passed a stone bridge over the Antietam and then branched off into the fields. Gen. Mansfield and his escort led the way, but it was so dark and the forests and woods so deep that I could not follow and was obliged to send ahead to stop our leaders repeatedly.

After a weary march we halted in some ploughed ground and I was told to put my division in column in mass. It took a long time as I had five new regiments who knew absolutely nothing of maneuvering. At length about two o'clock in the morning I got under the corner of a rail fence, but the pickets in front of us kept firing and as often as I got asleep Gen. Mansfield would come along and wake me with some new directions. At length I got fairly asleep and for two hours was dead to all sounds or sensations. I shall not, however, soon forget that night; so dark, so obscure, so mysterious, so uncertain; with the occasional rapid volleys of pickets and outposts, the low, solemn sound of the command as troops came into position, and withal so sleepy that there was a half-dreamy sensation about it all; but with a certain impression that the morrow was to be great with the future fate of our country. So much responsibility, so much intense, future anxiety! and yet I slept as soundly as though nothing was before me.

At the first dawn of day the cannon began work. Gen. Hooker's command was about a mile in front of us and it was his corps upon which the attack began. By a common impulse our men stood to arms. They had slept in ranks and the matter of toilet was not tedious, nor did we have time to linger over the breakfast table. My division being in advance, I was ordered to move up in close column of companies —that is a company front to each regiment and the other companies closed up to within six paces. When so formed a regiment looks like a solid mass. We had not moved a dozen rods before the shells and round shot came thick over us and around us. If these had struck our massed regiments dozens of men would have been killed by a single shot.

I had five new regiments without drill or discipline. Gen. Mansfield was greatly excited. Though an officer of acknowledged gallantry, he had a very nervous temperament and a very impatient manner. Feeling that our heavy masses of raw troops were sadly exposed, I begged him to let me deploy them in line of battle, in which the men present but *two* ranks or rows instead of *twenty*, as we were marching, but I could not move him. He was positive that all the new regiments would run away. So on we went over ploughed ground, through cornfields and woods, till the line of infantry fight began to appear.

It was evident that Hooker's troops were giving way. His general officers were hurrying toward us begging for support in every direction. First one would come from the right; then over from the center, and then one urging support for a battery on the left. I had ridden somewhat in advance to get some idea of the field and was standing in the center of a ploughed field, taking directions from Gen. Hooker and amidst a very unpleasant shower of bullets, when up rode a general officer begging for immediate assistance to protect a battery. He was very earnest and absorbed in the subject, as you may well suppose, and began to plead energetically, when he suddenly stopped, extended his hand, and very calmly said, "How are you?" It was Gen. Meade. He darted away, and I saw him no more that day. Hooker's troops were soon withdrawn and I think were not again brought into the field. Was it not a strange encounter?

I had parted with Gen. Mansfield but a moment before this and in five minutes afterward his staff officer reported to me that he was mortally wounded and the command of the corps devolved on me. I began at once to deploy the new regiments. The old ones had already gotten themselves into line. Taking hold of one, I directed Gens. Crawford and Gordon to direct the others. I got mine in line pretty well by having a fence to align it on and having got it in this way I ordered the colonel to go forward and open fire the moment he saw the Rebels. Poor fellow! He was killed within ten minutes. His regiment, advancing in line, was split in two by coming in contact with a barn. One part did very well in the woods but the trouble with this regiment and the others was that in attempting to move them forward or back or to make any maneuver they fell into inextricable confusion and fell to the rear, where they were easily rallied. The men were of an excellent stamp, ready and willing, but neither officers nor men knew anything, and there was an absence of the mutual confidence which drill begets. Standing still, they fought bravely.

When we engaged the enemy he was in a strip of woods, long but narrow. We drove him from this, across a ploughed field and through a cornfield into another woods, which was full of ravines. There the enemy held us in check till 9½ o'clock, when there was a general cessation of musketry. All over the ground we had advanced on, the Rebel dead and wounded lay thick, much more numerous than ours, but ours were painfully mingled in. Our wounded were rapidly carried off and some of the Rebels'. Those we were obliged to leave begged so piteously to be carried away. Hundreds appealed to me and I confess that the rage of battle had not hardened my heart so that I did not feel a pity for them. Our men gave them water and as far as I saw always treated them kindly.

The necessities of the case were so great that I was obliged to put my whole corps into action at once. The roar of the infantry was beyond anything conceivable to the uninitiated. Imagine from 8,000 to 10,000 men on one side, with probably a larger number on the other, all at once discharging their muskets. If all the stone and brick houses of Broadway should tumble at once the roar and rattle could hardly be greater, and amidst this, hundreds of pieces of artillery, right and left, were thundering as a sort of bass to the infernal music.

At 9½ o'clock Gen. Sumner was announced as near at hand with his corps.[12] As soon as his columns began to arrive I withdrew mine by degrees to the shelter of the woods for the purpose of rest, to collect stragglers, and to renew the ammunition. Several of the old regiments had fired nearly forty rounds each man. They had stood up splendidly and had forced back the enemy nearly a mile. The new regiments were badly broken up, but I collected about one-half of them and placed them in support of batteries. The regiments had up to this time suffered comparatively little. The 3rd Wisconsin and [the] 27th Indiana had lost a good many men, but few officers. I began to hope that we should get off, when Sumner attacked, with but little loss. I rode along where our advanced lines had been. Not an enemy appeared. The woods in front were as quiet as any sylvan shade could be. Presently a single report came and a ball whizzed close to my horse. Two or three others followed all in disagreeable closeness to my person. I did not like to hurry, but I lost as little time as possible in getting out of the range of sharpshooters.

I should have mentioned that soon after I met Gen. Hooker he rode toward the left. In a few minutes I heard he was wounded. While we were talking the dust of the ploughed ground was knocked up in little spurts all around us, marking the spot where musket balls struck. I had to ride repeatedly over this field and every time it seemed that my horse could not possibly escape. It was in the center of the line of fire, slightly elevated, but along which *my* troops were extended. The peculiar singing sound of the bullet becomes a regular whistle and it seems strange that everybody is not hit.

While the battle was raging fiercest with that division the 2nd Division came up and I was requested to support our right with one brigade. I started one over to report to Gen. Doubleday and soon followed to see what became of them.[13] As I entered the narrow lane running to the right and front a battery opened a cross-fire and Pittman and myself had the excitement of riding a mile or so out and back under its severest salutations. We found Gen. Doubleday sheltered in a ravine and apparently in bland ignorance of what was doing on his front or what need he had of my troops, except to relieve his own, but I left the brigade and came back. Finding a battery, I put it in position to meet the flank fire of the Rebel battery and some one else had the good sense to establish another farther in the rear. The two soon silenced this disagreeable customer.

It was soon after my return to the center that Sumner's columns began to arrive. They were received with cheers and went fiercely toward the wood with too much haste, I thought, and too little reconnoitering of the ground and positions held by us. They had not reached the road before a furious fire was opened on them and we had the infernal din over again. The Rebels had been strongly reinforced, and Sumner's troops, being formed in three lines in close proximity, after his favorite idea, we lost a good deal of our fire without any corresponding benefit or advantage. For instance, the second line, within forty paces of the front, suffered almost as much as the front line and yet could not fire without hitting our own men. The colonel of a regiment in the second line told me he lost sixty men and came off without firing a gun.

Sumner's force in the center was soon used up, and I was called upon to bring up my wearied and hungry men. They advanced to the front and opened fire, but the force opposed was enormously superior. Still they held on, under heavy losses, till one o'clock. Some of the old regiments were fairly broken up in this fight and what was left were consolidated and mixed up afterward with the new regiments. The 46th Pennsylvania, Col. Knipe, and the 28th New York, Capt. Mapes, commanding, were especially broken. Col. Knipe has just returned to duty from his wounds. He had but one captain (Brooks) in his regiment present and he was killed early. The 2nd Massachusetts, which had done excellent service in the first engagement, was badly cut up and its lieut. col. (Dwight), mortally wounded. At 1½ o'clock I ordered them back, as reinforcements were at hand.

While this last attack was going on, Gen. Greene, 2nd Division, took possession and held for an hour or more the easterly end of the wood—struggled for so fiercely—where it abuts on the road to Sharpsburg. A small brick school house stands by the road, which I noticed the next day was riddled by our shot and shell. Greene held on till Sumner's men gave way towards the left, when he was drawn out by a rush and his men came scampering to the rear in great confusion. The Rebels followed with a yell but three or four of our batteries being in position they were received with a tornado of canister which made them vanish before the smoke cloud cleared away. I was near one of our brass twelve-pound Napoleon gun batteries and seeing the Rebel colors appearing over the rolling ground I directed the two left pieces charged with canister to be turned on the point. In the moment the Rebel line appeared and both guns were discharged at short range. Each canister contains several hundred balls. They fell in the very front of the line and all along it apparently, stirring up a dust like a thick cloud. When the dust blew away no regiment and not a living man was to be seen.

Just then Gen. Smith (Baldy Smith) who was at Detroit on the light-house duty, came up with a division.[14] They fairly rushed toward the left and front. I hastily called his attention to the woods full of Rebels on his right as he was advancing. He dispatched that way one regiment and the rest advanced to an elevation which overlooked the valley on our left, where the left wing had been fighting for several hours. The regiment sent toward the woods got a tremendous volley and saved itself by rushing over the hillside for shelter. The rest of the brigade got an enfilading fire on a Rebel line and it broke and ran to the rear. One regiment only charged the front, as if on parade, but a second battery sent it scampering.

On this ground the contest was kept up for a long time. The multitude of dead Rebels (I saw them) was proof enough how hotly they contested the ground. It was getting toward night. The artillery took up the fight. We had driven them at all points, save the one woods. It was thought advisable not to attack further. We held the main battlefield and all our wounded, except a few in the woods. My troops slept on their arms well to the front. All the other corps of the center seemed to have vanished, but I found Sumner's the next morning and moved up to it and set to work gathering up our stragglers. The day was passed in comparative quietness on both sides. Our burial parties would exchange the dead and wounded with the Rebels in the woods.

It was understood that we were to attack again at daylight on the 19th, but as our troops moved up it was found the Rebels had departed. Some of the troops followed, but we lay under arms all day, waiting orders. I took the delay to ride over the field of battle. The Rebel dead, even in the woods last occupied by them, was very great. In one place, in front of the position of my corps, apparently a whole regiment had been cut down in line. They lay in two ranks, as straightly aligned as on a dress parade. There must have been a brigade, as part of the line on the left had been buried. I counted what appeared to be a single regiment and found 149 dead in the line and about 70 in front and rear, making over 200 dead in one Rebel regiment. In riding over the field I think I must have seen at least 3,000. In one place for nearly a mile they lay as thick as autumn leaves along a narrow lane cut below the natural surface, into which they seemed to have tumbled. Eighty had been buried in one pit, and yet no impression had apparently been made on the unburied host. The cornfield beyond was dotted all over with those killed in retreat.

The wounded Rebels had been carried away in great numbers and yet every farmyard and haystack seemed a large hospital. The number of dead horses was high. They lay, like the men, in all attitudes. One beautiful milk-white animal had died in so graceful a position that I wished for its photograph. Its legs were doubled under and its arched neck gracefully turned to one side, as if looking back to the ball-hole in its side. Until you got to it, it was hard to believe the horse was dead. Another feature of the field was the mass of army accouterments, clothing, etc. scattered everywhere or lying in heaps where the contest had been severest. I lost but two field officers killed, Col. Croasdale, 128th Pennsylvania and Col. Dwight, 2nd Massachusetts, several men wounded. Gen. Crawford of the 1st Brigade was wounded, not severely. I marvel, not only at my own escape, as I was particularly exposed, on account of raw troops to be handled, but at the escape of any mounted officer.

The newspapers will give you further particulars, but as far as I have seen them, nothing reliable. . . . The "big staff generals" get the first ear and nobody is heard of and no corps mentioned till their voracious maws are filled with puffing. I see it stated that Sumner's corps relieved Hooker's. So far is this from true that my corps was engaged from sunrise till 9½ o'clock before Sumner came up, though he was to be on the ground at daylight. Other statements picked up by reporters from the principal headquarters are equally false and absurd. To me they are laughably *canard*.

On the afternoon of the 18th I received orders to occupy Maryland Heights with my corps. They are opposite Harpers Ferry, and had just been surrendered by Col. Miles.[15] I marched till 2 o'clock in the morning, reaching Brownsville. Halted till daylight, men sleeping in the road. I slept on hay in a barn. Started by sunrise up the Heights and marched along a rocky path on the ridge to the Heights overlooking Harpers Ferry. I left my artillery and train at Brownsville. Occupied the Heights without opposition. Found there was no water there; left a strong guard and took the command down the mountain on the east side. Sent a brigade over the river and a regiment to Sandy Hook. This morning (Gen. Sumner's corps having come up) I have sent one division over the river to Loudon Heights and one part way up Maryland Heights in front. The Rebels are in sight in and about and this side Charleston and to the west toward Shepardstown. What is to be done next I know not. It will be my fate, I fear, to go a third time up the valley. Heaven forbid! The valley has been an unfortunate land for me. My friends think I shall get a major generalship. I should if I was of the regular army; but not being such nor a graduated fool I suppose I shall remain a brigadier. Gen. Banks never moves for any of his command, unless solicited personally. Nobody in his corps has received promotion, though he seems to have gathered some newspaper laurels. . . .

It is now nearly six weeks that I have hardly halted a whole day, and when I have it was under orders to be ready to move at a moment. I am so tired and uneasy of this kind of sleepless life. On the march up my command was one day eighteen hours under arms and marching most of the time. But I am well and bear it better than anyone.

Affectionately, my Daughters,
Your Father,
A.S.W.

◈

RETURN TO THE POTOMAC

Camp near Maryland Heights, Opposite Harpers Ferry,
Sept. 23, 1862.

My Darling Daughter:

I have written a long joint letter to you and Rene but have sent it for her first perusal. You will get it almost as early as this. I write just a line or so as I know you are anxious to hear that I am well. I have had no time for writing and indeed no pen, ink and very little paper. It is now nearly two months that we have been daily on the march, or under arms ready to march at a moment's notice. We have had neither tents nor baggage. I have done a deal of my excellent sleeping under fences and trees and occasionally in a hay mow. I am undergoing an excellent tuition for a loafer's life: ragged clothes and sleeping in the open air.

We came down here two days ago under orders to occupy the Maryland Heights, which Col. Miles had so ignobly given up. I marched my corps till 2 o'clock in the morning, let them sleep two hours in the road at the foot of the mountain range, ascended at daylight to the crest of the ridge, and then marched over the stoniest ground to the high bluff which overlooks the Potomac at Harpers Ferry. We had six miles' march over rough, jagged, and loose stones. Just before reaching the Heights we passed the recent battlefield between a portion of Miles' infantry and the Rebels. The country people were there picking up arms, and the stench proved abundantly what was said by them, that many bodies were still unburied. The position was a very strong one, amongst large rocks and crags on the top of a narrow ridge. Two thousand men ought to have kept 20,000 at bay. . . .

I sigh for a leave that I might see you and Rene for a few days. It seems to me that I have done a lifetime of labor and exposure in the past two months. But to all appearances, we have just begun a new campaign. If it goes on with the same bloody issues as the past two weeks have seen, there will be nothing left from privates to generals. It will be a Kilkenny cat affair—both sides used up. In the last battle we had, I think, some ten or eleven general officers killed or wounded. My only wonder is that anyone escaped. I was myself under fire from sunrise to nearly 2 o'clock P.M. We went in without breakfast and came out without dinner. The major generals with big staffs will gobble up all the glory, judging from newspaper reports. But there is an unwritten history of these battles that somebody will be obliged to set right some day. Generals are amazingly puffed who are not ten minutes on the field. Corps are praised for services done by others. Commands that were hours behind the line, when the battle raged fiercest, are carrying off the reputation (in newspapers) of saving other corps from defeat. These reports are got from staff officers of the absent corps. The reporters are often members of the staff. . . .

Poor Gen. Mansfield, who took command of our corps two days before the battle, was an excellent gentleman, but a most fussy, obstinate officer. He was killed just as the head of our column reached the battlefield and I, of course, had command of the corps for the rest of the day. I had not parted from him five minutes when he was reported to me mortally wounded. Gen. Crawford, who commands a brigade of my division, was also wounded but not very seriously. But my long letter—written very hastily—will give you all the details I can find time to write. We have been so long without a halt and so much disorganized by battle and marching that I have an infinite deal of work to get reports of present condition. . . .

There are so many major generals anxious to command corps that I shall probably have a new commander soon. It is only wonderful that I have held the command so long.

Your Affectionate Father,
A.S.W.

◆

REASONS FOR FAILURE AT ANTIETAM

Camp near Harpers Ferry,
September 24, 1862.

My Dear Lew:

For the first time for weeks, I have found time to look over old letters which have become marvellously dirty in my pockets. I find yours of 5 August, I will answer the business part. . . .

Your famous 24th Regiment was assigned by general orders to my division just as we reached Rockville on our way up, but it never reported, nor have I had any explanations.[16] If it had come along Col. Morrow would have had a chance to take that battery he promised your good people in his last speech. At any rate, he would have got a terrible baptism of fire and blood. I had five new regiments. Some of them were badly peppered, and it took hard work to keep them anywhere, when once broken. They went in very valorously, but as neither officers nor men knew the first thing of movements they could not change positions without breaking and being rerallied. They were of superb material, and if they had had the drill of my old brigade, would have done fearful execution.

What has become of the rest of the 300,000? We can't have over 20,000 of new troops with us, if as many. The 17th Michigan did nobly in the mountain fight on Sunday.[17] It was a free fight in the woods and hills. I met Gen. Willcox in the pass, who praised them greatly. They are in his division. The old Michigan 7th suffered severely at Antietam. They are in Sumner's corps and in a different part of the field from us, though our corps is a part of Sumner's command, two corps being put under one commander. We were detached the night before to support Hooker's attack. I enclose a copy of my report of the battle of August 9th at Cedar Mountain.[18] It comes rather late, but we have really been separated from everything for weeks. I wore one shirt about three weeks. We have marched every day but four, and on those days we were under orders for immediate movement.

We punished the Rebels severely in the last battle.[19] The number of dead they left on the field was enormous. In some places whole regiments seem to have fallen in their tracks. If McClellan's plan had been carried out with more coolness by some of our commanding generals, we should have grabbed half their army. But we threw away our power by impulsive and hasty attacks on wrong points. Hundreds of lives were foolishly sacrificed by generals I see most praised, generals who would come up with their commands and pitch in at the first point without consultation with those who knew the ground or without reconnoitering or looking for the effective points of attacks. Our men fought gloriously and we taught the rascals a lesson, which they much needed after Pope's disaster. They out-numbered us without doubt, and expected to thrash us soundly and drive us all pell mell back towards Washington. As it was, they sneaked out of "my Maryland" at night leaving their dead and wounded on the field. Even dead generals were left within their lines unburied. Their invasion of Maryland has been a sad business for them. If you can find any Detroit editor who desires to publish my report, you can give it to him *sub rosa*. I suppose I have no right to publish myself without authority. Still, I see others get into the papers, and I suppose this can be got in without coming from me. . . .

Yours Truly,
A.S.W.

◆

REORGANIZATION OF THE ARMY

Sandy Hook, Oct. 5, 1862.

My Dear Daughter:

I have had time to write you but once since I came here and I really cannot recall what I wrote you in that. We have had most beautiful weather: warm days and cool nights; some days as warm as summer. Although I have had hard work, the quiet and absence of constant marches has been delightful. I have *thirteen* new regiments sent to this corps, all, or nearly all, with green officers and most of them just out from the States. One from Connecticut (29); eight from New York (117, 123, 127, 137, 138, 140, 145, 149); one from New Jersey (13); and three from Pennsylvania (124, 125, 128). You can well fancy that these green regiments give an infinite increase of work to get them into shape. Besides this, the old regiments, from loss of records and officers—especially the field and staff—had got into a disorganized state, which required inspections, examinations, enforcement of discipline and orders. An immense number of reports about everything and everybody. I have not got through yet, for as fast as one thing is disposed of and daylight begins to appear, a new batch of labor is laid out by a new order. Gen. McClellan is an indefatigable officer in organization. Nothing seems to escape his attention or his anticipation. Every endeavor is made, and constantly kept up, to enforce drill and discipline and to create an *esprit de corps* and confidence. I have met no officer at all his equal in this respect. But he keeps everybody hard at work.

I have sent in my report of the battle of Antietam.[20] I was obliged to make it out on short notice and before the subordinate reports were all received. We had 1,744 killed and wounded, quite one-fourth of our whole number in action. Gen. Sumner came to see me yesterday and was quite complimentary, stating that he had mentioned my name and had recommended me for promotion. He commanded the center, or properly right, in the action. Gen. Hooker, whose corps we relieved in the morning of the battle, sent his aide for a copy of my report, with a message that he was greatly pleased with my disposition of the troops and hoped he should be so fortunate as to have my assistance if he ever had another battle. Gen. Banks has also written me that he has strongly urged my promotion and congratulates me upon the splendid conduct of the corps. All the general and field officers of the corps have petitioned for my promotion. So I think I may well hope, at length, to be a major general. I think I am more pleased, however, with the commendations I have received from our best generals than with the prospect of getting rank, though I don't despise the latter. I still have command of the corps, the only brigadier who has so important a position. I can hardly expect to hold it long with so many ranking officers seeking the place. The President was here a few days since. I had quite a long talk with him, sitting on a pile of logs. He is really the most unaffected, simple-minded, honest, and frank man I have ever met. I wish he had a little more firmness, though I suppose the main difficulty with him is to make up his mind as to the best policy amongst the multitude of advisers and advice. . . .

I have just heard from Rene. She has not received my long letter after the battle of Antietam. I fear it has miscarried, which I should much regret, as I cannot write another. I will send you the next long letter, but I hope we shall not have a second Antietam immediately, unless the salvation of the Union depends upon it. I think we are fighting and have fought battles enough to have saved this Union, if they had been properly directed. This corps alone (the smallest) has lost between 4,000 and 5,000 men in battle within two months. The sacrifice would be less to be regretted if one did not feel that half of it has been fruitless and useless. All of Pope's losses were worse than waste of human life or limb. It was an absolute encouragement to the Rebels and resulted in the sacrifice of thousands more. . . .

I have a new brigadier general, just reported. Brig. Gen. Kane, brother of Kane the navigator. He is a small man and very precise.[21] Here he comes on business and I must stop.

Your Affectionate Father,
A. S. Williams

◆

PREPARATIONS FOR A NEW CAMPAIGN

Camp at Sandy Hook, Md.,
Oct. 17, 1862.

My Dear Daughter: . . .

We are still, you see, at the same place. There are daily rumors of a forward movement and we have daily reconnoissances with the usual accompaniment of big guns and a great deal of noise; not much wool. With all our efforts it seems almost impossible to get the troops into good condition for the field. Old regiments are much reduced and disordered, if not demoralized by loss of officers, by battle and disease. Majors are commanding brigades and lieutenants, regiments. While this lasts an efficient force cannot be made, and if we advance we shall soon retrograde. Yet I see by the newspapers that an uneasy and impatient public are demanding an immediate advance. We have the same old story—"demand." Yet these anxious souls know nothing of our preparations, nothing of the force or resources of the enemy. It would seem as if they thirsted for blood; for stirring accounts of great battles. No sooner is one story of bloody fights grown cold than the outcry is for another. Men and women who groan and sigh over a railroad accident which kills two and wounds six, seem to delight in the glowing description of a battle which leaves upon a single field 20,000 killed and four times as many wounded. Strangely inconsistent is poor human nature! . . .

We have a good many Michigan regiments in the corps not many miles off, but it will seem strange to you to be told that old friends may be within a mile or two of one another and never know it, except by chance. But it is so; nobody knows anybody not of their immediate command. The white shelter tents cover now an immense area in this vicinity. As seen from Maryland Heights, which terminates in an abrupt bluff on the very edge of the Potomac, the view is really magnificent and grand. On the west side the whole valley of the Shenandoah spreads out between the two rivers and mountain ranges away up to the bluff near Strasburg and Front Royal, sixty miles away. For several miles along the interior slope of Bolivar Heights, which run across the triangle between the Potomac and the Shenandoah, the *tents d'bris* of Sumner's corps shine in the purest white. Away south on Loudon Heights, higher than Bolivar, are seen the tents of the 2nd Division of my corps. On the east, along up Pleasant Valley for four or five miles, are thickly dotted the camps of my corps and Burnside's. Half way down the Maryland Heights on a considerable plateau, where are the big-ship Dahlgren guns of one hundred-pound caliber and the thirty-pound Parrotts, are thickly posted two brigades of the 1st Division of my corps. On the very pinnacle of the Heights is an observatory, where are stationed the flagmen of the signal corps. From this prominence you can overlook all this, to say nothing of the many villages and towns that peep out from the grove patches through the Shenandoah Valley, nor of the narrow gap below where the Potomac seems to have burst through the Blue Ridge.

Oct. 22nd.

I wrote this far some days ago, since which I have been very busy turning over the command to Maj. Gen. Slocum, who has been assigned to it. He is a New Yorker, a graduate of West Point. Was on the Peninsula, of course. Nobody gets permanent command or promotion, I believe, unless he was on the Peninsula. However, while there are so many major generals commanding divisions, I could hardly hope to be left long as a brigadier in command of a corps. Our people complain some and there is a general regret amongst the officers that I could not retain command.

This morning while [I was] at breakfast Mr. Reuben Rice, Mr. Hammond of Chicago, and others out west peeped into the mess-tent. I was greatly surprised. They stayed but a few moments, on their way to Antietam battlefield. Mrs. Hammond was with them. In riding around yesterday I fell upon "John Brown's School House," so called, a small log building in a ravine of the mountain where John Brown hid his army when he seized Harpers Ferry. The people [here] about speak of him as a quiet, inoffensive man in his bearing and some say he was a very kind-hearted creature.

I enclose you a button I cut from a dead Rebel officer's coat on the battlefield of Antietam. I also send you a very puffy paragraph which somebody sent me anonymously. A letter from Rene says it was in the Philadelphia *Press*. I have no idea who the writer is, as I have seen no reporters and don't recognize the initials. I send you also a letter from Gen. Banks for safe keeping. I have only a carpet bag for all my effects. We are reduced to the smallest scale. . . .

I suppose we shall move soon. Such seems to be the impression, and the public pressure is terrible.

The public knows nothing of our actual strength or preparation. If we fail, that same dear public will howl our condemnation. . . . The paymaster has not yet come and I have nearly three months due me.

Your Affectionate Father,
A.S.W.

P.S. The paymaster has just arrived and says, "Take off that mark that I am not here."

◈

CLAMOR FOR A NEW CAMPAIGN

Sandy Hook, Md.,
Oct. 26, 1862.

My Dear Daughter: . . .

Our mails have never been more irregular than for the past ten days or so. Everything now goes to headquarters and is scattered to everybody's corps except the right one.

Yours of the 18th only came day before yesterday. I have been under orders for instant march ever since and have been constantly employed to get all the readiness possible. By some fatality, or by the general crowding, we are lacking much. There seems to be an unaccountable delay in forwarding supplies. We want shoes and blankets and overcoats—indeed, almost everything. I have sent requisition upon requisition; officers to Washington; made reports and complaints, and yet we are not half supplied. I see the papers speak of our splendid preparations. Crazy fools! I wish they were obliged to sleep, as my poor devils do tonight, in a cold, shivering rain, without overcoat or blanket and under one of those miss-named "shelter tents"; a mere sieve, which filters the water over one in a nasty mist and gives no warmth. I wish these crazy fools were compelled to march over these stony roads barefooted, as hundreds of my men must if we go tomorrow. When will civilians who know nothing of our preparation or the force and strength of the enemy learn to leave war matters to war men, who have means of knowing their duties, their capabilities, and their chances? We are driven "forward" by the popular outcry. I can only hope we shall not be driven back disgraced and the country fatally put in jeopardy.

This grumbling is for your eye alone. Here I say nothing and it won't do for a general officer to complain, even in private letters. But let me tell *you* that we cannot successfully invade Virginia from this point. We must have water transportation or large railroad carriage to subsist our troops the moment we leave our depots. There are but few passable roads in Virginia. We cannot now live on green corn. We are under orders and I shall do my best and hope for the best. . . .

Your Affectionate Father,
A.S.W.

EMANCIPATION OF SLAVES

Camp at Sandy Hook, Md.,
Oct. 28, 1862.

My Darling Daughter:

I have written to Larned and Uncle Lew so recently that I can give you little news of myself except that I am still here, part of our corps moving over the river and a great number of troops marching up and down. I am kept very busy with these changes, especially as there has been a reorganization of our corps. The 2nd Division had become, from a multitude of commanders and other causes, pretty much demoralized, and so our new commander has infused new life into them by transferring a part of my division and two of my best colonels to command brigades there. These changes have delayed us a few days, but I suppose we shall move in a day or so. . . .

The weather is getting very cool and our accommodations are not good. We have not made our usual fire places, as we have been anticipating a movement. The poor fellows in shelter tents, which are really no shelter, as they are made of thin cotton cloth, are suffering much and the new regiments are full of sickness.

I like our new corps commander very much so far, though he does not strike me as of wonderful capacity.[22] In my division I believe I have told you I have a new brigadier general, Kane. He is a brother of Kane, the Arctic navigator and the same man whom Uncle Lew will remember was sent *via* the Pacific by our government to settle the Mormon troubles, while our troops were marching toward Utah. He is a little man of rather *petit-maitre* manners, but full of pluck and will. He was badly wounded at Cross Keys and taken prisoner.

The rest of my brigades remain the same. I have tried hard to get some of the colonels made brigadier generals, but have not succeeded. Indeed, Gen. Banks' corps has never yet had a promotion except in the regiments made by states. We begin to think the general has either very little influence or very little courage to use it. The latter, I think. He is very fearful of losing power by an over-exercise of it. As he seems to have got considerable glory, we naturally think that his subordinates should have a little. At least, it is hard to see how a commanding general can gobble up all the credit of success. . . .

I see somebody has printed a pretended extract from one of my private letters approving of the President's proclamation.[23] I don't remember to have written any such sentence, though I have repeatedly said that I was prepared to sustain any measure I thought would help put an end to this cursed rebellion. I should dislike to see or hear of the promiscuous slaughter that would follow an immediate emancipation of slaves in the South. There is no fear, however, that slaves will be freed any faster than our troops get possession of Rebel territory, and this was the case before the proclamation. I don't think matters are much changed by that document. . . .

Love to all,

Your Affectionate Father,

A.S.W.

1. Orlando B. Willcox of Detroit, a member of the West Point class of 1847. He served in the regular army from his graduation until 1857, when he resigned his commission to begin the practice of law at Detroit. In 1861 he became colonel of the First Michigan Infantry (three-months) Regiment. At the battle of Bull Run, where he commanded a brigade, he was wounded and captured, remaining a prisoner until August 19, 1862, when he was exchanged. He was immediately promoted to the rank of brigadier general and assigned to Burnside's corps, with which he served at Antietam and subsequently throughout the war. Like General Williams, he frequently held higher commands than his rank called for. Unlike Williams, he was rewarded with promotion to brevet major general of volunteers, and in 1867 to the rank of major general in the regular service. Save for a short period in 1866, he served in the army until his retirement in 1887.—*Dict. Am. Biog.*

2. John G. Parke, a West Point graduate in the class of 1849, served in the engineer corps of the army until 1861 when he was commissioned a brigadier general of volunteers. He was closely associated with General Burnside, for whom he served as chief of staff at Antietam and Fredericksburg. He remained in the regular army until he was retired at his own request on July 2, 1889, after forty years of service.—*Dict. Am. Biog.*

3. Jacob D. Cox of Ohio, lawyer, politician, Union general, governor of Ohio, and Secretary of the Interior under President Grant. He achieved distinction both in military and in civil life.—*Dict. Am. Biog.*

4. The Seventeenth Michigan was one of the "new" regiments of the army, although it was not assigned to Williams' command. It was mustered at Detroit on August 21, 1862 and departed for Washington five days

later. As yet (September 12) it had seen no fighting. Its bloody baptism in the art came at South Mountain on September 14, and three days later it participated in the battle of Antietam, sustaining heavy losses in both battles.—*Record of Service of Michigan Volunteers*, Vol. XVII.

5. Israel B. Richardson, a West Point graduate in the class of 1841 and a veteran of the Mexican War. Following that war he served at various western posts until his resignation with the rank of captain, September 30, 1855. Thereafter until 1861 he was a farmer at Pontiac, Michigan. In May 1861 he became colonel of the Second Michigan Infantry. On July 4, 1862 he became a major general of volunteers. Mortally wounded in the battle of Antietam on September 17, he died at Sharpsburg, November 3, 1862. His military career was notable and nothing has been found in the published records to support the statements of General Williams concerning him.—*Dict. Am. Biog.*

6. John Mason Norvell of Detroit entered the service on April 22, 1861, as second lieutenant of Company I, Second Michigan Infantry Regiment. On August 30, 1861, he was appointed captain and aide-de-camp on General Richardson's staff, and on August 22, 1862, major and assistant adjutant general. He resigned his commission on June 21, 1865. He subsequently entered the regular army, serving as lieutenant and as captain until his retirement, December 27, 1890. He died on December 18, 1893.—*Record of Service of Michigan Volunteers*, Vol. II.

7. Here, also, he was destined to be a year later, still with "a crippled nation's defenders," enroute this time to Pennsylvania and Gettysburg.

8. This was the battle of South Mountain, September 14, 1862. On September 9, at Frederick, General Lee issued his famous "lost order," outlining his plan of operations. While his main army marched westward from Frederick through South Mountain, Stonewall Jackson was to detour southward, capture Harpers Ferry, and then hurry northward to rejoin Lee, when the combined army would advance by way of Hagerstown into Pennsylvania. Unfortunately for Lee's plans, a copy of the order fell into the hands of a Union soldier and was brought to General Williams' headquarters. Armed with its information, General McClellan pushed his pursuit of Lee, capturing the mountain gaps in the hard-fought battle of September 14, and compelling Lee to retire toward Sharpsburg, where the battle of Antietam was fought on little Antietam Creek on September 17. Although the immediate battle ended in a stalemate, it proved to be a Union victory, for Lee was compelled to abandon the invasion of the North and retire to Virginia. The uncertainty attending the movements of the army on the day of South Mountain is shown in General Williams' account of his efforts to reach the field of battle. Concerning the lost order see General D. H. Hill's defense and General Lee's estimate in the *Virginia Magazine of History and Biography*, LXVI (April 1958), 161–66.

9. Major General Jesse L. Reno, for whom see *Dict. Am. Biog.* Fort Reno, Wyoming, Fort Reno, Oklahoma, and the city of Reno, Nevada, were subsequently named in his honor.

10. Joseph K. L. Mansfield was a West Point graduate in the class of 1822. Assigned to the engineer corps of the army, he performed distinguished service in the Mexican War. In 1853, through the influence of Secretary of War Jefferson Davis, who also had served in the Mexican War, he was promoted to the rank of colonel and appointed inspector-general of the army. In July 1862 he became a major general, and upon McClellan's reorganization of the Army of the Potomac was given command of the Twelfth (Gen. Williams') Corps. He joined the army two days before the battle of Antietam, September 17, 1862 in which he was mortally wounded.—*Dict. Am. Biog.*

11. Colonel E. Parker Scammon, a graduate of West Point in the class of 1837. He served in the Mexican War and on various surveys and other engineering works until June 4, 1856 when he was dismissed from the army for disobedience to orders and other alleged misconduct. The New Mexico survey alluded to by General Williams occurred in 1855–56. He was appointed colonel of the Twenty-third Ohio Regiment on June 14, 1861, attaining the rank of brigadier general October 15, 1862.—Cullum, *Biog. Register of Officers and Graduates of the U.S. Military Academy.*

12. Edwin V. Sumner, born in 1797, entered the army in 1819 and served continuously until after the battle of Fredericksburg, December 13, 1862, in which he commanded the right grand division of the army. Relieved from duty with the Army of the Potomac at his own request, he died the following year (March 21, 1863). He was a favorite of General Scott in the Mexican War, and, apparently, of General McClellan in the Civil War. It has remained for General Williams' pen to record his mishandling and the consequent needless slaughter of his troops at Antietam. See *Dict. Am. Biog.*

13. General Abner Doubleday of New York, reputed "father" of the game of baseball. He was a West Point graduate in the class of 1842 and a veteran of the Mexican War. In April 1861 he fired the first shot at Fort Sumter in reply to the Confederate bombardment. Appointed brigadier general in February 1862, he succeeded to the command of a division at South Mountain when its commanding officer was wounded. He served with distinction in the battle of Gettysburg, where, upon the death of General Reynolds on the first day of the battle (July 1) he succeeded to the command during the remainder of the day. While stationed at San Francisco, 1869–71, he obtained the charter for that city's first cable street railway. See *Dict. Am. Biog.*

14. William Farrar Smith, a West Point graduate in the class of 1845, for many years served as a topographical engineer. At the opening of the

Civil War he was appointed colonel of the Third Vermont Regiment, and in August 1861 commanded a division of the Army of the Potomac. In July 1862 he became a major general and commanded a division in the battle of Antietam. Undoubtedly a brilliant engineer, his military career was marred by indulgence in indiscreet criticism of his superiors.—*Dict. Am. Biog.*

15. On September 15, immediately before the battle of Antietam.

16. The Twenty-fourth Michigan was a new regiment which was mustered into service at Detroit on August 15, 1862. It left for Washington on August 29, where for some reason not learned it was diverted from General Williams' command and had no part in the Antietam campaign.

17. The battle of South Mountain, September 14, 1862.

18. The report is printed in *Official Records*, Series 1, XII, Part 2, 145–49.

19. The battle of Antietam, September 17, 1862.

20. Printed in *Official Records*, Series 1, XIX, Part 1, 474–78.

21. Thomas Leiper Kane of Philadelphia, an ardent Abolitionist. At the outbreak of the Civil War he organized a regiment of hunters and backwoodsmen, an undertaking repeated by Theodore Roosevelt in the Spanish-American War of 1898. He was appointed a brigadier general on September 7, 1862. Illness compelled his retirement from the army on November 7, 1863. His brother, Elisha Kent Kane, was a West Point graduate in the class of 1841. Addicted to a life of adventure, he achieved great renown by his determined search (1850–55) for survivors of the Sir John Franklin Arctic Expedition. His book, *Arctic Explorations* "lay for a decade with the Bible on almost literally every parlor table in America."—*Dict. Am. Biog.*

22. General Henry W. Slocum. Upon further close association Williams became a warm admirer of his superior.

23. The preliminary Emancipation Proclamation, issued September 22, 1862.

V

Virginia Mud
and Winter Quarters,
1862-63

VIRGINIA MUD AND WINTER QUARTERS, 1862–63

Safely back in Virginia from his futile invasion of the North, General Lee prepared as best he might to repel another advance of the Army of the Potomac. But McClellan procrastinated, despite the proddings of President Lincoln, while the autumn weeks during which a campaign might be waged slipped away. At length, near the close of October he ventured to cross the Potomac with a newly-refurbished army, moving so deliberately that on November 7, the President relieved him of the command, which was given to General Burnside. The action marked the sunset of McClellan's military career, yet the appointment of Burnside brought no improvement in the situation. He was quite unfit to command the Army of the Potomac, which he accepted only in obedience to a military order. The sorry tragedy of Fredericksburg in December followed in due course, by which time the bottomless mud of Virginia's roads brought a halt to further operations. Meanwhile, the command of General Williams, marching to join Burnside, arrived too late to participate in the battle of Fredericksburg, and after a desperate struggle with the Virginia mud went into winter quarters at Stafford Court House, close to the lower Potomac and but a few miles north of Fredericksburg. Here it remained until April 1863, when under a new commander the Army of the Potomac once more resumed the road to Richmond.

PROSPECTS FOR A NEW CAMPAIGN

Near Sandy Hook, Md.,
November 16, 1862.

My Dear Lew:

Larned arrived last Monday bringing your letter, which was gladly received. He also brought Rene with him from Philadelphia, and I have had her on horseback for the whole week, visiting all points of interest in this romantic part of our country. Rene will probably give Minnie a full description of her visit to the battlefield and her numerous rides over the mountains and to the camps in this vicinity. So I will not bore you nor myself with them. I have deposited her in a farmhouse nearby, but about all she does there is to sleep and eat breakfast. The rest of each day she is in my camp or on excursions.

My division is now spread out from Point of Rocks to Opequan Creek, one brigade being in Loudon Valley on the south side of the Potomac. How long we shall remain in this diluted condition, I can't guess. Rumors are rife that Jackson and A. P. Hill are about to make a descent upon the line of the Potomac. We are too thin to make any considerable resistance except at Harpers Ferry or its vicinity. I hardly think the attack, if any, will be made here. But for the fact that Jackson is the most reckless and often foolhardy of men, I should hardly expect any Rebel movement in the direction of the Potomac.

Yet he has twice made these movements and escaped punishment right under the noses of our superior forces. He may do so again. Last winter, you will remember, he marched 15,000 men to Hancock and Romney and lost about half his command by cold and consequent illness. Last spring he chased us out of the valley and threatened this point while Fremont and McDowell lay on either flank with over 60,000 troops. The rascal escaped when all his own officers gave up all hope.

Our corps is left here but for how long no one can guess. I supposed we should move on Martinsburg as soon as our other corps had reached the Rappahannock, and I think this was McClellan's design. What will be done now I cannot imagine. I have no faith in a campaign in Virginia from this or any other overland route. The topographical features of the country, the miserable state of the country roads, the necessity of heavily guarding such a long and exposed line of communication must render success with a politic and shrewd enemy almost impossible. They have done and are still doing what I anticipated, falling back on their supplies and reserves, and thus extending our lines and weakening our force as we move towards the interior. Somewhere on the railroad where important communications are threatened they will fight, if attacked. Their policy has always been this, except that unfortunate (to them) invasion of Maryland. In doing this they were laboring under the same or similar difficulties that oppose our invasion. Their numbers were reduced, and they were sadly straitened for subsistence. The history of war proves that an united people can in the end overwhelm any superior invading force, if acting purely on the defensive. These Rebels had at Antietam at least 20,000 more men than we had. If they had been on the Rapidan instead of the Potomac their position would have been successfully defended and our army would have retired.

Burnside is a most agreeable, companionable gentleman and a good officer, but he is not regarded by officers who know him best as equal to McClellan in any respect.[1] I coincide in this belief, though I am personally far better acquainted with Burnside than McClellan. Perhaps McClellan has too much of the Fabian policy, but in judging of this one must not forget that he has been placed in circumstances where to lose the game would have been to lose all. My idea is that the cursed policy of this war has its origin at Washington. Old fogyism has ruled in every department. Trepidation for the safety of the Capital seems to have paralyzed all faculties of preparation and promptness.

Yours Affectionately,
A.S.W.

Rene is in my tent and sends love. She will write soon. I will write you again soon, but in these quiet times I have nothing of interest to say. You quite surprise me about the Antietam letter, as it was written in great haste amidst a multitude of duties.

◈

EN ROUTE TO THE RAPPAHANNOCK

Fairfax Station,
Sunday night, Dec. 14, 1862.

My Dear Daughter:

I am so far on my march, very fatigued and full of a thousand duties.

After you left me at Harpers Ferry I soon mounted to go to the front. I spent all the day in Loudon Valley in sight of Mr. Longbridge's barn and of my old camping ground. With all my looking through field glasses I could get no signs of any of you. About 4 o'clock, with a heavy heart—the heaviest I have had in this sorrowful war—I took up the line of march with the 3rd Brigade. As its wagons were not up I ordered it into camp about two miles west of Hillsborough shortly after dark. With a small escort of cavalry I proceeded on and overtook Knipe's brigade at Wheatland, about nine miles from Harpers Ferry. Knipe had a nice house for his headquarters and I slept comfortably with him under his blankets. On Friday I marched the first two brigades to Goose Creek, passing through Leesburg. The 3rd Brigade was left to wait its wagons. We found a good camping ground and my headquarters in a farmhouse.

At daylight we were on the march. Some rascally fellows set fire to three stacks of hay belonging to my farmer. I was intensely angry, as well as grieved for the distress of the family, as this was their only subsistence. It was the first of this kind of wanton destruction I have seen, and was occasioned by Knipe's refusing to let the men use the stacks for bedding. On Saturday we marched to the deserted mansion (Chantilly) of the Stuart family, connections by marriage of Washington's family. In his attic our men and officers found autograph letters of Washington, Mrs. Washington, and others of the family connections. The place, which was once magnificent, has been occupied by cavalry and its fine grounds utterly ruined. You can hardly conceive such a picture of destruction and desolation. It is one of the pictures of civil war.

This morning we left Chantilly at 9 o'clock, halting two or three hours at Fairfax Court House. Reached this point about dark. The roads this side of Fairfax Court House are abominable, and worse, they say, ahead. My 3rd Brigade has caught up. The weather has been fine, but it has thawed the snow and frost and left the roads almost impassable. Many trains passing over them have cut up deeply what never was very good. I am tonight trying to reduce the miles of wagons and reducing weight so as to pass through the sloughs ahead. You cannot imagine the difficulties of marches at this season, on short rations, short forage, bad roads, bad preparations, and the like. Think of moving a force of 10,000 men with all its supplies in wagons over a stripped country in the month of December. The thing looks impossible, and yet we have done it so far and I have no doubt I shall get through with a fagged command.

I am without intelligence from the active world for four days. We have rumors of great fighting at Fredericksburg and severe losses.[2] I suppose we are bound for the same place, as we go now to Stafford Court House. I shall be there within four days. Write me via Washington, 1st Division, 12th Corps. I am very anxious to hear from you. Tell Minnie that I will write her as soon as I get to a camp where I can stay one day. God knows when that will be. . . .

Your Affectionate Father,
A.S.W.

◈

DISCOURAGEMENT OVER FREDERICKSBURG

Camp near Fairfax,
Dec. 19, 1862.

My Dear Daughter:

After floundering four days in such roads as were never seen in the earliest days of the Northwest I am again back in camp with my division at this place. My leading brigade reached the Neabasco River four miles from Dumfries.

I wrote you Sunday P.M. a short note from this place. We left on Monday morning, having taken the precaution to reduce my trains as much as possible. I sent Augustine with the surplus ammunition and shells with all the extra baggage to Aquia Creek via Alexandria. With the rest of our baggage and my division I began the march early Monday morning and after a hard day's work reached Wolf Run Ford over the Occoquan and passed over it with all my division long before dark. I encamped myself about two miles beyond the Occoquan at a cross roads where stands the remnant of an old Baptist church known for years hereabouts as the "Beacon Corner Church." My brigades were all well up and we should have gone farther but for the rear of Geary's division, which I overtook here and which had delayed us the day before.

Before daylight the next morning my troops were in motion, Knipe's brigade leading. About 12 o'clock I received orders to halt until further orders. Knipe had reached the Neabasco at a point near the Potomac. Kane was about two miles behind, and Gordon's brigade (Murphy commanding) was two miles or so behind him. Toward evening I was notified that we were to countermarch the next morning. It had rained the night before and during the morning and the roads—red clay—were indescribable. Our long trains cut them up fearfully and it really seemed impossible to return. I ordered the troops to march before daylight and difficult as was the route the 2nd and 3rd brigades succeeded in reaching this place before night. Knipe's brigade and all our trains crossed the Occoquan and I spent the night in a house on the banks of that creek. The night before I was in a house on the Neabasco. The other nights I passed in tents.

Altogether I have never had so disagreeable and difficult a march. How my trains got over such roads I cannot now guess, but they have all returned safe, though shattered, with the loss of but one mule. I reached this place about 11 o'clock yesterday. Geary's division is returning today. Where we are going to it is difficult to say. I suppose we shall remain hereabouts as a reserve until the movements of the Rebels are known. The disaster at Fredericksburg affects us all deeply. From our standpoint it seems a most unaccountable sacrifice of life with no results. I am glad I was not there. I am as discouraged and blue as one well can be, as I see in these operations much that astonishes and confounds me and much that must discourage our troops and the people. Who is at fault I know not, as I am not in a position to judge. . . .

Your Affectionate Father,
A.S.W.

SKIRMISHING WITH GENERAL STUART

Camp near Fairfax Station, Va.,
Dec. 31, 1862.

[My Dear Daughter:]

Christmas has come and gone so gently and with so little of the circumstance of holidays that I was not made aware of its presence. A day or two afterward I was just sitting down to send you a remembrance, which would aid you in remembering others, when I was ordered to march my division towards Wolf Run Shoals as Dumfries had been attacked. So with three days' rations in our haversacks we started to find Stuart, leaving this depot (by orders) almost without a guard at all. At Wolf Run Ford I drew up my three brigades on the hill slopes in a most picturesque spot and occupied with my artillery the fortifications and rifle pits made by the Rebels last year and waited orders from Gen. Slocum, who had gone toward Dumfries with Geary's division to relieve Col. Canby, who was there with three regiments and had been assaulted all the day before by Stuart.

We could hear nothing of Canby's condition as the Rebel cavalry occupied the roads between us in force. Every now and then we could hear Geary's guns shelling the woods in his advance, a favorite mode he has of skirmishing with artillery. About 3 P.M. (Sunday) a runaway cavalryman brought us word that all our cavalry pickets on the Occoquan below to the village had been driven off and that Stuart had crossed with 4,000 men and two guns, making toward Fairfax Station.

Here was a pleasant fix. We had left all our personal luggage, to say nothing of the stores, at the junction unguarded. I at once dispatched a brigade back with four guns and before sundown occupied our camp here and the whole road from this to Wolf Run Ford. I dispatched messengers to Fairfax Court House to have the line of railroad between this place and Alexandria guarded. If this had been done we should have caught Stuart in a trap, as we held the Occoquan River and the whole west line. His only escape was by Burke's Station on the railroad between this and Alexandria.

Stuart came up as far as Mt. Carmel Church within two and one-half miles of my line and then struck off towards Burke's Station, where he cut the telegraph wire and damaged the railroad somewhat and then passed on around Fairfax Court House. I had no cavalry and could not find out his movements till too late. His men were all mounted. The authorities in Washington, where probably are 5,000 cavalry, were asked to send out on the railroad but I cannot hear that the least movement was made. On the contrary, it is reported here that they ordered our troops to defend Alexandria, as it was threatened by a cavalry raid!

I kept my whole division under arms or on the move for nearly forty-eight hours. Thus we let a few thousand cavalry ride through our lines while our cavalry is cut up into small parties of fifty or a hundred scouring around the country to little or no purpose. Although Stuart began to cross the Occoquan over a bad ford at 11 A.M. in the face of a hundred or more of our cavalry, no information was brought me, and then by chance, until nearly 3 P.M. The reason was that our cavalry pickets ran away, each man for himself, and took the most convenient route to a safe place. They did not even resist the crossing at a ford where but two men could pass at the same time. I marched my division back to its old camp day before yesterday, everybody much disgusted at the result. . . .

It is more than fifteen months since we parted at the Central Railroad with a heavy heart, both of us, and with that vast uncertain future overshadowing our souls. How I have longed to see you, my darling daughter, no one but an anxious parent can guess. But we must submit patiently to the allotments of life, trusting that a wise Providence will in His good time reunite us in happiness and health. . . .

Your Affectionate Father,
A.S.W.

❖

HORRORS OF THE MUD MARCH

Stafford Court House,
January 24, 1863.

My Dear Daughter,

Here I am at length at another of those old Virginia Court Houses, which means, generally, nothing but an old tumble down courthouse with a few dilapidated dwellings around it. I reached here through much toil and tribulation, Heaven only knows how, through seas and oceans of mud and over multitudes of angry, swollen streams.

We left Fairfax Station camp on the 19th, weather cold and road frozen in the roughest state. My division led. I encamped that night about two miles beyond Wolf Run Shoals, at Beacon Race Church, near the camp of our first march this way. The next day (20th) the road was still rough and the weather cold and threatening snow. We started by daylight and reached Dumfries (fourteen miles) before night, encamping on the south side of the Quantico Creek, one brigade on the north side. I took my headquarters at a house on the south side upon an elevation where Stuart had put his battery during his recent raid. In consequence the house had been greatly mauled by our batteries in Dumfries, receiving no less than nine shots, one of which tore down the chimney. The women and children of the house took to the cellar during the cannonading and were, of course, terribly alarmed, especially so when the chimney fell. We found nobody at the house but women and children, one married woman and her sister, who was very pretty. There was but one room which could have a fire. In consequence, we had not much spare room.

A cold northeast rain began before dark with a very tempest of wind. The few tents our men had were soon flattened. All night the cold rain dashed on the windows and the wind howled. In the morning we had a precious sight. The frost had all gone and mud of the stickiest and nastiest kind had taken its place. The rain was still pouring, but we began our march at 7 o'clock, and such a march! On either side of the road was the densest forest of scrub pines, a perfect thicket. There were no side roads, no turning out, no getting into fields, but right on-ward through the saturated clay man and beast were compelled to travel, every wagon deepening the profound depth and every drop of rain soft-ening the lower depth profound. After an infinitude of floundering, my infantry and artillery reached the Chopawamsic Creek early in the afternoon (five miles). We found it not fordable for ammunition wagons, and news was brought from the rear that the Quantico had risen above fording. So here we were between two rising streams, our supply train cut off, rain still falling, and the heavens indicating a continuation beyond a guess of fair weather.

Our only resource was to bridge the Chopawamsic. So at it went a hundred or two of our men, and at it they worked by details all night. In the meantime, I unloaded what wagons had arrived and sent back for the stalled ammunition train and other be-mudded vehicles. The five miles of miry clay back to the Quantico seemed like fifty, but by 9 or 10 o'clock the following morning all my trains except some ammunition wagons were up, and I began to cross the creek over our rough but stout bridge. We were, however, on our last day's rations, and the supply train, which is managed by the corps quartermaster, could not be heard from. At length, however, before the last of my division crossed it was reported as across the Quantico and coming up. So onward we went, full of hopeful appetites, and reached the Aquia Creek soon after 2 o'clock and found it not fordable! Here was another bridge to build, or wait till morning in hopes of sudden subsidence of the waters. Wait was the word, but preparations for bridging were made.

Fortunately, the water fell and early in the morning we were able to ford the artillery. By noon I began my march towards this place, moving forward my infantry (who were without rations) and leaving trains with small guards. I reached here in time to get one day's rations from Sigel's commissary and so was able to feed my men after 24 hours fasting. Horses and mules were worse off. Dozens died on the way, wagons abandoned, ambulances broken down, contents thrown away. But after all, the wonder is that a single wagon or gun was got through, but today I have got up my ammunition train and all other wagons except the broken-down ones and order begins to reign again. I fear, however, the effects on officers and men. For three days there has not been a dry foot nor dry skin nor shelter scarcely at night, and for one day and night the rain was so pelting and heavy that fires could not be built. Such exposure must produce more deaths and disability than two pitched battles.

We are here now in the mud, striving to get food and forage over such roads as I have described from Brooke Station on the railroad, or [Hope's] Landing five miles away on Aquia Creek. How we shall succeed is yet a problem, as, indeed, is the fact whether there is either to be had at either place. Such is campaigning in Virginia in the winter. If a few of our "Onward" people could try the experiment, I think they would vote backward till spring comes. Tonight it looks like more rain. If it comes, the Lord help us, for I don't exactly see how we can help ourselves. The roads will be literally impassable. In truth, they are so now. One can't go a mile without drowning mules in mud-holes. It is solemnly true that we lost mules in the middle of the road, sinking out of sight in the mud-holes. A few bubbles of air, a stirring of the watery mud, indicated the last expiring efforts of many a poor long-ears.

I don't know, of course, how the world's surface looked after the flood in Noah's time, but I am certain it could not have appeared more saturated than does the present surface of this God-forsaken portion of the Old Dominion. Our whole line of march, almost without exception, has been through pine barrens with scarcely a house, certainly not one to a mile, and those [there were] of the most forlorn look with starved-looking occupants. It is neither a decent country to fight in or to fight for. I would [not] accept as a gift the whole of Prince William County, and yet this was once a rich part of Virginia, the great tobacco-raising region, and Dumfries, now the most wretched of worn-out places, was once a great mart importing from Europe largely. There are traces now of splendid old estates, with enormous trunks of cherry and pear trees standing amidst the pine forests all along the road. One can hardly fancy, however, that so desert a region could ever have been fertile or populous. This Stafford Court House is a small group of poor houses and one dilapidated thing called a courthouse.

We are now within eight miles of Falmouth in the most direct line, and may be said to have joined Burnside. We belong to Sigel's grand division. His headquarters are here. Where we shall next go, no one knows. I suppose some grand movement is in contemplation. If we find, as I think probable, that the enemy has fallen back from Fredericksburg we shall have a tedious and exposed forward movement with a long line of supply communication, which the whole army could hardly protect. If we attempt this during the wet months it will be a dead, if not disastrous, failure. Indeed, the efforts already made to campaign in the winter have greatly destroyed the spirits of the men. Other causes have combined, but the exposure and hardships of such a camp life has done the most. In consequence, the desertions from Burnside's troops are very large. I arrested some thirty on the march, who were straggling in the wood. In truth, Rene, I fear it is done with the Army of the Potomac for any vigorous operation. I think the commander has very little confidence in himself and the army generally reciprocates the feeling. This is a critique not for the public. . . .

Love to all,

Your Affectionate Father,

A.S.W.

❖

VIRGINIA MUD AND SOLDIERLY AFFECTION

Stafford Court House, Jan. 27, 1863.

My Dear Daughter: . . . .

I wrote you as we were about to march from Fairfax Station. Our march on the 19th and 20th was tolerably fair; weather cold and roads exceedingly rough, frozen after having been cut up in the deepest mud. On the evening of the 20th a severe northeast cold storm began with wind and rain, prostrating the few tents we had, putting out camp fires, and exposing the whole command to the pitiless peltings. It was a savage night. In the morning everything looked afloat. The rain still fell heavily, the frost was all out of the ground, and the deepest mud was substituted.

We worked all day to get four miles; such floundering in bottomless holes; such whipping and hallooing and boasting and swearing. Many of our wagons stuck fast inextricably and many mules were drowned in the middle of the road, fairly swallowed up in the mud. It was, in places, really difficult to force a horse through the tenacious stuff. The road on both sides was for the most part hemmed in by dense and impassable pine thickets. Of course man and beast were obliged to flounder along the best way possible. Towards night the head of the column reached a stream called Chopawamsic. We had encamped the night before on the Quantico, opposite Dumfries. The rain had so raised the Chopawamsic that it was not fordable. So we sat down before it in the pine barrens, unloaded what wagons had got up, and sent back to relieve others and began building a bridge.

All night we worked at it and until 10 o'clock the next morning, when it was fit to pass. We got over the angry stream pretty well and worked on all day through similar mud and country to Aquia Creek. Here we found another unfordable stream and again encamped. I sent back wagons again and prepared to bridge, but the rain had stopped and the stream was falling, as they do rapidly in this country, so we waited for morning and found that we could ford. From Aquia to this place (five miles) we were nearly all day in getting through the men and a few wagons. It was not till next day that all my wagons got up and some of the supply corps train is, I believe, still behind. I say, 'all my wagons'; I mean all that were not lost in the mud. We had to abandon several wagons and ambulances broken down or from loss of mules. Such a march! such destruction of property, throwing away of loads, dying mules and horses, the old "Cyropedia" wasn't a circumstance! Black Swamp or the old Chicago Road twenty-five years ago was a pleasant race course [compared] to the quagmires of the Old Dominion.[3]

This part of Virginia, through which we marched, used to be its most fertile and populous portion. It was worn out by tobacco raising and fairly abandoned. All along in the midst of the pine barrens are traces of old estates and of splendid mansions; stumps of old cherry and pear trees; outlines of large gardens and ornamental enclosures. But the houses are now very few and very dilapidated, and what few farms there are are very sterile looking and the people apparently very poor. Northern people in several places began settlements some years ago and a few still remain. They say the land can be reclaimed, but the instances we saw would not warrant much outlay. Dumfries, now the most forlorn of all old towns, was once quite a mart for importation as well as exportation, one of the largest in the South, and in Colonial days second to but few in the country. They pretend to show the house where Patrick Henry made his great war speech before the Revolution. The present appearance of the town would chill the eloquence of Demosthenes!

This Stafford Court House, near which we are encamped, is like most of Virginia's "Court Houses," a place of three old homes, a small, dilapidated court house, and a jail about eight feet square. It is surrounded by the same interminable stunted pine and evergreen thickets, though now pretty well thinned out by Sigel's troops, here before us. There is, amongst other evergreens, a most beautiful one called the holly, the same that I saw in Tennessee two years ago. I wish I could send you a live plant.

We are now only eight miles from the main camp opposite Fredericksburg. There was to have been another crossing, but Burnside's army, after floundering two days in the mud, was obliged to return or starve. They could not draw an empty wagon through the roads after a few trains had passed. . . . We are five miles from the Aquia Creek at Hope's Landing. We have all we can do to draw supplies for man and beast. I would I could have some of the winter "Onward" people one day at work on these roads. They would get some faint idea of Virginia winter roads. . . .

Did I tell you of the handsome gift I received from the officers of my 'Old Third Brigade'? Though it had partly leaked out through Rene months ago, I had quite forgotten it and was quite taken aback the evening before we marched by being invited into the office tent by a committee and finding it lit up and decorated with evergreens and full of officers, some sixty. Col. Knipe, now commanding the brigade, received me with a very flattering speech, opened a box, and took out a most magnificent sword and a belt and sash, which he presented on the part of the officers. I was so taken by surprise, so affected by the manner and mode the testimonial was made, so filled with recollections of the past several months that this gallant brigade has been under my command, of the many changes that death has made, that I fairly broke down and for the second time since I have been in the service, tears flowed freely. You can hardly realize how attached I have become to many of these officers who have been with me through so many trials, privations, and dangers. Of course it makes me very happy to know that they love me, as I know they do, sincerely. The sword is the most gorgeous thing I have seen, costing nearly four hundred dollars. Nobody but the officers of my old brigade was permitted to subscribe. The sword has been sent to New York for some inscriptions and will then be sent to Rene for present safekeeping. It is altogether too fine for the field.

Perhaps almost a more touching compliment was started by this. The enlisted men of the brigade, hearing what the officers had done, got together, I am told, and resolved that they would make me a present and I hear they are busy in getting one up. A testimonial of privates is not a usual thing. I have had hundreds of occasions to know that those of my old brigade have great affection for me. I will give you two instances on the recent march. On the first day's march in rain and mud, I stayed behind to see the rearmost brigade start. Afterwards I went forward. On reaching the front, I found the old brigade just halting after a most fatiguing march. I was myself wet and cross as could be, hardly able to speak a kind word. As I rode down the hill where the men were lying, they all sprang up and gave me three cheers. This, from tired men with wet feet and wet skins, was something.

On the last day's march our rations gave out, as the supply trains were stuck in the mud. In riding by a rear regiment with the brigade commissary the men set up a cry of "Crackers, Crackers." The old brigade was just in advance and a halt was sounded soon afterward. As soon as it halted the men went back in crowds to this new regiment and told these cracker fellows if they ever insulted their general again they'd "lick the Devil out of them." The cry was undoubtedly intended for the commissary, but the men of the old brigade saw me only and thought I was being insulted.

I should hardly dare say these things to anyone but you, but I confess and feel that the love of these men, whom I have taken through snow and rain, [who] have marched thousands of miles for the last year and a half under all circumstances that try the temper and disturb the amiability, is worth a great deal. It is my chief support and encouragement amidst the trials and dispiriting circumstances that surround me. Poor fellows! Their ranks are terribly thinned. At Cedar Mountain nearly one-half of this brigade was killed or wounded, every field officer and every adjutant included. In one regiment every company officer was numbered in the casualties. At Antietam they lost every fourth man. Many of the wounded have come back, some quite disabled, but sticking to their ranks. I met one the other day whose left arm was so disabled at Antietam that he could only carry his musket in his right hand. Still he does not ask for a discharge.

I see another list of major generals and my name not included. Amongst them are several who have seen no service, one a captain on duty in my command six months ago. He has seen little or no service. I have been now nearly a year commanding a division, a major general's command, longer than any officer in the service. How long I shall be able to hold out under this oversloughing is very doubtful. Every such promotion over me, as Carl Schurz and the twenty others in the last list, is an insult.[4] Of course it greatly dispirits and discourages me. I am not so annoyed that I am not promoted, as I am that others are promoted over me, especially as the President has months ago announced in general orders, published to the Army, that no promotions to general officers would be made except for services in the field. And yet he promotes over my head men who have not seen a tenth part of the service I have. So much for grumbling! My officers swear worse than I do on this point and I hear are getting up a petition. Love to all. . . .

Your Affectionate Father,
A.S.W.

❖

DECAYING GRANDEUR OF VIRGINIA

Stafford Court House,
February 16, 1863.

My Dear Jule:[5]

Your kind and welcome letter enclosed in Minnie's last deserves a prompt answer. . . . We are still in the mud in this most God forsaken of all holes that human eye ever rested upon since Noah first looked out of the ark. I doubt if his prospect wasn't more inviting. He could have seen more mud, and if my memory serves, he had a hill or two and some rocks, like Ararat, to look upon. We have a broad waste, slightly rolling, once covered with a thicket of stunted pines, which have pretty much disappeared under the joint operations of Sigel's Teutonics and our own corps.

Houses, there are none in sight. What few decayed and dilapidated ones there were, have found their way into the cabins of the men and the bricks and stones have followed the boards. For example, my headquarters are on the site of what was one of Old Virginia's most stately stone mansions. Not one stone is left upon another, save one chimney which we use for an office fireplace and around which an Aroostook company from one of my Maine regiments have built me a very neat and comfortable log office. One tall brick chimney we tumbled down to accommodate the multitudinous little fires of our quarters. Our location is on the summit of quite a high knoll in the center of my fifteen regiments. There are still on its slopes traces of the garden paths and old adornments, solitary-looking fruit trees and other evidences of decayed wealth and grandeur. Gen. Kane, who has kindred hereabouts and who spent some boyish days in these parts, gives us great stories of its ancient wealth and of the pure blood of its former denizens. In my rides about I occasionally meet an old decayed mansion, with bushes and pine thickets growing up where was evidently once splendid parks and fruit yards. Often venerable old fruit trees are standing in the midst of these pine barrens.

Just over the hills east is what is called Stafford Court House. One old tavern, awfully used, one small courthouse, windowless, one smaller jail, a blacksmith shop for mule shoeing, and one tolerably looking house terraced in front, where "Mit Sigel" has his headquarters and around which barbaric Dutch is uttered with most villainous vehemence and gutturalness.

You probably think living in tents in the winter is a killing thing. But it is vastly more pleasant and comfortable than you in a warm house imagine. You are obliged to stoke the little stove pretty briskly, for the moment the fire stops the cold air slips in. It is something like living out of doors with something to keep the wind off. But I prefer the tent to one of these nasty houses, or one that has been occupied by some of our men. Those little creeping things will stick to the tenants in spite of water and soap.

[The remainder is missing.]

◆

BAD WEATHER AND CAMP LIFE

Stafford Court House, Feb. 22, 1863.

My Dear Daughter:

It is a most tempestuous day, snow, cold, and a very high wind. I have never seen at the North a more disagreeable day. I find it hard work to keep my tent comfortable and am kept very diligent at my little sheet-iron stove. The front of the tent, which is tied together by strings, is not easily kept tight in this gale. It is one of those storms when at home one would not willingly go out of doors. Think of my poor 600 men on picket out in front, and the thousands around so poorly sheltered. To add to our troubles, the wood has been so cut away that it is not easy to get a supply for our large camps. We consume fuel at an enormous rate with these large camp fires.

Today is the anniversary of Washington's birthday. We expected to have a grand division parade and review, with salutes. I hear now the big guns going in all directions (12 M.) but I ordered mine to be omitted on account of the weather. . . .

Yesterday I took a long ride to see a road I have 600 men corduroying toward Falmouth, I don't know for what purpose, unless we are about to corduroy up to the Rebel position. I dined with the Baron Von Steinwehr, a general in Sigel's corps, with whom I spent a couple of hours. He is a remarkably intelligent and agreeable person. I have not seen him since we were at Sulphur Springs last summer, where we passed through that terrific artillery fire. . . .

I rode yesterday my "Yorkshire." I have not been on his back for over a month, preferring to ride "Plug Ugly" over these rough and muddy roads. "Yorkshire" never looked so well as now. He has grown large and muscular since we left Detroit. Considering his thin skin and soft hair he stands exposure wonderfully, though Charley is as careful of him as a mother of a baby. The horse is admired by everybody and pronounced by all as the finest animal in the army.

Have I described to you our location? Our headquarters tents are pitched upon the summit of a pretty high knoll where once stood a large stone house, one of the mansions of the old F.F.V.'s. There is not a stone of it left now, save a chimney around which the Aroostook boys from one of my Maine regiments have built me a nice log cabin, which is used as an office. It is roofed with canvas, but is quite comfortable. When we came here the ground was saturated, I think, to the center of the earth, as I have not been able to get my ground floor dry. Yesterday some of the men got me boards enough to cover half my floor. Our tents are pitched in a square and we have some evergreen bushes outside to break the high winds, not very successfully.

I am almost in the center of my three brigades (fifteen regiments) and can overlook nearly every camp. Of course I get the benefit of all the calls and am awakened every morning by the reveilles on drums or trumpets on every side of me. The ground is so broken into short hills that we have no space for drill grounds, even when the mud partially dries up. These short hills, which two months ago were covered by a heavy growth of yellow or pitch pine, are now stripped and naked in all directions, save the log huts and shanties with the shelter tent roofs of the regiments, which are generally placed on the slopes. We have an old log barn for our private horses. All the rest, horses and mules, are obliged to stand out in this terrible snow storm. . . .

Your Affectionate Father,
A.S.W.

◈

MILITARY OPERATIONS AND OPINIONS

Stafford Court House, Mar. 7, 1863.

My Dear Daughter:

I am stopped on my application for leave, as the enclosed paper shows. Whether I shall succeed hereafter is very doubtful, and depends upon the weather, as we shall undoubtedly move as soon as the earth dries up. Spring is so rapidly advancing that this must come soon. Ergo, I think I shall not get leave. Besides, after the mud and exposure of our winter life there is much to do to prepare for a march. Everything gets out of order. Mules and horses are used up, harnesses destroyed, accouterments injured, guns and muskets need repairs. Everything is at sixes and must be looked to. We have a stupid old ass for chief quartermaster of the corps, through whom all these requisitions must pass and who makes no more headway than a man on a treadmill, always fussy and tramping but never getting ahead.

We are having the preparatory reviews. Day before yesterday I reviewed my division and yesterday Gen. Hooker was to be here to review it, but it rained and the affair is postponed. Today it is foggy and showery. Our duties continue arduous. I have 2,000 men on duty daily on pickets, road building, guards, etc., and the mud is so deep yet that we can hardly fix up. For a season I am obliged to cram my whole division into a space about big enough for a regiment, such is the broken nature of the country, full of deep ravines and rolling hills. . . .

Aunt Rene writes that Letty Larned (Mrs. some other name now) reports in Norwich that she saw letters of mine in Detroit in which I represent myself as greatly disgusted with the war and awfully discouraged. She says she saw them at Uncle Lew's. Now as I write to you all a good many things I don't wish to publish, I hope you will all be careful how you show my letters. I sometimes 'bile up' on first impressions, but it won't do to make the 'bilings' public. From what I hear you are all too excited up North and everybody is in an extreme state on one side or the other. I don't remember writing such doleful accounts, though I have felt irritated enough at times to say most anything in confidence. I suspect Mrs. Letty has exaggerated my opinions. I have never felt otherwise than fighting out this war to the bitter end, or at least to the point of teaching Rebels that there is a power of heavy chastisement amongst the loyal people of the country. Just now I feel like letting slip the dogs of war in any way that will most effectually subdue Jeff. and his myrmidons. Goodbye, and God bless you. Love to all.

Your Affectionate Father,
A.S.W.

◈

DETROIT RIOT AND MILITARY INSPECTIONS

Stafford Court House, Mar. 20th, 1863.

My Dear Daughter:

I have not heard from you for an unusual time but I get now and then a Detroit paper, in one of which I see you have had a great riot, which, however, looks to me from this distance to have been a very small one, and very easily stopped if there had been any efficiency and vigor in civil or military authorities. These mobs are generally composed of nine-tenths spectators, whose presence serves to encourage the rioters and to disperse them by their own flight when vigorously attacked. This Detroit riot was about as absurd an affair as I have read of, only equalled by the weakness and want of action on the part of somebody in power. The provost guard rather inflamed than quelled it.[6]

We are still having bad weather; quite a snow storm today. Our best weather so far has been cold, high winds, with gleams of sunshine. Still, we are preparing for good roads and a movement. Reviews and inspections are frequent. Yesterday Gen. Hooker reviewed my division and pronounced it a "splendid division." The regiments certainly never looked better or did better. The day before I was reviewed by Gen. Slocum, and the day before that I reviewed a brigade. Inspections of regiments go on when it don't rain or snow. There are so many things to look after by the way of supplies before taking the field that everybody must be active, each one above inspecting to see that those below are doing their duty. Among the multitudinous officers of a division of fifteen regiments it is not easy to keep all up to their duties. . . .

I suppose we shall move soon, or as soon as the roads are practicable for artillery. It looks very little like it today, as snow is falling heavily. We have symptoms of alarm almost daily now and as my division is on the right of the Grand Army I am expected to look out that we are not surprised and our flank is protected. It takes a large number of men to do picket and fatigue duty, nearly 2,500 men out at all times. The news today looks not as pleasant as I could wish from Yazoo and Vicksburg and Port Hudson. . . .[7]

Love to all,

Your Affectionate Father,
A.S.W.

◈

COMMENDATION AND PROSPECTS OF PROMOTION

Stafford Court House,
March 31, 1863.

My Dear Daughter: . . .

I wrote you last that Gen. Slocum was away to attend Gen. Sumner's funeral, and that Best was with him as far as Philadelphia, I supposed.[8] Do not believe all you hear about my modesty in applying for leave. I tried all manner of strings, private and official, and should have succeeded but that Gen. Geary got in an application when I was in command of the corps in the first absence of Gen. Slocum. I did not approve of his leave but was obliged to forward his application, hoping, however, it would die in the pigeon holes of the adjutant general's office. Unfortunately, my application unhoused his, and as he was ahead of me in date he succeeded. Before his return the weather began to look favorable and orders were issued for inspections etc. preparatory for a march. I applied privately to Col. Dickinson, adjutant general on Hooker's staff, who offered to help me, but it was decided that we should probably move before I could get back. In such a case, I did not wish to go. I enclose Williams' last letter, by which you'll see they were courteous if not obliging. I am sorry, for no one can tell how I weary to see Minnie. Indeed, it became a thing which made me very unhappy. However, my whole reputation depends upon my being on hand when the army marches. Did I tell you how highly my division was complimented by Gen. Hooker and staff at the recent review? He pronounced it the best he had seen in the army. The other day I called upon Gen. Meade and others six or eight miles away. He also spoke of the high praises we had received, as did other general officers. Gen. Butterfield, chief of staff, was especially flattering. I am glad I was not away. I should have lost some of the fame of a splendid division. Gen. Meade spoke of having passed you with Cousin[?] Brooks, but did not recognize you till he was by. He wonders I am not promoted, and says the fault must be with Gen. Banks. He owes his own, he thinks, to the recommendation (active) of his commanders. I feel, however, that there is something deeper, a want of army prestige and not having been on the Peninsular [Campaign]. The whole thing is so smothered in army influence that not to have its aid is quite death to one's hopes. Every military bureau in Washington is in the hands of army officers and Gen. Halleck thinks nothing else can be valuable.

However, patience and perseverance. I have a letter from Senator Howard who says he shall continue to urge my promotion. I met Parson Hunter at Gen. Meade's. He is chaplain to some regiment.

Capt. Beman has come back to me, so we are nearly all together again. Capt. Wilkins has tendered his resignation, but I doubt if it will be accepted. He acts foolishly just now, on the eve of a movement.

[*The remainder is missing.*]

1. He led the Army of the Potomac to senseless slaughter at Fredericksburg four weeks later.
2. The battle of Fredericksburg, one of the worst Union defeats of the war, occurred on December 13, 1862. About 10,000 Union soldiers and one-half as many Confederates were killed or wounded in the battle.
3. The infamous Black Swamp embraced portions of a dozen present-day Ohio counties at the western end of Lake Erie, occupying the drainage basin of the lower Maumee River. Prior to the construction of improved highways it was impassable for wheeled vehicles during a large part of the year, constituting an effective barrier to travel between southeastern Michigan and the settled portions of Ohio. The Chicago Road was the highway which followed the old Sauk Indian trail from Detroit to Chicago. See "The Black Swamp Road," *Burton Historical Collection Leaflet*, I (September 1922), 45–52, and M. M. Quaife, *Chicago Highways Old and New* (Chicago, 1923), Chap. II.
4. Carl Schurz, like General Sigel, was a participant in the German Revolution of 1848. In America he attained outstanding influence as a German-American spokesman and an enthusiastic advocate of Unionism and Emancipation. Without a background of military experience, on April 15, 1862, he was appointed brigadier general and within a few weeks was given command of a division in General Fremont's army. The feeling of such contemporaries as Williams is wholly understandable. It was Schurz' misfortune, perhaps, that his division was driven in panic flight by Stonewall Jackson at Chancellorsville. Controversy with General Howard, his superior officer, developed both here and at Gettysburg, two months later, in which the majority of authorities tend to exculpate Schurz. See *Dict. Am. Biog.*, sketches of Schurz and Howard.
5. Mrs. Lewis Allen, sister-in-law of General Williams.
6. The anti-Negro riot of March 6, 1863 has been characterized by Silas Farmer as "one of the darkest pages in the history of Detroit." It was precipitated by an alleged outrage by a mulatto named Faulkner upon a little girl. Although Faulkner was promptly tried and sentenced to prison for life, a mob which vainly attempted to lynch him vented its wrath upon the Negro residents generally, many of whom were beaten and their dwellings burned, some eighty-five buildings in all being destroyed.
7. The "news" concerned the efforts of General Grant, wholly unsuccessful as yet, to capture Vicksburg.
8. General Sumner, who had commanded the right grand division at the battle of Fredericksburg, December 13, 1862, died on March 21, 1863.

VI

To
Chancellorsville
and Back

TO CHANCELLORSVILLE AND BACK

The distance from Stafford to Chancellorsville is short, hardly a dozen miles as the crow flies. For an earth-bound army the distance was somewhat greater, of course. Like General Burnside, General Hooker, the new commander of the Army of the Potomac, was unequal to the responsibility of so large a command. Yet he proved to be an excellent leader of smaller military units, and not for nothing had he won his nickname of "Fighting Joe." With the renovated Army of the Potomac, 130,000 strong and, as he declared, the finest army on the planet, he set forth on April 27 in quest of Lee and Richmond. His initial maneuvers proved highly successful and May Day 1863 saw the main portion of the army united on the south side of the Rappahannock River. Chancellorsville was a single house whose place in history is due to its position at the crossing of two main highways. General Hooker made it his headquarters, and around it surged the terrific battle of May 1 to 3. With its progress General Hooker's self-confidence fell ever lower and because of this General Lee won his greatest victory, over an army twice the strength of his own. By May 7 General Williams was back at Stafford Court House, whence he had departed less than two weeks before. About the same time, too, General Lee was meditating a second invasion of the North. On June 3, only a month after Chancellorsville, he set his army in motion toward the Shenandoah Valley.

PREPARATIONS FOR A NEW OFFENSIVE

Stafford Court House, April 14, 1863.

My Dear Daughter:

We have had ten days of such continuous reviews that I have hardly written a letter. The President and Mrs. Lincoln and family and a long string of satellites came down and spent a week or more, reviewing the troops. First, all the cavalry that could be spared from duty— over 12,000—were reviewed together, then the artillery, then four corps (probably 60,000) infantry together, and then the other corps separately. Our corps was the last reviewed, as we are on the extreme right. We had difficulty in finding open ground enough in this broken and pine-barren country to get our two divisions into reviewing positions. As it was, we were obliged to mass each regiment by two-company fronts. But we made a very fine show, as the ground, from its undulating surface, gave a conspicuous and picturesque appearance to the masses moving over the crests and down the slopes.

The President and Gen. Hooker were greatly fagged, as they had been almost every day on horseback for hours and had on that day reviewed one corps (11th) before ours. Mrs. Lincoln and other ladies came over (in spite of bad roads) in ambulances. I doubt if any week in the history of our country has ever witnessed such a large display of fine troops. The army never looked better and but for the small regiments in some corps would certainly impress one with its invincibility. If properly handled I feel that it must carry everything before it.

I met a great many old acquaintances at these reviews; Gen. Meade, Col. Stockton, Gen. John C. Robinson, Col. Morrow and his field and staff officers, who are known in Detroit, besides many others.[1] I have been living for months comparatively near all these persons and yet have not met them before. Indeed, the roads have been so bad that it was quite an impossibility to look up your old friends, even when but a short distance off. It is often strange, too, that in the army you may be almost near neighbors to a friend without knowing it. For instance, I met H. G. Lacey, Gen. Witherell's son-in-law, who told me he was on duty as staff officer in the 11th Corps, which adjoins me on the left.

We have had several fine days and the roads were getting in good order for this country, but today it is pouring again and the mud will be back again. We shall move, I think, in a few days, as preparations have been ordered which indicate that we are to march; I have no idea in what direction, nor has any one beyond Gen. Hooker's confidential staff. The cavalry command is now up the Rappahannock and we hear firing in the direction they have moved. It is a mere reconnoissance, I think, to divert the attention of the enemy while we get ready to strike somewhere else. I shall write you as often as I can. Tell Uncle Lew that I shall write him before we march, probably tonight.

[The remainder is missing.]

April 16th, '63.

My Dear Daughter:

The jewel in the sword Maj. Sherman thinks is with the engraver in New York. It was replaced and sent to him. By observing you will see that the jewel can be removed with a small portion of the hilt. The sword made slow progress but it is now in your possession and I hope is safe. I sent you yesterday by Maj. Sherman, a box containing some papers which I wish to keep and a valuable military book with autographs of my officers mainly.

I sent you another lot of photographs. Did you get two I sent of Lt. Dutton and Maj. Blake, 5th Connecticut Volunteers, both killed at Cedar Mountain? I have been much occupied for the past ten days with Gen. Jackson commanding one of my brigades, who had his leg broken by his horse falling with and on him. He was going to his quarters from mine about ten o'clock of a very dark night. It is a very lamentable affair, as he is a superior officer and though with me but a few weeks was greatly liked. I send his photograph with others.

❖

THE ARMY COUNTERMARCHES

Stafford Court House, May 7, 1863.

My Dear Daughter:

You will be startled to see that I am back to the old camping ground. But so it is, and sadly so. After ten days of great hardship, exposure, and privations we are back again with a diminished and dispirited army.

177

We recrossed the Rappahannock yesterday morning, the whole army moving after midnight over two pontoon bridges. My division was the last to escape, except the rear guard.

I have not time to write you at length. I sent you a long pencil scrawl which I fear you will be troubled to read, as it was written after a week of watching and fasting and fighting and under the nose of Rebel pickets.[2] The mail carrier waits, so I must say goodbye. All my staff are well and safe except Wilkins, who, I think, is again in the hands of the Rebels. I have heard nothing as yet from any of our prisoners. I am by no means cheerful, because I think this last [battle] has been the greatest of all bunglings in this war. I despair of ever accomplishing anything so long as generals are made as they have been.

Love to all,

Your Affectionate Father,
A.S.W.

◈

CHANCELLORSVILLE

Stafford, May 18, 1863.

My Dear Daughter:

I have been reading over today the newspaper accounts of our recent operations south of the Rappahannock. Such pure fictions are not to be found even in this fertile age of romancers. Either they have most deliberately lied for hire, or not one of them saw what he describes and gets his story from some interested narrator. We had a reporter near us for a while, on the march; but as soon as we reached the sound of cannon he departed and was seen no more. We heard of him with our train on the north side of the Rappahannock. Yet his letters have been full and rich; the rehash of tales told by some skulking officer.

I promised you a detailed account of our ten days' campaign, and yet after so many days of fatigue and heat I undertake it with dread and fear that I shall make you a dry story. But as I can give you personal experience and the incidents of my own command, it will probably prove more interesting than these newspaper accounts, which really cannot be understood by those on the ground. I have seen in the illustrated news-papers and in the *Herald* diagrams and drawings of furious onslaughts made by troops which never fired a gun. Sickles' corps, which, as it was near me, I can speak of with confidence of being truthful, did less than any of all under fire, except the 11th Corps, I see carries off all the glory (if there was any) of the contests about Chancellorsville. Berry's division of this corps fought well. The rest of it ran from a position which enfiladed my whole line and cost my division hundreds of men, killed and wounded. But I will not anticipate, but take up the narrative of my ten days south of the Rappahannock seriatim.

April 27th: My division struck tents at daylight, carrying on the person of each man and officer eight days' light rations, which means hard bread, coffee, and sugar, which filled not only haversacks but knapsacks. All our trains were left behind with orders to follow, we knew not where, but wherever the chief quartermaster should order. Our ammunition was packed on seventy-odd mules, two boxes on each. I had had them in training for some weeks, but as they were jacks of the smallest pattern I anticipated nothing but a dead loss of mules and ammunition on the first day. The day was pleasant, but the roads, after we left the open country, were terrible, and my pioneer corps was busily at work cutting new roads all through the pines, which cover the whole face of this ragged and broken country. However, we reached Hartwood Church at 3 P.M. (twelve miles) and encamped, each brigade in the woods, on a pretty little rivulet. The 11th Corps, which took another route, reached the same point about the same time and encamped in advance of us, and about dark the 5th Corps (Meade's) came up and encamped on our left. It was rather a "bivouac," though most of our men carried their shelter tents. I had been informed before marching that our destination was Kelly's Ford, but with the exception of Gen. Slocum I think everybody else was ignorant of our destination.

April 28: We marched at sunrise, following closely the 11th Corps toward Kelly's Ford. I had not moved more than two miles before I ran against the rear (artillery and trains) of the 11th Corps (Howard's) and was obliged to halt for an hour and a half, massing my three brigades in some open fields where the 11th had bivouacked. Starting again, I reached about noon a place called Grove Church, from its situation (isolated) in a pretty grove of evergreens and poplars. Here I was crowding Howard's corps again, and massing my men I ordered them to cook dinners and make coffee, giving them an hour to do it.

I had just begun to move out when down the road came Gen. Hooker and a long staff train and the inevitable lancer escort. He didn't stop, but merely saluted me as he passed, wherein I was more lucky than others, for as he passed Geary's 2nd Division, our corps, he gave him a sound scolding for not being closed up, and when he overtook Gen. Slocum in advance he reversed the complaint, and seemed full of dire anger, swearing heavily at somebody or something [on] which he was not very clear headed. His general complaint, however, was that the 12th Corps had not kept its interval closed and that Meade's corps was delayed, when in truth I had crowded the 11th Corps all day, and in a half hour afterward overtook its rear guard and was obliged to halt for over an hour to have it clear the way.

Knowing of the anger of our commanding general, I despatched a note forward to the effect that my advance was greatly delayed by the artillery and trains and rear guard of the 11th Corps and begging that the road might be cleared. It had begun to rain and the roads were exceedingly slippery, but in spite of all delays and hard traveling I had my three brigades encamped in the woods near the ford by 3 o'clock P.M. (fifteen miles) and everything as comfortable as the misty, drizzling, cold rain would permit. We pitched a tent or two for headquarters and had the honor of *finding* two stray reporters of the *Herald* (Carpenter and Buckingham) and one artist of some illustrated paper (Lumley), which said artist, by the way, drew some very pretty sketches of our crossing the Rappahannock and fording the Rapidan, all of which he lost with his portfolio before reaching Chancellorsville.

After encamping, a general order was published which told with grand confidence the line and results of our further march. We were to cross the Rappahannock on pontoons, two corps ([the] 11th and 12th) taking the route to Germanna Ford on the Rapidan, and one (Meade's 5th) the route to Ely's Ford on the same river. Once at Chancellorsville the whole Rebel people were to submit or be at once overthrown, or words to that effect.

Two considerable rivers were to be crossed and several large and ugly streams in face of the enemy, or where it was believed the enemy's face would present itself. It was not a pleasant prospect, but obstacles always grow less as you approach them with confidence and vigor or with a feeling that you must meet and overcome them. We saw the pontoons going down and in the course of two or three hours it was generally known that the bridge was laid without much opposition and that Gen. Howard had passed over one brigade to protect it. Gen. Hooker was not to cross with us. Ergo, Gen. Slocum, as ranking major general, commanded the three corps until they were united at Chancellorsville, and I, for the sixth time, became commander of the 12th Corps. I was notified that my corps was to have the advance on the morrow, and that we must at all hazard pass the Rapidan.

April 29: I slept soundly, but I was up long before daylight and before it was fairly light my 3rd Brigade (Ruger's), which was to be the advance guard, was moving toward the bridge. As we approached the river the sound of cannon and small arms not far to our right up the river became more and more frequent and distinct. We were, however, all across by 6 o'clock and I hurried to see Gen. Howard to learn what was going on and to find guides to show me the road to Germanna Ford. He seemed in profound ignorance but had sent out a cavalry picket. Presently an officer reported that it was a Rebel cavalry attack with a battery of artillery, and that they were retiring.

As my whole corps (I was corps commander for three days) was massed in columns on the low ground bordering the river, around which rose an amphitheater of hills, the picture was indeed exciting. Across the river long lines of infantry were winding down toward the river and on the south side brigades were breaking masses and filing up the hills. Batteries of artillery and heavy columns of cavalry were forming large solid squares, which, seen from the elevations in advance, looked like great black blocks on the green surface, massed by some unseen power.

Something less than 200 cavalry preceded us as an advance guard, and soon began the crack of carbines with the cavalry pickets of the Rebels. I moved with a long line of skirmishers stretching a mile on either side of the road and then two regiments marching in the fields by the head of companies. Other regiments and brigades followed the road, which we found better than on the north side of the Rappahannock. The country, too, was less broken and hilly, but as usual, greatly wooded and not much cultivated, at least poorly cultivated, though with more farms.

A few miles out we had to ford a small stream swollen by yesterday's rain, wetting the feet of the men, but no obstacle to our march. Just beyond this Lt. Col. McVicar, 6th New York Cavalry, our advance, came hurrying back with a report that the enemy's infantry was massing in the woods in our advance. Columns were halted and infantry closed up, but it proved to be a false alarm. No masses of infantry were found, though the skirmishers in advance kept up a brisk popping of small arms. Our section of artillery, which followed the advance regiments, made no reply nor any challenge.

Poor McVicar! He was a bluff, red-haired Scotchman, somewhat excitable and apt to see mountains in mole hills; but the next afternoon he was shot dead while leading his fellows forward beyond Chancellorsville and thus gave the last best proof of his pluckiness and fidelity to his command. We had begun to laugh at him for seeing so many infantry where none were found, but when told of his gallant death our hearts paid homage to the bluff old trooper, if they did not upbraid us for injustice to his character.

About 2 o'clock we began to approach the hills which overlook the course of the Rapidan. The crack of the rifles increased in volume. Ruger was ordered to deploy his two leading regiments to the right and left and move rapidly down to the river bank. This was done with a rush, picking up some thirty prisoners, who had not time to ford. On the opposite bank a hundred or so of bridge builders and armed guards had posted themselves in the trench of a road which runs from the ford almost parallel with the stream up the bank to the plateau above. In this trench they supposed themselves safe and able to pick off our advance, but to their astonishment they found our deployed skirmishers were able to enfilade their hiding place, and that they were anything but safe. A few attempted to escape by running up the road, but our riflemen brought them down every time, and in a few minutes they hung out a white cloth and the whole batch surrendered, though they had a rapid and rocky ford between them and us. We counted 125 prisoners. Most of them were engaged in rebuilding a heavy and high bridge upon stone piers. The old bridge was burned a year or more ago. In the mill nearby we found a large quantity of new tools (English) and a pretty good supply of provisions and forage for a cavalry guard which had been there.

The Rapidan at this point is not very broad, but its banks are high and the ford deep, rocky, and rapid. I dashed in with some of the foremost cavalry to cross and tumbling over a rock came near being submerged in the angry flood. In the meantime the infantry came up and finding the shallowest track went in with a scream and a yell, holding one another's hands and wading to their armpits with cartridge boxes slung on their bayonets. Now and then one would tumble over in the rapid stream, but in all cases their companions fished them out and my division all passed without loss, except some wet ammunition.

The scene was a very spirited one and Lumley made a pretty sketch of it, which unfortunately was lost afterward. A foot bridge was afterward made on the feet of the piers, over which the 2nd Division and 11th Corps passed after dark and across which we backed our ammunition. It was after midnight before all was over and one of our headquarters wagons was found at daylight fast between two rocks in the middle of the river, with the rapid current flowing freely through the box. We got it out, however, without serious loss.

The rain began to fall before night, but as we were all pretty wet and my boots full of water, it mattered little and the men were as cheerful as in gayest sunshine. We had crossed the two rivers and were on equal terms. I posted my division in a strong position through the woods, across the peninsula formed by a sharp bend of the river at this point, but it was long after dark before I could leave my saddle, quite tired enough for a sound sleep on the bare ground with two blankets. We got up a tent, however, and were comparatively comfortable, even in wet feet, wet clothes, wet blankets, and on the wet ground. How much our comforts depend upon surrounding circumstances. I slept soundly till broad daylight, probably never with more real enjoyment of "nature's sweet restorer."

April 30th: "The morning lowered and heavily in clouds brought on the day." It was a dismal, drizzling morning, but at 8 o'clock I was ordered to start the advance toward Chancellorsville and feel carefully the way. Nothing definite had been heard from Meade's corps, which was to cross at Ely's Ford below and coöperate with us. We had heard the evening before of his arrival at the ford. Geary's 2nd Division led, followed by the 1st Division and then by the 11th Corps. We met with no opposition of consequence until near Old Wilderness Church. The road was an old, worn-out plank road, full of holes and gullies and very slippery from the rain, the mud on what planks were left being a foot or so deep. It was a very hard march, as on previous days, but the men bore up splendidly and there was absolutely no straggling.

Near Old Wilderness (which, by the way, is no wilderness but the best-cultivated part of Virginia I have seen outside of the valley), the enemy opened with artillery on our right. As I was in advance, I detached a regiment of infantry, which deployed as skirmishers and got up a very brisk engagement, in which we lost a few men and the Rebels more. A second regiment succeeded in brushing away both skirmishers and artillery and we were not further molested during the day. While this was going on I stopped at what had been a country store near Old Wilderness, on a strong elevation, where I could watch and supervise the skirmish on the right. The people had abandoned their store in some haste, but left little behind except quack medicines. We found, however, some curious letters to soldiers, one of which, from a clerk of Gen. Stuart, I have since seen published in the *Tribune*. The Rebels tried one shell on the house and made a very good shot.

We reached the vicinity of Chancellorsville about 3 o'clock and found that Gen. Meade had also arrived behind the place on the Ely Ford Road. Chancellorsville is (or was) simply a Virginia "ville" of one large brick house on the northwest corner of [two] cross roads, built by one Chancellor. You will see on most of the maps its situation, seven or eight miles west of Fredericksburg and on the plank-road route to Orange Court House and Culpeper. It is in close proximity to two good fords (in dry season; now ten feet deep) over the Rappahannock, the U.S. Ford six miles and Banks' Ford four miles off. They are of no advantage as fords at this season, except the advantage of roads leading to them. I will send you a sketch of the roads and our positions during the operations around this place as soon as it can be copied.

We commenced taking up position as soon as we arrived. Our left was directly in front of the Chancellorsville house in some rifle pits made by the Rebels, running in a circular shape through a belt of woods and crossing a deep ravine near a place called Fairview; ran through the woods beyond and struck the plank road, on which we had been marching, a mile and a half west of Chancellorsville. Geary's division occupied the left and my division the right of this line and the general direction of our front was southeast. Meade's corps was to continue the line eastward and the 11th Corps (Howard's) was to connect with us on the west and continue the line down Hunting River to the [blank in MS.]. Banks' Ford was still in possession of the Rebels, while we held and covered with our line the U.S. Ford. It was intended to cover Banks' Ford, too, and our trains and reserve artillery had been ordered there, but somehow the Rebs. got the start of us and seemed determined to hold possession. So our trains and artillery went to the U.S. Ford.

It was a pleasant, moonlight night. Chancellorsville house became the center of hundreds of officers (generals and staff). It was a gay and cheerful scene. We had successfully accomplished what we all supposed would be the great work of the campaign. Everybody prophesied a great success, an overwhelming victory. Everybody was full of enthusiastic congratulations. Gen. Hooker came over during the evening and issued a flaming order complimenting the splendid operations of the 5th, 11th and 12th corps. We began to think we had done something heroic, we didn't exactly see what, except we had put three of the smallest corps on the flank of the Rebel stronghold. But it was rumored that others were coming to help us, and that others had crossed and driven the enemy from his entrenchments at Fredericksburg. All was *couleur de rose!* How many joyous hearts and bright cheerful faces beat and smiled happily for the last time on that delightful moonlight night at Chancellorsville!

I went back to my division (my corps command was gone on the return of Gen. Hooker), pitched my tent near the old log house on Fairview, and went to sleep to the music of the rifle crack of the pickets and the sound of the axes and falling trees of men at work making barricades in the adjacent woods.

Friday, May 1st: The morning was foggy but soon cleared up before a strong sun. I went early to Chancellorsville house, where the headquarters of the army and several corps commanders were concentrated. Hundreds of horses held by orderlies filled the broad space in front, and the piazza and rooms were filled with general staff officers.

Everybody supposed it was the beginning of a day big with the fate of the nation. Meade, Sickles, Couch, Howard, [besides] corps commanders and dozens of division commanders were floating around talking anxiously but still confidently. It was known that Hooker had boastingly declared the night before that "God Almighty could not prevent his destroying the Rebel army." The blasphemy did not please the most irreligious as appropriate to any, and least of all to an, occasion so momentous, but allowance was made for excitement. Still, there was an uneasiness in the best military minds. There was too much boasting and too little planning; swagger without preparation.

At length I was ordered to move my division up toward the Chancellorsville house and to move out on the left-hand side of the main road towards Fredericksburg. I never saw my troops in better condition, never more anxious to meet the enemy. The poor fellows, marching on an average of fifteen miles a day over hard, muddy roads and carrying sixty pounds on their backs for four days, were not only not weary or disheartened, but they seemed panting to meet the Rebels. They had marched without stragglers and they went out to battle without skulkers. Such, I believe, was the condition of almost every corps of the army. Surely we had promise of success.

We marched out some two miles, my division on the left of the road, Geary's on the right. I had two brigades, Knipe's and Ruger's, deployed and Jackson's (Ross commanding) in reserve, moving through the densest kind of pine thickets and underbrush. The Rebels were throwing shells at us and their pickets popping away at our skirmishers, but on we went and finally came to an open field, across which Knipe rushed his brigade and seized a belt of wood beyond. Here the engagement on my right became brisk and I had halted Knipe to connect my line on the left and put the reserve in position. The Rebel earth-works were just ahead, and their forces were being marshalled to resist us. We had lost but few men, for luckily their shell and shot had gone over us, following generally the line of the pike. Ten of my regiments lay close behind the woods and the men were eager and cheerful to joking, when up came an order to countermarch and go back to my original position.

Everybody asked why, and the best accepted reply was that Meade, who had been pounding hard on our left, had driven the enemy from

Banks' Ford and the object of our advance was fully accomplished. Still the men went back disappointed, not without grumbling, and it really required some policy to satisfy them that there was not mismanagement somewhere. Back we went three miles or more to our old camp, and began again to cut logs and construct our barricades, but in trying to replace our picket line to the front, we had some severe conflicts and lost two field officers and several men. And the Rebels had brought up on an elevation to our left and front, which opened on our headquarters plateau, a few pieces of artillery and began shelling my position strongly.

They were soon silenced by my artillery, and my picket line cleared them out in front but not before they had planted several shells through my Fairview log hut and one through one flue of the chimney, the shell dropping down into the fireplace unexploded. As good luck would have it, there was no fire and the next morning the cooks built fires outside. Accidentally one of the staff officers, in a spirit of curiosity, discovered the unexploded shell in the ashes of the fireplace. If the cooks had, as they had done the morning before, used the fireplace for cooking, we should have had an explosoin which would probably have spoiled our breakfast and lessened the number of headquarters cooks materially. Such are the slight accidents that make or mar small as well as great matters.

The night passed as before with an almost constant popping of picket riflemen, but our tents were still up in front of the log cabin. I sat quite late enjoying the brilliant moonlight. A long line of artillery was in battery just in front, on the brow of the hill which overlooked the ravine and the woods beyond, in which lay two of my brigades. The whippoorwills, which are thicker here than katydids up north, were whistling out their "whip-poor-wills" as if there was nothing but peace on earth, and save the occasional crack of the rifle away off on the left there was a solemn stillness which was almost oppressive. Two immense hostile armies, over two hundred thousand armed men, lay within almost the sound of one's voice, and now and then away off in front I could fancy the sound of wheels and the tramp of men. It proved afterward to have been no fancy, for Jackson was then moving his artillery and infantry by a crossroad around our front towards the right and rear of the 11th Corps, which on the following day developed itself in a most disastrous discomfiture of our Dutch friends, "what fight mit Sigel," or did until Gen. Howard was made a major general and sent to teach these fellows how to fight after Sigel quit for want of more men.

Saturday, May 2nd: The morning was of the densest fog. We breakfasted, as on every morning during the operations, before daylight and as a battle seemed inevitable, we ordered our few tents struck and everything packed for a movement to clear the front. By sunrise I was out along my lines. The whole front was covered by a very good breastwork of logs. The map which I shall send you will show its direction. I also rode up the "dirt road" which runs south from a short distance in advance of my line on the plank road. Here I found Birney's division lying along the road with a battery or two of artillery, Birney himself stretched on the grass under an evergreen shade.

All night the noise of the enemy moving along our front was distinctly heard, and it was reported that his columns could be distinctly seen a short distance in advance. The rumor was that at Gen. Hooker's headquarters it was believed the enemy were retreating toward Orange Court House and quite a number of prisoners brought up the road was taken as evidence of the fact of haste and confusion amongst them. I went back to an unfinished church on the plank road, where Knipe had his headquarters, and as no orders came I took a long nap. I found Gen. Slocum there with his staff, and what with his and mine and Knipe's we formed a large group of officers and orderlies, all of us pretty much engaged in sleeping.

I was a disbeliever in the retreat, and finally made Knipe send out two or three well-known scouts of his command. They returned after an hour or so and reported that they had gone beyond the 11th Corps and by climbing into a tall tree had seen the columns of the Rebels passing across the Orange Court House road and massing to the right of the 11th Corps, the front of which, by the way, was nearly due west. I was then entirely satisfied that we were to be attacked from that point, and so reported to Gen. Slocum, who, I believe, reported the facts to Gen. Hooker.

Soon after, I saw Whipple's division moving down to the road on which Birney was found, but I fell asleep again in the shade of the church on a plank which I had given an easy inclination to on a sill of the building. My posture and an unlighted cigar in my mouth at-

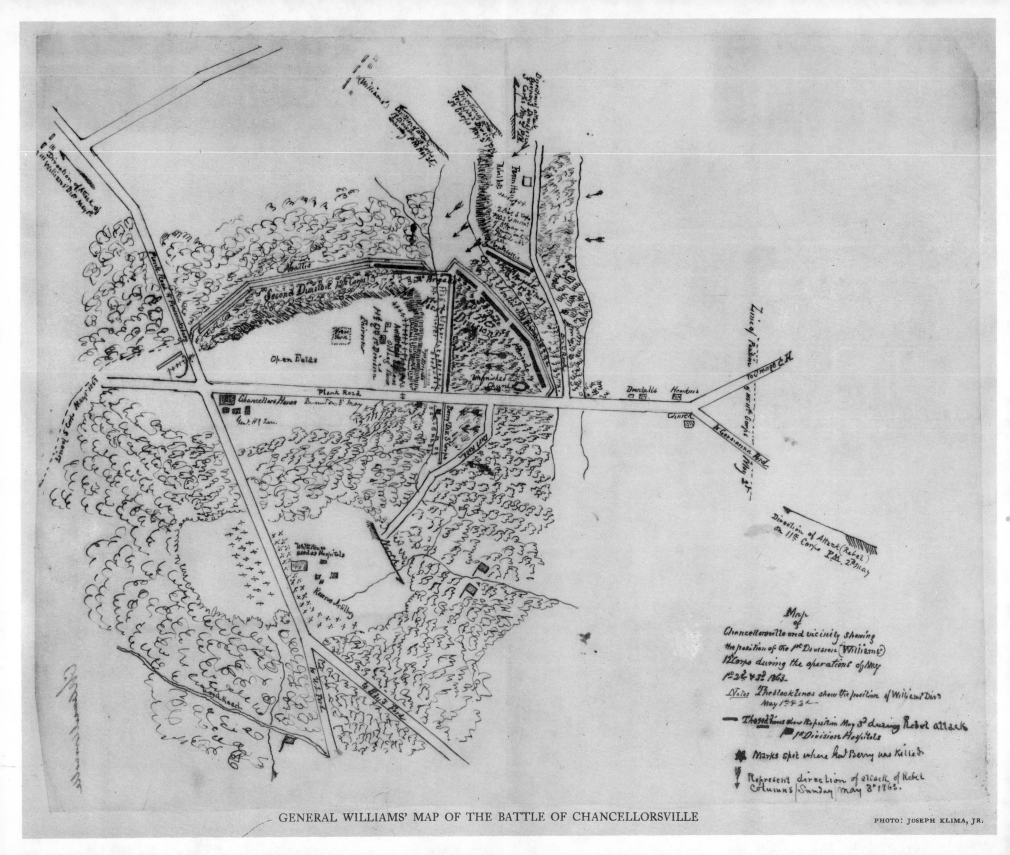

GENERAL WILLIAMS' MAP OF THE BATTLE OF CHANCELLORSVILLE

PHOTO: JOSEPH KLIMA, JR.

tracted the notice of a passing artist, who took a sketch of me as I slept and presented it to me on waking up. I enclose it that you may see me as reposing on the spot around which twenty-four hours afterwards lay thousands of dead and dying, Federals and Rebels, and as an interesting memento, as well as a striking evidence of how easily and carelessly the heart beats on the very eve of scenes of battle and carnage. Jokes were played; the laugh and the jest were as common as if we had been a party of picnickers instead of armed men awaiting the onslaught of thousands in deadly conflict.

Now and then those not asleep would speculate on the probable movements of the day or guess the cause of the rattling of musketry or the booming of cannon not far off. And so with sleep and talk the day wore through until after 1 o'clock P.M., when I was roused up and told to get my command under arms. I dispatched the orders and went off through the thick underbrush to see that my brigades were ready to move. Presently came another order to move out towards my left and front, go two or three miles down through the woods and strike the Fredericksburg plank road as far as possible from Chancellorsville, and then sweep both sides of the plank road towards the Chancellorsville house.

The intention was to strike the Rebel breastworks and entrenchments on this road in flank and rear and thus place them between two fires as I drove them towards Geary's barricades. The old story of a flying enemy was repeated to me, and I was to help "gobble" the Rebel rout. Geary had been sent out early in the day directly on the road, but he had found a force too large for him and was compelled to get back to his entrenchments. All these things did not prove to me a flying enemy. In moving out to my position in the open field at a point where I designed to enter the thick woods, mostly of stunted pines, I came in contact with Whipple's division.

You will remember Gen. Whipple as Capt. Whipple of the Topographical Engineers at Detroit, living for a while in Mrs. Campau's house on Woodward Avenue.[3] Finding I was to form on his left, he came to arrange with me the order of formation. My brigades were already deployed with two regiments front in line and the rest in reserve for each brigade. Poor Whipple was red with heat and excitement, and I fancied then, and have recalled my fancy often since, that he felt the shadow of the Dark Angel's wing over him. I am by no means superstitious, as you know, but it seemed to me that I could read in his face—misfortune! He was killed, you know, not that day but the next, and I never saw him again. From what I hear, his death was strangely accidental, or, more properly, unaccountable, occurring after the main action was all over and apparently by a stray musket shot.

To return to my attack: The underbrush was densely thick, almost impenetrable to man, and I had the greatest difficulty in finding a place to crowd my horse through. The skirmishers were soon engaged in front, showing that the Rebels were well posted on our movement. We had proceeded forward perhaps two miles from our camp; Knipe's brigade on the right was sharply engaged, and we were driving the enemy before us. I was in the act of getting Jackson's (3rd) brigade (Col. Ross, commanding) into shape, as it had fallen into some confusion, to push to the support of Knipe, when an order was brought me to return at once and reoccupy my old line.

I had for some time heard rapid firing in the direction of the 11th Corps, which in the direction we were attacking was almost directly in my rear, but until this order came it never once occurred to me that any disaster of a serious nature could have taken place. I had left the knapsacks of most of the regiments in our breastworks, as the day was hot and our probable duty severe. My apprehensions were now greatly aroused, though I had no definite information of what had taken place. With the one or two staff officers who had not been sent away on duty I hastened back to see what was occurring.

As I cleared the underbrush where the open space lies in front of Fairview and behind the woods where were my entrenchments, I saw the immense mass of fugitives and heard the yells of the pursuing Rebels. After some difficulty in getting over my own barricade, which lay between that point and the open ground, I rode rapidly to the right near the plank road, where some officers of the general staff had arrested a group of a few hundred men and were trying to get them into order. Lt. Col. Dickinson of Hooker's staff was riding fiercely about, pistol in hand, and occasionally discharging it at some flying Dutchman. Swords were out and flashing in the setting sun. Such a mixture of Dutch and English and oaths! Such a rolling in and out of frightened men (the first really frightened mass of men I ever saw)! Such a swinging of arms on the part of officers, who evidently were quite as much stampeded as the men!

I saw at once that all effort to organize such a body of men was fruitless. They were like a flock of scared sheep driven into a corner; not one thought of defense. In the meantime, the pursuing Rebels were rapidly advancing. The crack of the musket was close at hand. Fortunately my two leading brigades, as soon as they cleared the underbrush, saw the disaster and came down at a double-quick. I rode back to meet them, and leading them by flank along the inner edge of the woods at right angles to the line of the Rebel advance, they faced by the left flank and thus presented the front of a line of battle of two brigades directly towards the Rebels.

Without a halt, and with a cheer that made the woods and the open space ring, the whole line rushed into the woods. The Rebel advance was checked at once and fell back within fifteen minutes, almost without resistance. This is the true story of the first checking of Jackson's pursuit of the 11th Corps. The New York papers are giving immense glory to Sickles for this very act. But he was at least two miles away and did not get back to the vicinity of this affair till some time after dark.

I sent at once by Lt. Pittman to report to Gen. Hooker (Gen. Slocum not being at hand) that my right (north side of the plank road) was uncovered and that I should be flanked and driven out if not supported there at once. It was at this time that Gen. Berry was sent with his division to occupy the woods on the right in prolongation of my line. Gen. Berry was at Gen. Hooker's when Pittman reached there, and it was at least an hour and a half before he got into position on my right, and yet newspaper reports I see have given that division the credit of driving back, first of all, Stonewall Jackson's advance. What I have written to you is capable of proof in any court, except the court of reporters, but history will probably give the absent Sickles and the gallant 3rd Corps whatever of reputation belongs to that body of our troops; [4] and it was the 1st Division, 12th Corps, which stopped an exulting enemy pursuing a disorganized and broken corps and which had reached within half a mile or less of the headquarters of the commander of the army! So much for the truth of contemporaneous history at least!

Thus far all had gone well with my division, but unfortunately an order was now sent me to push into the woods and reoccupy my log entrenchments, which you will see by the map ran diagonally to the front and towards the line of Rebel advance. They were built with reference to an attack from the direction of Fredericksburg, which direction the Rebels had not seen fit to follow. I protested against the movement as useless and very risky. It was now quite dark, especially in the woods, dense with underbrush. There was quite a slough hole in the center of the road which would break my line of advance and separate my regiments. The enemy might conceal himself at any point on my right flank and thus take me in reverse. The order, I understood, was from Gen. Hooker, and there was no help. It must be tried. So, cautioning Knipe to push his skirmishers well out, and look to his right flank, he was ordered to move through the woods.

What I feared happened. No one could tell friend from foe nor see a hidden enemy a rod away. In consequence, the right regiment (128th Pennsylvania, Col. Mathews) got fairly enveloped and lost its colonel and lieutenant colonel (Smith) and nearly 200 men killed, wounded, and prisoners. The 5th Connecticut lost its colonel—Packer—prisoner, and a good many men. Maj. Strous commanding the 46th Pennsylvania (Knipe's old regiment) was mortally wounded. It was a conflict of great confusion and came near losing me all of Knipe's brigade. We had already lost Lt. Col. Cook, 28th New York, who was left as a guard in the barricades with four companies of his regiment. He had arrested nearly 2,000 fugitives of the 11th Corps and got them behind breastworks, but they fled at the first sight of the Rebels' approach and breaking through Cook's small guard left him to combat as best he could the exultant enemy.

Cook obstinately held on and lost nearly half his command. All these misfortunes had lost Knipe every field officer but one of his brigade and left him but three broken regiments. Of course, we withdrew as best we could to the north and south line of the woods in front of Fairview, where we had first entered. The Rebels attempted to follow, but we punished them severely. Best, whose batteries were on the Fairview Ridge, opened with his artillery, shelling the woods with appalling vigor, and our whole infantry line hailed upon them with a simultaneous storm of bullets. The Rebels fell back, and in fifteen minutes there was a silence that was almost painful, after the roar of the short combat.

It was in this advance of Knipe to recover our old position that Wilkins was made prisoner. He had gone with me to the right to help stop the fugitive Dutchmen, as I have mentioned, and when I returned to meet my brigades I remember him swinging his sword vigorously, especially at the time the cheer was given when my troops entered the woods. He writes me that I ordered him to follow Knipe's brigade and directed him to look towards his right flank and that he was dodging through the underbrush when he was surrounded by those he supposed were his friends and ordered to dismount. He writes me a piteous story of his forced march from Richmond to the gun boat and says his feet are blistered and his leg rheumatic. He is still, I believe, in Washington on parole and expects to be exchanged within thirty days.

To come back from this digression: Our new line being taken up (as shown by the red line on the map) the men were set to work making log breastworks. We knew there was hard work ahead. Our pack-team of ammunition was sent for and every man fully supplied. I went down to where my line crossed the plank road and had an interview with Gen. Berry, arranging the connection of our two divisions. I met him almost exactly on the spot where he fell the next morning. I had never seen him before, and it was too dark then to see him, but I had another interview with him early the next morning. He was a tall, heavy, coarse-looking man, but I believe a good officer and faithful to his duty. The result of my first interview was that I replaced two of his regiments on the south side of mine by two of mine, taken from my extreme left, where the line connected with Geary's division. He was anxious I should take up my headquarters with him that we might act in concert, and I should probably have done so but for after events which kept me till late in the night busy elsewhere.

Somewhere about 10 o'clock a staff officer came from Sickles' headquarters with information that he had reached the open hill seen to the left and front, about 400 yards across the ravine before Fairview, with Whipple's and Birney's divisions and that he should attack the enemy's right flank during the night with at least one brigade. Gen. Slocum was still absent at general headquarters, but the danger of such an attack, which would bring his troops directly in front of my line of infantry and artillery, was so palpable, and a great mishap and miscarriage so inevitable that I requested this officer to ask that the matter be deferred until the return of Gen. Slocum, who would probably arrange with Gen. Sickles so as to avoid doing injury to ourselves. Luckily, I dispatched messengers to my infantry line that such an attack might take place, and cautioned commanders to withhold their fire.

It was lucky, indeed, for scarcely could the staff officer have got back to his general before the tumult began. There was a faint, misty moon, just enough of its light to make darkness visible. A tremendous roll of infantry fire, mingled with yellings and shoutings almost diabolical and infernal, opened the conflict on the side of Sickles' division. For some time my infantry and artillery kept silent and in the intervals of the musketry I could distinctly hear the oaths and imprecations of the Rebel officers, evidently having hard work to keep their men from stampeding. In the meantime, Sickles' artillery opened, firing over the heads of the infantry, and the din of arms and inhuman yellings and cursings redoubled. All at once Berry's division across the pike on our right opened in heavy volleys and Knipe's next to the pike on the south followed suit. Best began to thunder with his thirty-odd pieces. In front and on the flank shell and shot and bullets were poured into these woods, which were evidently crowded with Rebel masses, preparing for the morning's attack.[5]

It was at this time, as we subsequently learned, that Stonewall Jackson received his mortal wound, and prisoners taken subsequently say that if we had continued the storm of fire a few moments longer the whole of Jackson's corps would have been stampeded. I can conceive of no spectacle more magnificently and indeed awfully grand and sublime than this night attack. Along our front and on Sickles' flank probably 15,000 or more muskets were belching an almost incessant stream of flame, while from the elevations just in the rear of each line, from forty to fifty pieces of artillery kept up an uninterrupted roar, re-echoing from the woods with redoubled echo from the bursting shells, which seemed to fill every part of them with fire and fury. Human language can give no idea of such a scene; such an infernal and yet sublime combination of sound and flame and smoke, and dreadful yells of rage, of pain, of triumph, or of defiance.

Suddenly, almost on the instant, the tumult is hushed; hardly a voice can be heard. One would almost suppose that the combatants were holding their breath to listen for one another's movements. But the contest was not renewed. It was after midnight and the air had become unpleasantly cold. I went back to my log shanty at Fairview. It was full of wounded, and around the fires were fellows boiling coffee in their large camp kettles. One poor fellow was moaning piteously that "he was so cold." His were probably death chills, but I directed some warm stones to be put to his feet. After awhile I got myself warm by an outdoor fire, behind the shanty. The night wore away rapidly as I dozed or half slept by this camp fire, roused every now and then by the rattle of picket firing. It had been a strange day of sleep and excitement of the highest character, winding up with a pyrotechnic display which furnished certainly a magnificent finale, and but for

"The shout and groan and saber stroke
And death shot falling thick and fast
Like lightning from the mountain cloud"

it would have been one of immense admiration and beauty.

Sunday, May 3rd: We breakfasted before dawn, as we anticipated at the earliest daylight we should have a very poor chance for meal-taking. We were not disappointed. Our appetites were not bad, considering the time and circumstances, and probably we were not without forebodings that it would be some time before we got the next regular meal.

The Rebels opened with infantry alone, pushing their heavy columns at the same time against my front and upon the two divisions of Sickles in the open fields to my left front (as marked on the map) and against Berry's division in prolongation of my right, across the plank road. I think the heaviest attack was against me, but as I was nearer and could see my own position best, and *hear* there the most, I may be mistaken. At any rate, the fire of musketry was incessant for quite four hours, almost without cessation or intermission. But in all that time they were never able to reach my front line. Three times they were driven back and their masses (in column) thrown into great confusion, but almost immediately replaced with fresh troops. Our batteries on the ridge a few hundred yards behind my line opened through the entire line of thirty-four pieces, I believe, and for a while Sickles kept up the fire with great animation. Soon, however, his division began to give way and some of his troops came back diagonally through our lines in great confusion. The Rebels captured one or more of his batteries and turned them upon our artillery and infantry at short range, besides bringing up several batteries of their own, which were placed in this commanding position.

It was a great misfortune to us, the loss of that position; as great, I think, as the discomfiture of the 11th Corps. They were able to enfilade our lines and place their infantry masses on our left flank. It was about half-past 2, I think, that they got full possession of this hill. The din of war was never more violent than for the next two hours. My division could do nothing but hold its own, and this it did splendidly. I had withdrawn two regiments from my left between the angle of my breastworks and Geary's division, both to strengthen my right center and because I supposed Sickles' division would hold the hill and hence prevent any infantry attack upon that point. But when they abandoned that position the Rebels followed down over the ravine in heavy masses and pitched in a run upon the line east of the angle. Only two regiments (20th Connecticut and 145th New York) were at hand to resist, but they drove them back in confusion, aided somewhat by a left oblique fire of Ruger's regiments, which held the angle. The strangest part was that the 145th Regiment had attempted to run and had actually marched away from its post without orders. I, fortunately, saw the movement and checked it in time to replace the regiment in its position before injury was done. It fought valiantly afterwards. The same thing happened to a New Jersey regiment, moving back without orders. I halted it and merely said they were disgracing the state of "Jersey blues." The regiment at once marched back and fought nobly.

No man can give any idea of a battle by description nor by painting. If you can stretch your imagination so far as to hear, in fancy, the crashing roll of 30,000 muskets mingled with the thunder of over a hundred pieces of artillery; the sharp bursting of shells and the peculiar whizzing sound of its dismembered pieces, traveling with a shriek in all directions; the crash and thug of round shot through trees and buildings and into the earth or through columns of human bodies; the "phiz" of the Minie ball; the uproar of thousands of human voices in cheers, yells, and imprecations; and see the smoke from all the engines of war's inventions hanging sometimes like a heavy cloud and sometimes falling down like a curtain between the combatants; see the hundreds of wounded limping away or borne to the rear on litters; riderless horses rushing wildly about; now and then the blowing up of a caisson and human frames thrown lifeless into the air; the rush of columns to the front; the scattered fugitives of broken regiments and skulkers making for the rear. If you can hear and see all this in a vivid fancy, you may have some faint idea of a battle in which thousands are fiercely engaged for victory. But you must stand in the midst and feel the elevation which few can fail to feel, even amidst its horrors, before you have the faintest notion of a scene so terrible and yet so grand.

My personal experiences, for which you will probably care more than for generalities were these: As soon as the battle opened I rode to the right to consult with Gen. Berry, for the maintenance of his line was my safety. Poor man! He was probably dead within fifteen minutes after I left him, killed by a rifle ball, and thus it happened that two general officers who had supported me on the right on two successive days were both victims of this battle. Leaving Gen. Berry, I rode down my line, giving such instructions as seemed necessary to my brigades. My line was well sheltered behind logs and a slight depression of the ground behind the woods. This artificial and natural protection saved me hundreds of lives.

I then took position on a knoll which overlooked my whole division from the left of the battery. Of course I remained stationary nowhere, as the changing tide of affairs kept me moving from right to left to see that all was firm and safe. In one of these movements I had a most extraordinary escape. I was passing from the left to the right when I saw one of Berry's regiments giving way, which I was afraid would expose my whole line to a flank movement of the enemy. I was passing through a low, muddy spot, when a shell struck in the mud directly under my horse and exploded, throwing up the mud like a volcano. I felt as if I was lifted ten feet in the air, and supposed, of course, my horse (old Plug Ugly) was clean gone in all his under-works. I dismounted in haste and found he was bleeding pretty freely, but strange to say not seriously wounded, and only in three or four places. It was probably a percussion shell which buried itself below the mud so deep till it reached the hard earth, that the superincumbent pressure gave a low direction to the pieces, and thus saved both horse and myself.

During this terrific contest I saw two or three small regiments coming up behind our batteries and in an exposed position. I rode to them to advise a better shelter, when I encountered two Michigan regiments, the 3rd, Col. Pierce of Grand Rapids, who was wounded by a musket ball as I talked with him, and the 5th, Lt. Col. Sherlock, formerly of the theater proprietorship, who came out from behind his regiment to shake hands with me. He was killed a few moments afterwards by a piece of shell. Indeed, it seemed a wonder that anything could live on that slope and hill-brow in front of Fairview. Shot and shell and musketry swept it from end to end and side to side, and the columns of destructive missiles seemed to increase every moment.

At length, after four hours or so of this incessant strife and turmoil, it was reported to me that every regiment was nearly out of ammunition. I sent a staff officer to Gen. Hooker or to Gen. Slocum, who was at general headquarters, with the report and that I should soon be flanked on both sides unless fresh troops came to my support and to replace my exhausted regiments, half of whom had been without food for nearly twenty-four hours. Hooker replied that I must furnish my own ammunition, which, of course, was not possible through that volcano of flame and roar with a mule pack-train. At length I saw Sickles not far in the rear, and as he had, or ought to have had, two divisions which had been but little engaged, I went to him and was told that he had just sent forward his troops to replace mine.

I hurried to the front to order my regiments to withdraw as soon as other troops came up, but the relieving troops never reached my line. The right (Berry's division) was giving way. The artillery was already nearly gone with empty chests. The Rebels had already occupied the woods far in front of my line on my left flank. There was no time for delay if I would save anything of my command. Oh! but for *one* of the four corps which lay behind me unengaged. But I do not intend to express opinions. I am giving facts. The getting away was worse than the staying. Our line of retreat was over the ravine, up an exposed slope, and then for three-quarters of a mile over an open plain swept by artillery and infantry of the Rebels as they pressed forward. There was no shelter on our side of the Chancellorsville House, and no reinforcements appeared to stay the pursuers. But we had punished them severely and the infantry pursuit was feeble, but the artillery thundered its best—or worst—upon us, and the mud of the slough holes over this plain was thrown up in huge columns on all sides from exploding shells and round shot falling in our midst. Many a poor fellow lost his life or limb in this fearful transit. You remember Lt. Crosby, commanding Best's battery, a young officer of superior merit and fidelity. He was shot dead by a musket ball just as we were leaving the front. In the confusion his body was left on the ground, but has since been recovered.

Reaching Chancellors House, I formed line behind some rifle pits made by the Rebels before we reached C. and facing down the plank road toward Germanna. Here I was ordered by a staff officer of Gen. Hooker to hold this place at all hazards, who to my protestation that I had no ammunition, replied with immense pomposity, "Use the bayonet"! As we were suffering hugely from artillery shells thrown from a half mile to a mile distant, I didn't exactly see how my bayonets were to be effective. No reinforcements or new troops had yet shown themselves.

I knew the 1st, 2nd, 5th and 11th corps were within a mile to three miles of us and yet here my poor devils were ordered to suffer, after a fearful conflict which had in reality kept them under arms all night and in which they had expended eighty rounds of cartridges per man. At length I found Gen. Slocum, and through his protest I was finally ordered to move down the U.S. Ford road and to pass the second line and halt in the woods beyond. The Chancellors House, set on fire by the Rebel shells, was already in flames. Eight or ten women who had been for three days hid in the cellar of the house made their escape, half-starved and half-dead. They were sent over the river and well cared for. The building was full of our wounded, but I believe every one was safely removed. Not so fortunate were the poor fellows lying wounded in the woods, which, taking fire during the battle, burned fiercely in all directions, covering the country for miles with dense smoke and flames.

At the White House, where is marked the reserve artillery, we met the 2nd Corps just moving into position to meet the Rebels. A few rods behind we formed line of battle in a crossroad and my poor fellows disposed themselves for rest, their first chance in twenty-four hours. I caught a stray team of pack mules, deserted by their drivers, and was thus able to replenish, in part, my ammunition. The day was very warm, and what with excitement, dust, and heat my tongue was parched by thirst. I found the hospital of my division and got the most refreshing drink of cinchona and whiskey that was swallowed by mortal throat.

All day we lay in line on our arms. The sound of battle pretty much subsided after we fell back. Now and then a brisk cannonade would open and a fusillade of infantry which, however, was always of short duration, showing that no real engagement was taking place but a mere encounter of opposing skirmishers or patrol parties. Towards evening we could distinctly hear the artillery combat between Sedgwick's corps and the Rebs. toward Fredericksburg, and yet no attack began on our side.

After dark we were ordered to relieve a portion of the 11th Corps on the extreme left of our line, our left directly on the Rappahannock. It was long after dark before we took up our position, but it was a strong one on two high bluffs, forming a kind of natural bastion, separated by deep ravines. We spread our blankets under some evergreens and slept with a soundness which might have been expected after our long fatigue and many nights of broken sleep.

May 4th: Another warm, sunshiny day. The men were put at work strengthening the rifle pits, partly made before, and making traverses for our artillery guns, of which we had sixteen pieces on the two bluffs. We determined to make an impregnable position, as we had one of great natural strength. As the 11th Corps was on our right, we thought it not improbable that the enemy might break through there and turn our right, thus separating us from the U.S. Ford. We made up our minds to hold our post at all hazards to the last. Nothing was seen of the enemy except a few cavalry and infantry pickets, with which ours exchanged occasional shots.

Early in the morning some artillery had opened fire from a high point formed by a short bend of the river a few miles below. We could not imagine at what it was firing. It turned out afterwards that they had the range of our train camp on the other side of the river, and pretty effectually stampeded all our non-combatant staff and made several wounded officers, who could only move on litters the day before, take to their legs with the speed of a scared Indian. It happened that several hundred Secesh prisoners were in the same camp. They set up a loud yell for Jeff Davis and, I fear, laughed somewhat at the general skedaddles on the part of our officers and men. However, it was a pretty sharp specimen of shell practice, and as it found most of them in bed, the notice to quit was to men unused to the sounds rather startling, it must be confessed. Three or four men were killed in the camp.

May 5th: This day passed pretty much as yesterday. It opened pleasantly. No one disturbed our front, but on our right the Dutchmen kept up night and day pretty frequent popping, varied now and then by heavy volleys. It was generally reported that they were firing at imaginary Rebels. It gave us no uneasiness. We constructed evergreen bowers for shelter under the slope of our natural bastions. For food, we broiled pork on the sticks and with hardtack (soldier's hard bread) we made the sweetest meal of the season. About 3 o'clock we had a heavy storm of thunder, lightning, and rain, and it ended off in a regular heavy, cold rainstorm.

Orders had been communicated to me to be ready to recross the river soon after dark, but as ours was the last corps to move, it would probably be 10 or 11 o'clock before we should fall in. The rain poured down heavily. Soon after dark our artillery moved to the rear, so as to clear the bridges early for the infantry. Some of my regiments had been ordered out of the trenches so that the division might be speedily formed. It was darker than Erebus. We gathered around a big camp fire and piled on the wood, but the cold rain poured, and done up in our rubber coats and hats we looked most forlorn and felt quite so. Gen. Slocum had gone about dusk, no one knew where. Finally, tired with waiting I dispatched a staff officer to Gen. Couch to get instructions about withdrawing pickets. He returned with the information that the bridges had been carried away by the flood and that our march was countermanded! Here was a fix. I ordered my regiments back to the rifle pits and sent for the artillery to return. Back came the messengers after an hour with information that the bridges would be repaired in an hour or so, and that I was to move when Gen. Howard sent me word that his corps had moved.

Wearily wore away the rainy, cold hours. At length, about daylight, came a messenger that Gen. Howard had marched. Silently and sadly we fell in and took the road to U.S. Ford. As I came out on the plateau overlooking the river bottom, a magnificent sight of three or four of our corps moving over the plain presented itself. There were two bridges, made out of four before the freshet. The river looked broad and angry. I was obliged to wait for at least three hours as my division was the last but the rear guard (Meade's corps) to pass the bridges. Time wore heavily and I was terribly anxious, as the guns were booming heavily in the direction of the enemy and our skirmishers were already engaged. Our rear regiment and line of pickets, [which] left a half hour after we marched, at length came up. The bridge was cleared, over went my division, and we took the shortest cut towards Stafford Court House, where we were all encamped by dark the same day. So ended the last day's campaign in Dixie.

I have written you a hurried and yet, as far as I can, a faithful account of this campaign. You will see how poorly it agrees with newspaper stories, which so far as I have seen are mainly fictions. Indeed, most of the pretended writers see nothing. They are safely in the rear. At least it was so with one who pretended to report for the 11th and 12th corps for the New York *Herald*. He went over the river on Friday and never appeared, as far as I could learn, on the south side again.

I have no time to read over what I have written, so you must make the best story you can of it. I have really so much to attend to that I have no thought nor time for outside work. Of thirty-one field officers engaged in these operations, fourteen are numbered with the casualties, nearly one-half. All are absent. All the adjutant generals (including my own) are wounded or missing. Almost all the adjutants of regiments and a great many of the line officers. In consequence, everything is deranged and it requires a great deal of work to get reports and to move things forward smoothly.

My aggregate of casualties in the division is nearly 1,700. I had less than 5,000 in the Sunday battle, consequently I have lost more than one man in three! The absence of many intimate friends and the sad results of our promising campaign have made me almost melancholy. I should like to get away, to restore my spirits, but I cannot just now, as I have but one brigadier left and very few field officers. Knipe [illegible] after the excitement was over and has gone home to Betsy, sick. My division has gone down to a zero of numbers by battle and the discharge of two-years' and nine-months' troops. I have less than half [the number] I had when we first encamped at this place. Heaven knows what are the intended future movements, but it requires no great genius to say that if with all the advantages of position and numbers in the recent operations we made a failure, our chances will not be regarded as promising with diminished numbers and a defensible river to cross. However, I do not propose to criticise the past nor speculate on the future. I have most decided opinions on both, but do not choose now to put them on paper. I enclose you several extracts from newspapers which please file with this letter. I shall need them sometime. Also the map and sketch of the sleeping brigadier! . . .

Your Affectionate Father,
A.S.W.

◈

LAURELS OF GENERAL SICKLES

Stafford Court House, May 23, 1863.

My Dear Daughter:

I will write you in a day or so. I send this note to let you know I am well. I shall come home if I can, but don't forget that I have lost half of my field officers, all my adjutant generals, more than *one-third* of all my command, and hence have unusual duties and difficulties to encounter. . . .

I shall write to Rene to visit Detroit this summer, but I don't know as I shall be able to get away. No one can 'weary for rest' more than I do, and I think I deserve a vacation, but these matters are not settled by merit but by impudence and brass and well paid reporters. A "Sickles" would beat Napoleon in winning glory not earned. He is a hero without an heroic deed! Literally made by scribblers. But justice is sure, if slow, and patience and perseverance will succeed. I think a man as old as Methuselah would on his death bed say he had to regret his short life, that he might see more of human character.

People at home are fancying this war is waged for the Union and for a stable and united government, but it is a mistake. It is carried on exclusively to make heroes of charlatans and braggarts!

Tell Aunt Jule that I lost not a single piece of my artillery, but that the major general whose name fills the New York papers shamefully abandoned his guns in my face and gave up to the Rebels a position which cost my division 500 lives. I'll write more soon.

Your Affectionate Father,
A.S.W.

DESPONDENCY OVER CHANCELLORSVILLE

May 29, 1863.

My Dear Daughter:

I have been hoping for some days to get leave for fifteen days to go to Detroit but am again disappointed. I applied a week ago, on the suggestion of Gen. Slocum, but was met, as before, by an order suspending all leaves except for five days; too short, of course, for me. . . .

I suppose now it is expected that Lee will cross and try his hand on us. At least, I cannot believe that the most extravagant self-conceit nor the wildest lunacy could bring anyone to the belief that with our reduced army we can, with the least prospect of success, cross the Rappahannock just now. We have lost physically and numerically, but still more morally, not by being dispirited, but by a universal want of confidence in the commanding general, growing out of the recent operations. I have not met the first officer who does not feel this, from the highest to the lowest. Of course, with such a feeling offensive operations are out of the question. . . .[6]

I am greatly dispirited and almost disposed to resign. "Whom the gods wish to destroy, they first make mad!" That our government shows symptoms now, as in the past, of being prepared in this way, as the instruments of our natural destruction, seems to me clearly manifested. I could tell you most astounding things, but cannot write them. I will write you again by next mail. Gov. Blair visited me yesterday and I rode all day with him to visit the Michigan regiments. . . .

Your Affectionate Father,
A.S.W.

◆

COMMENDATION OF GENERAL WILLIAMS

Headquarters, 12th Corps,
Army of the Potomac.
June 5th, 1863.

Sir:

Brig. Gen'l. A. S. Williams entered the service at the commencement of the war and has been constantly in the field ever since, and for more than a year past he has been the senior brigadier general in the U.S. volunteer force, has during all this time been performing the duties of a major general, having been in command of this corps at Antietam and for several weeks subsequent to that battle.

Since I was assigned to the command of the corps, Gen. Williams has been in command of the 1st Division. I have found him in camp as well as on the field a most valuable and efficient officer. I cannot speak too highly of his conduct during our late movements under Gen. Hooker. His division marched over sixty miles in three days, and forded the Rapidan during the time. In all our engagements with the enemy, his division did its full duty, as is attested by the loss sustained by it, which exceeded one-third of the number he took into the field. He, as its commander, was constantly at his proper post, both by night as well as day. I know of no officer in the service who has in my estimation so well earned promotion as Gen. Williams.

He has neglected to follow a custom which has become quite general in the army, that of calling the press to his aid, by employing reporters to sound his praise at the close of any engagement, in advance of official information on the subject, but I think in the estimation of every true soldier he will be more honored in the breach than in the observance of such a custom. I most earnestly hope he may be promoted.

I am Sir,
Very Respectfully,
Your Obedient Servant,
H. W. Slocum,
Maj Gen'l Vols. Comd'g

To his Excellency
A. Lincoln,
President of the United States.

◈

PROSPECTS OF PROMOTION

Stafford Court House, June 7, 1863.

My Dear Daughter: . . .

We have been under orders to be ready to move at a moment's notice for several days, but we don't move. Two regiments of my division went to the front yesterday, detached for some secret service. I think we shall have hot work very soon, but in which direction is very uncertain.

We have had the dustiest and warmest of days, so oppressive that it was fatiguing to sit under an awning. Today is cooler and pleasanter. I have kept very shady and to my tent. Indeed, I am almost without assistance. Not more than six or seven field officers out of thirty-three, and all adjutant generals gone. I am the victim of constant annoyance and anxiety, especially as my small division holds the extreme right and pickets a front of over four miles. My letter writing, ergo, is not brisk. Indeed, it is quite as much as I wish to do to look over papers and decide upon them. Knipe is still absent. I have not heard from him. Jackson does not get over his broken leg, and my only brigadier is Gen. Ruger. My command has run down to less than one-half [the number] I arrived at this camp with.

Gen. Slocum has *voluntarily* sent me a splendid letter recommending my promotion. I will send you a copy. It is a very gratifying testimonial from my corps commander.

I have been down to visit Krzyzenowski, commander of a brigade in the 11th Corps, and dined with him and Madame S. He is a Pole but a good officer and speaks English well. . . . I have received a very kind letter from Mr. J. M. Howard, U.S. senator from our state. He wrote to the Secretary of War urging my promotion and sent me a copy of his reply, which was as "wish a washy" as everything which comes from that Department. Just think of the promotion of *Birney* over me for the battle of Chancellorsville!! An officer who has been once tried for misconduct or something else in face of the enemy. I believe he was found not guilty and have no doubt he is patriotic and valiant enough, but he is my junior a year and a half and I have seen more service than he ever can.

All leaves are stopped now. I could go to Washington for five days and get an extension, doubtless, but in the judgment of honest men this practice is regarded as sneaking. I confess I desire still to keep my self-respect. Perhaps something may turn up by which I can get away before summer is over. . . .

Your Affectionate Father,
A.S.W.

1. John Stockton of Mount Clemens, who was appointed colonel of the Eighth Michigan Cavalry Regiment upon its organization October 3, 1862. John C. Robinson of Ann Arbor was appointed colonel of the First Michigan Infantry Regiment on September 1, 1861. He became a brigadier general on April 28, 1862 and a brevet major general on June 27, 1864. Henry A. Morrow of Detroit was appointed colonel of the Twenty-fourth Michigan Infantry upon its organization, August 15, 1862. It was attached to the famous Iron Brigade, in which on the first day of Gettysburg (July 1, 1863) it sustained a loss of 80 per cent of the 500 men engaged. Twenty of its twenty-eight officers were killed or wounded, among the latter being Colonel Morrow, who became a prisoner but was left behind when the Confederate army began its retreat.—O. B. Curtis, *History of the Twenty-fourth Michigan of the Iron Brigade* (Detroit, 1891).

2. The "scrawl," written on May 4, was a 2,400-word description of the campaign and battle to that time. Since its contents are necessarily repeated, in the main, in the more detailed narrative of May 18, it is not included.

3. Amiel W. Whipple, a West Point graduate in the class of 1841. From 1856 to 1861 he was engineer in charge of the ship channel through the St. Clair Flats, and of the channel through Lake George and Neebish Rapids in the Saint Marys River. Mortally wounded at Chancellorsville, he died on May 7, 1863, having been brevetted major general of volunteers the day before.—Cullum, *Register of Officers and Graduates of the U.S. Military Academy.*

4. It has. See sketch of Sickles in *Dict. Am. Biog.,* where we are told that (with the Third Corps) he "attacked the victorious Jackson and after bloody fighting stopped his advance."

5. They were crowded, also, with the Union troops whom Sickles had ordered to make the night attack upon the Confederates and who found themselves under fire from the enemy in front and from their own colleagues in the rear. General Slocum, in reporting the action, expressed the fear that they had suffered heavily from the fire of the latter.—*Official Records,* Series 1, XXV, Part 1, 670; General Williams' report, 679.

6. This analysis of the current situation proved entirely correct save for the forecast concerning General Lee's intentions. Instead of an assault upon the Army of the Potomac he detoured its position, beginning the march which led to Gettysburg.

VII

Gettysburg

Barely a month sufficed to determine the issue of the Gettysburg campaign and the war. In early June General Lee's army set forth from its encampment around Fredericksburg upon its second invasion of the North, hopefully anticipating the capture of Baltimore and Washington and the dictation of a peace on Confederate terms. To checkmate this design General Hooker also moved northward, keeping the Army of the Potomac as a shield between the invader and Washington. Whether he would lead it to another Chancellorsville and the probable loss of the war was the question at issue when on June 27, in response to his own request, he was relieved of his command. Upon General Meade, whom the President appointed to succeed him, now devolved the responsibility of defeating the invading Confederate army. How he did so at Gettysburg in the three-day battle of July 1–3 is known to the world. Less known, however, is the role of General Williams in the campaign, described in part in the letters to his daughters which follow. Once more in temporary command of an army corps, it was his lot to defend the right flank of the Union army, stationed on Culp's Hill. But for his successful performance of this task in a desperate struggle of several hours duration during the forenoon of July 3, there would have been no Pickett's charge and no Union victory. It is our present misfortune that the concluding portion of his narrative describing the battle is missing from his papers.

BACK TO MARYLAND AGAIN

Fairfax Court House, June 16, 1863.

My Dear Daughter:

You will be astonished at my locality, but our changes now are *magical*. Joseph says "presto" and to the charge! I doubt if he is any wiser with the operation than some of our traveling magicians by their legerdemain. I have no time to describe movements, but simply to tell you where I am. We left Stafford Court House Thursday night, (the 11th); marched all night to Dumfries; lay there all next day and left there yesterday morning at daylight; made a march of twenty-five miles with my division in the hottest, dirtiest day I ever saw and reached here last night. I lost a good many men, I fear, by sunstroke. It was a terrible day and my poor fellows suffered greatly.

We have all sorts of rumors and no facts; but I suppose, as the newspapers say, we shall have "stirring times."

Your Affectionate Father,
A.S.W.

❖

RETURNING TO MARYLAND

Leesburg, Va., June 20th [and 23rd], 1863.

My Dear Daughters:

I write to you jointly, as I shall probably have little time to write you separately for some time, at least if the past week is a specimen of what we are to expect. I sent to Rene a short pencil note from Fairfax Court House, but I will begin from our old camp.

Saturday, 13th: We received the evening before orders to take up a new line in rear of the old one, to cover the railroad from Aquia to Fredericksburg. The day was hot and we were busy moving the regiments from sunrise taking up a line from Aquia Creek some four miles long toward Potomac Creek and in establishing in front a long line of pickets. It was a hard job in a country so densely covered by thickets and broken by deepest ravines. I had just got to my new camp about

3 o'clock P.M., very pleasantly located on a grassy knoll near Brooke's Station, and was anticipating a day or so of freedom from dust, under cool shades, when lo! up came an order to put my division in march towards Dumfries without delay.

Here was a pretty duty, after a laborious day! A line of pickets four or five miles long to be taken up; our wagons over a line of encampments covering four miles to be repacked, and all the preparations for a permanent breakup and a rapid night march to be made by a wearied and heated body of men. All the long trains of regimental, brigade, division, and corps wagons, with ten days' supplies, were to be sent ahead. There was hurrying in hot haste and mounted orderlies stirred up a big dust in all directions. It was near sundown before I had massed my whole division around the barren-looking knoll, which had for so long a time been the site of my headquarters. It looked sad and forsaken, for in leaving it in the morning we had stripped everything portable for our new quarters and some of the men had made bonfires of the debris. Here we found the wagon trains blocking the way and it was hours before we could resume our march. And what a dark and dreary night march it was.

Almost the whole way to Dumfries is lined by the densest pine thickets and as the night was cloudy the darkness was as thick as that of a subterranean dungeon. The road in the daytime is at this season quite passable by avoiding the deep gullies of the water courses, but at night it was impossible to choose the side roads. In consequence we had a continuance of upsets in our wagon trains, causing vexatious delays in the marching column in the rear. It was over this route that we made our slow march through the mud last winter, through the worst of obstacles. We made more progress in the night march, but with a condensation of vexatious occurrences. Staff officers were tumbled into deep ravines; wagons went over steep ledges or turned bottom upward in deep gullies and were abandoned. We forded Aquia Creek and Chopawamsic Creek and about daylight, after various calamities and a sleepless night, the head of my column reached the Quantico Creek and pitched our shelter tents on the north side near the antique village of Dumfries.

This place, once so noted in the commerce and politics of Virginia, which boasted in colonial times of its dozens of importing warehouses, which was the theater where Patrick Henry made his great war speech, is nothing now but a straggling and deserted village of a dozen or so tumbling down houses, with not a store or a shop. Even its river, where heavily freighted vessels once unloaded their cargoes, has so filled up that our troops forded at the very landing place of olden times. It was a part of our program to have crossed at Occoquan village, the 3rd Corps passing us here and crossing at Wolf Run Shoals; but after staying all day Sunday (14th) at Dumfries we got orders to march to Fairfax Court House via Wolf Run Shoals over our old route of last winter. . . .

[*A four-page section is missing at this point.*]

June 17: We left Fairfax Court House just as day was breaking, my division leading. Our march was over a new route via Hunter's Mills near Vienna, and striking the turnpike from Alexandria to Leesburg. The morning was pleasant, but by 8 o'clock exceedingly warm again. We halted an hour at Hunter's Mills in a nice shady ravine on Difficult River, to let the men breakfast. The country through which we marched was more fertile and better cultivated and [had] a good many nice farm houses. It was a great contrast to the country from Fairfax to Stafford. We found a few cavalry pickets on the route as far as Hunter's Mills belonging to the 6th Michigan Cavalry. A Captain Weber from Grand Rapids, a very gentlemanly young man, introduced himself during our halt and gave me information as to [our] route.

We intended to pass Dranesville but were met by an order to halt short at a small stream about two miles south of Dranesville and found a good camping ground. We pitched our tents in the pleasant yard of a farmhouse where we found the unusual luxury of sweet butter and fresh milk. Our march was only ten miles and was completed about 11 o'clock A.M. The afternoon was intensely hot, so that we could not be comfortable on the green grass beneath the densest shade. Either by accident or design the dry old grass of the fields and woods got on fire, and filled the air with smoke and additional heat. Altogether it was an afternoon of great discomfort, and I was quite glad that our march was a short one.

June 18: I was ordered at 6 o'clock to move my division towards Leesburg. The early morning was the hottest we had felt. One per-

spired freely standing still at sunrise. We were ordered to reach Leesburg but as it was understood that we were not to march, there was
some delay, and it was past 7 o'clock before we were fairly on the
road. We had reached the pike, which was hard enough, but rough with
unbroken boulders and very hard on the feet of men and animals accustomed to dirt roads. We passed through Dranesville, a small, insignificant village, and made our first halt at Broad River, over which
we found a stout stone bridge. The country along the pike is well
cultivated and farmhouses are thick. We had all sorts of rumors of
Rebels in front, but none appeared except a few horsemen on our left,
which we paid no attention to.

About 1 o'clock a brisk shower relieved our tired and over-heated
soldiers and we soon reached Goose Creek, where we found a deep and
rocky ford, the bridge having been destroyed long ago. My division
forded at once, waist deep, with their usual yells and jokes. The storm
of rain, hail, thunder, and lightning had become terrific, but the men
felt new life from the cool wetting, and we marched directly on this
town, three and a half miles, which my advance reached about 4 P.M.
and found no enemy. The 2nd Division (Gen. Geary's) had fallen
behind and did not get over the ford until dark, and our trains were
unable to pass at all. This place we passed through last December on
our march from Harpers Ferry. It is a place of considerable importance
in peaceful times, though very old and not at all prosperous in appearance. It lies in a natural bowl or circular valley, around the rim of
which the Rebels built last year three or four strong forts. These we
have occupied, though they are somewhat dilapidated.

The famous Ball's Bluff is within four miles of this, as is Edwards
Ferry, to which you will remember I made my first march in October
1861. The original order of Gen. Stone to Col. Davis, upon which the
movement was made, is now in the possession of a landlord of this
town, named Williamson. He was at the time adjutant of a Virginia
regiment and in the battle, I think. He told me the order was found
in the hat of Gen. Baker, who was killed. I have seen the original when
we went through last winter and could not but feel that it exonerated
Stone from much of the blame put on him. A copy was made at the
time, by one of our officers and published. From the accounts of this
officer, I think that unfortunate disaster to our troops arose mainly from

the neglect or ignorance of green colonels who commanded our regiments and from the rashness of Gen. Baker himself. The government has restored Gen. Stone to duty and I suppose considers him blameless in the matter. It is quite certain from the stories of both sides that we ought not to have suffered the disaster we did and might have occupied Leesburg with ordinary care and sagacity.

As it was raining when we reached town I halted at the head of a street, while my advance passed through, and finally took up my quarters in the house, occupying two large rooms, one for a sleeping room for a dozen or so of us, and one for an office. I slept for the first time for months under a roof, but in my blankets on the floor. The woman of the house is named Grover. No men are seen, but lots of children, white and black. On returning from a ride through the town to see to the position of my troops I found a young lady dressed up very finely in white, with red and blue ribbons. She had come to see the general, and show one Union lady. It was indeed a rarity for a native in this state, where the women are the fiercest of all Secessionists. Her name is Honda, and her family live about a mile from town. As it was raining and very muddy I sent Pittman to escort her home, after doing her up in an India rubber coat, but I fear her Union finery was not a little drabbled in the mud and wet.

June 19th: Today we had the most unpleasant duty of shooting three deserters, about the first capital punishments which have taken place in the army for this offense. Two of them, of the 46th Pennsylvania Volunteers, deserted about two weeks ago when we were under orders to march towards the enemy. They bought citizens' clothes, but were apprehended while trying to get off by Aquia Creek. The other (13th New Jersey Volunteers) deserted a year or more ago and was sent back from home. He neglected to avail himself of the pardon offered by the President in April last. The sentence of court martial was approved by Gen. Hooker just as we were leaving Stafford, and they were ordered to be shot between 12 and 4 o'clock yesterday. Officers of regiments went to ask a commutation, but he would not see them and so the sad business had to go on. The whole corps was paraded in a large field and formed three sides of a square. By Gen. Hooker's orders the execution was under my direction as commander of the division to which the men belonged. The carrying out of details

I put, of course, on my provost marshal. Three graves were dug some two feet apart in a slight depression of the field, and on the gentle swell of the ground the troops were formed so that every man could see the execution. . . . [*The succeeding portion of the journal is missing. It was resumed by General Williams in a letter dated at Leesburg, June 23, whose opening lines are omitted.*]

Saturday [20th] was a calm day. No sound of guns, and I spent most of it in making disposition of my troops and establishing outposts and picket lines.

Sunday, June 21st: Firing began on our left early and seemed about 7 or 8 miles away. Our outer pickets could hear volleys of musketry. The cannonade was kept up all day at intervals, but seemed to recede towards Ashby's Gap, by which token we concluded our cavalry with an infantry support was driving the Rebels. I dined with Gen. Slocum at the hotel in town, kept by an ex-Rebel officer (Williamson). In my rides about town I find many pleasant residences and a great many indignant and explosive Secesh women, but very few men except old ones. The country about is very fertile and beautiful. I came through here for the first time with Alf Coxe in 1850 or '51 after visiting his sister—Mrs. Lewis—in the Shenandoah Valley. A great many years ago when I was a boy (eight or ten years old) an old shoemaker and farmer, with whom I boarded in Madison near the academy, had a son in Leesburg keeping a shoestore. Of course, I heard a great deal of the place and my boyish fancy was quite excited about Leesburg. It was at least forty years ago. Strange are the occurrences of our lives. My earliest ideas of Virginia towns were of a peaceful shoestore and here I am as a belligerent, in manhood, dictating terms of ingress and egress to its people!

Monday, June 22nd: I mounted my horse early in the morning to take a long circuit of the town on the out hills, which rise above the lesser hills near the village and command it. Indeed, all around the town there is an amphitheater of hills like seats which rise as they recede. Towards Edwards Ferry the country is more level, though spurs of mountains run towards the pass in that direction. For perhaps two miles towards Ball's Bluff the country is comparatively level, with immense fields of grass and corn, a very fertile soil and not looking like famine. One corn field we estimated had 400 acres planted. I rode down to the pontoon bridge which has been laid over the Potomac at Edwards Ferry, which is over a quarter of a mile broad. Indeed, in appearance nearly as broad as the river at Detroit.

I went over the scene of the contest which you may remember I described as taking place on Tuesday after the Ball's Bluff fight. From this I visited the scene of the Ball's Bluff disaster, which is some three miles higher up and opposite Harrison's Island. One is filled with astonishment that any man of the least military pretensions should have crossed at such a place and with such means. The island divides the river so that the stream on this side is narrow, but at the landing place the bluff is covered with woods and thickets to the river's edge and is cut deep with water courses, and gullied into deep ravines to the river's edge. It was with difficulty I could get my horse down the narrow footpath, where our troops went up. For three-quarters of a mile back, the woods and underbrush are very thick with small cleared patches, into which, after defeat began, our troops by a monstrous fatality were collected to make slaughter sure and certain from the adjacent woods held by the Rebels. Gen. Baker was killed near the river bank in one of these small clearings. I found a long trench without sign or headboard where our dead were buried. I confess I felt all through the ride over this unfortunate ground that somebody should have been exemplarily punished for permitting the slaughter that occurred there. It is a singular fact that while they were killing and taking prisoners of so many of our men, we had at Edwards Ferry, not over three miles distant and on the flank of the Rebels, a larger force than they brought into the fight. They made no demonstration to relieve our overwhelmed forces. . . .

I finished my day's ride by visiting Fort Johnson, where I have posted two regiments and a battery. It is on a very high hill north of the town. On the south we have Fort Beauregard and on the southeast Fort Evans, but they are miles apart and are nothing but dilapidated earthworks which we are repairing somewhat, though we don't know we shall stay here a day. On the west there is no work. The country slopes away gradually towards the hills and is a good deal exposed. Indeed, our location is by no means a strong one or easy of defense with the force we have. There are too many hills and we have too few men away up in advance of the other corps. But I suppose it is the post of honor, even if we get used up!

I have several times intended to send you an account of my visit to the division hospital after the battle of Chancellorsville, but other things have prevented. All our wounded—700 or 800—were taken back to Aquia Creek and put in large hospital tents on the high hills overlooking the Potomac River. They were made as comfortable as the severely wounded (and none others were kept in hospital) could be. It took me all day to go through and I saw and talked with every man of my division. I need not say that they all seemed pleased to see me, but I had a terrible surfeit of looking at amputated legs and arms, and of all imaginable kinds of severe wounds. It was wonderful how men could survive some of them. Several had been shot through the lungs; one through both eyes and was stone blind; many had had several inches of bone cut out of legs and arms (ex-section) and were doing well. One poor fellow had had his leg amputated by the Rebs. on the field and the flesh had sloughed off, leaving a long bone sticking out, and he was much reduced by secondary hemorrhage; but strange to say, with this one exception, all had healthful, and many cheerful faces, and talked to me cheerfully and happily. One poor fellow had been wounded through the hips, and his feet had lain in the water until they gangrened and more than half the flesh had fallen off, leaving the bones of the feet protruding fleshless, nothing but skeletons of toes and outer bones. I intended to have sent you a full account of these terribly wounded [men] and of the heroic manner they bore up under these distressing injuries, but it is too late now. I was gratified after my visit to get repeated messages from the surgeons from the wounded that my visit had done them so much good and that they had said that the general's medicine was better than the doctor's. It was four or five miles from my camp or I should [have] gone often. . . .

We have no certain information of our future movements. They depend upon the enemy, but I fancy we shall not be here long. When armies approach one another, fighting is sure to follow pretty soon. In this case there is a momentous issue, for if we are badly defeated there is but little hope, I think, of saving Washington. The troops held so sacredly about that "corruption sink" would make a poor show before the victorious Rebels. God save our Republic! For I sometimes think that human heads and arms are working for our destruction. I suppose, however, they are but instruments of divine will, though why He should use those who most blaspheme his authority, it is hard to imagine. I have seen dark times, but none where before I could not see some superior intellect that might probably be brought to our safety.

Your Affectionate Father,

A.S.W.

◆

FOREBODINGS OF DEFEAT

Frederick, Md., June 29, 1863.

My Dear Daughters:

I have a moment in the office of Dr. Steiner of the Sanitary Commission to tell you where I am. We left Leesburg on Friday last, the 26th inst., and marched across the river at Edwards Ferry on pontoons and encamped that night at the mouth of the Monocacy. The next day we marched to within a mile of Knoxville, which Rene will remember is within two miles of the Longbridges on the Baltimore & Ohio Railroad, where we generally took the railroad for Baltimore. The Saturday's march was too tedious and fatiguing for me to go to the Longbridges. Besides, I did not get my brigades in camp until after dark. The whole line of march was crowded by baggage wagons and trains. I expected to march through Sandy Hook towards Williamsport but during the night was ordered to march my division towards Frederick. I reached this [place] yesterday afternoon, when a change of commanders was announced, Meade superceding Hooker.

It was intimated that we should remain at this place a day or so, but at 2.30 this morning I was awakened by a messenger ordering my division to march towards Taneytown at 5 A.M. I was camped in a fine grove and had a great desire for sleep after three days' fatiguing marches, but there is no help under orders. Besides, we are filled with an idea that the Rebels are getting into Pennsylvania, and of course we are bound to go on, cost what of human flesh it may. For myself, I am rejoiced at the change of commanders. I have said very little in my letters, but enough for you to guess that I had no confidence in Hooker after Chancellorsville. I can say now, that if we had had a commander of even ordinary merit at that place the army of Jackson would have been annihilated. I cannot conceive of greater imbecility and weakness than characterized that campaign from the moment Hooker reached Chancellorsville and took command.

I am not much of a military genius, but if I could have commanded the Army of the Potomac at Chancellorsville I would have wagered my life on being in Richmond in ten days! All we are suffering now in shame and mortification and in the great risk of losing the whole fortunes of the war is the legitimate result of the weakness which characterized that campaign. Since then, and as the results of that campaign, our army has been reduced over 50,000 men, two-thirds by expiration of term of service of three-months' and two-years' troops, and yet not one soldier has been added to our forces. All winter, by the natural disintegration of armies, we have been running down at the rate of 20 per cent per annum; add to this 35 to 40,000 men discharged by expiration of service and 25,000 killed and wounded in battle and you have at least 85,000 men in this army less now than last December, and this, too, at the season when active field duties commence. I have in my division less than half the men I had in January last, when I reached Stafford Court House. I think my division is a fair sample of the Army of the Potomac.

You see we have a great task before us to preserve the Republic. It is reported that the Rebels are 110,000 strong in infantry, with 20,000 cavalry. I think the report is greatly exaggerated, but they have been all winter recruiting by conscription, while we have been all winter running down. Still, I don't despair. On the contrary, now with a gentleman and a soldier in command I have renewed confidence that we shall at least do enough to preserve our honor and the safety of the Republic. But we run a fearful risk, because upon this small army everything depends. If we are badly defeated the Capital is gone and all our principal cities and our national honor. That this dilemma could have been suffered by men deputed to care for the safety of the Republic is indeed disheartening. That our northern people could sit down in search of the almighty dollar, when their all is depending upon this conflict, is indeed passing strange. If we fail in this war, be assured there is an end of northern prosperity. The Rebels in Baltimore and Washington will dictate terms and these terms will humiliate and destroy us. I would I had an archangel's voice to appeal to the patriotism (if there be any left) in the North!

I sent you a sort of journal of a few days we were in Leesburg, excepting two or three of the last. Those were devoted to putting the forts in good condition for the Rebels and making several miles of rifle pits and breast works.

Love to all; my column has passed and I must follow. This is a hasty scrawl, but I know with you better than none. Keep writing me. I am full of faith and yet fearfully anxious. There must be a decisive battle, I think, soon, but you will hear of it before this reaches you, probably. Possibly the enemy may withdraw, and I am not without hope that we may strike them on a weak flank exposure.

Whatever may happen, be contented and resigned, and believe it is all for the best. In nations, as in individuals, we must believe there is a "Divinity which shapes our ends, rough hew them as we will."

Your Affectionate Father,
A.S.W.

◈

GETTYSBURG

Halt near Littlestown, Pa.,
July 6, 1863.

My Dear Daughters:

I wrote you a hasty note on the 4th from the battlefield in the rear of Gettysburg and previously a hasty scrawl from Frederick on the march up. I am now at this "halt," moving back over the same road we advanced, for the purpose, I suppose, of hanging on the flank of Lee's army, reported on the retreat. My division lies in the fields hereabouts, and I have borrowed a very poor pen and poorer ink to take advantage of the occasion, for the prospect of quietude is not promising. How long I shall remain at this temporary halt is very uncertain, as we are watching the Rebel movements, so may be off in an hour. There can be little rest until Lee is driven out of Maryland, or we are amongst the armies that were. I wrote you so hastily from Frederick, that I will briefly resume my journal.

Friday, 26th: Left camp at Leesburg and crossed the Potomac on pontoon bridges at Edwards Ferry four miles; marched to mouth of the Monocacy, passing 5th Corps near Edwards Ferry. Day drizzling and disagreeably sultry fifteen miles.

Saturday, 27th: Marched from Monocacy to within a mile or so of Knoxville through byroads which led near Jefferson. Abundance of cherry trees; day cloudy and not oppressive. Marched eighteen miles, the men coming in cheerful. After dark rode to headquarters in Knoxville for consultation on order to advance to Williamsport to burn pontoon bridges. Countermanding order came and we were directed to march for Frederick next morning. Headquarters at Mr. Tighlman Hillyear's—a fussy old fellow of seventy, who was greatly disturbed at the destruction of his rail fences. Got supper at Hillyear's, who has a splendid large brick farmhouse and is an old Secesh.

Sunday, 28th: Marched at 5 A.M. for Frederick, passing through Jefferson. Reached camp near the town. Twelve and a half miles; pitched headquarters tents in a nice grove and anticipated a nice day's rest. Worked all afternoon, after fifteen miles march. In the night got orders to march at daylight towards Taneytown, Md. Received, on arrival, news of the removal of Gen. Hooker and appointment of Gen. Meade to command the army. Very general satisfaction expressed in our division.

Monday, 29th: Marched through Frederick and took the road to Taneytown. March much obstructed by trains of different corps. Day cloudy and occasionally drizzling. Encamped on Little Pine Creek and got our supper at a farmhouse. Wagons behind. March eighteen miles.

Tuesday, 30th: Marched at daylight, my division in advance. Reached vicinity of Littlestown about noon, twelve miles. Found great excitement, growing out of cavalry charge upon our cavalry in the town. Moved through the town, the people turning out en masse with great curiosity and apparent joy that we had come in season to protect them. All along the road since leaving Frederick the people have assembled in country wagons to gratify their curiosity to see the Army of the Potomac. Their comments have been very entertaining. Our cavalry, having chased the Rebels off a few miles, returned, and Gen. Slocum came up and ordered us to encamp, which was done in the fields above the town.

Our whole march from Frederick, as indeed since crossing the Potomac, has been through a very rich and highly cultivated country. Indeed, it was not easy to find a lot upon which we could encamp, so universal were the cultivated fields by the roadside. On our march today we passed the line between Maryland and Pennsylvania. The inhabitants are Dutch descendants and quite Dutch in language. The country is full of Copperheads, more so than the southern part of Maryland, and the people are rich, but ignorant of everybody and [every]thing beyond their small spheres. They have immense barns, looking like great arsenals or public institutions, full of small windows and painted showily. Altogether, they are a people of barns, not brains.

Wednesday, July 1st: Marched at daylight towards Gettysburg, my division leading. Halted at Two Taverns, a small village, where my division massed in the fields. The people all along the road manifested great curiosity to see us and assembled at all road crossings. The country was beautiful and most richly cultivated. The same big barns and hayhouses. After an hour or so halt, got a dispatch that our troops of the 11th and 1st corps were engaged with the Rebels near Gettysburg. My division was at once put in march. Some two miles south of the town we turned off to the right on a narrow, winding path or country road, and after a couple of miles reached a dense wood, behind which was a high, bald hill on which a good position could be had in sight and rear of the town.

I had pressed my men for five or six miles over very muddy and slippery roads in order to reach the hill before the Rebels, who, it was reported to me, were advancing in that direction in heavy column. As I reached the woody screen, officers I sent forward reported that the enemy had possession. I, however, drew up in order of battle and went forward myself to reconnoiter under the cover of the woods. I reached the ravine at the bottom of the hill and from behind a tree (leaving my horse and staff behind) I could see Rebel cavalry on top, but no infantry. There might possibly be a battery there, but I determined at once to take it by assault. Some of my regiments were already at the foot, and the skirmishers were in advance, covered by bushes. I gave the order to advance at double-quick, when I was overtaken by a staff officer of Gen. Slocum's directing me to withdraw, as the Rebels had already driven back our troops in front of Gettysburg and occupied the town, and we were in danger of being cut off from our line towards the main road.

My men were halfway up the hill, but I withdrew them at once and returned to the vicinity of the main road to the town, where we had diverged. Here we passed the night without any information on the condition of the 11th and 1st corps, which we had very indefinitely heard had been repulsed. We had plenty of rumors, and had reliable information of the death of Gen. Reynolds, commander of the 1st Corps. I had been notified that I was in command of the 12th Corps, Gen. Slocum temporarily taking command of the right wing, in place of Reynolds. Gen. Meade had not come up. I was in considerable dilemma, as I could learn nothing of the 2nd (Geary's) Division of our corps.

At length a staff officer came with information that it had been ordered to the vicinity of Gettysburg to support the right of Wadsworth's division, 1st Corps. So I put out strong pickets in all directions, as it was dark and I literally knew nothing of the topography or geography of the country. In my rear was a broad, cultivated country, but all along the front and on both sides of the road I was on was a dense wood, and in front (toward Gettysburg) a considerable stream called Rock Creek; properly named, as it was built up on either bank by high hills of huge boulders; and farther on a high ridge, densely covered, and of irregular form, ran toward Gettysburg on our right.

The country people seemed stupidly ignorant of the Rebel movements, here, as everywhere on our route. They had plenty of stories of huge bodies of cavalry and infantry, from 100,000 to 1,000,000, and thousands of pieces of artillery. These stories, which are repeated and swelled through a long line of timid imaginations, become exceedingly laughable, especially when heard from the chattering lips of the frightened men and women. It is not strange that they are alarmed for their property and themselves. Their peaceful lives in these retired spots have not been calculated to prepare their hearts for "war's stern alarms," and the sound of cannon and the movement of troops on all sides must fearfully disturb their fancies. I pitched my bivouac (for I had neither tents nor blankets) under a big oak near the edge of the woods, and after making arrangements against surprise and "giving audience" to several farmers, rolled myself in an india-rubber poncho and slept most splendidly until daylight.

Thursday, July 2nd: Woke at daylight and soon after began to put my troops in better order than the dark permitted last night. Borrowed a little coffee from an orderly and a piece of hardtack, which made an excellent breakfast. Gen. Slocum came out from the front early with general directions as to the positions the 12th Corps was to take up. As I was placing the 1st Division, the head of the 5th Corps began to arrive and took up a position on our right, all of us facing to the east. I met for an instant on the ground Capt. Chipman, who is on Gen. Sykes staff.[1] We had scarcely got into position before I was ordered to change a couple of miles or so toward the town and form the 1st Division on the right of the 2nd, already in position along the wooded ridge I have before mentioned. I was soon there, following up the pike to within half a mile of Gettysburg and then taking a bridle path which led to about the center of the ridge. Here I found the right of Geary's division and I placed the 1st along the rocky crest, extending south until I struck Rock Creek, and then following it to a rocky knoll near the pike, where it crosses the creek.

This ridge was a wild position, full of great detached masses of rock and huge boulders. I ordered at once a breastwork of logs to be built, having experienced their benefits at Chancellorsville. Looking at the spot, it seemed almost absurd that the enemy could attack there, as the approach was so rough and broken. Besides, the creek, dammed near the pike bridge, became almost the whole length of our front a stream quite unfordable, as far as we had been able to follow it. Still, though ridiculous the work, we were there, and our men had learned to love entrenching with logs. So at it they went and in a couple of hours had covered themselves with a good, substantial breastwork.

Matters went on all day pretty quietly. I had lost a few men in the morning in my skirmishers, sent out to feel the enemy, and on our left towards the front the artillery had been occasionally exchanging shots. Nothing to indicate the intentions of the Rebels had occurred. They

had got the better of us the day before, rather through our own rashness, I think, as it was not intended to have a general engagement until
the several corps could concentrate from the many routes they were
obliged to take. Reynolds, I fancy, precipitated a large action by under-
rating the strength of his opponents. In consequence, both the 1st and
11th corps were badly cut up, and it is reported that a considerable
portion of the latter corps behaved badly, almost as much so as at
Chancellorsville, falling back without firing and thus uncovering the
flanks of that corps, which suffered terribly in killed and wounded.[2]

In consequence the two corps which fought in advance of Gettysburg
were driven nearly through the town, the Rebs. holding the north side
and we the south with our headquarters in the cemetery adjoining the
village. We had the considerable but gently rising ridges on the center
and left of the town; the Rebs. similar ones, with the high hill I spoke
of yesterday, on the right of the town. Wadsworth's division, 1st Corps
and 12th Corps held the wooded and rocky ridge from the town to
Rock Creek. Gen. Meade had concentrated to a narrow circuit all his
troops which had arrived. He held the center or interior lines, and the
enemy were on the outer lines or circumference. The diameter of the
circle was not two miles, I think, while the circumference, in its
irregular shape, was six or seven, or more. The Rebs. were for once at
a disadvantage, as we could reinforce any part of our line rapidly, while
the "Secesh" had a long outer line to march over to bring aid to an
overpowered point.

During the morning, as we were taking up a position, a new brigade
of two pretty large regiments, the 1st Maryland Home Guards and
the 150th New York Volunteers, reported to our corps. They were
under command of Gen. Lockwood, of whom I know as yet very little.
He appears to be a very pleasant gentleman and I believe has had some
command for a long time on the Eastern Shore of Maryland.[3] Another
regiment (1st Maryland Eastern Shore) will join the brigade tomorrow,
quite desirable reinforcements to our weakened corps in matter of
numbers, but I fear not very reliable, as none of them have seen much
active duty.

It was as late as 3 o'clock P.M. when the Rebels began heavily with
artillery at our front and then with infantry on our left, attacking at
first the 3rd Corps. The battle raged fiercely until dark and several

corps or parts were ordered up to reinforce our line; the 5th, part of the 6th, and finally my division of the 12th Corps. I was in command of the corps and could properly have left the division with Gen. Ruger, temporarily commanding, but as I had also the new brigade of Gen. Lockwood, I preferred to accompany the division. We took the route promptly and marched rapidly, following the sound of the battle, for I could find no one on the way to give me intelligence as to the point I was most needed.

On we went, therefore, following up the main line of the returning wounded and the skulkers. We soon came to signs of battle; broken-down fences, trodden fields, broken gun-carriages, scattered arms, knapsacks, blankets, and clothing of all kinds. I reached a considerable elevation upon the center of which heavy woods came down to a point, and in the rear spread out broad both ways. I followed the side where I heard infantry volleys, and as I came near the wooded apex an artillery officer rode rapidly towards me begging for assistance to protect his battery. It proved to be Maj. McGilary of Maine, who once commanded a battery in my division. He was delighted to see me and I heard, with the rapidity that such occasions require, that the infantry supports had just left him and that in the woods in front the Rebels had just captured several pieces of our artillery, or rather dragged them there after capture. I had the new brigade leading and one regiment of it had fallen behind. The 1st Maryland Home Regiment, Col. Maulsby, was ahead and I ordered him to pitch into the woods. So he did, indeed, without waiting to form line of battle, but rushing forward in column. Fortunately, he met little resistance, for the Rebs. ran and left the catpured guns, which were thus recaptured without firing a gun.

Leaving this regiment, I passed to the other side of the wooded triangle where the main road runs and after placing my 1st and 3rd brigades in the woods went forward to learn what was to be done, but it was fast growing dark and the battle was really over. I chanced, however, to meet Gen. Meade and a good many other officers on the field and to learn that we had successfully resisted all the Rebel attacks and had punished them severely. There was a pleasant gathering in an open field, and gratification and gratulation abounded. One must see these events and anxious scenes to realize the joy of a successful termination, even of a single day's work, no matter how uncertain may be the morrow.

I returned toward my entrenchments after dark and was met with the astounding intelligence that they were taken possession of by the Rebels in my absence! Gen. Geary (whom I left to guard them) had been ordered out after I left by Gen. Slocum, and though he did not reach the front, by mistaking his way, he was gone long enough for the Rebs. to seize upon two-thirds of our line, which we had prepared with so much care. Fortunately, Gen. Greene was left on this extensive left, adjoining Gen. Wadsworth, and on the highest part of the ridge at a point where our line made an abrupt angle, along a pretty high cliff. The angle of the line came almost to the edge of a low morass, or swale, leaving but a narrow, rocky pass for the Rebs. to move up against Greene's position. They tried hard to drive him out, but failed, though keeping up [the attack] until nearly my return. I had had experience in trying to retake breastworks after dark, so I ordered all the brigades to occupy the open field in front of the woods, put out a strong picket line, and waited daylight for further operations.

In the meantime as temporary commander of the 12th Corps, I was summoned to a council at Gen. Meade's headquarters. I found present, Gens. Slocum, Sedgwick, Hancock, Howard, Newton, Sykes and Gibbon. It was to decide upon the next day's policy. I have no right to tell others' opinions, but mine (the second given) was to remain the following day, hold a defensive attitude, and await events. This was the decision, as the day showed. It was rather a serious question for one great reason, if not many others. We had but one single day's rations for the army. Many corps had not even one. We had outrun our supplies, and as all the railroad lines which came near us were broken, there were no depots within reach. But it was thought that what with beef cattle and flour, which possibly could be got together, we could eke out a few half-fed days.

Few appreciate the difficulties of supplying an army. If you will calculate that every man eats, or is entitled to eat, nearly two pounds a day, you can easily estimate what a large army consumes. But besides what men eat, there are horses and mules for artillery, cavalry, and transportation in vast numbers, all which must be fed or the army is dissolved or made inefficient. There is another all-important matter of ammunition, a large supply of which for infantry and artillery must be carried, besides what is carried on the person and in the ammunition chests of guns and caissons. Our men carry forty rounds in boxes, and when approaching a possible engagement take twenty more on the person. Of this latter, from perspiration, rain, and many causes there is great necessary waste. It is an article that cannot be dispensed with, of course, and the supply on the person must be kept up. The guns cannot be kept loaded, therefore the diminution is constant from this necessary waste. My division, at present numbers, will require forty to fifty wagons to carry the extra infantry ammunition. You should see the long train of wagons of the reserve artillery, passing as I write, to feel what an item this single want is.

But to come back to my narrative! After returning from the council I met Gen. Geary and Col. Best and made arrangements for retaking our entrenchments in the morning. The plan was simply to open upon the ridge they occupied with several batteries of artillery at daylight, and after a cannonading of fifteen minutes to attack them from the left (Greene's position) while the 1st Division held a threatening position on the right and felt them cautiously by skirmishers. The cannonading was to be kept up on the right woods so long as it could be done and not interfere with the advance of our troops.

We had high and admirable positions for our artillery, but the defense of the Rebs. on our right (opposite the 1st Division) was quite impregnable for assault. There was, besides our log entrenchments along the crest of the ridge, a strong stone wall parallel to it about one hundred feet on our side, but inside the woods, which was also in possession of the Rebels. They therefore had two lines of strong defenses against a front attack and the flank toward the creek could not be turned, as a morass and impassable stream protected it; and across the creek they had filled the woods with sharp-shooters behind rocks and in a stone house near the bank.

Thus unfavorably stood matters. It was 3.30 o'clock at night before I got through duty and then got a half hour or so of sleep on a flat rock sheltered by an apple tree.

[*The remainder is missing.*[4]]

ONCE MORE ON THE POTOMAC

Pleasant Valley, Md.,
July 16, 1863.

My Dear Daughter:

I reached this place today from Williamsport. I have hurriedly continued my journal from where I left off at the halting place. I have been so long on marches and so much deprived of sleep and rest that I am obliged to send you a stupid account of our share of the great battle.

The newspapers will give you the intelligence that Lee has reached the Virginia shore with most of his army. His invasion has doubtless cost him 40,000 men in killed and wounded and prisoners. I doubt if he ever tries the game of invasion the third time.

I am now encamped within a few rods of my headquarters of last autumn. Rene will remember the rolling hills towards Sandy Hook, near Maryland Heights. I am on these.

I have not yet seen Miss Longbridge nor any of the family, but propose to go over today. I judge from the orders that we shall be here but a day or so and then cross into Virginia again, and so do the campaign over and over. Our troops require rest, shoes, and clothing. They have been some five weeks on the march. None but veteran troops could stand it, especially as we have not had a dry day for nearly three weeks. It is pouring in torrents today, but I think the Army of the Potomac is simmered down to the very sublimation of human strength and endurance. I will bring up my journal to date, if I stay a day or so. . . .

Love to all,

Your Affectionate Father,
A.S.W.

1. Henry L. Chipman of Detroit, who became lieutenant colonel of the Second Michigan Infantry upon its organization in April 1861. He served with distinction throughout the war, being brevetted for gallantry at Chancellorsville and again at Gettysburg. Following the war, he remained in the regular army until his retirement in 1887. In May 1881 he became lieutenant colonel of the Seventh Cavalry, General Custer's old regiment.—*Record of Service of Michigan Volunteers.*
2. In the battle of July 1 the First and Eleventh corps, commanded respec-

tively by General Doubleday and General Howard, were alone opposed to the vastly superior numbers of General Lee. Although they were driven from their positions and compelled to retreat through the town of Gettysburg to the new position selected by General Howard on Cemetery Ridge, the desperate fight they had waged made possible the assembling of the Union army in the favorable position it occupied during the second and third days of the battle. Although Pickett's charge on July 3 still captures the headlines, the fight made by these two corps on July 1 contributed as much as anything to the ultimate Union victory. The reports of Generals Doubleday and Howard concerning the action of July 1 do not support the statements of General Williams, who apparently was still smarting over the rout of Howard's Eleventh Corps at Chancellorsville, two months earlier. The losses sustained by the regiments of Doubleday's First Corps sufficiently attest the desperate nature of the fight they waged. The Twenty-fourth Michigan Regiment of the Iron Brigade, in particular, sustained a battle loss of 80 percent of the number engaged, of which 64 percent— practically two men out of three—were either killed or wounded. At the Gettysburg semi-centennial celebration fifty years later, survivors of the regiment welcomed their ancient foemen of the Twenty-sixth North Carolina Regiment, which had sustained a battle loss of over 800 of its total of 900 men engaged. For the reports of Generals Doubleday and Howard see *Official Records*, Series 1, XXVII, Part 1, 696– 711 and 243–257.

3. General Henry H. Lockwood of Delaware, a West Point graduate in the class of 1836. Following the Florida War of 1836–37 he resigned his army commission and in 1841 became Professor of Mathematics in the U.S. Naval Academy. His service here continued, save for the interruption occasioned by the Civil War, until his retirement in 1876. In August, 1861, he became a brigadier general of volunteers, continuing in the army until August 24, 1865.

4. The remainder of General Williams' letter, describing the action of July 3 in which the Confederates were driven from Culp's Hill after seven hours of continuous fighting, is unfortunately missing. A summary account of the action is included in Williams' report upon the battle, published in *Official Records*, Series 1, XXVII, Part 1, 772–76.

VIII

To the Rappahannock Once More

TO THE RAPPAHANNOCK ONCE MORE

For whatever reason, the will to fight displayed by General Meade prior to the battle of Gettysburg seemed to have vanished following that event. Contrary to President Lincoln's desire, General Lee was permitted to withdraw his army across the Potomac without interference by Meade, who continued to sadden the President by his procrastination throughout the autumn months of 1863. On October 16, Lincoln proposed that if Meade would attack Lee on a field "no more than equal" to the Union army, the honor, if successful, would belong to him, while the blame, if defeated, would be shouldered by Lincoln. Prior to this proposal, however, on September 29 an order was issued which brought General Williams' career with the Army of the Potomac to a sudden end. The Union defeat at Chickamauga (September 19–20) led the government to order the transfer by rail of the entire Eleventh and Twelfth corps (some 16,000 men) from the Army of the Potomac to the western arena, the operation constituting perhaps the largest transfer of troops over so great a distance that had ever been performed. The letters which follow relate General Williams' closing activities with the Army of the Potomac.

IN PURSUIT OF GENERAL LEE

Snickersville, Va., July 21, 1863.

My Dear Daughters:

The change of my whereabouts is almost as magical as the Rawls[?] performances, appearing through the stage floor in one instant and mysteriously disappearing in the scenic clouds above in the next. We literally have no rest now, for our stoppings are so full of duties that we can hardly be said to rest. We remained in Pleasant Valley two days, exclusive of the day of our arrival, one of them very rainy. I sent you my journal up to the 16th. I visited the Longbridges and took tea there. Miss Ella and the old folks were in good health, the former as sweet as ever.

The fields which we left last winter all forlorn and desolate-looking, are now planted all over with corn and grain, but are for the fifth time terribly cut up again, as two or three corps encamped on them and whole acres of wagon trains. I pity the poor people who live where armies encamp. Pleasant Valley has suffered worse than any other spot. This time our visit was especially destructive, as wheat, corn, and potatoes were all standing and as far as the eye could reach were being desolated by horses, herds of cattle, tramping men, and crushing wagon wheels. It is absolutely an impossibility to keep up in the minds of soldiers and employees the least respect for private property. They drive through fields of ripe wheat and over acres of growing corn without one thought of the destruction they are causing.

I sent you from Pleasant Valley a conclusion of our Gettysburg campaign and battle. It was stupidly done, as absolutely I could not get my fatigued mind up to the subject. I forgot also to tell you of a narrow escape I had on the road. I was passing a column of our soldiers and endeavored to take the side of the road, passing along a deep roadside or ditch on a narrow strip between a stone wall on one side and the deep ditch on the other. I finally came to the end of the wall where a rail fence had been partly thrown down. Here I tried to jump my horse over, but in turning him on the narrow ledge he slipped and tumbling down the bank landed flat on his back in the bottom of the ditch. Fortunately, as he slipped I jumped from the saddle and landed safely on the bank. Old

Plug Ugly must have fallen eight or ten feet and as he groaned hugely I supposed he was finished at last, after passing through divers[?] battles and one heavy fall into the pontoon boats. The men got his saddle off while he lay as quiet as a lamb and turning him round, with a big grunt he got to his feet and was led to the upper end of the ditch to terra firma, apparently as sound as ever. My saddle, which I supposed was crushed beyond repair, came out scarcely injured, saved I supposed by the overcoats and blankets strapped before and behind. Altogether, it was a lucky escape for man, beast, and saddle.

Old Plug was somewhat stiff the next day, but I rode him every day. He is a regular old soldier, however, and takes great advantage of my indulgence and his long service and five or six wounds. As we march along he grabs at every knot of grass, corn, shrub, or any vegetable substance that presents itself on his way. No amount of spurring or whipping can break him of this habit of laying in a supply against short rations. He is an odd, lazy old fellow, sometimes pretending to be very scary, especially after every battle, at other times apparently afraid of nothing. For a year and a half we have been daily companions. We get up a great love for even brutes under such circumstances. I should grieve to part with old Plug Ugly, with all his faults.

Sunday, 19th July: We marched from Pleasant Valley at 9 o'clock, the 2nd Division leading. The 2nd and 3rd corps had crossed the day before. We crossed at the same place as last winter, over the pontoon bridge into Harpers Ferry and round the foot of Loudon Heights. The corps trains in advance delayed us so that we halted for the night about eight miles up the valley.

The guerrillas troubled the advance considerably, coming down from the passes in the Blue Ridge. We sent out patrolling parties, and as some firing had been done from houses, we arrested several citizens and copying Lee's example we gathered up all the horses and cattle we could lay hands on. Our first camp was in the vicinity of the pass through "Short Mountains" near Hillsboro. From this point we went last winter through Hillsboro to Leesburg. Our present march will be toward Snickersville.

Monday, July 20th: Marched at 7 o'clock, in the rear as before; road very rocky, muddy, and crooked. Men and teams were obliged to find new paths through fields and woods. In an hour or so, ran against the trains of the 2nd Corps and halted for several hours. Day very hot and sultry.

At 2.30 P.M. marched again. Passed through Woodgrove, a village of half a dozen houses, and struck the Leesburg Pike about four miles from Snickersville. Encamped in the vicinity of Snickersville at 6.30 P.M.

This village is just in the mouth of Snicker's Pass through the Blue Ridge. It is the main route to Winchester from Washington.

You may remember that I marched my division up to the pass on the other side just before the battle of Winchester, and was obliged to go back and go through Jackson up the Shenandoah Valley. Years ago I passed over this same route from Berryville to Washington. It was before the days of pikes in this section. I found the most execrable roads, such as we came over yesterday; roads in which small mountain streams find their courses, making an alternation of rocks and mud as the nature of the soil changes. Roads are never repaired in this state, except the pikes.

It is now 9 o'clock A.M. and we have as yet no order to march today. Our destination was supposed to be near Warrenton. What the grand program is, I cannot say, but if it be another "onward to Richmond" we shall make another failure, simply because our army is still outnumbered by the Rebel army under Lee. He is constantly falling back on reinforcements and his base of supplies. We are moving away from both and daily decreasing in numbers. Besides, as an invading army, we must almost of necessity attack, and the odds are always greatly against the attacking party in two armies like those now opposed. We have, I hear, received some reinforcements, not as many as we lost men at Gettysburg, nor are they the same hardened troops, but rather of that kind which have been enervated by garrison life on the sea-coast. These long and daily marches will break them down in spirits and strength.

I see that our real strength at Gettysburg is greatly exaggerated in the public prints. I have no doubt the public generally think that our army wears longer than a railroad track, with not half the wear and tear! It never takes into account the fact that this army has lost nearly 40,000 men by expiration of term of service within the past two months. That in the same time at least 40,000 have been put "hors de combat" in battle and engagements, and that sickness and intercessions of friends are continually draining our ranks. It is a fact, I know, that at Gettysburg we had less than 60,000 fighting men. The lowest estimation of the enemy's force was 85,000, and from that to 120,000. I think they crossed the Potomac with at least 90,000 men, and they lost in killed and wounded, prisoners and deserters, at least 40,000, an expensive invasion, from which they cannot soon recover. It vexes us here, however, to see the constant disposition of people at home to overstate our numbers.[1] There never was a better army, because from long service and few recruits we are hardened down to the very sublimation of muscle, health, and endurance. The men can march twenty-five to thirty miles a day with sixty pounds—if necessary. They seldom grumble, and come to camp after a hard day's march with jokes and songs. They are absolutely without fear, and if ordered forward as skirmishers against entrenchments they go with cheerfulness and generally cracking jokes. Such an army can only be made by long service and exposure in the field and at a great loss of original numbers.

If recruits had been constantly sent to old regiments they would have [been] assimilated, in a good measure, to these old soldiers, and in a short time caught their spirit and daring. It is wonderful how soon a recruit becomes a good soldier when placed amongst old troops. Our government should never have relaxed for a minute its recruiting. It takes a great effort to keep a large army from decreasing, and it can be kept fully efficient only by constant additions. When regiments fall below a certain number their efficiency is greatly destroyed. The details and daily-duty men oppress the soldier, and their thin ranks discourage and dishearten him. But enough of this!

I hope a new policy is inaugurated of filling up old regiments who have experienced officers with the new drafted men, and that our armies will never again be permitted to lose half their men in the beginning of a campaign, and at a moment when the enemy has just filled his ranks with hordes of conscripts.

Love to all,

Your Affectionate Father,
A.S.W.

◈

STILL FOLLOWING GENERAL LEE

Camp near Warrenton Junction,
July 27, 1863.

My Dear Daughters:

I sent you my journalizings from Snickersville up to the 21st inst., I think. If the mail escaped the guerrillas, who watched our flanks and rear pretty closely, you have received the package before this.

We remained at Snickersville two days, expecting to move every hour and therefore uncomfortably packed up, ready for a start. We were encamped near the mouth of the pass over the Blue Ridge. Some of the officers went up the mountain ridge and found a splendid view of the Shenandoah Valley, embracing Winchester, Martinsburg, Front Royal, Berryville, and other towns of the valley. A sight of the Rebel camps and their moving columns and trains was also had.

On account of the repeated annoyances of the guerrilla bands, firing at our men from houses or their vicinity, we sent out scouting or patrolling parties to sweep in all cattle, horses, and forage that could be found. The country was pretty well cleaned out before, and our gleanings were of a poor character. Lame and worn-out horses, poor cattle, and mixed wheat, corn, and oats. But the gatherings were followed by all sorts of people begging for the return of horses and cattle, as the last left them to carry on their farms. Women (all widows, by their own accounts) were generally successful, as they gave piteous stories of their necessities. The men in some cases were handed over to the provost guard to be carried on a few days. They were generally in concert with these roving guerrilla bands, although they swore to entire ignorance of anything of the kind.

July 23rd: My division marched at 6 o'clock under orders to encamp at Paris, which is in the entrance to Ashby's Gap. These gaps, you know, are low places in the mountain range through which roads have been made. They are generally deep gullies or ravines cut by the passage of small streams or rivers; sometimes simply low depressions in the mountain. They occur in the Blue Ridge Range at pretty regular intervals, commencing within a short distance of Harpers Ferry in the following order, southward: Vestal, Hammond, Gregory's, Snicker's, Ashby's, Manassas, Chester, Thornton's, Swift, etc. If you have Lloyd's official map you can follow our lines of march pretty accurately, though the roads and relative positions of villages are by no means correctly laid down. For general purposes and for names of small places it is the best map you can get.

Our first halt today was near Upperville, a small village on the stone pike which runs through Ashby's Gap to Fairfax Court House and Alexandria. I halted here for several hours to avoid the heat of the day, myself and staff taking a nap under the shady oaks of a Mrs. Fitzhugh's lawn. It was a beautiful broad lawn of a very dilapidated old Virginia residence. Mrs. Fitzhugh was in great distress about the vegetables of her small garden, which I protected by a guard. Several grown daughters took observation of us from a rickety old stoop of the decayed mansion.

I moved on toward Paris at 3 o'clock, and when about half way to what I supposed would be my night halt, up came an order to counter-march through Upperville to Piedmont, and thence to Markham's Station on Manassas Gap, fifteen miles distant. I had already marched nearly fifteen miles in a very hot day. The order was not a pleasant one, but there was no appeal. I countermarched the whole command, in-fantry, artillery, ambulances, and ammunition trains, leaving the sup-ply train to follow the 2nd Division, which was going by the way of Paris. We had a pike road all the way to Piedmont, but a terrible one for the men as it was covered all the way with small boulders and sharp stones which cut their feet badly. As the side of the road every few rods was springy and miry, I was obliged to keep the stone pike.

About sundown we reached Piedmont, an abandoned railroad station with two or three ruined buildings. There was nobody about to give us information as to the route beyond, but after some delay one of my staff found the residence of a Mr. Marshall (who said he was a son of the late Chief Justice Marshall) from whom we got information as to the road to Somerset Mills, one of the designated points of my march.[2]

We found this road very bad. At its outset it ran along the bed of a creek, which recent rains had overflowed. It was very rocky and full of deep holes. Dusk had come pretty deep, and the very small crescent of a moon helped us but little. We splashed along this dismal way, wind-ing about in great uncertainty as to whether we were on the road or not, the troops going along the fields as much as practicable. After much labor the head of the column reached Somerset Mills. Regiments straggled in, having lost connection in the woods. It was 10:30 o'clock. There was just moon enough to find a campground. I massed the brigades in the field and having traveled twenty-five miles in the most sultry of temperatures I ordered a bivouac and reveille at 3 o'clock. I put myself on my rubber poncho under a thick sour apple tree with my saddle for a pillow and was asleep in five minutes.

July 24th: Reveille at 2:30 o'clock and marched at about 3:30, as soon as light showed me the road down a deep muddy ravine on toward Markham's. These Virginia roads wind about in all directions; seem to be the chance paths of farms connected by lanes; never repaired; and all the little brooks flow into and along them, cutting out gullies and forming immense mud holes. It is incredible that heavy loaded wagons get over them. The country is not well cultivated, though capable of high cultivation for the most part. The fields now are covered with the largest kind of blackberries, both the vine and the bush kind. We have been surfeited with them. For miles and miles in every day's march since crossing the Potomac the fields on both sides of the road have been, at every halt, covered with men gathering these berries. Before crossing the Potomac, we had feasts of all kinds of cherries. Our orderlies would break off limbs loaded with the most luscious of this fruit, which we ate as we marched along.

We halted at Markham's to issue rations to the troops. The trains which we overtook at Somerset Mills last night had passed on to this point. I found Capts. Whittlesey and Beman (who remain with supply trains) still in bed. They have comparatively easy times in these active campaigns. I went ahead and halted for the troops at a small church in front of Gen. Meade's headquarters. It was full of wounded cavalrymen from a skirmish yesterday. Now and then a gun boomed out of the mountain gap in our front, and it was generally understood that a strong attack was to be made by the 3rd Corps, which our corps was to support. Gens. Meade and Slocum had gone in advance.

I took a long nap and was awakened by a staff officer, with orders to march to White Plains via Rectortown. Took a road to the right, which led below the railroad at Piedmont, to Rectortown. Roads badly blocked by trains of three or four corps, all fighting for the right of way.

THE UNION RETREAT AT BALL'S BLUFF, OCTOBER 21, 1861
Reproduced from a sketch in *The London Illustrated News*, November 23, 1861.

CHARGE OF THE FIFTEENTH MASSACHUSETTS REGIMENT AT BALL'S BLUFF, OCTOBER 21, 1861
Reproduced from a sketch in *The London Illustrated News*, November 23, 1861. The accompanying article states that most of the officers of the regiment were students of Harvard College, whose conduct was "most praiseworthy."

An "incident" in the life of General Banks' Division in western Maryland. Reproduced from a sketch in Frank Leslie's *The American Soldier in the Civil War.*

MARCHING UNDER DIFFICULTIES

Reproduced from a sketch in *The London Illustrated News,* July 13, 1861. The accompanying article describes the tactics of the Secessionists in waylaying Union sentries and officers and mentions "our special artist" accompanied the party on the night when the incident illustrated occurred.

"ALL QUIET ALONG THE POTOMAC TONIGHT"

"CONTRABAND OF WAR" IN VIRGINIA

Slaves seeking refuge in the Union Army. Reproduced from a sketch by "our special artist" in *The London Illustrated News,* July 27, 1861.

Got bread and milk at the "house of a widow" in Rectortown. Bad roads to that point; better between Rectortown and White Plains. It was 10:30 o'clock when the head of my column reached the cross-roads from Salem to White Plains, [two and] one-half miles distant from the latter place.[3] The multitudinous mountain streams had all disappeared, and for hours my men were without water. Found a little stream and good spring at this point and bivouacked for the night, sleeping again under an apple tree, very soundly and very nicely. Marched today twenty miles, making forty-five miles in two hot days for my troops, over all sorts of roads from stony pikes to water courses, and fording lots of small streams.

July 25th: Made a late start, as my staff officer reported that corps headquarters had not arrived at White Plains and I had no orders. Went forward, however, to relieve a brigade of the 6th Corps (Gen. Russell) at the railroad depot. Halted on a broad plain near the village, forming two lines and breaking into column by the right of companies, the usual formation for camping. The men had their shelter tents up at once, supposing we were camped for the day.

Gen. Slocum came up in an hour or so and ordered me to move in my own time through Thoroughfare Gap to Haymarket, enroute for Warrenton Junction! I let the men remain quiet until 1 o'clock; sounded the "generale," a signal to strike tents and prepare for march. It was a sunny, hot day and over acres of ground covered in regular streets by the little white shelter tents you could hardly see a man, but when the drum corps on the right rolled out the "generale" the fields swarmed like a bee-hive with the "blue jackets" in a confused mass of moving humanity.[4] Soon the "assembly" is beaten and that confused and restless mass suddenly forms in regular columns. The acres of white tents have disappeared and motionless columns of men stand in their places. You hear the confused murmur of the roll calls and the responses of the men. Then comes the beat of "to the colors" and those columns wheel into two long lines and the head of it begins to stretch out over the fields towards the route of march, preceded by the colors of the different brigade commanders. In fifteen minutes this city of canvas has disappeared and is moving away as if by a magical power.

So in halting: The order of camp depends upon the space and nature of the ground. Sometimes in masses, sometimes in long lines, sometimes in a front line of battle, with a second line in column. Riding ahead or sending a staff officer, the order of encampment is determined and notice sent to the commanders of brigades. The formation is taken up without delay or confusion, and before you could fancy so many men could be put in position, you will see the little canvas tents formed in regular order and the fires built and suppers cooking. The practice of two years has taught the economy of time and the way to do it.

After leaving White Plains we found a tolerable country road to Thoroughfare Gap, a deep and famous pass through the Bull Run Range. It was through this gap that Lee sent most of his army last summer before the second battle of Bull Run. A stream called Broad Run, has its headwaters north of this gap and tumbles through it in a very tumultuous way. It is a very narrow pass and one cannot help wondering why Ricketts with his division of McDowell's corps did not hold Longstreet in check, when sent there last summer. Had he done so, Jackson's famous corps would have been destroyed. On the east side of the gap, at the base of very steep bluffs, is a considerable group of deserted stone houses and a very large mill, windowless and floorless, several stories high. I believe it was intended for a cotton mill. The road from the gap to Haymarket is a good pike, but the level, fine-looking country is wholly abandoned. We did not see one cultivated farm nor an inhabited dwelling. Even the fences have pretty nearly disappeared.

I encamped near where the village of Haymarket once stood, of which nothing is now left but chimney stacks. The houses were all burned last summer by Sigel's corps in a belief that one of our soldiers had been murdered in the village. On investigation, however, it turned out that the bloody clothes found were those of one of our cavalrymen, mortally wounded in a skirmish, who had been kindly cared for by the people whose houses were burned and who came near being hung by the infuriated soldiers. Such is one of the phases of war. March today, thirteen miles.

Sunday, July 26th: Marched at 6 o'clock via Greenwich, crossing the Warrenton pike two miles below. As we approached Greenwich a church bell rang. It was a sound we had not heard for a long time. The people did not know we were near, and stopped the bell at once. They seemed to fear that we would think it a signal for the Rebels. A very healthy and gentlemanly Englishman has a splendid country place here. As I was halting at one of his tenant houses he came out and invited me to his house, introducing me to his stout and very ladylike wife. On the gate post of his grounds he had a large placard, "This is the property of an Englishman and protected by safeguard," which safeguard he showed me and requested a guard, all which was furnished while my troops were passing. This Englishman was a cotton broker for several large Swiss and French factories, residing in the winter in Savannah and in the summer here. His name is Green. As few of our troops have been this way before, the people were both curious and agitated. I saw a good many female faces peering out of Mr. Green's windows, and Mr. Green was very short of breath when he introduced himself. However, he knew several officers of my acquaintance, had been a good deal in New York and in the North, and was very pleasant, setting out his good things with capital whiskey and ice water! Altogether I was sorry I could not stay longer with Mr. Green.

We reached Catlett's Station on the railroad. Here the whistle of the cars sounded like the tones of civilized life again and we found a newspaper, after a week's fasting. Two miles beyond Catlett's in a large open plain, almost surrounded by woods, we encamped about 4 P.M., from which I am at present writing. It is just south of Cedar Run. Good water is scarce, though we have contrived to find two or three tolerable springs. Two other corps (the 1st and 11th) are at Warrenton Junction, just beyond us. The 6th is at Warrenton. I know nothing of the others. Our march today was fifteen miles. The 2nd Division, which we have not seen since leaving Snickersville, arrived about dark and encamped opposite us.

We are now on our last summer's route of retreat under Pope. The face of the country has much improved in greenness and freshness, as the recent rains and the absence of troops have brought out the grass. Last summer everything was dry and dusty and desolate. There are no inhabitants about here now, but what with green, fresh foliage and herbage and the absence of dead mules and horses and general nastiness, things certainly look better than they did then. The affairs of the country look better, too, I think, though they ought to be much better than they are. But why complain? It is easier to grumble than it is to submit

245

with confidence and good nature. It is hard work, sometimes, to convince oneself that affairs are not most bunglingly conducted, and yet how few of us are on the proper standpoint to judge the best how things can be or ought to be conducted.

I will continue my journal from this point if we stay here, as I hope, a day or so. My men greatly need rest. They have been marched now for nearly six weeks, much exposed, up nights, and always on the march as early as 2:30 or 3 o'clock. It surprises me, often, how they stand it, carrying, as they do, over sixty pounds weight and marching over roads of the roughest and rockiest kind. But they do it, day after day, in the old regiments without a single man falling out. At the end of the two days' march of forty-five miles over the hardest roads, of the old regiments three men was the highest number reported as stragglers, and it is very probable that they were sore-footed or fell asleep on a halt, without waking.

But I must close for the day.

Your Affectionate Father,
A.S.W.

◈

Near Catlett's Station, July 30, 1863.

My Dear Daughter:

We have been here three days but I really have not gathered strength or resolution enough to do much letter writing, and now at 10 o'clock at night comes an order to march at 6 o'clock in the morning. I have just time to acknowledge yours of the 25th and to endorse a check for $100 as a birthday gift. After using what you need you can give the rest to Uncle Lew, as your trustee.

We march to Kelly's Ford, where we crossed in April last, and from there I know not where. My health is perfect, but I am somewhat fagged by six weeks' marching and by sleepless, or nearly sleepless, nights. This sleeping under a "sour apple tree" and being roused at 3 o'clock is not pleasant nor conducive to strong nerves and bright spirits. Love to Rene and all. I'll write you both from Kelly's if I have time.

I suppose some great event is in preparation. I hope it may not prove a repetition of my last summer's campaign on the Rappahannock. I cannot see the policy of our movement just now, but others have a higher standpoint and a broader view, and of course are better judges. We shall see!

Your Affectionate Father,
A.S.W.

❖

BACK AT THE RAPPAHANNOCK

Camp at Kelly's Ford, Va.,
Aug. 6th, 1863.

My dear Daughters:

I wrote you last from Warrenton Junction and enclosed a draft to Minnie for a birthday gift of $100, all of which I hope was duly received.

We left Warrenton Junction Friday, July 31st, marching at 6 o'clock A.M. via Elk River or Elkton and Morrisville to this point, a march of twenty miles on a very hot day. The roads were unusually good for Virginia, but the country poorly cultivated and thinly settled, as it has been since we crossed the Bull Run Mountains. We halted near Elkton for a long rest, and I rode over to a very antique-looking brick house to learn its history. I found it full of Negroes, dozens of which were children of all ages. It was a farm of about 900 acres formerly owned by a Mrs. Blackwell, who, dying a few years since, gave all her Negroes their freedom and the farm for their support. A half dozen or more families live in the family mansion and others are scattered over the estate. The land seems to be good, much of it lying along Elk River, but it is uncultivated except a small patch about the house, in corn, and the premises were sadly dilapidated.

I had a long talk with a very old Negress, who told me all about the family, but could not explain why so many Negroes free could not better cultivate. She insisted they were all fond of work, for their 'Missus' had brought them up to that. A brother of Mrs. Blackwell, a Mr. Fox of Foxville, above this, made the same disposition of his slaves and his estate. He had over 100 Negroes. It would be an interesting subject to look into. I should like to know how these communities of freed Negroes get along, where they have a large property left them. The outside appearances at Mrs. Blackwell's were not very creditable to this colony.

At Morrisville we passed the 2nd Corps. I saw Capt. Smith (formerly of Detroit) of the 7th Michigan Regiment. He is inspector general on the division staff. I have met him several times before. At Snicker's he came up several miles to call upon me. He did not reach the ford here until dark. The moon was just rising and gave light enough to make long shadows of woods and hills, quite a strange look to familiar localities. We encamped here one night last spring on our march to Chancellorsville, and crossed the Rappahannock at the very spot we have laid the present pontoon bridge. It is directly at the mouth of Marsh Run, on all the maps, which at its mouth is nearly as broad and deep as the Rappahannock.

The 2nd Division had the lead today and arrived before us. They were just crossing a regiment in the pontoon boats to cover the laying of the bridge. I was on a slope of ground in the angle between Marsh River and the river. It was reported that only two Rebel pickets had been seen. We supposed all was quiet, and would be, and I was forming my division by the moon-light on the side hill which slopes towards the south bank. All at once quite a volley of musketry belched from the opposite side of the river. The 2nd Division had a regiment in line and they opened in return and for a few minutes we had quite a lively fusillade. The low grounds lay in the shadow of the high hills on the north and east, and though we heard the whiz of the balls, nobody was hurt, nor did my regiments stop their movements into line for bivouac.

In ten minutes the whole hillside was blazing with the countless campfires for cooking coffee. As it was only a Reb. picket of twenty or thirty men, they did not stop to molest us, after one volley. But the cool and unconcerned way in which my troops took the affair, hardly asking what it meant, proves how strangely we get accustomed to all kinds of life of exposure and danger. If such a volley had been fired before our troops had seen the smoke of battle, it would have created an intense excitement, and in the night, as it was, probably great confusion. As it was, not a man moved nor halted to wonder even.

Saturday, August 1st: My division crossed the Rappahannock this morning at daylight, relieving five regiments of the 2nd Division bivouacked close to the stream. I deployed as skirmishers six regiments down and up the river and to the front to clear away the Rebel cavalry which showed itself here and there. We had some skirmish firing but no resistance. The day was intensely hot by 9 o'clock. I was obliged to ride along my whole extended front from the river above the ford, in a circle, to the river below the ford, a distance of several miles. I was ordered to halt my line and hold all this ground by a picket line. I got back to a small shaded hill near the center of my broad circuit well heated and was delighted to find that some of my staff had discovered an ice-house belonging to Mr. Kelly, with real ice in it! Was it not luxurious! Just fancy a day without a breath of breeze and the thermometer about ninety after a long ride, to find yourself most unexpectedly in possession of ice, somewhere where one had not even dreamed of the luxury. I immediately ordered a guard over the ice-house, the contents to be delivered on my order.

Pitched two tents for our headquarters near the small village of Kellysville, which is just above the ford. The Kellys, father and son (seventy and fifty years old) are rank old Rebels and the owners of great acres and vast property hereabouts. At the village is a large brick flouring mill and a woolen factory, both much dilapidated by nonuse for two years. They had over a hundred slaves on the breaking out of the war, most of which they have sent South. One old Negro, whose wife (now dead) was a slave of Kelly's, came in to visit his children, but he found that Kelly had sent them all off last week. The old man's voice was husky as he told me his story. I did not feel very bad that our soldiers had pillaged and destroyed most of Kelly's property and used his hay and grain. The younger Kelly, who looked very seedy and wore a very shocking, bad, white hat, pestered me greatly by his complaints. Today we gathered up all his cattle and horses we could find (some fifty of the former) and sent them to our commissary.

Sunday, August 2nd: Another very hot day. The south side of the Rappahannock here is a triangular shaped plain, a mile or so deep and perhaps three-quarters of a mile broad at its base, enclosed in thick woods. It is perfectly commanded by high hills which come almost to the riverbank on the north side. Our artillery is placed on these hills. Near the river on the south side the land is quite low and in places marshy. The land rises gently as it recedes from the river. Of course the ford and

the approaches to it are perfectly commanded from the north side, and
to hold it on the south requires a large picket force and an encampment
in the hottest and most unhealthy locations. So we have been ordered
back to the north bank. I removed the six regiments which have been
frying under their little shelter tents to the north side, and after dusk
the six regiments on picket quietly withdrew and we all took up a much
pleasanter camp ground. The 2nd Division has gone below to Ellis'
Ford, and our corps now pickets the river from Wheatley's (a mile
and a half above, where we connect with the 1st Corps) to below Ellis'
Ford, seven or eight miles. I have all my headquarters tents pitched and
my camp bed, a luxury I seldom enjoy nowadays. The river from
Wheatley's to the ford here is rocky and rapid, giving an immense
water power. There was formerly a canal around the rapids built by
the state for slack water navigation, but its locks are all decayed and
broken in. Part of the canal is still full of water and used as mill races.

We have been figuring up our month's work to make out the
monthly report and find that we have marched, last month, eighteen
days; engaged in skirmishing and battles five; in camp, but mostly
under arms or packed for march, eight days. Since leaving Stafford
Court House on June 13th we have marched over 440 miles, to say
nothing of entrenching work, side marches, and small movements. Besides this, we are often up until 11 or 12, and must be around again by
3 o'clock and our men have heavy picket duty which keeps 300 to 400
without sleep after long marches. None but hardened troops could stand
this. Their cheerfulness under it is wonderful.

Monday, August 3rd: In withdrawing to this side last night I
ordered the provost to bring off the younger Kelly and turn him over
to the corps provost guard. He has recently been to Richmond and
is a great scamp, I think. My pickets brought over a Negro slave, belonging to a Mr. James ("Jeemes" he pronounced it). His wife is a
slave of Kelly's and he had the usual Sunday pass to visit two of his
children at Kellysville. His wife and three other children have been sent
away by Kelly. The man stays on account of his wife. He was greatly
alarmed when first brought to me, for some reason or other, but I was
interested in his talk and kept him at it till he told the whole family
history of the Kellys and the "Jeemes." Two of his "young masters"
had been at home, hid in the woods, all the while we were over the

river. He thought they were all very tired of the war. They didn't talk much before the slaves, but he contrived occasionally to overhear what his "Massas" said to other officers. Old Kelly has but one arm. The other was lost by erysipelas caused by a wound on the hand received in giving a slave woman a blow in the mouth!

Righteous retribution!

The old Negro, who was of very pious temperament, kept me entertained by his talk until midnight, every now and then exclaiming, "Why de good Lord, Massa, I'ze had passes to see my chillun every Sunday for years and always back before breakfast, Monday morning. Now I'm here, and de Missus will be mighty anxious." I kept the Negro all night, but let him off in the morning after breakfast, with advice that he leave "Massa Jeemes" at the first chance, but he replied that his wife was the most precious thing to him in this life and he couldn't go without her and the children. When I suggested that his wife might have been sold south by Kelly, he turned away his head, with evident emotion, and after a while replied, "I is feared that, Massa, a long time, but I hope"; and he made some sensible remarks about the uncertainty of his future if he went amongst strangers, and though his "Massa" was only tolerable, he might be worse off elsewhere. There is a wonderful amount of strong sense in many of these uneducated Negroes.

Last evening, indeed all day yesterday, there was a severe cannonading not over five miles away toward Culpeper. It receded at first and then returned until we could hear the screech of the shell and the volleys of musketry. At one time I thought it would reach us and made some preparations for it. It stopped about dark near Brandy Station, five miles away. You will see an account of it in the papers. Deserters and contrabands say that Lee and most of his army is around Culpeper Court House, fourteen miles distant.

What the purpose of our commander is I cannot guess. We keep down the pontoon bridge and have built a rifle pit (very strong) on the opposite bank and have strong ones on this side and guard it vigilantly. We are also replacing the old permanent bridge over Marsh Run by a new one. Matters look like a further advance. If we do, we must attack Lee in his chosen position. Our reinforcements of troops never in action do not yet replace our losses in the recent campaign, and we have as yet no conscripts. People at home would be surprised if they knew how small some of our largest corps have become. Death, wounds, sickness, and discharges are rapidly reducing us to a skeleton army. We must be reinforced or the Army of the Potomac will be of the things that were. If we had 50,000 more men (and there is that number on the Peninsula, at Suffolk, and North Carolina, better here) we could, I think, finish Lee's army and the war within two months. . . .

Tuesday, August 4th: Rode with Gen. Ruger up the river to the right of our line and then to the left, fixing points for strong guards and rifle pits and other earthworks. I don't think I have said much of Gen. Ruger, though he is one of my especial favorites—commander of the 3rd Brigade. He is as modest as a girl but of the most thorough and sterling character. He graduated at the head of his class at West Point, was in the engineers for a while, resigned and went to Wisconsin, and came out lieutenant colonel of the 3rd Wisconsin Regiment. He was promoted last winter at the same time Knipe was. Ruger spends half his time with me.[5]

Did I tell you that Knipe, who has been absent since the Chancellorsville campaign, returned while we were at Warrenton Junction? He has been in command of the militia in Pennsylvania part of the time and tells most amusing stories of the crack New York regiments which were under his command. His health is not good. Gen. Jackson, who commanded the 2nd Brigade, and whose leg was broken before our Chancellorsville campaign, has not yet returned. He has got as far back as Washington. His aide was here and said the general would be up soon.

We have had a furious hot day and my long ride was a fiery one.

Wednesday, 5th: Another hot day, and I spent it under the shade trees in front of my tent. It was barely tolerable in the shade. Paymaster Freeman arrived about noon to pay off part of my division.

Thursday, 6th: National Thanksgiving day, which don't seem to be very generally observed.[6] The regiment directly in my front had some kind of service toward evening. I heard a man holding forth in regular Methodistical roar, and psalm singing and hallooing prayers. There was a considerable confusion of tongues, for the adjoining regiments were singing patriotic songs with uproarious choruses, and the drums of other regiments were beating the adjutant's call for dress parade. The day was very hot again, and I see by the New York papers, which we get now on the second day, that deaths by sunstroke have been large.

I have lost my favorite medical director, Dr. Chapel. He received an order as we were leaving Warrenton Junction to report to Gen. French as medical director of the 3rd Corps. It is a promotion, but the doctor left us with regret and was sorry for what most would have rejoiced at. He has been with us over a year and is, I think, one of the best surgeons and physicians I have ever met and withal a most agreeable and pleasant companion. I feel sad to lose such a staff officer. Dr. Love[?], of the 13th New Jersey Volunteers has been temporarily sent in his place.

I sent sometime ago for Minnie a melanotype group of officers and ladies taken at Stafford Court House and previous to that I sent a similar copy to Rene at Philadelphia. Neither of you have made allusions to them, and I fear they have miscarried. The one sent to Minnie was a laughing scene and we all thought very funny. . . .

Your Affectionate Father,
A.S.W.

❖

FAMILY AND PERSONAL GOSSIP

Kelly's Ford, Va.,
Aug. 31st, 1863.

My Dear Daughter: [7]

I have been rather dilatory in writing and can hardly remember the date of my last letter; but I remember that I was more than two weeks without hearing from you or Rene and that I wrote a short note of complaint. However, I believe your last letter sufficiently explains the delay. It was really too hot for work; but the weather is cooler here now.

I liked the photographs you sent much and it was rather curious that I was just then regretting that I had not asked you to have your photograph taken on your birthday. The full-faced is most liked, though it is not easy to decide. Capt. Pittman has seized upon the full face and several gentlemen have asked for them. Capt. Whittlesey especially wonders you don't send him one. So you'd better do it and send me a half dozen. I don't think your picture shows much change; a little [more] maturity, but I suppose when I get to see you I shall find a tall young lady! [8]

That reminds me that we have very stringent orders about leaves, and must not apply except on a surgeon's certificate of illness, though I judge from the number of general officers absent that the rule is not obeyed strictly. I have been waiting for Gen. Slocum to get off and back before I tried my chance. He has just got twelve days leave and went day before yesterday. I fear it will be too late for me when he gets back. Such has been my luck before. However, I shall try, if we do not get moving orders before.

Our daily routine is so void of interest that I can find hardly enough to make a readable letter. I have one agreeable piece of intelligence. One of my staff has just heard of the birth of a daughter, and he has named it "Minnie Williams Whitney." She is the first daughter of Capt. Whitney, 5th Connecticut Volunteers and provost marshal on my staff. The namesake was born on the 17th of August. You'll have to get up some present for the namesake. I have seen a photograph of the mother, which is beautiful. The father is a most gallant, energetic, and excellent officer, and an especial favorite of mine. So probably your namesake will combine many qualities. I hope she may prove as good a daughter as you have. I, also, have a namesake, for about the same day there was born unto Gen. Knipe a son, which he has named Alpheus Williams Knipe! So you see I have some gift making to do.

Capt. Wilkins has arrived but has sent in his resignation on account of his lameness. I suppose Capt. Pittman will take his place permanently.

Uncle Will Rumsey has a sutlership of one of our regiments. He comes up from Washington once a week or so. He brought up little Will the last time. Henry Colt spent Sunday with me a week ago. He is quartermaster of the 104th New York, in the 1st Corps, about four miles away. I send you photographs of three of my staff. The doctor is the new medical director in place of Dr. Chapel, promoted to a corps. Tell Rene I will write her in a day or so. I shall send the button you want and the Antietam bullets and some papers for safekeeping by Capt. Wilkins.

Your Affectionate Father,
A.S.W.

PROMOTIONS IN THE ARMY

Kelly's Ford, Sept. 4th, 1863.

My Dear Daughter:

I wrote you by Capt. Wilkins and sent a package of papers for safe-keeping. We were all sorry to have the captain leave us. He is exceedingly companionable and very popular as adjutant general with the subordinate officers, with whom he is officially brought much in contact. He has his peculiarities but is an admirable officer in the office, very systematic and thorough. The evening before he left we gave him quite an entertainment, at which the general and field officers "assisted." It was quite the most considerable set-out I have seen in camp. We even had watermelons!

There was a great deal of speech-making, most of which curiously and unexpectedly grew out of my own case on non-promotion. I was rather surprised to find how much feeling there was in my behalf. As a sequel to it all, the officers of the division held a meeting last night and appointed a committee to draw up a memorial to the President to be signed by every officer. I have no idea it will accomplish anything. Such a fellow as Crawford,[9] who skulked at Antietam and knows no more of military than that piebald dog I used to own, will be promoted before I am, simply because he has the impudence and falsehood of the devil, knows well the Secretary of War, is from Pennsylvania, and gives great dinners which he never pays for! He got a small puncture—self-inflicted, I think—(he was an assistant surgeon formerly) at Antietam and he nursed it so vigorously that he stayed away over six months, most of the time in Washington having small puffs prepared for the newspapers. He has recently got assigned to the Pennsylvania reserves and had a big time presenting a sword to Gen. Meade, for his own glorification. These are the fellows that get promotion. . . .

[*The concluding portion is missing.*]

❖

FOREIGN VISITORS AND MILITARY EXECUTIONS

Rapidan River, Raccoon Ford, Va., Sept. 20, 1863.
My Dear Daughter:

I received your letter of 12th inst. (no. 20) on the march to this place. It was indeed a nice long, agreeable letter and very acceptable. I answer it on top of a box, as we are all packed for a moment's move. . . . My command left our camp at Kelly's Ford Wednesday last (16th) and marched to Stevensburg. I pitched my tents in the front yard of a dilapidated F.F.V., who seemed very glad to have me about as a protector. He had a very smart and chatty daughter, to whom some of my staff made themselves very agreeable. I did not make her acquaintance, having absolutely lost all charms for maid or widow.

The cavalry crossed the Rappahannock the day before us and drove the Rebel cavalry beyond Culpeper. From Stevensburg I could see the line of the Orange Railroad down which we retreated from Culpeper last year. The village (a dozen houses or so) is on quite a hill, and the country around is very flat. As we encamped in the afternoon, the 1st Corps was on our right, but nothing on our left. We were the left of the whole army. On Thursday morning (5 o'clock) we marched for this ford. The morning was very foggy, luckily for us, for we struck the Rapidan and marched a mile or so under the Rebel batteries, not 500 yards distant. At length I found out our position from some cavalry and moved my troops into the woods before the enemy found out we were near them.

The whole line of country hereabout is very flat, while the opposite side is a series of high hills rising one above the other from the river bank. It is all fortified and the Rebs. are constantly digging on every hillside and crest. They have all the advantage, especially as a quite high mountain back of them serves as a lookout upon all our positions. Our picket line has been constantly fired upon and is exposed for hundreds of yards this side of the river. It took me all day Thursday, after reaching this, to get my pickets out to relieve the cavalry pickets. Every man who showed his head was sure to be a mark, and in some parts of the line I was obliged to wait until after dark before I could send forward my detail. In the meantime, the heavens opened on us in a terrific storm, which pelted us sadly. I was all day in the saddle and at night pitched my tent in the edge of the woods and by the advantage of some straw for a bed got a good sleep.

Friday (18th) was an equinoctial day, high wind and cold rain, a regular gale, which howled through the woods and poured in torrents. It cleared up about noon, partially, and I had the unpleasant task of calling out my division to shoot a deserter. It began to pour again in equinoctial torrents as my troops were forming, and the gloom of the weather was in concert with the melancholy duty. I have described for you the shooting at Leesburg. It was the same thing over. The poor fellow sat on his coffin and fell back stone dead at the discharge, like one going to sleep. It was his second desertion and the last after our execution at Leesburg and while marching toward Gettysburg. Of course, he had no hope of escape. I have over twenty conscripts who probably will die the same way.

Saturday, 19th: I rode along the whole of our front. The Rapidan is a very narrow stream, but its high banks are all on the side of the enemy. They are as busy as bees throwing up entrenchments and rifle pits. We count sixteen guns in position on my front from Raccoon Ford up to Somerville Ford, two miles or so. The firing has somewhat subsided, as I order my pickets not to reply unless they try to cross. I rode in plain view and at a fair musket-shot, and nobody fired at me, though I could see lots of officers on their works looking to see what was going on. I had with me two mounted officers, Gen. Knipe and Col. Hanley, 2nd Wisconsin, and two mounted orderlies. As I was riding up the river I heard a tremendous firing in our rear, which I supposed was distant artillery near Stevensburg. I hurried home and found an order for the troops to be under arms and the telegraph, which connects with us from headquarters, was working hard to find out the trouble. At length it was ascertained that the cavalry division at Stevensburg was discharging its pieces in volleys.

Sunday, 20th September: This was my birthday, an event which few of you at home remembered, I think. I was obliged to move camp from the wet woods to an open plain farther in the rear, but as I had received a present of a box of sherry I celebrated in the evening with my staff.

An Austrian captain with seven general staff officers called. He was on a mission to see the Army of the Potomac.

Monday, Tuesday, and Wednesday: Three sunshiny but cool days. We have been constantly packed expecting a movement. Night before last we were ordered to put five days' marching rations in knapsacks with three in haversacks. This indicates a long march away from our wagons. Today Sir Henry Holland, physician to Her Majesty, etc., Col. Townsend, and several staff officers, came to see our corps. I was obliged to unpack my only decent coat and do other things to put myself in a presentable look. Sir Henry is an old man. He remained but a short time, but went down to the front to see the Rebel line. . . .

You seem to have a gay time in Detroit. I have not yet learned how the concert went off. . . . Love to all. I have a good many letters to write and while so many things are on my mind I don't make much headway. The news from Rosecrans looks badly. I have feared that he was going too fast for that country. . . .

Your Affectionate Father,
A.S.W.

❖

LAST LETTER FROM THE ARMY OF THE POTOMAC

Raccoon Ford, Sept. 24, 1863.

My Dear Daughters:

We have just received orders to be ready to move on being relieved by the 1st Corps, I suspect to attack the enemy on the flank. The telegraph will tell you of coming events before this reaches you, but I write a word on the head of a box as it is very uncertain when I can write again. Don't be concerned if you don't hear from me. We are supplied with eight days' rations on the person. Love to all.

Your Affectionate Father,
A.S.W.

1. General Williams' statements, both here and elsewhere, illustrate a common tendency among soldiers to overestimate the strength of their opponents in relation to their own and the contrary tendency among

civilian and political observers to overestimate the strength of one's own army. At Gettysburg, the two opposing armies were fairly evenly matched, Lee having about 70,000 and Meade about 80,000 men. Of course many factors other than mere numbers operate to determine the outcome of a battle or a campaign.

2. The birthplace and boyhood home of John Marshall was in this vicinity. Descendants and collateral relatives of the chief justice lived in northern Fauquier County in the Civil War period. See W. M. Paxton, *The Marshall Family* (Cincinnati, 1885).

3. Salem and White Plains, both in northern Fauquier County, are now called respectively, Marshall and The Plains.

4. The "general," like many army customs, was probably an inheritance from the British army. Mrs. Lydia Bacon, who in 1812 accompanied her husband on the march of the Fourth U.S. Infantry from Boston to Vincennes and back (via Detroit as prisoners of war) recorded the words which accompany the tune: "Don't you hear your general say, 'Strike your tents and march away.' "—"Mrs. Lydia Bacon's Journal, 1811–1812," *Indian Magazine of History*, XL (December 1944), 374.

5. General Thomas H. Ruger, but thirty years of age at this time, ranked number three in the West Point class of 1854. Number one place was held by G. W. Custis Lee, son of General Robert E. Lee, who resigned his army commission on May 2, 1861 to uphold the fortunes of the Southern Confederacy. From 1856 to 1861 Ruger was engaged in the practice of law at Janesville, Wisconsin. In June 1861 he was appointed lieutenant colonel of the Third Wisconsin Infantry and remained in the army thereafter until his retirement in 1897 with the rank of major general.—*Dict. Am. Biog.*

6. On July 15, 1863 President Lincoln issued a proclamation appointing Thursday August 6, 1863 as a day of national thanksgiving of praise and prayers for the recent victories at Gettysburg and Vicksburg. In Detroit, as in the army, very little attention was paid to it, insofar as an examination of the *Free Press* discloses. Acting Mayor Francis B. Phelps issued a brief statement commending the observance to the local citizenry (dated August 5, but not published until August 6), and a thanksgiving service, to which the public was invited, was held in the Christian Church, corner of Jefferson and Beaubien. Meanwhile the Unitarian Society conducted an all-day excursion to Grosse Ile, featured by picnicking ashore and dancing on the vessel. The *Free Press* contains no further mention of the Thanksgiving service at the church.

7. This letter addressed to Minnie is included in the published collection as offering a sample of the domestic details dwelt upon by General

Williams, which, as far as practicable, have been deleted from most of the other letters.

8. He had not seen his daughter since the breaking-up of his family at Detroit upon entering active service two years earlier.

9. General Samuel W. Crawford of Pennsylvania, who entered the U.S. Army as an assistant surgeon in 1851, serving continuously, chiefly in Texas and the Southwest, until the outbreak of the Civil War. In 1860 he was stationed at Fort Sumter, where he commanded a battery during the bombardment of April 1861 which opened the Civil War. Contrary to General Williams' characterization, his wartime service was conspicuously distinguished. See sketches in Appleton's *Cyclopaedia of American Biography* and in *National Cyclopaedia of American Biography* (New York, 1904), XII, 232.

IX

Guarding
the
Railroad

With the Union army pinned in Chattanooga, besieged by General Bragg, and in imminent danger of starvation, some effective rescue measures had to be instituted promptly. The dispatch of 16,000 men from the Army of the Potomac was one such measure. More important, perhaps, was the appointment of General Grant, recently conqueror of Vicksburg, to the command of all military operations in the western theater of war. He promptly replaced Rosecrans, whose military competence seemed to have vanished, by General Thomas, who grimly promised that the army would hold Chattanooga until it starved. Yet starve it must if its line of communication with Nashville and Louisville, whence its supplies were drawn, were to be closed. From Nashville the railroad ran to Bridgeport in northeastern Alabama, distant fifty-five miles southwest from Chattanooga. From this point supplies had to be wagoned to Chattanooga over a shockingly villainous highway which was "strewn with the debris of broken wagons and the carcasses of thousands of starved mules and horses." October 23 witnessed the arrival of General Grant, who immediately approved the opening of a shorter and better route between Bridgeport and Chattanooga. With the more immediate danger of starvation removed, Grant turned his attention to raising the siege of the city, and in the actions of November 23–25 (Chattanooga and Missionary Ridge) General Bragg was defeated and driven in retreat, burning his depots and bridges as he withdrew. Early in March 1864 Grant arrived at Washington to assume his new position as commander of all the Union armies. The difficult task of guarding the railroad line from Nashville southward still remained. To this service General Williams had been assigned upon his transfer to the western theater. His letters depicting his experiences and his observations upon the country and its inhabitants comprise the present section of his correspondence.

REMOVAL TO TENNESSEE

OFFICE OF SUPERINTENDENT
MILITARY RAILROAD
DEPARTMENT OF THE CUMBERLAND

Nashville, Tennessee,
October 5, 1863.

My Dear Daughter:

I am stopped here by a guerrilla raid, which has broken up the track below. My troops are scattered everywhere and our horses and baggage are nowhere that I can hear of. In short, this transportation of large numbers of troops over long lines of different railroads is a tedious and uncertain matter. When my division will get together again in its excellence and unity, such as it was ten days ago on the Rapidan, is more than I can guess.

I wrote you a short note from our camp on the Rapidan on the 24 ult. We had been several days under marching orders and I supposed our destination was against the left flank of the Rebels. Indeed, I had my command under arms before I knew our route lay to the rear. We marched to Brandy Station on the Orange Railroad that afternoon, where we were ordered to turn in all our wagons and public property and prepare to take the railroad cars for Alexandria. Great was the speculation on our destiny and great the bustle and hurry all day Friday. But amidst all I was obliged to shoot a deserter, which [made] the circumstances of our march ten-fold more unpleasant.

Friday night, 25 September, I was ordered to march my command to Bealeton Station north of the Rappahannock. I reached that [place] about daylight and lay there until night waiting [for] cars. I took a train in the night and reached Washington Sunday morning. I was very busy all day, but dined with Maj. Sherman. At night I went as far as the Relay House to superintend my troop trains. I left there Monday morning on the express train, upon which I found Miss Lib Kirby and her cousin Mrs. Pratt, an authoress of some note and wife of an ex-secretary of legation at Paris.[1] Also Gen. Hooker, who took me into his private car and discussed by the hour . . . his military matters. He had been ordered to command the 11th and 12th corps, but Gen. Slocum demurred and sent in his resignation, but the President, I believe, decided to relieve one corps from Hooker's command. I expect that Gen. Slocum talked pretty plain to the President, but of that I can talk to you, not write. At any rate, Gen. Hooker and myself talked on the same subject. I believe you know what I think of Gen. Hooker, a gallant and chivalrous soldier and most agreeable gentleman, but as an army commander his signal failure at Chancellorsville under such advantages as no general officer has a second time will ever prevent any confidence in him as a great commander.

I stopped for the night at Cumberland, a romantic spot where the Alleghanies drop down into the lesser ranges of mountains. A committee called on me proffering a public reception in order to get a speech. I declined peremptorily and they threatened to follow me with a crowd; luckily my troop cars came up, and I escaped.

[*The remainder is missing.*]

❖

GUARDING THE RAILROAD

Decherd, Tenn., Oct. 12, 1863.

My Dear Daughter:

I was very low-spirited after parting from you at Louisville and had a tedious ride to Nashville, which we reached about 7:30 P.M. The country the whole way was without interest or attraction of any kind and seemed poorly cultivated. Perhaps it would have looked better if my feelings had been more joyous. Our reunion was too short for me to get over first impressions. I was really too full to talk; full of joy at seeing you, and full of regret that we were so soon to part, that mixed and conflicting state of the mind that keeps one in constant thought. I was glad, however, to see you for even that short time, after two years' separation.

I found Gen. Slocum and staff at Nashville, but Gen. Knipe and Ruger had gone on. I started to the depot the next morning to take the first train south, but was stopped by news that the Rebel cavalry were south of Murfreesboro and had destroyed a railroad bridge. I remained all day in the depot, but no trains ran and at night I was obliged to go to the hotel again. The next day (Tuesday) I spent the whole day watching the telegraph, receiving all kinds of rumors that the Rebs. were advancing towards Nashville, destroying the railroad as they moved. Toward dusk a train was sent out and we reached Murfreesboro about 10 o'clock without molestation. The town was full, no hotels, no stopping place. Fortunately I took letters from Capt. Irving, formerly of Detroit, to private families and to a quartermaster of the name of Williams, who found us comfortable quarters at the house of a young widow. . . .

I stayed Wednesday and Thursday at Murfreesboro waiting for repairs of the bridge. I was greatly impatient as I was separated from most of my division, which Gen. Butterfield had picked up and was marching up and down in pursuit of Rebel cavalry, which I knew had been chased away beyond Shelbyville by a superior force of our cavalry two or three days before. I left Murfreesboro Friday P.M. about sundown and after a most disagreeable night in a box car, picking up three of my regiments on the way, reached this point the next morning about eight o'clock. I had heard that Rebel cavalry was threatening this place, from which Butterfield had withdrawn all troops, leaving my baggage and Capt. Whittlesey without a guard, or a very small one.

However, I found all safe, except that the mountain tunnel six miles below had been somewhat obstructed by the Rebs. throwing rocks down the shaft. These were soon cleared away. As fortune would have it, a rock had lodged in one of the shafts and when the first train went through with Gen. Butterfield, down it tumbled, without, however, doing damage. Gen. Butterfield imagined the Rebs. were after him and telegraphed a firm order from the first station for watchfulness, etc. I had the whole country around scoured, but found no Rebs., though I am bored to death by incessant stories brought in by citizens that Rebel cavalry is moving to attack such and such points.

This is a monstrous line over which Gen. Rosecrans has to supply his army, over 300 miles of railroad, crossed every few miles by broad streams and valleys and running through and around and across high mountains from this [place] to Chattanooga. The bridge at Bridgeport (where the railroad crosses the Tennessee) has been destroyed and the railroad from that point to near Chattanooga, south of the river, is in Rebel possession. In consequence, all supplies must have land carriage over thirty miles over mountains and on roads of the worst description. This beggars anything we have seen of lines of operations in the Army of the Potomac, and I can't see how the army can be supplied at Chattanooga unless the Rebs. are driven off and the railroad opened in its whole length. Even then, it will be a most insecure line, liable to constant interruptions, and of a length that forbids protection. Even my command is now wholly out of forage and rations, except what I have been able to pick up with four or five wagons. All our transportation was turned in at Bealeton Station and we have received none here, nor do I hear of any.

My horses arrived yesterday. Old Plug Ugly has lost pretty much all his tail. His length is so great that he rubbed at both ends of the car and has bared the bones of his head and his tail, besides having had his neck badly bitten by some indignant horse. He looks worse than after the shell exploded under him at Chancellorsville. He looked at me with most sorrowful eyes on our first meeting. The stallion looks better, though he is badly rubbed on both hips by his two weeks railroad voyage. None of the horses are badly injured, however.

My command extends from Tullahoma south, half way between Cowan and Tantalon, so as to embrace the railroad tunnel which runs through the mountains six miles below this, a distance of twenty-two miles! Of course we can guard only the bridges, tunnels, culverts, water-tanks, etc. Gen. Ruger's brigade is from Tullahoma to Elk River, his headquarters at Tullahoma. Gen. Knipe's brigade extends the rest of the way to Cowan. His headquarters are here. The country about this is not well cultivated and the people who are left look shabby and forlorn. But there is a fine town two or three miles off (Winchester) and the country about it is said to be fertile and well cultivated. It has been pretty well stripped, for Bragg's and Rosecrans' armies have both encamped here. It was near Murfreesboro that the three-days' battle of Stone River or Murfreesboro took place. It was in the same town that Col. Duffield was made a prisoner with most of his regiment.[2] I am anxious to hear of your safe arrival home. Write me all about it and direct at present "Commander 1st Div. 12th A. Corps,

Decherd via Nashville, Tenn." All my staff are well and desire to be remembered. Give my love to all. If things don't move soon I shall apply for leave for twenty days.

Your Affectionate Father,
A.S.W.

❖

Tullahoma, Nov. 11, 1863.

My Dear Daughter:

I wrote Uncle Lew a hasty note yesterday after my return from Bridgeport. . . . I have so many posts now in the ninety miles of railroad I am guarding that my duties are greatly increased at home and away. It is no easy job to travel on this railroad, the way it is managed. The road is in a bad condition and the engines are old and worthless. It is a good day's work to get forty miles. There is a constant struggle to push forward freight cars with supplies for troops in front, but very little judgment is used in putting the road in condition to meet the demands upon it.

I was lucky this time in getting as far as Stevenson (forty-three miles) in one day. I believe I have written you that after leaving Cowan the road begins the ascent of the first Cumberland Range of mountains and passes through the rest of the ridge by a tunnel over half a mile in length. It then descends to the deep valley of Crow Creek, along which, deep down between the high mountain ridges, it follows to Stevenson in the valley or bottom land of the Tennessee River. At this point it unites with the Memphis, Chattanooga and Charleston Railroad and follows the valley of the Tennessee amidst stupendous mountains to Chattanooga.

Gen. Knipe joined our party at Decherd, his headquarters, so we had a quartette of Gen. Slocum, Gen. Knipe, Dr. McNulty, and myself. At Stevenson we found Col. Ross of the 20th Connecticut (whose regiment guards this place) comfortably located in the only decent house there and we were comfortably lodged with him. He had made ready a very stylish bedroom for Mrs. Ross, whom he was anxiously waiting for.

Luckily for us she was denied a pass and we had the benefit of the preparations.

We spent a day at Bridgeport where I have a regiment (123 New York), and where they are re-building a very long railroad bridge over the Tennessee, which was destroyed by the Rebs. in their retreat. The river is very broad here, and is divided into two streams by an island. The bridge makes slow headway as all the lumber is brought from Nashville. I met on my way down several Michigan officers. Amongst others Maj. Wm. Phelps, paymaster, who spoke of seeing you and "Mr. Allen." At Stevenson, Geo. Fellers, who used to keep a grocery store near the oil store, came to see me. He is with the 4th Cavalry, but, with all sutlers, is having a very hard time just now. At Bridgeport the famous Lookout Mountain, now in possession of the Rebs., is in full view, towering high over all the surrounding hills. It must be a grand lookout over the whole country, and I am more than surprised that it should have been given up to the Rebels. It will cost us many lives to regain it.[3] It has already cost some valuable ones to get hold of the valleys at the foot of the mountain.

In my first trip down with my division, when I expected to have been a part of Hooker's advance, I had as companions Capt. Atwell and Lt. Geary of Knapp's Pennsylvania Battery, and I relieved at Anderson a lieutenant colonel of the 111th Pennsylvania Infantry, all of whom were killed in the recent night attack upon Hooker's command. They were attached to the 2nd Division of our corps. It is hard to realize these sudden removals of one's friends, with whom but a few hours before one has talked in health and cheerfulness. But what a long list of them I can recall in this war!

Gen. Greene, whom I think I have spoken of to you, a very warm personal friend, was also badly wounded through the face. He for a while commanded a brigade in my division, and last year was in command of the 2nd Division while we were at Harpers Ferry, and previously at the battle of Antietam. He is a descendant of Gen. Greene of our Revolution. His wound, I hear, is not considered dangerous.[4]

In returning from Bridgeport we were obliged to stop a day at Stevenson where the officers of the 4th Artillery battery gave us an extensive supper. We had oysters and champagne! Just think of that, away down in northern Alabama and over these hard roads! The explanation is, that about fifty purveyors had been ordered away from the front and were all congregated at Stevenson with their unsold goods, and with some they had not been able to get farther toward the main army. It seemed strange, when our soldiers and officers, too, all along the railroad and in front were living on half and one-quarter rations, that oysters and champagne should be abundant at Stevenson. But by bribery and other tricks these sutlers contrive to get transportation often when men are starving for necessary supplies. What an immensity of rascality this war produces or develops!

It makes me sick, sometimes, to hear of the frauds and rascality that are practiced in all departments, often to the suffering and misery of those exposed in the field. These things are found, from the miserable pasted shoes that men pay high prices for to the food they eat. In everything there is proof of contractors' and government agents' fraud and cheating. I think it was Wellington who said that these things could be stopped only by hanging a contractor and inspector every Saturday night! I wish often it could be tried.

I sent you yesterday a few views I found at Stevenson. If I can get more I will send them. I am very comfortably situated now; have a nice cottage for officers and my own private room. The staff are in tents. You will think it strange, but I do not find my large room as comfortable as a tent with a stove. It is more convenient, that is all. . . . How long we shall stay on this railroad no one knows. I rather sigh for the field. I hate this kind of responsible and divided command, and yet those big mountains and rough roads look repulsive. Are we never satisfied?

I shall try to get leave before Christmas, though Gen. Thomas is one of those officers who never leaves himself and thinks nobody should. However, if we set down here for winter, I think I can accomplish it.

Love to all and accept oceans from,

Your Loving Father,
A.S.W.

◈

ROUTINE CARES AND UNFAIRNESS
OF GENERAL MEADE

Tullahoma, Nov. 20, 1863.

My Dear Daughter: . . .

I have nothing of interest to write. One day is like unto another. Only from the multitude of posts I have a greatly increased number of papers to examine and supervise and a great many more matters to think of. The weather has been for the most part mild and Indian summer-like, but from sleeping in a house I have caught a very bad cold, a thing that has never happened to me in the worst weather in a tent! Isn't it strange? Gen. Slocum has moved his headquarters here. Col. Rogers has gone home to get married, it is said; though I think not, for he is on a *real* sick leave and his lady love has been sick unto death's door.

Col. Best spent an hour with me this morning, discoursing about matters and things in general. . . . We are all just now terribly disgusted after reading Meade's report. He not only ignores me as corps commander, but don't even allude to the 1st Division, which lost more men on the morning of July 3rd than the 2nd Division to which he gives the whole credit of the contest on that part of the field. Gen. Slocum, who commanded the right wing, is not named and one brigade of my command is actually given to the 1st Corps! I have read botched reports, but I think Meade's beats all in blunders and partiality. When one reads the conclusion of a loss [of] over 23,000 men, one wonders how it could be from any description of a battle he finds in this report. I am not only disgusted and chagrined, but I am astonished, as I have regarded Meade as one of the most honorable and high-toned men, wholly incapable of unfairness or political bias.

I see, however, that he mentions Carl Schurz for being an hour or so in command of a corps, and Gen. Gibbon and Gen. Birney commanding corps [for] a few hours, but ignores me and my report, too, who commanded a corps the (entire) three days at Gettysburg. To make the matter worse, another Pennsylvanian, Gen. Geary, gets all the credit of the operations on the right during the morning of July 3rd, and myself, who spent a sleepless night in planning the attack, and my old division commanded by Gen. Ruger, which drove the

Rebs. from their double line of entrenchments, are not alluded to. Save me from my friends! I am pretty mad, but I think Gen. Slocum is a mile or so ahead of me in indignation. I do not remember to have passed forty-eight hours in a more vexed and annoyed state.

On the 27th I got back through that Cumberland tunnel, after many delays, and my forty-two miles (up and down eighty-four) seemed to me to have been a voyage equal to the passage to California by the Rocky Mountains. On coming back I changed my headquarters from Decherd to Tullahoma. I have hardly been quiet since I returned, for I am obliged to have a guard at every bridge, culvert, tank, and trestle on the railroad for over ninety miles. So I am kept going up and down to see how they are placed, what defense works, whether patrols are kept up, and generally if the railroad is as well guarded as possible. If important bridges are lost the whole army goes up, as they are just able to live now.

You see the responsibility is immense, without any possible credit. On this long road, bridged over mountain streams and trestled across mountain valleys and ravines for two or three hundred miles, the whole Army of the Cumberland now in and about Chattanooga must get its supplies for man and beast. The country is full of guerrilla parties and the Rebel cavalry are always menacing right and left to pounce in upon a weak point. I got back only yesterday from my last trip of four or five days, going with Gen. Slocum to Bridgeport. At this point the railroad stops by reason of a destroyed bridge where it crosses the Tennessee.

Until within a few days the whole supply of the army at Chattanooga has been carted over the most infamous mountain roads from this point, nearly sixty miles. The recent rains have raised the river so that the boats can now go part way up, to within eight or ten miles of Chattanooga. Gen. Hooker, with the 11th Corps and one division of the 12th Corps, has cleared the intermediate valley. They had quite a smart "skrimage" on the way, a night attack by part of Longstreet's men. Gen. Greene was badly wounded in the face and Capt. Atwell of the Pennsylvania Independent Battery mortally wounded. Lt. Geary, son of Gen. Geary, was shot dead. Both of these officers sat with me during the night I was trying to get over the mountain, as I have mentioned above. Geary's troops were on railroad trains and mine marching. For this reason, and perhaps a little partiality of Gen. Slocum for my division, was the reason mine was sent back to meet, as was supposed, a great cavalry raid. Geary gets the glory, but he suffers, as mine would, in loss of officers. It is singular, but after all and with these hazards, officers complain of being sent to inactive life and *losing* their chances! Strange animal is man!

In going down the other day there were thirty paymasters on the train. Among them, Wm. Phelps of candy store memory, who is now a P.M. I met several Michigan officers, but none from Detroit. At Stevenson on Sunday, Mr. Geo. Fellers, son of the former proprietor of the Exchange, now a sutler, came to see me. On my first trip I should have fasted for forty-eight hours but for a Michigan man who was the telegraph operator. He fed me quite nicely and could not do too much to aid me. Indeed, I find at all points the Michigan officers and men treat me with more than marked kindness and attention.

We have very beautiful moonlights just now and an immensity of whippoorwills, and there are two mocking birds which begin their imitations every night in apple trees close to my tent. They mock everything from a frog to a crow. Some of their notes are beautifully sweet. The boys have tried to capture them but without success so far. . . .

Your Affectionate Father,
A.S.W.

◈

GUERRILLA RAIDS AND POOR WHITES

Tullahoma, Nov. 31st, 1863.[5]

My Dear Daughter:

It is a cold, leaden, cloudy, snow-feeling day. My fingers are so stiff that I can hardly guide a pen; and yet I am away down in the sunny south, close to the Alabama line. Indeed, I have just come from Alabama. I don't see that the skies are more genial or the temperature much milder than in northern Michigan at this season. Indeed, the whole month of October has been mainly rainy and disagreeable, not half as pleasant as those misty, smoky, warm days we generally have up north. . . .

You see I have changed my locality and I must first tell you how. About a week ago I got orders by telegraph to put my division in march for Bridgeport, the place where the Chattanooga Railroad crosses the Tennessee River. They were in motion at daylight in the morning along my whole line. Between Decherd and Tantalon is the first high range of the Cumberland Mountains, and the road over it is nothing but a bed of high rocks and deep mud-holes. The ascent of the mountain begins just beyond Cowan. Having crossed this mountain the road runs down the deep valley of Crow Creek to Stevenson and then turns east toward Chattanooga. The railroad follows pretty much the same line, except that it pierces the mountain crest by a tunnel, three-fourths of a mile long.

I waited for my rearmost brigade to come up and then [went] to the cars, expecting to reach Bridgeport before the advance, but I found that such railroads run in such a way as this one is are not exactly to be relied on. The grades are tremendous, and the locomotives old, worn-out affairs. To this add the fact that no fuel is provided on the road. I started from Decherd in the afternoon and reached Cowan (four miles) without much trouble. But here began the heavy mountain grades and the tug of war. They keep at this point a locomotive called a "pusher" which pushes behind each train. The ascent to the mountain tunnel is about two miles. All night the locomotives tugged and pushed and screeched out signals and blew whistles, but it was "no go." We were obliged to go back to Cowan, where conductors and engineers and firemen all went to sleep. I didn't much blame them, for they had been out several nights without sleep. I rather envied them, as my seat was a board close to a broken window.

The night was very cold and (what is strange with me) I could not sleep. I had received a telegram that Wheeler, Roddey, Lee and other Reb. cavalry commands [6] had crossed the Tennessee to make another raid, and I was ordered to halt my command to meet them. Here I was, unable by rail to reach my command not ten miles ahead of me. I fumed and, I fear, swore, and walked the sidetrack for hours to keep warm and to keep down my indignant spirit. At length day-

GENERAL BANKS' DIVISION RECROSSING THE POTOMAC AT WILLIAMSPORT
TO ATTACK GENERAL JACKSON, AT THE BEGINNING OF MARCH 1862
The Forty-sixth Pennsylvania band in the foreground. This was under General Williams' command.
Reproduced from Frank Leslie's *The American Soldier in the Civil War.*

GENERAL BANKS' DIVISION ENTERING FRONT ROYAL, SPRING 1862
The Blue Ridge Mountains and Manassas Gap in the background. Reproduced from a sketch in Frank
Leslie's *Illustrated History of the Civil War.*

BATTLE OF CEDAR MOUNTAIN, AUGUST 9, 1862
Reproduced from a sketch by Edwin Forbes in Frank Leslie's *Illustrated History of the Civil War.* General
Banks' force, numbering 7,500 men, was defeated by Stonewall Jackson's army of 20,000. Each army
lost about 1,400 men. Jackson was so elated by his victory that he declared a day of thanksgiving for the
Confederate Army.

light broke on Cowan's Cove (a cove here is a tract of bottom ground in the mountain valleys) and I stirred up engineers, conductors, and stokers with a vengeance and insisted upon another trial. Wood was collected and we started up the grades, luckily made a successful effort, got through the tunnel, and went tumbling fiercely down the slopes into the Crow Creek valleys, where I found three regiments of Knipe's and all of Ruger's brigades. Part of the artillery, after three days' labor, had got over the mountain by the aid of a regiment to each battery. Ten gun-carriage wheels were reported broken and the horses used up.

I was obliged to go on to Anderson to find a telegraph station. Here I began a library of telegrams to Hooker on one side (Stevenson) and Slocum on the other (Wartrace) both sending conflicting orders, Slocum ordering me to move on to Bridgeport, Hooker (through his Chief of Staff, Butterfield) ordering me to relieve certain posts along the railroad. In the meantime, the telegraph wire was so constantly employed by headquarters of the department that it was only now and then I could get in a word. All my baggage, bedding, mess, etc., was left at Cowan. Anderson has a depot building and one or two shanties. Luckily the telegraph operator was from Grand Rapids (a Mr. Atwater) and he saved me from a fast of forty-eight hours, besides exerting himself professionally.

After much tribulation and after collecting my whole division within fourteen miles of Bridgeport, I got an order to retrace my steps, or rather to distribute my division from Bridgeport to Murfreesboro to guard the railroad bridges, tanks, culverts, etc. But the trouble was not over. Butterfield ordered the batteries at Tantalon to be shipped to Bridgeport. So I sent across the horses and put the guns on cars, when I was notified that my guns were not wanted. The messenger, with instructions from Gen. Slocum, was detained by a torpedo-blowing-up of track near the tunnel. I waited another night in the windowless depot, trying to get orders. Near morning a locomotive came along and I hitched on my train of guns and repeated the struggle to get up the grades and through the tunnel to Cowan, which, after many hours, was accomplished; to find, however, at Cowan written orders to leave the batteries at Stevenson and Bridgeport.

These orders could have reached me hours before and saved an immensity of trouble and annoyance if the staff officer of Gen. Slocum had done as he was ordered. My guns were brought on to Decherd and there they stand on the railroad "flats" waiting to be drawn back. My troops were marched back, and now occupy in small posts (just large enough to be gobbled) the railroad from Murfreesboro to Bridgeport, ninety-one miles. I changed my headquarters to this place as being more central, and because the buildings used at Decherd for my offices were occupied in my absence by cavalry officers.

How long this arrangement will last I can't guess. The 2nd Division of our corps has gone to the front and probably crossed the river at Bridgeport with the 11th Corps. They went down by rail, but as I was nearer Bridgeport than they were, with my whole command, I was somewhat annoyed at being countermarched. I went to Wartrace to see Gen. Slocum, and the only satisfaction I got was that he preferred to trust my division with the responsible duty of guarding the long channel of supplies for the whole Army of the Cumberland. Very complimentary, but I dislike this railroad guarding in small posts. The whole country is full of small guerrilla parties who can get to the track and tear it up in spite of anything that infantry can do, over a line ninety miles long. Besides, the posts at important bridges are too small to defend themselves against any serious attack. I prefer the field with my whole division to this kind of duty, and hope I shall get away soon, if I carry nothing but pork and hardtack on my saddle.

This town of Tullahoma, which you have seen in the papers as the headquarters of Bragg and oftimes of Rosecrans, consists of a hundred straggling houses of faded paint and retrograding look. Indeed, it reminds me strongly of some Michigan towns after the speculating fever of 1836 had subsided, a great town-plat with here and there a pretentious frame house of thin boards, half finished and destined to remain so for years. Judge Catron of the Supreme Court has a neat summer cottage in the suburbs, but it is badly soiled by the occupation of soldiers.

All the towns along this railroad excepting Murfreesboro are the veriest pretenses, most of them sounding names and nothing else, and the people—the "poor white trash"—are disgusting: the mere scum of humanity, poor, half starved, ignorant, stupid, and treacherous. The women all "dip" snuff; that is, rub their teeth and gums with a pointed stick dipped in Scotch snuff! If anybody doubts the damning effects of slave labor upon the poor whites, let him come into Kentucky and

Tennessee and see the poorer classes of whites. Of course, there is a rich and educated class, but they are mostly gone and the poor now stand out in bold relief, with not even a bright background. Travel through this country by rail and you will never see this poor class; none but the rich planters and traders. You must stay here and move through the country to see how many there are vastly inferior to the Negro in common sense, shrewdness, and observation, and in the comforts of life. Let us not grieve for the Southern Negro as much as for the poor Southern white man—covered with vermin and rags, and disgusting with the evidences of a cureless "Scotch fiddle," [7] which they dig at continuously. . . .

I must close my long letter as the carrier has just called. I am afraid I can't get leave, as we are expecting to do or suffer great things this fall. If we don't go ahead, and we can't in the present state of supplies, I think Bragg will come ahead on us. It will be an awful country to concentrate troops in, so full of pathless mountains and roadless valleys. How they ever got into Chattanooga is a marvel, and how they will ever get out now the mud roads have begun is a greater wonder. I hope we shan't get out, but things look squally for supplying an army down through this winter. . . .

Your Affectionate Father,

A.S.W.

◈

THANKSGIVING AND REBEL PRISONERS

HEADQUARTERS 1ST DIVISION, 12TH CORPS
ARMY OF THE CUMBERLAND

Tullahoma, December 8, 1863.

My Dear Daughter:

If my memories are correct, I have been very remiss in writing you. I intended to have sent you a letter on Thanksgiving Day, but as the day was very fair I had a crowded levee all the morning of the officers of my division on duty here. First came the general court martial, headed by the venerable-looking Col. Selfridge, and following them the corps and brigade staff officers and others of the command here. So my day was used up and I did nothing, except in the quiet of the evening sat before my fire and thought of absent friends. Of course, the good things and the good company at Uncle's had a prominent place in my reveries. Our anticipated feast of good things was delayed and almost lost by the very mysterious disappearance of our cook. It was nearly 8 P.M., before we got anything to eat. The cook, making an early beginning of his Thanksgiving, mistook a Nashville train for his kitchen and went off in it, not returning for a week nearly. He came back in a very penitential mood and has been restored to his pots.

Poor Dr. McNulty with a gay cavalcade started for a visit to a very large cave some seven miles away. The result was that his horse fell and the doctor was so stunned that he remained insensible for two days and is still in a very weak and imbecile state, hardly recognizing his friends. I fear he is done for duty at present. Singular how these things result. A day or two before, Gen. Slocum's horse fell with him catching his leg under it and going at a gallop. The general escaped without serious injury. You have not forgotten my fall with Old Plug into the Potomac pontoon and more recently his dropping into a deep ditch without injury to me.

We have had for a week past a continuous run of Reb. prisoners, long lines of railroad trains crammed with them, over 7,000 taken in the recent operations in front. They are a hard-looking lot of men without overcoats and very short of dirty blankets, marked generally "U.S.," showing that what they have are taken or stolen from us.

But you should see this "chivalry" to appreciate it. A more dirty, destitute, and diabolical lot of humanities cannot be conceived. We get in Dickens' novels and in similar works some fanciful sketches of English poorhouses and poor people, but no imagination can conceive nor words express the dirty and ragged condition of these prisoners. Their hands are as black as a Negro's and if their faces are not seen you would pronounce them Negroes. Such is the pure blood and the high status of these troops over the destruction of whom by foul Yankees you see the lamentations of the Southern papers. Their stolid, unexpressive, and almost idiotic features are quite in keeping with their dirty condition. I could not help comparing the neat and orderly appearance of our guards as they stood in the doorways of the boxcars with the stupid foul look of the men they were guarding.

[*The remainder is missing.*]

❖

ERRORS IN REPORT OF THE BATTLE OF GETTYSBURG

HEADQUARTERS, 1ST DIVISION, 12TH CORPS
ARMY OF THE CUMBERLAND

Tullahoma, Tenn., Dec. —, 1863.

Major General H. W. Slocum,
Comm'd'g 12*th* Army Corps.
General:

In forwarding the report of Brig. Gen. Ruger, Comm'd'g 1*st* Division, 12*th* A.C. at the battle of Gettysburg, (delayed to this late date for reasons stated in the letter accompanying the report) I embrace the occasion to call your attention to certain errors and omissions in Maj. Gen. Meade's official report of that battle, which I think do much injustice to some portions of this corps. These briefly stated are:

1*st*—In crediting Lockwood's brigade to 1*st* Corps.

2*nd*—In omitting all notice of the gallant defense by Greene's brigade of the left flank of our entrenched line on the evening of the 2*nd* July, after the other troops of the corps had marched out to support of the left.

3*rd*—In wholly ignoring the operations of the 1*st* Division.

4*th*—In repudiating most of the material statements of my report as temporary commander of this corps.

1*st As to Lockwood's Brigade.* The following is the notice taken of it in General Meade's Report.

"In the meantime perceiving great exertions on the part of the enemy, the 6*th* Corps (Maj. Gen. Sedgwick) and part of the 1*st* Corps (to the command of which I had assigned Maj. Gen. Newton) particularly *Lockwood's Maryland Brigade,* together with detachments from the 2*nd* Corps were all brought up, &c."

I cannot be mistaken in asserting that Lockwood's brigade was at no time during this battle a part of the 1*st* Corps, or under the command of Gen. Newton. It was a part of the 12*th* Corps, and was brought up under my immediate command, with the 1*st* Division of same corps, to the support of the left.

This brigade (composed then of the 150*th* New York Volunteers and 1*st* Maryland Potomac Home Regiment) coming from Baltimore or its vicinity, reported to me as temporary commander of the corps early on the morning of the 2*nd* of July, while the skirmishers of the 1*st* Division (still on the south side of Rock Creek) were engaged with the enemy. Gen. Lockwood being senior to Gen. Ruger, then comm'd'g 1*st* Division, and a stranger to the division, I directed him to take his orders directly from me as an unassigned brigade, during the pending operations.

When the 1*st* Division and Lockwood's brigade were ordered to support the left on the afternoon of same day, I went in command of the supporting column, leaving [the] 2*nd* Division to cover our entire entrenched line. On reaching the crest of the Cemetery Ridge, Major (now I believe Lieut. Colonel) McGilvery of Maine Artillery, in command of one or more reserve batteries, reported to me that he was threatened by the enemy and was without infantry supports; and that the enemy, but a few moments before, had drawn off into the woods in his front several pieces of our artillery. I ordered Gen. Lockwood to move into the woods indicated, which was promptly done, and our artillery, abandoned by the enemy, was almost immediately recaptured. The 1*st* Division at the same time was ordered into the woods on the left of Lockwood's brigade and both advanced for some distance and until halted pursuant to superior orders, meeting very little resistance at any point from the retiring enemy. Though we passed large masses of our disorganized men, we saw not one line or body of our troops in position. The enemy seemed to have a clear field in that part of our lines and were helping themselves to our artillery until interrupted by the approach of reinforcements from 12*th* Corps and 6*th* Corps, advancing at about the same time. These facts having been fully reported, I am at a loss to comprehend (when all other corps sending supports to the left are especially named) why the 12*th* Corps should be—not only not named—but deprived of the small credit of "Lockwood's Maryland Brigade," for the benefit of the 1*st* Corps.

2nd In omitting any mention of the gallant defense made by Gen. Greene's brigade on the left flank of the entrenched line of the 12th Corps on the evening of the 2nd of July.

Gen. Meade's report thus speaks of the manner in which the enemy got possession of our line of breastworks.

"During the heavy assault upon our extreme left, portions of the 12*th* Corps were sent as reinforcements. During their absence the line of the extreme right was held by a much reduced force, and was taken advantage of by the enemy, who, during the absence of Geary's division of the 12*th* Corps, advanced and occupied a part of the line."

It was the absence of the whole of the 1*st* Division and of Lockwood's brigade (supporting the left) and of two brigades of 2*nd* (Geary's) Division (marching towards Littlestown by mistake) that the enemy took advantage of—not only to occupy our line on the right and center, but also to attack, with great vigor, Greene's brigade of 2*nd* Division (the only portion of the corps left behind) on the extreme left of our entrenched line. Gen. Meade omits all mention of this gallant contest, which lasted full three hours, and resulted in our retaining this important part of our line of defenses and enabling us to resist for hours, with comparatively little loss, his heavier attacks on the following day and finally to expel him wholly from our line.

Gen. Meade speaks of another attack, in a different part of the field, at about the same hour, as follows;

"On the extreme left, another assault was, however, made about 8 P.M. *on the 11th Corps,* from the left of the town, which was repulsed with the assistance of the troops from the 2*nd* and 1*st* corps."

The similarity of time and circumstance leads me to think that there is a mistake in locality of this attack. It is quite certain that Greene was attacked and was reinforced by [the] 1*st* and 11*th* corps, about the same hour that the report says the attack on [the] 11*th* Corps was repulsed by aid of troops from [the] 1*st* and 2*nd* corps. Be that as it may; the defense made by Gen. Greene was eminently worthy of notice and commendation.

3rd In wholly ignoring the operations of the 1st Division, 12th Corps.

The active participation by the 12*th* Corps in the battle of Gettysburg was,

1*st* The marching of the 1*st* Division and Lockwood's brigade to the support of the left on Thursday afternoon, the 2*nd* of July.

2*nd* The defense of the left flank of the entrenched line on the evening of the same day, and

3*rd* The long contest on Friday morning (3*rd* July) to recover possession of our line of breastworks. I have spoken of both operations of Thursday. Of those of Friday morning Gen. Meade thus speaks in his report.

"On the morning of the 3*rd* Gen. Geary, having returned during the night, was attacked at early dawn by the enemy, but succeeded in driving him back, and occupying his former position. A spirited contest was maintained all the morning along this part of the line. Gen. Geary, reinforced by *Wheaton's* [a mistake for *Shaler's*] brigade, 6*th* Corps, maintained his position and inflicting very severe losses on the enemy. With this exception the lines remained undisturbed, &c"

This is certainly neither a full nor a fair statement of a conflict which was waged almost without cessation for full seven hours, and in which all the infantry and artillery of the corps were engaged. The idea conveyed by Gen. Meade's Report is a simple defense of one division of the corps. The engagement really began on our side by a heavy cannonading from guns placed in position after midnight. The plan of attack, arranged the night before to dislodge the enemy from our breastworks, was for Geary's division to follow the cessation of the artillery firing by an attack along the entrenchments which he held on our left, while the 1*st* Division was placed in preparation to assault over the marshy grounds on the extreme right, or attack the enemy's flank should he attempt to move beyond the breastworks. The enemy on the other hand had brought up strong reinforcements with the design of carrying the position of our entrenched line, which he had failed to drive Greene from on the previous night, and which would have placed him in the rear of our army and given him possession of our main line of communication, the Baltimore Pike. Both parties started at daylight with plans of attack, each with the expectation of expelling the other.

Not only, as Gen. Meade's report says, did Geary's division (or more

correctly the two absent brigades of it) return during the night, but
so also did the whole of the 1st Division and Lockwood's brigade, and
the whole corps (not Geary's division alone) artillery and infantry
"succeeded in driving the enemy back and occupying its former position." It is a noticeable fact, too, that the portion of the corps not mentioned by Gen. Meade lost more in killed and wounded in this contest,
from its exposed line of attack, and I think captured more prisoners,
than did the division which gets the entire credit in Gen. Meade's
report. The commendation given to Geary's division was justly merited,
but the same praise might safely have been extended so as to embrace the
conduct of the whole corps without doing injustice or giving offense
to any portion of it. The entire omission of the 1st Division is so marked,
and the report of the contest on Friday morning so meager and so at
variance with official statements of the superior officers of the corps,
that I am at a loss to conceive from what source Gen. Meade derived his
information. Not, I know, from my report as temporary commander of
the corps, and not, I think, from yours as commander of the troops of the
right wing.

4th The fourth item of omissions stated at the commencement of this
communication is sufficiently shown in the comments already made. Gen.
Meade either has not seen my report or he has intentionally repudiated
all its material statements as to the operations of the 12th Corps at Gettysburg. No commanding general can verify by personal knowledge all the
occurrences in his own command in a great battle. But so confident
am I of the truth of every material statement of my report in this instance that I could confidently submit its correctness to a decision on
proofs, in any respectable court of justice.

There is another omission which in connection with those I have
named has a significant bearing. Gen. Meade carefully names all general officers temporarily in command of corps—Maj. Gen. Schurz, in
command of 11th Corps for six hours, from 10:30 A.M. of July 1st
(when Gen. Howard assumed command of the field) to 4 P.M. same
day (when Gen. Howard was relieved by the arrival of Gen. Hancock)
is properly reported as such. So are Maj. Gen. Birney, 3rd Corps, and
Brig. Gen. Gibbon, 2nd Corps, (Maj. Gen. Hancock, commanding
the left center) named as temporarily commanding corps on different
days. I was in command of 12th Corps part of July 1st and all of 2nd

and *3rd* of July, and on the evening of the *2nd* (Thursday) attended a council of corps commanders on a summons conveyed to me by a staff officer of Gen. Meade. I may be pardoned, therefore, for expressing some surprise that my name alone of all those who temporarily commanded corps in this great battle is suppressed in Gen. Meade's report. I know Gen. Meade to be a high-toned gentleman and I believe him to be a commander of superior merit and of honest judgment, and I confess to have read that part of his official report relating to the 12*th* Corps with a mixed feeling of astonishment and regret. I submit these comments to you as the commander of the 12*th* Corps, not in the expectation that any adequate remedy can now be applied, after the official report of the commanding general has become an historical record, but because I deem a statement of the facts and grievances an act of justice to the corps with which I have been long connected, (and which I commanded on the occasion referred to), and especially to the gallant division which I have had the honor to command for nearly two years.

I have the honor to be, General,

Very Respectfully, Your Ob't Servant,

A. Williams

Brig. Gen'l of Vols.

❖

HEADQUARTERS, 12TH CORPS

ARMY OF THE CUMBERLAND

Tullahoma, Tenn., Jan'y 2nd 1864.

My Dear Sir:

I presume you have read Meade's report of the battle of Gettysburg.[8] I can imagine the feeling that its perusal has caused you. I have not met a sensible man who has read it, either a soldier or civilian, who has not felt disappointed on reading it. It purports to be the official history of the most important contest of modern times—a contest in which our troops fought with a valor and determination never before exhibited—and the only evidence in the entire report which tends to prove this heroism is contained in the closing sentence, "Our losses were very severe, amounting to 23,186." Your disappointment must have been greater from the fact that the true history of the operations on the right had already been made known to you by me,[9] and Meade's report is a plain contradiction of almost every statement I have ever made to you. It is in direct conflict with my official report and the reports of all my subordinate commanders. My first impulse on reading his report was to ask for a court of inquiry. I was prompted to this course not so much from personal considerations, as from a desire to have justice done to Gen. Williams and his division.

Although Meade professed the warmest friendship for me, and the utmost confidence in me, not only during the entire battle, but at all times subsequent to it while I remained in his army, yet in his report he utterly ignores me. That he did repose this confidence in me, and that he placed the right wing entirely under my control, I have abundant written evidence now in my possession. In proof of this I enclose a copy of an order sent me during the battle, showing that he had sent part of Sedgwick's corps to me, and that, without visiting me or my portion of the line, he wished me to place it in a central position where he could use it as soon as I could spare it. I also enclose a copy of an order received at 10:20 A.M. on July 2nd directing me to move from the strong position we then held, and the 5th and 12th corps, then under my command, and the 6th, which was hourly expected, to attack the enemy. The latter order was not obeyed because every general officer consulted on the subject deemed it unwise to leave the almost impregnable position we then held. I send you copies of these orders to convince you that although my name is not mentioned in the report, yet I really occupied the position, and had the commands mentioned in my former letters. At no time was I in command of less than two corps, during the entire campaign, and during all the battle the right wing was entrusted entirely to me—a position to which my rank entitled me. Williams commanded the 12th Corps, and was at all times during the battle treated as a corps commander by Meade. He was invited by him to the council with other corps commanders, and yet no mention is made of this fact in the report, nor is Williams' name or that of his division to be found in it.

I finally gave up the idea of asking for a court of inquiry, knowing that the interests of the service could not be promoted by such a course. I wrote a letter to Meade, however, asking him to correct his report, a copy of which I enclose.

There is much secret history connected with the Gettysburg campaign which will some day be made public. The proceedings of a secret council of the corps commanders held the night before the enemy crossed the river was at once divulged, and the remarks of Meade, Warren, and Pleasonton published to the world in full. It was for the interest of Meade that this publication should be made, and there is no doubt that publicity was given to it with his consent, if not through his direct instrumentality. There were other councils, however, the proceedings of which were not made public, and which never will be published with the consent of Gen. Meade. On the evening of July 2nd a council was called, and each corps commander was asked his opinion as to the propriety of falling back towards Washington that night. The majority opposed it, and after the vote was taken Meade declared that "Gettysburg was no place to risk a battle," and there is no doubt that but for the decision of his corps commanders the army on the 3rd of July would have been in full retreat, and the 4th of July, 1863, instead of being a day of rejoicing throughout the North, would have been the darkest day ever known to our country. This piece of history can be verified by the records of that council kept by Butterfield, and cannot have been forgotten by any officer present.

On the 4th of July nearly every corps commander urged an immediate movement, but my corps was kept three days in idleness. In the meantime the enemy had reached Hagerstown, taken up his new line, and had abundant time to fortify. At the council held on the 13th of July by which "Meade was overruled" the following question was proposed to each officer, viz., "Shall we, *without further knowledge of the position of the enemy,* make an attack?"

Previous to putting the question, Meade announced that he could get no knowledge of the position of the enemy. This announcement, together with the peculiar phraseology of the question, indicated the decision which the commanding general anticipated. He offered no remarks until a vote was taken and the question answered in the negative. He then made some general remarks about "the necessity of doing something," which were approved by all. Having "placed himself right on the record," as the politicians would say, he retired. This record he at once used to sustain himself at the expense of his brother officers, although the action of these officers was precisely what he anticipated when he framed the question.

You may think this a hard charge to bring against a soldier, but I believe I am fully justified in it. There are other circumstances which I will make known to you when we meet, which will convince you that I have not done him injustice.

As long as this war continues I shall pursue the course I have thus far followed. I shall ask for no court; enter into no controversy; write no letters. But when the present danger has passed from us, many facts will come to light giving to the public a better knowledge of the real history of this war than can be obtained through the medium of such reports as that written by Gen. Meade.

Very Respectfully,
Your Ob't Servant,
H. W. Slocum

Hon. L. R. Morgan
Syracuse, N.Y.

◈

GETTYSBURG REPORT AND DULLNESS OF RAILROAD DUTIES

Tullahoma, Feb. 25th, 1864.

My Dear Sherman:

I enclose you some correspondence (copies) relating to the battle of Gettysburg and Meade's report. Mr. Thos. M. Cook, formerly of Detroit and more recently of the New York *Herald*, will call upon you for the perusal of them. I have told him he could take notes of all the facts published, but that it won't do to have the letters printed nor extracts from them verbatim.

I do not understand that he wants the facts for the newspaper, but as part of the historical *res gestae* of the battle. At any rate, I do not think I could properly place them in the hands of gentlemen of the press, though I can give him, as I have already, the facts touching Meade's *defective* (unholy) report. Indeed, he was so unjust to me and my command and to Gen. Slocum and his command—so wholly ignored the operations on the right, which he committed to Gen. Slocum and never once took the trouble to look at himself—that I feel a great inclination to open a paper war on him myself. I shall do so if I live through this war. Having let Cook get out the bowels of these papers, will you please forward them to my daughter, Irene Williams, 1605 Filbert St., Philadelphia.

I shall send you tomorrow a copy of a private letter, which you can also show to Cook, and which please also forward afterward to Rene.

Well, I have been home on a thirty-days' leave; expected to have gone on to Philadelphia and Washington, but did not find time. It was the shortest thirty days I ever saw. The winter has been very dull. This railroad guarding is doleful. My command is scattered sixty miles or so, and I have only one small regiment at headquarters. I miss the parades, drills, music, and company of a concentrated division and I weary to get together again. . . .

This town is dolorous; a type of western map cities after the speculations of '36; thin, slabby and shabby houses scattered about, with broken windows and a deserted air. The people are like the houses, poor white trash. The Negro is the only gay dog, keeping up dances every night and having a good time at a cheap rate. . . .

No news not in the papers. Weather has been fine. We shall probably be doing something soon, though a great many of our best troops are out on furlough. All my old regiments re-enlisting. Five are at home; 46th Pennsylvania, 5th Connecticut, 2nd Massachusetts, 27th Indiana, 3rd Maryland.

Goodbye; write us.

Yours truly,

A. S. Williams.

Maj. Sherman.

P.S. Cook is at the *Herald* rooms, Washington.

◆

DEFENSE OF GETTYSBURG REPORT

HEADQUARTERS, 12TH CORPS
ARMY OF THE CUMBERLAND

Tullahoma, Tenn. Mch. 5th, 1864.

General A. S. Williams,
Comm'd'g 1st Divn 12th Corps,
The following is a copy of the letter from Gen. Meade, amending his report of the battle of Gettysburg,

Very Respectfully &c
H. W. Slocum
Maj. Gen'l Comm'd'g 12th Corps.

◈

HEADQUARTERS
ARMY OF THE POTOMAC

Feb'y 25th, 1864.

Maj. Gen'l H. W. Halleck,
Gen'l in Chief,
Washington, D.C.
General:
I transmit herewith the report of Brig. Gen. T. H. Ruger, Commanding 1st Division, 12th Army Corps, and those of his brigade and regimental commanders, of the operations of his division at the battle of Gettysburg. These reports were only recently received by me, owing to Gen. Ruger's being detached with a large portion of his command not long after the battle; and soon after his return the corps was ordered to Tennessee.

I beg these reports may be placed on file, as part of my official report of that battle. I embrace this opportunity to make certain corrections and alterations in my report, to which my attention has been called by Maj. Gen. Slocum. These alterations are as follows:

I. In relating the occurrences of the 2nd of July I state:

289

"In the meantime perceiving the great exertions on the part of the enemy, the 6*th* Corps. (Maj. Gen. Sedgwick) and part of the 1*st* Corps. (to the command of which I had assigned Maj. Gen. Newton), particularly Lockwood's Maryland brigade, together with detachments from the 2*nd* Corps, were all brought up, &c"

This should read:

"In the meantime, perceiving the great exertions on the part of the enemy, the 6*th* Corps (Maj. Gen. Sedgwick) and part of the 1*st* Corps (to the command of which I had assigned Maj. Gen. Newton), together with detachments from the 2*nd* Corps, were all brought up. Subsequently the 1*st* Division and Lockwood's brigade of the 12*th* Corps, under the immediate command of Brig. Gen. A. S. Williams, then temporarily commanding the corps, arrived at the scene of action; the service of Lockwood's brigade being particularly mentioned."

II. In relating the occurrences of July 3*rd*

"During the heavy assaults upon our extreme left, portions of the 12*th* Corps were sent as reinforcements. During their absence, the line of the extreme right was held by a much reduced force, and was taken advantage of by the enemy, who, during the absence of Geary's division, 12*th* Corps, advanced and occupied part of the line. On the morning of the 3*rd* Gen. Geary, having returned during the night, was attacked at early dawn by the enemy, but succeeded in driving him back, and occupying his former position. A spirited contest was maintained all the morning along this part of the line. Gen. Geary, reinforced by Wheatons' brigade, 6*th* Corps, maintained his position, inflicting severe losses on the enemy."

This should read:

"During the heavy assaults upon our extreme left, the 1*st* Division, and Lockwood's brigade of the 12*th* Corps, were sent as reinforcements, as already reported. Two brigades of Geary's division (2*nd* of this corps) were also detached for the same purpose but did not arrive at the scene of action, owing to having mistaken the road. The detachment of so large a portion of the 12*th* Corps, with its temporary commander, Brig. Gen. A. S. Williams, left the defense of the line previously held to the remaining brigade of the 2*nd* Division, commanded by Brig. Gen. Greene, who held the left of the 12*th* Corps, now become the extreme right of the army. The enemy, perceiving the withdrawal of our troops, advanced and attacked Gen. Greene with great vigor, who, making a gallant defense, and being soon reinforced by portions of the 1*st* and 11*th* corps contiguous to him, succeeded in repulsing all the efforts of the enemy to dislodge him. After night, on the return of the detachments sent to the left, it was found the enemy were occupying portions of the line of breastworks thrown up by the 12*th* Corps. Brig. Gen. Williams, in command, immediately made arrangements, by the disposition of his artillery, and instructions to both divisions, commanded respectively by Brig. Gens. Geary and Ruger, to attack the enemy at daylight and regain the position formerly occupied by the corps. In the meantime the enemy brought strong reinforcements, and at early daylight a spirited contest commenced which continued till after 10 A.M., the result of which was the repulse of the enemy in all his attempts to advance and his final abandonment of the position he had taken the evening before. During this contest Shaler's brigade, 6*th* Corps, was sent to reinforce the 12*th* Corps. With this exception the lines remained undisturbed."

I should be glad, as an act of justice, if this communication could be published.

Respectfully, Your Ob't Serv*,

Geo. G. Meade,

Maj. Gen'l Com'd'g

❖

SOCIAL FESTIVITIES AT THE FRONT

Tullahoma, March 26th, 1864.

My Dear Daughter:

Last night as I was reading Kinglake's Crimean War, the cry of fire was raised by the sentinels and looking out of my window I saw our only hotel, a good-sized wooden building, all in flames. It was midnight and raining. As the commissary's store was in the range and the stable of our horses near, I ordered out the provost guard and all was saved except the tavern. While the fire was fiercest, the passenger train from Nashville came in, and when I returned to my quarters I found your letter of the 20th inst., and this was after all the great event of the night! I was delighted with your long letter, especially so, as I have been some days anxious to hear the fate of my letter of the 6th inst. enclosing some photographs and $40 in *greenbacks*. . . .

The photographs were of several general officers of my acquaintance, which I thought good likenesses, but they can be replaced. The cash, in these times, I greatly regret the loss of. However, I will replace it by express in a few days. Somehow or other my salary oozes away very rapidly and I save nothing; what little I get over our expenses is melted on debts and interest money, without greatly reducing my indebtedness. I am pretty economical myself and none of us are very costly, yet it takes money to keep us all. I was unable to get drafts on my last pay, hence I trusted greenbacks to the mail. If I had left out the photographs it would doubtless all have gone safe. I hope it may yet turn up; but I fear not, as complaints are very frequent and safeguards from the army not great.

I wrote you an account of the ball in that letter, I think. I did not go to the first one, as I had no clothes. The last was not very elegant and I think I have greatly lost my taste for the gay world. Several officers' wives were there and some rather dashing ones. One, wife of Lt. Bartlett, 150th New York Regiment, is a daughter of Capt. Andrews on Gen. Morris' staff, a brother of my classmate, W. W. Andrews, a reverend gentleman who visited us once and preached in Dr. Duffield's church. A mild, gentle, classical man, of queer religious opinions, the peculiarity of which I cannot describe, but the main idea of which is, to unite all denominations in the church. He is a sort of bishop of this religious fraternity. Another officer's wife (Lt. Col. Rogers) is fresh from 5th Avenue, New York, a bride. The change must have been marked, but she is sensible and enjoys life as it comes. Aunt Hatty was there but not very well, and Mrs. Capt. Pittman, a little body about as big as a piece of chalk, also a Mrs. Capt. Greene of the 150th New York. The rest were all leather and prunella women who mostly dip snuff and look very thin and gaunt. Music, made up from two bands of the division, was very good.

This is about all I can remember of the ball, excepting that the landlady, a Mrs. Robinson of Kentucky, who entertained me with tales of her high relationship to a great many Kentucky bloods, was immensely chagrined that a private table set apart for herself and guests (myself one) was appropriated by the ignoble vulgar before we could get up the narrow stairway. All the silver and splendor and six bottles of champagne was lost to us and we were obliged to take seats in the very worst spot of the banquetting hall. Poor woman! She seemed greatly distressed, but I contrived to smother my disappointment in a very large quantity of boned turkey and the like. Last night poor Mrs. Robinson suffered a greater chagrin by being burned out, stock and fluke. She was obliged to take shelter in the hospital building. I hope she saved the spoons. Our ball room, not of the most superb dimensions, has gone up and we shall no more transgress in that way during Lent.

That reminds me. We received yesterday preparatory orders for the front. It will be a week or more before we get away, and I think much longer, as we are wanting many things for which we cannot get transportation and we must be relieved by other troops. I look for a long, sorry campaign amongst these barren and denuded mountains below us. As for our horses, I don't see how they can be fed. I wish my Yorkshire was at home, or on Uncle Lew's farm. He never looked so splendid as now, but what will he be beyond the reach of forage.

Mar. 27th: I was stopped here yesterday and could not resume until the mail closed. There is not much new. Capt. Whitney and five lieutenants have returned. Capt. Whitney brought me from Mrs. Whitney a very neat gold locket badge of a Royal Arch Mason. Mrs. Knipe also sent me a very fine military hat, with a gold general officer's hat band. So you see our namesakes' families do not forget me. I think I shall send you the old hat which I have worn so long and which you have so much admired. . . .

I suppose all the ladies will be obliged to decamp soon. I am afraid part of my division will have to remain behind, guarding the blockhouses now being built. Commands are badly mixed in this department. In trying to give places to officers not wanted in the field, a great many useless commands are carried out in the shape of military districts and independent posts. We have in this way a conflict of authority and a want of graduated command which is provoking and alarming, and subversive of good order and organization. I find somebody now and then trying to command some of my regiments on the ground that they fall within their military district. I notice they don't succeed well in this attempt. . . .

I have just got rid of a big job in the way of a personal listing with account of battles, etc., sent to the War Department by order. I have just received a letter from Gen. Greene, who had a talk with Gen. Meade. The latter expressed much regret at the oversight in his report. Said he thought I reported as a division commander and he had not read my report when he made his! I shall send copies of Gen. Slocum's letter to Gen. Meade, as well as mine, for safe keeping, also a copy of my report of services, a volume of some seventy-five pages. . . .

Love to all. I am working up my neglected correspondence to be ready for the front.

Your Affectionate Father,
A.S.W.

❖

ARMY REORGANIZATION AND COMMANDS

Tullahoma, April 15, 1864.

My Dear Daughter:

Yours of the 10th came to hand last night. I have been absent four or five days—two days in Nashville. I went up to see about supplies for my men. It is several months since we have been able to get clothing, for want of railroad transportation. Gen. Knipe went up with me. I saw nothing wonderful in Nashville. It is a very dirty and badly managed place. I met Maj. Fifield of Monroe and saw several Michigan officers. Col. Mizner was down here while I was absent.[10] I think I have writen you since the order consolidating the 11th and 12th corps. As you [may] imagine, we [are] not very amiable over it. Officers and men get much attached to corps names. It is the *espirit de corps* which is a great military power. Besides, we are all very much attached to Gen. Slocum and dislike greatly to lose him. What you say about our new commander may be all true, *though I hope you are all careful about expressing your opinion or judgments on this topic.* It would probably be sent back here by some kind friend, greatly to my injury. The inference would be that if my family said hard things that their opinions were founded upon something I have written or said. So express no opinion about my commanding officers, unless favorable. You will understand, and Uncle Lew, who is very judicious on such subjects, will explain what you may not see clearly. I hear that our new corps commander has not drank for some months, and if he ever was indiscreet that he is now the pattern of temperance.[11]

We have been a week waiting for the new organization. As we have several major generals, it is not at all improbable that I may lose my division. It is said Gen. Butterfield has come back expecting to get one. If so, he will be very apt to choose mine, which is the best in the new corps. Such is the fate of war. It is now over two years since I took command of this division! Would it not be strange if I was sent back to a brigade? [12] . . .

[*The concluding portion is missing.*]

❖

VISIT TO GENERAL HOOKER AND
LOOKOUT MOUNTAIN

Tullahoma, April 21, 1864.

My Dear Daughter:

I have been knocking about so much of late that I have not written you, since the breaking up of our old corps. We all feel pretty badly to lose our old name. The badge we shall retain, and Gen. Hooker has applied for the name of 12th Corps instead of 20th.

Gen. Slocum has left us for Vicksburg, taking with him Col. Rogers, Col. [blank] and Maj. Gordon [?] Capts. Mosley and Tracy. The rest of his staff are waiting orders. Col. Best, I fear, will be obliged to go back to a captaincy. We shall miss the general and his staff. Circumstances have thrown our quarters near together for a long time and intimacies and friendships become very strong under such circumstances as we have lived in for eighteen months.

I have been away for most of the past two weeks, first to Nashville for four or five days and last over to Gen. Hooker's headquarters in Lookout Valley this side [of] Chattanooga. I had a very pleasant visit there. The general was quite gracious and insisted upon our stay for a day or so. He went with us to the summit of Lookout Mountain and explained the recent military operations around. I think the prospect from this mountain exceeds in extent and grandeur anything I have ever seen and you know I have seen grand natural scenery. I found Mrs. and Col. Ross of the 20th Connecticut at corps headquarters. They were our companions on the trip to Lookout. I wished often that you were along. I came back yesterday.

In the new organization, I have still my old division (1st) with additions. I exchanged the 20th Connecticut for the 141st New York. I get one entire new brigade.

Gen. Hector Tyndale, an officer you wrote me about after Antietam, where he was wounded, [commands the brigade]. He is a Philadelphian. My division, I think, will number present nearly 9,000 and present and absent probably 14,000. Individually, I cannot complain of the new deal, but somehow I feel heavy hearted and not buoyant. I hope when the weather improves my spirits will amend. . . .

I expect to have a hard summer. The mountainous country in front is so poorly supplied for man or beast and we shall be so far away from supplies that I prepare for a season of deprivation. I really fear more for my horses than myself. We shall probably break up here next week and move to the front. When the fighting campaigning will begin I cannot guess. The season is very backward and grass hardly started, even down in this sunny South; peach trees and apple trees are blossoming. The weather is much like our April in Michigan.

I hear from Best that you are having great concerts. It must be over two weeks since I heard. . . .

[*The remainder is missing.*]

❖

END OF RAILROAD GUARDING

Tullahoma, April 26th, 1864.

My Dear Daughter:

I enclose a sprig of crocus taken from Top Lookout (Mountain), which place I visited lately in company with Gen. Hooker; also, a more acceptable memento of a $20 greenback, picked up in Washington. . . . I wrote you a few days ago. We are certainly off this week. I am glad of it, for I weary to be somewhere, I know not where. I am tired to death of this railroad life, out of spirits, for what I know not. It is a year ago since I started for Chancellorsville, full of hope and confidence. Today I feel sad and blue, though the weather is fine and spring-like. . . .

I have a letter from Mr. Jacob Howard, saying that Meade's supplemental report will be published by Congress. The President promised him that I should have the next promotion. Two have been promoted since. The making of fortunes I do not understand. I could have made one here if I had consented to have sold my self-respect and the good name of my children to the third and fourth generation. While somebody makes $700,000, somebody [else] loses a corresponding sum. The world's cash don't grow as fast as that. We hear of the successful, but of the poor devil who loses his all in the pocket of the other little is said. He returns to shady life. I long more than you can to be gathered with you all in some quiet home, but I don't see clearly how I can get out and not regret it. I want to see the end. . . .

> Love to all,
>
> Your Affectionate Father,
>
> A.S.W.

1. Apparently this was Mrs. Sarah Morgan Bryan Pratt, for whose career see *Dict. Am. Biog.*
2. The desperately-fought battle of Murfreesboro, December 31, 1862, to June 2, 1863, is regarded as a Union victory, since General Bragg's Confederate army retired from the field of combat. The capture of Colonel William W. Duffield with a portion of the Ninth Michigan Infantry Regiment at Murfreesboro on July 13, 1862 was another and minor affair.
3. On October 19, General Grant had replaced Rosecrans in command of the army and with the support of reinforcements assumed the offensive against the now discouraged Confederates. Contrary to General Williams' forecast, the recapture of Lookout Mountain on November 24, 1863, in the storied "battle above the clouds" was effected rather easily, marking the initial success of the Union army in the Chattanooga campaign.
4. General George Sears Greene, for whose career see *Dict. Am. Biog.* He attained the age of ninety-eight and in his later years took pride in his distinction as the oldest living graduate of West Point. In 1836

he had resigned from the army to devote himself to an engineering career. In 1894, then ninety-three years old, by special act of Congress he was given the rank of first lieutenant which he had held in 1836, and placed on the retired list—possibly a record of longevity in the American army.

5. Apparently an inadvertent error for November 30.

6. Joseph Wheeler, Phillip D. Roddey, and Stephen D. Lee. For sketches of those notable Confederate cavalry leaders see *Dict. Am. Biog.*

7. More commonly known as the itch, a parasitic infliction common among domestic animals and among certain economic strata of the human race.

8. This report is printed in the *Official Records*, Ser. 1, XXVII, Part 1, 114–19. General Meade's supplementary report, made in response to General Slocum's letter of protest, is in the same volume, pp. 120–21. General Slocum's report upon his role in the battle and campaign is on pp. 758–63. His subsequent letter of protest to Meade (December 30, 1863) and General Meade's reply (dated February 25, 1864) admitting some of the criticisms and rebutting others are on pp. 769–70. General Williams' own report of his operations is on pp. 770–76.

It is interesting to note that both General Slocum and General Williams were concerned over the judgment of future history upon General Meade's misleading report of their roles in the battle. Perhaps it would be a fair statement of that judgment (as of 1959) to say that General Meade, whatever his errors of detail may have been, waged a creditable campaign and battle, on the whole, in marked contrast with the performances of McClellan, Burnside, and Hooker, his predecessors in command of the Army of the Potomac. In particular, all of his forces were thrown into the battle, being moved from point to point as circumstances dictated, instead of permitting a large part of the army to lie idle while the enemy defeated the remainder in detail. Yet Meade was subjected to a storm of contemporary criticism, chiefly inspired by his failure to pursue and destroy Lee's army. One lengthy critique in particular, published in the New York *Times* on March 12, 1864 and signed by "Historicus" (whom Meade identified as General Sickles) stung him into requesting a court of inquiry upon his conduct of the battle. See *Official Records*, XXVII, Part 1, 127–36.

9. From 1858 until he resumed military life as colonel of the Twenty-seventh New York Infantry in May 1861, General Slocum had practiced law in Syracuse. LeRoy Morgan, to whom this letter was addressed, was Slocum's brother-in-law and a fellow-member of the bar of Syracuse, who in 1859 was elected justice of the Supreme Court. See sketch of Slocum in *Dict. Am. Biog.* and sketch of Morgan in D. H. Bunce, *Onondaga's Centennial* (Boston, 1896), I, 349–350.

10. Colonel Henry R. Mizner of Detroit entered the regular service as a cap-

tain in May 1861 and on November 11, 1862, was commissioned colonel of the Fourteenth Michigan Infantry Regiment. He served throughout the war and at its close remained in the regular service until he retired with the rank of colonel in 1891.—*Record of Service of Michigan Volunteers*, Vol. XIV.

11. General Joseph Hooker, who following his resignation of the command of the Army of the Potomac in June 1863 had been given command of the Eleventh and Twelfth corps, was assigned to the Army of the Cumberland, now consolidated as the new Twentieth Corps.

12. His forebodings were unjustified. General Butterfield was given command of the Third Division of the Twentieth Corps, and Williams, although but a brigadier, continued in command of the First Division.

X

To Atlanta
and
Savannah

TO ATLANTA AND SAVANNAH

Three years too late, President Lincoln had at length found a general whom he could trust to wage the war effectively. For himself Grant reserved the direction of the Army of the Potomac, whose repeated efforts since July 1861 to traverse the less than one hundred miles distance between Washington and Richmond had failed utterly. To General Sherman was assigned the task of reducing Atlanta, next to Richmond the most strategic point still held by a Confederate army. The two great invading hosts were to strike in unison, Grant with an army of 120,000 and Sherman with the slightly lesser force of 99,000. The advance from Chattanooga to Atlanta was begun by Sherman on May 6. His progress disputed at every turn by General Joe Johnston's army, 50,000-odd, and subsequently by General Hood, Johnston's successor, almost four months were consumed in the march from Chattanooga to Atlanta. From here, after a considerable delay, Sherman launched his much celebrated and much longer march from Atlanta to the sea (at Savannah) which was reached in time to present the city to President Lincoln as a Christmas gift. This section of General Williams' letters, the longest in the series, is largely devoted to the advance to Atlanta. The six-weeks' march from there to the sea was chiefly a festive military promenade, but since Sherman's army was cut off from all communication with the North no letters could be sent concerning its progress, although a typed copy of the "journal" he kept during the campaign (sent from Savannah to his daughter Minnie) still remains. With the letters written from Savannah in early January 1865, the present section concludes.

FORWARD TO ATLANTA

HEADQUARTERS, 1ST DIVISION, 20 CORPS
ARMY OF THE CUMBERLAND

Tullahoma, April 28, 1864.

My Dear Lew: . . . .

I am off tonight for the front and within the month of May you will hear of stirring events. Almost everything is adverse to us. The face of the country is almost impassably mountainous. I expect to live on hardtack and pork, without tents and roughly as a trapper. But I always feel in the best spirits when so living. So God prosper the right and let it come. . . .

Yours Affectionately,
A. S. Williams.

❖

ROSSVILLE AND CHICKAMAUGA VISITED

3½ miles south of Ringgold, Georgia,
May 6th, 1864.

My Dear Daughter:

I have sat down in the shadow of my tent to tell you of my whereabouts. It is near sunset and at my front canvas door the shadows are most agreeable after a hot day. A hot and busy day! Just in front of me, over the woods beginning to put on a deep green, is seen the almost straight line of Taylor's Ridge, at the foot of which along Middle Chickamauga Creek my brigades are encamped.

I left Tullahoma on Thursday afternoon (28th April) after putting all my troops in motion for the front. I stopped that night at Decherd and took the cars next day for Stevenson, where I passed a night in the "Soldiers' Home." The next morning I went to Bridgeport, opposite which, across the Tennessee, one of my brigades was encamped, the new 3rd Brigade of Gen. Tyndale. I found the general quite ill, troubled with his old wound at Antietam. He has received leave of absence and is now on his way home. His brigade is at present commanded by Col. Robinson of the 82nd Ohio. At Bridgeport I concentrated all my brigades, excepting the 107th New York (left to guard the supply trains which I had sent to Nashville, unfortunately, just before the order of march came) and the 3rd Wisconsin, which had been on duty at Fayetteville and had not come up.

We marched from Bridgeport to Shellmound on Sunday and on Monday to Whiteside. The whole of the route is quite mountainous, though it is spoken of as a valley. I had sent my equipage and staff (excepting Lt. Robinson, A.D.C.) by rail direct to Lookout Valley; my horses [went] with the brigade trains. My destination was quite uncertain and I got them as near corps headquarters as possible. We marched from Whiteside to Chattanooga Valley on Tuesday, passing my headquarters tents on the way, very pleasantly located. I also called at Gen. Hooker's headquarters in Lookout Valley and was very pleasantly received. Our day's march was over the Wauhatchie battle-ground and along the valley in front of Lookout Mountain.

On Wednesday we moved early across Chattanooga Valley to Rossville, crossing the Mission Ridge at that point and then turning south over the Chickamauga battleground to Gordon's Mills, where we encamped. We saw at Rossville the old residence of John Ross, the Cherokee chief.[1] It is, indeed, with its barns and granaries, all that remains of Rossville. On the Chickamauga battleground the torn trees and numerous graves pointed out the scenes of the heaviest fighting. We passed several wagons loaded with disinterred bodies of the victims of the battle. I was surprised to find the battleground so level and almost wholly covered by dense forests. . . . It was a poor spot for a great battle and I am not astonished that the reports show a series of defenses and isolated combats of which the rest of the army seem to have been in ignorance. I think our people must have been forced to accept the battle there, for a far more advantageous spot was near Rossville.

On Thursday (yesterday) we marched from Gordon's Mills to this place, a hot day and a dusty march, miles without water; but the men are in good condition and spirits. On my march I received your letter of 26th April, No. 12; also the *Advertiser* with a long account of the tercentenary. You must have had a rare time for Detroit. I fancy I see little Jule in the mass of young beauties, looking like a cherub, as well as a fairy.[2] So Kitty has gone. You must miss her vastly;

but such is life—meetings, pleasant moments, sorrowful partings! . . .

I send you a flower I picked from near some graves on Chickamauga battleground. We move tomorrow at daylight, I know not in what particular direction, but you will see that we are near where the enemy have held strong positions. Before this reaches you, you will know by telegram if anything has occurred.

God bless you my darling daughter and keep you in health and happiness. Love to all. I write on a box cover and amidst constant interruptions.

Your Affectionate Father,
A.S.W.

◈

CORRESPONDENCE UNDER DIFFICULTIES

Near Snake Creek Gap,
12 m. S.W. of Dalton, Georgia,
May 11th, 1864.

My Dear Daughter:

I write you a line to show you where I am. We are stripped of everything for a vigorous campaign and have few facilities for writing. Besides, we are kept constantly on the *qui vive*, marching nights and always ready to move at a moment's notice. I wrote you from Pleasant Church near Ringgold on the 5th. On the 6th we marched at daylight, crossing Taylor's Ridge on the Nickajack Trace, a rough and dangerous pass over a pretty sharp mountain. We encamped at Trickum Post Office. Gen. Kilpatrick's cavalry accompanied my command. The day was very hot. We were two days at Trickum. The enemy made but little demonstration but appeared strongly entrenched about Buzzard's Roost and toward Dalton, between which and us runs a strong mountain range.

On the night of Monday, the 8th, we marched about 12 o'clock towards this place, marching all night and reaching this at 8 A.M.[3] The whole country is a series of mountain ranges, with intervening valleys densely wooded, a hard country for campaigning. At Trickum

Post Office I received your letter of May 2nd, a most pleasant surprise, and Capt. Pittman received yours also and was greatly pleased with the hits. We have before us a hard campaign, I think, but I am well and can stand anything. I slept last night in the most furious storm of rain, lightning, and wind under a shelter fly. I am very moist this morning and am writing on my knees before a campfire, talking business and supplies while I write.

The enemy are near and we shall have stirring times soon. You will hear it all by telegraph. The postman waits. Love to all.

Your Affectionate Father,
A.S.W.

❖

THE BATTLE OF RESACA

Camp near Cassville, Georgia,
May 20, 1864.

My Dear Daughter:

For the life of me, I cannot recollect whether I have written you since I left Trickum Post Office or not. I scribbled a short pencil note from that place. Since then my mind has been so full of constant duties, responsibilities, and cares, and events have followed in such rapid and varied succession that my recollections are a jumble. Day and night we may be said to be on duty and under anxieties. No one who has not had the experience can fancy how the mind is fatigued and deranged (as well as the body) by these days and nights of constant labor and care.

We left Trickum Post Office on the night of the 9th after much reconnoitering and skirmishing toward Buzzard's Roost and reached the entrance of Snake Creek Gap in the Chattanooga Mountains in the morning. The whole march, as everywhere, [was] through woods, with hardly a clearing. On the 12th, moved the division through the gap about six miles and encamped. On the 13th moved towards Resaca, under arms always from daylight and lying ready for a fight all night. I carry nothing for myself and staff of a dozen but four tent flies and one wall tent for an office. All private baggage is left behind. The wagon with the tent flies is seldom up and consequently we roll ourselves in overcoats and what we can carry on our horses and take shelter under trees every night. The days are hot and the nights quite cold and foggy. Most of us have been without a change of clothing for nearly three weeks.

On the 14th we moved through thickets and underbrush to the rear and in support of Butterfield's division, and in the afternoon received a hurried order to move rapidly farther to the left to support Stanley's division of the 4th Corps. I reached the ground just in time to deploy one (3rd) brigade and to repulse the Rebels handsomely. They had broken one brigade of Stanley's division and were pressing it with yells and were already near one battery (5th Indiana, Capt. Simonson, Lt. Morrison commanding) when I astonished the exultant rascals by pushing a brigade from the woods directly across the battery, which was in a small "open" in a small valley. They "skedaddled" as fast as they had advanced, hardly exchanging a half-dozen volleys. They were so surprised that they fired wildly and didn't wound a dozen men. I was much complimented for the affair and Gen. Howard, commander of the 4th Corps, came and thanked me.

On the 15th we had a more serious engagement. Butterfield's division attacked their entrenched positions on the hills, short steep hills with narrow ravines. I was supporting. While his attack was in progress, information was brought to me that the Rebels were moving towards our left in force. I changed front and in luck had plenty of time to form my line and place my batteries in position before they attacked. They came on in masses and evidently without expectation of what was before them. All at once, when within fair range, my front line and the batteries (one of which I had with much work got on the ridge of a high hill) opened upon them with a tremendous volley. The rascals were evidently astounded, and they were tremendously punished. They kept up the attack, however, for an hour or so, bringing up fresh troops, but finally gave way in a hurry.

We captured one battle flag and the colonel of the 38th Alabama, several other officers, and several hundred prisoners. The flag was a gaudy one and covered with the names of battles in which the regiment had been engaged. It was the only flag taken during the day. But that I was not advised of any supports on the left, I could have charged them with great success. As it was, I did a good thing, and the division behaved splendidly. Not a man left the ranks unless wounded. In the language of a private of the 27th Indiana (one of my old regiments) we had a "splendid fight," and he added, " 'Old pap' (that is I) was right amongst us."

The fight ended about dusk and in the morning there was no enemy in front. I went out over the field in our front, not out of curiosity but to see what was in advance. There were scores of dead Rebels lying in the woods all along our front, and I confess a feeling of pity as I saw them. One old grey-headed man proved to be a chaplain of the Rebel regiment, and it is rather a singular coincidence that one of our own chaplains (3rd Wisconsin) was seriously wounded directly in front of where he was found dead. Early in the war I had a curiosity to ride over a battlefield. Now I feel nothing but sorrow and compassion, and it is with reluctance that I go over these sad fields. Especially so, when I see a "blue jacket" lying stretched in the attitude that nobody can mistake who has seen the dead on a battlefield. These "boys" have been so long with me that I feel as if a friend had fallen, though I recognize no face that I can recollect to have seen before. But I think of some sorrowful heart at home and oh, Minnie, how sadly my heart sinks with the thought.

I put parties to bury the dead Rebels but was ordered away before half were collected over the mile and a half in our front. I fear many were left unburied, though I left detachments to gather up all they could find. As I marched away, I was obliged to go along the line where my own dead were being collected by their comrades and interred in graves carefully marked with name, rank, and company. It is interesting to see how tenderly and solemnly they gather together their dead comrades in some chosen spot, and with what sorrowful countenances they lay them in their last resting place. There is much that is beautiful as well as sad in these bloody events. I lost in this battle between four and five hundred killed and wounded.

[*The remainder is missing.*]

◆

THE PILLAGE OF CASSVILLE

Cassville, Georgia,
May 22, 1864.

My Dear Daughter:

I wrote you on the 19th [17th?] from camp this side of Adairsville.[4] We moved from that camp at 12 M., hurried up to support Butterfield's division four miles in front. [We] found his skirmishers engaged and a good deal of artillery firing, so after I had formed [a] line of battle I was ordered to move to the front till I met the enemy. We drove his skirmishers before us over hills and down valleys, across creeks and marshes until after dusk when I halted and bivouacked, sleeping myself under a very dense thicket.

During the night I found we were within a few hundred yards of this place, which lies deeply embowered between two ranges of hills. On the hill beyond the town the Rebs. had constructed strong entrenchments and kept popping away until near midnight. They had all decamped before morning, though Johnston had most of his army here the day before and published an order that he should fight and retreat no farther. He had found his "last ditch."

During the night two regiments of another division were sent in to occupy the town. In the morning I was ordered to send in a strong guard and clear away the stragglers. The people had abandoned their houses leaving suppers on the tables. The Rebels fired from the close hill upon our troops in the town and what with vacant houses and irritation every house was dolefully pillaged. Hardly a thing was left not destroyed or carried away. The picture is painful enough. Just as I reached town some rascal had set fire to one of the principal buildings, which bid fair to finish the whole place as it was difficult to find water. I had a lot of New York firemen who wet sheets, etc. and tore down buildings and saved the place. A few women have come back to mourn over the desolation of their houses and the destruction of their household gods.

This was formerly Cass County and Cassville [was] named after Gen. Cass, but the legislature of Georgia in its Confederate wrath changed the county name to Bartow and the town to Manassas! It is still generally known as Cassville.

Gen. Sherman spent an hour or more with me yesterday. He was very frank, pleasant, and communicative, more so than any commanding general I have ever met. Gens. Hooker, Butterfield, and Geary also came to see me, and scores of colonels. It was our first day of real rest for nearly a month.

Tomorrow we are off again with preparations for a twenty days' march. The long line of fortifications (six to seven miles) running N.E. and S.W. beyond this town would seem to indicate that Gen. Johnston did intend to make a stand here. They ran the line straight through a handsome cemetery, cutting up graves and overturning tombstones. The few people who remain are very angry.

I have been very busy and am still preparing supplies of ammunition, forage, and rations for the twenty days, sending back sick, and am hourly interrupted. If my dates are not correct as to my writing before, it is because my head is too full of the thousand and one questions from staff officers, commanding officers, and the like. Captain Whittlesey is now by my side full of wants and queries. He has read your letter and is tickled.

   Love to all,

         Your Affectionate Father.

       ❖

BATTLE OF NEW HOPE CHURCH

      Camp near Rafer's Creek,
     4 miles north of Dallas, Georgia,
        May 31, 1864.

My Dear Daughter:

I wrote you last from Cassville. We left that [place] at daylight on the 23rd, marching a circuitous route to avoid the other corps. We crossed the Et-o-wah (accent on first syllable) on a pontoon bridge just south of the mouth of Euharlee Creek, and the whole corps encamped along that stream. The next day, the 24th, we moved forward to Burnt Hickory or Huntsville and encamped just in advance of it. Owing to delays and having troops and trains in advance, I did not get into camp until dark. We had a tremendous storm of thunder, lightning, and rain soon after, which lasted well into the night. Neither my wagon nor ambulance could get up. Luckily for me, Gen. Knipe had his with his command and I took shelter in his tent. My staff passed the night on a rather musty pile of straw, enveloped in their rubbers. Some of them got very wet, but all seemed pretty jolly in the morning.

The next morning (25th) my orders were to move in advance of Dallas and encamp to the right. I took a road leading south of the direct road; had rebuilt a bridge over Pumpkin Vine Creek, destroyed by the Rebels, and was within a mile of Dallas when an order came to me to countermarch and move back across the creek to the direct road to support Geary's division. He had met the enemy in force, and apprehended trouble. It was about 2 P.M., the day very hot, and my men much fatigued. Back I turned, and after a march of six miles or more came up with Butterfield and Geary's divisions occupying both sides of the direct route from Burnt Hickory to Dallas, four miles or more south of Pumpkin Vine Creek.

They were in dense woods with considerable underbrush and the ground full of small ravines enclosed in gently swelling hills, which evidently grew higher in front and [on which] was the entrenched line of the enemy. We could see but a few rods in front, but the constant rattle of the skirmish line showed that we had a stout enemy before us. I was ordered to the front with my division and told that I was to push forward and drive the enemy until I found out his force or chased him away from our front. I formed in three lines of brigade front, the 3rd, Robinson's brigade, leading, next Ruger's, and last Knipe's. Two regiments were thrown forward as skirmishers. The bugles sounded the "forward" and on went the three lines in beautiful order, though the ground was broken, bushy, and covered with small stones.

I followed just behind the leading line. We met the heavy supports of the Rebels in a few moments and the volleys of infantry firing became intense. Our lines never halted. As the opposition became intensified, I sounded the "double-quick" and all three lines pounded forward on the trot and the Rebels traveled back quite as quick. Soon we got within range of the enemy's artillery and they poured into us canister and shrapnel from all directions except the rear. My front line, after advancing a mile and a half or more, brought up against the enemy's entrenched line. They had expended pretty much all their ammunition, sixty rounds per man. I sent forward the second line to relieve it, and they expended their ammunition, and Knipe's line was sent to replace it, and thus under continuous shot and shell we held the line close up to the enemy's entrenchments until my whole division had nearly expended its ammunition.

After dark we were relieved by troops of Geary's and Butterfield's divisions and I withdrew my division some three or four hundred yards to the rear. Rain began falling. I found the campfire of Gen. Newton, where I met many general officers, among them Gen. Kimball, who was with us up the Shennandoah and whom I have not met since. Everybody congratulated me on the splendid manner my division made the advance. Gen. Hooker said to me, "It was the most magnificent sight of the war"; that in all his experience he has never seen anything so splendid. He has induced Dory Davis, the artist of *Harper's,* to make a sketch of it. If Dory is not too lazy he will do it,[5] though it will probably be some weeks before it will appear.

I lost about 800 men killed and wounded. Col. McDougall of the 123 New York lost his leg above the knee. I went to see him in the hospital. He seemed cheerful and I hope will recover. He has been a long time with me and I shall miss his pleasant face.[6] Several younger officers were killed, and a good many wounded. None of my staff were hurt. My horse got a ball in his hind leg. I was talking with Gen. Knipe at the moment, just behind the front, when I heard the "sug" and the horse made a tremendous leap. He was hit in the fleshy part of the leg.

We have been here now five days and have not advanced an inch beyond the point my division reached. On some points the troops sent to relieve us did not hold, and some of our dead lie there unburied. There is a constant rattle and has been all these five days on the skirmish line, and now and then tremendous volleys are poured in from one side or the other. Several batteries have been placed in the front in as favorable points as the woods and ground will admit. They occasionally join in the tumult of sounds.

On the 26th we opened with all our guns in position for three hours. I think Gen. Sherman intended to charge their lines. He probably came to the conclusion that the whole Rebel force, with strong reinforcements, were in front strongly posted and entrenched. Two nights ago they came out in some force to attack our position, not more than four hundred yards in front of where my division lies. There was a tremendous hubbub stirred up of infantry and artillery all along our front, extending for miles both ways. I had several men wounded by glancing balls. We have these affairs almost every night and there is not a minute of the twenty-four hours that popping is not going on. We are so near that it seems in our very camp. I have been along the skirmish line several times. Little can be seen through the dense forest. On the extreme right of our corps, from a hill I can see a long line of entrenched hills. The Rebs. have evidently a strong place and I suppose have collected all their forces in the South to give us a final meeting.

I thought I had got quite a hit the other day, but it turned out to be nothing. On the day after the fight I had fallen asleep in front of a tree with all my staff and Gens. Knipe and Ruger with me. A good many "Minnies" had passed over us with their peculiar buzz, cutting the leaves high up in the trees. All at once I was made wide awake by a sharp sting on my elbow joint; I thought somebody had hit me with a stick. Knipe was coolly looking around for the ball, which he soon found. It had struck a tree and spent itself so nearly that it only made a lump on the elbow, without breaking the skin. I had it well rubbed with spirits and have not suffered the least inconvenience. It hit so near the "funny bone" that it quite paralyzed my fore-arm for a while.

I suppose we shall move somewhere soon. It is a very tedious and worrying life as we are situated, for we are kept constantly on the *qui vive* ready for battle. Our rest, you can well fancy, is not of the most refreshing kind. We have had no mails since leaving Rossville.

Love to all,

Your Affectionate Father,
A.S.W.

◆

ADVANCE TO LOST MOUNTAIN

Jackson's House Near Lost Mountain, Georgia,
June 10th, 1864.

My Dear Daughter:

While we are waiting orders to march I pull over my wallet and find two photographs which I enclose. Also a flower plucked in the woods on my line for your herbarium collection.

I wrote you yesterday; nothing new. We are under orders to march towards Marietta. Goodbye, and love to all.

Your Affectionate Father,

A.S.W.

◈

June 10th, 1864.

My Dear Daughter:

I wrote you last on the 27th or 31st ult. in the woods after our engagement of May 25th. We lay in those woods from May 25th to June 1st. The days were exceedingly warm and the air filled with the noisome odors of the dead, man and beast. The tread of so many thousand men had destroyed all traces of vegetable life on the ground. The small stones so thickly strewn over the surface seemed to have been partly converted into powder, which every shuffling mule stirred up in our faces. All the days and nights the same incessant rattle of musketry [continued], so close to us that it seemed in our very camp. About midnight both parties would open in volleys, which in the reverberation through the woods would be redoubled in volume and sounded like a tropical thunder storm twenty times increased in noise.

Of course this was a great interruption to sleep, as when the great din of small arms and artillery began everybody stood to arms, not knowing whether the attack was real or feigned. I think I slept better than anyone. Nothing disturbed me, unless there was an unusual hubbub and artillery joined in the fray. It is wonderful how soon we get accustomed to such confusion and sleep straight through noises that otherwise would drive away our senses.

On the 1st of June I moved about four miles northeast and took position with my left on a considerable hill, which we called "Brownlow Hill" after the Parson's son, who commands a cavalry regiment.[7] From this hill we had a very extensive prospect, but not an inviting one. It was woods and mountain ranges as far as the eye could reach in the direction we wished to travel. To the east, the Kenesaw Hills near Marietta; at the southeast, the solitary Lost Mountain; north, the high Allatoona Range; and between all, nothing but woods, woods, woods!

We remained in this position until the morning of the 5th inst. Three days of it were very rainy and our gravelly soil, we found, had a very large portion of bad clay mixed with it. Brownlow's Hill was quite the resort of general officers. I have seen there, at one time, Gens. Sherman,

Thomas, Hooker, Schofield, Howard, Palmer, corps commanders, besides dozens of division and brigade commanders. A good many old acquaintances came to see me. Among them Gen. John King of the Brady family,[8] who told me to remember him to Aunt Jule; Col. Henry Mizner, who had just reached the army with his regiment; Col. Lum of the 10th Michigan Regiment, and scores of others who had known me at the camp of instruction. These almost always ask after my *little* daughter, whom they saw at the camp.

On the 5th inst. I moved about four miles and took position at the junction of the Marietta and Big Shanty Road fronting southeast. We passed one quiet night, without picket firing or midnight alarms. On the 6th my division took the advance down the Marietta Road two miles and then south two miles to this point. We met and drove in the Rebel skirmishers before reaching this [place] and followed them until I found a ridge running west to Allatoona Creek, where I took post and in half an hour my fellows, as usual, had made a mile or so of very formidable-looking breastworks. It is wonderful how rapidly they will entrench themselves after a halt.

In our front was a group of log houses and barns, from which the enemy's sharpshooters annoyed us much. I spent an hour or so on our line looking at them and being a target for their practice, keeping myself, however, pretty well under cover. After a while I got up a piece of rifled artillery and skedaddled the rascals by throwing a few shells amongst them. For the last few days our pickets have completely fraternized. They have been exchanging papers, coffee, tobacco, and the like. Yesterday morning I found them actually sitting together on the banks of a small stream, a branch of the Allatoona Creek. I was obliged to stop the fraternal intercourse. Isn't it strange that men in mortal strife one hour are on affectionate terms the next! and apparently fast friends. Strange are the commingled events and incidents of war!

I write this early in the morning. We are under orders to march at 9 o'clock. Did I tell you how near Pittman came to getting a bad hit? He had just risen from his blankets under the tent fly, while we were at Brownlow's Hill, when a bullet came through the fly and struck just where his head had been and expended itself on a stone inside, falling on Lt. Robinson, A.D.C., who pocketed the trophy. . . .

I have seen very few reports of our operations. Those I have seen disgust me with their lies. I see a Cincinnati paper gives Hovey's division the credit for what my division did, and yet it is a fact that this division could not get up until we had repulsed the Rebels. I went to Gen. Hovey myself to get him to support my left flank, and he confessed that his troops were new and could not be got through the line of artillery fire. Yet this Cincinnati *Commercial* gives a glowing description of a most gallant charge in which Hovey drove the Rebels like sheep. A pure lie! I see also that they are all careful to speak of a portion of Hooker's corps saving Simonson's battery, when every one of them knows it was my division which came to its rescue at the double-quick, arriving just in time to beat back the yelling and exultant Rebels, who were driving Stanley's division like a frightened mob. However, I have got used to these outrageous reports. They are got up by special scribblers, who are kept in many commands. I don't know but one reporter by sight, and he looks like a jailbird. I wish the whole crew were driven out.

I send you a flower plucked in the woods on my present position. I face south. Lost Mountain is just in front of me, a solitary knob covered densely with trees. The Rebs. have been cutting and digging on its sides for the past three days. My tents are by the side of a house of Mr. Harris Jackson, an old fellow with his third wife and his fourteenth child. He has lost two sons and has two [more who are] prisoners in our hands somewhere. He lives, as all do in this region, in a double log house with an open hall or passage between the two parts. He is a nabob and has two carriages, but lives filthily and ignorantly. . . . Love to all and kisses expressly to little Jule.

Your Affectionate Father,

A.S.W.

◆

DELINQUENCIES OF REPORTERS

In the field, 8 miles from
Marietta, Georgia,
June 12, 1864.

My Dear Daughter:

Yours of the 27th ult. reached me last night. I wrote you and Larned day before yesterday a joint letter. We were under orders to move, but did not until yesterday afternoon and then only a mile or two amid the rain, which pours in real tropical storms day after day with intervals of sunshine. Today it looks like a settled steady rain after pouring all night. The ground is saturated from surface to center and the roads, of course, "awful." It is so cold that I have on my winter coat. Of course, changing camp under such circumstances is no joke for man or beast. All of us have to take to the deeply saturated ground and as our bedding consists of blankets with now and then a buffalo robe you can fancy we sleep rather moist. If we don't all come out "rheumaticy" it will be indeed strange. You speak of not seeing any mention of my division. We don't see many papers out here, but the New York *Herald* of the 25th ulto. had a long and very complimentary notice of the division, and the New York *Post* of about that date another. I don't know by sight but one correspondent. He belongs to a Cincinnati paper. I have seen him once, inquiring about our movements. I never intended to say that I should employ or encourage reporters, but that I should see that the official reports did no injustice. I am not indifferent to the ephemeral praise of reporters, but I cannot sell my self-respect to obtain it. The only other New York report I have seen is the New York *Tribune*. I don't know who writes for that paper but he hardly tells a truth and a great many lies. He gives to Hovey's division, 23rd Corps, the credit of defending our left flank and capturing the gaudy flag of the 38th Alabama, when it is known all through the army that Hovey did not get into the fight and that my division captured the flag and the colonel and many officers of that regiment.[9]

Indeed, Gen. Schofield, who commands that corps, told me yesterday that Hovey did not lose in killed and wounded a dozen men on the day of that fight. Such is the reliability of the correspondent of that pious and patriotic paper, the New York *Tribune!* I see he wholly ignores my division and always speaks of it as "a portion of Hooker's corps," but is careful to name Geary's and Butterfield's divisions. Probably the fellow, whoever he may be, fancies I have neglected him sometime. I have no recollection of ever having seen him and don't know his name. But don't let us fret ourselves over this, Rene. Be assured that my division stands as high as any with those who know and that the truth will appear in the end.

I have lost over 1,200 men killed and wounded since leaving Chattanooga, and on the 14th of May, I believe, as do many others outside my division, that my opportune arrival and the gallant conduct of my troops saved our army from a great disaster. Gen. Howard, commander of the 4th Corps, thanked me in person for the services I had rendered his corps. It was one of his divisions that was being repulsed, leaving a battery in the Rebels' grasp. . . .

I send you the *Herald*'s letter, enclosed—the account of Knipe's charge is a good deal exaggerated. He was only slightly wounded and his nephew mortally.[10] The colors of the 38th Alabama were taken by Ruger's brigade. The account of the 14th is correct and mainly that of the 15th. I have seen no account of our battle of May 25th. Hooker says I made the most splendid charge he has seen in this war.[11]

I send you a photograph of Gen. Slocum which he sent me from Vicksburg, his new post. He writes that he is greatly amazed by speculators and sharps who do not hesitate to sell arms and ammunition to Rebels to obtain cotton. They will find Slocum a hard nut to corrupt.

Tell Larned I will write him a separate letter soon but as a general thing I shall be obliged to write you jointly. We are kept all the while packed and booted and spurred for a conflict. The enemy are doubtless very strong. The petty and miserable failures along our coast enable them now to withdraw everything to help Johnston's army. If these expeditions had started now, they could have drawn away from our front tens of thousands of men.

But I will neither speculate nor criticize, but hope for the best and that a speedy end may come to the rebellion and the war. . . .

Your Affectionate Father,
A.S.W.

◈

PINE MOUNTAIN AND GENERAL HOOKER

HEADQUARTERS 1ST DIVISION, 20TH CORPS
DEPARTMENT OF THE CUMBERLAND

Near Kolb's House 3 miles west of Marietta, Georgia,
June 24, 1864.

My Dear Daughter:

I wrote you last from the house of J. Jackson on the 10th inst. The weather has been so rainy since and our occupations so incessant that I have found no chance to write.

We left our quarters at Jackson's on the 11th and moved a mile and a half to the east, establishing a new line. The weather which had been for some days of alternating heavy showers and sunshine became a heavy northeast storm and lasted without intermission for two or three days, so cold that with big camp fires and overcoats one was hardly comfortable. The earth became saturated like a soaked sponge and the mud was intolerable. Our batteries were established on a ridge 800 yards or so from a prominent knoll called Pine Hill. It was on this hill that Bishop or Maj. Gen. Polk was killed by our shell.[12]

On the night of the 14th the enemy evacuated their line of entrenchments and the hill. We moved southeast and in a few miles came up with another line of the enemy's works. Geary's division was leading. I was obliged to put Knipe's brigade on his right and the other two on his left. We had quite a combat but my loss was not large. Geary lost a staff officer, Capt. Veale, I fear mortally wounded.[13] I was quite near him when he was shot, the ball passing into his right breast. I had gone to the left to look out a position for my command. Soon after, I returned towards the center where my troops were lying and was talking with Gen. Hooker when an enormous explosion burst out directly in front of us, within a few feet. We had heard no ball whiz, nor report of artillery. It was like lightning from a clear sky. It turned out that we were close to a Rebel battery which was concealed by the woods, and the shell bursting and the report of the cannon was probably simultaneous. The Rebs. kept the place all around very hot with musketry and artillery. We lost quite a number of men, as it was impossible to find a place of shelter for troops in reserve even.

320

All day, the 16th, we kept up an artillery duel, and the din of small arms went on as has been the custom for weeks past. In the night the Rebs. evacuated and early in the morning we marched over their works, which we found heavily constructed with flanking works and embrasures for artillery. We followed through the woods, my division being on the left, with orders to connect with the 4th Corps. I had a hard task through the underbrush, up hill and down vale. I finally found Gen. Hazen commanding the right brigade. Returning towards the center to find Gen. Hooker, I saw him ascending an open hill in front and followed with Gen. Knipe. Hooker had his escort deployed as skirmishers and was vigorously at work at the Rebel cavalry down in the valley in front. The Rebs. had a battery on a small hill to our right and front and were firing it over our hill pretty energetically. We at length got up a rifled battery and some infantry and were making pretty rapid work with what was in our front.

Suddenly we saw, half a mile or more on our right, a great cloud of Rebel cavalry flying in disorder to the rear. There must have been a brigade of them and every man was kicking and spurring for dear life. Many horses were riderless. We opened on them with artillery, which greatly increased the disorder. It was laughable to see Hooker's excitement. "Williams," he would cry out, "see them run. They are thicker than flies in a Mexican ranch." "See them go," and we all shouted, to the astonishment of our troops who had not got up. In truth our line of skirmishers that morning had one major general, two brigadier generals, and about fifteen poorly armed cavalry! We found the Rebel works a short distance in advance and took up a new line. The rain came down in torrents all the afternoon and night and the mud seemed too deep to ever dry up.

On the 18th, still in the mud. Our pickets, especially on the right of the 4th Corps, kept up a great noise.

19th. The enemy having withdrawn, we moved early to the southeast, crossing Mud Creek. Just after we had got over on a temporary [bridge] the torrents of rain began again, and our small creek swelled up in an hour to a respectable sized river. I moved my division and got possession of a high ridge.[14]

◈

OCCUPATION OF MARIETTA

[July 7(?), 1864]

[The first four pages are missing.¹⁵]

Entrenchments—the third very heavily and strongly constructed. In the march of three or four miles I struck a byroad which led to the Marietta and Powder Springs Road, not more than half a mile from Marietta. Here I put the division in mass and as the corps was waiting orders I rode into the town. The buildings and grounds in the suburbs looked very invitingly cool and shady though for the most part deserted. It was, indeed, pleasant to see signs of cultivated homes after my exile of two months in camps and woods. The town was almost wholly deserted, not more than seventy-five families remaining out of a population of several thousand, not an article of any kind left in the stores, nor the smallest piece of furniture in the abandoned dwellings. Every street is deeply shaded with pride of China and other large leafed trees. Cavalry horses were grazing in the public square, and altogether this once beautiful place wore an air of complete desolation. Our troops were marching through one end, but stragglers were not permitted.

Aunt Rene had written me that the children of an intimate friend of my youth (Miss Julie Denison, afterwards Mrs. Burr of Richmond) had been living in Marietta, but I found on inquiry that they had moved farther south some months ago.

Returning to my command, we continued our march south three or four miles until we were again brought to a stand before formidable looking works along a high ridge in our front. The Rebel cavalry opened upon us furiously but did very little damage. It was nearly dark before I got my division in camp in the woods.

July 4th I did a day of heavy riding. First over to Gen. Palmer's corps (14th) to see if I could connect lines with him. Then I rode with Gen. Hooker over hill and dale and across ditches and through thickets passing the barricades of pickets (23 corps) looking in all directions until we reached Ruff's and Daniel's mills on the Nickajack Creek. It was an intensely hot day and Gen. Hooker is a furious rider. As soon as I got back, I was obliged to put my division in motion to take a new position two or three miles west. It was nearly sundown before I got into camp, but I had the satisfaction of seeing a brigade of "blue jackets" occupy some heights away off on my right front and on the flank of the enemy's position of defense.

Early on the morning of the 5th we found the Rebels had again vacated their strong line of entrenchments. I followed across the valley and creek in my front and across their strongly constructed works until I struck a north and south road, which I followed for several miles, halting now and then to look after crossroads leading farther east. I met Capt. Poe on my rides, looking sound and cheerful. I did a great deal of riding in a very hot sun. Towards 5 o'clock by crossing over creeks on slight cowpaths we reached the crest of a densely wooded hill from which, over a new line of Rebel breastworks, we could see the tall spires and many of the buildings of the city of Atlanta, twelve to fifteen miles away, looking like a city set upon a hill, for it seems a good deal higher than our high position. Nearer, not over three-quarters of a mile away, heavy columns of "grey backs" with wagons and artillery were marching with a hurried pace towards the river and along their lines of defenses. They were, however, taking up a new position of defense, and between them and us lay a deep ravine and a miry creek. We could only reach them with artillery, and this was not effectively used.

We encamped on the high ridge until the afternoon of the 6th, when we moved towards the railroad in an easterly direction and took position on the right of the 14th Corps. Here the left of my division adjoined two Michigan regiments, the 14th Michigan, Col. H. R. Mizner, and the 10th, Col. Lum. Both of these officers and several others from Michigan have been to see me. Indeed, for the four days I have been encamped here in the woods I have had quite a levee of acquaintances and strangers. The weather has been intensely hot in spite of bowers and shades. The firing between our lines and the Rebs. has not been very active. Indeed, the pickets of my division and the Rebs. formed a truce to cease firing, but yesterday afternoon the 14th Corps opened with a battery of artillery and the rattle of the pickets began again soon afterwards. During the night the battle kept up, and in the stillness of camp seemed to be within a stone's throw of my headquarters.

At daylight this morning the general officer of the day reported that the enemy had evacuated again. I ordered forward the picket line, which reached the Chattahoochee River a mile and a half away without opposition. A good many Rebel stragglers and deserters have been taken on each abandonment of Rebel camps. On some days we have taken some hundreds. They give abundant proof that the Rebel ranks contain thousands who would gladly desert. They are carefully watched and it is a great risk to attempt to escape. These deserters have no especial love for us, but are tired of war, discouraged, and after years of absence anxious to see [their] home, which is generally within our lines. Still, the Rebel army has made a very clean retreat. They leave little behind. Even the inhabitants follow with their slaves, cattle, and furniture. I think we should have punished their army vastly more than we have. From my standpoint occasions have presented themselves during these tedious two months in which large portions of the Rebel army could have been destroyed and the whole virtually broken up. But after all, their losses must have been severe in desertions and killed and wounded. Their falling back has enabled them to recuperate by collecting reserves and guards, while our lengthened line has greatly weakened our numbers.

We have reached a point now where comes the "tug of war"—a broad river to be crossed—strongly fortified at all points, and an advance towards the objective point which has taxed the defensive purposes of the enemy for a year or more. I am not so confident as some, as our real base of supply is far away and the line we depend upon a very long and uncertain one, subject to accidents and to destruction by the feeblest party. And yet with the fair chances of war on our side, I think we will get Atlanta. There is much work and I can't help sometimes envying those who are peacefully sitting under their own vines and fig trees and have none of the heavy cares and anxieties that confront us. . . .

Love to all. I never was so impatient to hear from you and have never been so long without letters.

Your Affectionate Father.

◈

FROM KOLB'S FARM TO THE CHATTAHOOCHEE

On the Chattahoochee River
Near railroad from Marietta to Atlanta,
July 10, 1864.

My Dear Children:

You all complain that I do not write you, and yet if you have received my letters (and a reference to dates will inform you) by measuring the *quantity* you will see I have written more to you than all your combined letters would amount to. I have no easy chair in a nice room with pleasant surroundings to repair to while I write, but with all the cares and responsibilities of my place I am obliged to sit on the ground in the woods, generally amidst the rattle of small arms, the booming of cannon, the braying of mules, the rattle of wagons, and the universal din of large armies. If we halt for a few days it is always in readiness to move at a moment's notice; always in expectation that every mounted orderly bears the order to forward. Sleeping on the ground after a whole day in the saddle, roused up half a dozen times a night, up before daylight to be ready to march at daybreak; all these and a thousand matters, that you cannot imagine, nor have I room to repeat, don't prepare either the mind or body for letter writing, even to those we best love and oftenest think of. Yet if my letters to you all have come to hand you will find I have written a good many very sorry looking pages. . . .

Now for my movements since writing any of you. I wrote last to Minnie on the 24th ult. and to Larned or Rene, I cannot recall which, on the 27th or 28th, ult. My division was then lying on Kolb's farm in the same position in which it was attacked on the 22nd of June, and of which I gave you an account. We remained in the same position until the morning of July 3rd. The corps on our right and left made several efforts to do something, but without much effect, save the loss of men. On June 27th the 4th and 14th corps made a combined attack, but without success and with much loss, especially in officers. Brig. Gen. Harker was killed.[16] I see the papers report his name as Maj. Gen. Hooker.

Our corps was not engaged. We were held in reserve for a *coup de grace* in case the Rebel lines had been carried. But in truth they were very strongly built, with strong abatis and chevaux-de-frise. My division lost a good many men on the picket line, as their shelters were exposed in the open and they could scarcely move without exposure to sharpshooters. We had on one day a grand effort to drive them out of their works with artillery. There was a grand expenditure of ammunition, an immense noise, and great deal of smoke, without results.

On the morning of [July] 3rd we found that the Rebels had left. I immediately advanced my picket line and followed with the division over very rough country, full of thickets and deep ravines. We crossed three lines of theirs which the enemy kept disputing. They held a spur somewhat higher. I arranged a small column of attack and having got a battery in position I pounded the top of the spur and immediately charged it with not over fifty men and took it in ten minutes with a loss of only three men. I captured one young fellow who told me the hill was held by a regiment of Confederate Regulars, belonging to Gen. Cleburne's division. I have taken a good many prisoners from Gen. Stevenson's division. Uncle Lew will recollect him, Carter L. Stevenson, of the 5th Infantry.[17] He married a Miss Griswold of Detroit. The Rebs. tried hard to retake the hill, but did not succeed.

On the 20th I was relieved by Wood's division, 4th Corps and marched down across a broad valley to a wooded plateau beyond, then west along this to a larger plantation, where the elevated plateau drops down to the margin of Closed[?] Creek. We found Rebel pickets at a cluster of Negro houses, but they decamped in haste. We came up with a division (Hascall's) of the 23rd Corps, which lay considerably behind us. As our march was in some way to relieve this corps of a body of Rebs. disputing their crossing, we came to a halt for the night in another pouring rain.

There was no stately mansion on this plantation. A few decrepit Negroes were about, who told us that the master lived in Marietta and had carried off about sixty sound Negroes. The overseer, when here, lives in a very poor log house. There were crops of oats, wheat, and corn, all of which became the coveted food for our animals. All the crops very thin and poor. Wheat about ripe, corn half grown in length of stalk, oats in the milk. You can compare this with your crops.

On June 21st, we remained in camp at Atkinson's farm. It was the first day for weeks that it did not rain. We were expecting to move at any moment. I moved forward two regiments about a mile and took possession of a high ridge with a good deal of open country in front and the two twin mountains of Kenesaw clearly defined about six miles north. The enemy have batteries on the summit of both knobs and keep up a pretty brisk cannonading. McPherson's command (Department of Mississippi) is around its base.

June 22nd: Early in the morning I moved up my whole division and occupied in force the ridge taken yesterday and one in echelon to it, farther in advance, which is partly covered by woods in front. Two brigades, Knipe's and Ruger's, were put on the advance ridge and Robinson's brigade on the rear ridge. Robinson and Knipe and two regiments of Ruger had an open country in front, varying from 500 to 1,500 yards wide. I had previously occupied the Marietta and Powder Springs road several hundred yards on my right. There was savage skirmishing all day, especially on my left where the Rebs. held some log houses and had built rail covers all along the front of the woods.

Every time I attempted to advance my line the enemy would get a flank fire from my left. Geary's division was considerably behind mine and on my left a thousand yards or more. I could see his line of skirmishers, but they could not, or would not, advance so as to cover my left or connect with my advancing line. The enemy gave signs of being in great force in the woods in front. Gen. Hooker was impatient for an advance. I was opposed, until my flanks right and left were protected. I had put a battery of rifled guns on the rear hill and a battery of twelve lb. Napoleons on the advanced hill. Luckily, the rifled guns practiced on all the points in front and got superb range in trying to drive out the heavy skirmish reserves.

About 3 P.M. I rode over to the Marietta road to see Gen. Hooker at Kolb's house. He had just got information that the enemy was massing to attack us. The story was that the whole Rebel army had concentrated. No time was to be lost in getting into position and entrenching. I rode rapidly back along my brigades and in ten minutes my whole command was deployed in a single line and everybody piling up logs and rails for breastworks. Ruger and Knipe formed a continuous line of battle, as I have before mentioned, with open country before most of the line. Robinson was on a parallel ridge a few hundred yards in the rear, his right resting opposite Knipe's left, which fell back around the termination of his ridge towards Robinson. Just in front of Knipe's left was a dense patch of woods with heavy underbrush which I had ordered cut down.

We had just fairly begun to pile rails when the heavy skirmish line of the enemy poured out of the woods all along the open and advanced at a run. Three columns, massed, followed close and deployed in three and four lines. Our artillery opened upon them a most destructive fire. The infantry columns opposite Knipe and Ruger's left moved forward, but as they reached the brow of a ravine which ran parallel to our front, the whole line opened a withering volley. Some Rebs. went back, some scrambled down into the deep ravine, but none ever passed beyond it. One heavy column got hold of the woods in front of Knipe's left, and upon it I turned twelve pieces of artillery, sweeping it with canister and case shot until the devils found sufficient employment in covering themselves behind trees and logs.

Farther toward our left a huge mass of Rebels moved out to attack Robinson's brigade, but three rounds from the rifled guns set the whole mass flying in the greatest disorder. They never reached the fire of our infantry. The attack was kept up from 4 P.M. until near dark. The numbers were formidable, but the attack was indeed feeble. The Rebs. had been badly shaken by our artillery fire before they left the woods. All the prisoners say this. Indeed, after the first half-hour the men considered the whole affair great sport. They would call out to the Rebels who had taken shelter in the woods and in the deep ravines in our front, "Come up here, Johnny Reb. Here is a weak place!" "Come up and take this battery; we are Hooker's paper collar boys." "We've only got two rounds of ammunition, come and take us." "What do you think of Joe Hooker's Iron Clads?" and the like.

The fellows down in the shelters, I regret to say, generally answered with some very profane language and with firing of their guns. In the morning, however, over sixty of them lay dead there. Judging from those they left behind, and from the fact their wagons were all night carrying off dead and wounded beyond the ravines, with our consent, the Rebs. must have lost over a thousand men in this attack. My loss in killed and wounded was not far from 120, many of them, slightly. I was in a single line of battle without reserves, and had little or no breastworks. They had four lines of attack and a division in reserve in the woods. I captured one battle flag and could have taken a thousand prisoners, but that I dared not break my single line to advance, especially as I had been officially informed that the enemy was in great force in my immediate front. I took prisoners from Stevenson's, Stuart's and Cleburne's divisions. I lost but one field officer, a Maj. Becket of the 61st Ohio, killed. Several other officers were wounded, but none of the staff. Capt. Pittman had quite an independent fight of his own on the right, in moving up the skirmish line to occupy the Marietta Road. He accomplished the affair with great success.

Altogether, I have never had an engagement in which success was won so completely and with so little sacrifice of life. Considering the number of the enemy sent against my single division, the result is indeed most wonderful and gratifying. Dory Davis (T.R.) has been here making a sketch of the ground for *Harper's;* but he says that *Harper's* don't put in half he sends and those are bunglingly and incorrectly copied. He sketches beautifully and the pictures he has sent give a most correct idea of the field of fight, so far as landscape is concerned. We are now lying in the woods and have possession of the ground the enemy charged over. They have strong works not a mile in our front and our pickets keep up the usual popping of small arms. . . .

And now I'll close. The day is hugely hot, and as I write I circulate around a big oak to get the shadiest spot. Just think of two months of the campaigning we have had with the two weeks of deluging rain. Since the 1st of this month my division has been every night in line of battle and under fire. There has not been a night or day that Rebel musketry could not have reached my headquarters and hardly a day that the projectiles of their artillery and infantry have not made solemn music over my head. Love to all. . . .

Your Affectionate Father,
A.S.W.

◆

FRATERNIZATION AND LIES OF REPORTERS

Near the Chattahoochee, Georgia,
July 15th, 1864.

My Dear Daughters: . . .

Nothing particular has occurred since I last wrote you. I spent one afternoon, the day after I wrote you, along the river with the picket line. The Johnnies were pretty thick on the opposite side, a few hundred yards away, and kept us dodging behind our log defenses so briskly that our sight-seeing was by no means agreeable. One fellow, especially, was an excellent shot and would graze the top of our log defenses at almost every pop. We were quite safe, as we could drop at the smoke of his gun and hear the whiz of the bullet before it reached us. Since that, our "boys" have got up an armistice and they bathe on the opposite banks of the river and meet on a neutral log in the center of the stream and joke one another like old friends, making trades in tobacco, coffee, and the like, and exchanging newspapers. It is a curious fact that while the pickets on both sides of my front are popping away at one another, those of my division have not fired a shot for several days, but are on the most quiet and joking terms with the opposite Johnnies. I had a man mortally wounded yesterday in the picket reserve, which is kept quite in the rear. The fact was reported to the Rebel pickets, with a threat of retaliation. The Rebs. in front opened a volley of hard words on their reserve, which fired the shot, and an explanation was sent down that it was a mistake. The sharpshooter mistook the reserve for one of the 14th Corps, which keeps up its firing. I am always glad when picket-firing stops. It has no effect upon the results of war and is a miserable and useless kind of murder. Pickets are mainly intended to give notice of an advance or movement of the enemy. This constant popping obviates or destroys this valuable purpose. . . .

I have never seen more lying by the letter-writing fraternity than in this campaign. We have no correspondent in this corps, but we have had one division commander who, I judge, has kept a corner in the notes of every correspondent in the army, besides keeping his staff busy at the same work. He claims pretty much everything. I see the New York *Times* gives him the credit of my attack at Dallas. He was hardly near enough to hear my guns. He is not the only instance of lying humbugs in this army who contrive to keep their names connected with battles which they were not near.[18] It sickens one to see what efforts are made by officers high in rank to steal undeserved honors, and how much thirst for false fame preponderates over real love of country and an honorable ardor to serve the great cause, irrespective of personal reward.

Have you seen T. R. Davis' sketches in *Harper's?* He has drawn several of my division; one, the attack in the woods at Dallas, has been published. The other is the Rebel attack on my division on June 22nd near Kolb's farm. I see by the papers that everybody is claiming part of this defense; Geary and Butterfield's divisions and the twenty-third Corps. The truth is, that there was not a musket fired on the Rebels in this attack except by my division, and all the claim for artillery services from other commands is all bosh. My own artillery and infantry did the whole thing, for I stood on the slender rail piles in the front rank and saw all, directing even the fire of my artillery. But enough of complaint! I have been made exceedingly mad, I confess, to read the meanness which would rob another division of its well-earned reputation, to bolster up some ambitious fool to a major generalship. These stories in the press originate in the envy and jealousy of commanders, and I know them.

Gen. Butterfield, commanding the 3rd Division of our corps, has gone home. He says [he is] sick, but I think he was disgusted and tired. Brig. Gen. Ward of Kentucky commands the division. Butterfield was a much more honorable officer than Geary, but he "hankered" after newspaper fame, and was uneasy that as a major general he had a subordinate command to others he ranked. In many respects he is an excellent officer, but cannot stand the hard service of such a campaign as this. Indeed, few can. Many of our general officers are going home and more intend to go, but hope to hold out until we reach Atlanta.

Gen. Hovey, the officer whom the newspapers gave the credit of my defense near Resaca, resigned soon after that affair and started for Washington. I have it from a prominent staff officer of Gen. Sherman's that his only reason was that the President had promised to promote him, and had not, and he would not stand it any further. This he did in face of the enemy and within sound of his guns. I see he has been made a *brevet major general!* The same gazette announces the dishonorable dismissal of a captain for resigning in the face of the enemy, for reasons not satisfactory. Hovey is my junior by two years at least.[19] He resigns in face of the enemy and is promoted; I stay and am never thought of at the War Department.

I write all this for your private eye. I don't wish my grievances made public, but I have made up my mind to quit when I can do so honorably, when the present active campaign is over. The whole system of promotion is by the practice of a low grovelling lick-spittle subserving and pandering to the press, who can lie you into the favor and notice of the war authorities. I might stay a long life in hard service, as I have done for over three years, and I never could seek the polluted steps to preferment and should never reach it.

Theo R. Davis, the artist for *Harper's,* spends most of his time with us now. He sits sketching now, just before me, sketching "Vining Station" and the Chattahoochee River. A smooth-faced, handsome-looking youngster, full of good humor and wit. His sketches are beautiful, much better than copies seen in *Harper's,* and he does them with the rapidity of a ready writer. His mother is traveling in Europe. He reads me long passages from very long, well-written letters, descriptive of men and things. He is an only son, and she a widow.

I have written Minnie several times that Capt. Beman has been detached and is in charge of some commissary depot. I have not heard from him for several months. Capt. Whittlesey is here, as fat and jolly looking as ever, but rather grouchy at times on account of the trouble of large trains. I am going over to tea with him. He lives as only quartermasters can, very luxuriously, for the woods. Has *spring chickens* and soft bread and pies and *butter* (a thing I have not had for two months) and all other luxuries. Living behind us with large trains, they contrive to carry anything, while we eat hardtack and hog meat salted. . . .

Your Affectionate Father,
A.S.W.

◈

KOLB'S FARM AND AGGRESSIVENESS OF HOOKER

Near the Chattahoochee, Georgia,
July 17th, 1864.

My dear Lew:

We cross the river this afternoon, so I employ a few moments to tell you of my whereabouts, as you have not Minnie's letters now to inform you. I hope you opened my last to her as it would give you information of my movements up to the 25th ulto. or thereabouts including a "right smart" fight my division had on June 22, in which I licked Carter L. Stevenson's division and other Rebel troops right soundly.[20] Do you remember C. L. Stevenson of the old 5th Infantry, who married a Miss Griswold of Detroit? He is the man. His division is a part of Hood's corps. I had moved my division to a line of small hills in an "open" where Master Hood thought he had caught me, and he moved his whole corps straight on my front. But I had my twelve pieces of artillery admirably posted and my whole line was deployed before he could get out of the woods. I had no defenses save a few rails thrown down in a hurry, but before they could get within reach of my infantry their columns were awfully ploughed through and through and thrown into great confusion. Then his advanced lines became commingled and badly confused when they reached a point where one brigade could reach them. It opened a volley of two thousand muskets! The devils, what was left of them, took refuge in a deep ravine, into which I plunged shot and shell for an hour from a whole battery. Another huge column (covering ten acres, I should think) further to our left was broken up and thrown into a rolling mass by my artillery alone and finally fled like scared sheep back to the woods. The fight was kept up by fresh troops for nearly four hours. The Atlanta papers acknowledge a loss of three brigade commanders and 1,200 men. Another paper says one brigade lost over 700 men out of 900! I have no doubt their loss was over 2,000! *Mine was only 120!* That is what I call a glorious success. So few men lost and the enemy so badly punished. I could have taken a thousand or two of prisoners, but as I was deployed in a single line without supports and without connection on my left, and as I had been advised by Gen. Hooker that two corps were on my front, I dared not venture from my strong position to pursue their broken columns. Prisoners say that they thought to catch me before I could get into position.

We have had a hard and wearisome campaign. For more than a month we have been day and night literally under fire, and day and night the din of war has ceaselessly gone on. From our crossing the Etowah, the Rebs. have entrenched themselves every five miles. Driven from one line, they would fall back to another and each one seemed stronger than the last. If you could see the obstructions they place in front of their strong lines of dirt and log breast works you would wonder that any attempt should be made to carry them. The country is all woods, deep ravines, muddy creeks, and steep hills, the most defensible positions by nature I have ever seen, and they most skillfully bring art to aid nature. Rods and rods of abatis, trees, and bushes cut down and intertwined in front, and chevaux-de-frise of strong pointed stakes, fastened firmly in the ground in the midst of the abatis, making a network through which a man could hardly crawl in an hour. Just imagine a line of armed men making their way through and thousands of rifles firing upon it!

Our corps has had the fighting share. It seems to me we are always in advance. In truth, the impetuous Joseph, surnamed Hooker, hates to be behind—is restless, prompt, sometimes impatient, and always "Fighting Joe." He is not so reckless of his men as the world thinks but is exceedingly reckless of his own safety. You will always find him in the front. He sometimes drags us division commanders a little farther on to the advance picket or beyond than we would think it judicious to go. On one occasion, Hooker, Knipe, and myself encountered the Rebel line of skirmishers. Hooker deployed his fifteen or twenty mounted orderlies with carbines and actually drove a strong line of mounted infantry and we held a hill, notwithstanding the Rebs. opened a battery upon it!—until I could get up a battery and a regiment or two of infantry. Just as we had accomplished this, a whole brigade of Rebel cavalry came pouring from the woods on our right in the greatest confusion and disorder, every man spurring over the soft ground as if for dear life. We helped the confusion by pouring into their flanks salvos of case shot from our battery. Hooker was as tickled and excited as a boy and fairly shouted with delight. He is indeed a strange man, but the men like him as he is always seen when a fight is on. When we came from the Potomac, the troops here called us the "paper collar troops."

Now they call us the "iron clads," and I have requests from dozens of regiments and some brigade commanders asking transfers to our corps. I think none stands higher than Joe Hooker's corps.

I want to write you about the probabilities of this campaign, but I have a call and must mount horse. We are a long way from our base and if any loafer or body of Rebs. happens to burn an important bridge, we are in a bad way. We can thrash Johnston at all times if we can keep up supplies. The recent fuss in Maryland which gave "conniptions" to all Pennsylvania and the whole country makes one sick. A thousand old maids with broomsticks ought to have driven the enemy over the Potomac. It seems, however, that all the forces we have there are divided up into squads and put in charge of a lot of fussy and incapable major generals, decayed and fossil remains of political appointments. Love to all. I'll write you again when I have time.

Yours Affectionately,
A.S.W.

❖

INVESTMENT OF ATLANTA

Near Atlanta, Georgia,
July 26, 1864.

My Dear Lew: . . .

We are now *near* Atlanta, but there is a big gulf or gulfs I fear between us. Unless we can starve the Rebs. we have hard work ahead. I had a severe fight on the 20th, was attacked in the woods and lost nearly 700 men and six good officers, killed and wounded.[21] I have recently written to you but such are the occupations of my head and heart that I really cannot remember whether it was since the 20th or not. We have little rest, as my division lies near the Reb. entrenchments and the din of arms is kept up night and day. A battery of twenty pieces is posted near my headquarters and is booming away night and day into Atlanta. Every report cutting the air along a ravine in front of my entrenchments reverberates and gives out a volume of sound like the falling down of many houses. In the night it is particularly noisy and rest-breaking. In return, the Rebs. throw round shot and shell on all sides of my tents. Yesterday they spoiled one of my water buckets. I lost one of my aides (Capt. Newcomb) killed and one (Capt. Bennett) badly wounded in the head on the 20th. My veteran division has been sadly cut up, so that I am reduced in numbers to a brigade. We have had so wearisome and long continued a campaign that I sigh for rest. My health has been perfect until within a day or so. I begin to feel debilitated and broken down and am taking quinine to build. Shall be all right I hope in a day or so.

Love to all,

Yours Affectionately,
A.S.W.

❖

Outside Atlanta,
August 11th, 1864.

My Dear Daughter:

I have been unusually occupied for some days and have neglected to write you. . . . I have been in command of the corps since the 27th, which coming suddenly has put upon me a great deal of new duty, especially in our close proximity to the Rebel lines. I am obliged to be on the front line almost every day and it is an all day and laborious job. We are constantly moving up some part of the line, which for this corps extends over three miles along the northwesterly side of Atlanta. We are now face to face with the outer Rebel works, and one has to be very cautious of sharpshooters and very steady nerved to get into and out of our line of works through the picket bullets and the tornado of artillery missiles.

There is scarcely a cessation night or day, and as some very large guns are in position very near my headquarters on both sides, I have a constant irritation of the tympanum kept up through the twenty-four hours, to say nothing of that irritation in the shape of Rebel shells which are at times whizzing and exploding on all sides. I have twice been fairly shelled out, the rascals throwing projectiles of fifty and sixty pounds weight directly amongst my tents and wagons. It is strange how few, comparatively, are injured by these heavy guns. Now and then a shell explodes inopportunely and a few men are injured. The stray bullets and the sharpshooters do more damage. Still, I don't think one will ever get so used to the shrill and sometimes roaring sound of shot and shell as to enjoy it as a serenade. It is decidedly disagreeable, and the different varieties and calibers give every possible variation of unearthly noises.

The Northern papers speak of the country between the Chattahoochee and Atlanta as level and open. It is, on the contrary, full of deep ravines and steep, wooded hills, and directly around the town the elevations command each other. Tangled bushes and underbrush fill the gullies and obstruct the hillsides. In going to the front I am obliged to leave my horse in a deep ravine as near to the picket line as it is safe and then ramble through the tangled undergrowth over muddy rivulet banks and up steep hillsides under the hottest sun's rays, with occasional pouring showers, and in this way trace out the next best line for our advanced works.

It has been a most fatiguing business, but we have now reached hills on my front which stand face to face (but a few yards distant) with the more elaborate entrenchments of the Rebels. I am now principally occupied in straightening my line and seizing upon favorable advanced points held by the Rebel outposts. Almost every day we stir them up and drive back their pickets. A day or so ago I captured 138 in one haul by the picket line of one brigade. We have thus far always succeeded in dislodging them from their small entrenched picket posts and their stronger reserves. But they show no signs of yielding the town, though it must be a very uncomfortable place, as every day we treat the occupants or the vacant edifices to a thousand or so of shell and shot, and now we have several guns of very large caliber in position, within close range.

Last night they opened for the first time and made the woods and ravines howl with the heaviest reverberations. We had got used to ten pounders and twenty pounders but these eight and ten inch fellows throwing elongated shells of sixty-odd pounds are a new element in the general thunder. The Rebs. have thrown into my camp several

337

weighing over forty pounds, and of all varieties of French and English invention; some of about the shape of a large iron pot, though much more solid. They come with a noise of most portentous and ferocious import, and I notice that Christian and Sanitary agents and all non-combatants make rapid tracks towards the rear at the first sound thereof. . . .

Gen. Hooker left us on the 28th, much to the regret of the whole division. He asked to be relieved because Gen. Howard, his junior and often his subordinate in command, was placed over his head in command of the Army of the Tennessee, in place of Gen. McPherson, who was killed on the 22nd inst. He thought it was intended as an indignity. Gen. Hooker has certainly been a superior corps commander. He is full of energy, always courteous and pleasant, and has a great faculty of winning the confidence and regard of all ranks. It was a blue day when he left us so suddenly, after the many days of hard service we had been together.

I was placed temporarily in command [of the corps] until an assignment is made by the President. We hear now that Gen. Slocum has been ordered here. I hope it may be so, for my rank precludes a chance for myself, even if I desired it, which I really do not. I am satisfied with my old division and I have long given up all hope of promotion from the present powers. When officers can quit the army in the face of an enemy and get promotions in Washington, those who stay may well despair! . . .

I have seen several newspaper notices of my division in western papers and one in the *Herald,* but not the *Times* article. You had better keep it. I will send you some others. The division deserved all that was said of it, and more, for it saved one of the other divisions from a great repulse and flight. But it has deserved as much on five or six occasions during this campaign, for which others got the credit. All at once it seems to be discovered that it is a great fighting division. It has been so at Cedar Mountain, Antietam, Gettysburg, and dozens of other places, always fighting without skulkers and always repulsing or driving the enemy. I think it the best division in the army! A good portion of it has been under my command for more than two and a half years. If I had, as others have, paid puffers, it would have had a name of marvel and its commander would probably have been promoted! Did you see

THE BATTLE OF CHANCELLORSVILLE
Reproduced from a sketch by A. R. Waud in *Harper's Weekly*, May 23, 1863. The sketch shows General Couch's corps forming a line of battle to cover the panic flight of General Howard's Twelfth Corps on May 2, 1863.

VIEW OF DUMFRIES, VIRGINIA

Reproduced from a sketch by A. R. Waud in *Harper's Weekly*, August 29, 1863. The town was occupied alternately by Union and Confederate armies. "It has been the scene of many a savage skirmish," wrote artist Waud.

GENERAL HOOKER'S ESCORT CHARGING CONFEDERATES AT THE BATTLE OF DALLAS, MAY 25, 1864

Reproduced from a sketch by Theodore R. Davis in *Harper's Weekly*, July 2, 1864.

my likeness in the last *Harper's?* (dated the 13th). Capt. Pittman thinks your comments on it will be entertaining. I recognize nothing but my mustaches! I suppose Dory Davis sent it to *Harper's,* but I have no knowledge about it. . . . I send you some little trifles for your scrap book. No. 1, sample of maps sent to division commanders to indicate routes on march; No. 2, a note from Gen. O. O. Howard, written at Gettysburg and carried in my pocket until today. No. 3, sketch of position of my division (in red pencil) 21st and 22nd June. On last day was attacked by Rebels; see letter account. No. 4, sketch of my position of the 2nd Division taken a few hours before the attack at Peach Tree Creek, July 20th, '64. It was drawn to enable me to find the road through the division after I had crossed the creek. My division moved up the road towards what is marked "open fields" and was lying both sides of the road close to the house indicated in N.E. corner in the woods. My advance engaged with Rebel pickets, when the furious onslaught was made. I send you also a map of the vicinity of Atlanta, on which I have indicated as nearly as practicable the position of our corps relating to the town. *We stretch out over three miles.* These are not very valuable additions to your collection; but I have no doubt will greatly interest you, trifles though they be.

I am now at corps headquarters and have with me of my old staff only Capt. Pittman and Lt. Robinson. All the rest of the mess are new. We have three or four messes here and live more expensively than at the division. Indeed, one can hardly avoid living expensively in the humblest way, for we depend upon caterers and sutlers who bring everything from Nashville at enormous prices. I have seen green corn but once; new potatoes once; no butter for weeks. The country is stripped about this. We get what we call desecrated [dessicated] potatoes now and then, canned milk and fruits at outrageous prices. But all the fruits of the season as well as vegetables are not seen. I hear peaches and watermelons are plenty below this. I weary to get there. The postman waits and I must close. . . .

Your Affectionate father,

A.S.W.

OCCUPATION OF ATLANTA

In Atlanta, Sept. 3rd, 1864.

My Dear Daughters:

I have dated my letters so long from *Near* Atlanta that it is quite a change to write *"In* Atlanta." Most of our corps came in yesterday evening, the Rebels having evacuated the night previous. We remained in our old camp and works in front of Atlanta until the night of the 25th, when the 20th and the 4th corps on our right were withdrawn to cover important operations of the army. Our corps moved to three crossings of the Chattahoochee; Pace's and Furness' ferries and the railroad crossings. We did not march, except to move out of the trenches, until the 4th Corps had withdrawn across our front and taken a new position. It was after 2 o'clock at night before we got away. The Rebs. never fired a shot at us and we quietly took up our new positions on the south side of the Chattahoochee. We entrenched ourselves strongly and awaited the progress of events by the rest of the army, which moved southward to strike the Macon Railroad. We heard little from it, but every day we made reconnoissances in force toward Atlanta, getting up to our old line, where the enemy appeared in force.

On the night of the 1st inst. I was awakened from a dream of heavy thunder in which the earth seemed to tremble. Heavy reports of what I thought artillery firing followed in rapid succession, and for two hours or more the roll of artillery firing seemed to increase, while a red glare lit up the skies in the direction of Atlanta, with fitful shooting up through the clouds that hung over the town. After listening and wondering for an hour or more I concluded that Sherman had driven the enemy near the southeast part of the city and had attacked or was being attacked.

I was strengthened in this belief as toward morning the firing was renewed with more regularity. I inclined at first to the opinion that the reports were explosions, but I had heard distant firing so resembling this, and the line of sound seemed to recede, so my judgment settled down on artillery. We know now it was the explosion of powder shot and shell from eighty-two carloads of Rebel ordnance stores, and the burning of a large car factory. At daylight we started out reconnoitering parties and about noon our advance had entered and occupied the town. I brought up two brigades of my division, reaching this [place] after dark. We entered the town with bands playing. The people say that the Rebel army has gone toward Macon, avoiding the position of Sherman. A good many people are still in town, but my duties on the lines which the Rebs. built to protect the town have not yet given me much chance to see this town of greater distances than the original city of Washington. It appears to be scattered over leagues, having a thickly-built business center.

Many [residents] are said to be sincerely Union. As I was marching at the head of my column last night through the dark streets, made intensely so by the heavy shade-trees, I heard a window shoved up and a female voice cry out, "Welcome!" I cried back, "Thank you, and the more so as it is a rare sound down here." It did, indeed, seem strange, that voice of welcome where we have met little but battle and carnage, coming so suddenly from the impenetrable darkness. For more than a month we have lain face to face with the heavy works thrown around this city, and day after day have I peered over our trenches to catch some new idea of the position of affairs. Three high, broad parapets seemed to bid defiance, and my curiosity was generally met with sharp efforts to plug my head. Week after week their heavy guns and ours have kept up a roaring, during which we have thrown thousands of projectiles from the twenty-pounder Parrott to the sixty-odd-weight ball into this city.

It seemed, therefore, very strange to march unopposed, as I did last night, through these same hostile works, and especially right alongside of one of those frowning fortresses that lay in my original front and which had killed or maimed hundreds of men of my division. I rode along full of queer sensations and exciting emotions. It was too dark to see much, but there was the principal battlement which had caused so much trouble and injury and not a sound came from it. I could hardly realize that its strong and defiant voice had really been silenced.

I forgot to mention, in its place, that Gen. Slocum joined us just after we withdrew to the Chattahoochee. He brought with him his three aides, Maj. Guindon and Capts. Moseley and Tracy. I was glad to turn over to him my command and go back to my division. The general seemed to fear that I would be greatly disappointed in not getting command of the corps.

On arriving here last night I took quarters at a very imposing-looking house, as seen by the dim candle light. A very large room with a broad bed and white counterpane promised a splendid rest, after a fatiguing day. It was the first time in four months I had slept in a house. You will laugh when I tell you that I found the air oppressive and could not sleep. To add to the troubles, the bugs (bedbugs I suppose) worked on me from head to foot. I have never, during the campaign, sleeping under trees, on the ground, or in straw, suffered anything like it from the numberless variety of wood-ticks, jiggers, and other festering biters that fill every atom of the dirt of this section. The consequence was, of course, a very disturbed night and the getting up at daylight with a resolution to have my tent pitched and go back to the luxury of my cot and blankets.

I took a long ride at sunrise along my lines and came back in an hour or so to my breakfast, with a hearty appetite. This afternoon we have a huge storm of thunder, lightning, and rain, with a cold wind. I doubt if we have had as hot weather down here as you have had. Our nights are always cool. There has been but one or two that I have not slept under a blanket. The days are hot, very, outside the shade.

Capt. Pittman has sent in his resignation, which will doubtless be accepted. He will go home soon I suppose. [Illegible] left us day before yesterday for home, after three years' service with us. It made me homesick to say good-bye. He has been a very faithful and useful man. When Capt. Pittman goes, all my Detroit associations will be broken up. I shall have no one about me from home. These matters affect me very unpleasantly. But three years have taught me sad lessons of sudden and painful partings and of friendships swept away by hundreds in an hour of bloody battle. I don't know that the heart grows callous, but it learns to bear the heaviest blows with but a passing pang.

What a retrospect! What a mass of mixed recollections is embraced within the compass of three years! How merriment and agony and death; pomp and parade; the battle struggle; the excitement of the charge and rush; the despondency and sinking sensation of retreat; the proud feeling of success; the oppressive and disheartening thought of failure; the dead and dying friends; some with cheerfulness, crying you a "Farewell" as they are borne away; some—so many indeed—with the glassy eye and speechless tongue! How all these recollections and a thousand others fill the mind in an hour of meditation such as I have had tonight, looking out of my window into the dark night and forgetting the present and living alone in a retrospect of the now almost three years of my active war life! Who can tell, but he who has passed through such a weird life of excitement and joys and sorrows?

Sunday morning, 4th September: I got so far last night. Fearing I was getting rather too sentimental for a soldier, I stopped. Now the mail messenger says the bag goes in a minute. We hear the Rebs. have burned the Bridgeport bridge. If so, it is a very bad thing for us, and this letter may not reach you for weeks, if at all. Love to all.

Your Affectionate Father,
A.S.W.

◈

Atlanta, Georgia, Sept 21st, 1864.

My Dear Daughters:

Pittman left us day before yesterday [22] and I celebrated my fifty-fourth birthday by a review of my division. I don't think I should have called them out for that purpose, but Gen. Slocum's order did the thing, unconsciously. We had tried it the 18th in a big rain and so on the 20th the Heavens let up, though very cloudy, long enough to let us through. After the review the troops marched by the headquarters of Gen. Sherman and Gen. Thomas. Sherman came out in his careless manner, standing in the middle of the street and emphatically declaring that such soldiers could never be beaten. He is indeed a queer one. A genius indeed!

I feel pretty blue today. These changes of one's old comrades are not pleasant. Besides, we are having the meanest kind of rainy weather. I believe I shall never feel in good spirits while in the service, except on active duty. I think I shall journalize for a while, so adieu for today. The review was a good one and the division appeared well. I was surprised to see how neatly the fellows had got themselves up.

September 24th: Rain every day at intervals, pouring down. I was out almost every day, in spite of the rain.

343

25th: Geary's 2nd Division was reviewed and made a good show. From the high works of the Rebs. behind his review ground I could see our old line from which for weeks I had watched this same Rebel works. It looks less formidable inside, than out, but along the whole line is a very strong line of obstacles; sometimes three or four lines of abatis and chevaux-de-frise. It seems fortunate that we did not attempt a direct attack.

26th: The 3rd Division was reviewed and did not appear as well as the other divisions of the corps. It is of more recent organization and its principal officers are away. A colonel was in command of the division and seemed a little at loss. My old inspector (Lt. Col. Buckingham) was in command of a brigade. I forgot to say that Gen. Knipe left us on the 22nd, having been detailed as chief of cavalry of the Army of the Tennessee. I am grieved to part with him, after three years' service together.

October 1st: More rain; more cloudy, dull weather.

October 3rd: Rumors of trouble on the railroad. Have reports for several days that enemy was moving towards our communications. The 4th and part of the 14th corps moved toward the Chattahoochee. Railroad cut somewhere. All mail and papers stopped a day or so ago. Trouble ahead, unless we catch the rascals. Met Gen. Sherman today in front of corps headquarters. He was evidently uneasy. A day or so before I had been to his headquarters to call upon Mrs. Rousseau and daughter and two other ladies. Sherman was in a distressed state that ladies should intrude upon his precincts without permission. I have been riding all round the Reb. works twice in the past few days, no easy job, as it must be over ten miles. Took a look at several points where I had been to establish [entrenchments].

October 4th: Great moving of troops yesterday and today toward the Chattahoochee. This morning Gen. Sherman followed with all the corps but ours, and a few thousand convalescents, wagon guards, and the like. Day cloudy.

October 5th: Cloudy and more rain in the afternoon. Was obliged to ride half around the outer works to make new dispositions of my command, and to look out the many small camps and squads left by other corps.

October 6th: Raining all day. Out again on horseback. I have half the circle of the town to picket. The number of small squads left behind is very annoying.

October 7th: Clear and cool; first signs of frost and first real fires of the season. We had one early morning fire in September. More long rides; horses on half forage. Lt. Harbaugh came to see me.

October 8th: Clear and cool; no doubt that Hood has badly cut the railroad; have been days now without letters or papers. Two orderlies sent to the Peach Tree Creek were gobbled (Snow and Ransom), both mounted. Sent out a party and found that they had been taken prisoners by about twenty-five cavalry.

October 9th: Weather keeps cool, but pleasantly so. The rascally signal fellows sent in a story that Richmond was captured. Whereat there was great rejoicing and hurrahing all over the camps. A band came to serenade me, late in the evening. I didn't believe the story and didn't get up to rejoice. I have serenades now almost every night, as the moon is shining finely.

October 10th: The Richmond news is pretty much blown up by a report from Gen. Sherman. The Pennsylvania and Ohio regiments vote today for their state tickets. I stayed an hour or so at one of the polls. The vote seemed to be pretty much all Union. I think this army will vote strongly for Lincoln. I think full four-fifths, not counting the Missouri and Kentucky regiments. Something may work a change or the vote may be lost by Hood's impediments. Sent out a long train today for forage.

October 14th: We have actually got a mail. It was carted around the railroad break. Got letters from Rene, Minnie, Larned, Capt. Pittman, and others. Latest date from Detroit Oct. 1st, Pittman's letters. You will all be anxious to hear from me. I am anxious to hear from the railroad for I think Hood is on an audacious raid and will do great harm. No mails have gone forward north since Oct. 1st. I am told. It seems queer to be cut off from all news and all letters so long. It is like being at sea. No enemy has appeared near the town and we are all greatly mystified. I see Jeff Davis prognosticates a Moscow defeat for our army. I think he will find things different, even if we have to retreat!

Saturday October 15th: The Department photographer came and took a picture group of myself and staff, with headquarters for a background. After several trials made necessary by someone's moving his head at each trial, we finally succeeded in getting a picture pronounced satisfactory, though Capt. Whitney's face is badly blurred from movement. Col. Boughton had himself and all his officers (twenty-two) taken in one picture. In the afternoon went to see Col. Ketcham, 150th New York, off, going home to attend to his election to Congress. Found Lt. Duffield at the cars going home, mustered out. Went back to headquarters and made up two packages of pictures and a short letter with $200 Pittman's checks for my daughter. Reports from the rear bad. Hood seems to be getting hold of the railroad where he pleases.

Sunday October 16th: In all the forenoon, lots of officers called. In the afternoon called on Dr. Batewell, at 14th Corps Hospital and on Col. Inness, 1st Michigan Engineers. Evening at home. Col. Robinson, 3rd Brigade, in command of three brigades from different divisions and two batteries artillery left with over 600 wagons for foraging. Rather a lonely day. Telegraph from rear shows that Hood is still at work on railroad. Track all up from Resaca to Dalton. Day fine.

Monday October 17th: No further news this morning. Our suspense is great, and our condition by no means pleasant. We are pretty hopeful that Sherman will give Hood a big coup, but it is not pleasant in our isolated condition to reflect that if he fails, or Hood out-maneuvers him, we are badly isolated. The morning is very pleasant. Artist shows first impression of our staff group. Capt. Whittlesey could not be present, which I greatly regret. All the rest are in and good, save Whitney's. I close here as one of my clerks can send it outside mail. I saw Capt. Poe this P.M. Wrote to Rene yesterday.

❖

REASONS FOR THE RE-ELECTION OF LINCOLN

Atlanta, Georgia, Oct. 18th, 1864.

My Dear Daughter:

I sent you a special letter, though as things look just now it may be a long time getting to you. It was good and affectionate of you to remember my birthday. I forgot yours only for the day. Then I have a great deal more to think of than you, and expecially at that time while in command of the corps. . . .

Give my love to Syl. and tell her that I have hunted all along Marietta Street for that female who cried, "Welcome!" But the night we came in was so dark that I have never been able to locate the spot of female patriotic welcome. Most of the houses in the vicinity are small and of humble pretensions. Gen. Sherman's order was made necessary from the fact the people could not stay here and subsist. The moment we took the city all supplies from the country stopped. North of this there are no people left but the very poorest, and the country is literally stripped. South of this in Rebel hands. It became a matter of necessity and mercy, therefore, to send them away, north or south as they choose, where they could be fed.

You seem to be in doubt on political matters. I am no politician, nor have I been for some years. Fortunately, too, I have been for years at a distance from the political contests which excite the passions and prejudices of men and so dethrone their reason. I think I am, and have been, in just the position to make a dispassionate judgment between the contending parties. McClellan is patriotic enough, but the great weight of talent and energy and shrewdness of the party which is going to control him (especially in the western states) belongs to men who hold that one state can not coerce another or that the de facto government has no rightful power to compel a state to remain in the Union.

These kind of politicians control the Democratic party in a majority of the western states and they really controlled the Chicago convention. They did not dare present one of their own men, for it would have so shocked the masses that their game would have been up. They, therefore, yielded the man, but took the platform. They got in the clause for an immediate armistice, well knowing that an armistice or truce, unless sought for by the Rebels, is nothing more nor less than absolute submission to the Rebel government. They know that Rebels in arms must be so subdued by arms as to be driven to ask terms themselves; that no rebellion was ever put down by gentle means, after severe ones had been tried; and that especially in this rebellion the Confederate government and its President and Congress has repeatedly and officially declared that they will accept no terms short of absolute independence.

Now I think that to abandon the war now, to submit after all that has been done and suffered, would be disgraceful to us of the North, who now live, and would entail dishonor and disaster upon our posterity for many generations. We cannot stop now and concede all we have been fighting for without bringing upon our heads the contempt of foreign governments and of the Rebel government itself. Personally, I should certainly wish to find a home where the finger of scorn could not be pointed at me.

Now from what I have written you will understand that I do not favor the McClellan-Pendleton ticket. I have no particularly strong personal reasons for loving the existing Administration, nor do I, in everything, admire its policy or measures. Still its great aim, in the emergency which absolves small things, is right. It goes for fighting this rebellion until the Rebels cry, "Enough!" Therefore, without making pretensions to any very large amount of Roman virtue, which prefers country to self and forgets personal grievances in the thought of the general good, I do not hesitate to say that if I was at home I should vote for "A Linkum" and his party. So much for politics. I catch up these themes as I read over your letters. . . .

I have missed Capt. Pittman greatly. He was always near me and more a confidential officer and friend than any of the others. I sometimes get so *lonely* when surrounded by thousands that I feel sorry I did not resign and go home also. But for a great desire to see this war through, I should have done so long ago, and don't know but I shall do so now. I feel at times as if my duty to the government demands it, as well as my own self-respect. You will not appreciate the feeling, because you can never know all that I know of the facts of my case. It has become in my mind a question, often mooted, whether the discouragement and depression the government has put upon me is not unfitting me for that zealous and ambitious discharge of duty which is properly due from every man holding the responsible position I do. So you see I either feel, or am trying to argue myself into the belief, that on every account, public as well as personal, I ought to quit the service. Some fine morning you may see me at the front door a *citizen!* . . .

People at home can't see why a man's pride and spirit is wounded and diminished. Let them work and toil long months under every exposure, doing, in the written judgment of their superiors, their full duty in all respects, and then let them see dozens of sneaks and drivellers put over their heads. Ah, Minnie, in civil life honest labor and faithful services unrewarded or unacknowledged chill the heart and depress even the efforts of the benevolent Christian spirit, but there is something, especially in military life, where the gradations of command are violated and the shirking junior is foisted over the heads of long-serving and faithful officers, that falls with especial weight upon one's pride and self-respect. It can't be denied nor concealed, and he who does not feel it is not fit to hold a commission! . . .

Oct. 20th: No mails go out today. Several guns heard this morning toward the river. About 200 Reb. cavalry appeared on the track. Yesterday a train of cars was burned at Vining's Station, just beyond the river. Things begin to look rather mixed for us down here. However, we keep in good spirits and hope for better news. If this gets through you will know that matters are improving. Again love to Rene and family.

Your Affectionate Father.

The ring enclosed was made by Capt. Whittlesey's blacksmith out of the brass plunger of a percussion shell, thrown into my camp by Rebs. in Atlanta.

◈

GENERAL HOOKER'S OPINION OF SHERMAN

Cincinnati,
October 31, 1864.

Brig. Gen. Williams,
Dear General:

I have just received yours of the 23d and have only time to reply that [I] am rejoiced to learn that my letter was in every way satisfactory to you. It is not in [my] power to do as much for you as I would like to, or as much as it is my duty to do. If you were here, I could make application for you to be assigned to the command of the district of [?] Michigan, but until you are, it will do no good, as you know. It might not if you were here, but whether so or not it would afford me happiness to have an opportunity to press it. I leave for Detroit tomorrow and wish that you could be with me.

I am a good deal amused as well as annoyed at Sherman's cunning. He

349

is a fool or a knave. I think the latter, and I know that he is crazy. The superior administrative ability of Howard required him to discover. He knows better or ought to, and it is only made use of as a cloak to cover his d—d rascally treatment of me. This matter is not over. It will have a long tail to it. The indignation of the Army of the Potomac at the treatment I received from Sherman was deep and violent. Sherman's conduct is fully understood by all and his motive of action. The truth was he was afraid of me.

Excuse my writing so much of myself.

His excuse in his report for ordering the assault of the Kenesaw is rich—that the enemy might know we could do it. He ought to have known this from their experience with him in his first attack at Vicksburg, also at Missionary Ridge, in all of which he was whipped out of his boots. But damn him, let him go at present.

Adieu, Your Friend and Servant [?],

Joseph Hooker.

❖

EVACUATION OF ATLANTA

Journal, 1864:

November 5th: A beautiful day again. Sent box and letters home with pictures and a remittance in 7 2/00 and $250 to Lew Allen, and to Larned a check for $100 by Maj. Stone, paymaster. About 12 M. got an order to move the division on the McDonough Road about three miles out and encamp. Marched at 3 o'clock and encamped with trains and all before sundown. The order was unexpected and the hurry of packing up was great. I passed the night in a log-hut, occupying the *top* of a bed in a room full of men, women, and children.

November 6th: Was awakened at daylight by the firing on picket line and the beating of reveille along the whole line. The attack was on the 3rd Division just to the right of me. Our pickets ran in without much resistance, losing one man killed and one mortally wounded. The ground was at once recovered and the firing soon stopped. The morning was very cool and soon clouded over with high, disagreeable November winds, not very much like the pictures of the sunny South. It was not easy to keep comfortable around the largest campfires. At 12:30 M. received an order to move back into town and occupy our old camps. Moved at once. I went back to my old quarters. Sharp rain in the afternoon and pretty much all night. No news, but all manner of rumors about the future.

November 7th: Cloudy again and rainy at intervals. Temperature mild. Gen. N. J. Jackson, who is here awaiting orders, called.[23] Gen. Ruger left with the probability of commanding a division of the 23rd Corps. This leaves me without a general officer. All my brigades are commanded by colonels.

November 8th: Election day. Went with Capt. Whittlesey to the polls of the 1st Michigan Engineers and Mechanics and deposited my vote, the first time within four years or more, I think. I voted for Lincoln electors. After voting, went with Col. Robinson, 3rd Brigade to several Ohio and Pennsylvania regiments. Everything going on quietly and orderly.

Reports that the last train runs north to-morrow morning. We are then to be cut loose and find a new base of supplies. Doubtful if some weeks don't elapse before we hear the election news. The weather is quite mild, but showery, and the prospect of bad roads is not amusing. The roses have pretty much disappeared from our yard; now and then one blooms forth. I enclose one, very fragrant, which was solitary and quite alone.

There is a great scramble at the depot to get away. Thousands of Negroes are striving to get transportation. We sent away a family of blacks which came in about forty miles soon after we got here. Part of them have been with us. There are two women and one boy that I should like to get to Detroit. They are the best and steadiest Negroes I have ever seen. One of the women washed and sewed for our mess and cooked part of the time. She cooks, sews, and washes splendidly, and withal is a steady home body and a most excellent character. She calls herself "Pibby," not *Phoeby*. If anybody wants a superb house-servant let them get her or her sister also with her. I gave them a letter of commendation to Lew Forsyth at Louisville.

These may be my last notes for sometime. I will write as soon as possible. And so, Goodbye!

[A.S.W.]

BATTLE OF GETTYSBURG AGAIN

HEADQUARTERS, 12TH CORPS
ARMY OF THE CUMBERLAND

Tullahoma, Tenn., Dec. 30, 1864.

Major General George G. Meade
Commanding Army of the Potomac
General:

I enclose herewith the report of General T. H. Ruger of operations of
the 1st Division, 12th Corps, at the battle of Gettysburg, together with
the reports of his brigade and regimental commanders. General Ruger,
with a large portion of this division, was ordered to New York City soon
after the battle, and immediately after his return from New York the
corps was ordered to this department. The reports of General Williams
and myself were delayed with the hope of recovering General Ruger's
report in time to forward it with them. I deeply regret the necessity
which compelled me to send my report and that of General Williams un-
accompanied by any report of the operations of the 1st Division. For
although an account of the operations of this division was given in the
report of General Williams, who commanded the corps during the
battle, I think the absence of Ruger's report may account for some of
the errors contained in your report as to the operations of the 12th
Corps.

I enclose a letter from General Williams calling my attention to
these errors, to which I respectfully invite your attention, and if anything can be done at this late day to correct these errors I trust you will
do it. Your report is the official history of that important battle, and to
this report reference will always be made by our government, our
people, and the historian, as the most reliable and accurate account of
the services performed by each corps, division, and brigade of your
army.

If you have inadvertently given to one division the credit of having
performed some meritorious service which was in reality performed by
another division, you do an injustice to brave men and defraud them of
well earned laurels. It is an injustice which even time cannot correct.
That errors of this nature exist in your official report is an indisputable

fact. You give great credit to Lockwood's brigade for services on the evening of July 2nd, but state that this brigade was a portion of the 1st Corps, while it never at any time belonged to that corps, but was a portion of the 12th Corps, and was accompanied in its operations on the evening of July 2nd by General Williams in person. A portion of this brigade (150th New York Volunteers) is still in General Williams' division.

I copy the following statement from your report: "During the heavy assault on our left, portions of the 12th Corps were sent as reinforcements. During their absence, the line on the extreme right was held by a very much reduced force. This was taken advantage of by the enemy, who, during the absence of General Geary's division of the 12th Corps, advanced and occupied part of the line. On the morning of the 3rd, General Geary's division having returned during the night was attacked at early dawn by the enemy and succeeded in driving him back, and reoccupying his former position. A spirited contest was maintained all the morning along this part of the line. General Geary, reinforced by Wheaton's brigade of the 6th Corps, maintained his position and inflicted severe losses on the enemy."

From this statement it would appear that Geary's division marched to the support of your left—that Williams' division did not—that his (Williams') division, or a portion of it were guarding the entrenchments when the enemy gained possession—that General Geary returned and with his division drove the enemy back—that the engagement on the following morning was fought by Geary's division, assisted by Wheaton's brigade. This I know is the inference drawn from your history of these operations by every person unacquainted with the truth.

Yet the facts in the case are very nearly the reverse of the above in every particular, and directly in contradiction to the facts as set forth in the report of General Geary, as well as that of General Williams. Geary's division did not march even in the direction of your left. Two of his brigades under his immediate command left the entrenchments under orders to move to the support of your left, but through some unfortunate mistake he took the road leading to Two Taverns. Williams's entire division did move to the support of your left, and it was one of his brigades (Lockwood's) under his immediate command, which you commend, but very singularly credit to the 1st Corps.

353

Greene's brigade of the 2nd Division remained in the entrenchments, and the failure of the enemy to gain entire possession of our works was due entirely to the skill of General Greene and the heroic valor of his troops. His brigade suffered severely but maintained its position and held the enemy in check until the return of Williams' division. The "spirited contest maintained by General Geary reinforced by Wheaton's brigade" was a contest for regaining the portion of our entrenchments held by the enemy, and was conducted under the immediate command of General Williams, and was participated in by the entire 12th Corps, reinforced not by Wheaton's, but by Shaler's brigade.

Although the command of the 12th Corps was given temporarily to General Williams by your order, and although you directed him to meet at the council of other corps commanders, you fail to mention his name in your entire report, and in no place allude to his having any such command, or to the fact that more than one corps was at any time placed under my command, although at no time after you assumed command of the army until the close of this battle was I in command of less than two corps, and I have now in my possession your written orders dated July 2nd, directing me to assume command of the 6th Corps, and with that corps, and the two then under my command (the 5th and 12th) to move forward and at once attack the enemy. I allude to this fact for the purpose of refreshing your memory on a subject which you had apparently entirely forgotten when you penned your report, for you have not failed to notice the fact of General Schurz and others having held, even for a few hours, command of above that previously held by them.

I sincerely trust that you will endeavor to correct as far as possible the errors above mentioned, and that the correction may be recorded at the War Department.

I am General,
Very Respectfully Your Obedient Servant,
H. W. Slocum
Major General Vols. Commanding

◈

ARRIVAL AT SAVANNAH

Savannah, Georgia, Jan. 6th, 1865

My Dear Daughters:

I don't know when I shall be able to send you my promised description of our "promenade militaire" through Georgia. It seems as though I had not a moment to myself. What with visitors, business, reports, reviews, and what not, I have not a moment from getting up to going to bed.

We have been having a series of reviews by corps, all done in the broad streets of Savannah. My corps (or the 20th, more properly) was the last reviewed and all the world and his family came to see it. They call us the "paper collar and white glove fellows" and of course said we would beat them in show. And we did! Hundreds of officers have told me it was the finest and most splendid review they ever saw. Gen. Sherman confesses it was the best of all. The other corps commanders acknowledged the same. My old division (the 1st) was especially elegant. We have three or four of the best bands in the army, and we managed to have it all tell. I was quite a lion! Think of it—a lion! I—a lion!

We are without mails and almost without food for man or beast. This will sound strange to you, knowing that we have had communication with tidewater for nearly a month, but so it is. Few supplies have reached us. The country has none, and we are almost starving our animals on rice straw. And yet we are within three or four days' sail of New York.

While we were on the march through Georgia, supplying ourselves from day to day and not knowing whether tomorrow would furnish the supplies, the men used to say, "We can live on beef twenty days" (and we had plenty of it) "but when we get to the coast won't we find plenty. Lots of ships full of stores waiting for us." And yet, we have been poorer fed here than I have ever had my men during the war. I really begin to fear that we shall suffer for food with a dozen good ports close by us. I know that my artillery horses and wagon mules are already reduced to a dying state! I have in the corps 7,000 of them to starve and they can't be replaced here.

Tell Aunt Jule that I hear in this place of two daughters of Mrs. Clitz, wives of Secesh officers (Sallie Clitz one) [24] and a daughter of

355

John Kinzie of Chicago a *ditto wife*.[25] I have not been to see either, because I hear they are rabid "southrons." Old army officers talk of them.

I have just finished my official report and am having it copied. To-morrow I will begin a series of letters to you about our march. I hear Gen. Butterfield is coming back. If so he will rank me and command the corps. I shall ask to be relieved and probably shall get leave to come north. I have been strongly recommended by Gen. Sherman for promotion, but shall not accept brevets junior to the hundred who have recently been promoted. The mail leaves tonight and I write this merely to let you know I still live. Love to all.

Your Affectionate Father,
A.S.W.

◆

DEATH OF A SOLDIER

Savannah, Georgia Jan. 15th, 1865.

My Dear Minnie:

My dear daughter, your pious and hopeful spirit, as it breathes through your letters, gives me new strength for the labors and dangers which are before me. I shed tears sometimes when I read them, but I always feel refreshed and have a renewed vigor when I reflect what pure souls are praying for my safety. I ought, indeed, to be grateful that I have been so miraculously kept from harm. I have seen so many struck down by my side, so many who have fallen, as it seemed, in the very tracks I had left, that it seems like a miracle that I have always escaped.

The case of young Ahrett of my staff, a boy of twenty years, impressed me greatly. I had been over the same ground carelessly, trying to see the Rebel works and not imagining any particular danger. He goes out a few hours afterwards and in the same spot is struck dead by a ball through his heart and is brought back to my quarters a corpse. Accustomed as I have been for three years to like scenes, I know of no similar event as the death of this brave and beautiful boy, which has so long and so deeply impressed me. Dozens of times each day on the march he brought me messages, always with a cheerful face and a happy air, and always ready for any duty. It was not easy to believe that the boy with the curly hair and the smiling face could be so early a victim of war.

But goodbye. Love to all.

Your Affectionate Father,
A.S.W.

1. John Ross, notable chief of the Cherokees, had a white father and a mother who was three-fourths white. From early manhood he chiefly devoted his life to the public service of his tribe, of which he was principal chief from 1828 until its removal to Indian Territory in 1839. Thereafter, until his death in 1866 he served as chief of the united Cherokee nation. See F. W. Hodge, *Handbook of American Indians North of Mexico*, and Bella Armstrong, *History of Hamilton County and Chattanooga, Tennessee* (2 vols., Chattanooga, 1931), I, Chap. 5. The latter contains a picture of Ross's house at Rossville.

2. The celebration was in honor of the three-hundredth anniversary of the birth of William Shakespeare. The Detroit *Advertiser and Tribune*, issue of April 23, 1864 contains a nine and one-half column report of the elaborate day-long proceedings. Five addresses by eminent Detroit citizens were delivered, along with a musical concert and tableaus which the reporter characterized as "the finest exhibition ever gotten up in Detroit."

3. Here, as occasionally elsewhere, General Williams' chronology is inaccurate. Monday fell on May 9, 1864, instead of May 8. The succeeding letter (of May 20) correctly indicates that the march was made on Monday May 9.

4. This letter is missing from the collection. Presumably it described the desperate battle of Resaca, May 14–15, 1864, which is briefly described in his letter of May 20, 1864. His official report of the battle is in the *Official Records*, Series 1, XXXVIII, Part 2, 27–29.

5. Theodore Russell Davis, illustrator and artist-correspondent for *Harper's Weekly* during the war and afterwards for many years. See The New York Historical Society, *Dictionary of Artists in America, 1564–1860* (New Haven, 1957). The illustration showing the advance by General Williams' division was published in *Harper's*, July 2, 1864, p. 928.

6. Colonel Archibald L. McDougall died of his wounds in the officers' hospital at Chattanooga on June 23, 1864.

7. Colonel James P. Brownlow, commander of the First Tennessee Cavalry Regiment. His father was "Parson" William G. Brownlow of Knoxville, notable upholder of the Union cause, and subsequently Governor of Tennessee and U.S. Senator from that state.—*Dict. of Am. Biog.*

8. General John Haskell King of Detroit, whose son, Charles Brady King, developed the first automobile ever seen on the streets of Detroit (in 1896). In a letter of February 9, 1944 to Mrs. Elleine Stones, chief of the Burton Historical Collection, Detroit Public Library, Mr. King states that his father in boyhood lived for some years in the General Hugh Brady house on Jefferson Avenue at Hastings, where subsequently the former Detroit Museum of Art was built, and that this association with General Brady inspired him to adopt a military career. General King's wife was Matilda Davenport, member of an old-time Detroit family.—Data compiled from the Charles Brady King material in the Burton Historical Collection.

9. This was the battle of Resaca, May 14–15, 1864. General Ruger's official report of the action states that the flag, commander, and some thirty prisoners of the Thirty-eighth Alabama Regiment were captured by the Twenty-seventh Indiana Regiment of his command. Ruger's brigade formed a part of General Williams' First Division, Twentieth Corps. General Hovey, without mentioning the capture of the flag, affirms that his division fought brilliantly, rolling the Rebel force back "like smoke before the wind." Compare *Official Records*, Series 1, XXXVIII, Part 2, 29, 59, and 541. Obviously General Williams' statements and those of General Hovey are squarely contradictory.

10. The nephew, Lieutenant John H. Knipe, was a member of General Knipe's staff. The latter reported that his dying words were: "I have endeavored to do my duty. If you were satisfied with my conduct, I am ready and willing to die."—*Official Records, Series* 1, XXXVIII, Part 2, 44.

11. Described by General Williams in his official report in *Official Records*, Series 1, XXXVIII, Part 2, 29–30.

12. Leonidas Polk of North Carolina, a West Point graduate in the class of 1827, was "converted" through the influence of the chaplain, during his final year as a cadet. Following graduation he resigned his commission to devote himself to a religious career, in which he achieved marked distinction. A friend of Jefferson Davis and an ardent supporter of the Southern Confederacy, he resumed military life in 1861 with the rank of major general. Until his death in 1864 he was active in the western theater of warfare. On June 14 at Pine Mountain a Federal artilleryman fired a shell at a group of Confederates, and Polk, Episcopal bishop and Confederate lieutenant general, was slain. See *Dict. Am. Biog.*; report of General Geary in *Official Records*, Series 1, XXXVIII, Part 2, 127; Wm. H. Polk, *Polk Family and Kinsmen* (Louisville, 1912), pp. 181–83.

13. Although shot through the lungs, Captain Veale survived his injury.—*Official Records*, Series 1, XXXVIII, Part 2, 129 and 147.

14. The remainder of the letter is missing. Presumably it described Williams'

triumphant repulse on June 22 of the Confederate attack at Kolb's farm, which is also described, later, in his letter of July 10.

15. On June 27 at Kenesaw Mountain General Sherman made an all-out assault upon the Confederate entrenchments, only to be bloodily repulsed with a loss of 3,000 men. Resorting again to flanking movements, he compelled Johnston to abandon Kenesaw Mountain and Marietta in the night of July 2. The first four-page section of General Williams' present letter is missing. The remaining portion takes up the story as he entered Marrietta on July 3, 1864.

16. The battle of Kenesaw Mountain. General Charles J. Harker, a graduate of West Point in the class of 1858, colonel of the Sixty-fifth Ohio Regiment, November 11, 1861 and brigadier general of volunteers September 20, 1863. On May 14, 1864, he received a wound from a shell in the battle of Resaca. He was shot from his horse, mortally wounded, in the battle of Kenesaw Mountain on June 27, while leading his brigade and within fifteen paces of the Confederate entrenchments.—Cullum, *Biographical Register of Officers and Graduates of the U.S. Military Academy*, Vol. II; *Official Records*, Series 1, XXXVIII, Part 1, 369 and 888.

17. Carter L. Stevenson of Virginia was a West Point graduate in the class of 1838. From 1841 to 1844 and from 1847 to 1848 he was stationed at Detroit. Upon the opening of the Civil War he supported the Confederacy, attaining the rank of major general and of corps commander in the defense of Atlanta in 1864.

18. Apparently the officer alluded to was General Geary, commander of the Second Division, Twentieth Army Corps. His thirty-five-page report of the operations of his division during the Atlanta campaign contrasts markedly both in length and in tenor with General Williams' similar ten-page report. His one-page account of his role in the battle of Kolb's farm affirms that his artillery completely enfiladed the ranks of Hood's assaulting force, and "literally" swept them down by his "fearful" cannonade; yet Williams characterizes such claims as "all bosh." For the reports of Williams and Geary see *Official Records*, Series 1, XXXVIII, Part 2, 26–36 and 112–47.

19. Alvin P. Hovey, brevetted major general of volunteers, July 4, 1864. General Williams' official report of the battle of Resaca, May 14–15, 1864 is in the *Official Records*, Series 1, XXXVIII, Part 2, 27–29, General Hovey's report of the battle is in the same volume, pp. 541–42. Williams was made a brigadier general on May 17, 1861; Hovey, on April 28, 1862.

20. For the battle of Kolb's farm see the letter of July 10. For General Williams' official report of the battle see *Official Records*, Series 1, XXXVIII, Part 2, 31–32.

21. The battle of Peach Tree Creek, July 20, 1864. For General Williams'

official report of the battle see *Official Records*, Series 1, XXXVIII, Part 2, 33–34.

22. He had resigned his commission and left for Detroit. The official record shows that he was mustered out of the service on September 7, 1864. On March 13, 1865 he was awarded a brevet of major in the U.S. volunteers, and on the same day a second brevet of colonel. He had enlisted with the rank of first lieutenant in the First Michigan Infantry upon the reorganization of the regiment in September 1861. He served as aide to General Williams until May 1863, when he was promoted captain and assistant adjutant general U.S. volunteers. He died at Detroit, March 30, 1922 at the age of ninety-one. Much of his energy during his final decade of life was devoted to procuring the erection of the equestrian statue of General Williams on Belle Isle, whose unveiling he witnessed in October 1921. At his death the flag on the City Hall was displayed at half-staff, reputedly for the first time in honor of a civilian. Perhaps his foremost distinction in life was accidental. It was he who obtained the famous lost order of General Lee, outlining his plans for the invasion of the North in 1862, which, carried to General McClellan, led to the battle of Antietam.

23. Nathaniel J. Jackson, commissioned colonel of Fifth Maine Infantry, September 3, 1861; brigadier general of volunteers, September 24, 1862; mustered out of service, August 24, 1865; died, April 21, 1892.

24. The Clitz family story is a Detroit saga. John Clitz entered the army as an ensign from New York in 1814 and a year later was transferred to the Second U.S. Infantry, attaining the rank of captain, December 31, 1829. For many years prior to his death in November 1836, he commanded Fort Mackinac, then a place of much importance in the Great Lakes area. Following his death his widow removed to Detroit where she conducted a boarding house, which remained the family home for many years. From it came John M. B. Clitz who attained the rank of rear admiral in the U.S. Navy, and Henry H. B. Clitz, member of the West Point class of 1845, who attained the rank of brigadier general in the Civil War. In line with army tradition, Mary Clitz married Capt. Henry C. Pratt of the regular army. Hattie married Lieutenant Henry B. Sears, a West Point graduate in the class of 1846; Sally married Richard H. Anderson of Georgia who graduated from West Point in 1842 and during the Civil War became a lieutenant general in the Confederate Army; and Frances married another West Point graduate, Gustavus A. DeRussey, who became a brigadier general in the Civil War. The mother of this brood (several not mentioned here) lived to the age of ninety-one. Misfortune clouded the closing careers of two of her sons. General Henry H. B. Clitz disappeared from his Detroit home in October 1888 and supposedly committed suicide by drowning at Niagara Falls.

Admiral John M. B. Clitz late in life became hopelessly insane, and was committed to an institution in Washington.

25. John Kinzie, of early Detroit and Chicago background, popularly accorded the title "Father" of Chicago, had a son, John Harris Kinzie, who, following a varied career from infancy (1803) onward, settled permanently at Chicago in 1833, where he remained for a generation a well-known citizen. He married Juliette Magill of Connecticut, author of the much-celebrated narrative of frontier life, *Wan Bun the "Early Day" of the Northwest.* Their daughter, Eleanor, born at Chicago in 1835, who married William W. Gordon of Savannah, is the "ditto wife" of General Williams' letter. The lot of these Northern-bred women, now allied with the Confederacy, in opposition to their brothers and other relatives who were fighting in the Union armies, affords one of the poignant illustrations of the consequences of the Civil War.

XI

Through
the Carolinas
to Washington

THROUGH THE CAROLINAS TO WASHINGTON

In mid-January 1865, while Lee at Petersburg continued to baffle General Grant, Sherman set out from Savannah northward to rejoin his chief. Rain and Rebels conspired to make the march through the Carolinas a nightmare for the Union army. Despite both forces, however, the army moved northward as relentlessly as a glacier in its descent to the lowlands. Columbia occupied and burned, Charleston and Wilmington effectively separated from their interior bases of support, Raleigh, another state capital, taken—these were but landmarks high-lighting the success of the campaign. Meanwhile Richmond fell and Appomattox followed. With the surrender of Lee's army, the doom of the Confederacy was patent to all observers. The surrender of Johnston to Sherman followed in due course and for all practical purposes the war was over. It only remained for Sherman to continue the march to Washington, there to share in the pageant of the Grand Reunion. Upon its conclusion, with the heartfelt farewells of his official staff and the warm commendations of his superiors, weary warrior Williams sheathed his sword. Ended at last were his four years of service in the field with but a single leave of absence. Ended, too, were his letters home, written often times amid scenes of carnage such as only America's bloodiest war could produce. Hidden from the world for almost a century, they comprise a revealing picture of that war and an enduring monument to the memory of the man—soldier, patriot, and gentleman—who recorded it.

FLOODTIME ON THE SAVANNAH

Headquarters, Twentieth Corps,
Savannah, Georgia, Jan. 23rd, 1865.

My Dear Minnie:

Your journal letter to January 1st. was received last Wednesday, the 13th inst., while I was under orders to move and all packed up to go into South Carolina. . . . I sent you a long journal of our campaign down to the entrance here, but I fear you will find it dull. As I think it over, I am conscious that I left out the most interesting parts of such a march, especially for home reading. I am afraid it is too much for my own memoranda. I send you by this mail my official report, with maps of our daily camps, embracing each division of the corps. This is sent for safe keeping. It is of no consequence to you, except perhaps the statistical parts showing how much we punished Georgia. You must remember that this is only what one corps of four did, and all the estimations are understated.

Now I will give you a brief account of my three days' experience in South Carolina. For two weeks or more one of my divisions (Ward's) has been encamped on the opposite side of the river, beyond the rice plantations, some six miles inland. On Wednesday last Ward was ordered to move up to Hardeeville on the Charleston and Savannah Railroad and the 1st Division (Jackson's) to cross and take Ward's position; both to move forward the next day and take position from Hardeeville and Purrysburg on the Savannah River. Pontoon bridges had been laid from the upper part of the city to Hutchinson Island and from this across two other channels to the mainland, or rather the rice field, in South Carolina. Hutchinson Island and the intermediate one beyond are old, abandoned rice plantations and are kept from overflow solely by the dikes or banks of the old fields. The north bank of the river for three to four miles inland is equally low as the island and are the rice plantations of the Langdon Cheves, Huger, and other rich and old Carolina families. The only way we could make roads was to corduroy the dikes, which are barely broad enough for a single wagon.

Two of my divisions had been for weeks at work at this corduroy and had probably laid seven miles of it across the island and the low ground on the Carolina shore to the causeway road from [illegible]

Ferry to Charleston. The weather had been excellent and the road was pronounced all right. So on Wednesday, the 18th, Jackson's division crossed successfully. On the 19th the 15th Corps, or rather two divisions, were to follow, and I put my headquarters team in their train and started across in advance, expecting to encamp some ten or twelve miles inland. The river for days had been very high and well up to the tops of the banks or rice-field dikes, and the weather was threatening. Before we reached the woods on the Carolina shore, which skirts the broad belt of rice fields, it began to rain heavily. We hurried on, thinking to find a safe shelter for the night in the Cheves mansion, four miles ahead.

Alack for expectations! We found the Cheves house a heap, a mass, of smouldering ruins, hissing and laughing at our dilemma as the heavy rain poured on the mass of burning timbers. We were without blankets or overcoats except rubbers, and our only shelter was a Negro hut or shanty which had been occupied in turn by Reb. and Fed. soldiers, and would have been a very foul pigsty.

There was no alternative; outdoors in the cold rain and mud, or indoors in dirt and, possibly, vermin. We chose the latter; set the orderlies at work cleaning as far as practicable; built up a big fire in each of the three small compartments, and despatched the orderlies back for blankets and food. There were at least twenty of us, not counting servants or escort, and twice that number of horses, man and beast without food and most of them without shelter. About 10 o'clock of a very dark night the orderlies returned with some blankets, but no food. My pack of white blankets, carelessly enveloped in a rubber, had been dropped in the mud and badly besmeared, and the rain had pretty thoroughly saturated them. As the general, I was honored with the only bunk, and rolling myself in my only blanket and sheltering myself as well as possible by the rubber from the rain dripping through a bad roof, I went supperless and dinnerless to bunk!

I thought myself pretty fortunate, compared with the troops, the mules, and the mule drivers, who were stuck in the mud on the dikes of the rice plantation, and there were at least five miles of these unfortunate ones, not one of which could move forward over these greasy roads until the leading team was out of the way. You can get a pretty good idea of what these rice swamps are by imagining the Grand Marais in

Hamtramck [1] or the marshes in Ecorse spread out from three to four miles in width, and then ditched and diked by the fat, black unguinous soil. The river here, however, at high tides rises almost to the top of the dike and quite above the surface of the marshes or fields. Standing or lying on these narrow, slippery, and treacherous dikes were hundreds of wagons, including my headquarter's wagons, and thousands of men, who could not get past the vehicles or were left to help them out. A few broken-down wagons had greatly helped to obstruct the march, until the rain and darkness stopped all progress.

I slept soundly, waking up, however, now and then to hear the rain beating heavily on the shanty and drizzle in big streams down the timber near my head. It was one of those dismal nights that surroundings make more dismal, but I slept soundly in spite of weather and the occasional wakings to think of the poor devils on the muddy dikes. I mounted early without breakfast or face washing, for I had neither soap, towels, nor hardtack. Sending part of the staff forward towards Hardeeville, I turned my horse's head, with a dozen others, towards Savannah, to learn the prospects of my train. I felt an inward satisfaction that all the trains of two divisions were on what I supposed [to be] terra firma and that, excepting my own headquarters and Gen. Jackson's headquarters wagons, all the stalled trains belonged to other corps. So as I sploshed down the Union Causeway Road to the point where our dike road intersected it, I was thinking of the best method of getting up a cup of coffee when I should reach the wagons; and I thought, too, of the comfortable and delicious breakfast that was probably coming off at Aunt Jule's about that hour. I had been twenty-four hours without food, and my fancy was pretty active, to say nothing of my appetite.

Presently we began to find our farm path which led through the woods, the great, moss-bearing live oaks covered with water, and as we went forward it grew deeper and deeper and spread out wider and wider. Our wonder and concern grew fast, for, supposing that some one had cut the dike or destroyed a sluice, I saw that at least some days would pass before our road would be passable. But on we went, splosh, splosh, splosh, following one another to avoid the treacherous mudholes. In spite of all our caution, however, many a horse went down, pitching his rider to his middle in mud and water. After a couple of miles or so of this mysterious and perplexing aquatic equestrianism we came out upon the open rice field.

Just fancy our consternation when we saw before us, as far as the eye could reach, an almost uninterrupted sea of water. Nothing of land, but here and there the projecting points of the dikes, looking as one can fancy the backs of sea monsters may have looked in the great deluge. Away off, three miles distant, we could indistinctly see the white covers of our wagons, and in the background the upper portions of the tall storehouses of Savannah, like the great houses of sea-girt Venice over the Laguna. It was a rich spectacle, especially as the rain was still pouring, and more especially as from the broad canal, the bank of which we had reached, was pouring over its whole length a volume of water which was rapidly making its way to our road in the rear and making problematical whether our retreat was not doubtful.

Ahead no part of the long road we had passed over yesterday was visible above water. We drew up on the only semi-solid piece of ground we could find and after some consultation decided to try [to make] our way through to the pontoon bridges. We could see the corduroy sticks bobbing and floating ahead, but we were pushed to desperation by our empty stomachs, our wet feet, and the bad chance behind us. So we formed a *queue* again, and in single file tried to find the road over this waste of water. It was a bad beginning, for several orderlies' horses and one or two officers' went down into deep holes and riders were left floundering in the water before we had gone a hundred yards.

So I gave up the attempt, and ordered all to turn back. In turning round to get back, my horse, a tough, Canadian-looking racker, slid into a hole so low that the water ran into my boots. I sat quite still, and with wonderful sagacity the animal felt forward and sideways with his forefeet and finding a firm spot he planted it and making a spring we landed on the upper crest again, unharmed, but with my boots full of water.

A further consultation was had, and two or three staff officers determined to try again, taking the opposite side of the canal, which was crossed by a bridge. We watched them from our eyrie for a long distance, saw rider and horse repeatedly floundering in the water, and we shouted with great laughter, notwithstanding our real apprehensions and the very dolorous prospect of our next meal. I decided for the rest that we should turn back and overhaul some wagons I had seen stalled on the road toward Semmes [?] Ferry. There might be food for man and beast in them; besides I had made a water mark and saw that the flood was rapidly increasing. So back we turned into the woods and without serious mishaps reached beyond the sea, at a point where the Cheves family have built up a large village of Negro quarters for the slaves of their rice plantations. There were fifteen to twenty Negroes left and "the smoke that so gracefully curled" above these very dismal-looking pens reminded me that my feet were very wet and cold. So I dismounted, entered, unseated an "old Aunty," had a big fire stirred up, and entered into a long talk with a bright-looking Negress who had lost a right arm in a rice mill. A very smart old Negro soon joined in the conversation and about a dozen young ones snuggled close up to their colored people, gaping in wonder at a live Yankee general.

These people told me that we were witnessing the beginning of the annual freshet of the Savannah, larger this year than usual, but that ordinarily all the rice plantations were overflowed, and that in a day or so, probably, the high cause-way road from Semmes [?] towards Charleston would be submerged, and that last year they had lost over four hundred sheep by the freshet. On the whole, we were satisfied that we were just beginning to feel the rise of waters and that we should lose no time in getting our wagons on terra firma.

But how? As usual with these people, they talked a great deal of family matters; told me a history of matters about old Mr. Langdon Cheves, so long a member of Congress from South Carolina, and about Mr. Charles Cheves, who died before the war, and young Mr. Langdon Cheves, who was killed on Morris Island by a ball "that cut him right in two"; about the two widows and Mr. Langdon Cheves' daughters, who had not been on the plantation for years; about the extent of the rice plantation—over 3,000 acres; the ordinary annual amount of rice crop, over 90,000 bushels; or "ninety million thousand," as the woman said; of the hard life of incessant labor a rice-planter's slave lives; of the great amount of sickness amongst slaves, of which I expressed a doubt, but which she confirmed by opening a large cupboard or room and displaying an array of quinine bottles which she said they had to take in great doses. They told me that over 200 able-bodied slaves were worked on this plantation, and that most had been sent above Abbeville; that men and women labored alike in the field; that their only food since the war was rice, which they threshed and pounded clean themselves; that the Rebel troops had taken all their corn and drove away all the cattle from the place.

THE CAPTURE OF LOST MOUNTAIN BY GENERAL HOOKER, JUNE 14-16, 1864
Reproduced from a sketch by C. E. F. Hillen in Frank Leslie's *The American Soldier in the Civil War.*

THE MARCH TO THE SEA BEGINS
Sherman's Fourteenth and Twentieth corps moving out of Atlanta, November 15, 1864. Reproduced from a sketch by Theodore R. Davis in *Harper's Weekly*, January 7, 1865.

THE MARCH TO THE SEA ENDS

General Sherman's army entering Savannah "at sunrise," December 21, 1864. Reproduced from a sketch by Theodore R. Davis in *Harper's Weekly*, January 14, 1865.

I kept them talking for an hour while I dried my feet. At last I said to the old man, "Have you heard that they are going to put your people into the Rebel army?" He had heard of it, but he added, "Massa, they can't make us fight de Yankees, I habe heard de colored folks talk of it. They knowd all about it; dey'll turn the guns on the Rebs." "Then," I said, "you prefer the Yankees?" "Ah, Massa," and he said it with his hands raised and an expression of earnest feeling and a pious soul, "Efery night when me and my woman say our prayers we say the biggest part for de Yankees"!

I have no doubt there are hundreds of thousands of honest old pious Negroes all over the South who are nightly putting up the same heart yearnings and petitions for our success. I have been astonished to find how widespread amongst field hands, as well as house servants, the idea is that the Yankees are coming to set the captive free, and how long this feeling has existed. The Millerites [2] never looked with more faith for that certain and final ascension day than have these Negroes, especially the old ones, for their certain deliverance from bondage.

After my Negro confab we mounted, and learning on the causeway road that a portion of the 1st Division train was stuck in the mud toward Semmes [?] Ferry, where it had gone after subsistence stores, I turned my horse's head that way. I found a portion of the 5th Connecticut Regiment and some stalled wagons, with pork and hardtack. Perhaps I have eaten more sumptuous meals, but none with a heartier relish than that slice, or those slices, of pork, which I toasted myself on the point of a stick to a beautiful brown color, and then laid across a section of hard bread, as both plate and condiment, or vegetable accompaniment. Around a campfire, myself, [my] adjutant general, and two aides toasted and toasted, until I think we had made up, in quantity at least, for the previous long fasting. A tin cup of strong coffee finished the perfection of breakfast. I felt compassion for poor Billy, who wandered about near me cropping the leaves from a few stunted bushes and nibbling away at some rice straw in the road, as the best substitute that could be got up for his meal after nearly thirty-six hours of faithful unfed services.

I found some forty-odd wagons stalled, and the roads so bad that six mules could not draw through an empty wagon. Indeed, the mules themselves were nearly drowned in mud. It was now 2 o'clock, and we had fifteen miles to ride to the camp of the nearest division with unfed horses, over the heaviest road, and in regular pour-down rain, which, after a brief respite had begun again with renewed force. But on we went. Billy began to look upon spur and whip with indifference. Now and then, as some one tried to pass him, his pride would come up and he tried his best rack. The road was flat and marshy almost all the way, save now and then a sandy ridge upon which the Rebs. some time ago, probably about the [time of the] Port Royal capture, had constructed extensive field works.

Before reaching the point in the road where the Hardeeville road turns sharp to the left from the Grahamville Road, I met Gen. Smith of the 3rd Division, 15th Corps, going back to look after one brigade and a part of his train which had passed the night on the dikes. He was surprised to hear of the extent of the deluge, and expressed an opinion that he was in a bad fix, but he started to reach Savannah. I find since I got here that he has not reached it. What has become of him no one here knows.

I reached General Ward's headquarters at Hardeeville about dusk, found a good supper waiting, spread my blankets on the floor of a shell of a house, and I don't think I rolled over until daylight. My horses got a good feed. The venerable Yorkshire, who is generally carefully attended to, looked supreme disgust, as he was obliged to stand in the rain all night unblanketed, and for thirty-six hours un-fed. Major, the chestnut horse I have generally rode since last spring, as tough as a knot, looked quite resigned. The worthy and war-worn old Plug Ugly, I believe I have told you before, gave out last summer beyond even strength to be led, and was ignominiously sold for $50. I would cheerfully pay more for his bullet-bored skin, if I had it at home. I hear that he died soon after I disposed of him.

On the next morning (Saturday the 21st) I rode over to Purrysburg on the Savannah River; still raining and water all around. I found the two divisions (Geary's is still here) encamped wherever they could find some solid ground, and often obliged to move camp. In the river the "double ender" man of war *Pontiac*, Capt. Luce, was at anchor. I went aboard. He kindly gave me a boat and in it I descended the most unpicturesque Savannah in a dense fog and rain to this city, reaching this about 4 o'clock P.M. I was rejoiced to learn that my wagons had got safely out of the mud back to the city, and that my provost marshal,

Maj. Parks, whom I had sent across the river from Semmes [?] Ferry had them in charge. The staff officers who left me to try the submerged rice fields got safely through, after many mishaps and plunges. My supply wagons were still embargoed on the causeway and the [illegible] Whittlesey was transporting forage to the mules in boats! I took quarters in the comfortable apartments of the medical director of the corps, Dr. Goodman, and today have reestablished my own mess, only for a day or so until I can collect my scattered trains and troops. I shall probably go back to Purrysburg and Hardeeville on Wednesday, and if weather permits we shall soon advance again. I fear, however, we have a terrible job before us.

[*The remainder is missing.*]

◈

PUNISHMENT OF SOUTH CAROLINA

Fayetteville, North Carolina, Mar. 12, 1865.
My Dear Daughter:

After long and weary marches we entered this town yesterday. A gunboat came up this morning by which I am enabled to send you a line in pencil. As soon as we get our "base," or if we linger here long enough, I will copy my journal to this point.

Our campaign has been more arduous, weather worse, and roads infamously worse than on the Georgia campaign. We have had but little fighting, however, so far, the enemy always easily driven away from the strongest positions. He has evidently been confounded by the audacity of our movements. We swept through South Carolina, the fountain-head of rebellion, in a broad, semi-circular belt, sixty miles wide, the arch of which was the capital of the state, Columbia. Our people, impressed with the idea that every South Carolinian was an arrant Rebel, spared nothing but the old men, women, and children. All materials, all vacant houses, factories, cotton-gins and presses, everything that makes the wealth of a people, everything edible and wearable, was swept away. The soldiers quietly took the matter into their own hands. Orders to respect houses and private property not necessary for [the] subsistence

373

of the army were not greatly heeded. Indeed, not heeded at all. Our "bummers," the dare-devils and reckless of the army, put the flames to everything and we marched with thousands of columns of smoke marking the line of each corps. The sights at times, as seen from elevated ground, were often terribly sublime and grand; often intensely painful from the distressed and frightened condition of the old men and women and children left behind.

We saw no young men, save the deformed, the sick or wounded, and deserters (pretty numerous). Everybody else had been forced into the service, even to decrepit old men of sixty and upwards, lots of whom came to us to be paroled or to be sent home. Boys deserted to us, not over thirteen years old. The "Confederacy" has literally gathered its infancy and aged, [its] first and second childhood. If it fails now, all material for reinforcing its armies is gone, unless, indeed, they can make fighting men out of the Negroes.

Our line of march has been across the largest rivers, the broadest swamps, and the muddiest creeks of the state. I think I am within bounds in saying that this corps has corduroyed over a hundred miles of road. For the last fifty miles we have traveled over a shell of quicksand which would not bear up a horse, and through which a wagon would cut to the box. The country was much poorer than I expected to find. Even respectable houses are very rare, and superior ones rarer. The soil, never very fertile, is worn out. The people left at home, mainly sickly-looking and grossly ignorant. How even the politicians of South Carolina can boast a superiority over our hardy and industrious Northern people is more than I can imagine. Everything in that state presents evidence of decay and retrogradation. There is nothing new, nothing that looks flourishing, and the people look like "fossil remains."

So far into North Carolina the country, if possible, is worse and the people worser! This town, you know, is at the navigable headwaters of the Cape Fear River, and is second only to Wilmington in population. One of the largest U.S. Arsenals is here, which the Rebs. have used as their largest. Only one U.S. Arsenal stolen by Rebeldom now remains to them, that at Augusta. Our march in the rear of Charleston made necessary the evacuation of the first fort upon which the Rebels fired, and Wilmington and all their seaports follow as we interpose between them and their interior communications. How much more effectual this has proved than all the costly attempts to take these places from the sea front!

I suppose we shall move on tomorrow or next day. Gen. Sherman announces that we have new duties before us. I have no doubt that his great objective point is Richmond, but we shall probably halt this side to replenish and refit our army on the Charleston and Savannah Railroad. I received a letter from Rene of January 24th and Minnie's journal to January 17th. This is the last I have had from home. It was a pleasant surprise, brought to us from a rear corps.

I will write you again if I have time. We are sixty miles from Goldsboro and shall probably halt there for some days, if we get it, as I doubt not. Love to uncles and aunts and cousins, and believe me as ever,

Your Affectionate Father,
A.S.W.

P.S. My health has been and is excellent. No exposure seems to affect me.

◈

A TATTERDEMALION ARMY

Two miles north of Goldsboro,
North Carolina, March 27th, 1865.

My Dear Daughters:

Today brought us our first mail for sixty-five days; three from Minnie—regular journal series to February 17th, three from Larned, but *not one* from Rene! What is the matter with my eldest daughter? With the exception of one letter received on our march, I have not a line from her since the date of November 17th. I have written her several individual letters and she has a joint interest in all I send to "My daughters." Reflect, how much my mind is constantly engrossed with the care of nearly 20,000 men. No sooner do I reach camp after a most arduous campaign than my labors begin in making preparation for the next. No one who has not experienced it can comprehend the anxiety and watchfulness that this creates. Everything from wagon grease to the armament of artillery has to be attended to. With all the agents and assistance I have, I am still responsible that it is all done and done right. It must all be supervised. If it fails, or is neglected, I am the responsible man. In consequence, my mind is never at rest. My anxieties never cease. I dream of the work at night and I ponder and inquire and sometimes fret all day. I doubt if these stops to rest are not more harassing to me than the actual campaign.

You can see, therefore, that it costs me something to stop my cares and present responsibilities to write you long letters. I often think they must be very incoherent, as I catch myself, even while writing, thinking of something or other that ought to be at once attended to. Besides, I am every moment interrupted by all manner of applications, petitions, references, papers for approval, accounts to be examined and certified, and the thousand and one matters which the head of a large force must always supervise and decide. You must appreciate my letters, therefore, rather by the difficult circumstances under which they are written than by their intrinsic merits. I prove my love and constant remembrance somewhat, at least, in this way.

I wrote you a brief note telling you of my safe arrival here on the 23rd. Since then we have been daily changing camp and taking up positions of all the corps and making preparations to get supplies up from below, all of which we greatly need. We have had but little clothing since we left Atlanta, nearly six months ago. We started from Savannah with twelve days' rations of coffee, sugar, and hard bread (no meat) and were out sixty-seven days before reaching this base. All that we have had to support us, besides this, has been taken from the country. Our clothing is worn and torn. Many men are shoeless, and few have a decent pair of breeches. Every man's face is as black as a Negro's with the smoke of the pitch-pine fires. A more begrimed and war-worn looking army I fancy was never seen.

I doubt if your worthy "Pop" would have made a very presentable appearance in a drawing room. His pants, which were originally of light-colored corduroys, had assumed a very dirty and burnt-black color. The coat, torn in numerous places and badly patched, would have been an excellent "habit" in the *Beggar's Opera*. The vest had lost all but two buttons, and the shirt of brown woolen had undergone a three weeks' wear and tear. The hat, which was new in Savannah, having braved forty severe rain storms, had lopped down all round and the yellow cord turned to a dingy yellow gray. His beard, of a three-months' growth, never once in that time reflected from a looking glass, really seemed frightfully grizzly as first seen from a farmhouse mirror.

Altogether, it would have been gratifying if I could have sent you a true photograph of him and a panorama of the troops as they marched through town on the morning of our arrival, with the long train of pack mules, darkies, mounted bummers, and the thousand laughable and grotesque collections of a large army after a two-months' march. It was amusing to see the gaping wonderment of not only the few citizens, but of the 23rd Corps and other strange troops in the town. We were hardly conscious ourselves, I think, of the strangeness and war-worn appearance of our columns.

You can fancy something of the pleasure we felt at reaching a point where we could hear from home again, and yet, with what mingled feelings of apprehension, hope, and suspense. What calamities might not have happened to our friends at home during our two-months' wanderings. How we longed and watched for the first mail. How we pored over the few stray papers we could find, and when the mail came—tons of it—how impatiently we watched for the opening of each package, fretting at the seeming delay of the corps postmaster. How we grumbled that the mail was so old, a month and over! How eagerly letters are clutched at and torn open; read in silence, or rather skimmed over at first, to see if any sad event has occurred. And then follows the slow and careful reading, the exclamations that John Jones has married Fanny Smith. Tom Snooks has been brevetted for staying at home valorously. Peter Spike has resigned. Somebody has another heir or heiress; and alas! now and then the silent going aside with sad face tells of mournful and heavy tidings, such as unfit the heart for the general merriment and take away all the anticipated joy of getting, as it were, after toilsome marches, *near home!* Who can describe these scenes and these heart beatings? Not I.

But I shall send you my journal in a few days, if I can find time to transcribe it. In the meantime, I can only say that the fatigue and labor of the last campaign has far exceeded that of Georgia. The officers, especially, were well worn, though, like the men, looking tough and hearty. We were glad to get to a point where we could replenish and refresh our strength. Judging from Minnie's letter, you have had a gay winter, so in contrast to my life in the pine barrens and swamps that the description almost strikes one harshly. Still, yours is the season for rational amusements and I only ask that it be used and not abused. But are you not all, up North, running mad with a sort of ephemeral prosperity? Is everybody rich? We in the army feel poor, for as everything advances our salaries proportionally decrease. Our pay now, measured by prices, is not half [what] it was in the beginning of the war; our labors and exposures never half as great. It is a year now that I am absolutely without rest. How I weary for it; for absolute retiring in some most secluded spot where for months I should not see an army wagon nor hear the bray of a donkey nor feel that mental anxiety which sits perpetually upon me now. I might consent to go out to those fine operas, or musicales, or plays, but the parties and balls—no, I think I have had my day of these. . . .

I fear that my journal must have been sorry stuff to the reading club. I can't recall anything of it, except that I transcribed from brief notes in great hurry and under constant interruptions. Uncle Lew must be the judge as to reading these things, for you daughters are too partial and do not always see the fitness of Pop's productions as a more disinterested and cool eye would. The "curious letter" which you forwarded was from a colored servant girl, a most excellent cook, washer, and sewer. Indeed, the best colored servant girl I ever saw, pious, steady, industrious, and wonderfully intelligent. She came to my headquarters with her sister Ann and two brothers-in-law, and a nephew the day after we entered Atlanta, having walked thirty-odd miles with what worldly goods they could carry to get away from slavery. We took this girl as cook and the boy nephew as a servant. I tried to induce "Phibby," as she calls herself, to go to Detroit with the Michigan Engineers, but she has a husband, slave to an officer before Richmond, and a son eight to ten years of age, who was carried away into the interior of Georgia. She could not make up her mind to go so far away from them and lived in hopes to get them with her before we left Atlanta. At length the order came to evacuate the place, and with it her struggles of heart as to which way to go. I advised her to try to get North; got her a pass to Nashville for herself and sister and nephew; gave her Uncle Lew's address, and told her to write me if she got into any trouble. The boy nephew decided to go with us, but the attack of Wheeler's cavalry a few days after so disturbed his nerves that he gave up the idea. The brothers-in-law are still with the command and are excellent servants. I wish she and her sister could get to Detroit. The whole family is the best collection of Negroes I ever met, but "Phibby" is the leading spirit of them all. I see she calls me "Pap"; a term she got from the soldiers and no doubt thinks it both a respectful and affectionate expression of her gratitude and love. Her name is Phoebe Simms. "Old Tom" she speaks of is my Negro servant, whom everybody in this army knows for his grotesque costume, his cheerfulness, and his active and intelligent spirit. He is a great favorite, a decided character. If anybody in Detroit wants a steady faithful and most superior servant, let them get Phoebe from Nashville. When she wrote she was in a hospital, I judge, with somebody whose address was "Lock Box No. 75.". . .

I see by the papers that Gen. Willcox's brevet is dated August 1st, six months, nearly, before mine! The same paper has an abstract of the court of inquiry which censured him, I know not how justly or unjustly, but I can't help feeling that he had no claim for promotion over me and that the people at home and our delegation in Congress have done me great injustice and personal dishonor. But that my brevet is necessary to retain rank in my own corps, I would send it back. It is in other respects perfectly valueless. It gives the bauble of vanity to wear two stars! . . .

Love to all.

Your Affectionate Father,
A.S.W.

◈

DEMOTED ONCE MORE

Near Goldsboro, Apl. 5th, 1865.
My Dear Daughter:

I was right glad to get your two letters yesterday, one of March 7th and the other March 24th. I began to think you had cut me dead, but you see how irregular our mails are with a straight and quick communication with New York. . . . I have lost the corps again and go back to my old division tomorrow. You know I have been commanding the corps during the two last campaigns by *seniority*, Gen. Slocum being the regular corps commander assigned by the President. We have had a new organization, making the 14th and 20th corps into a new department, the Army of Georgia, of which Gen. Slocum was given the command. This made vacant the command of the 20th Corps and as we have a great many full major generals it of course threw me. It is one of the curses that I have to bear for not getting my proper rank years ago, but I shall go back to my division without grumbling. I was gratified yesterday, when the three brigade commanders called on me formally and announced that they spoke the wishes of every officer and man in the division that I would resume command.

Maj. Gen. Mower has command of the corps. He is a very pleasant, gentlemanly man of the old army and has been with Sherman during all his Mississippi campaigns. This is about the fortieth time that I have been foisted up by seniority to be let down by rank! But no matter. Sherman told my brigadiers yesterday that I should have a corps. I prefer my own division to any corps except the 20th. . . .

This morning (6th April) we got the news of the evacuation of Richmond. The regiments are cheering all around me. I do not feel so much rejoiced. I think if Lee had held on a little longer it would be better for us, as we should have made a junction with Grant. Now the whole Rebel army I fear, will get between us. I could have come home after being relieved, but it would have left me out in the cold and Sherman would have been angry. Besides, there was such a pressure from the old division for me to come back that I could not resist. At one time I made up my mind to go for thirty days. I have just finished my official report—will send a copy in a day or so. I am so busy and occupied that I really have found no time to copy my journal and now I have to do a great deal with the division in getting ready for a new move.

Your Affectionate Father.

◈

NEWS OF LEE'S SURRENDER

Raleigh, North Carolina, Apl. 15th, 1865.

My Dear Daughters:

I had so much to attend to, to meet our sudden march from Goldsboro, that I did not get the maps of my reports ready to send. . . . The news of the capture of Richmond and the retreat of Lee made it important that we should hurry towards Johnston, who lay in the vicinity of Smithfield on the Neuse, twenty-six miles from Goldsboro. Our corps left Goldsboro on the morning of the 10th inst., my division leading. We passed through the town and recrossed Little River, passed over the same road we went in on, as far as Beaver Creek, then north on Smithfield Road. We crossed the Moccasin Creek, after much opposition by Rebel cavalry. Indeed, we skirmished all day, but drove the enemy rapidly. At the Moccasin, which is a broad swamp with two deep streams, we were obliged to travel the men to their arm-pits to get possession of the bridges which had been thrown into the creek. Loss, two killed and three wounded. I got into a very hot place on one of the bridges, looking after the skirmish line. The day was drizzling and most disagreeable. Marched sixteen miles.

On the 11th we marched to Smithfield without much opposition. Found the large covered bridge over the Neuse on fire and was obliged to lay the pontoons. The country between Goldsboro and Smithfield is much better than any we have seen in North Carolina, better soil and better cultivation. The houses are of better character and the people at home generally profess to be Union and rejoice at the probable end of the war.

On the 12th we crossed the Neuse early. I had the rear, and before I got over heard of the surrender of Lee's army from a dispatch to Gen. Sherman. I have never seen Sherman so elated. He called out to me from a bevy of mules and as soon as I could reach him through the kicking animals he grabbed my hand and almost shook my arm off, exclaiming, "Isn't it glorious? Johnston must come down now or break up!" I confess that I felt and expressed a pretty large sized "Laus Deo" at the prospect of an early end of this great Rebellion and a return to my family. Our long and tedious marches, for now nearly a year, with but little cessation, has quite filled me with a yearning for quietude and repose.

We marched this day on the left road to Raleigh, twice crossing Swift Creek. It was a sultry, showery day and I don't know when I have seen the men so fagged and disposed to straggle. For old marchers of thousands of miles, it seemed singular. I think our new corps commander was a little too impetuous in his mode of marching. We encamped about sixteen miles from Smithfield. Road was heavy. Smithfield is a dilapidated old village.

On the 13th we moved at daylight, my division in advance. We hoped to reach Raleigh early, but we ran against the 14th Corps and had to flounder about on crossroads and byroads. We reached the southwest side of town about 12 M. Miles away we had heard that the enemy was gone and Kilpatrick in possession. We passed through some fine country today, our march over sixteen miles. We encamped near the Insane Asylum. While waiting orders Gen. Mower and myself visited the inmates. Dr. Fisher, the superintendent, was greatly distressed at the presence of our troops, but as we saw a strong line of Rebel works running directly through the asylum grounds we concluded he had other motives. Our men gathered pretty close about the building and were greatly entertained by the Union speeches and songs of several of the inmates. We saw a good many strange cases inside, several of whom made quite eloquent talks of the old flag. Indeed, the prevailing sentiment of these insane seemed to be for the old Union.

After the troops were encamped I rode into town with Gen. Mower. We found a large, straggling, well-embowered village, with a respectable State House in the center and a good many pleasant residences about, but no signs of commerce or manufacturing. I could not but feel that the place had got all its wealth and growth, whatever it may be, from the public pap.

The 14th we remained in camp, doing up what we could for a continued march, which it was intimated would be for a month, probably.

15th: This morning we were under orders to move at 6 A.M., marching in review order through town and then on a southwesterly road to—no one knew where, but it rained in torrents all night and poured this morning, and the march was countermanded after we had broken camp and got wet. So we pitched tents again and just now I heard a mail would be sent out this P.M.

Johnston and his whole army left this the day before we arrived, it is reported, for Hillsboro in expectation of meeting at least a part of Lee's army. No one seems to know or tell what his ultimate intention is. I doubt if he knew himself. He heard of the disaster to Lee the day he left but did not credit the extent of it, I think. He can hardly hope to make much headway against all of us, though I think he can, if he wishes, get away into Georgia. It would only prolong the war for a few months and bring great distress on the people of the South. . . .

I don't know and can't tell you where we are to go next. The telegram will let you know before this reaches you. The camps are full of rumors, but I credit nothing not official. Love to all.

Your Affectionate Father,

A.S.W.

◆

MURDER OF PRESIDENT LINCOLN

Raleigh, N.C. Apl. 21st, 1865.

My Dear Daughter: . . .

From a communication with Gen. Sherman yesterday I am satisfied that he has made such a negotiation with the military authorities as will surrender all the Rebel armies to the Rio Grande, if the powers at Washington approve the terms. You will probably have heard all about it before this reaches you. The terms, . . . which we doubt our government [will approve], relate to the state governments assuming power again and taking the oath to our government. Gen. Sherman don't seem to have doubts, as he has published an order that he expects to lead us to our homes again in a short time. The murder of Lincoln, tidings of which without particulars reached us a day or so ago, is likely, I fear, to complicate matters. The tidings were received here with a most solemn and sorrowful feeling on the part of officers and men, I fear not unmixed with bitterness that prompted deep revenge. The details have not yet come to hand. Should they implicate any of the Rebel authorities and this war goes on, woe to the people of the South! The reported assassination at Mr. Seward's would seem to indicate a most nefarious and wide-spread plot. It is to be hoped it will not so turn out. The news of the President's death came directly upon the news of Lee's surrender. I have never seen so many joyful countenances so soon turned to sadness. We have been expecting to march from day to day, waiting the result of negotiations going on between Sherman and Davis. Now we shall remain, at least until the terms are sent back from Washington.

We are fixing up camps which are a mile or two southwest of Raleigh. We shall probably march to Washington or Frederick, if the answer is favorable. . . .

Your Affectionate Father,
A.S.W.

◈

CONQUEST OF THE CAROLINAS

Raleigh, North Carolina, April 21, 1865.

My Dear Pitt:[3]

I intended to have written you from Goldsboro, but our stay there was comparatively short, and I had but just gotten through the reports of campaigns when we were ordered to march. I was greatly interested in your letter and for the element of it which you seemed to doubt would interest me—the talk about yourself and your prospects. . . . I think you did well to go to Chicago. Detroit is too old-fogy for an active youth, and it has nearly got its maturity, I fear.

We are likely to have peace soon now, I think, and with it will come the revulsions that always follow the expansions of war. So look out for a year or so, and be contented with direct profits on not very risky engagements.

Sherman told me yesterday that he expected to lead us homeward soon via Washington and Frederick in several columns. But it depends upon the approval at Washington of the terms of settlement that Sherman, Johnston, and Breckenridge have been fixing up for several days a few miles out of town. The only point of probable difficulty to an agreement is that the state authorities shall resume their powers on taking an oath of allegiance, or something to that effect. Nothing is said about Jeff Davis or his government. All troops and munitions of war to the Rio Grande are to be surrendered. But for the unfortunate and damnable murder of Lincoln (of which we have not yet the particulars) I think, and Sherman thinks, the whole subject would be peacefully settled, so far as the military authorities are concerned, within twenty days. Of course, there will be the great swell of the storm for years to come.[4]

I know not how often I have regretted you left us, but it is probably all for the best. It certainly looked so then. Our march through Georgia was altogether pleasant, a "big hunt," as a Wisconsin Indian recruit called it—A "promenade militaire," as a Frenchman would have named it. We swept up all forage, hams, turkeys, ducks, chickens, sheep—everything edible, and burned all the cotton and cotton gins and presses within a belt of from sixty to seventy miles wide. We had beautiful weather and but few days of very hard roads. Supplies were abundant, and we sat down before Savannah with at least one-fourth of the supplies we left Atlanta with. We had no fighting (except around Savannah) beyond some cavalry skirmishes.

At Savannah we lost a hundred men or so, killed and wounded. Col. Ketcham was among the wounded, was brevetted, and has since resigned.[5] Lt. Ahrett, assistant to Asmussen, was killed.[6] In Savannah we had quarters in town at Mr. Cuyler's house, railroad president, etc. and brother-in-law of Sproat Sibley.[7] The town was charming and the weather superb. Good wine of very old vintage abundant, and altogether it was a delightful winter residence. We had the grandest reviews, and by common consent the 20th Corps waxed them all. But, strange to say, we got no supplies of clothing, and on January 17th we crossed the river into the rice swamps of Georgia without stockings for the men and with but few shoes. The campaign of the Carolinas was a decided contrast to the Georgia march. It was all mud, swamps, treacherous quicksand and quagmires—cursed cold, rainy weather, hard work, much swearing, great wear and tear, short commons for days, and altogether a most irksome and laborious campaign. We wound up with two very considerable fights. That near Averysboro, N.C. on 16th March was wholly by our corps and the cavalry.[8] We drove them from two lines of works, captured three guns, and smashed them up sadly before the 14th Corps came up. It came off in the swampiest of country. The Rebs. got off in the night, leaving ambulances, caissons, and wagons sticking in the road toward Smithfield. That on 19th March was begun by the 14th Corps or rather two divisions, each corps having one division guarding trains eight or ten miles away. One division of the 14th got badly punished before we got up and was driven in some confusion. The Rebs. then undertook to carry a new line I established, in the angle of which I left a marshy interval commanded at canister distance by twelve pieces of artillery. They threw a mass into this interval and at the same time attacked in front. They were terribly punished, but tried it five times before nightfall and each time were repulsed in thirty minutes or less. They left lots of dead officers and men, especially when the canister swept them on the left front. It was a worse affair for them than Kolb's Farm, and somewhat reminded me of it. We sent during the night for the other divisions, and the 15th and 17th corps were moved toward their left on the following day. If they had stayed one day longer Johnston's army would have been finished then and there, but they put out in the night. Johnston's force, composed of the debris of Hood, Hardee's, and all the other armies outside Lee, was estimated by prisoners from 30 to 40 thousand. Our two corps, when attacked, had not together 10,000 present. I took nearly 400 prisoners on the 16th, and buried over 300. Lost, killed and wounded, 438. I lost about 250 on the 19th, but no officers of note killed.[9]

I can give you but a faint idea of the devilish nature of the country through which we passed. The streams (across all in the state our course ran) were generally in six to ten channels with the worst entangled swamps between, often three miles wide. Behind these the Rebs. would entrench, and it took a good deal of skirmishing in water waist-deep to get them out. We lost a good many men in these affairs. It rained twenty-one days during the campaign. The roads, mostly sandy loam with a quicksand substructure, would become so saturated that there was no bottom. Corduroy would sink, again and again. But we became expert road-makers, first piling on all the fence rails and then cutting the young pines of which there was an abundance everywhere. For days we corduroyed every mile, and moved the trains from eight to ten miles! Right glad were we after the fight of the 19th to get the order to make for what we knew was our base and resting place, Goldsboro. We reached there on the 24th of March and remained in camp until the 10th of April, seventeen days. We were joined by, or rather found there, the 23rd and 10th corps, Gen. Schofield, Terry of Fort Fisher memory commanding the 10th Corps. He has the only Negro troops (one division) in the command. We had but little rest at Goldsboro, but we got supplies of clothing for the first time since leaving Atlanta. We left Goldsboro on the 10th and reached this [place] on the 12th. Had much skirmishing at the swamps but no severe fighting.

Johnston evacuated this place two days before we got up. On the march we heard of the surrender of Lee's army. There was great hurrahing through the lines. It began to look like the beginning of the end. The day after our arrival Johnston began negotiations with Sherman. The result has gone to Washington. I send you by this mail a map showing the route of our march until we reached North Carolina.

Such in brief is our campaign history. It has been interesting, though often laborious. We have had a chance not often found of seeing the interior of Rebeldom. South Carolina will not soon forget us. A blackened swath seventy miles wide marks the path over which we traveled right through her center and sweeping in the march her capital and her chief commercial city.[10] The first gun on Sumter was well avenged. The state generally is miserably decayed and worn out. Its houses are comfortless and shabby, and the people at home rusty, ignorant, and forlorn. I think the tornado of war may do them good in the end. . . .[11]

Yours faithfully and sincerely,
A.S.W.

◈

END OF THE REBELLION

Raleigh, Apl. 29th, 1865

My Dear Daughters:

Johnston has surrendered his whole army east of the Chattahoochee River. We are back again from our march, and tomorrow we march toward Richmond and Alexandria. I expect to reach Alexandria by June 1st. Write me often via Washington, D.C. If I have a chance I will write you on the way. . . . The main body of Johnston's army is at or near Hillsboro and Greensboro. The newspapers will give you the terms of surrender before this reaches you. We move at daylight tomorrow morning. I expect to be at home by the middle of June. Love to all.

Your Affectionate Father.

◈

EN ROUTE TO WASHINGTON

Near Richmond, May 10th, 1865.

My Dear Daughters:

We arrived within eight miles of Richmond night before last, having marched about 170 miles in nine days. Yesterday we moved camp to this point about five miles south of Richmond. We had very pleasant weather but some hot days. We shall leave tomorrow morning for Alexandria and shall be from eight to ten days on the route. What will be our fate by then, we are not advised. Probably mustered out. . . .

I was visited by one of my classmates yesterday, who had been here nine days waiting to see me, Mr. Jansen Hasbrouck of Rondout, New York. We had not seen one another for thirty years. I did not recognize him at first. We spent most of the day together in Richmond. I am going in again this morning. The mail goes soon, so with love to all, I am as ever,

Your Affectionate Father.

❖

DRAWBACKS OF GRAND REVIEW

Near Alexandria, Va.,
May 21st, 1865.

My Dear Daughters:

We reached our camp some miles behind Alexandria night before last. . . . It was a great temptation that Capt. Poe made you to come here; but it wouldn't pay. Washington is overcrowded and has been for days. Alexandria is nowhere. In camp, as we are now situated, women could not live. I shall be so occupied during the reviews and a few days after that I could hardly see you. Besides, it is nothing but a march through Washington, and [the] tramp of masses, all looking alike, for hours and hours, till everybody will be tired to death of seeing soldiers. So far as show is concerned the review of a brigade or division would be far more agreeable. I say this to console you. You'd be bored to death, as we shall all be tired to death, with this grand show. I do not like the arrangement. One army (2 corps) only should have been reviewed in one day. As it is, I think our corps will pass the reviewing stand about midnight. One hundred thousand men cannot pass a given point in a short time.

I wish I had an available house near here. It is rumored that we are to change camps and to remain some weeks. If so, I may be tempted to get a short leave and bring you both to Washington or Georgetown *malgré* the paucity of pecuniary resources. We will see. As yet all is uncertainty. I have not been to Washington and have seen no superior officers since we arrived, except Gen. Meade, who seemed to know nothing of future policy. He inquired after Rene, and spoke feelingly of the death of his son.

After the review we shall probably know what is coming. As I am a poor figurer I fancy I shall retire to private life early. . . .

Love to all,

Your Affectionate Father.

◈

THE GRAND REVIEW

Near Bladensburg, Md.,
May 29th, 1865.

My Dear Daughters:

Since the "great review" I have been pretty much "horse de scramble" as Gen. McNeil used to interpret the used-up state. I got something into my stomach that has greatly distressed me ever since. Yesterday I was able for the first time to ride into town, with much pain, however, as every step of the horse was a pang. Today I am much better, and have been engaged on my report from Goldsboro to this place. Added to the discomforts of a sore stomach, the most dismal northeast rain storm has blowed and flowed for nearly three days.

I was in Washington a few hours during the review of the Army of the Potomac and saw lots of Detroiters. Amongst others I paid my respects to Mrs. Chandler. I did not see Chandler, as he was out.[12] I wanted to have a little talk with him. His intimate friends (Geo. Jerome amongst others) declare most positively that he has never opposed, but has repeatedly recommended, my promotion. I only know he has never written me a favorable line. The Detroiters and, indeed, hundreds of Michiganders received me with great cordiality. Everybody tells me that I am a greatly abused man. I shall begin to think, myself, that I am a *martyr!* However, it is gratifying to receive these evidences of appreciation, or of flattery. It seems to me I never met so many acquaintances. It took me an hour or more to get from Willard's to the National. . . .

The review of Sherman's Army was a great success. People doubtless thought us a military mob, but I believe it is generally conceded that we were in marching and military appearance at least equal to the Potomacs. I received whole armfuls of bouquets. Indeed, I could not carry them all. Some had names attached and some were sent out and delivered in the name of persons I had never heard of. One had Mrs. Gen. Willcox's name and was presented by a staff officer of the general. It was a very delicate compliment. I have not yet seen her to make my thanks, but shall do so as soon as I can get down town. He commands a district hereabouts. Several of the bouquets came from wives of my old officers. If you want to see the most flattering account of our display, you must read the New York *Herald*'s correspondent of Friday, I think. He says the "Red Star" division took the palm. Others (many) have said the same thing.

[*The remainder is missing.*]

◆

FRIENDSHIP OF SUPERIOR OFFICERS

Near Washington, June 5th, 1865.

My Dear Daughters:

As I have not heard from you for a week or more, I suppose you think I am on my way home, but I can't get away until the mustering out is completed and my remaining regiments are transferred. Nobody seems to know what will be done with us then. Gen. Slocum is an apathetic man in such matters, especially, and our corps commander is both modest and indifferent.

Gen. Geo. H. Thomas, our old commander of the Army of the Cumberland, is here. He sent for me on Saturday night and after telling me that after the campaign of Atlanta he had made a stronger recommendation of me for a full major general than he ever made before, asked me if I would like a command of troops embracing one of the Southern states. I said, "Yes!" He said that he should do all he could to get me such a position under him; that he had watched carefully my command while with him and was eminently satisfied with me; that he intended at Atlanta to ask to have me made a major general for the purpose of securing my command of the 20th Corps, which he thought was due me. He did not doubt that Gen. Sherman had acted for what he supposed was the best interests of the service, etc., etc.

Now to appreciate all this, you must know Gen. Thomas. He has all the gravity and solemnity (and I may add sincerity) of a Washington. Never pays a compliment unless he means it. An officer of great purity and most devoted to his duties, so much so that for four years he has never left the field and never seen his family, until he went back to Nashville just before the battles with Hood. I confess that I was overwhelmed with his good opinion, and could only express my thanks in some confusion. I knew that he had strongly recommended me at Atlanta and had often been told by his staff officers that he often spoke of my command of the corps in high terms, an unusual thing to be heard by his staff, as he talks but little and seldom with his staff generally. As Gen. Thomas is here to see the President on special summons, it is not improbable I may get the detail to report to Gen. Thomas.

I went to see Gen. Sherman to say good-by. He was very cordial and repeated several times, "Williams, if there is anything I can do for you, call upon me freely." It was too late then to ask his influence, and it is doubtful now if it would aid me with Stanton. Gen. Slocum promised to do it for me, but I fancy has said nothing. He is not marked for personal exertions of that kind. I have done nothing for myself because I don't know where to begin. It is dangerous to go high without the aid of those below.

Our corps will be entirely broken up this week, I think, and I shall soon know my fate. If I go west I shall soon see you. If not, I shall send for you when I get fixed. . . . Love to all. Keep writing until you hear that I am coming.

Your Affectionate Father.

FAREWELL OF STAFF MEMBERS

Headquarters 1st Div. 20th A.C.
Near Washington, D.C.
June 7, 1865.

Major General A. S. Williams
Commanding 1st Division 20th A.C.
General:

The members of your staff wish to present you before separating a slight testimonial of their esteem and affection. They, therefore, beg your acceptance of the accompanying album.

The marked impartiality, justice, and kindness with which our individual and collective claims and interests have been received and acknowledged, have animated us with feelings higher than regard for our commanding general.

The division is soon to be dissolved, but the officers of the 1st Division staff will ever remember with feelings of pleasure, gratitude, and veneration, one from whom they have always received the kindest personal consideration, and in whom they have had the fullest confidence as an able and energetic commander, and for whom they individually entertain the warmest feelings of affectionate regard.

May the remainder of your days be happy and their close glorious.

[*Letter signed by*]

James Francis, Major 2 Mass. Infantry
H. Z. Gill, Surg. U.S. Vols. Bevt. Lt. Col.
E. K. Buttrick, Capt. and Asst. Adjt. General
E. A. Wickes, Capt. and A.C.M.
S. V. R. Cruger, Capt. 150th N.Y. Vols. and A.A.D.C.
A. Y. Gavitt, Capt. 5th Conn. V.V. and Chief Pioneer
George Robinson, 1st Lieutenant, 23 [?] Aide-de-Camp
A. T. Mason, Capt. 123 N.Y. Vols. and A.A.D.C.
Wm. J. Augustine, Capt. 29 Pa. Vols. and Ord. Officer
C. M. Burke, Asst. Surgeon 46 Rt. P.V. Medical Inspector
H. A. Gildersleeve, Major 140 N.Y.V. and Pro. Mar.
Eugene Weigel, Capt. 82d, Ills. Vols, and A.A.D.C.

◆

COMMENDATION FROM GENERAL SHERMAN

Lancaster, Ohio,
August 5, 1865.

General E.O.C. Ord.
Comnd Dept. Ohio
Detroit
Dear General:

If you can favor General A. S. Williams in any way, I wish you would do so. He is an honest, true, and brave soldier and gentleman. One who never faltered or hesitated in our long and perilous campaign. He deserves any favor that can be bestowed.

Your friend,
W. T. Sherman
Maj. Genl.

1. The Grand Marais, or Great Marsh of early Detroit adjoined the opening of the Detroit River and the lower tip of Lake St. Clair. The "Hamtramck" of General Williams' letter was Hamtramck Township, from which the subsequent city of Hamtramck acquired its name.
2. The allusion is to the followers of James Miller, founder of the Adventist religious sect, who aroused widespread excitement by his predictions of the second coming of Christ, first in 1843 and subsequently on October 22, 1844.
3. Apparently the original manuscript of this letter belonged to Samuel E. Pittman. The present copy is from a typed copy of the letter on the letterhead of the Detroit Steel Products Company, with which Mr. Pittman was connected in his later years.
4. The terms agreed upon with General Johnston contemplated the surrender of all the remaining Confederate armies "from the Potomac to the Rio Grande" and the continuation in authority of the existing state governments. Although Sherman had thus assumed a political role, promptly repudiated by the Washington Administration, the nation would have been spared untold discord and misery if his program for reconstruction could have been accepted. For a revealing study of General Sherman's attitude toward the South throughout the war see E. Merton Coulter, "Sherman and the South," in *The Georgia Historical Quarterly*, XV (March, 1931), 28–45.
5. Colonel John H. Ketchum of the 150th New York Regiment, wounded near Savannah, December 20, 1864. He was promoted a brigadier

general on April 1, 1865. Heitman, *Historical Register . . . of the U.S. Army,* gives the date of his resignation as December 2, 1865.

6. For the death of Lieutenant Ahrett see *ante,* letter of January 15, 1865.

7. Ebenezer Sproat Sibley was the eldest son of Solomon and Sarah Sproat Sibley, founders of the well-known Detroit Sibley family. A younger brother of Ebenezer was Henry H. Sibley, notable early-day citizen of Minnesota. Ebenezer graduated at the head of the West Point class of 1827 and until 1864 devoted his career to the U.S. Army. In May 1831, he married Harriet Hunt, daughter of Judge Hunt of Washington. From 1838 to 1840 and from 1842 to 1844 he was stationed at Savannah, where, presumably, the family connection alluded to by General Williams was established.

8. The battle of Taylor's Hole Creek, or Averysboro. General Sherman's account of the affair is in *Official Record,* Series 1, XLVII, Part 2, 871. Contrary to his (and General Williams') statements, Confederate General Hardee on March 17 issued an order congratulating his soldiers upon their signal victory over vastly superior numbers, inflicting a loss of 3,300 men upon the enemy, at a cost of "less than 500 men" to themselves. Such are some of the oddities of warfare. For Hardee's order, see *Official Records,* Series 1, XLVII, Part 2, 1411.

9. This was the battle of Bentonville, in which General Johnston attacked the left wing of Sherman's army in a vain endeavor to stay its further northward march. Johnston's loss in the battle numbered "at least" 2,600 men. Some further fighting took place on March 20–21 by which time ample support had arrived to reinforce the Union left wing and Johnston withdrew his army.

10. That is, Raleigh and Charleston.

11. The remainder of the letter is devoted to personal news and gossip.

12. Zachariah Chandler, U.S. Senator from Michigan.

index

DESIGNED BY S. R. TENENBAUM

SET IN CASLON OLD FACE, BOLD, AND ANTIQUE TYPE FACES

PRINTED ON WARREN'S OLDE STYLE ANTIQUE WOVE PAPER

BOUND IN COLUMBIA BAYSIDE LINEN

MANUFACTURED IN THE UNITED STATES OF AMERICA